MW00964752

Adirondack Rock

A Rock Climber's Guide

Second Edition, Volume 1

Jim Lawyer
Jeremy Haas

Adirondack Rock Volume 1
A Rock Climber's Guide
Second Edition

Published by: Adirondack Rock Press, LLC
2795 Henneberry Road, Pompey, NY 13138
www.adirondackrock.com

First edition published 2008
Reprint, 2010
This edition published 2014

Printed in China
10 9 8 7 6 5 4 3 2 1

ISBN: 0-9814702-1-1
ISBN: 978-0-9814702-1-4

Written by Jim Lawyer and Jeremy Haas
Layout and design by Jim Lawyer and Jeremy Haas
Printed by Four Colour Print Group, Louisville, KY
Edited by Susan J. Cohan and Sara Catterall

Photographs by the authors unless noted otherwise.

Front cover: Art by Colin O'Connor.

Title page: *Avalanche Lake*. Watercolor by Lucie Wellner.

Read This First

Rock climbing is an inherently dangerous activity regardless of your level of skill and experience. It requires that you constantly assess and manage risk. You alone are responsible for your safety.

This book is not an instruction manual for climbing. Information in this book has been collected from a variety of sources, and, despite efforts to verify it, the authors and publisher make no guarantees as to its accuracy or reliability. The routes in the Adirondacks change—vegetation reclaims critical protection placements, rockfall alters sections of routes, the freeze-thaw action in winter loosens rocks, and once-open rock slides grow in and become unclimbable. Fixed protection is unreliable—pitons loosen and pull out; bolts rust and weaken; and anchors become old, rotten, sunbaked, or are removed by other parties.

THE AUTHORS AND PUBLISHER OF THIS GUIDEBOOK ASSUME NO RESPONSIBILITY FOR YOUR ACTIONS AND SAFETY.

If there is any doubt, if you are nervous and scared, then don't do it—seek instruction or hire one of the excellent local guides.

Emergency Information

Search and rescue is under the authority of the DEC forest rangers. In an emergency, call the DEC's 24-hour emergency dispatch center at:

518.891.0235

Make sure you have as much information as possible—name of the injured, time and location of the accident, nature of the accident, description of the injuries, who is present to assist, and what type of response to prepare for—high-angle rescue versus a litter carry.

Other important numbers include the following:

518.897.1300	Forest ranger headquarters
518.897.1200	DEC general information
518.897.2000	New York State Police in Ray Brook

You can call 911, but that requires extra rerouting of the information, and if you have a cell phone, depending on the receiving tower, you could be dialing 911 in Vermont.

Self-Rescue

Many of the remote cliffs in the park require that climbers be self-sufficient and get themselves out of tight situations. If you can safely evacuate the injured person to a vehicle, there are several hospitals in and around the park. Be warned that there are regions of the park where the nearest hospital is more than an hour from the trailhead. If you do self-rescue, be sure to let the DEC rangers know after the fact.

IN THE PARK

Here are the larger medical facilities in the park, each of which has a 24-hour emergency room:

Elizabethtown	Elizabethtown Community Hospital, 75 Park Street	518.873.6377
Lake Placid	Adirondack Medical Center, 29 Church Street	518.523.3311
Saranac Lake	Adirondack Medical Center, 2233 NY 86	518.891.4141
Star Lake	Clifton Fine Hospital, 1014 Oswegatchie Trail	315.848.3351
Ticonderoga	Moses-Ludington Hospital, 1019 Wicker Street	518.585.2831

OUTSIDE THE PARK

Just outside the park boundary are more options:

Glens Falls	Glens Falls Hospital, 100 Park Street	518.926.1000
Gloversville	Nathan Littauer Hospital, 99 East State Street	518.725.8621
Plattsburgh	Champlain Valley Physicians Hospital, 75 Beekman Street	518.561.2000
Potsdam	Canton–Potsdam Hospital, 50 Leroy Street	315.265.3300
Utica	St. Elizabeth Medical Center, 2209 Genesee Street	315.798.8100

MILEAGES BETWEEN GATEWAY CITIES AND DESTINATIONS IN THE PARK

Gateway City \ Destination	Lake George	Speculator	Old Forge	Keene Valley	Keeseville	Saranac Lake
Syracuse	166	113	94	194	217	222
Albany	61	87	143	121	145	148
Burlington	98	96	146	69	48	80
Montreal	164	184	206	110	80	112
Watertown	154	114	71	142	160	112
Potsdam	139	118	115	87	89	59

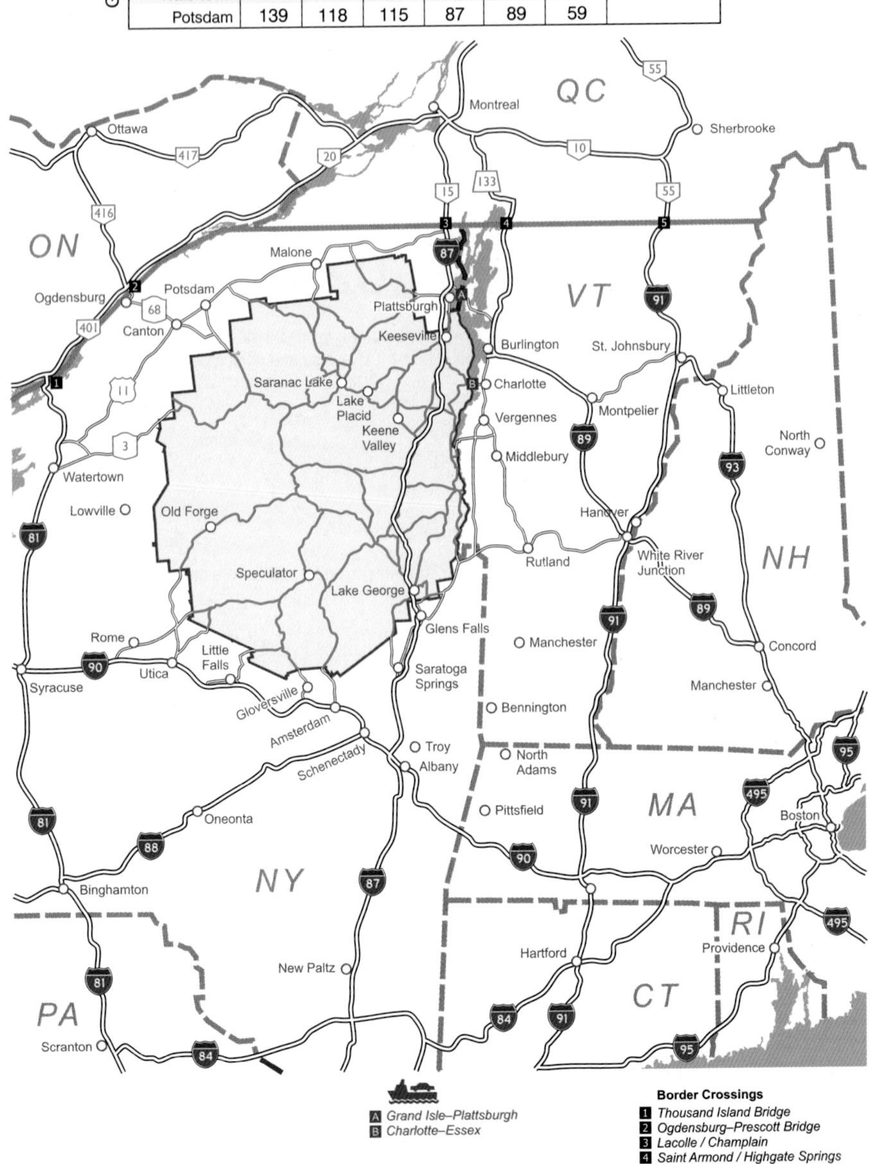

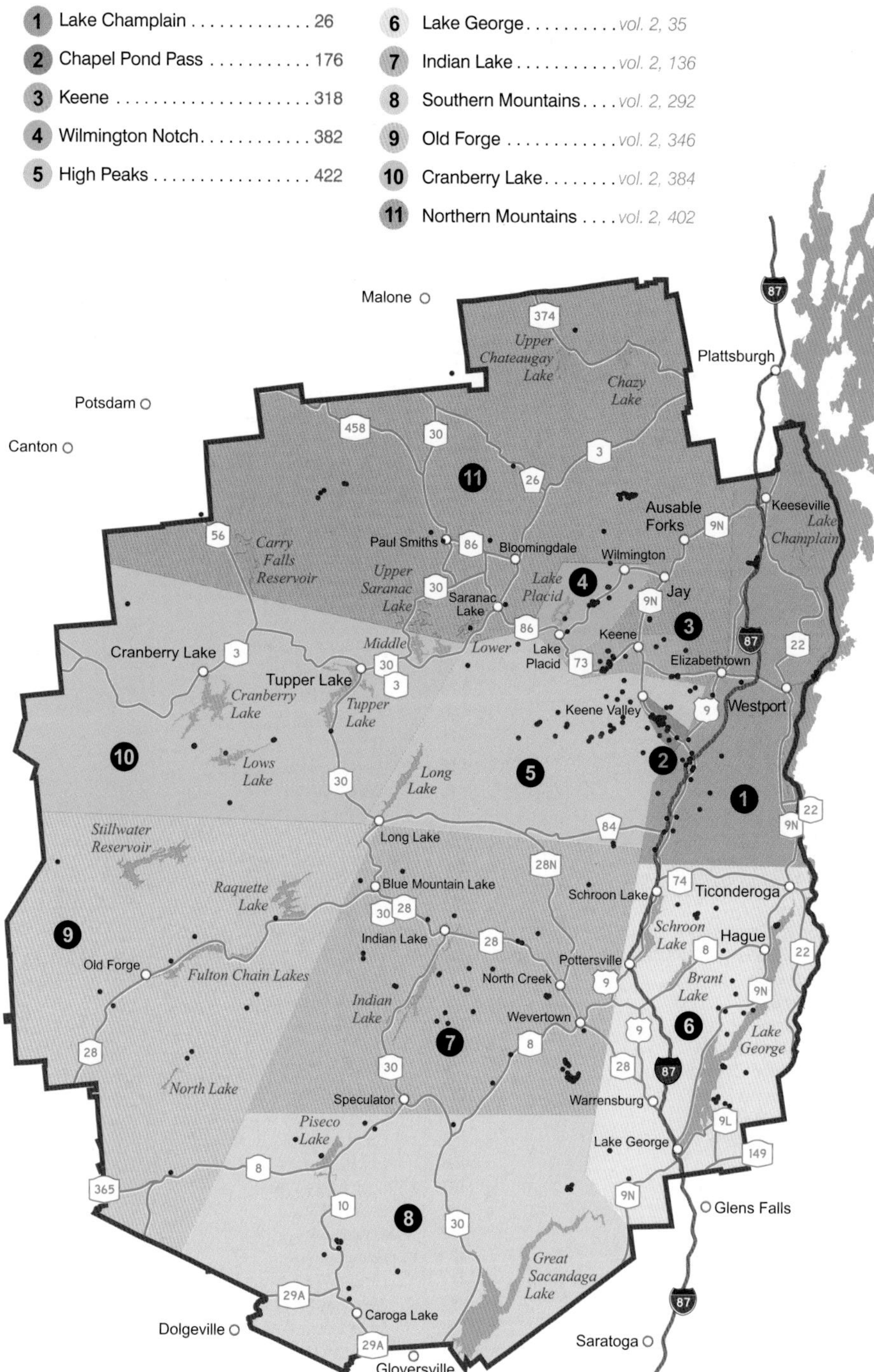

Malone
Plattsburgh
Potsdam
Canton
Upper Chateaugay Lake
Chazy Lake
Ausable Forks
Keeseville
Lake Champlain
Paul Smiths
Bloomingdale
Wilmington
Jay
Carry Falls Reservoir
Upper Saranac Lake
Saranac Lake
Lake Placid
Keene
Elizabethtown
Middle
Lower
Cranberry Lake
Tupper Lake
Keene Valley
Westport
Long Lake
Lows Lake
Stillwater Reservoir
Raquette Lake
Blue Mountain Lake
Schroon Lake
Ticonderoga
Hague
Indian Lake
Pottersville
Brant Lake
Old Forge
Fulton Chain Lakes
North Creek
Wevertown
Lake George
North Lake
Speculator
Warrensburg
Piseco Lake
Glens Falls
Great Sacandaga Lake
Caroga Lake
Dolgeville
Saratoga
Gloversville

Contents

Drawing by Tad Welch.

Foreword

By Tad Welch

Fingertips and eyelids burn from shards of brittle lichen and topsoil spindrift settles into creases of exposed flesh. Warm evening light sends an exaggerated petroglyph shadow across unclimbed rock from the first climber up. The tug of war with a rope zig-zagged by stunted cedars and Chouinard ovals has been won.

A slithering descent leads to a cave behind a truck-sized block that has fallen away from the cliff's base. It's easy to imagine the past in a place like this, where nature is so overwhelmingly present. Adirondack miners drilled rock from similar ceilings, albeit in shafts hundreds of feet from sunlight where ore hauling mules lived their subterranean lives and went blind. When eyesight adjusts to the half-light, recesses are revealed, like the one that held an ancient clay pot of Mohawk origin.

The return to the forest brings more history. Broken barbed wire sprouts from either side of an aged beech tree scarred by black bear claws. Farther along, a bramble-choked skidder road and double-bladed axe head attest to multiple logging generations. At last, packs are tossed in the station wagon's backseat and blackflies climb aboard.

As this new edition of *Adirondack Rock* makes clear, it's not only days spent exploring, bushwhacking, and cragging that multiply as the years go by. New cliffs are "discovered" and exploratory routes are put up. Some are gems, while others (I must accept responsibility here) are less so. The current generation adds lines to familiar walls, ascents that were overlooked or unimagined by earlier pioneers. The amount of activity and quantity of data can begin to overwhelm. After all, this is a six million acre park, a playground the size of neighboring Vermont. It would take a stack of volumes the size of *A Climber's Guide to the Adirondacks*, which was first published in 1967 and barely the thickness of a Power Bar, simply to list directions to every cliff, never mind the route descriptions.

Obviously, a thorough accounting of what is needed to get us to and up a route is essential. We're fortunate that *Adirondack Rock* sets a high standard here with its accuracy and detail. Once you choose the cliff with a suitable approach, the ideal range of route grades, preferred height, the right number of starred routes, and amount of sun or shade desired, all of which are easily found in the guide, it will be surprising if you can't find your way up a chosen line - the reason being that either Jeremy or Jim has been there and very likely climbed the route. Now, think about it. Spread over millions of acres are 330 crags, the majority with little more than cairns or a faint footpath leading to them. All told, those cliffs host 3,100-plus routes and a total of more than 4,000 pitches. (That's over 65 miles of climbing, in case you're wondering.) The first edition of *Adirondack Rock* tallied 1,900 climbs. In the intervening six years many rock walls previously unknown to climbers have appeared and more than 1,200 new routes and variations have been added to the Park total. It's an incredible time commitment to compile such vast amounts of information and present it in written and illustrated form in two guide book editions in a way that comes as close as is humanly possible to meeting every user's needs. Knowing this can leave you wide-eyed at how Jim and Jeremy have also managed to author a combined 374 first ascents!

But a climbing region is more than the sum of its routes and grades, a fact that some guide books overlook. A sense of our shared history – who climbed what and when, and, by extension, upon whom to exact revenge for your latest epic - adds a rich dimension of meaning to our efforts. From in-depth historical overviews to brief essays penned by some of the key players over the decades to one-liners inserted into route descriptions, Jim and Jeremy have given us a valuable passage to our past. While always entertaining, this aspect of their work also offers a broader lens through which we are encouraged to see the uniqueness of the region where we climb. Whether it's a day on Silver Lake Mountain, Wallface, Crane, or any of literally dozens of similar places, the experience can't help but foster an awareness of the positive mix of the wild and human that is the essence of the Adirondacks. Of course there are other rock climbing areas that are equally or more wild. And you don't need to look far for destinations where the mark of humankind lies heavy on the land. But, there's an unquantifiable something that comes with a region like ours where the two merge in a relatively seamless and mutually beneficial way. Perhaps the something is the way that the past, present, and future don't exist separate from one another in the Adirondacks, as is too often the case in the rest of our lives.

When we summit the routes on Gothics Mountain or climb from Panther Gorge to Mt. Marcy's peak, we've journeyed hundreds of miles north and over 10,000 years back in time. The arctic ecosystem of the High Peaks, a fragile symbol of the alpine climbing realm, followed the glaciers' retreat and lives a tentative life in its 87 acres refuge on the tallest summits. Most Adirondack species will seek survival, if they can, by migrating to higher and cooler habitats in response to hotter temperatures. The mountain top flora has nowhere left to go. But a special opportunity comes with this knowledge. It's a new and broader perspective that encourages us to expand our energies beyond climbing's ethical controversies to issues of global significance. Like the climbing we do, it demands the best from us.

With the publication 48 years ago of the first climbers' guide, which listed a very modest 70-plus rock routes (fewer than exist on half of Poke-O's Main Face today!), Jim Goodwin wrote that, "...rock climbing has come of age in the Adirondacks." In the five subsequent decades each generation of climbers has been privileged to experience a new coming of age for Adirondack rock climbing with every advancement on Trudy Healy's foundational work. Following Healy was Tom Rosecrans' *Adirondack Rock and Ice Climbs*. It reflected the environmental ethic of the 1970s with its emphasis on clean climbing and stated hope that a guide book would prove "more helpful than destructive." Next was - and is – Don Mellor, who continues to author the area's ice climbing guide in addition to other Adirondack and rock climbing-related books. His writing captured the spirit of the climbers' world inside the Blue Line with three editions of *Climbing in the Adirondacks*. At its heart, Don's message is an eloquent reminder to embrace Adirondack climbing on its own terms, to relish the adventure and avoid taming the vertical landscape for the sake of convenience or personal ambition.

We're fortunate that the maturation of Adirondack rock climbing and that of its community has been nurtured, inspired, and shown the way forward without forgetting the past for nearly half a century by Trudy, Tom, Don, - and now Jeremy and Jim. Thanks to their cumulative efforts, we can head confidently away from civilization's insistent chatter and into the forest solitude to the places where past, present, and future come together to create the potential for the unforgettable. And depending on the weather, bugs, our abilities and sense of direction, we may succeed - or fail - in getting to the top. But, no matter what the outcome, we are ultimately the ones responsible for our safety and quality of experience. On a handful of days we'll climb as if gravity doesn't exist and wish for the moment to go on forever. It's then that we should give special thanks to the authors of *Adirondack Rock* and to their predecessors. Their generosity has given access to some of the best days of our lives.

Tad Welch.

Les Adirondacks

par Loïc Briand

Le parc des Adirondacks, familièrement appelé « les Adis » par de nombreux francophones qui le visitent chaque année – et « the Dacks », par les anglophones – est un harmonieux mélange de terres privées et publiques réparties sur plus de 24 000 km^2 (6 000 000 d'acres), soit la taille approximative de l'état du Vermont. Créé en 1892 dans le but de préserver les ressources forestières et les plans d'eau de la région, il est traversé dans son axe nord-sud par l'autoroute 87, le prolongement 15 Sud au Québec. Les forêts y sont riches et denses. La multitude de sommets de plus de 1 200 m (4 000 pi), de vallées et de falaises en font un endroit très prisé pour la pratique de la randonnée et de l'escalade.

La philosophie de développement du parc est exemplaire. Hormis quelques exceptions, les rares villages qu'il contient n'abritent à peu près aucune habitation de plus de trois étages. Les publicités envahissantes des grandes villes ou de leurs autoroutes connexes y sont absentes. On y trouve un peu partout, au détour d'un sentier, au confluent de deux ruisseaux, dans une clairière ou au pied d'une majestueuse paroi, « des petits miracles de silence, échappés du progrès[1] ». Il est crucial et impératif que tout visiteur qui s'y aventure respecte cette philosophie qui rend l'endroit tout à fait singulier.

Dès 1967, les grimpeurs ont la chance de pouvoir consulter un livre guide d'escalade décrivant le parc. En 1975, Tom Rosecrans publie Adirondack Rock and Ice climbs. Don Mellor, le doyen de la grimpe aux Adirondacks, produit la première édition de Climbing in the Adirondacks en 1983. Ce livre est revu et augmenté, puis réédité en 1986, en 1989, en 1994 et en 1995. Mellor décide ensuite de passer le flambeau à Jim Lawyer et à Jeremy Haas, en 2008, qui révolutionnent carrément le monde du livre-guide sur la côte Est, en publiant la première édition de Adirondack Rock, en un seul volume. Ce premier ouvrage, qui décrit l'ensemble du parc, est consacré uniquement à l'escalade de rocher et au bloc. Exhaustif, facile à consulter et très précis, il comporte les coordonnées GPS des

1 La citation est tirée d'un article de Pierre Foglia (La Presse, septembre 2007)

parois, de nombreux détails historiques sur l'ouverture des voies et quelques récits des premiers ascensionnistes. Après une réimpression de l'ouvrage initial en 2010, ne reculant devant rien, forts de l'appui de nombreux collaborateurs motivés par l'incroyable travail de défrichage accompli, Jim et Jeremy poussent leur obsession jusqu'à de nouveaux sommets et décident en 2014 de scinder l'ouvrage en deux : le premier volume regroupe les régions de Keene, Chapel Pond, Wilmington, Lake Champlain et la région des High Peaks. Le second se penche sur les régions de Lake George, Indian Lake, Old Forge, Southern Mountains, Cranberry Lake, et les Northern Mountains. D'ailleurs, les auteurs ont accompli l'immense tâche de se rendre à la base de chacune des 3 100 voies réparties sur 330 sites et de les examiner toutes en détail. Il s'agit bien sûr d'un travail colossal ayant pris des années. De nombreuses photos aériennes et de multiples topos et croquis des parois rendent ces deux livres tout à fait remarquables. Si vous trouviez l'édition précédente déjà impressionnante, avec ses 672 pages, sachez que le nombre de parois développées et de voies ouvertes depuis lors a pratiquement doublé!

La proximité du parc avec la frontière canado-américaine en a fait un terrain de prédilection pour de nombreux Canadiens. Le développement de l'escalade aux Adirondacks a d'ailleurs largement été influencé par ces derniers au cours des décennies. De nombreux membres du club alpin du Canada, puis John Turner, Dick Wilmott, Claude Lavallée, Ben Poisson, Brian Rothery, Hugh Tanton, Dick Strachan, Rob Wood, Peter et George Bennett, Peter Baggaley, Peter Ferguson, François-Xavier Garneau, Bob Cartwright, Peter Gernassnig, Charles Pechousek, Pierre-Édouard Gagnon, Gelu Ionesco, Julien Déry, Louis-Philippe Ménard, Maxime Turgeon et Jean-Pierre Ouellet ont laissé leur empreinte sur la région en ouvrant de nombreux classiques.

La grimpe aux Adirondacks est surtout traditionnelle – c'est-à-dire protégeable avec des coinceurs – ou mixte. Ce n'est pas tout à fait le royaume de la moulinette, puisque la majorité des parois font plus d'une demi-corde. Pour bien apprécier les Adirondacks, il faut maîtriser l'art de poser tous les types de coinceurs. Cela dit, depuis la publication du dernier livre-guide de Don Mellor, les principaux ouvreurs ont équipé plus de voies que lors de tout autre époque. Les itinéraires sont à l'occasion très engagés, malgré tout, et nécessitent souvent un petit jeu de coinceurs. Une chose est certaine : bien que l'escalade sportive ou mixte soit en plein essor aux Adirondacks, il s'agit principalement d'un terrain de jeu d'aventure. De fait, en vertu des lois strictes de conservation du parc, il est interdit d'installer des protections fixes (plaquettes, scellements) dans la majorité des sites. Pour éviter toute interdiction de grimpe et par souci de préservation, veuillez respecter les règles concernant la modification permanente du milieu naturel. Le parc demeure un paradis des fissures classiques, parfois longues, sales, difficiles à protéger et soutenues. Les découvertes sont presque toujours au rendez-vous.

Les approches permettant d'accéder à plusieurs des parois décrites dans le guide sont parfois sauvages, impressionnantes, voire intimidantes. La pluie, les insectes et la recherche d'itinéraire sont régulièrement de la partie. Pour accéder aux parois de Wallface, l'une des plus hautes falaises des Adirondacks, avec ses quelques voies de plus de 250 mètres (800 pi), il faut marcher au moins 9 km par l'approche classique. Mieux vaut être bien préparé si on compte grimper l'une des nombreuses voies de la falaise et revenir à la voiture en une seule journée. Pour se rendre à Moss Cliff, il faut traverser un cours d'eau parfois glacial au printemps et à l'automne. Des voies sur les faces nord et sud de Gothics font près de 400 mètres (1 200 pi) de haut. Gravir de belles voies sur ces falaises rend l'aventure d'autant plus enrichissante.

Loïc Briand.

Comme ailleurs, les voies les plus courtes et les plus faciles d'accès sont aussi les plus populaires. Il faut apprécier les approches plus longues ou complexes pour se rendre aux plus belles parois et éviter les foules. Les itinéraires les plus intéressants ne sont pas nécessairement les plus faciles à trouver; façonnez vos aptitudes à lire votre livre-guide et le rocher. Plusieurs cordées se sont fait surprendre par l'ampleur de l'épopée dans laquelle elles s'étaient lancées... et par leur manque de préparation.

Les auteurs ont produit deux ouvrages exceptionnels, à l'image des régions qu'ils décrivent. Vous avez l'embarras du choix, et il ne vous reste plus qu'à définir vos propres projets, vos propres rêves. Le plus formidable terrain de jeu du Nord-Est américain vous attend.

Introduction

Splitter cracks, secluded crags, towering slabs and mazes of boulders— this is climbing in the Adirondack Mountains. The surrounding scenery of calm lakes, rocky stream beds and misty mornings carry you to the climbs, sometimes leading you across icy cold water to a high alpine face that sees only a handful of visitors each year. The variety, serenity, and solitude found here create a climbing experience that cannot be had anywhere else.

The year 1850 heralded the first technical climb on Adirondack rock—a bold solo on the remote Mt Colden. Much later, in 1916, John Case turned to the rope in order to safely seek out greater challenges, which marked the beginning of a steady increase in climbing activity. Presently there are more than 3,100 routes—1,240 new ones since the first edition—spread over 330 cliffs, 126 of which have multipitch routes, and 11 remote peaks with technical climbing.

Adirondack climbers are from all over—cosmopolitan cities, college towns, and neighboring Canada. This eclectic group's influence is felt at the crags with the array of cultures and climbing styles, yet the number of visitors remains low. The Beer Walls and Poke-O Moonshine are most popular, but at the peak of the season and even during a holiday weekend, the number of people at any one of these areas barely approaches 50. Perhaps the classic climb will have a queue of cordial and pleasant parties, but there are plenty more. This guidebook will direct you to them.

The Adirondack Park is a vast area, nearly 6 million acres, equivalent in size to Denali National Park in Alaska. Considering that half of the climbing destinations are located more than a half hour from the road, serenity reigns—the cliffs are as wild as the forests you pass through.

The Adirondack Park

The Adirondack Park was one of our nation's first protected areas (second to Yellowstone National Park). One of New York State's original missions in forming the park was to increase public landholdings until they comprised half of the total area. This goal, which promises more climbing opportunities, is getting closer with recent large land purchases. The blue line, as the park's boundary is called, surrounds public, private and municipal land—the towns located within have always been essential to the park's character. An early boom-and-bust period of logging and mining has now been replaced by tourism that consists of visitors who love the area's rich history and abundant outdoor activities. The small towns that have become popular vacation resorts struggle to provide year-round employment, living wages, and services for their residents, so by eating at the local restaurants, frequenting the gear shops, hiring one of the area's knowledgeable guides, or telling friends back home about your experience in the Adirondacks, you're doing your part to sustain this unique place.

Within the blue line, you find ski areas, colleges, factories, and busy towns. The park is unique in its capacity to encompass both the human and the natural and as metropolitan areas expand, the park's importance as a wilderness preserve becomes more apparent now than ever before. This is a place with remote expanses where you can hike for days without seeing another person.

This Guidebook

The number of cliffs and routes in the entire park far exceeds its climbers. Other than the popular spots in the park, the vast majority of cliffs have only a handful of visitors annually. If you want a wild experience, one that is far from the road and close to nature, you will have no difficulty finding such a cliff in this comprehensive book, and chances are you'll see little evidence that anyone else has ever visited.

Our primary goal is to get you to the base of a climb and give you the fine points of the ascent. You'll appreciate these details if you are a beginner climber or have chosen a route that is technically challenging. If you are a hardened adventurer, then our descriptions can be a springboard to your own explorations.

The climber's experience of the sport is captured by places visited, various partners, and challenges of particular routes, which add up to a rich backdrop of history. This guidebook continues the tradition established by previous guidebook authors by providing an extensive history inclusive of all routes—applauding and protecting the accomplishments of those who came before. With this clear documentation, you'll know where routes are located, their quality and grades, and who did the first ascents, allowing you to add new routes in a thoughtful and respectful manner.

This book shows the scope and potential of climbing areas in the park. There is a lot of undeveloped rock. By treading lightly on cliffs, it is possible to climb a route and leave little evidence of your passage. The Adirondack cliffs, like many natural resources, are finite and nonrenewable—they show scars much longer than a trampled forest, which can eventually regenerate. Many new crags discussed in this book are notable for their limited fixed protection and serve as a template, ideal, and guide for route development elsewhere in the park.

Undoubtedly there are undiscovered cliffs or ones that have been visited by climbers but whose history has been lost. We eagerly anticipate what the next generation of climbers will reveal.

The Area

Getting There

The Adirondack Park, roughly the size of Vermont, is hard to miss. It occupies nearly the entire upper portion of New York State. The primary points of entry are shown on the map (page 4) and accessed from the obvious interstate highways: the Northway (I-87), which runs north–south through the east side of the park; I-81, which runs north–south just west of the park; and the Thruway (I-90), which is to the south and runs east–west. Some popular tips and shortcuts are given here.

REFUEL OFTEN

There are few 24-hour gas stations, so plan accordingly.

NY 8 SHORTCUT

There are no fast east–west routes through the park: traveling from one side to the other can take 4 hr or more. (In other words, going through Old Forge is your last resort.) The exception is NY 8, the most convenient route for travelers coming from the west (e.g., Toronto, Buffalo, and Syracuse) aiming for the High Peaks and the southern areas. It is fast (shaving off an hour or more compared to going around the park through Albany), scenic, and has little traffic. There are few options for gas and groceries, though, so make sure you fill up first.

Take the Thruway (I-90) to Exit 33 in Verona, go northeast on NY 365, then northeast on NY 8 through Speculator and Wevertown. After Riparius, take US 9 north to Pottersville (24-hour gas), then get on the Northway (I-87).

DEALING WITH LAKE CHAMPLAIN

If you're coming from northern New Hampshire and Vermont, then all routes lead to Burlington. The Adirondacks beckon you from across the lake, but it takes more than an hour to get there. If you're going to Poke-O or Silver Lake, use the Grand Isle Ferry (www.ferries.com), as it is cheap, runs frequently, and avoids the hassles of south Burlington. Go north on I-89 to Burlington and continue north to Exit 17. Go east on US 2 to Grand Isle, then west on Ferry Road (VT 314) to the ferry dock. The ferry takes 12 min and runs every 15 min. Once you're in New York, follow NY 314 to the Northway (I-87) and go south. (This is Northway Exit 39 if you're reversing the route.)

If you're going to the Keene Valley area, head north on I-89 to Burlington, west on I-189 to its end, south on US 7 past Charlotte to Vergennes, south on VT 22A, then west on VT 17 to the Crown Point Bridge. Go north on NY 9N / NY 22 to Port Henry, west on Tarber Hill Road / Broad Street (CR 4), bear right onto Dugway Road (CR 4) to Moriah Center, northwest on Witherbee Road (CR 70) to Witherbee, then west on Tracy Road (CR 6) to the Northway and US 9 at Exit 30.

A popular alternative is to cross Lake Champlain on the Charlotte–Essex Ferry. In Charlotte, take Ferry Road (VT F5) west to the ferry dock. The ferry takes about 20 min and runs every 30 min; check the ferry schedule at www.ferries.com. Once you're in Essex, follow NY 22 to Wadhams, then take the Elizabethtown–Wadhams Road to US 9 in Elizabethtown.

COMING FROM CANADA

If you're coming from points along the northern shore of Lake Ontario, make your way to the Thousand Islands Bridge, then south on I-81 to Exit 48 in Watertown, east on NY 342, east on NY 3, east on NY 3A, then back on NY 3 to Cranberry Lake and Tupper Lake.

If you're coming from Ottawa, the best crossing is at the Ogdensburg–Prescott Bridge. Once you're across, take NY 68 to US 11 at Canton. Two options lead from here into the park: (a) south on NY 56, then east on NY 3 to Tupper Lake; or (b) east on US 11 to Potsdam, east on NY 11B, southeast on NY 458, south on NY 30 to Paul Smiths, then south on NY 86 to Saranac Lake and Lake Placid.

From Montreal, take AUT-15 south to the Lacolle–Champlain crossing. This is the largest border crossing and the delays can be considerable, with 20 min being typical. Early mornings are best, followed by late evenings. The alternatives (Rouses Point, Mooers) are less direct and usually not worth the extra time for the detour.

When to Come

Compared to the majority of the Northeast, the climate in the Adirondacks is wetter and colder than average—in fact, it's one of the coldest spots in the country. In the summer, the average daily temperatures are between 70°F and 80°F, with a range up to 25° (and as much as 30° in the High Peaks). Precipitation remains relatively constant throughout the summer at around 3"–4" per month. In general, it's wetter on the west side of the park than on the east side, and the High Peaks are colder and wetter than everywhere else.

The weather within the park can vary greatly, as conditions found online will illustrate. However, most of the current conditions that are reported at websites originate from stations located outside the park. Only a few locations, such as Old Forge and Saranac Lake, provide current conditions from within the park.

As early as April, although snow still blankets much of the region, climbing can begin at some south-facing cliffs. The Spider's Web always seems first on everyone's list, but there are plenty of other options—Hurricane,

Poke-O Slab, Potash Cliff, and Potter Mountain are great early season; see Appendix B, page 531, for more ideas). With no leaves on the trees, this is a good time to visit the harder-to-find cliffs, such as Lost Hunters, The Courthouse, or Pinnacle Mountain. Expect very wet approaches, and, for some cliffs, bring snowshoes. Optimal conditions continue until the middle of May, when the blackflies emerge.

The summer months range from perfect to hot and buggy. If it's hot, look for climbing up high (e.g., Wallface, Cascade Pass, Noonmark) or on north-facing cliffs (e.g., Avalanche Lake, Barkeater, Barton High Cliff, High Falls Crag, Cascade Cliff), or coordinate your climbing with the sun and chase the shade (Spider's Web and Upper Washbowl face toward the west; Poke-O Main Face and Chapel Pond Slab are oriented toward the east). South-facing slabs are best avoided on sunny days (e.g., Rogers Rock, Poke-O Slab). There's plenty of climbing near water (e.g., Bluff Island, Long Pond, Eagle Falls, Boquet River Crags, anything around Chapel Pond), providing ample opportunities to swim and enjoy the heat of the day (see Appendix B on page 531 for a complete list). Avoid bugs by sticking to the windy cliffs (e.g., Avalanche Pass, Poke-O Moonshine, Upper Washbowl, or Pitchoff Chimney Cliff) or those cliffs near BTI water treatment (anything near Chapel Pond). The insect population begins to decline in August.

The best months for climbing are September and October—the air is crisp and clear, all the cliffs are open, bugs are gone, snakes are hiding, summer vacationers have left, and daytime temperatures are perfect. Nights routinely dip below freezing. Even on cold days, the rock on the south-facing cliffs can be quite pleasant. As the season progresses toward winter, cliffs at lower elevations become better options (e.g., Potash Cliff, Stewart's Ledge, Shelving Rock, and Deadwater). The season continues into November with the occasional sunny day, but by Thanksgiving, it's time to break out the ice gear.

Rain and Rest Day Activities

If the rain is just starting, then the Spider's Web and King Wall stay dry longer than anywhere else. If it isn't absolutely pouring, you can go for a hike, perhaps investigating other cliffs. See Appendix B (page 531) for more ideas.

Summer recreational opportunities in the park are endless, and it seems only fitting to take advantage of what the region has to offer—mountains and lakes. You're really missing out if you haven't paddled down a remote winding bog or visited the alpine zones on the bare summits of the High Peaks.

For shopping, you can pass the time by visiting the shops in Keene Valley, Lake Placid, Lake George, and Old Forge. You can take the ferry to Burlington for shopping, restaurants, and a climbing gym.

The Keene Valley Library (518.576.4335, www.keenevalleylibrary.org) has a large collection of climbing-related materials contained in a special room in the basement, donated by John Case. It has computers, a copy machine, and free wireless high-speed Internet access. Check first, as its hours are unusual.

The Adirondack Museum at Blue Mountain Lake (518.352.7311, www.adkmuseum.org) is excellent, as is the Wild Center Natural History Museum (www.wildcenter.org, 518.359.7800) in Tupper Lake, and the Lake Placid Olympic Museum (www.whiteface.com, 518.302.5326). Historic forts are located at either end of Lake George: Fort Ticonderoga (www.fortticonderoga.org, 518.585.2821) and Fort William Henry (www.fwhmuseum.com, 518.668.5471). The Barton Garnet Mines in North River (www.garnetminetours.com, 518.251.2706) offer guided tours of this famous geologic site.

Layout of the Park

The Adirondack Park is unique in that it is a patchwork of private and public land. Out of approximately 5.8 million acres, roughly half the land is private. There is no climbing on private land unless you have the express permission of the landowner. Out of the remaining area, roughly 0.4 million acres are water (so no climbing there), and 2.5 million acres are public.

The public land is part of the New York State Forest Preserve, created in 1894 by a constitutional amendment, which requires that the lands be "forever kept as wild forest lands." There are several classifications of public land, broken down by the land's characteristics and ability to withstand use. The regulations are different for each classification. (The full set of regulations is contained in the Adirondack Park State Land Master Plan, on the Adirondack Park Agency website, www.apa.state.ny.us.) Even more confusing, each tract of land (wilderness, primitive, or otherwise) is managed according to a unit management plan (or UMP), and each one is different. (For example, climbing groups are limited in size and number of ropes in the Dix Wilderness Area but not in the High Peaks Wilderness Area.) The land classifications are as follows:

Wild Forest: Land that has a wild character but permits a higher degree of human use, such as biking, snowmobiles, and ATVs (although their use may be restricted by the UMP for the specific area).

Wilderness: Land where nature prevails and people are only visitors; land that has a primeval character, with the "imprint of man's work substantially unnoticed." Wilderness lands are the most regulated: no structures, no bikes, no motorized equipment, and tighter regulations on camping.

Primitive: Similar to wilderness but may have some inholdings (e.g., structures, roads, fire towers) or some other qualities that prevent it from meeting wilderness standards. Bikes are only allowed on existing roads and truck trails.

Intensive Use: Land where the state provides facilities for outdoor recreation, such as state campgrounds (e.g., Rogers Rock) and ski areas (e.g., Gore Mountain, Whiteface).

Where to Stay

There is a vast assortment of camping and lodging options that are simply beyond the scope of this book. Some general guidelines are offered here, with more specific options that are popular with climbers at the beginning of each chapter.

CAMPING

There is a basic set of rules for camping that apply to all forest preserve land. You can camp anywhere as long as it is 150' from a road, water, or a trail. Also, you can camp at any site designated with a yellow "Camp Here" disk. Fires are allowed using deadwood and downed wood, and you can bring pets as long they are under your control.

Groups up to 10 people can camp without a permit for up to three nights, beyond which a permit is required. Groups larger than 10 require a permit regardless of the length of stay. Camping is limited to two weeks at any location. Permits are obtained by calling the Forest Ranger Office in Ray Brook (518.897.1300) during business hours.

For disposal of human waste, the DEC encourages the use of the "leave no trace" principles (www.lnt.org)—e.g., 200' from a stream, buried 6"–8", toilet paper in the hole.

COMMANDO CAMPING

"Commando camping" is illegal camping, and every climber does it—sleeping at trailheads, pullouts, and other unsanctioned spots. The rangers know that climbers like to get an early start and probably won't bother you if you are discreetly sleeping a few hours *in your vehicle* before heading out at first light. Set up a tent, though, and you're asking for trouble. If you need to set up a tent or roll out a sleeping bag, then wander off 150' into the woods.

LODGING

A good resource for finding lodging is the Adirondack Regional Tourism Council (www.visitadirondacks.com). Its website has a search feature that allows you to narrow choices by a variety of criteria, including location and price.

The Adirondack Climbing Experience

Most of the cliffs in this guidebook have solid, climbable rock, but every cliff has its share of grunge—lichen; moss; pesky cedars; and grassy, dirt-filled cracks. The routes that see traffic stay cleaner, but even so, the Adirondacks have a way of reclaiming routes with alarming speed. Generally speaking, north- and west-facing cliffs are the dirtiest. For routes that aren't as well traveled, you should carry a wire brush to clean off the occasional key hold. For harder routes, you may want to inspect the line beforehand and do some cleaning. A nut tool for the leader is essential for excavating protection placements.

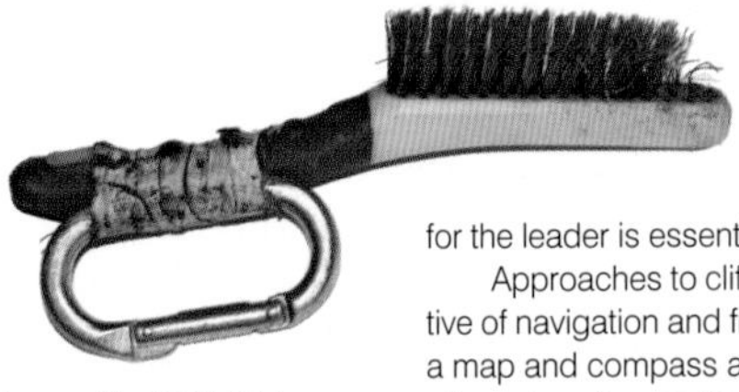

Approaches to cliffs in this guide can be a challenge, both from the perspective of navigation and from the sheer brutality of the bushwhack. For remote cliffs, a map and compass are essential and, for the gadget-minded, a GPS (or smartphone with GPS). Make sure you know how to use them. Unless you want scars, pants and a long-sleeved shirt should be considered for the more intense bushwhacks.

In the summer, there are the additional hazards of heat and insects. For the heat, check the aspect of the cliff so that you can avoid direct sun. For insects, a good repellent is essential; everyone has his or her own preference, but the ones with DEET tend to work longer. When the bugs are really bad, a long-sleeved shirt, pants, and thin socks work well. A head net is essential, especially for the belayer. The climate and terrain vary considerably in the park, as do the hatching schedules, so while climbers at Crane Mountain are hiding beneath head nets, those at the Spider's Web are climbing shirtless.

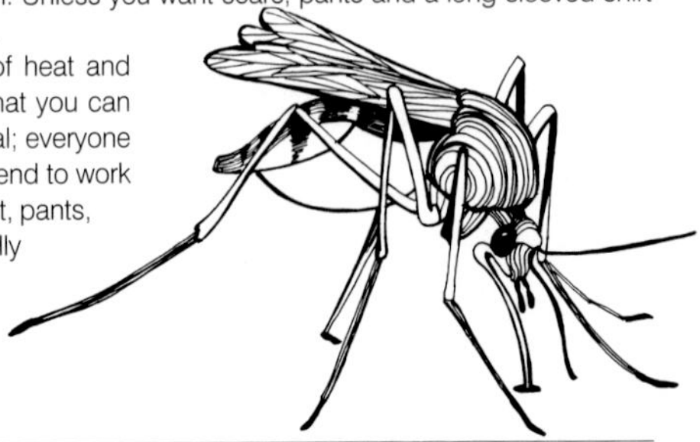

Black bears can be an issue when camping in the backcountry. Bear canisters are required for overnight camping in the High Peaks Wilderness Area. Outside that area, you'll still want to hang your food out of reach of bears. Poisonous snakes are a concern at some cliffs (see below), especially those around Lake George, and are noted in the cliff descriptions.

For remote climbs, hydration is very important, and you'll probably want more than you're willing to carry. Giardia bacteria have contaminated most of the water in the park, making it unsafe to drink without treatment. Backcountry climbers often carry a water filter or iodine tablets.

Poison ivy is a hazard at many lower-elevation cliffs, and it seems to be creeping in at the cliffs in the High Peaks as well. It's usually found in open, sunny areas near the base of cliffs and in the talus. Direct contact is required, but as little as a billionth of a gram of the oil is all that is needed to cause a rash, so know how to identify it and don't rub against it. The presence of poison ivy is noted in the cliff descriptions.

The Adirondack Rack: An "Adirondack rack" isn't all that unique, although, as with any other climbing areas, special gear is occasionally needed. For most climbing, a single set of cams up to 3.5", nuts, and microcams should suffice. For longer routes, double up on the cams. Specialized hardware includes larger cams (up to 6" for some of the off widths), slider nuts (especially at Rogers Rock), and RPs (especially at Poke-O).

Climbing and Endangered Species

PEREGRINE FALCONS

Peregrine sightings are one of the true pleasures of climbing in the Adirondacks. These majestic crow-sized falcons can be seen soaring around cliffs, diving at speeds up to 180 mph in pursuit of prey, transferring food midair, and performing aerial acrobatics during their courtship. They mate for life and often return to the same nesting site year after year, with a life span as long as 20 years. The peregrine population was all but wiped out due to exposure to DDT and other chemicals, and they were gone from the region by 1965.

Peregrine falcons returned to the Adirondacks as nesting birds in 1985, after an intensive, statewide restoration program. There are now over two dozen nesting pairs of peregrines present in the Adirondack region, which are closely monitored annually by the Department of Environmental Conservation (DEC) and by volunteer climbers and others. Rock climbers have been a great asset in this effort and have assisted the DEC with peregrine falcon protection and management for many years now by annually monitoring favored aeries (nesting sites) for occupancy; reporting new nest locations; advising on access points, climbing route designations, and cliff closures; and assisting with the occasional recovery of unhatched eggs or banding of young. Periodic cliff closures at some of the most popular climbing and nesting sites have been well respected and are essential to the successful nesting of the falcons. A single incidence of disturbance during the most sensitive period of incubation, or when a nestling is vulnerable to chilling, predation, or falling off the ledge before it can fly, can make all the difference between a successful and an unsuccessful nesting season.

In addition to heeding closure postings, the DEC asks that while climbers are climbing on open routes, they avoid disturbing peregrine falcons, not only for the sake of the peregrines but for climber safety as well. Peregrine falcons defend their nesting territories aggressively, vocalizing, circling overhead, and often diving at and even striking people (and predators) with their sharp talons. If you encounter such aggressive peregrine behavior, you should abandon your climb and report the incident to the DEC. The closures are generally posted on signs at trailheads, on approach paths used by climbers, and sometimes at the base of the cliffs, but consult the DEC website for more complete information. The closures sometimes apply to an entire cliff, or for larger cliffs like Poke-O, the signs may indicate a subsection of a cliff. All climbing activities are prohibited within the closed area. Access to the cliff or area immediately below for any purpose is prohibited when the area is closed, except for walking without loitering along the base to reach open areas or as otherwise specified by DEC.

The DEC makes every effort to ensure that the closures are focused on the cliff areas that affect peregrine activity and that cliffs are opened as soon as possible after the nesting season. Peregrine falcons are listed as an endangered species in New York State and are fully protected under state and federal laws. Climber assistance with this and other endangered species is vital for their continued recovery.

ROCK AND SNOW
Das ist der Hammer
This
Rock and Snow
original tee &
many others,
as well as
a great
selection of
climbing gear
at
rockandsnow.com
Also in
the Gunks
at one of the
oldest and wisest
climbing shops
in the country

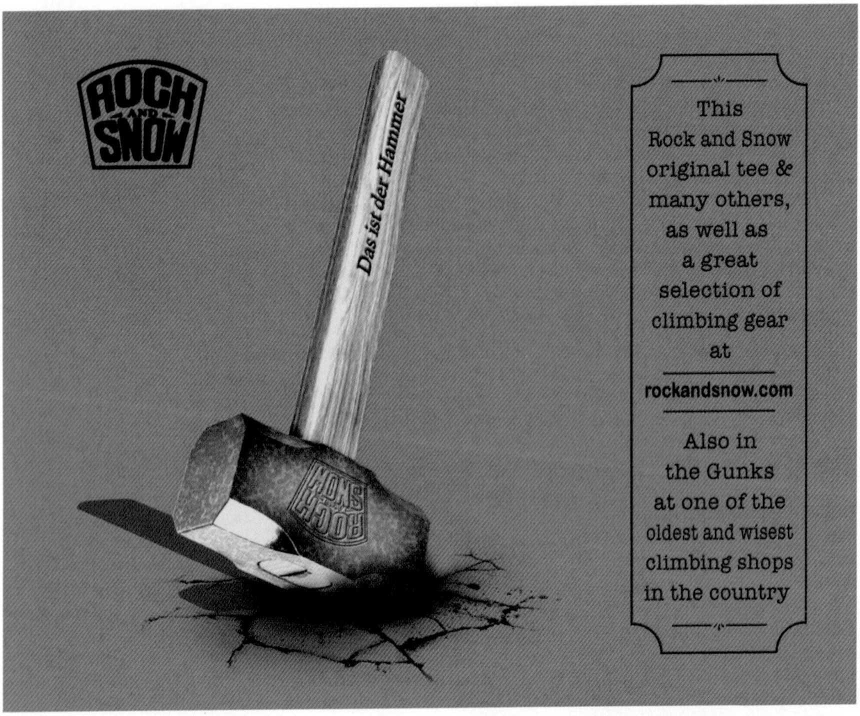

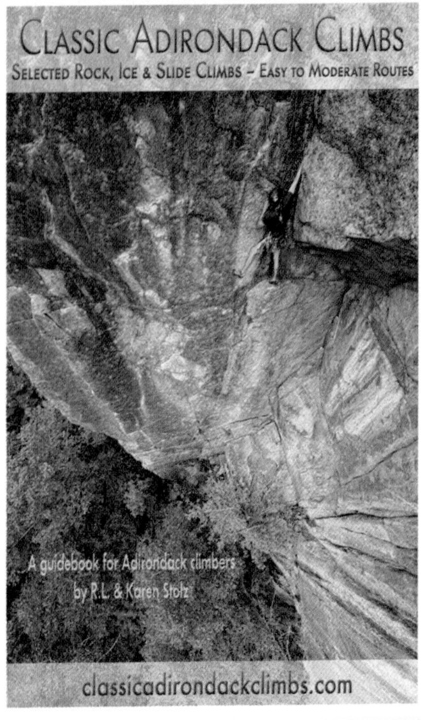

Classic Adirondack Climbs
Selected Rock, Ice & Slide Climbs – Easy to Moderate Routes
A guidebook for Adirondack climbers
by R.L. & Karen Stolz
classicadirondackclimbs.com

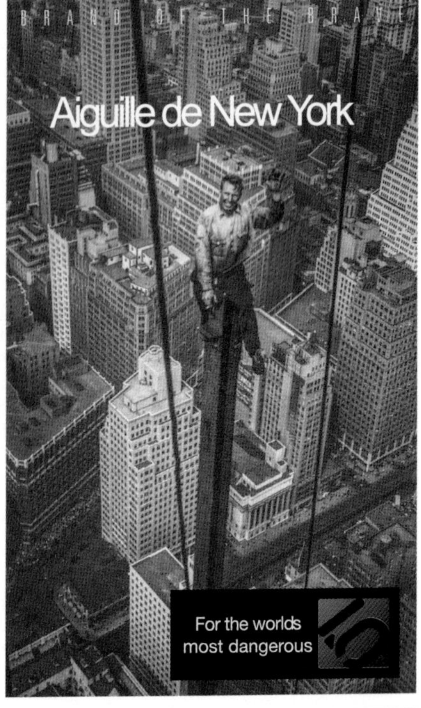

BRAND OF THE BRAVE
Aiguille de New York
For the worlds
most dangerous

Local Climbing Practices

by Dominic Eisinger

The Adirondacks, like many other climbing areas of the world, have seen a variety of trends and styles with regard to the use of fixed protection and route preparation. A common philosophy of minimizing human impact in the Adirondack Park is shared by the Adirondack climbing community and will help ensure that we maintain our freedom, which is by its nature individualistic and free-spirited.

NEW ROUTES

If you are contemplating a new route and you can climb it from the ground up without placing fixed protection, fantastic! If the route requires a little cleaning, then so be it. If the route requires complete excavation, then keep a few things in mind. It's dirty for a reason, and it will grow back. Will it be a popular addition to the repertoire of climbs at that cliff? Will it be worth your trouble and the disruption caused by your cleaning?

The decision to place fixed protection requires further soul-searching. Fixed protection should only be placed if there *are no options* for natural protection, and for the benefit of the community as a whole. For this reason, toprope the route first and make every effort to make an informed decision. Have your friends climb it to double-check your decision. Research the history of the area: respect the style of new-route development that has occurred in that area and check with local climbers and the guidebook to make sure it has not already been climbed. Ask yourself a few questions: Is it a place others will climb, or is the route destined for obscurity? Is the route independent from its neighbors? Is the route good enough, and will it stay clean enough, to warrant the fixed protection? Can people of different body sizes reach the protection? Is it an untouched area with no signs of human influence, far from the road? How much of your motivation is driven by an ephemeral pleasure—altering the rock for your own self-interest on a marginal route that nobody will repeat? Maybe it's better left as a toprope first ascent.

ROUTE PREPARATION

Scrubbing lichen from holds, cleaning dirt from cracks for protection, breaking the occasional branch to squeeze by a tree, or removing a dangerous loose block are all accepted practices. Scrubbing an 8'-wide swath and cutting trees are not only illegal but aren't accepted by the climbing community. There's a fine line between what's necessary for climbing and what constitutes excessive behavior in the eyes of the management agencies, and we should always err on the side of minimal impact.

Keep in mind, plenty of adventure can be had by reclaiming existing high-quality routes from relentless Adirondack lichen. There is no shortage of routes that are presently too dirty to climb. The adventure of such rediscovery can fulfill an undeniable motivation for why we climb—total absorption in challenging one's ability, with mind and body coming together on a tremendous route.

FIXED ANCHORS

For existing routes, no additional protection or fixed anchors should be added without the consent of the first-ascent party. Fixed anchors have been installed by the climbing community where necessary for safety and preservation of fragile terrain and trees. When replacing or adding new anchor slings, black and gray webbing certainly blends into the background better than the bright colors of the rainbow. This is especially true at highly visible areas such as Avalanche Lake, where 100 hikers a day will see your webbing and complain.

HARDWARE

When new or replacement fixed protection is needed, use high-quality stainless-steel hardware manufactured specifically for climbing. Hardware should match the color of the rock.

Photo by Joel Dashnaw.

HERD PATHS

For popular cliffs, land managers often see "herd paths" as a good thing, as they confine impact to one place. To the extent possible, use existing herd paths and refrain from adding additional markings such as surveyor tape and reflector disks—these are litter and ruin the wilderness experience for others. If a new herd path is created, it is recommended that it be direct (easier to sight along), narrow (less invasive, better defined), and marked discreetly only with natural materials such as rock cairns.

Please respect and pay attention to preserving the special one-of-a-kind place that defines the Adirondack Park, a quality that makes climbing here so exceptional.

TIMBER RATTLESNAKES

Occasionally, another rare New York State species, the timber rattlesnake, might also be encountered while you're climbing in the Adirondacks, specifically in the Lake George or southern Lake Champlain region. The snake measures from 3' to 4.5' and has a broad triangular head. Two color phases are commonly found: a yellow phase, which has black or dark brown crossbands on a lighter background of yellow, and a black phase, which has dark crossbands on a dark background. The most distinctive feature is the rattle at the end of the tail, although the rattles regularly break off.

Climbers should be aware that they may encounter rattlesnakes, take appropriate safeguards to avoid them, and understand that they are fully protected as a New York State threatened species and should not be disturbed. Timber rattlesnakes are most active and likely to be encountered from mid-May until early October. The rocky talus slopes below the cliffs and open canopied basking spots above the cliffs (i.e., the areas that climbers pass through to approach a climb or descend from one) are the most problematic areas.

As a precaution, be aware of where you walk and where you set your pack down, especially around talus, bushes, and logs. Consider wearing pants and boots. If you walk at a normal pace, the snakes will generally move away, hide, or issue a warning with their rattles. Bites are rare and usually occur when a snake is cornered or surprised. Staying back 3' is usually enough to avoid a strike. In the event of a bite, immobilize the victim and transport him or her immediately to the nearest medical facility. Suction, incisions, alcohol, or drugs are no longer recommended treatments.

REPORTING

To report activity, or obtain further information on these or other New York State endangered and threatened species, visit the New York State Department of Environmental Conservation (DEC) website (www.dec.ny.gov) or call the Ray Brook Wildlife Office (518.891.1291) or the Endangered Species Unit (518.402.8863).

Local climbing legends Tom Yandon (left) and Joe Szot (right), relaxing at Cascade Lakes in 2006.

Using This Guidebook

The park has been divided into 11, and split into two volumes for convenience. The master map in the front of the book will orient you to the various regions and how they are split into the two volumes. Each region begins with information specific to that region, including a locator map, crag planning table, general driving directions, amenities, camping and lodging options, common trailheads, and access issues.

The fundamental organizational unit of the book is the cliff (a continuous face of open rock), and a region is simply a collection of cliffs within the same geographic area. Cliffs are sometimes organized into groups—for instance, when several cliffs are referred to by a single name or share a common approach or trailhead, such as the Beer Walls. To assist in locating routes along the base of a cliff, a cliff is often divided into named sections—for example, Poke-O is divided into 15 sections, including The Waterfall, Luther Wall, Nose Apron, and so forth.

Cliff Descriptions

Each cliff has a summary table that provides a quick overview of the cliff with the following information:

Location: Brief description of the cliff's location and from where it is approached.

Aspect: Direction in which the cliff faces.

Height: Height of the cliff in feet (not the length of the longest route).

Quality: 0 to 5 stars, with 5 stars being the best.

Approach: Length (in time) of the approach and difficulty.

Easy	A short approach, not strenuous, with simple navigation.
Moderate	Involves some bushwhacking, requires some compass work, and is moderately strenuous.
Difficult	Usually long, very strenuous, and can involve blind bushwhacking with complex orienteering.

Summary: A very brief description of the cliff.

Route Table: Distribution of free-climbing grades at a cliff, including the total number of routes at the cliff. Each grade has two bars: the red bar shows the total routes of that grade, and the gold bar shows how many of these are high quality (three stars or above). The total number of routes listed in this summary includes aid routes and uncompleted projects, so the numbers may not add up.

The summary table is followed by some or all of these entries:

Description: In-depth discussion of the cliff, what the rock is like, the type of climbing, and other notes.

History: Brief discussion of the history of climbing on that cliff.

Camping: Options for cliffs commonly visited as an overnight (such as Wallface) or ones with noteworthy camping nearby.

Directions: How to get to the cliff, including driving directions to the trailhead and a description of the hiking approach.

Driving directions are given from easy-to-find landmarks, like an exit on the Northway (I-87) or a prominent town or road intersection. At the point from which mile markers begin, the expression "(0.0 mile)" appears in the text. Subsequent mileages are provided in the text and increase from that starting location. Mileages are from our own car odometers, and since odometer readings can be affected by tire size and whatnot, you should expect some minor deviations.

Official designations are used for road names: "I" for an interstate, "US" for a U.S. route, "NY" for a New York State route, and "CR" for a county route. Some roads have names and route numbers, both of which are given. Some roads have multiple designations, such as when a road crosses into an adjacent county, and are often noted.

Hiking distances are often described in terms of time rather than mileage. This is obviously subjective, but it is difficult to quantify a bushwhack by mileage. The approach times assume a reasonably fit individual hiking at a moderate pace with no breaks. The directions "left" and "right" are provided with respect to the direction of travel. Times are given in hours (abbreviated "hr") and minutes (abbreviated "min"), as in "1 hr 20 min." Times are often accumulated from a starting point, marked by the expression "(0 hr 0 min)" in the text.

Descent Options: Lists the various walk-off or rappel descents for the cliff, when known. Some routes have their own descents, which are indicated in the route description.

Maps

Approach maps are provided for cliffs with involved or obscure approaches. These maps are usually oriented with true north at the top and are created to scale. Magnetic north is 14° west of true north. The maps in this book differ from USGS (United States Geological Survey) maps. First, the topographical lines are de-emphasized to allow you to focus on other landmarks while still getting a sense of the terrain. Second, the contours aren't labeled, but most maps use a contour interval of 6 m. Third, only features that are needed to get oriented and find the cliff are included, reducing the clutter found on the USGS maps.

Download Free Topos

If you're tempted to photocopy the topos, maps, and aerial photos—don't bother. You can download many of these in Adobe Acrobat PDF file format format from www.adirondackrock.com.

Print them, fold them, shove them in your pocket, and take them up routes. There is no need to carry this heavy book up routes, tear pages out, or damage the spine of this book on a photocopier. Best of all, you can print them as large as you want.

A key to map symbols is provided on the inside back cover of the book.

Route Descriptions

The routes on a cliff are numbered and are always described from left to right, without exception. Admittedly, this is awkward for some cliffs, like those whose approach trail reaches the right end of the cliff. In these cases, you'll simply have to flip backward as you walk to the left. But at least you can open to any page and be sure of the orientation. The route numbers correspond to those used in the cliff photos and topos.

The typical entry for a route begins with a route heading with the route name, difficulty grade, protection rating, length, and quality. After the heading are entries for the start, each pitch (numbered P1, P2, and so on), gear list (if any), descent options, history, and first-ascent information. A difficulty rating, protection rating, and length are provided for each pitch. In some instances, this information wasn't available and is omitted. Toprope routes aren't described with the same level of detail and are shown in paragraph form, as are routes where information is scarce or where you can wander anywhere.

NCCS Grades

The National Climbing Classification System (NCCS), or commitment grade, indicates the time investment required for an average party to ascend the route. The scale goes from 1 to 7 and is always listed in roman numerals, I to VII.

The vast majority of the routes in the Adirondacks are grade I or II, which implies that they are less than five pitches in length and close to the road—not very committing. Many routes at Poke-O Moonshine, Moss Cliff, and Wallface are grade III—sustained and serious undertakings that can take the entire day to complete. Grade IV routes take a full day and are at least eight pitches in length with sustained and difficult climbing and may involve sections of aid climbing. There are several grade-IV routes, all on Wallface; these are the only routes in this guidebook shown with a commitment grade in the route heading.

There are no V, VI, or VII routes in the park.

Difficulty Ratings

The class system compares the technical difficulty of the hardest section of each climb. These grades assume dry conditions, clean rock, and favorable weather. At the least, the class system can offer a sense of difficulty relative to other sections for the climb. There are six classes: 1st class is hiking on and off trail; 2nd class is hiking on rough trails and low-angle slides; 3rd class is scrambling with exposure using holds, where a fall would be dangerous; 4th class is scrambling with exposure, where an unroped fall would be fatal; 5th class is technical free climbing using a rope for safety, further divided using the Yosemite Decimal System (discussed below); and 6th class is aid climbing, also further divided into an aid rating.

This book is concerned almost exclusively with 5th class climbing, although some noteworthy 4th class scrambles and 6th class aid routes are included.

Yosemite Decimal System (YDS): Routes and individual pitches are given difficulty ratings using the Yosemite Decimal System. The grades from 5.0 through 5.9 are further modified with a + or - for those pitches that are thought to be hard or easy for their grade. The grades 5.10 and above are subdivided with letter grades: a, b, c, and d (e.g., 5.11b).

The grade of a route is often that of the most difficult move on the most difficult pitch. For instance, P1 of **Gamesmanship** at Poke-O Moonshine has a short 5.8 crux move at the bottom, then decent rests for the remainder of the pitch, making the overall grade 5.8. As routes become harder, steeper, and more sustained, pump becomes an issue and is factored into the grade. For example, **On The Loose** at Spider's Web has no move harder than 5.9, but the sustained and pumpy nature of the climbing warrants a grade of 5.10a.

Older routes were not originally reported with letter grades; when no modern information is available for a route 5.10 or above, then the grade is shown without the letter subdivisions. Some routes were reported without pitch-by-pitch difficulty ratings, and in a few cases, we've simply omitted the pitch grades until this information becomes available.

Difficulty grades vary with the type of climbing. There is almost no correlation between a 5.10 crack climb and a 5.10 slab. Further, ratings are often relative to other routes on the cliff; for example, many believe Rogers Rock to have its own rating system.

Finally, ratings are highly subjective and provoke endless debate. The grades in this guide are often the result of our own personal experience and a consensus of other climbers. However, sometimes we have to rely on the raw data submitted by others with no verification. If the route feels too difficult and you cannot adequately protect it, then retreat and come back another day.

DON'T LET THE DIFFICULTY RATING LULL YOU INTO A FALSE SENSE OF SECURITY.

A grade-conversion chart, with international scales, is provided in Appendix A (page 530).

AID RATINGS

The rating of an aid pitch considers both the difficulty of making a protection placement and the fall potential if the placement were to fail. The grades in the park range from A0 to A4 and are further modified with a + or - for those pitches that are thought to be hard or easy for their grade. The sophistication of aid-climbing equipment increases as the grade increases. A climber can stand in slings on an A0 or A1 pitch but would need aiders, daisy chains, and hooks for A2 and harder. When a pitch has been climbed without using a hammer (i.e., no pitons, bashies, or rivets), then a C (for clean placement) is substituted for the A.

- A0 Pulling on a piece of protection, tension on rope, pendulums.
- A1 Aid on solid placements, including small wires and cams.
- A2 Awkward placements, or a few body-weight placements above solid placements.
- A3 Hooking, rivets, and thin pitons with a 30' fall potential.
- A4 Extreme aid, big fall potential, and the threat of hitting an obstacle.

PROTECTION RATINGS

Routes and individual pitches are given the now-standard protection ratings (G, PG, R, X). The ratings assume that you know how to place gear and have placed it correctly, that you have proper-sized gear at the right moment, and that you take advantage of the protection opportunities that are available. Protection ratings provide no information on how difficult or strenuous it may be to place protection, but rather the security offered by the placements.

- G Good protection, closely spaced; small falls possible.
- PG Fair protection; moderate falls possible but not likely to result in serious injury.
- R Poor protection with long falls possible; injury likely if you fall from the wrong place. Some well-protected routes have unfortunate ledge positions where even a short fall can be injurious; these get R ratings as well. An R rating can be due to a lack of gear or poor quality of the rock into which gear is placed.
- X No protection; ground fall possible, with death likely if you fall from the wrong place.

Needless to say, you should be very solid at the grade before heading up an R- or X-rated route. Some excellent routes have no protection and are perhaps better recommended as a toprope.

A route's protection rating is that of the most difficult pitch. For R and X routes, we have attempted to determine the difficulty of the section of unprotected climbing, and, when known, the protection rating is further qualified. For example, the rating of **Space Walk** is "5.9 G (5.7 X)," which means that the most difficult climbing is 5.9 with good protection, but there's a serious fall potential in a 5.7 section. If the climb says, for example, "5.10b R," then you should assume the unprotected climbing is in a 5.10b section.

Protection ratings vary with the type of climbing. On a slab, falling on an R or X route may not be lethal but is certain to be an unpleasant, skin-abrading affair that should be avoided. On these types of routes, R and X are more an indication of how frequently you can place protection and the length of a potential fall rather than how messed up you'll be after the fall.

If you are unable to arrange adequate protection, then **DON'T ASSUME IT GETS BETTER** just because this guidebook doesn't give it an R or X rating. Every route is potentially an R or X route if, for example, you skip opportunities for protection, get off route, place your protection poorly, or fixed protection fails. Retreat and come back another day.

Protection ratings are often subject to other factors, like body height, having the right gear at the right time, and so forth. Critical placements, when known, are often noted in the route descriptions.

Quality Ratings

We have adopted a five-star system for rating routes and cliffs. The more stars, the better. A rough translation is as follows:

No stars: Not recommended. Either it's a nasty route, or we simply don't know and can't find anyone who's climbed it. Often a route is too dirty to climb and might otherwise be recommended if it were cleaned.

★ Worth doing if you're at the crag.

★★ Should do it if you're at the crag.

★★★ Good route for the cliff, worth traveling to the crag for this route.

★★★★ Excellent route, a classic.

★★★★★ Highly recommended, one of the best in the park.

The criteria for a "good" route are very subjective and make for great debate. Our criteria are based on consideration of the following: consensus from other climbers, quality of the movement, quality of the rock, position, exposure, views, history, comfortable belays, and general atmosphere at the cliff. An average route next to a beautiful swimming hole would get a couple of stars, whereas an average route at the end of a long bushwhack with no views would receive fewer stars.

Finding the Start of a Route

Route starts are described relative to easy-to-locate features along the base of a cliff. We avoid the syndrome in which every route is described relative to some other route; relative distances between routes are important and we've included those measurements, but rarely are those measurements the only way to locate a route. Major features include obvious corners, large boulders, low roofs, or anything that is permanent and readily recognized. We avoid using vegetation (e.g., the "double-trunked oak tree") as the only way to locate a route, since this tends to change over time.

Route locations often refer to the terrain along the base of the cliff. The term *lowest point on the cliff* refers to where the terrain is at its lowest point, and moving in either direction along the base involves going uphill. Another terrain term is the *cone-shaped dirt slope,* where the ground spills out from an abrupt, high indentation along the base of the cliff.

Left and Right

In route descriptions, the terms *left* and *right* are from a climber's perspective while facing the rock. In approach descriptions, however, *left* and *right* are from a hiker's perspective and are referenced from the direction of travel. When an approach meets the cliff, these terms switch from a hiker's perspective to that of the climber. If there is any ambiguity, the terms are further qualified by a compass direction or by some other means. The terms become especially confusing when a climber finishes a route, then turns around to descend a gully, facing downhill like a skier. At these times, *left* and *right* are further qualified with *(climber's)* or *(skier's),* depending on whether you're facing the rock or facing downhill.

Other Climbing Terms

We use a collection of standard climbing terms to describe routes. Some of the important ones are listed here.

OVERHANGS

For overhangs, we've loosely adopted the terminology used by Dick Williams,[1] which takes the size of the feature into account:

overhang: A small overhang that protrudes 2' or less.
ceiling: A medium-sized overhang, roughly between 2' and 6'.
roof: A large overhang deeper than 6'.

CORNERS

There are many types of corners, and the terminology depends on the angle of the corner.
corner: The generic term *corner* refers to one whose angle is roughly 90°. A corner must face either left or right.
open book: A corner whose angle is obviously larger than 90°. An open book by itself faces out but can also be qualified as left- or right-facing.
V-corner: A corner whose angle is obviously less than 90°. A V-corner by itself faces out but can also be qualified as left- or right-facing.

1 Dick Williams, *The Climber's Guide to the Shawangunks* (2004).

CRACKS

Cracks vary from very narrow seams to chimney.
crack: A generic crack that could be any size.
seam: A faint crack that may take small protection, but you can't get your fingers in.
tips crack: A crack into which only the tips of your fingers can be inserted.
fingercrack: A crack that accepts fingers.
handcrack: A crack that accepts a hand.
fistcrack: A crack that accepts a fist.
off-width crack: A crack larger than your fist but smaller than your body.
chimney: A crack into which you can squeeze some or all of your body.
stem-box: A very wide chimney that is bridged with your legs.

LEDGES AND EDGES

Ledges vary from tiny edges to larger spacious forested terraces.
edge: A small edge, part of the rock face, that you can grab or stand on. An edge by itself is horizontal but can also be qualified as left- or right-facing.
rail: A long edge that you can shuffle your hands along.
flake: Same as an edge, but it's detached from the main rock face (i.e., there is space separating it from the primary surface of the rock).
ledge: A larger horizontal on which you can shuffle or walk.
ramp: A ledge that rises left or right. As a ramp steepens, it eventually becomes a leaning corner.
terrace: A very large ledge. Sometimes you can unrope and walk around on a terrace.

POCKETS

Pockets can vary from smaller than a fingertip to room-sized voids.
divot: A shallow indentation.
pocket: Will accept a finger.
hueco: Will accept a hand.
pod: Will accept an arm or more.

Variations

Routes sometimes have alternate sections or pitches. A variation tag, such as "(V1)," appears within the route description at the exact point where the variation begins. Variations are described after the normal route and are identified with the same tag. The difficulty rating of a variation applies only to the climbing on that variation, not to the entire pitch as climbed with that variation.

Gear Suggestions

When known, some routes have gear suggestions—for example: To 3", 2 ea 0.5"–0.75". This means a standard rack that covers placements up to 3", with double cams in the range between 0.5" and 0.75". (The "ea" means "each.") You should always use your own judgment when selecting gear, but our recommendations can help you decide what to haul in to those remote cliffs. Some routes have brand-specific gear beta offered by the first ascent party, which we've preserved in some cases.

Pitches entirely protected by fixed gear are marked with a solid blue circle ● before the P1 or V1 entry. The Adirondacks has precious few sport routes, and those with a blue dot come close. Be warned that despite having entirely fixed protection, many Adirondack routes can have dangerous runouts. For example, **Bill Route** (5.6+) at Roger's Rock is entirely bolt-protected, but has 30' runouts. The Adirondacks has its own style of "sport" routes. Older routes were often climbed ground up, meaning that the leader climbed to the next stance before drilling, creating routes with substantial runouts. Also, fixed protection is used as a last resort, and only if no natural placements are possible. Hence, there are relatively few pure sport routes.

There are many routes that come oh-so-close to being a "sport" route, but have an optional or required trad placement. These pitches are marked with a hollow blue circle ○ before the P1 or V1 entry, and the placements are mentioned in the gear list.

History and First Ascents

We believe that the history of a route adds an important perspective for those who follow. For this reason, each route has its own first-ascent information and occasionally a short history section. A historical summary for each cliff is also often provided. At a minimum, it adds an interesting human element to the route descriptions.

Route reporting is based on an honor system: if somebody says he or she did something, then, unless there's some obvious reason not to, we assume the claim is accurate. The first ascentionist names the route and provides the original description, difficulty rating, and other route details. (The difficulty rating may be adjusted by us or by community consensus.) Climbers are generally an agreeable lot, but even so, due to the lack of reporting, there are cases in which a route is known locally by one name but, upon further inquiry, it turns out that it was done years earlier and named something different. In these cases, the earlier name is used, and the more common local name is listed as an "aka" (also known as).

The first ascent (or "FA") of a route, when known, is provided at the end of each description. The date is given (as specific as is known) as well as the first-ascent party, listed in the order provided by the first-ascent party, which most often begins with the person who led the crux pitch. If the party shared equally in the climb, then we assume they've worked that out before submitting the route. A first free ascent (or "FFA") is listed when the first ascent is known to have been on aid. The term *as climbed by* (or "ACB") is used when the first-ascent party isn't sure if their ascent is the first, perhaps because they found some evidence of earlier passage (e.g., old pitons, slings on trees).

GPS Coordinates

This book contains GPS coordinates for every cliff and most parking areas. The coordinates are provided in UTM NAD-83 format. For example, the coordinate 619271,4917806 is UTM zone 18T (the entire park is in this zone), the x-axis (called "easting") 619271, and the y-axis (called "northing") 4917806. Coordinates are listed in the text next to the places to which they apply.

UTM coordinates are *x,y* values in a square grid of meters. They are easy to understand and use in equations; there's no degrees, minutes, seconds, or decimal values. The *x* and *y* values are in the same units (meters) in a square grid, not spherical polar coordinates. For example, 619272,4917806 is one meter to the right of 619271,4917806.

With a handheld GPS system, these coordinates can be used to assist in blind bushwhacking to remote cliffs. GPS coordinates can often be used with a car navigation system to help reach trailheads. The directions provided in this book do not rely on these coordinates; they are presented only for those who prefer using these tools. Be aware that when you're bushwhacking in a thick forest canopy, a GPS will lose its signal, rendering it useless. Navigating with a GPS almost always requires a compass as a backup.

GPS coordinates can also be used as an adjunct to other tools. The following tricks are particularly useful for planning trips into the Adirondack backcountry.

USGS Maps (www.adirondackrock.com/map.htm): On the maps page, type in the UTM coordinate to see a USGS topographical map with the coordinate centered.

Google Maps (maps.google.com): Convert the coordinate to decimal latitude/longitude (e.g., 44.40372269709332, -73.50216000198026), then type the comma-separated pair into Google Maps to display a map centered on that coordinate. The same feature is available at Bing Maps (www.bing.com/maps). There are plenty of online tools that perform UTM coordinate conversion, including the Adirondack Rock web site (www.adirondackrock.com/map.htm).

KML file (http://www.adirondackrock.com/cliffs.kml): The coordinates for all of the cliffs in this book are available in a KML file, a file used to display geographic data in earth browsers. Type the complete URL of the KML file into Google Maps to see a map of the entire Adirondack Park with markers for each cliff. This file can also be downloaded to your computer, then opened in Google Earth, allowing you to interactively browse the cliffs in the whole park.

SMARTPHONES

The popularity of smartphones with GPS has simplified backcountry navigation. Some popular apps are Topo Maps (by Philip Endicott, www.topomapsapp.com) and Gaia GPS (www.gaiagps.com). With these apps you can see your location on a USGS map, input GPS coordinates from this book, and navigate to them using the phone as a compass. Just like a normal GPS, though, watch the battery and your GPS signal in the forest canopy. Always carry a compass as a backup.

Be sure to check out the free topos available on www.adirondackrock.com.

Cliff Photos and Topos

Line diagrams (or "topos") are included for many cliffs to assist in finding and following routes, and to help you better understand the detailed terrain, fixed gear, and the spatial relationships among routes. With few exceptions, these diagrams were created from aerial photos and are drawn to scale.

A photo can sometimes be an effective tool for orienting yourself to a cliff, so we've included many cliff photos overlaid with route lines. For cliffs with a large number of climbs, such as Poke-O, we've included both a cliff photo with a few route lines (enough to get oriented, but limited to avoid obscuring the cliff features in the photo) and an accompanying comprehensive topo that was drawn from the same photo.

A key to topo symbols is provided on the inside back cover of the book.

Conduct

We climbers tend to be responsible land users with a full appreciation for the environment in which we play. With our expanding numbers and the increased scrutiny of land managers, it is imperative that we continue to portray ourselves favorably to the outside world and minimize the petty squabbles that plague other climbing centers.

The Department of Environmental Conservation (DEC) somewhat controls our conduct with general rules that prohibit cutting of vegetation and defacement of rock. The DEC also limits group size and restricts camping. This section adds to the formal rules with the following suggested behaviors:

Safety: First and foremost, don't get hurt. Nothing inhibits climbing freedoms more than the public's perception of irresponsible land users who make poor decisions and endanger others. If you see your fellow climbers make errors that affect their safety or endanger others, then speak up respectfully and offer to help.

Minimize your impact: The impact of the climbing community is most noticeable at the base of cliffs, so make every attempt to tread lightly. Avoid "pack dumps" that force everyone else to tromp off trail around your stuff. Stay on the established herd paths. Rappel from existing fixed anchors to avoid damage to the fragile cliff-top environment.

The Leave No Trace Center for Outdoor Ethics (www.lnt.org) is a nonprofit organization committed to minimizing environmental impacts by recreationists. Their tenets and commonsense guidelines are: (a) plan ahead and prepare, (b) travel and camp on durable surfaces, (c) dispose of waste properly, (d) leave what you find, (e) minimize campfire impacts, (f) respect wildlife, and (g) be considerate of other visitors.

Litter: Pack out what you pack in, and pick up the careless litter of others. If you smoke, take your butts with you.

Noise: The cliff is a shared environment where people go to enjoy the wilderness, so keep your voice down and shouting to a minimum. If you choose to bring music to the cliff, keep it to yourself and use headphones. At the few crags with cell-phone reception, keep your calls short and quiet. Turn off your ringer.

Beta: Don't offer unsolicited climbing beta. For many people, part of the game is figuring out the moves for themselves. Don't assume that someone is going to welcome your telling him or her how to do a problem.

Red tagging: On newer cliffs sometimes you'll find climbs with a small red tag on the first piece of fixed gear. This marks a new route that is somebody's active project. Ask around and find out more before jumping on it.

Courtesy: Be respectful of the climbers around you. Don't step on their ropes or kick their gear. If you have a pet, keep it under control and prevent it from stepping on the ropes and gear of others. If your intended route is occupied, then make a polite inquiry. While you're waiting, climb something nearby until they're finished. This does, however, mean you've given up your spot—no reserving routes.

If people are waiting for the route that you occupy, be accommodating and get on with your climb.

Passing: For longer routes, let faster teams pass you. You won't feel pressured, and the party behind won't get antsy. If you're the faster party, be patient and polite, and pass at a point that doesn't endanger others.

Rappelling: If you're rappelling, clearly yell "ROPE!" listen for a response, then throw your rope. If others are below you, they have priority—make sure you have their attention and permission before you throw. Use established fixed anchors when available and deemed safe. Avoid rappelling directly from trees, as repeated use kills a tree, especially birches. Instead, use dark-colored webbing and rappel rings. There are many options for rappel rings, the best being the stainless-steel rings made for climbing, and the cheapest being links of 7000-lb chain.

Toproping: Topropers have the same right to climb a route as do leaders, but nobody has the right to monopolize a route. If you're camped out on a route, be willing to share or move your rope aside if somebody wants to lead it. Don't leave your ropes unattended to reserve a route.

Avoid toproping through existing rappel anchors, and never toprope through webbing. Create your own anchor following best practices for anchor building. At fixed anchors, attach your own quickdraws to the anchor. Not only does this put the wear on your gear, but it allows other parties to share the anchor.

At cliff tops, use extreme care not to dislodge loose rock. Always assume there are people below you.

Chalk and brushing: If you use chalk, try not to overdo it. If you add tick marks, be sure to clean them off afterward. Use a nylon brush to remove excess chalk. Nylon brushes don't polish the holds as much as metal brushes do.

Landowner permission: If you want to climb on a cliff on private land, then get the landowner's permission. In general, landowners in the Adirondacks are accommodating, but only if you ask first. Some approaches in this guidebook cross private land. If you encounter the landowner, don't run away. Be respectful, listen, and do what he or she says.

Emergencies: Offer to help in the event of an emergency.

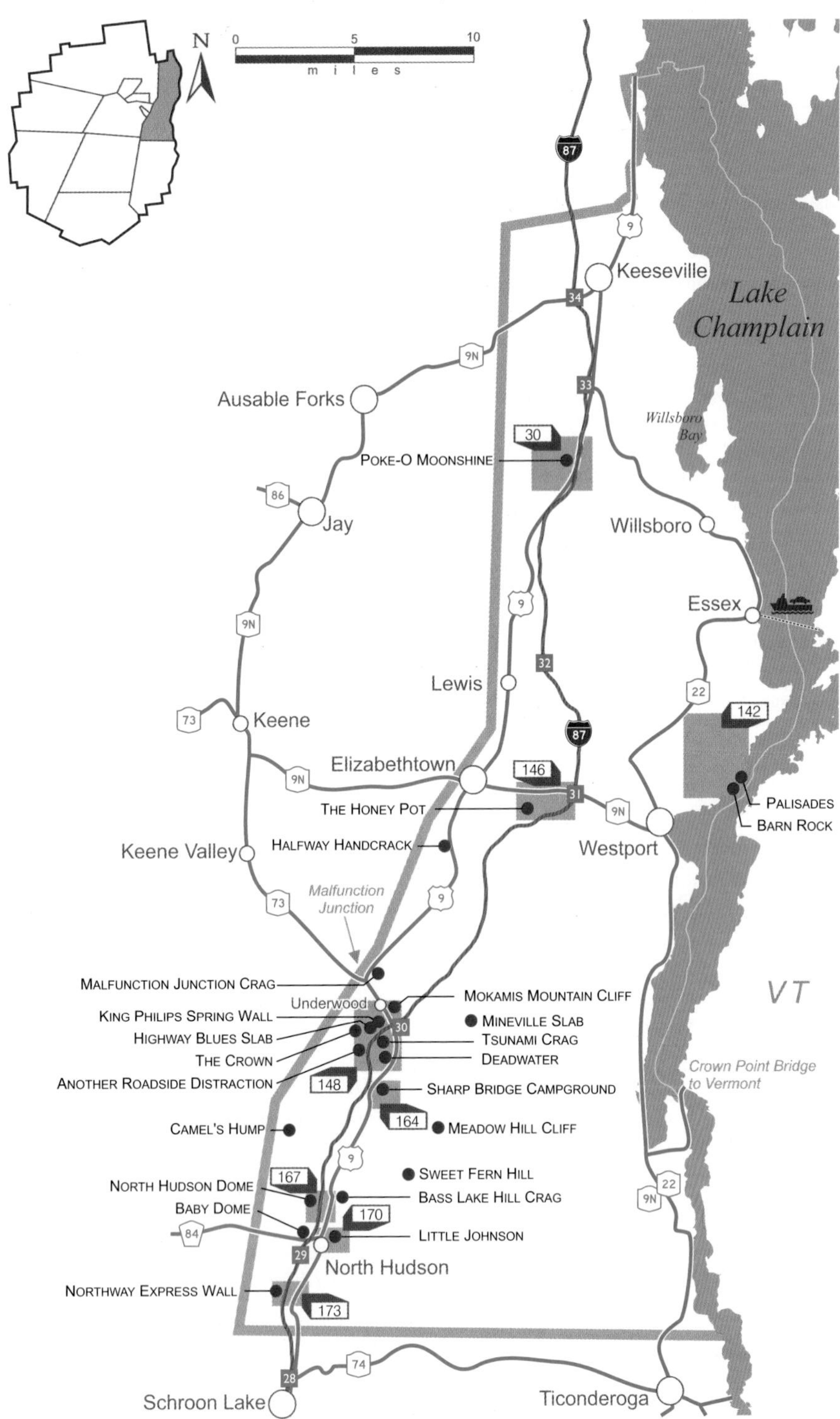

N
0
5
10
miles
Lake Champlain
Willsboro Bay
VT
Keeseville
Ausable Forks
Jay
Willsboro
Essex
Lewis
Keene
Elizabethtown
Keene Valley
Westport
Malfunction Junction
Underwood
North Hudson
Schroon Lake
Ticonderoga
Crown Point Bridge to Vermont
Poke-O Moonshine
The Honey Pot
Halfway Handcrack
Palisades
Barn Rock
Malfunction Junction Crag
King Philips Spring Wall
Highway Blues Slab
The Crown
Another Roadside Distraction
Mokamis Mountain Cliff
Mineville Slab
Tsunami Crag
Deadwater
Sharp Bridge Campground
Meadow Hill Cliff
Camel's Hump
Sweet Fern Hill
Bass Lake Hill Crag
North Hudson Dome
Baby Dome
Little Johnson
Northway Express Wall
30
142
146
148
164
167
170
173

Lake Champlain

This region straddles the US 9 / I-87 (Northway) corridor and extends eastward to the park boundary, at the rocky shores of Lake Champlain. Found here is a patchwork of farmland, low mountains, and shoreline communities. Most of the climbing is inland of the lake and clustered along the Northway.

Between Exits 32 and 33 is one of the centerpieces of Adirondack climbing, Poke-O Moonshine. Poke-O is a group of cliffs with a collective number of pitches that exceeds 500. There are long, difficult free routes on the Main Face, single-pitch cragging on the Upper Tiers, and low-angle multi-pitch friction routes of varying difficulties on the Poke-O Slab.

A little to the south near Exit 31 is the super steep Honey Pot with a three overhanging routes. Further south still near Exit 30 is the popular Deadwater Cliff (38 routes), a quick-drying cliff known for excellent moderate crack and face climbs on immaculate rock. Also near this exit is King Philips Spring Wall one of the most popular toproping sites in the park, and Mt Makomis with mostly steep, difficult routes.

A few miles to the south is Sharp Bridge Campground, a DEC campground with a convenient little wall nearby. Little Johnson near Exit 29 is a recently discovered cliff with ten, mostly difficult routes.

Scattered throughout the rolling forests around Exits 29 and 30 are many other cliffs, some largely unexplored with just a single route. These include the Tsunami Crag, Mineville Slab, Sweet Fern Hill, Baby Dome, Meadow Hill, Bass Lake Hill, North Hudson Dome, and the Northway Express Wall.

Finally, dropping into the deep waters of Lake Champlain are two "sea cliffs": the Palisades and Barn Rock.

SEASON

Located downwind of the High Peaks, this region is in the rain shadow and receives far less precipitation than the Lake Placid area. Additionally, this region has the lowest elevation in the park, which contributes to its long climbing season. Most of the cliffs face east and south.

ACCESS

Annual closures for peregrine falcon nesting affect the Poke-O Main Face—look for the signs posted at the climber herd paths. The North Hudson Dome, Northway Express Wall, Another Roadside Distraction, and King Philip's Spring Wall are in the Dix Mountain Wilderness Area, where camping and group size restrictions apply—the same as those for Chapel Pond Pass (see page 177).

DIRECTIONS **(MAPS PAGES 4 AND 26)**

Most of the crags are described relative to exits off the Northway (I-87). Poke-O, the northernmost cliff, is between Exits 32 and 33, the Palisades are at Exit 31, North Hudson Dome is between Exits 29 and 30, and the Northway Express Wall is between Exits 28 and 29.

There are several options to reach this region from Vermont that involve either using ferriess or going around the lake to the south (see page 12).

WHERE TO STAY

Details on primitive campsites in this region are limited, and the sites at Chapel Pond Pass are recommended—and coveted (see page 197).

Campgrounds: Sharp Bridge Campground (518.532.7538) is centrally located for the areas around Exits 29–31. Ausable Point Campground (518.561.7080), off Exit 35, has a beach on Lake Champlain and a boat launch. Unfortunately, the Poke-O campground is now closed.

AMENITIES

Both Keeseville and Elizabethtown have gas, groceries, and diners. Along the Northway there is gas at Exits 31, 32, and 34.

DIVERSIONS

One of the best swimming holes around—a three-tiered waterfall with large pools known as Split Rock Falls—is on US 9, 2 miles north of Malfunction Junction, on the right. Sea kayakers can find some excellent paddles around Valcour Island and along the Palisades shoreline of Lake Champlain with designated campsites that allow for multiday trips with climbing possibilities. A network of mountain bike trails is being developed at Split Rock Wild Forest, north of Westport. If it's raining, try The Crux (518.963.4646, www.climbthecrux.com), a climbing gym in Willsboro, not far from Poke-O.

Watercolor by Lucie Wellner.

PG	CLIFF	QUALITY	ASPECT	APPROACH		GRADES	#
31	Poke-O Moonshine Main Face	★★★★★	E	10–25 min	easy	.6 .7 .8 .9 .10 .11 .12 .13	171
106	Poke-O Moonshine Poke-O Slab	★★★	S	10 min	easy	.6 .7 .8 .9 .10 .11 .12 .13	14
115	Poke-O Moonshine Summit Cliff	★★	S	35 min	moderate	.6 .7 .8 .9 .10 .11 .12 .13	31
120	Poke-O Moonshine Headwall	★★★★	E & SE	25 min	moderate	.6 .7 .8 .9 .10 .11 .12 .13	47
131	Poke-O Moonshine The Lunar Wall	★	SE	25 min	moderate	.6 .7 .8 .9 .10 .11 .12 .13	6
133	Poke-O Moonshine The Sun Wall	★	S	30 min	moderate	.6 .7 .8 .9 .10 .11 .12 .13	5
134	Poke-O Moonshine Second Tier	★★	SE	20 min	easy	.6 .7 .8 .9 .10 .11 .12 .13	13
137	Poke-O Moonshine Third Tier	★★	E & SE	30 min	moderate	.6 .7 .8 .9 .10 .11 .12 .13	6
138	Poke-O Moonshine Fourth Tier	★★	E	1 hr	difficult	.6 .7 .8 .9 .10 .11 .12 .13	6
141	Poke-O Moonshine Beaver Wall	★	SW	1 hour	moderate	.6 .7 .8 .9 .10 .11 .12 .13	2
141	Palisades	★★★	SE	1 hr	moderate boat optional	.6 .7 .8 .9 .10 .11 .12 .13	6
145	The Honey Pot	★★★★	SE	20 min	moderate	.6 .7 .8 .9 .10 .11 .12 .13	3
147	King Philip's Spring Wall	★★★★	W	10 min	easy	.6 .7 .8 .9 .10 .11 .12 .13	2
149	Highway Blues Slab	★★★	E	15 min	easy	.6 .7 .8 .9 .10 .11 .12 .13	3
151	Makomis Mountain Cliff	★★	S	20 min	moderate	.6 .7 .8 .9 .10 .11 .12 .13	3
155	Deadwater	★★★★	SE	10 min	easy	.6 .7 .8 .9 .10 .11 .12 .13	23
162	Deadwater Way Left	★	S	10 min	easy	.6 .7 .8 .9 .10 .11 .12 .13	5
163	Sharp Bridge Campground	★	S	15 min	easy	.6 .7 .8 .9 .10 .11 .12 .13	8
167	North Hudson Dome	★★	SE	1 hr	moderate	.6 .7 .8 .9 .10 .11 .12 .13	2
168	Baby Dome	★	S	5 min	easy	.6 .7 .8 .9 .10 .11 .12 .13	6
169	Little Johnson	★★★	S	10 min	easy	.6 .7 .8 .9 .10 .11 .12 .13	10
172	Northway Express Wall	★	SW	45 min	moderate	.6 .7 .8 .9 .10 .11 .12 .13	18

POKE-O MOONSHINE

Location On US 9, south of Keeseville, just south of Northway (I-87) Exit 33

Summary A premier Adirondack climbing center with a wide range of single-pitch and multi-pitch climbing on excellent rock.

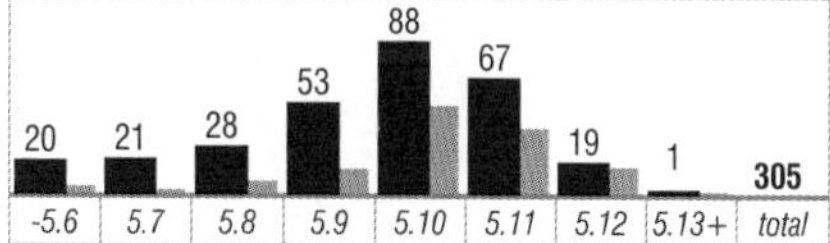

Poke-O Moonshine Mountain, located in the northeast section of the Adirondack Park, is one of the premier climbing destinations in the Northeast. The short, easy hike to the summit is popular because of its fire tower and many excellent viewpoints. For the climber, Poke-O offers a bit of everything, including multipitch slabs, one-pitch cragging, long free routes, and steep face and crack climbing. This mountain is furnished with an immense quantity of exposed rock.

The 400'-high east face of the mountain, known as the Main Face, rises above US 9 and the Northway and holds the bulk of the climbing. The south face, known as the Poke-O Slab, is lower-angled and has many excellent slab and friction routes. Below the summit are numerous steep bands of rock known as the Upper Tiers with many high-quality shorter routes up to 180'.

The state campground at Poke-O closed indefinitely in 2008. You can still park here during the day—and there is often a porta-potty—but there is no water. Don't camp here.

Poke-O enjoys strong cell reception due to the Frankenpine (a camouflaged cell tower) next to the highway in front of the cliff.

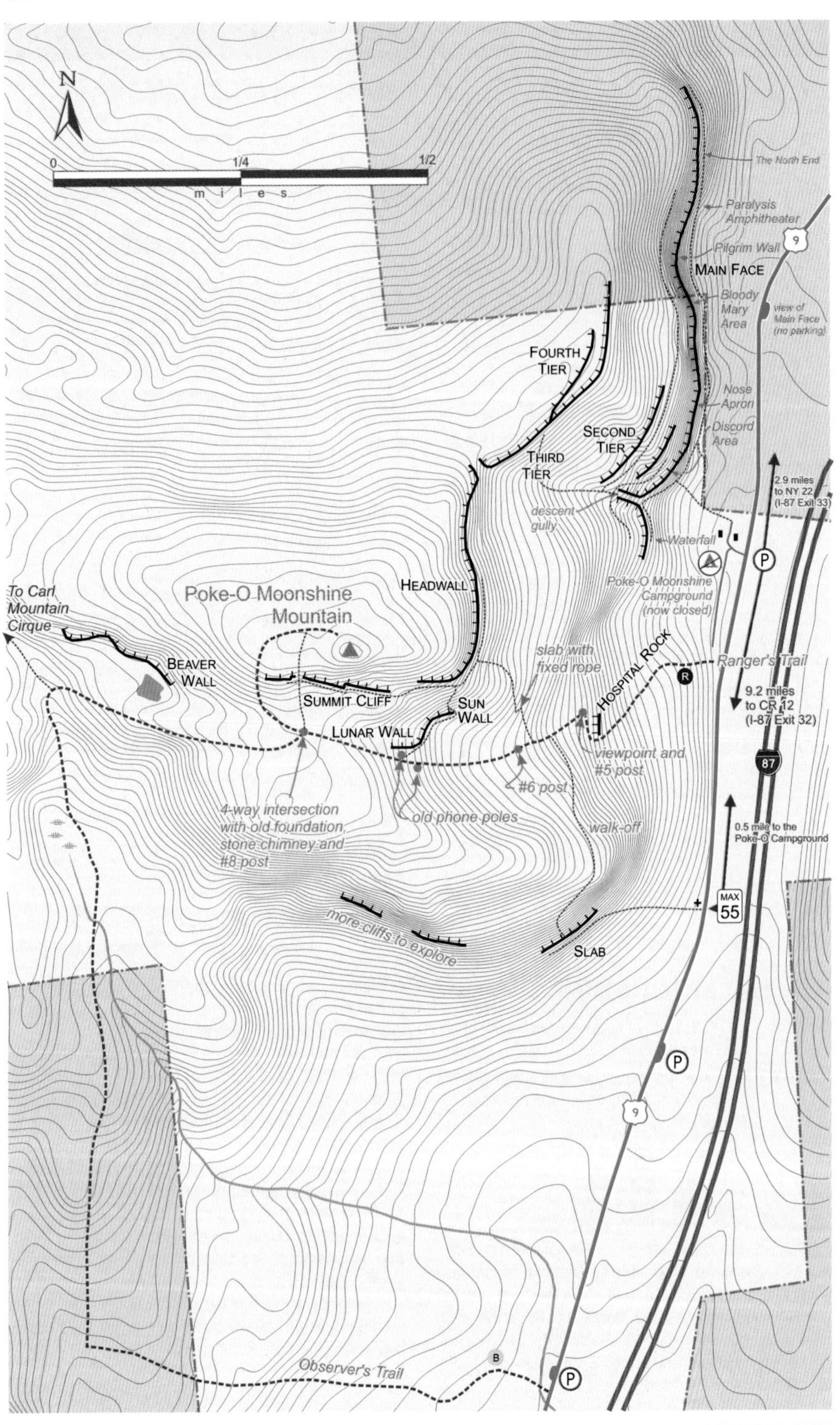
N
0
1/4
1/2
miles
The North End
Paralysis Amphitheater
Pilgrim Wall
9
Main Face
Bloody Mary Area
view of Main Face (no parking)
Fourth Tier
Nose Apron
Discord Area
Second Tier
Third Tier
2.9 miles to NY 22 (I-87 Exit 33)
descent gully
Waterfall
Headwall
Poke-O Moonshine Campground (now closed)
To Carl Mountain Cirque
Poke-O Moonshine Mountain
slab with fixed rope
Hospital Rock
Ranger's Trail
R
Beaver Wall
9.2 miles to CR 12 (I-87 Exit 32)
Summit Cliff
Sun Wall
Lunar Wall
viewpoint and #5 post
87
#6 post
4-way intersection with old foundation, stone chimney and #8 post
old phone poles
walk-off
0.5 mile to the Poke-O Campground
MAX 55
more cliffs to explore
Slab
P
9
B
Observer's Trail
P

DIRECTIONS **(MAP PAGE 30)**

Access to Poke-O is from the (now closed) Poke-O Moonshine Campground, on US 9, 2.9 miles south of the intersection with NY 22 (at Northway Exit 33) and 9.2 miles north of the intersection with CR 12 in Lewis (which goes east 1.7 miles to Northway Exit 32). Park on the road in front of the campground or, if the gate is open, in the campground itself. There is often a porta-potty here, but don't count on it 619271,4917806.

Poke-O Moonshine

MAIN FACE

Aspect	East
Height	400'
Quality	★★★★★
Approach	10–25 min, easy
Summary	The finest concentration of long, multipitch crack and face routes in the Adirondacks; some traffic noise.

-5.6	5.7	5.8	5.9	5.10	5.11	5.12	5.13+	total
5	8	12	27	47	48	16	1	171

The Main Face of Poke-O Moonshine is one of the crown jewels of Adirondack climbing. Located conveniently near the road and the Northway, the Main Face rises 400' above a talus slope with 164 free routes, 38 variations, and 349 pitches. In addition there are 6 projects and 8 aid routes. There are only a handful of moderate climbs 5.8 and under (25 routes); the cliff really shines starting at 5.9. The predominant route grades are 5.10 (47 routes) and 5.11 (48 routes), and even more telling is that 66% of the quality climbs (three to five stars) are in the 5.10–5.11 range; thus, a climber comfortable at the 5.10 to 5.11 level will feel right at home at the Main Face.

Despite the Main Face's reputation for cracks, many climbers have come away surprised by the "slab factor"—tiny edges on steep face. The climbing at Poke-O is unique and typically involves crack, corner, steep face, and slab climbing. There are relatively few ceilings and overhanging faces. The protection at Poke-O, especially 5.10 and up, can be tricky and often involves small wires, and the pitches are often long and require a range of passive and active protection. A typical Poke-O rack includes a full set of nuts, a double set of RPs or micronuts, and a double set of cams from TCUs through 3". Larger cams up to 4" are sometimes required as well, but rarely larger than 4". There are many bolts at Poke-O, but few pitches are completely bolt-protected; carry a small rack if you are unfamiliar with a route, even if it appears from the ground to be entirely bolt-protected.

Special mention should be made of the loose rock at Poke-O. The cliff is geologically active, with bits periodically dropping off. For example, a huge 40'-by-100' slab 20' thick (about 6,600 tons) peeled off of **Summer Solstice** in November 1998, and the "horrifying flake" on **Sailor's Dive** fell in 2006, erasing P1 of that route (which has since been rerouted). On most routes, you have to contend with stacked blocks and loose rock. Wear a helmet! It won't protect against a major cliff event, but it will save your head when other parties drop rocks.

Finding routes on the Main Face can be daunting at first. The cliff has been broken into sections, each of which includes notes on the various major landmarks and cliff features used to find routes in that section. The base locator diagram shows these landmarks and cliff features as well as the terrain that runs along the base of the cliff and where the trail rises and falls. You can find a rough location simply by tracking the ups and downs on the terrain map. The diagram also includes many obvious features that can be seen from the base, like the Nose, the fragile finger of rock of the **Pillar**, the pillar of **P.T. Pillar**, the **Thunderhead** roofs, various black water streaks, and so on. Once you are in the vicinity, you can use the cliff topos and route descriptions to pinpoint your route more closely.

When you view the cliff from the road, the most obvious features (apart from the Nose) are the right-rising dikes—narrow bands that are striped across the cliff. Sometimes these dikes are quite solid (as on the **Freedom Flight** traverse), and sometimes they provide rests, belays, and route terminations; more often than not, however, dike rock is chossy and vegetated. When you climb full-length routes at Poke-O, you can't avoid climbing through dikes. The dikes are shown on the topos and should provide good markers for finding your route from the road.

HISTORY

Compared to the other big cliffs, Poke-O escaped the attention of early climbers. Possible reasons for this are its location far from the High Peaks, most popular with vacationers in Keene Valley and Lake Placid, or perhaps the intimidating nature of the cliff discouraged early pioneers who may have lacked the skills necessary to ascend it. Its climbing potential was discovered in 1957, when John Turner and friends drove down from Montreal.

1957–61: The Turner years: Turner was considered reckless in his time, but posterity holds his ascents to be bold and visionary. The two first routes in 1957 were **The Snake** and **The FM**, in which order is not remembered. His best achievements were **Gamesmanship** (at 5.8, it's the most popular route on the cliff today), **Psychosis**, **Paralysis**, **The Body Snatcher**, and, of course, his masterpiece **Bloody Mary**, a route that took nearly ten years for a second ascent. Turner wrote a miniguide to the cliff—route descriptions and a photo with lines—that appeared in *Appalachia* in 1961.[1] Every route in the first official guidebook by Trudy Healy in 1967 has been credited to Turner and the Canadians.[2]

1 J. M. Turner, "Various Notes—Rock Climbing," *Appalachia* 33 (1960–61), [pp. 248–49.

2 Trudy Healy, *Climber's Guide to the Adirondacks,* Adirondack Mountain Club (1967).

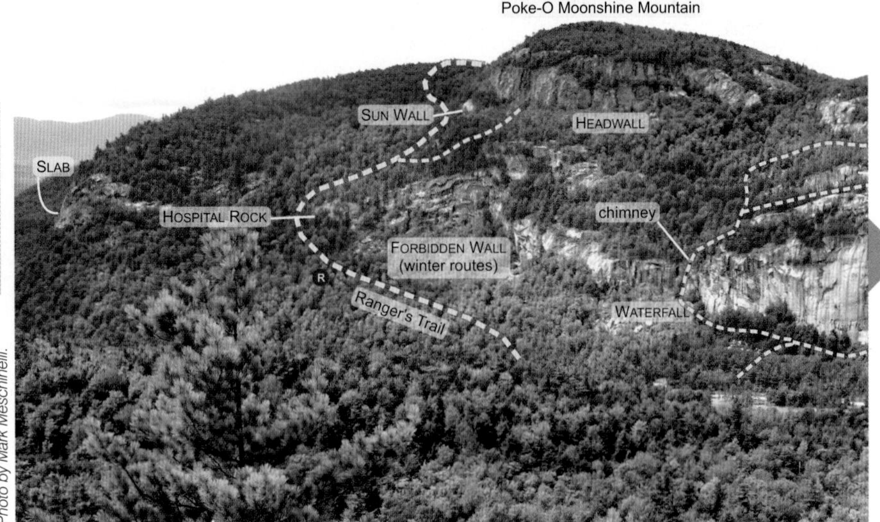

Photo by Mark Meschinelli.

In 1961, the Canadian visits ceased. They had completed all the lines they thought were within their capability and worth doing—excluding, or course, anything that required more than the odd piton for aid or that didn't go to the top of the cliff.

1961–74: Transition with the Gunkies: After the whirlwind achievements by the Canadians, things quieted down for nearly 10 years. No doubt everyone was playing catch-up with the Turner routes. At the time, the Gunks were in the midst of a renaissance, and a few Gunkies made the drive north—among others Jim McCarthy, Dick Williams, Richard Goldstone, Ivan Rezucha, and John Stannard, with routes that include **Psychosis**, **Bloody Mary**, **The Body Snatcher**, **The Great Dihedral,** and **Cirrhosis**.

1974–78: The Ski to Die years: Next on the scene was Geoff Smith along with his band of young protégés who called themselves the Ski to Die Club—a group that included Gary Allan, Dave Hough, Patrick Munn, and later Mark Meschinelli and Dick Bushey. With Smith's vision and drive, this group tore into Poke-O by first repeating Turner's routes, then adding their own. They began modestly in 1974 with **Opposition** (now very obscure) and **The Sting** (immensely popular), but later, as forays out West developed their skills, they forged ahead with a litany of major full-length routes. The list includes **Wild Blue**, **Summer Solstice**, **Microwave**, **Rattlesnake**, **Southern Hospitality**, **Sailor's Dive** (the first ascent of the Big Wall), and **It Don't Come Easy**. While some of these routes originally used aid, many were done free, including the first 5.11 pitches at the cliff—**Firing Line**, by New Hampshire visitor Jim Dunn, and P1 of **Southern Hospitality**. Smith and Dunn put in **Fastest Gun**, perhaps the most recognized achievement of this period, as it's one of the most sought after and popular 5.10 routes in the state.

The group was notoriously protective of the cliff and secretive about their achievements. Tom Rosecrans recalls that he

Mark Meschinelli. Photo by Don Mellor.

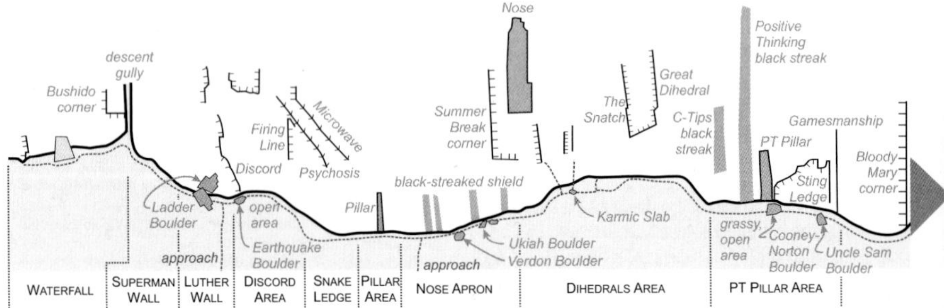

received little cooperation with route reporting for his 1976 guidebook[3]—the routes listed at Poke-O were the same as in Trudy Healy's 1967 guidebook. The next guidebook author was also kept in the dark and had to obtain his route information from New Hampshire (from Jim Dunn).

1978–82: After 1978, Geoff Smith took a hiatus from climbing, but his youthful followers—Mark Meschinelli, Gary Allan, and Patrick Munn—continued their work and added a few interesting lines, including **Royal Savage**, **Cooney-Norton Face**, **Scallion**, and **Snow Blue**. Their influence continues to this day, now going on 40 years.

1982–89: Visitors and style changes: In 1982, Don Mellor took an interest in the Main Face and focused on traditional full-length routes such as **Wild Blue** (freeing many pitches), **Snow Blue** (first free ascent to the top), and **Moonshine**. Mellor carried on the traditional customs that predated him—ground-up with minimal use of fixed protection. In the mid-1980s, a different style appeared, brought by visitors from the south (Dave Lanman) and a return of the Canadians from the north (Pierre-Édouard Gagnon, Gelu Ionescu, and Julien Déry). These "outsiders" recognized the potential of bolt-protected face climbing at Poke-O and exploited it enthusiastically, at first ground-up (e.g., **Maestro**), then on rappel (e.g., **Verdon**). Their stylistic differences were not really all that new, as Geoff Smith and his group had certainly experimented with bolt-protected faces (e.g., **Homecoming**, **Freedom Flight**, **Ukiah**, and routes on the Poke-O Slab). But they were visitors, and this fact caused a clash with the established protectionists. In 1989, they grew tired of the cold shoulder and removed all their own fixed protection, never to return. Eventually, many of these routes were resurrected and are now considered to be some of the best at the cliff—the new style, unwelcome at first, was there to stay.

The next guidebook, a quirky creation with a blue plastic cover, was published in 1983,[4] with 67 routes on the Main Face. This number jumped to 77 in the 1986 supplement,[5] then to 92 in the 1986 guidebook.[6]

3 Thomas R. Rosecrans, *Adirondack Rock and Ice Climbs* (1976).

4 Don Mellor, *Climbing in the Adirondacks,* Sundog Ski and Sports (1983).

5 Don Mellor, *1986 Supplement, Climbing in the Adirondacks* (1986).

6 Don Mellor, *Climbing in the Adirondacks,* Adirondack Mountain Club (1986).

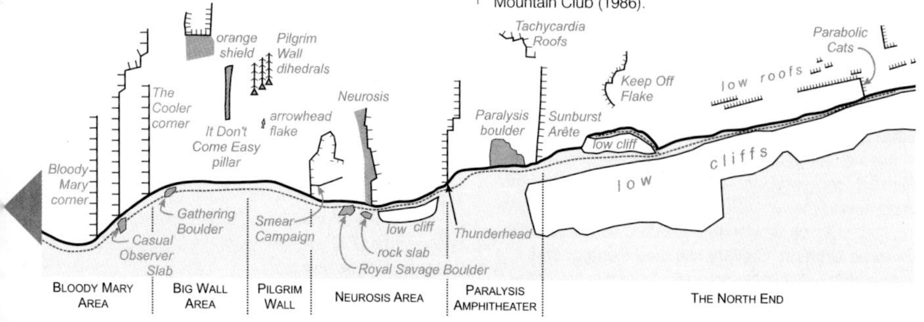

The year 1988 was important for the first 5.12 routes (**Parabolic Cats**, by Gunkie Bill Lutkus, and **The Howling**, by Gunkie Dave Lanman) and the first (and only) 5.13 (**Salad Days**, by Dave Lanman)—all put in by visitors.

The movement toward relaxed standards of new routing became more heavily debated beginning in 1988, both locally and across the country, as people disagreed on the role of bolts and their mode of installation. The Main Face was one of the many battlefields where routes were put in only to be removed. This lasted for several years, to around 1992, when finally a truce was declared, and today, climbers work out such disagreements amicably, off the rock.

*Gary Allan on P2 of **The Snatch** (5.10b) on the first ascent. Photo courtesy of Gary Allan.*

1989–96: Locals make it big: Once the new style was firmly established, local climbers made their mark: Patrick Purcell (**C-Tips**, **Home Rule**, and **Sinful Ways**); Gary Allan (**Forget Bullet**, **Karmic Kickback**, and **Sea of Seams**); and especially Patrick Munn, with his long, hard free routes. Munn clearly got really good. He would fix ropes the full height of the cliff to work and clean various lines. His creations are some of the best at the cliff—their exceptional quality is still being discovered today. Together with Dominic Eisinger, Mark Meschinelli, and a reemerging Geoff Smith, he put in **Calvary Hill**, **Psalm 32**, **Messiah**, **Amongst the Crowd**, **Deuteronomy**, **Remembering Youth**, **The Gathering**, **Extreme Unction**, **Raptor's Scream**, **Letting Go**, **God's Grace**, and **Resurrection**. That's a big list, but what's even more impressive is that they're all four- and five-star routes, and all between 5.11 and hard 5.12.

1996–2005: Pilgrim Wall: The cliff had a four-year break after the Munn-storm, but development picked back up again in 2000. Dennis Luther focused his attention on the left end of the cliff—the Luther Wall—a place under which people had walked for years. His routes on this wall stand as his legacy: **Static Cling**, **Air Male**, **Group Therapy**, **Bastard**, and **Son of a Mother**. The other big story of this period was the development of the Pilgrim Wall, a section of the cliff marked by a complex assortment of hanging dihedrals 200' up. Spearheaded by Patrick Munn and Dominic Eisinger, 20 new pitches were added, and they have proved to be extremely popular—**Pilgrim's Progress**, **The Rapture**, **Morning Star**, **Earthly Night**, **Ancient of Days**, **Smear Campaign**, and **Mayflower**.

2006 and onward: Very few routes have been added in the last few years, doubtless for want of giants like Patrick Munn and Gary Allan. However, there is something new in the air. More and more climbers are honing their skills on previously neglected hard routes, like **Extreme Unction**, **Calvary Hill**, and **Pentecostal**. It is to them that we must look for pioneering in the coming decade.

2013 Mini resurgence: Poke-O sat idle for 5 years until Royce Van Evera, a ski instructor from Lake Placid, climbed **Crux Capacitor**, resurrecting an older 1970s era route. This ascent sparked a resurgence of development on the newly developed Superman Wall, right of the Poke-O Waterfall. Geoff Smith sadly passed away that fall, making this the last place he climbed.

ACCESS

Most of the cliffs at Poke-O are on state land. The Main Face, however, is not entirely public. The land between the road and the cliff is private, so don't park along the road in front of the cliff and walk directly to the cliff base. (You can stop your car and scope out your projects, however.) Park at the (now closed) campground and use the approach trails from there to access the base of the cliff. The left end of the cliff is on state land—the property boundary runs close to the base of the cliff up to the route **Borderline**. Beyond **Borderline**, the base of the cliff and the cliff itself are on private property. It is important for climbers to treat the land with respect—especially so on the right end of the cliff.

Remember, park only in the campground or along the shoulder of the road in front of the campground. Do not wander into—or take shortcuts through—any neighboring properties. Restrict your walking to the approach path and along the base of the cliff.

Sections of Poke-O are closed during the summer months to protect the nesting of peregrine falcons. Starting in the spring, most of the Main Face is closed until the birds find their nesting sites. The DEC monitors the cliff (with cooperation from the local climbing community), and once the birds have chosen their nesting sites, the restriction is reduced to include only routes that are visible from the nesting sites. This includes some of the best routes at Poke-O, like **Gamesmanship** and **Fastest Gun**. If so, not all is lost, as you can always climb at the Upper Tiers. The closure notice is posted on the signboard at the (now closed) Poke-O Campground at the start of the approach trail. Closures are also posted online at the DEC website: www.dec.ny.gov (search for "peregrine route closures").

DIRECTIONS **(MAP PAGE 30)**

Walk to the north end of the campground and find the start of the climbers' path next to the information board, which is near the campsite with the huge boulder. Any cliff closures will be posted on this board. Follow the climbers' path uphill over a short slab and look for an unmarked turnoff on the right. If you're heading for any routes in the Discord Area, the Luther Wall, or the Waterfall, continue straight and meet the cliff at the base of **Discord** 619111,4917955; otherwise, turn right and meet the cliff near **Salad Days** and the Nose Apron.

It is tempting to park at the dirt pullout across from the Main Face and walk to the cliff using an old climbers' path. This approach is on private property, and the owners have requested that climbers use the approach through the campground.

DESCENT OPTIONS

For routes that reach the top of the cliff, it is always possible to walk off: walk left through the open woods and stay below the obvious 100'-high cliff (the Second Tier) until you come to the descent gully, a deep chimney that you can scramble down 619065,4917894. The walk-off makes sense if you reach the top in the dark or if you're completing a route at the left end of the cliff. Otherwise, there are several centralized rappels: Discord Rappel (page [44]), Central Rappel (page [65]), Neurosis Rappel (page [90]), and North End Rappel (page [96]).

Waterfall

The Waterfall is the almost-always-wet black wall on the far left end of the cliff, just left of the descent gully—the prominent deep gash that runs the height of the cliff. When dry, the rock is surprisingly clean and offers enjoyable climbing in a sunny location. The base of the Waterfall is open and grassy, but be on the lookout for poison ivy. In the middle of the wall is a large house-sized boulder that leans up against the cliff. You can walk under it to reach the climbs on the far left side.

To reach the Waterfall, walk left and uphill from where the approach trail meets the cliff at **Discord**. You'll pass the Luther Wall and the Superman Wall.

1 Opposition 5.8 G 100'

One of the more unpleasant-looking routes at Poke-O, **Opposition** climbs the off-width crack in the prominent right-facing corner high above and left of the Waterfall area. The location of this climb was once known as the Screwjob Area, and the route follows the line of the winter route **Goat's Butt**.

Start: At the far left side of the Waterfall, on top of slabs, is a large, black right-facing corner capped by a large, square roof 30' up (the ice route **Get a Job**). Begin 30' left of this corner, just right of a 20'-high right-facing chimney with a white chockstone at the top.

P1 5.8 G: Climb up an extremely vegetated right-facing, stepped ramp that trends left. At the top is a cleaner right-facing corner with an off-width crack. Up the crack to the top and step left to a grassy ledge, then up an easy slab to the trees. 100'

History: Significant in that it was the first first ascent of the 1970s Poke-O crew of Dave Hough, Gary Allan, and Drew Allan.

FA Jul, 1974, Dave Hough, Gary Allan, Drew Allan

2 Goat's Foot on Rock 5.10b PG 140' ★★

Takes its name from the ice route—**Goat's Foot on Ice**—that ascends the same line.

Start: Located on the far left side of the Waterfall on top of slabs that drop down into the woods. Begin on a grassy ledge, just left of a large right-facing corner capped by a large, square roof 30' up (the ice route **Get a Job**) and at the base of a smaller right-facing corner, the right wall of which is a lower-angled ramp.

P1 5.10b PG: Climb the right-rising ramp to a ledge even with the height of the large roof to the right. Up an open book to another ledge, then up cracks into a shallow left-facing corner that becomes right-facing. Finish with a slight runout to the top. Belay off trees set back from the top edge of the cliff. 140'

FA Jul, 2003, Nick Wakeman, Don Mellor

3 Falcon Free 5.10c PG 140' ★★

A drier line than **Bushido** or **Bushmaster**.

Start: On the left side of the Waterfall, 30' right of the large right-facing corner of **Get a Job** (winter route) just left of a large boulder.

P1 5.10c G: Climb straight up the face to a bolt (or climb the boulder and step left onto the face). Follow a seam (micro-cam crucial) straight up to a fragile flake and traverse a few feet right onto the face towards the second bolt. Go up to a small roof (avoid the tempting but unstable blocks on the left), over this (bolt) and up to a good ledge below the large, triangular roof. Break this on the left and follow a handcrack for 15'. Step left to a crack system that leads to a big leaning block (very stable) at the top of the cliff. At the block, move left and up the offwidth crack to the top. Belay at trees well back from the edge. 140'

Gear: Standard rack to 3".

History: The route was climbed during a falcon closure when the only section of open cliff was the Waterfall.

FA May 31, 2013, Michael Bauman, Royce Van Evera

4 High and Dry 5.9 PG 140' ★

Despite appearances, this route is pretty good, although often wet. It's a mixed bag of cracks—finger-, hand-, off-width, and chimney-cracks—that climbs right of an obvious cleft.

Start: 20' right of the house-sized boulder in the middle of the Waterfall is a cleft that runs the height of the cliff; begin on the face right of the cleft.

P1 5.9 PG: Up blocky rock to gain a narrow left-facing corner, then follow it to a crack that gains an off width. Power up the off width and crack above to a broken section under a roof. Step left into the left-facing corner, then up dirty rock to the top. 140'

FA Aug 30, 1985, Don Mellor, John Wald

5 Bushmaster 5.12a PG 120' ★★★★

An amazing section of high-quality rock and sustained climbing; often wet. Named after the largest New World pit viper, perhaps the deadliest snake on the planet.

Start: Downhill and left from **Bushido**, and just right of a large, flat block at the base, and below a left-rising seam with small grass tufts that begins just a few feet right of a 3'-high right-facing corner. This is the tallest part of the right-hand section of the Waterfall.

P1 5.12a PG: Climb up past the left-rising seam to parallel cracks with shallow pods, then reach up and left to a right-rising ledge. Up cracks in the black rock to a point even with the height of the **Bushido** ledge. Step left to a hole with two deep slots, then straight up the cracks to the summit. 120'

History: On the first ascent, Berzins rappelled to clean the cracks but ended up climbing a different line than the one intended.

FA Sep 4, 1989, Martin Berzins, Dave Lanman

6 Big Buddha 5.12b G 120' ★★★★

Start: Same as **Bushmaster**.

P1 5.12b G: Climb **Bushmaster** to the point where it traverses left to the hole. Move right a few feet to a shallow right-facing corner capped by an overlap, just left of a vertical white spot. Up the corner and through the overlap, following cracks—just seams at first, then widening, then pinching down again—to a final overlap. Break it on its left side. 120'

Gear: A #1 RP is vital at the crux.

FA Jul 28, 1991, Martin Berzins, Bill Griffith

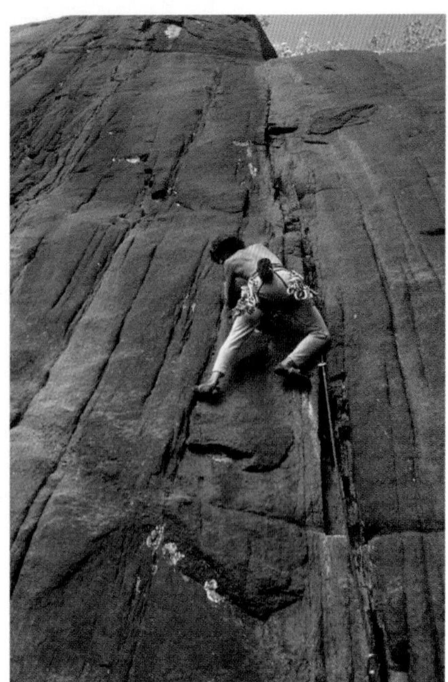

Nick Wakeman on P1 (5.10b) of ***Bushido*** *(5.11c). Photo by Mark Meschinelli.*

7 Bushido 5.11c G 130' ★★★★

This excellent route climbs the huge, chocolate-colored right-facing corner on the right side of the Waterfall. "Bushido" is the code of conduct of the Japanese samurai.

Start: 30' left of the descent gully at a hand- and fingercrack.

P1 5.10b PG: Climb the hand- and fingercrack through the black rock to a stance beneath the ledge. Frustrating face moves lead to the left side of the ledge and a fixed anchor in the huge right-facing corner. 90'

P2 5.11c G: Climb the corner to the top. Excellent gear but strenuous to place. 40'

Gear: Doubles in the small sizes; include nuts, RPs, and small cams.

History: The upper corner was originally climbed as a route by itself (either by rappelling to the ledge from the top or by climbing **Pearly Gates**) and named **Power of Soul**.

FA (upper corner, solo aid) 1984, Mike Heintz
FFA (upper corner) Jul 10, 1985, Dave Georger
FA (complete) Aug 15, 1987, Don Mellor, Bill Dodd

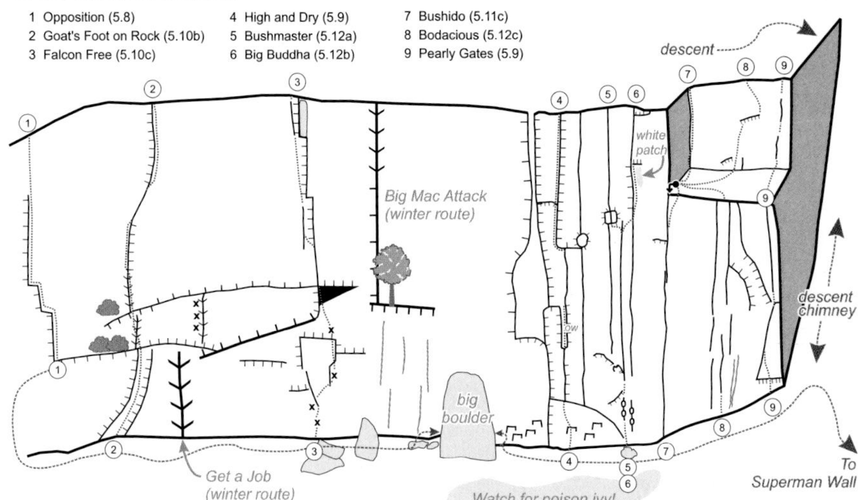

8 Bodacious 5.12c X 120' ★★★★

A difficult line, made even more difficult if you can't make the reach on P2. One of Berzins's superbold leads in the Adirondacks.

Start: 20' left of the descent gully below the thin seams in the black rock.

P1 5.12b R: Up the plethora of vertical seams that converge into just two seams, then follow them to the spacious ledge above. There is a fixed anchor on the left side of the ledge (as for **Bushido**). 80'

P2 5.12c X: About 14' right of the corner is a 4'-high crack. Start just left of this crack and climb straight up the unlikely blank wall; culminate in a long reach to a horizontal jug (the right end of this jug has a white point). Rail right to the white point, then up and left to the top. 40'

FA 1992, Martin Berzins, Richard Felch

9 Pearly Gates 5.9 G 130'

An uninspiring route but the easiest way to gain the **Bushido** ledge.

Start: 2' left of the arête formed by the left outside corner of the descent gully, below a crack that is black on the left side and white on the right side.

P1 5.9 G: Climb the crack to the **Bushido** ledge. It's best to rappel from the fixed anchor on the left side of the ledge; if you must continue, stay just left of the descent gully and climb the dirty cracks right of the black rock in the lichen-covered wall to the top. 130'

FA Jul, 1982, Todd Eastman, Don Mellor

10 Kaibob 5.8 G 70'

Often wet; wait until winter for this one.

Start: Scramble up the descent gully 80'. On the left wall of the gully, look for a ledge beneath a right-facing, right-leaning corner.

P1 5.8 G: Traverse left on a ledge to gain the base of the corner and climb it to the top. 70'

FA Aug 30, 1985, Don Mellor, John Wald

Superman Wall

This compact section of cliff extends from the Waterfall (immediately right of the descent gully) rightward to **Static Cling**. Most of the routes here are equipped with fixed anchors. The arête on the right side of the descent gully is a prominent landmark and has two routes—**Smallville Left** and **Smallville Right**. **Lex Luther** and **Time Jumpers** are located on the face just right of these.

To reach the Superman Wall, walk left and uphill from where the approach trail meets the cliff.

11 Battle Creek 5.10a PG 80'

The manky bottom crux section can be avoided with the **Waterloo** start.

Start: Find the opening to the descent gully; this route begins on the right wall, at a right-facing, right-leaning corner.

P1 5.10a PG: Climb the corner (crux) to the base of a handcrack on the right wall. Climb the widening crack to a fixed anchor on blocks. 80'

FA 1977, John Bragg, Dave Cilley

12 Waterloo 5.9 G 80' ★★★

A safe, moderate route and the best way to climb **Battle Creek**.

Start: Below a chockstone-filled slot, 10' right of **Battle Creek**.

P1 5.9 G: Go up to the base of the slot, work left on a smooth face (bolt) to a stance on an arête. Reach left to join **Battle Creek** at a crack that widens from tips to hand. Follow the crack and climb to a fixed anchor on blocks. 80'

FA Aug, 2013, Dave Hough, Dominic Eisinger

13 Smallville Left 5.9 G 80' ★★

A bit contrived, but surprisingly fun.

Start: Left side of the arête that forms the right side of the mouth of the descent gully.

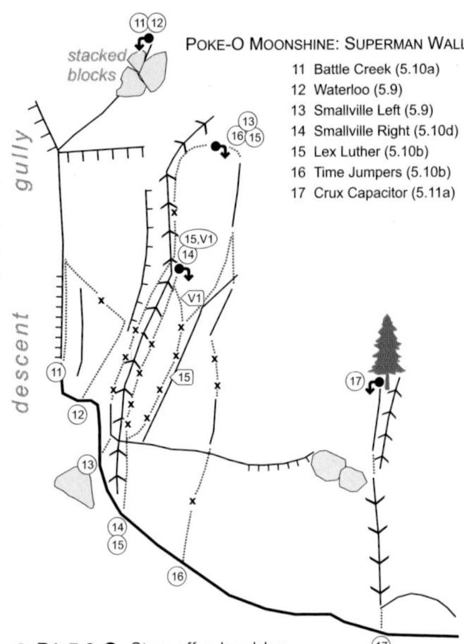

P1 5.9 G: Step off a boulder (small cam) and up a thin vertical crack. Use the arête to get onto a slab on the left, then climb easy rock to a ledge with a fixed anchor (for **Smallville Right**). Continue up the arête, then make an exciting hand-traverse right to a fixed anchor. 80'
Gear: Small cams.
FA Aug, 2013, Mark Meschinelli, Patrick Munn, Dave Hough

14 Smallville Right 5.10d G 50' ★★★

The start can be protected by stemming off of a boulder to the left.
Start: Right side of the arête that forms the right side of the mouth of the descent gully.
P1 5.10d G: Make a boulder move to a 0.5" horizontal crack 8' up. Move left to the arête and work up past horns to parallel right-rising seams. Do a strenuous pull on to the lower-angled section of the arête and climb to a fixed anchor on a ledge. 50'
Gear: 1 ea 0.5" cam.
FA Sep, 2013, Dominic Eisinger, Dave Hough

15 Lex Luther 5.10b G 80' ★★★

Start: Same as **Smallville Right**.
P1 5.10b G: Make a boulder move up to a 0.5" horizontal crack 8' up. Move right and follow a right-rising fracture up a steepening wall. (V1) Work right and join **Time Jumpers**: go up lower-angled rock to a sloping ledge (small wires), then up a handcrack on the right side of the wall to a fixed anchor. 80'
V1 5.11b G: Make a long reach left to a flake and finger rail, then make another long reach further left and climb to the fixed anchor of **Smallville Right**.
Gear: To 2", small wires.
FA Aug, 2013, Dominic Eisinger, Dave Hough, Geoff Smith

16 Time Jumpers 5.10b G 80' ★★★

Climbs an 8'-high fingercrack in the center of the wall.
Start: At a level spot along the base, beneath a right-facing scoop and a horn 12' up.
P1 5.10b G: Make a tricky move up the scoop to the horn. Work left to the fingercrack and climb it to a small ledge. Climb past a horizontal crack and up lower-angled rock to a sloping ledge (small wires). Go up a handcrack on the right side of the wall to a fixed anchor shared with **Smallville Left**. 80'
Gear: To 2", small wires.
FA Aug, 2013, Dave Hough, Dominic Eisinger

17 Crux Capacitor 5.11a G 50' ★★★

Start: 60' right of the descent gully, and 100' uphill and left of **Static Cling**, on a ledge below a left-facing corner system. There is a huge maple tree in front of the corner.
P1 5.11a G: Go up the dihedral and crack system through a small roof on good edges and finger locks. Continue up to a good stance below the second roof. Pull over this (crux) onto a sloping ledge with a fixed anchor on a pine tree. 50'
Descent: Rappel to the left to avoid a rope-eating crack.
Gear: Nuts and cams up to cams to 1.5".
History: The route was climbed on aid in the 1970s by the Ski to Die Club, who reported finding pitons and rap slings.
ACB (A2) 1974, Ski to Die Club
FFA Jul 25, 2013, Royce Van Evera, Michael Bauman

Luther Wall

The Luther Wall—named in memory of Dennis Luther, who developed many of the routes in this section—extends from **Static Cling** down to where the approach trail meets the cliff near **Discord**. For the most part, these routes are one-pitch and are equipped with fixed anchors for lowering off. The main feature in this section is the prominent right-facing corner with an off-width crack (**Phase III**) and a large boulder that leans up against the cliff below a left-facing corner (**Ladder**).

18 Static Cling 5.10c G 100' ★★★

Some chossy rock and fragile holds, but unusually good, gymnastic climbing.
Start: Begin 50' left of **Certified Raw** below a rotten alcove 10' up.
P1 5.10c G: Up into the alcove, then exit on the left side and up to a left-leaning, right-facing open book (crux) that leads to a scooped ceiling. Out the scooped ceiling on the right to juggy flakes on the face above and up to a fixed anchor. 100'
Gear: Optional finger-sized cam at the start in the alcove and just before the fixed anchor.
FA Jun 30, 2000, Dennis Luther, Kevin Boyle, Jay Kullman

19 Certified Raw 5.10b G 90' ★★★

An excellent corner climb, made more accessible by hidden face holds on the right wall.

Start: Just right of a huge, rotting tree in a right-facing corner with an off width immediately to the left.

P1 5.10b G: Up a right-facing open book into the more pronounced right-facing corner with some tiered overhangs. At the top of the corner is an A-shaped fragile flake-overlap; climb through this (carefully) to a jug and up to a fixed anchor. 90'

Gear: Singles to 2.5", doubles in the small sizes.

FA 1978, Gary Allan, Geoff Smith

20 Air Male 5.11c G 100' ★★

This one really packs a punch; another difficult, crimpy face climb. Named for the hidden "mail" slot, and for the airtime taken by all the male climbers at the crux clip. Once a toprope problem called **Wounded Knee**.

Start: 10' right of the right-facing corner of **Certified Raw** and 15' left of the right-facing corner of **Phase III**.

● **P1 5.11c G:** Climb the face, moving left then back right (crux) staying right of a ledge (the route previously ended here). Move delicately right up to a bolt (long runner), then go left and mantel to a ledge. Continue straight up on sidepulls and crimps to a fixed anchor. 100'

FA Aug 17, 2000, Dennis Luther, Kevin Boyle

FA (extension) Sep 23, 2008, Pascal Simard, Olivier Ouellet

21 Son of a Mother 5.10b G 100' ★★★★

Perhaps the best route on this section of cliff. It was first led without the bolts, which were added later by the first-ascent party (in 1998) to make the route safe.

Start: Same as **Phase III**.

P1 5.10b G: Up **Phase III** for a few feet, then left into a depression (protection good, but not visible from below). Work rightward (V1) to gain a left-rising flake and follow it to a fixed anchor. 100'

V1 5.11a G: At the second bolt, step left on small edges to a good handhold on the blunt arête. Join **Air Male** to the top.

Gear: Singles up to 3".

FA Jun 18, 1989, Dennis Luther, Tom Rosecrans

FA (V1) Sep 23, 2008, Pascal Simard, Olivier Ouellet

22 Phase III 5.9+ G 100' ★★

A burly off width in a right-facing corner with two small ceilings; much harder than it looks. This is one of Poke-O's two most-feared 5.9s (the other being **Psychosis**).

Start: Below the right-facing black corner in a little clearing 5' left of some large right-leaning blocks up against the cliff.

P1 5.9+ G: Up the corner system (V1) past two ceilings (crux). At the top of the corner, move right around a little bulge, then back left to a fixed anchor. 100'

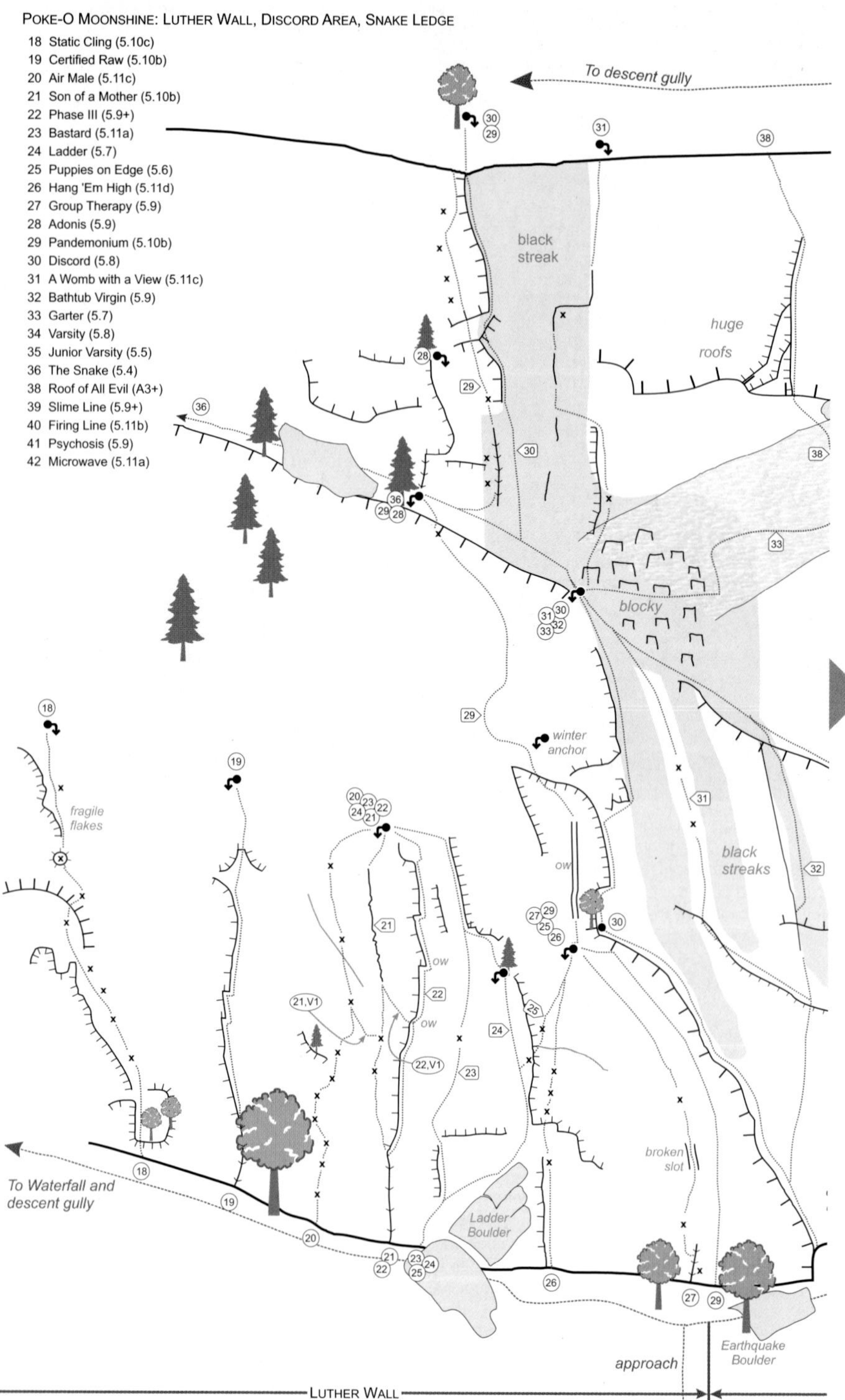

POKE-O MOONSHINE: LUTHER WALL, DISCORD AREA, SNAKE LEDGE
18 Static Cling (5.10c)
19 Certified Raw (5.10b)
20 Air Male (5.11c)
21 Son of a Mother (5.10b)
22 Phase III (5.9+)
23 Bastard (5.11a)
24 Ladder (5.7)
25 Puppies on Edge (5.6)
26 Hang 'Em High (5.11d)
27 Group Therapy (5.9)
28 Adonis (5.9)
29 Pandemonium (5.10b)
30 Discord (5.8)
31 A Womb with a View (5.11c)
32 Bathtub Virgin (5.9)
33 Garter (5.7)
34 Varsity (5.8)
35 Junior Varsity (5.5)
36 The Snake (5.4)
38 Roof of All Evil (A3+)
39 Slime Line (5.9+)
40 Firing Line (5.11b)
41 Psychosis (5.9)
42 Microwave (5.11a)
To descent gully
black streak
huge roofs
blocky
winter anchor
fragile flakes
ow
black streaks
broken slot
Ladder Boulder
To Waterfall and descent gully
approach
Earthquake Boulder
LUTHER WALL

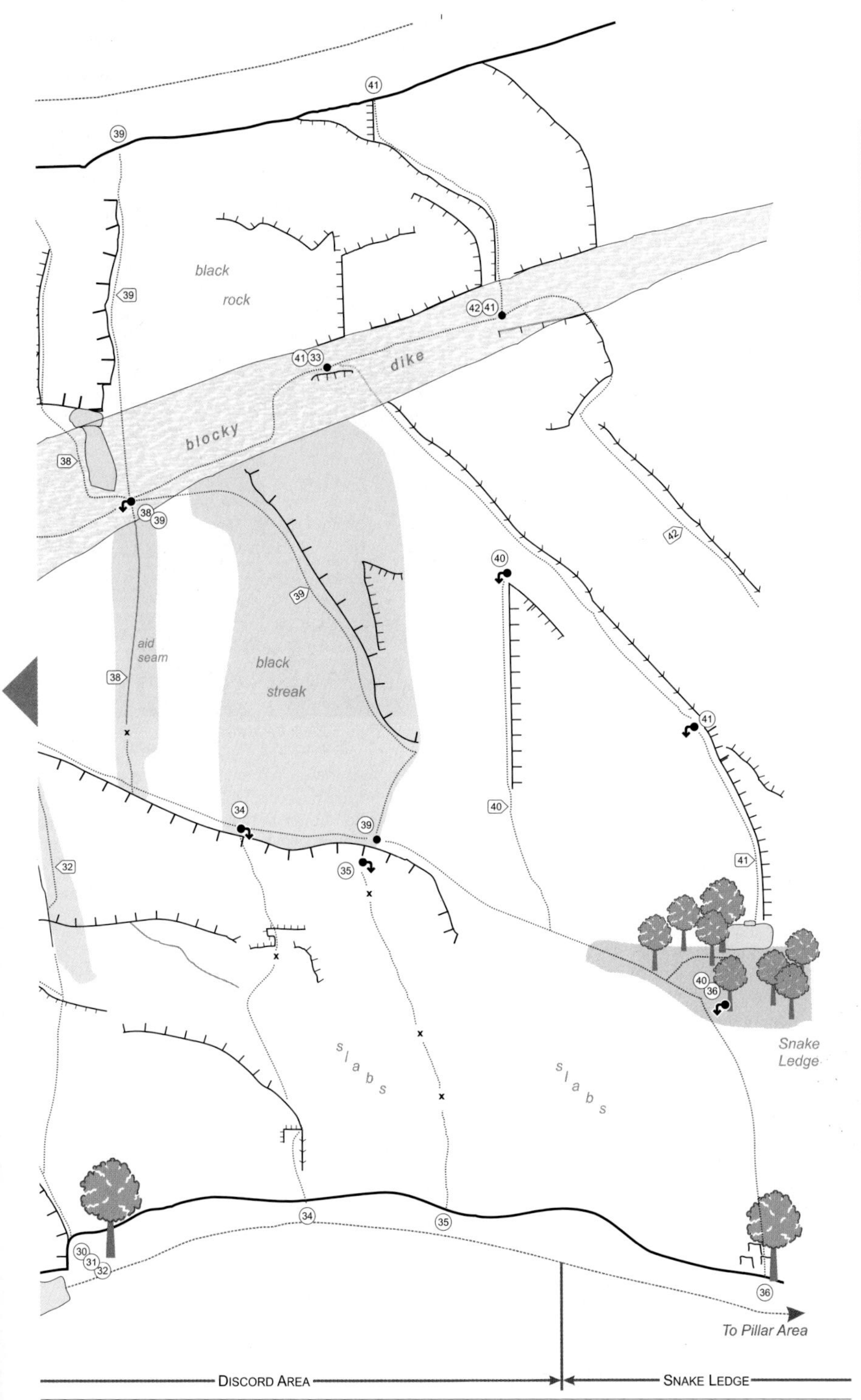
black
rock
blocky
dike
aid
seam
black
streak
slabs
slabs
Snake
Ledge
To Pillar Area
Discord Area
Snake Ledge

V1 Mother's Day Variation 5.9+ PG: Climb straight through the first overhang in the arête via a small right-facing flake, then move up and left to gain the left-rising finishing flake of **Son of a Mother** and follow it to that route's anchor.
Gear: Standard rack plus 2 ea 3.5", 2 ea 4".
History: On the day of the first free ascent, some visiting "Yosemite climbers" were looking for a route and were told this one was 5.8. The inadvertent sandbag resulted in a heated verbal exchange and some pushing. This incident speaks more to the isolation of the local climbers than any attempt at deception. Named for the "phase" in the first ascentionists' climbing careers; free climbing was the next phase (the third phase).
FA (5.6 A2) Jul, 1975, Patrick Munn, Dave Hough
FFA 1975, Gary Allan, Tom Schwarm, Dave Hough
FA (V1) 1977, John Bragg, Dave Cilley

23 Bastard 5.11a R 90' ★

Aptly named—the climbing is hard and the gear is sparse. Pretty good climbing, however, and worth doing, especially as a toprope from one of the routes that share the fixed anchor.
Start: Begin 5' right of **Phase III** at a right-facing corner below a little overlap at 10'.
P1 5.11a R: Climb the corner to the horizontal (gear), then up rightward to a lone bolt. Up a small pedestal (small nut), then stem right and straight up to join **Ladder** and easier climbing (5.7) to the fixed anchor (as for **Phase III**). Climbing directly above the bolt to the anchor is 5.12. 90'
FA Jul, 1988, Dennis Luther, Joe Szot

24 Ladder 5.7 G 220' ★★

P1 is popular. The top section is dirty and nondescript; much better to rappel from the fixed anchor on **Phase III**.
Start: On top of the huge right-leaning blocks right of **Phase III**, and below a large left-facing corner.
P1 5.7 G: Up the huge left-facing corner past a cedar with an anchor (possible rappel) at 60'. Go left under the overhang and into a smaller left-facing corner in a shallow chimney-box, then up to the anchor on **Phase III**. 90'
P2 5.5 PG: It is possible to continue by walking left on the large ledge past the anchors for **Son of a Mother** and **Certified Raw**, then moving up a handcrack in a block to a tree with an anchor and angling off left to the woods. 130'

25 Puppies on Edge 5.6 G 90' ★★★

Excellent climbing for the grade.
Start: Same as **Ladder**.
P1 5.6 G: Up the huge left-facing corner until a line of holds leads right to the arête; around the arête, then up the face to the fixed anchor (as for **Group Therapy**). 90'
FA Sep 17, 1990, Patrick Purcell, Andy Morcillino

26 Hang 'Em High 5.11d G 90' ★★★

A ceiling problem; easy to hangdog to work out the moves.
Start: Just around the arête from **Ladder**, at the right side of the huge right-leaning blocks and below a shal-

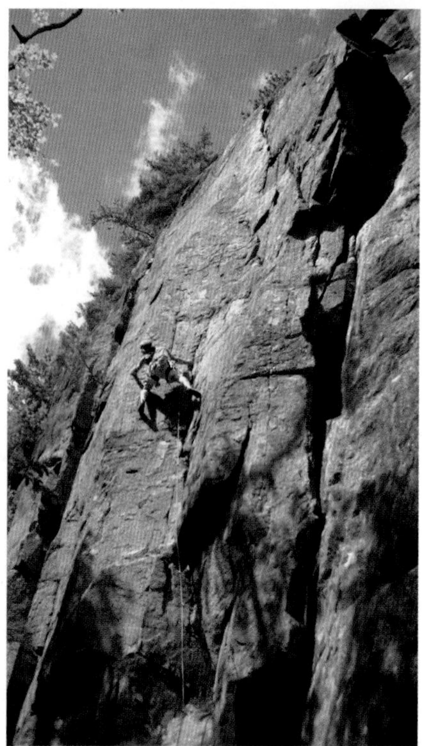

*Dennis Luther on **Son of a Mother** (5.10b). The large corner to the right is **Phase III**.*

low, broken right-facing corner beneath a ceiling.
⭘ **P1 5.11d G:** Up the broken corner to the ceiling, make tricky moves past the ceiling and left-facing flakes to a horizontal, then up the face to the fixed anchor (same as for **Group Therapy**). 90'
Gear: 1 ea 0.5"–1.75".
FA Jul, 2003, Patrick Munn, Mark Meschinelli

27 Group Therapy 5.9 G 90' ★

Quality face and slab climbing.
Start: In a flaring groove just above where the approach trail meets the cliff.
P1 5.9 G: Up the groove with a low bolt, then move left onto the face (crux) and up a broken slot (3.5" cam helpful) that leads to a slab and easier climbing up to a fixed anchor. 90'
FA Jul 20, 2002, Dennis Luther, Fred Schaefer

28 Adonis 5.9 G 30' ★★

Strenuous and mercifully short.
Start: At the large pine tree at the top of P2 of **The Snake**, below an open book.
P1 5.9 G: Up the open book to a ceiling (4" cam). Step right and up a shallow right-facing corner with a good jamcrack. 30'
Gear: To 4".
FA Jun 23, 2007, James Debella, Dennis Luther

*Opposite: Colin Loher on the exposed upper arête of P3 of **Pandemonium** (5.10b).*

The Next Level

In 1975, a small group of us had been climbing a couple of seasons on the cliffs at Poke-O Moonshine. We were frustrated 5.8 climbers, and we were very protective of our private rock playground. In those days, we had a morbid fear of outsiders stealing "our routes," so we kept information to ourselves.

On a particular day in 1975, we were messing around on the campground boulders when three climbers piled out of their car in front of us. They were a threat—confident, skilled, and well-traveled to fabled places like Yosemite and Alaska.

Their group's leader, Andy, confidently approached, and asked if we were the climbers from Plattsburgh putting up new routes at Poke-O. We reluctantly admitted to working on a few new routes. "Recommend a short climb to us," he said. Not wanting to spill too many beans, we gave up a small morsel. "We just finished a nice crack climb immediately left of the Ladder Route," we said. "We managed to get up it, and rated it 5.8+." They thanked us and moved off towards the cliff, not even bothering to ask for details. Impressive!

Hours later, as we were getting ready to leave, someone yelled, "Hey, I want to talk to you!" I saw Andy marching over, angrily yelling, and waving his arms. He positioned himself within an inch of my face, screaming so that I could see the blood vessels surging in his forehead. I was so taken aback that I could barely hear his words.

"You're going to get somebody killed with that bullshit rating," he yelled. I stammered out a few words, but this only intensified his anger. "5.8+? Is that some kind of fucking joke? That's a total sandbag. That route would be rated 5.10 in the Valley."

Behind me I hear Pat murmur, "You mean I lead a 5.10?" I saw his eyes move to Pat and then back to me, as he tried to digest this comment and decide if this was some kind of put on. His face finally softened as he realized that he was dealing with a bunch of North Country bumpkins who had never been outside the Blue Line. His yelling turned to stern warnings and fatherly advice about ratings. The moment passed, we shook hands, and they left.

This chance encounter stayed with me over the years. It was strangely satisfying to have ruffled the feathers of these hard-men. In a single moment, our group graduated from being mere 5.8 climbers. And, perhaps most importantly, we had learned a new word and concept: the "sandbag". A Poke-O tradition was born.

As a postscript, I ran into Andrew Embick several times over the next ten years. He always remembered the "5.8+ crack at Poke-O." Once, in the Wind Rivers, we shared food and stories about the Adirondacks and other places. For me, his sad departure ended a common thread that wove through the climbing fabric back to those boulders at Poke-O, when he opened the door, and we stepped through to the next level.

-Dave Hough

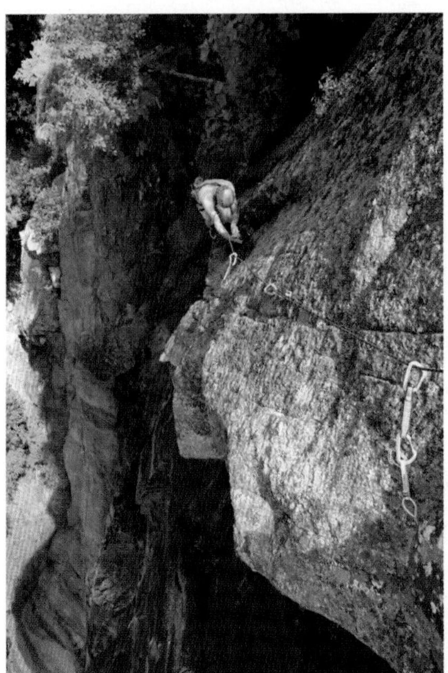

29 Pandemonium 5.10b G 310' ★★★

P3 is the real gem, with arête climbing and exposed positions. Access the 3rd pitch more easily by climbing P1-P2 of **The Snake**.

Start: 8' right of **Group Therapy** at a thin crack that begins at an overlap 7' up.

P1 5.9 G: Up a 10'-high bulge, then face-climb up a blunt rib to a wide crack and follow it to its end at a slab. Work straight up the slab to a critical nut placement, then up easier rock to the headwall. Step left to the fixed anchor as for **Group Therapy**. 90'

P2 5.8 PG: Step right to a thin, jagged crack (6' left of the **Discord** corner), then up this to a wide crack and climb it to its top, where the angle eases. Up a short right-facing corner, move left 10', up a low-angle face, then right to meet the ledge on **The Snake**. Walk left to a large pine tree belay. 120'

P3 5.10b G: Walk 20' down and right to a shallow V-groove in the black face. Up the V-groove (bolt) to a sloping stance at a horizontal. Up the overhanging stemming corner to a ledge. Step left and climb a face, staying left of the arête and the hanging block, up to a horizontal. Step right to the arête and climb it to a fixed anchor on a tree (as for **Discord**). 100'

History: P2 had been climbed earlier, and an unusually positioned piton was found on P3.

FA Jun 23, 2007, Dennis Luther, James Debella

Discord Area

The open, flat area where the approach trail meets the cliff is known as the Discord Area. The lower section is slabby, and the upper section has steep corners and overhangs. From the open area, there are good views of **Discord**, **Firing Line**, **Slime Line**, and other routes high on the wall. At the base of **Discord** in the open area is a large boulder, called the Earthquake Boulder, as it fell from **The Snake** during an earthquake.

Discord Rappel: An established rappel begins from an oak tree at the top of **Discord**. A 120' rappel takes you down the **Discord** corner; tension right to a fixed anchor. A second 200' rappel takes you to the ground.

30 Discord 5.8 PG 305' ★

A historic route with impressive climbing for the time—the first 5.8 on the cliff. More agreeable than the name implies. P2 is recommended, especially when combined with **Group Therapy** or **Puppies on Edge**.

Start: Uphill and right of where the approach trail meets the cliff is an open area where you can view the entire face. Begin on the left side of this open area, above a large boulder (the Earthquake Boulder) and at the base of a large, broken left-rising, right-facing flake system.

P1 5.4 PG: Ascend the left-rising flake system to a tree at the base of a prominent right-facing corner in black rock. 75'

P2 5.8 G: Up the right-facing corner, around a little overhang, and up to a flake that forms an overlap below a larger overhang 15' above. Traverse right and climb the right side of the flake and into the larger right-facing corner to a blocky area and a fixed anchor in dike rock. 110'

P3 5.8 PG: Traverse easily left to the base of a large right-facing corner above a pine; follow the filthy corner to the top. This pitch is best avoided. 120'

FA 1958, Brian Rothery, Bob O'Brien

31 A Womb with a View 5.11c G 260' ★★

A good route with a short but hard crux at the top.

Start: Same as **Discord**.

P1 5.10a G: Up the stepped low-angle rock of **Discord** for 30' to an open book. **Discord** angles leftward, whereas this route climbs straight up the open book, then up the short face with good holds to a vegetated right-facing, left-rising ramp at the base of a black streak (1 ea 2" and 3" cams). Follow the ramp up and left, then straight up the bulging slab to a fixed anchor in dike rock (shared with **Discord**). 160'

P2 5.11c G: Climb straight up a right-facing corner to its top, then traverse left to discontinuous cracks. Up these to a bolt, traverse right in a horizontal 6', then straight up (crux) to the top and a fixed anchor. 100'

FA Jun 14, 1990, Don Mellor, Jeff Edwards, Patrick Purcell

32 Bathtub Virgin 5.9 PG (5.8 R) 160' ★

Good climbing but a scary runout. Named for the lawn decoration that consists of a bathtub buried on end to form a shrine that holds a statue of the Virgin Mary.

Start: Same as **Womb with a View**.

P1 5.9 PG (5.8 R): Climb **Womb with a View** up to the base of the black streak, then straight up to a thin seam in the face with good gear at the base. Instead of climbing the seam, step right and up to a bucket on the face (crux; 5.9 PG), then run it out straight up the face using vertical edges and face holds to **The Snake** traverse. Traverse up and left to a fixed anchor in the dike (shared with **Discord**). 160'

FA Jun 12, 1990, Jeff Edwards, Don Mellor

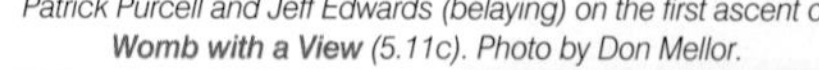

Patrick Purcell and Jeff Edwards (belaying) on the first ascent of ***Womb with a View*** *(5.11c). Photo by Don Mellor.*

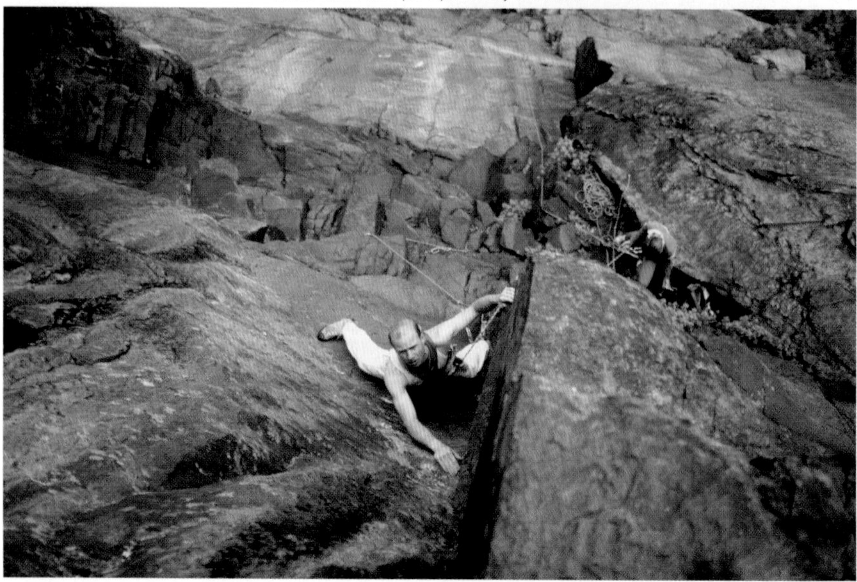

33 Garter 5.7 G 130' ★★

This historic route does a spectacular traverse above **Slime Line** following the featured dike. Historically, this is only a single pitch; you can join **Slime Line** (P2) or **Psychosis** (P3–P4) to finish.

Start: At the fixed anchor at the top of P2 of **Discord**.

P1 5.7 G: Traverse right in the dike to a small buttress; step down and around to the outside of this (spectacular 5.6) and up a bit until you can continue the traverse right. Proceed right to the next buttress and around the outside of this (crux; hidden pocket) to a fixed anchor below the huge right-facing corner of the last pitch of **Slime Line**. Continue rightward in the dike, where the climbing remains easy, and move up about 25' to a black ledge with a gear belay (same as **Psychosis**). This belay is just before the climbing in the dike gets more difficult (and is the base of the final pitch of the winter route **Midlife Crisis**). 130'

FA 1960, John Turner, Brian Rothery, Peter Thomson

34 Varsity 5.8 PG (5.4 R) 100' ★

Start: At a low-angle slab at the height of land, centered in the open area at the base of **Discord**.

P1 5.8 PG (5.4 R): Up the slab to a vague open book in black rock with a small overhang at head height. Through the overhang, laybacking a crack on the right, then up the slab to a bolt below two shallow right-facing corners at the left end of an overhang. Straight up through the corners and bulge above to a slot (crux; 3.5" cam critical), then up the unprotected slab to a fixed anchor. 100'

FA Sep, 2003, Plattsburg State Climbing Class

35 Junior Varsity 5.5 G 80' ★★

A candidate for the second easiest route at Poke-O. Take care to protect the opening moves.

Start: On the right side of the open area at the base of **Discord**, before the trail descends, at the base of an obvious black streak.

P1 5.5 G: Up the black streak for a few feet (crux), then step right to the slab. Climb past two bolts in the slab to a headwall; up this (bolt) to a fixed anchor below **The Snake** traverse dike. 80'

FA Sep, 2003, Plattsburg State Climbing Class

Snake Ledge

The routes in this section begin from the top of the Snake Ledge, a forested ledge 80' up accessed by climbing P1 of **The Snake**. There is a fixed anchor on a tree at the top of **Discord**; two double-rope rappels take you back to the ground.

36 The Snake 5.4 PG 380' ★★★

The Snake provides an easy but memorable traverse of an impressive section of cliff on clean rock; exposed and well situated. It is also the access route to Snake Ledge, the starting point for several other routes. It was so named because of the garter snake found sunning itself halfway across the ledge.

Start: From the open area beneath **Discord**, walk downhill to the base of a clean slab, 30' before the cliff becomes overgrown and vegetated.

P1 5.4 PG: (V1) Up blocky rock, then slither up a crack in a slab. At its top, step right (crux) and up to the trees on Snake Ledge. There is a fixed anchor on a tree. 80'

P2 5.1 G: From the left side of the tree ledge, follow dike rock left below a bulging black wall past the fixed anchors of other routes, to meet the right-facing corner of **Discord**. Climb up black rock and head left to a pine tree left of the base of the huge right-facing corner of **Discord**. 200'

P3 4th class: Scramble left to the forest and the descent gully. 100'

V1 Chik'n Garbonzo 5.6 PG: Start beneath a short v-slot 20' up and to the left of moss-covered rock. Scramble up to the slot, step left and go up a left-rising crack. Step right and climb a thin vertical crack to the tree belay for P1.

FA 1957, John Turner, John Brett

ACB (V1) Jun 23, 2013, Eric Bretthauer, Samantha Bretthauer, Tim Dufrane

37 7 Year Itch 5.9+ G 70' ★★

Climbs a clean, brown slab above stacked blocks.

Start: 75' left of **Pillar** at a sloping dirt ledge to the left of stacked blocks.

P1 5.9+ G: Layback up the blocks, then friction up the slab and climb a vertical crack that widens to hand size near the top. Belay at a tree with a fixed anchor. 70'

Gear: To 2".

FA Aug 21, 2013, Eric Bretthauer, Tim Dufrane

FFA Aug 30, 2013, Jake Hadden, Eric Bretthauer

38 Roof of All Evil A3+ 170' ★★★★

Start: On **The Snake** traverse, 50' left of **Slime Line**, just left of the fixed anchor on **Varsity**, below a bulging headwall with a bolt.

P1 A3+: Climb past the bolt to gain the aid seam with many fixed bashies. There is a fixed anchor just above in the dike rock (shared with **Slime Line**). 70'

P2 A2+: Above the anchor, 30' of 5.4 climbing in the dike leads to a 4' roof. Follow the thin crack through the roof and into a right-facing corner just above the roof; move up the corner past a small tree to a slab finish. 100'

Gear: Normal free rack plus many heads (mostly small to medium), many Bird Beaks, thin Leaper cam hooks.

FA Jun, 1997, Bob Cartwright, Patrick Wheatley

39 Slime Line 5.9+ G (5.8 R) 200' ★★★

A highly recommended route that climbs water-worn chocolate rock through an undulating left-slanting groove; exposed and sustained. Beware of wasps in the cracks above the belay.

Start: From the Snake Ledge, 4th-class up and left 40', following **The Snake**, to the right edge of the black streak above the anchors for **Junior Varsity**. (Access the start by climbing **Junior Varsity** or P1 of **The Snake**.)

P1 5.9+ G (5.8 R): Make unprotected moves rightward above the belay (RPs) to some good crack holds. Once in the corner, head leftward with good protection and ride the wave of undulating rock up to the dike area. Traverse left on a slab (unprotected but easy) to a fixed anchor just below and left of a huge right-

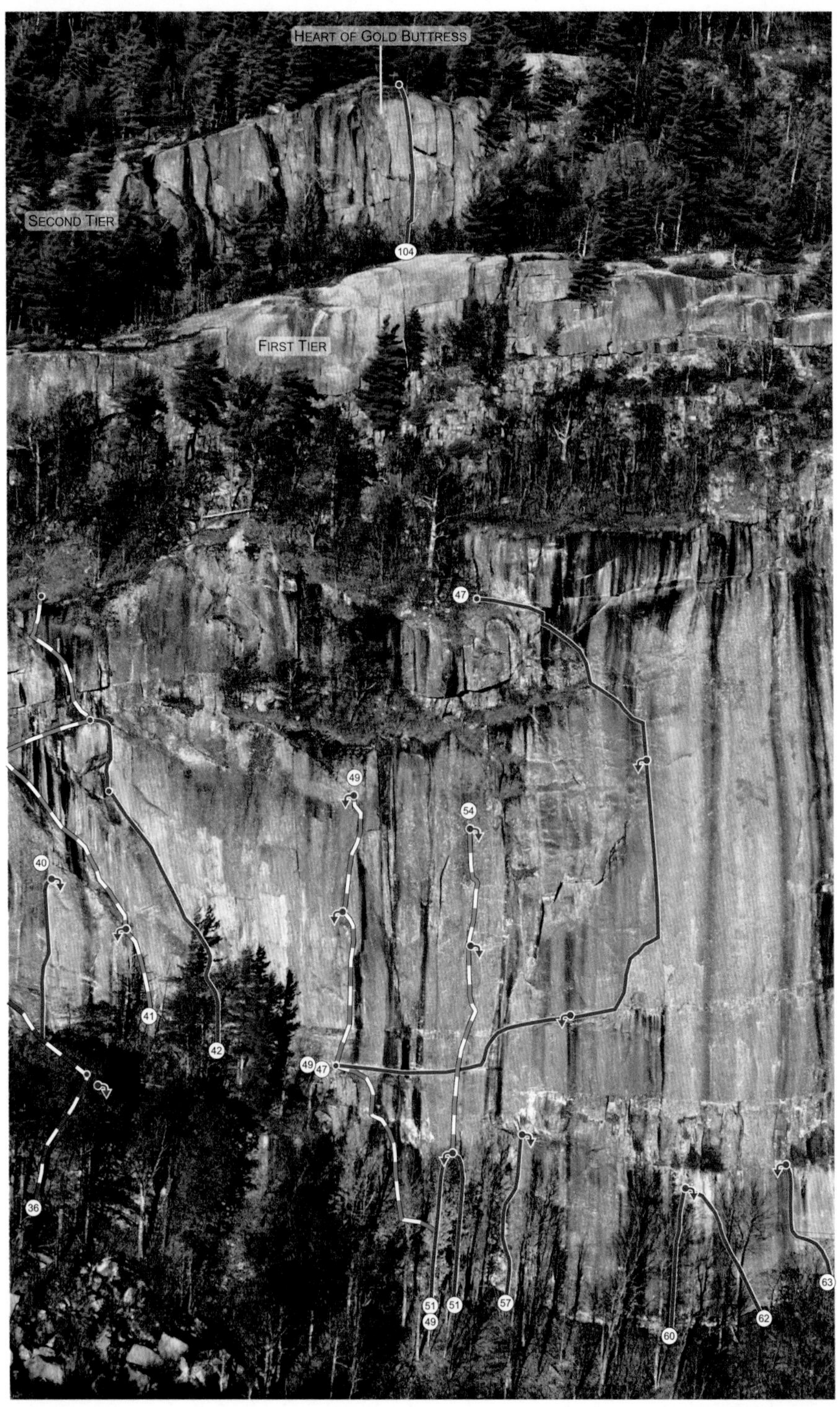

Heart of Gold Buttress
Second Tier
First Tier
104
47
49
54
40
41
42
49
47
36
51
49
51
57
60
62
63

Poke-O Moonshine: Snake Ledge, The Pillar, and Nose Apron

36 The Snake (5.4)
37 7 Year Itch (5.9+)
40 Firing Line (5.11b)
41 Psychosis (5.9)
42 Microwave (5.11a)
43 Creaking Wall (project)
44 Blinded by Rainbows (5.5 A3)
45 Forget Bullet (5.11b)
46 Rattlesnake (5.10b)
47 Freedom Flight (5.10b)
48 Project
49 Remembering Youth (5.12b)
50 Sound System (5.10d)
51 Pillar (5.7)
52 Autumn Flare (5.10d)
53 Katrina (5.11b)
54 Deuteronomy (5.11b)
55 Superstition Traverse (5.7)
56 Spooks (5.11d)
57 The Howling (5.12c)
58 Salad Days (5.13a)
59 Climb Control to Major Bob (A4+)
60 Pentecostal (5.12c)
61 Project
62 Verdon (5.11b)
63 Homecoming (5.9+)

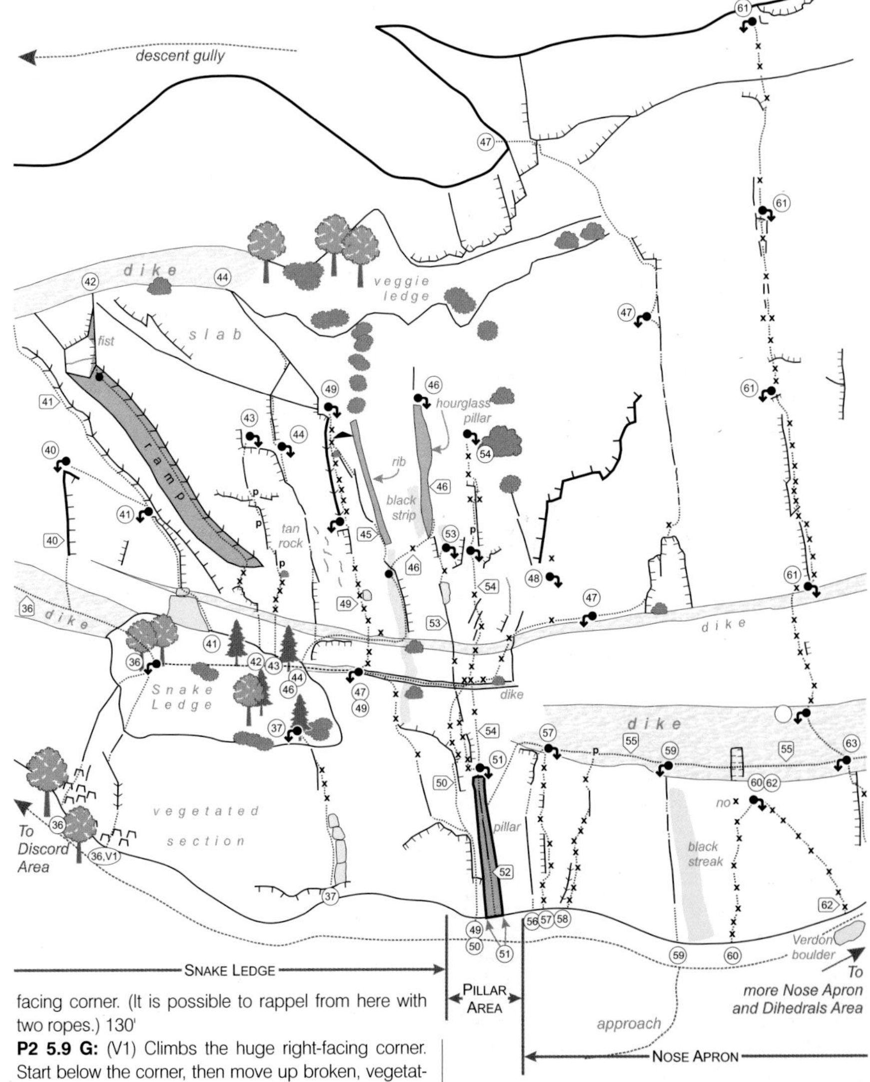

facing corner. (It is possible to rappel from here with two ropes.) 130'

P2 5.9 G: (V1) Climbs the huge right-facing corner. Start below the corner, then move up broken, vegetated rock into a chimney that narrows to hand size, then finger size. Step out left via a wild move to a jug, then proceed to the summit. 70'

V1 5.11b TR: On the left wall of the huge right-facing corner is a smaller, shallow corner. From the base of the main corner, traverse 10' left to gain the shallow corner, then follow it to the top.

Gear: Standard rack to 2", including many medium nuts and RPs.

FA Sep, 1987, Geoff Smith, Drew Allan

FA (V1) May, 1987, Patrick Munn, Patrick Purcell, Mark Ippolito

40 Firing Line 5.11b G (5.8 X) 100' ★★★

Poke-O's first 5.11 is an excellent tips power-layback problem that is well protected once you are established in the corner. **Firing Line** demonstrates how routes wax and wane in popularity, as this was once a standard route that everybody climbed but now rarely receives attention. Right of **Slime Line**, the upper wall is broken by the left-leaning ramps of **Psychosis** and **Microwave**. Just left of these on the steep face is a prominent left-facing corner that is obvious when seen from the base of **Discord**.

Start: At a tree on the far left side of the Snake Ledge. (Access the start by climbing P1 of **The Snake**.)

P1 5.11b G (5.8 X): From the belay, wander up and left on low-angled rock to just beneath the large left-facing corner. Climb unprotected rock (5.8 X; sometimes wet) to the base of the corner, then up the corner with excellent gear to a fixed anchor at the top near the low-angled, left-trending slab of **Psychosis**. 100'

*Dick Bushey leading P1 of **Psychosis** (5.9). Photo by Mark Meschinelli.*

Descent: Rappel from the fixed anchor at the top of the corner or join **Psychosis** to the top.

FA Sep, 1977, Geoff Smith, Jim Dunn, Gary Allan

41 Psychosis 5.9 G 375' ★★

Perhaps not as insanely difficult as once thought, although still one of Poke-O's two most feared 5.9s (the other being **Phase III**). A short layback and stemming problem up clean rock. P1 can be used to set a toprope on **Firing Line**.

Start: On the back of the Snake Ledge is a ledge on top of a large block (with another flat plate-block balanced on top) below the base of a left-arching yellow corner. (Access the Snake Ledge by climbing P1 of **The Snake**.)

P1 5.9 G: A short pitch climbs the yellow left-arching corner past a welcome rest at half height to a ledge with a bolt (rappel possible). (It is possible to continue up easy rock to the **Firing Line** anchor.) 50'

P2 5.7 G: Continue up the left-leaning ramp to the traverse dike under an orange wall beneath a huge, stepped roof. You can find a gear belay on a black ledge in the dike (same as for **Garter**). 150'

P3 5.8 G: From the right end of the ledge, climb up crumbly rock a few feet, then traverse directly right on orange rock, past an ancient piton, to a left-facing corner. Using a good ledge, traverse right around the outside of the corner (crux) to a ledge with a pedestal, then up rightward through brushy blocks to a gear belay at the base of a right-facing corner. 75'

P4 5.6 PG: Climb the right-facing corner directly above the belay. Step out left onto the face and follow a left-rising ramp for 30' past a small right-facing corner with good gear. The ramp levels to a ledge where you find a shallow right-facing corner. Up this (crux, hidden bucket) to the vegetated slab above. Finish on a runout easy slab for 50' to the trees. 100'

History: The climb was originally graded 5.9 A2 with the comment "The crack above may require two stirrups." Ironically, the route was freed at 5.9. The fact that it was one of the early 9s, and one used as the standard against which other 9s were compared, helps explain why some of the Poke-O 5.9s are really hard.

FA 1958, Claude Lavallée, John Turner
FFA Sep 23, 1967, Jim McCarthy, Richard Goldstone

42 Microwave 5.11a G (5.8 X) 215'

Climbs the rightmost of two left-leaning ramps above the Snake Ledge. It's an older route that is rarely climbed, so expect some dirty rock and old fixed gear. This route ends at the traverse dike; finish on the last pitch of **Psychosis**.

Start: 25' right of the **Psychosis** block at a large oak tree, below the right side of a left-rising flake system that ends in a steep wall below the ramp. This is also 15' left of the four-bolt start of **Creaking Wall**.

P1 5.11a G (5.8 X): Climb up to the left-rising flake (5.8 X), then up the headwall with two bolts (crux) to gain the ramp. Once on the ramp, climb the low-angled, left-rising crack to a belay at the base of the final right-facing corner at the top of the ramp. 175'

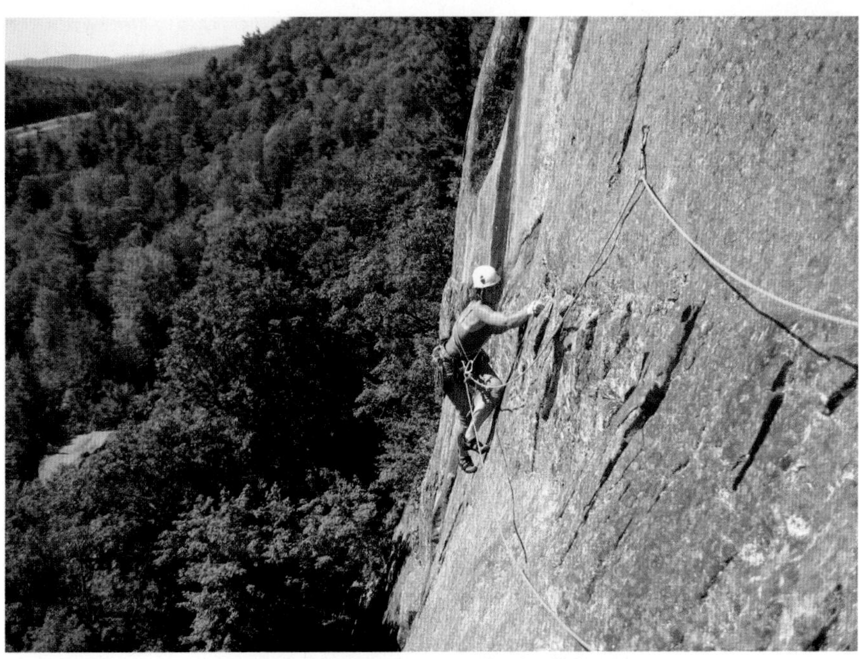

*Martine Schaer follows the P1 traverse of **Freedom Flight** (5.10b).*

P2 5.10a G: Climb the brutal fistcrack in the overhanging right-facing corner to the dike. Move left to a right-facing corner in vegetation (the base of the exit pitch of **Psychosis**). 40'
FA (5.10a A1) Sep, 1976, Geoff Smith, Patrick Munn, Dave Hough
FFA 1978, Geoff Smith, Gary Allan

43 Creaking Wall Project

Originally Patrick Munn's aid project, but he bailed when the wall creaked. The route appears to have been completed to the **Blinded by Rainbows** ledge and has its own fixed anchor, but nothing is known of the ascent. The route begins 15' right of **Microwave**, below a face with four bolts and a black streak that comes out of a shrub in a crack.

44 Blinded by Rainbows 5.5 A3 150' ★★

A worthwhile two-pitch route that requires the intricacies of modern aid. The route is dedicated to the memory of Tom Scheuer, the senior ranger at the Mohonk Preserve for many years, who died in an automobile accident a year before this ascent.
Start: 15' right of **Creaking Wall** below a shallow left-facing corner 8' above the black dike rock.
P1 5.5 A3: Climb a seam with three dowels that leads into the left-facing corner above the black dike rock. At its top, hook right to a thin splitter and follow it for 70' to a fixed anchor on the right side of a large ledge. 100'
P2 A2: Climb the left-facing groove above the belay. The slab above is the crux of this short pitch. 50'
FA Apr, 2000, Dave Lanman

45 Forget Bullet 5.11b G 90'

Seldom climbed and dirty, especially when eclipsed by the high-quality climbing of its neighbor **Remembering Youth**, which straightens out the line. "Bullet" is the nickname given to Gary Allan; he was several hours late for the climbing date, causing Munn to mutter "Well, forget Bullet, that S.O.B."
Start: At the belay at the end of P1 of **Rattlesnake**.
P1 5.11b G: Move up to a prominent rib and climb its left side (crux), then step left to a shallow left-leaning ramp that leads into the top of **Remembering Youth** and a fixed anchor. 90'
FA Aug, 1991, Gary Allan, Patrick Munn

46 Rattlesnake 5.10b R 170'

Climbs the detached hourglass pillar (shaped like a rattlesnake) pasted high on the wall. It has been described as "horrific" and "just plain bad"; it spooked Jim Dunn into placing bolts at the top of the pillar.
Start: At the right end of the Snake Ledge.
P1 5.10b R: (V1) Climb up to the black dike rock, then traverse the dike rock right for 30', cross **Remembering Youth**, and move past an old bolt to a vegetated left-facing corner in a black water streak. Climb the corner for 25' to a belay at its top, directly below a prominent rib feature. 90'
P2 5.10b R: From the belay, traverse right past a bolt to the hourglass pillar and climb it on its right side to the top and a fixed anchor. 80'
V1 5.10b G: From the fixed anchor at the start of **Freedom Flight**, climb the first section of **Remembering Youth** to meet the normal traverse in the dike rock.
FA Sep, 1976, Geoff Smith, Patrick Munn

47 Freedom Flight 5.10b G (5.7 X) 420' ★★★★★

Provides a good introduction to Poke-O discontinuous crack climbing. The quality climbing on the traverse pitch is also unique. The original ascent involved four straight days of cleaning on rappel, rehearsing, and then leading it free. It was the first 5.10 route on the Main Face of Poke-O. A lower pitch can be added by climbing P1 of **Remembering Youth** or **Sound System**, or by climbing **Pillar** and linking into the traverse by climbing the first section of **Deuteronomy** (this is especially good). Poison ivy grows in a patch on the P1 traverse ledge, and seems to persist year-to-year. Your body can avoid it, but not the rope: watch out!

Start: On the right end of the Snake Ledge, make 3rd-class moves on a ledge to a fixed anchor.

P1 5.10b G: Traverse right from the ledge and follow the dike. At the skyline, climb the face above the dike (bolts; crux) to gain the upper dike. Continue traversing right with mixed gear and bolts to a fixed anchor. 130'

P2 5.10a PG (5.7 X): Move right and climb the left side of the detached flake (5.7 X) to the top of the flake and an old bolt. (There is plentiful gear through this section, but it is in the detached, flexing flake and therefore highly suspect.) Gain the shallow, discontinuous crack and climb it to an anchor. Most parties rappel from here with double ropes. 150'

P3 5.6 R: Continue up the crack to its end, then up the slab left to an exit corner. 140'

History: Once known as **Freedom Fighter** but renamed **Freedom Flight** when Gary Allan took a big whipper on the crux traverse. Smith lowered him to the top of **Pillar**, which he solo-downclimbed, then soloed back up **The Snake** to the start of the route.

FA Sep, 1976, Geoff Smith, Dave Hough

48 Project

Gary Allan's project—for which there is an anchor and some other fixed gear in the roofs left of **Freedom Flight**.

Pillar Area

To the right of the open area at the base of **Discord**, the trail descends past a vegetated section to a narrow finger of rock at ground level that leans up against the cliff; this is **Pillar**. The routes in this section begin near this feature, and others start from the top of **Pillar**.

49 Remembering Youth 5.12b G (5.9+ R) 265' ★★★★

Some consider the upper corner of this route the best single pitch at Poke-O. The name comes from an 1800s epitaph found by Patrick Munn: "Remember youth as you pass by. / As you are now, so once was I. / As I am now, you soon will be. / Prepare to die and follow me."

Start: A few feet left of **Pillar** on vegetated ledges.

○ **P1 5.9+ R:** Climb up and left across an easy slab to a thin seam; a committing move (crux, 5.9+ R) leads to a bolt, then left to the headwall and interesting climbing to the traverse dike of **Freedom Flight**; move left 15' to the fixed anchor. 120'

○ **P2 5.11d PG:** Climb directly up from the belay past a dike and follow bolts up the steepening wall to the base of the final right-facing open book and a fixed anchor. 70'

P3 5.12b G: Climb the amazing corner with increasing difficulties. Step right (where **Forget Bullet** joins) to easier climbing up to a fixed anchor. 75'

Gear: A few small cams for P1.

FA Aug, 1993, Patrick Munn, Gary Allan

50 Sound System 5.10d PG 100'

This is a first-pitch option for those who want a more challenging start to **Deuteronomy** or **Freedom Flight**.

Start: Same as **Remembering Youth**.

P1 5.10d PG: Up a dirty crack past crumbly, bulging rock to three bolts. Follow them to the **Freedom Flight** traverse dike and a fixed anchor. (This route crosses **Katrina** and uses the mysterious paired bolts on **Deuteronomy** as an anchor.) 100'

FA 2003, Peter Gernassnig, Bob Cartwright

51 Pillar 5.7 PG 70' ★

A fragile-looking pillar that can be climbed on either side at about the same grade; popular, but not the best 5.7 around. Before the fixed anchor, climbers would simultaneously rappel down either side.

Start: Downhill and right of **The Snake**, and left of a sheer, black-streaked shield of rock, at the base of a fragile pillar.

P1 5.7 PG: Choose a side and climb the corner to the top at a fixed anchor. 70'

Gear: Standard rack to 3.5".

History:

ACB 1974, Geoff Smith, Gary Allan, Dave Hough

52 Autumn Flare 5.10d R 70'

Climbs the front of the pillar. Yikes! Perhaps better toproped.

Start: At the left side of **Pillar**.

P1 5.10d R: Start up the left side, then step right onto the front face and climb it to the fixed anchor at the top of the pillar. 70'

FA 1977, Gary Allan, Patrick Munn

53 Katrina 5.11b G 80' ★★★

Named for the hurricane that devastated the Gulf Coast in 2005. Difficult for the grade.

Start: On top of **Pillar**.

P1 5.11b G: Step up to the left and follow bolts to crack and face climbing, then break through two dikes to the base of the hourglass pillar on **Rattlesnake**. 80'

FA Sep, 2005, Patrick Munn, Gary Allan

54 Deuteronomy 5.11b G 120' ★★★

Excellent steep face climbing.

Start: On top of **Pillar**.

○ **P1 5.11a G:** Climb the technical face (RPs) past the traverse dike of **Freedom Flight**, then past the upper dike. Unusual face climbing leads past right-leaning slashes to a fixed anchor. 80'

P2 5.11b G: Follow a crack to an overhang; mantel this, then up to a fixed anchor. 40'

History: Originally led with two bolts by Geoff Smith, who called this his "last significant lead"—that is, until his comeback ten years later on **Ancient of Days**.

FA 1992, Geoff Smith, Patrick Munn

55 Superstition Traverse 5.7 PG 200'

Traverses the major dike system across the top of the Nose Apron. Interesting terrain with an easy walk-off. Begin at the right side of **Pillar**. Climb up the right side of **Pillar**, then out right across the face to gain the dike. Traverse right across the various fixed anchors for the other routes to eventually emerge through vegetation back at the base of the cliff below **God's Grace**.

History: This route was done back when 5.7 was the group's climbing limit.

FA Oct, 1975, Geoff Smith, Gary Allan, Dave Hough

Nose Apron

The Nose Apron is the sheer shield of rock with black stripes where the trail runs along the base up against the rock. The apron is positioned left of the Nose feature, the huge nose-shaped pillar of rock positioned high on the wall and perhaps the most eye-catching feature on the cliff; you can look up to the right and see the Nose. The right fork of the approach trail meets the cliff in the middle of the Nose Apron at the route **Climb Control to Major Bob**. The climbs on the apron are of a similar nature—face climbing with thin, finger-ripping holds.

Mark Polinski on ***Pentecostal*** *(5.12c)*
Photo by David Le Pagne.

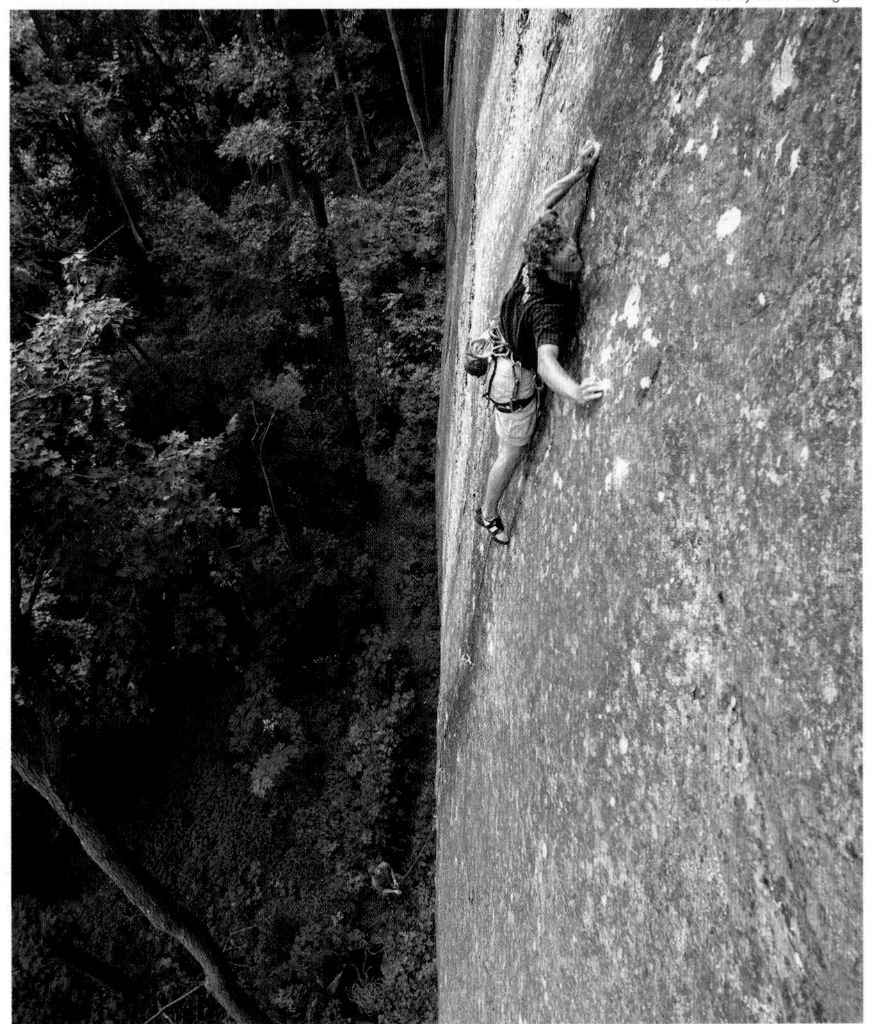

56 Spooks 5.11d R 70'

A thin crack testpiece just right of **Pillar**.

Start: 15' right of **Pillar** at the base of a straight-in seam.

P1 5.11d R: Climb the thin seam straight up and exit via a right-facing corner to the dike. 70'

Gear: Many RPs and small nuts.

FA Apr, 1981, Alan Jolley, Bill Diemand
FFA Aug, 1987, Dave Lanman

57 The Howling 5.12c G 70' ★★★

Start: 20' right of **Pillar**, below a seam that starts from a ledge 4' up.

● **P1 5.12c G:** Climb the face to discontinuous right-facing corners, then more face to a fixed anchor. 70'

FA Jun, 1988, Dave Lanman

58 Salad Days 5.13a G 100' ★★★★

Crimpy, sharp, and powerful. The first 5.13 in the park. The name refers to one's heyday, which Dave Lanman was certainly in.

Start: 35' right of **Pillar** below a right-leaning open book capped by a small, triangular overhang.

● **P1 5.13a G:** Climb the shallow technical open book to a rest at the top, then proceed up increasingly difficult moves over a bulge. An easy run-out slab leads to the dike. There is no fixed anchor; traverse left to the fixed anchor of **The Howling**. 100'

FA Sep, 1988, Dave Lanman

59 Climb Control to Major Bob A4+ 75' ★★★★

This space oddity provides a challenge for those looking for new-wave aid climbing with decking potential.

Start: Between **Salad Days** and **Pentecostal**, where the approach trail meets the cliff-base trail, below a thin seam that starts 15' up the wall. (If you look carefully, you'll find a deep finger-sized hole in the rock at head level, 15' right of the start.)

P1 A4+: Hook your way up to the seam with a fixed mashie. Continue up the thin crack to a small right-facing corner, then up to thin cracks. The route free-climbs the last 15' to the bottom of the dike, where there is a 3/8" stud with a rap hanger that serves as a top anchor. 75'

Gear: BallNutz, Beaks, BURPs, RURPs, Bat Hooks, numerous Bashies up to #1.

FA Aug 4, 1996, Charles Pechousek, Bob Cartwright, Connie Heessels

60 Pentecostal 5.12c G 90' ★★★★

This finger-ripping pile of fun will have you speaking in tongues. Features sustained microcrimp pulling and is a bit height-dependent. The route can be toproped by climbing **Homecoming** and tensioning over to the anchor.

Start: 15' left of the Verdon Boulder, before the trail heads uphill.

● **P1 5.12c G:** Climb the black rock with potato chip flakes and move right before the last bolt to the anchor on **Verdon**. Going straight up through the last bolt is extremely difficult (i.e., it hasn't been freed) and lands you on a bushy ledge with no way off. 90'

FA Aug, 1992, Gary Allan

61 Project

This project, bolted by Gary Allan in 2006, is a logical continuation of **Pentecostal** to the top of the cliff. When combined with that route's first pitch, it is the longest sport route in New York. Bring a rack of draws and some talent, as this has repulsed some good climbers. Begin at the top of **Homecoming** and diagonal up left 30' through the dike to a fixed anchor at the top of the dike (5.7). The next pitch steps right from the belay and climbs the face up and left past several flakes to a smaller dike, then traverses this dike right to a fixed anchor just left of a right-facing corner (5.12d; Pete Kamitses, 2006). The next pitch, dubbed the "Changing Corners Pitch," climbs the right-facing corner to its top, moves left over a small overlap and into the next right-facing corner, then up this to a stance at the top with a fixed anchor. The next pitch climbs straight up a faint discontinuous crack to a shallow overlap in lichen-covered rock. Straight through this to a slab (optional belay), then up to another patch of lichen-covered rock with a narrow foot ledge at its top and a fixed anchor. The final pitch climbs up to a bolt, then runs it out up a slab aiming for a left-rising overlap with a black streak on its left side. Over this to a horizontal, then up the steep headwall to a fixed anchor at the top.

62 Verdon 5.11b G 70' ★★

Another face-climbing exercise on supersharp flakes. The upper climbing is fun; the initial moves are just plain hard. Named for the resemblance of a key hold to those found in the limestone of Verdon, France, and for the tactic used for the first ascent (rappel-placed bolts).

Start: On the right side of the sheer wall with black streaks is a boulder where the trail is pinched against the cliff. This is the Verdon Boulder, positioned just before the trail goes uphill. This route starts on the uphill side of this boulder at a bolt in a shallow corner.

● **P1 5.11b G:** A bouldery move gains the shallow corner, which leads to a rising leftward traverse of the wall to a fixed anchor well below the dike rock. 70'

FA Nov 1, 1987, Julien Déry, Pierre Gagnon

63 Homecoming 5.9+ PG 60' ★★

Climbs the shallow right-facing dihedral that begins 15' up and continues to the dike above. Originally led with three bolts, this old-school style is still well preserved even with the additional bolt at the start. The first ascentionists had just returned from a trip out west, thus the name.

Start: 10' below and right of the dihedral.

● **P1 5.9+ PG:** Climb up to the low bolt, then traverse right and up the face on good holds to the second bolt. Traverse left to the dihedral and follow it to the dike and a fixed anchor. 60'

FA Aug, 1976, Geoff Smith, Dave Hough, Patrick Munn

64 Ukiah 5.10a PG 55' ★★

A nice, clean section of face climbing. Consensus has bumped this from its original grade of 5.9.

Start: At a boulder up near the cliff, right of the Verdon Boulder.

● **P1 5.10a PG:** Climb the face with a bouldery start past bolts to a reachy finish. Fixed anchor on the ledge. 55'
FA 1977, Geoff Smith, Mark Meschinelli

65 Raindance 5.9 G 55' ★

Certainly not the 5.7 it was once graded. A nice, short pitch, recommended if you're ticking off the single-pitch routes on this wall. It's also used as P1 of **Summer Break**.
Start: At the base of a left-facing corner with right-rising scoops on the face, directly below the **Summer Break** corner (the huge tan scar that deposited all the blocks at the base of the Nose Apron).
P1 5.9 G: Up the corner and scooped face on the left to a left-facing edge with a bolt. Layback up the edge (crux) to reach the dike. Walk left to the fixed anchor of **Ukiah**. 55'
FA 1977, Dave Hough, Geoff Smith, Patrick Munn

66 Libido 5.11a G 50' ★

A quality route, but short. Originally two bolts, now equipped with five.
Start: 15' right of the left-facing corner of **Raindance** at some pointy rocks below a chest-height hand slot with a hole above it.
● **P1 5.11a G:** Work up a difficult face to a ledge, then easier climbing to a fixed anchor. 50'
FA Aug 18, 1985, Julien Déry

67 Snake Slide 5.7 G 50' ★

The easiest way to gain the dike area below **Wild Blue** and **Summer Break**.
Start: 8' right of **Libido** at a left-facing corner.
P1 5.7 G: Up the corner to the top. Step left to the fixed anchor of **Libido**. 50'
FA 1976, Geoff Smith

68 Scorpion 5.11a PG 50' ★★

Start: At the right end of the Nose Apron before this section of cliff ends in vegetation.
P1 5.11a PG: Step onto the slab from the left and climb past a thin vertical crack to the dike. Walk off right (3rd-class). 50'
History: This was possibly the hardest thing that Smith had toproped up to that point; Dunn sent it with ease.
FA 1977, Geoff Smith
FFA Jul, 1978, Jim Dunn

69 Rodeo Man R.I.P.

This aid route climbed a left-facing corner formed by the now-missing section of rock on **Summer Solstice**. The route has since fallen into the talus (the memorial boulders lie at the bottom of the Nose Apron) but is mentioned for historical interest. There is an anchor left of the P2 anchor of **Summer Break** that belongs to this route. The route was named for a lasso maneuver that was used on the first ascent to reach the upper corner.
FA (5.7 A2) Sep, 1975, Geoff Smith, Dave Hough, Gary Allan

70 Summer Solstice R.I.P.

A huge section of this route fell into the talus slope in November 1998, leaving a clearly visible tan scar. P1 is shared with **Wild Blue** and described there. The first part of P2 face-climbs left with bolt protection but ends nowhere. The upper pitches are now climbed as part of **Summer Break**. Mark Meschinelli's fantastic photo of this route (and the now-missing section) appeared in *Climbing*.[7]
FA (P1–P2) 1977, Geoff Smith, Jim Dunn
FA (complete) 1977, Geoff Smith, Jim Dunn, Wendy White

71 Summer Break 5.12a PG 320' ★★★★

Ascends the left-facing corner formed when the left side of the off-width crack on **Summer Solstice** fell into the talus. Originally climbed as an aid route (named **Omi's Climb**), the free version has stellar corner climbing and perfect palming on nice rock with great exposure.
Start: Same as **Raindance**.
P1 5.12a PG: Climb the left-facing corner and scoops of **Raindance** to the dike (5.9). Continue up a crack through the dike to the ceiling. Break through the ceiling (3.5" cam) and climb 30' of difficult stemming up the dihedral (past two bolts) to a fixed anchor in the dike. 120'
P2 5.11c PG: Climb the second part of the dihedral to a big undercling. Make a difficult move to better holds and a bolt, then traverse right around the arête to a fixed anchor. 50'
P3 5.10c PG: The climbing above is the original line of **Summer Solstice**. Work up the continuous crack system, right-facing to start, past an optional belay on the left. The crack diminishes to a slab crux at a bolt, then up easier but unprotected climbing to a fixed anchor. 150'
Gear: Singles to 2", plus 1 ea 3.5".
FA (P3) 1977, Geoff Smith, Jim Dunn
FA (P1, P2, A2+) Sep, 1999, Dave Lanman, Kirstan Conley
FFA Sep 5, 2004, Maxime Turgeon, Philippe Lagacé

72 Wild Blue 5.11a G (5.10b R) 500' ★

A long and involved route that climbs the left side of the Nose feature; exposed, as in heading out into the wild blue yonder. Once known as **Shaky Flakes**. The P1 roof is recommended.
Start: At the fixed anchor at the top of **Libido**. Either climb **Libido** (or **Snake Slide**) or 3rd-class in from the right on vegetated ledges.
P1 5.11a G: This pitch climbs the **Summer Solstice** roof. From the belay, climb rightward through broken dike rock to the roof with odd geometry. Climb through the roof via an overhanging crack-corner to a fixed anchor just above. 50'
P2 5.10b R: Climb the crack to the fresh scar below a ceiling (the blocks from this area litter the base of **Scorpion**). Face-climb right across the scar (bolt) to the right-facing corner and climb it up to the dike and the base of a coffin-shaped pillar (V1). Climb the right side of the pillar to a fixed anchor at its top. 120'
P3 5.9 G: Traverse left across the face under the Nose toward a left-leaning crack. Follow this crack to a belay at the lower left side of the Nose. 80'

7 *Climbing*, no. 123 (Dec 1990), p. 85.

The Nose
71
72
73
74
75
76
63
64
65
67

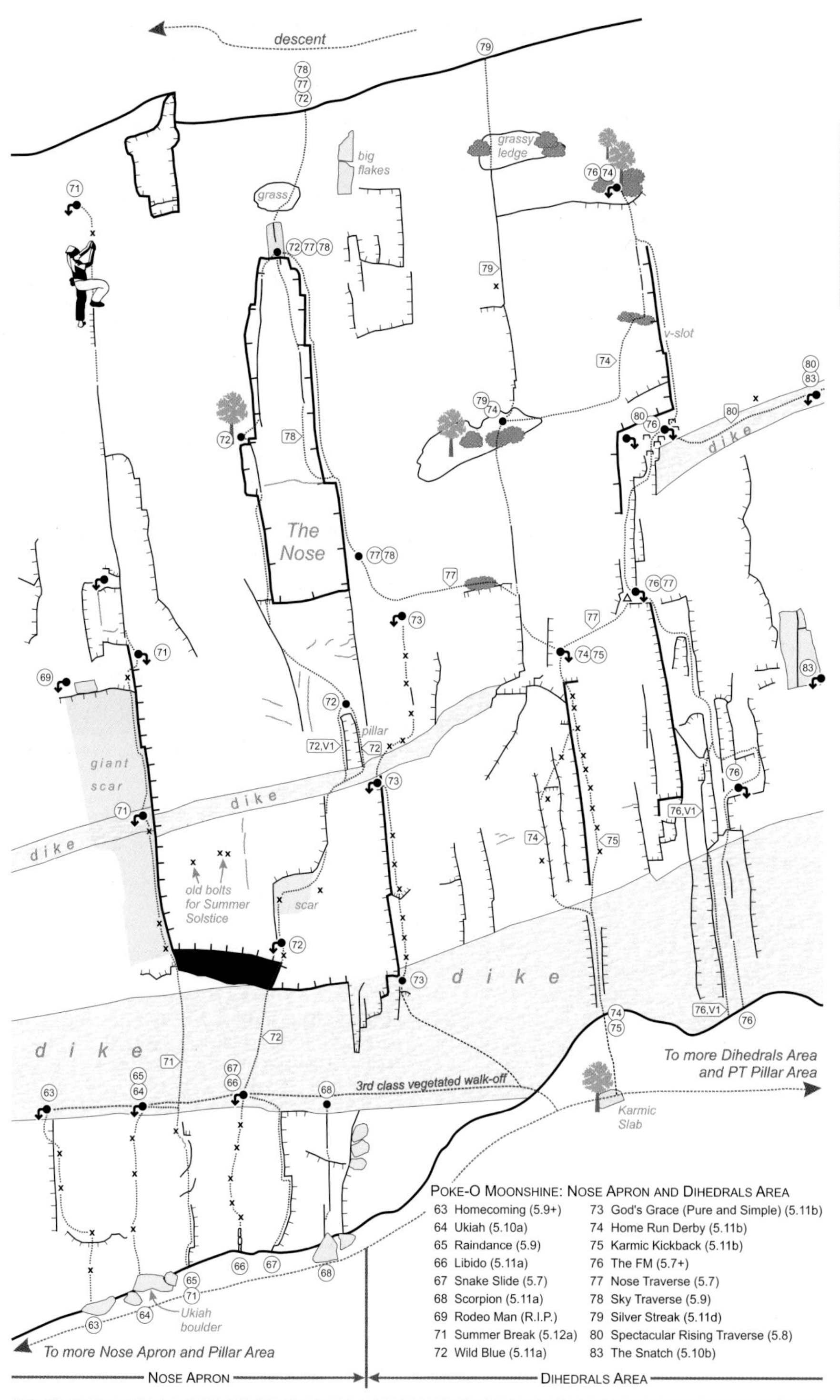
descent
grassy ledge
big flakes
grass
v-slot
dike
The Nose
pillar
giant scar
old bolts for Summer Solstice
scar
3rd class vegetated walk-off
To more Dihedrals Area and PT Pillar Area
Karmic Slab
Ukiah boulder
To more Nose Apron and Pillar Area
Nose Apron
Dihedrals Area
Poke-O Moonshine: Nose Apron and Dihedrals Area
63 Homecoming (5.9+)
64 Ukiah (5.10a)
65 Raindance (5.9)
66 Libido (5.11a)
67 Snake Slide (5.7)
68 Scorpion (5.11a)
69 Rodeo Man (R.I.P.)
71 Summer Break (5.12a)
72 Wild Blue (5.11a)
73 God's Grace (Pure and Simple) (5.11b)
74 Home Run Derby (5.11b)
75 Karmic Kickback (5.11b)
76 The FM (5.7+)
77 Nose Traverse (5.7)
78 Sky Traverse (5.9)
79 Silver Streak (5.11d)
80 Spectacular Rising Traverse (5.8)
83 The Snatch (5.10b)

P4 5.10b G: Climb a fistcrack on the right wall of the corner to gain an overhanging off-width crack formed by a huge block. Struggle upward to a belay at a tree just above. 75'

P5 5.9 G: Step right onto the face of the Nose and follow a crack just right of the arête to the top of the Nose and a ratty fixed anchor. 100'

P6 5.6 PG: From the top of the Nose, step back to the main face and climb vegetated rock to the top. 75'

V1 Pillar of Strength 5.9+ G: This variation stems up the left side of the pillar. Unusual and worth doing, according to the first ascentionists.

FA (P2) 1977, Dave Hough, Mark Meschinelli

FFA (P1) 1977, Geoff Smith, Jim Dunn

FFA (P2) May, 1978, Geoff Smith, Dave Hough

FFA (P3–P6) Jun 13, 1983, Steve Larson, Don Mellor

FFA (P2, after rockfall) Jun, 1987, Pierre Gagnon, Gelu Ionescu

FA (V1) Sep 6, 1987, Ken Nichols, Scott Reitsma

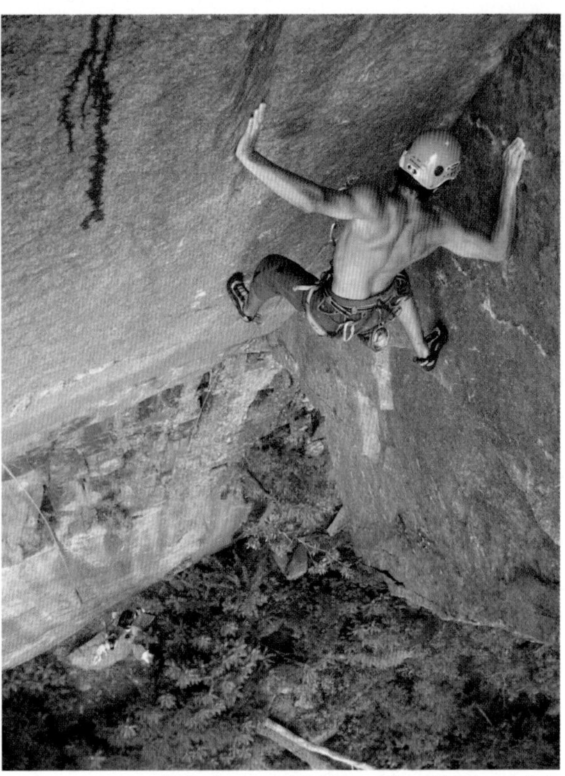

*Maxime Turgeon on P1 of **Summer Break** (5.12a) on the first free ascent. Photo by Louis-Philippe Menard.*

Dihedrals Area

To the right of the Nose Apron, the trail climbs uphill (past the slab of **Ukiah** and under the **Summer Break** corner) to a flat section in the woods—the Dihedrals Area. At the left end of this flat area, just uphill from the Nose Apron, is a table-sized rock slab buried in the ground; this is the Karmic Slab. Directly above this is crumbly chimney through the choss and vegetation that leads to the dihedrals of **Home Run Derby** and **Karmic Kickback**.

The climbs in this section are full-length routes, but all begin in corners above a steep, vegetated slope. This section ends where the trail drops steeply down into the open area near **Positive Thinking**.

73 God's Grace (Pure and Simple) 5.11b G 150' ★★★★

P1 is highly recommended; P2 is also good but not as popular.

Start: Approach **God's Grace** from the Karmic Slab by scrambling (3rd-class) up and left to the base of a right-facing corner directly below the right side of the Nose to a bolt belay.

P1 5.11b G: Up into the right-facing corner with a discontinuous fingercrack to a fixed anchor at the top of the corner. 70'

P2 5.10c PG: Move up into the dike and traverse to the right (wild) until you come to a line of weakness that heads up to a fixed anchor. 80'

Gear: To 2".

FA Oct 5, 1996, Patrick Munn, Dave Hough

74 Home Run Derby 5.11b PG (5.9 R) 335' ★★★

Interesting corner climbing on P1, which is joined by **Karmic Kickback**, a more direct line; most parties rappel from the end of P1. Named for the contest among top hitters in major league baseball to determine who can hit the most home runs.

Start: From the Karmic Slab, scramble up the steep, vegetated slope to the base of a broken chimney in dike rock.

P1 5.11b PG (5.9 R): Up the chimney to the top of the dike. Move left and into the bottom of the huge left-facing corner. Climb the corner with small gear, then traverse 8' right onto the arête (bolt, difficult to clip). Up the face through the overlap to a fixed anchor. 145'

P2 5.9 PG: Move left into a left-facing corner, then continue left to a vertical crack, right-facing at first, to reach a large, grassy ledge. 80'

P3 5.9+ PG: From the right end of the ledge, traverse directly right to a facing wall with a crack in a black streak. Up the crack to the left end of another ledge; traverse right to an arête and join the last 25' of P4 of **The FM**. 110'

FA Jun 30, 1989, Don Mellor, Jeff Edwards, Bill Dodd

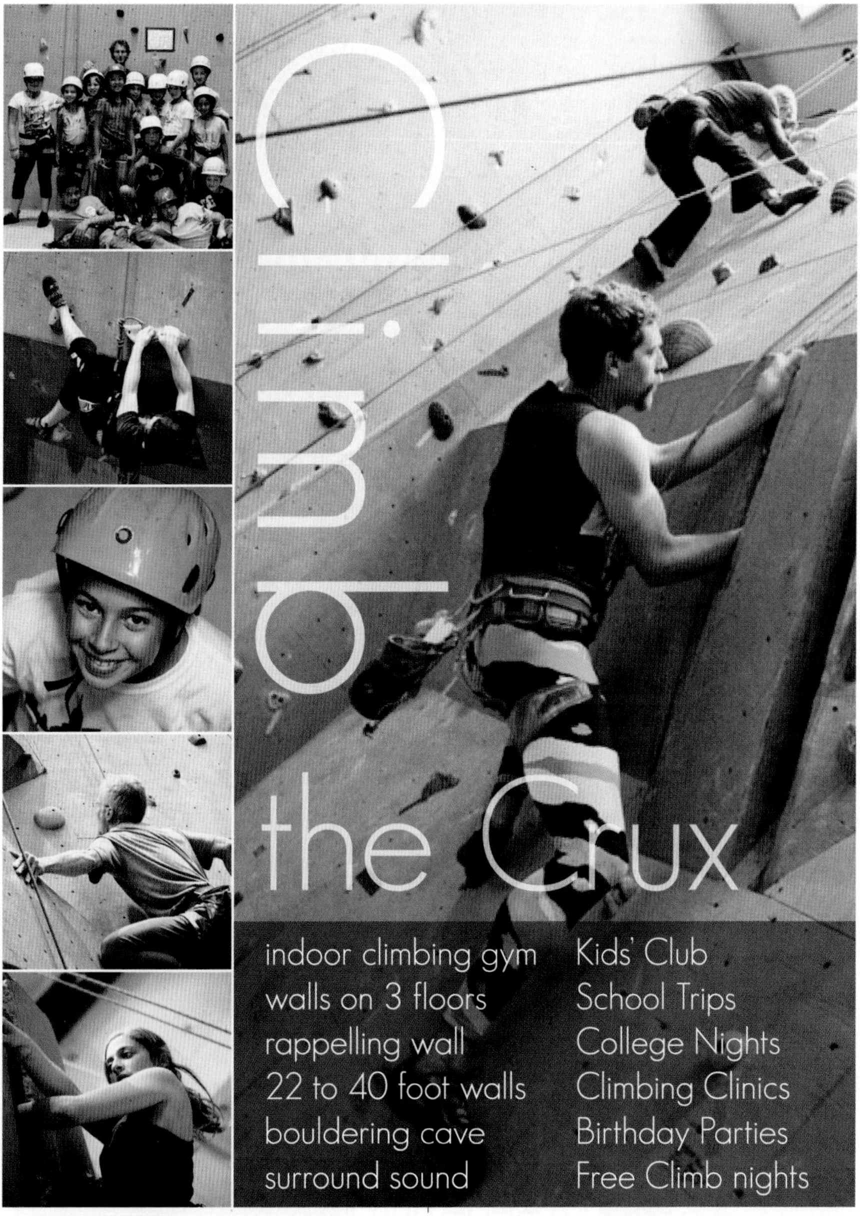
Climb
the Crux
indoor climbing gym
walls on 3 floors
rappelling wall
22 to 40 foot walls
bouldering cave
surround sound
Kids' Club
School Trips
College Nights
Climbing Clinics
Birthday Parties
Free Climb nights

Climber on ***TR*** (5.10a), *Spider's Web. Photo by Mark Meschinelli.*

75 Karmic Kickback 5.11b G 140' ★★★★

Start: As you walk uphill from the Nose Apron, the trail levels out at a table-sized slab—the Karmic Slab. From here, you can look up and see the dihedrals of **Karmic Kickback** and **Home Run Derby**, which form a rectangular buttress. Scramble up the slope to the base of a broken chimney in the dike rock.

○ P1 5.11b G: Climb straight up the chimney and into the right-facing corner, then face-climb and stem thin edges up the corner and arête and finish through the overlap of **Home Run Derby**. The pitch has good gear once you get to the first bolt. 140'

History: One of the first routes to break from the ground-up ethic; using such compromised tactics was considered cashing in one's accumulated points of karma.

FA Aug, 1991, Gary Allan, Patrick Munn

76 The FM 5.7+ R 370' ★★★

Thrilling and exposed with comfortable belays and a clean crux; at one time, this was the most popular route at Poke-O. P2 has several sections that traverse with poor protection, making it a route only for experienced 5.7 leaders and followers. Be aware that there is considerable loose rock at the third belay and on P4, and this is directly above the base of the route.

Start: 50' right of the Karmic Slab, in a small alcove formed by opposing corners capped by a small overhang 30' up.

P1 5.7 G: (V1) Up broken cracks in the back of the alcove to the overhang, then break it on the right side via a crack in a left-facing corner. Step right to a comfortable ledge with a fixed anchor. 70'

P2 5.7+ PG: (V2) From the right side of the belay ledge, climb up a left-facing corner for 10', then foot-traverse left to a shallow right-facing corner (scary for a second). Step down and left, across the face (crux; known as the "Lavallée Move") to a stance. Climb up the face toward a left-facing, broken corner, then up the corner to a large flake. Use the flake to step left to an opposing right-facing corner. Up the corner a few feet, then out left around the arête to a ledge with a fixed anchor, the Triangle Ledge. 90'

P3 5.7 R: Climb the right-facing corner directly above the ledge, and the arête to its left, to gain a right-rising ramp (crux; the moves off the ledge are committing; some RPs and nuts can be arranged). Follow the ramp up and right with good gear to a fixed anchor on a ledge covered with loose rock, below the deep V-slot. 60'

P4 5.7 G: Climb the deep V-slot directly above the belay (loose rock for the first 30') to the top, traverse left on the Gong Flake to the arête, then up the arête and face to the grassy ledge and fixed anchor. 100'

P5 5.2 PG: Climb a face left of a broken left-facing corner to the top. 50'

V1 The FM Direct 5.9 G: Climb the right-facing corner to the ceiling in the alcove, then work directly through the ceiling via a crack that joins **The FM** above the first belay ledge; continue up to the Triangle Ledge.

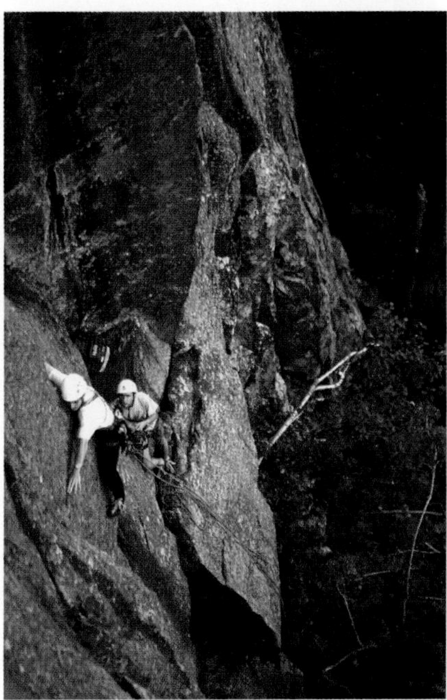

*A climber makes the crux move on **The FM** (5.7+). Photo by Mark Meschinelli.*

V2 5.9 R: Instead of moving right, face climb directly up and left and follow the normal line until the traverse left to the belay. Continue straight up to a dirty, right-facing corner-crack and follow it to a sloping ledge. Belay at the top of the ledge below the deep V-slot. Not recommended.

Descent: It is recommended to rappel from the top of P4 (angle left to avoid the V-slot) to the Triangle Ledge, then to the ground.

History: In Turner's words, "There had been a lot of hype about Poke-O; it was rumored in Montreal that the legendary Fritz Wiessner had pronounced it unclimbable, so Hugh Tanton and I approached what seemed to be the most amenable line with some trepidation. We missed the key foothold on the second pitch and took aid from a sling (Claude Lavallée and Mike Ward freed this pitch on the second ascent). After that, everything went well, and we reached the top pleasantly surprised. I said to Hugh 'What do you think of that?' He replied, 'All I can say is, "Fuck me!"'"

FA Jun, 1957, John Turner, Hugh Tanton

FFA ("Lavallée Move") 1957, Claude Lavallée, Michael Ward (surgeon and mountaineer, and medical linchpin of the successful 1953 ascent of Everest; credited with discovering the South Col route)

FA (V1) Sep, 1978, Geoff Smith, Dave Hough

FA (V2) 1976, R.L. Stolz, Dick Compton, Lisa Graves

V1
80
76
83
85
88

descent
dike
black streaks
leaning block
orange spot
Houdini Slot
dike
slab
To more Dihedrals Area and Nose Apron
To PT Pillar Area
POKE-O MOONSHINE: DIHEDRALS AREA
76 The FM (5.7+)
77 Nose Traverse (5.7)
80 Spectacular Rising Traverse (5.8)
81 The Body Snatcher (5.10a)
82 Piece of Snatch (5.11c)
83 The Snatch (5.10b)
84 Knights in Armor (5.10d)
85 Great Dihedral (5.9+)
86 Half Mile (5.7+)
87 Sea of Seams (5.12c)
88 C-Tips (5.10c)
91 Son of Slime (5.10a)
DIHEDRALS AREA
PT PILLAR AREA

77 Nose Traverse 5.7 PG 295' ★

Start: On the Triangle Ledge at the end of P2 of **The FM**.

P1 5.7 PG: From the Triangle Ledge, traverse down and left on a ledge to the P1 anchor for **Home Run Derby** and **Karmic Kickback**. Then follow P2 of **Home Run Derby** for a short distance (climb left into a left-facing corner and continue left to a vertical crack, right-facing at first) to reach an intermediate grassy ledge on the left. From here, traverse left on a ledge and onto the slab (crux) that leads left to the base of the right side of the Nose and belay on a vegetated ledge. 110'

P2 The Venezuela Pitch 5.7 PG: Climb the undesirable right-facing corner formed by the Nose and the main face to the top of the Nose and a fixed anchor. 110'

P3 5.6 PG: From the top of the Nose, step back to the main face and climb vegetated rock to the top. (Same as **Wild Blue**.) 75'

FA 1958, John Turner, Brian Rothery, Hugh Tanton

78 Sky Traverse 5.9 R 185' ★★★

Climbs the right edge of the face of the Nose. Spectacular climbing in an exposed position, but not for the meek. Good gear once you are on the face.

Start: At the end of P1 of **Nose Traverse**.

P1 5.9 R: Climb up the right-facing corner of the Nose to a series of fragile flakes on the left wall. Move left out the flakes (last protection) to the bridge of the Nose (crux) and a welcome crack, then up the face and crack to the top of the Nose and a fixed anchor. 110'

P2 5.6 PG: From the top of the Nose, step back to the main face and climb vegetated rock to the top. (Same as **Wild Blue**.) 75'

FA Sep, 1976, Geoff Smith, Patrick Munn

79 Silver Streak 5.11d PG 130'

Originally climbed from **The FM**, this route ascends the crack with a silver water streak coming out of the bottom. A horrible route, nothing good about it; an impressive lead for the era and probably hasn't seen a second ascent.

Start: At the end of P2 of **Home Run Derby**.

P1 5.11d PG: From the grassy ledge, go up a right-facing corner to a small overhang, then follow the silver-streaked crack above to the top. 130'

History: Geoff Smith placed the bolt at the base of the crack, then was scooped by Allan and Hough.

FA Oct, 1978, Gary Allan, Dave Hough

80 Spectacular Rising Traverse (aka SRT) 5.8 PG (5.7 R) 370' ★

This route follows one of Poke-O's dike features across the upper reaches of the wall to a final hanging chimney. The name was most likely derived from Turner's description, which appeared in *Appalachia:* "[The] variation starts from the foot of the final groove [of **The FM**] and follows a spectacular rising traverse to the right . . ."[8] Extra caution is warranted to protect those climbing the popular routes below you. The route offers some adventuresome climbing, and V1 is recommended.

Start: At the Triangle Ledge at the top of P2 of **The FM**.

P1 5.7 R: Follow P3 of **The FM**: Climb the right-facing corner directly above the ledge, and the arête to its left, to gain a right-rising ramp (5.7 R). Follow the ramp up and right with good gear. 10' shy of **The FM**'s P3 fixed anchor (and below the right side of the large roof), traverse right on dike rock that consists of blocks, ledges, bushes, and ramps to the jammed sling anchor of **Body Snatcher**. As you continue the traverse, an airy step right leads to a ramp, more bushes, then finally a spacious alcove with a fixed anchor at the top of **Great Dihedral** P2. 170'

P2 5.6 G: Continue the traverse up and right along the dike, past the anchor for **Sea of Seams** to a fixed anchor below a large left-facing corner, just left of a gigantic roof. 120'

P3 5.8 PG: (V1) Climb the left-facing corner to the roof, out left under the roof, then up the left-facing corner to the top. 80'

V1 5.9 G: Traverse right under the gigantic roof (spectacular 5.2) to a smooth-walled, hanging chimney. Squirm up the parallel cracks in the chimney, through a squeeze, then up a left-facing corner to a birch tree. Continue up a crack to the top.

Descent: From the birch at the top of the hanging chimney of V1, it is possible to rappel to the base of the chimney, reverse the traverse (5.2), then two 60-m rappels return you to the ground near the base of **C-Tips**.

History: Regarding V1, early ascents climbed a jammed block in the chimney. This dropped out in the late 1970s. Geoff Smith claims the first ascent sans block in 1978.

FA 1957, John Turner, Phil Gribben
FA (V1) 1957, John Turner, Dick Strachan

81 The Body Snatcher 5.10a PG 250' ★★

This historic route is more commonly climbed to access **Knights in Armor**. From the top of P2, it is possible to traverse left and join P4 of **The FM** (as the first ascent did) or finish as for **Spectacular Rising Traverse**.

Start: Same as **The FM**.

P1 5.10a PG: Angle up and right across easy but unstable dike rock to the large, bottomless left-facing corner of **The Snatch**. Climb the fingercrack in the corner (bolt, crux) past a small triangular overhang on the left, at which point the crack splits; **The Snatch** stays left in the corner, and **The Body Snatcher** veers right up to a block and stance (this is where **Knights in Armor** leaves off). Continue up and follow an insecure left-leaning ramp leftward to the fixed anchor in a blocky alcove (same as **The Snatch**). 150'

P2 5.9 PG: Climb the block left of the belay and into a long right-facing corner, then follow it to the dike rock and jammed-sling fixed anchor. 100'

Descent: There are two possible rappels: traverse left to the P3 anchor of **The FM** or traverse right to the fixed anchor on **The Snatch**.

8 J. M. Turner, "Various Notes—Rock Climbing," *Appalachia* 33 (1960–61), p. 249.

*Opposite: Jeff Edwards on P2 of **Great Dihedral** (5.9+). The tree just above the climber is gone. Photo by Don Mellor.*

History: Named for Burke and Hare, two serial killers from Scotland known as the Edinburgh Body Snatchers, who originally snatched bodies from graves and sold them for medical research but later found it easier simply to murder people. Turner originally referred to the route as **The AM** when he mentioned it in an article for *Appalachia* as a direct approach to **Spectacular Rising Traverse**.[9] The route was once graded 5.9, but was upgraded when a block pulled out of the lower corner on **The Snatch**.
FA (5.8 A1) 1960, John Turner, Wilfried Twelker
FFA 1968, John Stannard

82 Piece of Snatch 5.11c G (5.7 R) 140' ★★

Start: Same as for **The Snatch**.
P1 5.11c G (5.7 R): Climb dike rock (5.7 R) straight up to the shallow left-facing corner left of the triangular overhang. Climb a thin crack which widens, breaks an overhang, then becomes off-width before it reaches the fixed anchor (as for **The Snatch**). 140'
FA 2005, Dan Foster, Ty Mack

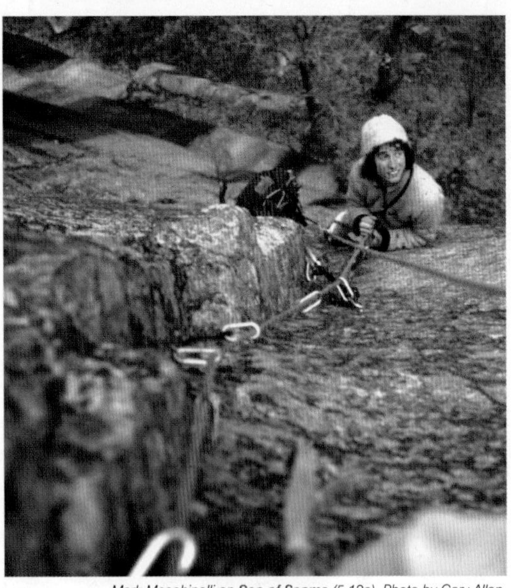

*Mark Meschinelli on **Sea of Seams** (5.12c). Photo by Gary Allan.*

83 The Snatch 5.10b G 240' ★★★★

Enjoyable climbing up a continuous finger- and hand-crack. Once you're past the dike rock, this climb is fantastic and well protected. The route is named because Allan "snatched" the lead from his partners on the plum P2. A block fell from the lower corner and a bolt was added; no change in grade.
Start: 50' right of **The FM** alcove where the trail comes right up to the rock face at the cleanest section of dike rock, below cracks in white, spotty rock.
P1 5.10a PG: Climb the crack in white, spotty dike rock (5.8 PG) to the base of a bottomless left-facing corner (unstable rock in this section). Climb the fingercrack in the corner (bolt) past a small triangular overhang on the left. Take the leftmost of two diverging cracks (crux). At the top, a hand traverse left on a rail leads to a ledge with a fixed anchor. 140'
P2 5.10b G: (V1) Reverse the hand traverse back right and into the left-facing corner. Work up an overhanging crack on the right wall until you can step back left into the main corner to the top of the dihedral and a fixed anchor. 100'
V1 Snatch It 5.9 PG: Climb the fingercrack in the face directly above the belay to the dike rock. Step right to the fixed anchor.
FA 1977, Gary Allan, Geoff Smith, Patrick Munn
FA (V1) Aug, 1991, Dominic Eisinger, Mike Wray, Anthony Smith (Geoff Smith's brother)

84 Knights in Armor 5.10d G 250' ★★★★

An incredible fingercrack, guarded by an involved approach. You can approach the base of the crack from **The Body Snatcher** using aid or by rappelling in from the traverse dike between **The Snatch** and **Great Dihedral**. (The **SRT** provides a moderate way to reach this point on the traverse dike.) P1 is popular, after which you can rappel from the fixed anchor on **Great Dihedral**.
Start: (V1) Climb P1 of **The Body Snatcher** to the stance after the cracks split. There is fixed gear above on the right that begins the first pendulum of the aid traverse (40') to a hanging belay at the base of the fingercrack (A1, 5.9+, RPs).
P1 5.10d G: Climb the steep crack to the ledge, then step right to the anchor on **Great Dihedral**. 100'
P2 5.8 PG: Step right to a large boulder and climb discontinuous fingercracks to a more prominent crack system that shoots to the top of the cliff. 150'
V1 Direct Start A4: The line of the original ascent climbed **Great Dihedral** to the roof, aided out left under the roof to the protuberance below the roof, then straight up through the roof (old bolt above the lip) to a faint crack with a couple of pitons 10' above the lip. An incredibly unlikely line.
FA 1977, Patrick Munn (rope solo)
FFA (P2) 1978, Gary Allan
FFA (complete) Sep 9, 1988, Patrick Munn, Don Mellor

85 Great Dihedral 5.9+ PG (5.8 R) 350' ★★★★

A testpiece of sustained difficulties and physical climbing; the Houdini Slot is especially memorable. The integrity of this Poke-O classic is somewhat marred by the proximity of a bolt-protected variation. A much better finish is **SRT**: climb P2 of **SRT**, then the V1 finish.
Start: At the right end of the Dihedrals Area where the trail is still against the rock and before it drops down into the P.T. Pillar Area below a bottomless right-facing dihedral 70' up.

9 J. M. Turner, "Various Notes—Rock Climbing," *Appalachia* 33 (1960–61), p. 249.

P1 5.8 PG: Easy steps in dike rock lead to a right-facing corner with a wide crack on the left wall. Continue up to the roof, then undercling right around the roof and up to a cramped stance in the corner. 80'

P2 5.9+ PG: Directly above the belay is a bombay chimney—the Houdini Slot—which you can gain by climbing, with thin protection, the vertical wall on the left. The security of the slot is short-lived, as the exit is both awkward and demanding. Take care to avoid rope drag. Secure and continuous finger jams lead to a stance below a section of off width (V1) (the bolts of **Changing of the Guard** are disturbingly close). A second crux is located near the top where you step right around a ceiling formed by a leaning block. Belay at fixed anchors on a dike ledge. 120'

P3 5.8 R: A rarely climbed pitch with an unprotected start. Make a short traverse right along the dike, then back left over the belay. Climb up to a bolt that protects 5.8 face climbing to perched blocks and an easier but dirty finish. 150'

V1 Changing of the Guard 5.9+ G: Below the off width, move left to a bolt-protected arête. Follow the arête, then move left to the face, then back to the arête at the left side of the leaning block. Up the block to the fixed anchor on the dike ledge.

History: Geoff Smith used one point of aid on P2, thinking that there was plenty of time to free it later. He was scooped when Goldstone climbed it the next year. This first free ascent is immortalized in Goldstone's article in *Climbing.*[10]

FA (P1) Oct, 1975, Geoff Smith, Dave Hough
FA (P2, 5.7 A1) Oct, 1975, Geoff Smith, Dave Hough
FFA (P2) Jul, 1976, Richard Goldstone, Ivan Rezucha
FA (P3) Aug, 1976, Geoff Smith, Dave Hough
FA (V1) Aug, 1993, Patrick Purcell, Gary Allan

86 Half Mile 5.7+ G (5.2 R) 750' ★

Start: At the right end of the Dihedrals Area, in the trees above where the trail drops down into the P.T. Pillar Area, 15' below a right-facing corner.

P1 5.4 PG: Climb straight up to dike rock, then traverse right to a left-facing corner at the base of a pillar that spans the height of the dike. 100'

P2 5.6 G: (V1) Climb the left side of the pillar—known as the Pendulum Pillar—to a fixed anchor at the top. Pendulum right to a fixed anchor (shared with **C-Tips**) 15' right of the base of the pillar's right side. 50'

P3 5.6 PG: Traverse rightward in the dike to the fixed anchor at the top of **Cooney-Norton Face**. 130'

P4 5.6 PG: Continue the rightward traverse in the dike to the fixed anchor on P2 of **Gamesmanship**. 110'

P5–P7 5.7+ G (5.2 R): Finish on **Gamesmanship** P3–P5. 360'

V1 5.9 PG: Face-climb across the front of the pillar to its right side.

History: The owner of the bar across the road (now long gone) once described how his non-climber son had soloed this route (roughly) with no equipment; if true, it ranks as one of Poke-O's great solos.

FA 1958, John Turner, Claude Lavallée

10 Richard Goldstone, "The Great Dihedral," *Climbing,* no. 123 (Dec 1990), p. 82.

87 Sea of Seams 5.12c G 170' ★★★★

Excellent, physical climbing on one of Poke-O's blank shields of rock. There is still quite a bit of metal around from the aid ascent. The route name is a nod to **Sea of Dreams** in Yosemite. Gary Allan gives this high marks as a free route, hence the four-star rating.

Start: Begin from the fixed anchor atop the Pendulum Pillar of **Half Mile**'s P2.

● **P1 5.12c G:** Climb the face left of a small overhang and trend left toward a suspect hanging flake. Pass this on the right and up into a left-facing corner and fixed anchor on the left wall. A bit sporty. 70'

● **P2 5.12a G:** Continue up the corner to a slab finish at a fixed anchor in a dike. 100'

FA (5.6 A3) Nov, 1978, Dave Hough, Mark Meschinelli
FFA (P2) Aug, 1993, Gary Allan, Patrick Munn

P.T. Pillar Area

Downhill and right of the Dihedrals Area, the base opens up into a grassy slope beneath the prominent black streak of **Positive Thinking**. Just right of this black streak is a 90'-high pillar of rock pasted to the face known as **P.T. Pillar**, with a flatish boulder at the base—the Cooney-Norton Boulder. Just right of this pillar is a right-rising flake, the top of which is known as the Sting Ledge; you can 4th-class up this ledge to reach the start of several routes.

Central Rappel: The Central Rappel is located in this section and begins about 200' left of the top of **Gamesmanship** and **Fastest Gun**. The top fixed anchor is on a large pine tree on the (climber's) left side of a slab that sits at the base of two large boulders perched on a slab. The first rappel is 150' and drops straight down the face to a fixed anchor near the left margin of the smooth, water-worn wall. (There is an alternative fixed anchor to the right, on the route **True Grit**.) The next rappel is 90' and takes you down to the major traverse dike at the top of **Ragtime**; there are several other anchors in this vicinity. The third rappel is 160' and takes you down to the Sting Ledge. A final rappel of 90' lands you at the base of **Save the Rock for Uncle Sam**, 40' left of **The Sting**. (Can be done with two 70-m rappels.)

88 C-Tips 5.10c G 120' ★★★★

"C-Tips" has been mistaken for "Sea Tips" but is really short for "Carbide Tips"—and you will indeed need carbide fingertips on this route's sharp holds.

Start: Walk out to the right end of the ledge system, just left of and uphill from the **Positive Thinking** amphitheater, at a fixed anchor below a black streak in the headwall.

○ **P1 5.10c G:** Climb up onto the slab, then straight up past bolts to a two-bolt anchor. 120'

Gear: Optional medium nut helps protect the moves to the first bolt.

History: The route is one of several that were climbed "ground up" with the drill on a separate toprope—an experiment to follow the ground-up ethic of the time. It didn't catch on.

FA 1991, Patrick Purcell, Mark Meschinelli

Positive Thinking
(winter route)
Central Rappel
Sting Ledge
88
91
90
91
93
96
100
105
106

POKE-O MOONSHINE: PT PILLAR AREA
slab
Central Rappel
black streak
black streaks
orange spot
wet chimney (yuck)
dike
pillar
rib
Pendulum Pillar
ski tracks
Sting Ledge
4th
grassy area
Cooney-Norton Boulder
Uncle Sam Boulder
To more Dihedrals Area and Nose Apron
To Bloody Mary Area
80 Spectacular Rising Traverse (5.8)
86 Half Mile (5.7+)
87 Sea of Seams (5.12c)
88 C-Tips (5.10c)
89 Project
90 Mogster (5.12b)
91 Son of Slime (5.10a)
92 Positive Thinking (5.9+)
93 P.T. Pillar (5.8+)
94 Macho (5.11a)
95 Holyfield & Foreman (5.8)
96 Cooney-Norton Face (5.10b)
97 Cosmopolitan Wall (5.10c)
98 Easy Street (5.11d)
99 Unforgiven (5.11c)
100 Ragtime (5.11a)
101 True Grit (5.11a)
102 Cosmo Cracks (5.9)
103 Excitable Boy (A2)
104 Save the Rock for Uncle Sam (5.12a)
105 The Sting (5.8)
106 Gamesmanship (5.8+)
DIHEDRALS AREA
PT PILLAR AREA

89 Project

One of Poke-O's last great projects, now abandoned. It was intended to extend **C-Tips** up the black streak above the anchor. There's a bolt just above the dike, an anchor in the middle of the wall above, and a final anchor below the final roofs of **SRT**.

90 Mogster 5.12b PG 165' ★★★★

This more difficult twin to **C-Tips** climbs an even more impressive section of vertical face. There is a runout section on the upper wall.

Start: Begin on a brown slab with a low bolt, just left of **Positive Thinking**'s black streak.

● **P1 5.12b PG:** Up the initial slab to a steeper headwall with several bolts. Cross the ramp of **Son of Slime** (and a shared bolt), then up the crux headwall, following the black streak. 165'

History: First toproped by Patrick Purcell and named **Edges to Heaven**. Purcell was scooped when the route was bolted and led before he could complete it. Named for Lanman's Newfoundland dog.

FA Jul, 1992, Dave Lanman

91 Son of Slime 5.10a PG 480' ★★★★

An incredible route up an unlikely section of rock; often wet, but not to be missed if it's dry. P1 and P2 are popular. Named after its parent, **Slime Line**, due to its similarity in rock color and texture.

Start: Same as **C-Tips**.

P1 5.10a PG: Up onto the slab, then traverse directly right 80' to a fixed anchor in black rock. There is gear in the break above the slab, and a bolt protects the most difficult moves. 80'

P2 5.9+ G: Straight up the black streak using discontinuous cracks, then face-climb left at first, then right (bolts; crux) to the dike and a fixed anchor. It's possible to rappel from here. 100'

P3 5.10a G: Staying left of the **Positive Thinking** abyss, climb dike rock to a small overhang, then up to the left-facing flakes above. Over the flakes, up a face (bolt) to a crack, then finally step left to a belay on a ledge. 150'

P4 5.9 G: Go up the crack above the belay to the large roof system and finish in the excellent bombay chimney of **SRT** V1. 150'

FA Aug, 1988, Mark Meschinelli, Patrick Munn, Ann Eastman

92 Positive Thinking 5.9+ G 440'

John Turner really had an eye for climbing ice routes in the summer. Often overlooked as a summer route, **Positive Thinking** is an extremely sought-after winter route, like its cousin **Repentance** in New Hampshire. P1 is technical and recommended, although watch for poison ivy up high. The name comes from P1, which, in Turner's words, "seemed elegant, unrelenting, and poorly protected, requiring a confident attitude."

Start: Same as **P.T. Pillar**.

P1 5.9+ G: Climb the squeeze chimney to the ledge, step left, and climb the crack to the overlap. Continue up the widening crack to a slab finish before the dike. Belay right on pitons or 20' left at the fixed anchor on **Son of Slime**. 180'

P2–P3 5.9 PG: Continue up the black, dripping abyss and through an overhanging section of shattered rock that leads to a chimney and low-angled crack right of the roofs at the top of the cliff. Nobody ever goes here in the summer. 260'

FA 1959, John Turner, Dick Wilmott

*Opposite: A climber on **C-Tips** (5.10c). The large right-facing corner to the left is **Great Dihedral** (5.9+). Photo by Mark Meschinelli.*

93 P.T. Pillar (aka Pee Wee Pillar) 5.8+ G 90' ★★

Another nice moderate pitch that is often overlooked. This route climbs the namesake pillar right of **Positive Thinking** and provides an easy way to set up a toprope on **Macho**.

Start: At a shallow squeeze chimney on the left side of the pillar, left of the Cooney-Norton Boulder.

P1 5.8+ G: Climb the left side of the pillar to a fixed anchor at the top. 90'

FA May, 1978, Dave Hough, Geoff Smith

94 Macho 5.11a PG 90' ★★★★

This route has been erased and restored at least three times. It is now an adequately protected testpiece of thin crack climbing.

Start: At the Cooney-Norton Boulder, in front of the pillar.

P1 5.11a PG: From the right side of a block that leans up against the cliff, step up to a ledge and clip a high bolt. Climb the face and trend left on good holds to a thin seam on the left. Up the seam with increasing difficulty; eventually move right to a parallel crack and follow it to the top. 90'

*Dennis Luther on **Macho** (5.11a), belayed by Nick Wakeman.*

History: A week after the first ascent, Patrick Purcell rope-soloed **Kato Crack** (A3), the left-hand crack straight to the top. **Macho** starts to the right, then goes left into the **Kato Crack**, then back right to finish in the right-hand crack.
FA Jun 7, 1986, Julien Déry

95 Holyfield & Foreman (aka P.T. Pillar Right) 5.8 G 90'

P.T. Pillar's ugly-sister route, which climbs the unappealing right side of the pillar. Named for a boxing match between George Foreman, then in his forties, and world heavyweight champion Evander Holyfield; Foreman went 12 rounds before losing the decision.
Start: Begin partway up the Sting Ledge, below the right side of the pillar.
P1 5.8 G: Climb up the right side of the pillar to the fixed anchor at the top. 90'
FA Apr 19, 1991, Patrick Purcell, Mark Meschinelli

96 Cooney-Norton Face 5.10b PG 420' ★★★★

Incredible climbing—sustained and technical, but never desperate. The final moves will knock you out. P1 is popular and superhigh-quality; the upper pitches are worthwhile but not as clean. Two ropes recommended. Another route named for a boxing match, this one in 1981 between Kenneth Norton and Gerry Cooney; Norton was annihilated in the first round, leading to his retirement.
Start: At the Cooney-Norton Boulder.
P1 5.10b PG: Climb up the left end of Sting Ledge, then up the face on positive holds, aiming for a piton between shallow opposing corners. Stem up the corners to an overhang, then climb rightward through slashes and unlikely terrain to a stance. Continue rightward to a bolt, then traverse left to a final bolt (V1). Move left into a left-facing corner (crux) and follow this to the top at a fixed anchor. 160'
P2 5.6 PG: Traverse the dike right 30' to stepped terrain in right-facing corners, then up to a block belay beneath a black ceiling. This belay is just below the Central Rappel anchor on the black face above the ceiling. 100'
P3 5.10a PG: This pitch climbs a left-leaning crack system on the left side of the water-worn face. Step up left on blocks in the dike and climb past the ceiling on its left side (bolt). Continue up, passing 6' left of a fixed anchor (the Central Rappel station), past a short right-facing corner, and through a bulge with slightly mossy rock. 160'
V1 5.10c PG: From the second bolt, climb straight up the bulge to the fixed anchor.
FA Jul, 1982, Mark Meschinelli, Dave Hough, Todd Eastman
FA (V1) May 4, 1988, Dennis Luther

97 Cosmopolitan Wall 5.10c G 140' ★★★★

Another masterpiece of steep face and crack climbing on the wall above the Sting Ledge.
Start: Scramble up the Sting Ledge 30' to a bolt below a crack just right of a prominent left-facing corner.
P1 5.10c G: Climb the crack right of a sharp, shallow left-facing corner to an overlap (stay right of the A-frame roof at the top of the sharp corner). Climb through the overlap (5.9 PG), protect in the crack above, then move 6' left to gain another crack. Climb the crack to its end, face-climb up to a rail (V1), then move left to meet the final bolts of **Cooney-Norton Face**. 140'
V1 5.11a G: Traverse right along the rail to join the upper three bolts of **Easy Street**.
History: The original line climbed to the last protection and lowered. After that, to get off, climbers simply moved left to join **Cooney-Norton Face**, which kept the grade at 5.10c. Gary Allan returned in 1992 to finish the route and added several bolts rightward to finish on a left-rising overlap (5.11a). In 1999, this finish was replaced with the finish for **Easy Street**, which keeps the grade at 5.11a.
FA 1978, Gary Allan, Geoff Smith, Dave Hough

98 Easy Street 5.11d G 140' ★★★★

"When life looks like easy street, there is danger at your door." Climbs the light-colored shield of rock right of **Cosmopolitan Wall**. **Easy Street** has been described as a collection of Poke-O face-climbing cruxes stacked into a single route. Thankfully the bolts minimize the pucker factor, and the ceaseless challenges remain amusing.
Start: Same as **Cosmopolitan Wall**.
P1 5.11d G: Climb the handcrack of **Cosmopolitan Wall** through the overlap and onto the thin face with numerous pinches and insecure stances. The wall steepens and finishes through a bulge below the dike. Traverse left to the anchor as for **Cooney-Norton Face**. 140'
FA Aug, 1999, Dominic Eisinger, Mark Meschinelli

99 Unforgiven 5.11c G 160' ★★★

Start: At the fixed anchors at the top of **The Sting**.
P1 5.10b G: Climb left to the highest point on the Sting Ledge. Climb the crack with a triangular pod, then move onto the face and head leftward to a bottomless right-facing corner. Climb up the corner, then head left and pass below a large flake to a small stance and fixed anchor. 90'
● **P2 5.11c G:** Move right to the top of the block and up the bulging headwall above, just right of the black streak, to reach the dike. Traverse right to the Central Rappel anchors. 70'
History: This line was originally attempted in the 1980s by some "Gunkies" using a top-down style but abandoned when they learned of the bottom-up ethic for first ascents of that era. Gary Allan led it on sight using the abandoned gear; later, bolts were added by other climbers who remain "unforgiven."
FA 1993, Gary Allan, Mark Meschinelli

100 Ragtime 5.11a PG 160' ★★★

Climbs the black streak at the right end of the P.T. Pillar wall. Although this route received an additional bolt on P2, it still climbs like an old-school route—committing, thrilling, and memorable. Think about the vertically challenged Munn stretching for the crux mantel hold before you curse this irreversible reach.
Start: At the fixed anchors at the top of **The Sting**.

*Opposite: Colin Loher on P1 of **Cooney-Norton Face** (5.10b).*

P1 5.8 G: Step right and climb a right-facing corner to gain a higher ledge with fixed anchors. 40'
P2 5.11a PG: A bolt above the belay safeguards the climbing of a hollow flake that arches left to a stance below an overhang. Climb up past the overhang, then choose the lesser of two evils: a traverse out right to the mantel with a bolt above, or a thin seam on the left. A short runout ends at the Central Rappel anchor at the dike. 120'
FA 1987, Patrick Munn, Dominic Eisinger

101 True Grit 5.11a PG (5.9 R) 270' ★★

Ascends the water-worn face right of the Central Rappel route.
Start: At the top of P3 of **Gamesmanship**. Take a belay on the left side of this ledge at an oak tree with a fixed anchor.
P1 5.11a PG: Step left off the tree ledge and up to a bolt (avoid the fixed piton farther left) in the headwall that gains a crack in a shallow left-facing corner. Up the crack to a bulge, past a dike, to a fixed anchor in dike rock. 90'
P2 5.9 R: Face-climb up and right, past a left-facing overlap, following the obvious weakness that continues up and right and eventually leads to an endless lower-angled slab. 180'
FA Jul 20, 1991, Dennis Luther, Steve Bailey

102 Cosmo Cracks 5.9 G 40' ★

These two overlooked cracks lead up to the beginning of **Cosmopolitan Wall**. They are fitting starts to **Cosmopolitan Wall** or a diversion of their own.
Start: 10' right of the Cooney-Norton Boulder is a chest-high ceiling. Both cracks begin at the left edge of this ceiling.
P1 5.9 G: (V1) The left-hand crack is 5.9 and a bit more popular. 40'
V1 5.11a G: The right-hand crack is harder.
FA Apr 18, 1991, Bill Dodd, Don Mellor, Mark Meschinelli
FA (V1) Apr 18, 1991, Don Mellor, Bill Dodd

103 Excitable Boy A2 60'

A short aid route that is unexceptional other than that it was named for Warren Zevon's third album. "Ah-ooooo, werewolves of London."
Start: On the right side of a chest-high ceiling, 30' right of the Cooney-Norton Boulder.
P1 A2: Aid the thin seam to the Sting Ledge. 60'
FA Sep 30, 1984, Tad Welch (roped solo)

104 Save the Rock for Uncle Sam 5.12a TR 75'

Climb the face 35' left of **Gamesmanship** and **The Sting**. Damn hard. Named for the conflict that took place at the time over first-ascent ethics; instead of bolting this face, the first ascentionist decided to avoid the controversy.
FA (TR) Jun, 1988, Julien Déry

105 The Sting 5.8 G 90' ★★★★★

One of the best moderate handcracks at Poke-O, although the start can be a little intimidating. Highly recommended. **The Sting** can be used for an alternate start to **Gamesmanship** and as an approach to **Ragtime**, **True Grit**, and **Unforgiven**. Named for the 1973 film *The Sting*.
Start: Same as **Gamesmanship**.
P1 5.8 G: (V1) Climb up the initial crack and pod of **Gamesmanship** for 6' until you can make a traverse left using a thin fingercrack. From the end of the traverse, follow the handcrack straight up until you can move left to a good ledge with a fixed anchor (the bottommost anchor for the Central Rappel). 90'
V1 5.9 PG: Starting 4' left of **Gamesmanship**, make a face move straight up (or lunge) to a series of incut buckets to gain the leftward traverse. This is a good alternative if **Gamesmanship** is occupied.
History: The route was soloed 50 times in one day by Patrick Purcell (using the Sting Ledge to walk off).
FA Aug, 1974, Geoff Smith, Gary Allan, Dave Hough

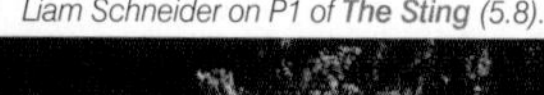
Liam Schneider on P1 of **The Sting** *(5.8).*

106 Gamesmanship 5.8+ G (5.2 R) 575' ★★★★★

Undeniably the most popular route at Poke-O. Although P1 is celebrated, the parallel cracks on P4 are the gift. Unfortunately, the aesthetic nature of these two pitches is diminished by the lesser quality pitches in between.

Start: 50' right of the Uncle Sam Boulder at the base of a handcrack that begins a few feet above the ground with a pod 8' up.

P1 5.8+ G: Up the crack through the initial pod (crux) to a rest just above. Continue up the crack, which widens from hands through off width, then back to thin hands, with the angle easing before the fixed anchor. Sustained and hard for the grade. 115'

P2 5.7+ G: Climb cracks in the face left of the left-facing corner for 20', then into the main left-facing, stepped corner (V1). Continue up the corner where it steepens with a handcrack, then up to a gear belay in dike rock. Either belay here or use one of the fixed anchors nearby (right is the fixed anchor for **Sportsmanship**; left is the fixed anchor for the Central Rappel). 115'

P3 5.4 G: Move straight up a clean swipe of dike rock just right of a fractured pillar to a point level with a tree ledge to the right. Traverse directly right to the ledge and continue to its highest point to belay on a pine at the base of a large left-facing corner. 115'

P4 Ski Tracks 5.8 G: (V2) From the belay, step right to the base of the laser-cut handcrack. Jam up the handcrack (crux), making liberal use of a parallel crack to the right. After 80', the crack enters a shallow, right-facing brushy corner. Follow it to a belay on a broad, grassy ledge with a sapling. 115'

P5 5.3 R: Climb straight up the slab above the belay to the trees. 115'

V1 Sportsmanship 5.10 A0 PG: Follow a right-rising ledge to the base of a series of thin, discontinuous cracks. Up these cracks to a fixed anchor in the dike.

V2 Direct Finish 5.8 G: Climbs the large left-facing corner that is split into segments by two roofs. The corner is aesthetic-looking from a distance but is extremely dirty, with several large bushes to make things interesting. Climb the corner to the first roof, out left around the roof and into the second corner to the next roof, then out left and up the third corner to a prominent pine tree with a fixed anchor. This pine tree is on the same ledge as the P4 belay.

Descent: From the top, scramble down leftward to the top fixed anchor of the Central Rappel. Alternatively, from the left end of the P4 ledge, you can rappel to an oak tree on the P3 ledge, then down to the **Sportsmanship** anchor, to the P1 anchor, to the ground.

Gear: Singles to 4", extra 2" pieces.

History: The route is named for Stephen Potter's book *The Theory and Practice of Gamesmanship: Or the Art of Winning Games without Actually Cheating,* published in 1947. Turner thought "the difficult first move to be a 'ploy,' intimidating future climbers as to the level of difficulty higher up."

FA 1959, John Turner, Brian Rothery, Wilfried Twelker
FA (V1) Aug, 2006, Dominic Eisinger, Dave Hough
FA (V2) 1975, Gary Allan, Dave Hough

Bloody Mary Area

To the right of the open, grassy slope of the P.T. Pillar Area, the trail drops down to a low point (the start of **Southern Hospitality** and **Psalm 32**), then rises steeply uphill past the starts of **Bloody Mary** and **Fastest Gun**, and levels off at the Big Wall Area. The high-quality full-length routes located here make this a popular section of the cliff.

There are several options for descent. From the top, walk left and use the Central Rappel. From various points, you can traverse to **Shark Week** and rappel that route with two ropes or traverse to **Casual Observer** and rappel that route with one rope.

107 Southern Hospitality 5.12a R 235' ★★★★

A devious route with delicious moves and sound rock. The route was straightened out (V1) with the addition of a couple of bolts, producing one of the best single pitches at Poke-O. P3, the crux of the route, is currently dirty and not recommended. From the top of P3, you can extend the route by climbing to the upper dike (5.8), then left to **Gamesmanship** or right to **Fastest Gun**.

Start: At the lowest point of the terrain, downhill and right of **Gamesmanship**, about 25' left of where the trail turns steeply uphill, below a short, thin, discontinuous fingercrack that begins 12' up in chocolate rock.

P1 5.11b G: (V1) Gain the fingercrack, then up the difficult, discontinuous fingercrack to a bulging overhang. (V2) Work 20' left (crux) using hands in the middle horizontal to a vertical crack in the bulging overhang, then up this 6' to a stance on square-cut holds just above the overhang. (2.5" cam helpful for the belay.) 60'

P2 5.10d G: Continue the vertical crack directly above the belay past two wide sections to where it pinches off. Traverse right 10' to the next crack (crux), then up this crack to a ledge with a fixed anchor. (Two ropes required to rappel from here.) 100'

P3 5.12a R: Climb the crack directly above the belay with increasing difficulty until you can make a tricky traverse leftward (crux) past a bolt and into a mungy corner. Then follow it to a fixed anchor tucked up under a bush. 75'

V1 Northern Inhospitality 5.12d G: Climbs directly up to the overlap and meets the original route at the end of the P1 traverse. Climb over a small ledge and crimp your way to a small diagonaling ramp to join a seam, then up to the bulging overhang to rejoin the regular route.

V2 5.11c G: Continue straight up past two bolts (crux) to a crack and follow it straight up to the P2 belay. Combining P1 and P2 this way avoids an uncomfortable hanging belay.

Gear: Gear to 2" (original P2 requires 3.5" cam), including triples in the small TCU range (up to yellow Alien).

History: This is one of several first ascents done in the winter. P3 was originally freed using a low traverse (5.12b). Later, a higher (and a little easier) traverse was worked out, which is how the route is climbed today. The route was named for Joe Yoist, a rodeo rider from Texas and former owner of the property at the base of

Central Rappel
Sting Ledge
V1
105
106
107
110
111
112
113
114

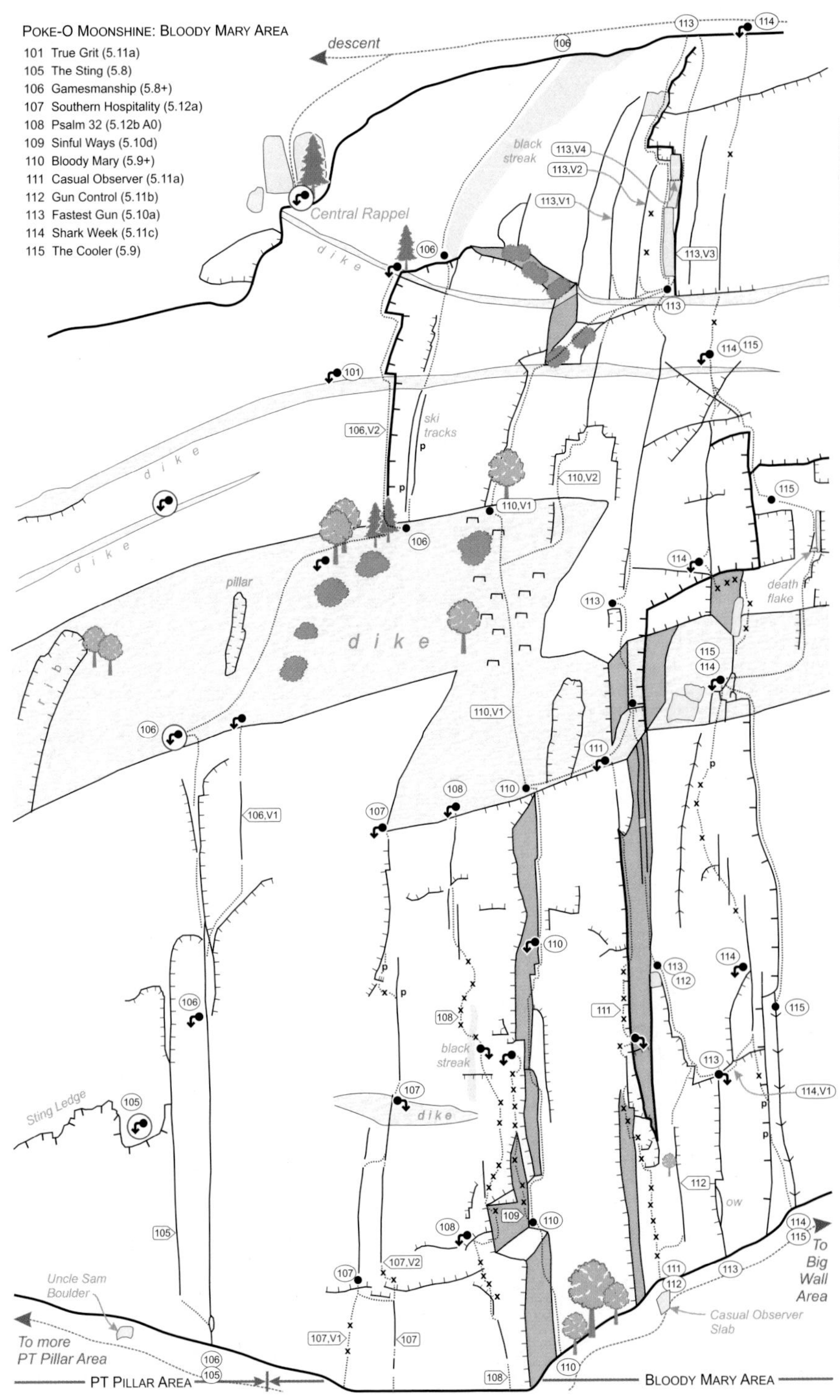
Poke-O Moonshine: Bloody Mary Area
101 True Grit (5.11a)
105 The Sting (5.8)
106 Gamesmanship (5.8+)
107 Southern Hospitality (5.12a)
108 Psalm 32 (5.12b A0)
109 Sinful Ways (5.10d)
110 Bloody Mary (5.9+)
111 Casual Observer (5.11a)
112 Gun Control (5.11b)
113 Fastest Gun (5.10a)
114 Shark Week (5.11c)
115 The Cooler (5.9)
descent
Central Rappel
dike
black streak
ski tracks
pillar
rib
death flake
Sting Ledge
Uncle Sam Boulder
To more PT Pillar Area
PT Pillar Area
Bloody Mary Area
To Big Wall Area
Casual Observer Slab
ow

the cliff, who showed considerable hospitality to the climbers in the 1970s with meals, drinks, and a place to crash.

FA (5.6 A1) Feb, 1976, Geoff Smith, Mark Meschinelli
FFA (P1, P2, combining both pitches into one pitch) Sep, 1977, Geoff Smith, Gary Allan, Drew Allan
FFA (P3, low traverse) Jul 29, 1989, Martin Berzins, Andy Gale
FFA (P3, high traverse) 1990, Patrick Munn, Mark Meschinelli
FA (V1) Oct, 2006, Louis-Philippe Ménard
FA (V2) 1992, Patrick Munn, Dominic Eisinger

108 Psalm 32 5.12b A0 210' ★★★★

Freeing the bolted section of P3 is one of Poke-O's great prizes. You can toprope P1 by climbing P1 of **Bloody Mary** and walking left on the ledge to a fixed anchor. Some consider P1 to be 5.11b, while others walk away sandbagged; you decide.

Start: 45' right of and downhill from **Gamesmanship**, at the lowest point on the cliff, 6' before the trail heads uphill, below a shallow right-facing corner with a crack in it.

○ **P1 5.12a G:** Climb the handcrack to a left-facing edge and the first bolt in a pinkish white scar. Follow the left-leaning edge left, then back right through a tricky bulge (crux) to a fixed anchor just above. (This anchor is on the far left side of the **Bloody Mary** P1 ledge.) If you can't pull the crux, you can traverse right at the bulge to a crack and up to the anchor. 50'

● **P2 5.12b G:** Step right into a right-facing corner and up to a ceiling. Break through the ceiling on the left and up the face, moving right to a blunt arête, then back left onto the face and a ledge with a fixed anchor, just right of a black streak. 90'

P3 5.12b A0 G: Climb the face, left at first, then back right to a right-facing corner, then back left to thin cracks that lead past a headwall to a fixed anchor at the base of the dike. 70'

FA 1994, Patrick Munn, Dominic Eisinger

109 Sinful Ways 5.10d G 70' ★★

Start: At the spacious ledge on top of **Bloody Mary** P1.

● **P1 5.10d G:** From the left side of the ledge, climb over a small overhang and into a left-facing corner. Follow bolts up the face to a fixed anchor. The crux is above the last bolt; the runout above the last bolt is tamed if you step right, then back left to the anchor. 70'

FA 1995, Patrick Purcell, Tom Yandon, Ian Osteyee

110 Bloody Mary 5.9+ G 200' ★★★★★

P2 is long and continuous, but never desperate; one of the best crack pitches at Poke-O. Turner was ahead of his time with this one, as it was considered the boldest and most difficult climb in the Adirondacks for more than a decade after its first ascent. From the top of P3, you can join **Fastest Gun** at the top of its P2 or finish on **Persecution**.

Start: 25' uphill from a low point on the cliff, in a small clearing in a large right-facing open book. Straight up is P2—a right-facing crack in white, spotty rock.

P1 5.6 G: From the block at the start of the corner, climb the corner to a belay on a flat ledge. 30'

P2 5.9+ G: Layback the crack past a small ceiling, then up until a left-facing, opposing crack appears on the right. Stem up between the cracks until you can make an unlikely move left to the white, spotty face, then up the face to an overhang and up to a fixed anchor on the left wall. (Rappel is possible from here with two ropes.) 120'

P3 5.8 G: Continue up the corner to the dike rock. (V1, V2) 50'

Nick Wakeman on P1 (5.12a) of ***Psalm 32*** *(5.12b A0). Photo by Mark Meschinelli.*

V1 Persecution 5.8 PG: Instead of joining another route, continue up and left through swag and brush for 90' to a large right-facing chimney, just left of a large pine tree that partially obscures the route (belay). Climb the chimney for 60'. (It narrows to off width, then finally down to 2".) From its top, traverse right to finish on **Goombay Finish** or any of the other variations to **Fastest Gun**.

V2 5.9: The stepped roofs below **Goombay Finish** and right of **Persecution** have also been climbed, reportedly in the 5.9 grade.

Descent: From the top of P3, traverse right 50' to the **Casual Observer** anchor or traverse left to the **Psalm 32** anchor; both routes can be rappelled.

History: In Turner's words, "At the first attempt, we abseiled off after Wilmott had vomited a surfeit of blueberries, and were met by Mary [one of the Montreal group], who had retreated from **Neurosis** with a scalp wound from a falling stone, which left her covered in blood. At the second attempt, Wilmott was flushed from the groove by a sudden thundery torrent, but at the third attempt, with the addition of Dick Strachan to the party, all went well." It wasn't until 1965 (or 1968, depending on whom you ask) that this route saw its second ascent by Jim McCarthy, Dick Williams, and Mick Burke.

FA 1959, John Turner, Dick Strachan, Dick Wilmott
FA (V1) 1995, Alden Pellett, Bruce Kilgore

111 Casual Observer 5.11a G 200' ★★★★

This mixed route makes its way up the right-facing dihedral between **Bloody Mary** and **Fastest Gun** and has become one of the more popular routes of its grade at Poke-O.

Start: 30' right of and uphill from **Bloody Mary**, at a large slab of rock at the base of the cliff, below a shallow right-facing corner with bolts.

⊙ **P1 5.10b G:** Climb the corner and outside arête, then move left (crux) to bridge a wet, vegetated gap beneath a steep corner in brown rock. Up the corner, right into the chimney, then exit into a crack above. From the top of the crack, move right around the arête to a fixed anchor. 90'

P2 5.11a G: Follow bolts up the arête, move right around the arête at a ceiling and into a corner system just left of P2 of **Fastest Gun**. Follow the crack-and-corner system, then move left to a fixed anchor. 110'

Descent: From the top anchor, make two rappels with a single 60-m rope.

Gear: To 2".

History: The route is a tribute to Geoff Smith, the man who added many of the best, most difficult, and most influential routes at Poke-O. It was named after the bust of Smith's father, which he placed atop a boulder to observe the cliff for many years.

FA (upper section of P2) Sep, 1996, Patrick Purcell, Dave Furman
FA Jul, 2001, Dave Furman, Mark Meschinelli, Nick Wakeman

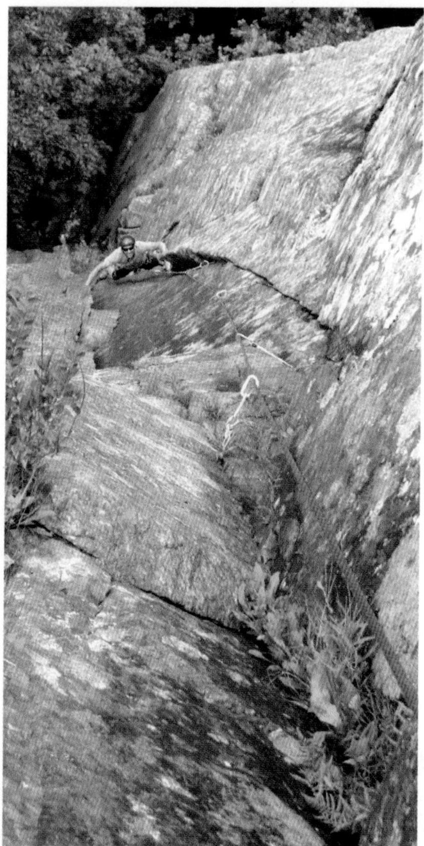

*David Buzzelli follows P2 of **Bloody Mary** (5.9+).*

112 Gun Control 5.11b G 70'

The first ascent didn't have the benefit of the bolts on **Casual Observer**. Good gear, but strenuous to place.

Start: Same as **Casual Observer**.

P1 5.11b G: (V1) Climb the first few feet of **Casual Observer**, traverse right to the superthin, sharp bottomless crack, and follow it to a corner a large, right-rising horizontal crack. Traverse right 5' to a fixed anchor. 70'

V1 Gun Control Now 5.11c G: Begin directly below the crack and stick-clip the bolt. Stand on a stack of cheater stones and make a hard move to gain the bottom of the crack. Avoiding the cheater stones involves a V6 sequence: two dyno slaps on slopers.

History: The original line continued on to a tree, then up the vegetated corner to a belay in right-facing blocks (the top of P1 of **Fastest Gun**). This is now too overgrown to climb.

FA Sep 3, 1988, Mack Johnson, Jim Shimberg, Paul Boissonneault
FA (V1) Sep 8, 2013, Dominic Eisinger, Mark Meschinelli, Dave Hough

113 Fastest Gun 5.10a PG 515' ★★★★★

Perhaps the most sought-after climb at Poke-O; a real prize. Every pitch is high-quality and demanding.

Start: At a fingercrack in a right-facing flake that shoots into the ground, above which is a short off width. As you move right from the low point of the cliff right of **Gamesmanship**, this crack begins halfway up the hill.

P1 5.9+ G: Work up the fingercrack and into the off width, then layback around a bulge and up the crack above to an anchor. Rappel from here or, if you plan to continue, walk left on ledges and climb left-rising flakes and blocks to a belay in a sheltered chimney formed by blocks. 100'

P2 5.10a G: Continue up blocks to the base of the parallel cracks; climb these through a shallow chimney capped by an overhang and up to belay at a ledge on blocks at the base of a large right-facing corner in dike rock. (You can climb down and left from here to the hidden fixed anchor of **Casual Observer** to rappel.) 100'

P3 5.10a PG: Go up the corner above the belay (5.8) to a perch on a block just above the dike (possible belay). Step right and make a committing move into a shallow, bottomless right-facing corner; up this corner and the thin seam above (RPs), then make a hard move to a bolt and proceed up to a shallow left-facing corner. Continue up thin seams and cracks with sparse protection to a ledge beneath the final corners and roof. 165'

P4 5.10a G: The corners above consist of car-sized blocks wedged under a roof; the blocks lean alarmingly away from the right wall to form an off width. (V1, V2, V3) Climb up the ceiling and make slippery moves left (crux) into a left-facing corner, then climb it to the large roof above (V4). Move left under the roof on a slab (often wet) and into a final left-facing corner to the top. 150'

V1 Goombay Finish 5.9+ PG: Climb the second crack left of the left-facing corner of the normal finish. Lots of small gear. Named for a chicken dish Mellor had in the Bahamas.

V2 The Cogito 5.11a PG: Climb the first crack left of the left-facing corner of the normal finish. Up the crack with technical protection past two bolts to join the normal finish.

V3 McCarthy Off Width 5.9+ R: Climb the off width that separates the leaning blocks from the face to the right and move up to a grassy finish. Small people fit into the slot, making this less traumatic. This was climbed in the 1960s and was originally described as the McCarthy finish to **Bloody Mary**.

V4 Dunn Finish 5.10a G: At the roof, make a spectacular hand traverse right (no feet) and around the corner (5.9+) to finish on grassy ledges. This variation avoids the slab of the normal finish, which is often wet.

History: Who was the fastest gun? None other than Geoff Smith. 25 years after the first ascent, Joe Szot passed by the base of the route and saw Geoff prying a chockstone out of the opening off-width crack. Joe prodded Smith, saying, "God put that stone there. What gives you the authority to remove it?"—to which Geoff replied, "There is no higher authority than me." This route sees a lot of traffic and speed ascents; one of the more impressive was 10 ascents by Patrick Purcell in 2.5 hr as training for **Astroman** (which he did in 4 hr with Peter Croft).

Gear: Doubles up to 2", 1 ea 3.5". A 4.5" cam is helpful for the off width on P1.

FA (P1, P2) Jan, 1977, Geoff Smith, Dick Bushey
FA (P3) Sep 1977, Jim Dunn, Mark Whitton
FA (P4) 1978, Gary Allan, Dave Hough
FA (V1) 1990, Don Mellor, Bill Dodd
FA (V2) Sep 12, 2006, Nick Wakeman, Marla Hayes
FA (V3) 1968, Jim McCarthy, Mick Burke (who died on the 1975 Bonnington expedition to the South Face of Everest)
FA (V4) Sep 1977, Jim Dunn, Mark Whitton

*A climber leads P1 (5.9+) of **Fastest Gun** (5.10a). Photo by Mark Meschinelli.*

Geoff Smith: The Visionary

First came John Turner, the pioneer, then Geoff Smith, the visionary: these two men figure most prominently in the development of rock climbing at Poke-O Moonshine. I first climbed with Geoff in the early 1970s, when he took me, Pat Munn, and Dave Hough under his wing as climbing partners. Together we repeated many of the Turner routes, then added a few of our own, such as The Sting, Pillar and Superstition Traverse. Little did we know that Geoff had a Big Plan for the next generation of new routes at Poke-O, and the Big Plan required man power, rope guns, and a commitment that turned into a lifelong hobby, at times pushing the limits of the sport.

In the mid-1970s, Geoff, Dave, and I moved out West to live The Dream—climbing and skiing. Geoff had already served a residency with rock-climbing legend Jimmy Dunn, and he passed that experience on to us in Yosemite and points west. Geoff served as our mentor and coach, motivating us to embrace rock climbing, the outdoors, and the camaraderie of the sport. But most of all, he showed us the excitement and adventure of first ascents. We returned each summer and applied our newfound skills to our "home" crag. Routes such as Freedom Fighter (soon to become Freedom Flight after I took a 25' flight on the second ascent), Microwave, Rattlesnake, and Homecoming went in during this period.

In 1977, Geoff moved back to Adirondacks and hit it hard. He studied the cliff with a passion, rappel-cleaning and inspecting every crack and corner of the huge face. He had a knack for spotting a line, and his vision led to the next generation of routes at Poke-O: The Snatch, Summer Solstice (now gone), Wild Blue, Fastest Gun, Southern Hospitality, Macintosh, It Don't Come Easy, and Sunburst Arête. Geoff pioneered techniques for new routing here—cleaning on rappel, using bolts, and fixing lines the full height of the cliff—long before these were considered standard, truly ahead of his time.

Geoff was diagnosed at age 10 with a backward heart, a condition with a grim life expectancy, and he was told to stay away from sports. In the face of this crisis, he made a vow that, should he live to 30, he would quit climbing and devote his life to God and family. True to his word, in 1979, he dropped out of climbing and started a family. But Geoff couldn't stay away and has remained influential to this day, with sporadic visits that resulted in brilliant lines such as Slime Line (1987), Deuteronomy (1992), and Ancient of Days (2002). The route Messiah, which he climbed with Pat, began the biblical naming trend at the cliff.

Without Geoff, Poke-O would not be the rock-climbing destination it is today. Personally, I never would have pursued the sport to the level I have without his guidance, inspiration, and endearing friendship. Thank you, Geoff, for your contributions to Poke-O, your effect on our climbing careers, and most of all your lifelong inspiration to the sport of rock climbing.

Geoff passed away November 15th, 2013 after a life long battle with chronic heart problems. His love of climbing and the camaraderie with his climbing partners continued right up to his passing.

- Gary Allan

114 Shark Week 5.11c G 420' ★★★★★

Regarded by some as one of the best routes at Poke-O; fun and well protected on clean rock all the way to the top. The **Fastest Shark** variation makes the route more approachable by reducing the overall grade to 5.11a. Like many routes at Poke-O, this one required considerable effort to unearth—a statement of dedication and vision by Dave Furman and various partners.

Start: 20' right of and uphill from **Fastest Gun** (but before the trail levels out), at the base of a right-facing corner with a small, triangular overhang at 25'.

P1 5.11c G: (V1) Up the corner (free-climbed earlier as the route **Pinhead**) past a triangular overhang to a good jam. Step left on a handrail and into a thin fracture on the arête with two pins. A hard move left (height-dependent) around the arête past a bolt leads to a fingercrack, then a fixed anchor on the left. 90'

P2 5.10d G: Continue the crack line, stepping left past a bolt to another crack, then step farther left to a stance below a steep slab. Bolts protect thin face moves (crux) to the dike. Step right to a belay. 90'

P3 5.8 G: Climb up to the 10'-high wedged orange flake in the corner. Once you are on top, traverse out the left wall to an airy ledge with a fixed anchor. 40'

P4 5.7 G: Up a crack through an overhang, then wander lower-angled rock to a fixed anchor below the final headwall. 100'

P5 5.11a PG: Face-climb to the thin crack and end the pitch with a hard move past a bolt. 100'

V1 Fastest Shark 5.10d G: Begin as for **Fastest Gun** and climb to the first anchor at the top of the corner, then traverse right under a ceiling to join the fingercrack on P1. Pumpy.

Descent: Rappel the route with two 60-m ropes.

Gear: Doubles from RPs through 1.5"; singles to 2.5".

FA (Pinhead) Jan 1977, Dave Hough, Mark Meschinelli
FFA (Pinhead) Jul 1985, Todd Swain, John Thackray
FA Sep, 1996, Dave Furman, Pete Cimasi
FFA Sep, 1996, Hobey Walker, Dave Furman
FA (V1) 1997, Dave Furman, Alden Pellett

115 The Cooler 5.9 G 360' ★

The worst route you'd ever want to climb: P1 and P2 are interesting and physical but would be much better with massive defoliation. Expect some tricky pro; loose flakes and blocks; and lots of moss, lichen, and hanging gardens of grass and thorny weeds. Despite all this, completing the route is remarkably satisfying. P3 has a death flake; a better option is to join **Shark Week** for P3 and P4, then rappel the fixed anchors of that route.

Start: 5' right of **Shark Week** at a 5'-high blocky pedestal, below a tree-filled crack system with a huge right-facing blade of rock at 60'.

P1 5.8 PG: Up a short off width formed by a block to a stance. Struggle up the next off width, moving left briefly onto the face, then through hanging weeds to gain the floor of a cave. Belay here or 10' higher at a good stance below the overhanging, acute corner. 50'
P2 5.9 G: Work up into the acute corner, overhanging at first, past some wedged blocks and flakes, for 80'. The crack opens wider to a chimney (fixed anchor on the left wall), then narrows to fists, then hands, then fingers. Step left to a flat ledge with a fixed anchor (shared with **Shark Week**). 150'
P3 5.8 G: Traverse dike rock rightward for 30' to a right-facing corner in the dike. Up the corner to the top of the dike and into a short left-facing corner, then up into a slot with a narrow pillar on the right side (which you can see behind) that has a death flake jammed below. Climb up the slot and flake and up to a bottomless left-facing corner beneath the roof. Traverse down and left to the larger opposing corner and belay beneath the roof. 80'
P4 5.8 PG: Up the roof, then hand-traverse out left to break the roof on its left side. Left of the roof is a large block; climb it on the right side. From its top, work up and left to the fixed anchor on **Shark Week** below a headwall. The route historically finished on **Gamesmanship**, but nowadays, that's idiotic, so rappel instead. 80'
Gear: Small nuts, doubles from 1–3", and 1 ea 3.5".
FA 1961, John Turner, Dick Strachan

Big Wall Area

On the right side of the Bloody Mary Area, the trail levels and the forest opens up below the Big Wall Area, the highest concentration of long, difficult free routes in the Adirondacks. The rock in this section is generally good, but it's sad to see that some of the routes have grown in higher up.

On the left side of the wall is a large slab that marks the start of **The Gathering**. Just right of this is a weakness that leads up and left, then cuts back right (making a "switchback") following a dike; several routes begin along this switchback. In the center of the wall and 100' up is the 130'-high pillar of **It Don't Come Easy**, which is a good landmark for finding routes. To the right, the trail enters the forest; look for a survey marker on the rock (centered in a painted yellow circle) that marks the right edge of this section of cliff.

116 The Gathering 5.11c PG (5.9 R) 410' ★★★★★

A full-length route up the left side of the Big Wall Area, with challenges on every pitch. The cruxes are well protected, and the route is equipped to rappel from any anchor. This is the most popular of the full-length routes in this section of cliff, as the rock is clean all the way to the top. Unfortunately, some of the anchors are uncomfortable and, in the case of the P2 anchor, occur in the middle of difficult climbing. (To truly free-climb P2 you must pass the anchor, move around the corner to the right, then downclimb easily to the fixed anchor on **Extreme Unction**, making the pitch 5.11d.) From the last anchor, rappel the route or step left and scramble up brushy ledges to the top. Named for the large gathering of friends who stopped to cheer during the first ascent.
Start: At the left side of the Big Wall Area, the trail crosses a large boulder at the base of this route (and thus called the Gathering Boulder); the route begins at the blocky left-facing weakness in black rock on the face next to this boulder.
P1 5.10b PG (5.8 R): Unprotected face climbing (RPs) leads to the bottom of a right-facing corner. Up the corner (bolt; crux) to the ceiling, then step left around the arête to another right-facing corner; up this (bolt) to an uncomfortable belay at a fixed anchor. 60'
P2 5.11c PG: From the right side of the belay, climb up the face to a bolt below a ceiling with a right-facing corner above. Pull the ceiling (5.11b) into the corner, then up the corner to an alcove beneath the next ceiling. Climb out right around the ceiling (crux) and past a bolt to a fixed anchor (and another uncomfortable belay). 90'
P3 5.9 G: Traverse directly right into a large right-facing corner, then up this until you can move left around the corner and onto the face. Up the face through the dike rock, then traverse right to a fixed anchor. 75'
P4 5.11c G: Climb straight up the face to an overlap, then undercling left to a shallow left-facing corner and crack. Up the crack (crux) and through a bulge to the left side of a block, then right to the belay. 75'
P5 5.9 G: Face-climb straight up and into a right-facing corner capped by a roof. Up the corner to the top, then break the roof on its left end to reach a ledge with a fixed anchor. 60'
P6 5.9 R: Above the belay are two right-facing corners (a small one on the left and a larger one on the right). Immediately to the left of these is a left-facing corner, just right of a black streak. Face-climb up and left to the left-facing corner, then up the corner to a fixed anchor on the wall right of a bushy ledge. 50'
FA (P1) 1992, Mark Meschinelli
FA Sep, 1993, Patrick Munn, Dominic Eisinger

117 Extreme Unction 5.11d G 140' ★★★★

A crimpfest crux. From the top of this route, you can rappel or continue up **The Gathering**. Named for the last rites, a sacrament administered to someone who is in danger of death.
Start: Same as **Sailor's Dive**.
P1 5.7 G: At the **Sailor's Dive** switchback, climb straight up the right-facing corner; at its top, step left to another right-facing corner and move up to a fixed anchor (this anchor has a bolt driven into each face of a right-facing arête). 60'
P2 5.11d G: Continue up the right-facing corner, which switches to left-facing, then up to a face. Bolts lead rightward across the face (crux at the last bolt) to a ledge and a fixed anchor. 80'
FA Sep, 1993, Patrick Munn, Dominic Eisinger
FFA (P2) 1998, Travis Peckham, Nancy Koenig Peckham

*Opposite: Gary Allan on P2 of **Calvary Hill** (5.12c). Photo by Mark Meschinelli.*

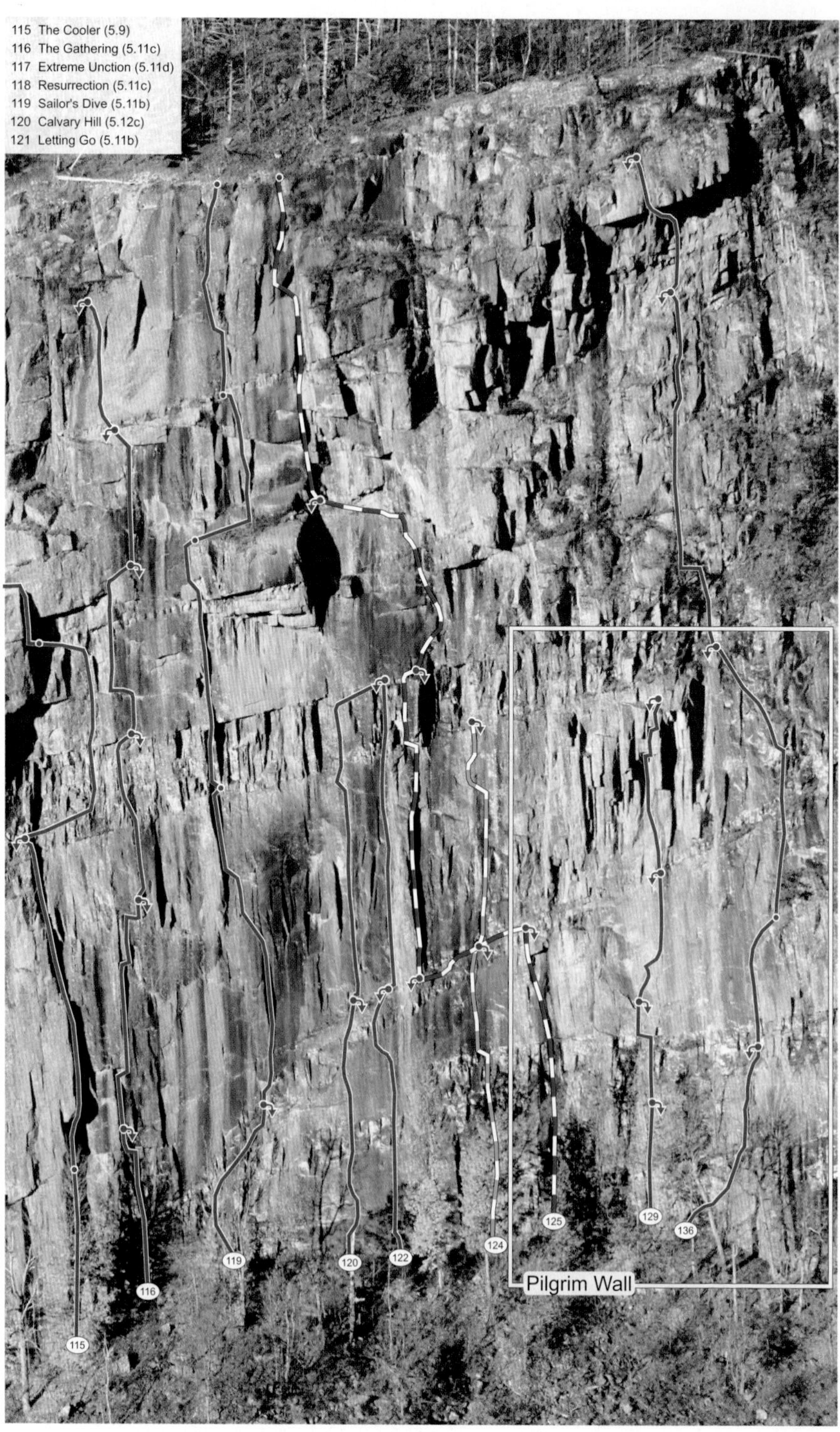
115 The Cooler (5.9)
116 The Gathering (5.11c)
117 Extreme Unction (5.11d)
118 Resurrection (5.11c)
119 Sailor's Dive (5.11b)
120 Calvary Hill (5.12c)
121 Letting Go (5.11b)
115
116
119
120
122
124
125
129
136
Pilgrim Wall

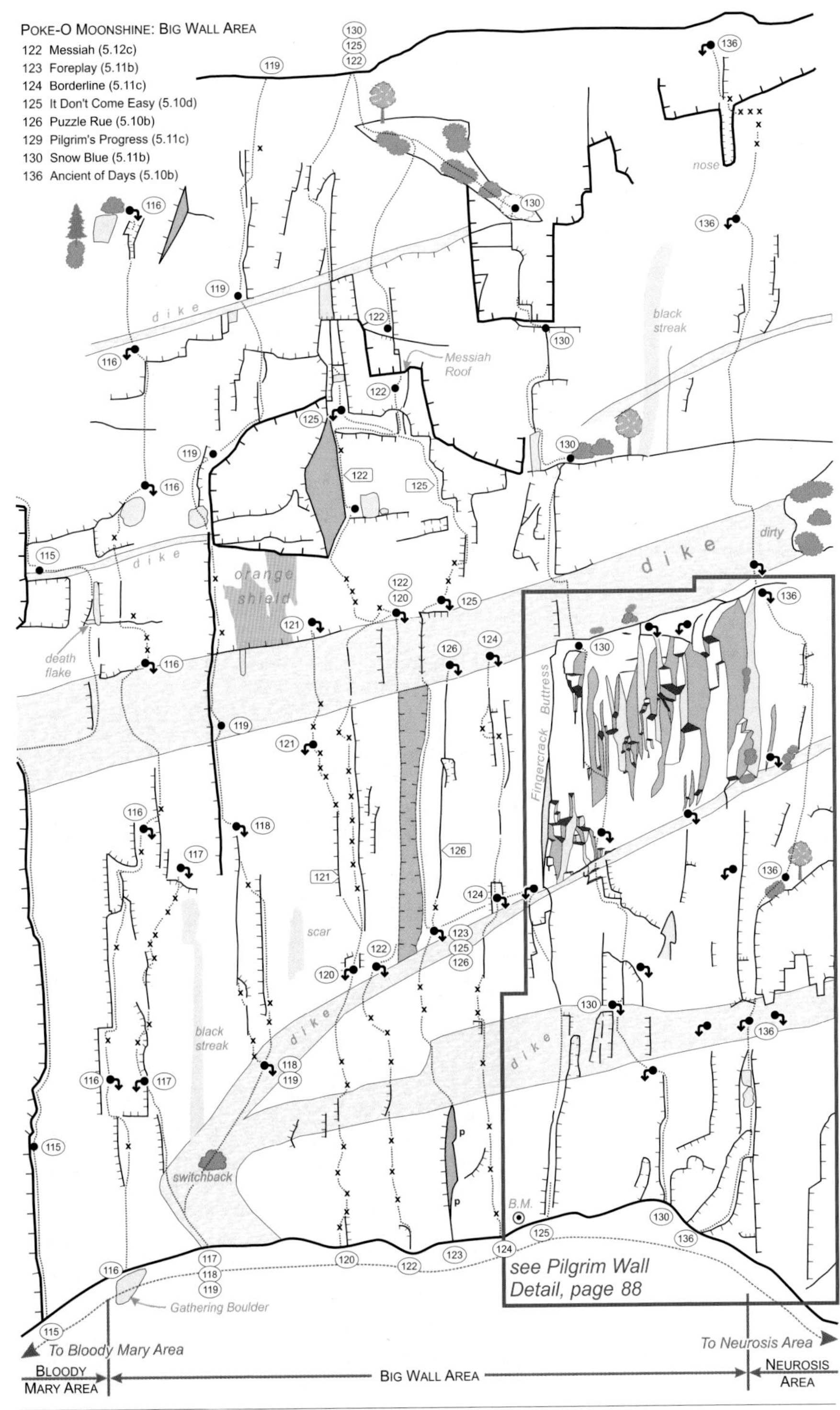

Poke-O Moonshine: Big Wall Area
122 Messiah (5.12c)
123 Foreplay (5.11b)
124 Borderline (5.11c)
125 It Don't Come Easy (5.10d)
126 Puzzle Rue (5.10b)
129 Pilgrim's Progress (5.11c)
130 Snow Blue (5.11b)
136 Ancient of Days (5.10b)
dike
nose
black streak
Messiah Roof
orange shield
death flake
dirty
Fingercrack Buttress
scar
switchback
B.M.
see Pilgrim Wall Detail, page 88
Gathering Boulder
To Bloody Mary Area
To Neurosis Area
Bloody Mary Area
Big Wall Area
Neurosis Area

118 Resurrection 5.11c PG 185' ★★★★

A super pitch with a well-protected crux and some sustained 5.10d to 5.11a climbing above. So good, you'll have to do it twice.

Start: Same as **Sailor's Dive**.

P1 5.7 G: Same as **Sailor's Dive**: From the **Sailor's Dive** switchback, climb right in the upper dike for 50' or so to a fixed anchor just right of a right-facing corner and below a blocky roof. 75'

P2 5.11c PG: From the belay, step up and left to break through the overhang to a face (crux), then a crack, past a small left-arching overlap, and up the crack to a right-facing corner and fixed anchor just above as for **Sailor's Dive**. 110'

Gear: To 2".

FA Aug 18, 1996, Patrick Munn, Chris Hyson

119 Sailor's Dive 5.11b G (5.10+ R) 515' ★★★

The route that gave the name "Big Wall" to this section of cliff—intricate and involved, requiring lots of small gear. Rockfall in 2006 changed the character of P2, rendering it unclimbable; the route described here was rerouted to avoid that section.

Start: 20' right of the Gathering Boulder is the start of two right-rising dikes. To access the upper dike, enter from the right on blocky rock, climb left-rising dike rock, then cut back right (known as the "switchback") into the upper dike.

P1 5.7 G: From the switchback, climb right in the upper dike for 50' or so to a fixed anchor just right of a right-facing corner and below a blocky roof. (The original P1 continued to a stance below a horrifying flake, which fell in 2006 leaving a tan rock scar.) 75'

P2 5.11b G (5.10+ R): Step right and climb straight up the face (bolt, runout) and into the right-facing corner above. Up the corner (crux; bolt, then RPs). At the top, move left across the face to a smaller left-facing corner and an optional belay shared with **Resurrection**. Step left and climb the right-facing corner to a belay at the base of the dike below an orange shield of rock. (You can easily see this shield from the road, directly below the largest roof system in this section of cliff.) 140'

P3 5.10b G: Climb right-facing corners through the dike rock to a roof below the left end of the orange shield. Through the roof (crux) and up the right-facing corner that defines the left edge of the orange shield to the next roof system at the top of the shield. Break left through the roofs and around an enormous block perched on a ledge below a left-facing corner. Up the left-facing corner, then out right to a belay on a sloped ledge. 140'

P4 5.10a G: Twin cracks begin in the middle of the ledge, just left of a long horizontal ceiling 15' up; climb these cracks past a small overlap and move left to the base of the huge low-angled left-facing corner. 60'

P5 5.11a G: Climb up the left-facing corner to where the wall becomes steeper; continue up until you can step right to a slab (old bolt), then move up to the top. 100'

Gear: Standard rack with extra small nuts and RPs.

History: Another winter first ascent over several days. The first continuous ascent required a bivy on top of P4. Around 1994, the route was climbed in under 4 hours with Gary Allen leading every pitch and Geoff Smith following; this was (and still is) very fast! The name was coined by Dick Bushey, who was demonstrating different diving techniques at a party, one of which was the "sailor's dive," a committing headfirst dive with arms behind your back; the name stuck.

FA (5.8 A3) Jan, 1976, Dave Hough, Mark Meschinelli, Geoff Smith

FA (continuous) 1977, Mark Meschinelli, Dick Bushey

FFA May, 1987, Don Mellor, Patrick Purcell, Mike Heintz

FA (P1, after rockfall) Aug, 2006, Rich Romano, Jamie Hamilton

120 Calvary Hill 5.12c G 200' ★★★★★

More sustained and higher-quality than P1 and P2 of **Messiah**. Both pitches are excellent.

Start: 40' right of **Sailor's Dive** at a left-facing edge below the thinnest of seams.

Dominic Eisinger on P1 of ***Border Line*** *(5.11c).*

● **P1 5.12b G:** Climb the left-facing edge and face above through the lower dike at a right-facing corner, then up more face to the upper dike. Belay in the dike at a fixed anchor below a small overhang. 100'
● **P2 5.12c G:** Go past the overhang on the right and into a right-facing corner. Follow bolts into a long, shallow left-facing corner that ends at dike rock. Up a crack through the dike, then traverse right at the top of the dike to the fixed anchor of **Messiah**. 100'
FA (P1) 1991, Patrick Munn, Dominic Eisinger, Mark Meschinelli
FA (P2) 1992, Patrick Munn, Bill Dodd

121 Letting Go 5.11b G 115' ★★★

Start: At the fixed anchor at the top of P1 of **Calvary Hill**. You can also reach the start by climbing to the start of **Resurrection**, then continuing the traverse in the dike.
P1 5.11b G: Start up P2 of **Calvary Hill** but instead of heading up and right into the left-facing corner, head up and left into a right-facing corner. Up the corner and, at its top, traverse left (dirty) to a fixed belay. 75'
P2 5.10d G: Work up the face toward a slot in the dike rock. Through the dike to a fixed anchor on the right end of the orange shield. 40'
History: This was supposed to be Munn's last climb, as he was "letting go" of climbing. But it obviously didn't take: look at the Pilgrim Wall.
FA 1995, Patrick Munn, Dominic Eisinger

122 Messiah 5.12c G 465' ★★★★

One of the East's biggest free-climbing objectives. P1 is recommended, but, unfortunately, the upper section of this route follows a drainage area and has grown in and is no longer recommended in its current condition. P1 can be toproped by climbing the dike from the left.
Start: On the right side of a 10'-high pedestal (the only pedestal along the base of this wall), 25' right of **Calvary Hill**, and directly below the left side of the **It Don't Come Easy** pillar, which begins 100' up.
● **P1 5.12b G:** Climb the right side of the pedestal to a high first bolt, then up the face with increasing difficulty to a fixed anchor on the left side of the pillar. 100'
P2 5.10a PG: Climb the left side of the pillar past dike rock at the top to fixed anchors. (Some loose rock. Mark Meschinelli swears he'll never climb this pitch again.) 100'
P3 Crystal Traverse 5.10d G: From the anchor, step down and left of a high bolt and traverse left below the black shield of rock. Move up and left, beneath a left-arching overlap, to reach the bottom of a large right-facing corner. Gain the corner via a long reach and follow it to a ledge. Step right to belay at a huge, precarious-looking block. This pitch has grown in. 80'
P4 Dodd Corner 5.11d PG: Step back left into the corner. Up the corner past an overhang at its top and on to a ledge. (This section is dirty and perhaps unclimbable.) Traverse right on the ledge to parallel cracks in tan-colored rock, then up these to a ceiling. Move right to break the ceiling at a left-facing slot to a stance below the Messiah Roof (the Horn of Plenty belay). 70'
P5 The Messiah Roof 5.12c G: No route finding required here: climb the roof via a downward-pitched fistcrack (crux) and up to a stance just above in a left-facing corner. (P4 and P5 are broken in this manner to reduce rope drag.) 25'
P6 5.9+ G: Climb up the corner (crux) for 30' to a grassy ledge, then follow nondescript vegetated ledges to the top. 90'
FA 1991, Patrick Munn, Geoff Smith
FFA (Messiah Roof) 1997, Rich Romano, Fred Yaculic (climbed with a broken blue Camalot)

123 Foreplay 5.11b G 120' ★★★

A nice linkup to **It Don't Come Easy**—starting **Foreplay** makes the pitch above come more easily. Varied 5.10 climbing with a height-dependent crux at the top of the pitch. Originally climbed as two pitches.
Start: Below right-facing corners with pitons, 25' left of a survey pin driven into the cliff.
P1 5.11b G: A flake gains the lower of two right-facing corners. Up past two pitons to broken rock below a dike (optional belay here). Move left and climb dike rock on positive holds and bad pins to a stance below the first bolt (difficult clip). At the second bolt, step left to gain the dike (crux) and a fixed anchor up and right at the base of the pillar (same as for **Puzzle Rue** and **It Don't Come Easy**). 120'
FA Jun 27, 1992, Dennis Luther, Dave Szot, Joe Szot, Tom Yandon

124 Borderline 5.11c PG 190' ★★★★

Named for its proximity to the survey marker just to the right; beyond this marker is private land.
Start: At a low bolt on the face 6' left of the survey marker in a yellow circle.
P1 5.11c G: Clip the low bolt, then make a difficult press up and right to easier rock. Continue past a headwall to a right-facing corner at the top of the dike rock. A difficult leg press left (crux) leads to a face, then follow a flared crack to a fixed anchor in an alcove in the upper dike. 100'
P2 5.11c PG: Out the alcove to heady climbing up thin cracks that lead to opposing shallow corners. Up the right side, then move left past bolts (crux) and back right to a handcrack finish and a fixed anchor in dike rock. 90'
Gear: Up to 3.5".
FA (P1) 2004, Patrick Munn, Mark Meschinelli
FA (P2) 2005, Patrick Munn, Dominic Eisinger

125 It Don't Come Easy 5.10d G 490' ★★★

Climbs the right side of the 100'-high pillar in the center of the Big Wall Area. There is nothing easy about getting to the top of this route, especially when you consider the condition of the upper pitches. However, the pitches to the top of the pillar are incredible; highly recommended. Other routes are conveniently located nearby, which allows for creative linkups.
Start: On the right side of the clearing at the base of the Big Wall Area, below a flared slot, one side of which is black and the other white.
P1 5.10a G: Climb the dirty flared slot, then up nondescript rock to an alcove (often wet). Exit the alcove on

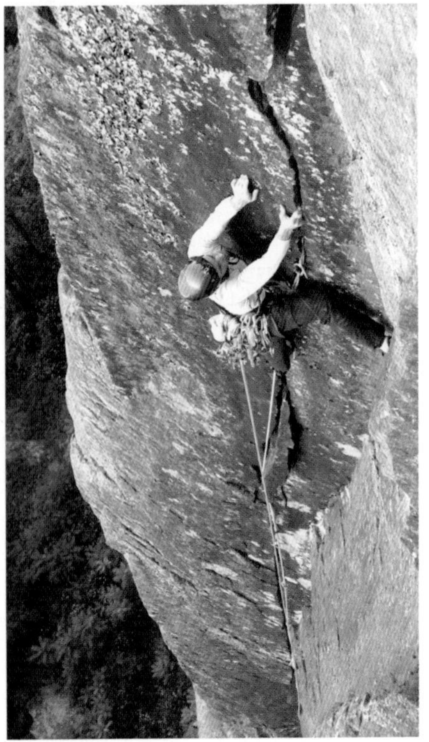

*A climber leads P3 (5.10b) of **It Don't Come Easy** (5.10d).*

the left via a steep, awkward handcrack (crux) and up to a fixed anchor. 100'

P2 5.4 PG: Traverse down and left on dike rock, past the fixed anchor for **Borderline**, to the fixed anchor at the base of the pillar (shared with **Puzzle Rue** and **Foreplay**). 50'

P3 5.10b G: Climb the crack in the right side of the pillar, past a low overhang, then up a wide section (crux). At the top, step left and climb a dirty crack in black rock to a comfortable, airy belay and fixed anchor at the top of the dike. 130'

P4 5.10d G: Two bolts protect face moves rightward to a right-facing corner. Up the corner into a series of three left-rising, left-facing corners, each capped by an overhang. From the last of these, move left past parallel cracks in tan-colored rock (**Messiah** P4 crosses here) to gain a ledge with a deep chimney above and a fixed anchor. This pitch is dirty and not recommended in its present condition. 90'

P5 5.9 PG: Up the chimney behind a chockstone, then exit left to a right-facing corner capped by a ceiling. Break the ceiling at a crack to gain a stance at the base of the large left-facing dihedral (optional belay). Climb the dihedral, then step left to a right-facing corner and follow it to the top. 120'

Gear: Gear to 6", extra 2–3".

FA (5.9 A1) Sep, 1976, Geoff Smith, Patrick Munn

FFA 1978, Geoff Smith, Gary Allan, Dave Hough

126 Puzzle Rue 5.10b G 90' ★★★

A crack climb with puzzling face climbing. Sustained.

Start: Begin at the fixed anchor at the base of the right side of the **It Don't Come Easy** pillar. You can climb **Foreplay**, **Borderline**, or **It Don't Come Easy** to reach this station.

P1 5.10b G: Climb the right-facing corner of the pillar for several feet until you can move right at a bolt to gain a stance below the thin crack. Climb the crack in a corner—left-facing at first, then right-facing—to a stance next to loose flakes. Continue up the crack, which becomes left-facing once again, until you can escape right to the fixed anchor. 90'

FA 2004, Patrick Munn, Mark Meschinelli

Pilgrim Wall

Right of the survey marker that delineates the right side of the Big Wall Area is the Pilgrim Wall, whose primary feature is the complex assortment of hanging dihedrals 150' up. From below, you can see the distinctive square and triangular roofs on the bottom of these dihedrals. Another feature, although you must look carefully, is an arrowhead-shaped flake 100' up (P2 of **Pilgrim's Progress**). The base is sloped and forested; to the right, the trail descends past the dihedral of **Raptor's Scream**, then goes around a corner to the Neurosis Area.

The routes in this section are newer and were developed during a flurry of activity in the 2002 and 2003 seasons. The reason for the spurt of development is best expressed in Patrick Munn's comment to Geoff Smith: "Our marriages are on the rocks, so we're on the rocks." In keeping with the Poke-O style, the routes in this section use bolts to link trad-protected features; thus, a rack is required. This style of climbing—bolts plus gear—is what Geoff Smith refers to as "modern trad." There are also many fixed anchors, which allow for one- to three-pitch cragging.

127 Mayflower 5.10c G 215' ★★★

Finds a moderate way to the top of the Pilgrim Wall. P3 is especially good. Named for the ship that carried the Pilgrims.

Start: 4' right of the flared slot of **It Don't Come Easy**, below a narrow ledge 5' up.

● **P1 5.10c G:** Mantel the small ledge and ascend right-facing features to horizontal slopers (crux). Move right to gain a crack and follow it to a fixed anchor on a ledge. 75'

P2 5.10a G: Step left and climb a left-facing corner, then continue up the face to a left-facing corner below ceilings. Up the corner, then angle rightward to a small stance and a fixed anchor. 70'

P3 5.10b G: A rising right traverse on good holds leads up into a hanging open book. Climb it to a fixed anchor at its top. 70'

FA (P1) 2003, Mark Meschinelli, Dede Johnston

FA (P2–P3) 2003, Patrick Munn, Dominic Eisinger

128 The Rapture 5.11d G 75' ★

Heaven awaits you at the top of Poke-O.

Start: Same as **Pilgrim's Progress**.

● **P1 5.11d G:** Face-climb up and left of the detached block to a stance below a small overlap. Move left (crux), then up to a crack finish (shared with P1 of **Mayflower**). 75'

FA 2002, Dominic Eisinger, Patrick Munn

129 Pilgrim's Progress 5.11c G 230' ★★★★

Three excellent pitches of climbing that get progressively harder. P1 is excellent face climbing, P2 climbs the alarming arrowhead flake, and P3 winds its way through a geometric maze of roofs and corners. The route takes its name from John Bunyan's 1678 book *The Pilgrim's Progress from This World to That Which Is to Come,* which he wrote in response to being jailed for his religious beliefs.

Start: At a right-facing, right-leaning flared corner formed by a detached block.

● **P1 5.10a G:** Up the detached block, then up the excellent face to a low anchor at 50'. Lower or continue up to a ledge, then up a handcrack through a vegetated section to a flake stance with a fixed anchor. 90'

P2 5.10c PG: Step right and climb the left side of the arrowhead (V1), then step right at the top to a shallow left-facing corner. Up the corner and crack through an overlap (crux) to a fixed anchor on the left. 60'

● **P3 5.11c G:** Step left from the belay (V2) and climb the face to a right-facing corner and up into the stem-box capped by a roof. Climb the roof on the right and into the next box, then through the final ceiling to a grassy ledge and a fixed anchor. 80'

V1 The Arch Crack 5.10a G: Traverse left from the arrowhead flake and undercling the left-arching overlap (strenuous) to reach a left-facing corner at its end. Finish through the ceilings as for **Mayflower**.

● **V2 Matrix 5.11c G:** Move left 8' from the belay and climb a steep face up to an open book that leads to a squeeze chimney. Exit via wild "matrix moves" to a left-facing corner (small nuts) that leads to a ledge with a fixed anchor (shared with **Mayflower**).

FA (P2) Jun 14, 1992, Joe Szot, Dennis Luther (led on aid, freed on second)
FA (complete) 2002, Patrick Munn, Dominic Eisinger
FA (V1, V2) 2002, Patrick Munn, Dominic Eisinger

130 Snow Blue 5.11b G (5.10a R) 590'

This route's distinguishing feature is the fingercrack that shoots up tan-colored rock on the buttress left of the Pilgrim Wall dihedrals. This buttress, known as the Fingercrack Buttress, is also distinguished by the huge boulder that overhangs its top. The lower pitches of this route are dirty and, in the case of P2, serious. However, climbing **Mayflower** straightens the line and provides access to the route's main feature. (P4–P6 are hopelessly dirty and not recommended.) Double ropes are recommended to overcome the hazard of the sharp edge on P2. Named by Munn for feeling blue after being dumped by Cindy Snow.

Start: Below a slightly left-leaning, right-facing flared corner beneath a larger right-facing corner. This is the next corner immediately right of **Pilgrim's Progress**, just before the trail descends right.

P1 5.8 G: Climb mossy corners to a ledge. Traverse the vegetated ledge up and left (crossing **Pilgrim's Progress**) to its high point and the fixed anchor shared with **Mayflower**. 80'

P2 5.10a R: Above the anchor is a handcrack in black rock. Up this handcrack, then runout the black face above to **The Arch Crack**. Undercling left to a left-facing corner, then up through ceilings to the fixed anchor shared with **Mayflower**. 70'

P3 The Fingercrack Buttress 5.11b G: Climb the corner above the anchor, then move left and reach blindly around the arête and into the fingercrack on the prow of the buttress. Shoot up the fingercrack (crux) and into the right-facing corner above. Belay at the top of the buttress in dike rock. 100'

P4 5.8 PG: Up to the left side of the large roof system above the belay, then into the deep V-groove. Belay in the treed ledge above. Best led by your partner. 100'

P5 5.7 G: From the left side of the ledge, climb either side of a pillar to its top, then up a left-facing corner to a grassy ledge. Up the straight-in crack to the next ledge beneath large roofs. 100'

P6 5.8 G: Out left is a clean crack in a corner on the bulging buttress, just right of some low roofs. Climb the crack 25' to the ledge above. Walk left on the vegetated ledge to the top. (This is where **Messiah** and **It Don't Come Easy** top out as well.) 140'

FA (P1–P3) 1982, Patrick Munn
FFA (complete) 1983, Don Mellor, Chuck Turner

131 Morning Star 5.10d G 270' ★★★

An even better line when combined with P1 of **Earthly Night**.

Start: On the right side of the Pilgrim Wall, just as the trail begins to descend downhill, is a series of large, stepped ledges that lead up and right to the base of two left-facing dihedrals. **Morning Star** climbs the leftmost of the two dihedrals.

P1 5.9+ G: Climb the stepped ledges to the base of the dihedral. Up the handcrack in the left-facing corner to a vegetated ledge with a fixed anchor. 70'

P2 5.10d G: Climb the dike up and right 10', then back left onto the face with long reaches. Work leftward into a left-facing corner; up the corner (RPs), then break out right onto the face and up to a fixed anchor on a ledge. 100'

P3 5.10b G: Go up the seam above the anchor to a ledge with a block at the base beneath a deep, vegetated V-slot (just left of the anchors on **Earthly Night**). Step left into a right-facing corner (this corner is right of a prominent triangular roof); up the corner and face on the left to a hard layback move that gains the grassy ledge with a fixed anchor. 100'

FA 2002, Patrick Munn, Dominic Eisinger

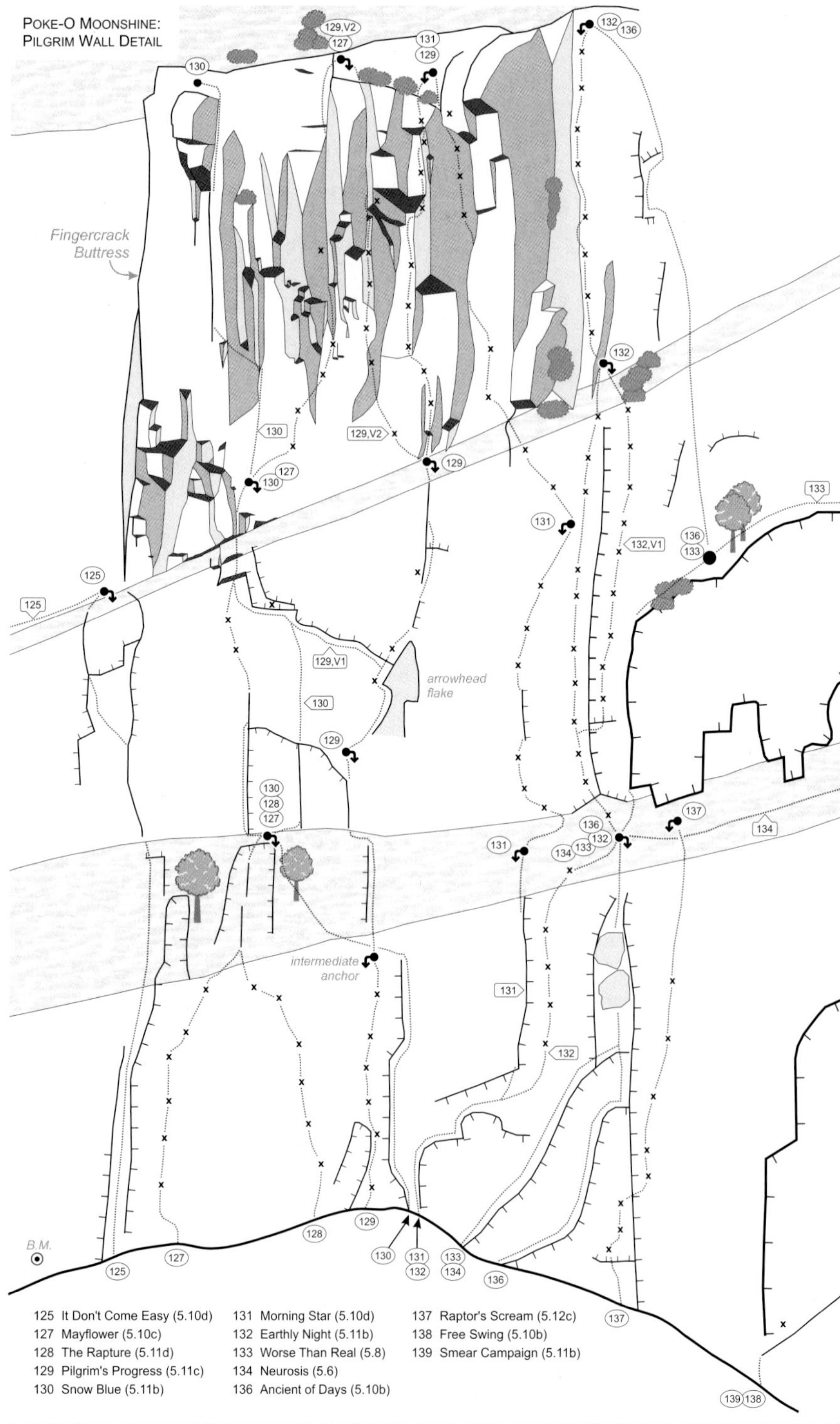
POKE-O MOONSHINE:
PILGRIM WALL DETAIL
Fingercrack
Buttress
arrowhead
flake
intermediate
anchor
B.M.
125 It Don't Come Easy (5.10d)
127 Mayflower (5.10c)
128 The Rapture (5.11d)
129 Pilgrim's Progress (5.11c)
130 Snow Blue (5.11b)
131 Morning Star (5.10d)
132 Earthly Night (5.11b)
133 Worse Than Real (5.8)
134 Neurosis (5.6)
136 Ancient of Days (5.10b)
137 Raptor's Scream (5.12c)
138 Free Swing (5.10b)
139 Smear Campaign (5.11b)

132 Earthly Night 5.11b G 270' ★★★★★

Three high-quality, bolt-protected pitches up the right margin of the Pilgrim Wall, featuring fantastic corner and arête climbing.

Start: Same as **Morning Star**.

● **P1 5.9+ PG:** Climbs the arête of the **Morning Star** dihedral: Up the stepped ledges to the ledge at the base of the arête. Up the arête (ledge fall potential if you botch the clips), then step right up to the treed ledge below a ceiling with a fixed anchor. 70'

● **P2 5.11b G:** Up to the ceiling below the endless left-facing dihedral. Crux moves through the ceiling gain the corner (V1). Follow it to the **Morning Star** ledge and its fixed anchor. Continue up the corner, break out right onto the face, then up to a ledge. Step left to a fixed anchor. 120'

● **P3 Raspberry Pitch 5.10c G:** Devious climbing on both sides of a blunt arête leads to a fixed anchor below vegetation. 80'

● **V1 Munchky Microarête 5.12a G ★★★★:** According to Munn, this pitch is "a small man's problem." After the fourth or fifth bolt (at a point level with an overhang around the corner), move right around the arête and undercling a square overhang to gain the face. Climb the face to the top, then move left to the fixed anchor below **Raspberry Pitch**.

FA 2002, Patrick Munn, Dominic Eisinger
FA (V1) 2003, Patrick Munn, Dominic Eisinger

133 Worse Than Real 5.8 G 170' ★

P1 and P2 are worthwhile and actually part of other routes now. After P2, however, the climb lives up to its name, as its features become overgrown and the historic description is vague. Only P1 and P2 are described; after that, the approximate line of ascent is shown on the topo.

Start: Right of the stepped ledges (the start of **Earthly Night** and **Morning Star**) are two right-leaning, left-facing shallow ramps. **Worse Than Real** begins at a handcrack in the leftmost ramp.

P1 5.6 G: Follow the ramp up and right to a left-facing corner and into a block-filled, flared chimney. Climb it to the tree ledge and the fixed anchor for **Earthly Night**. 80'

P2 5.8 G: Step right, then up a left-facing chimney with a handcrack in the back. At the top, step right and up to a vegetated ledge with trees. 90'

FA 1963, Brian Rothery, Bob O'Brien

134 Neurosis 5.6 PG 560'

An obscure summer route also known as the winter route **Italian Traverse**. The upper section is clearly a winter-only project.

Start: Same as **Worse Than Real**.

P1 5.6 G: Same as **Worse Than Real**. 80'

P2 5.6 PG: Traverse right around a buttress in dike rock. Continue in the dike and stay high, at times passing some fixed protection, until you reach the tree ledge with "gardens and other botany."[11] Belay on trees at a fixed anchor. 180'

P3–P4 5.6 PG: Continue right on the vegetated ledge and aim for the wettest rock around. Climb this for 250' to the acre-sized tree ledge beneath a headwall. You can find a fixed rappel left, at the low point on the tree ledge. 300'

FA 1957, François Garneau, Bernard Poisson, John Turner

135 Steptoe 5.6 PG 50'

Ascends the section of cliff above **Neurosis** and **Worse Than Real**. Since these routes are rarely (if ever) climbed, perhaps the best approach is to first climb **Paralysis**, then walk left to the start of this route.

Start: At an 18"-wide, 10'-high slot, at the left end of a low roof. The roof continues to the right, and 30' to the right, there is a fragile column that looks as though it's holding up the roof. The low roof is 180' right of **Neurosis Direct Finish** (the winter route in a deep depression of black rock left of a left-facing corner) and 65' right of **Hidden Pique** (another winter route that climbs a right-facing corner with three spikes of rock at the base).

P1 5.6 PG: Up the slot, then trend leftward on steps and slabs to a ledge with three cantilevered blocks. 50'

FA Sep 16, 1968, Rob Wood, Dave Keefe

136 Ancient of Days 5.10b G 550' ★★★★

Above the Pilgrim Wall is a high roof system with features similar to that of a human face—a forehead, an eyebrow, and a prominent nose. Such a distinctive feature escaped the interest of climbers until Geoff Smith's "comeback." This route packs an amazing variety of climbing—chimney, face with small gear, and a big roof—in a natural line that climbs to the top of the cliff in a location where few other routes top out. Nearly the whole family participated in the first ascent.

Start: Downhill 15' from the start of **Worse Than Real**, on the lower of the two left-facing, right-leaning ramps.

P1 5.9 G: Traverse right on the ramp to a broken left-facing corner. Up the corner and into a chimney (as for **Worse Than Real**) and the tree ledge above with a fixed anchor (as for **Earthly Night**). 80'

P2 5.8 G: Same as **Worse Than Real**: Step right and climb the left-facing chimney with a handcrack in the back. At the top, step right and up to a vegetated ledge with trees. 90'

P3 5.9+ PG: Above the ledge, climb the thin crack in the low-angled face and up to steep rock. You must make a devious step left to pass through this section. At the top of the face, move left to either of two fixed anchors shared with **Earthly Night**. Lots of small gear. 150'

P4 5.9+ PG: Up through the heavily vegetated dike, move left 10', then straight up past a right-facing corner (crux) and up to a fixed anchor on a slab directly below the nose. 160'

● **P5 5.10b G:** Up suspect blocks on the right side of the nose under the huge roof. Traverse left under the roof to the bridge of the nose and break through the roof at a small left-facing corner and a fixed anchor just above. A spectacular and airy pitch. 70'

11 Tom Rosecrans, *Adirondack Rock and Ice Climbs* (1976), p. 87.

History: Smith retired from climbing, then returned for this route, his last hurrah. He counted 60 trad placements on the route. This was Smith's last major contribution to Poke-O climbing.

FA Sep, 2002, Geoff Smith, Tim Smith, Silas Smith (Tim and Silas are Geoff's sons.)

137 Raptor's Scream 5.12c G 80' ★★★★

A stunning route. Named for the screaming peregrine falcons that frequent the cliff.

Start: Downhill and right of the Pilgrim Wall, halfway down the hill (50'), below a left-facing dihedral with three overhangs.

● **P1 5.12c G:** Physical climbing up the corner past the three overhangs, then move right onto the face with a prominent black streak. Here the climb changes character: up the technical slab (crux) to a fixed anchor in dike rock. 80'

FA Aug, 1993, Patrick Munn, Dominic Eisinger

Neurosis Area

Around the corner from the Pilgrim Wall is another open area with some flat slabs and a couple of large boulders that mark the start of Neurosis Direct. The routes in this section end at the traverse dike two pitches up, as the upper section of the cliff is dirty, loose, wet, and nondescript (the routes that climb through this upper section—Neurosis and Worse Than Real—are not recommended).

Some features to look for are the huge boulder that marks the start of Royal Savage, the buried slabs beneath Home Rule, the huge 160'-high left-facing corner of Neurosis Direct with the brown water streak to the left, and the narrow tree ledge up close to the cliff with the starts of Scallion, Green Onion, and other routes. The tree-covered ledge system at the top of Green Onion and Thunderhead is Calamine Ledge, named in honor of the poison ivy that grows there.

Neurosis Rappel: There is an established rappel line from the huge treed terrace at the top of End Game, Worse Than Real, Neurosis, Moonshine, Paralysis, and other routes. Walk left on the terrace to a deep, wet depression in the cliff above (this is the direct finish to Neurosis in winter). Continue down and left on the terrace to find a large oak tree near the edge with a fixed anchor. The first rappel is 120' and takes you to a small vegetated island with a lone oak tree and a fixed anchor. The next rappel is 100' and takes you to the vegetated ledge system with many trees (where Royal Savage and Home Rule finish; Neurosis also traverses this ledge system). The final rappel is 190' and lands you near the Royal Savage Boulder.

138 Free Swing 5.10b PG 175'

Originally climbed using a tree for the initial protection. The tree is gone, replaced by a welcome bolt for the opening moves. The bolt at the end of P1 is missing, which makes P1 serious.

Start: Downhill from the Pilgrim Wall, the trail goes around an arête to level ground. Begin at this arête below a crack that shoots rightward across the wall.

P1 5.10b PG: Climb up to the bolt (crux), then hand-traverse the steep face rightward in the good crack and pass beneath the bolt line for Smear Campaign. Near the crack's end, step up onto the slab and work back left to a bolt (missing) and up to a narrow ledge system, which leads back right. Then step around the corner and up to a belay tree. 100'

P2 5.9 G: Move back left around the corner and up to a crack on the face, then follow it to the top. 75'

FA Apr, 1977, Geoff Smith, Patrick Munn

139 Smear Campaign 5.11b G 90' ★★★★

A burly start, followed by a smearfest on a steep slab. The grade continues to be debated—some say 5.10b, others say hard 5.11.

Start: Same as Free Swing.

P1 5.11b G: (V1) Climb up to the bolt (5.10b), then hand-traverse the steep face rightward in the good crack for 20'. Step up onto the face through undulating waves of rock and follow features to the right, then move back left (crux) to a steep finish. 90'

V1 Direct Start 5.10b R: 30' right of the arête below the left end of a horizontal seam 20' up with a piton (missing), climb the face to gain the horizontal, then leftward to join the traverse crack.

FA Aug, 2002, Mark Meschinelli, Dominic Eisinger

FA (V1) May 29, 1988, Gelu Ionescu

140 Royal Savage 5.10b PG 180' ★★

Good climbing, although the initial crack is somewhat grown in. The traverse on P1 is unlikely-looking but protectable. The route is named after a restaurant in Plattsburg, now long gone, which, in turn, was named for Benedict Arnold's two-masted schooner that was used to deny the British the use of Lake Champlain in 1776.

Start: In the clearing below the Neurosis Direct corner is a slab (the Home Rule Slab). To its left is a right-angling crack that starts near a huge boulder (the Royal Savage Boulder).

P1 5.9 PG: Climb the right-angling crack (crux) to its end. Make tricky moves left across the slab to the tree-covered ledge. 100'

P2 5.10b PG: At the left end of the ledge is a large right-facing corner. Right of this is a smaller right-facing corner; climb this, step left around the arête, then back right to the finish. Belay off trees. 80'

Descent: Walk right and rappel Home Rule.

FA 1980, Mark Meschinelli, Drew Allan

141 Lost Chance (aka The Natural) 5.10a G 90' ★★★

Originally led with trad gear. A later team added the two bolts and named the route The Natural, not knowing that it had previously been climbed free. Regardless, the bolts make this a safe and enjoyable route.

Start: Same as Home Rule.

P1 5.10a G: Climb left to the left edge of the black streak. Follow a discontinuous crack past several bulges to the anchor shared with Home Rule. 90'

FA 1993, Gelu Ionescu

Swimming with Sharks

I don't recall how I came to notice it—the line didn't show up on the guidebook photo, but I knew with the conviction of inexperience there was a route there even before attempting it. I was in for a big surprise, though—although several sections of the route looked clear, the middle half was vague and there was no ignoring the giant roofs blocking access to the cracks above.

Discouraged, I decided to console myself with the last pitch first, a splitter crack visible from the road to the right of Fastest Gun. Armed to the teeth, I hiked to the top of the route and rapped over the crack. I half cleaned the pitch on the way down, then, after a cursory look below, spent the next few hours clawing and scrubbing my way back to the top on aid. On my way down, I ran into a Who's Who of Poke-O regulars in the campground. I tried to keep it a secret, but the huge pack and thick coating of lichen on my face gave me away. Pointing to the roofs, I admitted I didn't think the route would go.

Later that summer, I turned my attention back to the Pinhead corner with renewed faith and made agonizingly slow progress, aiding a few feet at a time. As I passed Pinhead's anchors, the seemingly blank wall above yielded splitter fingercracks and crisp edges just a few feet to one side. I worked alone through the rainy weather of late summer, more days than I care to admit. One day high on the cliff, I watched a circling peregrine cartwheel, then dive to within a few meters of me—a loud smack and a puff of feathers turned some hapless bird into lunch. At some point alone on the cliff, I decided on the name, knowing it wouldn't make sense to anyone else.

To finish the one remaining barrier, I finally found some bait—a friend of a friend who wanted to climb for the day. Poor guy. We jugged to the top of the second pitch, and he belayed for hours while I cleaned and aided past a car-sized flake lodged in the corner above him, then eased out the humongous roof above. Surprisingly the most intimidating section of the route turned into the most exposed 5.8 pitch I've ever done, and the remaining sections went easily. A week later, after falling on the first pitch with Pete Cimasi, I shouted beta to one of my climbing mentors, Hobey Walker, as he flashed the first pitch and we continued to the top for the free ascent.

Shark Week holds special significance for me, as it was a milestone that marked the end of one of my life's chapters and the beginning of another. I have since climbed harder routes and maybe even better routes, but none have gone from vision to reality or remained as significant in my life as Shark Week.

- Dave Furman

*Dave Furman on **Home Rule** (5.10b). Photo by Mark Meschinelli.*

142 Home Rule 5.10b G 190' ★★★

A beautiful face climb that ascends the distinct brown water streak left of the **Neurosis Direct** corner. The two pitches can be combined into one long megapitch of face climbing. Often wet. At the time this was climbed, locals were concerned about outside forces influencing local issues (from closing roads to chopping bolts); the locals wanted "home rule."

Start: On a slab, 4' left of the huge left-facing corner of **Neurosis Direct**.

● **P1 5.10a G:** Face-climb up the brown streak using small face holds between stances to a fixed anchor. The pitch wanders and steps right at several points. 100'

● **P2 5.10b G:** Continue up the face to a fixed anchor just left of the top of the corner, below the dike rock. 90'

FA Jul, 1992, Patrick Purcell, Bill Dodd

143 Neurosis Direct A1 190'

A direct start to **Neurosis**, this route climbs the obvious wet corner, rumored to be free at 5.9 or 5.10, but nobody wants to verify it. Another route best climbed in the winter.

Start: At the major left-facing corner in the clearing.

P1 A1: Climb the corner to a ledge with a tree. Step right and continue up the corner. At the top, jog left and up to the fixed anchor as for **Home Rule**. Rappel or join **Neurosis**. 190'

FA 1980, Mark Meschinelli (solo)

Neurosis
Rappel
Hidden
Pique
(winter route)
Neurosis
(winter route)
156
135
Calamine
Ledge
161
164
Paralysis
Block
139
140
142
145
147
152
154

Poke-O Moonshine: Neurosis Area and Paralysis Amphitheater

133 Worse Than Real (5.8)
134 Neurosis (5.6)
135 Steptoe (5.6)
138 Free Swing (5.10b)
139 Smear Campaign (5.11b)
140 Royal Savage (5.10b)
141 Lost Chance (5.10a)
142 Home Rule (5.10b)
143 Neurosis Direct (A1)
144 Pomme de Terre (5.10b)
145 Scallion (5.10a)
146 Macintosh (5.10d)
147 Green Onion (5.9)
148 Grapes of Wrath (5.11b)
149 A.S. (5.10c)

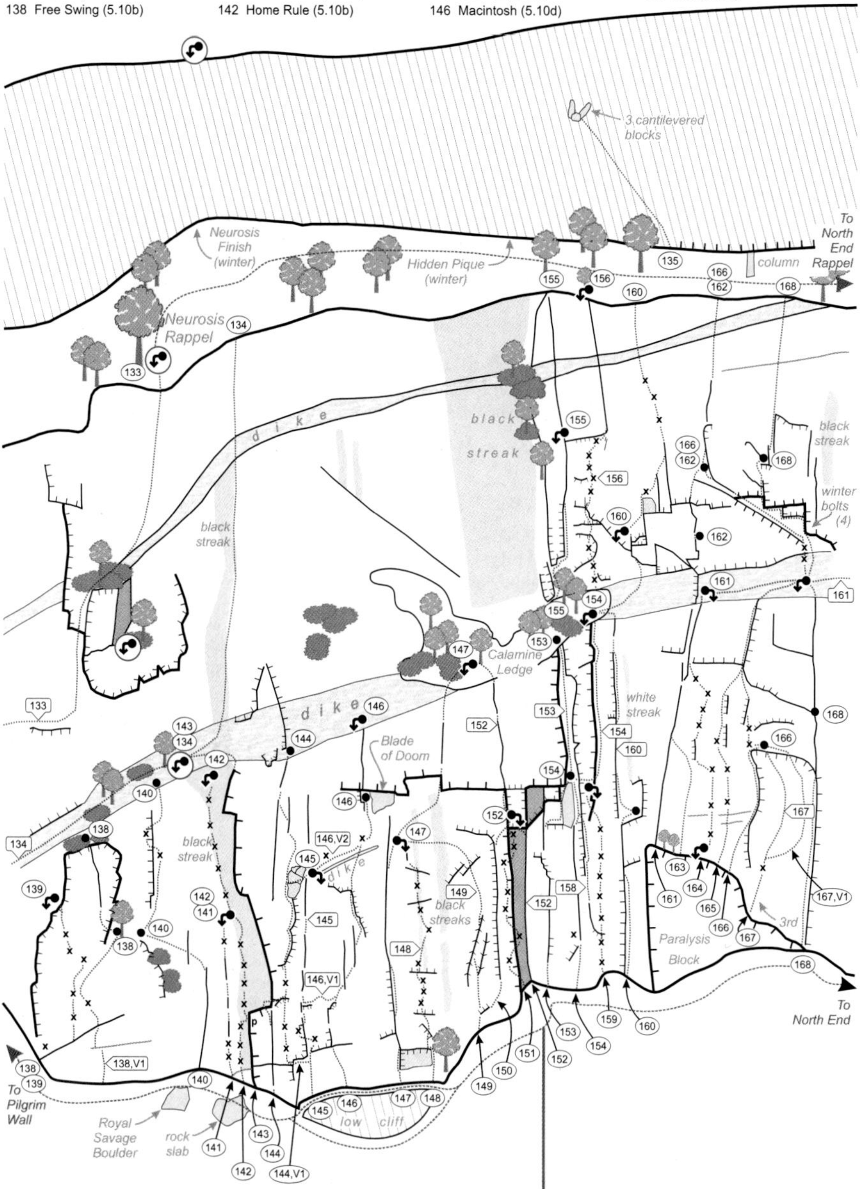

150 Quo Vadis (5.11b)
151 La Spirale (5.11b)
152 Thunderhead (5.10d)
153 Lightning (5.9)
154 Cirrhosis (5.9+)
155 End Game (5.10d)
156 Under the Influence (5.10d)
158 Dicentra (5.9)
159 Menace to Sobriety (5.10c)
160 Amongst the Crowd/Clouds (5.11a)
161 Paralysis (5.8)
162 Annie's Dilemma (5.11a)
163 Orchestra (5.10a)
164 Maestro (5.10c)
165 Macrobiotic (5.10a)
166 Moonshine (5.11a)
167 Watch My Bolt (5.9)
168 Tachycardia (5.12c)

Neurosis Area | Paralysis Amphitheater

144 Pomme de Terre 5.10b PG 100' ★★

Varied climbing up a difficult face and a beautiful arching corner in white rock, which unfortunately is shorter than it appears from below. The name means "potato," but more literally "apple of the earth," as this route was a gem excavated from the dirt.

Start: Just right of the brown left-facing corner of Neurosis Direct at a crack.

P1 5.10b PG: (V1) Follow the crack to the Neurosis Direct ledge (5.7; a tree with a long sling offers welcome protection), then traverse right on flakes to a stance below a bolt. Up the face (crux), then across easier terrain to the base of the left-facing, left-arching clean corner. Up the corner (RPs, or cheat and place a cam right in Scallion) to blocks. Move right to the fixed anchor on Scallion. (The original ascent continued up the face above the blocks to the dike area [5.7]; the climbing is short and there is no easy way off.) 100'

V1 Direct Start 5.11d G: Start as for Scallion, then move left in the horizontal below the initial overhang to a ledge. Up the clean face above to join the normal route after the traverse.

Gear: Include small TCUs and RPs.

FA Aug 30, 1984, Don Mellor, Bill Dodd

145 Scallion 5.10a G (5.7 R) 100' ★★★★

An absolute gem with a fun mixture of face, arête, corner, and moderate crack climbing. Named for the wild scallions that were weeded from the crack on the first ascent. Watch for wasps in the upper cracks.

Start: 40' right of the left-facing Neurosis Direct corner, on a rock ledge below a face that leads to a shallow, bottomless right-facing corner 15' up.

P1 5.10a G (5.7 R): Climb the face (5.7 R) to the base of the corner (good protection in the horizontal here), up the corner, then left onto the arête. Crux face moves at the top of the corner lead to a beautiful finger- and handcrack, discontinuous at first. Follow it to a fixed anchor right of three large, stacked flakes. 100'

FA Sep, 1980, Drew Allan, Patrick Munn, Mark Meschinelli

146 Macintosh 5.10d G (5.10c X) 200' ★★★★

A stellar face climb that features a thin corner with vertical edges just above, a stout runout, then a fingercrack headwall with an unusual move. Unfortunately, getting started is life-threatening; two variations are described that remove the hazard.

Start: (V1, V2) 20' right of Scallion, below a shallow right-facing corner above a horizontal 15' up.

P1 5.10c X: Climb up to the 4" horizontal crack, then run it out for 20' up the corner and face above to good gear. Traverse right 15', then up a series of parallel seams, working up and right to a shallow left-facing corner. Up the corner to the overlap, then straight up the face above using left-facing edges (crux). Continue up the face with no protection (5.7 R) to a 2"-high dike. Foot-traverse right to a bolt, then straight up the face to a stance below the roof, just left of the Blade of Doom (the gigantic pancake pasted to the face under the roof, one of the more terrifying features at Poke-O). Alternatively, at the bolt, you can continue the foot traverse right to the fixed anchor on Green Onion and a more comfortable belay. 140'

P2 5.10d G: Break through the ceiling via a fingercrack (crux) and follow it to a fixed anchor below the dike. 60'

V1 5.10c G (5.7 R): Climb Scallion to a ledge just above its crux (5.10a), then traverse right with good gear to join the normal route at the traverse. This avoids the 5.10c X climbed at the start while providing access to the amazing climbing above.

V2 5.10d G: Climbs P1 of Scallion, then traverses into Macintosh for the final pitch. From the fixed anchor at the top of Scallion, traverse right (bolt) on a thin 2"-high dike to a point below the fingercrack headwall; join Macintosh to the top.

FA 1977, Gary Allan, Geoff Smith

FA (V2) 1980, Mark Meschinelli

147 Green Onion 5.9 G 180' ★★★

An excellent P1 and a dirty P2.

Start: Find the block just above the trail 40' right of Scallion. The route begins on the left side of this block in a left-facing corner that is below a more prominent right-facing corner.

P1 5.8 G: Climb the left-facing corner to the top of the block, then up the shallow right-facing corner and follow it to a fixed anchor out left; this anchor is just below a boxlike break in the roof. The route looks unprotected, but cracks appear when needed. 100'

P2 5.9 G: Up the face rightward to the right side of the boxlike break in the roof. Climb the roof at the left-facing corner (the right side of the boxlike break), then up the steep crack to Calamine Ledge. 80'

Descent: Rappel from trees or walk right to the Cirrhosis anchor and rappel that route with two 60-m ropes.

FA 1977, Geoff Smith, Patrick Munn

148 Grapes of Wrath (aka Sour Grapes) 5.11b PG 100' ★★★

Excellent, sustained face climbing. The original route climbed the opening crux with three bolts, then climbed a weakness to join Green Onion to the anchor. The route as it exists today has been rerouted slightly to the right.

Start: On the right side of the block beneath the start of Green Onion, behind a large tree close to the rock.

● **P1 5.11b PG:** Climb to the top of the Green Onion block, then up a left-rising weakness to a fragile orange flake below an overlap. Over the overhang and up the face to the next overhang (crux), then right following the weakness (left of the black streak) to the fixed anchor on Green Onion. 100'

FA 1993, Joe Szot, Dave Szot

149 A.S. 5.10c PG 130'

Named for Alain Simard, who died soloing Hallunbeinbrunch in Grands-Jardins National Park, Quebec, in 1989. Bolts missing.

Start: Below a triangular roof 12' up, 40' left of (and downhill from) the Thunderhead.

P1 5.10c PG: Climb the steep slab left of the triangular roof up to a right-facing open book (5.10). Step left out of the book, around the arête (5.8), and up the face to the right-facing, right-rising overlaps. Traverse left to the fixed anchor on **Green Onion**. 130'
FA Sep, 1989, Gelu Ionescu, Pierre Gagnon

150 Quo Vadis 5.11b PG 90'

Latin for "whither goest thou," this name will acquire more meaning as you stand below and try to figure it out. Bolts missing.
Start: Same as **A.S.**
P1 5.11b PG: Climb up to the triangular roof and pass it on the right to gain a black right-facing corner. Up the corner to its top, then step right to the fixed anchor on **Thunderhead**. 90'
FA Jun 12, 1988, Gelu Ionescu, Pierre Gagnon

151 La Spirale 5.11b G 90' ★★

A pretty arête and a little spicy in sections. The climbing alternates between the faces on both sides of the arête, with boulder problems between good rests; some runouts. Save some pump for the 5.10b crux of **Thunderhead** at the top.
Start: Same as **Thunderhead**.
⭘ **P1 5.11b G:** Step left to the arête and follow it closely to a height-dependent reach below the fixed anchor of **Thunderhead**. 90'
Gear: RPs, 1" cams, 1 ea 4", 1 ea 3".
FA Aug, 1987, Gelu Ionescu, Pierre Gagnon

152 Thunderhead 5.10d G 150' ★★★

A burly, testosterone-laden route that features a huge roof and an overhanging fistcrack. Care must be taken to protect the second under the roof and also to ensure that the rope doesn't interfere with the gear in the roof crack. The first section is often wet. There is a demon-shaped outline of a head on the underside of the roof, dubbed the Thunderhead by the first ascentionist.
Start: At a black right-facing corner capped by giant roofs 60' up.
P1 5.10b PG: Climb the black corner using cracks in the left wall. Above, the corner becomes thin, and a couple of difficult moves gain a rail beneath the roof. Traverse left under the roof, then around its left end (crux) to an inconveniently placed fixed anchor. 90'
P2 5.10d G: Up the overhanging fistcrack with increasing difficulty to the Calamine Ledge. 60'
Gear: Standard plus 1 ea 3–4".
Descent: Walk right and rappel **Cirrhosis** with two 60-m ropes.
FA Sep, 1978, Gary Allan, Dave Hough

Paralysis Amphitheater

To the right of **Neurosis**, the trail goes uphill into an amphitheater capped by huge roofs 150' up. In the center of the amphitheater is the Paralysis Block, a house-sized block up against the rock, above which start several routes (e.g., **Paralysis** and **Maestro**). The amphitheater is bounded on the left by the roofs of **Thunderhead** and on the right by the large left-facing corner of **Sunburst Arête**.

DESCENT

There are several descent options. For routes that end on Calamine Ledge, there is a rappel at the top of **Cirrhosis** (two ropes required). For routes that finish at the top, you can walk right to the North End Rappel.

Poke-O Reverie

Every time I went from Quebec to New York, I got an ecstatic feeling while driving along I-87—the "highway to heaven." I felt as if I were being catapulted into an inexpressibly blissful climbing dream. Submerged adrenaline erupted the minute I laid eyes on Poke-O, a massive piece of rock right next to the highway. My desire to enter the unknown sparked an impulse to design creative lines: I was on a quest for nice moves and magic moments when excitement overwhelms doubt.

In the late 1980s, Pierre-Édouard Gagnon, Gelu Ionescu, and I were astute enough to recognize Poke-O's quality, height, and superb potential. We chose to begin our discovery the only way we knew—by exploring the few blanks spots that the locals considered unclimbable. Our game was face climbing, and we came from a place where, in that era, there wasn't much hesitation about using technology. In retrospect, it was challenging to introduce a new route-setting approach to Poke-O. It raised questions and sparked reactions among the locals. Climbing moves were by no means the only subject discussed.

The emptiness of the blank, virgin walls called for a revolutionary process, one that defied both ordinary philosophy and gravity while at the same time respecting the essence of climbing. My pursuit of new lines started with Libido (yeah, that type of spirituality). Next, I put in Maestro, placing all the bolts on lead. Originally named French Gravity, the route Verdon was a delight and epitomized the sheer beauty of movements on an incomparable wall. This namesake of a famous climbing area in France offered me ample support to justify a new kind of process. We moved on to Macrobiotic and Watch My Bolt, placing infrequent bolts on lead. The intense, run-out A.S., Quo Vadis, and La Spirale, by Gelu Ionescu, and Dicentra, by Pierre Gagnon, were done in the traditional, true-heroes style that has marked Poke-O's history. And finally, Macho, my favorite and last route, which revealed that although I was aging, I still had some testosterone left in me.

Writing about this evanescent period brings flashbacks of outings filled with thrilling experiences in a wild setting. By "stepping out of the beaten crack" at Poke-O, I experienced a rare level of excitement and awareness. Although I eventually reined in my craving for new and interesting climbs on this magnificent rock, I have no regrets. What I was unable to climb then, I will dream about forever. We ghosts who seek fame and recognition must finally conclude, "Off belay."

\- Julien Déry

North End Rappel: From the top, walk right and follow the open slab on the edge of the cliff for 250' to find an anchor 12' high in an oak tree. A 170' rappel over a slab lands on an island with another sizable oak tree (the finish to **In Vivo**), where another 170' rappel returns you to the ground.

153 Lightning (aka Zone X) 5.9 G 150' ★

A good-looking P1 that's filled with vegetables. P2 is even better.

Start: 10' right of the right-facing corner of **Thunderhead** below a bottomless crack with stacked flakes.

P1 5.9 G: Up the crack past a left-facing corner and up to a left-arching overlap. Through the overlap via a straight-in crack to the roof. Step right on a ledge and up a jamcrack to a flat stance on top of a block (as for **Cirrhosis**). 75'

P2 5.6 G: Climb the depression between opposing corners to the Calamine Ledge. 75'

Descent: Step right and rappel **Cirrhosis**.

FA Sep 21, 1984, Ken Nichols, Mike Heintz, Mark Meschinelli

154 Cirrhosis 5.9+ PG 160' ★★★

P2 is one of the best laybacks at the cliff and easily viewed from the ground. The route is in a shaded section of the cliff and is a good climb for a hot day.

Start: Midpoint between the **Thunderhead** corner and the Paralysis Block, below a weakness in black rock with a bolt, above the left side of a buried boulder.

P1 5.9 PG: Climb up to the bolt and follow the crack straight up to a right-facing corner formed by a block on the left. Up the corner to belay on top of the block. 80'

P2 5.9+ G: Traverse right from the block and into a right-facing flake. Jam and layback up the beautiful flake, which tapers near the top, to a fixed anchor on the Calamine Ledge. 80'

Descent: Rappel from the fixed anchor with two 60-m ropes, or make two 80' rappels.

FA 1972, Dick Williams, David Loeks

155 End Game 5.10d PG 150' ★

Hidden from view, this crack line is infrequently visited. P1 is recommended.

Start: Below a chimney with a ceiling on the right side, above and left of **Cirrhosis** on the Calamine Ledge. (**Cirrhosis** is the best way to reach this ledge.)

P1 5.10d PG: Move up to the right side of the ceiling and into the right-facing corner above. Continue in the crack through a bulge to a fixed anchor on the left. 75'

P2 5.10b PG: Continue in the increasingly dirty crack to the top. 75'

Descent: North End Rappel or Neurosis Rappel.

FA Jul 27, 1991, Dennis Luther, Dave Szot

156 Under the Influence 5.10d G 195' ★★★★

Excellent climbing with several difficult sections; the best route to break through this upper section of rock.

Start: At the P2 anchor of **Cirrhosis**.

P1 5.10d G: Climb up and right to a large suspect (but sound) flake. Climb the flake, then head left and up to a shallow right-facing corner–crack. Follow the crack up a left-facing corner to an overhang (3" cam helpful), through the overhang using a finger crack, to the face above. At the last bolt head up and right to a thin crack. Climb the crack and face above to the top. 195'

History: This is the completion of Dennis Luther's last route, and named by him in keeping with the theme of the lower pitches.

FA Sep 5, 2009, Bill Dodd, Chris Hyson, Nick Wakeman

157 Detox (linkup) 5.10d G 0' ★★★★★

This linkup is so good that it's worth mentioning as a separate route. The routes are stacked atop one another, so it's logical to think of them as a unit. Plus, the combination requires a variety of skills, from crimpy face to layback to thin crack. Climb **Menace to Sobriety** (5.10c), then P2 of **Cirrhosis** (5.9+), then **Under the Influence** (5.10d) to the top.

Descent: Two double-rope rappels return to the start.

158 Dicentra 5.9 PG 80'

Dicentra is the Latin name for bleeding heart, which was growing in the cracks above the corner. This route was chopped, but it is still possible to climb it using the fixed protection on **Menace to Sobriety**. Either finish on **Cirrhosis** or rappel from the **Menace to Sobriety** fixed anchor.

Start: Same as **Menace to Sobriety**.

P1 5.9 PG: Climb **Menace to Sobriety** to a left-rising, scooped ledge at 20', then follow it left to a right-facing corner. Follow the corner to the block belay of **Cirrhosis**. 80'

FA May 28, 1988, Pierre Gagnon, Jean-Luc Michaud

159 Menace to Sobriety 5.10c G 80' ★★★★

This one might drive you to drink. An amazing pitch of face climbing, made even better when combined with the upper flake of **Cirrhosis**. The route was put in on lead, three days before Pechousek went in for knee ligament surgery. Harder for short people.

Start: 15' right of the start of **Cirrhosis** and 20' left of the left-facing corner formed by the Paralysis Block, and directly beneath the long flake that forms P2 of **Cirrhosis**.

● **P1 5.10c G:** Meander up the face following bolts to a fixed anchor at the base of the **Cirrhosis** flake. 80'

Gear: Optional finger-sized cam up high.

FA Oct 9, 1995, Charles Pechousek, Bob Cartwright

160 Amongst the Crowd/Clouds 5.11a PG 360' ★★★★

P2, a trad climber's dream, ascends a discontinuous crack through wavy, streaked rock. P1 and P2 were climbed and thought to be squeezed in, hence the name **Amongst the Crowd**. These pitches can be climbed by themselves, by traversing left to the fixed anchor at the top of **Cirrhosis**. Later, the route was extended through some airy roofs and aptly named **Amongst the Clouds**, the first of four ways to break the roofs above the Paralysis Amphitheater.

*Opposite: Jeremy Haas and Robert Livingston (belaying) on P2 of **Cirrhosis** (5.9+). Photo by Tomás Donoso.*

Start: At the first right-facing corner (capped by a black roof) left of the Paralysis Block.

P1 5.10b PG: Climb up a slab and into the right-facing corner, then follow it to the black roof. Through the roof on the left using a flared fingercrack. Follow it to a ledge and belay on the right side. 75'

P2 5.11a PG: From the left end of the ledge, climb a crack in a series of right-facing open books in steep bulges for the entire pitch. At the top, step right to belay on a small ledge or step left to the **Cirrhosis** fixed anchor. 125'

P3 5.11a PG: This pitch climbs through the left-rising ceiling that begins at a hanging tooth. Step right to the white streaks in the black rock, then up to the ceiling and break through via a crack on the right side of the tooth to a fixed anchor. 40'

P4 5.10a PG: Face-climb up and right to a pasted flake, continue rightward past seams, then finally angle back left past a dike ledge to the top. 120'

Gear: Up to 3", extra 0.5" pieces.

Descent: Walk right to descend via the North End Rappel.

FA (P1–P2) Aug, 1988, Patrick Purcell, Herb George, Mark Ippolito

FA (P3–P4) 1991, Patrick Munn, Mark Meschinelli

161 Paralysis 5.8 PG 430' ★★★★

A historic route that travels through some dramatic terrain. It offers a bit of everything—a perfect 5.8 crack, a long traverse around an exposed arête, an exciting bulging headwall, and an off-width finish. The anchors are solid, and you can retreat from several points if desired.

Start: At the top of the Paralysis Block, the large block of rock against the cliff in the center of the amphitheater. Access the top from the right side by climbing a series of left-rising vegetated ledges (4th class). There is a fixed anchor on the face on top of the block.

P1 5.8 G: Beginning at the left end of the Paralysis Block, climb up steps to gain the crack. The crack is initially easy, then increases in difficulty past an off-width section to a steep finish. 130'

P2 5.7 G: Traverse right in the dike to the huge left-facing corner and the fixed anchor of **Moonshine**. 60'

P3 5.8 G: Continue traversing right and stay low in the dike under a black roof on the arête, move onto a slab under the roof, then step down around an orange corner. Continue right over a rectangular block to a fixed anchor on the left side of a pillar. 70'

P4 5.8 PG: (V1) Step back left to the top of the rectangular block, then onto the face and climb an unlikely bulge in broken rock via good holds. Work up and right to a steep, off-width crack with chockstones. Up the crack to the tree ledge. 100'

P5 5.7 G: Above the belay is a face between two opposing corners. Climb the left corner to the top. 70'

V1 5.9 PG: Directly above the belay is a clean right-facing groove with a black streak on the right side. Climb the groove to the top, then step left on the slab to join the normal route below the off width.

Descent: North End Rappel.

Gear: Cams to 5", plus extra hand-sized pieces.

FA 1959, John Turner, Brian Rothery, Dick Strachan

162 Annie's Dilemma 5.11a G (5.7 R) 145' ★★

This is the second of four routes that breach the roofs above the Paralysis Amphitheater. Presumably, Eastman had some trouble following through the roofs.

Start: At the fixed anchor on top of P1 of **Paralysis**.

P1 5.11a G: Directly above the anchor is a ceiling with a shallow crack. Climb up left to the bulge below the ceiling, then straight up through the ceiling into a discontinuous crack. This short pitch is required to reduce rope drag and to ensure that rope stretch for the follower is minimal. 25'

P2 5.11a G (5.7 R): Continue up the crack and through the next ceiling. Switch cracks right to **Moonshine** and follow that route to the top. 120'

Descent: Walk right to descend via the North End Rappel.

FA 1991, Patrick Munn, Ann Eastman

163 Orchestra 5.10a TR 130'

The first route on the shield of rock in the back of the Paralysis Amphitheater. This route was deemed contrived, as it was too close to its neighbors; the bolts were removed by the first-ascent party. The route is now climbed only by toprope. From the top of the Paralysis Block, above the fixed anchor, climb the face, then join either **Paralysis** or the upper section of **Maestro**.

FA (TR) Sep, 1987, Patrick Purcell, Ed Palen

164 Maestro 5.10c G 140' ★★★★★

The undisputed leader of the symphony of Poke-O face climbs—clean rock, good moves, and exposed position. This route has been erased several times, the unwitting victim of past ethics debates. Be aware that the route has a trad finish; more than one unsuspecting leader has climbed to the top of the bolts only to find 30' of 5.8 trad climbing to reach the ledge.

Start: Same as for **Paralysis**.

⊙ **P1 5.10c G:** From the anchor, climb up and right to a shallow right-facing corner (small nuts). Continue up the corner and face to below a horizontal break at the top of the shield. Work left to the **Paralysis** crack and finish on that route (5.8) to the fixed anchor. 140'

Descent: Rappel with two ropes.

Gear: Small nuts plus a couple of cams to 2" for the finish.

FA Jul 25, 1987, Julien Déry

165 Macrobiotic 5.10a R 150' ★★★

Another exposed, high-quality face climb, but absolutely terrifying to lead due to the serious runouts. Has the same trad finish as for **Moonshine**.

Start: Same as **Paralysis**.

P1 5.10a R: From the right end of the ledge, traverse up and right to the first bolt in white- and black-speckled rock. Continue straight up and stay just left of two stacked, shallow right-facing corners; then move right to finish to finish by following the left-facing corner of **Moonshine** to the fixed anchor. 150'

Descent: Rappel with two ropes.

FA Aug, 1988, Julien Déry

Opposite: Robert Livingston on ***Menace to Sobriety*** *(5.10c). Photo by Tomás Donoso.*

166 Moonshine 5.11a G (5.7 R) 325' ★★

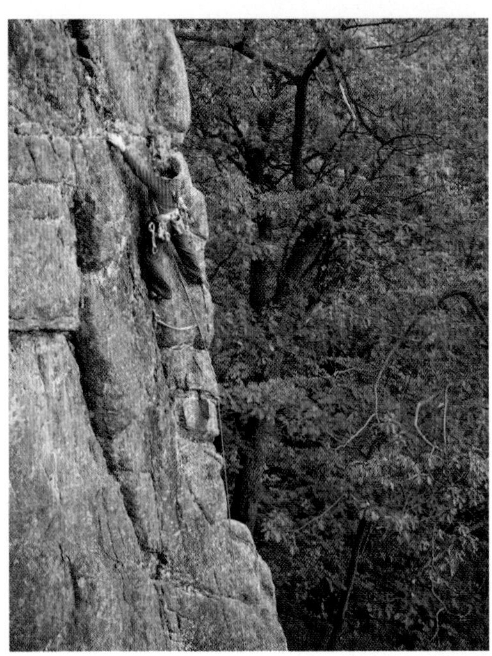

Jesse Williams on P1 of ***Sunburst Arête*** *(5.8). Photo by Tomás Donoso.*

The third route to break the roofs above the Paralysis Amphitheater. If it were cleaned and the manky bolts replaced, it would be highly recommended for its position, exposed terrain, and good moves. At the time of this writing, the bolts are 0.25" and desperately need replacement.

Start: Same as for **Paralysis**.

P1 5.7 R: From the right end of the ledge, traverse right with no protection into a scoop that leads to a left-facing corner. Follow the corner to a ledge and belay out right. 75'

P2 5.10d G: From the left end of the ledge, climb the difficult face up and left to a shallow right-facing corner with an intermittent crack. Up past an overlap, then to a left-facing corner where the climbing eases somewhat before you reach the dike ledge and a fixed anchor. 90'

P3 5.11a G: Stay left of algae (the consistency of yogurt) and climb up dike rock to the bulge below a left-rising 8" crack above a ramp. Up the bulge (bolts; crux) to gain the ramp, then follow it left and up to its end. Pull over a bulge to a cramped belay beneath a crack. 80'

P4 5.8 PG: Up a left-leaning crack on lower-angled rock to the top. 80'

Descent: Walk right to the North End Rappel.

History: The first two pitches were climbed prior to Dunn's free ascent by an unknown party.

FFA (P1, P2) Jun, 1977, Jim Dunn, Geoff Smith, Wendy White

FA (P3,P4) Sep 1, 1985, Don Mellor, Mike Heintz, Mark Meschinelli

167 Watch My Bolt 5.9 X 75' ★

Climbs the pretty face below the P1 belay ledge of **Moonshine**.

Start: 15' along the 4th-class approach to the Paralysis Block, below a shallow right-facing open book that is 20' up.

P1 5.9 X: Climb up to the open book (bolt) and crack above. Traverse diagonally right to the middle of the face (V1), then straight up to the first belay of **Moonshine**. 75'

V1 TAO 5.11a TR: Break farther right and up the face to the top.

History: Led ground-up; the hand drill broke, forcing Déry to run it out up the face.

FA Sep, 1988, Julien Déry, Daniel Vachon

FA (V1) Sep, 1988, Julien Déry, Daniel Vachon

168 Tachycardia 5.12c PG (5.7 R) 355' ★★★

Climbs one of the largest roofs in the region and is a recommended outing; the exposure is sure to get your heart pumping. The first couple of pitches are extremely dirty, but the P3 roof can be approached from **Paralysis** or any of its neighbors. It was originally an aid line with seven bolts, but these were removed; it was free-climbed using trad gear in a crack just to the right.

Start: At a huge left-facing broken corner in black rock, 10' right of the start of the 4th-class approach to the Paralysis Block.

P1 5.7 G: Up cracks in the broken left-facing corner (just right of the smooth wall), past the **Moonshine** ledge, to a stance on blocks below the steep fistcrack. 90'

P2 5.10c PG: Up the dirty, grass-filled fistcrack to the dike and a fixed anchor for **Moonshine**. 75'

P3 5.12c PG: Starting on the right wall, climb to a hanging tooth, then move left into a crumbly crack in a left-facing corner. Up the crack until you can step left into a V-groove, just below the deepest part of the roof. Undercling 12' left to the lip, around the corner, and up to the next big roof. Out this roof left via a handcrack to the lip; pull the roof and into a left-facing corner, then follow it a few feet to a ledge. 90'

P4 5.7 R: Up the crack to the right past a ledge to a low-angle slab, then past a horizontal to the top. 100'

Descent: Walk right to the North End Rappel.

FA (P1–P2, "Parallax") 1980, Mark Meschinelli, Patrick Munn, Drew Allan

FA (P3–P4) Aug 15, 1986, Don Mellor, Bill Dodd, Patrick Purcell

FFA (P3) Sep 5, 1992, Craig Smith

169 Sunburst Arête 5.8 PG 200' ★★★

A full-length adventure when combined with the top pitches of **Paralysis**; definitely worth the hike. The arête remains dry and sunny until late in the day.

Start: The right side of the Paralysis Amphitheater is defined by a huge left-facing corner and a broad arête. Begin on the left wall of the arête, below a horizontal fistcrack with a grassy ledge just above.

Opposite: A climber on ***Maestro*** *(5.10b). Photo by Mark Meschinelli.*

P1 5.8 PG: Ascend a handcrack in stacked blocks, then up the exposed secure face past horizontal breaks to a belay on a ledge with a wide crack just above. 120'

P2 5.8 G: A physical pitch: Up a 4" crack to a blocky finish before the dike. Step right to a fixed anchor on the left side of a pillar (shared with **Paralysis**). Rappel or join **Paralysis**. 80'

Gear: To 4".

FA Oct, 1978, Geoff Smith, Patrick Munn

The North End

The northern section of the cliff tends to feature lichen-covered rock and is therefore seldom visited. **In Vivo**, for example, has received high praise, but it's difficult to even find the bolts in the garden of flaky lichen. Unlike the other sections of the Main Face, the routes here spread out over a larger area (roughly 450').

The North End Rappel is located here and descends directly over the bolted finish of **In Vivo**.

170 The Real 208 5.9+ PG 150'

Start: 50' right of **Sunburst Arête** at a pedestal below parallel cracks that pass through orange lichen–covered rock capped by an overhang.

P1 5.9+ PG: Climb the cracks to a ledge below an overhang. Step a few feet left and belay below a bulging crack. 50'

P2 5.9+ PG: Break the overhang via the bulging crack and move into the dirty right-facing corner. At the top of the corner, follow the thin crack that arches right to a belay in dike rock. 100'

Descent: Traverse dike rock left to the **Paralysis** P3 fixed anchor and rappel.

History: In the 1983 edition of *Climbing in the Adirondacks,* the locator photo for route 208 (**Sunburst Arête**) erroneously pointed to a section of unclimbed rock. Two years later, Heintz and Mellor ascended this unclimbed line and named it **The Real 208**.

FA May 5, 1985, Mike Heintz, Don Mellor

171 Domingo 5.10c PG 100'

Domingo is Spanish for "Sunday," and appropriately enough, this route was climbed on a Sunday. Bolted on lead, this route seems to have been erased and has fallen into a state of extreme dirtiness. The original description is vague; this is our best attempt.

Start: 75' right of **Sunburst Arête** is a 30'-tall detached, horrifying orange pillar with chockstones behind it. This route is thought to begin on ledges just left of this pillar.

P1 5.10c PG: Climb a crack in the orange face 4' left of the pillar to a left-facing slot. Up the slot, through the overhang, then difficult face climbing rightward leads to a shallow right-facing edge. Move up the orange, lichen-covered face, then work back left to an improbable exit. 100'

FA Oct 15, 1989, Gelu Ionescu, Pierre Gagnon

172 Paper Walls 5.10d PG 340'

Climbs the attractive corners high above and to the right of **Paralysis**. Named for a Marc Cohn song and for the papery lichen that is so prevalent on this end of the cliff.

Start: On the left side of a jumbled pile of boulders up against the cliff, at the end of Keep Off Ledge (see **Keep Off Flake**).

P1 5.10d PG: Climb the straight-in thin crack in the black streak to a boulder on a ledge, up the groove above, then step left onto a grassy terrace. 80'

P2 5.9+ PG: Up the open book to a dike belay below big roofs. 60'

P3 5.10c PG: Go up to the right side of the roofs and into a tan-colored right-facing corner with a low bolt. Up the corner to the overhang, break this on the left, then up a runout slab rightward to a belay at a tree island with an overhang 30' above. 130'

P4 5.2 PG: Scramble the slab rightward to the tree at the top with fixed anchors (the top anchor of the North End Rappel). 70'

Descent: North End Rappel.

FA Oct 22, 1994, Jeff Achey, Patrick Purcell

173 Keep Off Flake A3 180' ★★★

A long-standing problem that seems to have been climbed earlier, as old pitons and nuts were found on the route. From the condition of the route and the fixed gear, the ascent occurred much earlier than that reported here.

Start: From **Sunburst Arête**, walk right along the cliff base until a point just past the right-arching **Keep Off Flake**, which you can see on the wall above. A short scramble up and left on a slab leads to a ledge directly below the flake; this is Keep Off Ledge. This route begins on the right end of this ledge, on top of blocks left of **In Vivo**, centered beneath the namesake flake high above.

P1 A2: From the block, aid past two 3/8" studs to a fixed anchor on a left-leaning ledge below the left end of the flake. (This pitch would reportedly go free at 5.9 if someone cared to add bolt hangers and lead it.) 50'

P2 A3: Aid the wild flake, moving delicately past the "gong" section, which rings like a 50,000-ton bell. At the end of the flake, turn the corner and continue up the face to a bushy ledge (and the North End Rappel tree). Long slings are helpful to reduce drag. 130'

History: Gary Allan attempted the line in 1978 and made it to the end of the flake (5.11). He then scratched into lichen the words "Keep Off," visible from the road, to keep other climbers off until he could complete the ascent, which he never did.

FA Jun, 1996, Peter Pechousek, Charles Pechousek

174 In Vivo 5.11d R 170' ★★★

The name refers to a method of experimental research that uses whole organisms, like animal testing. This gem of a route awaits the next guinea pig to resurrect it from the garden of lichen that has overtaken this section of cliff.

Start: Begin on the right end of Keep Off Ledge (see **Keep Off Flake**), just right of a boulder perched on some blocks.

● **P1 5.11d R:** Climb rightward up dirty rock to the first bolt, then back left to vertical cracks in pink rock to a triangular orange scar. Up a small left-facing corner to reach the right end of **Keep Off Flake**, then face-climb past several flexing flakes to the tree ledge of the North End Rappel. 170'

FA May 1, 1993, Gelu Ionescu, Pierre Gagnon

175 Rare Earth 5.9 PG 150'

Start: 170' right of Keep Off Ledge below a tight, steep left-facing V-groove above a boulder. This is also 150' left of **Parabolic Cats**.

P1 5.9 PG: Climb the left-facing V-groove to a horizontal break 25' up with a shrub-covered ledge. Up the left-facing open book to a slab, then step right and up a left-facing open book to the right end of a tree ledge. 150'

FA 1982, Dave Hough, Mark Meschinelli

176 Parabolic Cats 5.12a G 35' ★★

A short route that is always dry.

Start: 150' right of **Rare Earth** in the huge left-facing orange corner underneath large roofs 25' up.

P1 5.12a G: Up the perfect handcrack in the corner to the roof. Move left to the crack and go diagonally leftward through the roof; move out the crack to a fixed anchor just above. 35'

FA Jul, 1988, Bill Lutkus, Jim Damon

177 Lichenstorm 5.9 PG 150' ★★

Start: 50' right of **Parabolic Cats**, just after an exposed, low overhang on the trail, at the base of a slab with left-facing corners above.

P1 5.9 PG: Up a slab leftward to a break, then up an arching left-facing corner. At the top of this corner, break right into the next left-facing corner. Up the corner to the slab (V1), then traverse left to a left-rising ramp with a crack and follow it to the top. 150'

V1 5.9 PG: Climb straight up the friction slab (bolt) to the trees.

FA 1982, Mark Meschinelli, Dave Hough
FA (V1) 1988, Pierre Gagnon, Gelu Ionescu

Gary Allan on a free attempt of ***Keep Off Flake*** *(A3). Photo by Mark Meschinelli.*

V1
177
176
175
North End Rappel
174
173
172
169
161

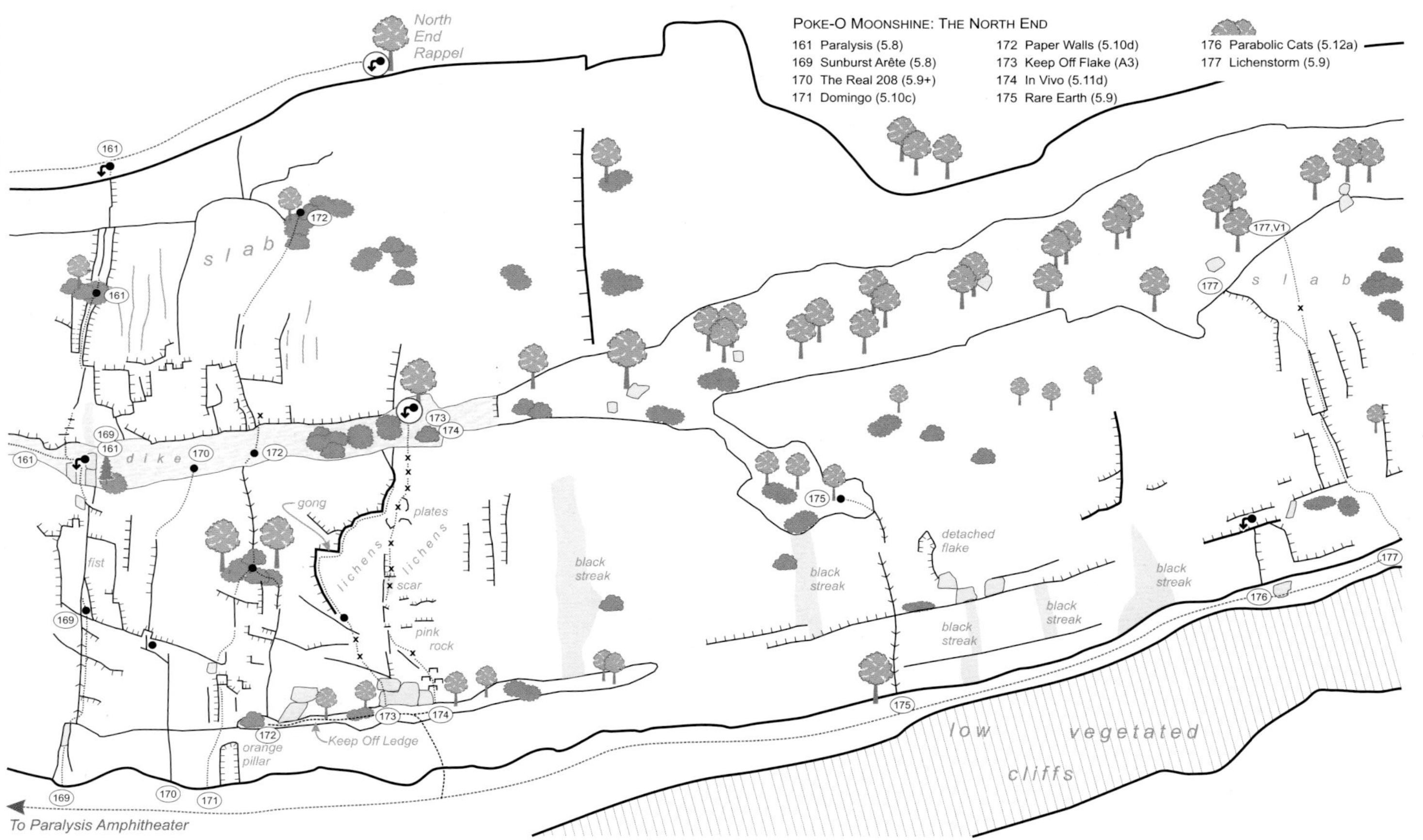
Poke-O Moonshine: The North End
161 Paralysis (5.8)
169 Sunburst Arête (5.8)
170 The Real 208 (5.9+)
171 Domingo (5.10c)
172 Paper Walls (5.10d)
173 Keep Off Flake (A3)
174 In Vivo (5.11d)
175 Rare Earth (5.9)
176 Parabolic Cats (5.12a)
177 Lichenstorm (5.9)
North End Rappel
slab
177.V1
dike
gong
plates
lichens
scar
pink rock
Keep Off Ledge
orange pillar
fist
black streak
detached flake
low vegetated cliffs
To Paralysis Amphitheater

Poke-O Moonshine

POKE-O SLAB

Aspect	South
Height	500'
Quality	★★★
Approach	10 min, easy
Summary	A south-facing slab with runout, multipitch face and friction routes. Home to one of the best moderate slab routes in the Adirondacks—**Catharsis**.

-5.6	5.7	5.8	5.9	5.10	5.11	5.12	5.13+	total
3	2	1	2	4	2			14

The Poke-O Moonshine Slab, also known as the South Face, is the first visible rock when you approach by car from the south. The face is characterized by off-vertical slab climbing on clean, textured rock and requires a combination of face-climbing and friction skills, as well as a cool head, as most of the routes have poor protection. Due to its orientation, the slab tends to bake in the summer and is best saved for an early morning or a cool fall day.

The slab's major physical feature is the giant curving overhang that arches horizontally across in the middle of the face, called the Visor (to avoid confusion with the generic term *arch* as well as the route **The Arch**). There are several places where you can break through the Visor to the upper section of the cliff, and most of the routes below the Visor funnel into one of these breaks. Due to the Visor's steeper angle, the climbing is more difficult below it than above.

Once you are above the Visor, there are only three routes to the top of the slab. You can rappel from a tree at the top of **Catharsis** or walk around the back side to the Ranger's Trail and return to the campground, about 0.5 mile from the approach trail. Plan accordingly when you climb at the Slab: either bring all your stuff up the cliff with you and climb to the top, or rappel with two ropes. Catharsis, **Last Chance**, and the more recent **A Fine Line** are the three routes that reach the top of the cliff.

Some other features of the Slab include the black water streak that runs from the ground up through the Visor to the trees above. This is the line of the route **Twilight**, and the easiest way through the Visor (**The Arch**) is just left of this streak. Left of the black water streak and midway up to the Visor is a large, wide ledge that is indistinguishable from below; this ledge has a fixed anchor and can be used for rappel from above. The routes **The Arch**, **New Star**, and **Inner Space** pass by this ledge. Finally, there are several tree ledges above the Visor, including Dead Oak Ledge (a landmark on **Catharsis**) and the Pine Tree Ledge, which has the fixed anchor and is the point where all the other routes converge.

HISTORY

Like Poke-O's Main Face, the Slab has a climbing history that dates back to the late 1950s. The first routes were uncovered by a multinational crew that lived in Quebec, including John Turner (United Kingdom), François Garneau (Quebec), Bernard Poisson (Quebec), Brian Rothery (Ireland), and Dick Wilmott (Canada). **Catharsis** was their major find and became a standard route for the time period; Poisson repeated this route in 2007, 50 years after the first ascent.

The only other group to develop routes on this cliff was the Ski to Die Club—Geoff Smith, Dave Hough, Patrick Munn, and Mark Meschinelli. Their efforts span more than 23 years, from 1974 (**Arch Traverse**) through 1997 (**Space Odyssey**). Some of their best efforts were **New Star** (the first route at Poke-O bolted on rappel, in 1976), **Space Walk** (1976), and **Twilight** (1988). Munn and Meschinelli climbed the cliff's most serious route, **Inner Space**, in 1990.

GEOLOGY

The Visor, the tall overlap in the center of the slab, is evidence of exfoliation. When the Adirondacks were rising from great depths below the earth's surface, pressure was released from the rock slab, and it separated into layers like the skin on an onion. Later, erosion removed earth materials and revealed this rock face. Portions of the layers have since broken off, leaving behind the overlap, through which several routes ascend.

DIRECTIONS (MAP PAGE 30)

Park alongside US 9 near the "SPEED LIMIT 55" sign, the first such sign south of the campground and visible to northbound travelers 619091,4916713. This is 0.5 mile south of the (now closed) Poke-O Moonshine Campground.

Alternatively, if you plan on climbing to the top of the cliff (e.g., **Catharsis** or **Last Chance**) and walking off, you can park at the campground (at the south end close to the start of the hiking trail), as this is where you descend. There is another parking area farther south on US 9 on the east side of the road that has great views of the Slab, but this adds unnecessarily to the approach walk.

The trail begins near a 6'-high rocky outcrop with a cairn on top on the west side of the road, across from the "SPEED LIMIT 55" sign 619204,4917037. Follow the trail through the woods to the base of the Slab (passing through several beds of poison ivy in the process) and meet the slab on its far right side. Walk along the base of the slab to an open area where you can see the lower section of the slab and the Visor; there is a large, flat boulder in the talus 50' back from the cliff. This open area is the start of **New Star** and its neighbors 618945,4916998.

DESCENT OPTIONS

The walk-off begins at the top of **Catharsis**. Head up and right to pick up cairns that contour northward, then downhill to reach the Ranger's Trail above the Viewpoint (the top of Hospital Rock and the #5 interpretive marker). Follow the hiking trail downhill to the campground. The descent from the top of **Catharsis** to the campground requires about 20 min.

To rappel, from the oak tree at the top of the climbing on **Catharsis**, walk right 15' to a large red pine and rappel straight down to the Pine Tree Ledge. From here, rappel down and slightly left to the ledge on **The Arch**, **Inner Space**, and **New Star**. (There are several bolted anchors below the visor, but this one has a spacious ledge for easy rope handling.) From here, another two-rope rappel reaches the ground at the open area (with the flat boulder 50' back from the cliff).

1 A Fine Line 5.6 R 580' ★★★

Compared to **Catharsis**, this route is nearly as good, but slightly more difficult and run-out.

Start: 40' left of **Catharsis** at a group of 3 oak trees, below a clean, featured, dark brown slab.

P1 5.6 R: (V1) Up the grey slab using friction and flakes for 20' until the angle eases, then continue on cleaner brown rock. Cross the right-rising crack at 60' (this is the last gear for 50') and, at a black streak, go up and very slightly left on immaculate, featured rock. Continue past horizontal cracks (good gear), then head left to a small oak clump to belay. (There's an oak above with a fixed anchor that offers an alternative belay position.) 160'

P2 5.5 R: Continue up the slab to a steeper section followed by an easier slab, aiming for a break in the overlap above. At the overlap, pass a large flake and move right up a short ramp–crack to a small left-facing corner (good gear). At the top of this corner traverse hard right across a ledge to a rounded nose which leads to the wide brushy ledge below a small overhang. Belay at a good crack. 190'

P3 5.3 G: (V2) Traverse right along the brushy ledge then up a right-facing corner to a stance at its top. 50'

P4 5.6 R: Diagonal right over the tiny overlap on easy black rock with no gear, aiming for the small slab above a short left-facing corner–groove. Climb the small slab then go back left slightly and around the left end of the final headwall on **Last Chance**. Climb up right to the slab and traverse right to the middle where unprotected friction (5.5) leads up a black streak. Belay at the crooked oak tree above. 180'

V1 5.6 PG: Start about 10' right and climb to the overlap, then move left to the regular route.

V2 5.8 G: Climb a crack straight over the bulge above the belay and onto a slab. Break through the short headwall above with good gear and belay at the overlap above or at the tree. Traverse right to rejoin the final pitch of the climb.

FA (P1, P2, to Dead Oak Ledge) Jul 20, 2004, R.L. Stolz, Jeffrey Ruiz

FA (P3, P3, from Dead Oak Ledge) 1987, R.L. Stolz, Stephanie Paradise

FA (V2) Aug 19, 2011, R.L. Stolz, Phil Doyle

2 Catharsis 5.5 PG (5.4 R) 490' ★★★★★

A wonderful slab climb with clean rock and good exposure; one of the best moderate slab routes in the park. There are some runouts, but these are generally in easy sections. The route was originally described as following the right-rising crack through the Slab. This crack is now quite overgrown; the description here reflects how the route is being climbed today.

Start: Starting at the open area near the low point of the Slab, directly beneath the center of the Visor, walk left on the climbers' path beneath a broken cliffband.

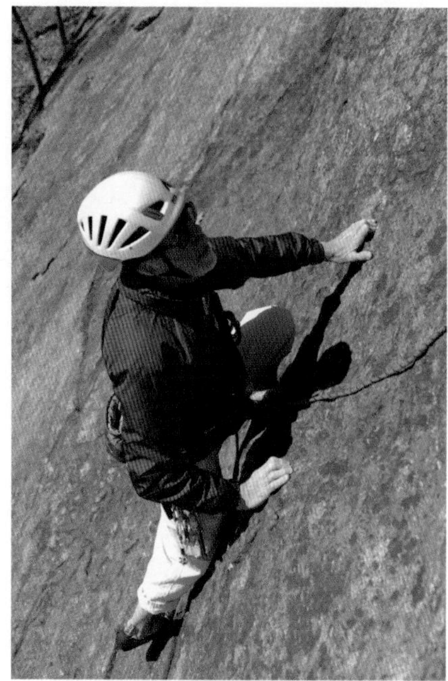

*Bernard Poisson on **Catharsis** (5.5), celebrating the 50th anniversary ascent.*

The path then scrambles up left of this broken area and cuts back right to gain a high, vegetated ledge at the base of the Slab, directly below an obvious right-leaning handcrack, the only crack in this section of cliff.

P1 5.4 R: Up the right-leaning handcrack, then straight up the orange, featured face to a ledge. This ledge is in the prominent, vegetated right-rising diagonal crack, at a point where it meets a vertical crack. There is an ancient, broken bolt about halfway up this pitch. 100'

P2 5.4 PG: Continue for 25' straight up the crack until it disappears, then diagonal right on low-angled rock (past an old bolt stud) to the base of a left-facing corner. Climb the corner and belay just above, at the base of another left-facing corner that arches left. 80'

P3 5.5 PG: Proceed straight up from the belay to a black, left-facing, slightly left-leaning corner at 80'. From the corner, traverse directly right another 40' to a vegetated ledge with a prominent oak tree. (This is known as Dead Oak Ledge; the dead oak has long since decayed and been replaced by its healthy descendant.) 120'

P4 5.5 PG: Move 40' right (4th class) to the base of a left-facing corner beneath the right edge of an overlap (optional belay). (From here, it is possible to 4th-class down right to a ledge with two pines and a fixed anchor—Pine Tree Ledge.) Step left, friction up to the overlap, and break through in the middle. Climb rightward up to the second overlap, then undercling around the left end of this and up to the series of yellow left-arching, left-facing overlaps. Friction up the face immediately left of these overlaps, then break right through the arch just before its end (immediately left of

UPPER TIERS: HEADWALL
1
3
2
13
Pine Tree
Ledge
Dead Oak
Ledge
Visor
4
10
13
9
7
1
2
3
12
9
10
7

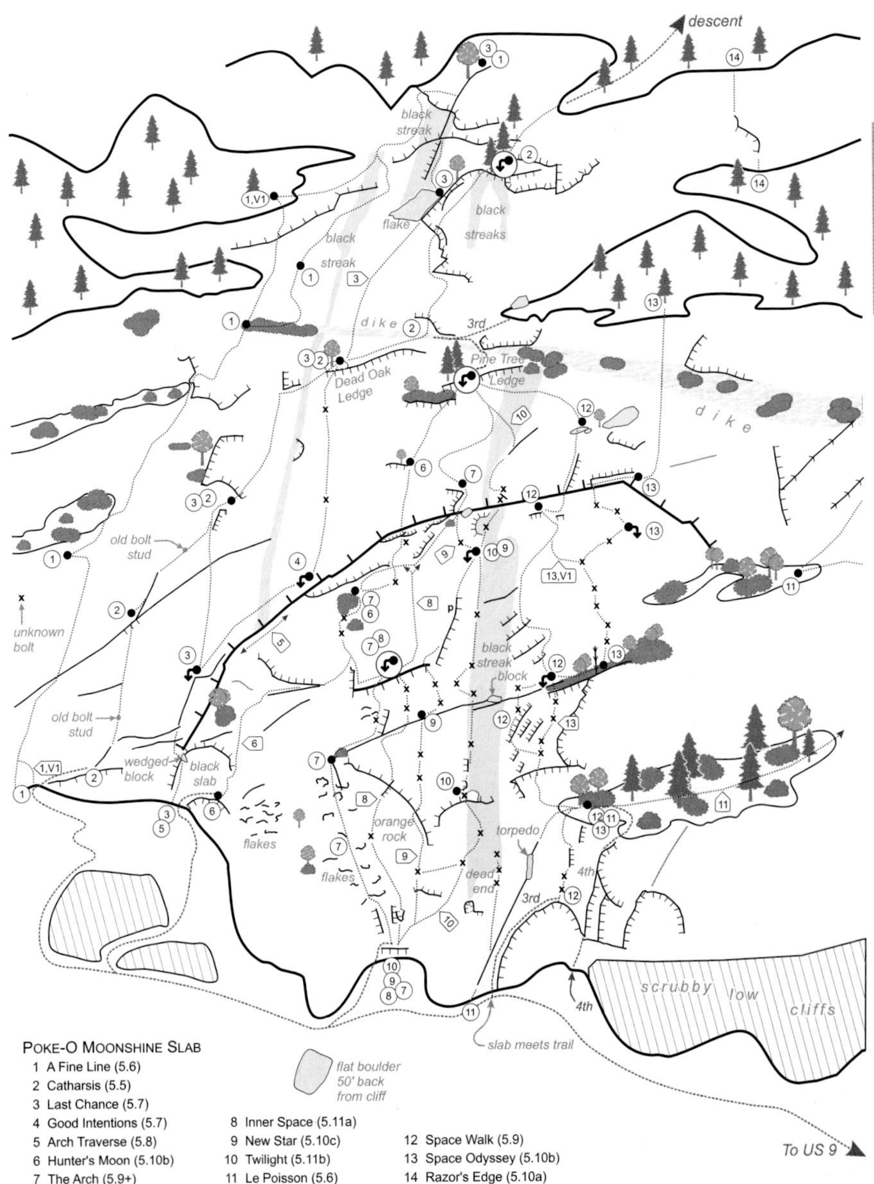

the tan rock) and climb straight up the face via friction and flakes (secure but unprotected) to the tree ledge on the right. 190'

Gear: Singles through 2", including small TCUs.

History: The bolts found on P1 and P2 are a mystery. Turner considered them immoral and laboriously removed the few he came across.

FA 1957, John Turner, François Garneau, Bernard Poisson

3 Last Chance 5.7 R 570' ★★

Start: Below the right-facing corner formed by the far left side of the Visor, on a black slab below a birch tree.

P1 5.7 G: Climb the corner and black slab past a birch to a wedged guillotine flake. Traverse left around the edge of the Visor to gain a wide crack and follow it to a fixed anchor where the wide crack joins a horizontal crack. 90'

P2 5.6 R: Straight up the face with no protection to meet the right-rising diagonal crack. Continue straight up toward the base of a left-facing corner, where the route joins **Catharsis** P2. Climb the corner to belay just above, at the base of another left-facing corner that arches left. 120'

P3 5.5 PG: Same as for **Catharsis** P3, ending at Dead Oak Ledge. 120'

P4 5.7 R: Work straight up from the ledge to a flake with a small right-facing corner. Friction up and right toward the top of the left-arching overlaps of **Catharsis**. Pass just left of the overlaps and belay in a right-slanting crack just above formed by the right side of a huge, greenish slab that rests on top of the black slab. 150'

P5 5.6 PG: From the top left of the greenish slab, climb a shallow right-facing overlap to the headwall. Break through the headwall via a crack and follow it to a large oak tree on the slab above. 90'

FA 1970, Rocky Keeler, Rick Weinert

4 Good Intentions 5.7 R (5.4 X) 220' ★

Climbs the face above the left side of the Visor. It was envisioned to be climbed from the bush belay below the Visor (accessed by climbing P1 of **Harvest Moon** or P1–P3 of **The Arch**), but this has proved difficult. The route described here instead traverses in from **Last Chance**. The route ends at Dead Oak Ledge; you can finish on **Catharsis** or traverse (3rd class) down and right to the Pine Tree Ledge and rappel (two ropes).

Start: At the fixed anchor at the top of P1 of **Last Chance**.

P1 Next to Last Chance 5.4 X: Traverse up and right above the lip of the Visor to a fixed anchor. The climbing is more difficult closer to the Visor. 90'

P2 5.7 R: Climb straight up to a bolt, move left to a crack, back right to a second bolt, then up to Dead Oak Ledge. 130'

FA 2006, Dave Sciole

5 Arch Traverse 5.8 PG 160'

Really a variation to **The Arch**, this route stays under the Visor and joins **The Arch** at the two-bush belay.

Start: Same as **Last Chance**.

P1 5.8 PG: Climb the right-facing corner of the Visor and continue under the Visor to the bush belay of **Hunter's Moon** and **The Arch**. 160'

FA Sep, 1974, Geoff Smith, Dave Hough

6 Hunter's Moon 5.10b G (5.7 X) 300' ★★

An interesting (i.e., devious and steep) and well-protected crux combined with some long runouts at a more moderate grade. Named for the big fall moon that provides enough illumination to allow hunters to stalk prey (and presumably climbers to climb serious runouts on a slab).

Start: Begin at the open area near the low point of the Slab, directly beneath the center of the Visor, and walk left on the climbers' path beneath a broken cliffband. The path then scrambles up right of this broken area 150' to a point that is 25' right of the Visor and 20' below an overlap that has a little left-facing corner on its right end.

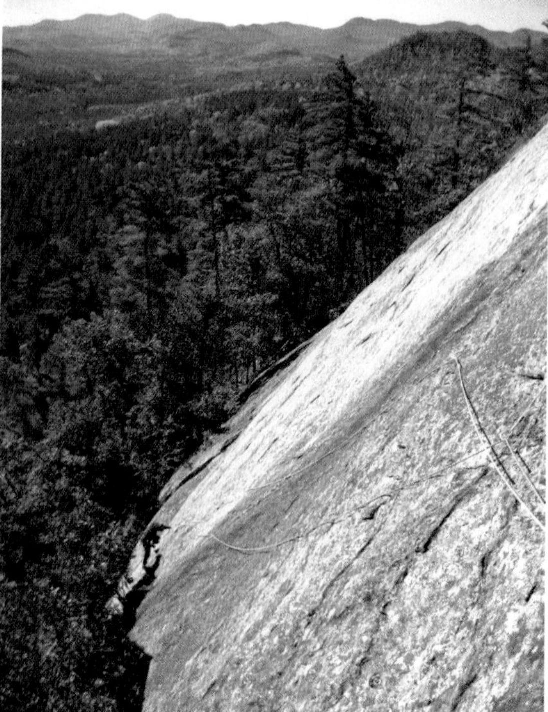

P1 5.8 R: This pitch traverses rightward to join **The Arch** at the stacked bushes. Above the ledge, climb up the left-facing corner, then break out right onto the black slab. Up this, move right to a horizontal ledge, and follow it right to its end. Continue right across the face to a crack just left of a right-facing corner (the left edge of the ledge for **The Arch**). Up the crack to its top, then gain the lower bush from the left (past two ancient bolts), traverse right, and gain the top of the upper bush from the right. 150'

P2 5.10b G (5.7 X): Traverse right to a bolt, then straight up the face to a second bolt below the double-tiered ceiling. Break through the ceiling (crux; small TCUs) to the unprotected face above (5.7 X) and on to a ledge with a tree (optional belay). Continue straight up to Pine Tree Ledge (a ledge with two pine trees and a fixed anchor, the same as for **Twilight** and **The Arch**). 150'

Descent: Rappel with two ropes.

FA Oct, 1987, Patrick Munn, Dave Hough, Mark Meschinelli

*Leslie Ackerman follows P1 (5.4) of **Good Intentions** (5.7).*

7 The Arch 5.9+ PG (5.8 R) 410' ★★★

The first route to break through the Visor and, as such, find the easiest way through—one that is shared by routes that came later. P1 was originally reported as "climb to the bulge," which you'll appreciate as you stand clueless below the slab. The route ends at Pine Tree Ledge; you can rappel from here with two ropes or head up and left to continue on **Catharsis** or **Last Chance**. The route contains some unprotected traversing and thus isn't recommended for a weak follower.

Start: From the open area near the low point of the slab, scramble up rightward to a fern ledge, the left side of which is below a small, orange left-facing corner. 6' left of this corner is an opposing corner; **The Arch** begins on flakes between these opposing corners.

P1 5.8 R: Climb the opposing corners, then step left at their top on fragile flakes. Traverse left 15' to a right-protruding flake; step up (crux) and continue up and left following positive flake-holds to a crack that leads to a horizontal left of a bush and a ledge. Belay. 110'

P2 5.9+ PG (5.8 R): Foot-traverse right 15' until you are below a bolt on the headwall, left of a shallow right-facing corner. Up the headwall (crux; bolt), then finish with a runout to a large ledge with a fixed anchor (shared with **Inner Space**). 40'

P3 5.7+ G (5.6 R): (V1) This pitch weaves between the two large bushes (actually, these are ledges with hanging shrubs), one above the other. From the left end of the belay ledge, climb the right-facing corner to its top. Gain the lower bush from the left (past two ancient bolts), traverse right, and gain the top of the upper bush from the right. 70'

P4 5.8 PG (5.6 R): Up and right to an overlap. Traverse right along this overlap to easier terrain (no gear) for 40' to a right-facing arch with a bush at the base. Climb up this through the overhang (5.5 fun), avoiding the death block on the right, to a small ledge and an adequate belay. 90'

P5 5.7+ G (5.4 R): Traverse left 10', then up to a flake (gear). Up the face (crux), then traverse right to a right-leaning crack (gear) and back left to Pine Tree Ledge (a tree ledge with two pine trees and a fixed anchor, the same as for **Twilight** and **Hunter's Moon**). 100'

V1 5.9 R: A good variation (and better climbing than the original line) moves right from the belay to climb the left-facing corner of **New Star** P2.

History: During the first ascent, Rothery climbed P1, and Wilmott followed by climbing the orange arching overlap, the same one crossed by **Inner Space** and **New Star**. It's difficult to imagine these slab routes being climbed in the 1950s in PAs (an early climbing shoe) and with virtually no protection. Rothery took a fall on the overhang but came through unscathed. According to Rothery, "[Turner] had considered **The Arch** still beyond us, so we were very pleased to go back to camp and tell him we'd done it."

FA 1958, Dick Wilmott, Brian Rothery

8 Inner Space 5.11a G (5.10a X) 340' ★★★★

Amazing rock—clean, featured, and sparsely protected.

Start: From the center of the fern ledge as described for **The Arch**, below a vertical crack on the right side of several downward-pointing flakes 10' above the ledge.

P1 (10b R) 5.11a G: Climb the vertical crack right of the flakes to cleaner rock and trend slightly left (5.9 R) to a bolt in orange rock. Continue up and slightly right to the orange arching overlap (last pro), over this, and make a substantial runout to the 2" horizontal crack below a headwall (optional belay). Hand-traverse right 20' until you are below a bolt on the headwall. Climb

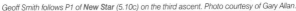

Geoff Smith follows P1 of **New Star** *(5.10c) on the third ascent. Photo courtesy of Gary Allan.*

the headwall, angling left (crux), and make a runout to a spacious ledge with a fixed anchor (same as **The Arch**). 140'

P2 5.10a X: 60' straight above the belay is a bolt; this is for **Hunter's Moon**. This pitch climbs (or rather solos) the face right of this bolt. Begin in the weakness above the fixed anchor. Climb pretty white rock past a triangular tan scar to easier face climbing. Either join **Hunter's Moon** at the bolt or head right and finish on **The Arch**. 200'

FA 1990, Patrick Munn, Mark Meschinelli

9 New Star 5.10c PG (5.9 R) 340' ★★★

The first two 5.10 pitches climbed at Poke-O and an early example of bolting on rappel. The route's name refers to the fact that it was the newest extreme route at the time—i.e., the "new star."

Start: At the right end of the fern ledge as described for **The Arch**, below a visible bolt 25' up, which is 6' above a small roof.

P1 5.10b PG (5.9 R): Climb up past several overlaps to a bolt, then up the face to the base of the left-facing, left-arching orange overlap. Follow the overlap (good gear), then break right onto a fragile flake and straight up the face (5.9 R) to a belay beneath a narrow ledge with a good crack (2"). 100'

P2 5.10c PG (5.9 R): Foot-traverse right 20' until you are below a bolt on the headwall. With good gear at your feet, make a hard move to the bolt, then angle up and left past quartz crystals (crux) to the large ledge (as for **The Arch** and **Inner Space**). From the right side of the ledge, climb a left-facing, right-leaning corner; at its top, go straight up the face (5.9 R) to the fixed anchor (shared with **Twilight**). 100'

P3 5.9 R: Traverse left to a small ledge with a bolt, then straight up the face to join **The Arch**. 140'

FA Sep, 1976, Geoff Smith, Dave Hough

10 Twilight 5.11b PG (5.9 X) 340' ★★★★

Very steep friction and face climbing characterizes this route, which follows the black streak below the center of the Visor, visible from the highway. In some positions on the route, it seems impossible to stand without sliding downward; imagine drilling these bolts on lead.

Start: Same as **New Star**.

P1 5.10a G (5.9 X): (V1) From the ledge, spy the hard-to-see bolt high and right. Aim for this bolt by underclinging out right on crumbly overlaps (before the first bolt of **New Star**) to a bolt just left of a prominent black streak (the streak runs from the top of the slab to the ground). Climb up and right across the black streak (bolt), then angle back left and follow a left-leaning dike to a bush with an old bolt to the left. Belay from the bolt with gear backup. 80'

P2 5.11b PG (5.9 R): A sustained pitch; the first-ascent notes say "a true friction pitch, 5.10+ or 5.11, depending on the humidity." Climb the discontinuous crack above the belay to a small right-facing corner. A difficult move at the first bolt leads to easier climbing and a prominent horizontal left of an unstable-looking block. Make another difficult move to the second bolt, then step left to a pocketed flake (very close to **New Star** at this point), then back right, past an intermediate anchor (crux). Runout but easier climbing leads to the last bolt, then to the fixed anchor above (shared with **New Star**). 120'

P3 5.10d PG (5.8 R): Climb up an unprotected face (5.8 R) to a bolt, then a hard move leads to a right-facing corner that arches right. Up this to the Visor (gear), then step right to below the first bolt on the Visor headwall. Make a big move straight up between good holds (crux), then up to the easier slab above and trend left to Pine Tree Ledge (a ledge with two pine trees and a fixed anchor shared with **Twilight**, **Hunter's Moon**, and **The Arch**). 140'

V1 5.10a G (5.8 R): You can reduce the seriousness of P1 by climbing to the first bolt of **New Star**, then traversing directly right 25' to the first bolt on **Twilight**.

FA Oct, 1988, Patrick Munn, Mark Meschinelli, Dick Bushey

11 Le Poisson 5.6 G (5.4 R) 140'

This historic route climbs an easy crack to reach the tree ledge as for **Space Walk**. It then reportedly continues another 260' (5.6 A1) on brushy ledges, finds its way through the treed ledge systems right of the Visor to the right-leaning dihedrals that are fairly obvious from the road, then climbs the lower of these two with some aid at the end. P1 is recommended and described here.

Start: 5' left of the 3rd-class ramp approach to **Space Walk** at the base of a right-leaning crack.

P1 5.6 PG (5.4 R): Climb the right-leaning crack with good protection to a 6'-high, torpedo-shaped flake balanced on end. Pass this on its right side and, from its top (last good protection), make hard friction moves (crux) to unprotected climbing (5.4 R) to the left end of the tree ledge as for **Space Walk**. 140'

FA 1957, Bernard Poisson, François Garneau

12 Space Walk 5.9 PG (5.7 X) 440' ★★★

Excellent climbing on clean rock with adequate protection makes this a good introduction to this slab. From the top (the ledge with two pine trees and a fixed anchor—Pine Tree Ledge), you can finish on **Catharsis** or rappel (one rappel 190' to the anchor on **Inner Space**, next rappel to the ground).

Start: Leave the approach trail at the first point where the trail comes within 3' of the base of the slab, just left of a pile of blocks and vegetation. Climb 3rd-class rightward up to a ledge at the top of the pile of blocks and vegetation.

● **P1 5.9 PG:** From the right side of the vegetated ledge, climb straight up the face past two bolts to a 6'-high left-facing flake. From the top of the flake, unprotected climbing (either left on edges or right to another flake) leads to the left end of a tree ledge. 60'

● **P2 5.9 PG:** From the left end of the tree ledge, climb up a slab to a ledge with a horizontal crack in the back. Make a hard move above the ledge (crux) to a bolt (shared with **Space Odyssey**), then traverse straight left 15' (necessary TCU placement here), up to another bolt and easier climbing to a ledge. There is an old bolt above the ledge (backed up with TCUs) that provides a directional; move right 25' to a fixed anchor. The pitch has G protection except for the move to the first bolt, where you would hit a ledge. 80'

P3 5.7 X: Climb up to a series of right-facing, right-leaning corners (which look like slashes from a distance) and follow the largest corner out right to its end (last gear). Move 15' left over the top of the other corners, then straight up to a belay under the Visor. The gear for the anchor is in the underside of the Visor. 120'

P4 5.7 R: Move right on ledges under the Visor to a point below a left-facing corner above the Visor. Unprotected moves up the slab lead to the Visor (good gear here). Pull through the Visor and into the left-facing corner. The corner narrows, then disappears, requiring a few friction moves to reach a sloped ledge with boulders and a tree. 80'

P5 5.4 R: Head left across easy slabs to reach Pine Tree Ledge. 100'

FA Sep, 1976, Dave Hough, Geoff Smith, Patrick Munn

13 Space Odyssey 5.10b G (5.9 R) 340' ★★★★

Perhaps the best protected of the routes below the Visor; P1 and P2 are recommended. Like its neighbors, this route offers a style of climbing that is blurred between face and friction.

Start: Begin on the tree ledge above P1 of **Space Walk**. This tree ledge can be reached by climbing P1 of **Space Walk**, P1 of **Le Poisson**, or by a 4th-class gully in a left-facing corner just right of P1 of **Le Poisson**.

P1: 5.10a G (sport): From the left end of the tree ledge, climb up a slab to a ledge with a horizontal crack in the back. Make a hard move above the ledge (5.9 PG) to a bolt, then head up and right to an overlap. Undercling right, then straight up the face on flakes, edges, and crystal knobs (crux) to a ledge with a fixed anchor (shared with **Space Walk**). 60'

● **P2 5.10b G:** Move the belay 25' right to a tree below a line of bolts that begins to the right of an open book. Starting on the face right of the open book, step up to a small left-facing flake and the first bolt. Climb the face leftward and follow the white streak (crux after the third bolt) to a mantel move in black rock (V1), then traverse right, across the white streak to a fixed anchor above a sloping ledge. 90'

P3 5.10a G (5.9 R): Work up the face above the anchor to a bolt, then traverse left to a second bolt. Unprotected moves up a dirty face lead to the underside of the Visor beneath a right-facing corner. Break through the Visor (good gear) and up the right-facing corner to the next ceiling, then undercling right to the right end of the ceiling and belay. 90'

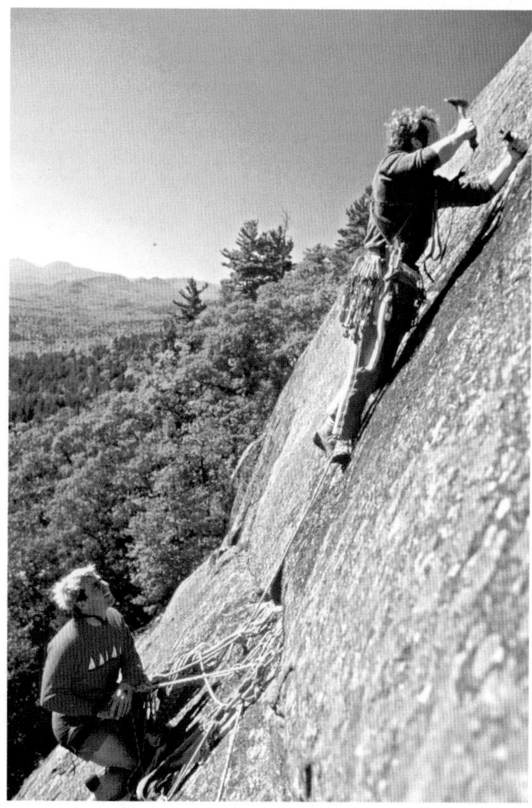

*Patrick Munn hand-drilling P2 on the first ascent of **Twilight** (5.11b), belayed by Dick Bushey. Photo by Mark Meschinelli.*

P4 5.7 PG: Traverse right from the belay for several feet to a faint black streak, then climb straight up to the vegetated ledge. 100'

V1 5.7 PG: From the mantel move, head left to join **Space Walk**.

FA (P1–P2) 1997, Dave Hough, Ann Hough
FA (P3–P4) 1997, Dave Hough, Patrick Munn

14 Razor's Edge 5.10a G 75'

Start: This route is located on a small 70' cliffband above a tree-covered terrace that sits above the right end of the Visor. You can access this terrace from Dead Oak Ledge by traversing directly right (3rd class) to the tree grove or from Pine Tree Ledge at the top of the other routes. The route climbs the right-curving crack in the center of the wall below a large, flat, overhanging wall.

P1 5.10a G: Climb the crack, vertical at first, through a bulge. Above, the crack curves up and right with unique climbing, as you can put your forearms down into the crack. The protection is also placed upside down (use long runners). 75'

Gear: Up to 4".

FA Nov 12, 1988, Dennis Luther, Tom Yandon

Poke-O Moonshine

SOUTHWEST FACE

The broken walls and slabs left of the Poke-O Slab have been explored over the years, and some routes have been climbed. Expect slabby, brushy rock with bulges; some corners and a few roofs; and a real wilderness feeling. The terrain is far from convenient, and getting oriented is difficult at best.

Poke-O Moonshine

UPPER TIERS

"Above every tier is yet another tier."

Location	High on the south and east slopes of Poke-O Moonshine Mountain, accessed from the Ranger's Trail and from the descent gully next to the Waterfall.
Summary	A group of several horizontal cliffbands that divide the south and east slopes of Poke-O Moonshine Mountain with mostly one-pitch cragging, but there are some two-pitch routes; the better-quality climbs tend to be of a high standard of difficulty.

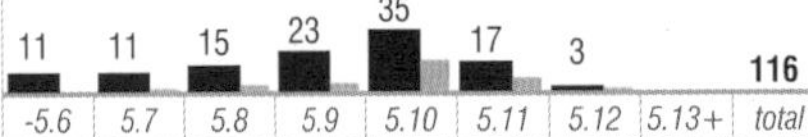

Poke-O Moonshine Mountain has many cliffs scattered on its forested south and east slopes known as the Upper Tiers in previous guidebooks. From the Northway (I-87), a quick glance at the upper mountain gives the impression that the area could hold hundreds of routes. The reality is that many cliffs lack clean, climbable rock, and others are still largely unexplored. There are, however, some gems concentrated in two areas of the mountain—the bands of rock above the Main Cliff (the Second Tier and the Third Tier) and cliffs below the summit (the Summit Cliff, Headwall, Sun Wall, and Lunar Wall).

Climbers have largely ignored the routes on these cliffs, which are perhaps overshadowed by the huge number of routes on the Main Face close to the road. Thus, despite good rock quality, many routes tend to be dirty and overgrown. Increased climber traffic will likely improve the situation, which may indeed occur given better cliff documentation and the frequent closures of the Main Face due to the nesting of peregrine falcons.

Currently, the atmosphere at the Upper Tiers is remote and adventurous. A wire brush should be standard equipment on your rack, and you should be prepared to replace ancient anchor webbing. The cliffs require at most 40 min of hiking, most of which is on a maintained hiking trail, and the final approach involves only a few minutes of off-trail hiking through open forest. They're just far enough away from the Northway to minimize the road noise.

Some of the noteworthy lines include the 100'-high knife edge of **Plate Tectonics** and the sustained face of **Born Ready**. Crack climbers should take notice of the many cracks, including **Fairview**, **Octoberfist**, **Fear of Gravity**, **Dutch Masters Direct**, **Jackal**, and **Bitter End**. More typical of Poke-O are the mixed face and crack routes, including **Enigma**, **Dill Pickle**, **Code Breaker**, **Crossfire**, **Perfect Storm**, and **Connoisseur**.

HISTORY

More than for other areas, the reports of climbing here are convoluted and conflicting. The lack of reporting

and route recording has resulted in routes with conflicting names and first-ascent information. For the most part, this has been sorted out, with one result being multiple names associated with various routes.

The earliest climbers to visit were the Ski to Die Club—namely, Geoff Smith, Dave Hough, and Gary Allan—whose members climbed various routes on the Second Tier above the Main Face around 1974. Hough recalls this cliff's being as much a hangout as a place to climb. Nobody knows for sure who led what, but they uncovered some gems, such as **Heart of Gold**, **Black Market**, and **After the Gold Rush**.

Two years later, Allan and Smith, now joined by Patrick Munn and a young Mark Meschinelli, explored the Headwall. Some of these routes are popular today, including **Fairview**, **Mechanical Hydraulic Control**, and the upper section of **Fear of Gravity**. After 1978, nothing happened for about eight years.

From 1984 to 1990, the Upper Tiers became a favorite spot for Ken Nichols, who, with various partners, quietly exhausted most of the natural lines. Only recently has the extent of his exploration here become more widely known, and it is impressive, climbing trad 5.12 in the 1980s. Nichols has a rocky relationship with the Adirondack community, but you can't fail to be impressed by the awesome **Plate Tectonics**, the overhanging crack of **Bitter End**, or the sheer number of routes he developed.

In the 1990s, Tim Beaman, a Vermont local who enjoys unearthing hard lines, made notable contributions. **Devotee**, **The Gauntlet**, **Connoisseur**, **Enigma**, and **Born Ready**, all in the solid 5.11 range, are testimony to his ability and perseverance. Dennis Luther and Mark Meschinelli continued their explorations as well, uncovering **Trilogy**, **Crossfire** (on the Lunar Wall), and **The Bandit**.

In 2006, after a 16 year absence, Ken Nichols returned to fill in some blanks at the Summit Cliff. Two years later he returned with Mark Bealor to explore the Third and Fourth Tiers high above the Main Face. They uncovered many gems including **Autumn Gold**, **Trick Move**, and **Perfect Pitch**.

DIRECTIONS **(MAP PAGE 30)**

There are several approaches to the cliffs of the Upper Tiers, all of which begin at the (now closed) Poke-O Moonshine Campground.

You can best access the Headwall, Summit Cliff, Sun Wall, and Lunar Wall from the Ranger's Trail that ascends Poke-O Moonshine Mountain, which begins at the south end of the [now closed] campground at the end of the fence 619208,4917560. A landmark on this trail is the Viewpoint, an open area on top of Hospital Rock with pretty views of the valley, also marked by the #5 interpretive marker. The Viewpoint is a 10-min hike from the road. Approaches to the various cliffs are described relative to this hiking trail and Viewpoint.

The First, Second, and Third tiers are located above the Main Cliff. To approach these, from the north end of the [now closed] campground, find the start of the climbers' path to the Main Cliff. This path goes uphill and meets the cliff at the Discord Area. Walk left along the cliff to the descent gully, a deep cleft that breaks the cliff just right of the Waterfall, and ascend this (3rd class) to its top. Approaches to the various cliffs are described relative to top of this gully.

Poke-O Moonshine • Upper Tiers

HOSPITAL ROCK

Aspect	East
Height	50'
Quality	
Approach	10 min, easy
Summary	Small cliff with two historic routes.

-5.6	5.7	5.8	5.9	5.10	5.11	5.12	5.13+	total
			1	1				2

This is the first cliff encountered along Ranger's Trail, and about 10 min from the road 618956,4917403. The #4 interpretive marker is positioned at its base. It is a relatively small cliff and presently has only two routes.

1 First Aid 5.9 R 50' ★

This route ends at the Viewpoint on the hiking trail.

Start: Below an overhanging handcrack that begins just over the lip of a ceiling on the left side of the crag, behind a boulder. This is the leftmost of two such cracks, and there is a boulder below the ceiling that points to the start of the handcrack.

P1 5.9 R: Climb the handcrack to a ledge (5.9 G; possible to walk off left back to the trail). Continue up the thin crack until it ends, diagonal up left, then move back right on a friction slab to the top at a pine tree. 50'

FA 1977, Mark Meschinelli, Dick Bushey

2 Incision 5.10b G 30' ★

Start: Below a large right-facing corner capped by a roof on the right side of the crag.

P1 5.10b G: Up the corner to the roof, then jam strenuously out left around the lip to the walk-off ledge. 30'

FA 1977, Gary Allan, Patrick Munn, Dave Hough

Poke-O Moonshine • Upper Tiers

SUMMIT CLIFF

Aspect	South
Height	120'
Quality	★★
Approach	35 min, moderate
Summary	

-5.6	5.7	5.8	5.9	5.10	5.11	5.12	5.13+	total
7	6	4	5	4	3	1		31

DIRECTIONS **(MAP PAGE 30)**

From the Viewpoint (at the #5 interpretive marker), continue on the Ranger's Trail to a four-way intersection at an old chimney, the site of what used to be the fire observer's cabin 618306,4917424. There is also a #8 interpretive marker here. From this intersection, take a sharp right onto the faint path and follow it uphill for 4 min, past the remains of a spring box, to a point where you can see the cliff in the woods to the right, just before a steep-walled constriction. From this point, walk left to a smaller crag with **Flashback Crack** 618304,4917529 or right to the Summit Cliff proper 618399,4917511. The approach takes about 35 min from the trailhead.

3 Lookout Crack 5.6 PG 60'

Start: 15' left of **Flashback Crack** at the base of a wide crack

P1 5.6 PG: Climb the crack past a horizontal on the left to a large ledge. Finish up a left-facing corner to the pretty summit area. 60'

FA Oct 6, 2006, Ken Nichols, Jim Lawyer

4 Flashback Crack 5.9+ G 60' ★

Nice climbing but needs cleaning.

Start: From the approach trail, just before the narrowing constriction, walk left 80' to the cliff. The route begins 6' left of a blunt arête at the lowest point on the cliff, 15' right of the wide crack (**Lookout Crack**).

P1 5.9+ G: Climb the left-leaning fingercrack up to a wide ledge. Up a thin crack in a lower-angled headwall (crux, height-dependent) to a pretty summit area. 60'

FA 1978, Mark Meschinelli, Patrick Munn, Dave Hough

5 Matt Finish 5.8 PG 75'

Start: At a prominent left-facing corner that angles up 45' to the right, 55' uphill to the left of **Morse Code**.

P1 5.8 PG: Climb partway up the corner to the obvious crack on the left wall, then follow the crack up left to a low-angle face above. Finish straight up the poorly protected face. 75'

FA Oct, 1989, Matt Rugens, Ken Nichols

6 Friction Finish 5.5 PG 75'

Start: Same as **Matt Finish**.

P1 5.5 PG: Follow the left-facing corner up right until it ends, climb over a short wall at a black water streak, then up a poorly protected low-angle face to the top. 75'

FA Oct, 1989, Matt Rugens, Ken Nichols

7 Runway 5.5 PG 75'

Start: Below a short, rounded ramp, 15' right of the **Matt Finish** corner.

P1 5.5 PG: Layback up onto the ramp and continue up a steplike left-facing corner to a steep friction bulge. Step up and left, then work up right above the bulge to a good bucket. Finish straight up the poorly protected low-angle face. 75'

FA Oct, 1989, Matt Rugens, Ken Nichols

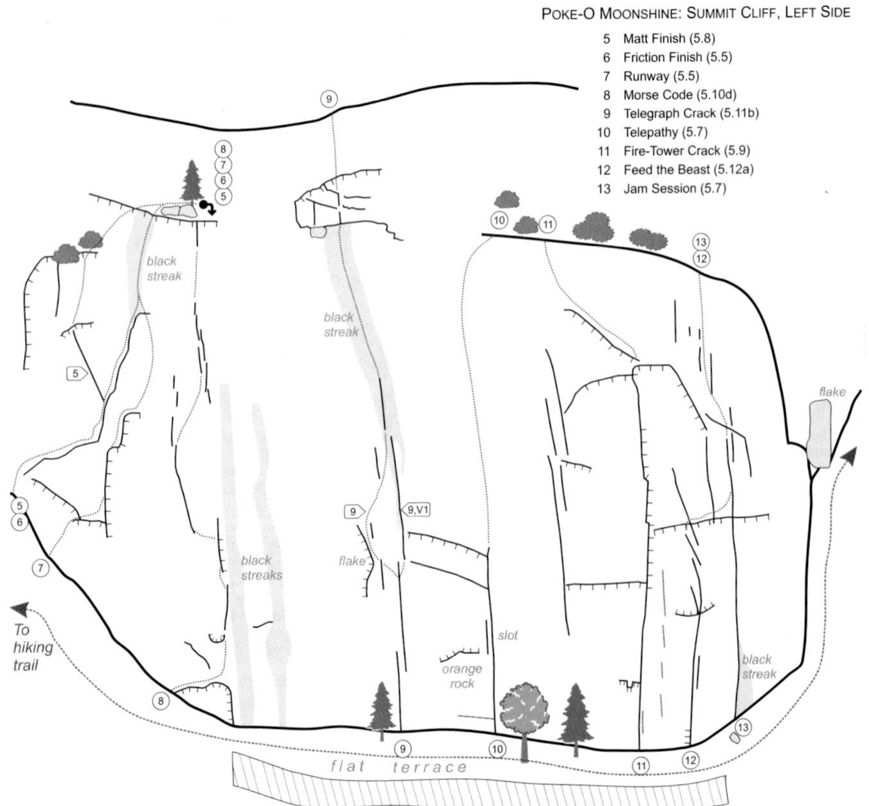

8 Morse Code 5.10d G 80' ★

Start: At the end of the flat terrace below the **Telegraph Crack** wall, 30' left of **Telegraph Crack**.

P1 5.10d G: Scramble up onto a ledge that is 7' above the ground and 7' below a small, rounded overlap. Layback up the crack above the right side of the overlap until it ends, then reach up and left and gain a stance in a shallow left-facing corner. Traverse left to a prominent jamcrack and follow this and a small right-facing corner to a horizontal flake on the face to the right. Step right and follow easy cracks up the low-angle face to a pine tree at the top. 80'

FA Oct, 1989, Ken Nichols, Matt Rugens

9 Telegraph Crack 5.11b G 100' ★★

Start: In the center of a 60'-long flat, open terrace that sits 15' above the forest floor, at a straight-in handcrack, 30' right of **Morse Code**.

P1 5.11b G: Climb the flared hand- and fingercrack to where it offsets to the right (V1); make a difficult traverse left to a flake that forms a small right-facing corner. Layback strenuously up the corner to the low-angle face above. Finish up a shallow crack in a black water streak and pull over a short headwall. 100'

V1 5.11 G: Move right at the offset and continue up the crack to the top.

FA Oct 7, 1984, Ken Nichols, Mike Heintz
FA (V1) 1988, Bill Pierce

10 Telepathy 5.7 G 100' ★★

Start: At a prominent handcrack that widens into a slot, 15' right of **Telegraph Crack**, just right of center on the open terrace.

P1 5.7 G: Climb the crack past the slot and finish up the hidden low-angle face above. 100'

11 Fire-Tower Crack 5.9 G 100' ★

Start: At a black strip that has shallow parallel cracks in it, 12' left of **Feed the Beast** and 30' right of **Telepathy**.

P1 5.9 G: Follow the cracks past a short left-facing corner and up the hidden low-angle face above to the top. 100'

FA Oct, 1989, Ken Nichols

12 Feed the Beast 5.12a G 100' ★

Nichols considered this route a real beast, as he fed it protection on the first ascent.

Start: At a short 4'-high right-facing corner with a crack that rises through a bulging overlap 20' up. This is 6' left of the **Jam Session** handcrack and 12' right of **Firetower Crack**.

P1 5.12a G: Follow the crack to a ledge, step right, and finish up the low-angle cracks of **Jam Session**. 100'

FA Oct, 1989, Ken Nichols

13 Jam Session 5.7 G 100' ★

Start: At the prominent handcrack in a black streak near the right end of the **Telegraph Crack** wall, 6' right of **Feed the Beast** and 6' left of a large corner.

P1 5.7 G: Climb the crack to a ledge and finish up a series of low-angle cracks that lead to the top. 100'

FA Oct, 1989, Ken Nichols, Gary Lundin

14 Deep Cover 5.7 PG 120' ★

Start: At a deep, V-shaped, right-leaning chimneylike corner with two ledges (one 10' up and the other 20' up), uphill and around the corner from the **Telegraph Crack** wall, approximately midway between **Jam Session** and **Crack of Despair**.

P1 5.7 PG: Follow the corner to a bushy ledge. Then continue up a series of cracks and small corners past several ledges to a short crack at the top, staying a few feet left of the arête. 120'

FA Oct, 1989, Matt Rugens, Ken Nichols

15 Crack of Despair 5.11 A1 170' ★★

An amazing-looking wall on P2; this would be a real prize to free. A key piece of protection on P1 was a 7" cam, placed by jumping up and popping it into position.

Start: Beneath a square roof, 10' down left from the **French Curve** corner.

P1 5.9 G: Reach up to the roof, undercling right, and continue up a jamcrack to the ledge. 40'

P2 5.11 A1 G: Follow the diagonal crack up the overhanging left wall of the **French Curve** corner to a horizontal fingerhold, aid up the crack about 10' to the arête, and finish up easy steps on the left side. 130'

FA (P1) Jul, 1989, Ken Nichols, Jack Wenzel
FA (P2) Jul, 1989, Ken Nichols

16 French Curve 5.7 G 130' ★★

An impressive feature that is difficult to imagine being 5.7. Named after a template used by draftsmen and architects, but inspired by the curving nature of the route.

Start: At the base of the huge right-facing corner with a right-arching chimney that goes through a pod, directly below the fire tower. **P1 5.7 G:** Follow the corner to the point where the low-angle right wall steepens. Traverse out right a few feet to a small flake and mantel up onto a stance. Then move back left into the corner and continue to the top. 130'

FA Oct, 1988, Ken Nichols, Jack Rankin

17 American-Russian-Chinese Route 5.9 R 140' ★★★★

According to Nichols, this is "probably the finest route on the Summit Cliff."

Start: At a large pointed block that leans against the face, 25' right of the huge **French Curve** corner.

P1 5.9 R: Step off the block and climb a short left-facing corner. Continue up left on narrow ledges to the end of an overlap. Follow a diagonal crack above the overlap up left to a long, narrow ledge and walk right to the obvious vertical crack. Work up the crack, hand-traverse 4' right along a horizontal crack, and pull up into a short left-facing corner. Continue straight up the lower-angle face above to a sloping ledge and ascend the right side of two large stacked blocks to a walk-off ledge. Finish up cracks on the lichen-covered nose at the top. 140'

FA Oct, 2006, Ken Nichols, Boris Itin, Yvonne Lin

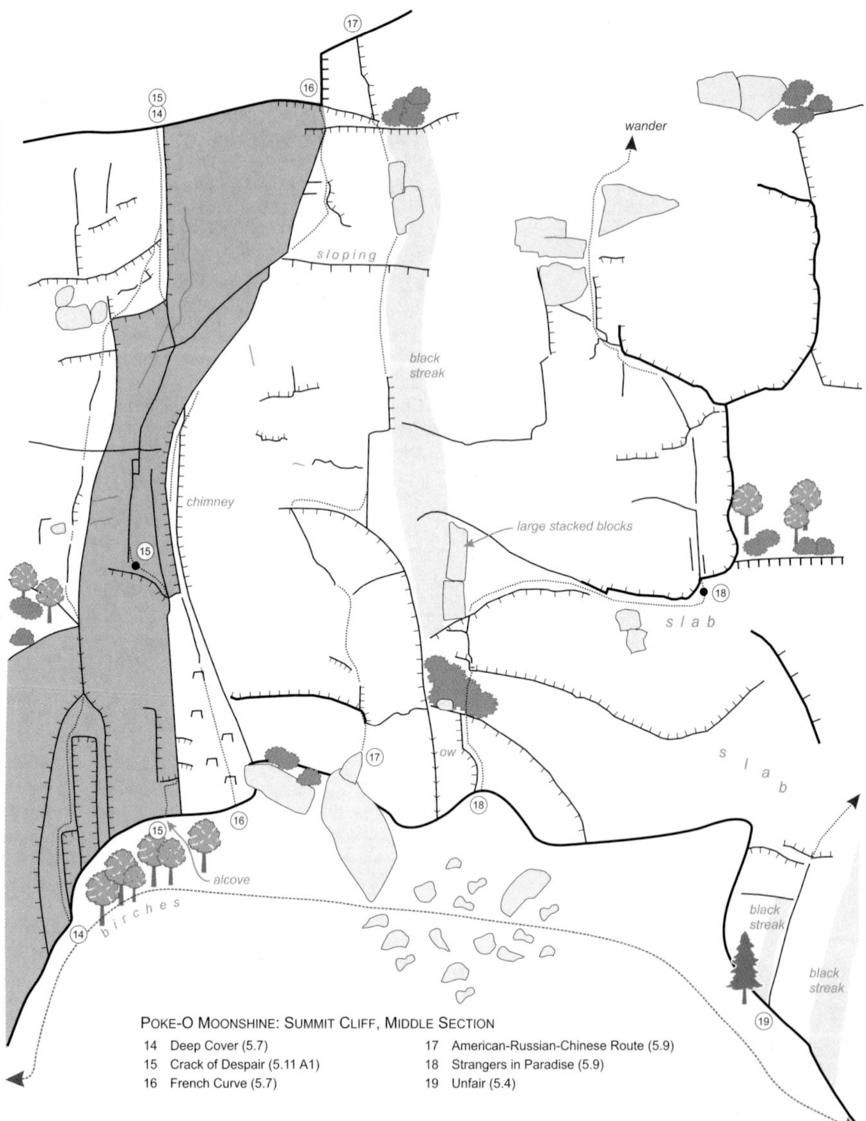

Poke-O Moonshine: Summit Cliff, Middle Section

14 Deep Cover (5.7)
15 Crack of Despair (5.11 A1)
16 French Curve (5.7)
17 American-Russian-Chinese Route (5.9)
18 Strangers in Paradise (5.9)
19 Unfair (5.4)

18 Strangers in Paradise 5.9 G 170' ★★

Start: At a short, rounded corner below and just right of some huge stacked blocks 20' up, 50' right of the huge **French Curve** corner, and just right of a large open book with a fistcrack in the back.

P1 5.9 G: Climb the corner and a short crack to the right side of the stacked blocks, then traverse right 50' on the obvious sloping ledge to a semihanging belay beneath the right end of an overlap, below a crack that breaks through the overlap. 80'

P2 5.9 G: Continue up a crack system to the main overlap higher up, traverse a few feet left, and follow another crack to the left end of the overlap. Step up and right onto a small ledge on the low-angle face above, step left, then climb up past a huge flake to a ramp system on the left that leads to the top. 90'

FA Oct, 1990, Ken Nichols, Al Carilli

19 Unfair 5.4 G 50'

Vastly inferior to **Fairview**, hence its name.

Start: At a crack behind a large pine tree, 125' right of the huge **French Curve** corner and 65' uphill from and to the left of **Fairview**.

P1 5.4 G: Climb the crack. 50'

FA Oct, 1989, Al Carilli, Ken Nichols

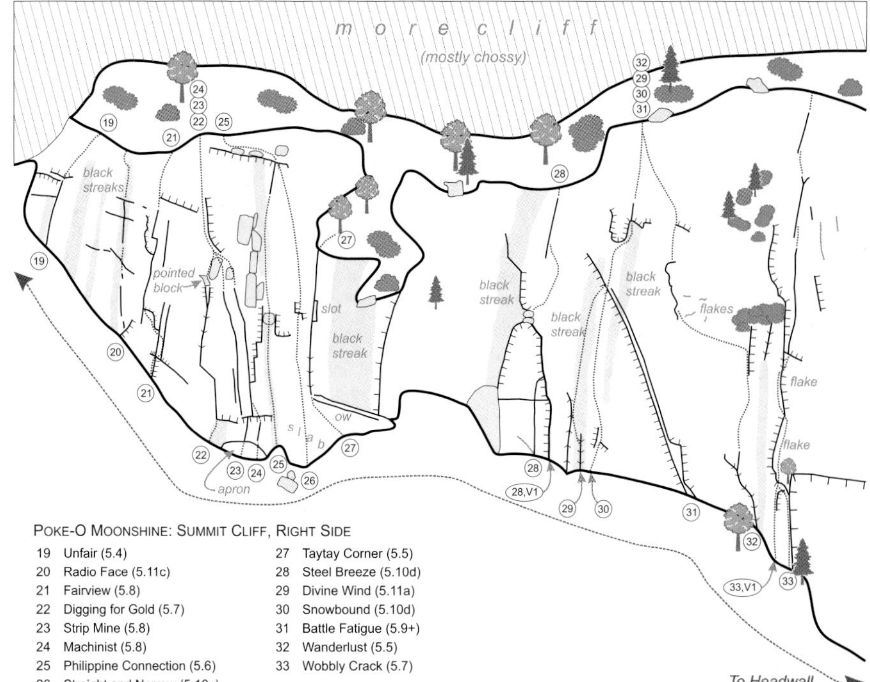

20 Radio Face 5.11c TR 80' ★★★

A high-quality toprope that makes a nice finish after you climb one of the neighbors. It begins at a short ramp just right of a prominent black water streak, 30' uphill from and left of **Fairview**. Step left to a shallow vertical groove in the black streak and continue up the streak past another shallow groove to the top of the wall. Traverse left to a flake just past the streak and pull over the top.
FA (TR) 1977, Geoff Smith

21 Fairview 5.8 PG 100' ★★★★

Start: On a face below the rightmost of a series of parallel cracks. (The rightmost crack comes to the ground, the next one to the left starts higher up, and the leftmost is a handcrack that begins even higher.) This face is uphill and left from the toe of the buttress that has a square roof 12' up.

P1 5.8 PG: Start in the rightmost crack, switch to the middle crack, then move farther left to the handcrack and follow it past a slight jog to an unprotected friction ramp that leads to the top. 100'
FA Apr, 1977, Geoff Smith, Don Layman

22 Digging for Gold 5.7 G 100'

On the first ascent, the crack was dug out and thoroughly scrubbed, hence the name. However, the precious metal turned out to be fool's gold.

Start: 17' right of **Fairview**, on black rock below the left end of a roof 12' up, and at a small downward-pointed flake.

P1 5.7 G: Climb up to the left end of an overlap. Follow the obvious crack up and then out left across the face to a wide vertical crack. Up the wide crack, past a large pointed block, and finish up the low-angle face. 100'
FA Oct, 1989, Al Carilli, Ken Nichols

23 Strip Mine 5.8 G 100'

Start: At a short, low-angle apron of rock, 16' right of **Digging for Gold**.

P1 5.8 G: Climb the apron, then up an obvious crack system, and finish up the low-angle face above. 100'
FA Oct, 1989, Ken Nichols, Al Carilli

24 Machinist 5.8 G 100'

Carilli is a machinist by occupation.

Start: At the second obvious crack system to the right of **Digging for Gold**, 10' right of **Strip Mine**.

P1 5.8 G: Climb the crack system and finish up the low-angle face above. 100'
FA Oct, 1989, Al Carilli, Ken Nichols

25 Philippine Connection 5.6 G 80'

Start: At a crack-and-corner system with a black water streak, 8' right of **Machinist**.

P1 5.6 G: Work up the crack-and-corner system to the top of some precariously stacked blocks, then step right and follow a crack to a walk-off ledge just below the top. 80'
FA Oct, 2006, Ken Nichols, Fausta Esguerra

26 Straight and Narrow 5.10c TR 120'

This route begins on the lowest point of a large low-angle apron of rock, just right of a white birch and 40' right of **Philippine Connection**. Follow a narrow black water streak straight up to a short but steep wall and work up left to a small left-facing flake. Step back right, then straight up the black water streak until just below the top. Follow a shallow groove up left to a walk-off ledge.
FA (TR) Oct, 2006, Ken Nichols

27 Taytay Corner 5.5 G 50'

Named for Esguerra's hometown in the Philippines.
Start: At a large, curving open book on the right side of an apron of rock, 30' uphill from and to the right of **Straight and Narrow**.
P1 5.5 G: Follow the corner and short crack to the top. 50'
FA Oct, 2006, Ken Nichols, Fausta Esguerra

28 Steel Breeze (aka Rainbow Crack) 5.10d R 90' ★

Start: 3' left of a huge right-facing flake that forms an off width on its right side, at the base of a thin crack split by a horizontal crack 18' up.
P1 5.10d R: (V1) Climb the thin crack up to the left-rising edge of the flake. Follow the flake up to some stacked blocks at the top. An unprotected friction move over a bulge (5.8 R) leads to lower-angled rock; there is a crack on the left should you want some gear. 90'
V1 Cold Hands 5.6 PG: Climb the off-width crack on the right side of the flake for 25' and join the normal route where it meets the flake.
FA (V1) Oct 30, 1987, Ken Nichols, Sarah Locher
FA Oct, 1987, Ken Nichols

29 Divine Wind 5.11a TR 75' ★★

This route begins at a shallow open book, 20' right of the **Cold Hands** corner and 7' right of a blunt arête. Layback up a short crack and diagonal up left on a black water streak just right of the blunt arête to a ledge below a crack with bushes. Step out right and work up the face just left of an indistinct vertical groove to a small left-facing corner. Then pull up onto the **Battle Fatigue** ramp and follow it up left to the top.
FA (TR) Oct, 2006, Ken Nichols

30 Snowbound 5.10d TR 75' ★★★

Another fine-quality toprope problem that begins at a short vertical crack, 15' right of **Divine Wind**. Layback up the crack to a small ledge, then to the top of some tiny right-facing corners. Step out to the right of a black water streak, move up a few feet, and step back left into the streak. Follow the streak straight up to the **Battle Fatigue** ramp, then up the streak past a left-facing layback edge to the offset in the prominent overlap near the top, and finish up the crack. You can avoid the initial crack (5.10d) by following **Divine Wind** to a stance 6' up, then traversing right (5.9) to the small ledge.
FA (TR) 1986, Mike Heintz, Mark Meschinelli

31 Battle Fatigue 5.9+ G 120' ★★

Start: At a left-rising off-width crack opposite a large white birch tree, 55' right of **Steel Breeze**.
P1 5.9+ G: Follow the off-width crack up left to a low-angle ramp. Up the ramp until you are below a large hanging flake, then up right to the flake and finish up its right side via a vertical crack. 120'
Gear: Cams up to 7".
FA Oct, 1988, Ken Nichols, Jack Rankin

32 Wanderlust 5.5 R 170'

Start: At a 12"-thick maple tree in front of the left end of an apron-slab of rock, below a shallow flaring corner that angles up and left, 50' right of **Battle Fatigue**.
P1 5.5 R: Follow the corner until the crack fades out, climb up right 10', and traverse back left 10' to a stance in a left-leaning, left-facing open book below a mass of bushes. Traverse 20' left to a small ledge, work up some rounded flakes and shallow vertical cracks, and diagonal up right to a small overlap. Step above the overlap and follow its edge up left to a small crack that runs up the center of the final low-angle face. 170'
FA Oct, 1989, Ken Nichols, Gary Lundin

33 Wobbly Crack 5.7 G 160' ★

Start: At a large but short left-facing corner 25' right of the **Wanderlust** maple tree.
P1 5.7 G: (V1) Scramble up the corner and follow the obvious bushy ramp up left to a right-facing flake. Continue up to a left-facing flake until you are just below a bushy ledge. Step right to a handcrack and follow it to the top. 160'
V1 5.9 R: An alternate, unprotected start begins on the slab 13' to the left. Climb up and slightly left (crux) to a small, shallow left-facing corner, then up to the right-facing flake of the normal route.
FA Oct, 2006, Boris Itin, Yvonne Lin, Ken Nichols
FA (V1) Oct, 2006, Ken Nichols

Poke-O Moonshine • Upper Tiers

HEADWALL

Aspect	East and southeast
Height	180'
Quality	★★★★
Approach	25 min, moderate
Summary	Highest and most developed cliff on the Upper Tiers.

-5.6	5.7	5.8	5.9	5.10	5.11	5.12	5.13+	total
2	2	4	9	19	10	1		47

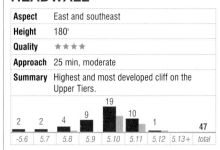

DIRECTIONS **(MAP PAGE 30)**

From the Viewpoint (at the #5 interpretive marker), continue up the Ranger's Trail for 3 min, then turn off the trail and into the woods, heading up and right 618814,4917410. There is sometimes a small cairn marking this junction, and there is a larger cairn 30' off the main trail; the junction is also just after the trail makes a left bend around an oak tree. From the junction, head up and right to a short vegetated slab, up this, then angle right to a small, slabby cliff. Follow a weakness up and left through the cliff (there is a fixed rope here

618789,4917457), then follow a good trail up and right through huge boulders to the base of the cliff, meeting it at the slab below Dark Lord, 8 min from the hiking trail or 25 min from the road 618687,4917569.

You can also approach the Headwall from Summit Cliff. Walk right along the base of Summit Cliff to its far right end, where the cliff diminishes into vegetation. Head up and right to meet the Headwall at Solar Energy.

34 Moonstruck 5.8 PG 70'

Named after the 1987 film with Cher.

Start: 8' left of Solar Energy corner.

P1 5.8 PG: Up a slab (no protection), then follow small corners and right-facing layback flakes to a stance. Step left and mantel to the top. 70'

FA Oct, 2007, Ken Nichols

35 Solar Energy 5.6 G 75' ★★

Start: Uphill and left of Gusto Crack is a shallow right-facing corner, above which the corner is larger with an off-width crack.

P1 5.6 G: Climb the corner past the off-width crack to the top. 75'

FA 1975, Gary Allan, Tom Caramia

36 Hot Saw 5.9 G 75' ★★

Start: 6' right of the Solar Energy corner, at a fingercrack on a face below the left side of a 12'-high perched flake. There is a 4'-high tan strip that comes out of the bottom of the fingercrack.

P1 5.9 G: Climb the fingercrack to the right side of a tan perched block below a roof. Go around the right side of the roof and up the fistcrack on the steep face above. 75'

FA 1978, Mark Meschinelli, Dave Hough, Patrick Munn

37 Jump Back Jack Crack 5.7 G 90' ★

Named after a route out West but inspired by Rankin's first name.

Start: Under Gusto Crack's big, low, left-arching chimney-roof, uphill from and to the left of Adirondack Crack, on the slab below and left of a long, thin right-facing flake. There is a brown water streak that runs down the slab from the bottom of the flake. Opposite the chimney-roof is a huge block.

P1 5.7 G: Climb up and slightly right to a thin flake and follow the flake to the big overlap. Pull over the overlap at the crack, continue up to a sloping grass- and tree-filled cleft, then finish up the crack in the corner to the right. 90'

FA Oct, 1988, Ken Nichols, Jack Rankin

38 Great Northern 5.10a G 100' ★★★

Named after the now-defunct Great Northern Railway.

Start: Under Gusto Crack's big, low, left-arching chimney-roof, uphill from and to the left of Adirondack Crack, at a thin crack on the face just right of the brown water streak that runs out of the Jump Back Jack Crack flake. Opposite the chimney-roof is a huge block.

P1 5.10a G: Follow the crack until it intersects the chimney at a point where the chimney narrows to an off-width crack in an inside corner. Up the corner to the impressive roof and undercling right (crux) to a small ledge just past the far end of the roof. 40'

P2 5.9 G: Step up left and follow a flaring crack to a long step out right to a good ledge. Up a short left-rising, right-facing ramp and step out left again to a horizontal crack below a left-facing corner. Instead of climbing up into the corner, follow a series of vertical cracks and layback edges up right to the top. 60'

FA Oct, 1988, Ken Nichols, Jack Rankin

Chuck Boyd on Raven (5.11b). Photo by Ken Nichols.

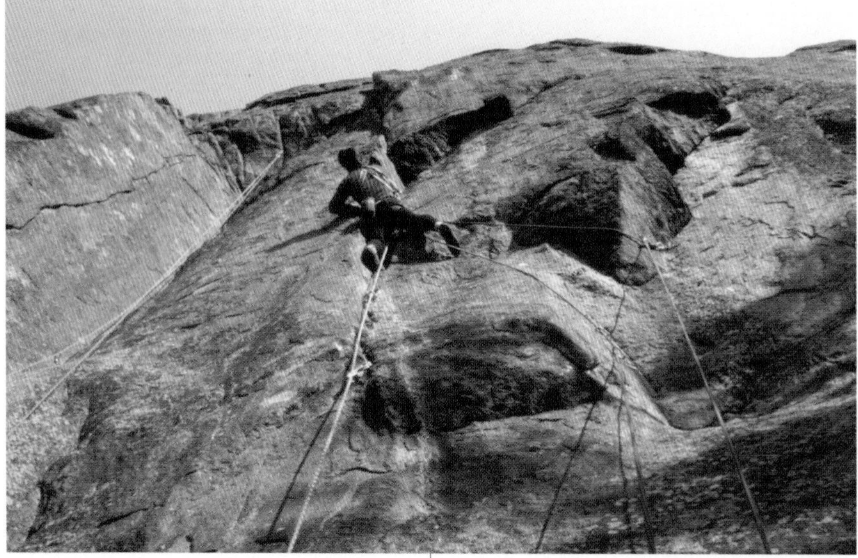

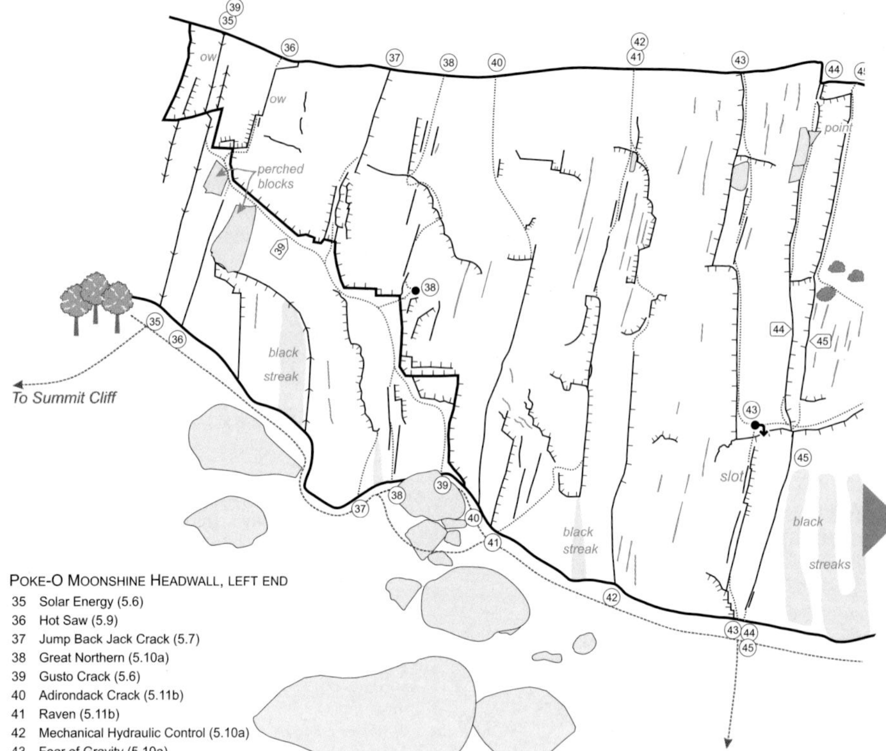

Poke-O Moonshine Headwall, Left End

35 Solar Energy (5.6)
36 Hot Saw (5.9)
37 Jump Back Jack Crack (5.7)
38 Great Northern (5.10a)
39 Gusto Crack (5.6)
40 Adirondack Crack (5.11b)
41 Raven (5.11b)
42 Mechanical Hydraulic Control (5.10a)
43 Fear of Gravity (5.10a)
44 Dutch Masters Direct (5.10a)
45 Thunderbolt (5.10a)
46 Hydrophobia (5.9)
47 Jumpin' Jack Flash (5.11b)
48 Project
49 The Bandit (5.9)

39 Gusto Crack 5.6 R 75'

For many years this route was confused with **Battle Fatigue**.

Start: At a big, low, left-arching chimney-roof, the only such deep feature on the cliff. The base is jumbled with boulders.

P1 5.6 R: Climb the left-arching chimney-roof for quite a distance, to the perched block of **Hot Saw**, then continue left under the roof to finish in the off-width crack of **Solar Energy**. 75'

FA 1976, Geoff Smith, Dave Hough

40 Adirondack Crack 5.11b G 100'

An exercise in difficult jamming in a flared crack.

Start: Just right of the big, left-arching chimney-roof of **Gusto Crack** below a crack.

P1 5.11b G: Climb the crack that leans a little to the right until it abruptly ends at a small overlap. Make a desperate reach up left to a small hold (crux) that leads to easy face climbing diagonally up left to the top. 100'

FA Oct, 1984, Ken Nichols, Marco Fedrizzi

41 Raven 5.11b R 100' ★★

The first ascent used three 9-mm ropes to reduce drag and left one behind at the vertical crack.

Start: The route climbs a crack in a shallow left-facing corner 25' left of **Mechanical Hydraulic Control** that doesn't reach the ground; a black streak extends from the bottom of the corner to the ground. Begin at a sloping step below a thin, groovelike crack, 20' left of the black streak and 10' right of **Adirondack Crack**.

P1 5.11b R: Climb up right to a shallow left-facing corner, move up, and traverse right (5.10c) to the prominent vertical crack, which begins 15' above the ground. Follow the crack past a bulge (crux) to a protruding ledge. Up a right-leaning crack, then up the parallel cracks above. 100'

FA Oct, 1988, Ken Nichols, Chuck Boyd

42 Mechanical Hydraulic Control 5.10a PG 100' ★★★

Lemmons is an engineer from St. Louis, which accounts for the rather unusual name.

Start: At a crack that leads to a prominent left-facing corner, 35' right of **Gusto Crack**'s big, low, left-arching chimney-roof.

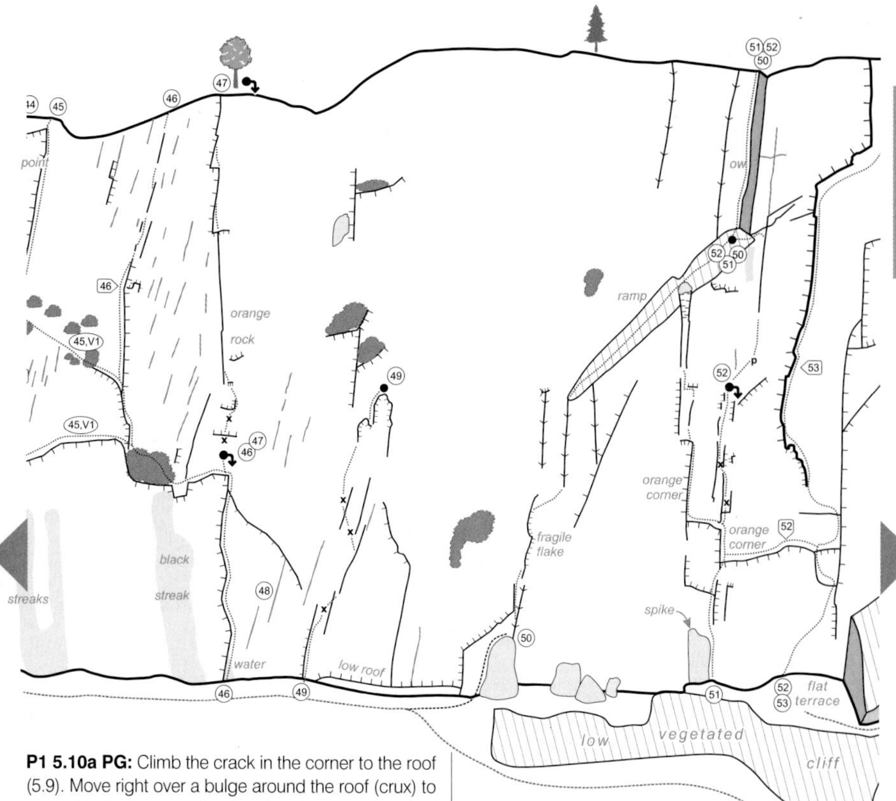

P1 5.10a PG: Climb the crack in the corner to the roof (5.9). Move right over a bulge around the roof (crux) to a small ledge (1" cam helpful). Continue in a series of right-facing corners and flakes (5.9) to the top. 100'
FA (TR) 1977, Mark Meschinelli
FA Oct 13, 1984, Mark Lemmons, Ken Nichols

43 Fear of Gravity 5.10a G 120' ★★★★★

Originally called **Fear of Flying**, but the first-ascent party found that this route name was already in use.
Start: At some steps below the left-hand of two short fingercracks that lead to the left end of a long ledge 40' up.
P1 5.9+ G: Climb the left-hand fingercrack through a 10"-high slot to the ledge with a fixed anchor. 40'
P2 5.10a G: From the left side of the ledge, climb the off-width, left-leaning crack in the right-facing corner (5.8) to a sloped ledge, then up through a right-leaning, flaring fingercrack in black rock (5.9+) to another sloped ledge with a large wedged block. Step back left and finish up a short right-facing corner. 80'
Gear: Doubles through 3.5", 1 ea 4".
History: The original route climbed **Hydrophobia** to the ledge at the top of P1. The direct line described here was added later and is considered the straighter, more aesthetic line.
FA (P2) 1976, Gary Allan, Geoff Smith, Dave Hough
FA (P1) 1984, Mark Lemmons, Ken Nichols

44 Dutch Masters Direct 5.10a G 100' ★★★

The name was a play on the Yosemite route **DNB** as well as a reference to the Dutch Masters cigar tubes used as a conveyance for "baking" supplies.
Start: This is the right-hand of two short fingercracks that lead to a long ledge 40' up (the left-hand crack is **Fear of Gravity**).
P1 5.10a G: Climb the right-hand fingercrack (crux) to the ledge (optional belay, fixed anchor). Continue up a left-facing corner with a handcrack and into a right-facing corner higher up that has an off-width crack. 100'
FA 1977, Mark Meschinelli, Geoff Smith, Patrick Munn

45 Thunderbolt 5.10a G 100' ★★

Named for the A-10 ground attack jet that flew overhead during the first ascent.
Start: Same as **Dutch Masters Direct**.
P1 5.10a G: Climb the right-hand crack to the ledge, then up to a bulge with a shallow groove. Up the groove, then finish in the obvious right-facing corner that increases in size toward the top of the cliff. 100'
History: The original route climbed P1 of **Fear of Gravity**, then traversed right on the ledge to a point near the left-facing corner of **Hydrophobia** and worked diago-

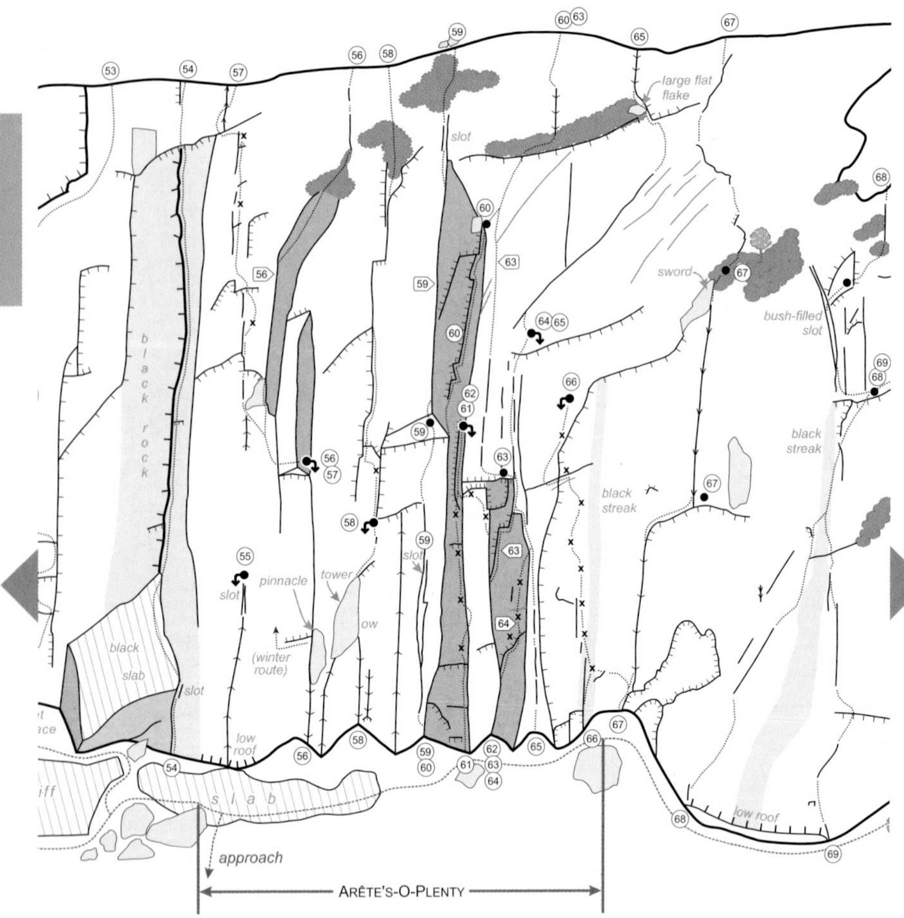

nally up and left to the main corner above. The direct line described here was added later and is considered a straighter, more aesthetic line.

FA Oct, 1984, Marco Fedrizzi

FA (direct) Oct, 1984, Todd Eastman, Ken Nichols

46 Hydrophobia 5.9 G 140' ★

Named in keeping with the "fear" theme, the wet rock, and intermittent rain during the first ascent. This route can be used to access the upper sections of **Fear of Gravity**, **Dutch Masters Direct**, and **Thunderbolt**. The upper section is often wet.

Start: At a right-facing wavy corner with a nice crack. There is a pink water stain that emerges from the crack 5' up. This corner is 6' left of two right-leaning seams in smooth rock.

P1 5.7 G: Climb the wavy right-facing corner to a good belay ledge with a fixed anchor. 50'

P2 5.9 G: Diagonal up and left for 30' to a left-facing corner, then climb it to some cracks that lead up the final face to the top. 90'

FA Oct, 1984, Chuck Boyd, Ken Nichols

47 Jumpin' Jack Flash 5.11b G 90' ★★★

The upper crack is dirty but still quite nice.

Start: At the top of P1 of **Hydrophobia**.

P1 5.11b G: Up the face above the belay to an overlap, then reach right to a shallow right-facing corner with a hidden hold. A big move gains a bucket and handcrack in pink rock above. Follow the nice handcrack (5.9) to a steep wall, then up the right-facing orange flake past big jugs to the top. 90'

FA 1990, Joe Szot, Dave Szot, Dennis Luther, Tom Yandon

48 Project

Right of **Hydrophobia** are some slanting seams with a fixed RURP. This is an abandoned project.

49 The Bandit 5.9 G 50'

Start: 60' left of and uphill from the boulder that marks the start of **Adirondack High** is a low overhang, 1' off the ground. This route starts at the left end of this overhang where it disappears into the ground, at a shallow right-facing, right-leaning black corner with a crack.

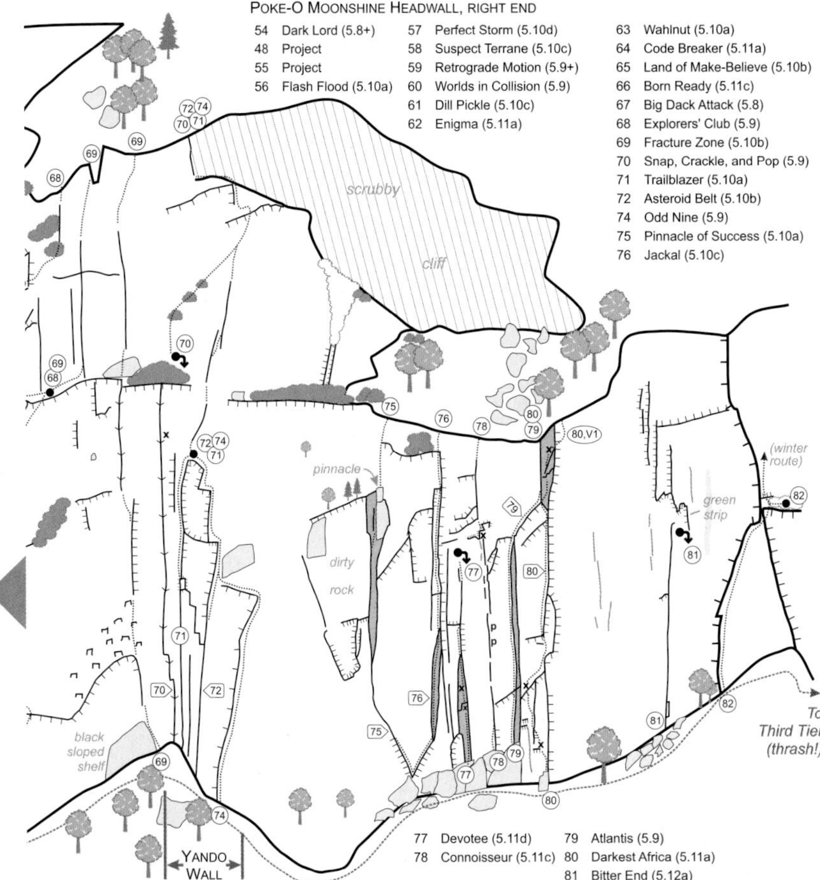

P1 5.9 G: Climb up the crack, then friction right to gain a handcrack. Up the handcrack to its top, then move left and up to a stance. Continue up to the top of a flake, then right into a left-facing corner and follow it to a spire. Rappel. 50'
FA 1991, Mark Meschinelli, Patrick Munn

50 Adirondack High 5.8 PG 170'

Start: Walk left from **Dark Lord** and pass though some large boulders. Continue left along the base steeply uphill with boulders between you and the cliff. At the far end of the boulders, scramble to the top of the leftmost boulder with a flat top. The route begins at a V-groove on the cliff in front of this boulder 618658,4917524.

P1 5.8 PG: Step across to the cliff into the V-groove, then out left and up to the thin left-facing flake pasted to the rock. Up the flake (crux) and onto a slab below an open book. Move right into the next open book (this is the middle of three open-book corners), then up the corner to the left end of a long, right-rising, sloped ramp. Climb rightward up the ramp to belay at the base of an off width in a left-facing corner. 130'

P2 5.7 G: Climb the off width to the top. 40'
FA 1975, Patrick Munn, Dave Hough, Geoff Smith

51 Continental Drift 5.10c G 180' ★★

Start: From the base of **Dark Lord**, scramble left on a narrow ledge to an open terrace. From the left end of the terrace, walk left 15' on a narrow vegetated ledge to a shallow left-facing corner covered with lichen. Just left of the start is a 15'-high flake-boulder.

P1 5.10c G: Climb the left-facing corner to gain a ledge at the base of a short orange corner. (A cleaner start is to climb the slab of **Plate Tectonics** to the ledge, then traverse left to the orange corner.) Climb the small orange corner to a ledge at the top, then traverse left to a larger, right-facing orange corner (possible belay). Up the corner to a ledge, then straight up some thin cracks to an overlap. Break out left to the arête and up the crack to the sloped ledge. Step right and belay at the base of an off-width crack in a left-facing corner. 140'

P2 5.7 G: Same as **Adirondack High**: climb the off-width crack to the top. 40'
FA Sep, 1987, Ken Nichols, Bruce Jelen (P2 only)

52 The Gauntlet 5.11d PG 190' ★★

Start: Same as **Plate Tectonics**.

P1 5.11d PG: Climb up the slab of **Plate Tectonics** to the first ledge, then traverse left to the orange right-facing corner. Up the corner, then continue straight up to a fixed anchor. 80'

P2 5.11d PG: Continue up and right to gain a finger-crack, then climb it to a horizontal with a dangerous-looking block. Rail left to the arête, then around to a sloped ledge beneath a left-facing corner with an off-width crack. 70'

P3 5.7 G: Same as **Adirondack High**: climb the off-width crack to the top. 40'

FA Jun 28, 1997, Tim Beaman, Dave Boyden

53 Plate Tectonics 5.10d R (5.7 X) 180' ★★★★★

Climbs the huge right-facing knife left of **Dark Lord**, directly above where the approach trail meets the cliff. In Nichols's words, this route is "the most spectacular flake in the Adirondacks" and "the most satisfying climb I've done in the Adirondacks." Despite the high praise, this route has seen only a handful of ascents due to its terrifying appearance. The main feature of this route is the huge flake, one of the biggest in the region, which looks as though it was formed by movement in the Earth's crust, hence the name.

Start: From the base of **Dark Lord**, scramble left on a narrow ledge to an open terrace. The route begins in the back of this terrace at the base of a slab with a black streak, below the ominous right-facing blade, the route's central feature.

*Ken Nichols on the first ascent of **Worlds in Collision** (5.9). Photo by Mike Heintz.*

P1 5.10d R (5.7 X): Climb the unprotected slab (5.6) up right to within a few feet of a large left-facing dihedral. Up the corner to another ledge, then step left to a fragile right-facing flake on the face (actually a continuation of the route's central feature). Up the flake and into the bottom of the blade with a 6" crack. Layback securely up the flake; at the top, the crack narrows to a well-protected, stemming crux to a roof. Traverse right under the roof to a short crack and broken rock to the top. 180'

Gear: A large cam for the bottom of the flake, then 5.5" and 6" tube chocks.

History: Mark Meschinelli and Geoff Smith climbed the first half of this route in 1978 and named it **Rest in Pieces**.

FA Sep 29, 1984, Ken Nichols, Marco Fedrizzi

54 Dark Lord 5.8+ PG 180' ★★★

Climbs the jet-black corner directly above a slab. The corner is a sought-after ice route, which means it is almost always wet; wait for dry conditions for this one. Much easier than it looks.

Start: At the base of the large, black left-facing corner with a squeeze chimney, at the upper left end of a slab (the large slab where the approach trail meets the cliff). Left of the corner is a pointed boulder, and right of the corner is a low roof.

P1 5.8+ PG: Climb the squeeze chimney through the initial bulge for 12' (crux) to a ledge. Continue up the large black corner, past a small ledge, and on to the top. 180'

FA Sep 29, 1984, Ken Nichols, Marco Fedrizzi

Arête's-O-Plenty

As you move right from the deep recess at the start of **Dark Lord**, there are six arêtes used to locate routes in this section. The first is the blunt arête right of the black recessed start of **Dark Lord**.

55 Project

The right wall of the first arête has a black strip that comes down the wall, 4' right of the arête. There is a fixed anchor on top.

56 Flash Flood 5.10a G 180' ★★★

Good crack climbing on P1. This route is also the start of the winter route **March Madness**.

Start: At a grassy terrace at the top of the slab right of **Dark Lord**, beneath a small left-facing corner between the first and second arêtes right of **Dark Lord**. On the left wall of the corner, about 25' up, is a 6" overlap.

P1 5.10a G: Climb the crack in the left-facing corner to the top of a small pinnacle. Continue up cracks on the face above, past a key downward-pointed flake, to a large ledge and a fixed anchor. 80'

P2 5.7 G: From the left end of the ledge, climb the large, left-facing black corner to a ramp and a final crack to the top. 100'

FA Sep 27, 1987, Ken Nichols, Bruce Jelen

57 Perfect Storm 5.10d G 100' ★★★★

Incredible climbing on an exposed upper wall, with clean rock and good protection throughout.

Start: On the ledge on top of P1 of **Flash Flood**.
P1 5.10d G: From the left side of the ledge, climb up the **Flash Flood** crack a few feet, then onto ledges on the left wall. Up a steep black wall to the next ledge. Continue up to another ledge, then up shallow facing corners on the next headwall to a horizontal. Step left around an arête to a stance, then finish on the rounded arête to the top. 100'
FA 1995, Tim Beaman, Sylvia Lazarnick

58 Suspect Terrane 5.10c G 170'

Terrane, another geological term, refers to a detached piece of the earth's crust.
Start: In a shallow broken corner that leads to a 3" crack, 8' right of **Flash Flood**, and between the second and third arêtes right of **Dark Lord**.
P1 5.8 G: Up the broken corner and nice crack to a fixed anchor on a slab. 60'
P2 5.10c G: Up an open book, then step left into the right-facing corner, past a small triangular roof, and angle right up the weakness to the top. 110'
FA 1999, Tim Beaman, Bill Dodd

59 Retrograde Motion 5.9+ PG 180' ★★

Quality crack climbing on P1.
Start: Same as **Worlds in Collision**.
P1 5.9+ PG: Climb a few feet up the corner to gain the cracks in the left wall (crux; some hollow rock here) and follow them to a ledge. (It's possible to traverse left to the fixed anchor on **Suspect Terrane**.) A short, unprotected friction ramp leads to a huge ledge on the right. 80'
P2 5.9 G: Continue up the corner past an awkward bulge to the top. 100'
FA (P1) 1977, Geoff Smith, Gary Allan, Dave Hough
FA (P2) Oct 6, 1984, Ken Nichols, Mike Heintz, Carold Nelson

60 Worlds in Collision 5.9 G 200' ★★

Start: In the V-corner between the third and fourth arêtes. There is a 2'-wide strip of jet-black rock left of the crack in the corner.
P1 5.9 G: Climb the corner to the top at the base of the sloping ledge. Just above, and on the right wall of the corner, is a smaller right-facing corner with two small ceilings. Continue straight up into the right-facing corner, past the two ceilings, to a ledge at the top of the corner next to a large boulder. 150'
P2 5.8 PG: Continue up a slab (which joins **Wahlnut**) to a grassy ledge. Step right and climb a short open book, then finish up a short black face (same as **Wahlnut**). 50'
FA Oct, 1984, Ken Nichols, Mike Heintz, Carold Nelson (P2 only)

61 Dill Pickle 5.10c G 80' ★★★

Named for Bob Dill, an early partner of Beaman's.
Start: At the toe of the arête (the fourth arête right of **Dark Lord**), 10' left of the deep V-corner of **Wahlnut**.
● **P1 5.10c G:** Climb straight up the arête using bolts on the left wall. The arête merges with a large roof on the right; move onto the wall above the roof to a fixed anchor (shared with **Enigma**). 80'
FA 1995, Tim Beaman, Dave Boyden (owner of Boyden Valley Winery in Vermont)

62 Enigma 5.11a G 90' ★★★

Start: At a deep V-corner capped by high, blocky overhangs, 25' right of **Worlds in Collision** and 10' left of **Land of Make-Believe**. This corner is between the fourth and fifth arêtes right of **Dark Lord**.
P1 5.11a G: Climb up the corner to the roof. Work out left under the roof, then up to a fixed anchor on the face above (shared with **Dill Pickle**). Watch the rope over the sharp edge of the roof. 90'
FA 1993, Tim Beaman, Sylvia Lazarnick, Bill Dodd

63 Wahlnut 5.10a G 170' ★

Start: In the deep V-corner, same as **Enigma** and **Code Breaker**.
P1 5.10a G: Work up the corner, then undercling out right under the lowest overhang. At its end, step up onto a small ledge on **Land of Make-Believe**, then up a few feet to a semihanging belay on a small, square ledge at the level of the lip of the top of the overhang. 70'
P2 5.8 PG: Traverse straight left at the lip of the large upper overhang to a series of vertical cracks near the arête. Follow the cracks and arête to the left end of a large, grassy ledge, up a short open book, then finish up a short black face. 100'
FA Sep, 1990, Ken Nichols, Eric Wahl

*Colin Loher on **Dill Pickle** (5.10c). Photo Mark Meschinelli.*

*Mark Meschinelli at the crux of **Code Breaker** (5.11a). Photo by Jeff Cochran.*

64 Code Breaker 5.11a G 100' ★★★

Climbs up to the fifth arête right of **Dark Lord**.

Start: In the deep V-corner, same as **Wahlnut** and **Enigma**.

○ **P1 5.11a G:** Up the overhanging V-slot and into the corner above (3" cam useful at the top). Move right onto the right wall of the corner, diagonal up and right to the right side of the face (crux), then up and right to join **Land of Make-Believe**. Up cracks and corners of that route to the fixed anchor. 100'

FA 1999, Tim Beaman, Diane Dodd

65 Land of Make-Believe (aka Your Anus) 5.10b PG (5.8 R) 180' ★★★

Climbs through a tight, unappealing constriction, which is much better than it looks. There is even a no-hands rest in the middle of this crux section.

Start: In the back of a flat, shady alcove, at the base of the flared chimney, between the fifth and sixth arêtes right of **Dark Lord**.

P1 5.10b PG: Climb through the constricting chimney (crux) to the top of the corner. Step out left and follow a series of cracks and shallow left-facing corners past a horizontally protruding flake to a large, sloping ledge on the right with a fixed anchor. 100'

P2 5.8 R: From the left end of the ledge, climb up to a diagonal crack and follow the crack up right for about 50' until you can gain a flake up to the left. Continue up to a small overhang, step left, and pull up onto a ledge with a huge flat flake. Finish up a short corner. 80'

Gear: Up to 4".

FA Oct, 1989, Ken Nichols, Gary Lundin

66 Born Ready 5.11c G 90' ★★★★★

Sustained climbing up a steep face; one of the best bolted face routes at Poke-O. The first clip is desperate and usually stick-clipped.

Start: 30' right of **Land of Make-Believe** is the huge open book of **Big Dack Attack**; this route climbs the left wall.

● **P1 5.11c G:** Stick-clip the first bolt. It's easier to climb a few feet up the corner to the right (**Big Dack Attack**), then move left across the face to the first bolt (taken directly, it's 5.11d). Continue up the face to a good horizontal at the top. Follow the horizontal left around the arête, then past another bolt and up to a fixed anchor. 90'

FA 1999, Tim Beaman, Mark Meschinelli

End of Arête's-O-Plenty

67 Big Dack Attack (aka The Sword) 5.8 G 160' ★★

Start: At the base of a huge open book, 30' around the corner from **Land of Make-Believe**. At the top of the cliff is a swordlike protrusion of rock.

P1 5.8 G: Follow the corner to a large, blueberry-covered ledge. 50'

P2 5.8 G: Continue up the corner to another bushy ledge (possible rappel here), work up past a fragile flake, then finish straight up the low-angle face. 110'

FA Oct, 1989, Matt Rugens, Ken Nichols

68 Explorers' Club 5.9 R 160'

Start: From the open grotto at the base of **Land of Make-Believe**, walk right past the deep corner of **Big Dack Attack**, then steeply downhill for 50' to the toe of the rounded buttress. This route begins at a block at the left end of a low overhang that is 3' above the ground on the toe of the rounded buttress.

P1 5.9 R: Step off the block, climb a few feet up some rounded grooves, step out right around the outside corner, and layback up a narrow edge to a sloping ledge. Follow a diagonal crack up right to the obvious black water streak and work up the face (20' runout) just left of the streak to a hidden incut flake. Traverse 15' right to lower-angle rock on the right side of the streak and climb up left to a bush-filled slot. Continue to the top of the slot, then step right into a triangular alcove with a down-curving floor. 140'

P2 5.6 G: Step out right from the alcove and climb up and left to the top. 20'

FA Sep, 1990, Ken Nichols, Eric Wahl

69 Fracture Zone 5.10b G 160' ★★

Start: At the toe of the rounded buttress of **Explorers' Club** is a low overhang 3' above the ground. The low overhang continues to the right and eventually merges with the ground, marking the start of **Fracture Zone**. Begin at a shallow 10'-high crack that leads to an undulating slab of black rock.

P1 5.10b G: Climb the undulating black slab diagonally up and right to a sloped ledge. From the left end of the ledge, climb a bottomless crack up a steep wall to another ledge, then up lower-angled rock to a high, clean sloped ledge. 100'

Colin Loher stuffs himself into the constriction of Land of Make-Believe (5.10b).

P2 5.9 G: Climb up and right 10' and follow a steep crack to the top. This crack is about 10' to the left of the finish crack of **Snap, Crackle, and Pop**. 60'
FA Oct, 1987, Ken Nichols, Chuck Boyd

Yando Wall

The Yando Wall is south-facing and has several vertical cracks, which start with **Snap, Crackle, and Pop** and end with **Odd Nine** on the right side of the face; it faces the trail as you approach from the left.

70 Snap, Crackle, and Pop (aka Along the Watchtower) 5.9 G 160'

A straight line that has considerable lichen, hence the name.
Start: On the face 10' left of the large left-facing corner, the right wall of which forms the Yando Wall.
P1 5.9 G: Climb up a crack to a set of stepped ledges, up a left-facing corner that becomes a larger left-facing open book, then up to a steep vertical crack near the top that leads to knobby face climbing and a short low-angle slab. 160'
FA Sep, 1989, Ken Nichols, Rick Orsini, Al Carilli

71 Trailblazer 5.10a PG 160' ★★★

A high-quality first section.
Start: Same as **Snap, Crackle, and Pop**.
P1 5.10a PG: Climb up a few feet and follow a small curving ramp up right to the base of the large left-facing corner immediately left of **Asteroid Belt**. Continue up the corner to a bushy ledge with a fixed anchor. Rappel or continue up right onto an unprotected friction slab, then traverse out right to a rounded ridge (which joins the upper pitch of **Asteroid Belt**). Follow the short ridge up and left, move left up onto a step, and finish up a short jamcrack. 160'
FA Sep, 1989, Ken Nichols, Al Carilli

72 Asteroid Belt (aka Tunnel Vision) 5.10b G (5.6 R) 160' ★★

Start: On the left end of the Yando Wall, on the top of a triangular slab beneath a right-facing corner.
P1 5.10b G: Climb up the right-facing corner a few feet, then into the crack on the right wall. Up the crack, angling slightly right, up to a square hole, then up into a left-facing corner. Follow the corner to its top at a large ledge. 100'
P2 5.9 G (5.6 R): Move left and follow a low-angle crack and an unprotected friction slab to the top. 60'
History: Likely not the first ascent, as Nichols found evidence of previous climbing on this route.
ACB Oct, 1987, Ken Nichols

73 Ten Even (aka Dennis' Demise) 5.10b G (5.6 R) 160' ★★

Start: At the crack 15' to the right of the **Asteroid Belt** crack.
P1 5.10b G: Climb the crack and continue up a tight handcrack in a right-facing corner system to its top. Traverse a few feet right on a ledge to an off-width crack (5.6) that leads to a large ledge. 100'
P2 5.9 G (5.6 R): Move left and follow a low-angle crack and an unprotected friction slab of **Asteroid Belt** to the top. 60'
FA Sep, 1989, Ken Nichols, Jack Wenzel

74 Odd Nine 5.9 G (5.6 R) 160' ★★

Start: On the right side of the Yando Wall, at a shallow right-facing, right leaning corner with a good crack. 18' right is a right-leaning off-width crack (just left of the right end of the wall).
P1 5.9 G: Climb the crack to a ledge, up to a tree, then move up and left to join **Ten Even** at a nice ledge below a right-facing corner with a crack. Up the crack (5.6) to a large ledge. 100'
P2 5.9 R: Move left and follow a low-angle crack and an unprotected friction slab of **Asteroid Belt** to the top. 60'
FA 1977, Geoff Smith, Gary Allan, Dave Hough

End of Yando Wall

75 Pinnacle of Success (aka Perseverance) 5.10a G 100' ★★★

RPs are needed for the described finish. Alternatively, it is possible to continue up the left-facing corner to the top.
Start: Below a left-leaning crack at the base of **Jackal**.
P1 5.10a G: Climb the left-leaning crack to a vertical crack (crux) and follow it up into a left-facing corner. Up the corner until you are just below the top, then step out right to a wide crack and climb up onto the top of a small pinnacle. Finish up low-angle friction steps. 100'
FA Sep, 1989, Ken Nichols

*Joe Szot on **Jackal** (5.10c), belayed by Will Mayo.*

76 Jackal 5.10c PG 100' ★★★★

First climbed by Nichols thinking he was on **Atlantis**; pretty stiff for 5.9, eh?

Start: Climbs the leftmost of two left-facing dihedrals. Begin on the left end of a boulder ledge (the same ledge from which **Atlantis** and **Connoisseur** start) below the dihedral.

P1 5.10c PG: Climb up the dihedral to a sloping stance. Follow the dihedral through a broken section with sustained climbing to the top. 100'

FA Jul, 1989, Jack Wenzel, Ken Nichols

77 Devotee 5.11d G 70' ★★

Start: Climbs the rightmost of two left-facing dihedrals. Begin in the center of the boulder ledge (the same ledge from which **Atlantis** and **Connoisseur** start) below the dihedral.

P1 5.11d G: Up the dihedral, past an overlap on the left side, to a fixed anchor on the face above. 70'

FA 1996, Tim Beaman, June Mendel

78 Connoisseur (aka Tommy's Climb) 5.11c PG 100' ★★★★

Start: On a boulder ledge, 3' left of the left-facing corner of **Atlantis**, at a shallow 4'-high left-facing edge below a thin seam.

P1 5.11c PG: Climb the face via good square cuts and follow the thin seam past pitons to a left-facing corner. Up the corner (which veers off to the right) to another shallow left-facing corner, then move left past a bolt (crux) to get established in the handcrack. Climb the handcrack through a bulge to the top. 100'

FA Jun 28, 1997, Tim Beaman, Dennis Luther

79 Atlantis 5.9 G 100'

The final corner is dirty and often wet.

Start: At the right end of a boulder ledge below a large left-facing corner, offset near the top, with a handcrack.

P1 5.9 G: Follow the corner to a sloping ledge that leads out right to the final, slightly overhanging V-corner. 100'

FA 1976, Geoff Smith, Gary Allan

80 Darkest Africa 5.11a G 100' ★★★

The **Atlantis** finish corner is horrible, but the **Trilogy** variation, which breaks onto the right wall at the top, is recommended.

Start: At the left end of the sheer wall with **Bitter End**, at 5'-high blocks stacked tightly up against the face, above which is a shallow left-facing corner, 5' right of the left-facing corner of **Atlantis**.

P1 5.11a G: Work up some tiny overhanging cracks and left-facing corners to a larger left-facing corner that leads straight up to a ledge. (V1) Climb the final left-facing corner to the top (same as **Atlantis**). 100'

V1 Trilogy 5.11a G: This variation avoids the super-wet final corner of **Atlantis**. From the ledge, climb out onto the right wall past a small overlap and into a right-leaning crack that leads to the arête. Around the arête to a slab that leads to the top.

FA Oct, 1989, Ken Nichols

FA (V1) Jun 5, 1999, Dennis Luther

81 Bitter End (aka Fear of Frogs) 5.12a G 60' ★★★★

An amazing crack to a fixed anchor in the middle of the wall. Hasn't yet been linked to the upper crack systems.

Start: At some boulders at the base of a relentlessly overhanging crack, 150' right of the Yando Wall and 30' left of a large, 30'-high left-facing corner. The crack breaks an otherwise sheer wall 618674,4917690.

P1 5.12a G: Climb to the top of the crack, which ends at a fixed anchor on the short, black face. 60'

FA Oct, 1987, Ken Nichols

82 Poodles Are Just Like Little Sheep 5.7 G 40'

Manky! Better off as the winter route **Hold the Mayo**.

Start: 15' right of **Bitter End** in a right-facing corner that forms a 30'-high triangular alcove with a larger left-facing corner. There is a chockstone 15' up.

P1 5.7 G: Climb up the right-facing, right-leaning corner to the apex, where it meets the larger left-facing corner. Step out and right to a ledge. 40'

History: Only the first names of the first ascentionists are known.

FA Sep 7, 1992, Jim, Rob

Poke-O Moonshine • Upper Tiers

THE LUNAR WALL

Aspect	Southeast
Height	100'
Quality	★
Approach	25 min, moderate
Summary	Small section of cliff very near the trail with several difficult routes; nothing easy here.

-5.6	5.7	5.8	5.9	5.10	5.11	5.12	5.13+	total
				5	1			6

The central features of the cliff are the high orange right-facing corner (the route **Cosmic Arrest**) and the slab that leans up against the cliff under which you can walk (which marks the starts of **Teamwork** and **V for Victory**). Right of this is a broken area, often wet, where the cliff bends to the right into the Sun Wall.

DIRECTIONS **(MAP PAGE 30)**

From the Viewpoint, continue on the Ranger's Trail uphill another 12 min. The trail begins to parallel a cliff on the right, which you can see through the trees. There are two abandoned telephone poles, the first on the left and the second on the right and marked with a trail marker. From the second pole, contour right 100' to the base of the cliff 618561,4917385 and meet it near **Crossfire**, about 25 min from the trailhead.

*Ken Nichols on the first ascent of **Smoke Signal** (5.11c). Photo by Mark Meschinelli.*

83 Snowballing 5.10a PG 30'

This route's only significance is that it was done early.

Start: This is the first climbable rock starting at the left end of the cliff, and about 300' left of **Crossfire**. It begins at parallel cracks below the left end of a low roof 15' up.

P1 5.10a PG: Climb the parallel cracks to a large horizontal, then up a single crack that disappears just shy of the top. 30'

FA Apr, 1976, Patrick Munn, Geoff Smith

84 Crossfire 5.10b G 100' ★★★

Start: Below the left end of a high roof (the right side of this roof system forms the bulge through which **Smoke Signal** climbs).

P1 5.10b G: Climb up onto a slab with an obvious flake. Move right to the first bolt, gain a crack that climbs to a left-facing scoop, then move up to another left-facing scoop. Over the overlap to the roof at a left-facing corner. Climb up the corner to gain the main roof, around this to the left, and up the left-facing corner to a grassy ledge. Rappel from trees 50' to the right. 100'

FA 2002, Mark Meschinelli, Patrick Munn

85 Smoke Signal 5.11c G 100'

Start: 50' left of the **Cosmic Arrest** orange right-facing corner and 30' right of **Crossfire**, at a straight-in crack, just left of a left-facing corner capped by a small ceiling.

P1 5.11c G: Up the crack through the bulge to a stance, then along a flared fingercrack through black rock (crux) to the top. 100'

History: Cleaned by Geoff Smith; scooped by Nichols.

FA Sep 22, 1984, Ken Nichols

86 Cosmic Arrest 5.10d G 100' ★★

Climbs the prominent right-facing orange dihedral capped by a roof.

Start: In a shallow right-facing chimney formed by a large 15'-high flake that leans up against the face. The flake is positioned directly below the right-facing, right-leaning orange dihedral with a black roof on the right wall at midheight.

P1 5.10d G: Climb up the flake into the orange corner. Use the crack in the left wall to gain the black roof at midheight. Continue up thin fingers in the corner to the triangular roof at the top of the corner. Hand-traverse out left to the top. 100'

FA Aug 26, 1987, Ken Nichols

87 Teamwork 5.10a R 100'

Start: 40' right of the orange corner of **Cosmic Arrest**, on top of the slab that leans up against the face (under which you can walk), below a series of shallow, steep left-facing corners in black rock.

P1 5.10a R: Up the first left-facing corner to a ledge at the top. Move left into the next left-facing corner and follow it to a ledge on the right. Up and right on blocky rock to an open book. Climb the right wall of the open book via a fingercrack to the top. 100'

FA Aug 16, 1987, Bruce Jelen, Ken Nichols

POKE-O MOONSHINE: LUNAR WALL
84 Crossfire (5.10b)
85 Smoke Signal (5.11c)
86 Cosmic Arrest (5.10d)
87 Teamwork (5.10a)
88 V for Victory (5.10c)
veggie island
black streak
narrow dike
black band
big flake
wide
To hiking trail
slot
alcove
orange strips
orange strip
slab
walk under
To Sun Wall

88 V for Victory 5.10c G 100'

Start: 10' right of **Teamwork**, on the ground beneath the slab that leans up against the face (**Teamwork** begins on top of the slab), at a right-facing slot.

P1 5.10c G: Climb up the slot, then up a crack to a right-facing corner, the right wall of which is covered with orange lichen. Follow the corner as it angles right to an awkward right-facing slot finish at the top. 100'

FA Sep 16, 1987, Ken Nichols, Bruce Jelen

Poke-O Moonshine • Upper Tiers

THE SUN WALL

Aspect	South
Height	100'
Quality	★
Approach	30 min, moderate
Summary	Known for the three parallel cracklines near **Octoberfist**.

-5.6	5.7	5.8	5.9	5.10	5.11	5.12	5.13+	total
			1	3	1			5

A short section of wall with three parallel cracks that each lean right, on a gently sloped hillside with open forest.

DIRECTIONS **(MAP PAGE 30)**

Walk right from the Lunar Wall to where the cliff bends to the right (the black wall straight ahead is **Black Crack**). Continue along the base of the cliff, uphill to the height of land, then downhill to the three cracks (**Octoberfist**, **Foam Flower**, and **Eastman-Kodak Crack**).

The cliff can also be approached from the Headwall: from the base of **Fear of Gravity**, walk downhill, scramble down a slab, then angle (skier's) right to the top of the Sun Wall; walk downhill until you can scramble down onto the slab at the end of the wall; walk uphill along the base of the wall to **Lazy Crack** and the other routes 618648,4917450.

89 Black Crack 5.11a G 100'

Start: At the obvious crack on the black wall, on the left side of the black streak, 100' right of the slab that leans up against the cliff (under which you can walk).

P1 5.11a G: Follow the crack, angling right at about half height, to a ledge. (V1) Above is an overlap with a right-leaning handcrack (5.8). 100'

V1 5.6 G: You can also traverse off right on the ledge, which is how the route was originally climbed.

FA (direct finish) Oct, 1988, Ken Nichols, Chuck Boyd
FA (V1) Sep 16, 1987, Ken Nichols

90 Octoberfist 5.10c G 75' ★★

This is the leftmost of three parallel cracks that lean right.

Start: At the right end of a bulging ceiling 6' up.

P1 5.10c G: Climb the crack past the ceiling and into a wide section, then back to hand size and on to the top. 75'

FA 1977, Mark Meschinelli

91 Foam Flower 5.10d G 75' ★

This is the middle of three parallel cracks that lean right.

Start: 15' right of **Octoberfist** at a left-facing open book with a crack in the back. On the left wall of the open book is a zigzagging horizontal overlapping flake.

P1 5.10d G: Climb the crack with increasing difficulty to the top. 75'

FA Jun, 1985, Don Mellor, Mark Meschinelli

92 Eastman-Kodak Crack 5.10b G 75' ★

Start: 5' right of **Foam Flower** at a crack that begins on top of a sloped shelf.

P1 5.10b/c G: Climb the strenuous off-width crack to a bushy thrash finish. 75'

Gear: To 5".

FA Oct, 1984, Ken Nichols, Todd Eastman

93 Lazy Crack 5.9 R 30'

Start: At the right end of the Sun Wall is a slab. Begin at the left end of the slab below a crack in the wall above the slab.

P1 5.9 R: Up the slab, then make unprotected moves to gain the crack. Up the crack to the thicket of weeds at the top. 30'

FA Sep 16, 1987, Ken Nichols, Mike Barker

Andy Zimmerman on ***Octoberfist*** *(5.10c). Photo by Don Mellor.*

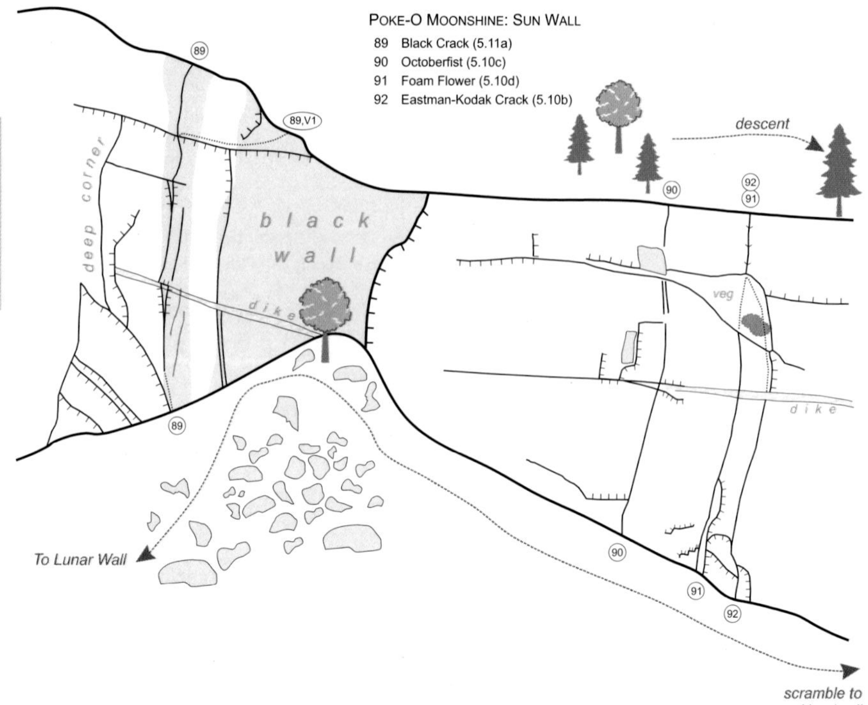

Poke-O Moonshine • Upper Tiers

SECOND TIER

Aspect	Southeast
Height	100'
Quality	★★
Approach	20 min, easy
Summary	Single-pitch cragging with two excellent routes and the potential for more.

-5.6	5.7	5.8	5.9	5.10	5.11	5.12	5.13+	total
1	2	3	5		1	1		13

This area is the second tier above the Main Face. If you walk off any full-length routes right of **The FM**, you'll walk directly under this cliffband. There is an intermediate cliff just below this—the First Tier—accessed by taking a hard right at the top of the descent gully; there are no reported routes, although there is some potential.

On the left end of the Second Tier is **Handcrack Boulder**, a small buttress with an attractive handcrack. 140' right is **Christmas Gully**, a winter route, just left of some wide roofs. On the right end of these wide roofs and 150' right of **Christmas Gully** is a left-facing corner with the routes **Bee's Knees** and **Pollen Junkies**. Just right is a gigantic, fern-covered boulder (the Separate Denialty Boulder) in a large right-facing corner; **Spider Biter**, **Patent Proof Roof** and **Separate Denialty** begin behind this boulder. Above the huge boulder are more large roofs, each higher than the preceding one as you move right. Right of this is a left-facing corner (the start of the excellent **Black Market**).

Further right still is the Heart of Gold Buttress with the distinctive deep chimney on the outside face, the only chimney on the wall.

DIRECTIONS **(MAP PAGE 30)**

Walk up the descent gully right of the Waterfall. At the top of the gully, head straight up to find **Handcrack Boulder**, a small buttress with a perfect 5.8 handcrack, and about 15 min from the car. **Handcrack Boulder** is at the extreme left end of this tier; walk right (past the winter route **Christmas Gully**) to find the other routes 619072,4918023.

Black Market Wall

This wall extends from **Handcrack Boulder** on the left, past the Separate Denialty Boulder to the route **Black Market**.

DESCENT OPTIONS

Rappel from trees.

94 Handcrack Boulder 5.8 G 25' ★★

This is the "handcrack boulder" used as a locator for the winter route **Christmas Gully**, 140' to the right.

Start: At a small left-facing corner with a perfect handcrack.

P1 5.8 G: Climb the crack to the top. 25'

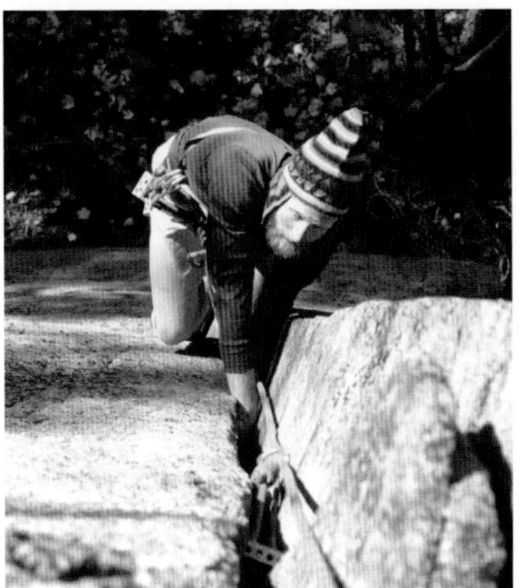

*Todd Eastman on **Handcrack Boulder** (5.8). Photo by Jim Cunningham.*

95 Bee's Knees 5.9 G 40' ★★

Tremendously fun.

Start: 15' left of **Pollen Junkies** at a crack in a left-facing corner capped by a large roof. This is just left of a black ramp–slab.

P1 5.9 G: Climb the short slab to gain the corner crack. Stem and jam the crack to the base of the roof (#4). Follow the crack through the roof (heel hook, lie back, and enjoy) and up to a fixed anchor on a tree. 40'

Gear: Small rack up to 1.5", plus a #4 Camalot for the roof.

FA Sep, 2012, James DeBella, Eric Bretthauer

96 Pollen Junkies 5.8 G 110'

Start: 20' downhill and left of the Separate Denialty Boulder at a 6'-long left-rising ramp that begins 2' up and ends at a handcrack with a pine tree 30' up.

P1 5.8 G: Jam the crack past the tree. The crack widens to 4"; at its top, move right across a slab and go up a fingercrack to its top. Step right and climb another fingercrack. Move right over bulges to a fixed anchor on a pine tree. 110'

Descent: Belay on top with a 60m rope, as there is insufficient rope to lower a leader. You can, however, rappel with a 60m rope.

Gear: Up to 4".

FA Sep, 2012, James DeBella, Eric Bretthauer

97 Spider Biter 5.8 G 80' ★★★

Some impressive terrain here.

Start: 40' right of **Pollen Junkies** and behind the Separate Denialty Boulder is a huge right-facing corner capped by large roofs. Begin on the left wall of the giant corner at a fingercrack that splits a 12'-wide ceiling 8' up.

P1 5.8 G: Climb the fingercrack to the left end of the huge roof, then up into a flared, overhanging corner (the "Harding Slot") to a roof (#00 TCU). Traverse left to the arête, then up to a good shelf with a fixed anchor on a pine tree. 80'

Gear: Standard rack up to 2". Double 1.5" helpful.

FA Sep, 2012, James DeBella, Eric Bretthauer

98 Patent-Proof Roof 5.11b PG 90'

Start: Same as **Separate Denialty**.

P1 5.11b PG: Climb up to the roof of **Separate Denialty**, traverse right and up into a right-facing corner to the next roof, then out the roof via a good crack up to a pine tree. 90'

FA Jun 29, 1987, Patrick Purcell, Bill Dodd

99 Separate Denialty 5.12c TR 100'

The route begins behind the Separate Denialty Boulder on a slab 4' right of the large right-facing corner. Climb scoops on the mossy slab to the 8' roof. Traverse right under the roof to a left-facing offset under the roof. Climb out the offset to a handcrack at the lip, then up the face to the top.

FA (TR) Jun 29, 1987, Patrick Purcell

100 Black Market 5.9+ G 100' ★★★★

Exciting traversing in a bomber handcrack.

Start: Locate the Separate Denialty Boulder. Behind this is a large roof that arches up and right to a point and meets another left-arching roof, almost touching it at the apex. Begin in the left-facing corner below the right end of the left-arching roof, 100' right of the Separate Denialty Boulder.

P1 5.9+ G: Climb up the left-facing corner to the roof, then traverse left (past a scary meat-cleaver flake, which you can pass without disturbing it) on good footholds to a crunched sloped stance. Continue traversing left in a good 3" crack above a smooth wall to a welcome sloped stance at the pointed end of the right-arching roof. Step up onto the point, then up left on an easy slab and slippery pine needles to a large pine tree. 100'

Gear: Standard rack plus 2 ea 3".

FA 1974, Ski to Die Club

*Jim Lawyer on the scrunched traverse of **Black Market** (5.9+). Photo by Leslie Ackerman.*

Heart of Gold Buttress

From the Black Market Wall, walk right 100' through a short section of large talus blocks to the base of a buttress with a chimney on the outside face; this is the route **Heart of Gold**. The most distinguishing feature is a huge 12'-high block that leans up against the cliff just right of the **Heart of Gold** chimney, a block that you can walk (or camp) under.

About halfway up the **Heart of Gold** chimney on the right is a large roof, visible from the road. On the left side of the buttress is a gold-colored left-facing wall with the routes **Gold Wall** and **After the Gold Rush**. The large corner formed by the left side of the buttress is the route **Homegrown**.

HISTORY

The routes here were climbed by the Ski to Die Club—Geoff Smith, Patrick Munn, and Dave Hough—in the 1970s. Nobody recalls who led what.

DESCENT OPTIONS

There is a fixed anchor 30' left of the Heart of Gold Buttress where an 80' rappel returns you to the ground.

101 Journey through the Past 5.1 G 70' ★★

Secure climbing on an exposed ramp. Can be used as a downclimb.

Start: 50' left of the Heart of Gold Buttress is a ledge gained from the right side. The route begins on the left end of this ledge.

P1 5.1 G: Follow the low-angle ramp up and left to the top. 70'

History: The first ascent isn't known, but old pitons (probably-1950s vintage) were found here in the 1970s.

102 Homegrown 5.9- G (5.5 R) 100' ★

Good layback and jamming moves and with good protection, but the rock is questionable.

Start: At the left-facing corner that forms the left side of the Heart of Gold Buttress.

P1 5.9- G (5.5 R): Climb up unprotected ledges and bulges to the slab, then follow it to the base of the main corner. Layback and jam up the corner to the top. 100'

Gear: To 3".

FA 1974, Ski to Die Club

103 Gold Wall 5.7 G (5.5 R) 100' ★

The main route has some loose, exciting blocks. The variation is recommended and has excellent jamming on an overhanging gold wall.

Start: At the left-facing corner that forms the left side of the Heart of Gold Buttress, at the base of a chimney.

P1 5.7 G (5.5 R): Climb up unprotected ledges and bulges to a square roof in the right wall. (V1) Climb out the left side of the roof into a block-filled crack and chimney in a corner and on to the top. 100'

V1 After the Gold Rush 5.9+ G (5.5 R) ★★: Move right from the square roof onto a ledge. Step right on the ledge to a left-arching crack (there is an old fixed anchor at the base of this crack). Up the crack (crux), then back right on good holds to the arête. Step right around the arête and climb an easy crack and ledge up and left through a leafy garden of lichen to the top.

FA 1974, Ski to Die Club

104 On the Beach 5.9+ G 100'

Climbs cracks in the front face of the Heart of Gold Buttress; extremely dirty.

Start: Same as **Heart of Gold**.

P1 5.9+ G: Climb the chimney a few feet to the orange block, then up the crack on the left side of the block to the overhang. Out the overhang on its left side and into the thin crack above. Up the crack to a horizontal, then left a few feet to a wide crack and follow it to the top. 100'

FA 1974, Ski to Die Club

*Tom Yandon on **After the Gold Rush** (5.9+).*

*Leslie Ackerman on **Heart of Gold** (5.7). Soloing this route was a rite of passage of the Ski to Die Club.*

105 **Heart of Gold 5.7 PG 100'** ★★★

This historic route climbs a deep chimney, the only one on the Second Tier. If you like chimney climbs, this one is spectacular for its grade. Soloing this route was once considered a rite of passage in the Ski to Die Club.

Start: Leaning up against the cliff at the base of the deep chimney is a block that you can walk (or camp) under. The route begins just left of that block.

P1 5.7 PG: Climb into the alcove (crux) and up the crack, which narrows to hand size, then into the chimney above. Up the chimney to a large roof (there is an old fixed anchor here). (V1) Work into the deep squeeze chimney using good edges on the left wall, then out to the mouth of the chimney and climb the two edges of the opening to the top. 100'

V1 Tempest 5.8 G: Move right under the roof around a jammed block and left-facing corner to a handcrack that rises from a triangular alcove. Climb the handcrack to the top. Very dirty.

Gear: To 2".

FA 1974, Ski to Die Club

106 **Harvest 5.9 PG 100'** ★

Some clean, interesting climbing down low with a dirty finish.

Start: 5' right of the leaning block (under which you can walk), at a crack in black rock, 2' left of a shallow left-facing corner.

P1 5.9 PG: Climb the crack to a left-facing corner capped by an overlap on the left wall. Up the crack through the overlap and to a sloped ledge. Continue up the crack in a shallow left-facing corner to the top. 100'

FA 1974, Ski to Die Club

Poke-O Moonshine • Upper Tiers

THIRD TIER

Aspect	East and southeast
Height	200'
Quality	★★
Approach	30 min, moderate
Summary	The highest band of rock above the Main Face with remote, high-quality trad routes; good potential for new routes.

-5.6	5.7	5.8	5.9	5.10	5.11	5.12	5.13+	total
		3	2	1				6

On the left side of the cliff at the lowest point of the terrain is a wide, low roof that forms a 20'-deep cave. Most of the established routes are located right of this cave. The cliff is split horizontally by an inaccessible ledge 100' up. The left end of this ledge is narrow, but to the right it becomes very deep, so deep in fact that the cliff above it is referred to as the Fourth Tier.

On the left side of the cliff is a giant, overhanging buttress cleaved in the middle to form a giant open book corner; P2 of **Rearview Mirror** ascends this feature. The left half of the buttress is especially distinctive, as it forms a left-leaning, left-facing corner, an old route reportedly in the 5.8 range.

The base of the cliff is relatively level and pleasant, and it's easy to locate the routes. The top is open with sections of flat, open rock and good views of Lake Champlain and into Vermont.

DIRECTIONS **(MAP PAGE 30)**

Walk up the descent gully right of the Waterfall. At the top of the gully, head straight up to find **Handcrack Boulder**, a small buttress with a perfect 5.8 handcrack, and about 15 min from the car. Walk up the left side of this short cliffband and up to another short cliffband with a very large, communal cave with a fire ring. Continue up the left side of this cliff through a low-angle chimney. At its top, continue walking uphill through open woods. Stay right of the large boulders and continue uphill to the cliff 0618813,4918000, about 10 min from the Second Tier, or 30 min from the car.

HISTORY

Not much is known about the early climbing here other than the large corner—**Old Route**—which was climbed in the late 1970s by Geoff Smith and Dave Hough. The cliff lay dormant until the 2008 explorations by Ken Nichols and Mark Bealor.

107 **Old Route 5.8 G 100'**

This route climbs the giant, left-leaning corner formed by the left side of the overhanging buttress 100' up. It's an amazing-looking feature, but it's dirty and has loose rock. From the base, walk left until you can scramble up ledges. Eventually you'll have to rope up to reach the horizontal ledge that splits the cliff. From here you can access this corner.

FA 1974, Geoff Smith, Dave Hough

108 Rearview Mirror 5.9 G (5.7 R) 150' ★★★
This route is located on the right side of a buttress, the left side of which is the huge left-facing corner of **Old Route**. A sub-par first pitch and good second pitch.
Start: 70' right (and slightly uphill) from the cave, at a large, left-leaning open book and below a towering prow of rock 80' up.
P1 5.4 R: Follow the shallow open book up left past a small white birch to a slab. Step up left onto the slab (5.7 R) and up to a deep horizontal below a towering prow of rock. Traverse 20' left to a large blueberry-covered ledge. 75'
P2 5.9 G: Follow an offwidth crack (crux) on the left side of stacked blocks to a ledge formed by the blocks. Finish up a jamcrack in the huge open book above. 75'
Gear: Standard rack plus some large cams.
History: Bealor just moved to the area, having left the Shawangunks behind in his rearview mirror.
FA Oct, 2008, Mark Bealor, Ken Nichols

109 Hand Therapy 5.8- PG 75' ★★
Harder for short climbers or those with small hands.
Start: 25' right of **Rearview Mirror** at short left-leaning cracks below an open book corner system in black rock. This is the left side of a large, triangular black slab, the top of which points up the open book corner.
P1 5.8- PG: Climb the cracks and corner system, then up a 4"-wide slot and finger crack to the top. 75'
FA Oct, 2008, Ken Nichols, Mark Bealor

110 Autumn Gold 5.9 PG 90' ★★★
Start: 100' right of **Hand Therapy** is a gigantic, spectacular, horizontal block 20' up, the left side of which forms a point. Begin below an undulating 3'-deep left-facing left-leaning corner, 35' right of a the block.
P1 5.9 PG: Up the undulating corner to a stance just right of a short right-facing corner. Angle up right into a right-facing V-corner (the left-hand of two corners), step left at the top of the corner, and pull over the top. 90'
FA Oct, 2008, Ken Nichols

111 Trick Move 5.10b G 90' ★★★
Start: At a slightly low-angle left-facing corner on the right end of a 20'-high black wall, 120 right of the **Autumn Gold** corner. There is a spruce tree above the left end of the black wall, 30' up.
P1 5.10b G: Up the corner to the first ledge, which is just below a broad ledge running to the left. Move up right onto the huge ledge at the base of a large left-facing corner. Follow the corner (3.5" Friend useful) to the top. 90'
FA Oct, 2008, Ken Nichols

112 Maiden Voyage 5.8+ G 90' ★★
Probably PG for shorter climbers.
Start: At a large left-facing, stepped corner with a 20'-high yellow spot on the right wall, 30' right of the **Trick Move** corner.
P1 5.8+ G: Follow the corner and crack that diverges left to a large ledge. Step out right and finish up a short jamcrack. 90'
FA Oct, 2008, Mark Bealor, Michelle Sirois, Ken Nichols

Poke-O Moonshine • Upper Tiers

FOURTH TIER

Aspect	East
Height	70'
Quality	★★
Approach	1 hr, difficult
Summary	A difficult-to-access cliff rising immediately above the Third Tier with several remote, good-quality trad routes; good potential for new routes.

-5.6	5.7	5.8	5.9	5.10	5.11	5.12	5.13+	total
1	1	1		2	1			6

As you move right along the base of the Third Tier, just right of **Rearview Mirror**, the cliff splits, forming a fourth tier. A tree ledge up to 80' deep separates the two tiers. There is potential for more routes, and the rock is generally clean.

DIRECTIONS **(MAP PAGE 30)**
The easiest and fastest way to access the ledge at the base of the Fourth Tier is to climb a route on the Third Tier. If you climb **Hand Therapy**, you arrive at the base of **Rockhound** and **Poke-O Pup** 0618852,4918049. It is possible, but not recommended, to walk right (beyond **Perfect Pitch**) and climb scary 5th class grunge to access the ledge. You can also walk left along the base, past the winter route **Run For Your Life** to a narrow notch that separates the Third Tier from the Headwall. Up this, then walk right across the top of the Fourth Tier until you can easily walk down onto the broad ledge at the base of the Fourth Tier. It's a long walk.

113 Rockhound 5.6 G 35' ★
Start: 30' uphill and right from the left end of the ledge where the Third Tier and Fourth Tier merge, at a right-facing, black open book on the left side of a short, black, water-stained wall.
P1 5.6 G: Up the corner, exit left near the top. 35'
FA Oct, 2008, Ken Nichols, Mark Bealor

114 Poke-O Pup 5.8 G 35' ★
Harder for short climbers.
Start: At a shallow right-facing corner below some vertical cracks in the black water-stained wall, 6' right of the **Rockhound** corner.
P1 5.8 G: Follow the corners and cracks to the top. 35'
History: Named for Bealor's dog, a stray found wandering below the Main Face of Poke-O.
FA Oct, 2008, Mark Bealor, Ken Nichols

115 Defiant Eyes 5.11d PG 40' ★★
The runout through the crux is above bomber nuts.
Start: At a vertical crack 20' right of **Poke-O Pup**. 7' up the crack leans left in a very shallow left-facing corner.
P1 5.11d PG: Climb the crack and a small left-facing corner, then up the face to a right-leaning, right-facing open book. Stretch up left to the arête and pull over the top. 40'
FA Oct, 2008, Ken Nichols

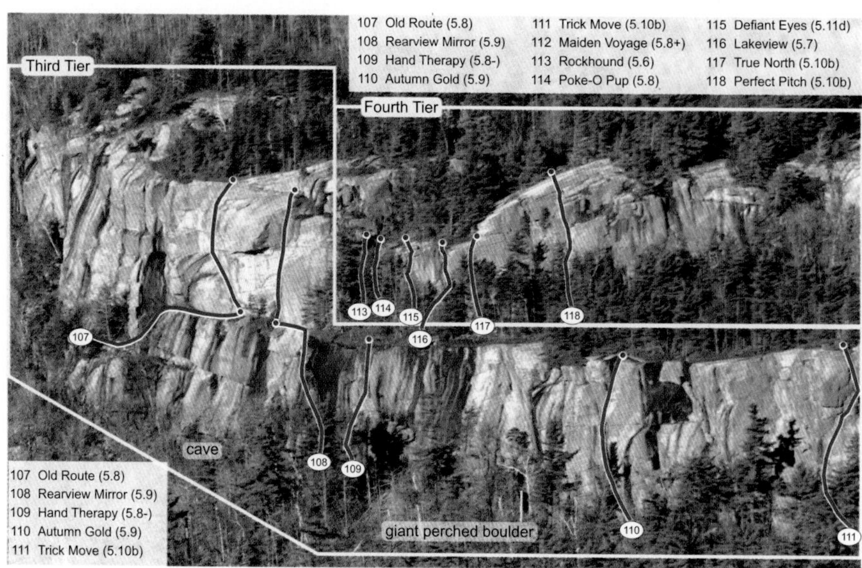

116 Lakeview 5.7 G 50' ★

Great views of Lake Champlain.

Start: 60' right of **Rockhound** is a large open book corner, the base of which has a boulder and perched triangular flake. Begin on the left side of the boulder at a left-facing crack.

P1 5.7 G: Up the crack to the ledge, pull up onto the perched flake, then follow a large open book to the top. 50'

FA Oct, 2008, Ken Nichols, Mark Bealor

117 True North 5.10b G 60' ★★★

Continually interesting and beautiful to look at. Requires skills in placing small nuts. Named for a book by Jim Harrison.

Start: At a thin crack below an attractive 5"-deep left-facing corner that curves up the face, 8' right of a prominent arête and 50' right of the **Lakeview** crack.

P1 5.10b G: Climb the crack and follow the corner up right to the top. 60'

Gear: Two #6 Crack'n Ups (hook-like pitons by Black Diamond) were used on the first ascent.

FA Oct, 2008, Mark Bealor, Ken Nichols

118 Perfect Pitch 5.10b G 70' ★★★★

Named for the aesthetic quality of this stunning corner.

Start: At a left-facing crack in an open book with a short offwidth section 15' up, 80' right of the prominent arête (the arête that is 8' left of **True North**).

P1 5.10b G: Up the corner until just below the top. Finish up a short vertical crack to the left. 70'

FA Oct, 2008, Ken Nichols, Mark Bealor

Poke-O Moonshine

WEST SIDE

Location	West side of Poke-O Moonshine Mountain, accessed from the Observer's Trail.
Summary	More single-pitch, largely unexplored cliffs with good potential for new routes.

-5.6	5.7	5.8	5.9	5.10	5.11	5.12	5.13+	total
1			1	2				4

Several small cliffs have been explored on the west side of Poke-O Moonshine, accessed from the Observer's Trail—a new trail that provides a more gradual and longer approach to the summit of Poke-O Moonshine Mountain. There are only a few routes so far and plenty of room for those willing to make a somewhat long approach.

DIRECTIONS **(MAP PAGE 30)**

Parking for the Observer's Trail is from a the new parking area on the west side of US 9 0618881,4916189, 3.9 miles south of the intersection with NY 22 (at Northway Exit 33) and 8.2 miles north of the intersection with CR 12 in Lewis. This is 1 mile south of the (now closed) Poke-O Moonshine Campground. The hiking trail marked with blue discs begins on US 9, 300' south of the parking 0618838,4916048.

Poke-O Moonshine • West Side

CARL MOUNTAIN CIRQUE

Location	Between the summits of Poke-O Moonshine and Carl Mountain accessed from the Observer's Trail
Aspect	Southeast and southwest
Height	160'
Quality	
Approach	55 min, moderate
Summary	An impressive horseshoe-shaped valley ringed with walls up to 160' in height; only two routes reported so far.

-5.6	5.7	5.8	5.9	5.10	5.11	5.12	5.13+	total
1				1				2

The Carl Mountain Cirque is a horseshoe-shaped valley located on the east-west ridge between Poke-O Moonshine and Carl Mountain. The Cirque is tucked in behind Deerfield Mountain, which makes it invisible from the valley and shields it from the road noise that plagues the other cliffs at Poke-O. The terrain around the rim of the Cirque has a distinctly alpine feel, enhanced by the quiet and isolation of the location.

The Cirque is ringed with walls up to 160' high, although most are smaller. The initial impression is of an undiscovered country. Closer inspection reveals many possibilities, but not quite the Mecca that one would hope. The southeast-facing wall of the Cirque is the largest; it's sheer with several clean sections but offers no obvious lines of ascent. The southwest-facing wall is broken into sections. The leftmost section has large orange roofs and corners, the location of **Dutchman's Britches**. To the right is a large left-facing, left-leaning black corner, the route **Chocolate Rain**. There are more cliffs to the right, but one of the more interesting cliffs is tucked down into the woods to the right, a severely overhanging cliff of roofs and smooth walls . . . and no routes yet.

There's a lot of exploration to do here. From various vantage points, you can see over an intervening ridge to the summit cliffs of Carl Mountain. Most of these look bushy and uninteresting, but there is a promising sheer wall directly below the summit.

HISTORY

The first known to have visited the Cirque were Patrick Purcell, Tim Beaman, and Sylvia Lazarnick, who climbed **Dutchman's Britches**. Many local climbers have wandered here, but nobody else climbed here until one of the authors during his reconnaissance to find the Purcell-Beaman-Lazarnick route. Not much has happened here until 2014; expect some cool routes here soon.

DIRECTIONS (MAP PAGE 30)

Follow the Observer's Trail to a wooden bridge 0617802,4917017 at 40 min. Continue steeply uphill to a sharp right turn to the east at 50 min; there is a stream on the left with a cairn 617731,4917534. Leave the trail here and follow the stream and marshy depression north to meet a small south-facing cliff at 50 min. Turn left on a bearing of 285° to reach the rim of the Cirque at 55 min 617420,4917620.

Wander along the rim of the Cirque until you find a flat rock ledge with a deep crack in the floor that runs parallel to the cliff; this pretty vista is the top of **Chocolate Rain**. There is a large tree here where you can rappel to the base of the cliff with a single 60-m rope. Another option is to walk back into the woods and contour along the rim of the Cirque to its "head," where the southeast and southwest walls meet. There is a gully that can be descended with a short rappel, after which you can walk along the base of either wall.

1 Dutchman's Britches 5.10d G 90'

Start: This route is located on the left end of the southwest-facing cliff in the Cirque, near where the southwest and southeast walls meet at the head of the Cirque. The major feature in this section of rock is large orange roofs located above open talus, 250' left of the large left-facing, left-leaning corner of **Chocolate Rain**. 20' left of the roofs is a steep right-facing corner that runs the full height of the cliff. This route begins 10' left of this right-facing corner below a smaller 10'-high right-facing corner that begins 8' up.

P1 5.10d G: Climb up to a ledge at 8', then up the short right-facing corner and up a right-facing flake to an overlap on the right wall. Pass the overlap on its left side into a large open book with a fingercrack. Up the crack to a small triangular ceiling; over this on the right and up a crack to a ledge. Easier climbing leads over a short wall (either to the left or right) to the top. 90'

FA May 8, 1993, Patrick Purcell, Tim Beaman, Sylvia Lazarnick

2 Chocolate Rain 5.5 G 90' ★★

A relatively clean corner with an open base and a flat summit area with great views of the Cirque.

Start: One of the major features of the southwest-facing cliff is a 20'-deep left-facing, left-leaning corner. There is an open area beneath the corner with some comfortable rock ledges. You can also approach the climb from the top. At the top of the southwest face, find the open ledge with a deep crack in the floor that runs parallel to the cliff and 10' back from the edge; from below, this crack makes the tower seem detached. There is a large pine tree from which you can rappel to a forested terrace 95' below, then walk left 30' to the base of the corner.

P1 5.5 G: Scramble up and right to a cluster of birch trees at the base of the corner, then up the corner to a jammed block 15' up. Continue up the corner (crux) to a ledge where the crack turns into a chimney. Chimney up to the top of the detached tower. 90'

Gear: To 5".

FA Aug 17, 2007, Michelle Burlitch, Jim Lawyer

Poke-O Moonshine • West Side

BEAVER WALL

Location	On the west side of Poke-O Moonshine, accessed from the Observer's Trail
Aspect	Southwest
Height	90'
Quality	★
Approach	1 hr, moderate
Summary	Backcountry cliff accessed by a new hiking trail with two trad routes so far.

-5.6	5.7	5.8	5.9	5.10	5.11	5.12	5.13+	total
			1	1				2

DESCRIPTION

This is a sunny cliffband with clean rock and decent route potential. It has a somewhat long approach, but it's just off a good, well-graded trail, and in a pleasant spot overlooking a beaver pond. A primary feature is a chimney in a deep, right-facing corner, 150' from the left end of the cliff. The left-hand wall of the corner is black-streaked and gently overhanging. The vertical main wall extends 150' to the right of the chimney.

DIRECTIONS (MAP PAGE 30)

Follow the Observer's Trail to a wooden bridge 0617802,4917017 at 40 min. Continue steeply uphill to a sharp right turn to the east at 50 min; this is where you leave for the Carl Mountain Cirque. Continue on the trail to a level section next to a beaver pond. The Beaver Wall faces the trail and is on the opposite side of the beaver pond. Leave the trail before the pond 0617814,4917519 and go around the left (west) side of the pond to reach the slabby left side of the Beaver Wall 0617925,4917536 at 1 hr.

DESCENT OPTIONS

A 110' rappel can be made from the pine tree belay shared by **Beaver Fever** and **Glass Ceilings**.

HISTORY

Mark Meschinelli visited the cliff during his routine fitness runs up the trail to the summit. He returned with Leslie McCarthy to establish **Glass Ceilings**, her first new route. The routes here accompanied the new route spree at the Superman Wall on Poke-O Main Face.

1 Beaver Fever 5.10d G 110' ★★★

Start: 30' right of the chimney is a right-facing corner. Begin on the arête of the corner below a fingercrack that starts 8' up.

P1 5.10d G: Boulder up to the fingercrack on the right side of the arête. Follow the crack to its end, then move left around the arête to a lower-angled face. Go up a vertical crack, then go right to belay at a pine tree. 110'

FA Sep, 2013, Dominic Eisinger, Dave Hough

2 Glass Ceilings 5.9 G 110' ★★★

Climbs the right-facing corner with a deep, parallel-sided crack.

Start: 30' right of the chimney in a right-facing corner, just right of **Beaver Fever**.

P1 5.9 G: Climb a fingercrack that widens to 4" at a ceiling 20' up. Pull over the ceiling and follow the corner to a second ceiling where the crack narrows to hand-size. Stem out left with good feet and climb easier rock to the pine tree belay shared with **Beaver Fever**. 110'

Gear: doubles to 5"

FA Sep, 2013, Mark Meschinelli, Leslie McCarthy

PALISADES

Location	West shore of Lake Champlain, north of Westport
Aspect	Southeast
Height	200'
Quality	★★★
Approach	1 hr, moderate; boat optional
Summary	Dramatically exposed, but minimally explored, lakeside cliff with compact rock.

-5.6	5.7	5.8	5.9	5.10	5.11	5.12	5.13+	total
1		2	2					6

The Palisades is a 200' cliff that rises dramatically out of the deep waters of Lake Champlain, on the west shore north of Westport. It's located in the Split Rock Mountain Wild Forest, which has the longest section of publicly owned shoreline on Lake Champlain. The area has most recently gained popularity for its high-quality, but fickle, ice climbing. In the summer, it's known as the northernmost breeding site of the timber rattlesnake and for nesting peregrine falcons.

This cliff has seen limited exploration for rock climbing. Results thus far have revealed two routes, one of which is especially noteworthy. Given the cliff's large size and complexity, additional routes will surely be revealed in the future. The cliff is featured with large corners, overhanging faces, and dirty cracks. The rock is compact, offering excellent angular holds but little natural protection.

HISTORY

Climbers have explored the Palisades for years, as evidenced by the ancient, rotten gear found on some of the routes, but not much is known. The earliest known route is **Birthday Route**, by Herb George and his son. Ed Palen recognized the potential of this cliff; he climbed several ice routes and put in **Lake Champlain Monster**, perhaps the best route here. Tom Yandon has made several exploratory forays, one with Chris Hyson and another with Will Mayo that resulted in the line **For the Birds**. Others have explored as recently as 2012.

DIRECTIONS (MAP PAGE 142)

Two approaches are possible. The land approach is easy but anticlimactic, in that you rappel over the route you're about to climb. The water approach is more adventurous and recommended in the right conditions.

Land approach: Parking for the Palisades cliff is at the Split Rock Mountain Wild Forest Trailhead. From the intersection of NY 9N and NY 22 in Westport, drive north on NY 22 for 0.4 mile. Turn right onto Lake Shore Road

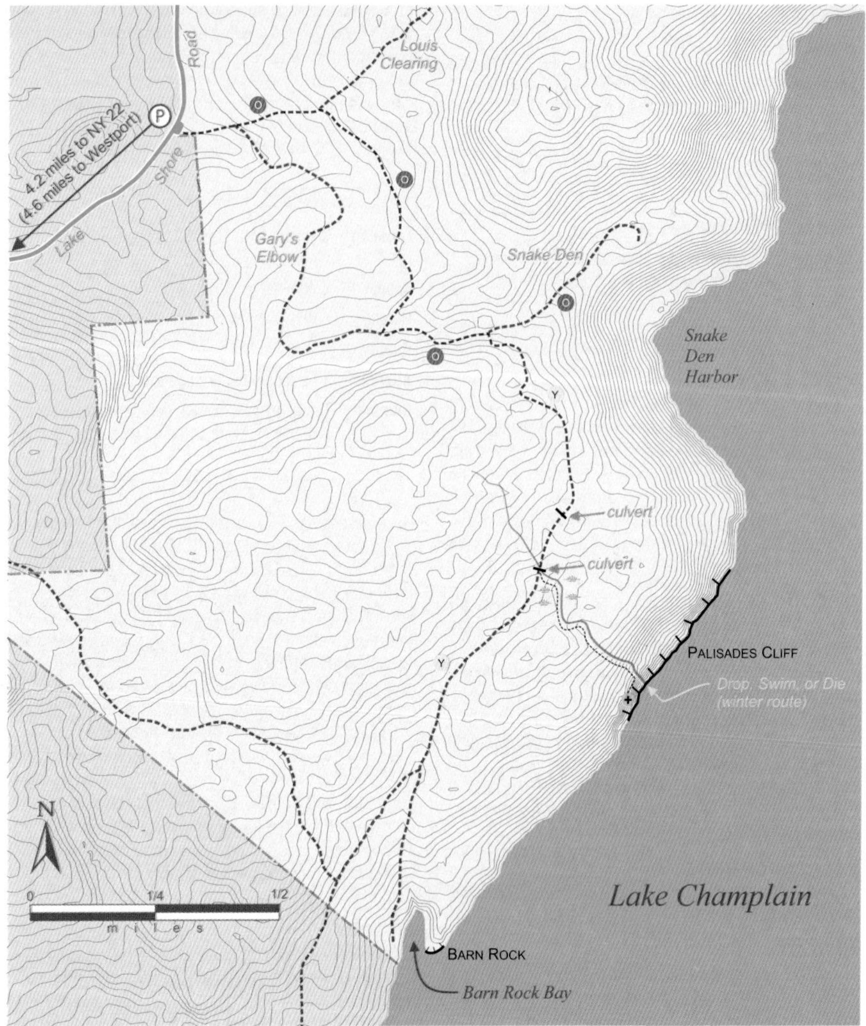

(CR 80) and drive 4.2 miles to the parking area on the right 629145,4899096.

Follow the hiking trail (marked with orange disks) from the parking lot. The trails aren't well marked, but they are heavily used and easy to follow. At 2 min, a lesser-used trail goes right; continue straight. At 6 min, the trail forks; take the right fork on orange markers, following the fork for Barn Rock and Snake Den. At 17 min, a trail merges in from the right; continue straight on orange markers. At 20 min, the trail forks: the left fork (marked with orange disks) goes to Snake Den, and the right fork (marked with yellow disks) goes to Barn Rock. Take the right fork for Barn Rock. The trail climbs to a height of land, then makes a long, gradual descent. When the trail levels, look for steel culverts; the first is generally dry, and the second feeds a marshy area. At the second culvert, head left on a bearing of 124° into a marsh. On the other side of the marshy area, follow a small stream, which eventually forms a 10'-deep ravine. Follow the ravine to the cliff. This stream forms the ice climb **Drop, Swim, or Die** and is the only place where a stream in a deep ravine meets the cliff 630632,4897393.

Water approach: The more adventurous may opt to approach in a boat. Be warned that the lake can be windy, with large waves; even in moderate conditions, the wave action at the base of the rock may prevent a landing. Check the Lake Champlain open waters forecast beforehand.

From the intersection of NY 9N and NY 22 in Westport, drive north on NY 22 for 0.3 mile to the boat launch on the right. Paddle north about 5 miles along the shoreline past Hunter Bay, Partridge Harbor,

Rock Harbor, and the sheltered Barn Rock Bay (campsites here). Continue along the shoreline to the cliffs.

You can also put in at Button Bay in Vermont. This is perhaps a bit shorter, but involves crossing the open water of Lake Champlain and can be challenging in a canoe. From the put-in, head toward Button Island, around the point, then north and cross the lake to the cliffs.

Jim Lawyer and Tom Yandon on Lake Champlain Monster (5.8). Photo by Lucie Wellner.

1 Lake Champlain Monster 5.8 G 170' ★★★★

A four-star route in a five-star location, and, as Tom Yandon put it, "5.8 climbing with a 5.9 feel." Clean rock, great moves, and exposed positions. The route follows the black rock under the ice climb of the same name.

Start: If you're approaching by land, from the ravine at the top of Drop, Swim, or Die, turn right (south) and follow the top of the cliff for 150' to a large cairn. Scramble down a 3rd-class section for 30' to a good ledge above a slab. There is a rappel tree on the (climber's) right end of the ledge. With a single rope, rappel 70' down the slab to the top of the vertical wall and find a fixed anchor. A second 100' rappel gains the fixed anchor near the right end of the large sloping ledge at the base of P1. If you're approaching by water, find the first large cliff that drops into the water. The large sloping ledge at the base of P1 can be seen from the boat. At its left end is a small rocky landing with a few trees where you can (barely) pull a canoe out of the water. Scramble up left, then step back right onto the ledge and traverse right 100' to a fixed anchor below P1.

○ **P1 5.8 G:** Step right and climb up and right to a bolt. A right-trending line on numerous layaway holds leads to a right-facing fin. Layback up the fin to its top, then climb up and left to a fixed anchor on a sloped ledge. 100'

P2 4th class: Scramble up the slab to a good ledge at the top. 70'

Descent: When you're approaching by water, rappel from the top of P1, then either jump into the water or reverse the traverse back to the boat.

Gear: Optional small cams.

FA 2001, Ed Palen, Mark Scott

2 Beating to North 5.9+ G 180' ★★

After the initial thrash up the offwidth on P1, this is a pleasant and relatively clean line. It ascends the most natural (albeit wandering) line between Lake Champlain Monster and the bottom-to-top chimney of Birthday Route.

Start: Approach by boat (as described here by the first ascent party) or by rappel from above. Begin 60' right of the ramp of Lake Champlain Monster below the highest part of the cliff. There is a small landing. From here scramble up (3rd class) to a tree-covered ledge to the left of a black-streaked corner, the right wall of which has brown stains behind a large tree.

P1 5.7 G: Climb a brushy offwidth crack in a corner for 10', then move right around the corner and follow a series of ramps up and right to a short headwall. 110'

P2 5.9+ G: Climb the headwall on its right (or go up expanding flakes in its center). Continue up ramps and, at their top, angle left and surmount a difficult, short fingercrack to a tree-covered ledge. 70'

Descent: Rappel with double ropes straight down to the starting ledge.

Gear: Small to mid-sized cams and double ropes.

History: The FA party was attempting to locate Lake Champlain Monster, and instead found this line. A bail sling was encountered in the initial offwidth, so it's possible others have climbed parts of this line.

FA Jul, 2011, Peter Helmetag, Tim Ramsey

3 Birthday Route 5.6 PG 210'

About 200' right of Lake Champlain Monster, beginning at water level, this route follows the winter route Drop, Swim or Die, the leftmost bottom-to-top depression in black rock.

FA 1985, Herb George (Sr), , Herb George (Jr)

4 For the Birds 5.8 G 240'

This route was later climbed in the winter and, done as such, is a much better outing. If you climb in the summer, expect poison ivy and loose rock. From the water, first locate the broad, sloping ledge 25' above the water on the left end of the cliffs; this is **Lake Champlain Monster**. Right of this is an amphitheater, the right side of which is black rock with a deep gully and chimneys; this is the line **Drop, Swim, or Die**. Right of this is a straight bottom-to-top straight-in crack with a large, sloping black ledge at half height. (Tom Yandon and Chris Hyson made some explorations here in 2000.) Right of this, the cliff is broken by four right-facing corners and depressions, each of which reaches a left-rising tree ledge at midheight. This route climbs the fourth corner.

FA 2002, Tom Yandon, Jeanie Garrison, Will Mayo

5 The Original Route 5.9+ G 80' ★★★★

The obvious corner to the left of **Atom Smasher**.

Start: On the ledge at the start of **Atom Smasher**.

P1 5.9+ G: Make moves over the water on good holds to a sketchy pull into the corner (optional belay). Jam and stem the amazing corner to a ledge. Hard moves up the hanging flake system lead to an offwidth and a fixed anchor. 80'

FA Aug 12, 2012, Mike Miletich, John Cohen, June Carter

6 Atom Smasher 5.10d A0 65'

This mixed line is on the far right side of the main face. It is best approached from the water, as there is a small landing platform near the base. The initial moves (presently A0) are estimated at V6. This is an open project.

Start: On the right end of the main cliff, about 200' right of **For the Birds**, on a small buttress with a small, right-rising ramp that serves as a landing platform at the base. There is a dark-colored horizontal band in grey rock that marks the start.

P1 5.10d G: Stick clip the first bolt and pull up the rope to reach a flake. Go up and right, then step back left on ledge. Move straight up a face to the top of the buttress. 65'

Gear: To 2".

FA May 30, 2012, Mike Miletich, Emily Butler

BARN ROCK
1 Barn Buttress (5.4)
2 Piton Route (5.8)
3 Gone Fishin' (5.8)
4 Too Much Chop (5.7)

Photo by R.L. Stolz.

BARN ROCK

Location	West shore of Lake Champlain, north of Westport
Aspect	South
Height	60'
Quality	★
Approach	1 hr, moderate; boat optional
Summary	Small cliff directly above the water with several lead-from-a-boat routes; most parties simply toprope.

About 0.5 mile south of the Palisades cliff is Barn Rock Harbor, protected by a rocky point with a 60' cliff known as Barn Rock, which has some of the best lake views of any cliff on the New York shoreline 629989,4896490. The cliff rises directly from the lake and is similar in character to Bluff Island in Lower Saranac Lake. Several routes have been led out of a boat, although this requires an especially calm day and a large boat with bumpers (one that won't swamp from the wake of other boats). There is a nose that forms the left end of the cliff (**Barn Buttress**; 5.4 PG; ACB Jul 7, 2005, R.L. Stolz, Jeffry Ruiz). The gem of the cliff is the route in the center—a face with discontinuous fingercracks that go straight up the cleanest part of the cliff. The route has a piton (**Piton Route**; 5.8 PG; ACB Aug 5, 2005, R.L. Stolz, Phil Nathan). Starting at the same place is a toprope route to the right (**Gone Fishin'**; 5.8 TR; ACB Aug 25, 2007, R.L. Stolz, Stewart Rosen). Right of this, and sharing the same start, is a right-diagonal crack that leads to a small pine two-thirds of the way up, then goes up and left through overhangs (**Too Much Chop**; 5.7 PG; ACB Aug 31, 2005, R.L. Stolz, Rene Ruel).

Barn Rock can be approached by boat, but unusually calm conditions are required to climb out of the boat. An alternative is to beach the boat in Barn Rock Harbor, then hike a good path to the top of the cliff. There are no fixed stations or stances above the water, so lowering a climber is the preferred method here.

THE HONEY POT

Location	Near Elizabethtown, close to the Northway (I-87) Exit 31
Aspect	Southeast
Height	70'
Quality	★★★★
Approach	20 min, moderate
Summary	Small cliff with a several spectacular routes that breach multi-tiered roofs.

-5.6	5.7	5.8	5.9	5.10	5.11	5.12	5.13+	total
					2	1		3

This is a smallish 80'-wide cliff with a low, sheer, vertical wall, a roof at mid-height, and an overhanging wall at the top. There is nothing moderate on this cliff. The rock is smooth down low, but otherwise high quality. The overhanging sections are split by horizontal seams and cracks.

The cliff is nestled in a tiny wooded valley and, due to the forest canopy, is a shady place to climb on a hot day. The base of the cliff is open, level, and pleasant, and there are decent views of the valley from the top. The Northway can be seen (and barely heard) from the top. Due to the sloped terrain at the top, water seepage is a problem.

ACCESS

The entire cliff and approach are on state land. Be aware, however, of the east-west property boundary running diagonally down the hill 75' in front of the cliff. Further southwest along the same aspect on Green Hill is another taller cliff visible from the Northway (I-87). This is clearly on private land.

DIRECTIONS (MAP PAGE 146)

From the Northway (I-87) Exit 31, drive west on NY 9N for 1.7 miles. Park on the south side of the road directly across from the former Mountain Shadows restaurant (now an apartment), just west and in sight of the Essex County Transportation Maintenance facility (shown as "gravel pit" on topo maps) 616423,4896311.

Locate an old forest road across the road from the

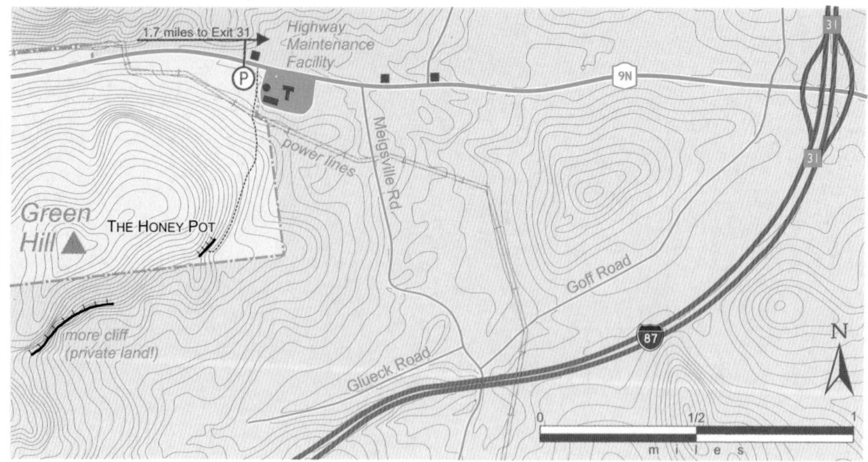

former Mountain Shadows building. Follow this south into the woods, roughly along the fence of the maintenance facility, to a power line. Go straight across the power line and pick up the forest road again. Follow this on a southerly course through generally open, pleasant forest, heading gradually uphill and contouring the hillside. The forest road is difficult to follow in places, but if you stay on course, it will lead you to the base of the cliff about 20 min from the car 616183,4895394.

HISTORY

The cliff was discovered by Tom DuBois in his never-ending hunt for new terrain. Finding limited potential, he turned over his discovery without attempting any routes. Jim Lawyer and Martine Schaer were the first to report a route here in 2011. They named the cliff The Honey Pot because it was "super sweet" and because the right end was dripping.

1 Honey Dipper 5.11b G 50' ★★★★

A direct (and the easiest) line straight up the impressive overhanging wall.

Start: 25' left of **Monkey Pump** directly below a hanging right-facing corner. There is a horizontal ledge at head height, and a rectangular chockstone wedged alarmingly (but solidly) at the top of the right-facing corner.

● **P1 5.11b G:** Go up to the right-facing corner and climb up the arête of the corner. Reach up to a large roof and (V1) hand traverse left 6', then mantel into the horizontal ledge–cave. Climb straight up the overhanging wall using great horizontal holds to a fixed anchor. 50'

● **V1 5.9 G:** Alternatively, you can climb up the right-facing corner, then squat into the ledge–cave using the chockstone.

FA Aug 11, 2013, David Buzzelli, Jim Lawyer

2 Urgent Fury 5.12c G 50' ★★★★★

This spectacular route finds its way up the steepest part of the wall; very unusual for the Adirondacks. It's got everything: dynos, heel hooks, slopers, jams, clean falls, and sustained desperation.

Start: 10' right of **Honey Dipper** at the most overhanging section of the cliff, below a black slab 10' up.

● **P1 5.12c G:** Go up some easy ledges, then up a short black slab to a nose in the lip of the lowest roof. Over this to a fist jam in a horizontal. Get psyched, then dyno for a bucket on the face above. Climb slightly right through the next roof to slopers at the horizontal break, then move 4' left to a "thank god" hand jam in a horizontal. A final overhanging crack leads to a fixed anchor. 50'

History: Jim Lawyer, Sarah Pancoast, and David Buzzelli worked the line for several days, the lead finally falling to Buzzelli.

FA Aug 17, 2013, David Buzzelli

3 Monkey Pump 5.11d G 50' ★★★★

This gymnastic route, the first on the cliff, finds its way up an unlikely wall capped by a roof. Getting through the roof involves two totally-horizontal body positions with both feet above your head.

Start: At a 2'-high pedestal just right of a boulder pile, located right of center on the cliff.

● **P1 5.11d G:** Stand on the pedestal, then follow horizontal edges up a smooth face to the roof. A few juggy reaches get you positioned below a shallow, overhanging right-facing corner. Monkey your way into the corner, then up to a ledge with a fixed anchor. 50'

FA Nov 7, 2011, Jim Lawyer, Martine Schaer

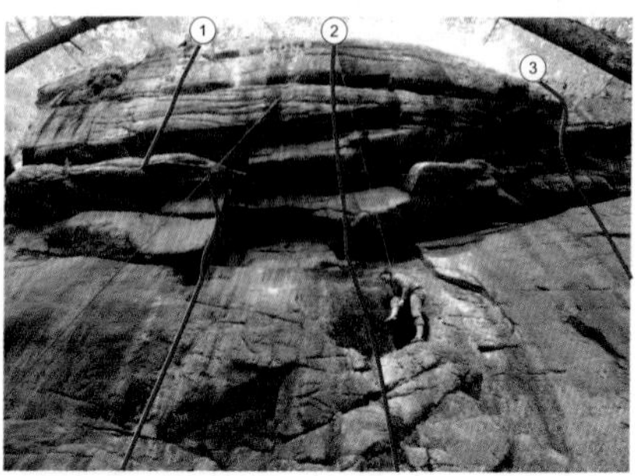

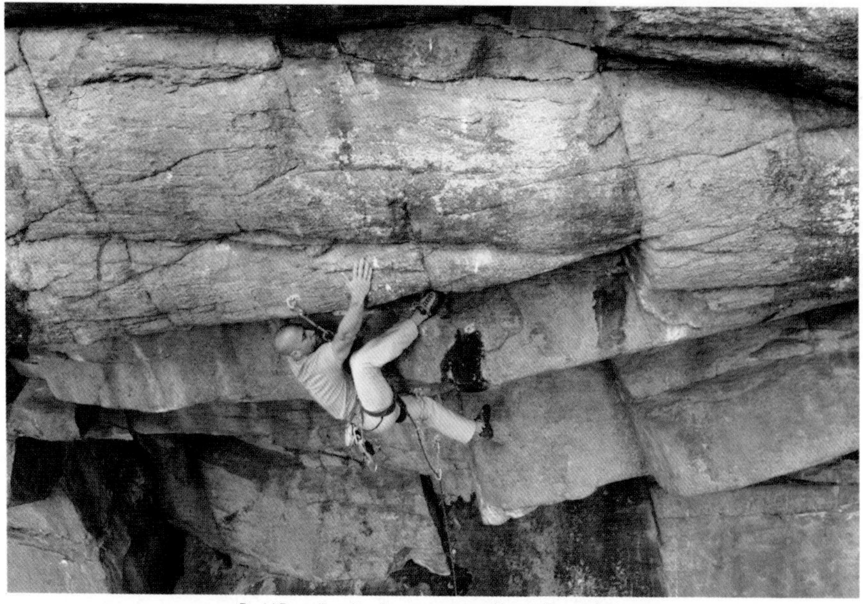

David Buzzelli makes the crux move on ***Urgent Fury*** *(5.12c).*

HALFWAY HANDCRACK

Location	On US 9 between New Russia and Elizabethtown
Aspect	East
Height	40'
Quality	
Approach	1 min, easy
Summary	A small cliff with a single steep crack.

DIRECTIONS

Parking for the Halfway Handcrack is on the east side of US 9, 2.4 miles south of Elizabethtown (from the intersection of US 9 and NY 9N) and 1.5 miles north of New Russia (from the post office at the intersection with Simmonds Hill Road). Some other locators are 0.1 mile north of the intersection of Otis Lane, and just south of a driveway marked "Crows Nest 6999."

The cliff is 25' from the road, hidden behind a narrow strip of trees 610618,4893016.

HISTORY

Nothing is known, other than that the area was listed in Don Mellor's 1983 guidebook as a good cliff for toproping.

1 Halfway Handcrack 5.9 G 40' ★★

Currently very dirty, but a good-looking crack otherwise.

Start: Below an obvious crack at the low point of the face, 5' right of a left-rising ramp and 10' left of a wide crack behind a large tree.

P1 5.9 G: Climb the crack to its end, then switch right to another crack and follow it to the top. 40'

KING PHILIP'S SPRING WALL

Location	Near Northway (I-87) Exit 30
Aspect	West
Height	100'
Quality	★★★★
Approach	10 min, easy
Summary	Very accessible crag with excellent rock and great toproping, but plagued by highway noise.

-5.6	5.7	5.8	5.9	5.10	5.11	5.12	5.13+	total
1		1						2

This west-facing cliff has long been a Mecca for toproping and group outings. The rock is excellent, off-vertical, and nearly every square inch of it is clean, coarse, and positive. The base of the cliff is open and communal, and the top has flat, open ledges with good views to the south and west. For some reason, the area has a reputation as a toproping-only destination and is, in fact, the most popular toproping locale in the park (so expect some crowds). But nothing could be further from the truth—there are many high-quality leads with excellent protection, most between 5.2 and 5.8. The routes described here should get you started.

The cliff is split into two sections by the approach gully. When you approach, to the (skier's) right is the North End, and to the (skier's) left is the South End, nearest the Northway. The most popular areas are self-evident, as the base is open and well used.

The only negative aspects of this cliff are the crowds and the noise from the Northway. Expect about the same noise level as at Poke-O Moonshine.

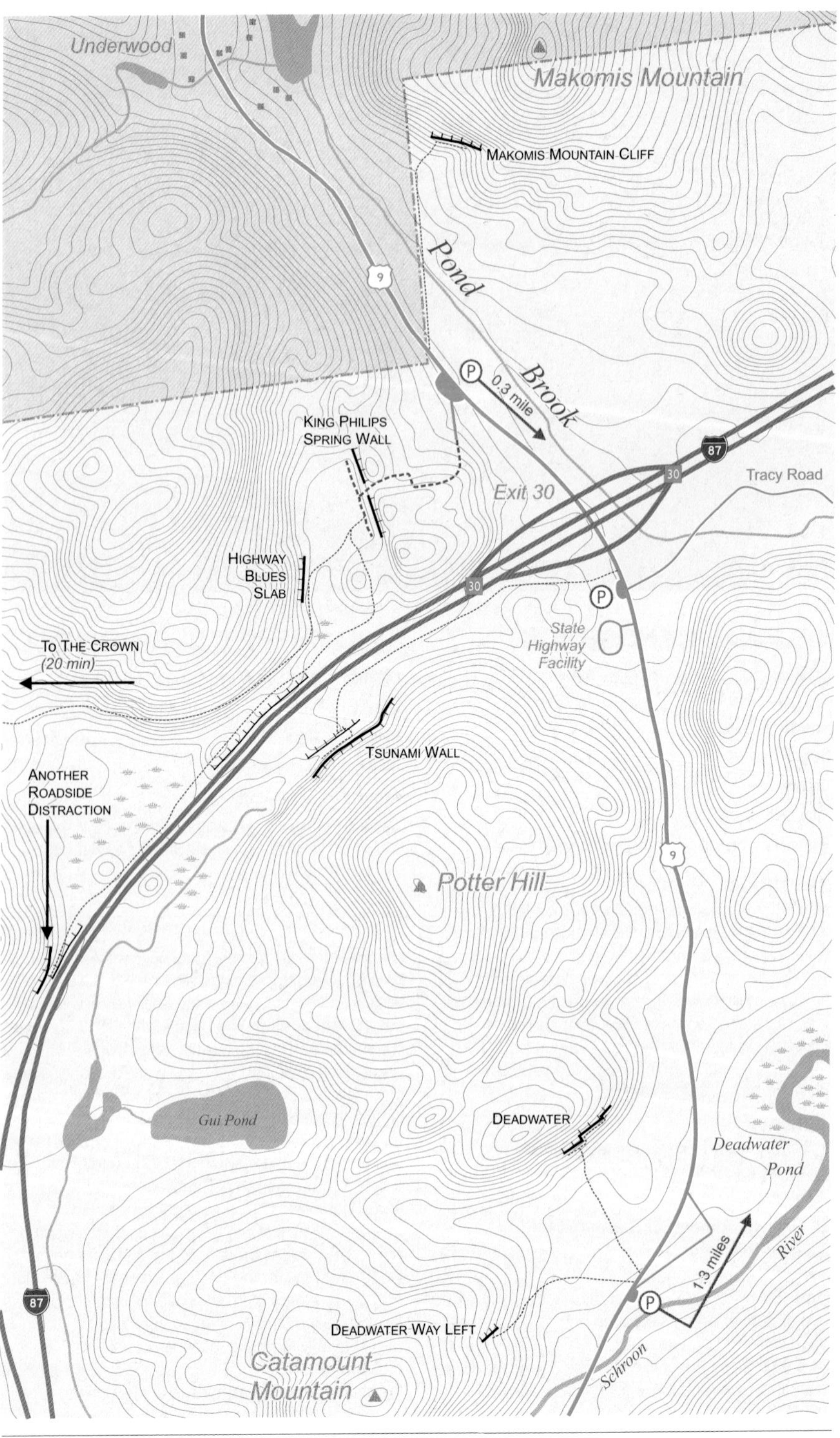
Underwood
Makomis Mountain
Makomis Mountain Cliff
Pond
Brook
9
0.3 mile
King Philips
Spring Wall
87
30
Tracy Road
Exit 30
Highway
Blues
Slab
30
State
Highway
Facility
To The Crown
(20 min)
Tsunami Wall
Another
Roadside
Distraction
9
Potter Hill
Gui Pond
Deadwater
Deadwater
Pond
River
1.3 miles
87
Deadwater Way Left
Schroon
Catamount
Mountain

For toproping, there are some tree anchors, but they are set far back from the edge. Long runners, short lengths of rope, and even some gear are required to set toprope anchors here.

There was a freshwater spring at the parking area, from a pipe installed at the far end of the parking lot, that served as the local fill-up spot for travelers. In 2009, the DEC closed the spring due to contamination.

HISTORY

The cliff is named after the spring, which was named for King Philip, the English name for Metacomet, the Massachusetts Wampanoag Indian leader of a 1675-78 war against colonial expansion. Legend has it that he fled north and drank from this spring. He and a band of followers are believed to have toproped on a "cliff just south of the spring" in mid-1675.

All joking aside, perhaps more interesting is that when the Northway was built, the state bought all the land around Exit 30 and decided that Exit 29 was going to be the oasis at the halfway point for travelers. This is the only location on the Northway where signs are permitted. The commercial enterprises at Exit 29 are now defunct, and, ironically, there is now a booming sandwich business that sets up at the King Philip's Spring pullout every summer weekend.

DIRECTIONS **(MAP PAGE 148)**

Park at a pullout on US 9 about 100 yards (toward Keene Valley) from Northway (I-87) Exit 30. The pullout is on the left as you drive toward Keene Valley 606608,4881577.

At the end of the pullout nearest the Northway, follow a dirt road that forks into the woods (the original US 9). After 100 yards, the road fades into a trail; follow it uphill to the top of the cliff. From the height of land, follow the trail down a gully that splits the cliff into two sections 606441,4881242.

North End

The North End extends for some distance beyond what is obviously popular, with considerable potential for more routes.

1 Metacomet 5.2 G 100' ★★★

Terrific climbing with cracks just about everywhere; a great route for the novice leader.

Start: 140' left of the gully that splits the cliff, at a large half-circle white spot at ground level. This is 12' right of a left-facing corner that begins on a ledge 6' up.

P1 5.2 G: Up a black slab with good holds to a ledge below three cracks that form a triangle. Over a bulge on beautifully textured white rock, then straight up to another ledge below a cluster of cracks. (V1) Follow a left-leaning crack out of the cluster, over a bulge, to a left-rising ramp. Follow the ramp to the top. 100'

V1 5.5 G: Traverse right following a right-rising crack system across a steep wall. The cracks end at a bulge; over this on buckets to the top.

Gear: Standard rack to 3".

South End

2 Springtime 5.8 G 130' ★★★★

Excellent crack climbing that rivals any of the leads at the Beer Walls.

Start: 150' right of the approach gully is a recessed amphitheater of chossy rock with white rock in the back. Just below the opening on the left side is a left-facing corner; this route begins 20' left of this left-facing corner and 130' right of the approach gully, at a right-rising series of vertical cracks and small stepped edges.

P1 5.8 G: Climb the discontinuous vertical cracks up and right to a shallow boxed alcove, then up a crack (crux) to a horizontal crack below a bulge (just right of a tree ledge). Step left and climb a crack through the bulge to the top. 130'

HIGHWAY BLUES SLAB

Location	Near Northway (I-87) Exit 30
Aspect	East
Height	120'
Quality	★★★
Approach	15 min, easy
Summary	Off-vertical face climbing on extremely textured rock.

-5.6	5.7	5.8	5.9	5.10	5.11	5.12	5.13+	total
			1	2				3

This beautiful, sheer, off-vertical slab has been completely overlooked, perhaps because its popular neighbor is considered a toproping-only beginner cliff. The face has excellent dimpled face climbing with hidden protection. The top of the cliff is burned and offers no natural anchors. There is potential for additional routes.

Walk left to reach the top of the cliff.

DIRECTIONS **(MAP PAGE 148)**

From the right end of King Philip's Spring Wall, walk away from the cliff onto open rock slabs parallel to the highway. Meander down some short cliffs, cross a stream, and walk over to the base of the wall, about 5 min from King Philip's Spring Wall 606210,4881049.

3 Road Trip 5.9+ G 130' ★★

Unlikely climbing at a moderate grade, followed by a brief (and well-protected) crux move at the top. You can keep the overall grade at 5.7 with the variation.

Start: 20' left of **Eighteen Wheeler** at a satellite dish-shaped scoop 3' up.

P1 5.9+ G: Mantel into the dish, then weave straight up the face past several horizontals aiming for the left side of a prominent black wave-like bulge at the top of the cliff. At the break below the overhang, (V1) clip a bolt above the wave-like bulge and pull up using crimps to a hidden hold. Heave over the bulge, then up a short crack to a ledge. Fixed anchor at the back of the ledge. 130'

V1 5.2 G: Traverse right 20' along the break to the midpoint anchor on **Eighteen Wheeler**. This keeps the

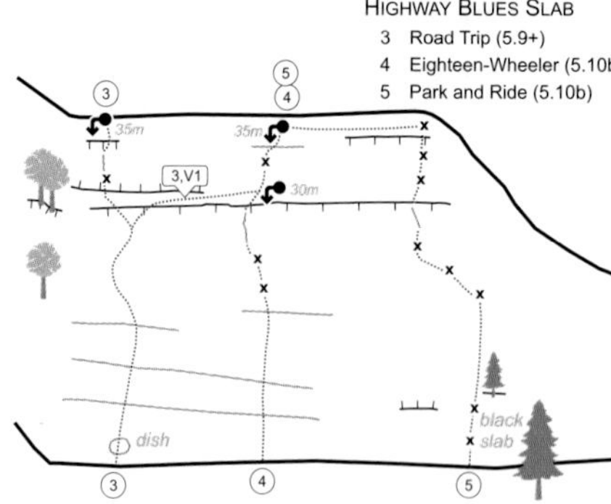

overall grade at 5.7. Rappel with a 60m rope from the mid-point anchor.

Descent: A 70m rope just makes it from here.

FA Jun 21, 2013, Leslie Ackerman, Jim Lawyer

FA (direct finish) Jun 21, 2013, Jim Lawyer, Leslie Ackerman

4 Eighteen-Wheeler 5.10b G 120' ★★★

Interesting climbing between horizontal cracks, with the crux being bolt-protected face climbing on very textured rock. Best climbed as a single pitch.

Start: In the middle of the face, below the fixed anchor at the horizontal break 90' up.

P1 5.10a G: Climb up past horizontals with good gear, trending left to a white slab. Up this (bolts; crux) to a left-leaning crack, then follow the crack to a horizontal break. Step right to a fixed anchor. 90'

P2 5.10b G: Hard moves past a bolt lead to a horizontal (small TCUs), then another hard move gains a slab. Follow the slab to a fixed anchor. 30'

Gear: Standard rack from small TCUs to 1".

Descent: Rappel with 70m rope.

FA May 8, 1994, Patrick Purcell, Mary Purcell

5 Park and Ride 5.10b G 140' ★★★

Great crimpy face climbing with very grippy rock on a sheer wall.

Start: 22' right of **Eighteen Wheeler** at a black slab, 10' right of a small black ceiling 15' up. There's a bolt 12' up.

P1 5.10b G: Go straight up the black slab to a good stance left of a scrawny cedar. Continue straight up with hidden protection to a smooth wall, then go up and left 15'. Stand into a pie-pan divot (first crux), then reach for a good thank-God short vertical crack. Up this to a break. Continue straight up to a final bulge (second crux) to a 6"-deep ledge. Traverse 15' left to the fixed anchor on **Eighteen Wheeler**. 140'

Descent: A 70m rope makes it from here.

Gear: From micro-cams up to .75".

FA Jun 21, 2013, Jim Lawyer, Leslie Ackerman

THE CROWN

Location	Near Northway (I-87) Exit 30
Aspect	Southwest
Height	70'
Quality	★★
Approach	1 hr, moderate
Summary	An overhanging wall with some steep cracks and a giant roof; there is good potential for high-end routes.

The Crown, so named by its position in a crown-shaped contour on the USGS map, is a long, super-steep wall with great potential for difficult routes. It's located just under a mile west of the Northway just before Exit 30, and virtually invisible from any vantage point.

On the left end of the cliff is an amphitheater capped by an enormous 25'-deep roof split by a crack. On the right end is a dramatically overhanging wall that rises above a right-rising terrace; this is where the dramatic **Crown Crack** is located. In between are several sheer, overhanging walls. On the far right end is a southeast-facing slab with potential for easier routes.

DIRECTIONS

Park as for King Philip's Spring Wall (0 hr 0 min) and walk to the Highway Blues Slab at 15 min. From here, walk (climber's) left along the base of the cliff and follow the contour southwest, parallel to the highway. At 25 min the contour bends to the west. Follow the contour west away from the highway (avoid the swamp parallel to the highway) and into a broad valley. Go northwest up the valley to the cliff, just before the height of land 604885,4880973. In the full foliage of summer, the cliff will be difficult to spot until you're very close; otherwise, you can see the elephant-shaped profile from quite a distance.

HISTORY

Ed Palen noticed the profile of this cliff—which he thought resembled an elephant's head—from the Northway in the mid 1990s (it's now obscured by trees). He brought students here to teach aid climbing (on **Crown Crack**), and beginner leading on the far right end slab. He also led two routes somewhere left of **Crown Crack**.

1 Crown Crack A2 70' ★★★★

This crack is begging to be freed.

Start: At the right end of the cliff, 30' from the right end of the right-rising terrace, below a left-leaning crack in a severely overhanging wall.

P1 A2: Go up the crack past two horizontal breaks (multiple pitons) to a ledge (bolt). Go right 8' to a fixed anchor. 70'

FA 1997, Ed Palen

MAKOMIS MOUNTAIN CLIFF

Location	Near Northway (I-87) Exit 30, west of US 9
Aspect	South
Height	100'
Quality	★★
Approach	20 min, moderate
Summary	Blocky steep cliff with three excellent routes and good potential for more.

-5.6	5.7	5.8	5.9	5.10	5.11	5.12	5.13+	total
				1		1	1	3

Known for the winter climb **Rites of Passage**, this cliff now has a few rock routes. It's 400' wide, overhanging, and since it's broken by ledges, there are few continuous full-height features. The rock is brittle, blocky and angular.

The winter routes are on the right end of the cliff on black rock next to an enormous full-height chimney with a large chockstone. Left of this is a most distinctive feature—a 10' wide, 20'-tall cavern 20' up the face. The rock routes are located on a 70'-tall, narrow, overhanging buttress just left of this hole.

HISTORY

When driving along US 9 from Exit 30, for a brief moment you can glimpse the ice line of **Rites of Passage**, which is what led Don Mellor, Mark Meschinelli, and Gary Spesard here in 1986. Several more ice lines were added 10 years later. In 2013, Jim Lawyer and David Buzzelli explored the rock climbing potential and came away with a couple of gems.

DIRECTIONS (MAP PAGE 148)

Park as for King Philip's Spring Wall—at the pullout on US 9 about 100 yards (toward Keene Valley) from Northway (I-87) Exit 30 606608,4881577.

From the pullout (0 hr 0 min), walk northwest on US 9 towards Chapel Pond for 200 yards. Keep an eye on the right side of the road for property markers. When you see the first red private property sign 606536,4881798, drop over the edge of the road and follow the property boundary north. At 1 min, cross New Pond Brook. At 10 min, go through a narrow trough and locate a pair of 4'-diameter white pines 6' apart, and a large moss-covered boulder 50' to the right. Leave the property boundary and walk northeast following the gigantic white pines to an open ridge. Follow this up to the left end of the cliff 606668,4882253.

1 Daughter of the Moon 5.12a G (5.3 R) 80' ★★★

Start: At the left end of the cliff below a slab—the only slab on the cliff—that leads to an overhanging, black-and-white wall.

● **P1 5.12a G:** Solo up the slab (5.3 R) to a perched boulder at its top. Stand on this, then move up and right on the overhanging wall to the highest ledge. Power up the overhanging wall (crux at the top) to a sloped ledge. Go up the left side of an overhanging arête to a jug; mantel this, then step right to a fixed anchor. 80'

History: On some maps, the name of the mountain is "Nokomis" rather than Makomis. This route name is the Iroquois translation for Nokomis.

FA Oct 20, 2013, Jim Lawyer, David Buzzelli

2 Coming of Age 5.10b G 60' ★★★

Start: On the right end of the cliff, locate the unusual 10'-wide, 20'-tall, cavern 20' up. Just left is a narrow, overhanging buttress of clean rock. Begin on the left side of the buttress at a 6'-high ledge with a perched flat boulder.

● **P1 5.10b G:** Get onto the ledge, then step up and right onto the face. Follow a narrow left-facing corner to its top, then make a few big moves left. Work back right, and mantel onto a sloping ledge at the top. There's a fixed anchor on the left-facing wall above. 60'

FA Oct 12, 2013, Jim Lawyer, David Buzzelli

3 Leap of Faith 5.13b G 60' ★★★★

An aesthetic, beautiful line up a sheer, overhanging buttress. Might be easier if you're tall.

Start: 20' right of **Coming of Age**, on the left wall of a large left-facing open book that defines the right side of the narrow buttress.

● **P1 5.13a G:** Stick-clip, then boulder up a short face to a horizontal crack. Work up the overhanging central face of the buttress following a shallow, left-facing edge in white rock. At its top, make a 6'-dyno right to a good bucket in black rock. Power over a chossy, overhanging bulge, then run up the overhanging face to a fixed anchor. 60'

FA Oct 20, 2013, David Buzzelli

ANOTHER ROADSIDE DISTRACTION

Location	On the Northway (I-87), south of Exit 30
Aspect	Southeast
Height	60'
Quality	
Approach	30 min, easy
Summary	A small cliff with good routes whose ambience is diminished by its proximity to the interstate.

-5.6	5.7	5.8	5.9	5.10	5.11	5.12	5.13+	total
	1		2	1				4

The routes on this cliff are quite good but, because of its inaccessibility, have become somewhat overgrown. If the cliff were more accessible and not 50' from a busy highway, it would be very clean and popular.

The wall is a high-angle face split by several long horizontal cracks. The most distinctive feature is the right-rising diagonal crack that crosses the better part of the main face, the line of **Traverse of the Climbing Gods**. Left of the main face is a right-leaning depression filled with trees and debris; left of this is another, smaller face with the route **Arc of a Climber**.

HISTORY

Patrick Purcell was the first to climb here, parking on the interstate faking a breakdown (don't do this). The cliff has seen few visitors since that time.

DIRECTIONS (MAP PAGE 148)

Park as for King Philip's Spring Wall—the large paved pullout 200 yards northwest of the overpass on the south side of US 9. There is a freshwater spring here. Begin the approach by walking to King Phillips Spring Wall: hike the dirt road toward the highway, which turns into a trail, which is followed to the top of King Phillips Spring Wall. Scramble down a gully between the two cliffbands, then turn left (toward the highway) and walk to the far end of the cliff. Turn right away from the cliff and follow a trail out onto slabs, then turn left and head directly to the highway. Follow the highway southwest, staying in the grass well off the highway. Walk over the top of a large road cut and down the other side, then continue in the grass off the highway. Just past a swamp is a second road cut; walk up this, then down the far side to the cliff, which is on the right 605511,4879989 facing the road.

ACCESS

Be sure to stay well off the highway, which means over the guardrail, in the grass at its margin with the woods. Scramble over the road cuts; not only does this get you off the highway, but it's more scenic. Even with these precautions, the State Police may question you, as they don't like pedestrians on the highway. They need to see that you're making an effort to stay off the interstate.

*Opposite: David Buzzelli setting up for the crux on **Leap of Faith** (3.13b).*

1 Arc of a Climber 5.9+ G 60' ★

Named for a 1980 Steve Winwood album, *Arc of a Diver.*

Start: 18' left of the right-leaning depression filled with trees below a grass-filled crack in a slab.

P1 5.9+ G: Climb up the crack past a prominent horizontal to the top. 60'

FA Sep, 1983, Patrick Purcell, Tom Skrill

2 A Better Place to Be 5.9 G 60' ★

Start: At the left end of the main wall 20' right of the right-leaning depression filled with trees. There is an oval patch of angular blocks pasted to the face 3' up that marks the start of a right-rising crack.

P1 5.9 G: Climb up the pasted-on blocks, then follow the right-rising crack right 12' to a thin crack in a black streak. Up the crack to a small bush at a horizontal, then through the steep wall above. 60'

FA Sep, 1983, Patrick Purcell

3 Traverse of the Climbing Gods 5.7 G 100' ★★

Start: Same as **A Better Place to Be**.

P1 5.7 G: Climb up the pasted-on blocks, then follow the right-rising horizontal crack to its end, where it meets a horizontal crack. Straight up a thin crack on the wall above past several horizontals to a wide horizontal break, then up through the bulge on good holds to the top. 100'

FA Sep, 1983, Patrick Purcell, Tom Skrill

4 A Midsummer Night's Frustration 5.10b G 60' ★

The name is a literary reference to a romantic comedy by Shakespeare.

Start: 18' right of the pasted-on blocks of **A Better Place to Be**, on the face below the rightmost of two vertical fingercracks that rise above the prominent right-rising horizontal crack (the left crack is **A Better Place to Be**).

P1 5.10b G: Climb up flakes on the blank face to the right-rising crack, then straight up the thin fingercrack to the next horizontal. Step right 6' to the next fingercrack, which is climbed through the steep face above (crux) past several horizontals and better holds to the top. 60'

FA Jul 24, 1986, Jeff Edwards, Patrick Purcell

TSUNAMI CRAG

Location	Off the Northway (I-87), south of Exit 30
Aspect	North
Height	140'
Quality	
Approach	30 min, easy
Summary	A very overhanging face on the east side of the Northway.

This cliff, known more for its winter routes (e.g., **Fecalator**, **Glass Pipe**), has only one rock route to date. With the well-equipped winter routes, though, the crag is primed for difficult free climbing. The top pitch of

Fecalator is a real prize—an amazing severely overhanging hand- and fingercrack.

The most obvious features on the cliff are the overhanging crack of **Fecalator** and, to its left, the "surfboard"—a visor at the very top of the cliff.

HISTORY

The cliff was first explored for its ice-climbing potential by Yvon Chouinard and Jim McCarthy in 1969. Dave Aldous was the first to see (and report) any rock climbing here, but his ascent was solo and not widely known. Development has really exploded in the early 2000s with high-end winter routes, but no other rock climbing has been reported.

DIRECTIONS (MAP PAGE 148)

Park at the dirt pullout on US 9 east of the Exit 30 overpass, across the street from the intersection with Tracy Road (CR 6). Walk toward the Northway, then turn south and follow the northbound off-ramp (staying well off the road). After about 10 min, when you are roughly even with the roadcut on the west side of the highway, turn left into the woods and walk to the top of a smaller cliff that faces the main overhanging wall; you can scope out the routes from here. Walk left and descend into the trough, then up through moss-covered talus to the base of the cliff 606298,48880580.

ACCESS

Be sure to stay well off the highway, which means over the guardrail, in the grass at its margin with the woods. Scramble over the roadcuts; not only does this get you off the highway, but it's more scenic. Even if you take these precautions, the State Police may question you, as they don't like pedestrians on the highway. They need to see that you're making an effort to stay well off the interstate.

1 Catch a Wave A3- 140'

Climbs the corner and wavelike visor (called the "surfboard") at the top of the cliff. It is positioned between the winter routes **Fecalator** (on the right) and the right-rising handcrack of the **Higher Education** finish to **Catatonic Immobility** (on the left).

Start: Below the surfboard at the highest part of the cliff, at a spike of rock 10' from the cliff and 1' left of a 2'-high boxed alcove, below a discontinuous handcrack. This is also 15' right of a low-angle left-rising ramp and 25' left of a cave (where **Fecalator** begins).

P1 A3-: Climb a handcrack (green and mossy) to a slab and follow it up to the overhanging wall. Up cracks in the overhanging rock (long reach) to gain the white left-facing corner. Follow the corner (rivet) to its top, then move right through roofs to an overhanging crack that breaks the surfboard on its left side. 140'

Gear: Normal aid rack plus thin pitons and bashies.

FA Jul 21, 1996, Dave Aldous (solo)

MINEVILLE SLAB

Location	Near Northway (I-87) Exit 30, off Tracy Road
Aspect	Southwest
Height	50'
Quality	
Approach	1 min, easy
Summary	A small cliff very near the road with a single bolted route.

-5.6	5.7	5.8	5.9	5.10	5.11	5.12	5.13+	total
2				1				3

This small cliff is located on the side of Tracy Road, a rural road with very little traffic. The right end of the cliff reaches the road and has been cut away for the road. The left side is untouched and is a steep slab with a single route.

HISTORY

The first route here, **Conveyor Belt**, was put in by Patrick Purcell. Locals have known about the cliff and recall it with contempt, but it's a good route.

DIRECTIONS

From Northway Exit 30, drive 0.1 mile south on US 9, then turn left onto Tracy Road (CR 6). Drive 3.9 miles and park at a dirt pullout on the right next to a pond (Newport Pond) 612359,4881717. The cliff is visible 100 yards down the road on the left (north) side opposite the pond 612379,4881716.

1 Conveyor Belt 5.10b PG 50' ★

Start: In the center of the slab, at the base of a shallow left-rising jagged overlap.

P1 5.10b PG: Climb up to the first bolt 10' up, then up and left, following wavy featured rock to a large shallow scoop. Up the scoop past a horizontal, then over a bulge to the top. 50'

FA Aug, 1991, Patrick Purcell, Ann Eastman

2 Zero Gravity Bella 5.2 R 60'

Start: Same as **Turd Ferguson Can Suck It**.

P1 5.2 R: Follow left-rising scoop features to the top of **Conveyor Belt**. 60'

FA May, 2009, Rich Balzano, Caitlin Balzano

3 Turd Ferguson Can Suck It 5.5 G 35'

Start: 30' right of **Conveyor Belt** below an obvious right-leaning crack system.

P1 5.5 G: Go up the vegetated crack to a low-angle section beneath a block headwall. Continue over this via a fistcrack (crux) to the top. 35'

FA May, 2009, Rich Balzano, Caitlin Balzano

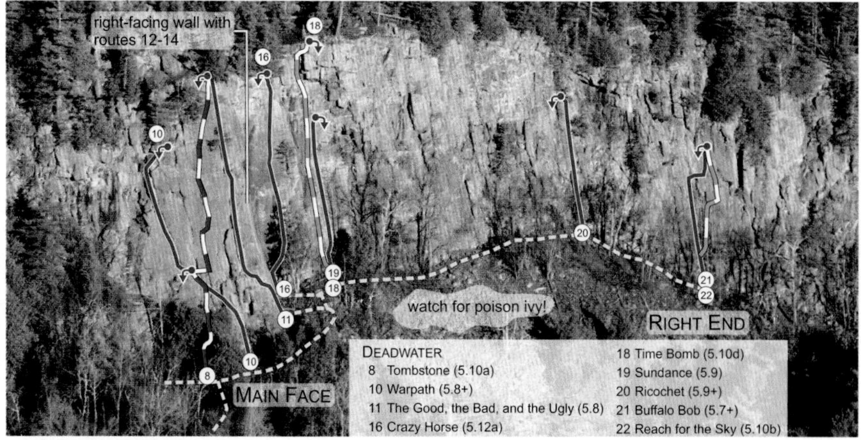

DEADWATER

Location	Near Northway (I-87) Exit 30, west of US 9
Aspect	Southeast
Height	90'
Quality	★★★★
Approach	10 min, easy
Summary	High-quality moderate routes very close to the road in a private, quiet, sunny setting.

-5.6	5.7	5.8	5.9	5.10	5.11	5.12	5.13+	total
1	3	6	3	7	2	1		23

The cliff is located very near US 9, just south of Northway Exit 30, on a knoll between Potter Hill and Catamount Mountain, and oriented to receive considerable sun. Despite its proximity to the road, the cliffs feel quiet and remote, with no discernible signs of human development visible from the pretty viewpoints. Much of the cliff sits above the trees and, with no drainage from above, dries very quickly after a rain.

Efforts have been made to prepare this cliff for climber use: erosion-control terraces and rock steps have been built around the cliff base, and lower-off anchors protect the cliff-top trees. Despite the friendly environment and many moderate, high-quality routes here, this isn't a cliff for toproping, as the top of the cliff is not accessible from below; you must be willing to lead the routes here.

Deadwater consists of three distinct areas. The Left End has a separate approach (although it is only about 2 min away) and has three routes, including the high-quality **WISWIG**. The Main Cliff is the primary attraction at Deadwater with the majority of the routes. The most obvious feature here is the huge right-facing corner (the route **Space Cowboy**) that sits above the erosion-control terraces. As you move right from the terraces, the rock deteriorates in quality, but about 200' to the right, the quality improves briefly with three more routes, in what is called the Right End.

The cliff has reasonable cell phone coverage.

HISTORY

"Dead water" was the name given to a long, flat section of the Schroon River, dammed by lumbermen sometime before 1829 to create Deadwater Pond. The settlement we call Deadwater was built around the Deadwater Iron Works in 1848 on the east side of the Schroon River near this pond. It eventually had a school and post office. The forge closed after the Civil War and the settlement declined and eventually disappeared leaving cellar holes you can still find in the woods. The last known commercial enterprise was the NYS Serpentarium (a reptile museum), located at the present parking area.[12]

Being a history buff, Ed Palen has traced old Adirondack roads. He discovered the cliff in 2001 while skiing across Deadwater Pond. He returned in the summer of 2002 and, with several others, including Steve Mergenthaler and Bob Starinsky, climbed many of the first routes. The long-ago settlement along with its western-sounding name Deadwater established a theme for route naming.

DIRECTIONS (MAP PAGE 148)

Parking for Deadwater is at a large pullout on the east side of US 9 607184,4879119, 1.3 miles south of the intersection with the Northway at Exit 30.

Cross to the west side of the road and walk north a few yards to find the start of the climbers' path. Follow the path uphill at first, then flat through open forest to a final short uphill section through talus to the base of the crag 607015,4879529, meeting the crag in the vicinity of **Tombstone**. The approach takes about 10 min.

DESCENT OPTIONS

The cliff is well equipped with lower-off anchors above most climbs, suitable for lowering with a single rope. A few longer routes require belaying on top and walking to an anchor where you can rappel with a single 60-m rope.

12 Richard E. Tucker, "Re: Deadwater History", email to Jim Lawyer, Apr 9, 2014.

MT Wall

Yet another cleaned buttress left of the Left End (i.e., the Real Left End). Named for the initials of the last names of the primary developers.

DIRECTIONS **(MAP PAGE 148)**

Walk left 30' from the Left End (the location of the routes **Doc Holiday** and **WISWIG**) to a pair of low-angle arêtes; this is the MT Wall.

1 Hoedown 5.8 G 70' ★

Worthwhile, although not quite as good as **Incognito** to the right.

Start: At the toe of the left-hand arête, 12' left of **Incognito**.

P1 5.8 G: Up the arête to where it steepens. Move left to a stance, then back right to a crack on the arête. Continue up the arête to a fixed anchor at the top. 70'

Gear: To 2".

FA May, 2008, Davis Trachte, Steve Mergenthaler

2 Dig It 5.8 G 70' ★★

This is the corner between the two arêtes. It has recently been cleaned, and is now quite nice.

Start: At the top of a dirt cone in the corner between the two arêtes of **Hoedown** and **Incognito**.

P1 5.8 G: Up the corner to a roof. (V1) Reach left and pull over the roof, then follow a finger- and hand-crack in the large corner to a fixed anchor. 70'

V1 5.10+ G: Climb the roof directly following a flared seam (deliberately avoiding the bigger holds to the left) to join the handcrack above.

FA Jul, 2006, Steve Mergenthaler

3 Bear 5.11a TR 70'

Climbs the face between **Dig It** and **Incognito** through a roof to the fixed anchor on **Incognito**.

4 Incognito 5.8 G 70' ★★★

Beautiful rock and great protection; a great addition to the moderate routes at Deadwater.

Start: Walk 30' left of **Doc Holiday** to a pair of arêtes, 12' apart. Begin at the toe of the right-hand arête.

P1 5.8 G: Boulder up the arête to a ledge. Continue up the arête to a ceiling. Break through this into a right-facing corner, step right, then climb the face to a fixed anchor. 70'

Gear: To 2".

FA May, 2008, Steve Mergenthaler, Davis Trachte

Left End

The Left End is a short cliff with left-leaning slashes and a small erosion-control terrace at the base. All of the routes share a common fixed anchor at the top.

DIRECTIONS **(MAP PAGE 148)**

Just after the approach trail starts uphill for the final climb to the Main Cliff, and just before the trail becomes rocky, there is a faint path that goes left and up to another cliff face. The turnoff is nondescript; the primary landmarks are two very large white pine trees about 50' off the main trail to the left.

5 Doc Holiday 5.10c G 80' ★★

Good climbing up shallow seams with strenuous small gear placements. Much harder than it looks.

Start: At the left side of the face below left-leaning cracks.

P1 5.10c G: Up the left-leaning cracks to an overlap, then up past a second overlap (crux) to a good stance. Easier climbing leads up cracks, then move up and right to a ledge at the top with a fixed anchor. 80'

Gear: Up to 1", small nuts, RPs, and a double set of TCUs.

FA (TR) 2004, Ed Palen, Bob Starinsky
FFA Oct 6, 2007, Jim Lawyer, Emilie Drinkwater

6 WISWIG 5.11a G 80' ★★★★

Start: Same as **Cowpoke Chimney**.

○ **P1 5.11a G:** Step into the chimney, then out left onto the face to the first bolt. Follow a left-leaning seam up the face. At the top, (V1) move right onto a smooth wall with monopockets through an overlap to the ledge with a fixed anchor. 80'

V1 5.6 G: An easier finish climbs the good crack just left of the smooth face.

Gear: 1 ea 0.5" cam.

FA Jul 27, 2007, Steve Mergenthaler, Michelle Berrus, Royce Van Evera

7 Cowpoke Chimney 5.7 G 80' ★★

Start: At the base of the chimney, the right side of which is a little tower.

P1 5.7 G: Climb the chimney to a left-leaning crack, then follow it through a bulge to a ledge with a fixed anchor. 80'

FA 2004, Bob Starinsky, Ed Palen

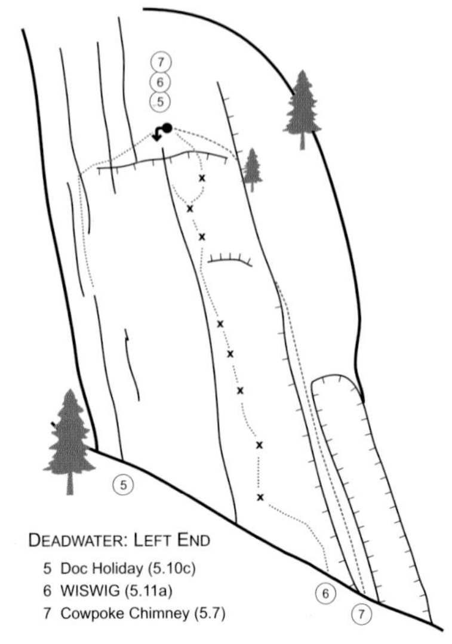

Main Cliff

You can reach the Main Cliff by following the approach trail to its end, meeting at the base of **Tombstone**.

8 Tombstone 5.10a G 170' ★★★★★

Stellar crack climbing with a clean face topout, excellent for the grade. This was the first route climbed at Deadwater. P1 can be used to access several variations on the upper wall.

Start: 25' left of the lowest point of the cliff (where the approach trail meets the cliff), left of the large left-facing, left-leaning corner, at some blocky left-rising steps below a crack with a bolt to the right.

P1 5.9 G: (V1, V2) Climb up to the crack, then up to the overhang. Move right and break the overhang at the V-notch. Above the overhang, step right to gain a left-rising crack, then angle up and left to a ledge with a boulder-seat and fixed anchor. 40'

P2 5.10a G: Climb up to the bolt, then traverse right below the bolt to the next crack. Up the crack, which jogs right past a hollow-sounding "tombstone flake," then continue up to a bulge with a piton (crux). Straight up the face past several horizontals to the top. 130'

V1 Welcome to Deadwater 5.10b TR: Right of the normal start is a prominent left-facing, left-leaning corner that begins at the base of the stairs. Climb the face left of the corner to a roof (crux), then up and left to the fixed anchor.

V2 5.9 PG: Right of the normal start is a prominent left-facing, left-leaning corner that begins at the base of the stairs. Up the corner to a ledge, then up and left to the fixed anchor.

Gear: To 3", small TCUs for the top.

FA Jul, 2002, Ed Palen, Mark Scott
FA (V1) 2004, Adam Crofoot, Matt Horner, Colin Loher (and a minikeg of Molson Canadian)
FA (V2) Aug, 2002, Bob Starinsky, Ed Palen

9 Bandito 5.10d PG 100' ★★

Climbs the crack straight up from the belay left of the **Tombstone** P2 crack.

Start: At the top of P1 of **Tombstone**.

P1 5.10d PG: From the belay, climb up to the bolt, then up the crack just right of the orange rock to a ceiling. Up the crack and through the ceiling to a fixed anchor (shared with **Warpath**). 100'

FA Aug, 2002, Mark Meschinelli, Dave Hough

10 Warpath 5.8+ G 130' ★★★

Very nice crack climbing on P2. The upper pitch is most often combined with P1 of **Tombstone**.

Start: At the lowest point of the cliff, walk right past a large left-facing, left-leaning corner to the base of the stone steps. Begin 5' right of this large corner below a smaller right-facing corner.

P1 5.6 G: A boulder move off the ground leads to a left-rising ramp. Follow the ramp up and left to the P1 fixed anchor on **Tombstone**. 50'

P2 5.8+ G: From the left side of the belay, bouldery moves lead to the right-facing, left-leaning corner. Up the corner to the top, then move right to a fixed anchor (shared with **Bandito**). 80'

FA 2003, Ed Palen, Bob Starinsky

11 The Good, the Bad, and the Ugly 5.8 G 100' ★★

Start: (V1) Same as **Bozeman Bullet**.

P1 5.8 G: Step left onto the face past a low piton, then continue left across the face and around the arête to a ledge. Foot-traverse left on the ledge to gain the bottom of a 4" crack; up the off-width crack to the top of the orange tower. Continue up the crack to its end, then step right onto the face and (V2) climb up past several horizontals to gain a right-rising crack. Follow the crack past a tree (possible belay) to the top. 100'

V1 5.8 G: Downhill from and left of the normal start at the base of the stairs, just right of the left-facing, left-leaning corner, climb up to a blocky orange roof, passing it on the right via a handcrack to meet the normal route at the end of the foot traverse.

V2 5.8 G: It is possible to continue right across the face to the midpoint anchor on **Bozeman Bullet**.

FA Aug, 2002, Ed Palen, Paul Brown, Bob Starinsky

*John Campbell on **Tombstone** (5.10a), belayed by his brother Thom Campbell.*

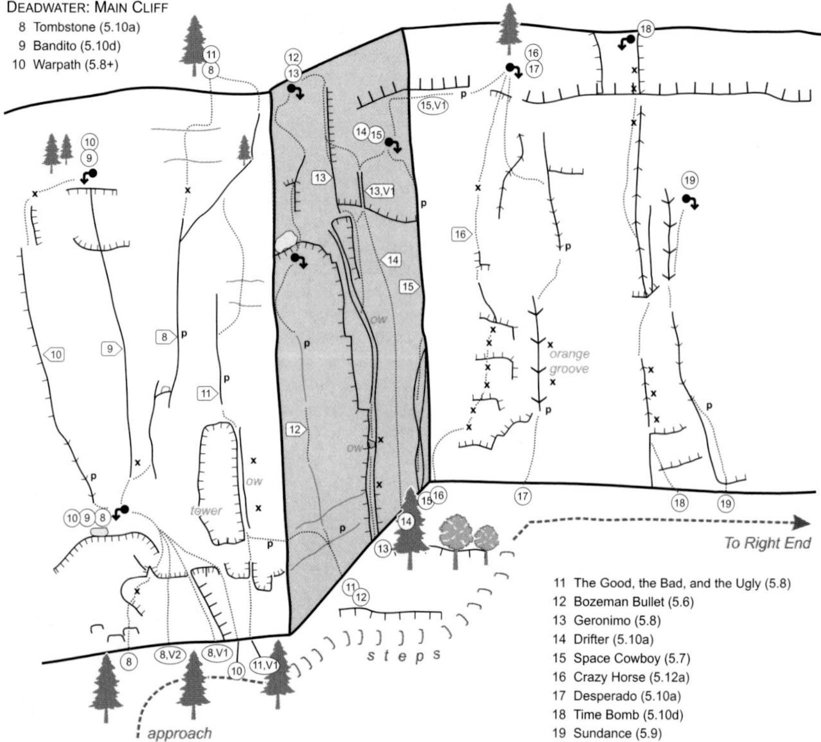

12 Bozeman Bullet 5.6 PG 100' ★★★★

Climbs the beautiful textured face and arête that form the left side of the huge right-facing corner at the top of the erosion-control terraces. Due to its aspect, it dries quickly after a rain.

Start: Below and left of the **Geronimo** off width at the lower of two terraces, below the beautiful textured face.

P1 5.6 PG: Step left onto the face past a low piton, then face-climb up to a crack, past a pod, out to the arête, then back onto the face to a fixed anchor (optional belay, 60'). Mantel onto the ledge with a large block, then up to a left-facing corner capped by a small overlap on the left. Climb up the steep Gunks-like corner to the face above and on to a fixed anchor. 100'

FA Jul, 2002, Bob Starinsky, Ed Palen

13 Geronimo 5.8 G 90' ★★★

The obvious off-width crack right of **Bozeman Bullet**.

Start: At the base of the off-width crack on the left wall of the huge right-facing corner above the terraces.

P1 5.8 G: Climb the off-width crack to an alcove. Angle up and right across the face to a large ledge 30' up (shared with **Space Cowboy**). Climb up an overhanging right-facing corner to just below the roof. (V1) Step left onto the face and up to a ledge, then angle up and right (making the "Geronimo move"; crux) into a left-facing corner. Follow the corner to its top. Step left to a fixed anchor (shared with **Bozeman Bullet**). 90'

V1 5.9 G ★★★: Climb the roof via the perfect hand-crack (same as **Drifter**), then step left to rejoin the original line above. It is also possible to climb rightward to the fixed anchor shared with **Drifter** and **Space Cowboy**.

FA Aug, 2002, Steve Mergenthaler, Bob Starinsky, Ed Palen

14 Drifter 5.10a R 90'

Start: Just right of the off-width crack of **Geronimo**.

P1 5.10a R: Climb the face between the **Geronimo** off width and the **Space Cowboy** corner to the right, deliberately avoiding either route. Finish through the right-hand crack in the roof (same as **Geronimo** V1) to the **Space Cowboy** fixed anchor. 90'

FA Sep, 2003, Steve Mergenthaler

15 Space Cowboy 5.7 G 90' ★★

Start: At the base of the huge right-facing corner above the terraces, and 10' right of the **Geronimo** off width.

P1 5.7 G: Climb the corner past a ledge and around a small roof to the giant roof at the top of the cliff. There is an optional fixed anchor on the wall to the left. An airy traverse right 20' leads up to a tree with a fixed anchor (shared with **Desperado** and **Crazy Horse**). 90'

FA Aug, 2002, Steve Mergenthaler, Ed Palen, Bob Starinsky

*Opposite: Tom Wright on **Bozeman Bullet** (5.6), Photo by Tomás Donoso.*

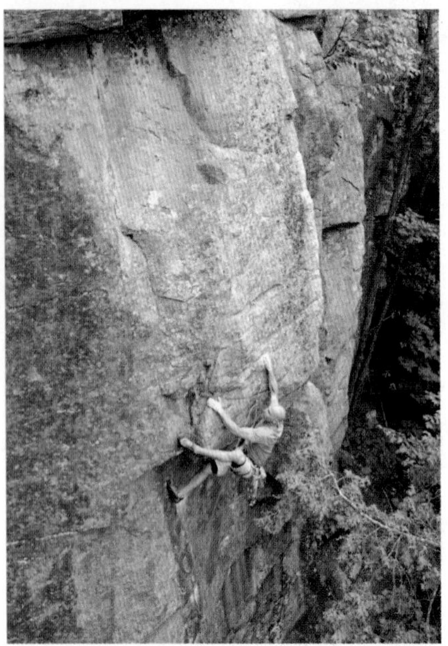

*David Buzzelli on **Crazy Horse** (5.12a).*

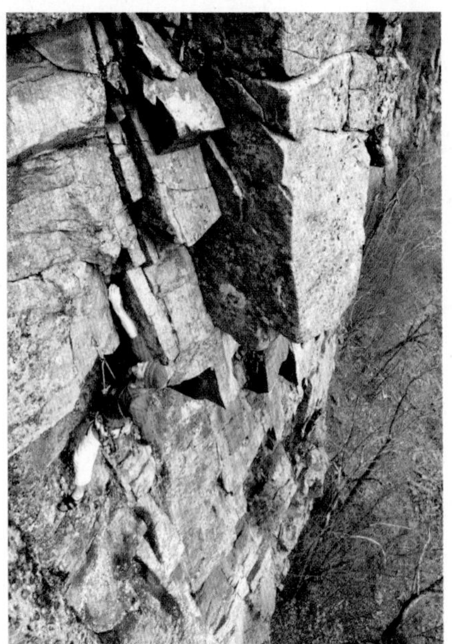

*James Armstrong on **Time Bomb** (5.10d).*

16 Crazy Horse 5.12a G 90' ★★★

A difficult route with two very puzzling cruxes. Some people find it hard for the grade.

Start: Same as **Space Cowboy**.

P1 5.12a G: Climb up the corner of **Space Cowboy** a few feet, then traverse right to the first bolt, then straight up to the first roof. Pull the roof and up to a second roof, through this and up to a third roof with a crack. Climb the crack to a small stance, then up the face to the tree at the top with a fixed anchor (shared with **Desperado** and **Space Cowboy** V1). 90'

Gear: To 1".

FA Sep, 2003, Steve Mergenthaler

17 Desperado 5.10a G 90' ★★★

Tricky climbing in the open book. Some swear they've been sandbagged—think stemming.

Start: 20' right of the large corner, below a clean orange open book that begins 12' up.

P1 5.10a G: Boulder up a blocky overhang and into the open book, then climb it to its top. Exit right around the arête and into a large right-facing corner system, then follow it to its top. Step back left around an arête, then up the face to a fixed anchor on a pine tree (shared with **Space Cowboy** and **Crazy Horse**). 90'

FA Aug, 2002, Ed Palen, Bob Starinsky

18 Time Bomb 5.10d G 100' ★★★

One of the more gymnastic routes at Deadwater. The unstable-looking blocks in the upper roof are what give the route its name; be careful! The huge pine tree that once stood at the top of this route succumbed to an ice storm and now makes a nice bench at the base.

Start: 10' right of **Desperado** on the arête just left of **Sundance**.

P1 5.10d G: Climb the arête with three bolts (5.10d) to easier rock and a horizontal break at 50' below the upper arête (which almost meets **Sundance** here). Climb up the arête and onto the left face (using a crack around the right for protection), then up into a small right-facing corner capped by a ceiling. Up the corner, then make wild, gymnastic moves through the upper roofs at a left-facing corner to an exposed stance on the right with a fixed anchor. 100'

Gear: To 3", many long runners.

FA Jul 6, 2006, Dennis Luther, Jim Lawyer

19 Sundance 5.9 G 70' ★★★

Secure crack climbing with interesting stemming at the start. The upper corner is often wet but still climbable.

Start: Just right of **Time Bomb**, at a large right-facing groove with a crack on the right wall.

P1 5.9 G: Stem up the corner and well-protected crack to a horizontal break at 50'. Continue a short distance up the upper corner to a fixed anchor on the right wall, just before the corner deteriorates in quality. 70'

FA Aug, 2002, Ed Palen, Mark Scott

20 Ricochet 5.9+ PG 60' ★★

Start: 100' right of **Sundance** (about halfway between **Sundance** and **Buffalo Bob**) at a 4'-high stepped block in the trail.

P1 5.9+ PG: Up blocky terrain to a right-facing corner. Climb the corner to its top, then make a tricky move left and follow a fingercrack through several overlaps to a fixed anchor. 60'

Gear: To 0.75", including several small nuts.

FA Aug 12, 2013, Michael Bauman, Royce Van Evera

*Opposite: Colin O'Connor on **Reach for the Sky** (5.10b).*

Right End

From the terraced area at the base of **Space Cowboy**, walk right 200' to a right-facing corner with a laser-cut handcrack; this is **Buffalo Bob**. There is a terrace at the base of this corner.

Be careful: right of **Sundance**, the base of the cliff and the talus below are sprinkled with poison ivy.

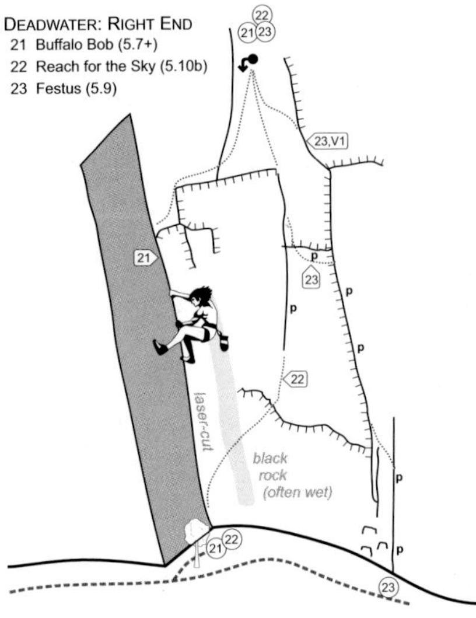

21 **Buffalo Bob 5.7+ G 70'** ★★

Start: At a terrace at the base of a black right-facing corner with a laser-cut handcrack.

P1 5.7+ G: Climb the handcrack to the top, then traverse right on ledges to a fixed anchor (shared with **Reach for the Sky** and **Festus**). 70'

Gear: To 3", extra 2"–3".

FA Jul, 2002, Bob Starinsky, Ed Palen

Watercolor by Lucie Wellner.

22 **Reach for the Sky 5.10b G 70'** ★★★★

Excellent climbing, but the start is often wet. Harder for short people—there's a long reach.

Start: Same as **Buffalo Bob**.

P1 5.10b G: Climb the black, often wet corner for 10', then move right to a bucket and continue right to a stance on the orange-colored wall. Up the crack using crimpers and holds on the face, past a piton (crux) to a ledge, then straight up more cracks to a fixed anchor. 70'

Gear: Small gear plus 1 ea 2"–3" for the start.

FA 2002, Ed Palen, Dennis Harrington

23 **Festus 5.9 G 70'** ★

Start: 15' right of the black right-facing corner of **Buffalo Bob**, in a depression with a spike of rock at the bottom and a piton in a crack 10' up.

P1 5.9 G: Climb up past the piton to gain a crack (some suspect rock here), which widens into a right-facing corner up to a ceiling. (V1) Below the ceiling, step left 5' to join **Reach for the Sky**, then follow it to a fixed anchor. 70'

V1 5.10d PG: Continue up the right-facing corner to the ceiling. Break the ceiling on the left via a crack, then step left to the fixed anchor.

Gear: Many pitons, plus gear to 3".

FA 2002, Ed Palen, Bob Starinsky

FA (V1) 2002, Kevin Boyle, Bill Dodd

DEADWATER WAY LEFT

Location	North Hudson, at the toe of Catamount Mountain, just south of the Deadwater
Aspect	South
Height	50' to 90'
Quality	★
Approach	10 min, easy
Summary	A raw cliff with some exploratory climbs and potential for more.

-5.6	5.7	5.8	5.9	5.10	5.11	5.12	5.13+	total
3			2					5

DESCRIPTION

While not physically connected to Deadwater, which is on Potter Hill, Deadwater Way Left is on neighboring Catamount Mountain and is best described as part of the Deadwater group. The cliff offers steep crack climbs with potential for several more routes. The cliff also features one of the larger horizontal roofs in the Adirondacks, split by a razor cut finger crack, as yet unclimbed.

The cliff is about 300' wide. It has a shorter section on its left end, a higher middle section featuring the obvious very large roof about 60' up, a very sheer wall below this to the right, and then lower-angled rock on the right end. It's fairly easy to hike up or down around the climber's left end of the cliff.

HISTORY

The cliff was located by Ellen and Tom DuBois in March, 2012. They saw rock on the west side of Catamount (the small hill south of Deadwater) from the Northway. Inspection revealed this cliff to be choss, but all was not lost, as they discovered this cliff on the hike out.

DIRECTIONS **(MAP PAGE 148)**

Park as for Deadwater. The herd path to Deadwater begins on the east side of US 9, about 100' north of the parking area, and goes northwest. The approach for Deadwater Way Left begins about 50' south of the normal Deadwater path, directly across Route 9 from the north end of the parking area, and goes generally west. (A very short way into the woods, a sign clarifies that this is not the approach for Deadwater.)

Follow the path easily through open woods, and you soon reach the brook that drains from between Potter Hill and Catamount Mountain. Cross this brook, then swing slightly southwest and climb into a small valley with open hardwoods. The cliff appears on the right soon after ascending into this valley 606738,4879012.

1 Do You Feel Lucky 5.9 G 50' ★★

Start: At a striking fingercrack that shoots up the middle of the short, gray wall at the left end of the cliff.

P1 5.9 G: Climb the crack. Many face holds remove the sting of the often-flared tips crack. 50'

Gear: To #1 Camalot; tiny cams are helpful in the slightly flaring crack above.

FA Mar 18, 2012, Tom DuBois, Ellen DuBois

2 Sister Sarah 5.9+ TR 70'

At the right end of the short gray wall 50' right of **Do You Feel Lucky**, the base of the cliff steps down about 15' to a lower base. Three parallel cracks about 6 feet apart rise from this lower base. Begin at the left-hand of the three cracks. Climb the crack. The low roof-block is shared with the middle crack. The protection for leading would be R.

FA (TR) Apr 14, 2012, Tom DuBois

3 Mule Project

An open project, this is the middle crack, just right of **Sister Sarah**. There is a fixed anchor on a tree at the top of this route.

4 Bonus Mule Project

Another open project begins at the base of the left-facing corner-slab, just right of the right-hand of three cracks (the left of which is **Sister Sarah**). This is directly under the left end of the big roof. Climb up and left into the crack line. The crack becomes a left-facing corner, and then transitions to a right-facing corner capped by a small roof. Step left around the roof to finish.

5 Josey Wales 5.6 G 70'

Start: At broken rock 8' right of **Bonus Mule**.

P1 5.6 G: Climb up and traverse right across 3rd class broken rock to a right-facing corner with a huge block sitting in it, under the right end of the roof. Go up the corner on the right side of the block, step right around the right end of the roof, and finish straight up. (A more direct start for this route would be better, but much harder.) 70'

FA Apr 14, 2012, Tom DuBois, Ellen DuBois

6 Every Which Way and Loose 5.5 G 55' ★

Start: 75' right of the right end of the roof, at the end of the sheer section, is a complex blocky area with easier climbing. Begin at the base of the blocky area at a rounded arête with a small chimney behind it.

P1 5.5 G: Climb the rounded arête and step right to the blocky rock. Climb delicately up to a fixed anchor. 55'

FA Apr 14, 2012, Tom DuBois, Ellen DuBois

7 Spaghetti Western 5.6 TR 45'

Begin at the base of a low-angled rounded arête, with obvious recent rockfall from its base, 35' right of **Every Which Way and Loose**. This route is a "forested scramble." Climb the arête to finish at a small platform about 6' below a very large tree with a fixed anchor. Walking up the slippery pine straw to the tree may be the crux.

FA (TR) Apr 14, 2012, Tom DuBois, Ellen DuBois

SHARP BRIDGE CAMPGROUND

Location	Near Northway (I-87) Exit 30, east of US 9
Aspect	South
Height	80'
Quality	★
Approach	15 min, easy
Summary	A small cliff with several high-quality short routes.

-5.6	5.7	5.8	5.9	5.10	5.11	5.12	5.13+	total
3	1	1	3					8

This small cliff seems overly riddled with cracks, which makes for nice climbing. For climbers staying at the campground, this cliff is a convenient place for an evening workout. It has an easy approach, and the top is easily accessible for toproping.

There are two right-facing corners on the cliff that can be used to locate routes. The right-facing corner on the left end of the cliff is used to locate **Rumble Strips** and **Guides Gift**, and the right-facing corner at the right end of the cliff (the route **Monkey**) locates the other routes.

ACCESS

The parking and access are via the DEC trailhead located at the entrance to the campground. Access to the cliff isn't affected by the campground, but do check if you want to stay here, as the DEC has flirted with closing it.

HISTORY

Inspired by the rock at Deadwater, Tom and Ellen DuBois scoured the landscape investigating every concentration of bunched-together contour lines. Nearly ready to give up, they found this little cliff in one of the last places they were looking, on the hill just outside the campground. They returned two weeks later and cleaned and climbed the best lines, beginning with **Monkey**.

DIRECTIONS **(MAP PAGE 164)**

The cliff is accessed from the Sharp Bridge Campground on US 9 605927,4877566, 2.6 miles south of Northway Exit 30 and 6.9 miles north of Exit 29. Park at the entrance to the campground on the left before the gated entrance; this is the trailhead for Round Pond and East Mill Flow.

Before the campground gate, bear right past a gate and downhill into a picnic area. Follow the dirt road parallel to a stream to a trail register. Continue on the trail to a wood bridge; 50' beyond the bridge, angle off left on a bearing of 105° for 10 min to the base of the cliff 606491,4877272. There is now a decent path to the cliff.

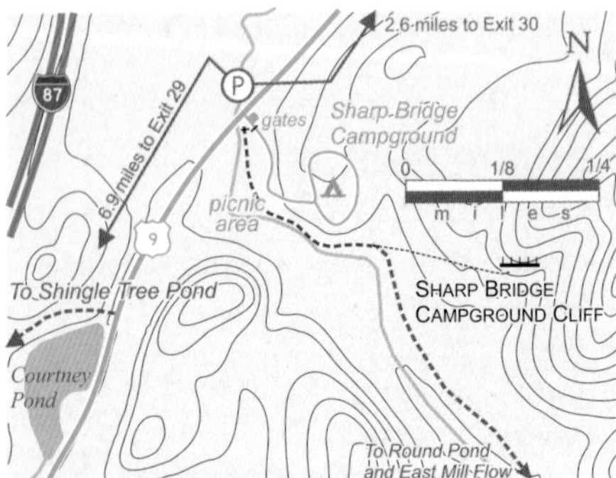

1 Short Sharp Shocked 5.4 G 40' ★

Start: At a large right-facing corner 50' from the left end of the cliff.

P1 5.4 G: Up the appealing fingercrack to a small overhang at midheight. Step easily left and up a slot with a handcrack to a block. 40'

FA Oct 7, 2007, Tad Welch, Bill Widrig

2 Rumble Strips 5.7 G 50' ★

Named for the rumble strips at the Border Patrol checkpoint on the Northway, which can be heard in the distance.

Start: 50' from the left end of the cliff is a large right-facing corner. This route begins 15' to the right at a shallow right-facing corner capped by a small ceiling 10' up.

P1 5.7 G: Up the corner to the ceiling, out the left side via a crack, and into an A-shaped slot. Up this to a shallow right-facing corner, then follow the corner to the top. 50'

FA Sep 16, 2007, Tom DuBois, Ellen DuBois

3 Guide's Gift 5.3 G 50'

Start: 30' right of the large right-facing corner (which is 50' from the left end of the cliff), at a right-facing, left-rising staircase of blocks.

P1 5.3 G: Climb the blocky staircase with a wide crack to the top. 50'

FA Sep 16, 2007, Tad Welch, Steve Jervis, Jim Lawyer

4 Not Tell Wife, OK? 5.9+ G 80' ★★

Start: At a shallow right-facing corner 15' downhill from and left of the large right-facing corner of **Monkey**.

P1 5.9+ G: Up the right-facing corner to its top, then up a crack to where the wall becomes steeper. A thin left-leaning crack leads through the bulging face past a small pine to a ledge. Move right to a tree with a fixed anchor (shared with **Sharp Bridge**). 80'

FA Sep 16, 2007, Jim Lawyer, Tad Welch

5 Sharp Bridge 5.9 PG 80' ★

Good climbing, although the route has some loose blocks and questionable flakes.

Start: At a thin crack 1' right of **Not Tell Wife, OK?**

P1 5.9 PG: Climb the crack straight up past a small triangular slot 8' up, through a bulge, and into a right-facing corner. Climb stacked blocks right of the corner through a slot. Step left and climb a short face to the top, at a tree with a fixed anchor. 80'

FA Sep 16, 2007, Tom DuBois, Ellen DuBois

6 Day-Tripper 5.9 G 80'

On the first ascent, the leader followed the Beatles' advice and took the easy way out.

Start: Same as **Monkey**.

P1 5.9 G: Up the thin right-leaning crack to the base of the right-facing corner. Step left under a ceiling to gain a vertical handcrack. Up the handcrack (crux) to a small tree beneath a square ceiling, then step right and climb a handcrack in the left wall of the **Monkey** corner to the top of a choss tower. Up and left over easy rock to the fixed anchor (shared with **Sharp Bridge**). 80'

FA Sep 16, 2007, Tad Welch, Jim Lawyer

Tom DuBois on the first ascent of **Sharp Bridge** *(5.9).*

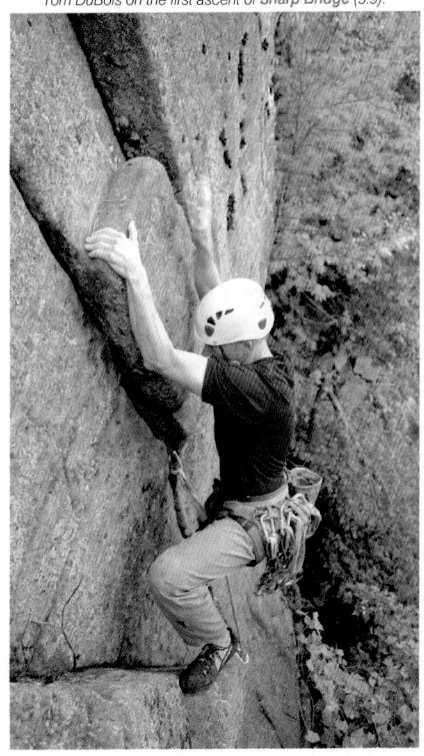

7 Monkey 5.8 G 80' ★★

Start: At the right end of the cliff where the terrain goes steeply uphill, below a large right-facing corner that begins 10' up.

P1 5.8 G: Up a thin right-leaning crack to gain the corner. Up the corner to the top, crux at the end. 80'

FA Sep 16, 2007, Tom DuBois, Ellen DuBois

8 Easy Monkey 5.5 G 70'

Start: 35' right of **Monkey**, at a right facing corner crack system.

P1 5.5 G: Up the corner and crack past a low crux (small TCU helpful). Easy moves continue up the crack to ledges and a short face at the top. 70'

FA Jun 19, 2011, Tom DuBois, Ellen DuBois

SWEET FERN HILL

Location	Hammond Pond Wild Forest, accessed from Ensign Pond Road
Aspect	South
Height	80'
Quality	
Approach	20 min, easy
Summary	A small, attractive wall that features vertical climbing on cracks and corners with good potential for more routes.

Sweet Fern Hill has several cliffs that overlook the scenic Hammond Pond. This is the first cliff to be explored and has the shortest approach. There is only one route to date but obvious potential for additional routes.

The cliff has a high south side with several cracks. A rounded arête transitions to a lower but steeper east side.

HISTORY

Tom and Ellen DuBois located this cliff while exploring the various areas of open rock on Sweet Fern Hill in 2007. They first become familiar with the area along Ensign Pond Road on a bike trip, and noticed many small cliffs in the area. They began a systematic exploration of all the little hills along that road.

DIRECTIONS

From Northway (I-87) Exit 30, travel south on US 9 for 6.8 miles to Caza Turn Road on the left. Turn left, then left again onto Ensign Pond Road.

From Northway Exit 29, travel north on US 9 for 8.5 miles to Caza Turn Road on the right. Turn right, then right again onto Ensign Pond Road.

Follow Ensign Pond Road (also known as North Hudson–Moriah Road) for 2.8 miles to the Hammond Pond Trailhead on the right side of the road 607385,4871917. There are several other trailheads in the area; this is the lot with the large "Hammond Pond Wild Forest" sign. From the parking lot, there are two trails. The right-hand trail leads to Berrymill Pond; take the left-hand trail to Hammond Pond, marked with red disks. The trail begins as a footpath but soon crosses a small bridge and joins a roadlike "handicap access" route. The total distance to the pond is 0.8 mile and may easily (and legally) be biked as an alternative to walking. At 15 min, the trail forks; take the left fork directly to the pond. Cross the wooden plank dam and the spit of land, then walk uphill through open woods for a couple of hundred yards to the cliff, which will be on your left, reached at 20 min 608198,4871767.

DESCENT OPTIONS

Walk around the left (west) end of the cliff.

1 Frosted Fern 5.8 G 80' ★

Start: At the right end of the south-facing section of the cliff, at a prominent dihedral with a consistent 0.25" crack.

P1 5.8 G: A bouldery start on small holds (crux) leads up a thin crack in the dihedral to its top. Scramble up large blocks to a tree with a fixed anchor. 80'

Gear: Wires, small cams (or Lowe Balls).

FA Oct 14, 2007, Tom DuBois, Ellen DuBois

BASS LAKE HILL CRAG

Location	East side of the Northway, near North Hudson
Aspect	West
Height	200'
Quality	
Approach	45 min, moderate
Summary	Large, complex, mostly unexplored cliff with potential for more routes.

This large and complex cliff can be easily seen from the old Frontier Town airstrip, and from the north-bound exit ramp of Northway Exit 29. The overall quality of the rock is reminiscent of Hurricane Crag—a bit of loose rock that can be pried off, and a sort of bristly, dry feel. The base is sloped downhill, but not unpleasantly so, with open vegetation. You can slightly hear the Northway.

The cliff is 150' wide and about 200' tall, but is broken by a ledge and some 4th class rock at the top. There is potential for more routes here.

Walking along the base of the cliff from left to right, after some broken rock, you'll reach a clean 60' x 60' black wall with a 12'-tall open book in the middle 25' up. Downhill and right of this 75' is a short black prow 15' up that juts out. Right of this is a flat terrace ledge 20' up—the most prominent feature on the cliff—above which is a sheer wall split by a horizontal. Most of the climbing potential is around these features.

DIRECTIONS

From Northway Exit 29 (North Hudson), follow US 9 north for 8.5 miles to Caza Turn Road on the right. Turn right and drive 0.15 mile (100 yards past the second house) and park where an old paved road forks to the right. This is the little known (and unsigned) Caza Trailhead. Park along Caza Turn Road 602976,4871116.

From the parking (0 hr 0 min) follow the blacktop road east 200' until it enters the woods and becomes a trail (there are DEC "Forest Preserve" and "No Live Bait in Bass Lake" signs). Even though there is no roadside sign or trail register, this is a wonderfully maintained DEC trail that leads to Bass Lake and beyond to Berrymill Flow. Follow the trail along Black Brook, and, at 5 min, cross a small brook. After this, the trail turns away from the brook and ascends uphill. At 15 min there is a cairn on the right side of the trail 604089,4870787. You've gone too far if you reach three tiny brooks that cross the trail in rock lined channels. Leave the trail and bushwhack 225° for 25 min to the top of the hill 603786,4870369, reached at 40 min.

Continue over the top of the hill and down the southwest side for 200' to the top of the cliff 603733,4870324. Walk (skier's) right around the side of the cliff to reach the bottom of the cliff 603685,4870298, at 45 min.

HISTORY

Tom DuBois saw this cliff from the Northway, but was unable to locate a trail for access (the DEC trail from Caza Turn Road is not on most hiking trail maps). Prepared for a difficult bushwhack, DuBois parked on Ensign Pond road, waded Black Brook, and began bushwhacking, only to come upon the excellent and well-maintained trail.

1 Snakeskin 5.7 R 95' ★

Start: 5' left of the black prow at a clean slab with a thin seam. This is 20' downhill and right of a broad open book with a slab at the base; there is a jumble of boulders on top of this slab in the open book.

P1 5.7 R: Go up the slab and seam to V-notch on the left side of the prow (no gear, 5.7 R), then up easier rock to a cleaned, left-leaning open book. At the top of the open book, step right of the arête and climb an attractive face for a few feet to an easy finish. Fixed anchor on the tree at the top. 95'

FA Aug 30, 2009, Tom Dubois, Ellen Dubois

MEADOW HILL CLIFF

Location	Hammond Pond Wild Forest, accessed from Ensign Pond Road
Aspect	Southeast
Height	50'
Quality	
Approach	8 min, easy
Summary	Small cliff with a single route and some potential for new routes.

This small cliff, about 50' high and 150' wide, faces away from the road and overlooks an attractive wetland and meadow, hence the name. It sits on a small subsidiary bump of Harris Hill off Ensign Pond Road. The woods in this area feature unparalleled natural beauty, so be especially vigilant to keep the area pristine. There are several unclimbed cracks near **My Pleasure**, and potential for more difficult routes on the left end. There is some loose rock, and the area is wet.

DIRECTIONS

From Northway (I-87) Exit 30, travel south on US 9 for 6.8 miles to Caza Turn Road (CR 4) on the left. Turn left, then left again onto Ensign Pond Road. From the Northway (I-87) Exit 29, drive north 2.4 miles to Caza Turn Road (CR 4) on the right. Turn right, then right again onto Ensign Pond Road.

Drive east on Ensign Pond Road for 5.8 miles to the Trout Pond trailhead on the left (south) side of the road. Turn around and drive west for 0.4 miles to a widened shoulder on the right side of the road with plenty of room for several cars 0609944,4874923. This is the first widened shoulder on the right past the yellow "35 MPH" sign.

Walk west on the road for 450' to where a stream runs up against the road on the south side. Cross at its narrowest point; there is a cairn on the far side. Turn right and proceed parallel to the road for a few feet under some overhanging outcrops. Step up into the woods (cairn), climb the hill, then hike across the flat top of the hill through open woods. As you descend the other side of the hill, you will reach the top of the cliff 610174,4874799. Turn (skier's) right to descend to the base of the cliff at its left end.

HISTORY

Tom DuBois found this little cliff during his systematic exploration of all the little hills along Ensign Pond Road.

1 My Pleasure 5.8 PG 45'

Fun moves and reportedly worth the short approach.

Start: Moving right from the left end of the cliff, the first major feature is a large right-facing corner capped by roof 35' up. 30' right is a pile of blocks detached from the cliff. Begin just right of this pile of blocks, below an obvious crack.

P1 5.8 PG: Climb the crack past a small overhang 15' up to the top. 45'

Gear: Mostly small: stoppers, small nuts, and cams to 0.5".

FA Sep 22, 2008, Tom DuBois, Ellen DuBois

CAMEL'S HUMP

Camel's Hump is located west of the Northway (I-87) between Exits 29 and 30. It is approached from US 9, across the Schroon River under the Northway, then up the Walker Brook Valley. From the head of the valley, bushwhack northeast to the col between Camel's Hump and Camel Mountain, then northwest to the summit of Camel's Hump. The approach requires about 3 hr and gains 2000' in elevation. The summit is an open rock dome much like Noonmark, and the climbing is on the west face, ending on the summit itself. The slabs are 300' wide and up to 250' high 600190,4874667.

The cliff was explored for climbing by Dick Tucker and Bob Hey, who climbed two routes on the right side of the slab. The rightmost route, **Child's Play** (5.3; 80'; Sep 23, 1990; Bob Hey) is pure friction, and 40' left is **Sunday Stroll** (5.4; 85'; Sep 23, 1990; Dick Tucker) that climbs a series of disconnected fingercracks. The left side of the cliff is longer, steeper, and holds good potential for routes. The remote setting combined with outstanding scenery make this a great place for further backcountry exploration.

NORTH HUDSON DOME

Location	West side of the Northway (I-87), 1.5 miles north of Exit 29
Aspect	Southeast
Height	300'
Quality	★★
Approach	1 hr, moderate
Summary	A slab with two excellent friction routes that face the Northway.

-5.6	5.7	5.8	5.9	5.10	5.11	5.12	5.13+	total
	2							2

As you walk along the base of this cliff, there is little to inspire you to climb it, as it's shrouded in trees, full of ledges, and has few continuous features. Once you're above the canopy, however, the cliff opens up, with large, unbroken spans of black, pocketed, sculpted rock that is so good for friction.

The cliff is on a hillside near the Northway positioned very similarly to the Poke-O Slab. This means you can hear the highway, but not offensively so. It is visible to northbound travelers between mileposts 95 and 96.

The cliff was originally accessed via the Northway, but since that approach is illegal, it's seen very few (if any) visitors. Walking along the Northway from the nearest exit is quite unpleasant, and you're likely to be stopped by the State Police. The approach described here minimizes interaction with the Northway and is completely legitimate.

HISTORY

This cliff represents yet another exploration by Patrick Purcell of cliffs that he could see from the Northway. He made a couple of trips here with various partners in the mid-1980s, but the cliff has seen little attention since.

DIRECTIONS (MAP PAGE 167)

Park at a dirt pullout on the east side of US 9 602667,4869323, 8.2 miles south of Exit 30 and 1.3 miles north of Exit 29 (where US 9 and Blue Mountain Road intersect). This pullout is 0.1 mile south of a funky old motel on the west side of the road (address: 3200 US 9).

From the pullout, walk south on US 9 for 100 yards to the yellow and blue DEC boundary markers (signs on the trees). Turn right (west) into the woods and bushwhack 5 min to the river. Walk right (north) along the river and find a crossing. The crossing is easy in low water—calf-deep.

Walk along the bank of the river until you're within 200' of the highway, then walk south about 200 yards, parallel to the highway, and find a marshy area; angle toward the highway and find the large rectangular concrete culvert that goes under the highway 602225,4869192. (There are actually two culverts here, one for animals and the other for the stream; the concrete culvert is better.) Walk through the culvert to the other side of the Northway, then up a short hillside to an open, flat wooded bench. Walk parallel to the highway for 10 min to a boggy section. Descend the hillside and go around the swamps next to the highway. On the far side of the swamps, find a deep ravine (which feeds the swamps) and follow this up to a level bench that sits below the cliffs, which are invisible on the hillside above. Walk up the hillside to the cliffs 601882,4870075.

The base of the slab is covered in a high forested canopy of oak trees but is relatively open beneath. The terrain at the base of the cliff is steep and covered with slippery oak leaves. The rock above is shrouded in trees with no major landmarks and no particular section all that inspiring. The distinguishing feature is a small slab that comes down into the woods bounded on its left side by a left-facing corner, filled with a couple of cedars. Just up from the base of the corner (and halfway up the left side of the slab) is a large oak tree very close to the corner whose trunk forks into two trunks about 6' up. The tree is the major landmark. On the uphill side of the base of the tree are two half-buried flat stones, one positioned on end. There is also a large cairn nearby.

Another feature to look for is a small buttress that sits in front of the cliff, about 80' right of the slab. The left side of the buttress has vertical 12'-high white rock, the lower left corner has a low, 8'-wide ceiling 5' up, and the front of the buttress is dark-colored rock.

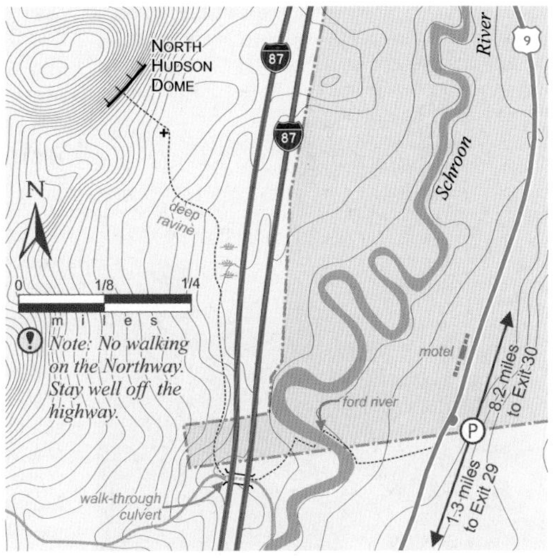

DESCENT OPTIONS

Both routes end on a tree island. A 200' rappel from the tree island, diagonaling slightly left, lands you on a small ledge 20' up from the base of the cliff. A 4th-class downclimb or another short rappel returns to the ground 40' left of **Easter's Force**.

1 Easter's Force 5.7 R 270' ★★★

Excellent climbing on P2 with a long runout on clean, dimpled rock with knobs.

Start: Just left of the left-facing corner and 8' left of the oak tree is a slab with a small left-rising 4"-deep overlap that rises to meet a more prominent left-rising corner.

P1 5.7 PG: Begin on the slab and climb up to the 4"-deep overlap. Follow the overlap up and left to a left-facing, left-leaning sharp-edged corner. (This corner sits just above a small island with pine trees.) From the top of the corner, angle up and left to a jagged crack, then up and left following the top edge of a good flake to the trees on the left. 80'

P2 5.7 R: Up and right to the first large right-facing corner, up to its top, then up and right to another shallow right-facing corner. At the top of the corner, step left and up to a good stance below a bulge of very positive white dimpled rock. Over the bulge on amazing rock (crux, no gear), then straight up to a very small seam (#00 TCU critical). Continue straight up the face to some right-facing flakes, then up and right to the tree island (shared with **Burton Birch Route**). 190'

FA Apr 7, 1985, Patrick Purcell, Mary Purcell

2 Burton Birch Route 5.7 PG (5.5 R) 250' ★★

This route sports clean rock, comfortable belays, and reasonable protection.

Start: At the left-facing corner above the oak tree.

P1 5.5 PG (5.2 R): From the oak tree, step right onto the slab and climb the face just right of the left-facing corner to a ledge. Continue up two left-facing corners, one stacked on top of the other, to a higher ledge. At the top of the second corner, step right 5' and climb a white streak up a slab to a nice ledge with a cedar on the right. 90'

*Jim Lawyer on P2 of **Burton Birch Route** (5.7). Photo by Simon Catterall.*

P2 5.7 PG (5.5 R): (V1) Traverse left on the face to the lower left end of a right-arching overlap. Traverse up and right under the arch to its right end, then over this on positive holds. Up the slab to a left-rising crack, then up to a good ledge. There is no gear here, but you can arrange a long leash to trees 20' to the right. 100'

P3 5.5 PG: Climb straight up the black textured rock face to an arched roof. (V2) Step left and up to a large tree island. 60'

V1 5.8 PG: Climb straight up the face to meet the top of the right-arching overlap.

V2 5.7 G: Step right and climb through the apex of the arch via a good crack.

History: The "Birch" on the first-ascent party is unknown.

FA Jul, 1984, Patrick Purcell, Burton Ryan, Birch
FA (V1) Jul, 2007, R.L. Stolz
FA (V2) Jun 23, 2007, Michelle Burlitch, Simon Catterall

BABY DOME

Location	North Hudson, at Northway Exit 29
Aspect	South
Height	70'
Quality	★
Approach	5 min, easy
Summary	Small cliff with an easy approach and several moderate routes.

-5.6	5.7	5.8	5.9	5.10	5.11	5.12	5.13+	total
4	2							6

This small cliff is located on a tiny round-topped hill near the Northway (I-87). The short climbs are reasonably pleasant and worth the very easy approach.

HISTORY

The cliff was located by Ellen and Tom DuBois in May, 2012. They thought that there was no state land access on the north side of Boreas Road, but while driving that road one day, Ellen noticed a DEC sign, so they began exploring the area.

DIRECTIONS

Park on Blue Ridge Road (CR 84), just west of the overpass on the Northway (I-87) Exit 29. Locate a path that starts near a culvert in the grassy shoulder on the north side of the road, 200' west of the Northway, and 70' east of a State Land sign. Enter the woods, and switchback up the steep bank. Go north across a flat area, and skirt a low area on the left (west) past two small boulders to reach the corner of the Baby Dome 601378,4867536.

The approach brings you to the south corner of the dome. Walk left about 150' to access the top of the dome.

On the wall left of the approach is a distinct left-leaning crack and flake system (the route **Well Now, That's Better**).

1 Pacifier 5.7 G 30' ★★

Start: Uphill and left from the toe of the dome is a black wall that rises above a large ledge. Walk left from the toe past the black wall, then back right to gain the ledge. Begin in the middle of the terrace below a bolt.

P1 5.7 G: Go straight up the face to a short, left-facing, right-leaning corner. A few more moves to the top. Step left to a fixed anchor. 30'

FA May 17, 2013, Simon Catterall, Jim Lawyer

2 Ankle Bruise 5.7 TR 50'

Not recommended. Just left of the approach are two left-leaning handcracks. This is the left-hand crack. Scramble up the crack, and then up the left-leaning rib of disintegrating rock. Stay clear of the base!

FA (TR) Jul, 2012, Tom DuBois, Ellen DuBois

3 Well Now, That's Better 5.6 PG 65' ★

Start: 50' left of the toe of the dome, below a crack in a series of large, left-facing flakes. There is a large boulder at the base.

P1 5.6 PG: Go up the crack in the left-facing V-corner, then past another large flake, then up the right side of the face to a small tree ledge. At the back of the ledge finish on a short black face. 65'

FA Sep, 2012, Tom DuBois, Ellen DuBois

4 Dome Arête 5.5 PG 45' ★

Start: 25' uphill and right from the toe of the dome, just right of a large white pine on a ledge 12' up.

P1 5.6 PG: Climb the face and blunt arête. 45'

FA Sep, 2012, Tom DuBois, Ellen DuBois

5 Little Corner 5.4 G 40'

Start: 10' right of **Dome Arête**, below a small left-facing corner that begin 9' up.

P1 5.4 G: Climb the face and corner to another blunt arête. 40'

FA Sep, 2012, Tom DuBois, Ellen DuBois

6 Easter's Bunny 5.5 TR 70'

From the approach path, walk right (southeast) around the hill for 300' to a low-angled slab. Begin right of the slab at a mossy arête with slanting ledges 25' up. Climb the mossy arête (first couple moves are hardest), then up steeper rock for a couple moves at the slanting ledges, and finish on low angled rock.

FA (TR) Oct, 2012, Tom DuBois, Ellen DuBois

LITTLE JOHNSON

Location	Near North Hudson accessed from the Northway (I-87) Exit 29
Aspect	South
Height	60'
Quality	★★★
Approach	10 min, easy
Summary	A wide, steep cliff with potential for short powerful routes.

-5.6	5.7	5.8	5.9	5.10	5.11	5.12	5.13+	total
		1	2	3	1	2	1	10

This 500'-long cliff barely rises above the tree canopy in a pretty valley with a brook and a smattering of bouldering. The cliff base is generally open and pleasant. On the left end is Big Red Wall, a small wall with several attractive lines. The center section is overhanging and has a prominent black cave with a fire ring used by hunters; the routes **Awesome Sauce** and **Mushu** are here, and can be climbed in the rain. At the right end of the cliff is a narrow wall with an unusual tan-colored patina; the route **Like a Boss** ascends this wall. In general, the rock quality is only fair.

Most of the routes are equipped with lower-off anchors. Due to the complexities of the terrain at the top of the cliff, it's difficult to set up topropes here.

*Adam Crofoot on **Juicy Fruit** (5.11b), belayed by Ben Cook.*

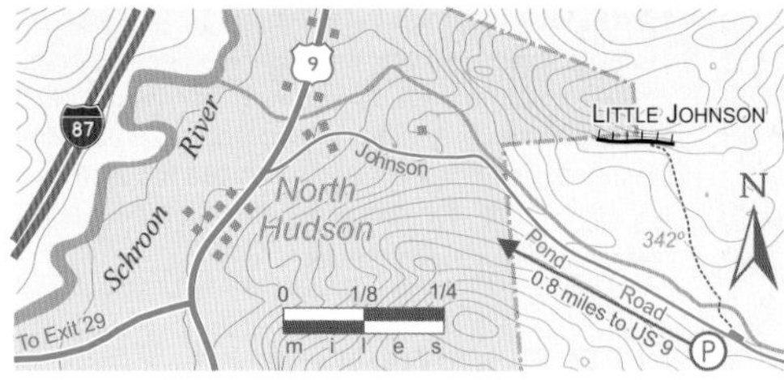

HISTORY

Todd Paris learned of the cliff from a boulderer who spotted the blocs from the road. Paris visited in 2008 with Jay Harrison and several others including Matt Hager and Jamie McNeill. After some initial cleaning and toproping success, they moved on to more fruitful pastures at Crane Mountain and never completed their routes. The chewing gum theme names were Paris' idea.

In 2013, while researching this book, Jim Lawyer made several visits with David Buzzelli, Colin O'Connor, Adam Crofoot, and Ben Cook. They freed some of the earlier topropes and added several routes, including the quality lines of **Like a Boss**, **Awesome Sauce**, and **Mushu**, which Buzzelli redpointed after many days of attempts.

DIRECTIONS (MAP PAGE 170)

From the Northway (I-87) Exit 29, drive east on Blue Ridge Road to the T intersection with US 9 (0.0 mile). Turn left (north) and drive through North Hudson. At 0.3 mile, turn right onto Johnson Pond Road (CR 78). At 0.4 mile there's a spring house on the right to fill up your water bottles. At 1.0 mile park on the left in a spacious pullout 603386,4867301.

From the left side of the pullout, go northwest through open woods (parallel to the road) and cross a stream. Continue northwest on a bearing of 342° following a rough herd path to the cliff 603096,4867757, 10 min from the road.

Big Red Wall

This is the first good rock wall at the left end of the cliff. It's about 60' tall, and the terrain rises gently as you walk right along the base. There's a large red pine 20' back from the face in front of **Beechnut**. 130' left is some fresh rockfall. Walk left (a bit of a thrash) to access the top.

1 Juicy Fruit 5.11b G 60' ★★

Start: 30' from the left of the wall at a left-facing left-leaning overlap.

P1 5.11b G: Undercling up the left-leaning overlap to its end, then layback up to a good crimp on a black, bulging face. Go over the bulge, then straight up to a good jug in a left-facing corner below the upper black bulge. Move left to a stance on the arête, then back right up the steep wall to a fixed anchor. 60'

FA Jul 20, 2013, Jim Lawyer, Adam Crofoot

2 Fruit Stripe 5.8 G 60'

Start: 10' right of **Juicy Fruit** at a full-height crack system in a shallow left-facing corner.

P1 5.8 G: Follow the crack up and left to a notch that breaks a ceiling. Go through this, then up right on a slab to a fixed anchor (shared with **Beechnut**). 60'

FA (TR) 2008, Todd Paris, Jay Harrison

FFA Jul 20, 2013, Adam Crofoot, Jim Lawyer

Jim Lawyer on the initial crack of ***Awesome Sauce*** *(5.12a), belayed by Royce Van Evera.*

3 Beechnut 5.10a PG 60' ★

Start: 10' right of **Fruit Stripe** in the center of a shield of reddish rock with a horizontal crack 8' up.

P1 5.10a PG: Go straight up the wall to a left-rising crack. Continue straight up the face to a fixed anchor. 60'

FA (TR) 2008, Todd Paris, Jay Harrison
FFA Jul 20, 2013, Jim Lawyer, Adam Crofoot

Geiko Cave Area

In the center of the cliff and 300' right of Big Red Wall is a black cave with a fire ring at its lowest point, and a large boulder on its left side.

4 Not Quite Geiko 5.10a TR 60'

Begin behind the boulder on the left side of the cave. Go up a crack, then step right onto the face. Follow a thin left-leaning crack to a broken open book; up this to the top. Some bad rock; not recommended.

FA (TR) 2008, Jay Harrison, Todd Paris

5 Awesome Sauce 5.12a G 50' ★★★★

A difficult fingercrack finishing on an overhanging wall with incut holds.

Start: In the cave below an overhanging, left-leaning fingercrack. The continuation of this crack is **Not Quite Geiko**.

P1 5.12a G: Power up the left-leaning fingercrack to a great jug at its top, where the angle relents. Go up the face right of the crack to a jug on a ledge, then up and left on sidepulls to another good jug. Traverse 6' right on incuts to some sidepulls (crux), then layback straight up to a fixed anchor. 50'

Gear: 1 ea #.5, #.4, #.75, #1, green Alien, #1. Once you clip the first bolt, downclimb, remove the gear above the overhanging crack, and place a #1 Camalot in the ledge–jug to keep the rope from getting stuck in the lower crack.

FA Aug 31, 2013, Jim Lawyer, David Buzzelli

6 Mushu (aka Raging Asian) 5.13d G 50' ★★★★

Demanding and gymnastic with multiple knee bars coming out of the belly of the cave. Bring knee pads! Might be easier if you're tall.

Start: 12' right of **Awesome Sauce** at the lowest point in the cave.

● **P1 5.13d G:** Stick clip the first bolt. Pull through the low roof to a cramped stance at an undercling crack. Move left into a shallow, overhanging left-facing corner (first crux). Slap and knee-bar your way up to a good hold, then up onto a ledge. Regroup, then dyno up the overhanging wall to a sloper (V10 crux). Join **Awesome Sauce** to the shared fixed anchor. 50'

FA Sep 14, 2013, David Buzzelli

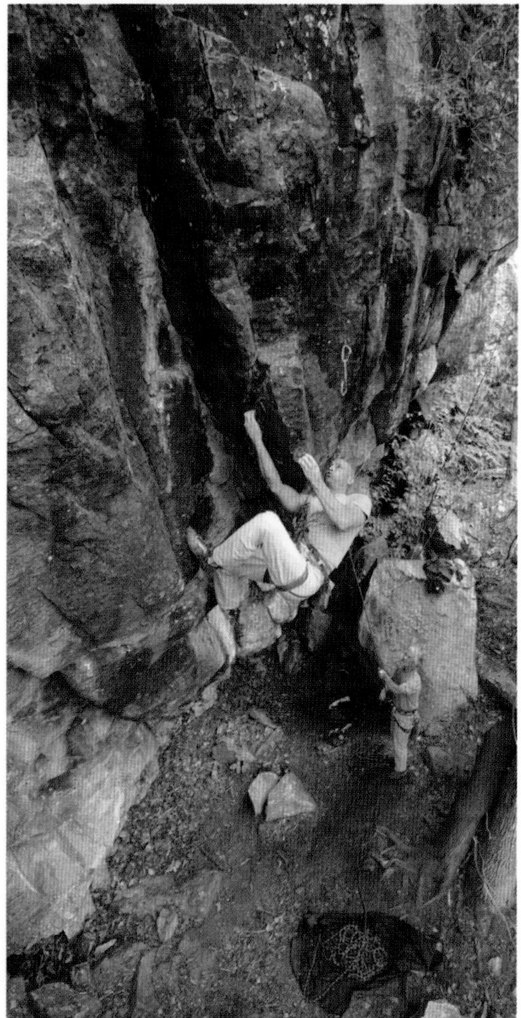

*David Buzzelli on **Mushu** (5.13d), belayed by Royce Van Evera.*

7 Boyz in the Hood 5.10c G 60' ★★★

Start: Uphill and right of the cave below a V-groove that leads to a large open book with a bottomless sharp arête in the middle capped by a roof.

○ **P1 5.10c G:** Up the V-groove, then up the open book to the bottomless arête. Go up the right side of the arête to a roof. Undercling the roof to its left side above crazy-sharp fins, then pull through the roof at a notch to a ledge. Traverse right, then go up a few overhanging jugs through a break to a fixed anchor on a tree. 60'

Gear: Optional #2 Camalot for the bottom.

FA Jul 27, 2013, Colin O'Connor, David Buzzelli, Jim Lawyer

Alligator Skin Area

On the right end of the cliff is a unique narrow wall with a tan-colored patina laced with vertical seams and flared cracks. This is the tallest wall on the cliff 603191,4867744.

8 Transplant 5.9+ PG 45' ★★★

Start: 40' downhill and left of **My Little Johnson** below a shallow left-facing corner in a right-facing wall.

P1 5.9+ PG: Go up the shallow left-facing corner to its top. Step left and make a hard move into a larger corner. Up this to a fixed anchor on the left wall. 45'

History: This is Cook's second new route. He's a transplant from Boulder, Colorado.

FA Jul 20, 2013, Ben Cook, Colin O'Connor

9 My Little Johnson 5.9 R 60'

Start: 15' left of **Like a Boss** and 4' left of a 4'-tall V-groove.

P1 5.9 R: Over a bulge and onto the slab. Up the slab to an open book left of a diamond-shaped roof. Up this to its top, then up the face to the top. 60'

FA 2008, Jay Harrison, Todd Paris

10 Like a Boss 5.12b G 70' ★★★★

Sustained and beta-intensive. The patina is friable and the cracks are flared and gravelly, but should clean up with more ascents.

Start: On the overhanging arête on the right side of the "alligator-skin" wall.

○ **P1 5.12b G:** Boulder up to parallel cracks. Make strenuous compression moves up the overhanging cracks to gain a good jug. Move right to the arête, then follow a left-trending line of cracks and holds to a final fingercrack. Fixed anchor. 70'

Gear: Optional yellow Alien for the final fingercrack.

FA Jul 27, 2013, Jim Lawyer, Colin O'Connor, David Buzzelli

Life is Short Wall

This short 30'-tall wall has several topropes in the 5.10 range. From the Alligator Skin Area, walk right along the cliff and onto a right-rising ledge. Continue along the ledge and into the forest. Walk back about 200' to this short, reddish wall with some left-leaning seams.

NORTHWAY EXPRESS WALL

Location	West side of the Northway (I-87) between Exits 28 and 29
Aspect	Southwest
Height	140'
Quality	★
Approach	45 min, moderate
Summary	A small cliff near the Northway with a number of single-pitch moderate routes.

-5.6	5.7	5.8	5.9	5.10	5.11	5.12	5.13+	total
4	3	3	6	1	1			18

The Northway Express Wall is a small wall on the lower hillside of Squaw Mountain. The rock is generally clean and high-quality, making this a good choice for single-pitch climbing, like a mini–Beer Wall. The routes are a mixture of cracks and faces.

The cliff can be seen from the Northway as you travel north past Exit 28 (just before milepost 92). You can hear the highway from the cliff, but, due to its orientation, it's not as bad as at Poke-O.

The cliff has three sections, with much undeveloped rock in between. The lower cliff, nearest the highway, is Pipeline Wall, a tremendous overhang wall with good potential for difficult routes. Spoof Wall has most of the routes and is characterized by a large roof with

*David Buzzelli at the crux of **Like a Boss** (5.12b).*

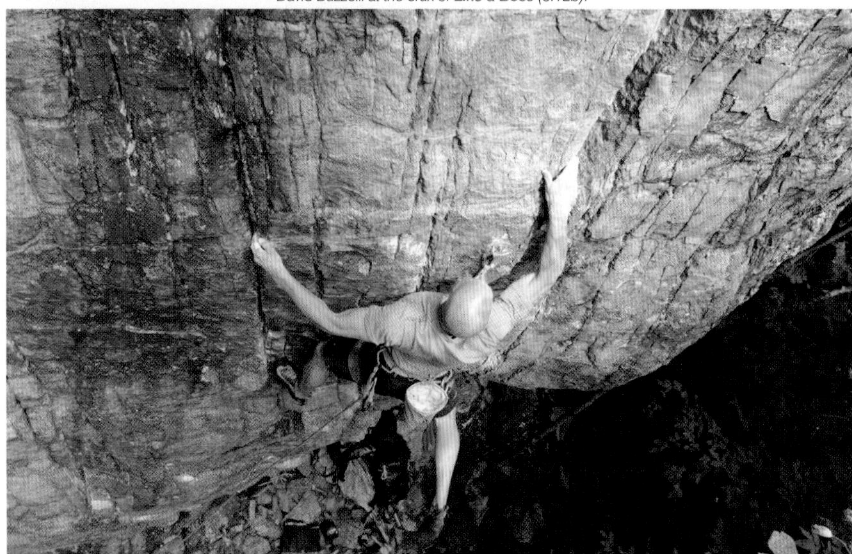

a broken leaning tower beneath it. Left of this is The Greenhouse, a face split by a long horizontal crack.

HISTORY

The cliff was first explored by Patrick Purcell, who made a couple of visits in 1984. Next to visit was Ken Nichols, who made several visits in 1988. Access has always been a problem: early visitors parked on the Northway and faked a breakdown, or pulled off on a hidden logging road and camped. Most people, unwilling to take such risks, have simply ignored this cliff, leaving it virtually untouched.

DIRECTIONS **(MAP PAGE 173)**

Access to the cliff has always been a challenge, as walking on the highway is long, unpleasant, and illegal. Obviously, you can't park on the highway (and don't try faking a breakdown). The approach described here is on state land, completely legal, and actually quite pleasant.

Park in a grassy area on the west side of US 9, at a hidden dirt road (an ATV Access Route for people with a qualifying disability) across from a house (address: 2504 US 9) 601196,4864542. This is 4.2 miles north of Exit 28 (and 0.2 mile north of the Blue Ridge Motel) and 1.9 miles south of Exit 29 (from the intersection of US 9 and Blue Ridge Road). The dirt road isn't well marked, but there is a small brown sign designating this as an ATV Access Route.

Follow the ATV Access Route for 15 min until it makes a 90° right turn to parallel the Schroon River. (Continuing down the road another 600' leads to a beautiful picnic area and campsite next to the Schroon River Weir. There is a plaque commemorating its reconstruction.)

Continue straight for 50' through the woods to the river, then turn left (downstream, as the river flows south) on the riverbank for about 100' to where the river makes a bend to the left. Ford the river here to the mouth of a small tributary on the opposite bank. The crossing is easy in the summer—the water is thigh-deep and moves at a moderate speed, and the bottom is sandy and flat. At times of high water, the crossing may be quite hazardous. (A second pair of shoes, ski poles, and a towel are nice to have.)

Follow the tributary upstream to the Northway, then cross underneath the highway though the 12'-diameter culvert. On the other side, stay in the woods and walk left (south) parallel to the highway, eventually working back toward the highway. After 5 min, you'll come to a deep ravine and a 24"-diameter culvert and a cairn. Turn right and follow the ravine on a bearing of 330° for 300' to a level section with ferns; you can see a wall to the right. This is Pipeline Wall, an overhanging 70'-high wall with a few minor routes 599749,4864128.

Continue uphill and left along the base of the wall about 10 min to reach the Spoof Wall, with the greatest concentration of routes 599608,4864252.

DESCENT OPTIONS

Rappel from trees.

The Greenhouse

This wall is on the left (west) end of the cliff, about 250' left of the leaning tower of Spoof Wall. The routes are located on a clean section of dark-colored rock that is split horizontally by a prominent long left-rising horizontal crack. The wall is located right of a large left-facing corner with a roof 25' up, and 30' right of a large left-arching scooped corner. The ground at the base is level but sloped away from the cliff.

1 Greenhouse Defect 5.11a TR 80'

Begin on the left side of the face at a dirty jagged crack. This is 4' right of a heavily vegetated left-leaning open book. Climb up the crack to the horizontal, then straight up the face, staying about 10' left of **Greenhouse Effect**.

FA (TR) Nov 30, 1990, Fred Abbuhl, Doug Douglas

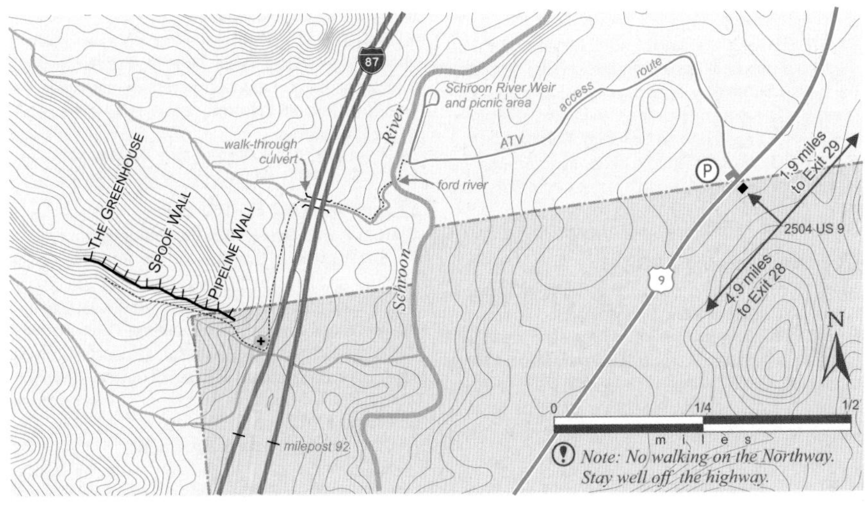

2 Strict Time 5.9 PG 80' ★★

After the first move, the rest of the route is 5.8+.

Start: 5' left of **Greenhouse Effect** at a left-leaning seam.

P1 5.9 PG: Climb up the left-leaning seam to the **Greenhouse Effect** horizontal. Traverse left 6' to a crack that begins above a bulge. Up the crack, then up the face, angling slightly left to finish in a very thin fingercrack that breaks a bulge. 80'

FA Apr 28, 1990, Fred Abbuhl, Sue Dearstyne

3 Greenhouse Effect 5.9 G 120' ★★

This route sports a long horizontal traverse and a good fingercrack. After the first move, the rest of the route is 5.7.

Start: On the right side of the face is a 20'-high V-groove that rises above a tree at its base. The left-rising horizontal crack that splits the face begins at this V-groove. Start 5' left of the V-groove at a very small seam that begins 3' up.

P1 5.9 G: (V1) Boulder up to the horizontal crack (crux), then follow the horizontal crack left for 30' to where it meets a vertical fingercrack. Up the fingercrack through bulges to the top. 120'

V1 Greenhouse Effect Direct 5.11a TR: Begin 20' left of the normal start at a shallow right-facing corner that starts 5' up. Climb up the corner to the main horizontal, traverse left 10', then follow the normal route to the top.

FA Apr 28, 1990, Fred Abbuhl, Sue Dearstyne

Spoof Wall

The Spoof Wall is the section of the cliff around the leaning tower—a two-tiered block-tower that leans up against the main face below a large roof. The tower looks as though it had just fallen out of the roof above.

4 Jackrabbit 5.9- PG (5.7 R) 140' ★

Start: On a steep left-rising slope beneath a slab, 20' left of the **Highway Patrol** V-corner and 56' left of the leaning tower, at a 15'-high vertical crack that doesn't reach the ground.

P1 5.7 R: Climb the crack and continue straight up the face past a right-leaning groove and the left end of the **Indian Summer** overlap to a ledge. Follow a right-leaning crack to a small overlap, then up a left-leaning crack to the large ledge as for **Indian Summer**. 110'

P2 5.9- PG: Walk 10' left to a cedar tree and work up a steep crack (crux) above to a larger cedar at the top. 30'

FA Oct, 1988, Ken Nichols, Jack Rankin

5 Indian Summer 5.8 PG 140'

Start: At some cracks 6' left of the **Highway Patrol** V-corner and 36' left of the leaning tower.

P1 5.8 PG: Follow the cracks until they end, then continue straight up the face past a small overlap and hole to a ledge. Climb up right onto a ramp that curves up left into a small right-facing corner. Continue up to a large ledge at the base of the headwall, then follow a right-leaning crack to a final short slab and the top. 140'

FA Sep, 1988, Ken Nichols, Anne Dal Vera

6 Highway Patrol 5.9- R 140'

Start: At a left-facing V-corner with a cedar tree 10' up, 30' left of the leaning tower.

P1 5.9- R: Climb the V-corner, follow the obvious crack system above, and continue straight up the face to a lone black water streak (left of the other water streaks). Climb up past several horizontals to a vertical crack out of which the streak emerges; follow the crack to the top. 140'

Gear: The crux is protected by a #2 RP turned 90° in a thin crack.

FA Sep, 1988, Ken Nichols, Anne Dal Vera

7 No Parking 5.7 G 140' ★

Start: At a crack 10' left of the leaning tower with a tree 4' up.

P1 5.7 G: Follow the crack up to the large roof. Over the roof, then angle up right along a crack system and move up to the lower left end of a right-arching overlap (the same arching overlap under which **Screams of the Primitive** climbs). Diagonal up left into the black water streaks, follow the streaks until just below the top, then finish up a crack that angles up right to the top. 140'

FA Sep, 1988, Ken Nichols, Anne Dal Vera

8 Screams of the Primitive 5.8 G 155' ★★

Start: At a chimney that splits the center of the leaning tower, with a flake-chockstone at two-thirds height.

P1 5.8 G: (V1) Climb the chimney to the top of the leaning tower to a ledge below the large roof. Reach across the abyss to the face above the tower and climb through the big roof on the left side at a crack. Climb the left-leaning crack to its top. Traverse left 6' and climb a right-leaning crack below and parallel to a prominent right-arching overlap. Work up this crack until just below a roof. Traverse 10' left, climb through the obvious notch, and continue straight up past ledges and a right-facing corner to the top. 155'

V1 5.8 G: Begin 5' left of the leaning tower below a shallow right-facing open book and crack through a low roof. Climb past the open book and follow the crack over the roof to join the normal route at the beginning of the traverse.

FA Aug, 1984, Patrick Purcell, Andy Zimmerman

FA (V1) Sep, 1988, Ken Nichols, Anne Dal Vera

9 Split Rock 5.7 PG 160' ★★

Start: Same as **Screams of the Primitive**.

P1 5.7 PG: Climb **Screams of the Primitive** up the chimney and through the large roof. Continue up and slightly right past a small overlap to a shallow right-facing open book capped by an overhang. Climb up to the overhang and traverse out left along a horizontal crack. Then climb up past the right end of another overhang, work up the face past the left side of a perched block, and finish up a low-angle slab. 160'

FA Oct, 1988, Ken Nichols, Jack Rankin

10 Freeze-Thaw Cycle 5.8 PG 140'

Start: Same as **Screams of the Primitive**.

P1 5.8 PG: Climb **Screams of the Primitive** up the chimney and through the large roof. Move up a few feet and traverse 15' right under the obvious overlap to its right end. Continue straight up a short right-facing corner and the face above to the middle of the overhang on the upper part of the wall. Pull over the overhang, step left, and work up a small right-facing corner and the face above to a ramp. Follow the ramp up left to the top. 140'

FA Oct, 1988, Ken Nichols, Bruce Jelen

11 Solid Rock 5.7 R 30'

This alternate start can be used with one of the other routes (**Freeze-Thaw Cycle**, **Split Rock**, **The Great Spoof**).

Start: On the arête at the bottom right corner of the leaning tower.

P1 5.7 R: Climb up the outside face of the leaning tower to the ledge at its top. 30'

FA Oct, 1988, Ken Nichols, Jack Rankin

12 The Great Spoof 5.9+ G 160' ★★

The first route climbed here.

Start: At a chimney formed by the right side of the leaning tower.

P1 5.7 G: Climb the chimney, which narrows to a crack, to a ledge on top of the tower. Traverse right on the face below the roof and move up to a small stance in the corner. 40'

P2 5.9+ G: Follow the prominent right-facing corner past a loose block, up a right-rising overhang (crux), then up cracks to the top. 120'

FA Jul 17, 1984, Patrick Purcell, Mary Purcell

13 Ace of Diamonds 5.10d PG 150' ★★

The most demanding lead at the cliff. It was originally climbed using the variation, then straightened out a month later.

Start: 30' right of the leaning tower are two right-facing corners. This route begins at some cracks on the face just left of the leftmost of these corners and 20' right of the leaning tower.

P1 5.10d PG: Follow the cracks up the low-angle face until they end below a bulging overlap. Traverse a few feet right, pull over the bulge, and (V1) reach left to a vertical crack. Work up the crack (crux) until it ends, continue straight up the blank face to a horizontal crack, and hand-traverse left to another vertical crack that leads to a large sloping ledge with a cedar tree. Finish up the short corner of **Dzelarhons** and the wide fissure above. 150'

V1 5.10b G: You can avoid the crux by stepping right into the **Dzelarhons** corner and following the corner for 15' to the beginning of the hand traverse out left.

Gear: RPs and HB offsets useful for the crux.

FA Oct, 1988, Ken Nichols, Bruce Jelen

FA (V1) Sep, 1988, Ken Nichols

14 Dzelarhons 5.4 G 150'

Named for a book by Anne Cameron about a legendary Salish Indian woman from Vancouver Island with supernatural powers.

Start: 30' right of the leaning tower, at the second right-facing corner.

P1 5.4 G: Follow the corner to the first small ledge, step right, and climb up into the main corner. Continue up the main corner past a blocky overhang to a large sloping ledge out left. Finish up the short corner and wide fissure. 150'

FA Sep, 1988, Anne Dal Vera, Ken Nichols

15 Freeway 5.6 PG 120' ★

Start: At a right-leaning crack that begins 3' up, 12' right of **Dzelarhons**.

P1 5.6 PG: Climb the crack past several horizontals to a cedar tree 20' up. Over a small bulge, then up a small left-facing corner. Move up and left, then continue straight up the undulating face to a right-arching overhang at the top of the cliff. Finish by climbing around the right end of the overhang to a pine tree at the top. 120'

FA Oct, 1988, Ken Nichols, Jack Rankin

Pipeline Wall

This steep, bulging 70'-high wall is impressive but currently has no routes that break the main overhanging section. There are several weaknesses that promise high-quality top-end routes. The currently reported routes climb the less imposing rock at the left and right ends of the wall.

The wall resembles the classic Hawaiian wave known as pipeline.

16 Ice Point 5.9 G 20' ★

Start: 30' from the left end of the wall below an overhanging left-leaning crack.

P1 5.9 G: Climb the crack to a small square-cut ledge, then to the top. 20'

FA Oct, 1988, Bruce Jelen, Ken Nichols

17 Ulluwatu 5.5 G 40' ★

Climbs the ramp to a point of rock. Named for an Indonesian surf break.

Start: 20' left of the deep V-chimney of **Grommet**, at a broken right-leaning crack.

P1 5.5 G: Climb the crack to a right-rising slab-ramp, then follow it to its top at a pointed spike. Over this to the top. 40'

18 Grommet 5.6 G 20'

An interesting feature but short. A "grom" is a young surfer.

Start: At a very deep V-chimney capped by a roof.

P1 5.6 G: Climb up the V-chimney to the roof, out left around the roof via a crack, then up a slab to the top. 20'

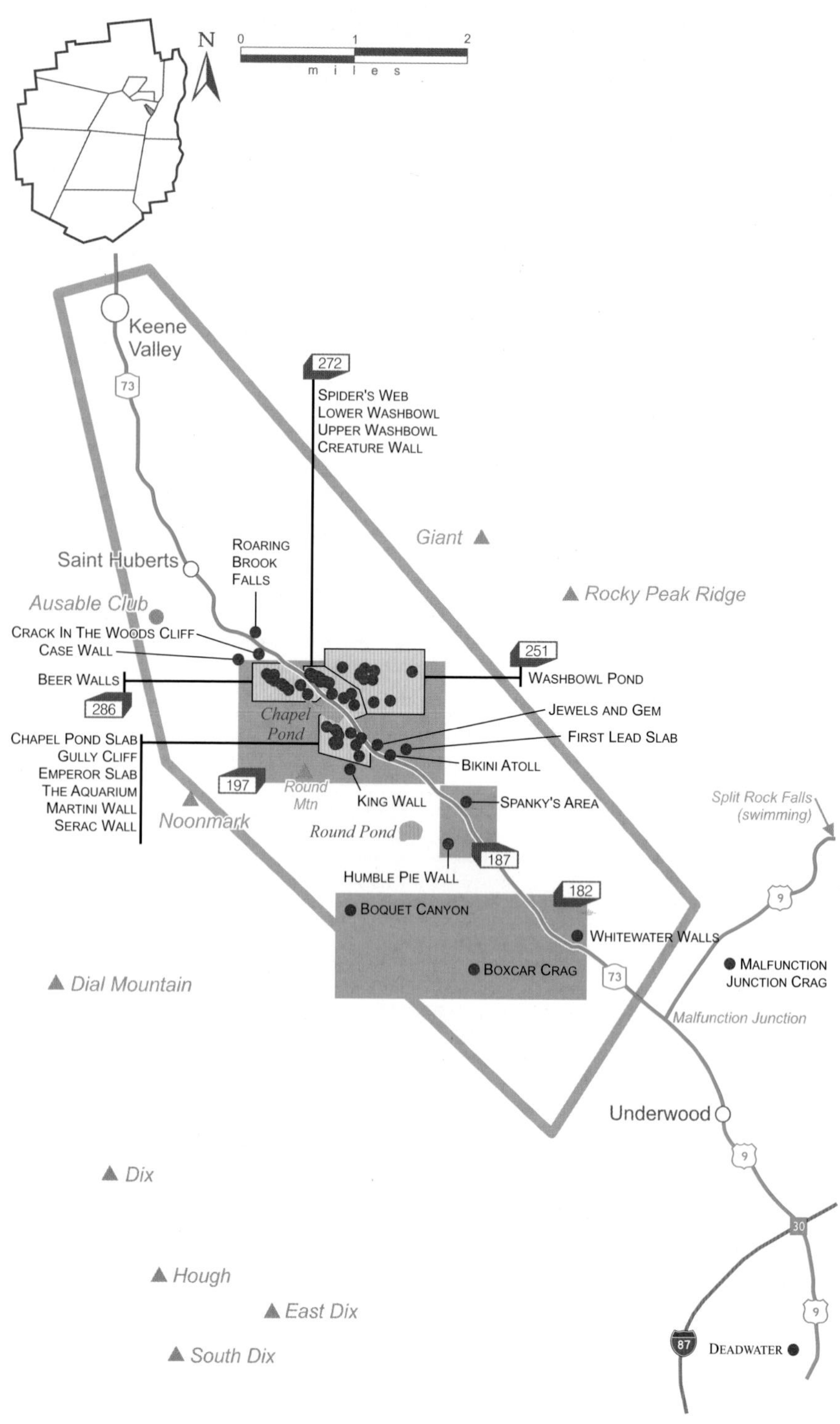

N
0 1 2
miles
Keene Valley
73
272
SPIDER'S WEB
LOWER WASHBOWL
UPPER WASHBOWL
CREATURE WALL
Giant
Rocky Peak Ridge
Saint Huberts
ROARING BROOK FALLS
Ausable Club
CRACK IN THE WOODS CLIFF
CASE WALL
BEER WALLS
286
251
WASHBOWL POND
JEWELS AND GEM
FIRST LEAD SLAB
Chapel Pond
CHAPEL POND SLAB
GULLY CLIFF
EMPEROR SLAB
THE AQUARIUM
MARTINI WALL
SERAC WALL
BIKINI ATOLL
197
Round Mtn
KING WALL
SPANKY'S AREA
Noonmark
Round Pond
Split Rock Falls (swimming)
187
HUMBLE PIE WALL
182
BOQUET CANYON
9
WHITEWATER WALLS
BOXCAR CRAG
MALFUNCTION JUNCTION CRAG
Dial Mountain
73
Malfunction Junction
Underwood
9
Dix
30
Hough
East Dix
9
South Dix
87
DEADWATER

Chapel Pond Pass

One of the major access routes to Lake Placid is through a narrow corridor between Giant Mountain and Round Mountain known as Chapel Pond Pass. US 9 leaves the Northway (I-87) at Exit 30 and winds northwest past the confusing intersection with NY 73 known as Malfunction Junction. From there, NY 73 continues up through increasingly rugged terrain to the height of the pass at Chapel Pond, an arresting tarn that reflects the surrounding cliffs in its waters. Both sides of the road, crowded with parked vehicles, are designated as wilderness areas—Giant Mountain Wilderness Area on the north and Dix Mountain Wilderness Area on the south. Chapel Pond is one of the trailheads for Giant Mountain (the Zander Scott Trail).

The cliffs in this section are described beginning at Malfunction Junction and working northwest, ending on the other side of the pass at Roaring Brook Falls and another trailhead for Giant Mountain (the Roaring Brook Trail). There are numerous pullouts on either side of the road. The cliffs are discussed relative to these parking areas and described in clockwise order on both sides of the road. Parking pullouts are measured from the major landmarks: Malfunction Junction, Chapel Pond, Roaring Brook Falls, and Keene Valley. Mileages are provided from one landmark *while driving toward* another landmark, which clarifies descriptions on NY 73, a southeast-to-northwest road.

You might feel overwhelmed by the wealth of rock in the pass, but it can be parsed down to something for everyone. Some of the best long and moderate slab climbs in the park are found here, 200' from the car, on Chapel Pond Slab. If you're looking for moderate single-pitch cragging, you'll find it at the Beer Walls, Creature Wall, and Spanky's Area. If you're itching for multipitch routes, try the Upper Washbowl, the King Wall, and the neglected Gully Cliff. Just down the road from these is the Spider's Web, with a dense collection of difficult crack climbs, considered to be incomparable in the Northeast. Want to get away from everyone else? Check out the gems on the Martini Wall, testpieces in the Amphitheater of the Overhangs, starred routes on the Lower Washbowl, and the long-overlooked Aquarium. Seeking the obscure? Lots of that, too: hit the Outlet Wall, P.E. Wall, Washbowl Pond, First Lead Slab, or the left end of the King Wall. Keep reading. There's much more.

SEASON

The weather patterns in the pass are influenced by its elevation (about 1300') and proximity to the High Peaks, so expect warm days and cool evenings in the summer, and be aware that frost customarily occurs every month of the year. You may be surprised at how local the climate is; for example, while Poke-O may be sunny and climbable, the pass may be foggy with intermittent showers. The area receives 40–60" of rain per year. If you get rained out, try other areas in the park, such as Deadwater to the east, Poke-O to the north, or any of the sites in the Lake George area to the south.

ACCESS

Annual closures for peregrine falcon nesting affect the Upper Washbowl and Lower Washbowl. Look for the signs posted at the climber herd paths. The wilderness designation imposes further restrictions on climbers, limiting groups to a maximum of 10 with no more than three roped parties at a time. Larger groups need to be separated into compliant groups at least 1 mile apart (similar rules apply for camping). Pets are allowed but must be leashed while on marked trails.

You are required to sign in before entering wilderness areas when a trailhead register is available.

DIRECTIONS (MAPS PAGES 4 AND 176)

Take the Northway (I-87) to Exit 30, then northwest on US 9 to Malfunction Junction where NY 73 begins. Go northwest on NY 73 into the pass.

WHERE TO STAY

Chapel Pond Pass is popular with tourists and hikers, as well as being a busy travel corridor, so roadside camping is limited. The accessible sites, prized by climbers for their proximity to the cliffs, are designated with yellow DEC "Camp Here" disks. There are several of these sites at Malfunction Junction, along the Boquet (near the parking for Boxcar Crag; map page 182), at the base of Chapel Pond Slab (map page 197), in the woods near Roaring Brook Falls, and at the outlet to Chapel Pond (map page 197).

The wilderness designation means that camping is restricted to groups with a maximum of 12 (soon to be 8, depending on when the DEC decides to enforce the limit). Larger groups need to be separated into compliant groups at least 1 mile apart. Fires are allowed only in existing fire rings at designated sites (marked with the yellow "Camp Here" disks). Primitive camping is allowed anywhere below 3500' as long as you are 150' from any road, trail, or water source. There are many bears, but unlike in the High Peaks, they are rarely seen here and there are currently no regulations regarding bear canisters.

Campgrounds: Sharp Bridge State Campground (518.532.7538), located near Exit 30; and Lincoln Pond Campground, off Lincoln Pond Road (CR 7) south of Elizabethtown (518.942.5292).

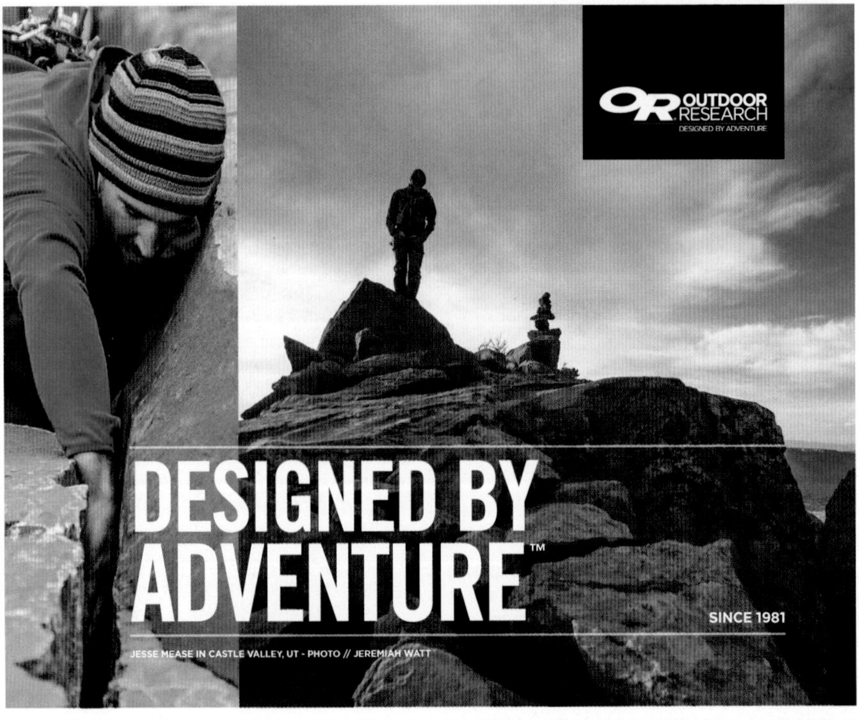

PG	CLIFF	QUALITY	ASPECT	APPROACH		GRADES	#
181	Malfunction Junction Cliff	★	NW	15 min	easy	.6 .7 .8 .9 .10 .11 .12 .13	1
181	Boquet River Crags Boquet Canyon	★	NW	1 hr 45 min	difficult	.6 .7 .8 .9 .10 .11 .12 .13	2
183	Boquet River Crags Boxcar	★	SE	30 min	moderate	.6 .7 .8 .9 .10 .11 .12 .13	1
184	Boquet River Crags Wall #1	★	SW	15 min	easy	.6 .7 .8 .9 .10 .11 .12 .13	6
184	Boquet River Crags Wall #2	★★	SW	15 min	easy	.6 .7 .8 .9 .10 .11 .12 .13	3
185	Boquet River Crags Wall #3	★	SW	15 min	easy	.6 .7 .8 .9 .10 .11 .12 .13	3
189	Spanky's Area Nestle Wall	★★	SW	12 min	easy	.6 .7 .8 .9 .10 .11 .12 .13	5
190	Spanky's Area Spanky's Wall	★★★★	SE & SW	12 min	easy	.6 .7 .8 .9 .10 .11 .12 .13	26
198	Jewels and Gem	★★★★	SW	1 min	easy	.6 .7 .8 .9 .10 .11 .12 .13	12
200	King Wall	★★★	E	20 min	easy	.6 .7 .8 .9 .10 .11 .12 .13	21
209	Emperor Slab	★	NE	20 min	moderate	.6 .7 .8 .9 .10 .11 .12 .13	5
213	Chapel Pond Slab	★★★★★	NE	1 min	easy	.6 .7 .8 .9 .10 .11 .12 .13	11
221	The Aquarium	★★	N	1 min	easy	.6 .7 .8 .9 .10 .11 .12 .13	8
223	Chapel Pond Gully Cliff	★★★	NE	5–15 min	easy	.6 .7 .8 .9 .10 .11 .12 .13	38
236	Martini Wall	★★	N	15 min	easy	.6 .7 .8 .9 .10 .11 .12 .13	2
236	Creature Wall	★★★	SW	10 min	easy	.6 .7 .8 .9 .10 .11 .12 .13	14
240	Upper Washbowl	★★★★	S	25 min	moderate	.6 .7 .8 .9 .10 .11 .12 .13	21
253	Washbowl Pond Banana Belt	★	SW, S, & E	45 min	moderate	.6 .7 .8 .9 .10 .11 .12 .13	6
258	Spider's Web	★★★★★	SW	15 min	easy	.6 .7 .8 .9 .10 .11 .12 .13	31
272	Lower Washbowl	★★	SW	15–45 min	moderate	.6 .7 .8 .9 .10 .11 .12 .13	48
274	Lower Washbowl False Arrow Face	★	SW	30 min	moderate	.6 .7 .8 .9 .10 .11 .12 .13	3
275	Lower Washbowl Lost Arrow Face	★★★	SW & SE	30 min	moderate	.6 .7 .8 .9 .10 .11 .12 .13	17
279	Lower Washbowl The Ticket	★	SW	45 min	difficult	.6 .7 .8 .9 .10 .11 .12 .13	5
281	Lower Washbowl Concave Wall	★★	SW	50 min	moderate	.6 .7 .8 .9 .10 .11 .12 .13	5
283	Lower Washbowl Eighth Wall	★★	SW	30 min	moderate	.6 .7 .8 .9 .10 .11 .12 .13	5
289	Beer Walls Near Beer Wall	★	SW	8 min	easy	.6 .7 .8 .9 .10 .11 .12 .13	2
289	Beer Walls Upper Beer Wall	★★★★★	SW	10 min	easy	.6 .7 .8 .9 .10 .11 .12 .13	28
299	Beer Walls Flailing Wall	★	SW	15 min	moderate	.6 .7 .8 .9 .10 .11 .12 .13	2
300	Beer Walls Lower Beer Wall	★★★★	SW	15 min	easy	.6 .7 .8 .9 .10 .11 .12 .13	51
315	Beer Walls Crack in the Woods Cliff	★	N	1 min	easy	.6 .7 .8 .9 .10 .11 .12 .13	1
316	Roaring Brook Falls	★★★★	SW	5 min	easy	.6 .7 .8 .9 .10 .11 .12 .13	3

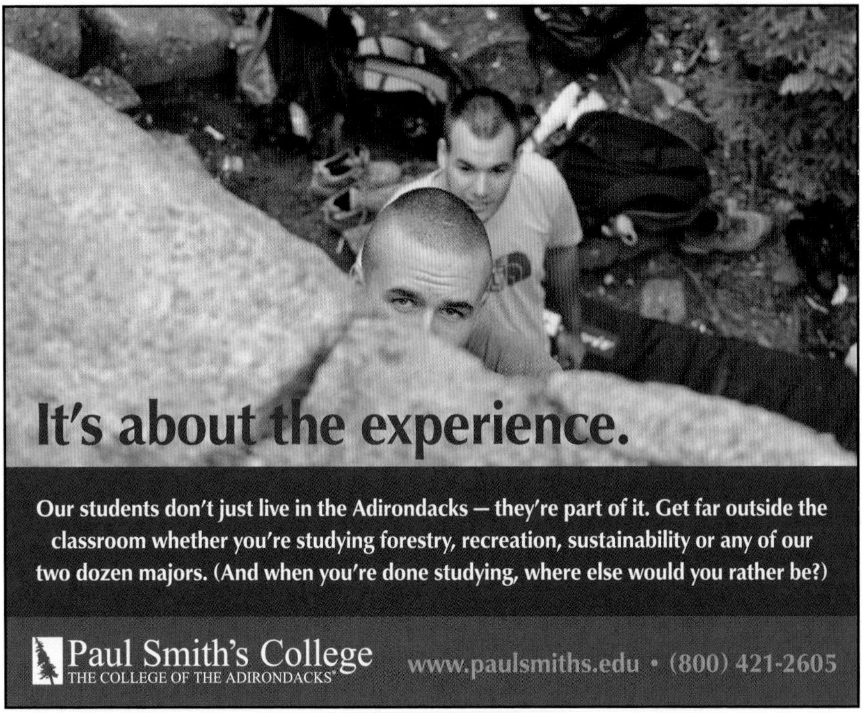

Bunkhouses: The Hostel, in Keene Valley (518.576.2030); and the ACC hut known as the Keene Farm or Keene Hut, in Upper Jay (www.accmontreal.ca).

Motels: The ADK Trail Inn (formerly The Ark), in Upper Jay (518.527.1155); and Brookside, in Upper Jay (518.946.8369).

B&Bs: Keene Valley Lodge, in Keene Valley (518.576.2003); Mountain Meadows Inn, in Keene Valley (518.576.4771); Trail's End Inn, in Keene Valley (800.281.9860); and Adirondack Rock and River, in Keene (518.576.2041).

Cabins: Dartbrook Lodge, in Keene (518.576.9080); and Mountain Manor, in Keene (518.576.9798).

AMENITIES

There is a large full-service grocery store (Tops) in Elizabethtown and a small one (the Valley Grocery) in Keene Valley. The nearest gas is the Stewart's Shops in Keene and Elizabethtown. There are a few restaurants in Keene and Keene Valley; be aware of odd hours in the off seasons. Favorites with climbers include the Cedar Run Bakery (518.576.9929), in Keene; and the Baxter Mountain Tavern (518.576.9990), near Hurricane Crag.

DIVERSIONS

There's great swimming at Chapel Pond from the beach on the way to Gully Cliff, and swimming holes are scattered on the nearby Boquet River (see page 182). One of the best swimming holes around—a three-tiered waterfall with large pools known as Split Rock Falls—is on US 9, 2 miles north of Malfunction Junction, on the right. On a rainy day, visit Keene Valley Library's special room devoted to mountaineering, dedicated by John Case (518.576.4335).

MALFUNCTION JUNCTION CLIFF

Location	Near North Hudson accessed from the Northway (I-87) Exit 29
Aspect	Northwest
Height	60'
Quality	★
Approach	15 min, easy
Summary	A small cliff with one exploratory route.

The cliff is 250' long and has a collection of roofs and overhanging faces with some potential for new routes. The single reported route is on the right end.

HISTORY

This cliff is another exploration by Tom DuBois, who was looking for ice routes (this cliff has several).

DIRECTIONS

Park on the east side of US 9, 0.6 mile north of Malfunction Junction, next to a grassy meadow with an oddly placed concrete wall and culvert in the middle 605714,4885048. The meadow is also 200 yards south of a small cluster of buildings on the west side of the road.

From the road, walk to the back of the meadow, then up a steep gully to rolling terrain at its top. Continue in a line perpendicular to the road to reach the cliff 606013,4884741; about 15 min of walking takes you to the cliff.

DESCENT OPTIONS

Walk right to return to the base of the cliff.

1 Traffic Engineer 5.9- G 60'

Start: At the right end of the cliff is an enormous 20'-long roof 15' up. This route begins 30' right of the roof below a jagged fingercrack. 4' left of the start is an overhang that rises from the ground up and left to meet the larger overhang.

P1 5.9- G: Climb the jagged fingercrack to the right-rising overhang. Climb around this on the right (crux) and up to a small tree. From here, you can scramble up slabs to the top of the cliff. 60'

FA Nov 25, 2006, Tom DuBois, Ellen DuBois

BOQUET RIVER CRAGS

Location	Along the North Fork of the Boquet River, accessed from NY 73
Summary	Remote cliffs where you can combine climbing with swimming and solitude.

-5.6	5.7	5.8	5.9	5.10	5.11	5.12	5.13+	total
14	4	2		1	1			22

The North and South Forks of the Boquet River flow from the remote northeastern slopes of the Dix Range. The Boquet River provides trail-less access to five of the peaks over 4000' as well as a paradise of narrow boulder-filled canyons, swimming holes, and idyllic camping.

Only a few crags have been reported here, each with its own charm and appeal. None of them can be considered a full-day climbing destination. Rather, each provides a day of swimming, bushwhacking, and solitude.

DIRECTIONS (MAP PAGE 182)

Park at a small pullout 603456,4885334 on the north side of the road 2.7 miles from the Chapel Pond pullout (when driving toward the Northway [I-87]) and 1.4 miles from Malfunction Junction (when driving toward Keene Valley). This pullout is just north of a stone bridge that crosses the North Fork of the Boquet River.

Specific approaches will be described from this common parking area. (Incidentally, there is a beautiful swimming spot about 1 min upstream from the parking area.)

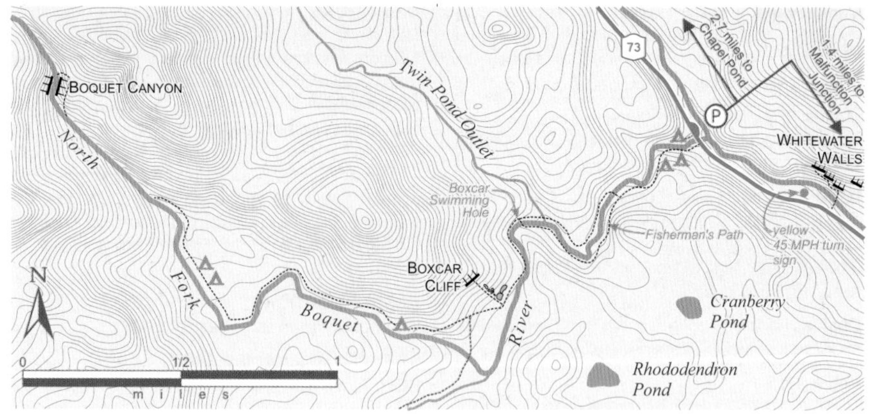

Boquet River Crags

BOQUET CANYON

Location	Dix Wilderness Area, North Fork of the Boquet River, accessed from NY 73
Aspect	Northwest
Height	100'
Quality	★
Approach	1 hr 45 min, difficult
Summary	A remote, narrow, and rugged river canyon with a couple of routes on clean rock; also a great location for swimming.

-5.6	5.7	5.8	5.9	5.10	5.11	5.12	5.13+	total
	1	1						2

This narrow canyon is far from any trail and is not easily reached from any direction. The approach described here is just one of several ways it can be reached. Either way, allow 1 hr 45 min for the approach and expect bushwhacking and some trouble getting to the base of the route, especially in high water.

The cliff is on the right (north) bank of the North Fork of the Boquet River; it drops into a deep rock ravine with large boulders, pools, and a pounding river. The cliff is split at its highest point by a huge left-leaning, left-facing corner that begins on the downstream side of a large pool. The route **Turbulescence** is on the wall right of this corner. There is potential here for more adventure routes in this remote, beautiful, and noisy setting.

With respect to swimming, there is a large pool at the base of the cliff. Upstream are three small waterfalls and several incredible dipping pools.

HISTORY

This canyon was first explored for rock climbing by Tom DuBois. He noticed on the map that the north bank of the river looked steep in that area and faced in a similar direction to the Beer Walls. The canyon was first approached from the Round Pond Trail near Round Mountain and turned out to be surprisingly scenic and rocky, but with only one area of good rock climbing. A little downstream is Boquet Country, the ice climbing area that area appears in Don Mellor's ice-climbing guidebook *Blue Lines*.

DIRECTIONS (MAP PAGE 182)

Walk across the stone bridge (0 hr 0 min) and follow a good fishermen's path on the left side of the river upstream. At 20 min, reach the Boxcar Swimming Hole, a flume that shoots into a narrow, deep boxcar-shaped trough in a large open area of rock slabs. Cross the stream to the right side and continue upstream on a good path to a split in the trail 602303,4884515, reached at 30 min. The main trail bends left and proceeds steeply downhill (to approach the Dix Range); instead, proceed straight on a less-used path to an excellent campsite at 35 min on the left above a section of narrow rapids 601982,4884423. Continue on the path with increasing difficulty, following the right bank of the North Fork of the Boquet River. Several more excellent tenting sites are reached at 50 min; beyond this, the path disappears altogether. Rock-hop up the river with increasing difficulty. As you go upstream, you will see wet black cliffs on your right and an interesting maze of talus on the riverbank—the location of the Boquet Canyon ice climbs. Eventually, you reach a narrow canyon, where further progress is stopped by pools and boulders. There are several options here: (a) continue in the stream, wading the pools as necessary to reach the base of the cliffs (fun and recommended); or (b) scramble up the right bank to a high open ledge at the top of the cliff overlooking the river 600500,4885451, continue upstream along the top of the cliff until it is possible to drop down a broad slope to the upstream end of the canyon, then rock-hop downstream to the base of the cliff, reached at 1 hr 45 min.

In high water, it may not be possible to reach the base of the routes from the river; you must rappel in from the top. There is also a difficult-to-find gully just downstream of the high open ledge, which can be descended (dirty 4th class) to reach the base.

1 Welcome to the Jungle 5.8 PG 90' ★★★

A cool corner and roof slot, followed by somewhat run-out, but clean, face climbing. Named for a Guns N' Roses rock anthem of 1987 and somewhat descriptive of the approach getting to this cliff.

Start: Below the large left-facing, left-leaning corner in the center of the cliff is a large pool that drains over a waterfall. 25' right of this waterfall is a right-rising slope of land starting at river level. This route begins 15' up the right-rising slope at a left-facing, left-leaning corner that leads to a slot in a ceiling.

P1 5.8 PG: Up the corner to the short A-shaped chimney that breaks the right end of the ceiling. At the top of the chimney, step right and climb up to the right end of an overlap, then straight up the face, using the arête to the left, then join the arête up to a tree anchor (shared with **Turbulescence**). 90'

Gear: To 1", small TCUs, and RPs.

FA Jun 30, 2007, Jim Lawyer, Colin O'Connor

2 Turbulescence 5.7 G 80' ★★★

Steep face climbing on beautiful black rock, similar in feel to **Pegasus** at the Beer Walls.

Start: At the top of the right-rising slope at a left-leaning fingercrack, 15' uphill and right of the left-facing, left-leaning corner of **Welcome to the Jungle**.

P1 5.7 G: Up the left-rising crack to some blocks, then work straight up the face to meet the top of a right-rising ramp. Step onto the top of the ramp, then up a short black face to a ceiling. Traverse left under the ceiling and to some trees. 80'

Gear: Cams to 1/2", small nuts, and small TCUs.

FA (TR) 2004, Tom DuBois, Ellen DuBois
FFA Jun 30, 2007, Jim Lawyer, Colin O'Connor

Boquet River Crags

BOXCAR

Location	Dix Wilderness Area, North Fork of the Boquet River, accessed from NY 73
Aspect	Southeast
Height	60'
Quality	★
Approach	30 min, moderate
Summary	A clean face with currently one single-pitch route and some good (hard) toproping.

This small crag is located near a popular swimming hole (also known as Shoe Box Falls) and, as such, makes a good destination on a hot day. The cliff is completely contained within the forest canopy.

HISTORY

Ed Palen discovered this crag while hiking to East Dix one winter (when the absence of leaves allows it to actually be seen).

DIRECTIONS (MAP PAGE 182)

Walk across the stone bridge (0 hr 0 min) and follow a good fishermen's path on the left side of the river upstream. At 20 min reach the Boxcar Swimming Hole, a flume that shoots into a narrow, deep boxcar-shaped trough in a large open area of rock slabs 602516,4884884. Cross the stream to the right side and continue upstream on a good path. At 25 min, the path heads away from the river, which can be seen off left meandering through some open meadows. On the right is a low ridge of rock and boulders; at the last boulder on the ridge (15' high with a cairn on top), turn right (on a bearing of 335°) and head uphill to the cliff 602309,4884638.

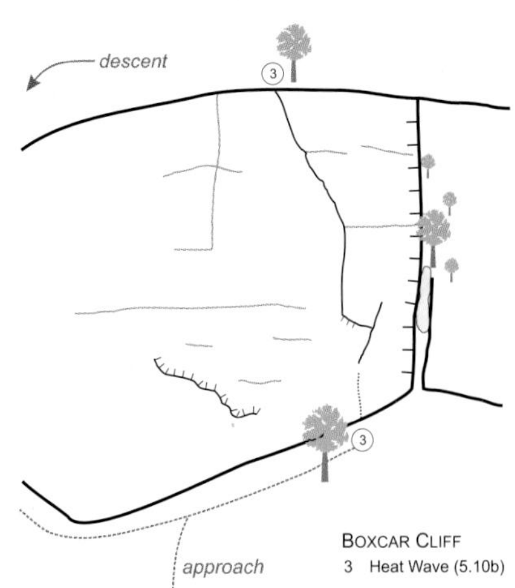

DESCENT OPTIONS

Walk left.

3 Heat Wave 5.10b G 60' ★★★

After the bouldery start, the route is 5.8.

Start: On the right side of the face, just left of a seeping right-facing corner and tree-filled chimney, below some slashes on the face.

P1 5.10b G: A bouldery start up the face leads to a good hold and a fingercrack. Climb up to a left-leaning crack, which is followed to the top. 60'

Gear: To 1".

FA Jun, 1994, Ed Palen, Chris Wolf

Boquet River Crags

WHITEWATER WALLS

Location	Giant Wilderness Area, North Fork of the Boquet River, accessed from NY 73
Summary	A collection of three walls near the Boquet River with mostly moderate, single-pitch lead routes.

These walls have long been considered a toproping area, but with its sloped base, annoying access to the top, and slabby topouts, it's not a very good toproping destination. Instead, the routes here are fairly easy leads (for the most part), moderately clean, and enjoyable due to the proximity to the river.

The walls are numbered from left to right as you view them from the road. Wall #1 is highest on the hill, and Wall #3 is nearest to the river. Access is fairly easy if you approach Wall #3, then move uphill and left to the other walls.

HISTORY

This was originally reported as a toprope area in the 1983 guidebook, then better details were provided in the 1986 supplement. For some reason, this area hasn't emerged as a toprope destination as originally anticipated, perhaps because the base of the cliff is sloped and messy. The primary activist here was Patrick Purcell, who visited with various partners in 1983.

DIRECTIONS **(MAP PAGE 182)**

Walk south (toward Malfunction Junction) across the stone bridge and down the road for 5 min until you can see the walls to the north on the other side of the Boquet River. Look for a yellow "45 MPH Turn" sign visible to cars traveling toward Chapel Pond; walk an additional 250' past the sign to a large cairn. Drop down through the woods to the river, cross the river (a simple rock hop in low water; there is a cairn on the far side), then up through the woods to Wall #3, the wall nearest the river 603792,4885116. Total time from the parking area is 15 min.

Boquet River Crags • Whitewater Walls

WALL #1

Aspect	Southwest
Height	100'
Quality	★
Approach	15 min, easy
Summary	Leftmost and highest wall on the hill with single-pitch routes.

-5.6	5.7	5.8	5.9	5.10	5.11	5.12	5.13+	total
5	1							6

Wall #1 is the highest wall on the hillside and sits uphill and left of Wall #2 by 100', separated by nondescript grungy rock on a left-rising slope.

4 The Great Escape 5.5 G 35'

Start: This route is on a small wall above Wall #1. From the top of the left side of Wall #1, walk straight back into the woods to a small cliff–boulder with a handcrack.
P1 5.5 G: Follow the handcrack to the top. 35'
Gear: to 2".
FA Jul 27, 2013, Eric Bretthauer, Tim Dufrane

5 Great Job 5.7 G 85'

Start: At a left-leaning crack on the far left end of the cliff, 30' uphill and left of **Route Number 1**.
P1 5.7 G: Climb the dirty, left-leaning crack for 40'. Traverse right to good holds on slab (crux), up 10', then back left to regain the crack that now leans right. Follow this to the top. 85'
Gear: To 4".
FA Jul 27, 2013, Eric Bretthauer, Tim Dufrane

6 Dragonfly 5.5 PG 90' ★★

Start: Same as **Route Number 1**.
P1 5.5 PG: Climb up the face into the trough, up the trough for 10', then work up a shallow left-facing, left-leaning corner with a good crack at its top. Continue up to another flake, then angle right to the top on good friction and knobs. 90'
Gear: To .75".
FA Jul, 1987, Tad Welch, Ali Schultheis

7 Route Number 1 5.4 PG 90'

Start: 6' right of the base of a right-rising trough or depression (with a few trees at the base) below a small 5'-high right-facing flake.
P1 5.4 PG: Climb the right-facing flake and scoops on the face to gain the trough. Up the trough (V1), which is followed up and right (broken, dirty, unpleasant rock) to the top. 90'
V1 5.6 G: Halfway up the trough, follow a right-rising horizontal crack to its end, then traverse right past some flakey rock to the left side of a large alcove with trees. On the left side of the alcove, climb up the crack and left-facing flake to the top.
FA May, 1983, Patrick Purcell, Mary Purcell

8 Corner In Out 5.6 PG 90' ★

Start: Walk right 40' from **Route Number 1** onto a dirty tree-covered slab. This route begins 10' right of the low point on the slab at a right-facing, right-leaning corner that tapers into the face 15' up.
P1 5.6 PG:. Climb the corner and right-leaning crack to an alcove (same as for **Wounded Knee**). Climb out left from the alcove to a good crack beneath an overlap; over this to the top. 90'
FA May, 1983, Patrick Purcell

9 Wounded Knee 5.5 PG 100' ★

Start: 10' right of **Corner In Out**, just before a drop on the right end of the dirty tree-covered slab, at several short right-facing corners.
P1 5.5 PG: Climb the flakes up and right to meet a left-rising crack, which is followed to an alcove beneath a bulge. Turn the bulge on the right following a right-rising crack, then up to an overhang, breaking this on the left. 100'
FA 1983, Patrick Purcell, Mary Purcell

Boquet River Crags • Whitewater Walls

WALL #2

Aspect	Southwest
Height	90'
Quality	★★
Approach	15 min, easy
Summary	Off-vertical face with several moderate routes and one good-quality hard route.

-5.6	5.7	5.8	5.9	5.10	5.11	5.12	5.13+	total
1	1				1			3

Downhill and right of Wall #1 by 100' is a wall whose major feature is a bulging ceiling that starts in the dirt on the right side of the face. Directly below the left side of the bulging ceiling is Bulging Smear. The other routes begin downhill and left at a right-rising fingercrack.

The top of the cliff can be accessed by following the base of the cliff uphill and right (actually on top of Wall #3), then back left to the top.

10 Looking for Mr. Goodhold 5.7 G 70'

Start: 40' uphill and right of the low point of the cliff below a right-leaning fingercrack.

P1 5.7 G: Climb the fingercrack to its end, jog left, then climb up and left to the top. 70'

FA 1983, Patrick Purcell, François Paul-Hus

11 BlueCross BlueShield 5.6 G 90' ★★

Start: Same as Looking for Mr. Goodhold.

P1 5.6 G: Climb the fingercrack, then step right to a right-facing flake and crack system. Climb the crack to its top, then up a very textured face to the top of the cliff. 90'

FA 1983, Patrick Purcell, François Paul-Hus

12 Bulging Smear 5.11a G 90' ★★

Perhaps the best route here, with a short, tough crux.

Start: 20' uphill and right of the fingercrack of Looking for Mr. Goodhold at a smooth face below the left side of a bulging ceiling 20' up. There are two bolts on the face leading to the ceiling.

P1 5.11a G: Climb the face to the bulging ceiling (small TCUs). Pull the bulging ceiling (bolt, crux), then climb nice but dirty rock to the top (5.5 PG), finishing left of a boulder. 90'

FA 1984, Patrick Purcell

Boquet River Crags • Whitewater Walls

WALL #3

Aspect	Southwest
Height	60'
Quality	★
Approach	15 min, easy
Summary	Off-vertical face with several very easy lead routes.

-5.6	5.7	5.8	5.9	5.10	5.11	5.12	5.13+	total
3								3

This wall is nearest the river and is characterized by two large roofs. The first roof is on the left side of the cliff, and the second is just right and lower to the ground (about 12' up). There is a narrow ledge that runs beneath the roofs from which the routes begin. There is a pretty summit perch on top.

Wall #3 is below and to the right of Wall #2. To reach Wall #2, walk left to the left side of the cliff, then uphill 50' to the base of Wall #2.

13 The French Spoof 5.4 PG 60'

Start: On a narrow ledge below the right side of the right-hand roof (the second large roof from the left end of the cliff).

P1 5.4 PG: A rough start on loose rock climbs up to a small birch, then up to the top. 60'

FA 1983, Patrick Purcell, François Paul-Hus

14 Walk on the Easy Side 5.3 G 60' ★

Start: 15' right of right side of the right-hand roof, at a slab that starts 4' up.

P1 5.3 G: Climb up rightward on a slab to some chossy blocks, then up and right on flakes, then up good cracks and bulges to the top. 60'

FA 1983, Patrick Purcell, François Paul-Hus

15 A Paris Parody 5.4 G 70' ★★

Start: 20' right of Walk On The Easy Side at a mossy slab. Up and left 6' is a barely-hanging-on spruce.

P1 5.4 G: Go up the mossy slab to a left-facing flake. Go up and right to a prominent, left-rising horizontal break. (V1) Go over a bulge to a single bolt, then straight up over bulges to the top. 70'

V1 5.5 R: Move right 10', then up a left-facing edge. Up this as it curves left and becomes an undercling, then go up right to a horizontal. Step right to a good crack and follow it up and left to an easy slab topout.

FA Aug 10, 2010, Todd Paris, Tom Lane
FA Aug 10, 2010, Jay Harrison, Tom Lane

Boquet River Crags • Whitewater Walls

BACKWATER WALL

Aspect	Southwest
Height	70'
Quality	
Approach	20 min, moderate
Summary	Hidden, off-vertical wall with some moderate crack routes in raw condition.

-5.6	5.7	5.8	5.9	5.10	5.11	5.12	5.13+	total
5	1	1						7

Backwater Wall is the fourth wall in the Whitewater Wall series. It's set back in the woods and cannot be seen from the road.

From Wall #3 (the rightmost of the walls), make your way to the top (go either left or right; both work), then walk straight back into the woods and up along a brook to a waterfall in a hollow. Turn right (east) out of the hollow and across the hill to the base of Backwater Wall 0603979,4885152. The approach takes about 5 minutes from the top of Wall #3.

16 Hydraulic 5.4 X 65'

Start: 15' left of the low point on the cliff, 12' left of a clump of three 8" maples, and 10' right of a 10'-tall 45° right-leaning ramp, below an 8'-tall promontory of rock.

P1 5.4 X: Climb the promontory. Step left and then run out the pleasant face to a horizontal crack 40' up (gear). Follow the diagonal feature up and right to finish in a flaring vertical crack. 65'

FA Aug 18, 2008, Tom DuBois, Ellen DuBois

17 Cool Water 5.7 G 65' ★

Perhaps the best route here, this climbs the right-leaning crack that begins at mid-height on the cliff.

Start: Same as Hydraulic.

P1 5.7 G: Climb the promontory. Step a few feet right to below a shallow, 4'-tall, left-facing corner (excellent

gear at its base). Climb up into the corner (crux) and up a couple easier, but unprotected moves above (5.5). Easier face and crack climbing leads up and right to the top. 65'
FA Aug 18, 2008, Tom DuBois, Ellen DuBois

18 Flume 5.5 PG 60'

Same: At the lowest point on the cliff, 2' right of a mossy area on the wall.
P1 5.5 PG: Face climb straight up 15' (V1), then move right to a small, 4'-tall, right-facing, right-leaning edge. Up this, then angle right to a right-leaning fingercrack which leads to the top. 60'
V1 Whirlpool 5.5 PG: Climb to a left-rising crack. Step left and follow the right-leaning crack of **Cool Water** to the top.
FA May 22, 2010, Kevin Heckeler
FA (V1) Aug 13, 2010, Todd Paris, Matthew Hager

19 Rock Hop 5.3 PG 60'

Start: 15' up and right from the low point on the cliff, at the base of a V formed by two ramps.
P1 5.3 PG: Climb the left-leaning ramp of the V to a small ledge with maples. (Alternatively, make one 5.5 move up a crack.) Move up into a shallow depression, then up and right on blocky terrain, then straight up to a birch tree centered at the top of the cliff. 60'
FA Aug 18, 2008, Tom DuBois, Ellen DuBois

20 Eddy 5.4 G 65'

Start: In the center of a triangular slab just right of **Rock Hop**. Two seams form an X in the center of the triangle.
P1 5.4 G: Go up the slab to its top, then up dirty rock to a left-rising break that splits the cliff and forms an arête. Follow the arête up and left to join **Rock Hop** at the top. 65'
FA Aug 21, 2010, Todd Paris, Gideon Paris

21 Swept Away 5.8- G (5.5 R) 70'

A one move wonder.
Start: Up and right 50' from the low point on the cliff is a left-rising break that splits the cliff. Begin 12' left of the bottom of this break, and just left of an 8" tree.
P1 5.8- G (5.5 R): Climb 8' up to an overhang, reaching it a couple of feet left of the crack in the overhang (which takes good gear). Break through the overhang and climb up an open-book depression to the top (5.5 R). 70'
FA Aug 18, 2008, Tom DuBois, Ellen DuBois

22 River Run 5.4 G 50'

Start: 25' right of **Swept Away**, just right of a 10" maple tree, below a blunt rounded section of lighter-colored rock with a network of crisscrossed diagonal cracks.
P1 5.4 G: Climb up, then trend left using the network of cracks. Continue up on good horizontals as the angle eases. 50'
FA Aug 18, 2008, Tom DuBois, Ellen DuBois

HUMBLE PIE WALL

Location	Near Chapel Pond, accessed from NY 73
Aspect	Southeast
Height	185'
Quality	
Approach	10 min, easy
Summary	A small, dirty cliff with several routes and excellent views of the valley and of Spanky's Area.

-5.6	5.7	5.8	5.9	5.10	5.11	5.12	5.13+	total
1			2	1				5

Humble Pie Wall is situated across the valley from Spanky's Area. Although originally deemed too dirty, persistence has paid off with a few routes. The cliff has a scrubby base with some slabs and low roofs. The tallest section has a high shield of white-colored rock, bounded on the left side by a left-facing corner (**Metatarsal Opportunity**) and on the right by a right-facing, right-leaning corner (**I Don't Need No Doctor**).

HISTORY

The cliff was first visited in the late 1980s by Ian Osteyee and Patrick Purcell, who thought it wasn't worth the trouble. Jim Lawyer, Colin Loher, and Tom Yandon did some cleaning but never finished their work. Their efforts were completed by Jay Abbey and Mark Arrow in 2007, resulting in **Metatarsal Opportunity**. Arrow returned to add several other routes.

DIRECTIONS (MAP PAGE 187)

Park at a pullout on NY 73, 1.8 miles from Chapel Pond on the left (when traveling toward Malfunction Junction) and 2.3 miles from Malfunction Junction on the right (when traveling toward Chapel Pond) 602445,4886290. When you're driving from Chapel Pond, it is the second official pullout on the left.

From the parking area, cross the road to a "State Forest Preserve" sign on a tree. Follow a trail parallel to the road, up a hill and around the right side of Bullet Pond, then up to the base of the cliff 601922,4886388, meeting the cliff at the base of **Smoking Jacket**. Long pants are recommended for the stinging nettles.

DESCENT OPTIONS

Walk left and down a steep gully to return to the base of the cliff near **Metatarsal Opportunity**.

1 Metatarsal Opportunity 5.9- G 140' ★★

Named for the broken bone in the foot of local guide Ian Osteyee, which prevented him from joining the first ascent.
Start: At the left end of the cliff is a steep gully (used for descent) that rises along a left-facing wall. Begin 20' downhill and right at a low-angle left-facing open book.
P1 5.9- G: Up the open book to its top, then rightward to the left end of a large roof. (V1) Work up a crack in a left-facing corner to a ledge on a block. Struggle up a prominent left-facing off-width crack (#00 TCU helpful) to a ceiling at its top. (V2) Traverse right to a

ledge below a headwall with twin vertical cracks. Up the cracks to a narrow, sloping ledge, then move left and up a slab to a tree ledge with a fixed anchor. 140'

V1 5.9- G: Traverse left and up the left side of the block to the ledge at its top. Step back right to the off-width crack.

V2 5.7 G: Traverse left under the roof and up to the belay.

FA Sep 20, 2007, Jay Abbey, Mark Arrow
FA (V1, V2) Sep 29, 2007, Jay Abbey, Mark Arrow

2 Desi's Misery 5.7 A1 185'

Start: In the center of the cliff, at an obvious depression with stepped ledges, 40' left of **Smoking Jacket** and 50' right of **Metatarsal Opportunity**.

P1 5.7 PG: Climb the stepped ledges in the depression, past two pitons, up and right to reach a wide ledge. Step up and right to belay beneath a right-leaning crack in a headwall. 100'

P2 5.7 A1: Climb the right-leaning crack to a right-facing corner formed by a block, then exit left at the top of the block. 85'

FA Oct 13, 2007, Mark Arrow, Jan Wellford

5 Smoking Jacket 5.6 G 165' ★★

Start: At the right end of the cliff at a low-angle left-facing, left-leaning open book with a crack.

P1 5.6 G: Up the left-facing open book to a ledge on the left (optional belay). Continue up the open book to its top, move right, then up a crack in a left-facing corner to a fixed anchor on a tree. 165'

Descent: Rappel or scramble to the top of the cliff.

FA Sep 21, 2007, Mark Arrow, Jay Abbey

SPANKY'S AREA

Location	North side of NY 73, east of Chapel Pond
Summary	Several small walls with excellent moderate face climbing and several challenging roof climbs.

-5.6	5.7	5.8	5.9	5.10	5.11	5.12	5.13+	total
12	4	10	2	2	5			35

This terrain, on the north side of NY 73, just east of Chapel Pond, has no shortage of cliffs, as there are many scattered through the talus-covered hillside,

3 I Don't Need No Doctor 5.9+ G 110'

The most prominent feature of the cliff is the giant right-facing, right-leaning corner.

Start: From the top of P1 of **Desi's Misery**, walk 15' left to a birch tree below the major right-facing, right-leaning corner.

P1 5.9+ G: Climb the corner to the roof, pull the roof, then exit right to the top. 110'

Gear: 2 ea 3", 4 ea 4", 3 ea 5".

FA Oct 18, 2007, Mark Arrow, Nathan Burkholder

4 Tarsal Grinder 5.10c G 70'

Often wet, and a bit on the dirty side.

Start: At the birch tree at the base of **I Don't Need No Doctor**. You have to climb P1 of **Desi's Misery** to access the start.

● **P1 5.10c G:** Step right and climb the low-angle face up and right to a prow. Up the prow (crux) to a fixed anchor below a ceiling. 70'

FA May 24, 2008, Seth Arrow, Mark Arrow

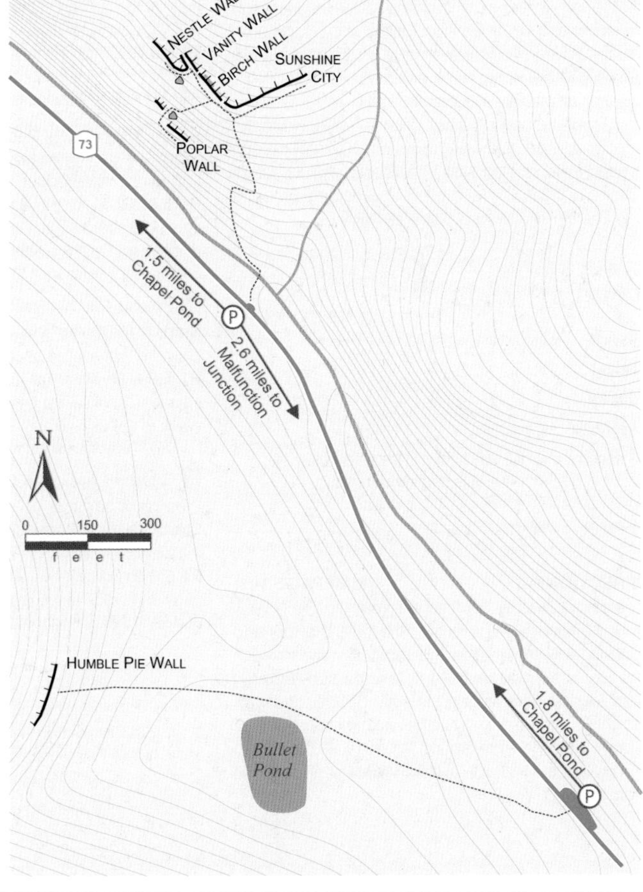

starting near Jewels and Gem and extending east for more than a mile. Most of these are small, insignificant lumps of choss, but occasionally there's a hidden gem. Spanky's Area is such a find, located very near the road with a wide range of features (slabs, cracks, and roofs) and difficulty (from 5.3 to 5.12).

The main attraction here is the bolted routes on the right end of Sunshine City and through the roofs on the Birch Wall.

HISTORY

Patrick Purcell climbed the first route here in 1983, **Dancin' Buckwheat**, thus starting the Little Rascals naming theme. Ian Osteyee, just out of high school, added a few routes in the mid-1980s, as did Tad Welch with **Arrested Development**. The cliff was documented in the 1988 guidebook with an enticing statement about the "unclimbed line of roofs" on the left end. In 1995, perhaps inspired by these roofs, a group of local climbers, led by David Lent and Kevin Crowl, resurrected the cliff. They put in some impressive routes here, all by "fair means"—i.e., ground-up and hand drilling.

DIRECTIONS **(MAP PAGE 187)**

Park at a pullout on NY 73, 1.5 miles from Chapel Pond on the left (when you're traveling toward Malfunction Junction) and 2.6 miles from Malfunction Junction on the right (when you're traveling toward Chapel Pond) 602126,4886772. When you're driving from Chapel Pond, it is the first official pullout on the left.

From the parking area, follow a trail down to the stream, cross it, then walk upstream 100' and pick up a good trail that diagonals uphill past a switchback to reach Sunshine City between **Let Sleeping Bats Lie** and **Dancin' Buckwheat** 602103,4886959.

Spanky's Area

POPLAR WALL

Aspect	Southwest
Height	45'
Quality	
Approach	12 min, easy
Summary	A small wall hidden in the trees below the Birch Wall with four short routes.

-5.6	5.7	5.8	5.9	5.10	5.11	5.12	5.13+	total
1		3						4

DIRECTIONS **(MAP PAGE 187)**

The Poplar Wall is approached from the Birch Wall. From beneath the large roofs, at the route **Thunder and Lichen**, walk straight downhill about 30 yards to reach the top of the wall, marked by a large spire-boulder. Turn (skier's) right around the spire-boulder and walk downhill to the base of another wall (the Spring Wall, always wet), then turn (skier's) left and walk downhill to the base of the Poplar Wall 602056,4886910, about 2 min from the Birch Wall.

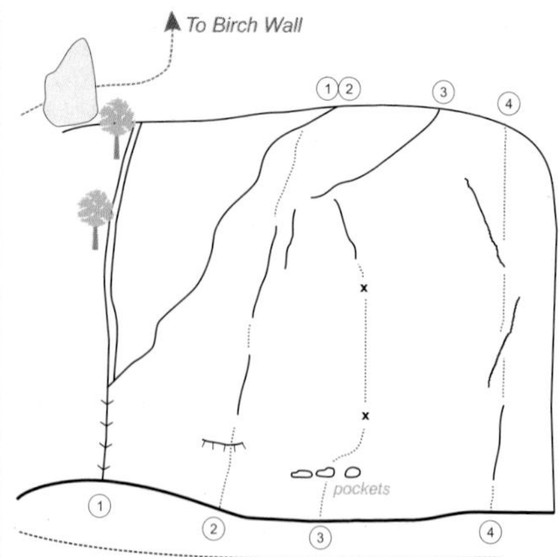

SPANKY'S AREA: POPLAR WALL

1 Unpoplar (5.6)
2 A Poplar Climb (5.8-)
3 Poplar Mechanics (5.8+)
4 Seams Poplar (5.8)

1 Unpoplar 5.6 G 45'

Start: 20' uphill from and left of the lowest point on the face, at the left end of the wall below a very mossy and wet V-groove and chimney.

P1 5.6 G: Climb up the V-groove for 6' to gain the right-rising crack, then follow it to the top. 45'

FA May, 1999, Rosanne Lent, David Lent

2 A Poplar Climb 5.8- G 40' ★★★

Start: 4' left of three pockets in the wall at a sharp-edged horizontal ledge 1' up.

P1 5.8- G: Tricky moves lead up to a horizontal slot, then up a short crack. Continue up seams to a finish in a right-rising crack (same crack as **Unpoplar**). 40'

FA May, 1999, Rosanne Lent, David Lent

3 Poplar Mechanics 5.8+ G 40' ★★★

Start: At the lowest point on the face below three pockets in front of a large poplar tree.

P1 5.8+ G: Move up to the pockets, then right to a stance. Continue up past two bolts and a horizontal crack to the top. 40'

FA May, 1999, David Lent, Rosanne Lent

4 Seams Poplar 5.8 G 40' ★★

Presently a bit dirty.

Start: 5' right of **Poplar Mechanics** at the right end of the wall below vertical seams.

P1 5.8 G: Follow several thin vertical seams with good jams and holds to the top. 40'

FA May, 1999, David Lent, Rosanne Lent

Spanky's Area

NESTLE WALL

Aspect	Southwest
Height	100'
Quality	★★
Approach	12 min, easy
Summary	A large wall with a single crack route and the potential for more routes.

-5.6	5.7	5.8	5.9	5.10	5.11	5.12	5.13+	total
2	1	2						5

The left side of this wall is home to the winter route **Sheik of the Burning Sands**. It is located down from and left of the Vanity Face.

DIRECTIONS (MAP PAGE 187)

From the base of **Sirloin Tips** on the Vanity Face, turn around and walk downhill and (skier's) right, contouring around the base of a cliff on the right. After 120', this brings you to a passage between a large boulder and the cliff on the right, which is the right end of the Nestle Wall. It takes about 1 min to reach this point from the Vanity Face.

DESCENT OPTIONS

If you have to walk, go right. It's a long way and involves traversing slabs, getting lost, and eventually coming down near Sunshine City. Much better to rappel **Sheik of the Burning Sands**: go to the top of the cliff and make a short rappel to a ledge with a giant pine tree with a fixed anchor, then another 30m rappel to the base.

5 No Regrets Coyote 5.8- G (5.4 R) 115' ★

Named for a Joni Mitchell song, and the fact that the first ascent party found the remains of a coyote near the base of the route.

Start: From the boulder on the right end of the cliff, walk left along the base towards the open wet face with the winter route **Sheik of the Burning Sands**; 30' right of that route, locate a 30'-tall boulder-buttress with a jagged crack in the front face above a ledge with two small trees. Gain this ledge from the left and begin below the jagged crack.

P1 5.8- G (5.4 R): (V1) Gain the mossy ledges below the crack. Up the crack (tight hands and fists) to the top of the boulder-buttress. (V2) Stem up a large, offwidth, right-facing corner with good faceholds on the right wall (5.4 R, 4" cam helpful) to a large belay ledge. (Or scramble up 20' to a scenic belay with views of the King Wall.) 115'

V1 5.7 G: Begin down and right below the ledge of the normal start in a large left-facing corner with two trees growing down low. Up the corner, then step left to gain the splitter crack of the normal route.

V2 5.4 G: Better protected than the original finish. Traverse up and right to a fingercrack, then follow this using plentiful holds on the face to the right. Belay at a large birch on top of the face.

Descent: Rappel from a pine tree on the ledge with a single 60' rope.

FA May 8, 2009, Sam Hoar, Jon Campbell
FA (V1) Jul 17, 2009, Duncan Lennon, Sam Hoar
FA (V2) Jul 17, 2009, Sam Hoar, Duncan Lennon

6 Black and Tan 5.7 G 70' ★

Start: 20' left of **Nescafé**, at the right end of a ledge, below another ledge 7' up with two perched boulders. To get to this high ledge, from the large boulder on the right end of the cliff, walk left 90', then scramble up and right onto a ledge, then walk back right to its right end.

P1 5.7 G: Scramble up onto the ledge 7' up, then up a left-leaning handcrack and follow it to a ceiling. Break through the ceiling on good jams up to a niche below a crumbly boulder; pass the boulder on either side. 70'

FA Oct, 1995, Kevin Crowl, Jonas Morelli, Neal Knitel, Jared Thayer

7 Morsel Line 5.8 PG 75' ★

Start: Near the right end of the wall, at a small nose in front of a slanting boulder, below a short ramp 3' left of **Nescafé**.

P1 5.8 PG: Climb to the ramp, then up flakes and cracks running up a steep wall (crux) on the left that follow a short, left-facing corner. At its top, (V1) step left to a rounded, left-facing corner and up it to the outside of a prow. 75'

V1 5.7 G: Traverse 4' right to a thin vertical crack, follow it to its end, then step left back onto the main line.

FA Oct 20, 2010, Jay Harrison, Todd Paris

8 Nescafé 5.5 PG (5.3 R) 230' ★★★

Start: On the right end of the cliff, at the base of the boulder close to the cliff and below a right-rising ramp.

P1 5.5 PG (5.3 R): Go up the right-rising ramp to its top. Go up a fingercrack (next to a flared vegetated crack), then up a textured face past a sill and a couple of pockets. Belay on a tree ledge on the left. Great views from here up the canyon and of the King Wall. 100'

P2 5.5 G: Step right, up a slab, then up a short 10'-tall handcrack. Step left and go up a narrow slab just left of a vegetated open book. At the top, watch the precarious block. Scramble up ledges to the top. 130'

FA Sep 29, 2010, Todd Paris, Mike Prince

9 Chock Full O' Nuts 5.6 PG 230' ★★★

Start: 30' right of **Nescafé** at the right side of the cliff in a dirty corner.

P1 5.6 PG: (V1) Climb up the dirty corner, step left onto the slab, and climb this to a small ledge. Make a few slab moves (crux) to reach a crack in a left-facing corner, and follow this to its top. 100'

P2 5.5 G: Up a crack in a small headwall, then wander up over the series of shorter walls and ledges to the top of the cliff. 130'

V1 5.9 TR: Begin 8' left of the normal start and climb a face to a right-rising rail, then move up and left around a small overhang via a rounded, small, left-facing corner to join the standard route.

FA Sep 29, 2010, Todd Paris, Mike Prince
FA (V1) Oct 20, 2010, Jay Harrison, Todd Paris

Spanky's Area

SPANKY'S WALL

Aspect	Southeast and southwest
Height	130'
Quality	★★★★
Approach	12 min, easy
Summary	Good collection of moderate-to-hard sport routes and some easier lead routes.

-5.6	5.7	5.8	5.9	5.10	5.11	5.12	5.13+	total
9	3	5	2	2	5			26

Spanky's Wall is a long wall with several distinct sections. The left end is southwest-facing and begins with an off-vertical face, the Vanity Face. To the right is a large roof, the Birch Wall. Right of this the cliff bends to become southeast-facing; this is Sunshine City. The approach trail meets the cliff on the left side of Sunshine City.

Vanity Face

From the point where the approach trail meets the cliff, walk left to an impressive roof 25' up—the Birch Wall. At the far end of the roof is a left-leaning chimney (**Ominous Chimney**) that marks the right end of Vanity Face. The aspect is southwest.

10 Little Chimney 5.5 PG 35'

Start: Walk uphill along the base of Vanity Face to enter a secret 15'-wide slot-gully with a dramatically overhanging left wall (some future lines, perhaps). This route begins at the height of the slot-gully below a wide crack and chimney capped by several chockstones.

P1 5.5 PG: Climb the wide crack to the top. 35'

FA Oct, 1995, Kevin Crowl, Jared Thayer

11 Jaredtol 5.6 G 55'

Start: 15' uphill from and left of **Crowley Cream Cheese** below a V-slot that begins 15' up.

P1 5.6 G: Up blocky rock to gain the V-slot, then follow it past a parallel-sided slot and up to a ledge below a blocky ceiling. Step right and climb more blocky rock to the top. Walk left to a large poplar tree with a fixed anchor. 55'

FA Oct, 1995, Kevin Crowl, Jared Thayer

12 Crowley Cream Cheese 5.7 PG 70'

Start: Just left of **Carbohydrate** is a shallow, 10'-high right-facing corner. Begin 10' uphill from and left of this corner below a fingercrack that starts 18' up in black rock.

P1 5.7 PG: Climb up onto a sloping chocolate-colored edge (TCU placement), then climb grainy rock up and right to gain a fingercrack. Follow the fingercrack to its end at a 1'-wide slot. Continue up and left on broken, blocky rock to the high point of the cliff. Walk left to a large poplar tree with a fixed anchor. 70'

FA Jul 13, 1995, Kevin Crowl, David Lent

13 Carbohydrate 5.8 PG 70' ★

Start: 8' left of **Lentil Beans** at a straight-up vertical crack that rises above a small shelf 2' up.

P1 5.8 PG: Climb the crack and shallow right-facing corner to a ledge. Work up and right following minibulges in black rock to join a right-leaning crack. Follow the crack to a ledge to finish on **Lentil Beans**. 70'

FA Jul 14, 1995, David Lent, Rosanne Corbo

14 Lentil Beans 5.9 G 70' ★★★

Start: 15' left of **Ominous Chimney** at the base of a left-leaning crack.

P1 5.9 G: Climb the left-leaning crack into a shallow left-facing corner and follow it to its top. Continue up the crack to a good ledge. Step left into a right-facing corner, through a bulge, and up to a fixed anchor. 70'

FA Jul 14, 1995, David Lent, Kevin Crowl

15 Sirloin Tips 5.11c G 75'

A hold has broken on this route, making it considerably more difficult; it hasn't been freed since the hold broke, so the grade is unknown (it was 5.11c).

Start: At the base of the slab 4' left of the chimney.

P1 5.11c G: Crimp hard and make several difficult moves past the first two bolts, then continue up easier ground past a third bolt. Continue straight up the face, then angle left to the fixed anchor of **Lentil Beans**. 75'

Gear: Several small TCUs and nuts

History: There are very hard FAs by women in the Adirondacks. This is perhaps the most difficult.

FA Apr, 1999, Rosanne Lent, David Lent, Kevin Crowl

16 Chili Pepper Arête 5.5 R 70' ★★

Start: Same as **Ominous Chimney**.

P1 5.5 R: Climb the blunt arête on the left side of the opening of **Ominous Chimney** on good holds, move out left to a good ledge, then traverse left 12' to the

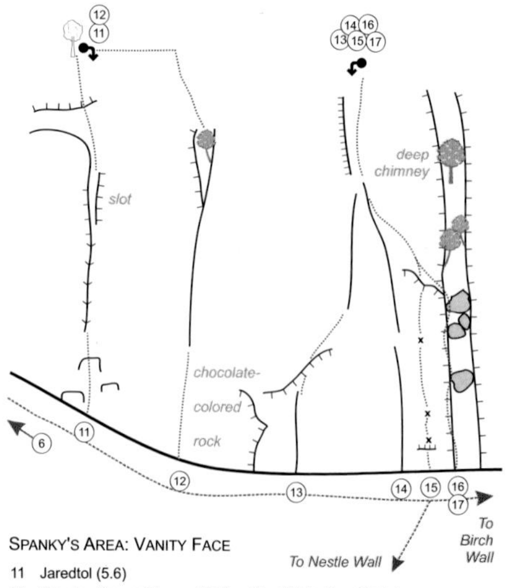

SPANKY'S AREA: VANITY FACE

11 Jaredtol (5.6)
12 Crowley Cream Cheese (5.7)
13 Carbohydrate (5.8)
14 Lentil Beans (5.9)
15 Sirloin Tips (5.11c)
16 Chili Pepper Arête (5.5)
17 Ominous Chimney (5.4)

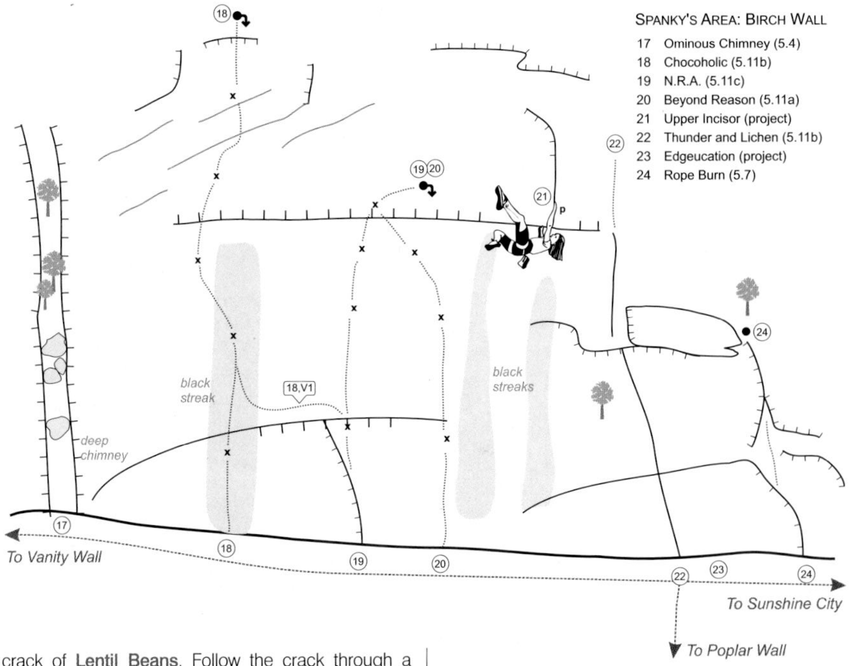

SPANKY'S AREA: BIRCH WALL

17 Ominous Chimney (5.4)
18 Chocoholic (5.11b)
19 N.R.A. (5.11c)
20 Beyond Reason (5.11a)
21 Upper Incisor (project)
22 Thunder and Lichen (5.11b)
23 Edgeucation (project)
24 Rope Burn (5.7)

black streak
black streaks
deep chimney
18,V1
To Vanity Wall
To Sunshine City
To Poplar Wall

crack of **Lentil Beans**. Follow the crack through a bulge to a fixed anchor. 70'
FA Aug, 1995, David Lent, Ian Osteyee

17 Ominous Chimney 5.4 G 70'

This is the winter route **Awwwh Yeah**; not recommended in the summer.

Start: 70' uphill from and left of **Chocoholic** and the right end of the Vanity Face, below a deep left-leaning chimney with a chockstone 70' up.

P1 5.4 G: Climb the dirty chimney past trees and loose chockstone. Move left at the top to a good ledge, then traverse left 12' to the crack of **Lentil Beans** and follow it through a bulge to a fixed anchor. 70'

Birch Wall

The central feature of this southwest-facing wall is a large roof 25' up. Three excellent, gymnastic routes climb this roof.

DIRECTIONS (MAP PAGE 187)

From the point where the approach trail meets the cliff, walk left to an impressive roof 25' up; this is the Birch Wall.

SPANKY'S WALL

17 Ominous Chimney (5.4)
18 Chocoholic (5.11b)
19 N.R.A. (5.11c)
20 Beyond Reason (5.11a)
22 Thunder and Lichen (5.11b)
24 Rope Burn (5.7)
25 Kristin (5.4)
26 Hangover Direct (5.4)
27 No Bats Here (5.4)
28 Let Sleeping Bats Lie (5.4)
29 Dancin' Buckwheat (5.9-)
30 Contos (5.3)
31 Diamonds Aren't Forever (5.10c)
33 Bee Hold (5.8)

18 Chocoholic 5.11b G 60' ★★★★

Fantastic climbing, pumpy, and spicy at the top (big air if you fall).

Start: Below the left end of the roof at a prominent chocolate-colored streak that shoots straight up to the roof.

P1 5.11b G: (V1) Climb the chocolate-colored streak past a ledge, then up a vague right-facing, left-leaning open book to the roof (optional 4" cam). Step left, up to a rail, right to a bolt, then up to gain a right-rising crack (crux). Continue up the face past two more horizontal cracks to a fixed anchor. 60'

V1 Hershey Squirt 5.10a G: If the bottom is wet, it is possible to climb the left-leaning ramp of N.R.A. to the ledge, then move left to join this route.

FA Jul 14, 1995, David Lent, Kevin Crowl

19 N.R.A. 5.11c G 50' ★★★

Spectacular moves through the roof. Taken directly, the roof is solid 5.12.

Start: 12' right of Chocoholic at a white right-facing, left-leaning ramp.

P1 5.11c G: Climb up the ramp to a ledge, move up and right on a white face to the roof, then make a wild move out right to a fixed anchor above the roof. 50'

FA May, 1999, David Lent, Kevin Crowl

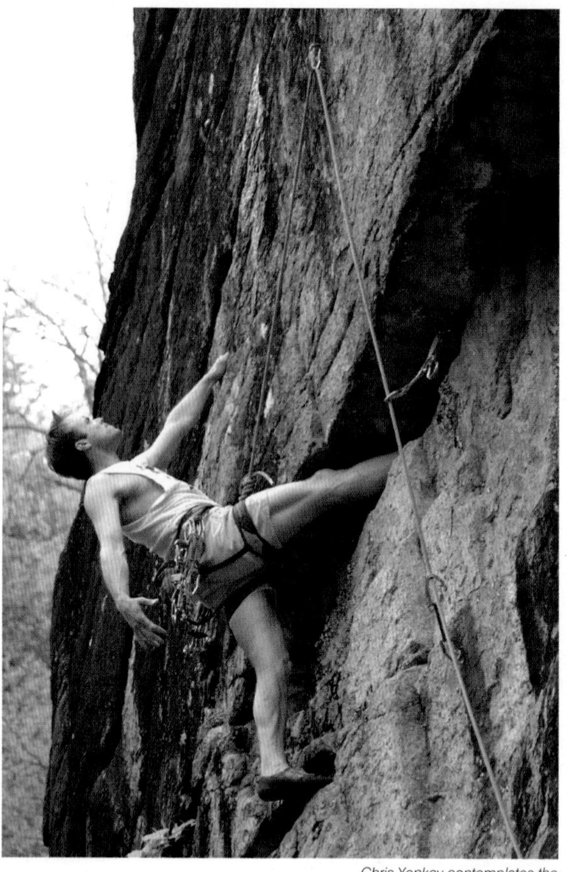

Chris Yenkey contemplates the crux on Chocoholic (5.11b).

20 Beyond Reason 5.11a G 50' ★★★

Start: At a short overhanging wall 15' right of N.R.A., at a section of white rock just left of a prominent black streak.

P1 5.11a G: Climb up on great holds to a ledge. Work up and left across the face to the roof, then make a wild move out right (same as N.R.A.) to a fixed anchor above the roof. 50'

FA May, 1999, Kevin Crowl, David Lent

21 Upper Incisor Project

This open project is right of Beyond Reason at a crack that breaks the roof on its right end above a black streak.

22 Thunder and Lichen 5.11b PG 85'

This route hasn't been led free; probably needs a cleaning before such an attempt.

Start: 30' left of Rope Burn below a left-leaning seam that leads to a horizontal crack 12' up.

P1 5.11b PG: Climb the steep face up to a wide horizontal crack, then up an overhanging off-finger crack on the left margin of a white wall sparsely dotted with orange lichen. Belay at a good ledge in a left-facing corner. 45'

P2 5.10b G: Continue in the same line through a bulge to another ledge. 40'

Gear: Small wires and TCUs, plus 1 ea 4.5" cam.

FA Jul 15, 1995, Kevin Crowl, David Lent

23 Edgeucation Project

Another open project. 20' left of Rope Burn and 5' right of Thunder and Lichen is a line of edges. Climb the black face on good edges to a large horizontal, then follow a black streak up to a ceiling with another horizontal crack. Pull through the ceiling and up to a sloping ledge. Reported in the 5.10 range.

24 Rope Burn 5.7 G 120'

Best done as two pitches, as the first-ascent party inadvertently cut a rope in two over some sharp holds.

Start: 35' left of the right end of the wall below the right end of a black left-rising ramp.

P1 5.7 G: Climb up and left following the ramp, then up a left-leaning crack in a right-facing corner to a ledge. 60'

P2 5.5 G: Follow slabs up and right to the top. 60'

FA Aug, 1995, Neal Knitel, Jared Thayer, Kevin Crowl

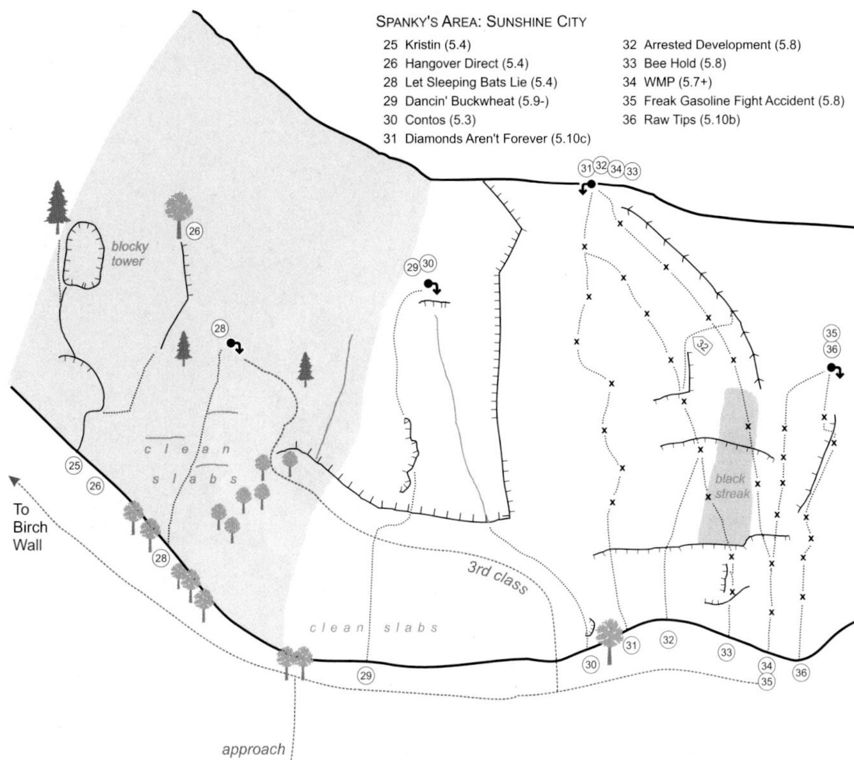

Sunshine City

Some of the best sport routes in the Chapel Pond area are located at the right end of this southeast-facing wall.

DIRECTIONS **(MAP PAGE 187)**

The trail from the parking lot meets a cliff and forks. This is Sunshine City. To the left are the routes **Kristin**, **Hangover Direct**, and **Let Sleeping Bats Lie**, and to the right are **Dancin' Buckwheat** and the other routes.

25 Kristin 5.4 G 90'

Start: 80' left of where the trail meets the cliff and forks, and 20' left of **Let Sleeping Bats Lie**, at a left-rising vegetated crack that rises above a boulder. This is 20' right of the Birch Wall.

P1 5.4 G: Climb the vegetated crack to a bushy ledge, step left, and climb a crack to a tree on the left side of a blocky tower. 90'

FA Oct, 1985, Ian Osteyee, Tom Skrill

26 Hangover Direct 5.4 PG 80'

Start: Same as **Kristin**.

P1 5.4 PG: Climb the vegetated crack, then up rightward across the face to a crack that leads to a left-facing corner. Climb the corner to a tree at the top. 80'

FA 1987, Ian Osteyee, Scott Daley

27 No Bats Here 5.4 G 90' ★★

A better-protected version of its neighbor to the right.

Start: Same as **Kristin**.

P1 5.4 G: Step right onto the face and follow a right-leaning crack to its top. Go up a ledge in a black streak to a shallow depression on the right side of the black streak. Follow a right-leaning crack up to the anchor shared with **Let Sleeping Bats Lie**. 90'

FA Oct 3, 2013, Royce Van Evera, Dustin Ulrich

28 Let Sleeping Bats Lie 5.4 G (5.2 R) 90' ★★

Well protected at the bottom, but the easier climbing higher up is slightly run-out.

Start: 60' left of where the trail meets the cliff and forks is a slab that rises above a small headwall. This route begins on the left side of the headwall at a point where it is only 4' high.

P1 5.4 G (5.2 R): Climb up onto the slab, work up and right to a right-rising horizontal, then wander up the slab to a fixed anchor above a sloped ledge. 90'

Gear: Up to 0.75".

Descent: Rappel, or scramble down and right on slabs and ledges to the base of **Contos**.

FA May 24, 1997, Steven Cherry, Kerry Flynn

29 Dancin' Buckwheat 5.9- PG 130'

Start: 60' uphill from and right of where the trail meets the cliff and forks, below a clean slab of rock directly above the trail. There are several solution dikes that cross the face; this route begins in the center of the clean slab at a pocket 4' up that is intersected by one of these solution dikes.

P1 5.9- PG: Up the low-angle slab to a large horizontal break below a wide ceiling. Walk right and pull through the overhang to a right-facing black fin. Up the fin and black streak on the headwall to a sloped ledge beneath a headwall with a fixed anchor. 130'

FA Aug, 1983, Patrick Purcell, Matt McKenzie

30 Contos 5.3 G 80' ★★

Named after Dave Contini, a classmate of Osteyee's.

Start: At the height of the terrain, 5' left of **Diamonds Aren't Forever**, below a crumbly flake 7' up.

P1 5.3 G: Climb up the crumbly flake to a sloped ledge, step left through some bushes, and follow a good left-leaning crack up and left to a headwall with a fixed anchor. 80'

FA Mar, 1986, Ian Osteyee, Dave Contini

31 Diamonds Aren't Forever 5.10c G 80' ★★★

Climbs the face crisscrossed with downward-pointed flakes. It looks much easier than it is, as the holds all face the wrong direction. Something may have broken on this route—at the crux, unless you move right to **Bee Hold**, it's hard 5.11.

Start: At the height of the terrain, 40' uphill from and left of the right end of the face at its lowest point, below a downward-pointed flake 1' above the ground.

● **P1 5.10c G:** Boulder over a bulge on left-facing edges to lower-angle rock. Climb up and right to a bolt, then straight up the face to the top. 80'

FA 2004, David Lent, Nick Gulli

32 Arrested Development 5.8 R 90'

A wandering line but totally trad.

Start: 10' right of **Diamonds Aren't Forever**, on the right end of a small chest-high ceiling, at a very shallow open book below a right-facing black flake 12' up.

P1 5.8 R: Up the shallow open book and right-facing flake to a ledge on the right. Climb up and right on good holds to join **Bee Hold**, then follow it up and left to a ledge and on to a shallow left-facing corner. **Bee Hold** continues up and left, whereas this route traverses right across the face to lower-angle rock (joining **WMP**). Follow **WMP** up and left to the fixed anchor at the top. 90'

History: **Arrested Development** has been relegated to obscurity with the existence of three new lines that climb sections of this route. In this case, it's for the better, as the newer lines are well protected and popular.

FA Oct 24, 1987, Tad Welch, Jim Lawyer

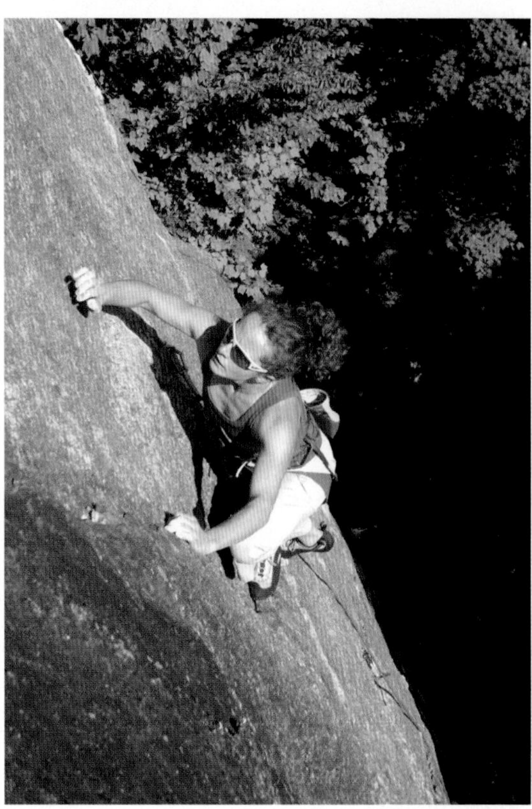

*Michelle Burlitch on **Freak Gasoline Fight Accident** (5.8).*

33 Bee Hold 5.8 G 90' ★★★★

Excellent face climbing on good holds and clean rock.

Start: 8' left of **WMP** below a black right-facing flake 10' up.

● **P1 5.8 G:** Climb up the right-facing flake to a ledge, then up and left on good holds to another ledge. Continue up a face to a shallow left-facing corner, then up and left to a short left-facing bulge; over this to a ledge with a fixed anchor. 90'

FA 2004, David Lent, Nick Gulli

34 WMP 5.7+ G 100' ★★★

The name stands for "What management plan."

Start: At the right end of the cliff, 10' uphill from and left of the toe of the cliff at its lowest point, below a white spot.

● **P1 5.7+ G:** Climb up to the white spot, then up through a bulge to a ledge. Up and left aiming for another ledge, then continue straight up a black streak to the blunt arête on the right margin of the face. Angle up and left on lower-angle rock to a fixed anchor at the top of the face. 100'

FA 2004, David Lent, Nick Gulli

35 Freak Gasoline Fight Accident 5.8 G 80' ★★★

A nice addition to the sport climbs on this wall.

Start: Same as WMP.

● **P1 5.8 G:** Climb WMP for 25' to the ledge. From here, WMP goes up and left; instead, go straight up a short wall, then slab to the fixed anchor (shared with Raw Tips). 80'

FA Jul 4, 2012, Colin O'Connor, Jim Lawyer, Michelle Burlitch

36 Raw Tips 5.10b G 80' ★★★★

Start: At the right end of the cliff at its lowest point, at the base of a toe of clean slab.

● **P1 5.10b G:** Climb straight up the prow to a right-facing flake, then up past a small dike 15' up (bolt). Continue straight up the slab to gain a right-facing, right-leaning corner. At its top, swing left around the corner onto the face and climb up to a fixed anchor. 80'

History: The route was originally climbed on Sep 2, 1988 by John Thackray and Tad Welch, who took a more wandering line at the bottom to gain the corner.

FA Aug 15, 2007, Ian Osteyee, Justin McGiver, Shyloah Nilsen

37 Simon 5.8 G 80' ★★

Start: At the right end of the cliff, 20' uphill and right from the lowest point below a right-facing corner formed by a flake.

P1 5.8 G: Climb the flake-corner to a large grassy ledge. Up the face (bolt) and through a roof (crux) to a good stance and fixed anchor. 80'

FA Oct 31, 2007, Jay Abbey, Mark Arrow

THE PEASANT CRAGS

Location	South side of NY 73, accessed from the Round Pond Trailhead
Summary	Collection of small, mostly undeveloped cliffs on the south side of Round Mountain.

-5.6	5.7	5.8	5.9	5.10	5.11	5.12	5.13+	total
5			1					6

DESCRIPTION

From the Chapel Pond pullout, Round Mountain is the cliff-covered land mass that you gaze at across Chapel Pond. These north-facing slopes are home to the King Wall, Chapel Pond Slab, and the Gully Cliff, as well as most of the ice climbing in Chapel Pond Pass. The Peasant Crags are located on opposite (south) side of Round Mountain in a hidden valley; they cannot be seen from any trail or road. The Peasant Crags are smaller and harder to get to than those above Chapel Pond, but this guarantees solitude and some great views.

There's intermittent cell reception at the cliff.

HISTORY

The cliffs were located by Ellen and Tom DuBois in 2011. DuBois had always suspected worthwhile rock on this "back door" of Round Mountain. A pre-existing herd path in this small valley suggests that this area is also visited by the occasional bushwhacking hiker, as it offers an interesting route to the summit of Round Mountain.

The Peasant Crags

THE CITADEL

Aspect	South
Height	100'
Quality	
Approach	1 hr, moderate
Summary	Raw, broken, remote cliffband with several routes on good rock.

-5.6	5.7	5.8	5.9	5.10	5.11	5.12	5.13+	total
5			1					6

This is a fortress-like cliff that forms a large outside corner, or prow. The prow is the low point on the terrain, and the location of Peasant's Toehold. To the right, the southeast-facing cliff rises 350' steeply uphill, reminiscent of the Live Free or Die Area of the Lower Beer Wall. To the left of the prow is a steep wall that continues for 60' to a wet, black corner.

The climbing here is scenic with wonderful views from the tops of the climbs, and the rock is textured and grippy.

The only practical approach to the top of the formation is a left-rising break in the cliff 215' right of the prow (at the start of Malfeasance).

DIRECTIONS

Park on NY 73 at the Round Pond Trailhead, at a paved pullout 1.0 mile from the Chapel Pond Pullout (when driving toward Malfunction Junction) and 3.1 miles from Malfunction Junction (when driving toward Chapel Pond) 601531,4887257.

From the trailhead (0 hr 0 min), follow the Dix Mountain trail (blue markers) to Round Pond. Go around the pond on the right, then ascend steadily to the height of land 600143,4886278 at 40 min, about 1.6 miles from the trailhead. Continue for 75' past the height of land to where the trail bends left. Veer right off the trail on a bearing of 300° and contour around the hillside to the northwest through open woods to reach a stream that drains this little valley. Go upstream, stay on the right. You will begin to see rock on the right and at 52 min you reach an open area in front of a more substantial cliff, the Gateway Crag 0599871,4886508. There are no routes here.

Continue upstream past a 10'-high waterfall (bypass on the right) to a small, seasonal tributary that comes in on the right. Follow this tributary upstream through rocky talus to reach some ledges. Before the ledges, hike left uphill out of the drainage, then contour left to reach the cliff of The Citadel at 1 hr 599796,4886756.

DESCENT OPTIONS

Best to rappel for most routes.

1 Storming the Tower 5.6 G 100' ★★

Start: From the prow (at **Peasant's Toehold**), hug the rock and walk 40' left to a ledge with birch trees. Begin at a broken, right-facing corner, above which is a nice, orange right-facing corner. This is 20' left of a prominent diving board flake 40' up, and 15 right of a black, wet wall.

P1 5.6 G: Go up the broken corner, then up the orange corner to a ledge. Continue up lower-angled rock to a shallow, vertical corner capped by a small overhang. Move up over this to a superb rectangular ledge, then up a little further to the top of the formation. 100'

FA Nov 11, 2012, Tom DuBois, Ellen DuBois

2 Peasant's Toehold 5.6+ G 75'

Start: At the base on a distinct, low-angle, right-leaning, right-facing corner on the prow of the formation.

P1 5.6+ G: Up the corner past two roofs (the first is 10' up) and a stunted birch to its top. Step around right and finish on easier rock. Walk back 40' to trees. 75'

FA Oct 7, 2011, Tom DuBois, Ellen DuBois

3 Guillotine 5.9 TR 55' ★

Begin 25' uphill and right of **Peasant's Toehold** at a short crack right of a large "nose" in black rock. There is a large roof 30' up broken in the center by a pair of cracks about 3' apart. Climb the crack and nose to a stance. (Go up and left from here to join **Peasant's Toehold**, 5.4.) Follow the pair of cracks through the large roof, then up easier rock to the same finish ledge as **Peasant's Toehold**.

FA (TR) Oct, 2011, Tom DuBois

4 Bastille Day 5.5 TR 55'

Begin 10' uphill and right of **Guillotine** at a system of steps and slashes in the black rock. Climb straight up past the right end of the large roof of **Guillotine** to the same finishing ledge as **Peasant's Toehold**.

FA (TR) Oct, 2011, Ellen DuBois

5 Malfeasance 5.6 G 95' ★★

Start: Walk 150' uphill and right from **Bastille Day** and locate a left-rising, tree-covered ledge that breaks the cliff (20' up this ledge is a short length of rope that protects a step up while traversing to the top of the cliff). Begin on the right end of this ledge at a wavy, low-angled crack system, 2' left of a brushy, right-facing corner capped by an offset roof.

P1 5.6 G: Go up 10' to gain the crack, the climb this to a roof. Step right and climb through the offset roof to a fixed anchor at a lone pine tree. 95'

FA Nov 11, 2012, Tom DuBois, Ellen DuBois

6 Armistice 5.6 G 65' ★★

Start: 75' right of **Malfeasance** (and past a low-angled section) at a final steep, black wall with a fingercrack on its left side.

P1 5.6 G: Climb the steep crack that's easier than it looks due to the excellent rock. Continue to the top on lower-angled rock. 65'

FA Nov 11, 2012, Tom DuBois, Ellen DuBois

FIRST LEAD SLAB

Location	North side of NY 73, accessed from the Round Pond Trailhead
Aspect	Southwest
Height	60'
Quality	
Approach	25 min, moderate
Summary	A small, off-vertical slab with several moderate crack and face routes.

-5.6	5.7	5.8	5.9	5.10	5.11	5.12	5.13+	total
4	1							5

As the name suggests, the First Lead Slab is an acceptable slab of rock for moderate leads. The top offers a unique view of the cliffs on Round Mountain, including the King Wall, which is difficult to see from other vantage points.

It's located on the north side of NY 73, up from and right of Bikini Atoll. The cliffs on this slope are notoriously difficult to find, as it's littered with outcroppings of rock, and the terrain is steep and heavily vegetated, reducing visibility to 30' or less. The directions here should remove much of the ambiguity.

The cliff's main feature is a giant block, just left of center, that rests on a narrow ledge and forms an overlap 6' up. **First Lead** is left of this block, and the other routes are downhill and to the right. The cliff is positioned on a left-rising hillside (so any cliffs you find with a flat base are not it).

HISTORY

The cliff was discovered by Tom DuBois while scouting for cliffs. Having forgotten his hiking shoes, he cleaned the routes in the rain in his dress shoes.

DIRECTIONS (MAP PAGE 197)

Park on NY 73 at the Round Pond Trailhead, at a paved pullout 1.0 mile from the Chapel Pond Pullout (when driving toward Malfunction Junction) and 3.1 miles from Malfunction Junction (when driving toward Chapel Pond) 601531,4887257.

Walk up the road toward Chapel Pond. On the right side of the road, 30' after the end of the guardrail, is a hidden concrete culvert that drains a small stream 601199,4887478. This is directly across the road from the mile marker 73/1201/1419. Follow the streambed up into a deep ravine. Stay on the left bank and continue steeply uphill to reach a large, flat, relatively open area with a cairn. From here, continue on a bearing of 91° to a scrappy cliff. Contour right along the base of this cliff to its right end, then uphill 50' to the base of the cliff 601264,4887683.

1 First Lead 5.4 G 45' ★★

Start: 10' uphill and left of the large block that rests on a narrow ledge 6' up, below a right-leaning crack.

P1 5.4 G: Climb the crack to where it meets a left-rising crack, then follow the left-rising crack to the top. 45'

FA Jul 21, 1996, Tom DuBois

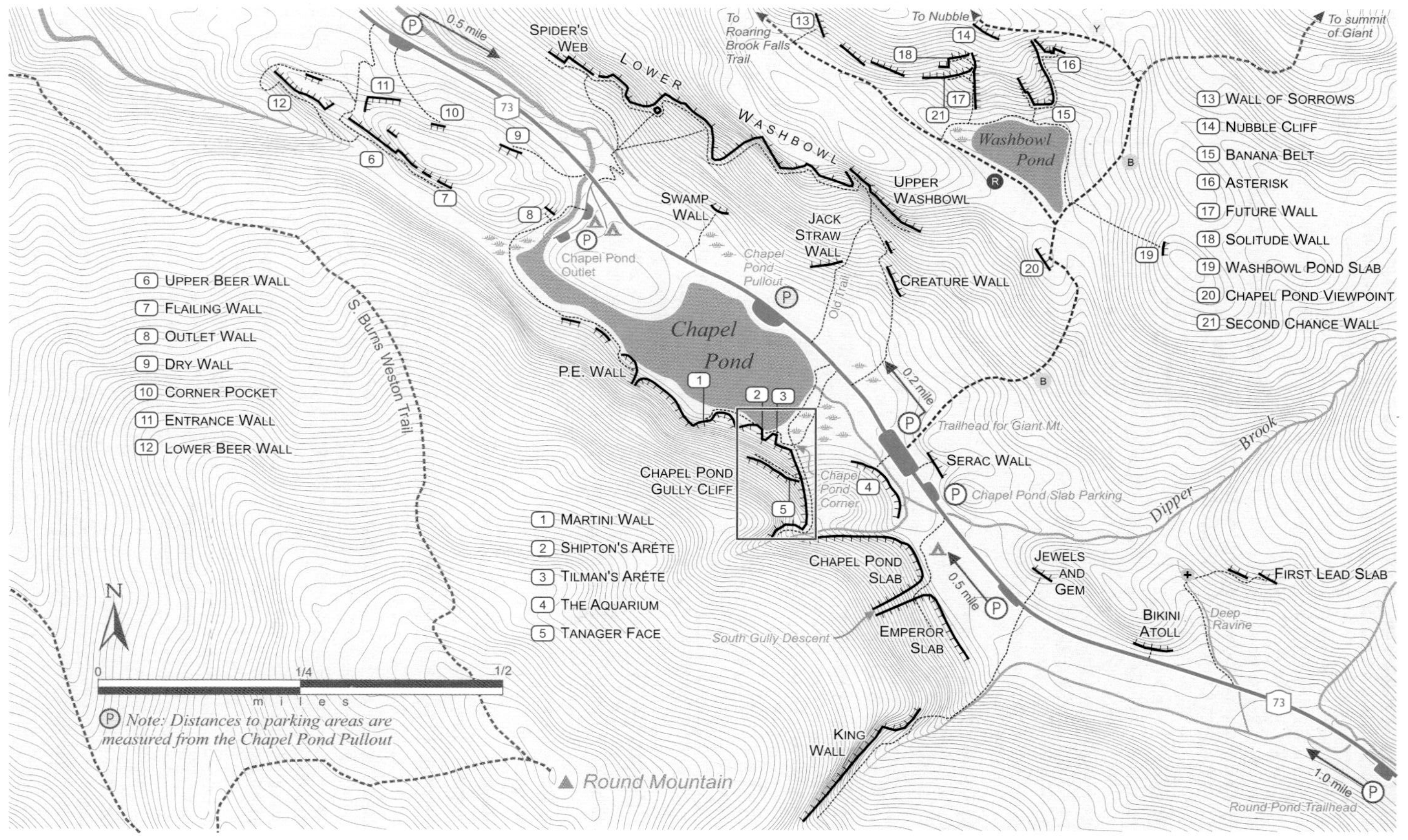
13 Wall of Sorrows
14 Nubble Cliff
15 Banana Belt
16 Asterisk
17 Future Wall
18 Solitude Wall
19 Washbowl Pond Slab
20 Chapel Pond Viewpoint
21 Second Chance Wall
6 Upper Beer Wall
7 Flailing Wall
8 Outlet Wall
9 Dry Wall
10 Corner Pocket
11 Entrance Wall
12 Lower Beer Wall
1 Martini Wall
2 Shipton's Arête
3 Tilman's Arête
4 The Aquarium
5 Tanager Face
Spider's Web
Lower Washbowl
Upper Washbowl
Swamp Wall
Jack Straw Wall
Creature Wall
Washbowl Pond
Chapel Pond
Chapel Pond Outlet
Chapel Pond Pullout
Old Trail
P.E. Wall
Chapel Pond Gully Cliff
Chapel Pond Corner
Chapel Pond Slab
Emperor Slab
South Gully Descent
King Wall
Serac Wall
Trailhead for Giant Mt.
Chapel Pond Slab Parking
Jewels and Gem
Bikini Atoll
First Lead Slab
Deep Ravine
Dipper Brook
Round Mountain
Round Pond Trailhead
S. Burns Weston Trail
To Roaring Brook Falls Trail
To Nubble
To summit of Giant
73
0.5 mile
0.2 mile
1.0 mile
0
1/4
1/2
miles
N
Note: Distances to parking areas are measured from the Chapel Pond Pullout

2 Second Lead 5.2 G 60'

The vertical crack is currently sprouting many saplings, so no stars for now.

Start: 20' downhill and right of a large block that rests on a narrow ledge, 10' uphill and left of **Scary Lead** and 25' uphill and left of the low point of the cliff, at a section of blocky rock that trends left.

P1 5.2 G: Follow the blocky rock up and left, then move 5' right and climb a vertical crack to the top. 60'

FA Jul 21, 1996, Ellen DuBois

3 Scary Lead 5.7 G 50' ★

Start: 15' uphill and left from the lowest point of the cliff at a shallow 5'-high right-facing stepped corner and a thin right-leaning crack that begins 10' up.

P1 5.7 G: Climb up to the thin crack and follow it up and right to where it intersects a left-leaning crack. Follow the left-leaning crack to the top. 50'

FA Jul 7, 1996, Tom DuBois

4 No Lead 5.6 TR 50' ★★

Begin as for **Second Lead** and climb up and right following right-rising discontinuous seams to join the left-leaning crack of **Scary Lead**, then follow it to the top.

FA (TR) Jul 7, 1996, Tom DuBois

5 Last Lead 5.6 PG 45' ★

Start: At the low point of the terrain near the right end of the cliff, left of a black streak and below a left-facing rounded flake 12' up.

P1 5.6 PG: Up the face to the left side of the rounded flake, then climb a crack up and right to a blocky arête (loose) and follow it to the top. 45'

FA Jul 21, 1996, Tom DuBois

BIKINI ATOLL

Location	North side of NY 73 using the same parking as Jewels and Gem
Aspect	South
Height	60'
Quality	
Approach	5 min, easy
Summary	A small crag, close to the road, with a single route.

DIRECTIONS (MAP PAGE 197)

Park on the right side of NY 73 (not at a prepared parking area) 0.5 mile from Chapel Pond as you travel toward Malfunction Junction, just before a guardrail (same as for the King Wall and Jewels and Gem) 600753,4887609.

Walk down the road (toward Malfunction Junction) to the end of the guardrail, then continue to a point 100' before the next guardrail 601026,4887513. Cross the road and head up to the cliff 601039,4887526, about 120' from the road.

1 Life's a Beach 5.9 PG 60'

Start: 25' up from the base of the cliff is a flat vegetated ledge, approached from the right, with a face above. The route begins at the base of a dirty fingercrack behind a tree on the ledge.

P1 5.9 PG: Climb the fingercrack and face above to the top. 60'

FA Aug, 1983, Alan Jolley, Roger Jolley

JEWELS AND GEM

Location	North side of NY 73, 0.5 mile east of Chapel Pond
Aspect	Southwest
Height	70'
Quality	★★★★
Approach	1 min, easy
Summary	Small wall that offers several clean cracks and face routes; extremely popular for toproping.

-5.6	5.7	5.8	5.9	5.10	5.11	5.12	5.13+	total
3	1	2	2	3	1			12

One of the more popular small crags in the Chapel Pond region due to the moderate grade of the routes, clean rock, and open communal area at the base. It is a good crag for beginning leaders, as there are several moderate leadable routes as well as a place to toprope.

DIRECTIONS (MAP PAGE 197)

Parking for Jewels and Gem is on the side of NY 73 (not at a prepared parking area) 0.5 mile from Chapel Pond as you travel toward Malfunction Junction. Park on the right just before a guardrail (same as for the King Wall) 600753,4887609. The approach trail begins across the road and is well worn and easy to follow, requiring about 1 min to reach the crag 600820,4887690.

HISTORY

This small cliff was the brainchild of Patrick Purcell, who climbed the bulk of the routes here in 1985, including the popular **North Country Club Crack**. Don Mellor added a few routes the next year. The cliff became very popular for guiding, but nobody bothered looking around the corners until David Lent in 1995 (**Shaky Spider**), then again in 2004 (**Family Jewels** and **Little Black Book**).

DESCENT OPTIONS

There are often several fixed anchors on trees, or you can walk right and descend a climbers' path back to the base of the cliff.

1 Sorcerer's Stone 5.2 G 40'

Quite clean with good pro.

Start: Walk left from the main face past boulders for several hundred feet to a low-angle, dirty cliff. Continue further and locate a bulging face with an arête partially obscured by cedars on its left.

P1 5.2 G: Climb the arête past a birch, then up a wide crack to the top. 40'

FA Jun, 2012, Tad Welch, Chloe Schultheis, Samantha Schultheis

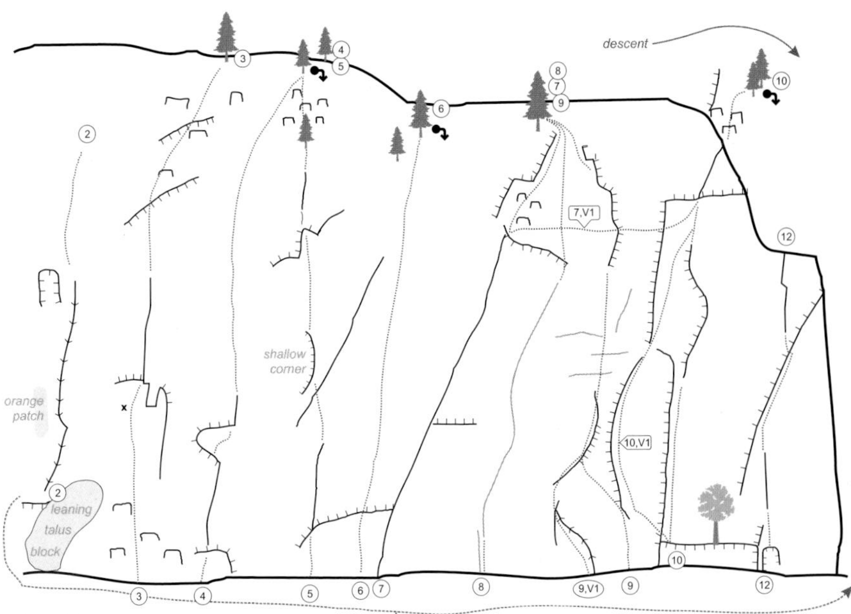

JEWELS AND GEM

2 Little Black Book (5.10a)
3 Family Jewels (5.8+)
4 Coal Miner (5.9+)
5 Pearl Necklace (5.8)
6 D1 (5.11c)
7 North Country Club Crack (5.6)
8 Gold Digger (5.10c)
9 Diamond and Coal (5.6)
10 In the Rough (5.7+)
12 Hidden Gem (5.9+)

2 Little Black Book 5.10a G 60' ★

Good pro but loose at the top.

Start: 50' left of the broken rock of **Family Jewels** is a large right-angled talus boulder. Scramble around to the left side of this talus boulder and up to a small vegetated platform at the base of a large right-leaning open book.

P1 5.10a G: Climb the open book to the right side of a small block-tower. 60'

FA 2005, David Lent, Ian Osteyee

3 Family Jewels 5.8+ G 65' ★★

Well protected at the bottom but run-out at the top.

Start: At the left side of the open area below a section of broken chossy black rock just above a rotting birch stump.

P1 5.8+ G: Climb up the black, chossy rock into a series of small overhangs with a bolt. Up past the bolt to a handcrack, then up easier rock to a tree at the top. 65'

Gear: To 2".

FA 2004, David Lent, Nick Gulli, Jeremy Degroff

4 Coal Miner 5.9+ PG 65' ★

Start: Just right of a section of broken rock at a head-high 1' overhang.

P1 5.9+ PG: Climb through the overhang at a bulge with a crack to a right-facing V-shaped flake just above the bulge. Undercling around right and wander up the face above to the top. 65'

Gear: To 1.5".

FA 1985, Patrick Purcell

*Colin O'Connor on **North CountryClub Crack** (5.6).*

5 Pearl Necklace 5.8 PG 65' ★★★

A quality route. The protection is good, but it's spaced and hidden.

Start: 15' left of **North Country Club Crack**, at the left end of the low overhangs, above which is a 6'-high crack.

P1 5.8 PG: Climb over the overhang and up the crack to a face with a couple of seams, then up to a shallow right-facing corner. More face moves lead to a triangular roof. Take the roof directly (crux) to a crack above. Follow the crack past a tree and up easier blocky terrain. 65'

FA Apr 19, 1986, Don Mellor, Alan Hobson, Patrick Purcell

6 D1 5.11c TR 65'

Begin in the center of the low overhangs at a thin seam and climb directly up the face, straight to the top at a tree ledge.

FA (TR) Apr 19, 1986, Don Mellor, Patrick Purcell

7 North Country Club Crack 5.6 G 70' ★★★★

A beautiful crack and extremely popular; if only it were longer! Named for a bar in Keeseville called the North Country Club.

Start: At the right end of the low overhangs at the base of a right-leaning crack the height of the cliff—the most obvious crackline on the cliff.

P1 5.6 G: Climb the handcrack to a ledge. (V1) Continue up blocky rock in a right-facing corner to the top, then step left to a tree. 70'

V1 5.8+ G: When the cliff was first developed, the top of **North Country Club Crack** had many loose blocks, which were avoided by traversing right across the thin face and horizontal crack, around a right-facing corner to a position under an overhang. Break through the overhang at a right-leaning handcrack (as for **In the Rough** and **In the Buff**).

FA May 8, 1985, Patrick Purcell, Mary Purcell
FA (V1) 1985, Patrick Purcell

8 Gold Digger 5.10c TR 60' ★★

Begin 8' right of **North Country Club Crack** at a seam that splits the face. Follow the seam with increasing difficulty to a ledge, then straight up to the top.

FA (TR) 1985, Patrick Purcell

9 Diamond and Coal 5.6 G 70' ★★★

The first ascent finished on V2 of **North Country Club Crack**, but it is more common today to climb the route as described here.

Start: Find the hourglass-shaped flake that is 20' up and 25' right of **North Country Club Crack**. This route begins on the right side of this feature.

P1 5.6 G: (V1) Climb up, then step left into the hourglass flake and climb it to its top. Continue up past nice horizontals to a left-facing flake system and follow it up to the tree ledge at the top of **North Country Club Crack**. 70'

V1 Ruby Star 5.7 G: Climb directly up to the left side of the hourglass flake.

FA Jul 9, 1985, Patrick Purcell, Bill Dodd
FA (V1) Jul 13, 1985, Patrick Purcell, Mary Purcell

10 In the Rough 5.7+ PG 70' ★

Start: At a ledge with a large birch on the right end of the cliff, at the base of a right-facing corner.

P1 5.7+ PG: (V1) Climb up the corner and off-width crack above, which turns into a right-facing flake. Climb the flake up to the roof (joining **In the Buff** here), breaking it at a right-leaning crack; then follow the crack up right to blocky rock and a couple of trees that serve as an anchor. 70'

V1 In the Buff 5.9 PG: Step left to a shallow right-facing open book that forms the right side of the hourglass flake (of **Diamond and Coal**). Up the flake to a right-angling crack, then follow the crack to a right-facing corner; climb the corner to a roof and join **In the Rough**.

FA 1985, Patrick Purcell
FA (V1) 1985, Patrick Purcell

11 Shaky Spider 5.10b R 70'

Start: Same as **In the Rough**.

P1 5.10b R: Climb up the right-facing corner of **In the Rough**, then traverse right onto the face and climb it straight to the top. 70'

FA Jun, 1995, David Lent, Kevin Crowl

12 Hidden Gem 5.9+ PG 60' ★

Start: 17' right of **In the Rough** at a right-facing open book with a pod–ledge at head height.

P1 5.9+ PG: Follow a crack to a stance, then step left to a right-facing, right-leaning corner. Up the corner 15', then break left around the corner using a blind crimp and up onto edges. Gain a fingercrack and follow it to a ledge. 60'

Gear: Small nuts, micro cams to 1".

FA Apr 15, 2010, Judson Arnold, Bobby Donahue

KING WALL

Location	South side of NY 73 using the same parking as Jewels and Gem
Aspect	East
Height	300'
Quality	★★★
Approach	20 min, easy
Summary	An overhanging wall with mostly difficult bolt-protected routes and several aid lines.

-5.6	5.7	5.8	5.9	5.10	5.11	5.12	5.13+	total
1	2	1	2	6	3	3		21

Tucked up in a hidden notch next to the Emperor Slab, the east-facing King Wall is one of the more impressive features in the region. The 300'-high wall is slightly concave, sheer, nearly crackless, covered with black stripes, and overhanging. You feel giddy excitement when peering around the corner to catch a first glimpse of this striped and magnificent wall.

The King Wall is one of the more peaceful cliffs in the Chapel Pond valley, in that it is removed from road noise and, on its right end, has an open, level base with flat boulders, tall ferns, and a running stream nearby. On the far right end is a vegetated slab that runs

perpendicular to the wall, insulating it from NY 73. As you move left, the terrain rises steeply along the base of the cliff until, at its far left end, the cliff becomes lower-angled until it eventually sinks into the hillside.

Due to the overhanging crackless nature of the rock, routes at the King Wall don't come easy. The routes here were climbed ground-up in a true adventurous style, arduously bolting from hooks. The wall will undoubtedly yield to those with the imagination and mind-set for such endeavors.

HISTORY

Todd Eastman was one of the first to consider the King Wall for climbing, having spied it from a car. He realized that the wall would require "at least a bolt or two," and given the antibolt ethic of the time, he went on to other projects. In 1979, he showed the wall to Patrick Purcell, who went on to become the primary protagonist here. His first climb in 1982, **Elusive Dream**, is a statement of single-minded dedication bordering on the obsessive, involving solo aid climbing over many days. In his words, "Warren Harding was renting space in my head," and it was in Harding style that Purcell experimented here. His gear list included, among other things, 19 drill bits, a homemade portaledge, homemade hangers, lengths of chain, a radio, Walkman, and, of course, some beer. He returned many times with various partners to establish, ground-up, many testpieces, the best being **Kingdom Come**. Recent additions such as **The Keep**, **The King and I**, and the freed **Another Wack and Dangle Job** demonstrate more potential here.

GEOLOGY

The colored streaks that are so prominent on the King Wall are the result of several different processes. The black streaks are biological colonies of cyanobacteria and other single-celled organisms. The white streaks are calcite deposits due to minerals dissolving out of the rock. Other cliffs have red- and orange-colored streaks, formed by iron in the rock, which rusts when exposed to air and water. Sometimes streaks are formed by lichen of various colors (grays, blacks, and sometimes orange) and indicate a watercourse, a nutrient-rich medium, or textured rock.

DIRECTIONS **(MAP PAGE 197)**

Parking for the King Wall is on the side of NY 73 (not at a prepared parking area) 0.5 mile from Chapel Pond as you travel toward Malfunction Junction. Park on the right just before a guardrail (same as for Jewels and Gem) 600753,4887609. The approach trail begins at the guardrail and runs south 300' or so through level forest into a steep drainage that is followed uphill to the base of the wall. The herd path stays mostly on the right side of the stream but often requires rock hopping up the stream itself. Eventually the herd path leaves the stream and climbs a steep hillside to a black wall (with the ice route **Cheese and Crackers**), then continues left along the base of this wall back to the stream, around the end of this cliff, and into the open, level talus at the base of the King Wall at its right end—near the base of the route **Kingdom Come** 600477,4887418. Hiking time from the road is 20 min.

DESCENT OPTIONS

Very few routes reach the top of the cliff. For those that do, rappel from trees and use the fixed anchors on the face.

Peasant Wall

The left end of the cliff, known as the Peasant Wall, is reached by a stiff uphill scramble along the base. The **Slave Labor** corner is a good feature, but the climbing is generally dirtier than the rest of the cliff.

DESCENT OPTIONS

Rappel from trees for routes in this area.

1 Black Plague 5.4 G 80' ★

Start: Same as **Slave Labor**.

P1 5.4 G: Up the corner and step left onto the sloped large ledge below a black face. Scramble up and left to the left end of the face and climb a shallow right-facing corner up to its top, then up the slab to the top. 80'

FA May 22, 1989, Don Mellor, Jeff Edwards, Patrick Purcell

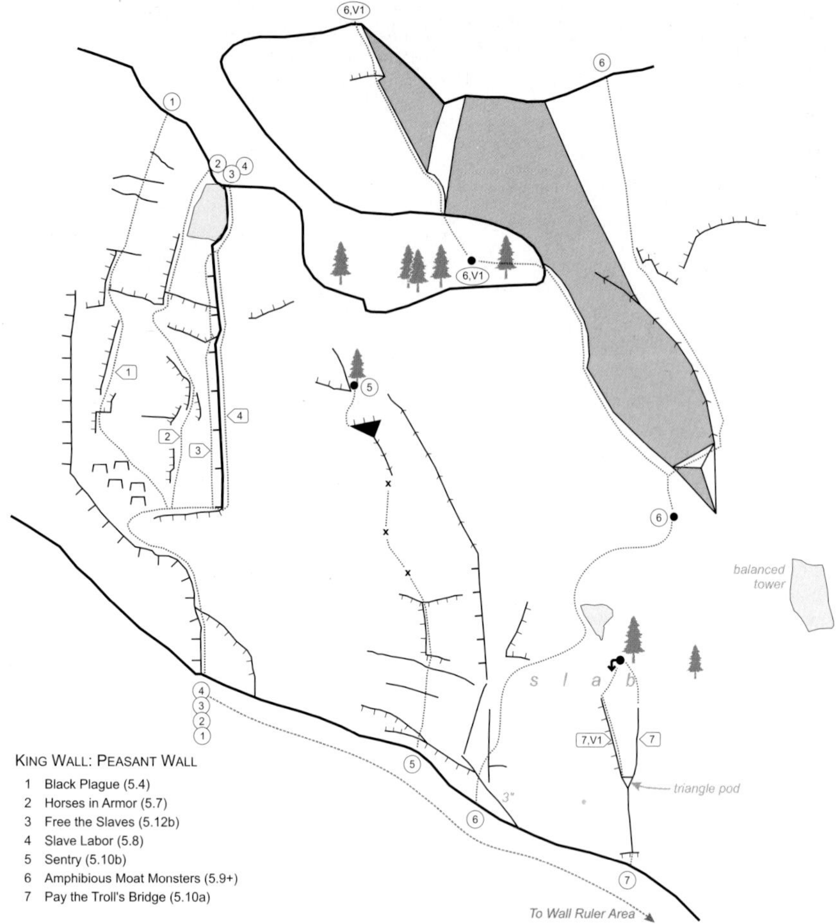

KING WALL: PEASANT WALL

1 Black Plague (5.4)
2 Horses in Armor (5.7)
3 Free the Slaves (5.12b)
4 Slave Labor (5.8)
5 Sentry (5.10b)
6 Amphibious Moat Monsters (5.9+)
7 Pay the Troll's Bridge (5.10a)

2 Horses in Armor 5.7 PG 90' ★

Start: Same as **Slave Labor**.

P1 5.7 PG: Climb up the corner and step left onto the sloped large ledge below a black face. In the center of the face, climb right-facing flakes and edges to an overlap. Step left to a ceiling, then back right into a shallow right-facing corner. Up the corner to the top. 90'

FA May 22, 1989, Patrick Purcell, Jeff Edwards, Don Mellor

3 Free the Slaves 5.12b TR 90'

This route climbs the arête of the **Slave Labor** corner.

FA (TR) Aug, 1990, Patrick Purcell

4 Slave Labor 5.8 G 90' ★

This attractive corner is a prominent feature. It is currently a bit mossy with an especially dirty topout.

Start: At a broken, deep, 20'-high right-facing corner, 70' uphill and left of the 3" slanting crack of **Pay the Troll's Bridge**. This is below and slightly left of a more prominent right-facing corner that starts 25' up and runs the height of the cliff.

P1 5.8 G: Climb the large corner to a good ledge, then traverse up and right on a sloped ledge to the base of the prominent right-facing corner. Up the corner past a ledge on the left wall to a roof at the top. Up the right side of the roof to the top. 90'

FA May 22, 1989, Patrick Purcell, Jeff Edwards

5 Sentry (aka Controversial Midgets) 5.10b PG 90' ★

Interesting climbing after a mossy start and an exciting roof finish.

Start: Uphill and left of the base of the 3" crack of **Amphibious Moat Monsters**, below a 10'-high ledge with a triangular block.

P1 5.10b PG: Dirty climbing gains the triangular block, then up the face to a good horizontal. Continue up to a shallow right-facing 10'-high open book with a crack. At its top, climb onto a tiny ledge, then step left and climb white rock to an open book, then up to a triangular roof. Break the roof on the left and climb to the top. 90'

FA Sep, 1990, Patrick Purcell, Patrick Munn

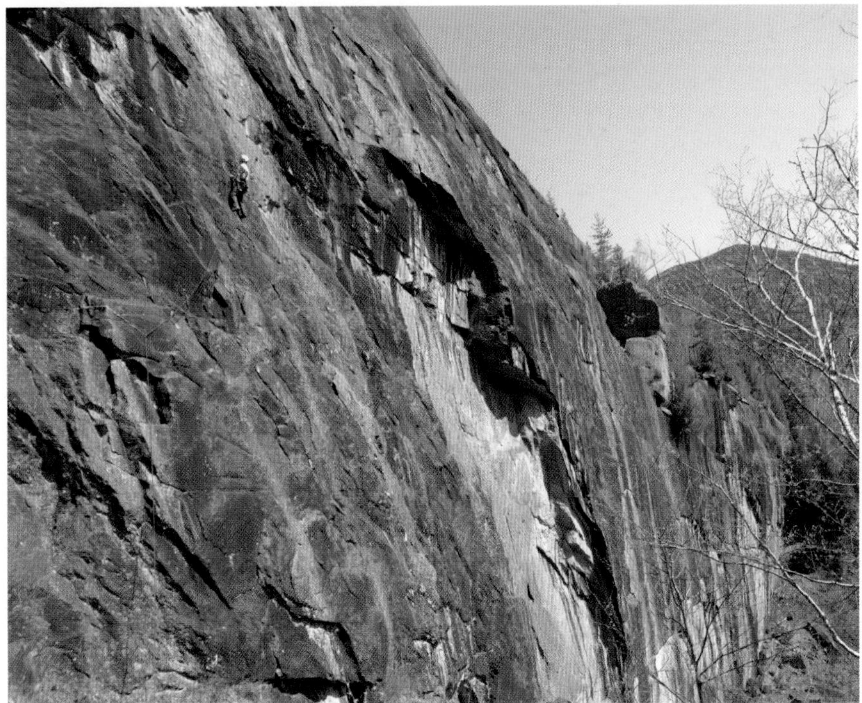

Don Mellor links together P1 and P2 of **Prince** *(5.7).*

6 Amphibious Moat Monsters 5.9+ G (5.4 R) 200'

The upper portion of this route features excellent pocketed face climbing on an exposed arête, but it's dirty and needs an easier start (hint).

Start: At a dirty right-facing, left-leaning corner with a 3" crack, 15' left of **Pay the Troll's Bridge**.

P1 5.9+ G: Climb up the dirty 3" crack for 10', then straight up the clean face to a horizontal. Make a long reach to a horn at the second horizontal, then pull up flakes onto the slab. Angle up and right for 50' (easy 5.4) to a slab below the left side of a prominent arête. 100'

P2 5.6 G (5.4 R): (V1) Climb a crack on the left side of the prow to a ledge on the arête with a cedar and pesky birch. Step right and climb the knobby face on the right side of the prow to the trees at the top. 100'

V1 5.8 G: At the top of the slab, climb the large corner to the trees and belay (40'). (Another pitch is possible by continuing up the large corner past a small overhang to the top.)

FA May 21, 1989, Patrick Purcell, Herb George, Herb George Jr.

FA (V1) May 21, 1989, Tim Beaman, Sylvia Lazarnick

7 Pay the Troll's Bridge 5.10a G 100' ★

Start: 150' uphill and left of **Prince**, below a handcrack that leads to a distinct triangular pod 20' up.

P1 5.10a G: Climb the handcrack to the triangular pod, (V1) then out the right-hand crack to a ledge. Continue up a bulging black wall to its top at 50'. Continue up and right across the low-angle slab to cedars. 100'

V1 Trolls in Hiding 5.9 G: Climb out the left side of the pod into a shallow right-facing, left-leaning corner and onto the slab; angle up and right to the cedars.

FA May 21, 1989, Tim Beaman, Sylvia Lazarnick, Patrick Purcell

FA (V1) May 21, 1989, Tim Beaman, Sylvia Lazarnick

Wall Ruler Area

The center section of the cliff has several longer routes, including the moderate **Price**, as well as several more difficult sport routes. The main features here are the large left-arching roofs; **Wall Ruler** makes its way through these.

8 Working Wives 5.12a G 120' ★★

This very thin slab crux has puzzled many leaders.

Start: Same as **Prince**.

P1 5.12a G: Climb up the left-facing corners to their top. Continue up and left on black rock to meet the left end of a wide overlap. Step around the left end of the overlap and up a bulging slab (crux) to a large sloped ledge. Climb up the face to a bolt and onto the blunt arête, following up above it on good ledges, then straight up the black face to an overlap and a fixed anchor just above. 120'

Gear: Small gear helps in the upper section.

FA May, 1992, Patrick Purcell, Bob Martin

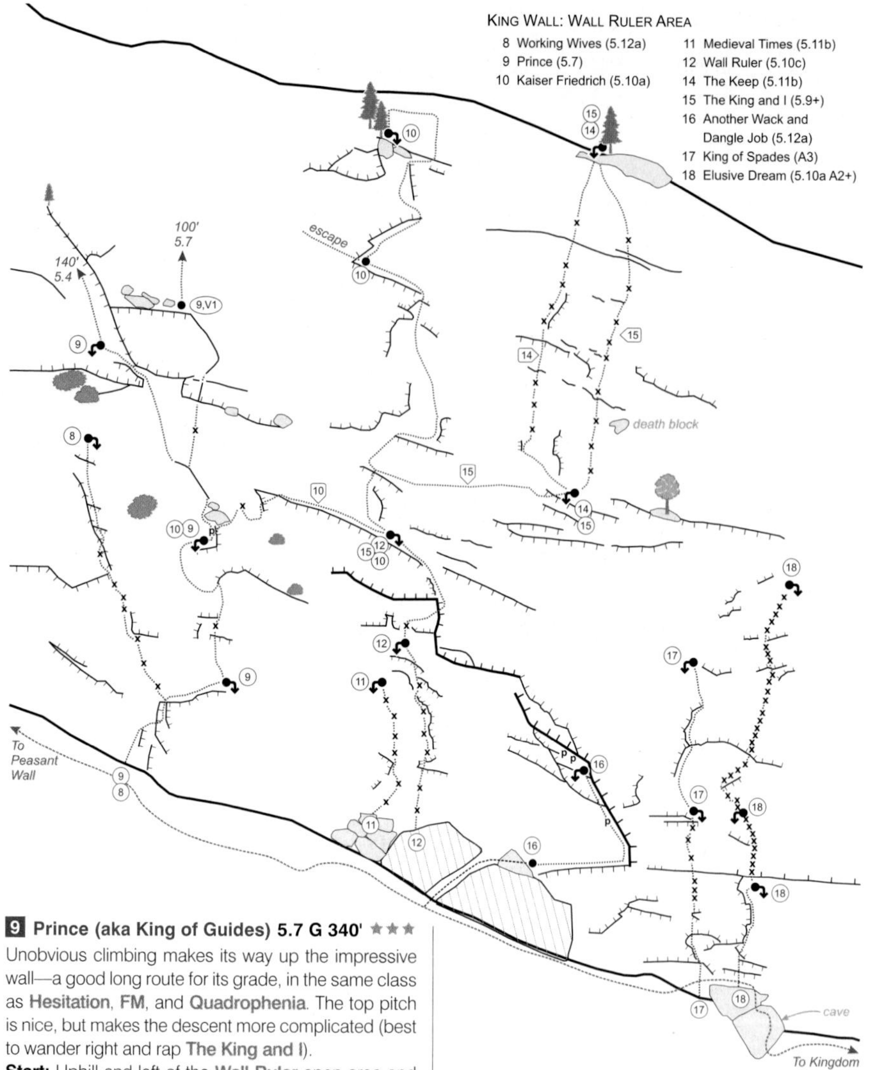

9 Prince (aka King of Guides) 5.7 G 340' ★★★

Unobvious climbing makes its way up the impressive wall—a good long route for its grade, in the same class as **Hesitation**, **FM**, and **Quadrophenia**. The top pitch is nice, but makes the descent more complicated (best to wander right and rap **The King and I**).

Start: Uphill and left of the **Wall Ruler** open area and ledge is a jumble of short left-facing corners with a ledge on top at 30'. This route begins below a 6'-high ledge beneath the left-facing corners, just right of a black streak on the wall above.

P1 5.5 G: Boulder up onto the ledge (or walk in from the left), then up the left-facing corners to their top. Traverse right on good ledges to a fixed anchor. 50'

P2 5.7 G: Continue straight up to an overlap (bolt), around the overlap on buckets, then trend left on the face, then back right onto a ledge with a fixed anchor below a left-facing open book below a huge balanced flake. P1 and P2 can be combined with good rope management. 60'

P3 5.7 G: (V1) Climb up the left side of a balanced flake, then follow a left-leaning fingercrack aiming for a large horizontal spike of rock. Climb in behind the spike (crux, large cam) and out left easily through the roof. Move up and left to a fixed anchor. 90'

P4 5.4 G: Rappel (200') or wander up the slab to the summit. 140'

V1 5.9+ R: Climb straight up the black face past a bolt to a handcrack in the roof. Out the crack, then follow a right-leaning crack as it bends back left to a broken ledge at 80' and belay. Wander up the slab (5.7) for another 100' to the top.

FA Mar 7, 1989, Patrick Purcell, Mary Purcell, Don Mellor

FA (V1) Jun 7, 1989, Don Mellor, Patrick Purcell

*Opposite: Matt McCormick on **Another Wack and Dangle Job** (5.12a). Photo by Dax Sommerfeld (daxopus.com).*

10 Kaiser Friedrich 5.10a G (5.7 R) 320' ★

This route extends **Prince** and **Wall Ruler** to the top of the cliff.

Start: At the end of P2 of **Prince**.

P1 5.8 PG: Climb out right under the balanced flake (crux) to a good foot edge (one hesitates to even touch this perched flake of doom; it is possible to do the moves without touching it). Face-climb up and right (bolt), then down and right to a shallow left-facing corner. Swing right around the corner on jugs and up to a ledge. Traverse down and right on ledges to a fixed anchor (shared with **Wall Ruler**). 90'

P2 5.6 PG: Move left along the traverse ledge, then up and right following left-facing flakes to a good ledge below a ceiling. Up a black face on good holds to another large sloped ledge. Step right to a shallow left-facing corner, then face-climb up and left, past an overlap, to the right end of another ledge. Walk left 20' to a belay beneath a right-arching ceiling. 130'

P3 5.10a G (5.7 R): (V1) Face-climb up and right following the underside of the right-arching ceiling. At its end, make a hard move over a bulge (crux, #00 TCU critical), then straight up to an overlap with good gear (about 6' right of a cammed hotdog-shaped flake). Climb an unprotected friction slab (5.7 R) to a short headwall, then walk left and downclimb to a large cedar tree. 100'

V1 5.6 PG: Up and left on the slab to escape. 90'

Descent: A 170' rappel returns you to the fixed anchor at the top of P1, then another dramatic free rappel 130' returns you to the ground.

FA Aug 19, 1989, Don Mellor, Friedel Schunk

11 Medieval Times 5.11b G 70' ★★

Quality face climbing. Originally called **Chariots and Race Cars**.

Start: At the left end of the ledge described for **Wall Ruler**.

P1 5.11b G: Climb up the black rock using good right-facing flakes and some edges. Continue up into white rock, then angle left to a fixed anchor in the middle of the wall. 70'

FA Oct 2, 1993, Patrick Purcell, Chris Hyson

12 Wall Ruler 5.10c G 130' ★★★

An adventurous route through an imposing roof system, which appears to be the easiest thing on the route. At the top, you can rappel or continue on **The King and I** (5.9+) or **The Keep** (5.11b) to the top.

Start: Up and left of the black slab (with the black triangular block on top) is another black slab with a flat ledge on top. Walk onto the ledge from the left. This route begins in the center of the ledge below a black face with two bolts.

P1 5.10c G: Climb the black face past two bolts to a ledge. Continue straight up the face to a left-facing flake (this flake defines the margin of the black and white rock). Follow the flake to a bulge and up to a ledge with a fixed anchor. 80'

P2 5.10b G: Continue up and right to a bolt, then traverse right across orange rock to the large left-facing corner beneath the roof. Break around the corner to the right on good buckets (surprising 5.4), then angle up and left to a fixed anchor on a good ledge. 50'

FA 1990, Patrick Purcell, Patrick Munn

13 Wall Ruler–King and I (linkup) ' 5.10c G 0' ★★★★★

An amazing linkup, one of the best in the region. Climb **Wall Ruler**, then finish on **The King and I**.

Descent: Two rappels with double 60m ropes.

14 The Keep 5.11b G 140' ★★★★★

Immaculate pocketed rock, sustained climbing, and several cruxes characterize this off-vertical face. Absolutely superb.

Start: At the fixed anchor at the end of P1 of **The King and I**.

○ P1 5.11b G: Step left from the anchor, mantel a ledge, then walk left 15' to a pocketed black wall with a bolt. Work straight up the amazing pocketed wall (5.9) to a sloping ledge below a shallow white open book. Boulder into the open book (first crux) and climb to its top, then up the super thin face past a key nipple (second crux) to another sloping stance below a scooped headwall. Friction up the scoop to a difficult mantel (third crux), surmount an overlap, then run out to the trees and fixed anchor shared with **The King and I**. 140'

Gear: RPs, and 1 ea 1" cam.

FA Aug 27, 2008, Jim Lawyer, Don Mellor

15 The King and I 5.9+ G (5.5 R) 215' ★★★★

Located above **Wall Ruler** and right of **Kaiser Friedrich** is a large, open, off-vertical face with naturally clean, pocketed rock, completely hidden from the cliff base. The wall is bordered on its right side by a perched house-sized boulder. This was the first new route at the King Wall in over 10 years.

Start: Begin on the good ledge at the top of **Wall Ruler**. This is accessed by climbing **Wall Ruler**, or (more easily) the first two pitches of **Prince** (5.7), then the P1 traverse pitch of **Kaiser Friedrich** (5.8).

P1 5.5 R: Go up and left 15' (easy, no gear), then straight up an excellent, clean slab right of a right-facing corner to a large ledge. Walk right 40' on a clean flat sidewalk with little pro to step-down (4th class, no protection) and obvious fixed anchor out right. 75'

○ P2 5.9+ G: Climb straight up the face through an unlikely-looking black headwall to the top. 140'

Gear: Cams through 2".

Descent: Two 60m double-rope rappels return to the ground near **Another Wack and Dangle Job**.

FA Jun 25, 2008, Don Mellor, Jim Lawyer

16 Another Wack and Dangle Job 5.12a G 60' ★★★★★

This route climbs the prominent left-facing, left-arching corner-roof. The face right of the corner is black, and the face left of the corner is white. The route was intended to be extended up through the arch, but Purcell never got around to it.

Start: 30' left of the base of the prominent left-arching corner-roof on top of a large black slab leaning against the cliff with a triangular block on top.

P1 5.12a: Foot-traverse right for 30' on a sloped ledge to the base of the left-facing, left-arching corner. Up the corner past a two-tiered ceiling to a fixed anchor beneath the arch. 60'
FA (5.8 A2) Oct 1, 1985, Patrick Purcell, Mary Purcell
FFA Jun 5, 2009, Matt McCormick

17 King of Spades A3 160'

Start: 20' left of **Elusive Dream** at the right end of a low roof 8' up. At the right end of the roof is an unusual horizontal pointed shelf.
P1 A3: Aid straight up a shallow right-facing flake to a stance, then straight up to a fragile left-facing tan-colored beak-shaped flake. Continue straight up the steep black face (rivets and hooks) to a fixed anchor. 80'
P2 A3: Move left into the arches and follow these past more rivets and fixed bashies to a fixed anchor. 80'
Gear: All Black Diamond hooks and Leeper hooks, bashies, and fixed thin blades.
FA Aug, 1996, Dave Aldous (roped solo)

18 Elusive Dream (aka Porcelain Forest) 5.10a A2+ 250'

In the words of Purcell, a "great adventure." P1 is a very popular free route, and the rest is a bolt and rivet ladder up an impressive wall.

Start: 150' left of **Chronic Fixation** is a cave formed by some large boulders leaning up against the cliff. This route begins on top of the slab that forms the cave.
P1 5.10a G: Climb up two ledges and into a right-facing white-colored flake. Up the flake to its top at a fixed anchor beneath a ceiling. 60'
P2 A2+: Climb over the roof and follow a line of bolts and rivets straight up to a fixed anchor. 40'
P3 A2+: Aid up and left, then back right, then over a shallow overlap. Continue up and right past two overlaps to a fixed anchor. 150'
Gear: P1 takes cams to 2".
History: P1 was climbed in 1981 to the first roof, then a short distance up P2. The route was extended up the wall to the next belay and partway up P3 in 1987. The first complete ascent was climbed solo over two days, bivying on the wall.
FA (P1) 1982, Patrick Purcell, François Paul-Hus
FA Jul 19, 1989, Patrick Purcell

Kingdom Come Area

This is the first section of cliff reached on the approach and has some popular sport routes that stay dry in the rain.

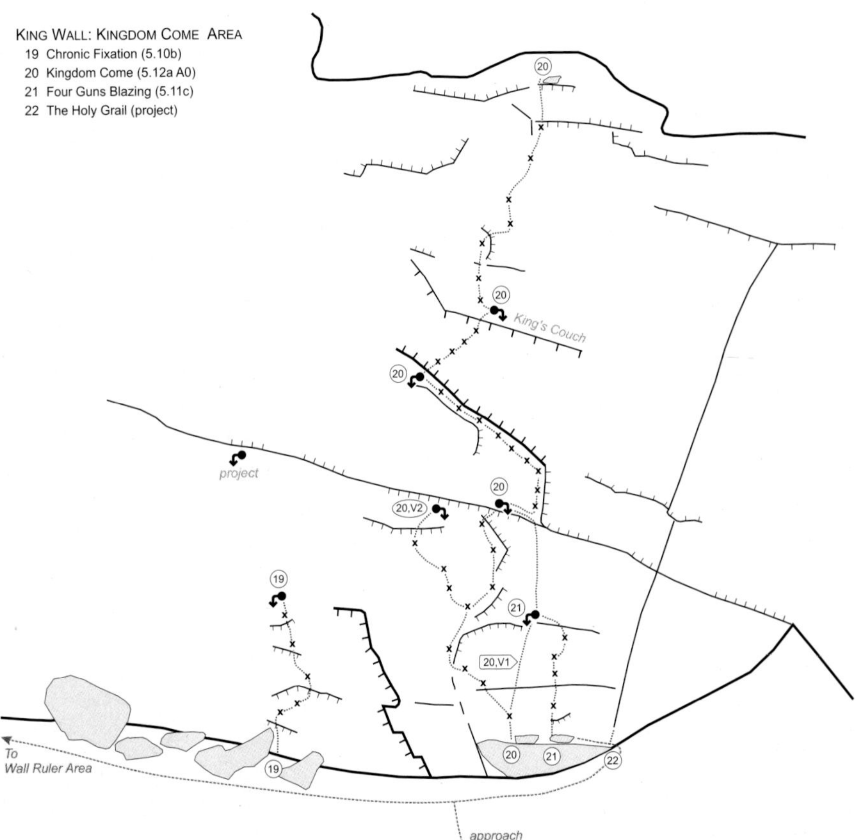

19 Chronic Fixation 5.10b G 60' ★★★

A short, steep route on good rock with positive holds. In an attempt to push the route farther, there is an additional anchor 50' above the P1 fixed anchor; this is an open project. Once known as **Feeding the Fix**.

Start: 30' left of a left-leaning, right-facing corner-flake (and 50' left of the ledge where **Kingdom Come** starts), on the right side of an 8'-high pointed boulder that leans up against the cliff.

● **P1 5.10b G:** Climb up to a slanted ledge and the first bolt, then move right on positive holds and up to another good ledge. Work back left, then straight up to a fixed anchor. 60'

FA Sep, 1992, Patrick Purcell, Patrick Munn

20 Kingdom Come 5.12a A0 270' ★★★★★

An incredible route on steep rock, sustained and very photogenic. P2 is unique, requiring unusual body positioning. The P2 anchor is very uncomfortable. (Hint: with a single rope, the leader can be lowered to the ground; the second can then follow on toprope, then be lowered to the V2 anchor, then pull the ropes and rappel to the ground.) Most parties stop after P1 or P2. P3 is a bolt ladder; freeing this pitch is one of the real prizes in the region. The last pitch is recommended and can be reached from rappel by hiking around the right end of the cliff. The bottom two pitches stay dry in the rain. Purcell believes this to be his best offering to the climbing community.

Start: At the right end of the cliff just before the terrain slopes up is a 10'-high ledge with two boulders (walk onto the ledge from the right). This route begins at the left of the two boulders (the one with the bolt) below a steep white wall.

● **P1 5.11b G:** (V1) Climb straight up on incut buckets on the overhanging wall, then up and left to a vertical seam. Follow this up (crux) to a right-rising, left-facing shallow ramp system. (V2) Climb up and right following the ramp to a final slanted ceiling; over this to a fixed anchor. 80'

● **P2 Under Thunder 5.11c G:** Traverse right on the sloped ledge to a left-facing black corner. Up the corner to the large left-rising roof. Climb up and left under the roof (some creative back smearing here) to a final crux before a fixed anchor at the left end of the roof. 80'

P3 A0: Climb the bolt ladder over the end of the arching roof, then up and right to a good ledge (the King's Couch) with a fixed anchor. Often wet. 20'

P4 Clipping in Space 5.12a G: A mean little boulder problem leads to beautiful climbing. Named because Purcell missed a clip, leaving him dangling in space. Step left and climb up to a good horizontal (crux after first bolt), then up a left-facing crescent. At the top of the crescent, the angle eases to a slab; go up and right across the slab to a bulge with a right-facing edge; over this to a balanced block. 90'

V1 5.12a TR: Climb up and right to meet the anchor of **Four Guns Blazing**.

Opposite: Colin Loher on P1 (5.11b) of ***Kingdom Come*** *(5.12a A0). Photo by Tomás Donoso.*

● **V2 All the King's Men 5.11c G:** Climb straight up the face to a fixed anchor at the break.

FA (P1) Jul 20, 1989, Patrick Purcell, Don Mellor
FA (P2) Aug, 1992, Patrick Purcell, Dominic Eisinger
FA (P4) 1993, Patrick Purcell, Dominic Eisinger
ACB (V1) Kevin Boyle
FA (V2) 1998, Patrick Purcell

21 Four Guns Blazing 5.11c G 50' ★★★

Originally called **Hiking on Hooks**. The first ascent was done on the lead and in the rain with perfectly dry rock. The route has been extended on toprope from the anchor to meet the end of the traverse on P2 of **Kingdom Come** (5.12a, ACB Kevin Boyle, Jay Kullman, late 1990s).

Start: 10' right of **Kingdom Come** at the right of two boulders resting on the ledge.

● **P1 5.11c G:** Climb up the left margin of the black streak following a line of bolts. Move right, then back left to a fixed anchor in the middle of the wall. 50'

FA Aug, 1992, Patrick Purcell, Chris Hyson

22 The Holy Grail Project

At the right end of the ledge (where **Kingdom Come** and **Four Guns Blazing** start) is a very thin right-leaning aid seam in black rock. It was tackled by Patrick Purcell in the early 1980s, but to no avail.

EMPEROR SLAB

Location	South side of NY 73, accessed from the Giant Mountain Trailhead at Chapel Pond
Aspect	Northeast
Height	700'
Quality	★
Approach	20 min, moderate
Summary	Long run-out friction routes on clean rock with very little protection.

-5.6	5.7	5.8	5.9	5.10	5.11	5.12	5.13+	total
1		3		1				5

The climbing on the Emperor Slab has long been shaded in mystery, as nobody seems to have climbed here. Perhaps this is due to the unprotected nature of the climbing or that slab climbing is out of fashion. The fears over protection are justified (some pitches have no gear, and some of the belays are poor), but the rock is excellent and the friction is secure. Further confusion over just where the lines go has also kept visitors at bay; after all, nobody wants to runout 5.7 friction for 180' and be unable to find a belay. The slab is a vast expanse of open rock, and at 5.7, you can climb just about anywhere. If you are comfortable on **Thanksgiving** on Chapel Pond Slab, then the Emperor Slab is the next step up (and you'll have the entire slab to yourself). For first-time visitors, you can climb P1 of **Tone-Boneparte**, traverse right to Second Tree Island, and set up a toprope on numerous lines.

Regardless of the chosen line, there are only a couple of ways to break through the upper roof that spans the width of the cliff. **Führer** breaks this at a notch on its left end, and **Tone-Boneparte** breaks it in

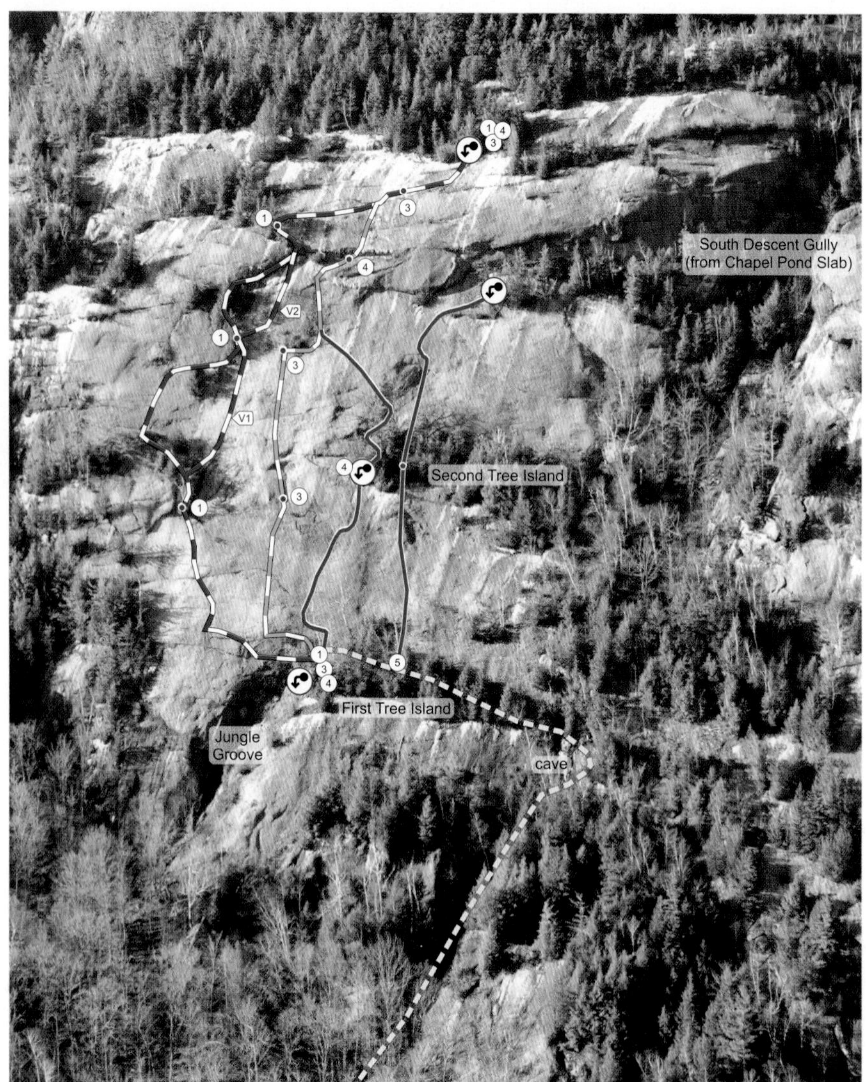

the center via devious scoops and knobs.

The routes begin on the left end of First Tree Island, a narrow band of trees and vegetation that spans horizontally across the slab from its right side. Below and left of this tree island is a deep right-leaning gully known as Jungle Groove. Above First Tree Island is Second Tree Island, a secure ledge of trees with a rappel anchor. On the right side of the slab is the South Descent Gully, which separates the Emperor Slab from Chapel Pond Slab and is one of two descents used from Chapel Pond Slab.

DIRECTIONS **(MAP PAGE 197)**

Park as for Chapel Pond Slab and walk to the base of the slab. From there, walk left through the woods to the South Descent Gully, by locating a giant V-groove filled with a couple of logs. Scramble up the V-groove, then up the gully (3rd-class) to a cave. Walk right, then back left along the base of a slab to a position above the cave. Continue straight left following a steeply sloped vegetated ledge (First Tree Island) for 150' (4th-class) to its end. There are several large trees here (one with a fixed anchor), and the position is on top of a nasty right-leaning gully (Jungle Groove) and below a clean slab.

DESCENT OPTIONS

There is a fixed anchor at the top of **Tone-Boneparte**. A 120' diagonal rappel (to climber's right) reaches a tree ledge below the roofs. The next rappel is 120' straight down to Second Tree Island. Walk left to a fixed anchor

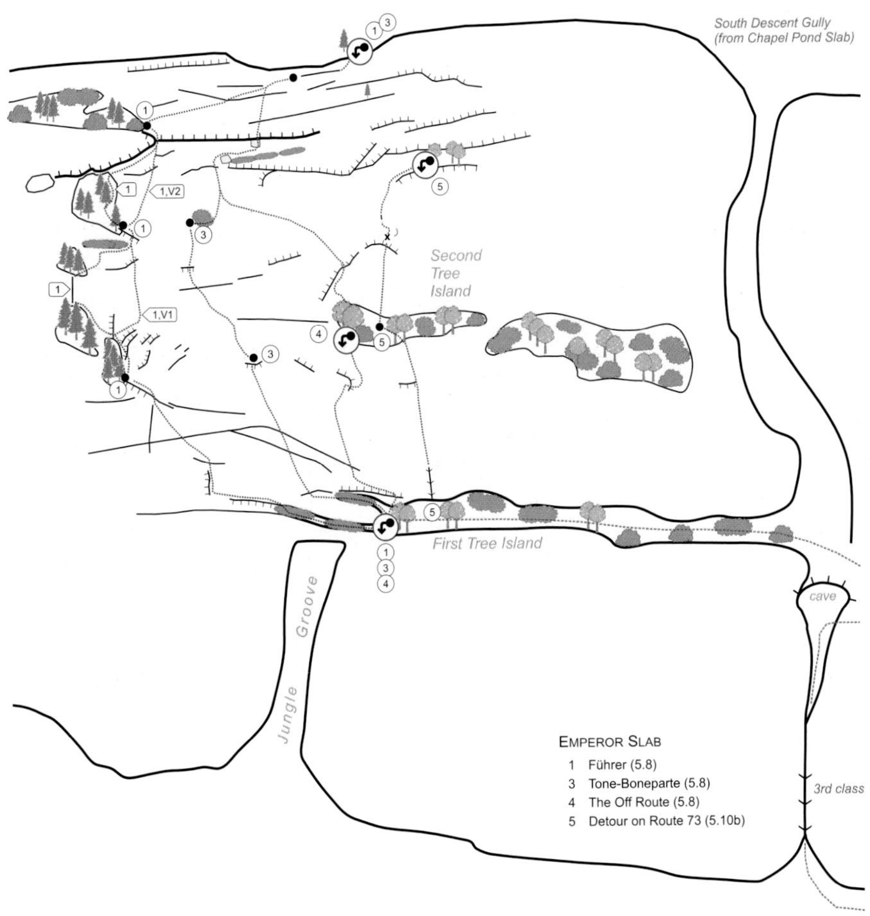

on its left end, then rappel 200' to First Tree Island and a fixed anchor on its left end. A final rappel of 200' down the slabs right of Jungle Groove reaches the bottom.

HISTORY

Tom Rosecrans recalls that this slab was known as the Emperor Slab even before he climbed the first route with Tony Goodwin in 1974. The name's origin isn't known, but it was probably derived from the route **Empress**, the next climb over on Chapel Pond Slab, perhaps by Yvon Chouinard, who is believed to have climbed the Emperor Slab during his visit in the winter of 1969 when he introduced the curved pick and front-pointing. After the first few routes here in the 1970s, nothing new has been climbed, with the exception of Patrick Purcell's obscure variation in 1991, **Detour on Route 73**.

1 Führer 5.8 G (5.5 R) 630'

A smorgasbord of friction with comfy belays. P1 is quite good, but the subsequent pitches degenerate into cedar pulling. The final moves through the roof are quite a puzzle. Although two high-quality variations are included that avoid the tree pulling, these should be attempted only by those extremely familiar with the slab and confident on friction—they are devoid of protection.

Start: From the left end of First Tree Island, two vegetated ribbons extend leftward into the slab, where they end. The upper vegetated ribbon is the start of **Tone-Boneparte**, and the lower vegetated ribbon is the start of **Führer**. Begin at the low point of First Tree Island just above the Jungle Groove gully.

P1 5.5 R: Follow the vegetated ribbon left across the top of Jungle Groove and onto the slab, aiming for a shallow, 15'-high right-facing corner. Up the corner (TCUs), then straight up to a horizontal crack (small cams). Continue straight up to a 4"-high rust-colored dike, then up the face on good, clean friction (5.5 R) to the right end of a left-rising crack full of grass. Follow the crack up and left, where it becomes a ramp. There is a fixed anchor on trees at the upper left end of the ramp. 200'

P2 5.6 PG: Work up the slab right of the vegetation past two right-facing, right-leaning overlaps. Go over these to a shallow right-facing open book with good

*Dennis Luther on P1 (5.8) of **Detour on Route 73** (5.10b).*

gear. (V1) Instead of climbing the open book, traverse up and left to the top of the tree island and climb a dirty straight-up crack with numerous pods to the next tree island. Friction up and right to the next tree island, traverse right to its right end, then up to a left-rising ramp. Belay at good trees. 160'

P3 5.8 G: (V2) Go up and left in the vegetation, then straight up through the jungle to the lower left end of a right-rising roof. Follow the slab under the roof up and right to where it joins the large horizontal roof. Make a very puzzling move through the roof at a left-leaning V-slot (crux), then step up and left to belay in trees. 100'

P4 5.2 R: Follow right-rising horizontal cracks rightward across the top of the slab to a fixed anchor on a cedar tree (shared with **Tone-Boneparte**). 170'

V1 5.7 PG (5.5 X): Traverse 8' right and climb an amazing chocolate-colored streak with knobs, edges, and pitted rock straight up for 80' (5.5 X) to a flake with good gear. Move up a smooth slab (crux) to a ledge, then up and left to a left-rising ramp and belay at good trees.

V2 5.8 X: Head up and right on small edges, then straight up past a blank section (crux), aiming for the left end of the roof (where the right-rising roof joins the horizontal roof). Pull the roof as for the normal route.

FA Sep 4, 1975, Tom Rosecrans, Joel Clugstone

2 Heel and Toe, Heel and Toe, Heel and Toe. Slide, Slide, Slide 5.6 X 700'

This route was another exploration of Steve Baker and Frank Abissi, two high school kids out for a day of fun. Their route begins at the bottom of the cliff at a disconnected block and zigzags up the "naked rock" between **Führer** and **Tone-Boneparte**. It doesn't involve any especially unique climbing as such. In Abissi's words, "We tried to go straight up from there. We hip-belayed in some scooped depressions. It was absolutely unprotected except for a couple #1 stoppers Steve put in. There were no anchors at the belays; that's why we hip-belayed because we hoped it would provide a very dynamic belay in case of a fall. We named it thus because we both had to take a lame square dancing class in high school, and the way we were climbing and sliding, it seemed to match the song we both heard many times." They used a 100'-long 9-mm rope purchased from EMS in Westchester County, where they met Royal Robbins, who was their inspiration for their climb on Wallface, **Right Place, but Must Have Been the Wrong Time**.

FA Jun 28, 1975, Steve Baker, Frank Abissi

3 Tone-Boneparte 5.8 G (5.7 R, 5.5 X) 510' ★★★

Good rock, long runouts, and an unlikely roof move characterize this route. Goodwin, a master of friction, went by the nickname Tone Bone, and, this being the Emperor Slab, a Napoleonic name was chosen. This was the first reported route on the Emperor Slab.

Start: At any tree at the left end of First Tree Island.

P1 5.5 X: Traverse left to the very left end of the upper vegetated ribbon and step left onto rounded holds on the slab. Climb straight up the slab to a good scooped ledge. 170'

P2 5.7 R (5.5 X): Climb up a carrot-shaped flake, then up a bulge to more pure friction, running it 30' up to a ledge with good gear. Continue straight up (crux) to the next tree island. A barely adequate belay can be arranged here (0.5" cam critical). 130'
P3 5.8 G (5.5 R): Traverse right on good holds, then up dirty but well-featured rock to the left end of a wide strip of blueberry bushes below the roof. Traverse right 30' to a white block positioned below the roof. Small scoops and knobs facilitate the pull through the roof (crux) and onto the slab above. Belay at a good horizontal up and right. 170'
P4 5.4 PG: Traverse right 30' on the dirty slab to a fixed anchor on a pine tree. 40'
FA 1974, Tony Goodwin, Tom Rosecrans

4 The Off Route 5.8 G (5.7 X) 480'

This route was the result of an attempt to climb **Tone-Boneparte** and, like the other routes, is a smorgasbord of unprotected climbing.
Start: 25' right of the left end of the vegetated tree ledge at a bulge 5' left of where the slab goes into the dirt, 20' left of the V-groove of **Detour on Route 73**.
P1 5.6 G (5.5 X): Climb up the clean slab, aiming for the left end of the next tree island. There is one piece of gear (#0 TCU) at 150' in a left-facing scallop flake, just before the crux. Belay at a fixed anchor on a double-trunked oak tree at the left end of the tree island below a right-facing, right-leaning shallow corner. 190'
P2 5.7 X: Climb up right-leaning, right-facing flakes (last protection). Before the last flake, step left onto the slab, then angle up and left, aiming for the left end of a wide strip of blueberry bushes below the roof. From here, climb onto the ledge with the blueberry bushes (joining **Tone-Boneparte**) and traverse right 30' to belay below the roof at a white block. 190'
P3 5.8 G: Small scoops and knobs facilitate the pull through the roof (crux) and onto the slab above. Traverse right in horizontal cracks to a fixed anchor on a pine tree. 100'
FA Aug, 1978, Geoff Powter, Jacquelyn Pidany

5 Detour on Route 73 5.10b R (5.8 X) 310'

This route has the only bolt on the slab.
Start: On the tree ledge at a left-rising 20'-tall vegetated V-groove.
P1 5.8 X: Climb up the V-groove, then straight up to a good flake at 30'. Run it out (crux), avoiding the moss, to the tree island above. 190'
P2 5.10b R: Step right and climb up chossy rock to the apex of the arch (5.7). Clip the bolt, then run it out straight up the slab to a thank-god edge. Step up onto the vegetation, then walk right to the trees. 120'
FA (P2) Jun, 1991, Patrick Purcell
ACB (P1) Jun 8, 2007, Dennis Luther, Joe Szot

CHAPEL POND SLAB

Location	South side of NY 73, accessed from the Giant Mountain Trailhead at Chapel Pond
Aspect	Northeast
Height	800'
Quality	★★★★★
Approach	1 min, easy
Summary	A historic slab with long, run-out friction routes and a trivial approach.

-5.6	5.7	5.8	5.9	5.10	5.11	5.12	5.13+	total
6	2		1	1				11

Slab climbing seems to be out of fashion, but Chapel Pond Slab continues to attract frequent visitors, perhaps because of a very short approach; long, moderate routes on clean rock; good belays; and excellent views of Giant and Chapel Pond Pass. **Empress** and **Regular Route** are two of the most popular slab routes in the Northeast. Several of the routes and variations have become very popular solos, especially with the easy North Descent.

The routes on the slab have a common start, then diverge as the slab fans out above. This can lead to some congestion, which can be frustrating as beginning climbers struggle with their first multipitch route. Some variations are possible at the start (described as variations to **Regular Route**), and once you are up on the slab, there are many variations, and you can pass other parties without undue interference.

The upper right side of the slab adjoins a steep buttress of rock known as Bob's Knob, named in

Donald LeBeau laybacking on the left side of Bob's Knob in 1951. There are no documented routes at this location, which further shows that every square inch of rock on this slab on Chapel Pond Slab has been climbed at some point. Photo by Stanley Smith.

Bob's Knob
1
5
6
5
6
5
1
5
1
1

South Descent Gully
North Descent
Bob's Knob
fixed rope
S-crack
descent
great belay
chimney
mossy moon rock
Twin Cracks Belay
split ledge
pancake flake
North Descent
to South Descent Gully and approach to the Emperor Slab
approach
Chapel Pond Slab
1 Empress (5.5)
2 Greensleeves (5.6)
3 Victoria (5.6+)
4 Thanksgiving (5.7)
5 Regular Route (5.5)
6 Bob's Knob Standard (5.3)
7 Dog's Breakfast (5.11 A0)
9 Hamburger Helper (5.9)
10 Eagle Crack (5.7)

memory of Bob Notman; **Thanksgiving**, **Regular Route**, and **Bob's Knob Standard** all finish on this buttress, topping out on its minisummit with great views. There are several short one-pitch routes on the front side of this buttress: **Dog's Breakfast**, **Hamburger Helper**, and **Eagle Crack**. The upper left side of the slab has a long, jagged offwidth crack that rises through a steep egglike buttress; **Empress** climbs this crack. Just right of the crack are the two long right-facing corners of **Greensleeves** and **Victoria**. A landmark low on the slab is the large left-facing corner that arches into a roof; **Empress** traverses under this roof, emerging onto a collection of four rounded knobs, or "hummocks," that mark the starts of **Thanksgiving** and **Victoria**.

Every climb on the slab involves runouts of some sort (the exception is **Regular Route**) on clean rock. Nearly every square inch of rock has been climbed and in every style imaginable—e.g., with packs, in hiking boots, barefoot, naked. For example, on P1 of **Thanksgiving**, after the corner, there is no protection, so why climb to the Twin Cracks Belay? Why not work left to **Victoria**? You can, and the grade doesn't change. One note about the protection grades: the angle of the slab is such that a fall, although long, often involves tumbling with lots of skin abrasions. A 60' fall here may seem unthinkable, but you probably won't die. Tad Welch once fell soloing **Pringles** and rode down to the hummocks on his hands, removing all the skin on his palms. He then drove to a bar using his wrists. Thus, for the slab, the R and X protection ratings are more an indication of how often protection is available on the line as described.

Aside from the odd piton, Chapel Pond Slab is completely lacking in fixed protection—i.e., not a single bolt—and local climbers prefer to keep it that way.

DIRECTIONS (MAP PAGE 197)

Park at the paved pullout on the north side of NY 73, 0.3 mile from the Chapel Pond pullout (when driving toward Malfunction Junction). Walk up the road toward the height of the pass, across a bridge, then over the guardrail, following a path 200' to the base of the slab.

DESCENT OPTIONS

There are several descent options.

South Descent Gully: This descent was once much cleaner but is now dirty and quite nasty when wet. If you rappel, it will also take longer than the North Descent.

At the top of **Empress** is a large rectangular boulder that rests on the slab. Walk left following a path across an exposed slab and into the trees on the far side. There are several rappel anchors here. If you are a competent climber (and if the rock is dry), you can downclimb the 4th-class sections; otherwise, several rappels interspersed with downscrambling lead to the top of a cliff (actually, the top of a cave). Walk (skier's) left, then cut back (skier's) right and reenter the gully below the cave. Continue scrambling and/or rappelling down a final V-notch to the woods.

North Descent: This is the easiest way off the slab, but it's a little difficult to find the start, and, once it's found, the uninitiated will have to hunt around to find the best way. To confuse things, there are many false paths and rappel anchors scattered through the woods on this side of the slab. Suffice it to say that all of these lead easily to the gully between the slab and the Gully Cliff, and all but one involve at least one rappel.

From the top of Bob's Knob, walk up and right through trees, then follow cairns across a slab to reach a narrow tree-filled gully. Scramble down the gully and fixed handrail to a broad tree slope. Where the path splits, take the left fork, and scramble down and left to a cliff with fixed rappel anchors. To the (skier's) right is a hidden fixed handrail around a tree; descend this, then rock-hop down the streambed, which curves back (skier's) right and can be followed to the base of the slab.

HISTORY

Little is known about the first ascents of the major routes on this cliff. For example, it is known that the members of the Alpine Club of Canada climbed **Greensleeves**, **Victoria**, and **Thanksgiving**, but which members were involved and when remain a mystery. (Considering the time period when the ACC was active, an educated guess would be between 1958 and 1964.)

As a side note, the ACC climbed in the Adirondacks starting in the 1940s, with John and Elizabeth Brett, founders of the Montreal section. A frequent camp spot was in the field by the brook below Roaring Brook Falls—that is, until the slides of June 29, 1963, destroyed the area and buried several of their cars in debris. The need for proper lodging prompted the ACC to purchase the ACC Keene Farm on Styles Brook Road in 1966. Sadly, this burned down in the 1970s due to an overheated wood stove. All the old files documenting early club activities in the Adirondacks were stored there.

Bob's Knob Standard was the first route climbed on the slab, by John Case and Bob Notman around 1933, as speculated by Laura and Guy Waterman,[1] the

1 Laura Waterman and Guy Waterman, *Yankee Rock and Ice* (1993), p. 39.

same year as John Case's ascent of **Case Route** on Wallface. John Case began climbing at Indian Head (above Lower Ausable Lake) in 1916, so it is conceivable that he ventured out onto the slab before then, though.

Despite the lack of first-ascent information, we do know that nothing new has been reported on Chapel Pond Slab since 1984. Perhaps this will change when somebody frees **Dog's Breakfast**.

1 Empress 5.5 X 865' ★★★★★

P1 is often wet, in which case you can climb the first section of **Regular Route** (to the good ledge at the base of the left-facing, left-arching corner on P2) and join **Empress** from there. The route links some of the major features on the slab—the initial left-facing corner; the left-facing, left-arching corner in the center of the slab; the three rounded knobs (or "hummocks") left of the arching corner; then the jagged off-width crack high on the left side of the slab. After a rain, there is often water running down the face just right of P4; this water seldom interferes with the climbing, and you can step over the water at the hummocks.

Start: At the open area beneath the slab is a low roof with some cracks above and a long, 100'-high left-facing corner to its left; **Empress** begins at the base of this corner.

P1 5.3 G: (V1) Climb up the corner past a few pitons (or the slab just to its left) for 120'. Before the bushes at the top of the corner, step right around the corner and belay in cracks just above. 145'

P2 5.2 G: (V2) Traverse right to stepped rock and follow it up and right, then break out left on beautiful white pocketed rock and run it out up to a ledge with a cedar at the base of the large left-facing, left-arching corner. (Some of this is shared with **Regular Route** P2.) 130'

P3 5.4 G: Up the huge left-facing, left-arching corner until it overhangs, then break out left across the slab to a groove on its left side, just above a vertical line of bushes. Step over the groove and across the base of a fragile pancake flake, then walk up and left on 4th-class ledges to the top of the first of three hummocks (rounded knobs). (This hummock is the start of **Thanksgiving**.) Step down and traverse left under a second hummock, then up and left to the top of a third hummock. 150'

P4 5.5 X: (V3) An incredible pitch climbs straight up the slab with no protection for 90' to reach a left-rising groove. Several cracks lead up and left to a good belay ledge. 130'

P5 5.5 G (5.4 R): (V4) Climb the obvious off-width crack to a good ledge (optional belay, but a fall from the next pitch would come directly onto the belay). Step right onto the face at a good foot ledge, then friction straight up (5.4 R) to an overlap. 130'

P6 5.3 PG: Climb a good crack and, at its end, friction straight up to a large block that rests on the slab (and that looks as though it could slide off); the easy friction is unprotected but 4th-class. Belay here or at the top of the tree island to the right. 120'

P7 4th class: From the tree island belay, another 4th-class pitch leads either straight up to the top (for the South Descent Gully) or straight right on a ledge to the trees (for the North Descent). 60'

V1 Leila's Line 5.7 R: Similar to the climbing on **Thanksgiving**. Ascend V1 of **Regular Route** to the right-rising dike. Move up and left onto the slab until 5' right of the huge left-facing corner of **Empress**. Staying close to the corner, work up the slab until the angle eases. Belay as for **Empress**.

V2 5.4 G: This variation continues 170' straight up the right-facing corners to the P3 belay. Although not as good as the normal route, it can be used when the route is congested. Climb up the crack and right-facing corner system to some bushes. Step left onto the face and climb up to a good ledge with boulders and debris. Continue up cracks and right-facing flakes past some bushes to the left side of a hummock; belay on top. 120'

V3 5.5 PG: A somewhat safer alternative to the run-out friction pitch, but inferior climbing. For this pitch, it is best to belay from the ledge down from and left of the hummock. From here, follow a left-leaning crack to its end, then move up into a shallow left-facing corner and climb it to its top. Traverse right to the left-rising groove and cracks of the normal route and follow these to the belay.

V4 5.8 X: Step right of the off width and climb the unprotected face up to the overlap at the top of P5. In Jolley's words, "What was I thinking?"

Descent: For the South Descent Gully, from the tree island belay, friction up and left to a large rectangular block perched at the very top of the slab, then walk left to the top of the South Descent Gully. For the North Descent, from the right side of the tree island belay, step down to a ledge and follow this rightward to its end. A few friction moves up and right lead to the trees. From here, you can unrope and walk right to some slabs, then down some slabs to the summit ledge of Bob's Knob.

FA 1933, Fritz Wiessner, George Austin
FA (V3) 1982, Alan Jolley (solo)

2 Greensleeves 5.6 G 350' ★★★

A good-quality variation that is better protected than its neighbors.

Start: At the top of P4 of **Empress**.

P1 5.6 G: Traverse right 15' across a steep slab to a left-facing corner. Up the left-facing corner to where it becomes right-facing. Belay at a bulge where the corner steepens. 150'

P2 5.6 G: Continue up the corner and crack above to its end. Friction up and left to a tree island. 140'

P3 4th class: From the tree island belay, another 4th-class pitch leads either straight up to the top (for the South Descent Gully) or straight right on a ledge to the trees (for the North Descent). 60'

FA Alpine Club of Canada

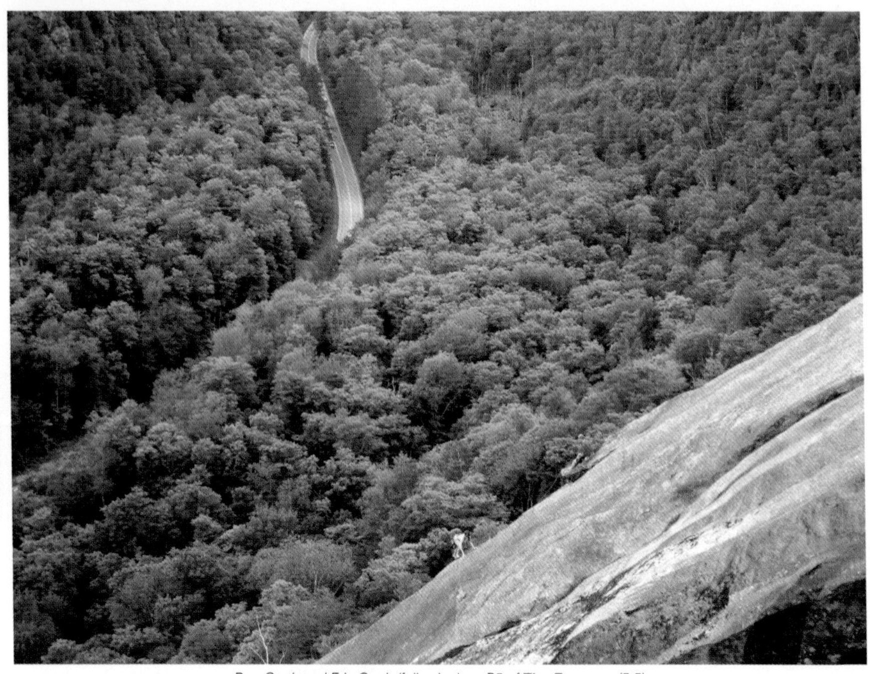

*Ben Cook and Erin Cook (following) on P5 of **The Empress** (5.5).*

3 Victoria 5.6+ R 410'

This route aims for the left side of a prominent roof in the upper section of the slab. P1 has some bad rock, but better protection the higher you go. The upper corner pitches are a little dirty, but climbable. A good alternative for climbing the better-protected upper pitches leaves from the Twin Cracks Belay (at the end of P3 of **Regular Route**) and frictions up and left on excellent pocketed rock to the stance at the end of P1. Named for the Canadian holiday Victoria Day.

Start: At the top of the middle (and highest) hummock on **Empress** below a shallow left-facing corner capped by an overlap.

P1 5.6+ R: Climb the left-facing corner to the overlap (piton), step left around the overlap (V1) and runout 25' to a crumbly overlap directly above. Up the left side on frustratingly crumbly rock (some marginal small cams), then up and left into a long, shallow left-facing corner. Up this to its top, then friction straight up and slightly right to a decent stance at a right-facing, left-leaning flake. 180'

P2 5.5 G: Up the flake and right-facing corner to the roof. Over the roof into a larger right-facing corner. Belay in a scoop in the right-facing corner. (Resist the temptation to climb higher, as you'll end up with nowhere to belay.) 150'

P3 5.4 G: Continue to the top of the right-facing corner at an overlap, then over this to some trees. Friction up and right across a slab to a break in the trees. 80'

V1 Pringles 5.7 X: From the overlap, climb up a few feet, then traverse right (crux) on fragile potato-chip flakes and scoops to a mossy strip. From here, climb excellent dimpled rock straight up the mossy streak (5.5) to the stance at a right-facing, left-leaning flake (same as **Victoria** P1). Once you get to the dimpled rock, the climbing is quite nice.

History: This could be the "direct route left of the normal route" that John Turner recalls, climbed by "a group of Irish." He's referring to Brian Rothery and Phil Gribbon in 1959 (and maybe Doug Sloan and Keith Millar as well). Recalls Rothery, "In those days of proper attire, Phil specialized in dressing in rags, and on that particular day, one whole leg protruded from his torn trousers. As was common back then, motorists stopped on the road to look up and photograph us. Phil began to shout down, 'Yankees, go home!' which was particularly bizarre seeing that we were in New York."

FA Alpine Club of Canada
FA (V1) 1982, Alan Jolley, Jim Cunningham

4 Thanksgiving 5.7 R (5.6 X) 540' ★★★

Climbs high-quality sparsely protected friction for several pitches, then through a climactic roof to the very top of Bob's Knob.

Start: At the top of the first hummock on **Empress** P3, just after the pancake flake, below a shattered left-facing corner.

P1 5.7 R: Climb the shattered left-facing corner to a left-arching overlap with good gear (V1), then up an open book to its top. Step right to a grapefruit-sized hueco, move up to a flake (TCU), then follow coarse friction up and right to a sloped ledge. Traverse right on the sloped ledge to the Twin Cracks Belay (at the end of **Regular Route** P3). 150'

P2 5.6 X: (V2) Traverse to the left end of the sloped ledge and friction straight up over a bulge, then up and left to the right end of the **Victoria** roof. 160'

P3 5.5 PG: (V3) Climb the slab right of the wide crack to its top, then straight up to a good right-facing flake. Angle up and right to the huge left-facing corner formed by Bob's Knob and the slab, then follow it to a tree belay below a roof. 140'

P4 5.7 G: Climb up to the roof, then traverse right to a good crack that breaks the roof on its right side. Continue up and right to the nice ledge at the top of Bob's Knob. 90'

V1 Palm Sunday (aka New Rubber) 5.7 X: Clean rock and better climbing than **Thanksgiving** P1, but with less protection. After the good gear in the left-arching overlap, climb up onto the highest hummock, then traverse right and up to a pie-pan–sized dent. Mantel this, traverse right 10', then climb a vague, blunt prow of rock straight up. At the top of the prow, continue straight up the face, staying right of a green streak, and eventually work rightward to the Twin Cracks Belay (at the end of **Regular Route** P3).

V2 Dangerous Game 5.7 X: Follow the diagonal crack of the **Regular Route** to its end, then go straight up the face to a bulge. Pull over the bulge (crux), then straight up the whitish face (100' runout, 5.6) until even with the top of the right-leaning corner of P3. Traverse 10' left to belay at the top of the corner. This is a long pitch (200').

V3 Roast Turkey 5.7 X: Go up the wide crack for a few feet, then step left around the corner (crux) onto a blank face. Go straight up the face to belay at a flake just below the birch trees.

History: Every square inch of rock on Chapel Pond Slab has been climbed and soloed at some point, and very little is known about who did what and when.

FA Alpine Club of Canada

FA (V1) Jun 1, 1984, Don Mellor, Gill James

5 Regular Route 5.5 PG 775' ★★★★★

The most popular and best-protected route on the slab, with clean rock, good friction, some exposed sections, and an incredible crack-in-a-corner pitch.

Start: Same as **Empress**.

P1 5.0 G: (V1, V2, V3) Climb up the corner for 15' to a block split by a jagged crack. Follow a right-rising dike to its end, then follow a good groove up and left to its top. Scramble up and right on lower-angled rock to belay on a small ledge in a shallow open book with a good crack in a sea of left-facing flakes. 150'

P2 5.4 G: Up and right on the stepped rock with cracks, then break out left on beautiful white pocketed rock (just left of a good crack) up to a ledge with a cedar at the base of the large left-facing, left-arching corner (optional belay here; **Empress** and **Regular Route** meet here, then diverge). Climb the huge left-facing corner for a few feet to an old ring piton, then move right over the bulge (5.4) and onto a low-angle face and up to a good ledge. 140'

P3 5.5 PG: An incredible pitch. Climb a shallow left-facing corner to a break in the bulge above. Step through this to the right to a scooped ledge just above. Climb up and right on sculpted rock for 20', then angle up and left to the base of a crack that leads to a left-facing corner. Up the corner and crack above to the Twin Cracks Belay—a sloped ledge below two parallel right-angling cracks in the wall. 165'

P4 5.5 PG: (V4) Climb the right-hand crack to its end, then make a few friction moves right to a gravel ledge at the base of Bob's Knob on its left side below a giant boulder. Climb up the left side of the boulder (or friction up the slab farther left) to its top. Continue up the corner another 30' to a perfect bathtub-like belay slot with three sides, a flat floor, and a birch tree. 120'

P5 5.5 G: Climb the corner to a position 25' below a black cave (the cave has a giant bathtub-sized block wedged into the bottom). Angle up and right on good holds to gain the left end of the large terrace on Bob's Knob. 50'

P6 5.2 G: (V5) Walk right on the terrace and scramble up some ledges (joining **Bob's Knob Standard** here) to the base of a small face with an S-shaped wide crack. (V6) Then climb the crack to its top (5.2) at a good ledge. Climb up a short, 8'-high face with a good crack split by a horizontal, then climb low-angle ledgy rock straight up to meet the top of a left-rising wide crack at a ceiling. Break this on the left and up a low-angle left-facing corner, then easy friction straight up to the top. There is a nice ledge on top where you can unrope, kick back, and have lunch. 150'

V1 5.2 G: Begin 6' right and climb a slab to a left-facing blade, through a little notch, then up a crack to join the right-rising traverse dike.

V2 5.6 G: Begin 25' right, 5' left of where the low roof rises from the ground. Climb up the slab to a good handcrack, then follow it to lower-angled rock. Join the right-rising dike at its right end.

V3 5.7 G: Begin 30' right where the low roof rises from the ground. Climb the hand- and fingercrack up the low-angled buttress to a small ledge, then up lower-angled rock to meet the right end of the right-rising dike.

V4 5.6 G: The left-hand crack above the Twin Cracks Belay is a bit harder. At its end, friction up, then straight right to join the normal route.

V5 Cave Finish 5.7 G: Step left into a chimney and climb this to a right-facing corner with a handcrack. Step right and belay at trees. Join the normal route by scrambling up easier 4th-class terrain to the top. (Most parties combine **Cave Finish** with P5.)

V6 Li'l Sebastian 5.6 G ★★★: This excellent variation follows an obvious crack on the right side of Bob's Knob when seen from the opposite side of the valley (like from the Upper Washbowl). From the high ledge below the S-shaped crack, walk right 30' to an offwidth crack. On your right at waist level is a horizontal crack that disappears around a corner. Follow this crack as it shoots up and right for 140'. At its end, follow a slab straight up to trees and the intersection with the north descent. Great handjams and scenic views of Chapel Pond.

History: Not much is known about the climbing on this route, except that it was originally a short variation to **Bob's Knob Standard**. Over time, more interesting

climbing has been added to the mix to produce a continuous collection of quality pitches. It has been speed-soloed car-to-car in 12 minutes (7 up, 5 down).
FA (V5) 1960, Bernard Poisson

6 Bob's Knob Standard 5.3 G 840' ★★★

This route, the original on the slab, begins as for **Regular Route** and then veers right to climb easy rock, avoiding most major difficulties or exposed features. Portions of this route are commonly used as a 4th-class downclimb.

Start: Same as **Empress**.

P1 5.0 G: Same as **Regular Route**. 150'

P2 5.2 G: Up and right on the stepped rock with cracks, then break out left on beautiful white pocketed rock (just left of a good crack) up to a ledge with a cedar at the base of the large left-facing, left-arching corner (**Empress** and **Regular Route** meet here, then diverge). 80'

P3 5.1 PG: Traverse right 20' under some vegetation past a couple of cracks, then up and right on clean rock between sets of trees into an arched depression (optional belay here at 80'). Follow the handcrack in the left wall of the depression up onto a blunt low-angle prow of rock and follow it to the forest. The final friction moves into the forest are often wet. 175'

P4 3rd class: Unrope and scramble up through the trees to a bulge; over this, then traverse right and slightly up (staying just above the forest) to the split ledge—a ledge split by a long horizontal chimney spanned by a block. Continue rightward across the top of the horizontal chimney to its end, then walk 30' right on ledges and set a belay on a slab below a shallow cave just left of a short prow. 150'

P5 5.3 G: Step right to the prow and make a tricky mantel move onto the ledge at its top. Traverse 15' right to the base of a chimney-slot (two pitons here). Climb the easy chimney (sometimes wet) on jugs to its top at a fixed anchor in the forest above. Continue straight up through the trees to a wide crack, then climb it for 15' to a wide terrace. 100'

P6 5.2 G: Up a slab to a ledge (**Regular Route** joins here), then up the wide S-shaped crack to another ledge (optional belay here at 100'). At the back of the ledge is a short wall with a handcrack; up this to a ledge, then up slabs broken by ledges aiming for a short left-leaning wide crack in a bulge. Climb the wide crack up and left, then up a slab to the top of Bob's Knob. 185'
FA 1933, John Case, Bob Notman

Bob's Knob Routes

These routes are located on Bob's Knob on the wall that faces the road, 20' above the split ledge (a ledge split by a long horizontal chimney spanned by a block) on **Bob's Knob Standard**. You can get here by climbing **Regular Route**, then walking right on the gravel ledge on P4, or by climbing **Bob's Knob Standard** to the split ledge.

7 Dog's Breakfast 5.11 A0 120'

A tremendous route in a cool setting and one of the long-standing free-climbing problems in the region. Unfortunately, the start has poor rock. Recent free attempts peg it in the 12+ range.

Start: On a slab 4' left of the right-facing dihedral of **Hamburger Helper** at an overhanging left-leaning crack in a shallow left-facing, left-leaning corner.

*Liam Schneider and Monica Wormald soloing **Regular Route** (5.5), shown here on P5.*

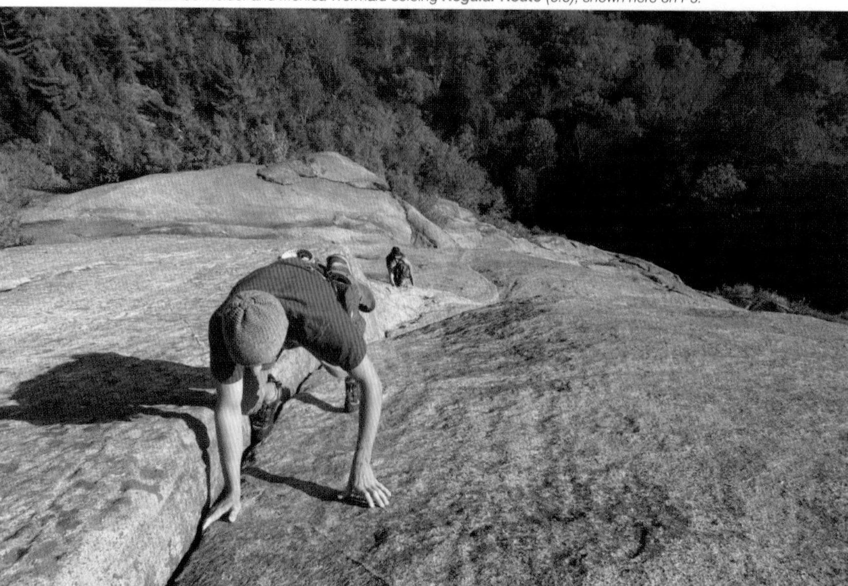

P1 5.11 A0 G: Climb up the crack and swing around left on a white bulging face. Continue the left-angling crack to a square overlap, over this, and up to a scooped break. A handcrack leads through a final bulge to a slab, then up to a ledge. Traverse right to a tree or farther right to a tree with a fixed anchor. 120'
FA 1982, Don Mellor, Bill Diemand

8 Dead Dog 5.10- R 90'

Not recommended.
Start: Same as **Dog's Breakfast**.
P1 5.10- R: Begin up **Dog's Breakfast**, and continue straight up stucco-like rock past a left-rising ramp and discontinuous cracks to the top. 90'
FA Jul 20, 2012, Conor Cliffe, Tom Wright

9 Hamburger Helper 5.9 PG 120'

Start: At the base of a right-facing open book, the bottom of which is obscured by trees. The open book is 4' right of **Dog's Breakfast** and just right of where a low roof rises left from the slab.
P1 5.9 PG: Climb up the corner through an overhanging thin-fingers section (crux) to a sloped stance. Climb through an overhanging handcrack (5.8), then up easier cracks to a tree ledge with a fixed anchor on its right end. 120'
Descent: Climb down and right 15' to a path that leads right, then up to a cairn on the North Descent. You can also scramble up a short slab to join **Regular Route** at the S-crack on P6.
FA 1980, Rick Davis

10 Eagle Crack 5.7 G 120'

Start: At the base of a crack that begins on the ledge above the 7'-high buttress with a tricky move on **Bob's Knob Standard**. (From the split ledge, walk 30' right to the small, 7'-high buttress, mount this, and belay at its top.)
P1 5.7 G: Climb the black crack to a triangular pod, step left, and climb the left side of boulders to their top. Climb up some easy ledges, then up a short face with positive scooped holds to a friction slab with three horizontals (5.6 PG); up this to a good tree ledge with a fixed anchor on its right end. 120'
Descent: Climb down and right 15' to a path that leads right, then up to a cairn on the North Descent. You can also scramble up a short slab to join **Regular Route** at the S-crack on P6.
FA 1980, Helen Hibbert, Andy Helms

North Gully

The North Descent travels along the base of a wide slab which has mostly escaped interest. There's potential here for more routes.

11 Bailey–Bolliger Route 5.5 PG 60' ★

A nice flake, and excellent views of the Chapel Pond Gully Cliff to the right.
Start: 20' above the lower handrail and 25' up and right from a rappel anchor below an attractive, 18'-tall, left-facing flake.
P1 5.5 PG: Climb the left-facing flake to a small ledge, then up a second left-facing flake to its top. Wander up a slab to a ceiling. Break this on the right to a tree island. 60'
FA Jun 7, 1987, R.L. Stolz, Geoffrey Bailey, Steven Bolliger

THE AQUARIUM

Location	South side of NY 73, accessed from the Giant Mountain Trailhead at Chapel Pond
Aspect	North
Height	100'
Quality	★★
Approach	1 min, easy
Summary	A small number of short routes on a slab above the stream that feeds Chapel Pond.

-5.6	5.7	5.8	5.9	5.10	5.11	5.12	5.13+	total
3	1		2	2				8

Despite its proximity to the trailhead for Giant, this area has been virtually ignored. There are now several good climbs here, and it makes a great spot for squeezing in a few more pitches before heading home. The wall gets its name from a creek that feeds Chapel Pond and runs along the base of the rock—so close, in fact, that high water makes some of these climbs inaccessible. The water creates a nice atmosphere, though, and completely masks the activity at the nearby trailhead.

Several of these routes require smearing on tiny crystals and rippled dikes. Due to the north-facing aspect and vegetation above the slab, you should probably carry a small wire brush to clean off key holds.

During the aftermath of Irene, the course of the stream was significantly altered by machinery. The water was directed to run up against the cliff face, making it near impossible to access the routes. Climbers responded by piling rocks near the base of the routes to create dry launching platforms.

HISTORY

Climbing first occurred here in the late 1960s by visitors to the Canadian Alpine Club Hut in Upper Jay, but these routes never appeared in any guide. The prolific Patrick Purcell visited this cliff in 1989 and climbed a few routes, including a toprope ascent of **Get Up, Stand Up**, but, like many of his climbs, these went unreported and fell into obscurity. Tad Welch resurrected several routes and added some of his own in the late 1990s. This picture isn't complete, as there are also several bolts and anchors of unknown origin scattered about the cliff.

DIRECTIONS (MAP PAGE 197)

Park at the Giant Trailhead at Chapel Pond on NY 73. Just opposite the trail, walk into the woods on one of several herd paths.

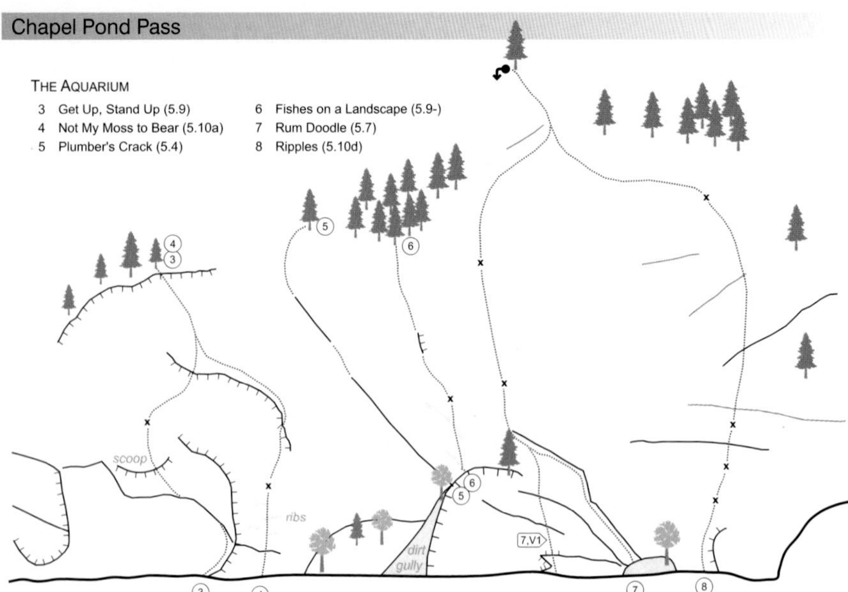

1 Marjory 5.6 PG 100' ★

This route description was resurrected from some early notes from the Canadian Alpine Club Hut. The start and finish of **Marjory** are currently a bit dirty, but the crack and bulge are good. The route, originally described as a "practice climb," is named after Peter Baggaley's wife.

Start: Ascends the first section of open rock that you encounter near the stream. Begin on a slab with a prominent overlap 30' up.

P1 5.6 PG: Up the dirty slab to an overlap, step left 6', and climb a 2" crack up to a stance. Pull through the bulge using a sidepull jug and small divots. Up and right on a slab, then break over dirty bulges to a good ledge with several pine trees. 100'

FA Apr 27, 1968, Peter Baggaley, Peter Ferguson, Ray Johnson

2 Juliet 5.3 G 60'

Another route resurrected from the Canadian Alpine Club Hut notes.

Start: Just right of **Marjory** is a right-leaning wet, broken section of rock, and right of this is a cleaner buttress of rock very near the water. The route begins on this buttress, 40' right of **Marjory** and 240' left of **Get Up, Stand Up**.

P1 5.3 G: Up the buttress to right-leaning mossy cracks; follow them up and right to a tree island. 60'

FA Apr 27, 1968, Peter Baggaley, Peter Ferguson

3 Get Up, Stand Up 5.9 G 40' ★★

The name is a reference to a Bob Marley song as well as the crux move.

Start: At a shallow left-facing, right-leaning bulge below a prominent left-rising crack. As you walk right from **Juliet**, this is the first climbable rock where the water runs right up against the rock. Just left of this route and 6' up is a car-sized block with a cedar tree growing out of the top; the block forms an off-width crack.

P1 5.9 G: Smear up the bulge, then climb the crack up and left to a tricky mantel move into a scoop. Exit the scoop on the right to an edge, then left up the slab and bulge to the trees. 40'

FA Nov 1, 1999, Tad Welch (roped solo)

4 Not My Moss to Bear 5.10a PG 40' ★

Start: 4' right of the left-diagonaling crack of **Get Up, Stand Up**.

P1 5.10a PG: Climb up a series of crystal edges past a bolt to a right-rising crystal edge that leads a few feet right to a right-facing, left-rising flake (gear). From the top of the flake, climb straight up a bulge in the slab, then left to the trees (same as **Get Up, Stand Up**). 40'

FA May 22, 1999, Bill Widrig, Tad Welch

5 Plumber's Crack 5.4 G 40'

Start: 30' right of **Not My Moss to Bear** is a tree ramp that faces left. Scramble up the ramp to the base of a left-facing corner.

P1 5.4 G: Up the left-facing corner with a left-slanting wide crack at its top. 40'

FA Apr, 1989, Patrick Purcell

6 Fishes on a Landscape 5.9- G (5.7 X) 100' ★

After the crux, it's possible to avoid the runout section by going right to the top bolt of **Rum Doodle**.

Start: At the top of the tree ramp, just right of **Plumber's Crack**, below a clean face with crystal dikes.

P1 5.9- G (5.7 X): Climb the clean face up to a jug, then foot traverse up and left along a ripple rail (bolt, crux) to better holds and a left-facing flake (gear). Continue straight up a slab to a final bulge (5.7 X) to the trees. 100'

FA Nov, 1999, Tad Welch (roped solo)

7 Rum Doodle 5.7 PG 100' ★★

This route is named after a fictitious 40,000'-high mountain, Rum Doodle. The variation makes for a cleaner, more interesting route.

Start: 40' right of **Fishes on a Landscape**, beginning at the stream at a dirty left-rising handcrack.

P1 5.7 PG: (V1) Climb the left-rising handcrack and the face to the left to a sloped ledge with cedars. Move right to a bolt, then make tricky moves up to a hidden handhold, then straight up the face to a second bolt. Move right, then back left through a bulge to a ledge with a fixed anchor on a pine tree. 100'

V1 Rum Doodle Direct 5.7 PG: Begin 10' left of the normal start at a sideways V-notch. Climb up the face using incut horizontals for 20', then join the left-leaning handcrack just before the ledge.

FA Sep 28, 1999, Tad Welch (roped solo)
FA Sep 9, 2006, Tad Welch, Jim Lawyer, Leslie Ackerman

8 Ripples 5.10d G (5.4 R) 100' ★★★

Excellent climbing on small, crimpy holds.

Start: At the right end of the cliff, 25' right of **Rum Doodle**, at the base of a slab that reaches down to the water, at a 5'-high right-facing corner.

P1 5.10d G: Climb up the face just left of the corner using rippled features and crystals of rock to a prominent horizontal at 20'. Mantel this, move up past another horizontal, then up right to a good crack (1"). Easier slab climbing heads left under some tree islands to a fixed anchor on a pine tree (same anchor as for **Rum Doodle**). 100'

FA Sep 9, 2006, Jim Lawyer, Tad Welch, Leslie Ackerman

*Jim Lawyer on the first ascent of **Ripples** (5.10d). Photo by Leslie Ackerman.*

CHAPEL POND GULLY CLIFF

Location	South side of NY 73, accessed from the Giant Mountain Trailhead at Chapel Pond
Aspect	Northeast
Height	500'
Quality	★★★
Approach	5–15 min, easy
Summary	A huge piece of rock broken into sections by trees and sections of poor rock; many good routes here, including several long adventure routes.

-5.6	5.7	5.8	5.9	5.10	5.11	5.12	5.13+	total
15	4	4	5	5	5			38

The Gully Cliff is a complex assortment of faces and slabs that sits above the south end of Chapel Pond. The cliff is separated from Chapel Pond Slab by a deep gully that provides access to the many routes.

There are five major clusters of routes on the Gully Cliff, each with its own character: Amphitheater of the Overhangs has the most overhanging routes at Chapel Pond; the Old Route Area has longer historic routes; the Cheap Date Area has mostly single-pitch routes 5.9 or harder; the Tanager Face offers mostly single-pitch cracks that can be toproped; and the lakeshore arêtes (Tilman's and Shipton's) have mostly single-pitch moderates.

If you are lucky enough to top out on this cliff, the summit is open and slabby, offering unique views of the Upper Washbowl, Giant Mountain, and Chapel Pond.

DIRECTIONS (MAP PAGE 197)

Park at the Chapel Pond pullout or at the Giant Trailhead. Follow herd paths to the south end of Chapel Pond and walk along the beach (or stay in the woods near the beach if the water level is high) and cross several feeder streams to reach the cliffs on the other side of the lake, opposite the road. This spot is known as Chapel Pond Corner 600313,4887955; from here, you can walk right (north) to Tilman's Arête, Shipton's Arête, and the Martini Wall or walk uphill to the left (south) to reach the other areas.

DESCENT OPTIONS

For those routes that reach the top of the Chapel Pond Gully Cliff (such as those starting in the Amphitheater of the Overhangs or the Old Route Area), walk toward Chapel Pond Slab and find a cairn at the top of a steep ramp. Scramble down the ramp, which bends to the (skier's) right, to another ramp that leads down to the top of a short wall broken by a 12'-high chimney. Scramble down the chimney to the base of the Amphitheater of the Overhangs. Walk downhill along the base of the cliff to its low point, then scramble down to the stream. Boulder-hop downstream and pick up the trail that runs beneath the Old Route Area climbs. You can follow this trail along the base of the cliff back to Chapel Pond.

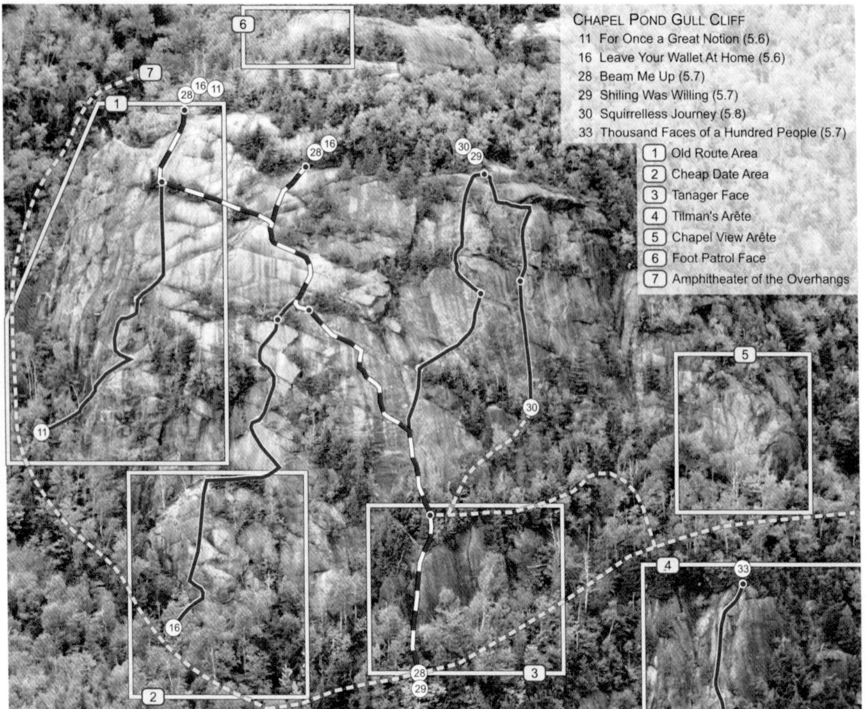

HISTORY

The first route climbed on the Gully Cliff was most likely climbed by Fritz Wiessner (**Old Route**), although it isn't known exactly when. Development was spotty over the next years, with more long routes added, such as **Right-Hand Route** (1958), **For Once a Great Notion** (1970), and **Beam Me Up** (1978). These were most likely climbed by those seeking out long routes like those available on Chapel Pond Slab just across the gully.

It wasn't until 1986 that local climbers took an interest in the cliff. In a brief span of four years, almost all of the routes were climbed: Patrick Purcell and Tim Beaman tackled the huge roofs and overhanging cracks in the Amphitheater of the Overhangs (1987–88); Tad Welch and Bill Pierce developed the Tanager Face (1987–88); and Don Mellor, Jeff Edwards, Mark Meschinelli, and Tad Welch developed the routes in the Cheap Date Area.

Foot Patrol Face

Foot Patrol Face is a small southeast-facing wall that sits at the very top of Chapel Pond Gully Cliff (above the Amphitheater of the Overhangs). It can be recognized by a crack in the top center of the face.

DIRECTIONS **(MAP PAGE 197)**

From Chapel Pond Corner, walk left (south) and follow the steep gully along the base of the cliff past the Cheap Date Area and the Old Route Area until it reaches the stream (at **Left-Hand Route**). Enter the stream and boulder-hop through a constriction in the gully, then walk uphill to the base of the Amphitheater of the Overhangs. At the right end of the large overhangs, find a left-facing corner with a chimney in the right wall; ascend this to a right-rising ramp and follow it up and right (past **Dodder**) to the summit area. Scramble up ledges and easy slabs to the summit and the base of this small wall.

1 Foot Patrol 5.11b TR 50'

Locate the fingercrack that breaks the top third of the face and begin on the face to its right. Climb up and left to a horizontal, then up a vertical seam to reach another good horizontal. Climb the fingercrack to the top.
FA (TR) Jul 29, 1987, Patrick Purcell

Amphitheater of the Overhangs

This small amphitheater contains the most overhanging routes at Chapel Pond. It is hidden high and left on the Gully Cliff and provides a shaded place to climb on hot days. No lines here, as the ferocity of the routes will keep all but the most persistent suitors at bay.

DIRECTIONS **(MAP PAGE 197)**

From Chapel Pond Corner, walk left (south) and follow the steep gully along the base of the cliff past the Cheap Date Area and the Old Route Area until it reaches the stream (at **Left-Hand Route**). Enter the stream and boulder-hop through a constriction in the gully, then walk uphill and right to the base of the amphitheater, about 200' left of the Old Route Area.

2 Tennessee Excursion 5.11b G 60' ★★★★

This route is on Purcell's "Nothing but the Superb Best" list. It climbs an amazing multitiered roof system, more akin to the giant roofs found in Tennessee sandstone than the Adirondacks.

Start: At the left side of the amphitheater at a flat area, just before the gully on the left side, at a left-facing corner below a multitiered roof.

P1 5.11b G: Climb up the corner to the first roof; over this via the obvious crack with a chockstone in the lip, then up a right-facing corner to the next roof. Clear this roof via the good crack and into a short chimney, then follow the chimney to the top. 60'

FA Jul 30, 1987, Patrick Purcell

3 Chattanooga Choo-Choo 5.11c G 60' ★★

This is the leftmost of two parallel cracks that break through the roof system with white blotches.

Start: 25' right of Tennessee Excursion and 5' left of a 12'-high left-facing corner with a chimney in its right wall.

P1 5.11c G: Climb a crack in a face up to a multitiered roof system. Climb through the lower roof to parallel cracks and follow them to the top. 60'

FA Jul 16, 1988, Tim Beaman, Don Mellor

4 Pardon Me, Boy 5.10d G 60'

This is the rightmost of the two parallel cracks that break through the roof system with white blotches. The name is the first three words of the big-band/swing song "Chattanooga Choo-Choo."

Start: At a 12'-high left-facing corner with a chimney in its right wall.

P1 5.10d G: Climb up the right-facing corner and into the wide crack that leads to the roof. Break through the roof through a squeeze to the top. 60'

FA Jun, 1988, Tim Beaman

5 Chewing on Balloons 5.8+ G 60' ★★

Climbs the face below the descent ramp, topping out 10' right of the start of Dodder.

Start: Right of the huge overhangs is a left-facing corner with the descent chimney in its right wall. This route begins 70' right of this corner at a steep wall, 8' right of a small, 15'-high right-facing corner.

P1 5.8+ G: Climb up and left on ledges to a thin crack. At its top, move left to a left-angling seam and follow it to a ceiling. Break through the ceiling at parallel fingercracks and climb to the top. 60'

History: The route was cleaned (and perhaps climbed) by unknown climbers prior to Sep 2005, when Amelia Zagorski and John Whalen climbed the lower portion.

ACB May 26, 2007, Jim Lawyer, Leslie Ackerman

6 Dodder 5.6 G 30' ★

This short crack begins halfway up the descent ramp.

Start: From the base of Pardon Me, Boy, scramble up the chimney to a ramp. Dodder begins 10' from the right end of the ramp at the base of a vertical fingercrack.

P1 5.6 G: Climb the vertical fingercrack in coarse black rock up to a tree on the left with a fixed anchor. 30'

FA Jun, 1988, Bill Dodd, Diane Dodd

Martine Schaer topping out on the Chapel Pond Gully Cliff.

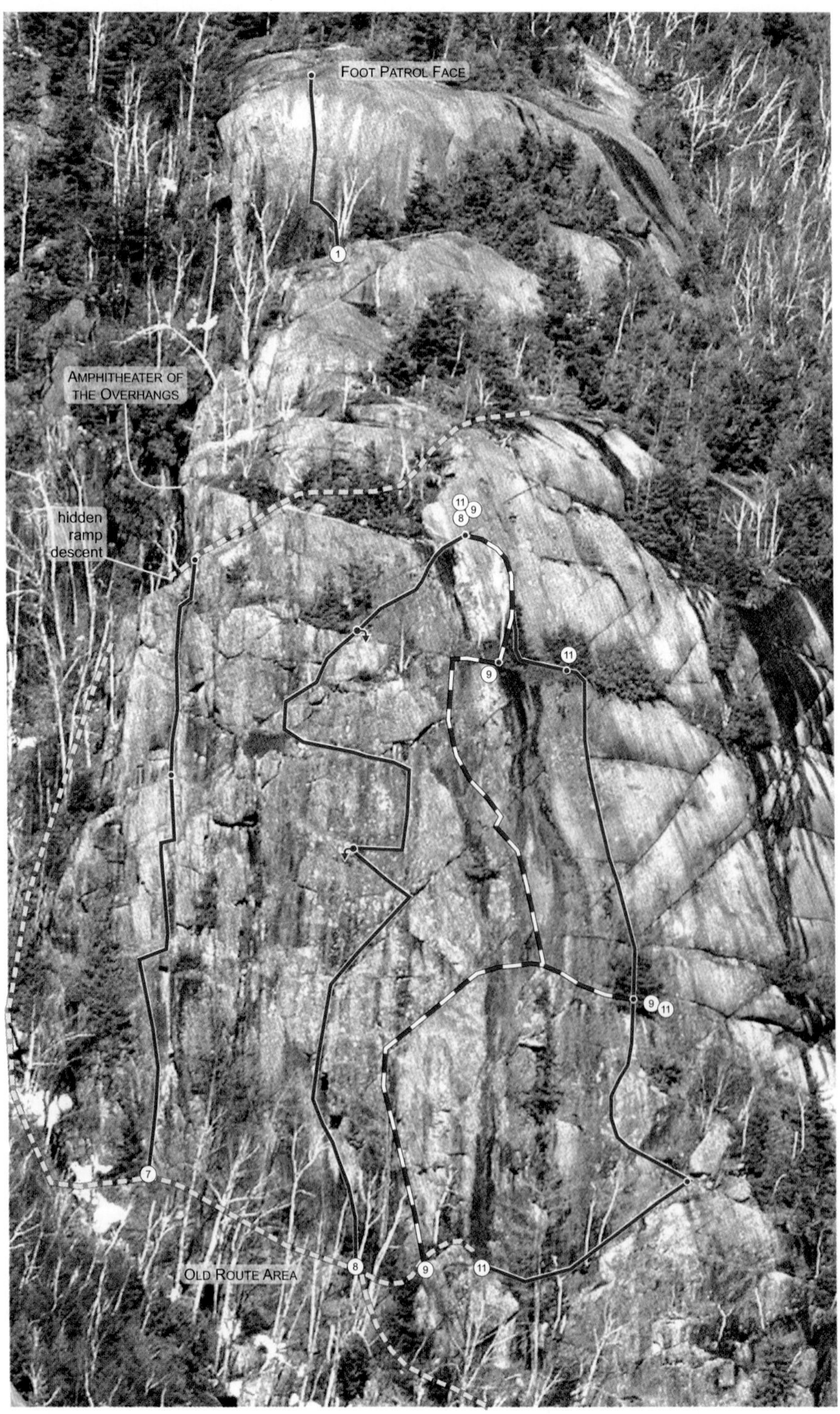
Foot Patrol Face
1
Amphitheater of the Overhangs
hidden ramp descent
11
9
8
9
11
9
11
7
Old Route Area
8
9
11

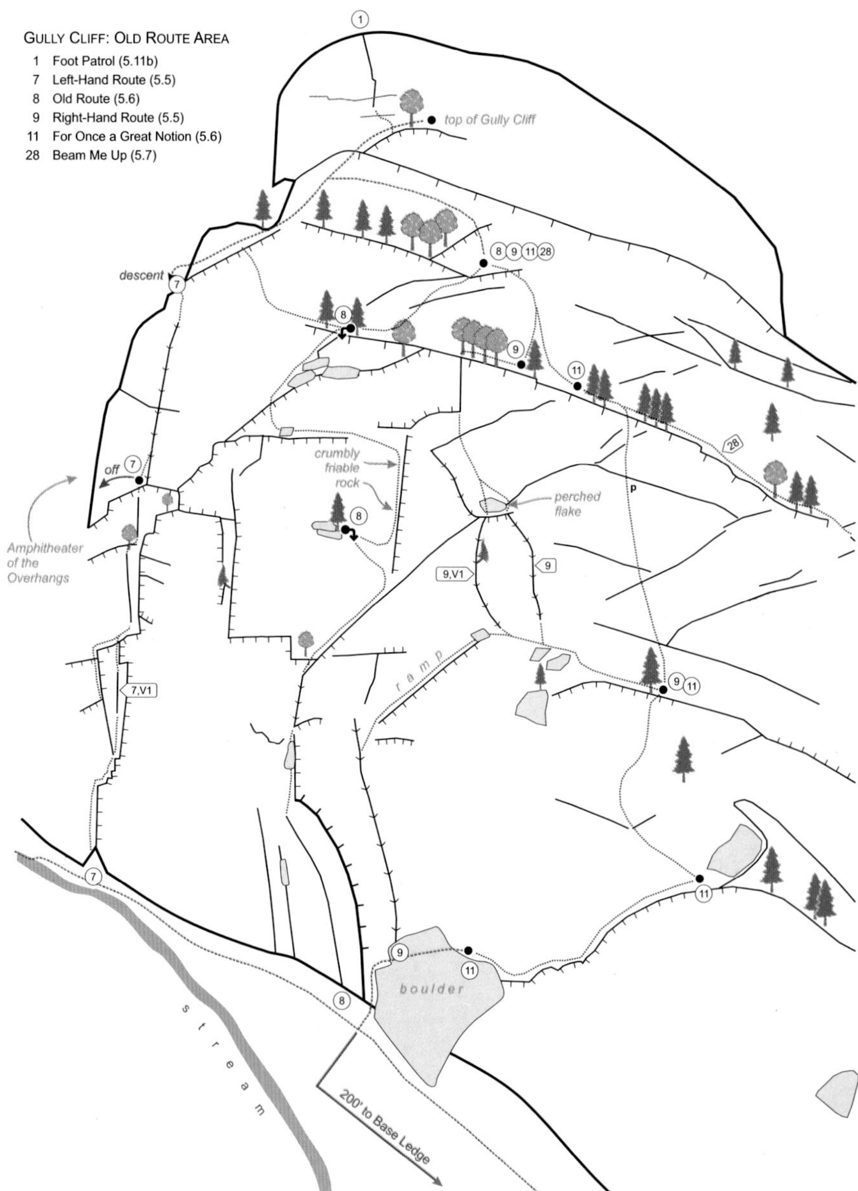

Old Route Area

The Old Route Area contains a collection of historic routes (including yet another Fritz Wiessner route), each of which finds its way to the top of the cliff. There are several good linkups here, with **The Right Notion** linkup getting special mention.

DIRECTIONS **(MAP PAGE 197)**

From Chapel Pond Corner, walk left (south) and follow the steep gully along the base of the cliff past the Cheap Date Area to Base Ledge, a distinctive right-rising ramp that breaks the cliff. 200' uphill from and left of this is a large pointed boulder up against the cliff with a long tunnel behind it. This boulder is a landmark for finding the routes in this section.

7 Left-Hand Route 5.5 G 170' ★★

From the end of P1, you can walk off left down ramps to the right end of the Amphitheater of the Overhangs (near the route **Chewing on Balloons**) or continue up

and right following easy 3rd-class ramps and ledges to the top of the cliff.
Start: 80' left of the large pointed boulder with a small tunnel behind it, at a point where the main trail meets the stream, below a large left-facing corner with a square roof 40' up.
P1 5.5 G: Up the left-facing corner to a sloped ledge. (V1) Left of the corner, climb the 3" crack in the left wall to another ledge (level with the square roof), then step right 10' across the top of the roof and climb another 3" crack left of a left-facing corner up to a ledge. Climb the left wall to another ledge and belay. You can walk off left from here. 110'
P2 5.5 G: Continue straight up a series of corners to the top. 60'
V1 Left-Hand Direct 5.8 G: Up the 3" crack for a couple of feet, then step right into a smaller crack. Climb the crack and corner to the square roof; over the roof on its left side to join the normal route.
History: The first ascent is unknown, but the route was described in a letter to Trudy Healy from Fred Gemmill in the 1960s.
ACB (V1) Bill, Kathy

8 Old Route 5.6 R 190'

This route isn't Wiessner's best work, as it climbs extremely friable rock on P2. Not recommended.
Start: 20' left of the large pointed boulder with a small tunnel behind it, at a crack in a black face that is 4' left of a left-facing, left-leaning corner with some orange lichen spots.
P1 5.5 G: Climb the crack on good face holds to where the left-facing corner turns vertical. Stem up the corner to a dirty groove, then up and right on a short ramp with increasingly friable rock to the base of a left-facing corner. Step left to a ledge and belay at blocks and a cedar tree. 80'
P2 5.6 R: Step right and climb the left-facing corner with horribly friable rock. At its top, climb up and left on a ledge to a large blueberry patch, then back right on another ledge to a very unstable chest-sized block. Climb up to the next ledge to a tree with a fixed anchor. The pitch has PG protection . . . if it holds. 70'
P3 4th class: Walk right and climb up and right on friable rock to the ledge of **Right-Hand Route**. Scramble to the summit from here. Alternatively, from the left end of the ledge, you can climb up a short wall (5.2) to the descent ledge. 40'
History: There seems to be some confusion as to where this route actually goes. The original description written by Wiessner suggests that at the top of the groove on P1, you should step left to a ledge with a small tree. From there, the line continues left into a left-facing corner, then straight up this corner to a right-rising ramp, which leads to easier terrain. This line looks even worse than the dangerous friable rock of P2.
FA Fritz Wiessner, Douglas Kerr

9 Right-Hand Route 5.5 PG 300'

This is a quality route when combined with P3 of **For Once a Great Notion**. You may want to split P1 into two pitches to avoid dragging the rope over loose rock.
Start: On the left side of the large pointed boulder with a tunnel behind it, below a left-leaning open book.
P1 5.5 G: Climb up the open book to its top, then make an airy step right onto a right-rising ramp. Up the ramp to its top, then traverse right 15' to some blocks below a groove. Continue right another 15' to a comfortable belay on a ledge with trees (shared with **For Once a Great Notion**). 110'
P2 5.4 PG: Traverse back left to the blocks (V1) and climb the groove up to a perched flake at a right-rising crack. Go up a slab past another right-rising crack to a vertical crack and follow it to a tree ledge. 140'
P3 5.2 PG: Step right and climb an easy slab to the top. 50'
V1 5.4 PG: Go left to the block at the top of the ramp and climb a left-leaning groove past a pine tree, then rightward to join the normal route at the perched flake.
FA 1958, Fred Gemmill

10 The Right Notion (linkup) 5.5 PG 270' ★★★

This excellent linkup provides a nice tour of the cliff on sound rock and with comfortable belays.
Start: Same as **For Once a Great Notion**.
P1 5.5 G: P1 of **Right-Hand Route**. 110'
P2 5.5 PG: Combine P3 and P4 of **For Once a Great Notion**. 160'

11 For Once a Great Notion 5.6 R 320'

P3 is quite good, but the lower climbing isn't. It's best to link into this route from **Right-Hand Route**. The name is a reference to the Ken Kesey novel *Sometimes a Great Notion*.
Start: On top of the large pointed boulder with a small tunnel behind it, at a gap with a level dirt floor.
P1 4th class: Traverse right on vegetated ledges with loose rock, first down, then steeply up to the top of the ledge. 50'
P2 5.6 R: Climb out left on the slab, then angle back right to a comfortable ledge with trees (shared with **Right-Hand Route**). 70'
P3 5.5 PG: Starting on the right side of the ledge, climb straight up the face with good horizontals to the left end of a long right-rising horizontal. Runout straight up the slab to a left-rising horizontal (fixed bong). Climb straight up the face above to a tree ledge. 160'
P4 5.2 PG: Continue up easy slabs to the top. 40'
FA 1970, David Lovejoy, Dwight Bradley

Cheap Date Area

This small section of cliff is the first climbable rock you come to in the gully and has a number of single-pitch routes, all of which are cracks that lean right. If you tire of right-leaning cracks, then switch to the Tanager Face, where all the cracks lean left. All of the routes end on a sloped ramp-ledge covered with gravel and loose rocks, called Base Ledge.

DIRECTIONS (MAP PAGE 197)

From Chapel Pond Corner, walk left (south) and follow the steep gully along the base of the cliff. The first rock encountered is an unappealing sheer black face that

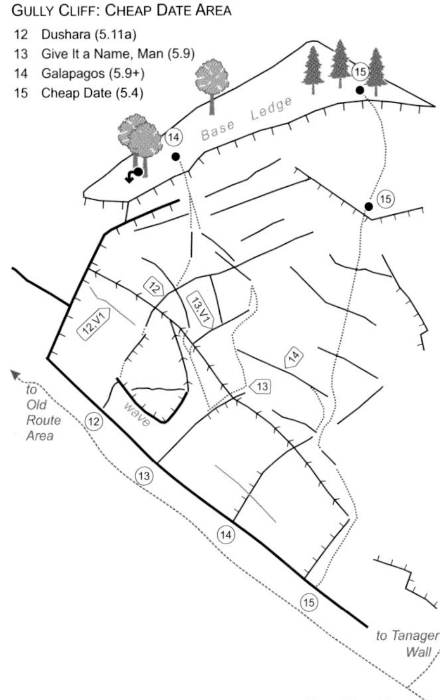

is often wet, the winter route **Crystal Ice Tower**; the annual sloughing of ice and debris from above keeps the base of this wall (and the gully below) clear of trees. Continue up and left along the base of the wall to a low, shallow cave on the right with a roof 6' up. 30' beyond is the turnoff for the Tanager Face. 40' beyond the turnoff is the Cheap Date Area (the first appealing rock you come to) and the route **Cheap Date**.

DESCENT OPTIONS

For the routes that end on Base Ledge, scramble to the low point on the ledge and rappel 30' from trees to the base.

12 Dushara 5.11a G 100' ★

Named for the Greek goddess of stone.

Start: 20' uphill from and left of **Give It a Name, Man** at a crack that meets the left end of the wavelike roof that is 12' up.

P1 5.11a G: Climb up the crack and over a bulge to a good stance. Continue up a right-leaning crack to a bulge (V1), then though the bulge onto the slab. Wander up to Base Ledge. 100'

V1 5.11a R: From the base of the right-leaning crack, follow a thin crack out left beneath a steep wall to the arête. Climb up and right onto the slab up to Base Ledge.

FA May 14, 1988, Don Mellor
FA (V1) Aug 18, 1988, Kris Klein, Mark Abbott

13 Give It a Name, Man 5.9 G 120' ★★

Start: 25' left of and uphill from **Galapagos**, and just right of a wave-shaped roof, below a right-leaning crack that begins 6' up.

P1 5.9 G: Boulder up to the crack, then follow it up and right to a right-rising ledge. (V1) Continue up and right around the lip and onto the slab, joining **Galapagos** to Base Ledge. 120'

V1 5.9 G: From the right-rising ledge, climb up and left in an open book for 10'. (V2) Follow a short right-leaning fingercrack out onto the slab, joining **Galapagos** to Base Ledge.

V2 5.9 G: Continue up the open book following a thin crack to a good horizontal at its top. Join **Dushara** up to Base Ledge.

FA May 14, 1988, Mark Meschinelli, Don Mellor

14 Galapagos 5.9+ G 130' ★★

Start: 20' uphill from and left of **Cheap Date** at a shallow right-facing, right-leaning corner that leads to a crack.

P1 5.9+ G: Climb up the right-leaning thin crack (small nuts) to an awkward jug, then out the gnarly right-leaning crack (crux) to a stance on the slab. Rail right, then zigzag left, right, and left again to the top at Base Ledge. 130'

Gear: 2 ea 2" cams.

FA May 14, 1988, Jeff Edwards, Don Mellor

15 Cheap Date 5.4 PG 150' ★

Start: The first climbable rock where clean rock comes right down to the gully, 50' beyond the turnoff to the Tanager Face, at a right-facing, right-leaning corner with a 4'-high, 4"-wide crack at the bottom. This is just uphill from two left-rising ceilings.

P1 5.4 PG: Step right onto the face and climb good holds on clean rock to the top of the corner. Up left onto the slab, then wander up and right to a tree ledge. 100'

P2 5.2 G: Scramble up to Base Ledge. 50'

FA Jun 11, 1987, Tad Welch, Ali Schultheis

16 Leave Your Wallet At Home 5.6 PG 500'

This route climbs some new terrain in order to link **Cheap Date** to the top of the cliff.

P1 5.4 PG: Same as **Cheap Date**. 150'

P2 5.3 G: Step right of belay and friction up then right through a tree island to gain a left-rising crack. Climb the crack to a nice ledge above and right of base ledge. Tree belay. 80'

P3 5.6 PG: Go straight up the face using a series of horizontal cracks until it is possible to step left above a large tree island with an vegetated offwidth crack at its right end. Climb the tricky face (crux) just left of the offwidth to a horizontal. Step right and friction above the offwidth to another tree belay. 70'

P4 5.6 PG: Step though tree island to a right-rising crack. Follow this right to a left-rising crack, joining P3 of **Beam Me Up**. Make the dicey friction move to a horizontal then friction straight up to the top on easier terrain. 200'

ACB Aug 3, 2012, Ben Brooke, Tina DeSanto

Tanager Face

This small north-facing cliff holds a good concentration of short, difficult crack routes, with **Lifelong Affliction** being the most popular. The defining feature of the cliff is a left-facing corner that begins 12' up; this is **Brightly Colored Males**. Left of this is a high-angle slab with a patchwork of excellent left-leaning seams and finger-cracks.

The base is slightly sloped and open with a few trees. The routes can be toproped by walking right to the first chimney-gully that breaks the cliff. Scramble up this gully (4th-class), then walk left on a tree ledge with one exposed move to the top of the face. There is a fixed anchor at the top of **Brightly Colored Males**.

HISTORY

The wall was first developed by Tad Welch and named after Tanager Lodge, a children's camp located on Upper Chateaugay Lake. Bill Pierce returned the next year and climbed the bulk of the difficult crack routes.

DIRECTIONS (MAP PAGE 197)

From Chapel Pond Corner, walk left (south) and follow the steep gully along the base of the cliff. The first rock encountered is an unappealing sheer black face that is often wet, the winter route **Crystal Ice Tower**; the annual sloughing of ice and debris from above keeps the base of this wall (and the gully below) clear of trees. Continue up and left along the base of the wall to a low, shallow cave on the right with a roof 6' up. 30' beyond is the turnoff for the Tanager Face. Turn right from the gully trail and scramble uphill for 40', then level another 100' on a good path to the base of the wall 600306,4887891.

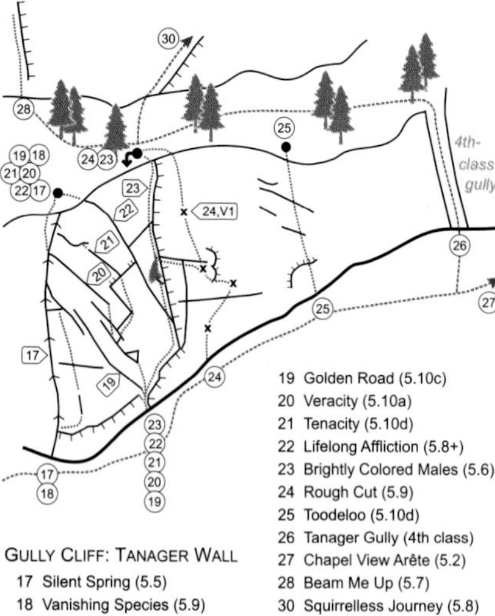

GULLY CLIFF: TANAGER WALL
17 Silent Spring (5.5)
18 Vanishing Species (5.9)
19 Golden Road (5.10c)
20 Veracity (5.10a)
21 Tenacity (5.10d)
22 Lifelong Affliction (5.8+)
23 Brightly Colored Males (5.6)
24 Rough Cut (5.9)
25 Toodeloo (5.10d)
26 Tanager Gully (4th class)
27 Chapel View Arête (5.2)
28 Beam Me Up (5.7)
30 Squirrelless Journey (5.8)

17 Silent Spring 5.5 PG 50' ★★

Start: 50' left of the **Brightly Colored Males** corner at the left end of the wall, below a clean arête that comes down to the trail. The left side of the arête has two wave-shaped bulges.

P1 5.5 PG: Climb the flakes and cracks on the arête past the right end of the wavelike bulges. After the second bulge, angle right on a low-angle slab to the top. 50'

History: Named for the book of the same name by Rachael Carson that launched the environmental movement.

FA Sep 18, 1989, Tad Welch, Bill Widrig

18 Vanishing Species 5.9 G 50' ★

Start: 5' right of the arête of **Silent Spring** at the left end of the wall.

P1 5.9 G: Climb up the face using face holds and hidden fingercracks to the top. 50'

FA Oct 1, 1989, Tad Welch, Bill Widrig

19 Golden Road 5.10c G 50' ★

This is the discontinuous thin crack left of **Veracity**.

Start: Same as **Brightly Colored Males**.

P1 5.10c G: Climb the crack left of the triangular pod until it fades. Switch left to the next crack and follow it to the top. 50'

FA Aug, 1988, Bill Pierce

20 Veracity 5.10a G 50' ★★★★

Good moves that switch from jamming to layback.

Start: Same as **Brightly Colored Males**.

P1 5.10a G: Climb up to a triangular pod, then up the left-leaning discontinuous cracks to the top. 50'

FA Aug, 1988, Bill Pierce

21 Tenacity 5.10d G 50'

Start: Same as **Brightly Colored Males**.

P1 5.10d G: Climb up to a triangular pod (as for **Veracity**), then up the **Veracity** crack for 4'. Finger-traverse right to another left-leaning crack, climb it to a small right-rising overlap, then climb the left-rising seam to the top. 50'

FA Aug, 1988, Bill Pierce, Don Mellor

22 Lifelong Affliction 5.8+ G 50' ★★★★

Excellent crack climbing, although short.

Start: Same as **Brightly Colored Males**.

P1 5.8+ G: Follow the right-rising ledge to the base of the left-facing corner of **Brightly Colored Males**. Up the corner for 5' to a left-rising crack on the left wall, then follow the crack to the top. 50'

FA May, 1987, Tad Welch, Jamie Savage

23 Brightly Colored Males 5.6 G 70' ★★

Start: 15' downhill from and left of the prominent left-facing corner that begins 12' up and has a cedar tree at midheight.

P1 5.6 G: Scramble onto a right-rising ledge and follow this rightward to the base of the corner. (V1) Up the corner to its top, then up and right on a slab to a fixed anchor on a tree. 70'

V1 5.8 PG: Climb the crack right of the arête to a left-rising horizontal, then follow it back into the corner above the cedar.

FA 1986, Don Mellor

*Opposite: Rob Griffiths on **Lifelong Affliction** (5.8+).*

24 Rough Cut 5.9 G 80' ★★

Quality face climbing with a tricky traverse.

Start: On the face 10' right of the **Brightly Colored Males** corner (and 25' right of the start of that route) below a bolt.

P1 5.9 G: Climb the face on good incut edges, angling right to a horizontal. Move left to a left-facing shallow crescent, (V1) then follow a left-rising horizontal crack to the arête of the **Brightly Colored Males** corner. Step around the arête (just above the cedar tree) and finish in the corner. 80'

V1 A Touch of Gray 5.12a G: Very thin face climbing on this one. From the left-rising horizontal, climb straight up the face to the top.

History: The route was put in on lead by Welch and Lawyer, then erased. Bill Pierce later climbed the direct variation, but his lower bolt was removed and the route fell into obscurity. The route has been resurrected so that both the original line and the variation can be led.

FA Oct 24, 1987, Tad Welch, Jim Lawyer

FA (V1) 1988, Bill Pierce

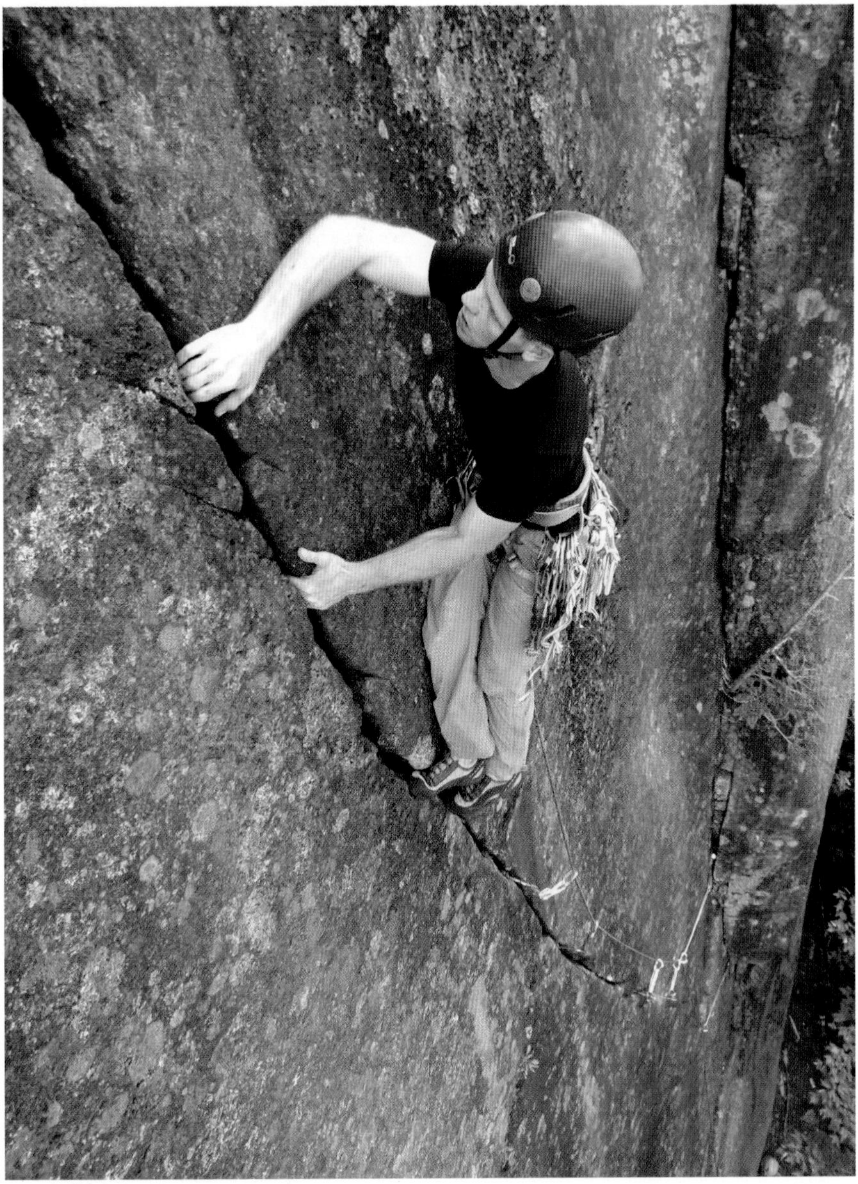

25 Toodeloo 5.10d R 50'

Very mossy in its current condition.

Start: At the top of the hill 30' right of the **Brightly Colored Males** left-facing corner at a face below a small overlap 7' up, which is just right of a black half-crescent overlap.

P1 5.10d R: Climb up with no protection past the overlap to a second overlap (the horizontal above this is the first protection). Continue straight up the face past several more horizontals to the top. 50'

FA 1988, Bill Pierce

26 Tanager Gully 4th class 50'

About 100' right of the **Brightly Colored Males** left-facing corner is a break in the cliff that provides access to the top of the Tanager Face.

27 Chapel View Arête 5.2 G 100' ★★

A pretty arête littered with cracks and holds, with a boulder move at the bottom.

Start: 240' right of the **Brightly Colored Males** left-facing corner is a clean buttress and blunt arête with white spotty rock on its left side and a left-facing, right-rising 20'-high corner on its right side. Begin on the toe on the left side of the arête or 10' right at a short left-facing corner with cracks.

P1 5.2 G: Climb up and right to the arête, then follow it to the trees at the top. 100'

FA Aug, 1988, Don Mellor (solo)

28 Beam Me Up 5.7 R 440' ★★★

The long Gully Cliff climbs are concentrated on the left side of the face; this route was an attempt to open up the right side of this face. The first ascent is believed to have come in from Base Ledge, but that ledge is more of a landslide and quite horrible. A much better approach has been uncovered that begins from the top of the Tanager Face, which makes this the longest route on the Gully Cliff. The route has excellent climbing and exposure, following amazing diagonal incut cracks across a slab, interspersed with spicy friction.

Start: Same as **Silent Spring**. If **Silent Spring** is wet, then scramble up **Tanager Gully** to the top of **Brightly Colored Males**, or climb any of the other routes on the Tanager Face.

P1 5.5 PG: Same as **Silent Spring**: Climb the flakes and cracks on the arête past the right end of the wave-like bulges. After the second bulge, angle right on a low-angle slab to the top. Belay from trees below a crack in a left-facing corner in the slab above. 50'

P2 5.5 PG: Climb a fingercrack in the left-facing corner to its top. Work your way straight up easy rock with good protection to some deep horizontal cracks. Follow these up and left for 100' and belay at a fixed anchor in bushes on the right side of an opening where the lower slab connects to the upper slab. One tricky 5.5 move is required to span a blank section (small TCU helpful). 190'

P3 5.7 R: Up a short, dirty left-leaning crack that leads to a good left-rising horizontal crack. Rail left and break through the bulge above at a small broken flake, then friction moves lead to the next left-rising horizontal crack. Continue up and left on friction to the left end of a tree island (a convenient loop of rope hangs here for

Bernard Poisson on P2 (5.5) of ***Beam Me Up*** *(5.7).*

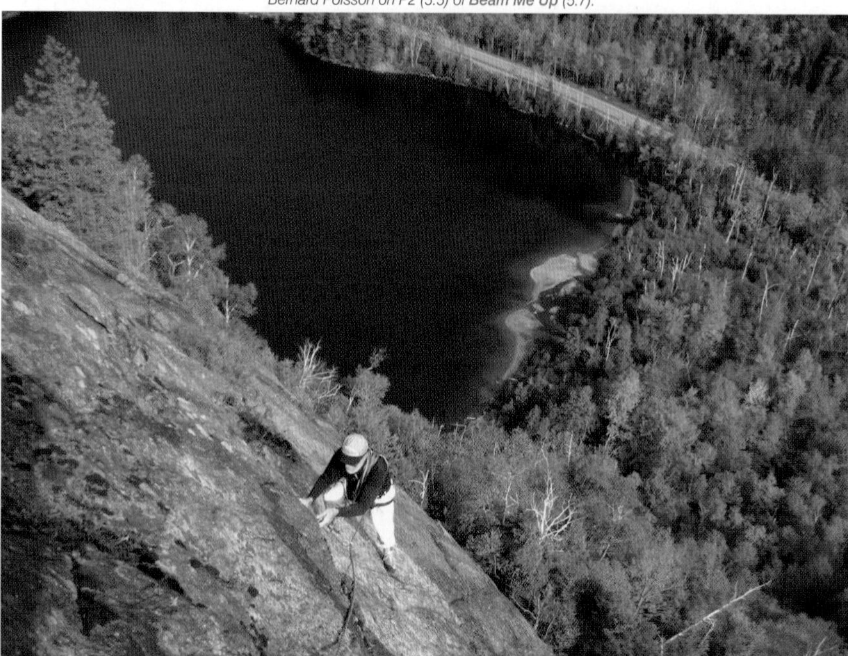

protection). Friction straight up to the top, or thrash left on the tree ledge and finish on easy slabs. 200'

Gear: Standard rack up to 3".

History: This route appeared in Mellor's 1983 guidebook but was dropped when nobody could figure out where it went, due either to a poor description or to changes in the cliff vegetation. The route described here matches the features of the original description, more or less. Who knows?

FA May 5, 1978, Geoff Powter, Jacquelyn Pidany

29 Shiling Was Willing 5.7 PG (5.4 R) 390'

Start: Same as **Silent Spring**. If **Silent Spring** is wet, then scramble up **Tanager Gully** to the top of **Brightly Colored Males**, or climb any of the other routes on the Tanager Face.

P1 5.5 G: Same as **Silent Spring**: Climb the flakes and cracks on the arête past the right end of the wavelike bulges. After the second bulge, angle right on a low-angle slab to the top. Belay from trees below a crack in a left-facing corner in the slab above. 50'

P2 5.4 PG: Follow the corner of **Beam Me Up** to its top, then trend right to a belay at the left end of a cedar island. (This is the left end of the same cedar island in which **Squirrelless Journey** begins.) 120'

P3 5.6 PG: Make a right-rising traverse on good face holds (5.4 R) to a left-facing left-leaning corner. Move up through lichens and follow the left-facing corner and flakes to a belay at a cedar. 140'

P4 5.7 PG: Climb straight up on good rock for about 20', then up a broken crack (#2 Friend) to a small ledge. Move right and up on more loose rock to belay at cedars above (same topout as for **Squirrelless Journey**). 80'

FA Aug 6, 2008, R.L. Stolz, David Shiling

30 Squirrelless Journey 5.8 R 220' ★★

This route sits 100' above the top of Tanager Face and ascends a pretty face with excellent climbing. The crux pitch has G protection, but some gear low is in questionable flakes. The name is a play on the route **Perilous Journey** (in Eldorado Canyon) and the fact

that Purcell (aka "the Squirrel") overlooked this obvious line.

Start: Scramble up Tanager Gully to the top of Brightly Colored Males (or climb any of the routes on the Tanager Face). Climb up a short slab, then claw your way up a right-rising ramp through some tight trees to a ledge. Walk left, then continue in the right-rising line up to a second ledge beneath a clean slab. Begin below a 7'-high left-rising 2"-deep overlap that starts from the ground.

P1 5.8 R: Climb up the face over the overlap (crux) to a flake (first gear). Step left, then back right, then straight up on left-facing flakes and slopers to better gear. Belay at the base of a left-facing corner with a birch tree and loose blocks at the top. 100'

P2 5.5 G: Continue up the corner, step right at its top, and climb up the depression to a roof. Step left to avoid the friable choss beneath the roof, climb straight up to some slabs, then up to the trees. 120'

Gear: Standard rack to 0.75".

Descent: Walk left through the trees to the top of the cliff and the normal descent.

FA May 8, 1992, Don Mellor, Brad Hess, Jason Piwko

Tilman's Arête

This buttress of rock sits above the south end of Chapel Pond. The buttress's left wall (which faces east) contains the immensely popular Tilman's Arête (whose P2 is a sharply defined arête), in addition to several other routes located on the wall adjoining the buttress on the left.

DIRECTIONS **(MAP PAGE 197)**

From Chapel Pond Corner, walk right following a path to the first buttress of rock 600277,4887956. Some large boulders separate the toe of the buttress from the water.

31 Miller Time 5.11b TR 50'

This route begins 30' left of Tilman's Arête at a low overhang 5' up. Climb up the face past a prominent horizontal 20' up and up to three cedars. To toprope this route, gain the three cedars by climbing the first section of Thousand Faces of a Hundred People.

FA (TR) May, 1989, Patrick Purcell

32 Otherwise Normal People 5.8 G 130' ★★★

An excellent and unusual route in that it never breaks out of the trees. After 130', you can lower to the ground 40' below.

Start: At a slab 6' left of the large corner of Ectoplasmic Remains.

P1 5.8 G: Climb up the slab and ledges to gain a horizontal crack. Traverse straight left 50' (crossing Miller Time after 15') to where the upper side of the crack forms an overlap. Some crunched moves under the overlap (crux) gain a left-facing, right-rising flake. Climb up past the flake, friction straight up to a horizontal crack (gear), traverse left 15', then up to a tree ledge. Walk left on the tree ledge to a large tree with a fixed anchor. 130'

Gear: Standard rack to 2", doubles in the medium-sized cams.

FA Jun 26, 2007, Jim Lawyer, Michelle Burlitch

33 Thousand Faces of a Hundred People 5.7 PG (5.4 R) 360'

Climbs two very pretty arêtes, but the climbing between them is uninspiring. With some traffic, this could be a good route. P1 of this route zigzags over the winter route Necktie Party, and P2 climbs the arête right of the winter route White Line Fever.

Start: In the large corner as for Ectoplasmic Remains.

Ben Cook on P2 of Tilman's Arête (5.7), belayed by Erin Cook.

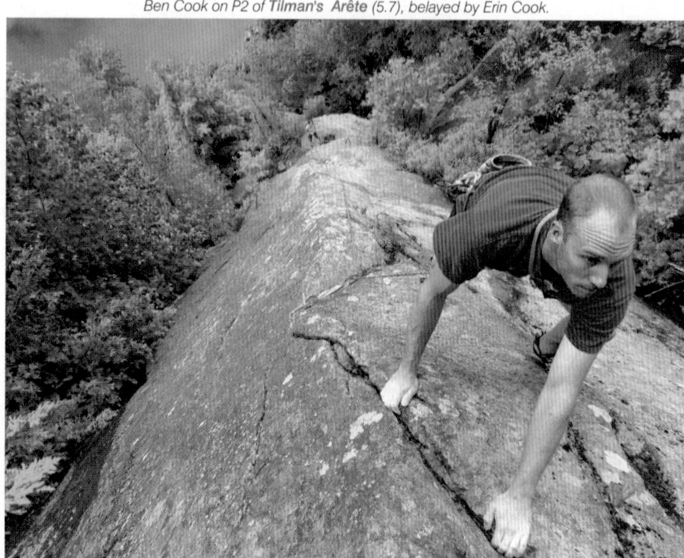

P1 5.6 G (5.4 R): Climb up the main corner for 15', then step left onto the face at a good hand edge. Mantel onto the edge, then move left to a ledge with a cedar. Traverse 30' left past a grouping of three cedars (the top of **Miller Time**) to the left end of the slab, then climb a slab (5.4 R) up and right to some cedars at the base of a right-leaning arête. Pass the cedars on the left and climb the clean arête to a fixed anchor at the next cedar island (the same anchor as for **Necktie Party**). 160'

P2 5.7 G: Traverse left on a slab using a good foot ledge for 40' to near its left end, then climb up and left to some cedars. Climb up the left side of a good flake, step left to the blunt arête, and move up to a good ledge (optional belay, 120'). (V1) Climb the excellent clean crack in the arête to its top, step left to avoid some trees, and cedar-pull onto the tree island. 200'

V1 5.12a TR: Move right from the optional belay ledge and onto the face, then climb it to the top.

Descent: Scramble up through the trees 40' to a path below the next band of cliffs (this is 75' left of **Chapel View Arête**). Walk left beneath Tanager Face to return to the gully, then follow it down back to Chapel Pond.

FA (P1) Jul, 1988, Patrick Purcell, Mary Purcell
FA (complete) Aug 11, 1988, Patrick Purcell, Mary Purcell, Jay Holtz
FA (V1) Aug 18, 1988, Patrick Purcell, Jeff Edwards

34 Ectoplasmic Remains 5.9+ PG 100' ★★★

An often-overlooked gem, this quality route sports a committing bulge and some steep face climbing.

Start: In the large corner formed by the left wall of the buttress of **Tilman's Arête** and the adjoining face to the left, at the height of land on the left side of the arête.

P1 5.9+ PG: Climb up the main corner for 15', then step left onto the face at a good hand edge. Mantel onto the edge, then move left to a shallow left-facing, right-rising corner with a crack. At its top is a crack through a bulge; this puzzling move requires an awkward mantel with protection at your feet. Continue up and right on easy slab to a bolt on the headwall above. From here, climb up the steep face to a horizontal, rail right to good gear, then up the steep bulge to a fixed anchor. 100'

FA Aug 18, 1988, Patrick Purcell, Jeff Edwards

35 Tilman's Arête 5.7 PG 150' ★★★★

An excellent route in a scenic position above the lake, with quality rock, adequate protection, and a moderate grade. Don't miss the sharp arête on P2! A very popular route for guiding. P1 has several worthwhile variations.

Start: 6' left of the nose of the arête and 15' right of the large corner, at a short, 4'-high right-rising ramp that leads to a right-rising crack.

P1 5.3 PG: (V1, V2, V3) Climb up the crack to the arête, then up and left following the blunt nose of the arête up to a good ledge with a fixed anchor. 75'

P2 5.7 PG: Climb the well-defined arête, past a bolt at midheight, to a ledge with a fixed anchor. 75'

V1 5.6 PG: Start in the large corner as for **Ectoplasmic Remains** and climb the corner for 12', then move out right on a good horizontal to a crack leaning 45° to the right. Climb up the crack (crux; good protection) to the arête to join the normal route.

V2 5.5 G: Start in the large corner as for **Ectoplasmic Remains** and climb the corner to reach a crack on the face that parallels the corner to its end at some bushes in the main corner. Make a slab move right to reach the ledge with the fixed anchor.

V3 5.4 G: Start in the large corner as for **Ectoplasmic Remains** and climb the corner to the bushes, then make a slab move right to reach the ledge with the fixed anchor.

History: The route was originally climbed by Karen Stoltz . The fixed anchors and the bolt on P2 were placed by Patrick Purcell a week later.

FA Jul 13, 1988, Karen Stolz, Cindy Dohl

Shipton's Arête

This is the second prow of clean rock that sits above the pond. The right end of this prow dips into the water, thereby preventing any further hiking access along the shoreline. The routes are located on the east face of the prow, perpendicular to the shoreline. The routes share an anchor, so it is possible to toprope the other two after leading one of them.

DIRECTIONS **(MAP PAGE 197)**

From Chapel Pond Corner, walk right to Tilman's Arête, then scramble down boulders to the shore. Continue walking right to the base of this prow 600258,4887970, reached when you can't walk any farther.

36 China Grove 5.5 PG 100'

Start: 20' uphill from and left of the toe of the arête, below a blocky groove with left-leaning cracks.

P1 5.4 G: Up the cracks to a flared left-leaning crack, then climb it to its end. Move up and right with less protection to the tree ledge at the top with a fixed anchor. 100'

37 No Picnic 5.6 R 110' ★★

Nice climbing with little protection if you strictly avoid cracks to either side.

Start: At the clean face between **China Grove** and **Shipton's Voyage**.

P1 5.6 R: Climb the face past several horizontals to the top. 110'

38 Shipton's Voyage 5.4 G 120' ★★★

Excellent climbing at a moderate grade—clean rock, great position, numerous holds, and interesting protection slots.

Start: Just left of the arête on the last chunk of land before it drops to the water, below a series of short left-leaning cracks.

P1 5.4 PG: Climb up left-leaning cracks to the arête, then follow the arête, moving left onto the face just before the top to gain a tree ledge and fixed anchor. 120'

MARTINI WALL

Location	South side of NY 73, accessed from the Giant Mountain Trailhead at Chapel Pond
Aspect	North
Height	200'
Quality	★★
Approach	15 min, easy
Summary	Two recommended, but rarely climbed, face routes.

-5.6	5.7	5.8	5.9	5.10	5.11	5.12	5.13+	total
			1	1				2

This wall, located just left of the winter route **Power Play**, contains two excellent face routes. The difficulty is in reaching the wall.

DIRECTIONS **(MAP PAGE 197)**

From Chapel Pond Corner, walk right under Tilman's Arête and Shipton's Arête to where the cliff plunges into the water. Wade across on submerged ledges (about thigh-deep in high water), then walk right for 200' under the cone-shaped slope (the top of which is the winter route **Chouinard's Gully**) to an overhanging black wall with a chimney-cave on its left end. Follow the base of this wall right, then steeply up a gully to an open, flat terrace below these two routes 600135,4888011. The Power Play Amphitheater is to the right—a large open area beneath wet, towering black walls and ramps.

1 Bond Girls 5.10a G 70' ★★★

Start: At the height of land below the leftmost of two lines of bolts. There is a small, 8"-wide horizontal 5' up.

● **P1 5.10a G:** Climb up to the first bolt, then left to a good jug (crux). Continue up the face past several good ledges to a short right-facing corner near the top with a fixed anchor just above. 70'

FA 2000, Jeff Edwards, Jeff Martin

2 Shaken, Not Stirred 5.9 G 70' ★★

Start: 8' right of the height of land and 20' left of large black right-leaning ramps, below a short, tilted right-facing edge 7' up.

● **P1 5.9 G:** Climb straight up the face, moving left to a fixed anchor. 70'

FA 2000, Jeff Edwards, Jeff Martin

View from Chapel Pond Slab. Photo by Monica Wormald.

CREATURE WALL

Location	North side of NY 73, accessed from the Giant Mountain Trailhead at Chapel Pond
Aspect	Southwest
Height	90'
Quality	★★★
Approach	10 min, easy
Summary	A collection of moderate, one-pitch crack routes on clean rock; well traveled and good for toproping.

-5.6	5.7	5.8	5.9	5.10	5.11	5.12	5.13+	total
1	2	7		3	1			14

The Creature Wall is one of the hidden gems of the Chapel Pond area. The cliff lies low in the trees, just above the level of the road, and has a quick, easy approach. It is a popular destination for toproping because of the moderate grades and easy rope setup, but every route can be safely led.

The predominant features on this cliff are the handcracks, most of which lean to the left. There is a high concentration of routes on a short section of cliff, meaning that every crack and variation has been named and climbed countless times. Several of the lines are squeezed-in, allowing you to "cheat" and stem to a neighboring route. For first-timers, the cliff can be difficult to figure out, as all the crack lines are parallel and look similar. The key features to watch for are the triangle face just above the approach trail, the arching roof on the right end, and the stacked chockstones at the start of **Arachnid Traction**.

HISTORY

Don Mellor's 1983 guidebook mentioned "a good, steep wall [that] stands about 80' high and is split by vertical cracks."[2] Tom Rosecrans, always the explorer, took note and immediately climbed **Pet Cemetery** in January of 1984. He recognized the potential here and, with various partners, exhausted most of the route possibilities within a couple of years. He began the Stephen King theme in route naming because of "all the bats, snakes, and other stuff."

DIRECTIONS **(MAP PAGE 197)**

You pass this cliff on the approach to the Upper Washbowl. Park at the Giant Mountain Trailhead on NY 73, 3.9 miles northwest of Malfunction Junction and 0.2 mile southeast of the Chapel Pond pullout (Chapel Pond is 4.5 miles southeast of Keene Valley, from the intersection of NY 73 and John's Brook Road). From the parking area, hike 100 yards northwest (toward Chapel Pond) along the road to the start of a guardrail on the north side of the road. Pick up a good trail 600435,4888088 that heads downhill over the embankment and across a marshy area. This trail continues uphill to the base of the cliff, meeting the base at the route **Gob Hoblin** (about 10 min) 600530,4888317.

2 Don Mellor, *Climbing in the Adirondacks* (1983), p. 49.

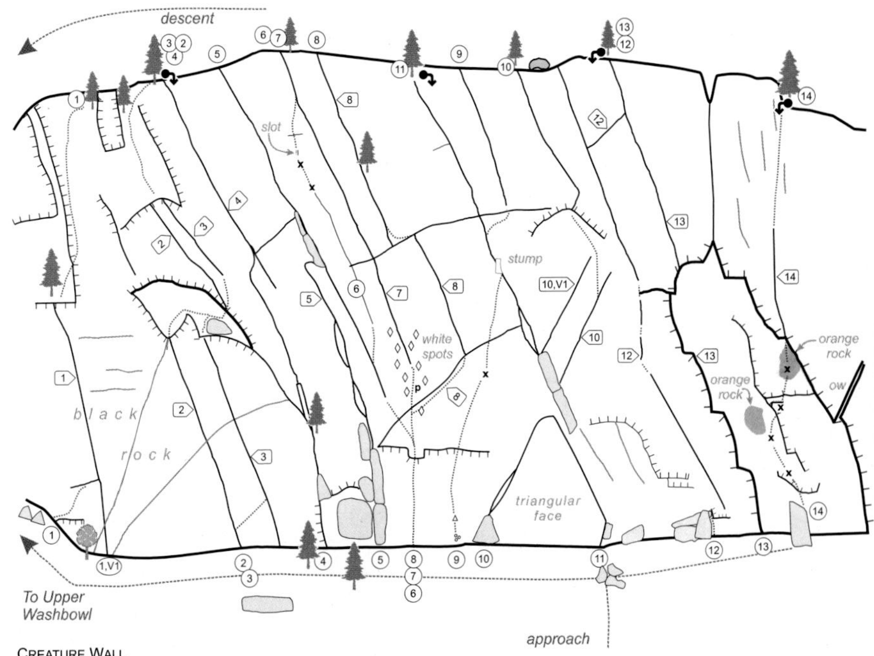

CREATURE WALL

1 Fire Starter (5.5)
2 Night Mare (5.8)
3 Octo-Pussy (5.7)
4 Jump Bat Crack (5.8)
5 Arachnid Traction (5.8)
6 Arachnophobic Reaction (5.10c)
7 Diamondback (5.8)
8 Black Moriah (5.8-)
9 The Shining (5.10a)
10 Christine (5.10a)
11 Gob Hoblin (5.7)
12 Pet Cemetery (5.8)
13 Cujo (5.8)
14 Crispy Critter (5.11a)

DESCENT OPTIONS

There are several fixed anchors on trees at the top of the crag for rappel or topropes. There is also an easy walk-off to the left: stay near the face and find a narrow ledge that drops down to the open talus on the left end of the cliff.

1 Fire Starter 5.5 G 60'

Start: 45' right of the descent gully at the left end of the cliff is a V-notch formed by two triangular boulders sitting at the base. Just right of the V-notch is an orange spot 10' up. Begin at the 6"-wide foot-traverse ledge below the orange spot.

P1 5.5 G: (V1) Traverse right across the 6"-wide ledge to gain a left-rising crack. Follow this crack to a cedar tree perched on a ledge. Continue up and right through easy rock to a final left-facing corner. 60'

V1 Tarantula 5.9+ PG: Begin downhill and 20' to the right (at a mossy grotto with a chockstone in the bottom) and climb the left-rising crack from the ground (instead of traversing in from the left). This is the line of the winter route of the same name and is therefore often wet.

FA Jun 22, 1984, Tom Rosecrans, Dave Szot
FA (V1) Jul, 1984, Dennis Luther

2 Night Mare 5.8 G 70'

Start: Set back from the cliff about 30' is a car-sized block with a flat landing in front. This route begins on the cliff in front of the block, which is distinguished by two left-diagonaling cracks that end at a large alcove with a large boulder on the right side. **Night Mare** begins in the leftmost of these cracks.

P1 5.8 G: Climb the leftmost of the two cracks to the alcove (crux just before the alcove) and enter the alcove on the left side of the point in the floor of the alcove. Step right to the top of the boulder and climb up onto the face with good jugs to a second set of left-diagonaling cracks; climb the leftmost of these cracks to a ledge, then more easily up and right to a tree with a fixed anchor. 70'

FA Jun 26, 1984, Tom Rosecrans, Mike Hay

3 Octo-Pussy 5.7 G 70' ★★

Climbs the right-hand of two parallel cracks (the left crack is **Night Mare**) and is the better of the two routes.

Start: Same as for **Night Mare**.

P1 5.7 G: Climb the **Night Mare** crack for a few feet, then traverse right to the next crack. Follow the crack to the alcove and enter it on the right side of the point in the alcove's floor. Move onto the boulder and climb up onto the face with good jugs to a second set of left-diagonaling cracks; climb the rightmost of these cracks to a ledge, then more easily up and right to a tree with a fixed anchor. 70'

FA Jun 22, 1984, Tom Rosecrans, Mike Hay

4 Jump Bat Crack 5.8 G 80' ★★★

Start: On the left side of the level area along the base of the cliff, at a 2'-deep right-facing corner capped by a triangular 4'-high chockstone 10' up. Above this is a cedar tree, the only cedar growing on the lower section of the entire wall.

P1 5.8 G: Climb up the right-facing corner past the chockstone to a wide slot with a cedar. Continue in a left-angling line to a clean handcrack that diagonals across the clean upper section of rock and ends at a large cedar with a fixed anchor. 80'

FA Jun 2, 1984, Tom Rosecrans, Chris Knight

5 Arachnid Traction 5.8 G 90' ★★★★

Exceptional hand jamming in the final section.

Start: Begin in the left-hand of two parallel vertical cracks formed by two chockstones stacked on top of each other and just right of a low overhang 15' up.

P1 5.8 G: Climb up the chockstones and angle left in a wide crack. At the top, switch to the parallel handcrack to the right, which angles left across a clean upper section of rock with increasing difficulty to the top. Step left to the large cedar with a fixed anchor (same as for **Jump Bat Crack**). 90'

FA May 28, 1984, Tom Rosecrans, Dave Szot, Dennis Luther

6 Arachnophobic Reaction 5.10c PG 100' ★★★

Climbs the face right of **Arachnid Traction**. It was originally equipped with two bolts, which were removed; despite this, it is still a safe lead and perhaps the best of the 5.10 routes at the cliff, with more sustained climbing.

Start: Same as **Diamondback**.

P1 5.10c PG: Climb up the face through the square notch in the ledge. Angle left to a crack that parallels **Arachnid Traction** and up this until you can move right 5' to the bottom of a very thin fingercrack. Follow the fingercrack to where it ends (good gear), then straight up a blank face (crux) to a 6"-high vertical slot. Climb past the slot to a horizontal, then make a big move up to some jugs that lead right to the upper crack on **Diamondback** and climb it to the top. 100'

FA Jul, 1988, Tom Rosecrans, Ken Wright

7 Diamondback 5.8 PG 90' ★

Named for the diamond-shaped spots on the rock.

Start: 3' right of **Arachnid Traction** below a faint vertical crack (which takes protection after 10') that leads to square notch in a ledge 15' up.

P1 5.8 PG: Climb up the face through the square notch in the ledge, then straight up to the right-rising horizontal crack. Move right a few feet to a piton above the horizontal, then up and left on layback edges (crux) to gain the bottom of a left-leaning crack. Climb up the crack past a wider section to the top. 90'

FA Jul 29, 1984, Dennis Luther, Dave Szot, Tom Rosecrans

8 Black Moriah 5.8- G 90'

Start: Same as for **Diamondback**.

P1 5.8- G: Climb up the face through the square notch in the ledge. A long right-rising horizontal crack begins above the left end of the ledge. Follow this crack up to a dark streak, then straight up the dark streak with crack and face climbing to a prominent horizontal. Step left in the horizontal to a left-diagonaling crack and follow it past a cedar to the top. 90'

FA Jul 22, 1984, Dave Szot, Dennis Luther

*Solo on **Arachnid Traction** (5.8). Photo by Colin O'Connor.*

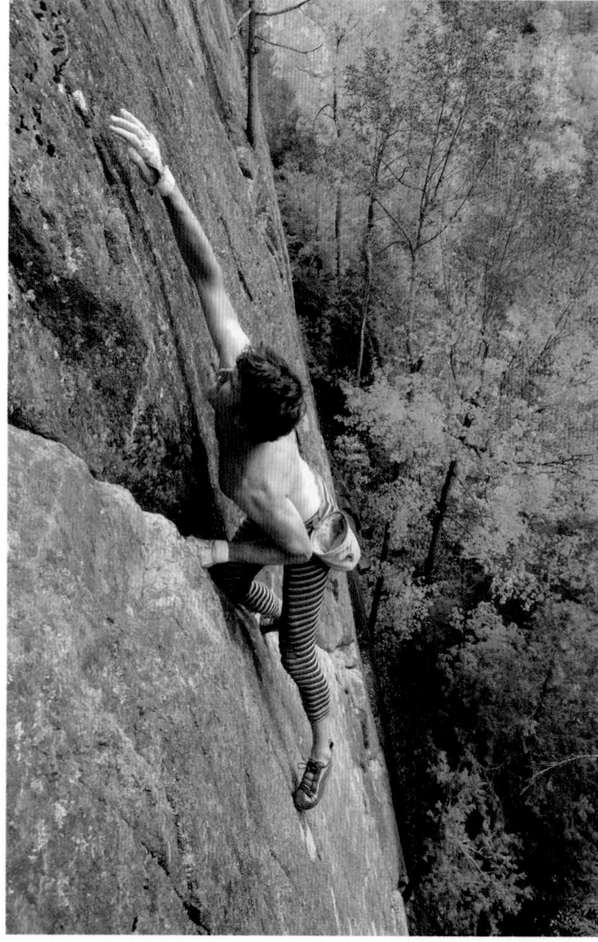

9 The Shining 5.10a PG 90' ★★★

Excellent face climbing with less than obvious protection.

Start: 6' left of a triangular 4'-high chockstone 2' up, at a black strip on the face. This is 20' left of where the approach trail meets the cliff. The start also has three small finger pockets at hip level.

P1 5.10a PG: Boulder up the face past two triangular holds (crux) to a ledge. From the right side of the ledge, angle up and right across the face with thin horizontals to a bolt, then above the bolt to a prominent right-rising horizontal crack. Continue straight up the face above the horizontal and angle slightly right to join the prominent left-leaning crack of **Gob Hoblin** just below the stump. Climb the **Gob Hoblin** crack for a few feet to a horizontal on the right. Step right in the horizontal and climb a left-leaning crack to the top. 90'

FA Jul, 1988, Ken Wright, Tom Rosecrans

10 Christine 5.10a G 110' ★★★

Start: Begin at a giant, 7'-high triangular chockstone 2' up, above which is a right-leaning crack that marks the left side of the triangular face. (The right side of the triangular face is formed by the **Gob Hoblin** crack, which begins just above the approach trail.)

P1 5.10a G: Climb up past the triangular chockstone and up the right-leaning crack (5.8, awkward jams) to the top of the triangular face. (V1) Cross the parallel cracks of **Gob Hoblin** and continue in the same rightward line by following the lower of two parallel right-leaning cracks across the face (crux) to a good rest beneath a left-facing flake-overlap that arches left into a ceiling (which you can see behind to the other side). Climb up the flake and the juggy face, angle right to gain a left-leaning crack, and follow it (5.8) to the top. 110'

V1 5.9 G: At the top of the triangular face, climb up **Gob Hoblin** for a few feet and take the upper of the two right-leaning cracks, then join the normal route at the ceiling.

FA Jun, 1984, Dave Szot, Tom Rosecrans, Dennis Luther

11 Gob Hoblin 5.7 G 90' ★★★

Start: Where the approach trail meets the cliff, at a table-sized boulder 5' in front of the cliff and at the left end of a low blocky ledge. Begin in a crack that forms the right side of a triangular face.

P1 5.7 G: A bouldery start leads to a left-leaning, right-facing corner that forms the right side of the triangular face, then up to parallel cracks formed by wedged blocks. Continue in the left-leaning crack line past an old stump and on to the top at a cedar with a fixed anchor. 90'

History: Fixed gear was found during the first ascent.

FA Jun 6, 1984, Tom Rosecrans

12 Pet Cemetery 5.8 G 90' ★

Start: At the right end of the low blocky ledge or just below the right end of this ledge at a chimney-slot formed by a right-facing corner and a low roof on the right.

P1 5.8 G: Either step right into the left-leaning crack or climb the chimney-slot below the ledge to gain the crack. Follow the crack until it disappears, then straight up to gain the bottom of another left-leaning crack. Climb this crack to a small alcove (V1), then traverse right and follow a diagonaling crack across the black face to gain the top of the **Cujo** crack. Follow it to a fixed anchor on a tree. 90'

V1 5.9 G: Continue straight up the crack above the alcove.

FA Jan 24, 1984, Tom Rosecrans, Mike Hay
FA (V1) 1996, Tom Rosecrans, Dave Aldous

13 Cujo 5.8 G 90' ★★

Start: At the right end of the wall beneath a right-facing corner that arches right into an orange roof 50' up.

P1 5.8 G: Climb up the stepped right-facing corner that forms the left side of the arch. At the roof, swing left onto the face. Make a few well-protected face moves to gain a flared crack and follow it past a ledge to a tree with a fixed anchor on top. 90'

Gear: To 3".

FA Jun, 1984, Dave Szot, Tom Rosecrans, Dennis Luther

14 Crispy Critter 5.11a G 80' ★★

A steep face climb—more typical of Rumney than the Creature Wall. Bolts missing.

Start: At the right end of the cliff below the double-tiered left-rising ceilings, at a prominent 5'-high boulder that forms a small pinnacle that stands 4' from the base of the cliff.

P1 5.11a G: Climb over a small overlap and onto the face, then trend left into a left-facing, left-leaning 5'-high orange corner. From the top of the corner, head up and right over the ceiling to the larger left-rising ceiling. Climb it via a crack (the only crack that breaks the roof) and onto the face above. Move up the face, using many vertical cracks and staying left of the black water streak, to a prominent bushy pine tree at the top. 80'

FA Jul, 1996, Dave Aldous, Scot Carpenter

Pen and ink by Colin O'Connor.

UPPER WASHBOWL

Location	North side of NY 73, accessed from the Giant Mountain Trailhead at Chapel Pond
Aspect	South
Height	350'
Quality	★★★★
Approach	25 min, moderate
Summary	Steep, multipitch routes, including the Adirondack classics **Hesitation**, **Wiessner Route**, and **Partition**.

-5.6	5.7	5.8	5.9	5.10	5.11	5.12	5.13+	total
2	2	4	2	4	5	2		21

Situated high above Chapel Pond, with its sunny exposure and alpine views, is the Upper Washbowl cliff, home to the best multipitch, moderate routes of Chapel Pond Pass. The rock quality isn't quite that of the Beer Walls, but the unique geometry of the Upper Washbowl provides the necessary ledges, corners, and cracks for routes to snake their way up this vertical cliff. The steep hike, disorienting base, and exposure enhance the "big cliff" experience, which can't be obtained at the lower crags.

The Upper Washbowl is divided into a left and right side. Conveniently, the approach trail arrives at the middle below a prow where the cliff is at its greatest height. The P1 corner of **Hesitation** and the massive roofs above are distinctive landmarks that will signal that you have reached the base of the correct cliff.

Due to its aspect, the Upper Washbowl has a long climbing season but is often closed at midseason due to the nesting of peregrine falcons.

Helmets and sturdy approach shoes are recommended.

Watch for poison ivy in the open talus below **Hesitation**, and along the approach trail just before **Wiessner Route**.

DIRECTIONS (MAP PAGE 197)

Parking for the Upper Washbowl is at the Giant Mountain Trailhead on NY 73, 3.9 miles northwest of Malfunction Junction and 0.2 mile southeast of the Chapel Pond pullout (Chapel Pond is 4.5 miles southeast of Keene Valley, from the intersection of NY 73 and John's Brook Road). From the parking area, hike 100 yards northwest (toward Chapel Pond) along the road to the start of a guardrail on the north side of the road. Pick up a good trail 600435,4888088 that heads downhill over the embankment and across a marshy area. This trail continues uphill to the base of the Creature Wall (about 10 min). From here, go up and left along the base of the cliff and through large talus blocks, veering right to the base of another steep wall. Go left along this minor wall and continue steeply uphill through talus to the base of the cliff 600487,4888474. Here the trail splits; go right to approach **Hesitation** or left for routes on the left side of the cliff. Total hiking time is 25 min.

There is an old trail that approaches the cliff directly across the road from the Chapel Pond pullout. Although it is well cairned, this approach is now overgrown and not recommended, especially considering that the Creature Wall approach is so well traveled.

HISTORY

The Upper Washbowl has a long climbing history, dating back to 1938. During an epic three-day weekend, Fritz Wiessner, Bob Notman, and M. Beckett Howorth climbed three new routes: the **Wiessner Route** on Wallface, the **Wiessner Route** at Indian Head, and the **Wiessner Route** at the Upper Washbowl (at that time known as the Nubble Cliff, or simply the "cliff at Chapel Pond"). Their route became a standard outing for climbers in those days and continues to be popular today, as it finds a moderate pathway up an impressive piece of rock.

Twelve years passed before the first surge of activity starting in the early 1950s with **BBC** and **Partition**, then in the late 1950s with the Canadians John Turner, Brian Rothery, and friends, perhaps better known for their exploits at Poke-O. The 1970s saw some route development by various groups, but it wasn't until the 1980s that things really got going, mostly through the efforts of a group of locals (the usual suspects: Don Mellor, Chuck Turner, Patrick Purcell, Bill Dodd, and Bill Simes).

Many of the difficult routes on the cliff are located above the Slanting Ledge and were climbed in the mid- to late 1980s by Mellor, Purcell, and visitor Harry Brielmann. The most difficult route, **Northern Revival**, was put up in 2008 by Matt McCormick and marked the beginning of his spree of difficult new routes.

DESCENT OPTIONS

There are several descents from the top of the cliff, with the Right End Rappel being the most recommended.

Walk off: It is possible to hike off of either end of the cliff. Both ends have steep loose sections, and approach shoes are recommended.

Partition Rappel: This rappel line is not ideal for several reasons: it's difficult to locate from the top, and there's the potential for stuck ropes on the second rappel and for dropping ropes on other parties. Find the rappel tree at the top of **Partition** (20' from the vague trail at the top of the cliff). Rappel with two ropes to the large tree on the edge of the Slanting Ledge (the top of **Mastercharge**). A second rappel with two ropes takes you to the cliff base; care must be taken to avoid jamming the ropes in the slot just below the tree. (Hint: Jam a stick into the slot.)

Right End Rappel: Walk east (climber's right) on open rock along the top of the cliff and drop down 40' to a lower tree ledge. Continue right along the ledge to a facing wall; follow the wall down to a slab. A 3rd-class descent on this slab for 40' leads to a second tree ledge. The rappel tree is located at the (skier's) left end of this ledge. A 100' rappel leads to the ground, about 150' right of **Prelude**.

The First Adirondack Locals

In the early history of Adirondack climbing, there are precious few "locals." The earliest Adirondack climbers were outsiders, that is, people who did not live year-round in the Adirondacks: Robert Clarke, Newell Martin, John Case, Fritz Wiessner and Jim Goodwin. This makes Stanley "Bud" Smith, Donald LeBeau, and David Bernays of Saranac Lake the earliest-known, home-grown, local climbers to explore Adirondack crags until Geoff Smith's Ski-to-Die group appeared in the mid-1970s at Plattsburgh.

This trio of locals began climbing while they were still students at Saranac Lake High School in the late 1940s. They learned the basics of technical rock and ice climbing from books and magazines and somehow convinced their high school shop teacher to let them forge and temper iron pitons in their shop class. With such home-made implements, they began exploring and climbing the crags and cliffs outside Saranac Lake. They soon became competent, self-taught rock climbers, which they saw as the first step toward becoming mountaineers.

Bernays briefly came under the tutelage of Jim Goodwin. Together, they climbed several rock and ice routes, and Bernays came to realize he had a real talent for ice climbing. However, Smith was the acknowledged leader of this group because he was slightly older. He considered Bernays somewhat off-putting; in his words "a chest-beater," "a blow-hard," someone he could stand only "in small doses." He preferred to climb with the more bearable LeBeau on one day of the weekend, and with Bernays on the other.

Their focus was on the obvious crags seen from Route 73: Cascade Pass, where they explored routes at Pitchoff Chimney, Pitchoff Chimney Cliff and across the road at Cascade Cliff; and down the road at Chapel Pond Pass, where they explored the Washbowl Cliff from upper to lower, spending the most time around the Lost Arrow Pinnacle. On these crags, they put up new routes using aid techniques, all of which have since been freed. Of their routes, today's climbers might be most interested in Pete's Farewell at Pitchoff Chimney Cliff; and Partition, and BBC at Upper Washbowl Cliff.

They did not put up a large number of routes. Oddly, at the time, no one did. From 1940 until John Turner arrived in 1957, a total of only 14 new routes were put up in the Adirondacks, and seven involved Smith, LeBeau, and Bernays. In New Hampshire during this same time period, not a single new route was established until 1954, when Dave Bernays and Andrew Griscom put up a bold ice route, and the first winter ascent, at Whitehorse Ledge. However, in the grand scheme of things, Smith, LeBeau, and Bernays were more active than most.

After high school, Smith went to Paul Smiths College just down the road, and continued to climb with LeBeau and Bernays at every opportunity. While at Paul Smiths, Smith and LeBeau used the nearby Charcoal Kiln Quarry as a practice area.

In the fall of 1950, LeBeau went off to the NYS College of Forestry at Syracuse University, and Bernays to MIT. This meant fewer opportunities to climb together, but they managed to reunite for significant climbs. LeBeau and Smith made the earliest known winter ascent of the Case Route on Wallface Mountain in 1951.

Dave Bernays at the top of the Upper Washbowl, ca 1950. Photo by Stanley Smith.

After 1951, the trio dispersed. LeBeau changed his focus from forestry to x-ray technology, and eventually relocated to Washington State, where he remained an active climber in the North Cascades. In 1962, at 29 years old, he and his climbing partner, Dr. Charles B. Andrews, were swept to their deaths in an "enormous" avalanche on Granite Mountain in the Cascade Mountains. David Bernays went on to make a name for himself in the climbing and mountaineering world: he is clearly the most accomplished of this trio. He made significant ascents in the Alaska Range, in Canada's Cirque of the Unclimbables and Bugaboos, and in Peru. He eventually relocated to Massachusetts, and died suddenly in 1980. Smith stayed in the Adirondacks, but his climbing career ended when the trio dispersed.

It is true that they only put up a few new routes, and it is equally true that they were locally active for only a few years. But one must understand their world at the time. They were just high school kids, and as climbers, they were mostly self-taught. There were no climber paths or guidebooks. They bushwhacked to cliffs that they could see from the road. Most people considered climbing to be a dangerous, dare-devil sport. Smith, LeBeau, and Bernays were bucking the social norms of the time when everyone else was playing it safe, though they probably did not think much of it—they were young and having fun, exploring and challenging themselves on the local cliffs.

\- Dick Tucker

Slanting Ledge

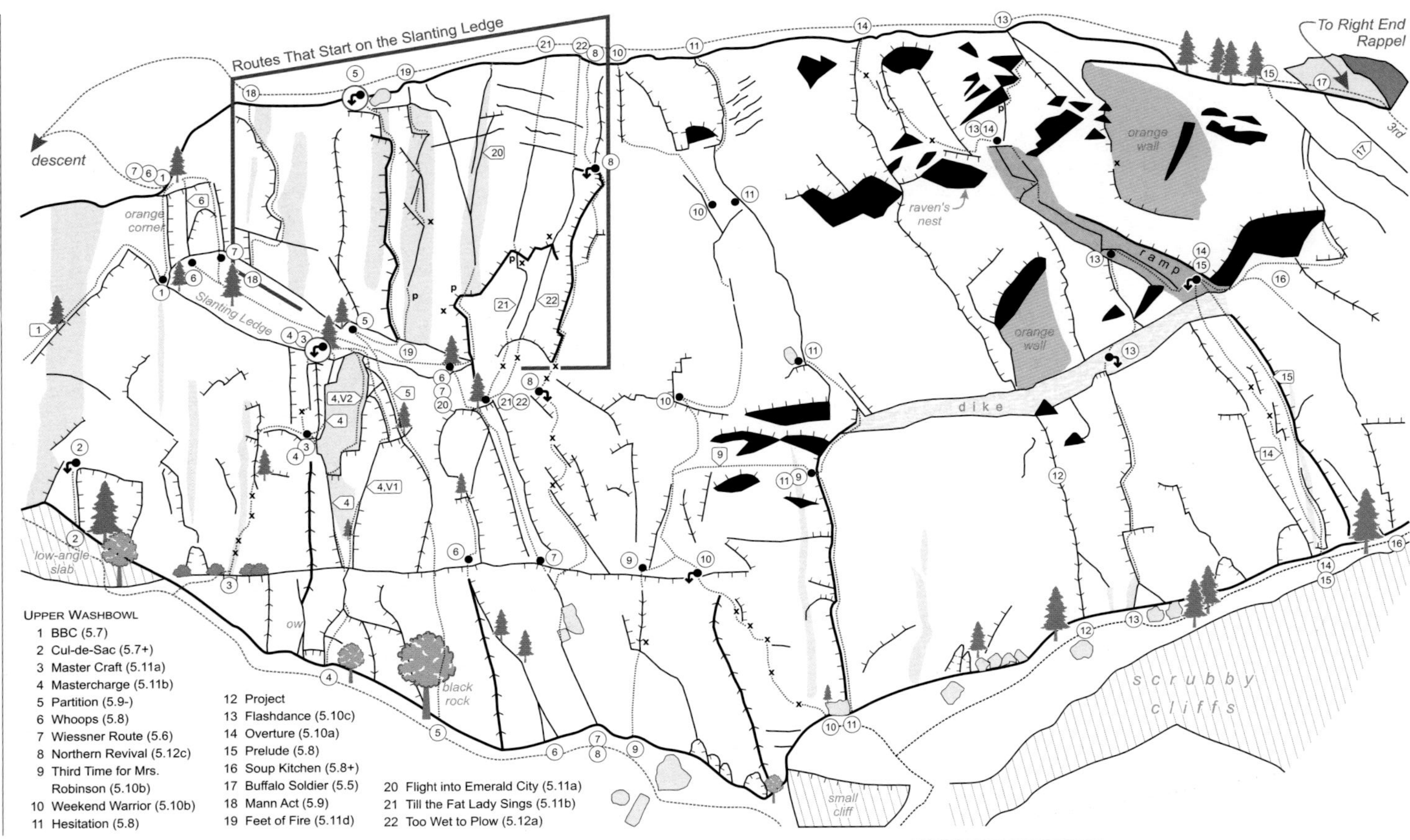
Routes That Start on the Slanting Ledge
To Right End Rappel
3rd
descent
orange corner
Slanting Ledge
raven's nest
orange wall
ramp
orange wall
dike
low-angle slab
ow
black rock
small cliff
scrubby cliffs
UPPER WASHBOWL
1 BBC (5.7)
2 Cul-de-Sac (5.7+)
3 Master Craft (5.11a)
4 Mastercharge (5.11b)
5 Partition (5.9-)
6 Whoops (5.8)
7 Wiessner Route (5.6)
8 Northern Revival (5.12c)
9 Third Time for Mrs. Robinson (5.10b)
10 Weekend Warrior (5.10b)
11 Hesitation (5.8)
12 Project
13 Flashdance (5.10c)
14 Overture (5.10a)
15 Prelude (5.8)
16 Soup Kitchen (5.8+)
17 Buffalo Soldier (5.5)
18 Mann Act (5.9)
19 Feet of Fire (5.11d)
20 Flight into Emerald City (5.11a)
21 Till the Fat Lady Sings (5.11b)
22 Too Wet to Plow (5.12a)

1 BBC 5.7 PG 180' ★

Despite a hard and somewhat desperate start, **BBC** climbs steep features with moderate difficulty. The top pitch, albeit short, is very good. Once known as **RPI-OC**.

Start: At the left end of the cliff is a low-angle slab with the scree-filled descent gully to its left. Scramble to the top of the slab and set up a belay at a cedar island left of a huge right-facing corner. Begin below a right-facing corner on the left wall of the huge corner.

P1 5.7 PG: Climb a right-facing corner past an old piton 20' up that protects the crux. At the top of the corner, traverse right to the sheer black wall. Hand-traverse right past two pitons to easier climbing and a belay at the left end of a long ledge. 90'

P2 5.2 G: Go right across the ledge, step around the edge, and go down a ramp to a tree belay beneath an orange corner. 60'

P3 5.6 G: A boulder problem start gains the orange corner. Climb the corner—which is sustained, exposed, and has a tricky exit—to its top. 30'

FA Jul 30, 1950, Richard Bailey, Dave Bernays, Tris Coffin

2 Cul-de-Sac 5.7+ G 25' ★

Climbs the left side of a large flake; the right side has been climbed at 5.9+.

Start: 20' right of and downhill from **BBC** at the base of a 25'-tall left-facing dihedral.

P1 5.7+ G: Excellent hand jamming leads to a fixed anchor at the top of the dihedral. 25'

3 Master Craft 5.11a G 120' ★★

A steep route with exposed face climbing, a fantastic belay ledge, and a fingercrack finish.

Start: At the left end of the cliff is a low-angle slab with the scree-filled descent gully to its left. At the base of the slab, cut back right onto a tree-covered ledge; begin on the right end of this ledge 30' above the cliff base, below a bolt 10' up.

○ **P1 5.10b G:** Up the steep face to the arête. Step right and climb a right-facing corner behind a tree to a belay ledge. 80'

P2 5.11a G: A demanding face move (bolt-protected) gains a fingercrack just left of the arête that ends at the tree belay shared with **Mastercharge**. 40'

FA Jun 10, 1994, Patrick Purcell, Bob Martin

4 Mastercharge 5.11b G 150' ★★★

The **Mastercharge** wall has excellent climbing and several variations. The height-dependent crux of **Mastercharge** tackles the short headwall at two vertical cracks. Most parties opt for the **Butterflies Are Free** variation, which exits up from and right of the stellar handcrack.

Start: Hike left along the base of the cliff from the approach trail to the second of two prominent right-facing corner systems (the first corner system is the **Wiessner Route**). The left wall of the corner has a long off-width crack on the left side. Begin in the corner.

P1 5.9- G: Up the corner (or the face to the right) to a ledge 30' up. Continue in the corner for a few moves, (V1) then traverse left to a crack on the left wall. The crack widens to perfect hands and leads to a small ledge. (V2) Go left around an arête and belay on an exposed ledge. 90'

P2 5.11b G: Climb the arête to a fingercrack on the right and follow it to the overhanging headwall. Move right and up the twin vertical cracks to the tree belay on the Slanting Ledge. 60'

V1 I'm Committed 5.8+ PG: Continue up the corner toward a tree, then up a crack on the right wall to a tree ledge. Climb the leftmost of two right-facing corners to the Slanting Ledge.

V2 Butterflies Are Free 5.8 G: Go right and up to a ledge beneath a left-facing flake in an orange right-facing corner. Up the corner and flake to the Slanting Ledge.

FA Aug, 1970, David Lovejoy, Dwight Bradley, Ray Crawford
FFA Aug 27, 1985, Don Mellor, Patrick Purcell
FA (V1) May 22, 1994, Peter Ulrich, Mark Rechsteiner
FA (V2) Aug 27, 1975, Greg Newth, Wayne Palmer

5 Partition 5.9- G 260' ★★★★

P2 of this route is the best on the cliff and a classic Adirondack climb. Bring extra hand-sized protection. P1 is seldom climbed; **Butterflies Are Free** is the recommended approach pitch. Promoted to easy 5.9, the **Partition** corner demands sustained jamming and a puzzling offwidth finish.

Start: Midway between the right-facing corner systems of **Mastercharge** and **Wiessner Route** is a blocky buttress that is low-angle to start. Begin in the rightmost right-facing corner on the buttress.

P1 5.7 PG: Up the corner for 40' to a ledge with a wide crack in the left wall. Continue up the steep corner to a broken ledge system that goes up and left to a tree-covered ledge. Climb the rightmost of two right-facing corners to the Slanting Ledge. Belay at a small cedar tree 15' left of a towering right-facing corner. 160'

P2 5.9- G: No route-finding issues here. The towering corner begins with tight hands (crux), relents a bit, and finishes with an intimidating off-width flare. 100'

History: At the top of P2 was a huge foot-thick flake, 4' by 7'. Climbing past this obstacle involved underclinging right under the flake, then grabbing the upper edge to stand on top. (Old descriptions said to "watch the large loose flake at the top.") In 1993, a crowbar removed the flake with surprising ease, creating the off width found today.

FA 1951, Donald Lebeau, Stanley Smith
FFA 1960, John Turner

6 Whoops 5.8 PG 350' ★

A better route than expected. Although the exit move from the P1 slot may be the crux, the start to P2 is committing.

Start: As you hike up and left from the approach trail, this route begins 20' left of the first major corner system (**Wiessner Route**) at a flared slot that leads to a ledge 30' up.

P1 5.8 G: Up the slot and 4" crack (5.8), then cedar-pull to a sloping ledge out left. Climb up and right past perched blocks to a spacious belay at a thin vertical crack. 80'

P2 5.8 PG: An unprotected start (5.8) above perched blocks gains a shallow left-facing corner. Up the corner and vertical crack on the right to a stance with loose flakes. Ascend the obvious right-rising handcrack (much easier than it looks) and join **Wiessner Route**. Belay at the higher of two cedar trees. 90'

P3 Slanting Ledge 3rd class: Traverse the Slanting Ledge up and left to its end beneath a short headwall. Belay beneath the leftmost of two right right-facing corners in the middle of the wall. 150'

P4 5.8 G: A very short pitch of finger jamming in the shallow right-facing corner leads to the top. 30'

FA Sep, 1979, Joe Szot, Tom Rosecrans, Rob Norris

*Jan Wellford on the **Butterflies Are Free** variation (5.8) to **Mastercharge**. With this popular variation, the overall grade of the route is 5.9 . Photo by Drew Haas.*

7 Wiessner Route 5.6 G 335' ★★★

When **Wiessner Route** is viewed from Chapel Pond, it is hard to imagine an easy route to the top of such a steep, tall wall. Wiessner's 1938 ascent of this route is impressive, and its quality continues to lure climbers to its base.

Start: 150' left of where the approach trail meets the cliff is a deep right-facing corner with a low-angle left wall. Begin in the deep corner below a short chimney in the left wall of the corner.

P1 5.6 G: Up the narrowing chimney to a ceiling formed by a rectangular block. Pull on the left side of the block and belly flop (crux) onto its top. Belay immediately after the crux or at a ledge 20' higher. 75'

P2 5.4 G: Work up the depression formed by the main wall on the right and an opposing corner on the left. Exit left (5.4) when the depression ends. Belay at the higher of two cedar trees. 75'

P3 Slanting Ledge 3rd class: Traverse the Slanting Ledge up and left to its end beneath a short headwall. Belay beneath a depression formed by the main face and an opposing right-facing corner. 150'

P4 5.5 G: (V1) Up the right-facing corner that opposes the main wall. Exit left. 35'

V1 5.5 G: Up the left-facing corner that is immediately left of the exit corner (and right of the final corner of **Whoops**).

History: Wiessner, like many climbers, was challenged by the rectangular block on P1. Howorth's comments: "Having observed his labors in circumventing the block, and being naturally lazy, I found a way to traverse from the sloping slab to the top of the block, thereby avoiding the crack, much to Fritz's disgust, and Bob followed." In 1948, Wiessner wrote that this was one of two "technically best rock climbs in the Adirondacks."[3]

FA May 28, 1938, Fritz Wiessner, M. Beckett Howorth, Bob Notman

3 Fritz Wiessner, "Rock Climbing in the Northeast," Intercollegiate Outing Club Association, *IOCA Bulletin* (Winter 1948), p. 46.

8 Northern Revival 5.12c PG 360' ★★★★

Follows the right-facing corner system just right of **Too Wet to Plow**. Amazing position and unique movement with steep bouldery sequences on pinches and slopey crimps, requiring many small cams in a row. Be mindful of the protection, as several gear placements make the difference between this being reasonable and R-rated. With proper rope management you can combine P1 and P2.

Start: Same as **Wiessner Route**.

P1 5.5 G: Climb P1 of **Wiessner Route** to the first big ledge. Traverse to the right end of the ledge below a left-leaning, left-facing corner and belay on small cams. 70'

P2 5.10c PG: Follow the left-facing corner system up and left using many long slings to reduce drag later in the pitch. At the top of the corner, step back right past a bolt and continue up past small cam placements and another bolt to a fixed anchor on a hanging ramp. (Note: A red Alien or large HB offset protect the moves to the anchor.) 80'

P3 5.12c PG: Work up and right past two bolts (crux) and follow the corner until the crack runs out below a small roof (black alien under the roof is the only piece that will fit). Run it out up and right to a shallow left-facing corner and good gear. Pull out right around the corner and up the face to a beautiful ledge and fixed anchor. 150'

P4 5.9 PG: A wonderfully exposed pitch up the very prow of the wall: head up and left and pull around the left side of an arête. Stay just left of the arête past small gear placements to the top. 60'

Gear: RPs, double set of cams to 2", 5 ea 0.4" (#00 C3 or black Alien). Although the gear is thin in the corner, it is solid.

History: The name comes from McCormick getting reinvigorated from climbing in the north country.

FA (P1-P2) Aug 2, 2008, Matt McCormick, Will Roth
FA (P4) Aug 7, 2008, Dave Vuono, Matt McCormick
FA (complete) Aug 16, 2008, Matt McCormick, Naomi Risch

9 Third Time for Mrs. Robinson 5.10b PG 170'

Left of the cliff's prow (just left of the lowest point) is an impressively steep wall. This route climbs beneath the steep wall but escapes out right onto less steep terrain to join **Hesitation**.

Start: 150' left of where the approach trail meets the cliff is a major right-facing corner system (**Wiessner Route**). This route climbs up the steep wall on the right. Begin left of some large blocks.

P1 5.10b G: Up to a low overhang with a small right-facing corner; up this (bolt) to lower-angle rock and a belay at a fixed anchor on a cramped ledge. 70'

P2 5.10b PG: Step right and join **Weekend Warrior**: climb up to a steep right-facing corner. At the top of the corner, climb the right wall (good holds) to a stance left of massive roofs. **Weekend Warrior** continues left, whereas this route traverses right onto a ledge system that passes beneath the massive roofs to the P1 belay on **Hesitation**. 100'

FA (P1) Apr 30, 1984, Michael Stone, Ian Wedmore
FFA Aug 27, 1985, Don Mellor, Patrick Purcell

10 Weekend Warrior 5.10b PG 360'

This route attempts to climb the prow of this cliff. P1, added after the first ascent, is high-quality and popular; above that, the climbing degenerates into loose, dirty face and crack climbing with marginal protection.

Start: From the base of the cliff, where the approach trail arrives, hike right around the low cliffband, then head back left to the base of the cliff where a boulder sits beneath a large right-facing corner with an off-width crack and a ceiling 40' above the base. The right-facing corner is **Hesitation**, and **Weekend Warrior** begins 15' to its left beneath the sheer, bolt-protected face.

● **P1 5.10b G ★★★★:** Increasingly difficult climbing leads to a thin leftward traverse into a left-facing corner. Climb the corner and make a crux move left to a ledge with a fixed anchor. 80'

P2 5.10a PG: Step left and climb a left-rising ramp to a steep right-facing corner. At the top of the corner, climb the right wall (good holds) to a stance left of massive roofs. Step left and climb a dirty face (careful: loose rock) to a sloping belay ledge beneath stepped ceilings. 90'

P3 5.10b PG: Traverse right 20' to a bulging face with a boulder problem move (small gear). Angle right and into a right-facing corner, then follow the corner until it is possible to escape right onto easy slabs. Belay, up and left, in a right-facing corner with shrubs. 90'

P4 5.6 G: Traverse left around an arête and onto a slab. Climb the slab and the left-facing corners above. Step left and climb a tree-filled slot to the top. 100'

FA (P1) Patrick Purcell
FA (P2–P4) Oct 16, 1988, Tim Beaman, Patrick Purcell

*Climber on P1 of **Weekend Warrior** (5.10b).*

*Opposite: Matt McCormick on P3 of **Northern Revival** (5.12c) on the first ascent, belayed by Naomi Risch on the portaledge. Photo by Dave Vuono.*

11 Hesitation 5.8 G (5.5 R) 325' ★★★

John Turner plucked the direct line on this cliff. **Hesitation** has consistent quality, varied climbing, and an exposed traverse under a large roof. Turner's moment of hesitation happened before he committed to the exposed traverse beneath the roofs.

Start: From the base of the cliff where the approach trail arrives, hike right around the low cliffband, then head back left to the base of the cliff where a boulder sits beneath a large right-facing corner with an off-width crack and a ceiling 40' up.

P1 5.8 G: Ascend the 4" crack to an overhang; pass this on the right. Continue up the corner until it is possible to climb a steep crack on the right. Above the crack, easier climbing leads a fixed anchor beneath the massive roofs. 80'

P2 5.7 PG (5.5 R): Move up to the roofs, then hand-traverse right on a positive rail. Continue right until the roof becomes an overhang and you encounter a piton in a small right-facing corner above the lip. Pull up into the corner (3/8" gear) and then run it out up and left to a belay at a good ledge with a vertical crack. 85'

P3 5.5 G: Better than it looks. The vertical crack above the belay leads to low-angle rock past a perched block to a belay beneath a steep right-facing corner. 90'

P4 5.6 G: Up the steep corner to the top. The right wall offers an abundance of good holds. 70'

History: P1 is believed to have been climbed by Fritz Wiessner, date unknown. John Turner recalls climbing the route in 1958 with Brian Rothery, Bob O'Brien, and Irwin Hodgson. Brian Rothery remembers events differently, having led the route with Irwin Hodgson as second. This was particularly memorable for Rothery because, as with **The Arch** on the Poke-O Slab, it gave him the "satisfaction of doing something that [Turner] had not yet done." Incidentally, Rothery credits Turner with making him such a good leader: he always led to "avoid the fear of seconding Turner, so great were the risks that he appeared to take."

FA 1958: John Turner, Brian Rothery, Irwin Hodgson

12 Project

This project attempts to climb the depression left of **Flashdance** to the final corner of **Overture**. Reports of bad rock have prevented completion of this project through the upper steep corners. The route begins left of **Flashdance** below an open book.

13 Flashdance 5.10c PG 275' ★★★

A favorite among local climbers who are looking for a more sustained linkup to P3 of **Overture**. Steep corners and strenuous jamming abound.

Start: Where the approach trail arrives, head right and follow the switchback around the low cliffband to the start of **Hesitation**, then continue right along the base of the cliff. 20' right of an open book with bail slings (the previous project) is a small right-facing corner. Begin below this corner, which starts 8' up and has a water streak coming out of it.

P1 5.9 G: A strenuous start in the right-facing corner ends at a ledge with a left-rising crack. Up the left-rising crack to an overlap. Move right around the overlap and up the right side of an enormous flake. Belay at fixed anchors atop the flake. 75'

P2 5.9+ G: Reach above the belay to a ledge, then hand-traverse right beneath a ceiling and onto a left-rising ramp. Follow the ramp to a vertical fingercrack (5.9+) and a belay on the **Overture** ramp. 60'

P3 5.6 G: There is a vertical step on the ramp with a 4'-high vertical crack. A strenuous jam gains the next step on the ramp, then follow this step to a left-facing wall. Traverse left, climb the wall, and continue left to a belay on a flat ledge with a 0.5" crack in its base. 70'

P4 5.10c PG: Up the vertical crack in an orange, lichen-covered wall to an alcove beneath tiered roofs. An old piton protects the undercling right around the first roof. Move right past a second roof and scramble to the top. 70'

FA (P2) 1983, Chuck Turner, Bill Simes
FA (P4) 1982, Chuck Turner, Bill Simes

14 Overture 5.10a G 300' ★★★

Dramatic entertainment. From the belay for the last pitch, the climbing looks very unlikely, but a masterpiece of route finding reveals an excellent, exposed, committing (yet well-protected) pitch. The scenery isn't too bad, either. Many parties avoid P1 by climbing the excellent P1 of **Prelude**, keeping the overall grade at 5.8. Bring a double set of small cams.

Start: Where the approach trail arrives, head right and follow the switchback around the low cliffband to the start of **Hesitation**, then continue right along the base of the cliff. The right end of the cliff has two left-leaning, right-facing ramps. **Overture** climbs the right-hand ramp. Begin beneath a small left-facing corner 15' up with horns in chocolate-colored rock just out of reach.

P1 5.10a G (5.8 PG): An unprotected start (5.7) leads to the left-facing corner. At its top, step left and gain another short left-facing corner. A bolt protects the left exit (crux) from the corner. Continue to a second, bolt-protected move (possible escape right to **Prelude**). Easy but unprotected climbing leads to a fixed anchor (shared with **Prelude**). 100'

P2 5.6 G: Climb a low-angle left-facing corner left of the belay. At its top, step left to a 4'-high vertical crack. A strenuous jam gains the next step on the ramp, then follow the step to a left-facing wall. Traverse left, climb the wall, and continue left to a belay on a flat ledge with a 0.5" crack in its base (same as **Flashdance**). 100'

P3 5.8 G: Drop down and left from the belay (protecting the second is possible with a microcam). Traverse left across a shelf to a low-angle face where a bolt protects a 5.8 move up to an exposed arête. Up the arête until you can step left into a hidden left-rising ramp. At the top of the ramp, a bolt protects a thrilling foot traverse left into a bottomless dihedral and an easy climb to the top. 100'

FA (P1) Mar 11, 1990, Patrick Purcell, Don Mellor
FA (P2–P3) Jul 10, 1990, Don Mellor, Bill Dodd, Jeff Edwards, R.L. Stolz

15 Prelude 5.8 G 230'

P1 is high-quality and popular. The upper pitches are seldom visited and not recommended.

Start: Where the approach trail arrives, head right and

follow the switchback around the low cliffband to the base of **Hesitation**, then continue right along the base of the cliff. The right end of the cliff has two left-leaning, right-facing ramps. **Prelude** climbs the corner of the right-hand ramp. Begin beneath a left-facing corner 15' up with horns in chocolate-colored rock just out of reach.

P1 5.8 G: An unprotected boulder problem (5.7) gains a left-facing corner and easy climbing to the main corner above. A low crux, at the steepest part of the corner, is followed by more relaxing climbing up the corner to a fixed anchor. 100'

P2 5.6 G: Climb the right-rising crack beneath the enormous roof on the right. Move around an edge, onto a low-angle face, and continue the traverse to a left-facing corner. Belay above the corner at a small stance. 60'

P3 5.7 G: A crack above the belay ascends a low-angle face that leads to a chimney finish. 70'

FA 1975, Grant Calder, John Wald, Mike Leverson

16 Soup Kitchen 5.8+ G 90' ★

This route ascends the new rock that was exposed when **Green Beer** fell into the talus in 2008.

Start: 15' right of **Prelude** at an open book with freshly exposed, white rock. There is a small ceiling 20' up.

P1 5.8+ G: Face climb the left wall of the open book, then up the crack in the open book to a ceiling. Over this to a larger wide ceiling. Break this on the left and continue up left-leaning, blocky terrain to the traverse line on **Prelude**. There are some old, sketchy pitons at the top. 90'

Descent: Either join **Prelude** and finish that route, or climb down and left to the **Prelude** P1 anchor and rappel. 90'

FA (Green Beer) Mar, 1985, Mark Saulsgiver, Terry Saulsgiver

FFA (Green Beer, 5.8) 1986, Joe Szot, Tom Rosecrans, Mike Hay

FA (post rockfall) Oct, 2011, Mark Pugliese, Keith Madia, Billy Morgan

17 Buffalo Soldier 5.5 G 160'

P2 is a pleasant handcrack in a low-angle face with terrific views of Chapel Pond Slab and Emperor Slab.

Start: From the base of **Prelude** and **Overture**, walk right along the base of the cliff for 25' and scramble up onto a ledge. Continue right another 20' to the extreme right end of the cliff, then uphill for 40' to a large left-facing black corner with a protruding fin on the left wall 15' up. The route begins below the left side of this fin, 8' left of the large black left-facing corner (which is the bottom of the Right End Rappel).

P1 5.5 G: Up the crack to the left side of the protruding fin. Continue up the crack through choss to a sloped ledge. Step left and climb straight up aiming for a right-facing corner on the right side of a protruding nose. Up the corner in a shallow 4'-wide chimney to the tree island. 110'

P2 5.5 G: From the left side of the tree island, climb an obvious shallow handcrack in a low-angle slab to a tree belay at the top. 50'

Descent: Walk right 15' and downclimb the slab to the anchor of the Right End Rappel.

FA 1992, Dave Brzykcy, Tony Kozlowski, Pete Cimasi

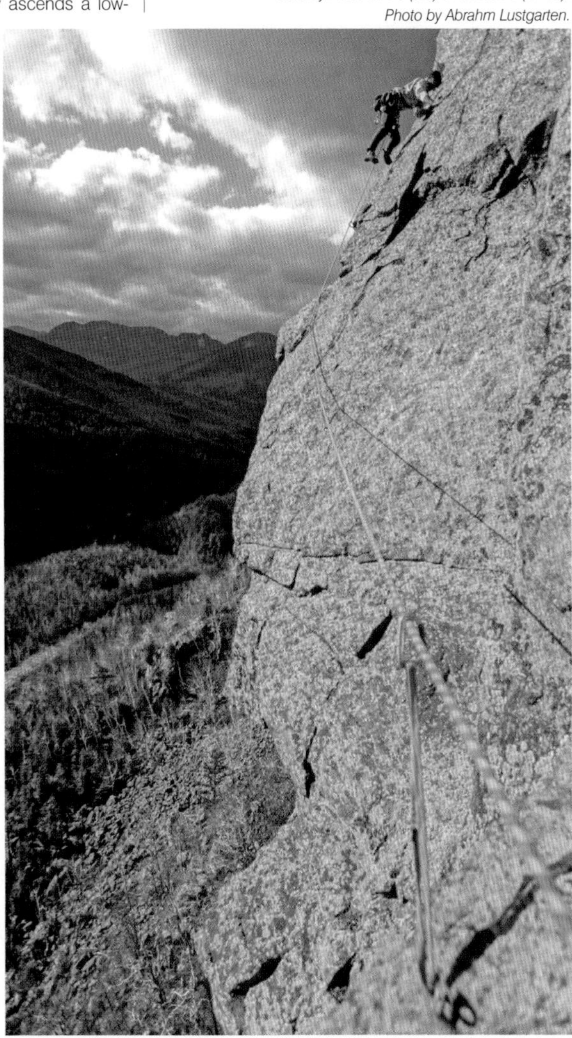

*Jeremy Haas on P3 (5.8) of **Overture** (5.10a). Photo by Abrahm Lustgarten.*

Routes That Start on the Slanting Ledge

These single-pitch routes are on the upper left side of the cliff (above the Slanting Ledge on **Wiessner Route**). They are approached by climbing **Wiessner Route** or any of the other routes that lead to the Slanting Ledge.

18 Mann Act 5.9 R 90'

Short climbers beware! The initial traverse is several grades harder to climb and protect if you can't keep your feet on the ledge. Loose and dirty with tricky protection.

Start: 10' down from and right of the exit pitch of **Wiessner Route** beneath the left end of a horizontal crack that slopes downward to the right.

P1 5.9 R: Climb up and left to big holds. Protect, then traverse down and right following the slanting crack; good gear at the end of the traverse. Pull up into the right-facing, left leaning corner. Follow the stepped corner to an easier finish. 90'

FA Oct 14, 1984, Don Mellor, Bill Simes

19 Feet of Fire 5.11d G (5.10c R) 90'

A very dangerous start that rewards the climber with unrelenting difficulties. The route is brilliantly juxtaposed to the secure handcrack of **Partition** a few feet to its left.

Start: 15' right of the base of the **Partition** exit corner at a vertical seam with a left-facing flake beneath a piton 20' above the Slanting Ledge.

P1 5.11d G (5.10c R): Demanding and unprotected climbing gains a cluster of pitons. Thin face moves (crux) above the pitons lead to a narrow ledge with a bolt. Traverse left, then climb a thin vertical crack (5.11b) to a ledge beneath exit cracks. 90'

FA Jul 27, 1990, Patrick Purcell, Don Mellor

20 Flight into Emerald City 5.11a G 90' ★★★

A great pitch on an exposed face with climbing similar to that of the Spider's Web. Old and unusable fixed gear protects the original start from the left. The recommended start begins 15' to the right.

Start: At the right end of the Slanting Ledge at a right-facing corner beneath a ceiling 20' up.

P1 5.11a G: Up the corner, clip a piton, then climb positive (but friable) rock through the ceiling. Move right to the base of a left-leaning crack. A short crux leads to pleasant jams and a fork in the crack. The easier fork heads right into surprisingly moderate climbing with secure jams and big holds. The finish is a bit dirty. 90'

FA Sep, 1983, Patrick Purcell, Mary Purcell, Tom Skrill
FFA 1985, Harry Brielmann, Tony Trocchi

21 Till the Fat Lady Sings 5.11b G 120' ★★★

Climbs the most continuous crack on the face, offers the best protection, and is more popular than the neighboring climbs.

Start: Below the right end of the Slanting Ledge at the lower of two cedar trees, at a crack that leads to the left end of an arching ceiling.

P1 5.11b G: Climb the crack, then left across friable rock (crux) to a stance beneath the ceiling. Pull over the ceiling and into a right-leaning crack. Sustained climbing up the crack eventually relents to more featured rock near the top. 120'

FA Jul 11, 1990, Don Mellor, Bill Dodd

22 Too Wet to Plow 5.12a G 100'

The most difficult pitch on the cliff follows an incredible crack across the sheer face above **Wiessner Route**. Impressive.

Start: Same as **Till the Fat Lady Sings**.

P1 5.12a G: Climb friable rock (bolt) to a pair of right-rising cracks that lead to the right end of an arching ceiling. Follow the cracks to the ceiling, where a crux reach (bolt) leads to another right-rising fingercrack. Finish up the fractured face left of the cliff's prow. 100'

FA Jul 27, 1990, Don Mellor, Patrick Purcell

WASHBOWL POND

Location	On the Zander Scott Trail (formerly the Giant Ridge Trail), accessed from the Giant Mountain Trailhead at Chapel Pond
Summary	A number of seldom-visited cliffs scattered on the hillside above Washbowl Pond.

-5.6	5.7	5.8	5.9	5.10	5.11	5.12	5.13+	total
3	2	6	5	1	1			18

The Washbowl Pond cliffs are a mixed bunch. There are a few quality routes, but the development thus far has been somewhat disappointing. There is certainly potential here, with the Future Wall being the most promising.

HISTORY

The first visitor to the area was Jeff Edwards, who explored the largest and most obvious cliff, the Banana Belt, in 1989. Tom DuBois was the next to record routes here, in 1993 and '94. He spent hours thrashing through brush examining nearly all of the exposed rock. If you have any doubts about his dedication, go find and climb **Solitude**. Various other people have climbed here, and there are rumors of other routes, backed by some evidence (anchors on dirty cliffs).

DIRECTIONS (MAP PAGE 251)

Park at the trailhead for Giant Mountain, 0.2 mile from the Chapel Pond pullout (when you're driving toward Malfunction Junction). Follow the Zander Scott Trail (formerly the Giant Ridge Trail), marked with blue disks, uphill for 30 min (0.7 mile) to Washbowl Pond. There is a three-way intersection here 600830,4888428 from which all other approaches are described. (From the three-way intersection, the signs indicate 0.7 mile to Chapel Pond, 1.0 mile to Roaring Brook Falls Trail, 0.8 mile to the Nubble, and 2.2 miles to the summit of Giant.)

Washbowl Pond

CHAPEL POND VIEWPOINT

Aspect	West
Height	20'
Quality	
Approach	30 min, moderate
Summary	A short, overhanging wall with a single lead route.

DIRECTIONS **(MAP PAGE 251)**

This is the first major viewpoint on the Zander Scott Trail and about 230' before you reach the three-way trail intersection at the south end of Washbowl Pond. Walk (skier's) left to scramble down to the base of the wall 600816,4888359.

1 Panorama 5.9 G 20'

Jokingly described by Mellor as "reminiscent of the Yellow Spur and other fine lines."

Start: In the center of the wall below a shallow left-facing corner that begins 6' up, and 3' right of a large, 10'-high open book.

P1 5.9 G: Climb up the shallow corner and angle right to the top. 20'

FA 1997, Don Mellor

Washbowl Pond

WALL OF SORROWS

Aspect	West
Height	100'
Quality	
Approach	45 min, moderate
Summary	A steep black wall that is disappointingly dirty, although it does have potential.

The Wall of Sorrows has several right-leaning cracks; **Manic Depression** climbs the rightmost of these. Uphill on its left end is a black, smooth shield of rock. The base of the cliff is open and pleasant.

DIRECTIONS **(MAP PAGE 251)**

From the three-way trail intersection at the south end of Washbowl Pond, follow the trail marked with red disks toward the Roaring Brook Falls Trail for 0.4 mile to the height of land. After you pass the north end of the pond, there are numerous cliffs that can be glimpsed through the trees on the right. This is the last such cliff: about 150' before the trail descends is a cairn on the right; turn right here and contour 200' to the base of the wall 600357,4888841.

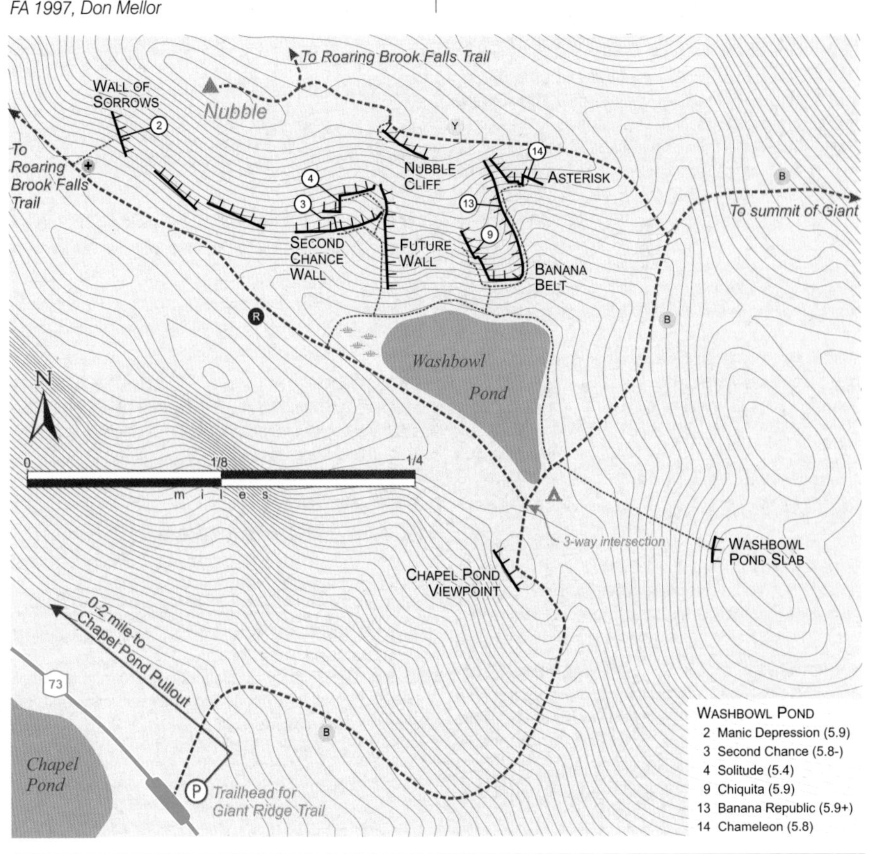

2 Manic Depression 5.9 G 80'

Climbs the obvious crack system and angles up and right behind a very tall pine tree. It looks much better than it is. Named for a Jimi Hendrix song.

Start: 30' downhill from and right of a large black face and 10' left of a spruce that grows up against the rock below a thin crack in a black streak. This is 4' right of a broken right-facing corner capped by a small blocky ceiling 20' up.

P1 5.9 G: Climb the crack to a small sloped ledge, then up a smaller crack to a larger ledge. Step right behind the tree and follow the right-leaning crack to its end in the middle of the headwall. Step down and traverse right on small holds to another crack (very dirty), then climb it to a ledge. 80'

Descent: Rappel from trees.

FA Jun 16, 2007, Jim Lawyer, Don Mellor

Washbowl Pond

FUTURE WALL

This west-facing wall holds the greatest potential for new routes at Washbowl Pond. It is a sheer wall, perhaps 90' high, with an attractive flat base and very clean rock. Across the middle is a right-rising horizontal crack. The right side has a left-facing scooped corner.

DIRECTIONS **(MAP PAGE 251)**

From the three-way intersection at the south end of Washbowl Pond, follow the trail marked with red disks toward the Roaring Brook Falls Trail. At the end of the pond, hike up the hillside to the base of the wall 600672,4888679. You can also contour left for a few minutes from the base of the Banana Belt.

Washbowl Pond

SECOND CHANCE WALL

Aspect	Southwest
Height	40'
Quality	
Approach	45 min, moderate
Summary	A short, steep black wall with a single route.

This wall faces the Future Wall; the two walls meet to form a nasty 4th-class gully (the approach to the Solitude Wall). The base of the cliff is open, sloped away from the rock, and covered in weeds.

DIRECTIONS **(MAP PAGE 251)**

To approach, first find the Future Wall. Walk left to the gully and cross it to the opposite wall, then walk downhill and left along its base to reach the route at a very black wall 600607,4888735, just right of a wall with orange lichen.

3 Second Chance 5.8- G 40' ★

A short route on black rock, named because it took DuBois two visits to get it.

Start: 25' right of a 15'-high pointed white tower, on top of some ledges on the right side of the black face below a left-facing black corner.

P1 5.8- G: Climb up and left across the face to a slot formed by a right-rising ceiling. Angle up and right following cracks to the top. 40'

FA Sep 18, 1994, Tom DuBois

Washbowl Pond

SOLITUDE WALL

Aspect	East
Height	40'
Quality	
Approach	50 min, difficult
Summary	A short wall with a nice crack (albeit short and easy) but very difficult to reach.

DIRECTIONS **(MAP PAGE 251)**

To approach, first find the Future Wall. Walk left to the gully (where the Second Chance Wall and the Future Wall meet) and ascend this to the next tree ledge through a brief 4th-class section. On the tree ledge, walk downhill and left along the base of the wall to an east-facing wall with a crack in it 600618,4888763.

Better yet, climb Second Chance.

4 Solitude 5.4 G 40' ★

Start: 15' downhill from and left of the large left-facing corner formed where the two walls meet, below a right-leaning crack.

P1 5.4 G: Climb the right-leaning crack for 10' to a triangular pod, then straight up the crack to a cedar. 40'

FA Sep 18, 1994, Tom DuBois

Washbowl Pond

NUBBLE CLIFF

Aspect	Southwest
Height	100'
Quality	
Approach	1 hr, moderate
Summary	A cliff of corners and arêtes with some loose rock, situated high on the Nubble ridgeline.

-5.6	5.7	5.8	5.9	5.10	5.11	5.12	5.13+	total
1	1	1						3

The Nubble Cliff is up on a ridge near the Nubble, a small summit on the side of Giant. From Washbowl Pond, the cliff is visible high above and left of the Banana Belt, up by the ridge. This cliff is accessed via an offshoot trail that goes to the summit of the Nubble.

The cliff presently has only a few routes, but it has a pretty summit with views of Washbowl Pond and the Chapel Pond valley.

DIRECTIONS **(MAP PAGE 251)**

From the three-way intersection at the south end of Washbowl Pond, follow the trail with the blue markers toward the summit of Giant. After 0.3 mile (and 1.0 mile from the road), the trail reaches an intersection with the Nubble Trail; turn left and follow the trail with the yellow markers toward the Nubble, uphill and onto the ridge. The trail descends into a small notch on the ridge; just after the notch is a large viewpoint and the top of the Nubble Cliff.

From the viewpoint, continue on the trail another 200' to where it meets a low wall in the woods. Leave the trail and follow the base of the wall down and left into a steep gully, eventually breaking (skier's) left to the base of the wall 600682,4888830. The first corner is the base of High Anxiety.

5 High Anxiety 5.5 G 80' ★★★

This pretty arête is enhanced by its position high on the Nubble ridge.

Start: In a large open book sheltered in the trees with a wide crack and many horizontals on the left wall. The right wall of the corner is 12' high and has a large ledge on top.

P1 5.5 G: Climb up the corner, then straight up the arête using good cracks and big holds to a lone pine tree at the top. 80'

Descent: Rappel, or scramble up easy rock to the top of the cliff.

FA Oct 3, 1993, Tom DuBois

6 Steve's Flakes 5.7 G 90' ★

Start: Same as High Anxiety.

P1 5.7 G: Climb up the corner to the large ledge on the right. Climb up right to left-facing flakes (about 10' right of the High Anxiety arête), then climb the flakes to the lone pine. 90'

FA Sep, 1993, Steve Adler

7 Howdy, Hiker 5.8 PG 110' ★

Start: Same as High Anxiety.

P1 5.8 PG: Climb up the corner to the large ledge on the right. Walk right to the next corner and climb it to the top, ending just below the hiking trail. 110'

FA Sep, 1993, Tom DuBois

Washbowl Pond

BANANA BELT

Aspect	Southwest, south, and east
Height	110'
Quality	★
Approach	45 min, moderate
Summary	Largest formation in the Washbowl Pond with climbing on two sides.

-5.6	5.7	5.8	5.9	5.10	5.11	5.12	5.13+	total
	1	1	2	1	1			6

The Banana Belt is the largest exposed rock at Washbowl Pond. From the south end of the pond, the south face of the Banana Belt is obvious above the opposite side of the pond. The south face, however, has no routes; the existing routes are located on the off-vertical Left Side (which faces southwest) or the surprisingly sheer Right Side (which faces east).

The best climbing at Washbowl Pond is on the Left Side 600797,4888673.

DIRECTIONS **(MAP PAGE 251)**

From the three-way intersection at the south end of Washbowl Pond, contour halfway around the pond until you're below the cliff, then bushwhack uphill 300' through the forested talus to the base of the wall. Go left or right as desired.

Left Side

The Left Side of the Banana Belt faces southwest and offers the best climbing at Washbowl Pond. The base of the cliff is sloped, but open and pleasant. The most obvious feature on the face is the large right-facing corner of **El Niño**.

8 Dole Me 5.8+ PG 75' ★

Start: 30' uphill from and left of the large arête of **El Niño** is a big cedar. This route begins on the mossy off-vertical face in front of the cedar below a right-diagonaling broken crack that starts 4' up.

P1 5.8+ PG: Climb the crack up and right to meet a left-leaning crack, then follow it to a prominent right-rising horizontal. Climb up and left, aiming for a prominent cedar left of a block ceiling. 75'

Gear: Include RPs and small TCUs.

FA May 18, 1990, Jeff Edwards, Patrick Purcell

9 Chiquita 5.9 PG 60' ★★★

Very good face climbing that ends on a ledge with a sick-looking cedar; needs a new anchor.

Start: 5' left of the large right-facing corner of **El Niño** below a thin vertical crack.

P1 5.9 PG: Climb up the crack, then straight up the face to a ledge below a broken ceiling. 60'

FA May 18, 1989, Jeff Edwards, Patrick Purcell

10 Banana Hammock 5.11a G 60' ★★

Quality moves on an arête. The critical tricky placement was rehearsed on rappel and involved inserting a medium-sized nut into a hole and turning it 90°; bomber.

Start: Same as **El Niño**.

P1 5.11a G: Climb the **El Niño** corner for 15', then traverse left to a small left-facing corner on the arête. A blind placement (#00 TCU) allows you to get established on the arête, then climb past a black face (crux, tricky gear placement) to a fingercrack. At the top of the crack, step left onto the face to a ledge below a broken ceiling. 60'

FA Jun 16, 2007, Jim Lawyer, Don Mellor

11 El Niño 5.7 G 120' ★

Start: At the large, clean right-facing corner, 120' uphill from and left of the toe of the buttress.

P1 5.7 G: Climb the right-facing corner, then angle up and right on the slab below the right-leaning corner, aiming for a spike of rock. Belay at a good crack. 80'

P2 5.5 G: Climb up a left-leaning crack to trees. 40'

Descent: Go up and right through trees to a good ledge. Walk right to the right side of the buttress and rappel.

FA Apr 11, 1995, Don Mellor, Chuck Bruha

Right Side

The Right Side of the Banana Belt faces east and is surprisingly sheer (and surprisingly dirty).

12 Banana Splitter 5.10 G 90'

Very dirty and virtually unclimbable now. Rumored to have been climbed by Tim Beaman.

Start: 200' up the slope from the toe of the buttress is a very large pine tree 10' from the cliff. This route begins 50' right of the pine tree at a crack that arches left in a V-groove.

P1 5.10 G: Climb up the crack, then up to the parallel "bear-hugging" cracks and follow them to the top. 90'

13 Banana Republic 5.9+ TR 60' ★

150' downhill from the right end of the wall is a wide tree-filled depression with a clean arête on its right side. This route climbs the arête, beginning 15' right of the depression and just right of a shallow, mossy grotto. 15' to the right is a very large double-trunked birch tree. Climb broken cracks, then up through angular compact rock to a tree at the top.

FA (TR) May 18, 1989, Jeff Edwards

Washbowl Pond

ASTERISK

Aspect	Southwest
Height	80'
Quality	
Approach	50 min, moderate
Summary	A single adventure route on an otherwise unappealing cliff.

The Asterisk is a small rock outcropping, visible from the pond, positioned right of and even with the top of the Banana Belt. It is said that the cracks intersect to form an asterisk, but from the pond, the cliff simply looks diamond-shaped, split by a vertical line (which is the corner and crack of **Cameleon**).

DIRECTIONS **(MAP PAGE 251)**

Walk up the right side of the Banana Belt. Just before the height of the slope, and 30' above a large double-trunked birch tree (which marks the start of **Banana Republic**), walk right over large boulders to a small amphitheater with a low "nose" of rock on the right side. Uphill from and right of this nose is a face and the start of **Cameleon** 600823,4888797.

14 Chameleon 5.8 G 80'

One of the loosest-looking corners around (the left wall looks as if it would crumble if touched), but the rock is more solid than it appears. Oddly enough, one is strangely compelled to climb it.

Start: The left side of the face has a right-rising roof that meets an opposing left-rising roof. At their junction is a short right-facing corner, below which is a thin crack in a white face. Begin directly below this crack.

P1 5.8 G: Climb up the thin crack in the white face into the corner and through the junction of the notch formed by the right-hand roof. Continue up the crack in the right-arching corner to a tree with a fixed anchor. 80'

FA Oct 9, 1993, Tom DuBois

Washbowl Pond

WASHBOWL POND SLAB

This small slab lies above the south end of Washbowl Pond. Although it looks good from a distance, there are only a couple of hard moves at the bottom (dirty 5.9), then 5.2 to the top. The slab does offer unique views of the other cliffs scattered around the pond as well as those at Chapel Pond from the King Wall rightward to the Gully Cliff.

From the three-way intersection at the south end of Washbowl Pond, walk up the trail toward the summit of Giant for 200', then bushwhack up the hill on a bearing of 116° to the base of the slab 601055,4888381. The slab is a narrow feature, so there's a good chance you'll miss it and have to hunt around for it. The route **Slab with a View** was climbed by Tom DuBois (Sep 1993).

Washbowl Pond

GIANT'S SECRET

Aspect	Southwest
Height	45'
Quality	★
Approach	1 hr, moderate
Summary	Several short routes in a unique slot canyon high on the Zander Scott Trail.

-5.6	5.7	5.8	5.9	5.10	5.11	5.12	5.13+	total
1		2	1					4

The Giant's Secret offers several short climbs in a unique slot canyon filled with ferns and birches, high on the Zander Scott Trail. The canyon slopes gently downhill to the southeast, and the climbs are located on the left wall of the canyon as you approach. The first obvious feature will be the bolt on **Little Secret**. On the right wall of the canyon is a fingercrack 2' right of an arête; across from this is **This, Too, Shall Pass**.

DIRECTIONS **(MAP PAGE 251)**

From the three-way intersection at the south end of Washbowl Pond, continue on the Zander Scott Trail (blue markers) for 0.3 mile to the turnoff to the Nubble (1.0 mile from the road). Continue on the trail steeply uphill for another 0.4 mile, up some new switchbacks, to the first open rock ledges. At this point, the trail passes a large bread loaf–shaped boulder that sits on a slab below a headwall. At the point where the trail meets the slab 601305,4888832, contour right through thick vegetation, staying below a cliff face. After 5 min, the cliff face becomes the left wall of a secret 40'-wide slot canyon; the climbs are on the left wall 601376,4888787.

15 Little Secret 5.9 G 40' ★★

Start: Below a bolt, 10' to the right of and downhill from a pointed boulder that sits on the ground in front of the face.

P1 5.9 G: Good holds lead up the face (crux, bolt) to a ledge. Step right and finish in an awkward left-leaning off width to the trees. 40'

FA Jun 18, 2000, Tom DuBois

16 Nobber 5.8 G 60' ★

Start: 50' right of **Little Secret** at overhanging left-leaning, right-facing stepped corners with a blocky knob 6' up.

P1 5.8 G: Struggle up over the knob, then straight up to the top of the corners. Step right, then follow left-rising ramps to trees at the top. 60'

FA Jun 18, 2000, Tom DuBois

17 Let It Dry 5.6 G 50'

Tends to be wet in the spring.

Start: 20' right of **Nobber** on the left side of a chocolate- and black-colored wall, at a vertical crack that begins above three ledges.

P1 5.6 G: Climb the ledges to the crack, up the crack, then up through an easy section to a short headwall. Finish just left of an overhanging perched pancake-block. 50'

FA Jun 25, 2000, Tom DuBois, Ellen DuBois

18 This, Too, Shall Pass 5.8 G 80'

Start: At a shallow, blocky right-facing corner, left of a short wall with right-rising cracks, and 20' right of the steepest part of an overhanging black wall. On the opposite wall of the slot canyon is a fingercrack 2' right of an arête.

P1 5.8 G: Climb the corner to a ledge 15' up, then up several more dirty ledges to the base of an overhanging 20'-tall black face with a handcrack. Climb the crack (crux) to the top, finishing just left of a large boulder on a ledge. 80'

FA Jun 25, 2007, Michelle Burlitch, Jim Lawyer

SERAC WALL

Location	North side of NY 73, accessed from the Giant Mountain Trailhead at Chapel Pond
Aspect	Southwest
Height	70'
Quality	
Approach	1 min, easy
Summary	An easily accessed scrappy cliff with a couple of routes.

-5.6	5.7	5.8	5.9	5.10	5.11	5.12	5.13+	total
1		1	1	1				4

This is the overlooked cliff adjacent to the Giant Mountain Ridge Trailhead and directly across the road (NY 73) from The Aquarium. It is a short (1-min) approach from the parking area. An offshoot of Dipper Brook runs between the road and the cliff.

DIRECTIONS **(MAP PAGE 197)**

Park as for Chapel Pond Slab, then walk to the end of the parking area toward Chapel Pond. Walk into the woods perpendicular to the road until you come to a cliff. Walk left to reach a distinctive fin of rock, the route **Edge of the Valley**. About 100' left through the talus is another section of rock with the routes **Paradise Now** and **Stagger and Swerve**.

1 Paradise Now 5.8+ G 60' ★★

This route and the next one are on the far left end of the cliff, nearest the hiking trail.

Start: 30' from the stream at the toe of the buttress, below a V-groove with a handcrack in the back. Leaning up against the left wall of the V-groove is an 8'-high spike of rock with a pointed top. About 15' right of the route is a large roof 30' up.

P1 5.8+ G: From the top of the spike, step left and follow the prominent 3'-wide rib to beneath the first bulge. Step left into the chimney and up this a few feet, then out right onto the rib again. Climb through the second bulge (crux; piton) to the top. 60'
History: Slings found on the first ascent indicate previous activity.
ACB Oct 7, 2007, Tad Welch, Bill Widrig

2 Stagger and Swerve 5.6 G 60' ★

Start: Same as Paradise Now.
P1 5.6 G: Follow the handcrack in the back of the V-groove immediately right of Paradise Now up to an overhang with a birch tree and a dangerous-looking chockstone (very solid, though) at midheight. Move out left to avoid the seraclike flake to a fixed anchor at the top on a cedar tree. 60'
FA Oct 6, 2006, Tad Welch (roped solo)

3 Edge of the Valley (aka The Shark's Fin) 5.10d TR 70' ★★

Climbs an amazing blade of rock. First, find the obvious fin of rock, about 100' right of Stagger and Swerve: on the left side of the fin is a deep V-chimney with a towering block that leans across the gap and touches the fin, and to the right is a giant dead birch. Begin at the toe of the buttress below the fin and climb broken, chossy rock to gain the fin, then follow it to the top.
FA (TR) Apr, 1989, Patrick Purcell, Paul Nelson

4 Cheap Money 5.9+ PG 50'

Start: On the face 5' right of the fin and left of a shallow chimney.
P1 5.9+ PG: Climb up the face and through the roof to gain cracks, then follow the cracks to the top. 50'
FA Apr, 1989, Patrick Purcell, Paul Nelson

OUTLET WALL

Location	South side of NY 73, accessed from the Chapel Pond Outlet
Aspect	Southwest
Height	50'
Quality	
Approach	2 min, easy
Summary	A steep wall with several face routes in a shady location near the camping area of Chapel Pond.

-5.6	5.7	5.8	5.9	5.10	5.11	5.12	5.13+	total
			1	1	2	1		5

Descriptions: This was once a popular spot, but the bolts have been removed on two of the good routes, relegating this to toproping. Regardless, this is a nice place if you're camping and need an evening pump.

DIRECTIONS (MAP PAGE 197)
Park at the Chapel Pond Outlet 599915,4888423, cross the stream at the camping sites, and walk upstream (toward Chapel Pond) until you reach the face on the right 599853,4888463, directly above the beaver dam.

1 Lessons in Guiding 5.9 G 30'

Start: 6' uphill from and left of Pepé Le Pew below some knobby ledges.
P1 5.9 G: Climb up the knobby ledges, then up the crack to the top. 30'
FA 1988, R.L. Stolz, Karen Kelch

2 Pepé Le Pew 5.10a TR 40'

This route begins 25' uphill from and left of the lowest point on the wall below right-facing cracks that lead to a 1'-wide fissure 15' up. Climb up to the fissure, then up the shallow cracks directly above to a final crux move before the top.
FA (TR) Aug 16, 1995, Christian Buckley

3 Silver Chicken 5.11b R 50'

The bolts have been removed.
Start: 10' uphill from and left of Mother Nature, below a short, shallow, 5'-high left-facing corner that leads to a left-leaning crack.
P1 5.11b R: Climb the crack to its end at a small triangular pod, then up the face past a bolt to the top. 50'
FA Sep 2, 1988, Bill Pierce

4 Mother Nature 5.11b PG 50' ★

The bolts have been removed.
Start: At the low point in the center of the face, 10' left of Rasp, below a left-facing flake 15' up.
P1 5.11b PG: Climb up to a bolt, then up the left-facing flake past a second bolt and up and left to the top. 50'
FA Jun 27, 1988, Patrick Purcell, Bill Pierce

5 Rasp 5.12 TR 45'

This route begins at the right end of the cliff just before the right-rising slabby ramp on the right below a faint crack. Climb this straight up through left-facing flakes (crux) to a second set of left-facing flakes. Head up and left to a detached block at the top. You can avoid the crux by moving left before the flakes, then straight up to the detached block, called Passing By (5.11a).
FA (TR) Aug 9, 1997, Kenny Clarke

P.E. WALL

Location	South side of NY 73, accessed from the Chapel Pond Outlet
Aspect	Northeast
Height	100'
Quality	
Approach	20 min, difficult
Summary	Some rarely climbed routes in a scenic setting above the pond guarded by a nasty approach.

-5.6	5.7	5.8	5.9	5.10	5.11	5.12	5.13+	total
	2	1	1					4

The P.E. Wall, located above the outlet of Chapel Pond, is a large cliff with a collection of corners at its right end. The routes J.E. 26, Synchronized Swimming, and Badminton 101 climb these corners. In the center is a large right-leaning depression (the winter route As You Like It), and left of this is a more unbroken section with the route Crab Soccer.

The cliff can be observed from the shore below the Chapel Pond pullout. With some effort, this cliff could have several more routes, especially on its left side.

Despite appearances, the cliff is difficult to reach.

HISTORY

The cliff was first explored by Patrick Purcell and Jeff Edwards in 1988, and the wall's name reflects their initials.

Upper P.E. Wall

DIRECTIONS (MAP PAGE 197)

To approach the Upper P.E. Wall, you must reach the base of the central section of the wall. A boat makes this trivial: simply paddle to the shore at the base of the wall, then bushwhack up and left along the base of a small amphitheater (this has several winter routes, including **Laceration**). You can also approach this as for **Synchronized Swimming**, then bushwhack down and left (horrible 4th-class in sections) to reach the base of the wall left of the **Laceration** amphitheater. Either way, continue up the gully to a waterfall where some 4th-class moves are required. Continue up the gully above the waterfall for 40' to the base of a black wall.

At the left end of the black wall is a very wet area (the start of the winter route **H14**).

1 Crab Soccer 5.7+ PG 150' ★★

In terms of quality, this route has been compared to **Pegasus** (almost).

Start: Just right of center on the black wall is a right-leaning crack-flake with two cedars. (This is the same start as the winter route **Spike**.)

P1 5.7+ PG: Climb past the cedars, then up into a left-facing shallow corner in white rock with a crack. Follow the crack, which continues up and angles left to the top. 150'

FA Jun, 1995, Don Mellor, Jeff Edwards

Corners Area

As its name implies, this is an area of corners, located on the upper right end of the cliff. From the correct viewpoint, you can see that these corners are separated by 18" cracks.

DIRECTIONS (MAP PAGE 197)

From the Chapel Pond Outlet, cross the outlet stream and contour around the marshy north end of Chapel Pond. Thick bushwhacking over boulders near the shore of the lake leads under a 60'-high wall with an open area below. About 70' past this, heinously clutch and claw uphill following a vague gully (Dead Rabbit Gully). Another way to find this gully is to continue along the shoreline until you get cliffed, then turn around and find the first gully, which should be Dead Rabbit Gully. Either way, head up the gully to a sheer orange wall, then turn left and slightly downhill to find the starting corner. The vegetation here is thick, especially in the middle of the summer, so expect to do some hunting around to find the initial corner. It takes about 20 min from the outlet to reach the base of the wall.

DESCENT OPTIONS

There is a fixed anchor on a tree at the top of **Badminton 101**; a 100' rappel returns to the base of the starting corner.

2 J.E. 26 5.8 R 120' ★★

Well-protected cruxes with run-out squeeze-chimney climbing in between; easier than it looks, with hidden edges on the left wall. The climbing is secure if you're small and can squeeze parts of your body into the crack. The route name is derived from Edwards's initials and the fact that he had just turned 26.

Start: Same as **Synchronized Swimming**.

P1 5.5 G: Climb the handcrack on the right wall of the corner for 20' up to a stance. Make an awkward step left onto the large tree ledge that sits above the left wall

of the corner. Walk left 25' to a black face on the far side of the tree ledge and climb a very dirty crack past a cedar to a comfy cave belay on a ledge with a birch tree. 60'

P2 5.8 R: Above the belay, climb around the first ceiling with the chockstone and up to the second ceiling. Climb out left under the ceiling to a bolt, then up the 15" crack using positive features on the left wall for 30' to a second bolt on the right. Continue up the 15" crack to trees at the top. 60'

Descent: Climb down and right 6' to a ledge with a fixed anchor on a tree (the top of **Synchronized Swimming**).

FA Aug 13, 1988, Patrick Purcell, Jeff Edwards

3 Badminton 101 5.9 G 110'

Start: Same as **Synchronized Swimming**.

P1 5.9 G: Follow **J.E. 26** to the large tree ledge. Walk 10' left on the tree ledge to an overhanging corner with jammed flakes. Climb up the corner and around a pointed nose, then up the 20" crack to the fixed anchor at the top (shared with **Synchronized Swimming**). 110'

Descent: Rappel from the fixed anchor, 100'.

FA Aug 2, 1988, Patrick Purcell, Mary Purcell

4 Synchronized Swimming 5.7 G 100' ★

Start: At a corner that faces left (when viewed with your back to Chapel Pond) filled with scrubby cedars and moss. The corner sits on a steep dirt slope with trees that show signs of recent pruning. The dirty left wall of the corner is 20' high, on top of which is a broad tree ledge. The route begins on the narrow right wall of the corner at a clean handcrack 4' right of the corner.

P1 5.5 G: Climb the handcrack 10' to a stance, then step left and climb a thin fingercrack to another ledge. Move left into the corner and follow it to a ledge. 60'

P2 5.7 G: (V1) Climb the right-leaning finger- and handcrack to the top. 40'

V1 5.5 G: This variation climbs the handcrack on the face around the corner to the left of the belay ledge. From the ledge, downclimb to a narrow ledge with trees, traverse left into the large corner of **Badminton 101**, then climb up a few feet until you can move right to a handcrack on the face. Follow the handcrack past a cedar to the fixed anchor at the top.

Descent: Rappel from the fixed anchor, 100'.

FA Aug 2, 1988, Patrick Purcell, Mary Purcell

Watercolor by Lucie Wellner.

SPIDER'S WEB

Location	North side of NY 73, accessed from the Chapel Pond Outlet
Aspect	Southwest
Height	160'
Quality	★★★★★
Approach	15 min, easy
Summary	Overhanging finger- and handcracks on a sheer wall; extremely popular, as it is perhaps the only cliff of its type in the Northeast.

-5.6	5.7	5.8	5.9	5.10	5.11	5.12	5.13+	total
		1	3	7	13	5	2	31

Housing some of the cleanest, purest, and most difficult cracks in the Adirondack Park, the Spider's Web is one of the best cliffs in the Adirondacks. The sheer overhanging face is virtually unbroken by ledges and crisscrossed with a web of vertical cracks. For this reason, before any routes had even been climbed here, the face was known as the Spider's Web.

Climbing at the Web is relentless and pumpy. The hand jams and finger locks can be very secure, but linking an entire pitch of overhanging jamming is a real test of your endurance.

Due to the aspect, the Web gets climbed year-round. On a sunny day in March, you can warm up by climbing ice at Chapel Pond, then posthole up to the Web and climb sunny cracks in the afternoon. Another unique feature of the cliff is that it stays relatively dry in the rain.

The cliff has several major features that will assist you in getting oriented. It has a shorter wall on the left that is separated from the larger wall on the right by the huge right-facing corner of **Slim Pickins**. In front of the shorter wall is a low cliff that makes an excellent perch for photographing routes such as **It's Only Entertainment** and **Esthesia**. Along the base of the cliff's central section is a boulder-filled trench—a deep gash from which routes such as **Mr. Rogers' Neighborhood** and **Drop, Fly, or Die** begin. Above the right end of the boulder-filled trench is a vertical fracture of giant blocks and cracks—this is the line of **The Key**; right of this is the steepest section of the cliff, home to **Romano's Route**, **White Knight**, and **On the Loose**. The Traverse Ledge, between **Esthesia** and **Mr. Rogers' Neighborhood**, has several fixed anchors that facilitate one-pitch cragging as well as provide a convenient walk-off.

HISTORY

Tom Rosecrans, one of the early visitors to the cliff, recalls that the Spider's Web was originally used as a practice cliff for aid climbing. The first route, **Yvonne**, climbed by members of the Canadian Alpine Club in 1968, was an aid route, as were many of the early routes (**Esthesia**, **Zabba**, **Lycanthropia**, and **White Knight**). Free climbing took hold in the 1970s, and many of the plums fell to Todd Eastman and visitor Henry Barber, including several of the best lines on the cliff: **Drop, Fly, or Die**, **Esthesia**, and **On the Loose**. Development continued strong through the 1980s for those solid at 5.11, including names that we see throughout the region during this period—Don Mellor, Chuck Turner, Ken Nichols, Tim Beaman, and Patrick Purcell. Notable contributions were made by Martin Berzins, who raised the standards to solid 5.12 in 1989–91, and Dave Aldous, who led the most sought-after and difficult crack, **Zabba**, in 1996.

The most difficult route on the cliff, and one of the most difficult pure trad routes in the park, is **Wheelin' N' Dealin'**, put up by Matt McCormick in 2009. The route required enormous effort and many big falls, some of which were captured on film and are quite horrifying.

DIRECTIONS **(MAPS PAGES 197 AND 272)**

Parking for the Spider's Web is at the paved pullout at Chapel Pond on NY 73, 4.1 miles from Malfunction Junction on the left (when you're driving toward Keene Valley) and 4.4 miles from Keene Valley on the right (measured from Adirondack Street, when you're driving toward Malfunction Junction). Additionally, you can park at Chapel Pond Outlet—the hidden camping spot 0.3 mile from the Chapel Pond pullout (when you're driving toward Keene Valley) on the pond side of the road. There is room for several cars on the other side of the road across from the outlet, but it's a little too close to the road to be recommended.

From the Chapel Pond Outlet, cross the road and guardrail to a flat, grassy, circular area, the site of an old vehicle pullout and viewpoint. The climbers' path begins here, and there's an information board that lists cliff closures, if any. From the viewpoint, follow the switchbacks down into the deep-freeze canyon, then up into the talus on the other side. There is no distinct trail through the talus, as you can see the cliff. Simply head up and left through open talus to the base of the cliff, for about 15 min 599882,4888751.

DESCENT OPTIONS

Several routes, such as **Drop, Fly, or Die** and **On the Loose**, have fixed anchors at the top of their first pitch. For routes on the left end (i.e., routes left of **Esthesia**, such as **Dacker Cracker** and **Entertainment**), you can simply walk off left. For routes that intersect the Traverse Ledge (such as **TR**, **Zabba**, and **Mr. Rogers' Neighborhood**), you can 3rd-class scramble to the left or use one of the fixed anchors located above **Esthesia**, **Zabba**, and **Mr. Rogers' Neighborhood**. Climbers topping out at the right end of the cliff can scramble right down a loose gully or rappel from a tree near the top of **Eternity** with a single 60-m rope.

1 Retrograde 5.11b G 30'

Named for all the back-and-forth motion required to get the crux.

Start: At the leftmost crack on the wall, the one with a vertical 8"-high slot at midheight on an orange wall.

P1 5.11b G: Climb up some blocks, reach out right to a jam slot, then work up two thin cracks at the left. 30'

Gear: To 3".

FA 1988, Bill Dodd

Chris Thomas on ***Ku Klux Ken*** *(5.12c), belayed by Chris Yenkey.*

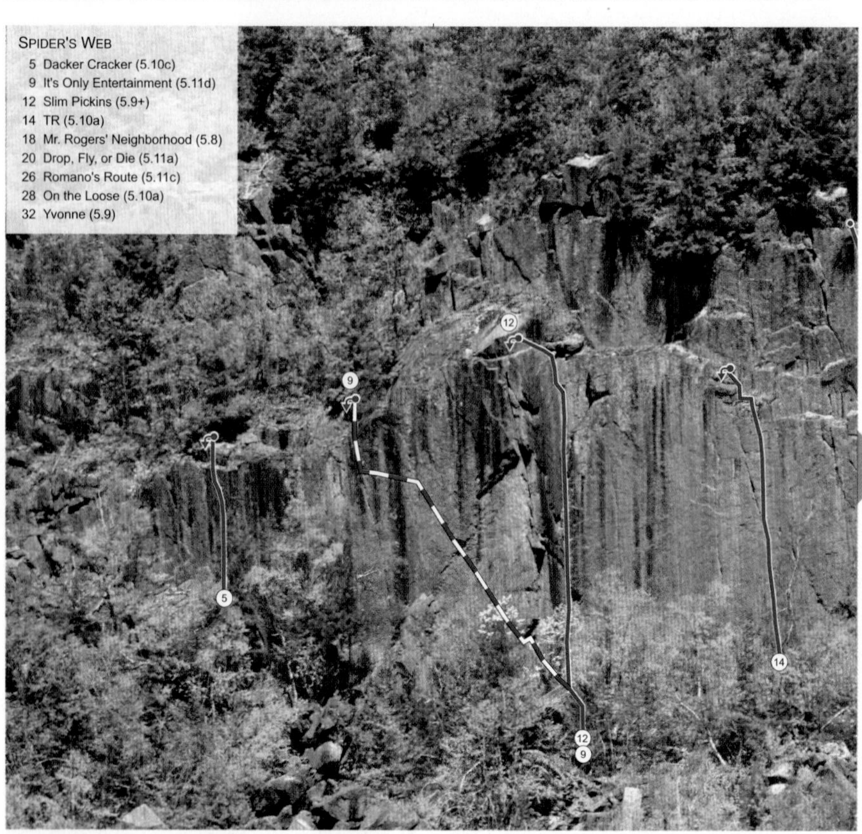

2 Wrong Again, Chalkbreath 5.11a G 35' ★

Start: At the second crack left of **Bird's Nest** and 4' right of **Retrograde**, which goes up the left side of a black water streak, directly below the left side of the protruding block at the top and above a hole in the ground.

P1 5.11a G: Up the crack to a 3" horizontal that makes a cross, then straight up to a block overhang at the top. 35'

FA 1988, Tim Beaman, Herb George

3 Bird's Nest 5.10d G 35' ★★

Start: On the top of some blocks 20' right of the end of the cliff, 25' left of **Dacker Cracker** at another vertical crack that runs the height of the cliff.

P1 5.10d G: Climb the crack to the top. The crux is off the ground. 35'

Gear: To 1.5" with an optional 4" piece at the top.

4 Five Hundred Rednecks with Guns 5.11c TR 45'

Begin 4' left of **Dacker Cracker** at the base of a series of left-rising, right-facing edges with a bolt 8' up. Angle left to a shallow, vertical right-facing corner in very dirty rock, then climb the corner through a V-notch.

FA (TR) 1986, Patrick Purcell

5 Dacker Cracker 5.10c G 50' ★★★

The name is in keeping with the rhyming of other well-known routes, like **Sacherer Cracker**, **Bachar Cracker**, and so on.

Start: On a slab of rock at the base of an obvious vertical crack that runs the height of the cliff. There is a V-slot at half height with some stacked blocks.

P1 5.10c G: Climb the crack to the top. The crux is at the start, and there is a knee-bar rest at the V-slot. 50'

Gear: To 2".

FA May, 1982, Don Mellor

6 Jelly Arms 5.11b PG 55' ★

Chuck Turner once claimed this as his most difficult first ascent, in which he supposedly wore out a rope because he fell so many times.

Start: 4' right of **Dacker Cracker** at right-slanting cracks that join a vertical crack.

P1 5.11b PG: Climb the slanting cracks with awkward protection to the vertical crack. (V1) Continue rightward following the obvious right-slanting flared crack, which finishes in a small chimney. 55'

V1 Hit by a Car 5.11d TR: Start as for **Jelly Arms**, but where the crack angles right, continue straight up the face to the top.

FA Oct, 1982, Chuck Turner
FA (V1) 1993, Bill Dodd

7 Chicken Wire 5.11d PG 55' ★

Mellor wire-brushed the route at first but then couldn't quite reach the first wire placement, which is crucial. Bill Dodd, being taller, tiptoed up on the base ledge and, just as he dropped in a sinker RP, slipped and hurt his leg and was unable to climb. So Mellor got the lead—a truly chicken accomplishment.

Start: 15' right of **Dacker Cracker** is a left-leaning broken crack that finishes in the **Jelly Arms** chimney.

P1 5.11d PG: Climb up the face and broken crack to an easier finish in the **Jelly Arms** chimney. 55'

FA Jun, 1985, Don Mellor

8 Peace in Our Climbs 5.12c R 70' ★

Climbs the bottomless crack that leads to the finish crack of **It's Only Entertainment**.

Start: In orange rock directly below the finish crack of **It's Only Entertainment** at a high bolt that is 3' below a 3" overlap. It's also 15' right of **Chicken Wire** and 45' left of the huge corner of **Slim Pickins**.

P1 5.12c R: Stick-clip the bolt (amazingly, placed on lead from a hook), then climb up the orange face (crux) to gain the crack. Follow the difficult flared crack to the top. 70'

FA 1991, Chris Gill

9 It's Only Entertainment 5.11d PG 100' ★★★★★

Perhaps the most sought-after prize at the Web, this route breaks the orange wall left of the large **Slim Pickins** corner via an awesome left-rising crack. The climbing is fairly sustained at 5.10d–5.11a, but it's the traverse that provides the real challenge. Most climbers run it out to the tempting handcrack oasis at the far side only to take the big whipper, but there are a few choice placements along the way.

Start: Same as for **Slim Pickins**.

P1 5.11d PG: Climb up the right-facing corner, which becomes a left-leaning ramp. Up left on the ramp to the base of the **Esthesia** corner, then break out left around the arête and climb the left-rising fingercrack with excellent gear until the crack ends. (V1) Traverse left 15' (crux) to a vertical crack and follow it more easily to the top. 100'

V1 Captain Hooks 5.12a PG: Climb straight up the crack, which pinches off, then opens back up.

Gear: Up to 2", double in finger size. #1 TCU for the traverse.

FA 1988, Tim Beaman, Bill Dodd
FA (V1, A3) 1984, Chuck Turner
FFA (V1) Jul, 2006, Dan Foster

Spider's Web

1 Retrograde (5.11b)
2 Wrong Again, Chalkbreath (5.11a)
3 Bird's Nest (5.10d)
4 Five Hundred Rednecks with Guns (5.11c)
5 Dacker Cracker (5.10c)
6 Jelly Arms (5.11b)
7 Chicken Wire (5.11d)
8 Peace in Our Climbs (5.12c)
9 It's Only Entertainment (5.11d)
10 Esthesia (5.10a)
11 Jungle Fever (5.12b)
12 Slim Pickins (5.9+)
13 Zabba (5.13a)
14 TR (5.10a)
15 Pumpernickel (5.11c)
16 Only the Good Die Young (5.11c)
17 Fear and Loathing in Keene Valley (5.11b)
18 Mr. Rogers' Neighborhood (5.8)
19 Monkey See, Monkey Do (5.11a)
20 Drop, Fly, or Die (5.11a)
21 Lycanthropia (5.12c)
22 Normal Route (5.11d)
23 Wheelin' N' Dealin' (5.13c)
24 The Key (5.9)
25 Skeleton Key (5.10c)
26 Romano's Route (5.11c)
27 White Knight (5.12a)
28 On the Loose (5.10a)
29 Grand Hysteria (5.12a)
31 Eternity (5.10d)
32 Yvonne (5.9)

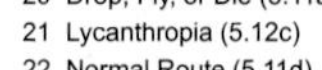

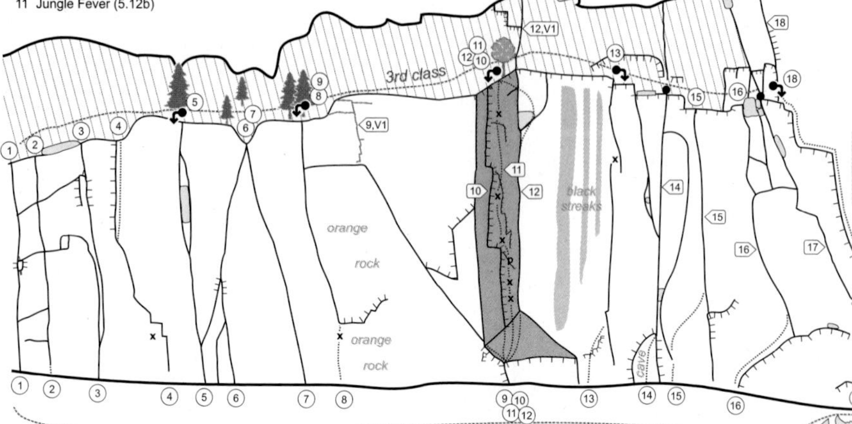

10 Esthesia 5.10a G 80' ★★★★

Climbs the inside corner in the arête left of the **Slim Pickins** corner. The wide crux crack can be protected with a 4.5" cam. The name was originally spelled **Aesthesia**, but misspelling took.

Start: Same as for **Slim Pickins**.

P1 5.10a G: Climb up the right-facing corner, which becomes a left-leaning ramp. Up left on the ramp to the base of the inside corner. Climb up the inside corner to a small ceiling, around this, and up the wider crack past a second small ceiling. Jam or layback around this (crux), then up the wide (3") handcrack to the top. Step right on a ledge to a fixed anchor (shared with **Slim Pickins**). 80'

Gear: To 4.5".

FA Jul 28, 1976, Grant Calder, John Wald, Dave Cilley
FFA Apr, 1977, Todd Eastman, Dave Cilley

11 Jungle Fever 5.12b PG 80' ★

This tip-ripping face climb ascends the black rock between **Slim Pickins** and **Esthesia**. It has two issues: first, the climbing is a little contrived, as it's easy to climb into the neighboring routes, and second, the bolt hangers have been removed. It makes an excellent toprope after you climb one of its neighbors.

Start: Same as for **Slim Pickins**.

P1 5.12b PG: Climb up to the slab, then up to the base of the black face (the left wall of the **Slim Pickins** corner). Up the black face using the arête, through some left-facing shallow corners to an overlap, then up the final face to the top. 80'

FA 1992, Patrick Purcell, Jeff Edwards

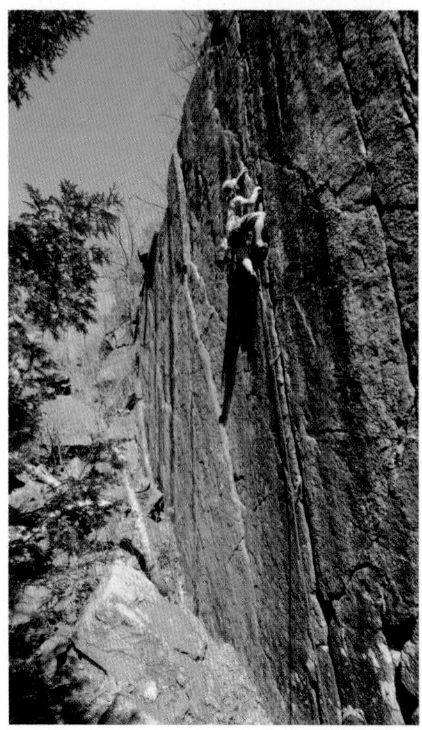

*Adam Crofoot on **Dacker Cracker** (5.10c).*

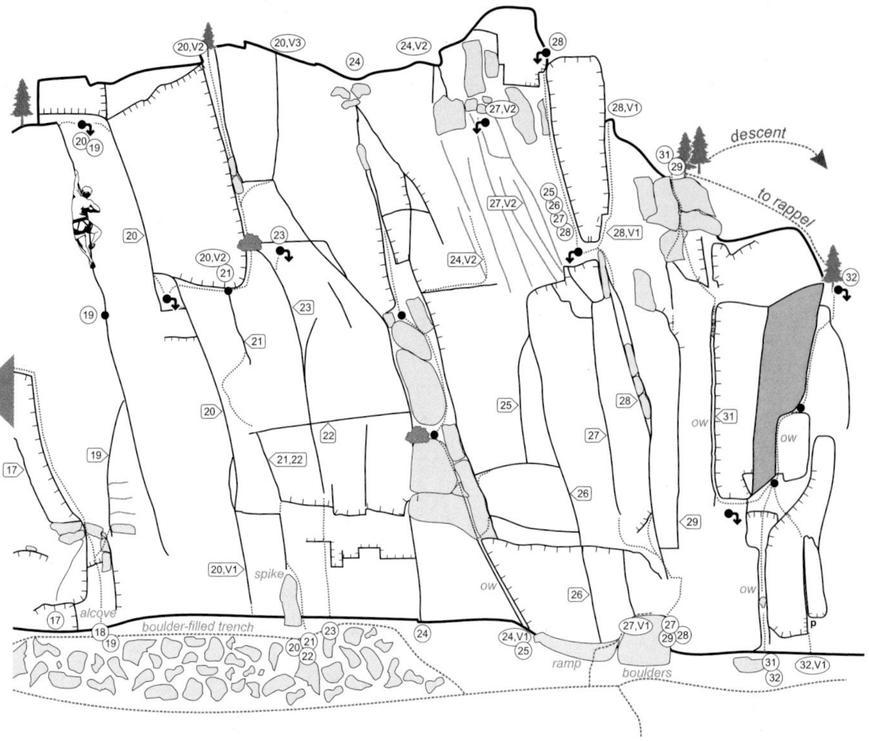

*Matt McCormick at the crux pinch of **Zabba** (5.13a). Photo by Dave Vuono.*

12 Slim Pickins 5.9+ G 80' ★★★★

Climbs the large right-facing corner, one of the most obvious features on the cliff. The route is out of character for the cliff, as it climbs a stemming corner rather than a steep fingercrack. In Henry Barber's words, this is "a classic by any stretch of the imagination."

Start: At an 8'-high right-facing corner that leans left into a ramp, below the huge right-facing corner.

P1 5.9+ G: Climb up the right-facing corner to gain the slab, then follow it to the base of the huge right-facing corner above. Up the corner, past a jammed block, to a ledge (crux just below the jammed block). Go up a handcrack in the corner, then step left onto the face for the final moves to the ledge and fixed anchor (shared with **Esthesia**). (V1) 80'

V1 Not for Love or Lust 5.10b G: From the top of the stacked flakes on the right end of the ledge, climb a crack up to the left of three overhanging summit blocks.

Gear: Optional 4" cam.

FA Apr, 1977, Henry Barber
FA (V1) 1986, Patrick Purcell

13 Zabba 5.13a PG 80' ★★★★

A testpiece of flared crack climbing. Also a popular clean aid route.

Start: 8' left of the **TR** cave, below a flared thin fingercrack that begins 10' up.

P1 5.13a PG: (V1) Begin to the left, then work up right to the flared crack (blind placements), then switch cracks right (past a bolt) and up to the Traverse Ledge with a fixed anchor. 80'

Gear: The bolt is worthless, but there is good gear just below and a good RP after that.

V1 5.13b G: The direct start.

History: Originally an aid route with a hanging belay! The name "Zabba" was yelled repeatedly by Bushart on the first ascent. The route was first climbed free, on toprope, by Chris Gill in 1991. The first known redpoint was by Dave Aldous, who placed gear on lead (and clipped the bolt); this was after three weeks of work—rehearsing the moves and practicing gear placements.

FA Jul, 1979, Bob Bushart, Bill Diemand
FFA Aug, 1996, Dave Aldous
FFA (V1) Jul 23, 2010, Nathaniel Popik

14 TR 5.10a G 120' ★★★★★

A popular warm-up with good jams and excellent protection. A couple of horizontal jams provide some key rests. The name represents the initials of the first ascentionist, not the acronym for "toprope."

Start: In the cave with a crack that comes out of the top right side, 50' right of the **Slim Pickins** corner.

P1 5.10a G: Chimney up the initial cave, exit on the right side into the crack, then climb the crack straight up to the Traverse Ledge. From here, step left to a fixed anchor (as for **Zabba**), walk off left, or continue with the next pitch. 80'

P2 5.9 G: Climb the crack above to a ledge at the base of a right-facing corner, then up the fistcrack to the trees. 40'

Gear: A 3.5" cam protects the start.

FA (TR) 1973, Tom Rosecrans, Paul Laskey
FFA Apr, 1980, Steve Hendrick, Jay Philbrick

15 Pumpernickel 5.11c PG 80' ★★★

A short but powerful exercise in shallow jams. It is possible to avoid the difficult start (broken hold) by starting on **TR**. The beginning is contrived, as you must deliberately avoid using the holds on **TR**. The original aid line was named "Pump-Her-Nickel."

Start: 4' right of the **TR** cave at a shallow, 4'-high left-facing corner.

P1 5.11c PG: (V1) Difficult moves off the ground lead to a narrow ledge; move right to a shallow left-facing corner. Continue up the left-facing corner to its top, then up the parallel cracks to the Traverse Ledge. From here, walk left to a fixed anchor above **Zabba** or walk off left. 80'

V1 Black Widow 5.12c PG: Climb a thin crack 10' right of the **TR** cave to the base of the shallow left-facing corner.

FA Jul, 1982, Alan Jolley, Bill Simes, Chuck Turner
FFA Jun, 1987, Patrick Purcell, Don Mellor
FA (V1) Oct, 1991, Ken Nichols, Jared Fleury

16 Only the Good Die Young 5.11c PG 80' ★

This route's only prominent feature is the left-leaning fingercrack, a more difficult version of **Fear and Loathing in Keene Valley**.

Start: Begin 12' right of the **TR** cave at the base of a right-rising broken ramp.

P1 5.11c PG: Climb the right-rising ramp to a small horn, then up and right across white rock to gain a left-leaning crack. Up the crack (crux), then straight up, joining **Fear and Loathing in Keene Valley** for its last few moves to the Traverse Ledge. 80'

FA 1982, Chuck Turner, Alan Jolley, Roger Jolley
FFA Sep 17, 1984, Ken Nichols, Mike Heintz

17 Fear and Loathing in Keene Valley 5.11b G 130' ★★★★

Excellent climbing with an unlikely start and superb finger locks through the crux.

Start: Right of the **TR** cave is a boulder-filled trench that runs along the base of the cliff. On the left end of this trench is a sloping shelf with a white wall above, just left of the broken area of **Mr. Rogers' Neighborhood**.

P1 5.11b G: Climb a thin crack in the white wall up to a small, 6"-by-6" square overhang, then angle right across the face (small TCUs and nuts) to the broken area of **Mr. Rogers' Neighborhood**, just below that route's right-facing orange corner. From the base of the corner, traverse left and into a left-leaning fingercrack. Up the fingercrack (crux) and continue in the left-leaning line to the Traverse Ledge. Move right to a fixed anchor (as for **Mr. Rogers' Neighborhood**). 80'

P2 5.10 G: Step back left and continue up the left-leaning crack to a ledge, then up a chimney with a block to the top. 50'

FA May, 1980, Steve Hendrick, Jay Philbrick

Opposite: Jim Lawyer on ***It's Only Entertainment*** *(5.11d). Photo by Adam Crofoot.*

Brian Kim on **Esthesia** (5.10a
Photo by David Le Pagne.

18 Mr. Rogers' Neighborhood 5.8 G 140' ★★★

One of the few moderate routes on the cliff; this one is actually pleasant climbing. The start is often wet and not to be underestimated.

Start: At the left end of the boulder-filled trench that runs along the base of the cliff, at a shallow, broken, square-sided depression with orange powdery lichen on the rock and some black streaks, on top of a pointed boulder.

P1 5.8 G: Climb up the broken depression and angle left through a small overhang (crux). Continue up and left to the base of a right-facing, left-leaning corner. Up this (5.6) to the Traverse Ledge and a fixed anchor. 90'

P2 5.8 G: Climb the crack (the one just right of the fixed anchor) in the shallow right-facing corner on the right side of the orange tower to its top, then up the left-facing corner past a cedar to the top. 50'

FA (P1) Apr 24, 1982, Don Mellor, Chuck Turner, Rich Leswing

FA (P2) 1985, Mark Saulsgiver, Terry Saulsgiver

19 Monkey See, Monkey Do 5.11a G 150' ★★

Start: Same as **Mr. Rogers' Neighborhood**.

P1 5.10b G: Climb up through the initial broken depression of **Mr. Rogers' Neighborhood**, then right to get established in a crack. Up the left-angling crack to a horizontal below an orange bulge (at a height even with the Traverse Ledge). Traverse left in a horizontal to the fixed anchor (as for **Mr. Rogers' Neighborhood**). 80'

P2 5.11a G: Reverse the traverse back right to regain the crack. Follow the wide crack through a bulge, then up the handcrack to a fixed anchor on the right below summit blocks (a 70-m rope required to lower off). 70'

History: Eastman recalls this climb as the highlight of his climbing career, saying "Barber calmly climbed removing dirt and loose rock as he made confident runouts between his hex or stopper placements. I've never seen anyone climb as well as Henry."

FA Sep, 1978, Henry Barber, Todd Eastman

20 Drop, Fly, or Die 5.11a G 160' ★★★★★

One of the top cracks in the Adirondacks—and perhaps on the planet—with perfect finger and hand jams, exposed position, and a rich history. As the story goes, Barber climbed the route in a single pitch, ran out of rope, and called down to Dave Cilley to tie on another rope. A 70-m rope is required to lower off P2.

Start: At the right end of the boulder-filled trench at an 8'-high spike of rock that is separated from the main face.

P1 5.11a G: (V1) Climb up the spike, then make a hard move into a right-facing corner-alcove under a roof. Traverse 6' left and into a slot, then straight up into the left-leaning finger- and handcrack to an alcove with a fixed anchor. 90'

P2 5.10c G: (V2) Up the left side of the alcove and into the left-leaning crack to a left-facing corner capped by a roof. Traverse left to a fixed anchor. 70'

V1 Direct Start 5.11b PG: Start 4' left of the spike and climb broken rock to a crack that joins the main route at the slot after the traverse.

V2 Captain Chips Traverse 5.10a G: From the alcove, traverse right under a roof to its right side. Climb cracks right of the shallow right-facing corner and into broken rock, then up this to a square roof. (V3) Up the jammed blocks on the left side of the roof and into the left-facing corner above to the top.

V3 5.9 PG: Step right and climb the right-facing corner to the top.

Gear: To 2.5".

FA Apr, 1977, Henry Barber

FA (V1) Jun 5, 1991, Don Mellor, Hans Johnstone

FA (V2) May, 1980, Steve Hendrick, Jay Philbrick

21 Lycanthropia 5.12c PG 90' ★★★

According to Berzins, the line is "a little artificial due to the proximity of **Drop, Fly, or Die**," but the first-ascent party avoided placing any protection in that route. The upper section is sustained and worthwhile. Named for the werewolf state of mind necessary to deal with a scary block at the top.

Start: Same as **Drop, Fly, or Die**.

P1 5.12c PG: Climb up to the corner-alcove under the roof as for **Drop, Fly, or Die**. Continue straight up, through the overhang, and up the steep crack to a horizontal. Step left into the **Drop, Fly, or Die** crack, up 4', then back right on great holds to a straight-up seam. Follow the seam up (crux, sustained) to belay below the **Captain Chips Traverse** roof. 90'

Descent: From the top, you can climb left to the anchor on **Drop, Fly, or Die** or right to finish on one of the variations to that route.

FA Jul, 1977, Todd Eastman, Chris Hyson

FFA Aug 5, 1991, Martin Berzins, Richard Felch

22 Normal Route 5.11d G 180' ★★★

Connects sections of other routes by an intimidating traverse. The route is "normal" in the mathematical sense, in that it is perpendicular to the vertical lines of its neighbors.

Start: Same as **Drop, Fly, or Die**.

P1 5.11d G: Climb up to the corner-alcove under the roof as for **Drop, Fly, or Die**. Continue straight up, through the overhang, and up the steep crack to a horizontal as for **Lycanthropia**. Follow the horizontal crack straight right for 30' to **The Key**. Finish on **The Key**. 180'

FA Sep 3, 2007, Nick Wakeman, Bill Dodd

FFA Sep 14, 2007, Nick Wakeman

23 Wheelin' N' Dealin' 5.13c R 100' ★★★★★

Climbs the beautiful seam bisecting the **Normal Route**; the hardest all-gear-protected route in the park. The first ascent required 3-1/2 months of work and close to 20 big falls, including a "cartwheel whipper" for which the route is named.

Start: 15' right of **Drop, Fly, or Die** below tiered overhangs.

P1 5.13c R: Pull the initial roof with some burly campus-like moves to a nice rest out right. Step back left into the seam, place small gear, then punch to a horizontal and good rest. Climb to a strenuous stance (improbable offset nut and green-yellow hybrid alien in the same pod). Gun up through an extremely insecure crux

(tiny feet) to reach a jug (two tiny RPs). Follow easier but runout ground to a fixed anchor. 100'

Gear: Extremely specific and includes three hybrid aliens and several micro RPs, some good and some questionable. Toproping prior to a lead is advisable due to the specific nature of the gear.

FA Oct 17, 2009, Matt McCormick

24 The Key 5.9 G 160' ★

An overlooked route that climbs one of the more obvious features on the cliff—stacked blocks and cracks that run the height of the cliff. Some people love this route; others absolutely hate it.

Start: (V1) At the right end of the boulder-filled trench, just uphill from the spike of **Drop, Fly, or Die**, is a jumbled pile of boulders. This route begins on the right side of this jumble of boulders in a small alcove below a shallow left-facing corner with orange lichen on the arête. There is a V-slot 20' up with a handcrack that shoots out the top.

P1 5.8 PG: Climb up the left-facing corner to an angled ceiling, then up into an alcove below the V-slot in the next ceiling. Through the V-slot and into the handcrack above to a ledge with a bush (optional belay). Continue up the cracks and blocks to a block-filled alcove. 100'

P2 5.9 G: (V2) Climb the left crack out of the alcove, then up through dirtier terrain to the summit. 60'

`**V1 5.8 G:** Begin as for **Skeleton Key** and climb the left-leaning fistcrack to join the normal route at the optional belay at the bush.

V2 Deviant Finish 5.10a G: From the alcove, climb out right using a horizontal to a series of cracks that leads to the summit. 70'

FA Jul, 1976, Grant Calder, John Wald
FA (V1) Sep, 1977, Jerry Hoover, Chris Hyson
FA (V2) 1988, Tim Beaman, Bill Dodd, Herb George

25 Skeleton Key 5.10c G 100' ★

Start: 8' left of **Romano's Route** and at the left end of the **Romano's Route** slab, on top of a pointed boulder, at a left-leaning fistcrack in a left-facing corner. This fistcrack is 25' right of and slightly downhill from **The Key**.

P1 5.10c G: Climb the fistcrack to a ledge. Step right, then up to a parallel crack in white rock and up to a high horizontal. Traverse right to a crack, then straight up the white face to join **Romano's Route**—move right on the ledge to the fixed anchor as for **On The Loose**. 100'

FA 1987, Tim Beaman, Herb George, Sylvia Lazarnick

26 Romano's Route 5.11c G 100' ★★★★

A very technical crack and a real pumper to lead. The route changes character after 40'; you can climb the quality 5.10 upper section by traversing in from **On the Loose**.

Start: At the right end of the cliff is a pile of boulders, on top of which starts **On the Loose**. This route begins on a short slab on the left at the base of this pile of boulders, at a thin crack that leans left.

P1 5.11c G: Climb the thin crack (crux) to a stance. Reach right to a second crack and climb up to a broken area at the base of a steep crack above (optional belay, 40'). Continue up the overhanging crack (5.10c)—fingers at first, then hands—to a ledge, then follow the ledge right to a fixed anchor (as for **On the Loose**). 100'

Gear: Standard rack plus small TCUs for the start.

FA 1978, Rich Romano

27 White Knight 5.12a G 90' ★★★★

An unrelenting fingercrack and a real prize as an onsight. Perhaps the purest fingercrack in the Adirondacks. On the original ascent, the white rock led to a discussion of chess, which led to the name of this route.

Start: (V1) Same as **On the Loose**.

P1 5.12a G: Climb up and right on the foot ledge, then up to a ledge and back left to an alcove, the same as for **On the Loose**. Traverse left 8' on a sloping ledge, then up the fingercrack in the white rock to an overhang at the top of the crack. Break the overhang up and left following a left-leaning crack to a ledge, then (V2) back right to a fixed anchor (as for **On the Loose**). 90'

V1 Ku Klux Ken 5.12c G: From the left end of the top of the boulder pile, follow the superthin crack up to the sloped ledge, joining the normal route at the base of the fingercrack.

V2 Ku Klux Who? 5.10d G ★★: Continue up the same crack system—rattly fingers to thin hands with multiple "finger buckets" along the way (much like the lower half of the route). Fixed anchor; lower with a 70m rope.

Gear: Extra gear up to 1".

FA 1979, Bob Bushart, Bill Simes
FFA Sep 19, 1984, Ken Nichols, Mike Heintz
FA (V1) Aug 6, 1989, Martin Berzins, Richard Felch

28 On the Loose 5.10a G 160' ★★★★★

An imposing, steep, and pumpy handcrack with comfy round-edged jams; one of the most popular routes in Chapel Pond Pass. If it hasn't been raining long, this route can be climbed in pouring rain. The first-ascent party found a lot of loose rock wedged in the cracks, hence the name.

Start: On top of the boulder pile at the right end of the cliff, at the base of a right-rising foot ledge.

P1 5.10a G: Climb up and right on the foot ledge, then up to a ledge and back left to an alcove beneath a left-leaning handcrack. Up the crack (wide hands) to parallel cracks that lead to the right side of a small overhang. Step right and climb a short right-facing corner that leads to a ledge with a fixed anchor. 90'

P2 5.9 G: Climb up to the square ceiling, (V1) then left into a left-facing, left-leaning corner to a chimney-slot. Up this to a fixed anchor on the left below summit blocks. 70'

V1 5.8 G: Climb out right from the square ceiling and into a right-facing corner-slot. Up this to a handcrack, which leads to a sloping ledge at the top. 50'

FA Apr, 1977, Henry Barber, Dave Cilley

29 Grand Hysteria 5.12a G 150' ★★★

Named for the psychiatric term, since Felch was in that profession.

Start: Same as **On the Loose**.

*Opposite: Nick Weinberg on **Slim Pickins** (5.9+).*

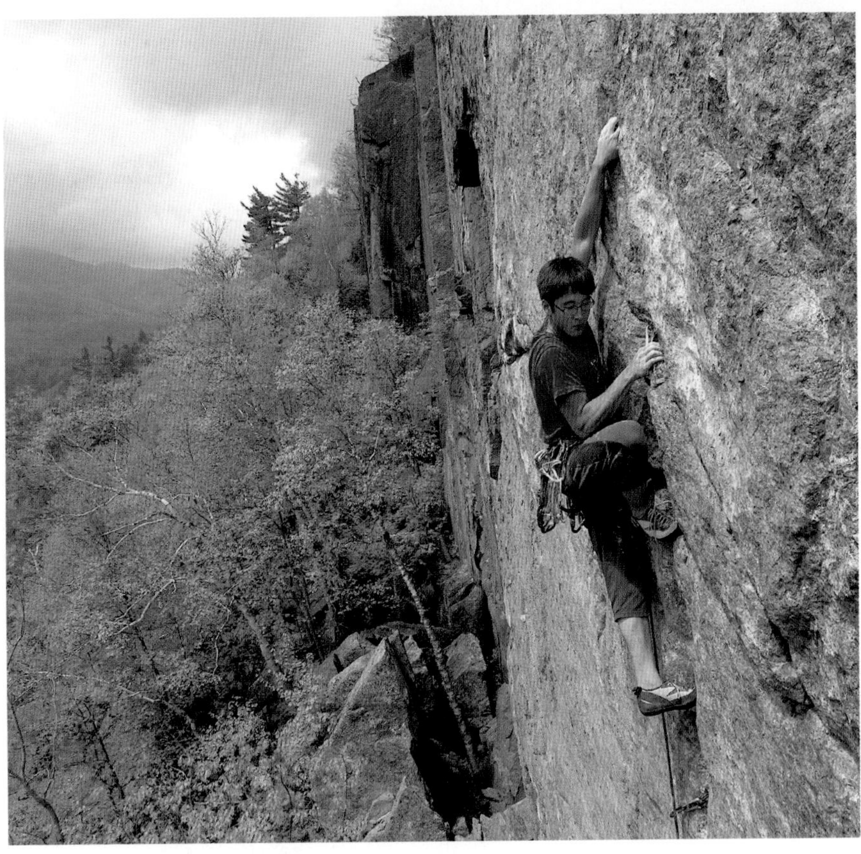

Brian Kim on the upper section of ***Romano's Route*** *(5.11c). Photo by David Le Pagne.*

P1 5.12a G: Climb up and right on the foot ledge, then up to a ledge and back left to an alcove beneath a left-leaning handcrack, same as for **On the Loose**. Traverse right 10' to a crack, then up to some small overlaps where the crack ends. Up the seam to a good hold, then right into another crack, which arches left into an overlap. Over the overlap to an easier finishing groove and tree 30' up and left. 150'
FA Aug 16, 1989, Martin Berzins, Richard Felch

30 Project

There is a fixed anchor below the traverse on **Eternity**. The route climbs left of the start of **Yvonne/Eternity** (5.10c), then climbs directly up the face above the fixed anchor, right of the **Eternity** off width.

31 Eternity 5.10d G 160' ★★★

The off-width testpiece of the cliff.
Start: Same as **Yvonne**.
P1 5.10d G: Climb the off-width crack past a chockstone to a sloped ledge. Traverse left from the ledge beneath a ceiling (above a fixed anchor) and into the off-width crack in the left-facing corner. Off-width crack climbing (crux) leads to some chockstones and fist jams on easier terrain. Step left around a ceiling, then up a very loose flare to the top. 160'
Gear: Double large cams up to 6".
FA Apr, 1977, Henry Barber, Dave Cilley

Opposite: Colin Loher on P1 of ***Drop, Fly, or Die*** *(5.11a). Photo by Tomás Donoso.*

32 Yvonne 5.9 G 125' ★★

Start: At the right end of the cliff, at an off-width crack that begins at a flat area in front of a large boulder.
P1 5.6 PG: (V1) Climb the off-width crack past a chockstone to a sloped ledge in a right-facing dihedral. 40'
P2 5.8 G: Layback and stem the off-width crack in the corner to the next ledge. 35'
P3 5.9 G: Up the corner, and just shy of the top, make an awkward move right (crux), then up to a ledge where you can traverse off right to the trees. 50'
V1 5.10a PG: Begin 5' right of the off-width crack at a shallow right-facing corner below a ceiling 15' up. Climb a crack in the corner (piton), clearing the ceiling on the left side, and into a shallow left-facing corner. Up the corner to a final unprotected friction move up and left to the ledge.
FA Apr 7, 1968, Rob Wood, Dave Thomas, Bob Rice
FFA Jun, 1976, Grant Calder, Todd Eastman

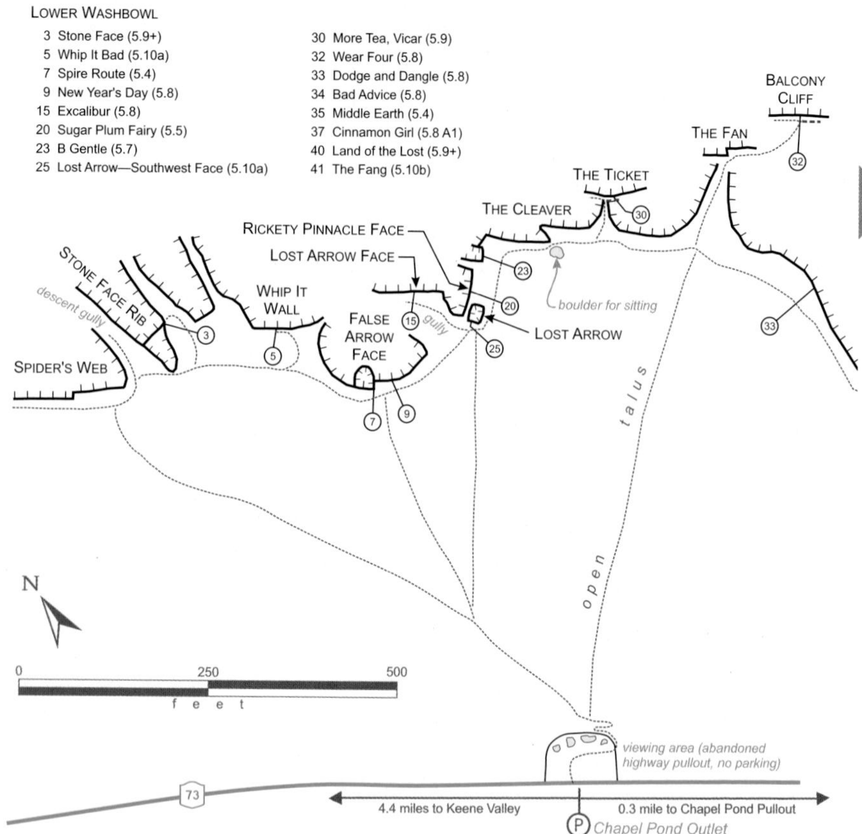

LOWER WASHBOWL

Location	North side of NY 73, accessed from the Chapel Pond Outlet
Aspect	Southwest
Height	200'
Quality	★★
Approach	15–45 min, moderate
Summary	Mostly chossy cliffs with isolated good routes and adventurous approaches, and the only true "pinnacles" in the region.

-5.6	5.7	5.8	5.9	5.10	5.11	5.12	5.13+	total
11	9	10	6	6	3	1		47

Sitting high above Chapel Pond and high above one of the largest talus fields in the park, the Lower Washbowl cliffs span from the Spider's Web to the Upper Washbowl. The aspect of these cliffs ensures plenty of sun, which therefore makes them a great late-season destination. On a cool day in November with snow on the ground, there is no better place to explore.

The Lower Washbowl was once very popular, with the pinnacles and moderate routes being the main attraction. In recent years, cliffs like the Beer Walls and the Creature Wall, with shorter approaches and cleaner rock, have usurped Lower Washbowl's popularity.

The main difficulty with the Lower Washbowl is the discomfort of the approach: when the leaves are off the trees, the navigation is easy, but with leaves, it takes a clever nose to sniff them out. There are many minicliffs (which look not unlike the "good" cliffs) that will further confuse you. In addition to navigation, the terrain is a real hazard—mostly steep, loose talus with low shrubbery and prickly plants. Some of the cliff bases are steep and uncomfortable. An ideal time to visit is early in the season when the snow still blankets the north-facing slopes; unfortunately, at this time, the Lower Washbowl is invariably closed due to the nesting of peregrine falcons, and, by the time it's open, the cliffs are baking in midsummer sun.

The most popular cliff in the Lower Washbowl is, by far, the Lost Arrow Face. It's easy to get to and has a good selection of routes in the 5.8–5.9 range, including the recommended **Excalibur**, **Virgin Sturgeon**, and the amazing **Bigger Than Jesus** arête. On its right end is the Lost Arrow, a freestanding spire that makes a fun

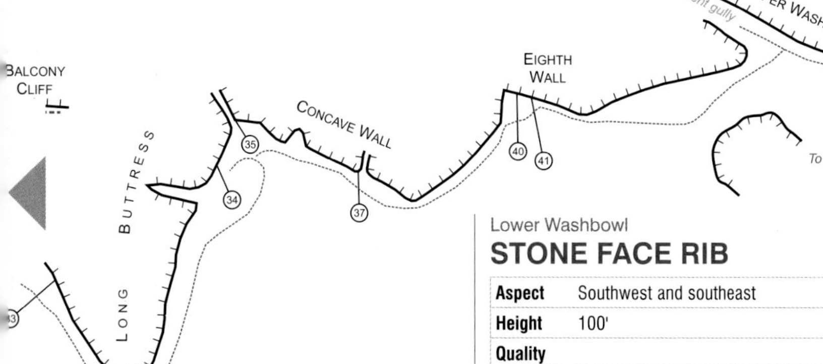

outing. The second best cliff is probably The Ticket, if you wish to brave the approach. Be warned that all the cliffs have unstable rock.

HISTORY

There is a long history of climbing on the Lower Washbowl, beginning with the freestanding pinnacles, which were considered somewhat of a novelty for the area. Dave Bernays, Stanley Smith, and Donald Lebeau are known to have climbed the Lost Arrow, False Arrow, and Rickety Pinnacle in the late 1940s and early 1950s. Nearly 20 years passed before more routes were reported, this time by visitors from the Canadian Alpine Club Hut, including Rob Wood, Peter and George Bennett, Peter Baggaley, and Peter Ferguson, among others. In the spring of 1968, they added about 10 routes on The Ticket and the Lost Arrow Face. Another 20 years elapsed before the cliffs again saw attention, this time by locals Don Mellor, Alan Jolley, Chuck Turner, Jim Cunningham, and Mark Saulsgiver, who added routes to The Ticket, Long Buttress, The Balcony, Concave Wall, and the Eighth Wall. A flurry of new route development was done later in the 1980s by Patrick Purcell and Jeff Edwards, mostly on the Whip It Wall, Swamp Wall, and Stone Face Rib. More recently, and after a 16 year gap, activity picked up at the Eighth Wall (Sam Hoar) and the Concave Wall (Conor Cliffe).

These 20-year gaps between development are most likely the result of climbers' failing to report routes. The pitons scattered around the cliffs tell of a more thorough exploration than what's recorded here.

The cliffs were named by Don Mellor and friends in his 1983 guidebook. (In the 1960s, they were known as the "first wall," "second wall," and so on.) They chose names based on similarity in appearance to real-world objects, such as a fan or a ticket . . . or, in some cases, just made them up (e.g., the Eighth Wall).

DIRECTIONS **(MAPS PAGES 197 AND 272)**

The best approach for the Eighth Wall, the Concave Wall, and the upper right side of the Long Buttress is from the Upper Washbowl, near the base of the **Wiessner Route**. Parking for the other walls is as for the Spider's Web.

Lower Washbowl

STONE FACE RIB

Aspect	Southwest and southeast
Height	100'
Quality	
Approach	18 min, easy
Summary	A narrow rib with some exploratory routes on both sides.

-5.6	5.7	5.8	5.9	5.10	5.11	5.12	5.13+	total
	2	1	1					4

Right of the Spider's Web is a rib of rock separated from the Spider's Web by the steep descent gully. The end of the rib forms a narrow, 10'-wide face with several climbs. The terrain around the base is steep and uncomfortable.

DIRECTIONS **(MAPS PAGES 197 AND 272)**

Stone Face Rib is best approached from the right end of the Spider's Web (near **Yvonne**) by hiking up and right into the descent gully. The right side of the descent gully is the southwest face of Stone Face Rib with the route **Made In The Shade**. Walk right from the base of the descent gully, around the toe of the rib (where there is a giant patch of poison ivy) with the route **Stone Face**, then steeply uphill on tree- and brush-covered talus into the next gully that separates the rib from the cliffs to the right. **Running on Empty** begins a short distance up this gully.

1 Made In The Shade 5.7 G 45'

A pleasant route; on a hot day, you'll be made in the shade.

Start: 20' uphill and left from the toe of the southwest face, at a deep alcove, the top of which begin two cracks. This is the left-hand left-leaning crack.

P1 5.7 G: Go up the alcove, then follow the left-hand, left-leaning, stepped crack to where it becomes vertical. Continue up a fingercrack over a bulge to a tree-covered ledge. 45'

FA Apr 25, 2009, Michael Gray, Aaron Donnelly

2 Nothing We Bailed 5.8 TR 40'

Begin as for **Made in the Shade**. At the top of the alcove, go straight up the crack through an offwidth section to the ledge.

FA (TR) Apr 25, 2009, Michael Gray, Aaron Donnelly

3 Stone Face 5.9+ G 100'

Good-quality rock.
Start: On the right edge of the face at the end of the fin, on a small ledge below a large birch. Watch for poison ivy in the talus here.
P1 5.9+ G: Climb the arête using horizontals for protection to a cedar that grows right on the arête next to some blocks. Over the blocks, then step left to an open book and follow the rib of the rock to the top. 100'
FA Apr, 1989, Patrick Purcell

4 Running on Empty 5.7+ PG 100'

Start: On the face to the right of **Stone Face** (facing northeast) at the first prominent crack to the right of the arête, 15' uphill from **Stone Face**.
P1 5.7+ PG: Climb the crack up to the block ledge with the cedar that sits on the arête, step right to a small cedar, then up a crack to a block, step right and climb past ledges to the top. 100'
FA Apr, 1989, Patrick Purcell, Mary Purcell

Lower Washbowl

WHIP IT WALL

Aspect	Southwest
Height	75'
Quality	
Approach	30 min, moderate
Summary	Short face with right-leaning cracks.

-5.6	5.7	5.8	5.9	5.10	5.11	5.12	5.13+	total
				2				2

The Whip It Wall, known for the ice route **Whip It Good**, is a short face with right-leaning cracks.

DIRECTIONS **(MAP PAGE 272)**
Walk steeply uphill and left from the False Arrow Face. Alternatively, from the right end of the Spider's Web, walk right to the descent gully, then angle steeply uphill and right, passing under the Stone Face Rib, to reach the base of the wall. The base is marked by a prominent right-facing corner.

5 Whip It Bad 5.10a G 75'

Start: At a right-facing corner, the only corner at the base of this narrow cliff.
P1 5.10a G: Climb up the right-facing corner to a ledge at its top. (V1) At the right end of the ledge are two right-leaning cracks that merge into a single right-leaning crack. Climb these out right to the top. 75'
V1 5.9+ G: Walk left on the ledge behind a large pine to a right-leaning crack and climb it to the top.
FA Apr 27, 1989, Patrick Purcell, Bill Dodd

6 Whips and Chains 5.10b G 50'

Start: Same as **Whip It Bad**.
P1 5.10b G: Climb up the right-facing corner and, at half height, climb the right-leaning crack to the top. 50'
FA May, 1989, Patrick Purcell, Dennis Luther

Lower Washbowl

FALSE ARROW FACE

Aspect	Southwest
Height	70'
Quality	★
Approach	15 min, moderate
Summary	A narrow face with a free-standing top.

-5.6	5.7	5.8	5.9	5.10	5.11	5.12	5.13+	total
2		1						3

The False Arrow is a small spire of rock that pokes out of the woods and is often mistaken for the Lost Arrow, which is farther up and right hidden in the trees. What appears to be a spire is actually a narrow face, the top 10' of which is in fact freestanding.

The face sits on a left-rising hillside, and the base has a large right-facing corner. **Spire Route** begins on the outside edge of this corner. The other routes are on the face right of this corner.

DIRECTIONS **(MAP PAGE 272)**
As you cross the talus heading for the Spider's Web, you can see the face straight up an open section of talus; simply walk straight up to the face. Or, from the Spider's Web, walk right to the base of the descent gully, then contour another 200' right and slightly uphill to the base of the face. (The face sits 100' higher than the base of the Spider's Web.)

7 Spire Route 5.4 G 70' ★★

Worthwhile for a climber in this grade.
Start: At the lowest point of rock on the right side of the spire.
P1 5.4 G: Climb chossy blocks stacked in the outside corner of the arête up to a ledge. Step left and up a crack to another ledge. Step right around a block and follow the prominent crack straight up the center of the spire past a small cedar to the top. There is a wedged boulder jammed into the crack at the very top. 70'
Descent: A short 10' downclimb on the other side of the spire leads to the talus at the base of the Lost Arrow Face. Walk right to return to the base of the face.

8 Short Order 5.5 G 40'

Start: The right side of the spire forms a right-facing corner. This route begins just right of the corner below a wide crack, 20' uphill from the low point of the face.
P1 5.5 G: Up the crack past the stuffed-in flakes, then a chockstone, and on to a large cedar at the top. 40'

9 New Year's Day 5.8 G 40' ★★

Although short, this is a quality fingercrack.
Start: 25' downhill from and right of the cone-shaped slope at the base of **Short Order**, 8' left of the right side of the face, at a small ceiling that is "held up" by a pedestal of rock.
P1 5.8 G: Step up to the ceiling and climb the fingercrack to an edge 15' up. Straight up to a ceiling, then break through the ceiling at a left-leaning crack that leads to the top. 40'
FA Dec 31, 1984, Don Mellor, Mike Heintz, Bill Dodd

Lower Washbowl

LOST ARROW FACE

Aspect	Southwest and southeast
Height	150'
Quality	★★★
Approach	30 min, moderate
Summary	Best collection of routes at the Lower Washbowl, and the region's only free-standing pillars.

-5.6	5.7	5.8	5.9	5.10	5.11	5.12	5.13+	total
6	3	4	1	1	1			17

The Lost Arrow Face is a southwest-facing cliff that has on its right end a freestanding pinnacle known as the Lost Arrow. This face sees the most traffic of all the Lower Washbowl cliffs, as it has relatively easy access, clean routes, moderate grades, and of course, the freestanding pinnacle that is so unique to the region.

The Lost Arrow Face sits just above the False Arrow Face, separated from it by a wide talus slope. A landmark for finding routes on the face is the sharp left-facing corner that begins 40' up with an orange spot just below it. This is the **Sergeant Pepper** corner.

DIRECTIONS **(MAP PAGE 272)**

Go to the False Arrow Face, walk to its right end, then continue straight uphill to the next cliffband. (When you approach from the road, you can simply aim for the right end of the False Arrow Face.) Total time from the road is about 20 min.

10 Robbed 5.7 G 150' ★

Start: From **Sergeant Pepper**, walk left 30', then scramble up and right to a pointed boulder that makes a good seat. This boulder is 20' left of the start of **Sergeant Pepper** and is below a broken right-facing open book.

P1 5.7 G: Climb the broken open book to a V-groove, then follow it to a triangular ceiling. Step left and climb a crack to a sloped ledge. Climb a handcrack up a steep wall to its top, then up to a belay at a cedar. 120'

P2 5.6+ G: Step right and climb a crack to the top. 30'

FA May 11, 1968, Peter Bennett, Dave Thomas

11 Chunga's Revenge 5.6+ G 150' ★

This was once a very popular 5.6 route but now sees very little traffic. The route has suffered substantial rockfall from the upper corner. Named for Frank Zappa's 1970 album.

Start: Same as **Sergeant Pepper**.

P1 5.6 PG: Climb up the left-facing, left-leaning flake to the orange spot. Step left to a large ledge with a pine and fixed anchor. 40'

P2 5.6+ G: Up and left on blocks to the right-facing corner, then follow the corner to a ceiling. Climb through the ceiling on its left side (joining **Robbed** here) and up a crack to the top. 110'

Descent: Scramble right to the fixed anchor at the top of **Bigger Than Jesus**.

FA Aug 9, 1974, Tom Rosecrans, Rob Norris

12 Sergeant Pepper 5.8 G 150' ★★

Start: On the left side of the face is a sharp-edged left-facing corner that begins 40' up just above an orange spot. This route begins 15' right of the corner on top of the blocky terrain below a shallow sharp-edged left-facing, left-leaning flake-corner that leads to the orange spot.

P1 5.8 G: Climb **Chunga's Revenge** past the orange spot to the ledge. Step right and climb the obvious left-facing dihedral to a roof, out this on the right, and continue in the left-facing corner to the top. There is an anchor just right on the face. 150'

History: On the first ascent, some pegs were used "whilst half a ton of earth was removed from the cracks and also to move round the overhang." The first free ascent is therefore unknown.

FA 1968, George Bennett, Rob Wood

13 Bigger Than Jesus 5.11b G 150' ★★★

An amazing arête climb. The name refers to a quote by John Lennon comparing the Beatles' popularity to that of Jesus.

Start: Same as **Sergeant Pepper**.

P1 5.11b G: Climb **Chunga's Revenge** to the orange spot. Step right onto the face to a good horizontal. Up the face to gain a faint seam (3' right of the arête); up the crack to its top, step left to the arête, and climb past several overlaps to a fixed anchor at the top. 150'

History: The origin of this route, which appeared prior to 1995, is unknown.

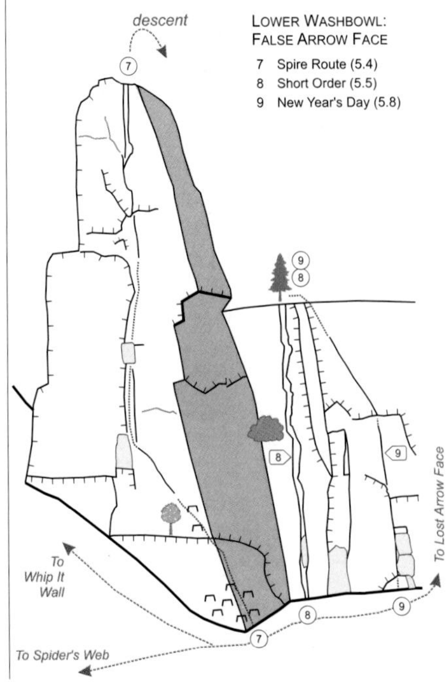

14 Virgin Sturgeon 5.9 G 150' ★★★

This route doesn't look obvious from below but comes together as you get higher. The first ascentionist wrote, "Difficulties sustained due to unrelenting verticality." The name comes from a ceremonial sturgeon song filled with innuendo: "Caviar comes from the virgin sturgeon. / Virgin sturgeon's a very fine fish. / Virgin sturgeon need no urgin'— / That's why caviar is my dish!"

Start: Same as **Sergeant Pepper**.

P1 5.9 G: Just right of the start is a short left-facing corner with a crack that comes out of the top. Climb up this crack system past several blocky overlaps to two parallel cracks with a bolt between them. Climb the right-hand crack to a wide slot, then up into a right-facing corner. Up the corner, then up a crack to a ceiling with some right-facing corners in it. Step right to the rightmost of these corners, then up this to the top. 150'

History: The first ascentionist wrote that the cracks "take pitons which were used discreetly (i.e., as in handholds, footholds, and teeth and any other parts of the body which still have any strength left to stay in contact with the rock)." Thus, the first free ascent is unknown. This same year, Rob Wood and Mick Burke went on to climb the Nose on El Capitan, making the 18th ascent, and the first all British ascent.

FA Apr 21, 1968, Rob Wood, Dave Keefe

15 Excalibur 5.8 G 120' ★★★

Climbs the interesting pillar of rock on the right side of the face. The name is derived from the Latin phrase *ex calce liberatus*, "liberated from the stone."

Start: Same as **Sergeant Pepper**.

P1 5.8 G: Traverse easily right to the base of the left-facing corner. Up the corner to the top of the blocky pinnacle. Follow the crack straight up to a tree with a fixed anchor. Stop here or continue in the line to the right edge of the ceiling with several right-facing corners. Finish up the rightmost of these corners (same as for **Virgin Sturgeon**). 120'

FA Jul, 1981, Alan Jolley, Scott Provost

16 Cozy Corner 5.4 G 120'

Start: Same as **Sergeant Pepper**.

P1 5.4 G: Traverse up and right on easy rock to the base of the left-facing corner of **Excalibur**. Up the corner for a few feet, then break right around the arête to a small cedar, past this, and into the right-facing corner above. Move right to a left-facing corner and up this to a ledge with an expansive cedar. From the left side of the ledge, climb a vertical crack (which is left of a large left-facing corner) up to the next ledge, then up and left to the trees. 120'

History: Tony Goodwin is the son of the well-known rock-climbing pioneer Jim Goodwin, and Steve Healy is the son of Trudy Healy, the author of the first rock-climbing guidebook to the park.

FA Apr 20, 1968, Tony Goodwin, Steve Healy

17 Hummingbird 5.7 PG 150'

Start: 15' below and left of the notch that separates the Lost Arrow from the main face, at a 12'-high clean slab with a crack on its right side.

P1 5.4 G: (V1) Climb up the slab to the ridge, then up to an obvious large pine. Up a right-facing corner to a cedar. 75'

P2 5.7 PG: Step right to a crack in a 4'-high left-facing corner. Up the crack to a groove that leads to the lower of two cedars. Thrash past the cedars and into the right-facing corner above. Climb up a crack in orange rock (just right of the corner) to a horizontal in the left wall (V2) and follow it left around the arête to the expansive pine tree on **Cozy Corner**. Continue up **Cozy Corner** to the top. 75'

V1 4th class: P1 can be avoided; starting from **Sergeant Pepper**, scramble up a right-rising ramp to the top of P1 at a comfy ledge with cedar trees.

V2 5.9 G: Continue up the corner into a square notch in a ceiling. Over the ceiling via two parallel cracks, then follow the cracks up the buttress to the top.

History: On the first ascent, a peg was used for balance to gain the lower of two cedars on P2. The first free ascent is unknown.

FA May 3, 1968, Peter Bennett, Peter Baggaley, Peter Ferguson

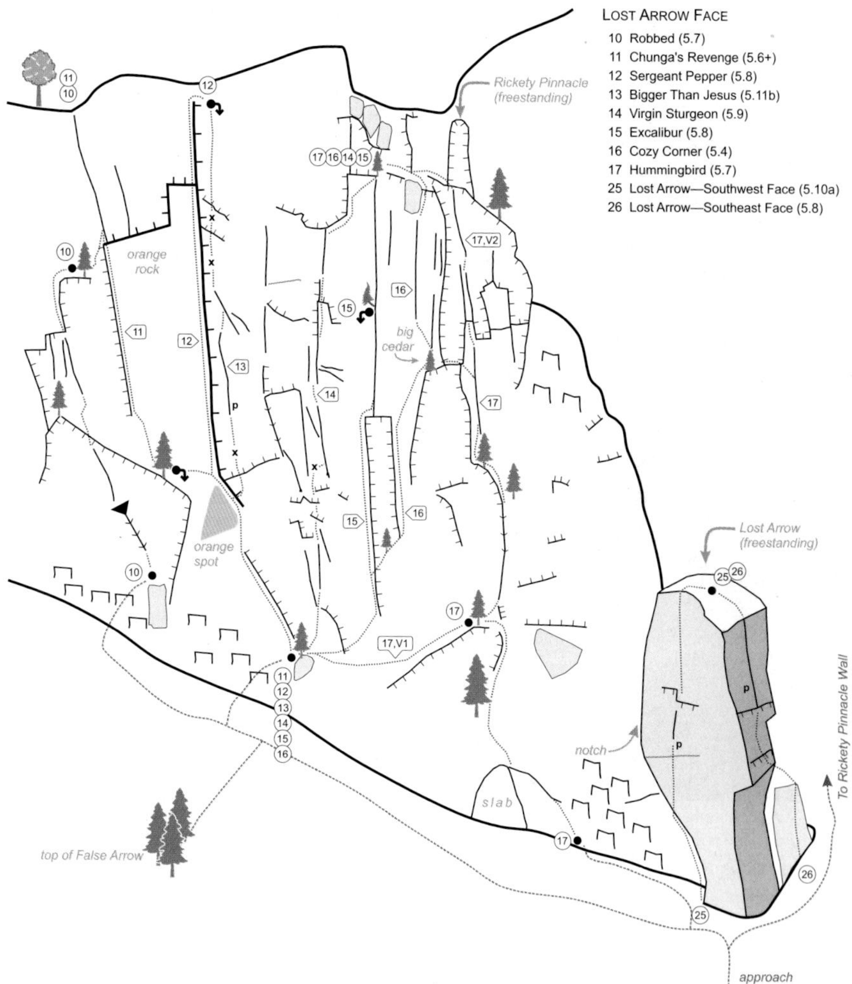

Rickety Pinnacle Wall

On the right side of the Lost Arrow Wall is the Lost Arrow, a freestanding pinnacle of rock. The face that runs behind the spire and uphill is the Rickety Pinnacle Wall, which faces southeast. The wall takes its name from the hidden freestanding pinnacle that sits atop it.

18 Recital 5.8 G 60' ★

Start: From the base of the southeast face of the spire (at the low point on the wall below the pinnacle), scramble into the opening of the notch. This route begins on the main wall below a fingercrack that starts 15' up. The fingercrack is 5' right of a giant orange cleaver-flake.

P1 5.8 G: Climb a short slab to a slot that narrows to a fingercrack. Up the crack to a cedar at the top. 60'

FA Apr, 1985, Don Mellor, Ian Osteyee

19 Rope Toss Wall 5.5 G 100'

Named by Don Mellor, as he reasoned that this was where Stanley Smith threw the rope over the Lost Arrow for its first ascent.

Start: Same as Recital.

P1 5.5 G: Climb up and right on blocky rock to a good crack system (old ring piton, perhaps one of Stanley's originals). Up this to a lower-angled area between two opposing corners; the left-facing corner on the right is larger and orange. Up the left-facing orange corner to a fixed anchor on a tree. 100'

Descent: Rappel from the tree or scramble down the 3rd-class gully on the right.

History: The lower section of this route was climbed in order to toss the rope over the Lost Arrow on its first ascent.

*Evelyn Comstock on **Rickety Pinnacle** (5.2), 1952. Notice the homemade ring piton. Photo by Stanley Smith.*

20 Sugar Plum Fairy 5.5 R 100'

Start: On the uphill side of the spire at the base of a slab with a crack with two cedars.

P1 5.5 R: Climb up the crack and step left onto the arête. Climb the narrow arête (the arête of the orange left-facing corner of **Recital**) to a fixed anchor on a tree at the top of Rickety Pinnacle Wall. 100'

Descent: Rappel from the tree or scramble down the 3rd-class gully on the right.

FA May 4, 1968, Peter Baggaley, Peter Ferguson, John Leggett

21 Irene 5.3 PG 150'

Start: 50' right of and 50' up from the Lost Arrow, just right of an arête.

P1 5.3 PG: Climb up to a vegetated ledge, then up a crack (dubbed the Half Moon Crack) in the face to the right, then up and left on easy rock to the notch. 130'

P2 5.2 PG: Continue up and left to the top. 20'

Descent: Rappel from the tree or scramble down the 3rd-class gully on the right.

FA Jun 2, 1984, Mark Saulsgiver, Terry Saulsgiver

22 Rickety Pinnacle 5.2 G 90' ★★

This historic route climbs one of the hidden pinnacles of Chapel Pond Pass, as described by Dave Bernays.[4] The pinnacle sits on top of the wall; you can climb **Rope Toss Wall** or **Sugar Plum Fairy** to get to the base of the pinnacle or scramble up this route.

Start: Just right of **Irene** at the base of a 25'-wide depression.

Route Description: Scramble up the depression on surprisingly solid rock (3rd-class) to the fixed anchor of the other routes. The pinnacle sits just above near the edge of the cliff. A couple of 5th-class moves gain the top of the pinnacle. 90'

FA 1949, Dave Bernays, Stanley Smith

23 B Gentle 5.7 R 170'

An appealing start but lots of loose rock after that. The first ascentionist wrote, "Resist the temptation to place pro behind loose blocks." Yikes.

Start: Walk uphill from the Lost Arrow until you are level with the top of the Lost Arrow. There is a clean low-angle buttress with a cedar on its right side, below a white spot high on the wall behind. This route begins in the middle of this slab, right of a 25'-wide ugly depression.

P1 5.7 R: Face- and slab-climb the low-angle buttress with scant protection to a ledge with several cedars. (You can avoid the run-out section at the start by scrambling in on a ledge from uphill to the right.) From there, blocky corners and ledges lead up the face to below the white spot. Traverse 20' right to a cedar. 100'

P2 5.6 PG: Climb up to the second cedar, then out right to the blocky arête; up this to the top. 70'

FA Jun, 1984, Mark Saulsgiver, Terry Saulsgiver

24 The Nutcracker 5.7 A2 180'

This "lost" route climbs a long diagonaling crack on the right side of the Rickety Pinnacle Wall. According to the first ascentionist, this is an excellent route and well protected.

Start: Scramble up to the high point of the terrain where Rickety Pinnacle Wall meets The Cleaver. This route begins on a ledge 20' left of this high point, below a broken right-leaning crack with a nifty orange spike 10' up.

P1 5.7 A2: Climb the crack to an alcove, then up through a bulge to a roof. Move around the roof and continue in the same line to a tree belay. 120'

P2 5.6 G: Continue in the crack to the top. 60'

FA May 11, 1968, Peter Baggaley, Peter Ferguson

Lost Arrow

The Lost Arrow is a unique freestanding pinnacle of rock situated on the right end of the Lost Arrow Face. There are two routes up the spire, no obvious anchors on the top, and no easy way off.

The pinnacle was dubbed "Lost Arrow" by Dave Bernays after its larger sibling in Yosemite.

4 David Bernays, "The Pinnacles of Chapel Pond Notch" *Adirondac* 9, no 4 (Jul–Aug 1950), pp. 76-77.

25 Lost Arrow—Southwest Face 5.10a R 50' ★★

Start: At the lowest point on the south side of the spire at the base of a crumbly crack that defines the base of the spire.

P1 5.10a R: Climb the crumbly crack up left, then onto the face at a rail. Up the face past a horizontal with a piton, then up a thin vertical crack to the next horizontal break. Thin face climbing leads to the top. 50'

History: Originally a toprope, this has been led.

26 Lost Arrow—Southeast Face 5.8 PG 40' ★★★★

Although very short, this climb is highly recommended due to the uniqueness of the formation and the history behind its first ascent.

Start: On the southeast side of the spire at a large block separated from the spire by an off-width crack.

P1 5.8 PG: Climb the block, step left on small ledges onto the spire and up the face to a second ledge, then up the thin seam, past a piton, to the top. There is no easy anchor on top; you can loop the rope around the far corner for an anchor. 40'

Descent: Leave a rope anchored below and rappel off the other side. Or, for a more thrilling descent, rappel simultaneously off each side of the pinnacle.

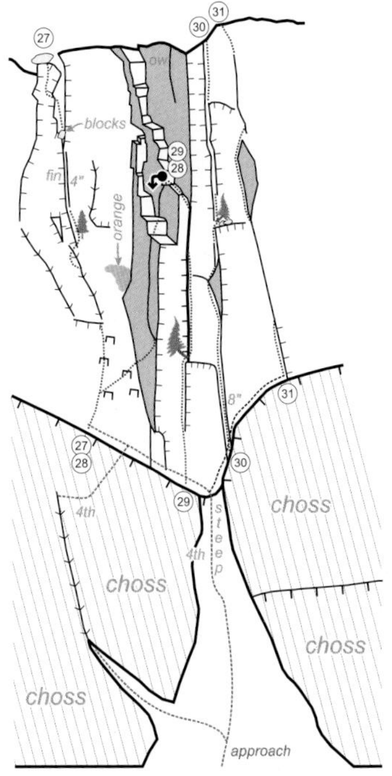

LOWER WASHBOWL: THE TICKET

27 Vogel (5.6)
28 Swept Away (5.9+)
29 Winter's Tale (5.10b)
30 More Tea, Vicar (5.9)
31 Chocolate City (5.7)

History: On the first ascent, Bernays and Smith tried direct aid but found the formation "devoid of holds or piton cracks." They returned two weeks later with a different tactic: Smith climbed a short way up **Rope Toss Wall** and threw a rope over the top of the pinnacle. After anchoring the line, they hand-over-hand climbed the rope to the summit. The first free ascent isn't known.[5]

FA Apr 16, 1950, Dave Bernays, Stanley Smith

Lower Washbowl

THE CLEAVER

At the top of the slope above the Lost Arrow and Rickety Pinnacle Wall is a slab of rock that faces the road, the right side of which forms an arête; there is a comfortable boulder at the base of this arête on which to sit. This wall has seen some exploration, with at least one party reporting pitons of unknown origin, although it has no reported routes.

Lower Washbowl

THE TICKET

Aspect	Southwest
Height	100'
Quality	★
Approach	45 min, difficult
Summary	A difficult-to-access cliff with two noteworthy cracks.

-5.6	5.7	5.8	5.9	5.10	5.11	5.12	5.13+	total
1	1		2	1				5

This cliff has the distinction of being the most difficult to get to of the Lower Washbowl cliffs.

DIRECTIONS **(MAP PAGE 272)**

At the top of the slope above the Lost Arrow, contour right to a position beneath the arête on the right end of The Cleaver. There is a comfortable boulder on which to sit. Continue contouring right to the base of a steep cone-shaped tree slope. There are two alternatives here: (1) scramble straight up the steepening slope, which becomes desperate weed pulling 4th-class; or (2) from the base of the slope, scramble left up a V-gully to its top, then make a 4th-class move right on clean rock to easier terrain at the base of the wall. The first climbers to visit this wall didn't like it either, calling this steep terrain P1.

27 Vogel (aka Sunday Funnies) 5.6 PG 120'

Start: Same as **Swept Away**.

P1 5.6 PG: Climb blocky rock straight up until it is possible to move right into the right-facing V-groove. Climb the wide crack past a chockstone into an alcove with some scary blocks at the base. On the left wall of the corner is a zigzag crack; follow this below the roof to the prow, then up to the top. 120'

FA May 11, 1968, Peter Bennett, Dave Thomas

5 An account of the first ascent of this pinnacle and other pinnacles in the area appeared in *Adirondac* 9, no. 4 (Jul–Aug 1950), "The Pinnacles of Chapel Pond Notch", pp. 76-77.

28 Swept Away 5.9+ PG 75' ★★★

An excellent crack and a "real route," according to Mellor. Named for a 1975 film by Lina Wertmüller.

Start: Up from and left of the low point of the face is a large left-facing corner, the right wall of which has a crack just left of the arête. Begin 15' uphill from the base of the corner.

P1 5.9+ PG: Traverse right across easy rock to the right wall of the corner. Hard moves right gain the crack; then follow the crack to a ledge at the top. 75'

Descent: Rappel from a horn as for **Winter's Tale**.

FA Dec 30, 1984, Don Mellor, Bill Dodd

29 Winter's Tale 5.10b G 100' ★

Start: At the lowest point on the cliff, at a crack directly below a cedar. This is also below the left end of a 10"-deep overlap 6' up.

P1 5.10b G: Climb up the dirty crack in the left-facing open book to a cedar. Battle through the cedar and into the dirty lichen-filled crack to the orange headwall in a right-facing corner. Climb through the headwall via the fist-sized off width and onto a sloping ledge. 100'

Descent: Rappel from a horn.

FA Dec 27, 1982, Don Mellor, Chuck Turner

30 More Tea, Vicar 5.9 G 120' ★★

You'll need some gas to get up this route.

Start: 10' up from and right of the low point on the face at an 8" crack.

P1 5.9 G: Climb the 8" crack to a ledge, then up a fist-crack to the base of a steep orange wall in a left-facing corner. Climb twin cracks through the steep wall (crux) to a ledge with a cedar and some blocks (possible belay here). Continue up a deepening chimney to the top of the tower on the right. A right-facing corner leads to the summit. 120'

History: The first ascent actually climbed a variation, moving left at the first ledge to **Winter's Tale**, then back right to the base of the orange wall, where "three pegs were used to climb the wall above (a supercharged maniac could do it free)."

FA May 5, 1968, Dave Keefe, Dave Thomas
FFA Jul 5, 1981, Chuck Turner, Mike Young

31 Chocolate City 5.7 G 100'

The name comes from an incident in the Gunks in which a climber asked Mellor for directions to **Chocolate City**; the climber had gotten the name **Shockley's Ceiling** wrong.

Start: 30' uphill from and right of the low point of the cliff at a short, broken, shallow left-facing corner; this corner is left of a larger left-facing corner.

P1 5.7 G: Climb up the left-facing corner to a crack through dark rock and into a large left-facing corner. Up the corner past a fistcrack, then wander to the top. 100'

FA Oct, 1983, Don Mellor, Paul Carlson

Lower Washbowl

THE FAN

The Fan has no reported routes (although it looks promising) but is included because it is a landmark for finding the Balcony and the other cliffs to the right. The cliff is roughly circular in shape with cracks radiating out from the center, like a fan.

DIRECTIONS **(MAP PAGE 272)**

To approach this cliff from the overlook, drop into the gully and climb up onto the talus. Traverse left toward the Spider's Web. After about 200', instead of going straight uphill as for False Arrow and Lost Arrow, angle up and right following the widest open slope of talus, the head of which is The Fan. At the top of the talus, you can (1) continue straight up an increasingly steep slope to the base of The Fan, then on to the Balcony; (2) contour left to The Ticket; or (3) walk right to reach the Long Buttress.

To approach from the Lost Arrow, at the top of the slope above the Lost Arrow, contour right to a position beneath the arête on the right end of The Cleaver. There is a comfortable boulder on which to sit. Continue contouring right to the base of a steep cone-shaped tree slope (the approach to The Ticket). Drop down around the toe of a scrappy cliffband, then contour right to the tree slope beneath The Fan. Follow the increasingly steep slope uphill to the base of The Fan.

Lower Washbowl

BALCONY CLIFF

Aspect	Southwest
Height	80'
Quality	
Approach	50 min, difficult
Summary	One historic route and some potential for more.

There is a lot of rock here but only one reported route. The cliff is high up on the mountain, wide, and has two right-rising ledges on its upper left end. From the base of The Fan, walk right along the base of the cliff to its right edge, then diagonal up and right to the base of the Balcony.

32 Wear Four 5.8 G 80'

Start: At the low point of the face beneath a crack that begins 5' left of a deep alcove.

P1 5.6 G: Climb the crack to a good ledge (known as the Balcony). 40'

P2 5.8 G: Climb the leftmost of two parallel cracks through the steep wall to a ledge. Step left and up into an alcove, then angle up and left following a crack to the top of the cliff. 40'

FA Dec 27, 1982, Chuck Turner, Don Mellor

Lower Washbowl

LONG BUTTRESS

Aspect	Southwest and southeast
Height	230'
Quality	
Approach	45 min, moderate
Summary	A tall ridge of blocky, discontinuous rock and two adventure routes.

-5.6	5.7	5.8	5.9	5.10	5.11	5.12	5.13+	total
		2						2

The Long Buttress is a tall ridge of blocky rock that extends from the right edge of the Balcony all the way down into the talus. The ridge is complex, with many ledges, corners, ramps, and just enough evergreens to make finding routes next to impossible. There are two routes reported here, neither of which begins at the toe of the ridge. **Dodge and Dangle** begins up the left side of the ridge, and **Bad Advice** begins way up on the right side, actually facing southeast. There is potential for new routes on the lower right portion of this buttress.

DIRECTIONS **(MAP PAGE 272)**

There are two approaches to the Long Buttress: (1) contour left from the Eighth Wall, meeting the buttress on its upper right side; or (2) walk downhill and right from the steep slope beneath The Fan, meeting the buttress on its left side; to reach the right side of the buttress, walk downhill and right around the toe of the buttress, then back uphill on its right side.

33 Dodge and Dangle 5.8 G 230'

This mountaineering-style route begins high on the left side of the buttress.

Start: There are several tree-filled gullies that diagonal up and right to the crest of the buttress. This route begins below the highest of these gullies on a stepped ramp that leads diagonally up and right below the wall that forms the right side of the gully.

P1 5.6 G: Climb up the right-rising stepped ramp to a large broken corner that leads to the crest of the buttress. Scramble up and left to the highest position on the crest in the trees. 120'

P2 5.7 G: Traverse right on the ledge, then up a face to gain a right-facing corner with some trees. Thrash through trees and find a belay in the corner. 50'

P3 5.8 G: Climb the corner to the top. 60'

FA Aug, 1983, Jim Vermeulen, Eric Dahn

34 Bad Advice 5.8 PG 200' ★

A tree once obscured the wide section on P2, so Mellor, believing that no wide gear was needed, convinced Turner to leave the big gear behind. Oops.

Start: Hike uphill on the right side of the buttress to the high point of the terrain. Just downhill from this high point is a wall that faces southeast with several cracks, just right of a steep gully. This route begins at a crack below the right side of a low roof 8' up, 10' left of a 12'-high alcove in white rock.

P1 5.8 G: Climb up the crack into a right-facing corner and follow it to its top. Walk left on the ledge, then up and left to a pine tree at the base of the orange corners above. 80'

P2 5.8 PG: Climb the fingercrack in the orange rock to a small ceiling, around this to the left, then follow the large left-facing corner to the roof. Out the roof via the fist crack, then up to the trees. 120'

FA 1982, Chuck Turner, Don Mellor

Lower Washbowl

CONCAVE WALL

Aspect	Southwest
Height	200'
Quality	★★★
Approach	50 min, moderate
Summary	Mostly obscure routes with a couple high-quality—and hard—recent additions.

-5.6	5.7	5.8	5.9	5.10	5.11	5.12	5.13+	total
1	1				1	1		4

When viewed from the Chapel Pond parking lot, the Concave Wall is seen nearly in profile and appears overhanging at the top, similar to a cresting wave. The most obvious feature on the wall is an orange right-facing corner at half height; this is **Cinnamon Girl**. To the right and below the orange corner is a deep, narrow gash, the base of which marks the start of **Cinnamon Girl**. The orange corner sits on the most solid part of the buttress (and there is a huge boulder that sits on top on the left side of this solid section); left of this solid section is a more broken, stepped, black-colored section, the left side of which has a deep chimney up high. Left of this is a more solid section with the routes **Middle Earth** and **Tubular Bells**.

DIRECTIONS **(MAP PAGE 272)**

Walk uphill along the right (southeast) side of the Long Buttress to where it meets the next wall. From this height of land, to the left is the start of **Bad Advice**, straight ahead is a steep gully that leads to **Middle Earth** and **Tubular Bells**, and 150' right is **Cinnamon Girl**.

An alternative approach is from the Eighth Wall: walk downhill and left around a broken toe of cliff, then contour left until you reach the deep, narrow chimney that marks the start of **Cinnamon Girl**.

35 Middle Earth 5.4 G 160'

A mountaineering adventure, named for J.R.R. Tolkien's concept of the real earth, into which you will crawl to ascend this route.

Start: At the height of land on the upper right side of the Long Buttress where it meets the left side of the Concave Wall is a steep gully. Climb up the steep gully (3rd-class) to a sloped stance at its top, below a large roof, the left side of which forms a chimney-cave. The route begins at the base of a slab with orange lichen that leads to the chimney-cave.

It's All About Perspective

When I described to friends and family what I was doing, they were shocked and concerned. In contrast, my climbing friends expressed awe and envy. It was simple, really. I was working at a local restaurant, sleeping in a tent, cooking over a fire, and climbing a lot. Critics would call me a climbing bum, but I didn't care. I was on an extended camping trip. And I was climbing, because that's just what climbers do. I was easily able to trade my regular lifestyle for this alternative one, living out a fantasy that others struggle to fathom.

The first time I met Don Mellor was at the Web. I had just finished Grand Hysteria, and Don said "Jesus kid, nobody's climbed that route in probably 15 years." The route was actually only 13 years old, but you get the idea. "Wow, that's a long time," I said. "I think the moves are pretty fun...just needed some TLC, that's all." Not sure if he believed me, but he was happy that some life had been restored to the route.

Shortly after moving into the area, I heard about a selection of unfinished projects, routes awaiting first free ascents. I recall Colin Loher and Jim Lawyer telling me: "Yeah, there's this route that a bunch of people have tried, but no one has done it." My curiosity led me to check out several of them. If I liked what I saw, I pounced. Jenga, Flying Buddha, and Beavers Taste Like Wood were some pretty sweet lines.

Then I became interested in routes and areas I knew nothing about. "Doubtful potential," everyone said. I saw something different, something overlooked, and decided to find out for myself. None of the routes were far off the beaten path and in fact several could be seen from the road. The exposure of Cinnamon Girl's last pitch, which I named Big Brother; the unrelenting climbing on The Great Escape; and the wildly fun Bookmaker's Variation: in my opinion, these are some of the best lines in the Park, and I will forever take pride in establishing them.

Two years ago, when I first began climbing, and the summer before I lived in the Adirondacks, I was given a powerful piece of advice by my friend Steve Larson, a true pioneer of climbing. We had just finished The Possessed at Cathedral and were surveying a nearby route. What he told me was simple: "Yeah, the whole climbing thing, it's all really just about perspective." With this nugget of wisdom, he granted me the key to climbing. I took one step back from the cliff and tilted my head.

- Conor Cliffe

Route Description: Climb up the slab and into the chimney-cave, then emerge into the gully above. Various options lead from here to the top.
FA 1981, Jim Cunningham, Chuck Turner

36 Tubular Bells 5.7 G 170' ★

A good-looking P1 with an unpleasant approach. Named for Michael Oldfield's most famous album.

Start: The route begins 25' right of **Middle Earth**. To reach the start, approach up the gully as for **Middle Earth**. Near the top, the gully splits: the left fork leads to **Middle Earth**, and the right fork climbs an unpleasant, steep, narrow slot (4th-class) to the height of land at a narrow ridge with exposed ledges and good views. The route climbs the open book above (with a square roof at 50'), which is the second open book right of the roof that forms the chimney-cave of **Middle Earth**.

P1 5.7 G: Scramble up a ledge 6' up, then up a sharp-edged crack in the left wall of the open book. At its top, climb a left-leaning crack in the right wall of the open book to the square white-colored roof. Around the roof on the left, past a bush, up to a V-slot, then up and left to a ledge. 110'

P2 5.4 G: Step left to a left-rising ramp and climb it past loose rock to the top, just left of a large block-tower. 60'

FA 1981, Chuck Turner, Jim Cunningham

37 Cinnamon Girl 5.11c G (5.10 R) 230' ★★★

Quite an achievement on some super exposed terrain. The "bear-hug block" at the top is precarious.

P1 5.7 G: Climb the left-facing flake to the roof. Step left around the roof and up to a ledge with a cedar. 70'

P2 5.6 G: From the right side of the ledge, ascend a deep V-slot into a right-facing corner with a crack that leads to a ledge below the orange corner. 40'

P3 5.11a G (5.10 R): Go up the orange corner to its top (where the original route stopped), then move up and right around stepped roof to a corner. Up this (crazy runout) to next roof. Exit right to belay. 60'

P4 Big Brother 5.11c G: Angle up and left to a crack in the zebra-striped, overhanging wall. Follow the crack to a "bear-hug block"; pull left around this to the top. 60'

History: The original ascent, which stood for 21 years, stopped at the top of the orange corner. Conor Cliffe picked off this plum during his north country mop-up.

FA (5.8 A1) 1981, Chuck Turner, Rich Leswing, Jim Cunningham
FFA (P3, P4) Jul 3, 2012, Conor Cliffe

38 Bonnie and Clyde 5.12a G (5.7 R) 60' ★★★

This route follows the crack through orange rock just right of P3 of **Cinnamon Girl**.

Start: At the ledge at the top of P2 of **Cinnamon Girl**.

P1 5.12a G (5.7 R): Go up the crack to its top, then reach way right to another crack. Up this to the P3 belay of **Cinnamon Girl**. 60'

FA Jul 3, 2012, Conor Cliffe

Lower Washbowl

EIGHTH WALL

Aspect	Southwest
Height	200'
Quality	★★
Approach	30 min, moderate
Summary	Some good—but very dirty—cracklines.

-5.6	5.7	5.8	5.9	5.10	5.11	5.12	5.13+	total
	1		2	2				5

The Eighth Wall, the farthest right of the cliffs in the Lower Washbowl, sits below the upper left end of the Upper Washbowl. The wall has been compared to the Spider's Web, although this is a stretch given the level of dirt. The base of the cliff near **The Fang** and **Land of the Lost** is level and open; the routes **PR** and **Pantless Phenom** are up and right from this level terrain.

DIRECTIONS **(MAP PAGE 272)**

You can reach the Eighth Wall easily (less than 5 min) from the base of the Concave Wall by contouring right for several hundred feet, then up and right to the base of the Eighth Wall.

From the road, you can reach the Eighth Wall more directly by approaching as for the Upper Washbowl. From the base of the **Wiessner Route** walk downhill 120', then turn (skier's) right and contour into the open talus. Across the talus is a small rock buttress with a gully on its left side. Ascend this gully and go left down the other side, then contour (skier's) right to the base of the Eighth Wall. Time to the Upper Washbowl is 25 min, then another 5 min to the Eighth Wall.

39 Hoar–Horovitz 5.10a PG 75' ★★

Climbs the crack just left of the headwall top pitch of **The Fang**, and could make a logical extension to **Land of the Lost**. It's steep, sometimes puzzling, and has excellent exposure, positions, and scenery.

Start: At a tree ledge on top of P2 of **The Fang** or **Land of the Lost**, at a vertical crack broken at mid-height by a horizontal ledge, 15' left of P3 of **The Fang**. (Given the current conditions of these other routes, it's perhaps easier to rappel in from above. To do so, go up the decent trail on the left side of the Upper Washbowl until it turns sharp right, and just after a large boulder. Turn left and head slightly uphill to the height of land. Go right, then back left to reach the open summit ledges.)

P1 5.10a PG: Climb the thin crack system through some strenuous moves to the horizontal ledge (small gear; be mindful of falling onto the spiky dead cedar tree). Continue up the final corner to the open summit ledges on top of the Eighth Wall. 75'

FA Aug 27, 2011, Sam Hoar, Ari Horovitz

40 Land of the Lost 5.9+ G 160'

Start: At the left end of the cliff at a right-facing corner formed by a block with a ledge on top below a crack on the main wall that leads to the left side of a nose 40' up.

P1 5.9 G: Climb up the crack to a large left-facing corner with blocks. Continue up the wide slot in the corner to a ledge with a cedar tree. 90'

P2 5.9+ G: There are two parallel crack lines here, about 8' apart, the rightmost of which is directly behind the tree. Both are the same grade and lead to a tree ledge. 70'

FA 1989, Jon Barker, Chris Smith, Ward Smith, Jim Ainsworth

41 The Fang 5.10b G 210'

A nice-looking crack but extremely dirty.

Start: The left end of the wall has some blocks that form a ledge and a right-facing corner (the start of **Land of the Lost**). Begin 12' right of this corner at a straight-up finger- and handcrack. At the base of the crack is a 7'-high, 8"-deep right-facing corner.

P1 5.10b G: Climb the slot into a fingercrack, through a triangular pod, then up the handcrack to a fist-sized finish at overhanging cedar hell. 70'

P2 5.10b G: Climb straight up to the left end of a ledge, then up parallel cracks through a slot and up to a ledge, meeting it just left of a perched block. 70'

P3 5.10b G: From the ledge, step left and climb up to a ceiling, through some blocks, and up a crack in the headwall above. This very exposed pitch ends on a nice, open summit. 70'

FA Aug 14, 1983, Tim Beaman, Sylvia Lazarnick

42 Pantless Phenom 5.7 G 220'

Start: At a large, block-filled, right-facing corner up and to the right of the lower terrace that holds the routes **The Fang** and **Land of the Lost**, and 10' left of **PR**.

P1 5.0 G: Scramble up the block-filled corner to the broad, dirt- and tree-covered ledge and a belay at a large aspen. 30'

P2 5.7 G: Walk left along the dirty ledge to an 8'-high vertical crack that ends at a small ledge. Move to the right end of the ledge at a small left-facing corner, then climb the corner and adjacent fingercrack until it is possible to step right onto another ledge system. Continue straight through this small ledge system to a large offwidth, which is climbed to its top at a broad, flat ledge. From here, climb either the crack just above (or the next crack to the right shared with **PR**) to a small, treed ledge with a fixed anchor on a cedar. 130'

P3 5.6 G: Head left to a right-facing corner–crack. Follow the crack until it fades just below a small evergreen tree. Head up and left to the summit ledges. 60'

Descent: Walk straight back from the cliff, then down and slightly right to reach the Upper Washbowl descent trail after about 1 minute. Alternatively, rappel with 2 ropes to reach the ground at the base of **PR**.

FA Jul 15, 2010, Sam Hoar, Ari Horovitz

43 PR 5.9+ G 100' ★★★

An excellent route featuring 100 feet of steep, sustained crack climbing with solid rock, exposed positions, and spectacular scenery. This route is mentioned on page 233 of *Adirondack Rock*: "A good cleaning here will undoubtedly yield stellar crack routes, especially the unclimbed line on the right side of the wall (which has some unexplained fixed gear)." The name is short for "Paying Respects", as it was climbed the day following Dennis Murphy's tragic accident on the Upper Washbowl.

Start: 10' right of the large, block-filled, right-facing corner used to access the aspen ledge (the start of **Pantless Phenom**), behind a small hemlock and a small cedar, at a long fingercrack.

P1 5.9+ G: Follow the fingercrack through some thin sections to jugs and a good rest 30' up. Continue up the crack to a left-facing corner just left of an impressive tooth of rock. Climb the corner to a small ceiling at it's top, then step right to the parallel crack system. Up this crack for 15' to a horizontal break, then step back to the left-hand crack to an intimidating (but not overly difficult) offwidth. Go up the offwidth to a large ledge with a gigantic, gaping crack at its back, then climb the handcrack directly across the ledge past a perched boulder to a cedar tree with a fixed anchor. 100'

FA Aug 17, 2010, Sam Hoar, Hillary Gerardi, Brad Carlson

Lower Washbowl

JACK STRAW WALL

Aspect	Southeast
Height	80'
Quality	
Approach	10 min, moderate
Summary	Obscure cliff with a single exploratory route.

The Jack Straw Wall is a minor cliff that faces southeast and sits directly below the route **Hesitation** on the Upper Washbowl, about one-third of the way up to the Upper Washbowl on the old approach trail.

DIRECTIONS **(MAP PAGE 272)**

Park at Chapel Pond pullout and walk 120' toward Malfunction Junction, over the guardrail on the north side of the road, and down into the marsh. Cross this, then follow cairns up through the talus to a short double-tiered cliffband. The lower tier is short and has a roof 15' up on its right side. The trail goes uphill to the right along the base of the lower tier to the right end of the upper tier, where there are three prominent open-book corners. The left corner has white and yellow rock and a ceiling before the top, the middle corner has a ledge at the same height as the ceiling of the left corner, and the right corner has a prominent pine tree at the top and some black rock on the right wall. Hiking time from the road is about 10 min.

The trail continues up the right side of the Jack Straw Wall and on to the Upper Washbowl. Despite some blowdown, the trail is still sufficiently cairned and discernible.

44 Jack Straw 5.6 G 80' ★

Named for a Grateful Dead song.

Start: At a small slab beneath a roof 10' up, 20' left of a flat rock that sits beneath the three dihedrals.

P1 5.6 G: Up the slab, then up and right on a broken ramp to its top. Mount the right side of a large block to gain the corner, then climb up the corner to a pine tree. Walk right on a ledge to the top. 80'

Descent: Walk right to the path.

FA Apr 29, 1989, Don Mellor, Ben Kremers

Lower Washbowl

SWAMP ROCK

Aspect	Southwest
Height	80'
Quality	
Approach	15 min, moderate
Summary	Tiny rock with a very hard route and a couple historic easier routes.

-5.6	5.7	5.8	5.9	5.10	5.11	5.12	5.13+	total
	1	1			1			3

This small wall is not on the same cliffband as the other Lower Washbowl cliffs and has a separate approach. It sits above the level of the road and below the Concave Wall (down from and right of the toe of the Long Buttress) and can be seen from the road only when the leaves are off the trees.

DIRECTIONS **(MAP PAGE 272)**

From the pullout at Chapel Pond, walk along the road (toward Keene Valley) to the northwest end of the pond. On the right-hand side of the road is a small pullout near a rock outcropping. Continue following the road to the end of the guardrail and, at the "Falling Rock Zone" sign, turn right into the woods and descend to the northwest end of a swamp. Cross the end of the swamp, then scramble straight up the steep talus to the base of the wall 600208,4888473. Total time from the pullout is about 15 min.

45 **Swamp Gas 5.8 G 80'**

Start: At the low point on the face, just right of the huge left-facing corner with a chockstone at the bottom.

P1 5.8 G: Climb up the face just left of two left-rising thin cracks on the orange face and into a 1'-deep left-leaning, left-facing corner with a bush at the bottom. Up the crack in the left-leaning corner to a ledge, then climb up a right-leaning dihedral to the top. 80'

FA Jun 25, 1986, Jeff Edwards, Patrick Purcell

46 **Swamp Thang 5.11d G 30'** ★★

Start: At a large oak tree several feet right of the low point on the wall, below a horizontal crack.

● **P1 5.11d G:** Climb to the horizontal, then up the blank face to a fixed anchor in the middle of the face (about halfway up the formation). 30'

FA Aug 15, 1994, Dave Furman

47 **Swamp Arête 5.7 G 60'**

Looks like a good climb but a tree has fallen against the route, which obscures most of the start.

Start: Steeply uphill 25' from the low point on the face in a shallow cave with a handcrack in the back.

P1 5.7 G: Climb up the crack through a V-notch formed by a block, over the block, then up the arête to the top of the wall. 60'

FA Jun 25, 1986, Jeff Edwards, Patrick Purcell

BEER WALLS

Location	South side of NY 73, 0.5 mile west of Chapel Pond
Summary	A good collection of single-pitch routes—many 5.10 cracks and a large collection of moderates, with a couple of very popular toproping spots.

-5.6	5.7	5.8	5.9	5.10	5.11	5.12	5.13+	total
18	12	14	18	25	10	4		101

The Beer Walls, also known as Chapel Pond Canyon, is a collection of cliffs situated along the northeastern hillside of a deep drainage area that runs northwest from the outlet of Chapel Pond, parallel to NY 73. Unlike other roadside cliffs in the Chapel Pond area, the Beer Walls is separated from the road by a forested ridge and thus offers a quiet atmosphere in which to climb.

The cliffs are roughly broken into two major sections, the Upper and the Lower. The Upper Beer Wall's assets include the popular toproping cracks **Seven Ounces** and **3.2**, an amazing collection of straight-up 5.10 cracks on the appropriately-named "5.10 Wall," and one of the best 5.9 corner cracks around, **Frosted Mug**. Separated from this cliff is a lower cliff of equal proportion, the Lower Beer Wall, which includes the toproping area **Afternoon Delight** as well as a number of top-quality moderates such as **Pegasus**, **Rockaholic**, and **Clutch and Cruise**, mixed with more challenging lines such as **Blacksmith** and **Turbocharge**. With some exceptions—such as the Clutch and Cruise Cave, which houses several 5.12s and even a 5.13—these cliffs can be thought of as a place for moderate, one-pitch cragging.

*Isabelle Ménard on **Rockaholic** (5.8).*
Photo by Patrick Cadieux.

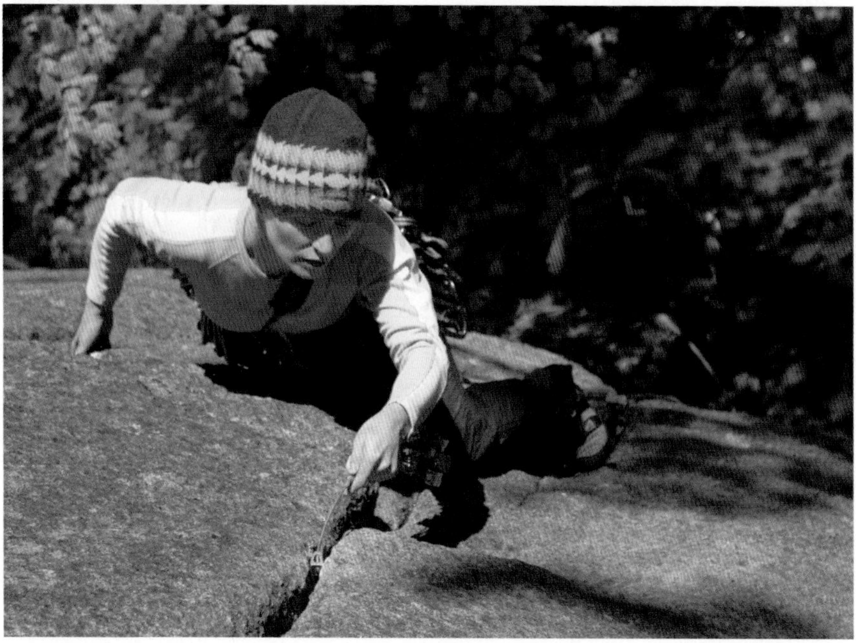

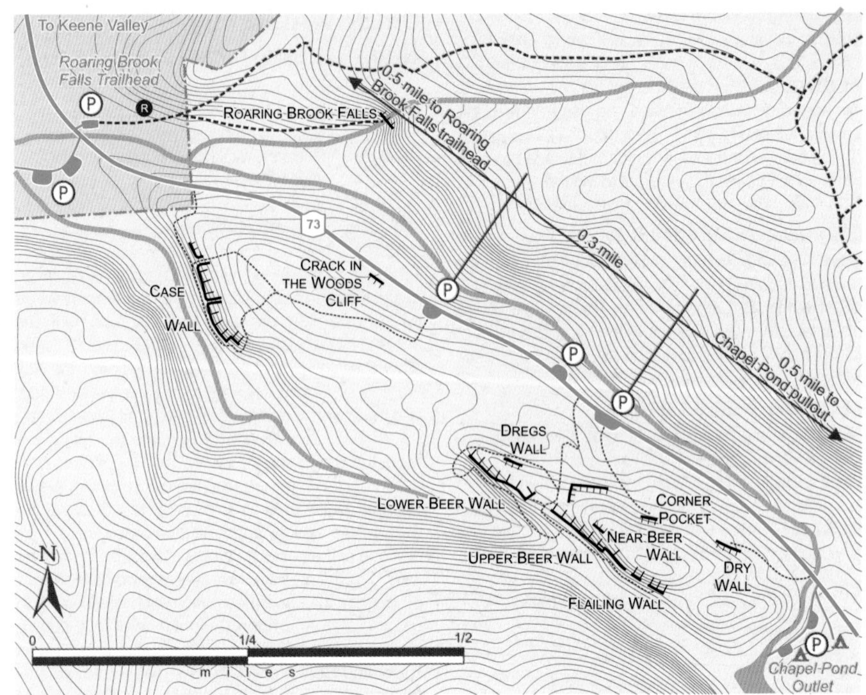

DIRECTIONS **(MAPS PAGES 197 AND 286)**

To reach the Beer Walls, park on NY 73 at a paved pullout 0.5 mile from the Chapel Pond pullout on the left (when driving toward Keene Valley) and 0.8 mile from the Roaring Brook Falls Trailhead on the right (when driving toward Chapel Pond from Keene Valley). From the lot, walk 200' down the road (toward Keene Valley) to a log bridge that spans the ditch on the same side of the road 599550,4888793; this trail leads uphill to the height of land on the ridge above the road 599440,4888644. Do not take the trail directly above the parking area, as this leads to Corner Pocket, a separate cliff.

There is an alternate, more spacious parking area on the other side of the road, 0.1 mile toward Keene Valley 599451,4888877.

From the trailhead, hike up the drainage area to a switchback and steps that lead to the height of land; about 5 min. This height of land sits between the Upper Beer Wall (to the left) and the Lower Beer Wall (to the right) and is the point from which most of the cliffs are accessed. Specific directions to the various cliffs are provided from this height of land.

There is an outhouse on the right just before the height of land.

HISTORY

In March 1980, Bill Simes, Bob Bushart, and Bill Diemand were flying around the High Peaks in a Cessna four-seater (with pilot "Captain [Mike] Quirk") looking for cliffs. They flew down Chapel Pond Canyon at about 100' and were all duly impressed by the rock. The following year, Bushart and Simes walked in for a closer look and made a feeble attempt on what was to become **Frosted Mug**, starting directly from below in what is now part of **Dark Horse Ail**. Simes was impressed and thought it incredible that no other climbers had made their mark here. Word got around, and, in 1982, Don Mellor and one of his students climbed **Positive Reinforcement**, an ice route across the canyon from the Lower Beer Wall. In the spring of that year, Simes returned, this time with Chuck Turner, to have another look. From above, Simes cleaned **Frosted Mug** and Turner cleaned **Labatt-Ami**; then they swapped lines (so no preinspection) and led them. These two routes began the beer-naming trend, and the walls became known as the Beer Walls.

Route development continued at a rapid pace in 1982 and 1983, with the main emphasis from the Red House Gang, including Jim Cunningham, Rich Leswing, Pete Benson, Alan Jolley, and Chuck Turner, who picked many classic lines, including **Pegasus**, **Turbocharge**, **Sword**, and **Rockaholic**, among others. Development nearly stopped after the Red House Gang dissolved (three routes in 1984 and six in '85) but picked back up again in 1988 for a few years as Patrick Purcell, Don Mellor, Jeff Edwards, and others combed through the remaining lines, including the amazing 5.10 Wall. Since 1999, development has virtually ceased, with only a couple of new routes.

A noteworthy achievement occurred in 1995 with the first free ascent of **They Never Recognized Me** by Michael Christon, the first 5.13 to be led in the Chapel Pond region. Located in the Clutch and Cruise Cave,

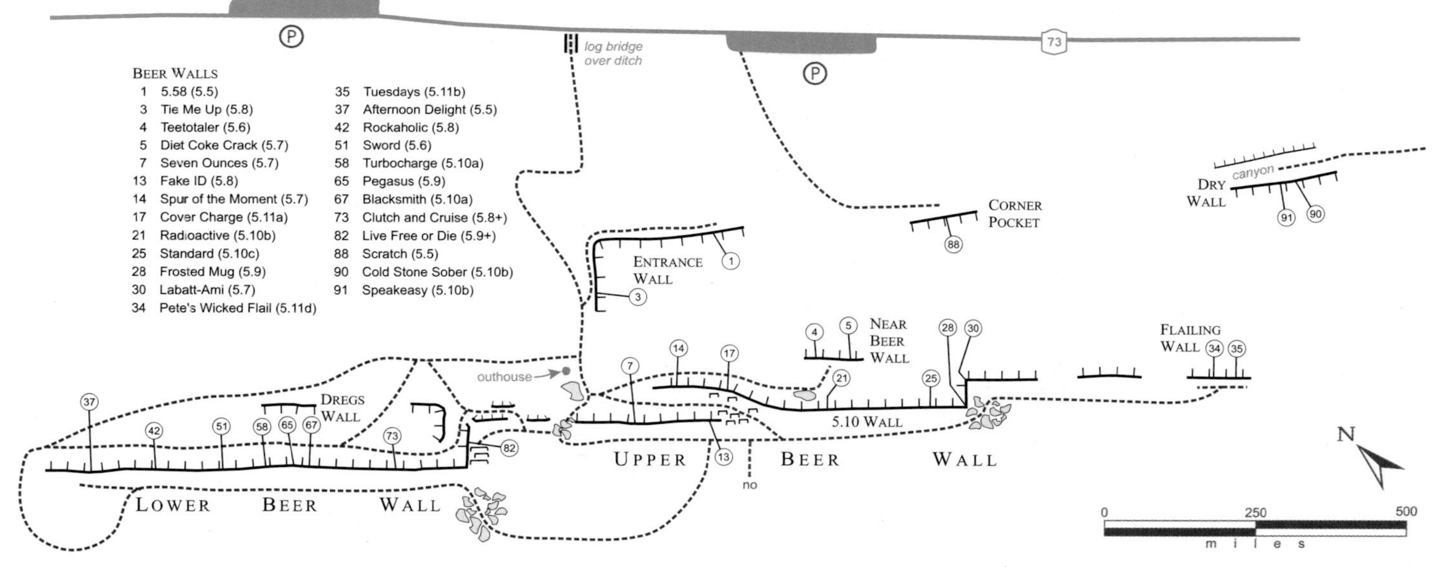
Beer Walls
1 5.58 (5.5)
3 Tie Me Up (5.8)
4 Teetotaler (5.6)
5 Diet Coke Crack (5.7)
7 Seven Ounces (5.7)
13 Fake ID (5.8)
14 Spur of the Moment (5.7)
17 Cover Charge (5.11a)
21 Radioactive (5.10b)
25 Standard (5.10c)
28 Frosted Mug (5.9)
30 Labatt-Ami (5.7)
34 Pete's Wicked Flail (5.11d)
35 Tuesdays (5.11b)
37 Afternoon Delight (5.5)
42 Rockaholic (5.8)
51 Sword (5.6)
58 Turbocharge (5.10a)
65 Pegasus (5.9)
67 Blacksmith (5.10a)
73 Clutch and Cruise (5.8+)
82 Live Free or Die (5.9+)
88 Scratch (5.5)
90 Cold Stone Sober (5.10b)
91 Speakeasy (5.10b)
P
P
73
log bridge over ditch
Entrance Wall
Corner Pocket
Dry Wall
canyon
Near Beer Wall
Flailing Wall
outhouse
Dregs Wall
5.10 Wall
Upper Beer Wall
Lower Beer Wall
no
N
0
250
500
miles

The Red House Gang

The Red House Gang—no club here, just a bunch of barely employed climbing bums and weekend warriors looking for a place to crash and party down. The original core was Mike Young, Peg Collins, Ben (a ranger), and myself. We had all worked for Vermont Voyageur Expeditions (VVE), based out of Montgomery Center, Vermont, at one time or other, and I was their main climbing instructor (1981–winter 1982). We had a base located about half a mile below Malfunction Junction on Route 9 just before Split Rock Falls where there was a house and a bunch of cabins. VVE scaled back operations in the spring of '82, so I was looking for a place to live and work. I ended up living in a tent on the upper level of the Chapel Pond outlet for about two months until Pete Fish ran me out of there! It was then I began The Adirondack Mountain Climbing School and Peg, Ben, and Mike began a guide service. We teamed together and rented what became "The Red House," a house on the other side of the river from the Mountaineer—it's no longer red and looks way more gentrified now. I guess the name got coined after I (and Bob Hey) put up and named Red House Ramp on the north side of Pitchoff. I was able to struggle through with my climbing school (along with odd jobs) until the time I left for Boston in the fall of 1984. The guide service never really got off the ground. Luckily the rent was right, at $50 per month including heat!

Photo by Jim Cunningham.

Ben and Peg married and divorced all in that summer. I was soloing routes on Chapel Pond Slabs barefoot when I befriended Ken Reville, who became our major weekend warrior and was responsible for bringing in Bob Hey, Dave Flinn, and Jake Piscowski. Tim Broader also joined us. Dave and Tim worked at the Mountaineer, and Bob had a string of odd jobs in Lake Placid. Interestingly, Dave was the mastermind behind Adirondack Alpine Journal, a quirky little local rag, with Bob doing some writing and editing.

The Red House became a magnet for transient climbers we would befriend on the crags and friends of my housemates. Many of my clients would stay over as well. Tim Beaman and Sylvia Lazarnick were regulars. The local crowd of climbers would come and hang out, too (mostly Chuck Turner, Rich Leswing, and Todd Eastman). Most weekend nights, a party was going on, people crashing on the floor or putting up tents in the backyard. It was a wild and wonderful time. Often we all would go solo up Bob's Knob on moonlit nights to hang out smoking dope and carrying on. It's a wonder none of us got hurt! Afternoons, after climbing we would spend long sessions playing hacky sack, drinking beer, listening to Bob Marley, The Who, The Clash, Neil Young, and Pink Floyd. Ahhhh, the life of the young and reckless. All this was in the framework of climbing and occasionally putting up new routes.

- Jim Cunningham

this overhanging buttress saw more activity in 2006, including another 5.13 by Mark Polinski: **Mark's Blue Ribbon**. These two routes, combined with **Zabba** and **Wheelin' N' Dealin'** at the Spider's Web, represent the most difficult climbing in the Chapel Pond area.

Several outlying crags have been discovered in the canyon and developed over the years, such as the Case Wall, developed in the late 1980s by Mellor and Tad Welch; the Dry Wall, discovered by Simes in 1996 and home to a couple of quality (but overgrown) 5.10s; and Corner Pocket, the work of Jeff Edwards and the Northwood School Outing Club in the mid-1990s.

DESCENT OPTIONS

There are very few established rappels on these cliffs, which are small enough that walking around back to your pack isn't really an issue. From the top of the Upper Beer Wall, walk left back to the height of land, down the 20' scramble through the notch, then back along the base of the cliff. From the top of the Lower Beer Wall, it is faster to walk left toward **Afternoon Delight**.

There is a fixed anchor at the top of **Frosted Mug** that requires you to downclimb an exposed, 4th-class slab and is therefore not generally recommended. Regardless, it does provide a good rappel for the routes on the 5.10 Wall.

Beer Walls

ENTRANCE WALL

Aspect	West and north
Height	40'
Quality	
Approach	5 min, easy
Summary	A tiny, mossy wall that was once cleaned with creative routes.

-5.6	5.7	5.8	5.9	5.10	5.11	5.12	5.13+	total
1		1	1					3

On the approach trail, just before you reach the height of land, is a short cliff on the left, facing the trail. Walk left and downhill along the base of the cliff to access the routes. This was once known as the Billboard Wall due to the cleaned stripe of rock on the **Zig-Zag** traverse; this has since completely grown in with thick, healthy moss.

1 5.58 5.5 R 40'

A nice face but requires some cleaning before it can be recommended. Depending on how you climb it, it's either 5.5 or 5.8, hence the name.

Start: From the approach trail, walk downhill along the base of the cliff to the lowest point on the cliff (the start of Up and Over). Walk around the toe and uphill along the base of the cliff for 110' to the first left-facing, 1'-deep, dirty corner on a slab.

P1 5.5 R: Climb the slab left of the left-facing corner to a tree that marks the top. 40'

FA Aug, 1983, Jim Cunningham, Dan Golpentia, Jan Kubli

2 Zig-Zag 5.9 G 60'

Looks like good climbing, but incredibly moss-covered and in need of a good scrubbing.

Start: This route is the horizontal crack that traverses left across the wall from the base of Tie Me Up.

P1 5.9 G: (V1) Traverse left across the face 30' to a stance at its end. (V2) Climb up the slab to a corner with an overhang; up this corner and overhang to a grungy slab and follow it to the trees. 60'

V1 Up and Over 5.6 G: From below the left end of the traverse and immediately to the right of the outside corner of the buttress, climb directly up to the stance and on to the top.

V2 5.8 G: From the end of the traverse, belay, then traverse back under the long overlap, cross Tie Me Up to a small vertical crack, and downclimb it to the ground.

FA Aug 25, 1983, Alan Jolley, Jim Cunningham
FA (V1) Aug 25, 1983, Jim Cunningham, Ken Reville
FA (V2) Aug 26, 1983, Jim Cunningham, Ken Reville, Tim Broader

3 Tie Me Up 5.8 G 40' ★

Start: At the highest part of the cliff, 30' left of where the approach trail meets the cliff, at the base of a handcrack and directly in front of a sizable birch tree.

P1 5.8 G: Climb the broken handcrack split by a horizontal break at midheight. 40'

FA Aug, 1983, Alan Jolley, Kathy Bright

Beer Walls

DREGS WALL

On the approach trail, just before the height of land, a trail leads right (northwest). Hike for 420' through open forest to the base of the Dregs Wall, a 75'-long, 25'-high wall that faces the road (north) 599361,4888730. It is mostly covered in moss and unappealing, but it has a cleaned section that makes a fair toproping and teaching spot.

Another landmark for finding this wall is that it sits directly behind the popular route Pegasus on the Lower Beer Wall (simply walk toward the road from the top of Pegasus).

Beer Walls

NEAR BEER WALL

Aspect	Southwest
Height	25'
Quality	★
Approach	8 min, easy
Summary	Tiny cliff with some quality cracks.

-5.6	5.7	5.8	5.9	5.10	5.11	5.12	5.13+	total
1	1							2

A 25'-high cliff located in the woods above the Upper Beer Wall. From the height of land on the approach trail and just before the scramble down through the notch, walk left (southeast) and uphill following the top of the cliff. There is a large boulder perched on a slab, and just beyond is an open slab marking the top of the 5.10 Wall; walk back in the woods away from the cliff 50' to the base of this short wall.

4 Teetotaler 5.6 G 25' ★

Start: At a vertical handcrack near the left end of the cliff just before the cliff turns into brushy slabs.

P1 5.6 G: Follow the right-leaning shallow crack that narrows to finger size up and right to the top. 25'

FA Aug, 1988, Ken Nichols

5 Diet Coke Crack 5.7 G 25' ★

Nichols's drink of choice.

Start: At a handcrack formed by a left-facing flake, 50' right of Teetotaler.

P1 5.7 G: Follow the crack up and right to the top. 25'

FA Aug, 1988, Ken Nichols

Beer Walls

UPPER BEER WALL

Aspect	Southwest
Height	120'
Quality	★★★★★
Approach	10 min, easy
Summary	Steep cliff riddled with stellar cracks.

-5.6	5.7	5.8	5.9	5.10	5.11	5.12	5.13+	total
2	3	2	5	9	5	2		28

From the height of land on the approach trail, continue straight (southwest) down a short 20' scramble through a notch, then turn left (or climber's right, since you're now at the base of the cliff) along the base of this cliff. The first recognizable route encountered is the straight-in crack of Seven Ounces.

6 Underage Drinking 5.9 R 35'

This route, which is easier for tall people, has reportedly been led, but nobody seems to claim it.

Start: 12' left of the straight-in crack of Seven Ounces, at the right end of a wide, 4"-deep ledge that is 4' up.

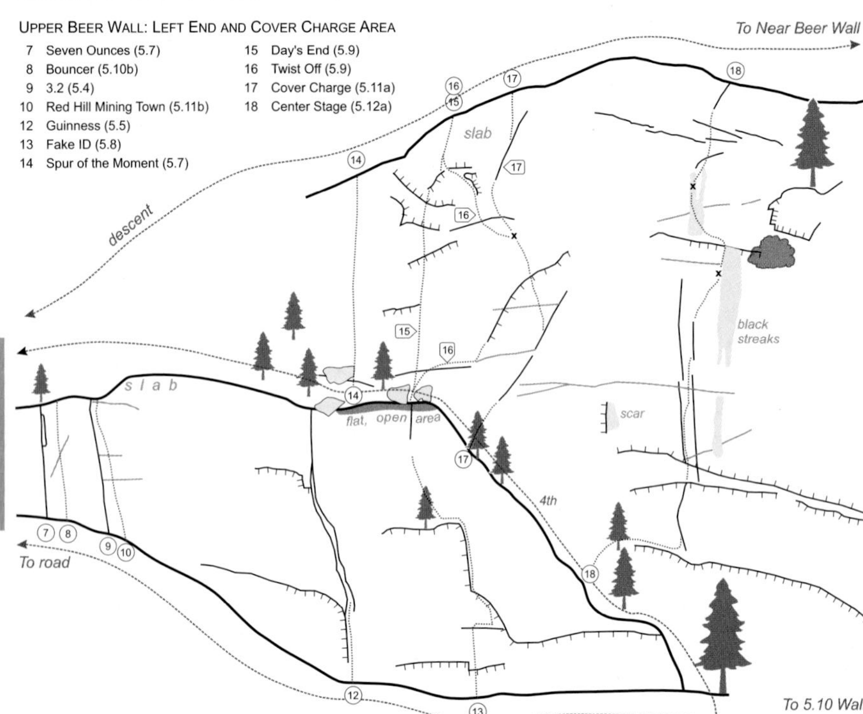

P1 5.9 R: Mantle the ledge and make delicate, unprotected face moves to a good slanted horizontal and left-facing flake. Climb up to the prominent horizontal (first gear), then up the face above to the top. 35'
FA (TR) 1988, Tom DuBois

7 Seven Ounces 5.7 G 40' ★★★★

Perhaps the most popular toprope route in the Adirondacks, although it's a nice lead for the grade. The heavy traffic has polished the holds a bit.
Start: From the left end of the cliff (where the approach trail scrambles down through a small notch), walk 80' right to the base of two obvious cracks 12' apart. This route begins below the left crack.
P1 5.7 G: Climb the handcrack past a wide slot past a ledge to the top. 40'
FA Jun 2, 1982, Jim Cunningham, Pete Benson

8 Bouncer 5.10b R 40' ★★

A very popular toprope after you climb one of the neighboring cracks.
Start: On the face between **Seven Ounces** and **3.2**.
P1 5.10b R: Climb the right-leaning slashes up the face, being sure to avoid the tempting handcrack to the left. 40'
FFA Oct 9, 1984, Ken Nichols, Chuck Boyd

9 3.2 5.4 G 40' ★★

Start: 12' right of **Seven Ounces** at the base of a broken left-leaning crack.
P1 5.4 G: Climb the crack, past many steps that offer rests along the way. 40'
FA May 4, 1982, Don Mellor

10 Red Hill Mining Town 5.11b TR 40'

Climbs the face just right of **3.2** but deliberately avoids using the crack to the left.
FA (TR) 1987, Jim Belcer

11 40 Oz. to Freedom 5.8+ X 45'

Start: 7' left of **Guinness**.
P1 5.8+ X: Climb the face just left of **Guinness** via finger pockets, but deliberately avoid the **Guinness** crack. Once on top of a blocky stance, step left and climb the face (crux) to a pine tree. 45'
FA Jun, 1997, David Lent (solo)

12 Guinness 5.5 G 40' ★★

Start: 50' right of **3.2** at a right-facing corner that forms the left side of a wide crack, and at the right end of a long horizontal ledge that begins near **3.2**.
P1 5.5 G: Climb the corner into the wide crack, through a pod where the crack narrows to hand size, then move right past a cedar tree and on to the top. 40'
FA Oct, 1982, Chuck Turner

13 Fake ID 5.8 PG 90' ★

Start: 15' right of **Guinness** on the "brick wall," a highly featured section of low rock that roughly resembles bricks. This is also at the intersection with the trail to the Lower Beer Wall.

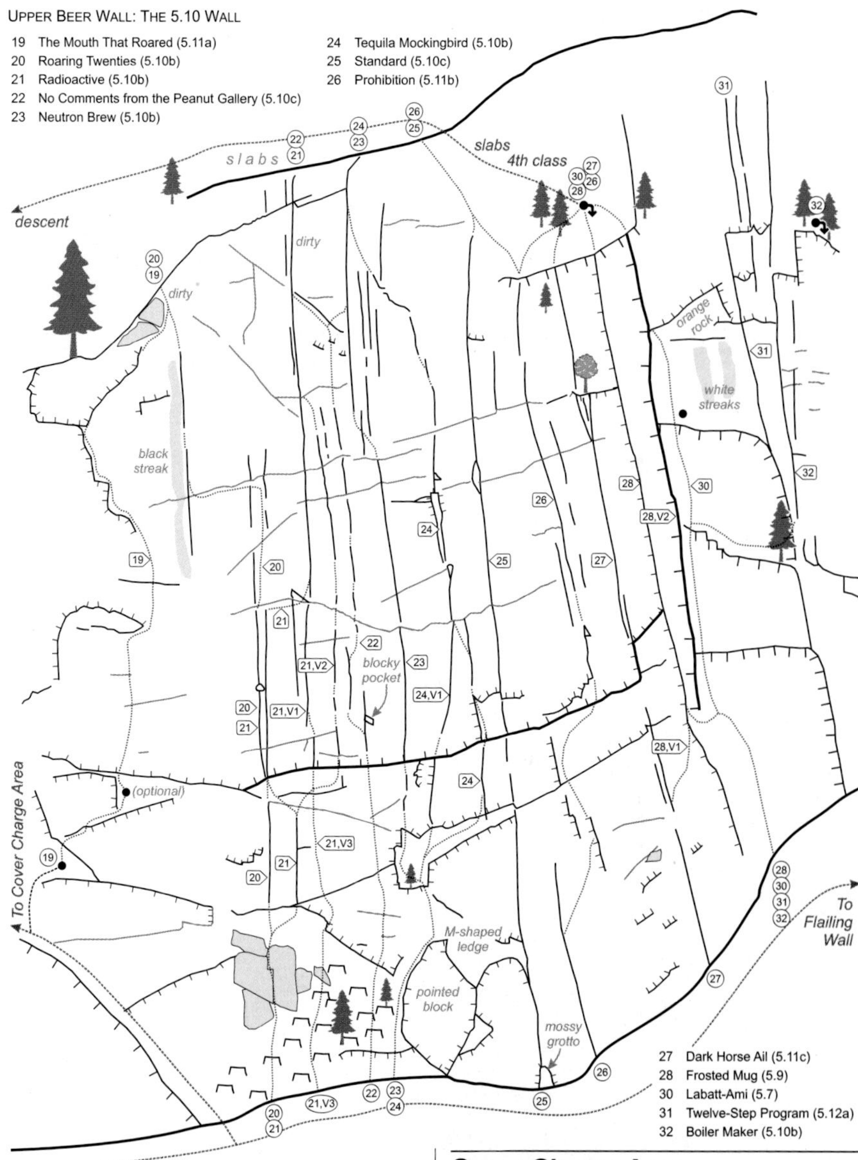

P1 5.8 PG: Climb the bricklike wall to a horizontal, step right, then up the face just left of the arête to a good ledge. Move up and left to a larger ledge with a tree. Step left 10' and climb the face via a thin flake to a jug. A short crack leads to the open area at the base of the Cover Charge Area. 90'

FA May 19, 1994, Don Mellor, Jake Bader, Joe Briggs, Dan Hart, Jeff Erenston, John Connell, John Beatty

Cover Charge Area

This area, which is actually part of the main Upper Beer Wall, has a separate approach because the routes begin from an upper ledge. From the height of land on the approach trail and just before the scramble down through the notch, walk left (southeast) 80' to an open area at the top of **3.2** and **Seven Ounces**. Continue another 40' to an exposed, open ledge with boulders 599470,4888604.

The rock quality on this wall is extremely good—clean and textured; unfortunately, the protection isn't.

Home Rule

"So you're Pat Purcell!"

"What do you mean by that?" was the response.

I had just run into Purcell while hiking near Chapel Pond, my first summer in the Adirondacks. He was always a little suspicious of people who knew him but whom he didn't know, perhaps from his work as a cop or maybe from a guilty conscience. His demeanor changed after I dropped a few names. We made plans to climb.

I don't have a chronological memory of when we did what, but climbing with Pat was usually an adventure, with cleaning lichen-covered routes the norm. He kept track of potential lines in his journals and put them in at a feverish pace. He would often hang ropes at night, prep the route, then go through his extensive list of partners—his little black book—and choose the right partner for that route, enticing them with the standard spiel "This is gonna be the best line in the Dacks." If it was a new route, then he saw it as "good."

One of our bigger projects was an ascent of Pan Am. Pat was training for big-wall climbing, and I was sort of interested. I had done some short aid climbs but never more than a pitch, and never A3. Pat led the first pitch, which looked just about impossible to my eyes, masterfully using a few RURPs and a ground-down fifi hook. He taught me what could be done with small gear, although he took most of the day to climb the first pitch. The next day, we jugged to our high point, and I took the sharp end. Now, Patrick is rather a small guy, and I'm . . . well, let's say bigger. The higher I climbed, the more gear he plugged into the belay. Good thing, too, as I took a 30' fall while leapfrogging a nut and pulled him right up against anchors. He took over the lead, but, to my satisfaction, not without some stress—he would beat in a RURP and shout down, "Don't bother to get this one out."

His small stature gave him an advantage that we tall people envy—the ability to scrunch up into a little ball by high-stepping his foot next to his hip. Anniversary Waltz was one such climb, one that I fell from repeatedly on the second ascent.

Pat was very organized and planned climbingwise, almost to the point of obsession. He had lists of routes he had done, lists of routes he wanted to do, lists of gear used on a route; he had a hand-drawn diagram of Center Stage complete with annotations of every body movement and gear placement. His vocation, however, was always a question mark. I was constantly working around Pat's schedule as a DEC ranger, cop in Saranac Lake, rock-climbing guide, or ski coach. There was one summer when he was at least three of the above.

Patrick Purcell on the first ascent of ***Tequilla Mockingbird*** *(5.10b). The route was originally climbed as two pitches. Photo by Don Mellor.*

His modus operandi was eccentric and spirited. For instance, he thought the upper floors of his house were wasted space. No problem. He just chainsawed the supports and yanked off the upper floors. Mowing the lawn? Easy, a 10-minute job with a weed whacker. He had a creative solution to many problems. . .

In the late 1980s and early 90s, the political climate in the Adirondacks was heightened, with downstate interests trying to overrule local governments. A "home-rule" movement was under way and spilled over into climbing when an out-of-state climber dictated our mode of new routing. This was at a time when Pat was almost fanatical about establishing new routes, and he didn't like being told how to play the game. Pat's solution? Ground-up, but with the drill on its own toprope. Always pushing the envelope, Pat was. Route names from this time reflect the conflict—Home Rule, Wandering Lunatic, and The Mouth That Roared.

One of my favorite days with Pat was at Poke-O. We started out on Firing Line. I had trouble at the crux, and Pat ended up leading the pitch. We rapped and walked over to Freedom Flight, an absolute delight, cruising it. At the top, Pat said, "That's the nice thing about working on hard climbs a lot. You can cruise up the really great routes like this."

- Bill Dodd

14 Spur of the Moment 5.7 R 35' ★★

Start: On the left side of the open ledge with boulders, at a tree close to the face.

P1 5.7 R: Several bouldery moves off the ground lead up to a bucket. Climb up past a 4'-long left-rising (first gear), right-facing edge 12' up, then up to a white face and the top. 35'

FA May 14, 1988, Steve Adler (solo)

15 Day's End 5.9 G 45' ★★★

A beautifully textured and clean face. Bolts missing.

Start: At the open ledge with boulders at the left end of a long, horizontal foot-traverse ledge, directly below a roof at the top.

P1 5.9 G: Climb straight up the face to the roof and break it via a right-rising groove or make an easier finish left. 45'

History: The route was originally toproped by Steve Adler on May 8, 1988, then bolted and led by Purcell. The bolts were chopped, then the route was led (or soloed, 5.9 X) by Don Mellor sans bolts.

FA 1988, Patrick Purcell

16 Twist Off 5.9 R 50' ★★★

Climbs the right-rising sloped ramp across the wall on excellent rock.

Start: Same as **Day's End**, at the left end of a long foot-traverse ledge.

P1 5.9 R: Foot-traverse right on the ledge with increasing exposure to the right-rising ramp (tricky gear here, including a bomber, blind TCU at your feet out right). Move a couple of feet past the ramp, then up onto the ramp via good holds (excellent gear). Follow the right-rising ramp to the top (meeting **Cover Charge** here), move left to the bolt, then up and left to a horizontal. Face moves left lead to a crumbly but excellent left-facing flake; swing left on this and up to the exit slab. 50'

History: The route was originally toproped and called **Pop Top** (Tom DuBois, May 4, 1988).

FA Sep 6, 2006, Jim Lawyer, Thom Campbell

17 Cover Charge 5.11a PG 70' ★★★

Very nice climbing, although a bit unprotected at the start. The exposed start can be tamed by slinging a tree for the first few moves.

Start: Begin 15' downhill and to the right of the open ledge (which marks the base of the Cover Charge Area), at a narrow ledge with a couple of cedar trees and below a bucket at 6' that marks the beginning of a right-rising thin crack.

P1 5.11a PG: Climb the right-rising crack with RPs to better finger locks. Move past two horizontals to gain a nice ledge at the top of a left-facing, right-rising ramp (**Twist Off** climbs this ramp). Step left to a bolt and climb up and left to a horizontal, then straight up to a right-leaning handcrack that gains the exit slab. 70'

FA Jun 11, 1988, Patrick Purcell, Mary Purcell

The 5.10 Wall

A collection of difficult, pumpy crack routes that break the central shield on the Upper Beer Wall. These routes begin practically on the trail at the base of the cliff and climb through a loose section to a bulging ceiling that breaks the wall across its entire width. This bulging ceiling represents the crux of most of these routes, but don't underestimate the climbing below, which can be loose, unprotected, and much harder than it appears; double ropes allow you to wander a bit through this section to select the best-protected line. Once established above the bulging ceiling, each route takes a distinct line to the top, although you can climb just about anywhere. In fact, nearly everyone you talk to climbs these upper sections differently.

The 5.10 Wall extends from the black streaks of **The Mouth That Roared** all the way to **Dark Horse Ail**, just before the huge right-facing corner of **Labatt-Ami**. Another distinguishing feature is that the trail is at its lowest point along the base of this wall.

18 Center Stage 5.12a PG 150' ★★★★★

From the trail at the base of the cliff, just left of the 5.10 Wall, you can spot twin thin cracks that break through a bulge and up onto a headwall, left of a collection of prominent black streaks. This route, one of Purcell's favorites, climbs these twin cracks.

Start: Just left of the start of **The Mouth That Roared** is an overhanging short, black face with brush on top. From the left side of the 5.10 Wall, scramble up (3rd-class) and left to the base of this black face and take a belay at a cedar tree to its left (10' left of the ledge where **The Mouth That Roared** starts).

P1 5.12a PG: Climb up the overhanging black face to a stance with cedars. Break through the bulging wall via the twin cracks, past a horizontal, then angle slightly right to a bolt positioned just left of the leftmost of the black streaks. (There is a crucial, but good wire placement below and right of the first bolt.) Climb straight up to a ledge, then step left to another black streak. A difficult move up the black streak (bolt) leads past two horizontals and a final short right-angling crack to the top. 150'

History: The route was originally bolted and led by Purcell, then the bolts were removed. It was led without the bolts (Aug 24, 1989, Martin Berzins, Richard Felch, Steve Andreski); like all of Berzins's routes in the region, it was led without toprope rehearsal. The bolts have since been replaced.

FA 1988, Patrick Purcell, Don Mellor

19 The Mouth That Roared 5.11a PG 150' ★

This route, which defines the left end of the 5.10 Wall, is clearly distinguished by the collection of dark streaks on the upper wall. It climbs these black streaks via holds that are virtually invisible from the trail. The route is a little dirty, and the two difficult sections could stand some minimal cleaning (moss in key TCU cracks). The name refers to a climber who exchanged strong words with Nichols over climbing style during the first ascent.

Start: From the left end of the 5.10 Wall, scramble up and left on vegetated ledges (3rd-class) to a clean, flat ledge on white rock (about 40' up) with a horizontal crack at 5' that diagonals out right.

P1 5.11a PG: Climb out right 15' on the horizontal crack, which cuts away underneath, to another ledge in a deep depression (optional belay). Move up the bulge in the black streaks via a thin crack (crux) and good horizontals, then up the seemingly blank-looking face above to a point under the right end of an arching overlap, 15' right of a prominent right-facing corner visible from below. Step right and up the steep face (just left of **Roaring Twenties**), past a horizontal, and up to a right-facing, left-rising stepped corner. Follow it up and left to the base of a right-diagonaling flake-crack. Climb out the flake-crack to its end, then up to the trees, and top out at the same point as **Roaring Twenties**. 150'

Gear: To 3".

FA Sep 9, 1988, Ken Nichols, Bruce Jelen

20 Roaring Twenties 5.10b G 150' ★★★★

Start: On the left side of the 5.10 Wall are two parallel cracks (4' apart) that break a clean, bulging white wall below the bulging ceiling. Begin directly below the leftmost of these cracks.

P1 5.10b G: Climb up blocks and take the left-hand crack straight up the headwall to a stance below the bulging ceiling. Break through the ceiling at parallel cracks in dark-colored rock and move up to a good horizontal. Continue in the parallel cracks up the wall above until the cracks fade, then traverse left to a vertical crack in the right side of a black streak. Follow the black crack to the top and finish at the same point as **The Mouth That Roared**. 150'

FA Sep 7, 1988, Ken Nichols, Bruce Jelen

21 Radioactive 5.10b G 130' ★★★★

This route and its variations climb the right-hand of the two parallel cracks (4' apart) that break a clean, bulging white wall below the bulging ceiling. From there, the variations diverge and break through the bulging ceiling at various points, only to meet again high on the headwall above. The most popular independent line is **Radioactive Direct**.

Start: Same as **Roaring Twenties**.

P1 5.10b G: Climb up blocks (V3) and take the right-hand of two parallel cracks (4' apart) straight up the bulging white wall to a stance below the bulging ceiling. (V1, V2) Step left 4' and break through the bulging ceiling at parallel cracks in dark-colored rock (same as **Roaring Twenties**), then move up to a good horizontal. Continue straight up the headwall in the parallel cracks for 20' to the next prominent horizontal and traverse right to the main crack system (where **Radioactive Direct** joins). Follow it straight to the top. 130'

V1 Radioactive Direct 5.10d G: Step right 5' to a shallow, short left-facing corner in the bulging ceiling; break through the bulging ceiling here and move up to a good horizontal. Above there are two parallel cracks; when the left crack fades, stay in the right crack straight up to the top.

V2 Isotope 5.10d G: Step right 10' (about 5' past **Radioactive Direct**) to where a short, thin RP crack goes through the bulging overhang; break through the bulging ceiling here with several long reaches to the right end of a long horizontal above the ceiling. Follow the discontinuous thin crack up the upper wall and eventually move left to join **Radioactive** to the top.

V3 Radioactive Direct Direct 5.10d TR: Climb the lower wall about 5' right of the right-hand crack to meet **Radioactive Direct** at the point where it breaks through the bulging ceiling.

History: At some point in the mid- to late 1980s, the local climbers began using the 5.10 Wall as a workout wall, dropping fixed lines down several routes and taking laps with solo devices. The variations to **Radioactive** were all climbed during this time, but nobody knows when or by whom.

FA 1987, Bill Dodd, Tim Beaman

FA (V2) 1992, Bill Dodd, Patrick Munn

22 No Comments from the Peanut Gallery 5.10c G 130' ★★★★

This route, whose early description was apparently incorrect, has been a mystery for some time. It follows a faint black streak from the low face all the way to the top of the cliff, making a completely independent route with excellent face and crack climbing and good protection.

Start: 10' left of the left side of the pointed block of **Neutron Brew**, on a ledge 10' up with a cedar tree, and just right of the blocky area that marks the start of **Radioactive** and **Roaring Twenties**.

P1 5.10c G: Climb up the steep, committing face with tricky protection (good gear, but you have to search for it) and stay in the black streak about 4' left of a left-facing corner (which forms the left side of the "alcove" described for **Neutron Brew**). Continue up a crack in a steep wall and straight through the bulging ceiling to a "blocky pocket" (a small tan-colored horn in the crack). Traverse left a few feet on good holds to a crack. Go up a few feet, move back right in line with the crack below, then straight up the crack to the top. 130'

FA Sep 2, 1985, David Smart, Dave Georger

23 Neutron Brew 5.10b G 130' ★★★★

Although the top can be wet after a rain, it doesn't really matter, as you can move left to finish in the cracks of **No Comments from the Peanut Gallery**.

Start: In the center of the 5.10 Wall is a 15' high pointed block, the top ledge of which forms the left point of the letter *M*. The bottom right side of this M-shaped feature is the wet grotto at the start of **Standard**. This route begins on the left side of the *M*.

P1 5.10b G: Climb to the top of the pointed block, then up into an alcove—a shallow, boxed area capped by an overhang with opposing corners on either side and a small cedar at the base. Climb up the left side of the alcove and into a crack above that leads to the bulging ceiling that splits the 5.10 Wall. Continue straight through the ceiling and follow a well-defined crack that leads to the top. 130'

Gear: To 3".

FA Jun 2, 1985, Don Mellor, Bill Dodd

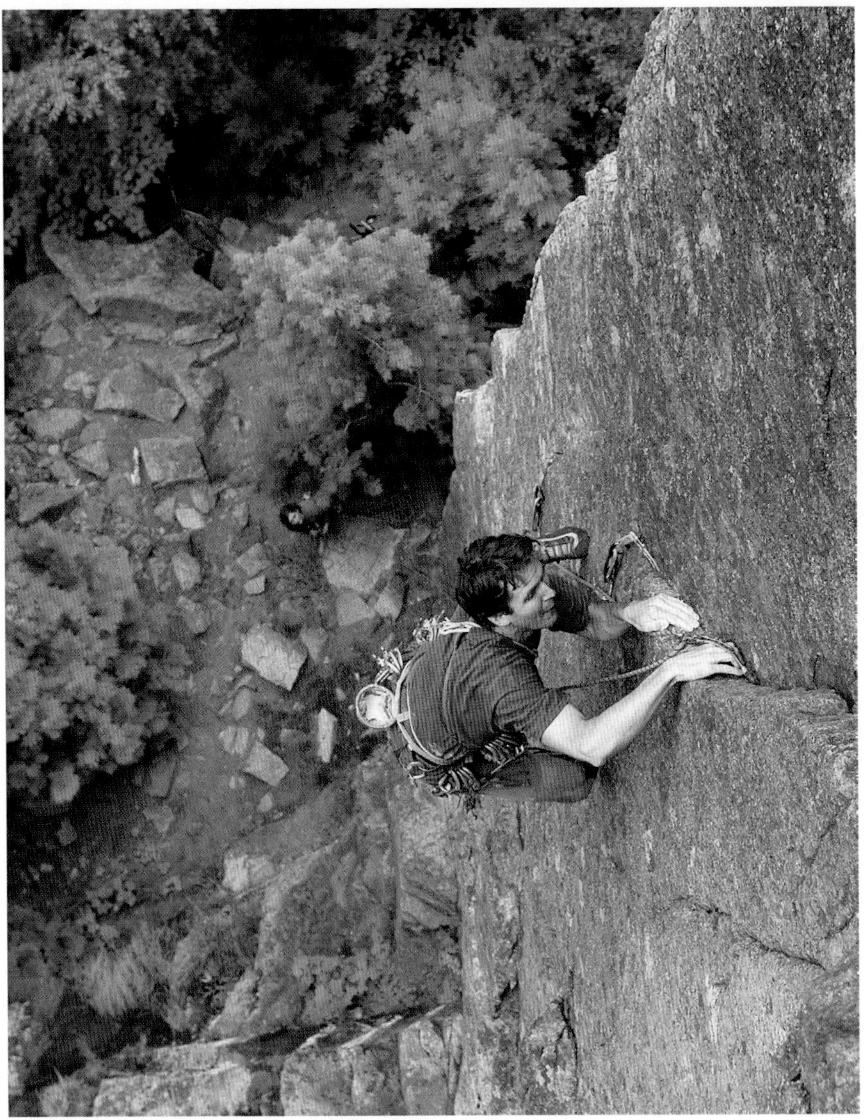

*Jim Lawyer on **Flying & Drinking and Drinking & Driving** (5.10a). Photo by David Le Pagne.*

24 Tequila Mockingbird 5.10b G 130' ★★★★★

Start: Same as **Neutron Brew**.

P1 5.10b G: Climb to the top of the pointed block, then up into an alcove (the same alcove as for **Neutron Brew**)—a shallow, boxed area capped by an overhang with opposing corners on either side and a small cedar at the base. Move out the right side of the alcove and (V1) traverse right 10' to gain a crack that leads straight up to the bulging ceiling, directly below a shallow right-facing corner capped by a overhang. Up the corner and out the left side of the overhang to the crack above. Follow it straight up to a horizontal. Move left a few feet to the next crack and climb this straight up through a wide section and up to a point where the crack fades. Work up and left across several cracks to the top, and finish as for **Neutron Brew**. 130'

V1 Tequila Mockingbird Direct 5.10b G: From the right side of the alcove, continue straight up and break the bulging ceiling via a right-leaning crack. Then follow the crack for 20' or so until the normal route joins in from the right.

FA Apr 20, 1985, Patrick Purcell, Don Mellor, Bill Dodd

25 Standard 5.10c G 130' ★★

One of the more obvious lines on the wall, as it follows a crack from the bottom of the cliff all the way to the top. The crux can be avoided by traversing in from **Tequila Mockingbird**.

Start: On the right side of the 5.10 Wall at a wet, mossy 3'-high grotto. This grotto is at the base of the right side of an M-shaped ledge at 15'.

P1 5.10c G: Climb out the top of the grotto into a hand- and fistcrack and follow it straight up (crux) to a break. Continue up another short crack to the bulging ceiling that splits the 5.10 Wall. Climb the crack through the ceiling (this point is about 7' right of the right-facing corner of **Tequila Mockingbird**) and through the center of a shallow overhang. Above, the crack is black and widens a bit but continues in a straight line to the top. The crack ends just left of the **Frosted Mug** ledge; either continue up a slab to the trees or move right onto the ledge and fixed anchor. 130'

FA Jun 30, 1983, Don Mellor

26 Prohibition 5.11b PG 130' ★★★

Start: Begin 5' right of the mossy grotto of **Standard** below a thin crack that goes up the face and dead-ends.

P1 5.11b PG: Climb up the crack to its end and move right to good stance. Then go back left and up several shallow right-facing corners that lead up to the bulging roof. Move right 10' and break the roof below the black cracks that can be seen on the upper wall (crux). Follow the cracks straight up the face to finish on the **Frosted Mug** ledge. 130'

Gear: Double sets of small gear through 2".

FA Sep 9, 1988, Ken Nichols, Bruce Jelen

27 Dark Horse Ail 5.11c PG 130' ★★

The last route on the 5.10 Wall. Larson saw himself as the "dark horse ailing away," hence the name.

Start: On the right side of the 5.10 Wall, just as the approach trail begins to go uphill to the **Frosted Mug** open area, below a set of left-leaning cracks through broken rock with many small overhangs.

P1 5.11c PG: Climb up the cracks to the ceiling. Break this on the left side with a very difficult reach and move up into a crack. Up the crack, past a tree, to the ledge with a fixed anchor (shared with **Frosted Mug**). 130'

FA Aug, 1983, Steve Larson

Frosted Mug Area

At the far right side of the Upper Beer Wall is an open area in the talus beneath a deep right-facing corner 599508,4888578. The left wall of this corner is black and sheer, and the right wall has four large stepped ledges and is capped by a large triangular roof. **Frosted Mug** climbs the inside corner on the left side of the left wall; **Flying & Drinking and Drinking & Driving** climbs the left wall, and **Labatt-Ami** climbs the corner itself.

28 Frosted Mug 5.9 G (5.7 R) 100' ★★★★★

A megaclassic corner climb, one of the best of its grade in the Adirondacks. Beware of the unprotected start, though. The second route climbed at the Beer Walls.

Start: In the open area, begin at the base of a left-facing corner just right of the arête.

P1 5.9 G: (V1) Climb up the corner to the flake at the top. Move left across the face under the overhang to the arête (5.7 R), then around onto the left wall to a stance with good protection at the bottom of the corner. (V2) Climb straight up the corner, stemming, layback, and jamming to the ledge with a fixed anchor. 100'

V1 Direct Start 5.10a PG: As an alternate start, climb the beginning of **Dark Horse Ail**, then move right into the bottom of the **Frosted Mug** corner.

V2 Frosty Edge 5.10d TR: Climb the arête right of **Frosted Mug** (i.e., the arête between **Frosted Mug** and **Flying & Drinking and Drinking & Driving**).

Gear: Singles to 3".

FA May 1, 1982, Chuck Turner, Bill Simes

29 Flying & Drinking and Drinking & Driving 5.10a G (5.7 R) 100' ★★★★★

One of the best climbs at the Beer Walls and definitely not a horror show as once believed. The route features impeccable black rock with excellent friction properties, a thin crack, and a spectacular and exposed jug haul up the final bulging face. Double ropes helpful.

Start: Same as **Frosted Mug**.

P1 5.10a G (5.7 R): Climb 10' up the left-facing corner at the start of **Frosted Mug**, then move right almost to the **Labatt-Ami** corner. Up the corner to a horizontal, (V1) then traverse left across the face 10' (about 3' shy of the arête). Make a hard move up to the next horizontal and gain the crack above, which runs up the face just right of the arête. At the top of the crack, move up and right on a shallow left-facing corner (crux) to a blocky section below the final bulging wall. From the right side of the blocky area, climb straight up the face and use reachy jugs to the top (5.7 R). 100'

V1 Flying & Drinking Direct 5.10d R: A popular toprope problem after you climb any of the neighbors. From the beginning of the horizontal, climb straight up the face past a unique hole to gain several ledges, then up to a left-facing corner. At the top of the corner (loose block), make a tricky move straight over the left-rising ceiling and join the regular route up the juggy face to the top.

Gear: To 2", double small TCUs.

FA May, 1985, Don Mellor

30 Labatt-Ami 5.7 G 120' ★★★

Originally named **Labattomy**, this was the first route climbed at the Beer Walls.

Start: 4' right of **Frosted Mug**. The start is sometimes wet, which you can avoid by coming in from the right.

P1 5.7 G: Climb the corner past several large ledges. From the topmost ledge (optional belay), (V1) climb up the corner below the orange triangular roof. Move left

Opposite: Todd Eastman on ***Frosted Mug*** *(5.9). Photo by Kennan Harvey.*

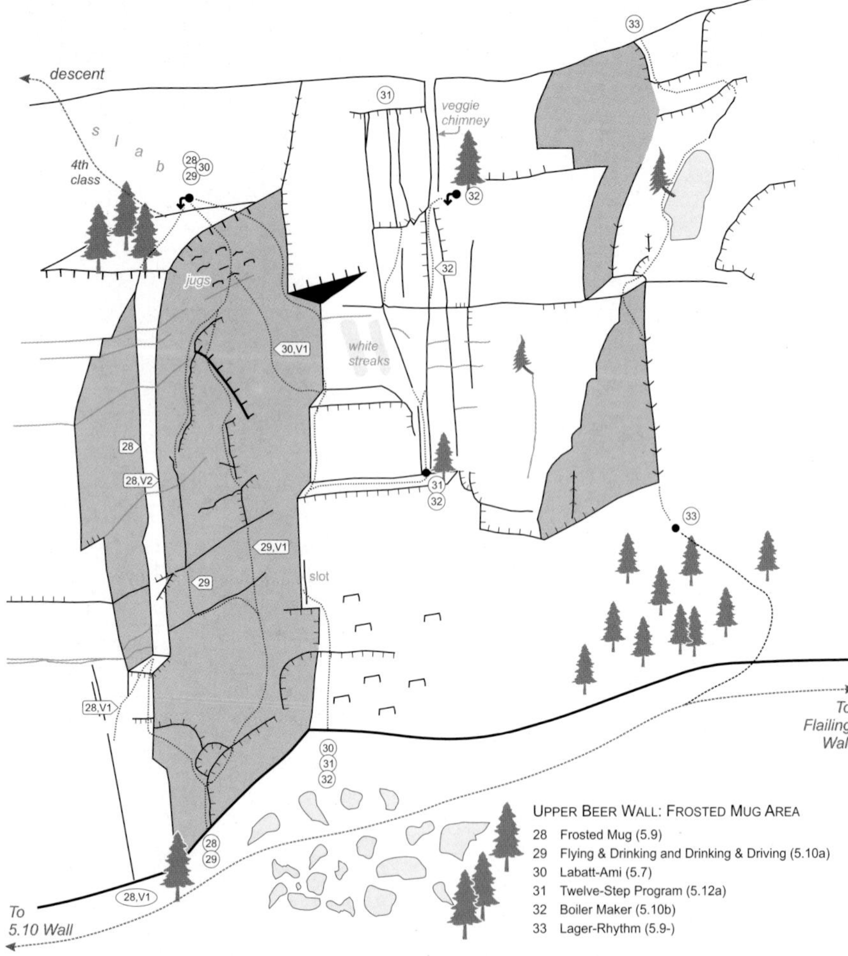

onto the face around the roof, then back into the corner to finish on a spacious ledge with a fixed anchor. 120'

V1 Buddy of Bradour 5.7 G: Move left from the ledge on flakes, then up and left to join the last 10' of **Flying & Drinking and Drinking & Driving**.

FA Apr 30, 1982, Bill Simes, Chuck Turner

FA (V1) May 23, 1989, Don Mellor, Dave Everhart, Ben Kremers

31 Twelve-Step Program 5.12a PG 100'

Climbs the cracks on the orange wall just left of **Boiler Maker**. Reported as a "piece of shit" with potato-chip jams, although the crux is clean.

Start: 4' right of **Frosted Mug**, the same as for **Labatt-Ami**.

P1 5.12a PG: Climb up **Labatt-Ami** to the second ledge (the ledge with a cedar on the right side). From the cedar, move right and make a boulder move up to a handcrack, which changes to a flared crack. Move up to crux face-climbing below the first overlap. Jam the beautiful 5.10 handcrack through the overlap to a tricky sloping exit over the upper overlap. 100'

FA Jun 27, 1999, Don McGrath

FFA Jul 12, 2012, Conor Cliffe, George Clark

32 Boiler Maker 5.10b G 80' ★★

When originally climbed, this was a fingercrack; subsequent removal of all the loose flakes has resulted in a secure hand- and fistcrack.

Start: 4' right of **Frosted Mug**, the same as for **Labatt-Ami**.

P1 5.10b G: Climb up **Labatt-Ami** to the third ledge (the ledge with a cedar on the right side). From the cedar, move right and into the steep hand- and fistcrack, then follow it through two flared sections to a chimney section. Up the chimney to a ledge on the right with trees. 80'

FA 1984, Tim Beaman, Sylvia Lazarnick

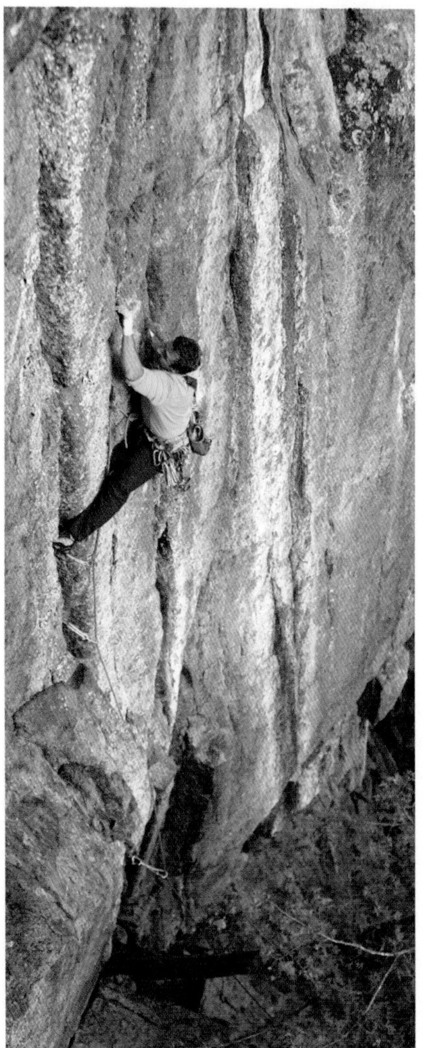

*Jesse Williams on **Boiler Maker** (5.10b).*
Photo by Tomás Donoso.

33 Lager-Rhythm 5.9- G (5.7 R) 150' ★★★

Start: 50' right of the huge right-facing corner of Labatt-Ami is another right-facing corner. Begin below this corner on a vegetated ledge.

P1 5.9- G (5.7 R): Climb 40' of nondescript, dirty rock to the clean dihedral. Up the corner with good protection to just below black rock, then make an exposed hand traverse out left to a large ledge (optional belay). From the ledge, make a puzzling step back right across the top of the corner (5.7 R) and aim for a large block with a tree on its left side. Climb to the top of the block, then up a corner to a sloped ledge below opposing corners; up the right-facing corner to the top. 150'

FA Jul, 1982, Don Mellor, Alan Jolley

Beer Walls

FLAILING WALL

Aspect	Southwest
Height	60'
Quality	★
Approach	15 min, moderate
Summary	Obscure cliff with several difficult sport routes.

-5.6	5.7	5.8	5.9	5.10	5.11	5.12	5.13+	total
					2			2

A short wall with a couple of sport routes lying upstream from the Upper Beer Wall.

From the height of land on the approach trail, continue straight (southwest) down a short 20' scramble through a notch, then turn left (climber's right since you're now at the base of the cliff) along the base of the Upper Beer Wall and pass under the 5.10 Wall to the Frosted Mug Area. Continue bushwhacking along the base of the cliff an additional 375' through increasingly thick vegetation, past a small cliffband (a steep black wall with a second tier above with huge roofs) to a second cliffband with a 2' overhang 15' up 599572,4888524.

A landmark for finding these routes is to locate the large pointed tooth that hangs from the overhang 15' up. Below this is a 6'-high, slender spear of rock that leans up against the cliff and points up to this hanging tooth.

34 Pete's Wicked Flail 5.11d G 50' ★★

A one-move wonder route with a really hard move.

Start: 6' left of the spear that leans up against the cliff.

P1 5.11d G: Climb up to the highest ledge and clip the first bolt. Move through the roof and straight up the face above to a fixed anchor. 50'

FA Jul, 1994, Frank Minunni

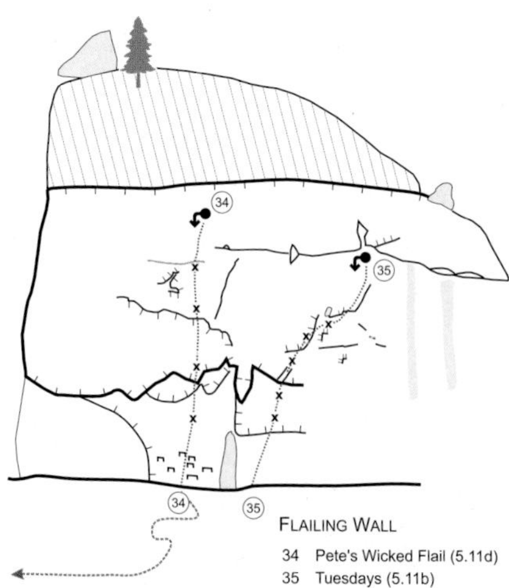

35 Tuesdays 5.11b G 60' ★★

Start: 3' right of the slender spear that leans up against the cliff.

P1 5.11b G: Climb up to the low overlap, then up and right through the overhang and take a right-rising line past two more bolts and an easier runout to a fixed anchor. 60'

FA Jul, 1994, Dave Furman

Beer Walls

LOWER BEER WALL

Aspect	Southwest
Height	120'
Quality	★★★★
Approach	15 min, easy
Summary	Good collection of moderate routes (**Rockaholic**, **Sword**, **Lichenbräu**) and a couple excellent harder routes (**Turbocharge**, **Blacksmith**).

-5.6	5.7	5.8	5.9	5.10	5.11	5.12	5.13+	total
9	4	9	12	12	3	2		51

The Lower Beer Wall can be approached from either end. For routes left of **Pegasus**, it is faster to approach via the left end (i.e., the end toward Keene Valley); first-time visitors may find it easier to approach from the right end (i.e., the end nearer the Upper Beer Wall).

To approach from the Upper Beer Wall, continue straight (southwest) from the height of land on the approach trail, go down a short 20' scramble through a notch, then turn left (which is climber's right, since you're now at the base of the cliff) along the base of the Upper Beer Wall. The first and most obvious routes you pass are the straight-in cracks of **Seven Ounces** and **3.2**; 60' past these cracks is a trail that heads back right and down. (Just past this trail is another false trail that heads in the same direction.) The trail you want goes steeply down, then works its way back uphill. The first climbable rock you come to is the route **Cue Ball** on a short wall with a piton 12' up. A little farther left is the distinctive cave area with the overhanging crack **Clutch and Cruise**.

To approach from the left end, turn right (northwest) just before the height of land on the approach trail (in front of the outhouse) and walk through open forest; keep the top of the cliff to your left. At the far end of the cliff, various paths lead down and around the left end of the cliff to its base near the route **Rockaholic**, the left-slanting fingercrack.

Afternoon Delight Area

Defined by the collection of climbs at the far left end of the cliff, which are accessed from an inconvenient, eroded gully just left of the Rockaholic Area. This was once the approach gully but is now so eroded that it requires some 3rd-class moves. An alternate path was engineered that runs from the base of the gully around the wooded knoll away from the cliff and then loops back to the top of the route **Afternoon Delight**.

36 CWI 5.6 G 50' ★★

A nice crack climb, although short. The acronym stands for "climbing while intoxicated."

Start: At a left-facing, left-leaning handcrack partway up a gully at the far left end of the Lower Beer Wall, 10' left of **Afternoon Delight**.

*Colin O'Connor on **Rockaholic** (5.8).*

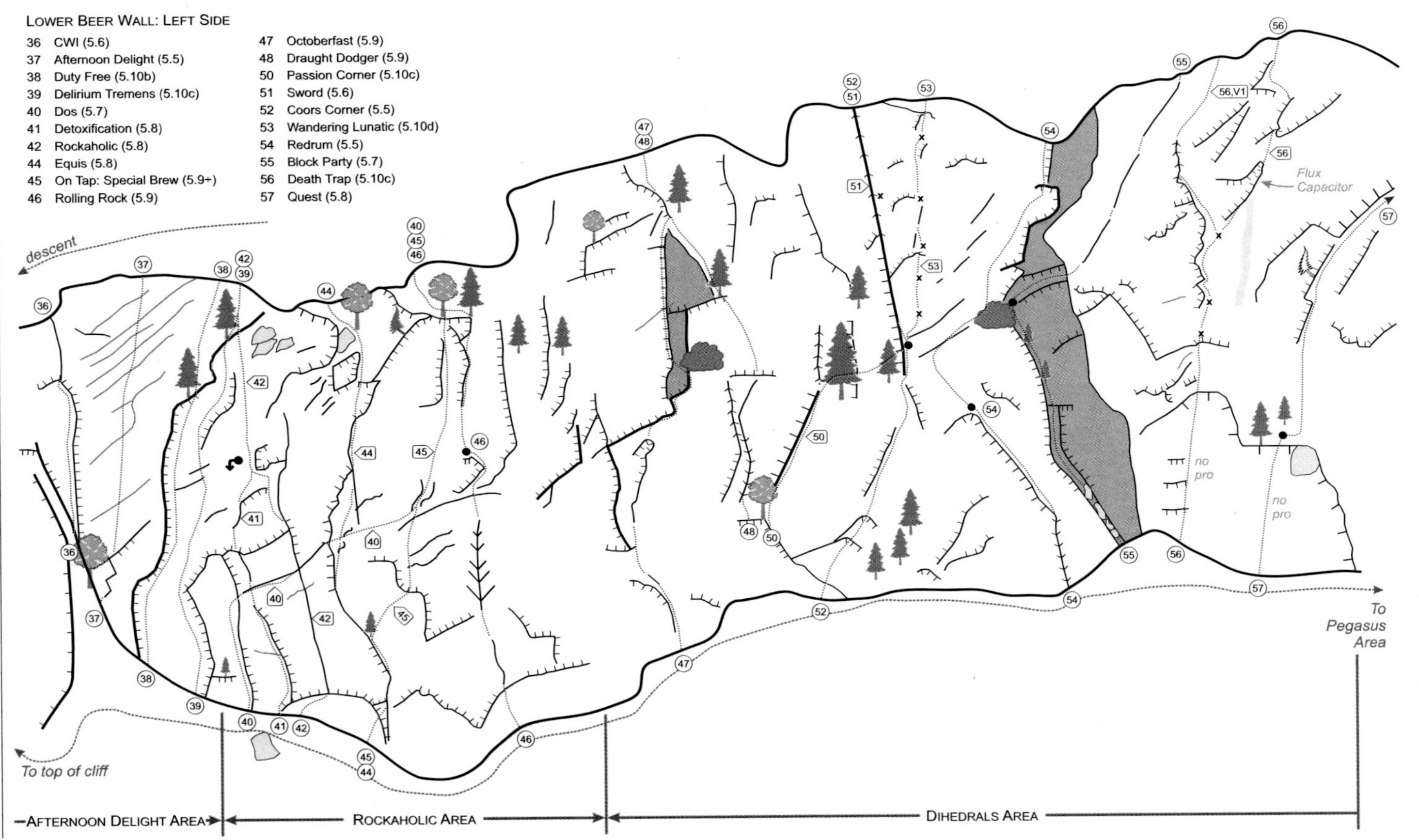
Lower Beer Wall: Left Side
36 CWI (5.6)
37 Afternoon Delight (5.5)
38 Duty Free (5.10b)
39 Delirium Tremens (5.10c)
40 Dos (5.7)
41 Detoxification (5.8)
42 Rockaholic (5.8)
44 Equis (5.8)
45 On Tap: Special Brew (5.9+)
46 Rolling Rock (5.9)
47 Octoberfast (5.9)
48 Draught Dodger (5.9)
50 Passion Corner (5.10c)
51 Sword (5.6)
52 Coors Corner (5.5)
53 Wandering Lunatic (5.10d)
54 Redrum (5.5)
55 Block Party (5.7)
56 Death Trap (5.10c)
57 Quest (5.8)
descent
Flux Capacitor
no pro
no pro
To Pegasus Area
To top of cliff
Afternoon Delight Area
Rockaholic Area
Dihedrals Area

P1 5.6 G: Climb the handcrack in the corner past several small ceilings to an easier finish. 50'
FA Jun 27, 1982, Jim Cunningham, Pete Benson

37 Afternoon Delight 5.5 G 60' ★★★★

This wide, steep face looks serious but is broken by numerous hidden horizontal cracks that moderate the grade. Combined with a pretty summit with views of the Great Range, this is justifiably one of the most popular toprope locations in the region. **Afternoon Delight** is a wide area of climbing rather than a single route, so several lines are possible. The aesthetics of this spot are somewhat diminished by the base, which is an eroded, steep, cramped gully.
Start: At a wide face partway up the steep gully at the far left end of the Lower Beer Wall, left of a left-facing dihedral and beneath a zigzag flake.
P1 5.5 G: Climb the zigzag flake (or easier just left if you step off the tree) onto a fantastic face crossed by numerous right-rising horizontal cracks. 60'
FA Sep 26, 1982, Mike Heintz, Ron Briggs (the student, not the Essex County D.A.)

38 Duty Free 5.10b TR 50'

Right and downhill of **Afternoon Delight** is a buttress with a left-facing corner on the left and a right-facing corner on the right. This route climbs the left arête of this buttress.
FA (TR) Aug 30, 1990, Jeff Edwards

39 Delirium Tremens 5.10c TR 50'

This route climbs the right side of the buttress right of **Afternoon Delight**. Climb up the outside edge of the right-facing corner and onto the face above through very steep face climbing and a finish just left of the arête at the top.
FA (TR) Aug 30, 1990, Jeff Edwards

Rockaholic Area

The open area around the obvious left-leaning handcrack of **Rockaholic** at the left end of the cliff 599256,4888739.

40 Dos 5.7 PG 170' ★

This route performs a girdle traverse of the Rockaholic Area.
Start: At the base of a left-facing, left-leaning corner 20' left of **Rockaholic** where the trail begins to climb steeply left to the end of the cliff.
P1 5.7 PG: Climb up easy ledges just left of the left-facing corner for 15' to gain a continuous right-rising crack and flake. Follow this crack across the **Rockaholic** fingercrack to a right-facing corner. Step around this corner and cross **Equis**, then continue rightward across the face above the roof of **On Tap: Special Brew** to join **Rolling Rock** at the right-facing, right-leaning corner above the open book. Take a belay at this corner. 120'
P2 5.4 G: Join **Rolling Rock** to the top: break around the right-leaning corner on the right, move past it to a tree, then up the right-facing chimney to the top. 50'
FA May 6, 1983, Jim Cunningham, Don Mellor

41 Detoxification 5.8 R 90' ★★

Start: 4' left of **Rockaholic** beneath a left-facing, left-arching irregular overlap.
P1 5.8 R: Follow the shallow arch and thin vertical crack (crux) to large holds and a fixed anchor on a tree (as for **Rockaholic**). 90'
FA Oct 19, 1986, Tad Welch (roped solo)

42 Rockaholic 5.8 G 80' ★★★★

Super climbing, although watch for slippery holds at the start. There was once an anchor on a tree after the good climbing; the quality of the route is now marred by the mandatory junky finish.
Start: At the left end of the low head-high overlap below a straight-in fingercrack that leans left.
P1 5.8 G: Make a bouldery start to gain the crack and a good stance. Some hard initial moves up the crack (crux) lead to easier climbing, past an overlap on the left. The crack ends at a block; move left around this block and up to a ledge. Continue up easier terrain to the tree. 80'
FA May 6, 1983, Mark Meschinelli, Dave Hough, Chuck Turner

43 Don's Toprope 5.10b TR 100'

This route begins just right of **Rockaholic** below the ceiling 6' up. Climb over the ceiling and up the face; trend left and follow the line of **Rockaholic**. The face steepens; stay just left of the right-facing crescent of **Equis** to the top.
FA (TR) Jul, 1997, Don Mellor

44 Equis 5.8 PG (5.4 R) 100' ★★★

Climbs the right-facing crescent above and right of **Rockaholic**.
Start: Same as **On Tap: Special Brew**.
P1 5.8 PG (5.4 R): Make a bouldery, unprotected move off the ground (crux) and proceed through the overlap to the base of a right-facing, left-rising ramp with a cedar 15' up (same as for **On Tap: Special Brew**). Continue up left and follow the ramp to a right-facing crescent. Climb the face and positive flakes right of the crescent to a point where a crack meets the top of the crescent (in the shape of an *A*; crux). Above, climb the magnificent layback flake (hollow but secure) to a cedar tree. Rappel from here or scramble to the top. 100'
FA May 7, 1983, Jim Cunningham, Rich Leswing

45 On Tap: Special Brew 5.9+ PG 110' ★

Start: 15' right of **Rockaholic** at a low point in the trail, below the center of a head-high arching overlap.
P1 5.9+ PG: Make a bouldery, unprotected move off the ground and proceed through the overlap to the base of a right-facing, left-rising ramp with a cedar 20' up. Climb the ramp up left to the cedar, then head right to a ceiling and left-facing corner, which is turned on the right side (crux). Continue up the face, tending right, to the top. 110'
FA Jul 8, 1983, Jim Cunningham, Hank Andolsek, Mark Eckroth

46 Rolling Rock 5.9 G 140' ★

Start: From the low point in the trail at the right side of the Rockaholic Area, walk uphill to the right for 20', then up a brushy slope to the base of the cliff at a position below the left end of a low, chest-high overlap.

P1 5.9 G: Climb the slab and thin crack into a 20'-high open book that narrows at its top. From its top, climb up to a right-leaning, right-facing corner, around this on the right and up to a tree, then up the right-facing chimney to the top. 140'

FA Oct 19, 1982, Don Mellor, Alan Jolley

Dihedrals Area

This section of the cliff contains the dihedral climbs, the most popular of which is the **Sword**, a sharp, exposed arête high on the cliff. From the base of the cliff, the area is complex, and it's difficult to get your bearings. The most prominent feature in this section is **Passion Corner**, a sharply defined, 25'-high right-facing, right-leaning corner that starts 15' above the trail.

From the Rockaholic Area, hike uphill on the trail; these routes begin where the trail levels out.

47 Octoberfast 5.9 G 120' ★★

Climbs a black- and white-streaked wall under a roof with some cool undercling moves. Named for the fact that Chuck Turner was on a weight-loss diet.

Start: 20' left of **Passion Corner** at a point where the trail drops steeply down left to the Rockaholic Area, at the right end of a 4"-deep left-rising ledge, 30' below a ceiling with a prominent white flake-horn on the face just below. (The ceiling and white flake can be seen when you stand below **Passion Corner**.)

P1 5.9 G: Climb up flakes that are right of a right-facing dihedral to the white flake-horn beneath the roof. Up this to the roof, undercling right around the first roof, up 4' to a second roof, and around this on the right (crux) to a stance in a large right-facing corner with a tree. Step left to the arête and climb it (5.6) to the top. 120'

Gear: To 2", 2 ea 0.5", long slings under the roof.

FA Sep 26, 1982, Chuck Turner, Don Mellor

48 Draught Dodger 5.9 G 100' ★★

Climbs the V formed by two opposing off-vertical faces. The back of the V is an overhanging face with a right-leaning fingercrack in the center.

Start: Same as for **Passion Corner**.

P1 5.9 G: Climb out left and into a corner, then follow it straight up to the V. Climb the fingercrack (crux) on the overhanging face in the center of the V. From the top, climb easy rock up and left to a ledge, then up to finish near **Octoberfast**. 100'

FA Oct 19, 1982, Don Mellor, Alan Jolley

49 Another Beer Walls Black Streak 5.9- PG 100' ★★

Start: Same as **Passion Corner**.

P1 5.9- PG: Up to the main corner of **Draught Dodger**, then traverse left to a triangular ledge on the arête. Up the arête over a bulge, and up face to top. 100'

FA 1999, Steve Adler, Tom DuBois

*Colin O'Connor on **Sword** (5.6).*

50 Passion Corner 5.10c PG 60'

Difficult corner climbing; not as good as it looks.
Start: The most obvious feature visible from the trail in this section of cliff, this is a sharply defined, 25'-high right-facing, right-leaning corner that begins 15' above the trail. Start below the corner at twin birch trees.
P1 5.10c PG: Climb the corner. From the top, traverse right to cedar trees at the base of the **Sword**. 60'
FA 1987, Patrick Purcell, Jeff Edwards

51 Sword 5.6 PG 60' ★★★★

Climbs a sharp edge of rock on the upper section of the wall. Short but highly recommended.
Start: At the top of P1 of **Coors Corner**. Some parties rappel in from the top, but P1 of **Coors Corner** isn't all that bad; even better is P1 of **Redrum**.
P1 5.6 PG: Climb up the arête to a bolt. Switch to the left face and climb to the summit. 60'
FA May 7, 1983, Jim Cunningham, Alan Jolley

52 Coors Corner 5.5 G 120'

P1 is used as an access to several routes and has been cleaned up a bit over the years. P2 is as uninspiring as they come and not recommended.
Start: Below **Passion Corner**.
P1 5.2 G: Climb broken rock rightward to a short right-facing, right-leaning corner. Climb up and around this corner, then angle up and left to belay at a blocky area with trees. 60'
P2 5.5 G: Climb a tree-filled right-facing corner. 60'
FA Jul, 1983, Jim Cunningham, Hank Andolsek

53 Wandering Lunatic 5.10d G 90' ★★★

Technical and sustained face climbing. Once a good toprope, now a good lead, although the bolts are somewhat misplaced for shorter climbers. The route climbs the V-shaped face right of the **Sword** and **Coors Corner**. Named for a particular climber known for chopping bolts in the region.
Start: At the top of P1 of **Coors Corner**.
● **P1 5.10d G:** Step right from the belay and onto the face, then climb past six bolts to the top. 90'
FA Sep 8, 1988, Patrick Purcell, Bill Dodd
FFA May, 2003, Steve Mergenthaler, Todd Morgan

54 Redrum 5.5 PG 110' ★★★

The best approach to the base of the **Sword** climbs P1 of this route. P2 is quite nice—an airy arête with interesting moves at the top. The route name is *murder* spelled backward, taken from the 1980 film *The Shining*.
Start: On the arête formed by the left wall of the deep right-facing corner left of the Pegasus Area is a left-rising ramp-corner. Begin at the base of this ramp-corner, which is somewhat hidden by trees.
P1 5.4 G: Climb the left-rising ramp-corner to the top (this is actually a giant detached flake). Traverse left 15' and belay in the corner. 40'
P2 5.5 PG: Climb up and right, and follow right-rising horizontal cracks to the arête. Up the arête to a final right-facing, right-leaning corner. Make a well-protected funky move to gain the corner, followed by a final mantel move to the top. 70'
FA May 7, 1983, Jim Cunningham, Rich Leswing

55 Block Party 5.7 PG 150'

An unappealing line that climbs the deep, nondescript right-facing corner left of the Pegasus Area. The corner is hard to discern from below, as it is broken and tree-filled, and the left wall is blocky and complex, with many ledges and cedars.
Start: At a table-sized boulder 6' uphill from the trail, below a flake-filled chimney-slot on the left side of the left wall of the corner.
P1 5.7 PG: Climb up the chimney-slot to belay on a ledge with bushy cedars at their top. 70'
P2 5.7 PG: Head right on ledges across the deep corner to the right wall and climb a thin crack with several bushy cedars to the top. 80'
FA Sep, 1982, Alan Jolley, Scott Provost

56 Death Trap 5.10c R (5.7 X) 150' ★★

The route is named for the questionable pointed flake (aka "the Flux Capacitor") on P2. The variation **Death Trap Lite** allows you to enjoy the quality climbing and avoid the death flake.
Start: On the left side of the black slab (the same black slab as for **Quest**).
P1 5.10c R: Climb up the clean slab with no protection (5.7 X) to a ledge with a cedar. Step left and go up the white rock and over a ceiling to a bolt. Diagonal up and right across the pretty white rock to a right-facing, left-stepping corner (bolt). Up the corner to a third bolt on the right wall; (V1) step right across the face and climb a right-facing, right-leaning black flake to its pointy top. Continue moving right to a right-rising ceiling, then to a final right-leaning crack, and follow the crack to the top. 150'
V1 Death Trap Lite 5.10a PG: From the third bolt, head up and left, and follow a left-leaning corner and arête to its top. Step right and climb the face to the summit. Small wires are critical on this variation.
FA 1986, Patrick Purcell, Andy Zimmerman

57 Quest 5.8 G (5.7 X) 150' ★

Climbs the large right-facing dihedral that joins the V-groove finish of **Turbocharge**. The lower face is featured and low-angle, making a good spot for teaching.
Start: In the center of a black slab that has a ledge at 30' with cedars. This slab is just above the trail and 25' left of **Turbocharge**.
P1 5.7 X: (V1, V2) Climb up the black slab with no protection to the ledge with cedars. 30'
P2 5.8 G: From the right side of the cedar ledge, climb up shallow right-facing corners to gain a larger right-facing, right-leaning dihedral. Move out right under the dihedral, past a short section of loose rock and unstable blocks, to a V-groove on the left side of a large roof (where **Turbocharge** joins in from below). Up the V-groove (crux) and left-facing corner above to the top. 120'
V1 5.5 G: Climb the unappealing right-facing corner to the right side of the black slab to gain the same ledge.
V2 5.7 X: Climb the left side of the slab (i.e., the first section of **Death Trap**); still unprotected, but the rock is cleaner.
FA Sep, 1982, Alan Jolley, Scott Provost

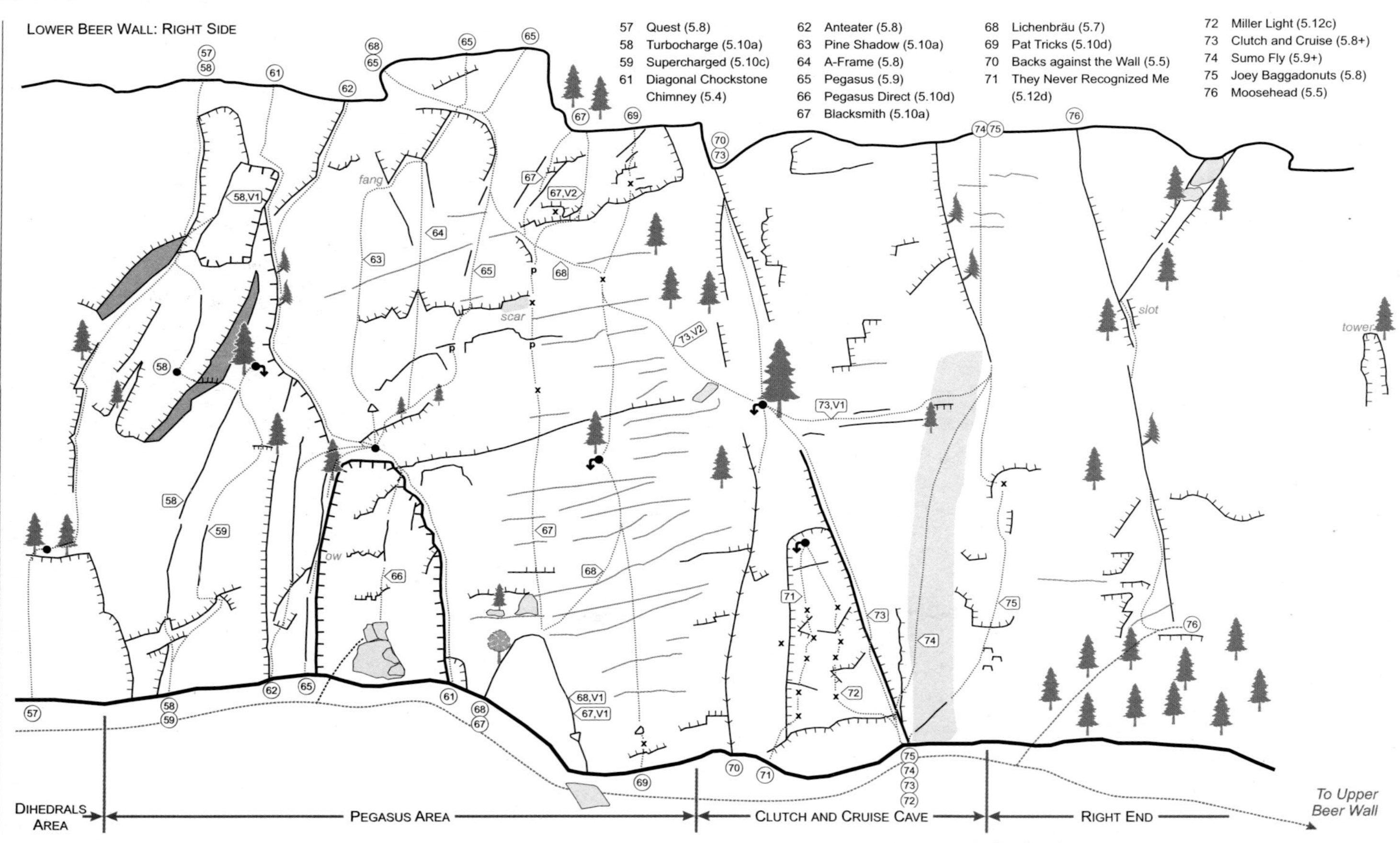
LOWER BEER WALL: RIGHT SIDE
57 Quest (5.8)
58 Turbocharge (5.10a)
59 Supercharged (5.10c)
61 Diagonal Chockstone Chimney (5.4)
62 Anteater (5.8)
63 Pine Shadow (5.10a)
64 A-Frame (5.8)
65 Pegasus (5.9)
66 Pegasus Direct (5.10d)
67 Blacksmith (5.10a)
68 Lichenbräu (5.7)
69 Pat Tricks (5.10d)
70 Backs against the Wall (5.5)
71 They Never Recognized Me (5.12d)
72 Miller Light (5.12c)
73 Clutch and Cruise (5.8+)
74 Sumo Fly (5.9+)
75 Joey Baggadonuts (5.8)
76 Moosehead (5.5)
fang
scar
slot
tower
ow
58,V1
67,V2
73,V2
73,V1
68,V1
67,V1
DIHEDRALS AREA
PEGASUS AREA
CLUTCH AND CRUISE CAVE
RIGHT END
To Upper Beer Wall

Pegasus Area

Home to all the routes on and around the awesome sheer black shield of rock that dominates the center of the Lower Beer Wall. Several of the routes begin on the Pegasus Ledge, a good ledge about 40' above a clearing in the talus, most easily accessed by P1 (5.0) of **Diagonal Chockstone Chimney**.

The Pegasus Area is on the highest point in the terrain that runs along the base of the cliff 599309,4888685. The most distinguishing feature is the start of **Diagonal Chockstone Chimney**—a well-defined right-facing chimney that starts about 5' up.

Incidentally, you can get an excellent view of the Pegasus Area by bushwhacking across to the other side of the valley and up to the rock ledges on the winter route **Positive Reinforcement** (approach this from the steep wooded hillside on the left). It takes about 10 min, but the photographic opportunities make the trip worthwhile.

58 Turbocharge 5.10a G 150' ★★★★

A nice climb and a popular one to fall off, as the crux is tricky but well protected. This was originally thought to be 5.8!

Start: 25' left of the **Pegasus** open area at a right-facing, sharp fin of rock below a small overlap at 12'. The fin points to a bottomless S-shaped crack that begins at the overlap.

P1 5.10a G: Climb up to the overlap to gain the crack (crux) and follow it up right (5.8) toward a cedar with a fixed anchor just right of a right-facing corner (you can lower off from here). Before the cedar, traverse left to a giant flake in a roof in the dihedral. Move left around the arête to a stance on the left wall. 90'

P2 5.8 G: Climb a crack in the face to a V-groove on the left side of the large roof above. Up the V-groove (crux; V1, V2) and left-facing corner above to the top. 60'

V1 Turbocharge Direct Finish 5.11b G: From the bottom of the V-groove, climb through the roof on the right and into the crack that runs through a slot and on to the top of the buttress—the nose left of the **Pegasus** face. Finish on the ledge (the same ledge as for **Mother Mantel** and **Diagonal Chockstone Chimney**).

V2 5.8 G: Climb up the V-groove for a few feet, then move right easily to the outside of the buttress to gain the fingercrack (the same as for **Turbocharge Direct Finish**), and follow it to the top.

FA Aug, 1982, Chuck Turner, Alan Jolley, Mark Meschinelli
FA (V1) Patrick Munn

59 Supercharged 5.10c G (5.9 X) 80' ★★★

An unlikely line up the face and thin crack right of **Turbocharge**. After the thin crack, you can step left into **Turbocharge** to avoid the runout.

Start: Same as **Turbocharge**.

P1 5.10c G (5.9 X): Climb up and right on the slab following the underside of the right-rising roof (#00 TCU helpful) to the A-shaped orange flake at its end. Move left over the roof onto the face (hidden TCU) to gain a faint crack. Follow the crack to its end. Continue up and right up the unprotected face to a small ledge (5.9 X), then up to the fixed anchor on **Turbocharge**. 80'

FA May 29, 2007, Jim Lawyer, Lori Crowningshield

Opposite: Emilie Drinkwater on ***Blacksmith*** *(5.10a).*

60 Mother Mantel 5.9 G 100'

An unlikely-looking route that climbs the right side of the overhanging nose high above and left of the **Pegasus** face. (**Turbocharge Direct Finish** climbs the outside face of this same feature.) During the first (aid) ascent, which climbed past the cedar at the top of P1 of **Turbocharge**, Williams attempted the mantel move at the top but then decided to place one last piece, which expanded the crack, zippered his gear, and sent him for a ride. Beware of the expanding flake!

Start: On the Pegasus Ledge, most easily gained by climbing P1 of **Diagonal Chockstone Chimney**.

P1 5.9 G: From the left end of the ledge, climb up the large right-facing corner for a few feet until you can move left to the arête. Climb up the arête with a clean crack on the right (a bit contrived due to its proximity to the corner). Struggle past a tree to a detached pillar and up the overhanging face via a hidden, thin crack. Make a final mantel move to the top. 100'

FA 1989, Stuart Williams, Eric Dahn
FFA 1990, Patrick Purcell

61 Diagonal Chockstone Chimney 5.4 G 140'

P1 is often used as an approach to the upper pitches of **Pegasus** and **Anteater** as well as the routes that begin on top of the Pegasus Ledge (**Pine Shadow**, **A-Frame**, **Mother Mantel**).

Start: At the highest point in the terrain at the base of the cliff where the trail is level and relatively open, below a right-facing chimney formed by a huge flake, which is the most obvious feature in this section of cliff.

P1 5.0 G: Climb the chimney to a good ledge. 40'

P2 5.4 G: From the left end of the ledge, climb the tree-filled, loose right-facing corner to the top. 100'

History: On P2, the route once had a large chockstone that formed a chimney. The first-ascent party reported finding an old piton en route.

FA Jul 6, 1982, Jim Cunningham, Rich Leswing

62 Anteater 5.8 G 150' ★★★

P1 is recommended and is a good alternative for reaching the Pegasus Ledge. Named for the biting ants that attacked the first ascentionists.

Start: Find the start of **Pegasus**—a left-facing corner 20' left of the right-facing chimney. This route begins at an opposing right-facing corner 10' to the left of **Pegasus**.

P1 5.8 G: Climb the fingercrack that breaks through a ceiling at 15', then breaks a bulge and continues straight up to a point level with the Pegasus Ledge. Traverse right to belay on the ledge. 50'

P2 5.7 G: From the left end of the ledge, climb the large right-facing corner (of **Diagonal Chockstone Chimney**). At a point above the tree in the corner, climb out right in a smaller right-facing corner that leans right and leads to the top. 100'

FA Jul 11, 1982, Jim Cunningham, Rich Leswing, Hal Coghill

63 Pine Shadow 5.10a R 140' ★★★

Quality face climbing on P2 that requires you to make difficult moves with RPs at your feet. P1, however, is a candidate for the most contrived line at the cliff; much better to climb P1 of Anteater or Pegasus.

Start: 2' left of the left-facing corner of Pegasus, at a greenish white rock capped by a roof 10' up.

P1 5.9 G: Climb up a contrived line straight up the face to the ceiling; break directly over this and up to the Pegasus Ledge. (The G protection rating comes from the ability to place protection in either of the neighboring routes.) 40'

P2 5.10a R: From the start of the Pegasus traverse, make an unprotected move straight up to gain a good, triangular hold (RP and TCU). Move up and left to a good bucket, then straight up the face to a small overlap (2.5" cam). Continue up to the face under the left side of the "fang" (the large triangular flake that hangs down from the top of the cliff, somehow adhering to the face), then traverse right under the point of the fang and climb up its right side to the top. 100'

Gear: Many RPs, TCUs, Lowe Balls, cams to 1", including one 2.5" cam.

FA (P2) May, 1983, Don Mellor, Chuck Turner

FA (P1) Mar 26, 1985, Don Mellor, Ian Osteyee, Patrick Purcell

Ken Reville on P2 of Pegasus (5.9), late in the season. Photo by Jim Cunningham.

64 A-Frame 5.8 TR 100'

Climbs left of P2 of Pegasus through the A-shaped notch in the roof. Move partway out the traverse on Pegasus, then straight up the face through the notch, and join either Pegasus (to the right) or Pine Shadow (to the left) to finish.

65 Pegasus 5.9 R 140' ★★★

A former classic of the region, with excellent face climbing in an exposed position on P2. In 2008 the ceiling on P2 fell leaving a large scar and a lone, unstable tooth that fell in 2014. It's now more serious and harder than it's original rating of 5.7. The route is named for Peggy Collins.

Start: At a left-facing corner 20' left of the right-facing chimney that marks the start of Diagonal Chockstone Chimney.

P1 5.7 G: Climb the crack on the left wall of the left-facing corner, which becomes off-width before reaching the belay ledge. Alternatively, climb P1 of Diagonal Chockstone Chimney to reach this ledge. 40'

P2 5.9 R: Step up onto a right-rising ledge and traverse right behind two scrawny cedars, then up the face past a piton to a hanging tooth. Step right and face climb straight up past the scar, over an overlap, then up and left on easier rock with good protection to a ledge just shy of the top. From here, you can walk off left or make a hard friction move straight up a slab to the top. 100'

FA Jul 21, 1982, Rich Leswing, Jim Cunningham, Peggy Collins

FA (after rockfall) Apr 6, 2008, Jim Lawyer, Jim Cunningham, Michelle Burlitch, Shahab Farzanegan

66 Pegasus Direct 5.10d R 40'

Climbs the face directly below the Pegasus Ledge. A proficiency in placing small nuts is required.

Start: At the top of a block on a slab halfway between the left-facing corner (the start of Pegasus) and a right-facing chimney (the start of Diagonal Chockstone Chimney).

P1 5.10d R: From the top of the block, climb up a short right-facing corner to a thin crack. (V1) Move right and up to another crack, follow it rightward to the chimney on the right side of the wall, then up easily to the top. 40'

V1 5.11b R: Move up, make a hard move up and left to gain some better holds, then finish up the center of the face.

Gear: RPs and small cams.

67 Blacksmith
5.10a G 140' ★★★★★

Incredible face climbing—one of the best face climbs in the pass. Originally toproped in 1986 and named **Brown Stain**.

Start: Same as **Lichenbräu**.

P1 5.10a G: (V1) Climb up the right-leaning crack past a birch to a ledge at 20', then move straight up the face across many horizontals. After the crux (bolt), proceed via thin climbing up the face past a piton, another bolt (just right of a fresh, tan scar), and several more pitons to eventually reach the left end of a ceiling. (V2) Break through the ceiling on its left end via a right-leaning fingercrack, then up more easily to the top. 140'

V1 5.10a G: Start in **Lichenbräu Dark** (5.9+), the next crack downhill and right. This straightens out the line and increases the difficulty of the start.

V2 5.10c G: Instead of breaking the ceiling on the left, move right to a bolt above the ceiling and pull the ceiling just right of the bolt via a thin right-rising crack on the wall above. Easier face climbing leads to the top.

Gear: Large rack to 3", including small TCUs.

FA 1992, Patrick Purcell, Bob Martin

FA (V2) 1992, Mark Meschinelli, Patrick Munn

68 Lichenbräu 5.7 PG 170' ★★★

Terrific face climbing. The pitches can be combined with good rope management.

Start: 10' right of the right-facing chimney of **Diagonal Chockstone Chimney**, at a crack that arches right with a birch in it.

P1 5.6 G: (V1) Climb up the crack past the birch to a ledge. Continue up and right across the steep wall that bulges between good horizontals to a cedar with a fixed anchor. 60'

P2 5.7 PG: Climb straight up the face above the tree, then up past a bolt. The first ascent angled right to finish in the left-leaning dihedral of **Backs against the Wall**. For a much better finish, angle left across the face and under the ceiling (crossing **Blacksmith**) to finish in easier rock on **Pegasus**. 110'

V1 Lichenbräu Dark 5.9+ G: Climbs the normal route but with a different start and finish. Downhill and right of the initial crack is another crack that doesn't quite reach the bottom. Climb up this crack for 20' to join the normal route. At the ceiling at the top, break through on the left via a right-leaning fingercrack, then proceed more easily to the top (same finish as **Blacksmith**).

FA Aug, 1982, Jim Cunningham, Rich Leswing, Mike Young

FA (V1) Aug 1, 1982, Jim Cunningham, Rich Leswing, Chuck Turner

Jim Cunningham on the first ascent of ***Lichenbräu*** *(5.7), belayed by Rich Leswing. Photo Jim Cunningham Collection.*

69 Pat Tricks (aka Hangover)
5.10d PG 150' ★★★

Good face climbing with a puzzling crux through the high ceiling.

Start: 20' left of the Clutch and Cruise Cave, at the base of a wall with a low bolt and a pocket just above it.

P1 5.10d PG: Up past the bolt to the pocket (3" cam here), move right, then back left and straight up the face, past many horizontals. Continue up the face, past the right side of a cedar with a fixed anchor (the P1 anchor for **Lichenbräu**), then up the face to a bolt. Move slightly right with no protection and aim for the ceiling and steep face in white rock on the right margin of the wall. Pull through the ceiling (crux; bolt) and up the steep face to the top. 150'

FA 1993, Patrick Munn, Patrick Purcell

Clutch and Cruise Cave

This section contains the routes in and around the Clutch and Cruise Cave, which is an open area beneath an overhanging buttress and the first major landmark as you approach from the Upper Beer Wall.

70 Backs against the Wall 5.5 G 145' ★★

P1 is nice climbing. Rappel from the top of P1 or finish on P2 of one of the neighbors.

Start: 3' left (and around the arête) of the overhanging wall that defines the Clutch and Cruise Cave, at the base of a handcrack in the back of a flared groove.

P1 5.5 G: Climb the handcrack up the V-groove up to a large cedar tree on the right with a fixed anchor (shared with **Clutch and Cruise**). 65'

P2 5.2 G: Step left and climb broken rock up to join **Clutch and Cruise** above the deep chimney. Finish in the left-facing, left-leaning dihedral of **Clutch and Cruise**. It is much better to finish on one of the **Clutch and Cruise** variations (**Cruisin' with Joey** or **Clutchin' the Bräu**). 80'

FA Jul 16, 1982, Jim Cunningham, Peggy Collins

71 They Never Recognized Me 5.12d G 60' ★★★

Start: At the left side of the Clutch and Cruise Cave, just left of the arête.

● **P1 5.12d G:** Work right to the first bolt, (V1) then move straight up the face and stay right of the arête, to a fixed anchor (shared with **Miller Light**). 60'

● **V1 Mark's Blue Ribbon 5.13a G ★★★★:** At the second bolt, cross right to finish on **Miller Light**, which eliminates the no-hands rest.

History: This was the original route on the buttress, climbed directly from the bottom by stick clipping the second bolt and climbing directly to the top (5.13b, crux at the bottom). The effort required two weeks' work. In 1996, Patrick Munn and Patrick Purcell climbed the route by starting from the right (**Pat's Blue Ribbon**) and adding the variation around the arête to the left; this stood as the only reported route on this wall for many years. In 2006, Mark Polinski added a first bolt, starting a few feet to the left (5.12d), and called it **Mark's Blue Ribbon**; this is the line as described above.

FA 1995, Michael Christon, Russ Boudreau
FA (V1) 2006, Mark Polinski

72 Miller Light 5.12c G 60' ★★★★

Start: At the right side of the Clutch and Cruise Cave, just left of the overhanging crack of **Clutch and Cruise**.

● **P1 5.12c G:** Move up left to the first bolt, (V1) then up and right through a big-move crux at the third bolt and into some pumpy spiciness before you reach the fixed anchor (shared with **They Never Recognized Me**). 60'

● **V1 Pat's Blue Ribbon 5.12b G ★★★:** From the first bolt, follow jugs left across the overhanging wall to join **They Never Recognized Me** to the top. It is possible to move around to the left side of the arête, which would make the grade 5.11d.

FA 2006, Mark Polinski
FA (V1) 1993, Patrick Munn, Patrick Purcell, Bob Martin

73 Clutch and Cruise 5.8+ G 165' ★★★

The overhanging handcrack on P1 is very popular; the incredibly loose rock above isn't. Most parties lower from the cedar or finish on one of the variations. The grade of P1 evokes much discussion, as some believe this to be the most sandbagged route in the Adirondacks.

Start: On the right side of the overhanging buttress of the Clutch and Cruise Cave, at the base of a left-facing corner with an overhanging handcrack.

P1 5.8+ G: Climb the handcrack in the overhanging left-facing corner (crux). At the top, continue up the corner, now right-facing, to its top. Step left and climb a broken slot to a cedar on the left with a fixed anchor. 65'

P2 5.2 G: (V1, V2) Continue up an obvious deep chimney behind a chockstone to finish in a left-facing, left-leaning dihedral. 100'

V1 Cruisin' with Joey 5.6 G: Step down and traverse right 25' (5.4, airy and exposed with some questionable rock) to an arête. Join **Joey Baggadonuts** from here to the top.

V2 Clutchin' the Bräu 5.7 PG: From the belay, step down and foot-traverse left to a cedar—the end of P1 of **Lichenbräu**. Join **Lichenbräu** to the top.

Gear: 2 ea 3" cams for the lower crack.

FA Jun 2, 1982, Rich Leswing, Jim Cunningham

74 Sumo Fly 5.9+ TR 150' ★

Begins on the right wall of the Clutch and Cruise Cave, at a large left-facing, pointed white flake. Climb the flake to gain the black streak on the right, then straight up the black streak to join the juggy face on **Joey Baggadonuts**. The route is named for the fat cluster flies that buzzed around the first ascentionists, who thought they looked like sumo wrestlers with wings.

FA (TR) Sep, 1983, Jim Cunningham, Todd Eastman

75 Joey Baggadonuts 5.8 G (5.7 R) 150' ★

A little-traveled route that sports excellent climbing and a thrilling runout on jugs, finishing on a featured, well-protected face. The topout is an open bare-rock area with pretty views.

Start: 6' right of the overhanging handcrack of **Clutch and Cruise**, at a right-diagonaling crack in black rock.

P1 5.8 G (5.7 R): Follow the right-diagonaling crack to a large white spot, then up to a ledge below a right-facing corner. Climb the steep face left of the right-facing corner up to the right-arching ceiling with an orange spot and a bolt just below. Step left to jugs and climb the face past the ceiling on the left. At the top of the face, gain the bottom of a crack with a scrawny cedar, then up this to the base of a right-facing dihedral. Climb the beautifully textured face right of this dihedral to the top. 150'

FA Aug 9, 1989, Don Mellor, Patrick Purcell, Bill Simes

Right End

The nondescript section of cliff to the right of **Clutch and Cruise**. This terrain at the base of the cliff drops down to the right to a low point immediately below the Live Free or Die Area.

76 Moosehead 5.5 PG 130'

Start: From **Clutch and Cruise**, walk right 30', then steeply up a treed slope to the highest point on the terrain, 20' above the trail. The start is 3' right of a white, fragile right-facing flake and just below a right-diagonaling crack on the black face.

P1 5.5 PG: Climb up the wall past the right-diagonaling crack to the right side of an A-frame formed by two leaning corners. Above this, (V1) stay in the crack line and trend slightly left through a steep wall to a slot with a cedar on the left (optional belay). From the top of the slot, continue up the left-leaning crack to the top. 130'

V1 5.5 PG: From the top of the slot, change direction and head right, then follow a crack to a right-leaning chimney chocked with cedars and blocks; up this to the top.

History: This route was incorrectly described in the first edition of *Adirondack Rock* as going right after the slot (now the variation). In fact, the route continues angling left to the top. Despite being recently resurrected, it's still of dubious quality.

FA 1983, Tom Rosecrans, Chris Knight

77 Barstool Direct 5.9 R 50'

An uninspiring route. From the ledge at the top, you can walk right to the base of the Live Free or Die Area.

Start: 40' uphill and left from the low point in the trail, below a right-facing corner capped by a ceiling 30' up.

P1 5.9 R: Climb parallel white cracks through broken white rock to a right-facing corner capped by a triangular ceiling. Climb through the roof on the left to a face and up to a spacious tree ledge. 50'

FA May 7, 1983, Dave Gillette, Chuck Turner

78 Cue Ball (aka Three Stooges) 5.9+ PG (5.6 R) 110'

Climbs past two ledges, or steps, on its way to the top. P1 is worthwhile (that is, if you've climbed everything else), but the remainder is dangerous and loose.

Start: At the low point in the trail, below a black face with a piton 12' up.

P1 5.9+ PG: Starting on the right, climb up to the horizontal and make awkward moves into a shallow crack, then follow the crack to a ledge. Step left and climb a chimney with very unstable chockstones to a second, more spacious ledge (the same ledge as for **Barstool Direct**). From here, you can walk off right to the base of the Live Free or Die Area. 60'

P2 5.6 R: From the ledge, continue climbing up a white wall with incut buckets and no gear (or step left and use the low-angle ramp) to a cedar (gear), then up and right on unstable rock to the arête and on to a pretty, open, flat summit. 50'

FA (P1) May, 1992, Patrick Purcell, Kevin Birk, Brad Hess

FA (P2) Aug, 2006, Jim Lawyer, Lori Crowningshield

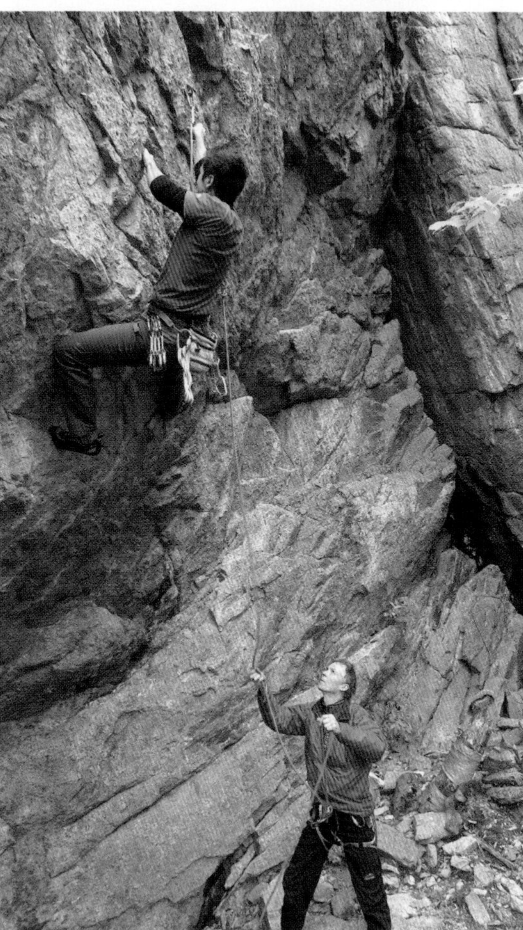

Colin O'Connor on ***Pat's Blue Ribbon*** *(5.12b), belayed by Tad Welch.*

Live Free or Die Area

This area is actually the right end of the Lower Beer Wall but has a separate approach. It is a popular destination for toproping as well as home to several good leads, including the classic **Live Free or Die**. From the height of land on the approach trail, continue straight (southwest) down a short 20' scramble through a notch, then turn right and walk 200' to the base of this east-facing wall on a steep hillside 599370,4888649. The base of the cliff has been built up with erosion-control terraces.

79 Crazy Fingers 5.11b PG 60'

Start: At the left end of the wall, just left of **Fast and Furious**.

P1 5.11b PG: Climb the seam-ridden face to a lower-angled finish at shrubs just below the ledge system at the top. 60'

FA 1988, Bill Pierce

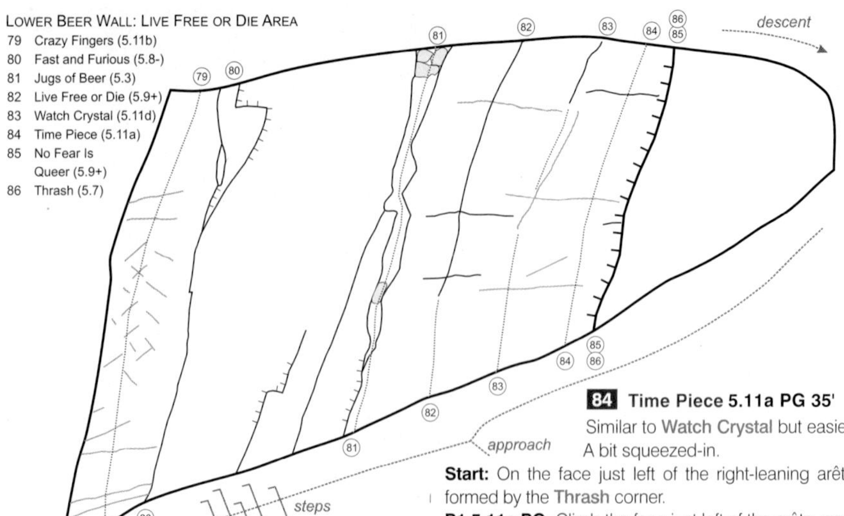

80 Fast and Furious 5.8- G 55' ★★

Start: Below the erosion-control terraces on the left side of the face, at the base of a right-slanting crack.

P1 5.8- G: (V1) Climb the crack, through a flared section at 25' (crux), to an easier topout. 55'

V1 5.11b TR: Climb the face right of the crack to the easier topout above the flared section.

FA Jun 27, 1982, Rich Leswing, Jim Cunningham, Pete Benson

FA (V1) 1988, Bill Pierce

81 Jugs of Beer 5.3 G 40' ★

Start: At the top of the erosion-control terraces, beneath a blocky right-leaning crack in the center of the face.

P1 5.3 G: Climb the blocky crack and exit on face holds to the right. 40'

FA Jun 27, 1982, Jim Cunningham, Pete Benson

82 Live Free or Die 5.9+ G 40' ★★★

A high-quality fingercrack with bomber locks and good protection; sustained. Unfortunately, gaining the crack requires some bold moves off the ground. A popular toprope.

Start: 5' right of a blocky crack, beneath a right-leaning fingercrack that begins 15' up.

P1 5.9+ G: Boulder up an unprotected thin face on small, polished face holds to gain the fingercrack. Follow it past several horizontals to the top. 40'

FA Jul 5, 1982, Jim Cunningham, Rich Leswing

83 Watch Crystal 5.11d PG 40' ★

Climbs the unlikely face right of **Live Free or Die**. The first ascent used a tie-down Logan hook.

Start: 6' right of **Live Free or Die**.

P1 5.11d PG: Follow thin vertical seams up the face past several horizontals to the top. 40'

Gear: RPs and small TCUs.

FA Oct 10, 1984, Ken Nichols, Todd Eastman, Chuck Boyd

84 Time Piece 5.11a PG 35'

Similar to **Watch Crystal** but easier. A bit squeezed-in.

Start: On the face just left of the right-leaning arête formed by the **Thrash** corner.

P1 5.11a PG: Climb the face just left of the arête, past several horizontal cracks along the way. 35'

FA Sep, 1990, Ken Nichols

85 No Fear Is Queer 5.9+ PG 25'

Another squeezed-in route that fully utilizes the real estate on this short wall.

Start: At the base of the overhanging arête on the right end of the wall.

P1 5.9+ PG: Climb the arête and use several horizontals on the arête for protection. 25'

FA Sep 24, 1996, Dan Wolfe

86 Thrash 5.7 G 20'

An insignificant, short corner.

Start: At the short right-facing corner on the right end.

P1 5.7 G: Thrash up the dirty right-leaning corner. 20'

FA Sep, 1990, Ken Nichols (solo)

Beer Walls

CORNER POCKET

Location	South side of NY 73, 0.5 mile west of Chapel Pond
Aspect	North
Height	50'
Quality	
Approach	5 min, easy
Summary	A small, cleaned wall with several moderate routes.

-5.6	5.7	5.8	5.9	5.10	5.11	5.12	5.13+	total
2	1							3

The cliff, which is great for beginners, is easily identified as a clean slab crisscrossed with faint seams in a clearing with ferns and a giant pine tree on top. There is a low bolt on **Natural English** to help you get oriented.

DIRECTIONS (MAP PAGE 286)

Follow the trail from the main Beer Walls parking lot that leads directly uphill and up a gully. At the top, walk leftward to the base of the cliff. Another approach is from the Dry Wall: walk right about 400' and follow the cliff line to the clean buttress in the open forest.

DESCENT OPTIONS

Rappel from the fixed anchor on the large tree.

87 Natural English 5.7 G 50' ★

Climbs the left side of the wall. There are several variations, although they all need some cleaning.

Start: At the lowest point on the buttress, below a low bolt 10' up and just right of a shallow, 4'-high left-facing corner.

P1 5.7 G: Climb up the face that is crisscrossed with faint cracks, then straight up to a left-rising crack. Follow the crack to a short, shallow left-facing corner and on to the top and a fixed anchor on a large pine tree. 50'

FA 1996, Northwood School Outing Club

88 Scratch 5.5 G 50'

Start: 5' right of **Natural English**.

P1 5.5 G: Climb up a heavily vegetated crack past several small birch trees, then straight up the buttress to a short zigzag crack that leads through the steep section at the top. 50'

FA 1996, Northwood School Outing Club

89 Snooker 5.6 G 50'

Extremely dirty.

Start: Uphill and right of the previous routes, 18' right of **Scratch**, at some moss-covered ledges.

P1 5.6 G: Climb up to a bolt on the face left of a shallow left-facing corner (and a large bucket up and right). Straight up to some left-facing flakes with some cracks, then up to the top. 50'

FA 1996, Northwood School Outing Club

Beer Walls

DRY WALL

Location	South side of NY 73, accessed from the Chapel Pond Outlet
Aspect	North
Height	50'
Quality	
Approach	3 min, easy
Summary	A small wall with a couple of routes, which are good but totally overgrown.

-5.6	5.7	5.8	5.9	5.10	5.11	5.12	5.13+	total
				2				2

This wall is on the original road through Chapel Pond Pass. The canyon was once a pleasant climbing area with clean rock, but it wasn't well known and hence became overgrown. The floor of the canyon is boggy, flat, and brushy, with trees leaning up against the rock.

DIRECTIONS (MAP PAGE 286)

Park at the Chapel Pond Outlet—the hidden camping spot 200 yards from the Chapel Pond pullout (as you're driving toward Keene Valley) on the pond side of the road. There is room for several cars on the side of the road across from the outlet, but it's a little too close to the road to be recommended.

Return to the road and walk northwest (toward Keene Valley) 150' across the small bridge over the creek, then head into the woods and angle away from the road. You'll immediately come to a rocky hillside; follow it rightward (parallel to the road) to the entrance to the wide opening of a canyon on the left. Continue parallel to the road for another 200', then angle leftward into the second canyon; this canyon is 50' wide and the entrance is more defined, with a sheer 30'-high wall on the left and a shorter 10'-high wall on the right. The left wall of this canyon is the Dry Wall 599746,4888591.

The first route is located about 150' into this canyon on the left wall.

DESCENT OPTIONS

There are several trees from which you can rappel. You can walk left and down through the woods back to the entrance to the small canyon.

90 Cold Stone Sober 5.10b G 70'

This route would get three stars if cleaned.

Start: At a face with an arching horizontal 6' up, the left side of which forms a large sideways V-slot. There is a buried mossy, slug-shaped boulder that pokes into the cliff just left of the start.

P1 5.10b G: Up the horizontals to a bolt (just right of a left-facing corner), then up to a second bolt below the ceiling. Move slightly left and break the roof at a horizontal (midsize cam), then make a long reach to a small handhold to get established above the roof. Climb the face (5.9), ease back to a slab, then up to the trees. 70'

FA May, 1996, Bill Simes

*Opposite: Mike Cross follows **Live Free or Die** (5.9+).*

91 Speakeasy 5.10b G 70'

This route, like its neighbor, needs a good scrubbing. If this were done, it would merit two stars.

Start: 25' right of **Cold Stone Sober** at a left-rising vegetated ledge with a birch tree on its right end.

P1 5.10b G: Climb up the left-rising vegetated ledge for 6', then onto the face past a shallow right-leaning overlap to a bolt. Up to a horizontal (crux), then make another hard move to gain a bucket left of the second bolt. Straight up to a ledge, then increasingly easier rock (5.7) to the top. 70'

FA May, 1996, Bill Simes

Beer Walls

CASE WALL

Location	South side of NY 73, 0.8 mile west of Chapel Pond
Aspect	Southwest
Height	50'–140'
Quality	
Approach	10 min, easy
Summary	Two small walls with a collection of moderate routes. Very dirty rock for the most part.

-5.6	5.7	5.8	5.9	5.10	5.11	5.12	5.13+	total
3	3	2		1				9

The Case Wall consists of two smaller walls farther down Chapel Pond Canyon (to the northwest). The cliff was named to commemorate John Case, one of the leading alpine climbers of his day and a major contributor to early rock climbing in the region, the **Case Route** on Wallface and the **Case Route** on Indian Head being two of the most noteworthy. (Unfortunately, the Case Wall is not as inspiring as John Case's actual contributions.)

DIRECTIONS **(MAP PAGE 286)**

Access the Case Wall from the Lower Beer Wall by walking farther down the canyon (downstream, toward Keene Valley) from the Lower Beer Wall for about 15 min. An easier approach is from NY 73: park at the large, paved pullout 0.8 mile from Chapel Pond (when you are driving toward Keene Valley) and 0.5 mile from Roaring Brook Falls Trailhead (when you are driving toward Chapel Pond from Keene Valley) 599209,4888973.

From the parking area, walk straight back into the woods and uphill to the crest of the ridge. Turn right (northwest, parallel to the road) and follow the ridge for 5 min or so. Drop down left into a ravine, which can be descended into the floor of the canyon. Since there are some minor ridges and gullies to confuse things, it is likely that once in the canyon, you'll have to explore left or right to find the major identifying feature of the cliff—**Gunpowder Corner**, a huge 90'-high right-facing corner. Its left wall is overhanging and lighter-colored, and its right wall is an off-vertical black slab.

Lives of the Hunted Area

A minor, hidden, uninspiring cliff about 400' left of **Gunpowder Corner** and separated from that cliff by a deep, narrow cleft in the rock. Left of this cleft is this small cliff, whose primary feature is a left-facing corner with a large hemlock tree welded to the rock (the marker for **Gev's Tree**). On the left side of this cliff is a broad, steep gully of tree-covered ledges. The right wall of the gully has the routes **Lives of the Hunted** and **Mule Kick**, and the left wall has **Tita U. Assol** 598843,4888941.

92 Tita U. Assol 5.8 G 40'

The name comes from Wallace's accented command for Mellor to take up rope: "Tighter, you asshole."

Start: On the left side of the gully is a small cliff with a prominent roof above a very black, mossy face. Begin on the slope right of the roof.

P1 5.8 G: Move out left on horizontals to below the roof. (V1) Climb a groove right of the roof to a ledge with a small cedar. Step right and follow a fingercrack to the top. 40'

V1 Tanks of Beer 5.10b TR: Move left and break the roof at a horn, then up to a bucket and on to the ledge with the cedar. Step right and join the normal route.

FA Aug 23, 1988, Don Mellor, Jeff Stewart, Ben Wallace

FA (V1) Aug 23, 1988, Don Mellor, Jeff Stewart

93 Lives of the Hunted 5.8+ G 50' ★

Start: On the right side of the gully, at a left-diagonaling fingercrack in orange rock behind a huge pine tree 3' from the face.

P1 5.8+ G: Climb the fingercrack up past a pasted flake and on to the top. 50'

FA May, 1988, Tad Welch, Jamie Savage

94 Mule Kick 5.10b TR 75'

This route begins on ledges 5' downhill and right of **Lives of the Hunted**. Climb up the arête, move left to a large bucket, then back right and up the face to the top.

FA (TR) Jun, 1988, Tom DuBois

95 Gev's Tree 5.4 G 60'

Seriously stretches the definition of a rock climb.

Start: Left of the narrow cleft that separates Lives of the Hunted Area from the Shotgun Face at a hemlock tree welded to the rock.

P1 5.4 G: Climb the face right of the tree, making use of the branches for protection. Eventually transfer to the tree itself and climb to its top. 60'

Descent: Rappel the tree.

FA May, 1989, R.L. Stolz, Gev Shai

96 Climb Free or Die Trying 5.7 G 50'

Start: Walking right from the Lives of the Hunted Area, you pass a deep cleft that breaks the cliff with an overhanging wall on the right side. This is also 200' left of **Gunpowder Corner**. Begin just left of the mouth of this ravine.

P1 5.7 G: Follow the slanting inside corner within the prominent outside corner. At its top, pull over onto the face and up the easy cracks to the trees. 50'

FA Sep 27, 1988, Bill Widrig, Tad Welch

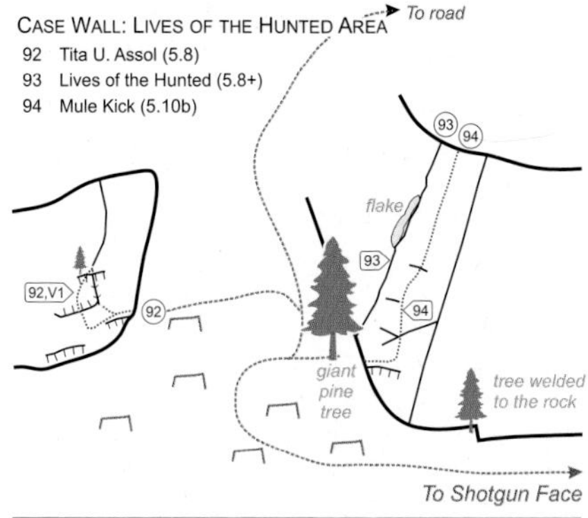

Shotgun Face

This cliff is characterized by the large right-facing corner of **Gunpowder Corner**, the left wall of which is overhanging 598843,4888941. It is separated from the Lives of the Hunted Area by a deep, narrow cleft. The terrain around these cliffs is inconvenient—sloped, vegetated talus with deep holes.

97 Standing Room Only 5.7 PG 140'

Start: Just left of the toe of the buttress formed by the left wall of **Gunpowder Corner** at the base of a cleaned slab.

P1 5.4 G: Face-climb up the right side of the slab past a flake and through the overhang to a ledge with a cedar and a fixed anchor. 50'

P2 5.7 PG: (V1) Step up, then traverse right to the airy arête. Follow big holds on the arête to the top. 90'

V1 Bone Games 5.6 PG: Climb straight up the right-facing corner, step left onto a ledge, then up another right-facing, right-leaning corner. At its top, climb the easier face to the top.

History: The fixed anchor was in place prior to the first ascent, most likely from Patrick Purcell.

FA Sep 23, 1988, Bill Widrig, Steve Jervis, Ali Schultheis, Tad Welch, Chuck Yax
FA (V1) Oct 29, 1989, Tad Welch, Ali Schultheis

98 Gunpowder Corner 5.5 TR 90'

Climbs the chimney in the huge right-facing corner. From the top of the vegetated cone at the base of the cliff, move up into the chimney and follow it to a point where it pinches down and becomes vegetated. Break out right onto the face and up to the top.

FA (TR) Jun, 1985, Tim Broader, Bob Hey, George Carroll

99 Last Swim or Dive 5.7 R 140' ★★

Start: A few feet right of the **Gunpowder Corner** chimney.

P1 5.7 R: Mantle onto a large hold several feet right of the chimney, then up and slightly left to a small flake (poor protection). Follow an obvious traverse right, then go up the face just left of the stacked blocks (as mentioned for **Amateur's Edge**). (V1) Head up and right past tiny trees and join the arête of **Amateur's Edge** just below the top. 140'

V1 5.7 R: From the left side of the stacked blocks, continue straight to the top.

FA Jul, 1988, Tad Welch, Ali Schultheis
FA (V1) Sep 27, 1988, Tad Welch, Bill Widrig

100 Amateur's Edge 5.5 PG 140' ★

A nice route in a fine position. The start is dirty, so the unprotected V1 of **Last Swim or Dive** is recommended.

Start: On the right side of the black wall that forms the right wall of the huge right-facing **Gunpowder Corner**, at a vertical crack with a birch 10' up, just uphill from the toe of the buttress.

P1 5.5 PG: Climb the wide crack and traverse right to the arête. Proceed past wide ledges (easy climbing) to the large stacked blocks. At the blocks, make a move on the right side of the arête to gain the enjoyable and narrow crest. Follow square-cut holds and a short crack to the top. 140'

FA May, 1988, Tad Welch, Jamie Savage

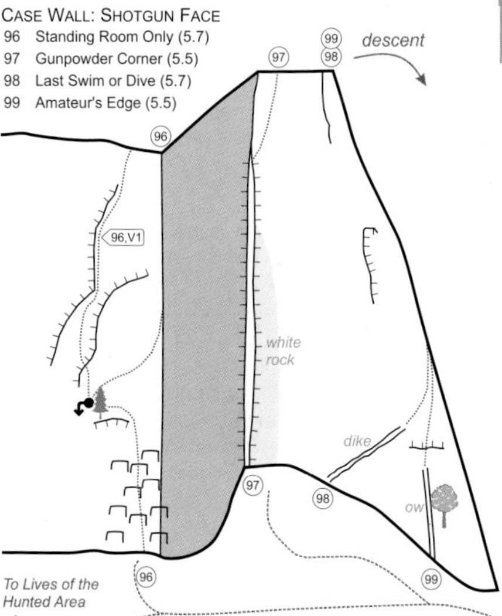

Beer Walls

CRACK IN THE WOODS CLIFF

Location	Directly next to NY 73 near the Case Wall parking.
Aspect	North
Height	40'
Quality	★
Approach	1 min, easy
Summary	A small outcropping with a single route.

This small outcropping has a single, difficult, offwidth crack. The proximity to the road detracts somewhat from the experience.

DIRECTIONS **(MAP PAGE 286)**

Park as for the Case Wall, at the large, paved pullout 0.8 mile from Chapel Pond (when you are driving toward Keene Valley) and 0.5 mile from Roaring Brook Falls Trailhead (when you are driving toward Chapel Pond from Keene Valley) 599138,4889019. Walk toward Keene Valley for 450' to a cliff that is visible 40' in the woods to the left, 60' beyond a concrete culvert in the road.

101 Crack in the Woods 5.10d G 40' ★★

A nice route but not nearly as good as its namesake in New Hampshire.

Start: At the base of the 4" crack with a triangular ceiling at midheight.

P1 5.10d G: Climb the crack through the ceiling to the cedar trees on top. 40'

Gear: To 4".

FA 1978, Mike Endicott, Dave Hough

ROARING BROOK FALLS

Location	North side of NY 73, accessed from the Giant Mountain Trailhead in St. Huberts
Aspect	Southwest
Height	500'
Quality	★★★★
Approach	5 min, easy
Summary	A mountaineering route with loose rock and minimal protection in a stellar location.

-5.6	5.7	5.8	5.9	5.10	5.11	5.12	5.13+	total
2	1							3

Roaring Brook Falls, visible to cars on NY 73, pours through a narrow trough, then cascades down in a many-layered flume to its base 500' below. In the drier summer months, the water volume diminishes, exposing superclean rock. Unfortunately, the action of water erosion has sculpted the rock such that there are very few protection opportunities. For those prepared for such challenges, climbing this waterfall is a great mountaineering outing. And where else can you climb *up* to take a swim?

HISTORY

The first ascent of the falls isn't known, but in 1938, Jim Goodwin referred to it as one of Keene Valley's "principal climbs." He described several practice climbs on the lower section below Roaring Brook Outlook (the flat area in the middle of the falls with the fresh rockfall debris), characterized the upper section as being "more difficult," and told of actually climbing in the water on blocky, angular holds.[6] More recently Butch and Jeanne Kinnon submitted details of their route **Keep Your Powder Dry, Ranger** (5.7+, Jul 16, 1991) that seems to find a reasonable way to the top. The line described here borrows pieces from the Kinnon's route and seems to be the easiest, safest, and most spectacular way to the top.

6 James A. Goodwin, "Rock Climbs in the Adirondacks", *Bulletin of the Adirondack Mountain Club* 2, no. 4 (Jun–Jul 1938), pp. 8-9.

ROARING BROOK FALLS
1 Roaring Brook Falls (5.7)

In 2011, Hurricane Irene scrubbed several more lines on the lower slab, thoroughly removing all the vegetation and choss. These were climbed by R.L. Stolz.

DIRECTIONS **(MAP PAGE 480)**

Parking is at the Giant Mountain Trailhead 598569,4889323, of which there are several. This particular trailhead is known as the Roaring Brook Falls Trail and is located on NY 73, 3.2 miles from Keene Valley (from the intersection with Johns Brook Road, when you're traveling toward Chapel Pond) and 5.4 miles from Malfunction Junction (when you're traveling toward Keene Valley).

Hike the Roaring Brook Falls Trail (red markers) for 100 yards to a fork. The left fork goes to the top of the falls (where you descend), and the right fork goes to the base of the falls. Take the right fork, following a good trail to the base of the falls 599088,4889322.

DESCENT OPTIONS

Walk down the Roaring Brook Falls Trail to the car.

1 Roaring Brook Falls 5.7 PG (5.6 R, 5.2 X) 520' ★★★★

The lower portion of this route has excellent rock, sculpted by eons of water erosion, with good square-cut holds and a somewhat polished texture. The upper portion has some loose, wet rock and is very exposed with sparse protection. The fantastic setting with the views of the Great Range and the pounding water makes this a great adventure, but one that should be undertaken only by those ready for its challenges.

Start: At the base of the falls and left of the flume is a white slab. This route begins in the middle of the slab below a smile-shaped ledge 15' up.

P1 5.7 PG (5.2 X): Up the white slab to its top below an overlap (100', optional belay at trees on the left). Clear the overlap in the center, then follow a right-rising rib (actually a blocky ramp) to its top below a 5'-high headwall with a wide overhang at half-height. If you're tall, some secure RPs can be arranged above the headwall (several feet right of the overhang) and the move is 5.7 G. If you're short, the headwall move is 5.9 R. An easier alternative is to traverse left and break the headwall left of the overhang. Above the headwall, go up to a spacious ledge with a fixed anchor on a tree. 200'

P2 5.2 PG: Step right across a chockstone-filled chimney with water, then up a small buttress to a flat area with many giant fresh boulders (from a recent rockfall) and a soaking pool. (V1, V2) Stay left of the stream and proceed up a slab to chocolate-colored rock. Scramble up the chocolate rock to a ledge just left of the water. Cams to 1" for the belay. 160'

P3 5.6 R: Step down 15' to a constriction in the waterfall. Step across (slimy) to the other side and climb unprotected blocky semisolid rock for 20' to another constriction in the waterfall. Step back to the left side and climb the wall just left of the water to the top. 160'

V1 Too Shallow for Diving 5.5 PG: An alternative to the top pitch is to climb the clean 40'-tall buttress-rib (on the road-side of the brook) to a large white pine. You can walk off right through the woods from here.

V2 Cedar Corner 5.7 G (5.6 R): Above and left of the soaking pool are 2 hidden bolts driven down; belay here. (V3) Climb up the low-angle rock to a tree island, around this on the left, then up a hidden corner to a ledge with trees. Traverse right and join the normal route to the top.

V3 Schwartz's Ridge 5.6 PG: This route has fallen down. From the bolt belay, work up the buttress-rib on the left side of the pool.

Gear: To 1", including RPs and 1 ea 4" cam.

ACB (V1) 1987, R.L. Stolz

ACB (V3) Jul, 2003, R.L. Stolz, Nancy Schwartz, Howard Schwartz

2 After Irene 5.6 R 170' ★★★★

This route was climbed the day after storm damage repairs to NY 73 were completed and the road was reopened.

Start: Just left of the pool where the lowest waterfall terminates is a rounded buttress. Belay at water's edge on gravel and rocks.

P1 5.5 R: Climb the buttress to a white slab and follow it to a small stance on a rib slightly left of the start. There is a small crack at the belay for gear. 120'

P2 5.6 G: Step up and move right to the base of a right-facing corner. Climb the corner to its top then trend right, close to the water, and up to belay at a dead cedar just left of the water. (This is the same belay as commonly used for P1 of the winter route.) 50'

Descent: Join the regular route or cross the stream and walk off right.

FA Sep 26, 2011, R.L. Stolz, Geoffrey Bailey

3 Hipster 5.6 R 190' ★★

Start: At a flat spot on the right side of the waterfall at the base of an obvious broken corner-gully.

P1 5.5 R: Climb the face just left of the corner for 30' until you can traverse left. Move left over corners and flakes to a small belay stance 15' below a break in the overhang and 10' right of the waterfall. 70'

P2 5.6 PG: Step up and traverse delicately back right for about 25' to good holds. Continue straight up a slab, then up a groove to a large ledge with a good tree. (It is also possible to climb through the overhang directly above the belay then move right to the top, but expect some loose rock.) 50'

P3 5.2 PG: Climb the steep, dark rib that is essentially in the stream, then move left to a belay near the soaking pool. 70'

Descent: Continue on one of the other routes to the top.

FA Sep 17, 2013, R.L. Stolz, Phil Nathan

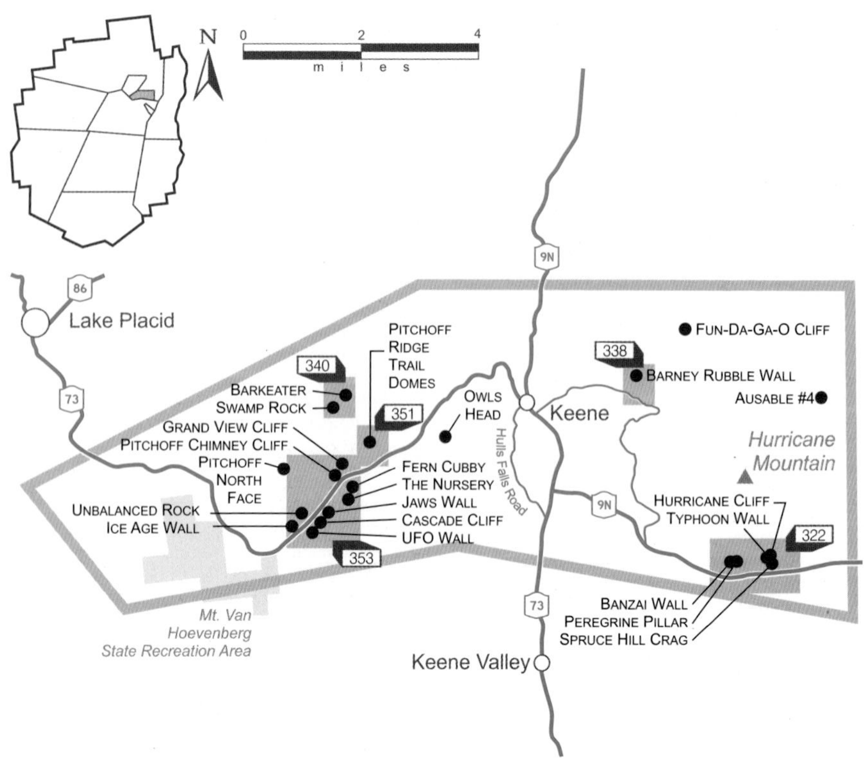
N
0
2
4
miles
9N
86
Lake Placid
73
340
Barkeater
Swamp Rock
Pitchoff Ridge Trail Domes
351
Owls Head
Grand View Cliff
Pitchoff Chimney Cliff
Pitchoff North Face
Fern Cubby
The Nursery
Jaws Wall
Cascade Cliff
UFO Wall
Unbalanced Rock
Ice Age Wall
353
Hulls Falls Road
Keene
338
Fun-Da-Ga-O Cliff
Barney Rubble Wall
Ausable #4
Hurricane Mountain
Hurricane Cliff
Typhoon Wall
322
9N
73
Banzai Wall
Peregrine Pillar
Spruce Hill Crag
Mt. Van Hoevenberg State Recreation Area
Keene Valley

Keene

This region, centered around the town of Keene, includes the climbing areas close to town (Barkeater Cliff and Little Crow Mountain), on NY 73 between Keene and Lake Placid (such as Pitchoff Chimney Cliff, Cascade Cliff, and Owls Head Mountain), and on NY 9N between Keene and Elizabethtown (such as Hurricane Crag and Peregrine Pillar). This is a diverse collection of well-developed crags, which are close to the road and popular with local climbers. Whether it be from a ledge high on Hurricane Crag or a belay in the birch grove beneath Barkeater Cliff, the scenery in this region is simply tremendous. There are climbs for all abilities, from the toproping at Spruce Hill and Owls Head to the moderate cracks and demanding face climbs at Pitchoff Chimney Cliff.

SEASON

Facing south, Hurricane Crag is one of the first places to go in early spring (as shown by some early first-ascent dates) but can be unbearable on hot, sunny days. In the heat of summer, the breezy crags atop Cascade Pass and the shaded Barkeater Cliff are as cool as it gets in the Adirondacks. Despite late-season ice in the pass, Pitchoff Chimney Cliff can be climbed on mild winter days.

DIRECTIONS (MAPS PAGES 4 AND 318)

From outside the park, Keene is best approached from the Northway (I-87): from the south, take Exit 30, then go northwest on US 9 to NY 73; from the north, take Exit 34, then follow NY 9N southwest.

WHERE TO STAY

This is a busy travel corridor with congested trailheads and limited roadside camping.

CAMPING

Two options that are adjacent to this region are Chapel Pond Pass (page 177) and the free car camping along South Meadow Road (from NY 73 in Keene, drive 10.8 miles toward Lake Placid, turn left onto Adirondack Loj Road, drive 3.9 miles, then turn left onto South Meadow Road).

Campgrounds: Campgrounds popular with climbers include Whispering Pines Campground, in Wilmington (518.523.9322); Wilmington Notch State Campground (518.946.7172); Sharp Bridge Campground, near Exit 30 (518.532.7538); Lincoln Pond Campground, off Lincoln Pond Road (CR 7) south of Elizabethtown (518.942.5292); and the Adirondack Loj, outside of Lake Placid (518.523.3441).

Bunkhouses: The Hostel, in Keene Valley (518.576.2030); Jackrabbit Inn and Hostel, in Lake Placid (518.523.0123); and the ACC hut known as the Keene Farm, in Upper Jay (www.accmontreal.ca, then search for "Keene Farm").

Motels: The ADK Trail Inn (formerly The Ark), in Upper Jay (518.527.1155); and Brookside, in Upper Jay (518.946.8369).

B&Bs: Keene Valley Lodge, in Keene Valley (518.576.2003); Mountain Meadows Inn, in Keene Valley (518.576.4771); Trail's End, in Keene Valley (800.281.9860); and Adirondack Rock and River, in Keene (518.576.2041).

Cabins: Dartbrook Lodge, in Keene (518.576.9080); and Mountain Manor, in Keene (518.576.9798).

AMENITIES

There are large grocery stores in Lake Placid and Elizabethtown, and a small one in Keene Valley. Gas is available in Keene, Elizabethtown, and Lake Placid. There are a few restaurants in Keene and Keene Valley; be aware of odd hours in the off seasons. Favorites with climbers include the Cedar Run Bakery (518.576.9929), in Keene; and the Baxter Mountain Tavern (519.576.9990), near Hurricane Crag. Lake Placid has many options for eating out and spending money (page 318).

DIVERSIONS

There's a great swimming spot at the picnic area between Upper and Lower Cascade Lakes (see map page 353) and another one outside of Keene, about 1.6 miles south on Hulls Falls Road. There are many great hikes around Keene, including Pitchoff Ridge, Hurricane Mountain, Little Crow Mountain, and Nun-da-gao Ridge.

Watercolor by Lucie Wellner.

PG	CLIFF	QUALITY	ASPECT	APPROACH		GRADES	#
321	Hurricane Crag	★★★	S	30 min	moderate	.6 .7 .8 .9 .10 .11 .12 .13	21
330	Spruce Hill Crag	★	S	10 min	easy	.6 .7 .8 .9 .10 .11 .12 .13	3
331	Typhoon Wall	★★★	S	25 min	moderate	.6 .7 .8 .9 .10 .11 .12 .13	11
333	Peregrine Pillar Area Peregrine Pillar		S	15 min	moderate	.6 .7 .8 .9 .10 .11 .12 .13	10
335	Peregrine Pillar Area Banzai Wall	★★★	S	20 min	moderate	.6 .7 .8 .9 .10 .11 .12 .13	2
336	Fun-da-ga-o Cliff	★	SW	50 min	moderate	.6 .7 .8 .9 .10 .11 .12 .13	6
337	Little Crow Mountain	★★	S	20 min	easy	.6 .7 .8 .9 .10 .11 .12 .13	7
339	Barkeater Cliff	★★★★	NW	25 min	easy	.6 .7 .8 .9 .10 .11 .12 .13	42
349	Owls Head Mountain	★	W	20 min	easy	.6 .7 .8 .9 .10 .11 .12 .13	5
351	Pitchoff Ridge Trail Domes Lower Dome		SE	30 min	moderate	.6 .7 .8 .9 .10 .11 .12 .13	1
351	Pitchoff Ridge Trail Domes Upper Dome	★	SE	50 min	moderate	.6 .7 .8 .9 .10 .11 .12 .13	3
352	Pitchoff Chimney Cliff	★★★★★	SE	3 min	easy	.6 .7 .8 .9 .10 .11 .12 .13	45
369	Grand View Cliff	★	SE	25 min	moderate	.6 .7 .8 .9 .10 .11 .12 .13	4
370	Fern Cubby	★	S	25 min	moderate	.6 .7 .8 .9 .10 .11 .12 .13	2
371	The Nursery	★★	SW	45 min	moderate	.6 .7 .8 .9 .10 .11 .12 .13	3
372	Between the Lakes Jaws Wall		NW	25 min	moderate	.6 .7 .8 .9 .10 .11 .12 .13	1
372	Between the Lakes Cascade Cliff		NW	15 min	moderate	.6 .7 .8 .9 .10 .11 .12 .13	14
379	Between the Lakes UFO Wall	★★	NW	10 min	moderate	.6 .7 .8 .9 .10 .11 .12 .13	3
380	Between the Lakes Ice Age Wall	★★	SE	15 min	moderate	.6 .7 .8 .9 .10 .11 .12 .13	3
380	Unbalanced Rock Cliff		SE	30 min	easy	.6 .7 .8 .9 .10 .11 .12 .13	2

HURRICANE CRAG

Location	North side of NY 9N between Keene and Elizabethtown
Aspect	South
Height	300'
Quality	★★★
Approach	30 min, moderate
Summary	A multipitch cliff with many moderate routes, including **Quadrophenia**, one of the most popular 5.7 routes in the Adirondacks.

-5.6	5.7	5.8	5.9	5.10	5.11	5.12	5.13+	total
3	5	8	3	2				21

Hurricane Crag stands high above the north side of the road and near a sub-summit of Hurricane Mountain. Along with Poke-O, Moss Cliff, and the Upper Washbowl, this is one of the best multipitch cliffs that is near the road. It is especially popular for its moderate climbs and sunny location, but beware of the black flies—this pass can be miserable during bug season.

The rock isn't the cleanest, in many sections even a little loose. Even so, there is new route potential.

HISTORY

The cliff was originally known as Pitchoff 9N. However, because there are too many Pitchoff Mountains with climbing on them, to avoid the confusion it was rebaptized with the name of the larger neighbor to the northwest, Hurricane.

The first visitor was, of course, Fritz Wiessner, who as usual picked the most striking feature of the cliff (the deep chimney of **Old Route**). Craig Patterson, in his explorations in the mid-1960s to help Trudy Healy with the original guidebook, was the next visitor, climbing another obvious feature, the large right-facing corner of **PSOC**. Ten years later, in the mid-70s, the duo of Long and Rubin made their mark with **Handle with Care**, the only route to break the featureless shield of rock on the highest part of the cliff. In the same decade, Parker and Radford established **Quadrophenia**. The final surge of activity was from Jim Cunningham in 1984, who with various partners, exhausted the last obvious lines, such as **Look, Roll, and Fire**, **Spring Equinox**, and **Schizophrenia**.

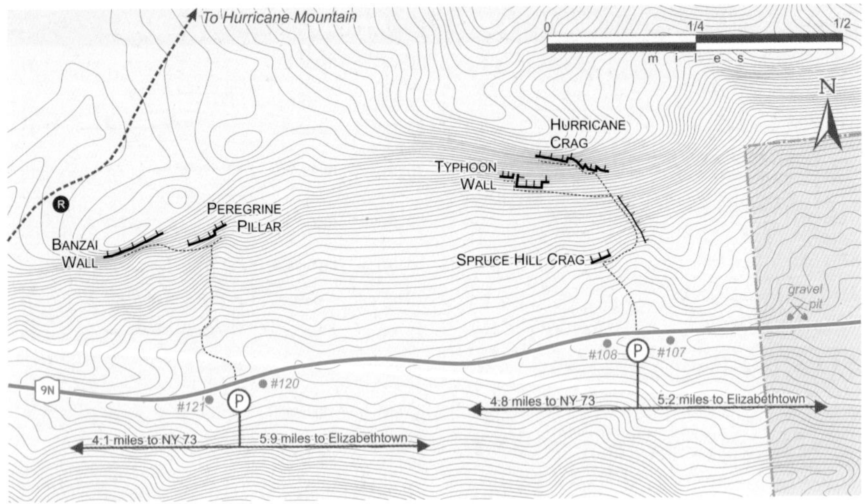

DIRECTIONS **(MAP PAGE 322)**

Park on the north side of NY 9N, 5.2 miles west of the intersection with US 9 in Elizabethtown and 4.8 miles east of the intersection with NY 73 near Keene (and 1.3 miles east of the Hurricane Mountain Trailhead). The herd path begins on the north side of the road between power poles 107 and 108. There is a large gravel shoulder and room for many cars 604056,4896204.

The approach follows a well-beaten path, staying on the left (west) side of a drainage. Within 10 min of the road, the path reaches the right end of Spruce Hill Crag, a small crag with several short worthwhile routes 603976,4896367. From the base of Spruce Hill Crag, hike right through some talus boulders to a band of cliffs that rise up the hill to the left. Follow a good path steeply uphill along the base of this cliffband to its top. From the top, continue straight uphill to the base of Hurricane Crag, hitting the cliff at its lowest point that is on the right end, which is about 50' left of **New Route** 603927,4896620.

The cliff has several major features that are used to locate the routes. The first is a deep chimney at the right end of the cliff (just right of **New Route**) and 50' right of where the approach trail meets the cliff. Moving left from where the approach trail meets the cliff, there is a higher, deeper chimney on top of a dirt cone. This is Wiessner's **Old Route** and is the landmark for **Afraid of the Dark**, **My Generation**, **Schizophrenia**, and **Spring Equinox**. Walking uphill and left of the **Old Route** chimney, you'll find a broken and nondescript section of cliff bounded on its left side by a huge, 100'-high right-facing corner that marks the start of **PSOC** and **Forever Wild**. The cliff base to the right of the corner is steep, loose, and uncomfortable, and is where the routes **Quadrophenia**, **Look, Roll, and Fire**, **Xenolith**, and **Hooligans** start.

DESCENT OPTIONS

Don't walk off the top; it's long and involves lots of bushwhacking. The rappel is easy, however. From the summit, walk (climber's) right (east), staying near the cliff face, then back (climber's) left (west), descending a forested ledge system beneath some slabs to the top of P2 of **Old Route**. From here, an 80' rappel deposits you at the blocky terrain at the top of the huge chimney (P1 of **Old Route**). Walk left (3rd class) with some exposure to a tree with a fixed anchor at the top of P2 of **Hooligans**. A second rappel (100') angles left toward the start of **Look, Roll, and Fire**.

1 Why Did I Fall for That 5.8 G 170' ★★

The first pitch is recommended (and much better than it looks), and the second pitch is simply awful; it is possible to rappel after P1. Named for another song by The Who from the *It's Hard* album.

Start: 150' uphill and left from the large right-facing corner of **PSOC** is a large left-facing corner with orange rock on its outside face. The top of the corner (about 100' up) forms a free-standing tower. Begin 15' left of the corner below a prominent right-facing flake that begins above and right of a 20'-tall boulder stack.

P1 5.7 G ★★: Up some stacked blocks into the right-facing flake. Stem up the flake to a ledge with two large, very unstable perched blocks. Traverse right, and belay at a comfortable tree ledge. 90'

P2 5.8 G: Traverse left (staying well above the scary perched blocks) to a 4" crack, and follow this straight up to a large tree on a grassy ledge. 80'

Descent: Walk left and rappel into a gully with a single rope.

History: The first pitch was initially climbed in the winter of 2008. Recognizing the potential for a good summer route, the pair returned in the spring. An anchor on the trees of P1 indicated a possible earlier ascent.
ACB May 10, 2008, Michelle Burlitch, Jim Lawyer

2 Squeeze Box 5.8 G 90' ★★★

A high-quality pitch, but often wet. Named for yet another song by The Who, and for the sweet stem box.

Start: Below the large left-facing corner described in the start of **Why Did I Fall for That**.

P1 5.8 G: Bypass a brief chossy band on the left, then enter the corner and climb the beautiful stem box to a ledge. Up a short finger crack that widens to tight hands, to another ledge. 90'

History: The route, being often wet, first attracted climbers as a winter destination.

FA (M5) Jan, 2008, Rayko Halitschke, Jim Lawyer
FA (as a summer route) May 10, 2008, Jim Lawyer, Michelle Burlitch

3 Happiness Is a Warm Belay Jacket 5.7 R 260'

Intricate climbing on the buttress left of **PSOC**. Watch for suspect rock at the start of P1 and the crux of P2.

Start: About 150' uphill and left of the large right-facing corner of **PSOC** is a large left-facing corner with orange rock on its outside face. Just downhill from this is a 15'-high, wide flake separated from the cliff by an 18" gap. Begin on the left side of this flake.

P1 5.7 PG: Climb to the top of the flake, up to the open book (with orange lichen on the right wall) to a ceiling. Below the ceiling, follow a crack out right, then up past the right side of the ceiling to a ledge with a block. Step right and climb a left-facing, broken open book to its top, then step right and climb a left-facing corner past

3
4
13
7
6
1
7
10
11
1
2
3
4
6
7
8
10

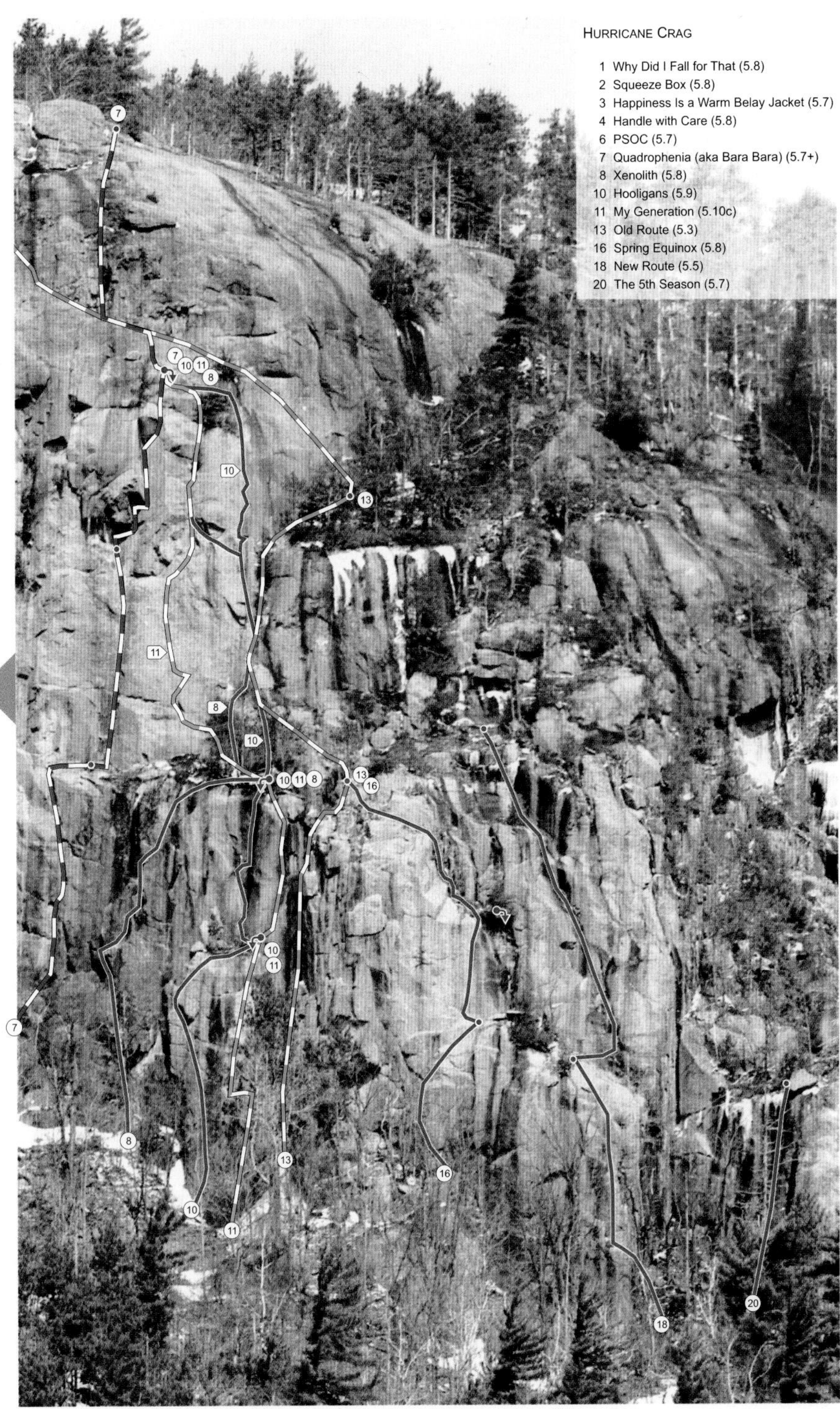
HURRICANE CRAG
1 Why Did I Fall for That (5.8)
2 Squeeze Box (5.8)
3 Happiness Is a Warm Belay Jacket (5.7)
4 Handle with Care (5.8)
6 PSOC (5.7)
7 Quadrophenia (aka Bara Bara) (5.7+)
8 Xenolith (5.8)
10 Hooligans (5.9)
11 My Generation (5.10c)
13 Old Route (5.3)
16 Spring Equinox (5.8)
18 New Route (5.5)
20 The 5th Season (5.7)

a bush to its top. Traverse right 10' and climb a thin crack up to some blocks with a tree, then up left to the rock ledge adjacent to trees (midpoint on P2 of **PSOC**). 100'

P2 5.7 R: From the right side of the tree ledge, climb up a thin crack to a flake, then onto a small ledge. Continue up the left-hand side of the face until you can cross right to a shallow left-facing, left-leaning corner. Above, follow a flared fingercrack to its end, then move upward on crumbly rock to a large boulder. Finish right and belay on a large ledge. 70'

P3 5.7 PG: Step right at the end of the ledge and climb a crack up the face. Scramble the low-angle slab up and right to the summit. 90'

FA Oct 30, 2005, Eric Gessner, John Best (aka "Johnny Appleseed")

FA (P2) May 4, 2007, Eric Gessner, John Best, Jacalyn Gniewek

4 Handle with Care 5.8 R 250'

Breaks the buttress above the **PSOC** corner and follows cracks and grooves. Much loose rock and poor protection.

Start: 15' uphill and left of the large right-facing corner of **PSOC**, at a left-facing open book 4' right of a large forked oak tree.

P1 5.8 G: Climb the crack in the open book past a pine, through a bulge, and up to a cedar growing out of the crack. Continue up and slightly left to an overhang, break through on the left into a dirty left-facing corner, which is followed to the tree-covered ledge (common with **PSOC**). 90'

P2 5.8 R: From the left end of the tree ledge, climb up and left (same as P2 of **PSOC**) until you are level with a foot ledge on the face to the right. Traverse right across the face, up on some flakes, then continue rightward with increasing delicacy heading to a tiny shrub and crack just beyond. Climb straight up the crack, switch right to a second crack and up past a small overlap on the left to a ledge on the left. Traverse left, then head straight up to a right-facing flake with a stunted tree, then back right to a stance with a pasted-on flake. 110'

P3 5.4 R: Climb up and left, then wander easily to the top. 50'

FA 1975, Al Long, Al Rubin

5 Forever Wild 5.10b G 100' ★★★★

Excellent crack climbing and deservedly popular.

Start: Beneath a large 100'-high right-facing corner (the most distinctive corner on the cliff) at the left end of a steep, blocky slope, at an oak 15' up the corner.

P1 5.10b G: Scramble up blocky terrain past an oak tree 15' up, then up a steep dirt cone to reach a horizontal on the left wall of the corner and the base of a fingercrack. Climb up the crack (finger and tight hands), through a flared section, up to a horizontal. Continue up to another horizontal, (V1) then hand-traverse right and climb up a fistcrack through a bulge (crux) to the tree-covered ledge and fixed anchor (common with **PSOC**). 100'

V1 5.9 G: A less committing finish steps left in the horizontal to blocky terrain near the arête and up to the top. Somewhat loose.

FA 1987, Don Mellor, Mark Meschinelli, Bill Simes

6 PSOC 5.7 G 310'

The Penn State Outing Club (PSOC) put up several new routes in the 1960s, around the same time as Trudy Healy's first guidebook was published in 1967. P1 is recommended, but the remaining pitches are a cedar-pulling nightmare.

Start: Same as **Forever Wild**.

P1 5.7 G: Scramble up blocky terrain to the oak tree 15' up, then move right to a left-facing corner. Up the corner and a ledge with a birch (optional belay). Step left into the main corner, over an overlap, and up the cedar-filled corner to the tree-covered ledge. 120'

P2 5.7 G: From the left end of the tree ledge, climb up a 10' crack and into a tree-filled weakness, which is followed to another tree ledge. Continue up and left following a weakness that becomes a horrible brush-filled right-facing corner, ending on a ledge covered with boulders. 110'

P3 4th class: From the left end of the ledge, climb up and left to the base of a tree-filled right-facing corner, which is followed to the summit. 80'

FA 1966, Craig Patterson, Fred Cady

*Jim Cunningham on **Quadrophenia** (5.7+) in 1985. For 30 years this was believed to be the first ascent. Photo Jim Cunningham Collection.*

7 Quadrophenia (aka Bara Bara) 5.7+ G (5.6 R) 350' ★★★★★

Spectacular climbing on P3 and one of the most popular moderate routes in the Adirondacks. Many parties link P2 and P3 together. The climbing at the start of P2 was once protected by a piton, which is now gone.

Start: 30' downhill and right of the large right-facing corner of **PSOC** below a crack that begins 25' up.

P1 5.7+ G: Scramble up blocky terrain, then step right to the base of the crack with a small pine. Up the crack to a crux that is just right of a small orange ceiling. Stay in the crack, then left across a small slab. Break right over a short wall to a sloping ledge, then right to a belay at a small pine below an open book. The gear for the P1 belay is not straightforward—but can be made bomber—and is located at your feet, adding to the inconvenience should one fall before the first piece on the next pitch. 80'

P2 5.6 R: Up the shallow groove and face with no protection to a horizontal break (5.6 R). Step right to another open book with a crack; up this to an uncomfortable stance below the roofs. 70'

P3 5.7 G: A fantastic pitch. Up to the roofs, then undercling right into a right-facing corner. Up the corner to the next roof, which is passed on the right, and up to a ledge. Step left to a pine and fixed anchor. 60'

P4 5.6 PG: Better than it looks. Climb up a couple of ledges to a short left-facing corner to the traverse dike. Traverse left 20' to a short chimney in the choss; up this chimney, then follow a slight weakness straight up through the choss to the top. 140'

History: This route was climbed by Jim Cunningham and Bob Hey on Mar 27, 1985 and named for a The Who album. However, the route had been ascended nine years earlier and named **Bara Bara** (a Swahili word for "road" or "route") by Radford and Parker, who reported that P1 had been climbed earlier (as evidenced by the fixed gear they found)—by whom isn't known, although it was generally known at the time that there was a "great 5.8 pitch" at Hurricane. Radford went on to become an accomplished mountaineer, climbing an early ascent of Fitzroy in the 1970s. He later died in an avalanche when skiing in Alaska. Also, the last pitch (through the choss) was first climbed by Wiessner as the original finish to **Old Route**.

Descent: Two ropes (or a single 70-m) are required to rappel from the end of P3 to the ledge of P1, then from there to the ground.

FA (P2, P3) May, 1976, Geoff Radford, Richard Parker

8 Xenolith 5.8 PG (5.7 R) 240' ★

This worthwhile two-pitch route ends at the P3 belay of **Quadrophenia**. Either rappel from the fixed anchor (two ropes) or continue to the top following **Old Route** or **Quadrophenia** P4. P2 is recommended.

Start: 25' downhill and right of **Quadrophenia**, just left of a double-trunked oak tree, below the left end of a ceiling 10' up.

P1 5.8 G (5.7 R): Climb up to the left end of the ceiling, then up a shallow left-facing corner to its top (5.7 R). Over a bulge, then traverse 8' right to a thin crack in water streak, up this, then up the face to the large tree ledge. Belay at a tree with a fixed anchor. 90'

P2 5.8 PG: From the tree, step left and climb a slab to a broad left-facing open book, which leads past a horrible loose block to a sloping ledge, joining **Old Route** at the large flake with a pine tree on the right. Up the 10'-high crumbly section, then before the cedar, step left into a thin crack in a left-facing open book; elegant climbing up the open book leads to a point level with the large tree ledge on the right; traverse left 10' on sharp buckets (crux, watch rope drag) to another open book with a crack. Up the open book past a cedar; at the top is another very obtrusive cedar, which is bypassed on the left. Climb leftwards to the top of **Quadrophenia** and up to its fixed anchor. 150'

FA (P1) May 1, 1993, Don Mellor, John Connell, Jeff Erenston

FA (P2) Oct, 1993, Ed Palen, Bob Martin

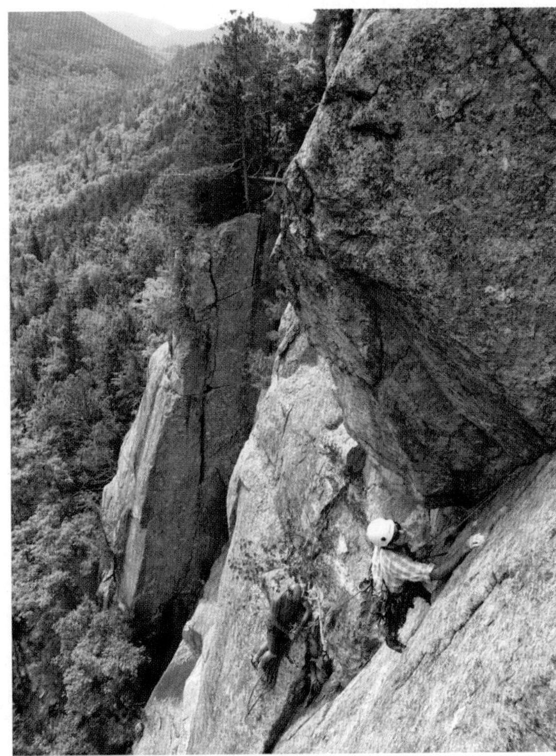

*A climber negotiates the roofs on P3 of **Quadrophenia**. The crack in the background is **Forever Wild**.*

9 Look, Roll, and Fire 5.9+ PG (5.7 R) 350'

A full-length route with some serious climbing.

Start: 10' right of Xenolith's double-trunked oak tree at a left-facing flake that begins 6' up and forms a shallow left-facing chimney.

P1 5.8 G (5.7 R): Climb up to the flake, (V1) then left and up flakes on the face, up through the top of the initial wall. (V2) Move up to a right-facing corner (staying left of the larger arête to the right), and follow the zigzag corner up and right, then back left, then up and right to its top. Move left and run out up the face to the large tree-covered ledge. Walk left to the Quadrophenia belay (at the small tree below a shallow open book). 100'

P2 5.7 PG: Same as P2 of Quadrophenia. 75'

P3 5.8 PG: Traverse left 10' on a sloping ledge and poor rock to a broken right-facing corner, then up the corner to the top of a rock pedestal on the arête. 25'

P4 5.9+ PG: Step left into the cedar-chocked open book. Thrash up this to an overhang with three cracks. Break through using the right-hand fingercrack to the unprotected face above, reaching the traverse line of Old Route, which is followed to the summit. 150'

V1 Tommy 5.7 G: Climb the left-facing chimney to its top at a large sloped ledge, then join the regular route. (It is also possible to rappel from the fixed anchor on the right end of the large sloped ledge.) Easier than it looks, as there are fins on the right side of the chimney. Named for rock opera by The Who.

V2 Bats and Bird Vomit 5.7 R: Move up right to a boulder on the left end of the large sloped ledge (optional belay). Continue up the increasingly steep corner, climbing wide, flat flakes. Make an awkward pull left onto a ledge (last pro), then move left and mantle onto another ledge, joining the normal route on the arête to the tree ledge.

FA Apr 3, 1984, Jim Cunningham, Ken Reville
FA (V1) Apr, 1984, Jim Cunningham, Dave Flinn
FA (V2) Apr 22, 2007, Jim Lawyer, Lori Crowningshield

10 Hooligans 5.9 PG 250' ★★

P3 combines some terrain from other routes and is quite good. The name, following The Who theme, is the title of their 1981 compilation album.

Start: 30' downhill and right of Xenolith's double-trunked oak tree and 20' uphill from the toe of the face is a left-facing, left-leaning corner. This route begins 3' to the right of this corner below a tiny sloped ledge 10' up with a piton.

P1 5.9 PG: Climb up the face to the tiny sloped ledge, then up the face (bolt) to the right to gain a left-rising crack. Follow the crack left to a bulge, then up a face to its top at a right-rising ledge. Climb up and right to a boulder, then step right onto a large ledge and a fixed anchor on its right end. 60'

P2 5.9 G: At the height of the ledge, climb a crack in a shallow right-facing corner up to a cedar. (V1) Step right and climb the unlikely black face with many square-cut holds to a thin seam, which is followed to a tree ledge and fixed anchor. 50'

P3 5.8 G: From the clump of trees, climb a short left-leaning crumbly crack to a broad sloped ledge. Join Old Route for a few feet (climb up to the top of the large flake, then up a crumbly crack to the first tree), then move left and climb the beautiful open book of Xenolith to its top. Xenolith traverses left, whereas Hooligans continues straight up the zigzag crack directly above. At the top, walk left to the fixed anchor as for Quadrophenia P3. 140'

V1 5.9- PG: Continue up left into a discontinuous, flared fingercrack. When the crack disappears, make a few tricky face moves (crux) to gain the ledge. Small gear needed.

FA Sep 9, 1990, Bill Widrig, Jim Lawyer, Tad Welch
FA (V1) Mar, 2009, Chris Duca, Nicole Doner

Bill Widrig, Tad Welch, and Jim Lawyer, the hooligans.

11 My Generation 5.10c G 280' ★★★★

This excellent route combines hard crack climbing with a puzzling steep face on its arête. Named for another song by The Who, this first new route in 13 years announces, with irony, a new generation.

Start: 25' downhill and left of the deep chimney of Old Route, just right of the toe of the buttress at a right-leaning crack.

P1 5.10c G: Up the right-leaning crack until it disappears, then move left onto a sloping ledge on the arête, which is followed (crux) to the large sloping ledge and fixed anchor. 100'

● **P2 5.10a G:** This fantastic pitch continues up the arête directly above the belay to the tree ledge. 40'

○ **P3 5.10b G:** Begin as for Xenolith: Step left and climb a slab to a broad left-facing open book. Traverse left on a sloping shelf to a shallow left-facing corner that is climbed to its top. Move out left onto a footrail on the face (crux), up past a left-facing edge, then step left to a stance. Work up into a broad open book below a white blocky ceiling. Out the right wall of the open book on good holds to join Xenolith at the end of the traverse on P2. Finish as for Xenolith: Up the corner past two cedars to a ledge, then move left to a fixed anchor. 140'

History: The initial cracks were climbed by Lawyer in 1990 with Tad Welch and Bill Widrig but failed to go higher due to lack of protection on the arête. P3 was originally climbed on toprope by Jim Lawyer and Lori Crowningshield on Apr 22, 2007.

FA (P1) May 13, 2007, Jim Lawyer, Lori Crowningshield, Leslie Ackerman
FA (P2) May 25, 2007, Jim Lawyer, Lori Crowningshield, Dennis Luther
FA (P3) Oct 5, 2007, Jim Lawyer, Tad Welch

12 Afraid of the Dark 5.8 G 70' ★★

Start: At a handcrack 4' left of the mouth of the chimney of **Old Route**.

P1 5.8 G: Up the handcrack and stay just left of the mouth of the chimney until it is possible to stem right to the chockstone. Continue up the mouth of the chimney, exiting left onto a large sloped ledge and fixed anchor (shared with **Hooligans**). 70'

FA May 23, 1991, Tad Welch

13 Old Route 5.3 PG 330' ★

P1 is incredible—perhaps the largest, highest, deepest, most continuous chimney of its kind in the Adirondacks. Here Wiessner once again picked the plum feature, which finishes with a bold bifurcation of the top of the cliff.

Start: At the base of the large, deep, 100' chimney in black rock, which sits on top of a dirt cone uphill from the toe of the cliff by 100'.

P1 5.3 G: Climb the chimney. The faces on the inside are liberally peppered with square-cut holds and protection cracks. Various exits are possible. Belay in trees above the final chockstone barrier. 110'

P2 5.3 PG: From the chockstones at the top of the chimney, cross to the left side and up a slab to ledges. Traverse left to a large flake with a pine tree on the right side. Up the flake, then straight up a short crumbly section (shared with **Xenolith** and **Hooligans**) to gain a groove with two cedar trees. Work up the groove to a large forested ledge (better than it looks, with good stances on the arête to the left). Walk up and right on the ledge for 30', following the base of the slab to belay near the base of a minor depression in the slab. 70'

P3 5.3 PG: Traverse left out to a white dike with little steps, then follow this dike up and left across the face. This rising traverse line crosses **Quadrophenia**, eventually reaching a crack in a short left-facing corner. Follow this corner and crack up and right to the summit. 150'

FA George Austin, Fritz Wiessner

14 Chimney Variation 5.8 PG 310' ★★

Start: Same as **Old Route**.

P1 5.3 G: Same as **Old Route**. 110'

P2 5.6 G: Follow the line of the chimney to a left-facing low-angle corner. Up the corner, past a shrub, and over a bulge to the large tree ledge above. 80'

P3 5.8 PG: From the left end of the tree ledge are two cracks 5' apart. The left crack zigzags and is formed by right-facing flakes (P3 of **Hooligans**), and the right crack is straight in. Climb the right-hand crack (5.8 G) up to a ledge, then make an unprotected move to the next ledge (optional belay off left at the fixed anchor on **Quadrophenia**). Continue straight up to a horizontal with a 10'-high crack, then up to a second horizontal, then up the slab leftward to the summit. 120'

FA Jun 4, 1975, Al Long, Al Rubin

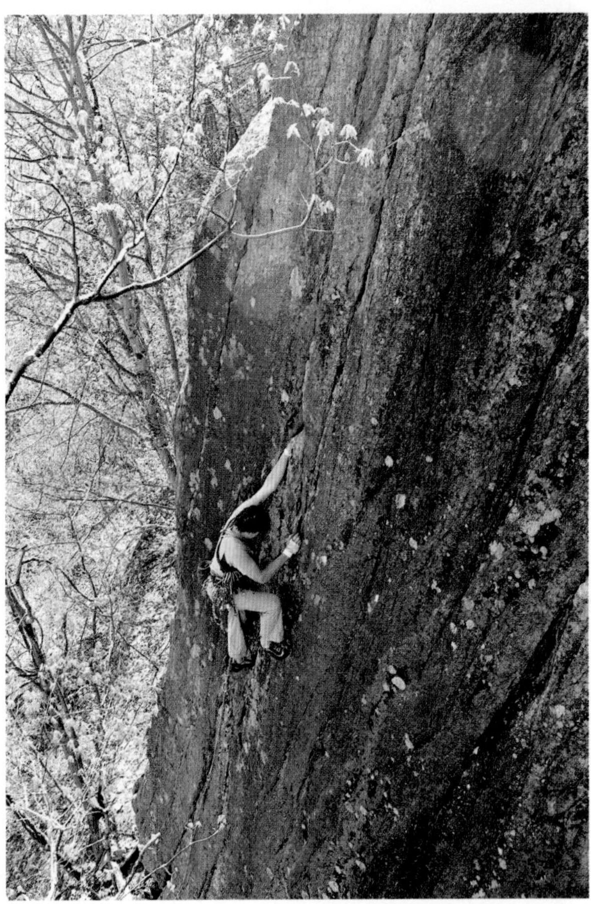

*Jim Lawyer on P1 of **My Generation** (5.10c) on the first ascent. Photo by Leslie Ackerman.*

15 Schizophrenia 5.9 G 100' ★

Start: 3' right of the deep 100' chimney of **Old Route**, at a left-facing corner formed by a pile of blocks.

P1 5.9 G: Scramble to the top of the boulder pile, then up to the left end of a ceiling formed by a large flake. Work left under the flake and up the left-facing corner formed by the flake to its top. Straight up a crack in a shallow groove to a position below a triangular overhang. Traverse right to a ledge, then up to a tree belay at the top of the **Old Route** chimney. 100'

FA Mar 28, 1984, Jim Cunningham, Bob Hey, Dave Flinn

16 Spring Equinox 5.8 G 130' ★★

The variation combined with P2 makes a nice linkup.

Start: Right of the chimney of **Old Route**, and right of the boulder pile marking the start of **Schizophrenia**, is a broad tree-covered ledge. Begin on blocky terrain right of a ceiling (formed by the **Schizophrenia** flake) below a short left-facing corner.

P1 5.6 G: (V1) Up a sharp-edged flake, then step right to the base of a left-facing corner; up this to its top, then head rightward on lower-angled rock to a ledge with boulders. 60'

P2 5.8 G: From the ledge, step left and climb a snaking crack to its top (fixed anchor on tree to the right), then scramble up and left on a blocky, left-rising ledge system to its top. Belay near the top of the deep chimney of **Old Route**. 70'

V1 5.8 G: Start 20' right at the base of a left-facing corner formed by a flake that has a cedar tree 10' up. Climb up the corner to its top, then up lower-angled rock to the ledge with boulders.

FA Mar 24, 1984, Jim Cunningham, Bill Dodd
FA (V1) Mar 28, 1984, Jim Cunningham, Bob Hey, Dave Flinn

17 March Magma (linkup) 5.8 PG 420' ★★

This linkup combines pitches for a sustained 5.8 tour of the cliff.

Start: Same as V1 of **Spring Equinox**.

P1 5.8 G: Climb V1 of **Spring Equinox** and string together with P2 up to the belay at the top of the **Old Route** chimney. 130'

P2 5.8 PG: Move the belay left to the tree ledge at the base of a slab below a broad left-facing open book, then climb P2 of **Xenolith** to the **Quadrophenia** P3 fixed anchor. 150'

P3 5.3 PG: Rappel, or climb up to the traverse line of **Old Route** and join that route to the summit. 140'

18 New Route 5.5 PG 150' ★★

Named in true Wiessner fashion.

Start: 50' right of where the approach trail meets the cliff is a second deep chimney that begins on top of a dirt cone. This route begins on the left wall that leads up to the chimney, just uphill from its toe.

P1 5.5 PG: Climb up to a ledge on the arête, then step left and follow a black-streaked face and slab to a large ledge (the same ledge as for **Spring Equinox**). 60'

P2 5.5 PG: Climb up and right to gain a left-slanting weakness, which is followed over streaked bulges to the ledge area at the top of the chimney of **Old Route**. 90'

FA Mar 26, 1984, Jim Cunningham, Bob Hey

19 Contact Buzz 5.7 PG 60'

Climb the well-featured wall left of the deep chimney. The rock looks interesting but may be rotten, with a cedar fight at the top. From the ledge at the top, you can finish on P2 of **New Route** or P2 of **Spring Equinox**.

Start: At a crack in the black, broken face on the left wall that leads up to the deep chimney described for **New Route**.

P1 5.7 PG: Climb the face past a cedar to the ledge. Walk left up the ledge to trees (the same as for **New Route**). 60'

FA Mar 28, 1984, Ken Reville, George Carroll

20 The 5th Season 5.7 G 60' ★

Start: On the right side of the cone-shaped tree slope that leads to the deep chimney (described for **New Route**), on a slab 10' left of a wide crack.

P1 5.7 G: Climb the face to a faint seam that leads to an overlap. Over this, then up a crack to a shallow left-facing corner which is climbed to its top. Step right and climb another crack to the top just right of a perched boulder. 60'

FA Nov, 1994, Tad Welch (roped solo)

Way Right Slab

The Way Right Slab is located to the right of the main cliff. More routes are possible in this area.

DIRECTIONS **(MAP PAGE 322)**

From the base of **The 5th Season**, walk down and right along the base of the cliff for 300' to a black slab with an overlap 100' up 604114,4896599.

21 After Ireland (5.5)

21 After Ireland 5.5 R 170' ★

Start: Below the apex of the overlap 100' up.

P1 5.5 R: Follow good holds to the overlap, then traverse right and break through the overlap at its apex. Continue up and right to a belay stance. 120'

P2 5.2 R: Continue up and left to a tree ledge. 50'

Descent: 100' rappel from a large pine tree on the left, or continue left and scramble down.

FA Jul 29, 2008, R.L. Stolz, Phil Nathan

SPRUCE HILL CRAG

Location	North side of NY 9N between Keene and Elizabethtown
Aspect	South
Height	50'
Quality	★
Approach	10 min, easy
Summary	Small crag with two prominent cracks; good for toproping.

-5.6	5.7	5.8	5.9	5.10	5.11	5.12	5.13+	total
1	1	1						3

This small 50' cliff is located about 10 min from the road 603976,4896367 on the normal approach to Hurricane Crag. Thoroughly cleaned and climbed in the early 90s by Ed Palen, it has been a popular toproping spot ever since. It's easy to walk around and set toprope anchors on the huge pine trees that line the top, and the base is slightly sloped and open. It can be buggy here.

There are two prominent cracks with about 5 more routes squeezed between ranging from 5.7 to 5.10.

22 Day of Madness 5.8+ G 50' ★

Start: 6' left of **Rasputin** at a small boulder on the ground below a fingercrack just left of a left-facing corner.
P1 5.8+ G: Follow the fingercrack to a layback flake 12' up. Up this awkwardly to gain a small ledge on the right. Follow the fingercrack to its top, then (V1) step left and friction up to an oak tree and dead pine. 50'
V1 5.10c G: Continue straight up into a second shallow fingercrack and follow this to the top.
Gear: Standard rack, from small cams to 2".

23 Rasputin 5.5 G 50' ★

Start: At the left end of the cliff at the base of a crack that begins 2' left of a 10'-high mossy shallow chimney with a block at the base.
P1 5.5 G: Follow the crack through a wide section, then through a chimney at the top. 50'

24 Figaro 5.7 G 50' ★

Start: On the right end of the cliff, 30' right of **Rasputin**, is another prominent crack, just left of a large tree growing next to the rock.
P1 5.7 G: Climb up the crack system to a left-facing corner then to the top. 50'

TYPHOON WALL

Location	North side of NY 9N between Keene and Elizabethtown
Aspect	South
Height	100'
Quality	★★★
Approach	25 min, moderate
Summary	Unique arêtes on the right end, steep central section with no routes, and a cluster of nice cracks on the right end.

-5.6	5.7	5.8	5.9	5.10	5.11	5.12	5.13+	total
1		3	2	1	3	1		11

This impressive collection of routes—three awesome arêtes, and six cracks—is located down and left of the Main Face of Hurricane. Established climbing is clustered on walls to the far left (the Ward Cleaver Buttress) and to the right (Typhoon Right). The crack routes here are uncharacteristically difficult, short, and steep.

DIRECTIONS **(MAP PAGE 322)**

Follow the approach to Hurricane Crag. From the top of the left-rising cliffband (where the cliff disappears into the ground), contour directly left and slightly uphill for 5 min to the base of the cliff 603813,4896543. There is no trail, but the bushwhacking is fairly easy. If you miss it, you might thrash around the steep forest for hours, so it is important to head left at the correct point.

HISTORY

The cliff was first visited by Jim Cunningham and Bill Dodd in 1984 when hiking back to their car after climbing **Spring Equinox**. They returned sometime later that summer with Don Mellor and made a failed attempt on **Wimp Crack** (finally climbed four years later by Don Mellor). Intrigued by the neighboring lines, Dodd and Cunningham returned a few days later and climbed the cracks around **Wimp Crack**. Finally, Purcell made his mark here in 1988, climbing the routes on the far left end. In 2008, Jim Lawyer with various partners made several visits, adding three excellent arête climbs on the left end.

The Main Face has been explored by Kevin Boyle, toproping several lines. He reported evidence of previous climbers.

Ward Cleaver Buttress

This is a small buttress separated from the Main Face by a steep cone-shaped talus slope. To approach, walk up the talus slope into the gully on the left side of the Main Face. At the head of the gully are some large boulders preventing further upward progress; break out of the gully to the left onto a tree ledge and walk left to the deep chimney of **No Name**, the primary landmark for these routes.

25 Sweat Man 5.10d G 50'

A good-looking route, although the topout needs some cleaning. Strenuous and overhanging.
Start: Around the corner to the left of the chimney is an overhanging yellow-colored wall. This route begins 20' left of the arête at a right-rising diagonal handcrack.
P1 5.10d G: Climb up the crack to a triangular alcove where the crack divides. Go left up to another triangular alcove, then up the increasingly wide slot to the top. 50'
FA May 15, 1988, Patrick Purcell

26 Ward Cleaver 5.11c G 60' ★★★★

Only the rare climber can reject the magnetic allure of this incredible arête. Multiple barn-door cruxes.
Start: Below the bladelike arête 10' left of the **No Name** chimney.
○ P1 5.11c G: Up the arête to a tree at the top with a fixed anchor. 60'
Gear: Optional 0.5" cam.
FA Oct 10, 2008, Jim Lawyer, Jeff Gilroy

27 No Name (aka I Didn't Give It a Name) 5.3 G 60' ★

The third prominent chimney of Hurricane (the other two being **Old Route** and the chimney right of **New Route**).
Start: At the base of a very deep 1'-wide chimney in a deep V-groove, capped by a marblelike chockstone.
P1 5.3 G: Up the chimney, staying on the outside edge and using a dirty fingercrack on the right wall for protection. 60'
FA May 1, 1988, Patrick Purcell

28 Master of the Flying Guillotine 5.11b G 70' ★★★

Climbs the orange arête high on the right side of the gully; the arête resembles a ship's prow. Intricate and unlikely with fantastic exposure. Named for a classic 1975 martial arts film of the same name, and for the blade-like arête that is the central feature of the route.

Start: 25' uphill from **Tsunami Slap-Up**, on the right side of the gully, below a 6'-high left-facing corner that begins above a shelf 6' up.

P1 5.11b G: Mantel onto the shelf, climb the corner, then up to the top of a right-rising ramp. Step left onto an orange face and work left to the prow-like arête. Up the overhanging arête using both faces (crux) to a ledge at the top with a fixed anchor. 70'

Gear: 1 ea 0.75" cam.

FA Nov 7, 2008, Jim Lawyer, Mark Bealor

29 Tsunami Slap-Up 5.12b G 70' ★★★★

Climbs a beautiful overhanging prow on the left side of the Main Face. Technical, sequency, and pumpy. Great photo opportunities from a shelf on the opposite side of the gully.

Start: On the left side of the Main Face is a steep, rubble-filled gully that separates the Main Face from the Ward Cleaver Buttress. Begin below the striking overhanging prow on the right side of the gully at a short staircase of incut holds.

P1 5.12b G: Up the staircase of holds, then up an orange face to a triangular incut bucket on the arête. Bump and slap up the overhanging arête to a fixed anchor at the top. Hint: don't clip the last bolt. 70'

FA Oct 18, 2008, Jim Lawyer, Emilie Drinkwater, Rayko Halitschke

FFA Nov 6, 2008, Jim Lawyer, Will Mayo

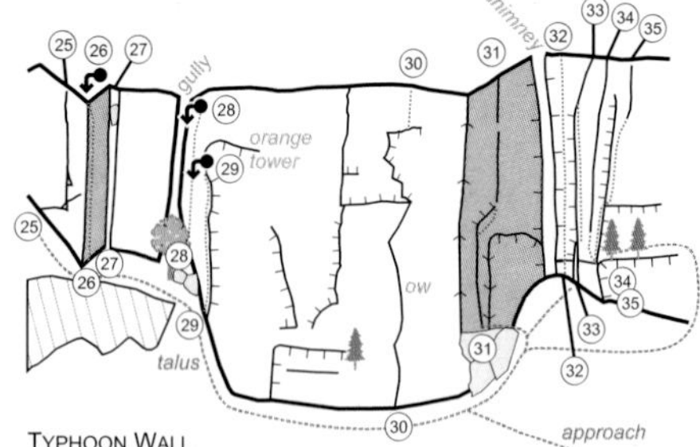

TYPHOON WALL

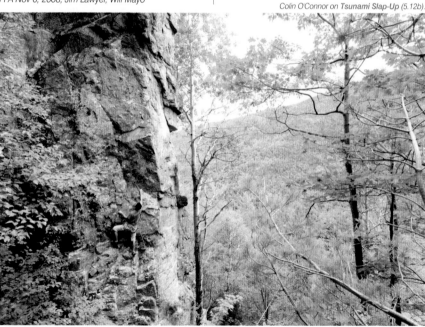

25 Sweat Man (5.10d)
26 Ward Cleaver (5.11c)
27 No Name (5.3)
28 Master of the Flying Guillotine (5.11b)
29 Tsunami Slap-Up (5.12b)
30 Land of the Little People (5.8)
31 Sports Psychology (5.8)
32 Some Things Considered (5.9+)
33 Force Nine (5.9)
34 Wimp Crack (5.11c)
35 Small Craft Advisory (5.8)

Main Face

The Main Face is quite impressive, 100' tall, with a wide crack on the right in a left-facing flake-corner and a good crack on the left. In between is a toproped line **Unfinished Business** (5.12; TR; Kevin Boyle; 2004) that ascends a discontinuous crack through some overlaps to a steep slab finish (like **Working Wives** at the King Wall). A little work could transform these projects into top-quality routes. The only reported lead route is the obvious crack around the corner on the right, **Sports Psychology**.

Colin O'Connor on ***Tsunami Slap-Up*** *(5.12b).*

30 Land of the Little People 5.8 PG 120'

Bummer if you're not tiny—take the Normal People variation.

Start: At the low point on the main face, downhill and left of Sports Psychology, below an obvious S-shaped offwidth crack.

P1 5.8 PG: Up the offwidth crack to an overhanging flake that forms a chimney. (V1) Squirm up the tight chimney to the top of the flake. Continue up and right, then straight up a crack to a lichen-covered slab, to the top. 120'

V1 Normal People 5.9 PG: At the base of the overhanging flake, step right and climb the outside of the flake to its top, then continue with the normal route.

Gear: To 6".

Descent: The route ends on a tree-covered ledge; rappel from trees.

FA Oct 18, 2008, Leslie Ackerman, Scott Ulrich, Rayko Halitschke

31 Sports Psychology 5.8 G 60' ★★★

Start: At the right end of the Main Face on a ledge 20' up with a lone birch, at the base of an open book with a handcrack on the left side.

P1 5.8 G: Climb the crack to a ledge, step right, and continue up the crack in the headwall to a lone tree, then through some loose rock to the top. 60'

FA 1985, Don Mellor, Bill Dodd, Alan Hobson

Typhoon Right

At the right end of the Main Face is a large chimney. The wall right of the chimney has three parallel crack routes, all within 10'.

32 Some Things Considered 5.9+ TR 90'

Begin 15' left of Force Nine, and climb the left-facing corner and open book to the sloped ledge.

FA (TR) Nov 7, 2008, Mark Bealor

33 Force Nine 5.9 G 50' ★★★

Start: Below the left end of the ledge where Wimp Crack begins and 20' right of the chimney that separates Typhoon Right from the Main Face, at the base of a wide crack.

P1 5.9 G: Up the wide crack past several horizontals to where the crack narrows in a shallow right-facing corner. Continue up the crack to the top. 50'

FA 1984, Jim Cunningham, Bill Dodd

34 Wimp Crack 5.11c G 40' ★★

The original attempt was thwarted by wet jeans 10' below the top.

Start: 25' right of the chimney that separates Typhoon Right from the Main Face is a tree ledge 25' up that is approached from the right. This route begins on the left end of this ledge (directly above the start of Force Nine).

P1 5.11c G: Step left to gain the thin crack and power up the steepening wall to the top. 40'

FA Aug 12, 1988, Don Mellor, Bill Dodd

35 Small Craft Advisory 5.8 G 40'

Start: Same as Wimp Crack.

P1 5.8 G: Up a fingercrack in a shallow left-facing corner to gain a ledge. Now in a large facing corner, continue up the handcrack to the top. 40'

FA 1984, Jim Cunningham, Bill Dodd

PEREGRINE PILLAR AREA

Location	North side of NY 9N between Keene and Elizabethtown
Summary	Two walls, one narrow and tall, the other wide with only a couple routes.

-5.6	5.7	5.8	5.9	5.10	5.11	5.12	5.13+	total
3	3	3	1		2			12

The Peregrine Pillar Area, on NY 9N between Keene and Elizabethtown, has two walls positioned below the crest of a ridge 0.6 mile due west of Hurricane Crag. The cliffs are just barely visible from the road in the summer.

DIRECTIONS **(MAP PAGE 322)**

Park on the south side of NY 9N between telephone poles #120 and #121. This is 5.9 miles west of Elizabethtown (from the intersection with US 9) and 4.1 miles east of the intersection with NY 73 near Keene. There is no formal pullout, but it's easy to get your vehicle off the road 602963,4896073.

Another landmark for the parking is that it's1.6 miles west of the Giant Mountain Trailhead, which is well marked with a DEC sign.

Peregrine Pillar Area

PEREGRINE PILLAR

Height	150'
Aspect	South
Quality	
Approach	15 min, moderate
Summary	Adventure-style climbing (loose and dirty) on a small (but tall) wall close to the road.

-5.6	5.7	5.8	5.9	5.10	5.11	5.12	5.13+	total
3	2	3	1		1			10

The Peregrine Pillar is a tall south-facing cliff with typical Adirondack adventure-style climbing. The wall isn't really a pillar as the name would suggest but just a narrow, tall cliff. The name comes from a peregrine falcon nest right of Weird Science.

Most of the climbing here is moderate with little to recommend it. The exception is Talons of Power, a steep and excellent fingercrack. The longest and most direct line on the cliff is Storm Warning.

HISTORY

Don Mellor and Jeff Edwards saw the cliff from the car and walked up. Hearing peregrines, they didn't climb anything and reported the nesting site to the DEC, which confirmed a nest there. Mellor returned with Purcell in 1986 to climb the first route, A Felony

in Georgia, which gave them a taste for the gravelly, the crumbly, and the loose; they didn't return. Activity picked up in 1990 with Tom DuBois, who climbed with Clint and Beth Telford to investigate the peregrine activity at the cliff. DuBois returned with his wife, Ellen, and Steve Adler to climb the remaining lines.

DIRECTIONS (MAP PAGE 322)

From where you park, cross the road at telephone pole #120 at a small cairn on a boulder. Hidden in the woods just beyond is a large, 6'-tall boulder, about 100' from the pavement. Walk perpendicular to the road, cross a stream, then turn left following cairns. The cairns wander through the most open sections of the woods, reaching the cliff in 15 min. If you lose the cairns, simply head straight uphill (north) to the cliff 602892,4896427.

DESCENT OPTIONS

Rappel from trees or walk off left.

1 Gale Force 5.9+ PG 110'

Start: 70' uphill from and left of the low point of the face, at a broken left-facing corner (the bottom of the corner is formed by a block 5' up). This is just left of a 4'-wide overlap.
P1 5.9+ PG: Up the broken left-facing corner to its top just left of a cedar. Continue up a smaller left-facing corner to a ceiling in the corner. Move right around the corner to a right-leaning fingercrack, then climb it to an alcove. Out the alcove on its left side via a crack, then straight up to a ledge with trees. 110'
Descent: Rappel from trees.
FA Sep 1, 1991, Tom DuBois

2 Storm Warning 5.8 G 170'

A long pitch with adventure-style climbing.
Start: 10' left of the low point of the face at a wet, shallow triangular alcove with a left-rising undercling crack at head height.
P1 5.8 G: Stem up the alcove, up the overhanging crack, then step left to a vegetated groove. Climb a few feet up to a crack, then step right and follow a right-rising ramp and shallow left-facing corner to a ledge at 50' (optional belay on a tree to the left). Continue up a short crack in an overhanging wall (crux) to an alcove, then up a handcrack that leads to jugs and blocky rock. Continue straight up steep, loose rock in a chimneylike weakness past several small ceilings to a precarious perched boulder-tower. Step right and climb unprotected easy bulges on cleaner rock for 30' to the top, then walk right 20' to belay at a good tree. 170'
Descent: Walk up and right to a lone pine and rappel with a single 60-m rope to Seagull Ledge (100'), then another rappel reaches the ground.
Gear: Double cams to 3".
FA Aug 18, 1990, Tom DuBois, Steve Adler

3 A Felony in Georgia 5.8 G 130'

Off-width, dirty, and loose . . . Sound good? The first route on the face.
Start: 30' uphill from and right of the low point on the face, at a widening vertical crack that starts at the ground. There is a short left-facing corner 4' to the right.
P1 5.8 G: Up the widening crack, which becomes off width in size, to a ledge below an overhang (optional belay). Up to the next ledge and into a slot (dubbed the "Kor Slot"). At its top, move left on loose holds to a single 1" crack and right-facing corner. Continue up and right to a cedar. 130'
FA Apr 2, 1986, Don Mellor, Patrick Purcell

4 Seagull 4th class 50'

The cleanest and easiest way to access the routes on the Seagull Ledge.
Start: 50' uphill from and right of the low point of the face at a shallow, 8'-wide depression.
P1 4th class: Take a right-leaning line up ledges and blocky terrain to a large pine tree at the left end of Seagull Ledge. 50'
FA Jul 22, 1990, Tom DuBois, Steve Adler, Clint Telford, Beth Telford

Seagull Ledge Routes

These routes begin on a ledge reached by climbing **Seagull**. The ledge is broad, deep, and covered in trees; you can unrope here and move about. The routes above this ledge are impossible to see from below.

DESCENT OPTIONS

Walk left to a lone pine, well positioned on the edge of the cliff. Rappel to the Seagull Ledge (100'), scramble down to the pine tree at the top of **Seagull**, then rappel another 50' to the ground.

5 Ornithologists from Hell 5.8 G 100'

Start: At the highest point on the Seagull Ledge is a large left-facing, sharp-edged corner that arches left into a ceiling. Begin 4' right of this corner in a shallow, blocky open book.
P1 5.8 G: Climb up blocks to the open book, then follow it to a small tree and block. Continue straight up a left-facing corner with a gnarly crack past two ceilings to its top at a cedar garden. Finish up and left on extremely dirty rock, or up and right as for **Weird Science**. 100'
FA Jul 28, 1990, Tom DuBois, Steve Adler

6 Weird Science 5.7 PG 130' ★

Climbs a large open-book corner that begins 40' up and has two blocky towers on the right.
Start: Same as **Ornithologists from Hell**.
P1 5.7 PG: Climb up blocks to the open book, then follow it to a small tree and block. Step right to a large pine tree that sits below a huge open-book corner. Climb up the corner to its top, then up gravelly bulges to the top. 130'
FA Jul 22, 1990, Tom DuBois, Steve Adler, Clint Telford, Beth Telford

Talons of Power Wall

120' right of the low point of the face, the wall turns uphill, facing southeast. The most prominent route is **Talons of Power**, a fingercrack that snakes its way up an overhanging wall with two ceilings.

7 Deep Cleanser 5.5 G 40'

Start: 40' downhill from **Talons of Power** at a right-facing corner with perched blocks 12' up.

P1 5.5 G: Up the vertical crack in the dirty corner past the perched blocks to a tree at the top. 40'

FA Jun, 1991, Tom DuBois, Ellen DuBois

8 Talons of Power 5.11b G 120' ★★★

P2 is reported to be very good.

Start: In the center of the southeast-facing wall, 30' downhill from and left of the height of land, at a right-leaning thin crack that has a short, shallow right-facing corner 8' up.

P1 5.10a G: Up the crack to a ledge 35' up. Continue to a higher ledge beneath orange ceilings. Belay at cedars on the left. 40'

P2 5.11b G: Follow a thin crack past changing corners and several overlaps to a ceiling. Over the ceiling following a thin discontinuous crack through a high bulge and on to the top. 80'

FA 1991, Eric Wahl, Ann Eastman

9 Nameless Corner 5.6 PG 60'

Start: At the uphill right end of the Talons of Power Wall beneath a dirty open-book corner.

P1 5.6 PG: Climb the open-book corner past horizontals to its top below some ceilings, then step right to a tree ledge. 60'

FA Aug, 1990, Tom DuBois, Steve Adler

10 Fledgling 5.7 G 35' ★

Start: From the highest point on the upper right end of the Talons of Power Wall, drop down and right 40' to the toe of a small buttress. Begin on the south side of the buttress at a left-leaning open book.

P1 5.7 G: Climb the left-leaning open book, then up the blunt arête to a belay next to a large perched block. 35'

FA Jun, 1991, Tom DuBois

Peregrine Pillar Area

BANZAI WALL

Aspect	South
Height	100'
Quality	★★★
Approach	20 min, moderate
Summary	A very long wall with only a couple of routes so far, but with good potential for more.

-5.6	5.7	5.8	5.9	5.10	5.11	5.12	5.13+	total
	1				1			2

The wide Banzai Wall sits up from and left of Peregrine Pillar. The rock is a mix of steep faces, corners, and seams, with a distinct lack of natural protection. It is difficult to toprope here, as the top is convoluted with minicliffs and steep, vegetated ledges; from the top, you need to do rappels or exposed 4th-class down-climbing to reach the edge of the main wall.

The cliff is quite wide; a good locator for routes is near the center—a large orange A-shaped roof, the apex of which is 20' up. This roof is situated above a pile of boulders interspersed with poison ivy. 70' right of the orange roof is a pointed boulder 6' back from the cliff, another good locator.

HISTORY

Several climbers have scoped out this cliff, including the authors in 2007 during a reconnaissance trip. Lawyer returned a few weeks later with Leslie Ackerman and Dennis Luther and climbed several lines. They discovered at least one rappel anchor at the top, below the upper band. The wall and routes are named for the 1984 cult science fiction film *Buckaroo Banzai.*

DIRECTIONS **(MAP PAGE 322)**

From the left end of Peregrine Pillar, contour left, staying in open woods and talus for 300', then walk uphill to the base of the wall, about 5 min 602691,4896416.

11 Black Lectroids 5.7 G 90' ★★

Quality climbing up cracks in a clean face. Named for peace-loving alien reptiles.

Start: 40' left of the orange A-shaped roof, below a cluster of fractured blocks and flakes 7' up. This is 4' right of a large boulder up against the cliff.

P1 5.7 G: Climb a short face to the blocks, then up a left-leaning open book with a crack to where it meets a right-rising crack. Step right and climb a face to a bush. Step left to ledges, then back right to a tree. 90'

FA Aug 5, 2007, Leslie Ackerman, Dennis Luther, Jim Lawyer

12 Oscillation Overthruster 5.11b G 120' ★★★★

Excellent climbing with a bit of everything—cracks, ceilings, ramps, and a climactic overhanging face with big moves. Broken into two pitches to avoid rope drag from the zigzag corner. Named for a device that allows one to travel through solid matter.

Start: 30' left of a pointed boulder that sits 6' back from the cliff below a 50'-high right-facing zigzag corner. This is also 40' right of the orange A-shaped roof.

P1 5.9 G: (V1) Climb up the ramp to the first ceiling, around this on the right (crux), then up to the next ceiling. Some high gear under the ceiling allows you to step back down and traverse right 10', then up over a bulge on black incut holds. Step back left into the corner to a fixed anchor that sits below the top of the zigzag corner, which is actually a detached tower (you can 4th-class to the top of this tower from the left). 50'

○ P2 5.11b G: (V2) Mount the tower, then work up and right over ramps and angular holds (#3 nut and green Alien) to a stance below a large left-facing, left-leaning corner. Step right around the corner and climb a shallow left-facing corner on the exposed overhanging wall (crux) to the top. 70'

V1 5.9 G: Useful if P1 is wet. Begin 6' left of the normal start and climb the outside face of the tower past a hole, then up a left-leaning crack to the top of the tower. Step down and right to the P1 fixed anchor.

V2 Yoyodyne 5.8 R: Angle up and right on a ramp for 40', past a freestanding block, to where the ramp ends. Make an unprotected move up to gain dirty jammed blocks. Step right to a tree ledge and belay. A 100' rappel returns you to the ground.

Gear: Cams and nuts to 1.5", including small TCUs.

History: The route was originally climbed via the **Yoyodyne** variation, which isn't recommended due to bad rock and lack of protection. The better finish was added the next day, and was the last new route completed by Dennis Luther.

FA (V1) Aug 1, 2009, Joe Szot, Don Mellor, Jim Lawyer
FA (P1, V2) Aug 4, 2007, Jim Lawyer, Leslie Ackerman
FA (P2) Aug 5, 2007, Jim Lawyer, Dennis Luther, Leslie Ackerman

AUSABLE #4

Location	Hurricane Mountain Primitive Area, accessed from NY 9N between Keene and Upper Jay
Aspect	South
Height	35'
Quality	
Approach	3 hr, difficult
Summary	A remote cliff with short routes; not worth the approach.

-5.6	5.7	5.8	5.9	5.10	5.11	5.12	5.13+	total
1		1	1					3

This cliff is located on the remote summit of Ausable #4, northeast of Hurricane Mountain. The cliff is a disappointment given the horrendous bushwhack approach, one of the most difficult in this book, and is included here to dissuade would-be adventure seekers enticed by the cliff photo in Barbara McMartin's book.[1] On the positive side, there is an enjoyable open summit with excellent views of Hurricane Mountain.

DIRECTIONS

From the intersection of NY 9N and NY 73 in Keene (0.0), follow NY 9N north toward Upper Jay. At 2.9 miles, turn right on Styles Brook Road (CR 52) and follow this to its end, where it Ts into Jay Mountain Road at 7.0 miles. Turn right and follow this to a parking area at 8.8 miles and the beginning of the seasonal road. Continue straight over a very rough road (high-clearance 4WD vehicle required) to reach a parking area (room for one vehicle) on the right at 10.2 miles, 120 yards after a stream crossing 606806,4904060.

Enter the woods and bushwhack uphill on a bearing of 195° for 1 hr to a summit. The vegetation becomes extremely tight near the summit and for the remainder of the approach—2 more hours of pants-shredding hand-and-knees-style bushwhacking. Follow the ridge on a bearing of 230° for 1 hr to an intermediate summit, then continue along the ridge, keeping the steep part to your left for another hour on a bearing of 245° to the end of the ridge. If you've aimed correctly, you'll come out on top of the cliff 605475,4901265.

DESCENT OPTIONS

A gully on the west end of the cliff allows you to descend to the base of the cliff.

1 Curb Your Enthusiasm 5.8 G 30'

Start: 20' from the left end of the cliff are two left-leaning open-book corners. This route starts in the rightmost open book that begins at a shelf 5' up.

P1 5.8 G: Up the open book to a bulge. Step left (crux) around the bulge to a short handcrack, which is followed to the top. 30'

FA Sep 14, 2007, Emilie Drinkwater, Jim Lawyer

2 False Advertising 5.9 G 35'

Start: Below a wide ceiling formed by two pancake flakes 15' up.

P1 5.9 G: Up a left-leaning crack and right-facing corner to meet the ceiling at its left end. Around the ceiling on the left and up a fingercrack to the top. 35'

FA Sep 14, 2007, Jim Lawyer, Emilie Drinkwater

3 Barbara's Fault 5.1 PG 30'

Start: At the right end of the cliff at a deep left-leaning chimney.

P1 5.1 PG: Up the arête that forms the left side of the opening of the chimney to its top, then up some 3rd-class terrain to the top. 30'

FA Sep 14, 2007, Emilie Drinkwater, Jim Lawyer

FUN-DA-GA-O CLIFF

Location	Soda Range, accessed from Hurricane Road outside of Keene
Aspect	Southwest
Height	70'
Quality	★
Approach	50 min, moderate
Summary	Small cliff with great views; climbing is ledgy and broken.

-5.6	5.7	5.8	5.9	5.10	5.11	5.12	5.13+	total
1	3	1	1					6

Located at the high point on the Nun-da-ga-o Ridge, this small cliff has excellent views spanning from the Dix range to Whiteface. The cliff is 500' wide, although the left end is ledgy and broken. The climbing is fairly good with cracks and featured faces on generally high-quality rock. Many of the obvious lines have now been climbed, but there is potential for those willing to climb less well-protected faces. There are no trees near the edge, so gear anchors are generally required.

DESCENT OPTIONS

Walk right to the trail and follow it to the base of the cliff.

DIRECTIONS

From NY 73 / NY 9N in the center of Keene near the fire barn, drive 2.3 miles up Hurricane Road (CR 13) to a

1 Barbara McMartin with Dennis Conroy and James C. Dawson, *Discover the Northeastern Adirondacks*, 2nd ed. (Lake View Press, 2000), p. 136.

90° bend to the right, and the intersection with O'Toole Lane. Turn left and drive to the end of the road at Crow Clearing, and the trailhead for Hurricane, Lost Pond, and Big Crow.

Hike the trail toward Big Crow for about two-tenths of a mile (about 10 min), steeply at times, to near the summit of Big Crow. Look for a trail on the right marked for Nun-da-ga-o Ridge (this ridge is marked "Soda Range" on the USGS maps); the intersection is obvious, but, as of 2011, the Nun-da-ga-o sign is very faded. Follow this trail, unmarked but in good shape and easy to follow, for 40 minutes over a series of bumps with beautiful views. Near the high point on the ridge the trail reaches the base of a 40'-tall cliff that wraps around the summit 601288,4903288. The hiking trail meets the cliff at the route **Mint Marcy**; this route, as well as **Crumbs Along the Mohawk** and **Samboneparte** are climbed directly from the hiking trail.

HISTORY

The cliff was noticed for climbing in 2009 by Sam Hoar while working for the Adirondack Trail Improvement Society (ATIS). He returned with Duncan Lennon, Annie Boucher, and Robbie Goodwin, and climbed several routes, naming them after Stewarts ice cream flavors. During a later conversation with Jim Goodwin, Robbie's 99-year-old grandfather, Jim recalled that John Case had done some climbing somewhere on Nun-da-ga-o Ridge, perhaps at this cliff.

Left End

To reach the Left End, bushwhack along the base of the cliff through thick balsam growth, or go back down the trail into the notch and through less thick growth to the base of the cliff (this is the easier approach for reaching **Peanut Butter Pandemonium**).

1 Peanut Butter Pandemonium 5.7 G 70' ★★

Start: 150' yards left of the trail below a winding crack on a right-facing arête.

P1 5.7 G: Follow a winding crack to a ledge below a short fingercrack. Pull the crack past a bulge and climb the face directly above it (crux), which can be avoided by moving right into a chimney-flake. 70'

FA Jul 18, 2009, Duncan Lennon, Annie Boucher

2 Caramel Chasm 5.7 G 40' ★★★

Start: At a prominent chimney-crack, 150' left of the trail.

P1 5.7 G: Access the hanging chimney via bouldery moves on the right-hand face. At half height, step across to the juggy left-hand edge of the crack and follow this to a loose topout. 40'

Gear: 4" cam useful.

FA Jul 18, 2009, Duncan Lennon, Annie Boucher

3 Fudge Brownie a la Mode 5.6 G 40' ★★

Start: Begin 75' left of the trail at a clean face beneath a small overlap.

P1 5.6 G: A tricky start leads up the face to the overlap. Over this, then up past several small wire placements. 40'

FA Jul 18, 2009, Duncan Lennon, Annie Boucher

Right End

This is the section of cliff where the trail reaches the base.

4 Mint Marcy 5.7 G 40' ★

Start: Where the trail reaches the base of the cliff, at a system of small flakes below a ledge 15' up.

P1 5.7 G: Climb the flakes to the ledge, then up a thin crack to the top. Scramble up ledges to set up a belay. 40'

FA Jul 18, 2009, Sam Hoar, Robbie Goodwin

5 Crumbs Along the Mohawk 5.9+ G 40' ★★★

Start: At a left-facing corner 10' right of **Mint Marcy**.

P1 5.9+ G: Climb the corner onto a small ledge (small cam essential), then up some insecure tips-locks into a handcrack. Exit onto the summit ledges with a gear belay. 40'

FA Jul 18, 2009, Sam Hoar, Robbie Goodwin

6 Samboneparte 5.8 G 40' ★★★★

A superb climb, if only it were longer!. Sports an excellent thin crack, and a clean face topout.

Start: 10' right of the **Crumbs Along the Mohawk** corner, behind some brush, at a set of small corners below a thin fingercrack that breaks a small roof.

P1 5.8 G: Up the corners past some hollow jugs, and through the roof via the fingercrack. Near the top of the crack, step right and continue up the face. Belay on the summit ledges. 40'

History: The route is named similar to **Tone-Boneparte**, done by Robbie's father Tony Goodwin 35 years earlier.

FA Jul 18, 2009, Sam Hoar, Robbie Goodwin

LITTLE CROW MOUNTAIN

Location	North side of Hurricane Road outside of Keene
Aspect	South
Height	40'
Quality	★★
Approach	20 min, easy
Summary	An obscure crag with cracks, unusual knobby faces, and a short approach from a hiking trail.

-5.6	5.7	5.8	5.9	5.10	5.11	5.12	5.13+	total
1	1		1	4				7

Various crags on the Crows were visited briefly by local guides who once lived along Hurricane Road. Despite the lack of traffic, the routes are remarkably clean, and the cliff bases are comfortable and open. There is no parking lot at the trailhead and the trail passes among homes, so be mindful where you park and stay on the trail during the approach.

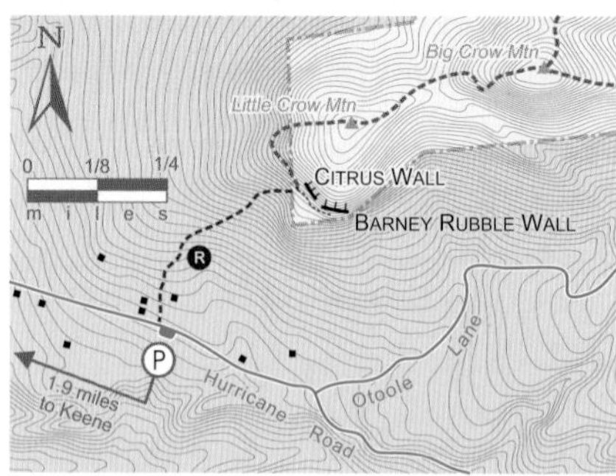

DIRECTIONS **(MAP PAGE 338)**

From NY 73 / NY 9N in the center of Keene near the fire barn, drive 1.9 miles up Hurricane Road (CR 13). The trailhead for Little Crow Mountain (orange blazes) is on the left (north) side of the road. Park on the shoulder of the road 599535,4901314, taking care to obey the "No Parking" signs and not block any driveways.

Located beneath the summit ledges of Little Crow Mountain, this breezy crag has excellent views of Keene Valley. The routes are face climbs on clean, highly featured vertical rock. A beautiful band of colorful crystals sandwiched between dark-colored anorthositic rock rises across the wall.

The trail to Little Crow Mountain begins on private land; take care to stay on the marked trail.

Hike for 10 min to where the trail goes beneath a 30'-tall black slab with three parallel vertical cracks. (Note: This slab and others in this area are on private property and closed to climbing.) Continue up the trail another 5 min to a "State Land Primitive Area" sign. The trail follows the contour of the hillside here; about 200' past the sign, the trail makes a left bend and begins a steep climb and a 40'-tall cliff is visible 150' to the right (east). Leave the trail and contour to the cliff, an attractive wall with a great-looking steep handcrack through orange lichen; this is the Citrus Wall. From its right end, continue right for 100' along the base of a slab to the left end of the Barney Rubble Wall, a short wall of unusual pebbly rock with black crystals 599862,4901795.

*Colin Loher on **Orange Crush** (5.10c)*

Citrus Wall

This is a steep sheer wall with a flat, open, grassy base, named for the distinctive orange lichen that graces the route **Orange Crush**. The cliff, like its neighbor, Barney Rubble Wall, has an open rocky top with excellent views of the Giant, Hurricane, Dix, and the Great Range.

DESCENT OPTIONS

Walk left.

1 Orange Crush 5.10c G 60' ★★★★

Steep crack climbing with an overhanging finish on jugs; juicy and delicious.

Start: At a steep handcrack through orange lichen-covered rock, 4' right of a prominent right-facing corner that defines the left end of the cliff.

P1 5.10c G: Jam up the handcrack to where it widens (4" cam helpful). Hand-traverse right and mantel onto a ledge, then step back left to the crack line. Move up to a slot (crux) and finish on steep jugs. Belay from large pine trees on top. 60'

Gear: To 4".

History: A route this sweet couldn't possibly have escaped notice. Anyone want to claim it?

ACB Aug 28, 2008, Jim Lawyer, Jeremy Haas

2 Plumb Line 5.9 G 60'

Start: On the right side of the wall, 40' right of **Orange Crush**, below a handcrack that defines the right side of a black streak.

P1 5.9 G: Up the handcrack to its top, step left, and continue up another crack to lower-angled rock, which is climbed more easily to the top of the wall. Belay from large pine trees on top. 60'

Gear: To 2".

FA Aug 28, 2008, Jeremy Haas, Jim Lawyer

Barney Rubble Wall

DESCENT OPTIONS

Rappel from the large pine tree or scramble down a gully on the left that is before the slab that you passed on the approach.

3 Hollyrock 5.0 R 60' ★★

An easy solo that provides access to the top of the Citrus Wall and the Barney Rubble Wall. The unique rubble is surprisingly solid with many holds.

Start: Halfway between the Barney Rubble Wall and the Citrus Wall below a slab with glued-on rubble.

P1 5.0 R: Climb up the slab to the rubble, then angle left to the top of the wall. 60'

4 Yabba Dabba Doo 5.10d G 45' ★★★

Strenuous and height-related; exceedingly difficult for short climbers.

Start: 5' uphill and left of the left end of the Barney Rubble Wall, just right of a black streak.

○ **P1 5.10d G:** Thin face moves lead to a left-facing edge (crux), then move up and right to a good stance. Work up the face past several good horizontal cracks to a final puzzling mantel into a scoop, then step up to the summit. 45'

Gear: 1 ea 1", 0.25".

FA Oct 4, 2008, Jim Lawyer, Tad Welch

1 Welcome to Bedrock 5.10a G 40' ★★★

Start: Where the right edge of the crystal band meets the ground, beneath a bolt 12' up.

○ **P1 5.10a G:** Climb through the crystal band and finish on a slab with a flared seam. Belay at the pine tree. 40'

Gear: 1 ea 1" cam.

FA Apr 27, 1988, Patrick Purcell

2 Pebbles and Bamm Bamm 5.10a G 40' ★★

Start: 4' right of where the right edge of the crystal band meets the ground, at a black streak.

● **P1 5.10a G:** Up the black streak and through the crystal band to the sloping ledge beneath a bulge. Over the bulge to a belay at the pine tree. 40'

FA Apr 27, 1988, Patrick Purcell

3 Betty Is a Klepto 5.7 G 50' ★★

Start: 10' right of where the right edge of the crystal band meets the ground, at the left-facing corner.

P1 5.7 G: Up the crack in the corner, then up a right-rising scoop in the crystal band to the sloping ledge beneath a bulge. (V1) Step left to easy ground, then back right to belay at the large pine tree. 50'

V1 5.9 G: Finish straight over the bulge.

Gear: Cams to 2".

FA Apr 27, 1988, Patrick Purcell

BARKEATER CLIFF

Location	North side of Pitchoff Mountain, accessed from the Jackrabbit Trail
Aspect	Northwest
Height	140'
Quality	★★★★
Approach	25 min, easy
Summary	An idyllic remote setting with mostly single-pitch routes that span a range from high-quality moderates to some challenging cracks and faces.

-5.6	5.7	5.8	5.9	5.10	5.11	5.12	5.13+	total
9	6	5	8	8	3	2		42

The Barkeater Cliff sits above the Jackrabbit Trail on the northwest flanks of Pitchoff. It was originally referred to as Pitchoff Northeast, but with so many Pitchoff cliffs with climbing, the name was changed to Barkeater. With its short approach and pleasant atmosphere of house-sized boulders, shady trees, and a nearby stream, this cliff has become very popular especially during the heat of the summer.

The base of the cliff is a jumble of large boulders, the largest being the huge Dog House Boulder, 80' high, which leans up against the center of the cliff forming a large cave (the Dog House). The Dog House Boulder is a barrier that divides the cliff roughly into two sections, each with a separate approach. When the main trail first reaches the boulders, you can duck left through a cave to access the routes left of the Dog House Boulder. Continuing on the main trail through a triangular archway accesses the routes right of the Dog House Boulder.

HISTORY

The cliff was first spied by Chuck Turner and Bill Simes while on an off-trail ski descent over South Notch in the Sentinel Range. They originally weren't impressed but thought it worthy of further exploration once the snow melted. They returned in the spring with Don Mellor and climbed **Overdog**, then came back a few days later and climbed **Mr. Clean** and **Finger It Out** (then rated 5.9). As is typical of the Adirondacks, the cliff had no trails, dirty rock, and the boulders at the base gave the cliff an overgrown feeling, so nothing happened for a few years. Exploration picked up again in 1985, with Jeff Edwards being the main protagonist, then surged in 1988, with Patrick Purcell being the driving force. There were other contributors, most notably Ed Palen, who, with the Rock and River guides, spent endless hours maintaining the trails and cliff. The cliff has remained virtually quiet since 1997, with no new routes.

The dog theme for route names comes from the first route **Overdog,** where Mellor left his dog (named Biner) in the cave (dubbed the "Dog House"). As Mellor describes, the "great Overdog" (as referred to in Robert Frost's poem "Canis Major") was seen as looking over "all us underdogs."

As an aside, the Jackrabbit Trail is an old stagecoach route and the first road from Lake Champlain into the interior of the Adirondacks. Some of the original stonework is evident after you leave the parking lot.

DIRECTIONS **(MAP PAGE 340)**

Parking for Barkeater Cliff is at the trailhead for the Jackrabbit Trail. From the split of NY 73 and NY 9N in Keene, drive 1.3 miles north (toward Lake Placid) to Alstead Hill Lane (CR 40). Turn right and drive 1 mile to where the pavement ends, then another 1.9 miles to the end of the road. There are several buildings here for the Adirondack Rock and River Guide Service 591706,4902125.

Hike west from the parking lot and follow a wide, flat trail (occasional yellow disks) for 15 min to a large cairn on the left 590645,4901483, 2 min before a beaver pond and 100 yards after a good wood bridge. Turn left and follow a climbers' path across a stream, then uphill to the house-sized boulders at the base of the cliff. The trail enters the boulder field at an 8'-high triangular arch where two boulders touch. Just through the arch, the boulder on the right has an overhanging fingercrack (**Little Rascals**). Continue over boulders to reach the base of the cliff right of the Dog House Boulder near the route **Mr. Clean** 590716,4901084.

Little Rascals Boulder

Little Rascals Boulder is the large house-sized boulder that forms the right side of the 8'-high triangular arch formed by two pinched boulders through which the trail passes to reach the cliff.

1 Little Rascals 5.12a G 35' ★

Painful and sandbagged (perhaps more in the V8 range).

Start: On the side of the boulder that faces the cliff (in front of the route **Mr. Clean**), at the base of an overhanging fingercrack.

P1 5.12a G: Climb up the fingercrack over a bulge past a wedged flake to the top. 35'

FA (5.8 A1) Jul 17, 1987, Jeff Edwards, Adam Clayman
FFA Oct, 1992, Ken Nichols

Barkeater Cliff.

Left End

The far left end of Barkeater Cliff is nondescript and has a few routes that need more traffic. The wall is approached from the main trail just before you reach the large boulders by hiking up through the woods for 20 yards. The routes are just left of the Lick It Up Wall, but the large boulders prevent you from simply walking along the base of the cliff from one wall to the other; you must return to the main trail.

Left of the Lick It Up Wall is a cone-shaped slope that leads to a deep chimney with giant chockstones. The right-hand wall has a distinctive red color, and the left-hand wall has the two routes **Pronged Again** and **Wronged Again**. Left of these around the corner is the route **Friends in Business**.

2 Friends in Business 5.8 G 50'

Start: From the low point of the cliff left of **Pronged Again**, walk 30' uphill and left to the base of this route. It begins at the base of a left-leaning flared crack and ramp that leads to a large triangular alcove 10' up.

P1 5.8 G: Climb up the crack angling left past the alcove to the left side of a 10'-diameter oval block. Climb up a left-arching sharp-edged corner to a vertical crack that leads to the top. 50'

FA May, 1988, Patrick Purcell, Ed Palen

3 Pronged Again 5.4 G 70'

Start: 20' left of **Wronged Again**, below a crack system with a large backpack-sized block 10' up.

P1 5.4 G: Climb up over the block, then up a left-leaning crack to the crest, then up and right on low-angle slab to the top. 70'

FA May, 1988, Tom Dodd, Patrick Purcell

4 Wronged Again 5.9 PG 50'

Start: At a flat boulder 20' downhill and left from the height of the cone-shaped slope, beneath some horizontal cracks that lead to a right-facing corner.

P1 5.9 PG: Climb up the horizontals to the right-facing corner, then follow a long, low-angled fingercrack up a slab to the top. 50'

FA May, 1988, Patrick Purcell, Tom Dodd

Lick It Up Wall

The Lick It Up Wall is located just left of the Dog House Boulder. It was once *the* place to climb at Barkeater but has lately become less popular for some reason. There are several good lines here.

To approach, from the main trail just before the 8'-high triangular arch where two boulders touch, turn left and squat under a boulder, following a trail that leads to the upper end of this wall near the mouth of the Dog House Cave and the route **Canoes for Feet** (the Dog House Cave is not accessible from this side). Alternatively, where the main trail first reaches the boulders, you can see a cave off left. Duck under this cave to reach the lower end of this wall near a chimney, which marks the start of **Way Hairball**.

5 Traverse City 5.11a PG 60'

Start: Same as **Way Hairball**.

P1 5.11a PG: Climb the chimney to a horizontal in the left wall. Make a long reach left to a horizontal crack that traverses the front face of the giant flake. At the end of the crack, step up and left to a sloped ledge. 30'

P2 5.7+ PG: Climb the face to the top. 30'

FA May 8, 1988, Patrick Purcell, Jeff Edwards, Tom Dodd

6 Joshua Climb 5.5 G 60' ★

Start: Same as **Way Hairball**.

P1 5.5 G: Climb the crack into the chimney, which is followed to a small ledge. Step left onto the outside face of the giant flake and climb a nice crack up to the top. 60'

Descent: Rappel or downclimb **In the Chimney**.

FA Sep 6, 1986, Tad Welch, Mike Cross

7 Way in the Chimney 5.5 R 30'

Start: Walk into the chimney; this route begins about 20' in the chimney.

P1 5.5 R: Climb up the chimney to a lone bolt. 30'

FA Jun, 1988, Patrick Purcell

8 In the Chimney 5.5 G 60' ★

Start: Same as **Way Hairball**.

P1 5.5 G: Climb the crack into the chimney. Continue deep into the chimney and emerge at the top of the giant flake. 60'

9 Way Hairball 5.9 G 70'

Start: At the downhill side of the Lick It Up Wall is a huge flake that you can walk behind. This route begins 5' right of the opening at a crack in a shallow left-leaning, left-facing corner.

P1 5.9 G: Climb the crack into the chimney, which is followed to a small ledge. From here, **Joshua Climb** goes left and **Way Hairball** goes right, following a right-arching off width to its top. Follow a crack up and right to finish as for **Dog Eat Dog** and **Canine**. 70'

FA 1983, Tim Beaman, Herb George, Sylvia Lazarnick

10 Canine 5.9 PG 70'

Start: Same as **Way Hairball**.

P1 5.9 PG: Climb 15' up the chimneylike recess and undercling 12' right along the obvious horizontal crack to a very small left-facing corner. Follow the corner to a ledge at the base of the flared right-curving crack. Continue up the flared crack and join **Dog Eat Dog**, following its rising hand-traverse line to the top. 70'

FA Sep, 1990, Eric Wahl, Ken Nichols

11 Dog Eat Dog 5.8+ PG 70'

Start: At a small left-facing edge 4' left of an obvious vertical groove and 8' left of the **Finger It Out** crack.

P1 5.8+ PG: Work up the corner and a thin crack to a ledge. Step right and climb past a hollow block to the edge of a flake that leads to a sloping ledge above the flared right-curving crack of **Canine**. Then follow a rising hand-traverse line up left to the notch on the skyline and hand-traverse up right along a flake to the top. 70'

FA Sep, 1990, Eric Wahl, Ken Nichols

12 Finger It Out 5.10a G 60' ★★★

Start: The other obvious crack on the wall, 30' uphill of the chimney of **Way Hairball** and 20' downhill from **Lick It Up** at a 2'-high finger slot that is 6' up.

P1 5.10a G: Climb the fingercrack to a torpedo-shaped flake stuck in the crack, then up to a large horizontal. Step right and climb over a triangular block and up a crack to the top. 60'

FA May, 1982, Chuck Turner, Bill Simes

13 Wipe It Off 5.10d R 60'

Start: On the face 5' left of the **Lick It Up** crack at a small seam.

P1 5.10d R: Work up the face past a hollow flake to a rounded flake at the top that provides a good anchor. 60'

Gear: Include two tie-down hooks (cliffhanger and a narrow-point Palmer) and psychological gear behind the hollow flake.

FA Sep, 1990, Ken Nichols, Eric Wahl

14 Lick It Up 5.10a G 60' ★★

Start: 25' downhill and left from the height of the terrain at a crack in a very shallow right-facing corner with a flared pod 10' up.

P1 5.10a G: Climb up the crack through the pod, then out the left-arching fingercrack. Make a jog to the right, then continue up the crack to the top. 60'

FA Jul 24, 1985, Adam Clayman, Jeff Edwards

15 Pump It Up 5.8+ G 90' ★

Start: Just left of the Dog House Boulder is a very steep orange wall. This route starts on the left side of this wall at a left-leaning, right-facing corner, just right of the large, ugly corner.

P1 5.8+ G: Climb up the crack in the corner to where it turns vertical. Jam and stem up the dirty vertical crack to an alcove belay. 90'

Descent: Rappel.

FA Sep 6, 1986, Tad Welch

16 Canoes for Feet 5.9 TR 50'

This toprope begins just left of the Dog House Boulder at the base of the arête that forms the left side of the entrance to the Dog House Cave. It climbs the arête to the large marble chockstone, then up onto the top of the Dog House Boulder.

FA (TR) Jul, 1988, Patrick Purcell, Mark Abbott

Dog House Wall

The Dog House Wall includes routes from the Dog House Boulder rightward. The main trail ends at this wall in the vicinity of **Mr. Clean**. At the left end of this wall is the most distinctive feature on the cliff—the huge cave formed by the Dog House Boulder, which leans up against the cliff. (There's an amazing crack inside the cave, on the overhanging wall of the boulder, aided by Patrick Purcell. There's a fixed nut, but no reports on this going free.) **ASPCA** climbs the outside of the Dog House Boulder, **Overdog** and **Hair of the Dog** begin in the Dog House Cave, and **On the Leash** begins just right of the cave entrance.

17 Hair of the Dog 5.10a G 140' ★★★

This route is much better than the amount of traffic it receives. It sports two Gunks-style roofs with heel hooks and good protection.

Start: Same as **Overdog**.

P1 5.10a G: Climb up the broken rock as for **Overdog**, then traverse left over easy terrain across the wall to gain the huge marble-shaped chockstone. Climb up onto the chockstone, then onto the face up to a stance

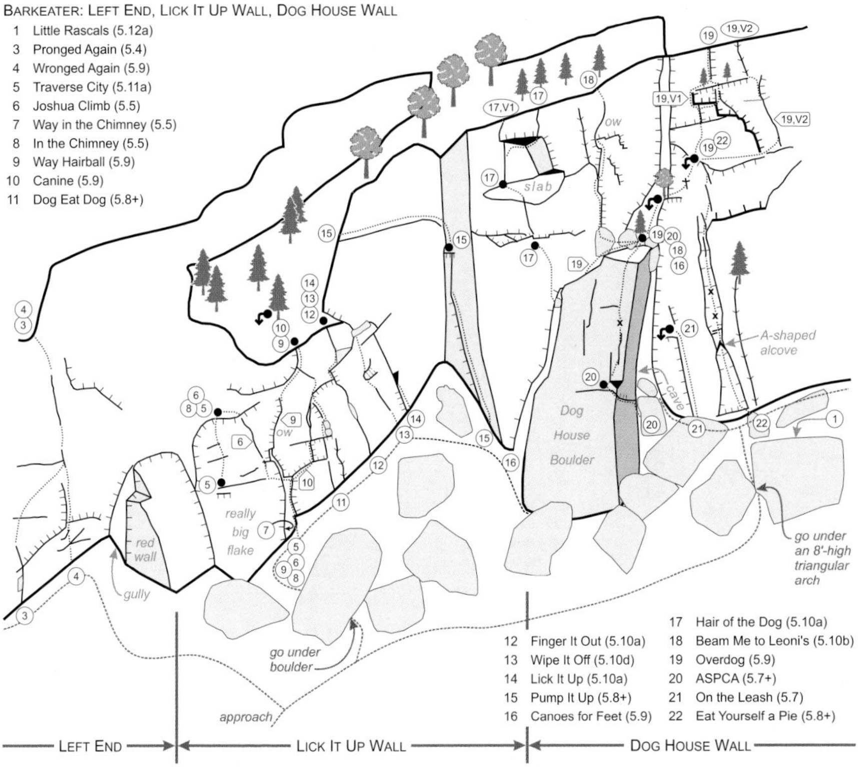

Barkeater: Left End, Lick It Up Wall, Dog House Wall

1 Little Rascals (5.12a)
3 Pronged Again (5.4)
4 Wronged Again (5.9)
5 Traverse City (5.11a)
6 Joshua Climb (5.5)
7 Way in the Chimney (5.5)
8 In the Chimney (5.5)
9 Way Hairball (5.9)
10 Canine (5.9)
11 Dog Eat Dog (5.8+)
12 Finger It Out (5.10a)
13 Wipe It Off (5.10d)
14 Lick It Up (5.10a)
15 Pump It Up (5.8+)
16 Canoes for Feet (5.9)
17 Hair of the Dog (5.10a)
18 Beam Me to Leoni's (5.10b)
19 Overdog (5.9)
20 ASPCA (5.7+)
21 On the Leash (5.7)
22 Eat Yourself a Pie (5.8+)

slab, ow, A-shaped alcove, cave, Dog House Boulder, really big flake, red wall, gully, go under boulder, approach, go under an 8'-high triangular arch

Left End | Lick It Up Wall | Dog House Wall

below the wide ceiling (optional belay with gear in the roof). Traverse left 10' and break through the roof at a good crack. Follow the crack to a good ledge. 110'

P2 5.10a G: (V1) Step right and climb a crack to the large roof, then traverse right under the roof (crux) and break through it at the twin cracks on its right end. 30'

V1 5.6 G: Escape up and left to the trees.

FA (P1) Sep, 1992, Patrick Purcell, Ed Palen, Ann Palen
FA (P2) Aug, 1993, Ed Palen, Chris Wolf

18 Beam Me to Leoni's 5.10b G 90'

Start: On top of the Dog House Boulder. To get here, climb P1 of **Overdog** (5.5). The route begins on top of blocks on the left wall of the huge corner, beneath a left-facing corner.

P1 5.10b G: Climb the left-facing corner to a break. Step right around the corner into a right-facing sharp-edged flake, up this to the left end of another ceiling. Follow the right-arching off width up to the top. 90'

FA 1985, Greg Koop, Hugh Rose

19 Overdog 5.9 G 150' ★★★★

Start: On the left wall of the cave formed by the Dog House Boulder, below three cracks that pass left of the contact point where the Dog House Boulder touches the main cliff face.

P1 5.5 G: Climb up broken rock to gain the three cracks on the left wall, which are followed to the top of the Dog House Boulder. 60'

Liam Campbell surmounts the roof on P3 of ***Overdog*** *(5.9). Photo by Peter Whitmore.*

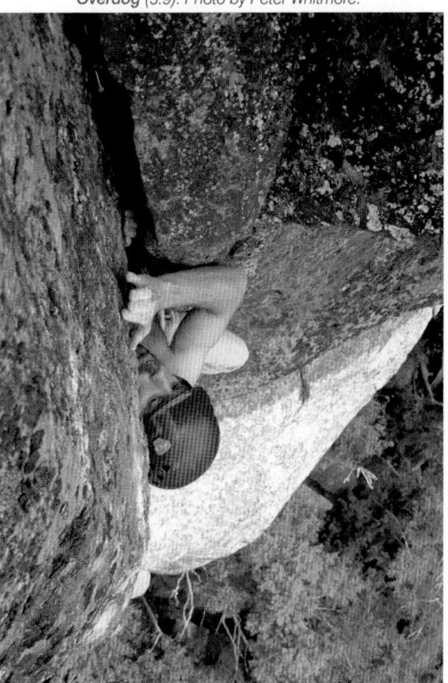

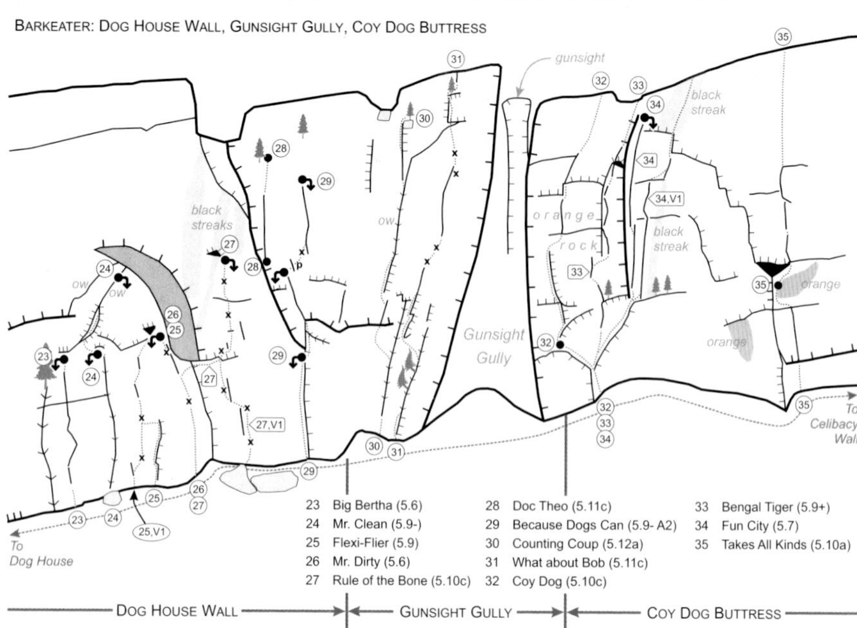

P2 5.7 G: Climb up the ugly corner to the birch, then up and right on a ledge (bolt). One awkward move gains the fixed anchor (shared with **Eat Yourself a Pie**). 40'

P3 5.9 G: Climb up the slab to the large square alcove beneath the roof. Up the left side, (V1) then switch to the right crack and break through the roof on its right side and up to a ledge with a tree. Step left and climb a short left-facing corner to the top. 50'

V1 5.10b G: Break through the roof on its left side, then join the regular route.

V2 5.11a PG: Traverse right on the sloped ledge to its right end, then climb a crack up an exposed wall to a shallow left-facing corner. Up this, then step left to a ledge and climb an open book to the summit.

FA May 2, 1982, Don Mellor, Chuck Turner, Bill Simes
FA (V1) Jul 10, 1988, Don Mellor
FA (V2) Jul 10, 1988, Don Mellor

20 ASPCA 5.7+ PG 100' ★★★

Unusual climbing on this route involves a scrunched traverse on solid holds, then a hard slab move on the upper section.

Start: On a large boulder on the right side of the Dog House Boulder and on the left side of the opening to the Dog House Cave.

P1 5.7+ PG: Drop down into a little chimney between the large boulder and the Dog House Boulder. Step onto the Dog House Boulder (green Alien), then climb up and left to reach some good buckets. (V1) A scrunched traverse left on good holds leads to the arête. Climb a crack in the slab to a bolt (crux), then up to the top of the Dog House Boulder. 100'

V1 5.8 PG: At the start of the traverse, reach up to a good horizontal, then into the corner above with a short crack, which is followed to an amazing jug. Pull over onto the slab at the bolt and continue up to the top.

Descent: Either rappel from the fixed anchor on the birch or do a short second pitch (**Overdog**) to the fixed anchor on **Eat Yourself a Pie** and lower from there.

FA May, 1988, Patrick Purcell, Tom Dodd, Jeff Edwards

FA (V1) Aug, 1993, Ed Palen, Chris Wolf

21 On the Leash 5.7 G 35' ★★

Start: 10' right of the mouth of the Dog House Cave at the base of a left-leaning, right-facing corner.

P1 5.7 G: Climb the crack to a stance at the top with a hidden fixed anchor. 35'

FA May 27, 1988, Patrick Purcell

22 Eat Yourself a Pie 5.8+ PG 100' ★★★★

Awesome position, solid rock, and good protection make this one of Purcell's best achievements at the cliff. A good linkup is to finish on P3 of **Overdog** (5.9).

Start: On top of a boulder 40' right of the Dog House Cave on the right side of the first arête you come to.

P1 5.8+ PG: Up knobs leftward to gain the arête. Up the arête to an A-shaped alcove (crux), then up the narrow face on the arête past more arête (bolts), then to a crack in a small right-facing corner. Up this to a fixed anchor on the left (shared with **Overdog** P2). 100'

Gear: Up to 2".

FA Apr 5, 1988, Patrick Purcell, Tom Dodd

23 Big Bertha 5.6 G 60' ★★

Start: 6' right of **Eat Yourself a Pie** is a deep, vegetated V-groove full of pine trees. This route begins 4' right of the V-groove at a slab 10' left of **Mr. Clean**.

P1 5.6 G: Climb up the slab to gain a crack that zigzags up the buttress to a fixed anchor below a small ceiling that is 15' below a large roof. 60'

Gear: Up to 2".

History: The route once had a large, precariously perched block—known as Big Bertha—the size of a washing machine, held on by 1" of rock barely stuck in a crack. Thus, nobody repeated the route until the rock was pried out (1994). It now lies near the base of the climb.

FA 1988, Patrick Purcell

*Opposite: Leslie Ackerman on **Eat Yourself a Pie** (5.8+).*

24 Mr. Clean 5.9- G 90' ★★★★

A pure, clean handcrack. P1 is highly recommended and extremely popular.

Start: 20' right of **Eat Yourself a Pie** (and 60' right of the Dog House Cave), and 30' left of the left-facing, left-arching off width, on top of a boulder that sits below an open book with a clean handcrack.

P1 5.9- G: Climb the handcrack past a wide section (crux) to its top at a small bush and a fixed anchor on the left wall. 60'

P2 The Kodiak Bear 5.9 G: Step left from the anchor to a short chimney. Climb up the chimney and right-leaning off width to a fixed anchor just before the end of the crack. 30'

Gear: Single set of cams, doubles in 2" and 3".

FA (P1) May, 1982, Chuck Turner, Bill Simes

FA (P2) May 8, 1988, Patrick Purcell, Jeff Edwards

*Simon Catterall on the clean-cut corner, **Mr. Clean** (5.9).*

25 Flexi-Flier 5.9 PG (5.7 R) 70' ★★★

Start: 15' right of the **Mr. Clean** handcrack and 15' left of the left-facing, left-arching off width, below a shallow sharp-edged left-facing corner that begins 8' up. The upper section is easier, but has some friable flakes for gear.

P1 5.9 PG (5.7 R): (V1) Climb up to the left-facing corner (crux), then up to its top, where the crack and corner disappear. Traverse left to a bolt, then up to a left-leaning seam. Move up and right to another seam and some hollow flakes (RPs) to a final tricky mantel at the top. 70'

V1 Radio Flier 5.11b G: Begin 7' left and climb to a vertical finger slot, then shuffle right (crux) to a bolt. Continue up the face to the next bolt to join the regular route. The runout between the bolts is tamed using the crack of the normal route.

Gear: Nuts, RPs, and cams to 3/4".

FA Aug 8, 1988, Patrick Purcell, Bill Dodd
FA (V1) Jul, 1991, Patrick Purcell

26 Mr. Dirty 5.6 G (5.4 R) 70' ★

Despite its name, this route sports clean rock and good face climbing.

Start: 10' downhill and left of a left-facing, left-arching off width at a clean face with pockets.

P1 5.6 G (5.4 R): Climb up the face, angling slightly right to an orange spot (bolt), then up and left following a thin seam to a fixed anchor (shared with **Flexi-Flier**). 70'

FA Aug 8, 1988, Bill Dodd, Patrick Purcell

27 Rule of the Bone 5.10c G (5.4 R) 100' ★★★★

Incredible climbing with a little bit of everything—thin face, fingercrack, a juggy ceiling, and some spicy traversing. The route was originally climbed by traversing in from **Mr. Dirty**; a direct start was added later, making a high-quality independent line.

Start: Same as **Mr. Dirty**.

P1 5.10c G (5.4 R): (V1) Climb up **Mr. Dirty** for 30', then step across the left-facing off width and traverse right (5.8), following a crack under a ceiling to a tiny left-facing corner in the ceiling. Bust through the ceiling with long reaches between buckets (crux), then step right on a good ledge to a mail slot (2" cam helpful). Climb up to a bolt, then 6' left and up to a thin seam. Move left once again to a good flake, then up and right onto the face. Thin face climbing past fragile flakes leads to a fixed anchor. 100'

V1 5.10b G: Begin 15' uphill and right of the left-facing, left-arching off width, above a large boulder-slab that pinches against the face. Climb up to a bolt, then up a left-leaning crack. Traverse left (hard) to another seam, which is followed up to a ceiling below a tiny left-facing corner in the ceiling where it joins the normal route. Quality climbing, but some friable rock.

Gear: Small TCUs, double set of cams to 0.5" and a single 2" cam.

FA Aug, 1994, Ed Palen, Ron Konowitz
FA (V1) 1998, Jeff Edwards

*Lindsay Duca belays Ara Finlayson on **Bachelors and Bowery Bums** (5.7). Photo by Liam Griffin.*

28 Doc Theo 5.11c G 50'

Start: This route is reached by rappel. It starts at a fixed anchor just right of the base of a thin crack that begins just over the lip of the left-facing, left-arching off width. The start is just left of the P2 anchor of **Because Dogs Can**.

P1 5.11c G: Climb the thin crack that arches left to the top. 50'

History: The route was named for Theo Dewitt, a psychiatrist and a client of Purcell's, who was convinced to belay Purcell on this route.

FA Sep 25, 1990, Patrick Purcell

29 Because Dogs Can 5.9- A2 110'

P1 is a nice jam and stemming corner and is recommended.

Start: 40' right of the left-facing, left-arching off width and 25' right of the **Rule of the Bone** where a large boulder-slab pinches against the face, at a left-facing corner with some orange rock.

P1 5.9- G ★: Climb up the crack in the corner to a fixed anchor just below where the wall steepens. 40'

P2 A 2 Brute? A2: Follow a thin left-angling crack up a severely overhanging wall to a fixed anchor. The name is a morph of the famous Caesar quote "Et tu, Brute?" 30'

P3 A2: Move up and right past a fixed piton and bolt to gain a crack (hook needed), which is followed straight up to a fixed anchor at the top. 40'

FA (P1) Aug 8, 1988, Patrick Purcell, Bill Dodd
FA Oct, 1993, Ed Palen (roped solo)

Gunsight Gully

Uphill and right of the left-facing corner of **Because Dogs Can** is a gully with a tower in the middle that resembles a gunsight. The routes begin on the left wall of the gully.

30 Counting Coup 5.12a G 130'

More of a high-altitude boulder problem. The name comes from a practice that Native Americans used to show their bravery by entering an enemy camp and stealing something (a horse or weapon perhaps), then running away unharmed; in this case, the theft was a route.

Start: On the left wall of the gully are two grooves: the right one is full of trees, and the left one is cleaner and leads to a small orange ceiling. This route begins in the left groove.

P1 5.12a G: Climb the groove for 20', then break left on knobs to a stance beneath a large roof. Break through the roof at a crack that splits the lip (crux), then up a crack to a stance. Step left and climb an easy groove past a wide section to a ledge, then on to the top. 130'

FA 2001, Karl Swisher, Frank Minunni

31 What about Bob 5.11c G 130'

Start: On the left side of Gunsight Gully in a groove filled with trees. (This is the rightmost of two grooves, the left one being the start of **Counting Coup**.)

P1 5.11c G: Climb the slab adjacent to the groove to some small left-facing corners in orange rock. Up the middle of these corners to a bolt, then move up and right past another bolt (no hanger or nut!) to gain a crack. Up the crack to a slab with two bolts, then angle left to gain a crack system at the left end of a ceiling. Up the crack to the summit. 130'

FA Oct 26, 1993, Patrick Purcell, Bob Martin

Coy Dog Buttress

Right of Gunsight Gully is a square orange buttress. The routes are approached from the right side of the buttress near the route **Fun City**.

32 Coy Dog 5.10c G 90' ★★★

This high quality line is a little dirty, but has sustained jamming, and is worth more traffic.

Start: From **Fun City**, scramble up and left onto a ledge at the base of a left-facing corner with a splash of orange lichen. (You can also gain this ledge by scrambling up Gunsight Gully, then breaking right to the base of the corner.)

P1 5.10c G: Climb the fingercrack in the left-facing corner through a bulge. Step right and continue up the crack past an overlap and onto a slab, which is followed to the top. 90'

FA May 27, 1988, Tim Beaman, Patrick Purcell

33 Bengal Tiger 5.9+ R 110'

Start: Same as **Fun City**.

P1 5.9+ R: Climb straight up a crack to a tree, then out left to a thin crack. Foot-traverse right on a bulge to an orange right-facing corner with a thin crack. Up the crack through two bulges and a final ceiling to a slab. Run out up the slab to the top. 110'

FA Sep, 1992, Ken Nichols, Al Carilli

34 Fun City 5.7 G 100' ★★★★

An extremely attractive crack and the second most popular route at the cliff.

Start: On the right side of the Coy Dog Buttress is an open area below two parallel "ski track" cracks, the leftmost of which is in a large right-facing corner. Begin below and left of these cracks.

P1 5.7 G: Climb easy rock up and right to the base of the cracks. (V1) Climb the cracks to a small ledge. Step left and continue up the crack in the corner to a fixed anchor on the left wall. 100'

V1 Fun Country 5.10a G: Climb the right crack through a bulge. Step right and finish up the large left-facing corner (or step left to the **Fun City** anchor).

Gear: Cams to 3.5", doubles of 2" and 3".

FA May, 1982, Rich Leswing, Pete Benson
FA (V1) Jul 24, 1985, Jeff Edwards, Adam Clayman

35 Takes All Kinds 5.10a G 80'

A good line, although pretty dirty.

Start: 40' right of **Fun City** is a low roof system with two parallel cracks on its left end. The left crack is very dirty and has a birch tree 15' up. This route begins on top of a block below the right-hand crack.

P1 5.10a G: Climb the fingercrack, then step left to a right-facing corner (optional belay). Climb up to the roof, then hand-traverse right 15' to a crack that breaks through the right end of the roof. Climb up the dirty crack past a tree to a slab, then up to the top. 80'
FA May 27, 1988, Tim Beaman, Patrick Purcell

Celibacy Wall

Moving right from **Fun City**, you'll find a low roof system. To reach the Celibacy Wall, walk right under the 100'-wide roof system and duck under a boulder to emerge at the left end of the Celibacy Wall. There is a huge flat boulder (Lunch Rock) in the open area at the base of the wall. The top of the Celibacy Wall is an open rock slab with terrific views of the valley.

This is a popular wall for toproping. The top can be accessed by walking right along the base of the cliff and picking up a good hiking trail that circles around to the top of the wall.

36 Parenthood 5.3 G 150'

Start: 15' uphill and right of the right end of the low roofs.

P1 5.3 G: Climb up 10', then traverse left 30' over the low roof on knobby rock to a ledge beneath a handcrack. 40'

P2 5.3 G: Climb the crack to a ledge with two trees. Work up left and climb slabs to the summit. 110'
FA Jul 26, 1990, Jeff Edwards, Ryan Van Loon

37 Skillyabuda 5.7 R 120'

Start: On the right end of the Celibacy Wall and just uphill and right of the low roof system are two tree-filled V-grooves separated by a clean buttress. This route begins at the toe of this clean buttress in front of Lunch Rock.

P1 5.7 R: Climb the face past two horizontals to a right-angling crack. Traverse off or continue up a mossy right-facing corner into a horrible tree-filled crack system that is followed to the top. 120'
FA Jul 26, 1990, Jeff Edwards, Ryan Van Loon

38 Yakapodu 5.6+ G 90' ★★★

This is the most obvious route on the Celibacy Wall. The name is a misspelling of the Tibetan word for "good", Yakpudo

Start: 6' right of a vegetated groove (the rightmost of the two V-grooves described for **Skillyabuda**) at a clean crack in a slab. This is just above and right of Lunch Rock.

P1 5.6+ G: Up the crack, then into the top of the V-groove, which leads to a right-facing corner. Up the corner, then follow a crack through an orange V-slot to a water runnel. Step right to another crack in a shallow right-facing corner, which is followed to the left end of an overlap, then up cracks straight to the top. 90'
FA Jul 16, 1985, Adam Clayman, Jeff Edwards, Todd McDougall

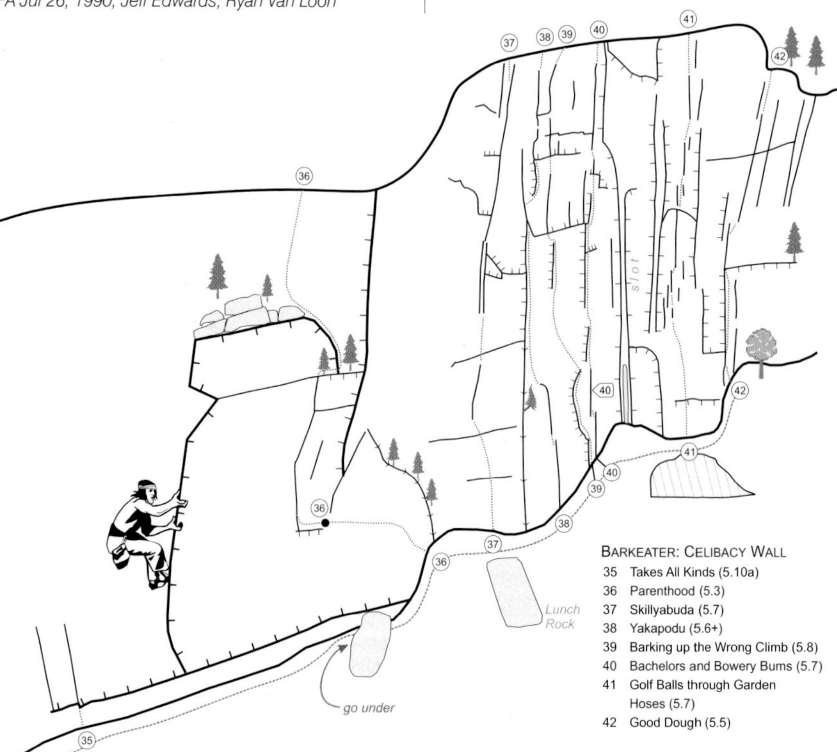

39 Barking up the Wrong Climb 5.8 R 90'

Start: 3' left of Bachelors and Bowery Bums below the shallow right-facing arch that fades at its top.

P1 5.8 R: Climb up the arch, then face-climb up and left to the steeper wall with a right-facing corner. Up the corner to its top, then step left and climb a shallow right-facing corner through a bulge to a crack in the slab, above which leads to the next overlap. Climb through the overlap and finish in the Yakapodu crack. 90'

FA 1993, Don Mellor, Brian Ballantine, Ed Ballantine

40 Bachelors and Bowery Bums 5.7 PG 90' ★

Start: 10' uphill and right of Yakapdu at two cracks in the slab, just right of a shallow right-facing arch that fades at its top.

P1 5.7 PG: Climb up the cracks in the slab and into a shallow right-facing corner. Up this, then step left to a large right-facing corner and up the orange rock where the wall steepens. Climb through a square ceiling via a crack and onto the face to another roof broken by many cracks, then up a wider crack just left of the arête. 90'

FA Jul 24, 1985, Jeff Edwards, Adam Clayman

41 Golf Balls through Garden Hoses 5.7 PG 60'

Start: Halfway across the ledge approach to Good Dough in the center of the clean buttress.

P1 5.7 PG: Climb up the slab to a ledge, then follow slash cracks up the center of the buttress, staying right of the deep fissure to a ledge, then on to the top. 60'

FA Aug, 1998, Jeff Edwards, Penny Beck

42 Good Dough 5.5 G 80' ★★

Start: From the height of land at the right end of the Celibacy Wall, walk right on a narrow ledge with trees for 40' to the base of a prominent right-facing, right-leaning corner.

P1 5.5 G: Climb the large right-facing corner to its top, then up one of two parallel cracks in the upper wall to the top. 80'

FA Jul 26, 1990, Jeff Edwards, Ryan Van Loon

SWAMP ROCK

Location	North side of Pitchoff Mountain, accessed from the Jackrabbit Trail
Aspect	North
Height	120'
Quality	
Approach	25 min, easy
Summary	Dirty cliff, with one quality route in need of scrubbing.

This north-facing cliff sits above the beaver swamp on the Jackrabbit Trail, 2 min beyond the cairn that marks the turnoff for the Barkeater Cliff. It is easily viewed from the beaver swamp. The most obvious feature on this cliff is a huge overhanging left-facing corner on its left end (climbed by Purcell at 5.10d).

DIRECTIONS **(MAP PAGE 340)**

To reach the cliff, hike to the beaver swamp (2 min beyond the turnoff for Barkeater Cliff) 590471,4901357. Continue on the trail an additional 2 min, then turn off left and bushwhack on a bearing of 170°, across a stream, and uphill steeply to the cliff. Aim for the left end of the cliff and find the huge left-facing, left-arching corner 590513,4901078. It takes about 10 min to reach the cliff from the beaver pond.

43 County Route 40 5.10b G 120'

This route is presently very dirty and needs some cleaning before it can be recommended; a quality route otherwise on a very textured face with good edges.

Start: From the huge left-facing corner, scramble right on a forested ledge for 40' to an obvious left-facing corner capped by a small ceiling. There are two pines at the base.

P1 5.9 G: Climb up the corner, around the ceiling, step right, and follow a shallow left-facing, right-leaning corner until it disappears. Several face moves gain a tree ledge. 80'

P2 5.10b G: (V1) Climb the face on good edges following bolts straight up the face to an overhanging moss cornice. The route ends at an anchor hanging over the moss cornice from above. 40'

V1 5.9 G: 15' uphill and right is a right-angling crack. Up the crack for 20' to meet a left-rising crack. Zigzag back left following the crack to a fingercrack finish.

FA Aug, 1991, Patrick Purcell, Ann Eastman, Kevin Birk

FA (V1) Aug, 1991, Patrick Purcell, Ann Eastman

OWLS HEAD MOUNTAIN

Location	South side of NY 73 between Keene and Cascade Pass
Aspect	West
Height	50'
Quality	★
Approach	20 min, easy
Summary	Short, easy crack climbs on top of a low summit; very popular with toprope groups and guides.

-5.6	5.7	5.8	5.9	5.10	5.11	5.12	5.13+	total
4	1							5

Commonly known as a toproping destination, Owls Head has some good leads and clean crack climbs. Expect to share this cliff with guides and outdoor groups. Owls Head is a pleasant, albeit low, summit that dries quickly and offers a cool breeze. Due to its popularity, trail erosion is an issue, and it is recommended that climbers avoid trampling the vegetation on the south side of the summit and instead walk off on the hiking trail to the north. The cliff base is accessed via a rock-walled chasm that is between the cliff and a rock ledge. Most of the routes begin on a rock ledge that extends along the base. A 4th-class corner and left-rising ledge cut across the cliff.

HISTORY

Climbers rig topropes at Owls Head Mountain.

Harry Eldridge took campers here in the 1950s on rock-climbing outings, although no one knows for sure whether he was the first. Eldridge was a counselor at Camp Treetops and eventually the headmaster at North Country School, a boarding school for children located near Cascade Pass. He was an enthusiastic mountaineer and rock climber and took young students on various adventures in the backcountry, including the Trap Dike, and ski descents of Marcy and Tuckerman's Ravine on Mt Washington in New Hampshire. Since the 1980s, Owls Head has become one of the premier toproping and learning locales in the High Peaks.

DIRECTIONS

Parking for Owls Head is on Owls Head Lane, 3.1 miles from the intersection of NY 73 and NY 9N in Keene on the left (when you're driving toward Lake Placid) and 1.8 miles from the Pitchoff Chimney Cliff parking area on the right (when you're driving toward Keene from Lake Placid) 593377,4900069. Drive 0.2 mile up Owls Head Lane to a side road on the left. Park on the side road and locate the signed trailhead that is at the intersection of Owls Head Lane and the side road. Hike up the trail for 20 min to the summit cliff 593936,4900115.

DESCENT OPTIONS

Walk off left (north) along the hiking trail. Rappelling Breeze Crack is recommended.

1 Owl Crack 5.6 G 40' ★

Start: 10' right of the left end of the cliff, in a rock-walled chasm at a vertical handcrack.

P1 5.6 G: Up the handcrack to a stance, then follow converging cracks, and a tricky exit, to a ledge. Belay on the top. 40'

2 Wind Song 5.6 G 40' ★

Start: 20' right of the left end of the cliff, just right of a rock-walled chasm, at a right-rising crack.

P1 5.6 G: Up the crack, then left across the ledge to a vertical flare. Up the flare to a large ledge, then up either of the two vertical cracks to the top. 40'

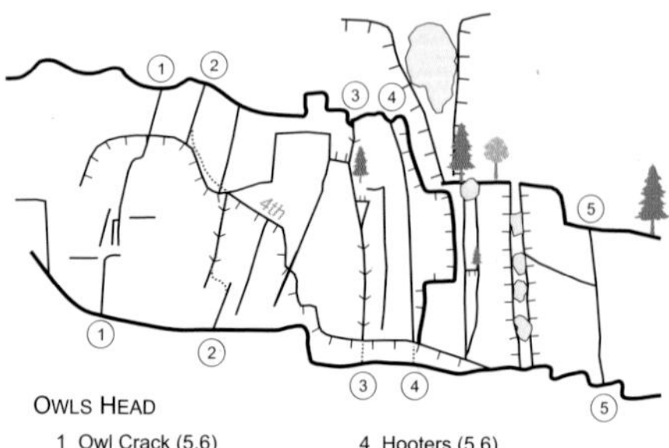

3 Central AC 5.6 G 50' ★

Start: On rock ledges to the right of the right-facing 4th-class corner, at a flared squeeze chimney.

P1 5.6 G: Up the chimney to a ceiling. Out the left side of the ceiling and up to an undercling flake. Step left to a flared vertical crack and follow it to the top. 50'

4 Hooters 5.6 G 50' ★

Start: At a vertical handcrack left of a 10'-tall shallow right-facing corner that is capped by an overhang.

P1 5.6 G: Climb the handcrack, past voluptuous jugs, to the top. 50'

5 Breeze Crack 5.7 G 30' ★

Start: 30' left of the right end of a rock ledge at a vertical handcrack.

P1 5.7 G: Up the crack to a large ledge. 30'

Descent: Traverse the ledge to the right and rappel from the tree.

PITCHOFF RIDGE TRAIL DOMES

Location	North side of NY 73 in Cascade Pass
Summary	Seldom-visited domes with moderately good rock in a scenic location.

-5.6	5.7	5.8	5.9	5.10	5.11	5.12	5.13+	total
2	2							4

The Pitchoff Ridge Trail Domes are open, rocky minisummits on the eastern end of Pitchoff, an open, rocky ridge above Cascade Lakes. The ridge has exceptional views and is a very popular destination for hikers. The rock looks especially appealing in the fall and spring when the leaves are down; when summer's green comes on, they are harder to find.

HISTORY

The domes were explored by Don Mellor with students from the Northwood School in Lake Placid in 1984, then again by R.L Stolz in 1988. It took 24 years for somebody to return, which Stolz did in 2013. Such a gap is odd given the location and amount of visible rock.

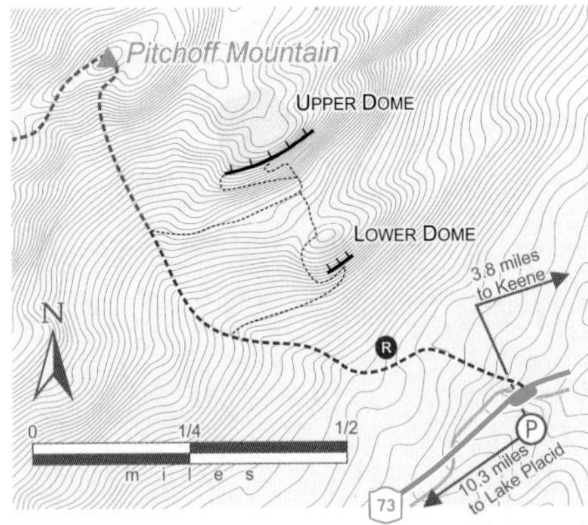

DIRECTIONS (MAP PAGE 351)

The Pitchoff Ridge Trail Domes are accessed from the trailhead for Pitchoff Mountain East 592162,4899577. This is at a paved parking lot on NY 73, 3.8 miles from Keene (where NY 9N and NY 73 split) on the left (when you're driving toward Lake Placid) and 10.3 miles from Lake Placid (at the intersection of NY 73 and NY 86) on the right (when you're driving toward Keene). The trail, marked with red disks, begins across the road with a sign for the Sentinel Range Wilderness Area.

Pitchoff Ridge Trail Domes

LOWER DOME

Location	North side of NY 73 in Cascade Pass
Aspect	Southeast
Height	375'
Quality	
Approach	30 min, moderate
Summary	

This dome is decidedly unimpressive but has an excellent open rocky summit.

DIRECTIONS (MAP PAGE 351)

Hike up the Pitchoff Ridge Trail to reach a stream crossing at 10 min. The trail crosses the stream, then crosses it again, staying on its right side. At 15 min, leave the trail and contour right for 10 min, bushwhacking through semiopen forest to the base of the slab. The base of the slab is a nondescript vegetated slope with trees that finally gives way to open rock 591656,4899811; there is no open, clear base.

A longer but perhaps easier approach is to hike up the trail for 30 min, then contour right (northeast) to a col. You should see some rock partially visible uphill to the left (the base of the Upper Dome) and a small minisummit (the top of the Lower Dome) to the right. Scramble to the minisummit at the top of the Lower Dome 591630,4899923. This is the top of **Sunshine Slab**. To reach the base, descend the (climber's) left edge of the slab until you find the bottom of the clean, most continuous section of rock 591656,4899811.

1 Sunshine Slab 5.3 PG 375'

This is a generally clean slab, although some rock is covered by a patina of powdery green lichen.

Start: Wander back and forth along the base of the steep slopes to find a clean, open section of rock.

P1 5.1 PG: Go up the slab, stay right of center, then traverse left into the center to belay at a 3" crack. 175'

P2 5.3 PG: Climb up the crack, then left over a bulge. Continue up the slab to belay at its top. 100'

P3 4th class: Wander via nondescript scrambling to the top of the dome. 100'

FA May 7, 1984, Alan Hobson, Don Mellor, Rusty Geh, Kevin Kearns

Pitchoff Ridge Trail Domes

UPPER DOME

Aspect	Southeast
Height	300'
Quality	★
Approach	50 min, moderate
Summary	Seldom-visited dome with a notable crack and slab route.

-5.6	5.7	5.8	5.9	5.10	5.11	5.12	5.13+	total
1	2							3

The Upper Dome has more exposed rock, and the **N.O.C. Route** takes the most direct line to its top. There is a surprising amount of exposed rock here, with good potential for more routes.

DIRECTIONS (MAP PAGE 351)

Hike up the Pitchoff Ridge Trail for 30 min, then contour right (northeast) for 10 min to a col. You should see some rock partially visible uphill to the left and a small minisummit (the top of the Lower Dome) to the right. Scramble to the minisummit at the top of the Lower Dome 591630,4899923 for an excellent view of the Upper Dome (and of the entire Cascade Pass). The **N.O.C. Route** climbs the slabs just left of a large left-facing, left-leaning corner that dominates the upper part of the dome. Locate the route and bushwhack directly to it.

2 NS Gauche 5.7 G 140' ★

Great position and nice climbing, but quite dirty.

Start: From the minisummit, bushwhack hard left toward the leftmost buttress on the upper dome. Stay below a steep headwall blocking a direct approach, and ascend to its left. Once above the headwall, bushwhack back to the right, eyeballing the route as you go. Begin on the left side of a sloping buttress below an obvious face 591404,4900036.

P1 5.7 G: Traverse right through tight trees (yuck) 10' to gain the toe of the buttress, and a nice crack. Follow the crack for 40' over dirty rock to a ledge with a small birch. At the birch, step right and down, then move further right across a small alcove, and back up to a hidden crack. Climb the crack until it ends, then step left and continue up the exposed face on knobs to the top. 140'

FA Aug 3, 2013, R.L. Stolz, Nancy Schwartz

3 N.O.C. Route 5.6 G 280' ★★

Start: From the minisummit, drop into the col and bushwhack uphill towards the dome. Below the start of the route is a scrappy cliff barrier. From its right end, take a left-rising line on vegetated ledges through the cliff barrier (3rd-class) to the top of a chimney, then straight up a vague gully to a slab. Walk right 50' along the base of the slab to an open, sandy, sloped area. Begin at the height of the terrain at a left-leaning crack, 10' left of a prominent black streak 591528,4900097.

P1 5.6 G: Climb the left-leaning crack (crux at the bottom) to its end at some flakes. At the top of the flakes, reach right to gain a right-leaning crack and follow it to a tree island. 160'

P2 5.5 PG: Climb a 30'-high shallow right-facing flake to a ledge at its top. Step right to some flakes, then up and right on good knobby orange rock. Traverse left 10' (2" cam), then straight up over a bulge to a low-angle slab. Follow the slab to the top at a cozy alcove near the top of the large left-facing, left-leaning corner that dominates the upper part of the dome. 120'

Gear: To 3".

Descent: Two double-rope rappels from trees return you to the top of the route. One more single-rope rappel returns you to the ground.

FA May 17, 1984, Don Mellor, Rusty Geh, Kevin Kearns, Sabine Weber, Jim Williams, Ian Osteyee

4 Don't Kill The Client 5.7 G 150'

The first ascent attempted the right-leaning roof crack, but, due to a dangerous block above the belay, opted for the easier exit. Named for the #1 rule in guiding.

Start: The top of the cliff on its right side is dominated by large roofs broken by a lone right-leaning crack. Begin at a slab with a lone birch 20' up, and just right of a right-leaning, tree-filled gully that leads the right-leaning roof crack. This is 200' uphill and right of N.O.C. Route.

P1 5.6 PG: Climb the slab past the birch tree, staying right of the tree-filled depression, to a ledge below the large roofs. 90'

P2 5.7 G: Traverse 25' right to the right end of the ledge and climb a crack in a left-facing corner to a ledge with a tree. Step right, and scramble to the trees. 60'

FA 1988, R.L. Stolz, Jeffrey Ruiz

PITCHOFF CHIMNEY CLIFF

Location	North side of NY 73 in Cascade Pass, above Lower Cascade Lake
Aspect	Southeast
Height	140'
Quality	★★★★★
Approach	3 min, easy
Summary	Face and crack routes that span the range of difficult grades, crowded into a small cliff very close to the road.

-5.6	5.7	5.8	5.9	5.10	5.11	5.12	5.13+	total
3	1	8	9	10	10	2		45

Pitchoff Chimney Cliff is a small cliff with excellent rock that squeezes in a large number of routes. Perhaps due to its short approach or proximity to Lake Placid, this cliff has seen considerable development, with nearly every crack, face, and overhang climbed and named. It sits just above NY 73 and the Lower Cascade Lake near the height of Cascade Pass, about 9 miles from Lake Placid.

Climbing in Cascade Pass is very scenic, with the enchained pristine lakes and gorgeous views of Cascade and the valley toward Owl's Head and Keene. Unfortunately, like Poke-O, the ambience is somewhat blemished by the road noise. Invariably during the day, passing motorists will see climbers on the wall and

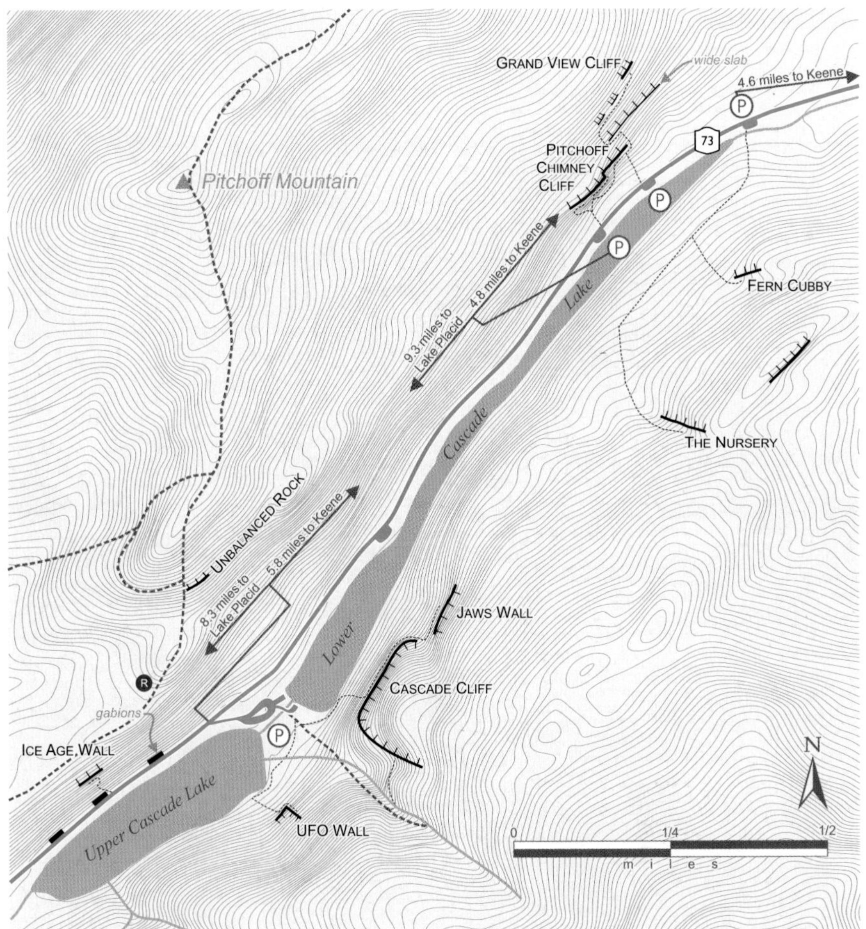

voice their "hellos" with repeated use of their horns.

An interesting feature of the cliff is that it isn't really attached to the mountain behind it. Rather, it is a giant slab of rock separated from the mountain by a boulder-filled chimney that forms the **Great Chimney** route. You can fully appreciate this geologic anomaly when using the Chimney Descent, which takes the climber under some boulders and into the chimney behind the very routes that were just climbed. The cliff's other major features are the waterfall on the far left end; the Roaches Terrace on the left end, from which many routes begin; the large, low orange roofs in the center of the cliff; the Practice Wall in the woods on the right; and finally the left-rising roofs on the right end of the cliff.

The cliff has some extremely good climbing, the most popular routes being the moderates **Pete's Farewell** and **The El**, which rank high on the list for visiting climbers. Some of the better cracks include **Star Sailor**, **Rock and Roll Star**, and **Brrright Star**. Face climbers can edge their way up the awesome overhanging face of **Raging Raven**, **Run Higher, Jump Faster**, or **Running of the Bulls**. And you can't miss arguably the best route on the cliff, **Roaches on the Wall**. There are 67 pitches of climbing on this cliff, the predominant grades being in the 5.8 to 5.9 range.

The bad news about Pitchoff is that many of the routes are becoming overgrown and unclimbable in their current state. On **Brrright Star**, for example, Doug Madera was once heard saying "Man, the feet are really small. But at least they're covered in lichen." Every couple of years, somebody cleans **Wald-Calder Route**, only to have it revegetate by the next year. Before you head up on any of the less frequently climbed routes (and it will be obvious), be prepared by carrying a wire brush and perhaps inspecting the route on rappel; the climbing is definitely worth it.

It should also be mentioned that Pitchoff has a number of "partial" routes—routes that end halfway up the cliff (e.g., **Raging Raven**, **Chuting Star**) or, even more confusing, begin high up the cliff at some landmark of another route (e.g., **Roof**, **Eurotech**, **PF Flyers**, **Hidden Constellation**, **Star Sailor**). Some of

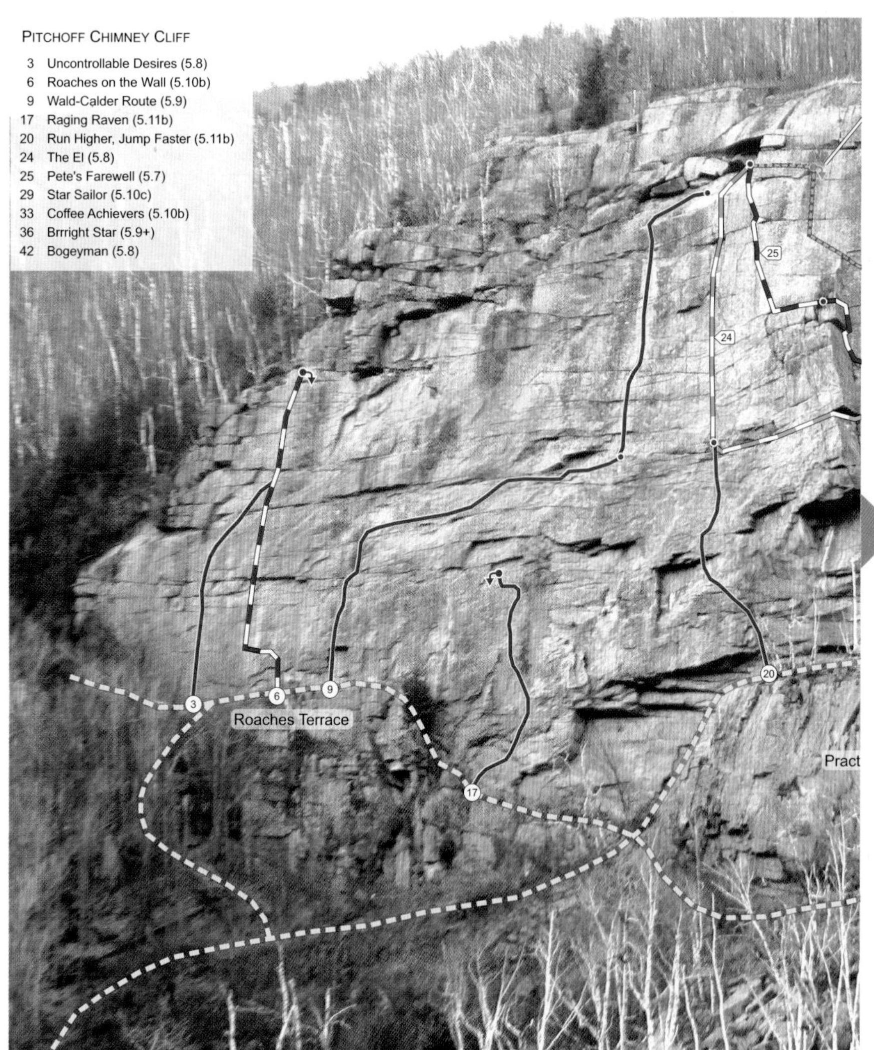

the confusion has been removed by combining bottom and top pitches into a single route (by consensus support of the local climbing community). The topo can help here, as will the "Start" section of each route description.

A final note about the weather: the environment here can be cooler and windier than other venues in the region, which is good for summer climbing (when the cliff is cooler and the bugs are kept at bay) but bad for the fall (when the cliff falls into shade early).

HISTORY

The False Face of Pitchoff, a name given to the cliff by some early climbers, was first climbed in 1949 by the **Great Chimney** route. Credit has been given to Fritz Wiessner and Jim Goodwin for this route, although other climbers recall climbing the chimney around the same time. The only other route believed to have been climbed in that period was **Pete's Farewell**, by Donald Lebeau and Tommy Condon, then 14 years old. One would think, due to its accessibility, that the cliff would have been an early bloomer, but it quietly slumbered for 26 years, waking back up in 1976 to the clanging gear of John Wald and Grant Calder with **The El**, one of the better moderates in the region. Things really got going in the 1980s, first with the Lake Placid crew (including, among others, Don Mellor, Bob Bushart, Chuck Turner, Bill Dodd, and Jeff Edwards) picking off some of the remaining obvious lines, then Patrick Purcell with various partners for the more obscure lines. Development slowed in the mid-1990s with the general thinking that the cliff was "climbed out." Developmentwise, the cliff

has sat nearly idle for the last 10 years, but it remains extremely popular among climbers for its moderate crack and face climbs.

GEOLOGY

With the intense faulting that occurs during continental collisions, it is possible for an isolated block of rock to surface. Such is the case with Pitchoff Mountain, which is composed of gneiss and is surrounded by anorthosite. This explains the different rock texture found at Pitchoff Chimney Cliff when compared to the Cascade Cliff across the pass.

DIRECTIONS (MAP PAGE 353)

The cliff is located on NY 73, 9.3 miles from Lake Placid (measured from the intersection of NY 73 and NY 86) and 4.8 miles from Keene (from the fork where NY 73 and NY 9N split). When driving from Keene, once you reach the first lake (Lower Cascade Lake), park at the second pullout on the left—the pullout near the left end of the cliff. There is a pullout directly below the cliff, but the trail begins at the second pullout. When you're driving from Lake Placid, drive past the first lake until you can see the cliff on your left and park at the pullout nearest the left end of the cliff.

There are several pullouts, so if the desired pullout is full, just park at one of the others. The correct pullout where the trail begins is the one with the sign that reads "Pitchoff Walls" and has a symbol of a rock climber 590710,4898727.

The trail begins directly across the road from the parking area. Hike uphill to a fork; the left fork continues uphill to access the Roaches Terrace at the left end of the cliff, and the right fork accesses the Practice Wall and routes at the right end of the cliff. It takes about 3 min to reach the cliff from the road 590719,4898829.

DESCENT OPTIONS

There are several descent options:

Walk-off: From the top, walk left and follow an obvious path down around the far side of the waterfall and back to the base of the cliff.

Roaches Rappel: There is a fixed anchor above the Triple Cracks of **Rock and Roll Star**. A single 60-m rope returns you to the Roaches Terrace.

Chimney Descent: From the top of **Pete's Farewell**, you can enter the **Great Chimney** (either directly or by squirming under boulders), then walk along the floor toward the cave opening. There is a fixed anchor here from which a single-rope rappel returns you to the base of the cliff near the start of **Pete's Farewell**.

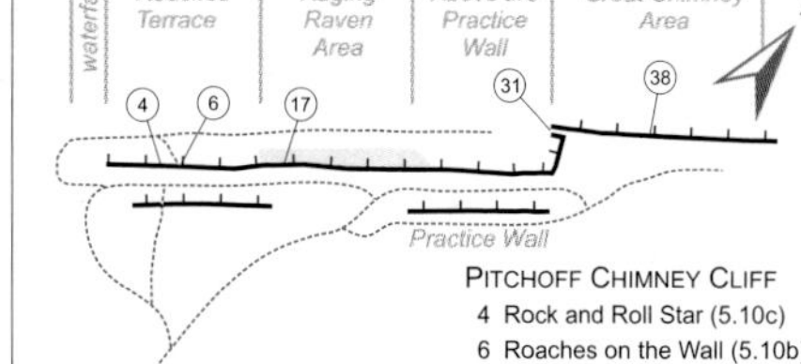

PITCHOFF CHIMNEY CLIFF
4 Rock and Roll Star (5.10c)
6 Roaches on the Wall (5.10b)
17 Raging Raven (5.11b)
31 Great Chimney (5.6)
38 Rugosity (5.8+)

Roaches Terrace

The Roaches Terrace is a tree-covered ledge at the left end of the cliff, just right of the waterfall. To access the ledge, take the left fork on the approach trail and hike to the waterfall, then walk right along the base of the cliff onto this ledge.

The most obvious route on this section of cliff is the chalked crack on the left end, **Rock and Roll Star**.

1 Vermontville Redneck 5.10c TR 60'

At the far left end of Roaches Terrace behind some trees is a once-clean face that's now covered in a jellylike ooze. Thin moves lead to horizontals and a good ledge. Continue straight through a bulge to good holds and the top.

FA (TR) Jun 22, 1986, Patrick Purcell, Steven Bailey

2 Anniversary Waltz 5.10c G 75'

Another face route that would be recommended (two stars) if cleaned.

Start: 10' left of the wet spot of **Uncontrollable Desires** at a shallow right-facing corner.

P1 5.10c G: Up the face to a horizontal, then make a long reach to the next horizontal and a bolt. Angle left to right-facing flakes, up these, then continue up the face, trending left to the top. 75'

FA May 28, 1986, Patrick Purcell, Ian Osteyee

3 Uncontrollable Desires 5.8 PG 100' ★

A seminal route.

Start: Just left of the low wet spot, which is just left of the fingercrack of **Rock and Roll Star**.

P1 5.8 PG: Face-climb up to a horizontal, then up the face to the second horizontal with a large piton. Trend right to a fingercrack that is 3' right of an off width. Up the fingercrack to a cedar, then join **Rock and Roll Star**: angle up and right across the face to the Triple Cracks (5.7) and up to a ledge with a fixed anchor. 100'

FA May, 1981, Bob Bushart, Bill Simes

*Rich Leswing on **Roaches on the Wall** (5.10b). Photo by Jim Cunningham.*

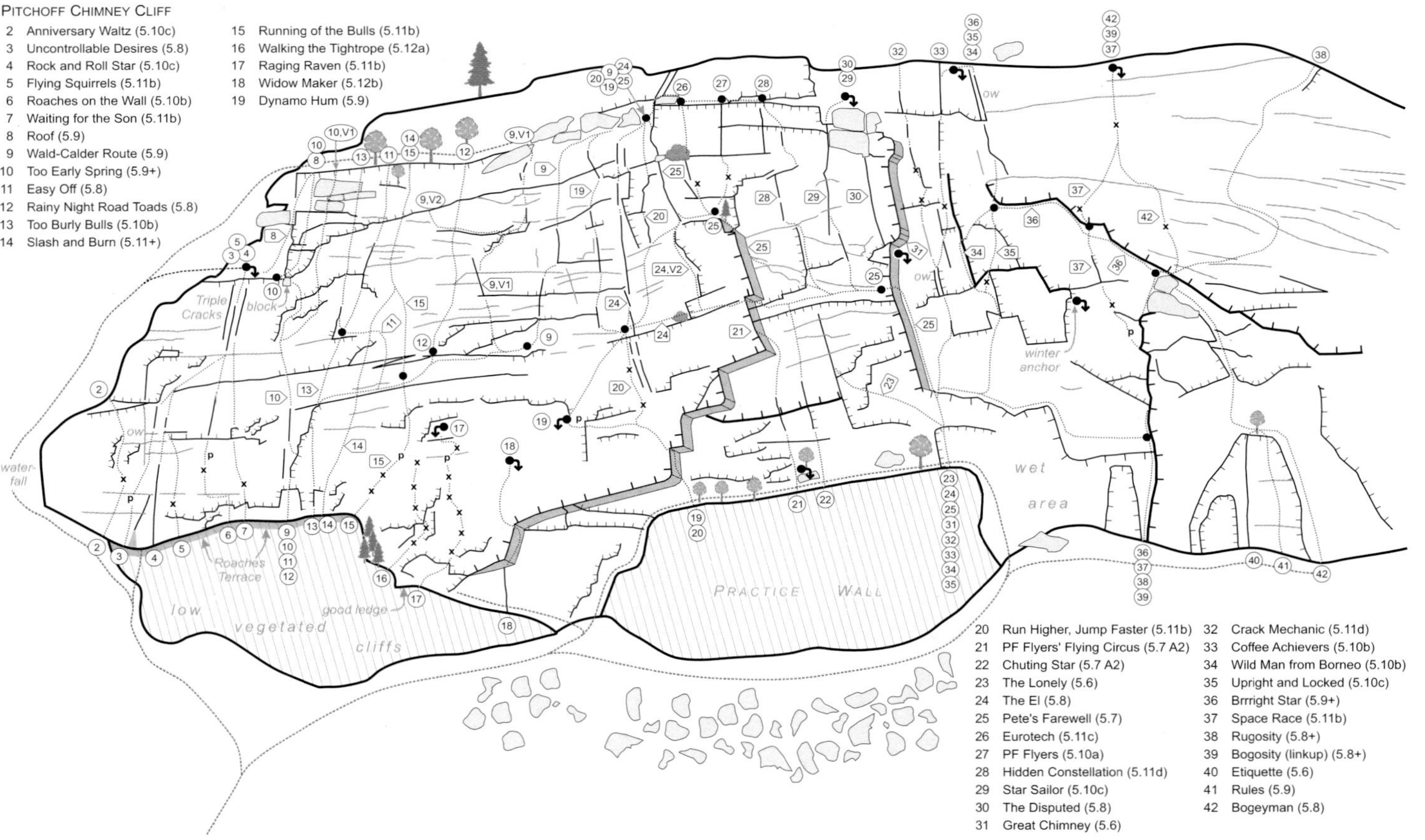
PITCHOFF CHIMNEY CLIFF
2 Anniversary Waltz (5.10c)
3 Uncontrollable Desires (5.8)
4 Rock and Roll Star (5.10c)
5 Flying Squirrels (5.11b)
6 Roaches on the Wall (5.10b)
7 Waiting for the Son (5.11b)
8 Roof (5.9)
9 Wald-Calder Route (5.9)
10 Too Early Spring (5.9+)
11 Easy Off (5.8)
12 Rainy Night Road Toads (5.8)
13 Too Burly Bulls (5.10b)
14 Slash and Burn (5.11+)
15 Running of the Bulls (5.11b)
16 Walking the Tightrope (5.12a)
17 Raging Raven (5.11b)
18 Widow Maker (5.12b)
19 Dynamo Hum (5.9)
20 Run Higher, Jump Faster (5.11b)
21 PF Flyers' Flying Circus (5.7 A2)
22 Chuting Star (5.7 A2)
23 The Lonely (5.6)
24 The El (5.8)
25 Pete's Farewell (5.7)
26 Eurotech (5.11c)
27 PF Flyers (5.10a)
28 Hidden Constellation (5.11d)
29 Star Sailor (5.10c)
30 The Disputed (5.8)
31 Great Chimney (5.6)
32 Crack Mechanic (5.11d)
33 Coffee Achievers (5.10b)
34 Wild Man from Borneo (5.10b)
35 Upright and Locked (5.10c)
36 Brrright Star (5.9+)
37 Space Race (5.11b)
38 Rugosity (5.8+)
39 Bogosity (linkup) (5.8+)
40 Etiquette (5.6)
41 Rules (5.9)
42 Bogeyman (5.8)
Triple Cracks
block
ow
waterfall
Roaches Terrace
good ledge
low vegetated cliffs
PRACTICE WALL
winter anchor
wet area

4 Rock and Roll Star 5.10c G 100' ★★★

A quality fingercrack, although some find the barn-door crux awkward and unpleasant. This is the most obvious line on the Roaches Terrace.

Start: At the chalked-up vertical crack, the only vertical crack that comes down to the ground.

P1 5.10c G: Up the fingercrack (crux) for 30' to some horizontal breaks. Through the breaks and up to a right-facing corner, then trend right across the face to the Triple Cracks—three cracks that break the upper face and lead to a ledge with a fixed anchor (5.7; the rightmost crack is the easiest). 100'

FA 1977, Eric Rhicard, Morris Hershoff, John Deladucca

5 Flying Squirrels 5.11b PG (5.9 R) 100' ★★★★

Yet another fine creation by Purcell, whose friends know him as the Flying Squirrel because he owned a pet flying squirrel.

Start: 10' right of the fingercrack of **Rock and Roll Star**, at an undercling flake 6' up.

P1 5.11b PG (5.9 R): Climb up the face and make a long reach past the undercling flake. Continue up the face past a bolt 20' up (difficult clip), then step left to RP seams that lead to horizontals 30' up. A final difficult move left through a bulge (crux) gains the upper face, then join **Rock and Roll Star**: angle up right across the face to the Triple Cracks (5.7) and up to a ledge with a fixed anchor. 100'

FA Jun 7, 1986, Patrick Purcell, Jeff Edwards

6 Roaches on the Wall 5.10b G 100' ★★★★★

This high-quality route sports delicious rock, a reachy face, a thin fingercrack, and a pleasant crack finish. Very popular.

Start: 30' right of the fingercrack of **Rock and Roll Star**, on top of a long horizontal boulder beneath an overlap 6' up.

P1 5.10b G: (V1) Climb up to a horizontal above the overlap, then hand-traverse 10' left until you can reach up to the next horizontal break. Climb up the face to the ceiling, over this (easier than it looks), then up the thin crack (crux) to a horizontal. Continue straight up to the Triple Cracks of **Rock and Roll Star** (5.7) and up to a ledge with a fixed anchor. 100'

V1 5.11b PG: Starting below the left end of the low overlap, boulder directly up to the end of the traverse (below the bolt). The crux is very close to the ground.

Gear: To 2".

FA Sep, 1979, Jerry Hoover, Bob Bushart
FFA May, 1980, Rick Fleming

7 Waiting for the Son 5.11b G (5.10 R) 110' ★

A very committing face climb that is also a popular toprope. Now in need of cleaning. Named by Edwards, who was anticipating the birth of his son Nicholas.

Start: On top of the long horizontal boulder beneath an overlap 6' up, 4' right of **Roaches on the Wall**.

P1 5.11b G (5.10 R): Climb over the overlap to the horizontal, move right to a bolt, then up the face (crux) to the ceiling. Step left a few feet and break through the ceiling right of **Roaches on the Wall**. Run-out climbing up the face leads to a prominent horizontal, then up left to the Triple Cracks of **Rock and Roll Star** (5.7) and up to a ledge with a fixed anchor. 110'

FA Jul, 1993, Jeff Edwards, Don Mellor

8 Roof 5.9 G 40'

This route breaks through the roof system above the previous routes. This can be done as a separate climb by approaching by trail from below or as an extension to any of the routes that end at the fixed anchor above the Triple Cracks of **Rock and Roll Star**.

Start: At the fixed anchor at the top of the previous routes.

P1 5.9 G: Walk right on the ledge to the large left-facing corner capped by a roof. Up the corner to the roof, then out the crack through the roof to finish in the blocky terrain above. 40'

9 Wald-Calder Route 5.9 PG 190' ★★

Very nice climbing and well protected after the first boulder move off the ground. P1 is very unobvious from below, as you cannot see the traverse or the belay ledge, and everything looks covered with lichen.

Start: At the right end of the Roaches Terrace, where the ledge narrows and becomes more exposed, is a shallow three-sided box with orange rock; the roof of the box is 7' up. Begin in the right-facing corner that forms the left side of this box.

P1 5.9- PG: Boulder up the left side of the box and make a long unprotected reach over the top of the box to a bucket (5.8), then up into a left-facing, right-rising flake. Climb the flake almost to its top, then traverse right 70' with good protection, following horizontals, past a thin section (crux) and on to a comfortable belay on a ledge (with blocks to sit on) at the right end of a low roof system. 100'

P2 5.9 PG: (V1) Straight up from the belay, climb up a crack through two overlaps to a horizontal. Step right to the next crack, then follow it past a hard move to a flexing flake, then up to a bulging headwall. Grunt through the bulge on perfect finger locks to the top. 90'

V1 Drawing Mustaches on Dangerous Dogs 5.9 PG: From the belay, move left 10' to a point under the ceiling at a right-facing offset. Climb through the ceiling at the offset and up to a good horizontal. Climb the face following a faint left-leaning seam to its end, then move up and right to a short right-facing corner with a horizontal on top. (V2) Move right, then up, following a thin vertical crack past several horizontals to the top.

V2 Barbecued Dogs 5.9 PG: Hand-traverse left along the horizontal, across a bulging wall to just before a grassy ledge, then up the face (the same line as **Rainy Night Road Toads**) to the top.

FA 1976, Grant Calder, John Wald
FFA Jun, 1979, John Wald
FA (V1) Jul 1, 1985, Bill Dodd, Patrick Purcell
FA (V2) Jul 26, 1987, Patrick Purcell, Jeff Edwards

10 Too Early Spring 5.9+ PG 140' ★★

The name comes from the fact that the route was discovered by toprope in February. Looks dirty, but clean enough where it needs to be.

Start: Same as **Wald-Calder Route**.

*Emilie Drinkwater on P2 of **Wald-Calder Route** (5.9). Photo by David Le Pagne.*

P1 5.9+ PG: Begin the same as **Wald-Calder Route**: Boulder up the left side of the box and make a long unprotected reach over the top of the box to a bucket (5.8) and up to a left-facing, right-rising flake. Up the flake to a horizontal, then traverse left to a point beneath a series of small vertical seams. Up the seams through a bulge to a prominent horizontal, then on to a ledge below a right-facing corner. (V1) Work up the corner to where it makes an angular bend right. Continue straight up to a ledge just left of a cantilevered block. Belay here or walk left to the fixed anchor as for **Rock and Roll Star**. 100'

P2 5.7 G: From the cantilevered block, climb onto the nose, then up the lichen-covered blocks to the top. 40'

V1 Pine Cone Eaters 5.10b R: Step right from the corner and up a right-rising ledge for a few feet, then straight up the face past dirty, fragile flakes; past a right-rising overlap; and into a right-facing corner (the right side of the nose feature). Up the corner and around a ceiling, finishing on dirty blocks. Probably as good as it sounds.

FA (P1) May, 1981, Don Mellor, Bob Bushart, Bill Simes
FA (P2) Jul, 1983, Don Mellor, Mark Ippolito
FA (V1) Aug 31, 1987, Jeff Edwards, Adam Clayman

11 Easy Off 5.8 PG 140'

Start: Same as **Wald-Calder Route**.

P1 5.8 PG: Begin as for **Wald-Calder Route**: Boulder up the left side of the box and make a long unprotected reach over the top of the box to a bucket (crux), then up into a left-facing, right-rising flake. Climb the flake almost to its top, then traverse right along a horizontal for 15', then up to a more prominent horizontal. Work up past this, then left to a belay ledge (shared with **Too Burly Bulls**). 70'

P2 5.5 PG: Move up and right to a left-facing corner capped by a small square block. From the top of the corner, follow a handcrack to a horizontal ledge below a ceiling, then over this through chunky terrain to the top. 70'

FA Jun, 1981, Bob Bushart, Bill Simes

12 Rainy Night Road Toads 5.8 PG 140' ★

Start: Same as **Wald-Calder Route**.

P1 5.8 PG: Begin the same as **Wald-Calder Route**: Boulder up the left side of the box and make a long unprotected reach over the top of the box to a bucket (crux), then up into a left-facing, right-rising flake. Climb the flake almost to its top, then traverse right along a series of horizontals for 35' to a hanging belay at a point where the traverse switches to the upper horizontal, left of the ceilings. 65'

P2 5.8 PG: Face-climb up and right, then straight up, connecting various horizontals through a bulge at the top. 75'

FA Jul 27, 1989, Don Mellor, Patrick Purcell

13 Too Burly Bulls 5.10b PG 140' ★★

P2 isn't recommended; it's much better to connect up with **Easy Off** or the top section of **Running of the Bulls**, making the route 5.9+. The name is a clever combination of the names of two other neighboring routes, and the fact that the first ascentionists were burly football players.

Start: At a shallow right-facing corner 4' right of the **Wald-Calder Route** box.

P1 5.9+ PG: Climb the corner past a small overlap, then up a face to a flake (the top of the left-facing, right-rising flake of **Wald-Calder Route**). Continue straight up past some brown, flaky rock to a roof. Pull through the roof on jugs and up to a ledge. 70'

P2 5.10b PG: Straight up the face from the belay, staying left of the left-facing corner of **Easy Off**, past an overlap in chocolate-colored rock, to a ceiling. Pull over the ceiling to dirty, blocky terrain. 70'

FA Bob Bushart, Bill Simes

14 Slash and Burn 5.11+ TR 150'

Begin 8' right of the **Wald-Calder Route** box and 4' right of a small right-facing corner. Climb straight up the face 15' to a slightly rounded horizontal fingerhold, then make a very long reach to a better horizontal fingerhold to the right and lunge up right to an inch-deep horizontal hold. Work up the face to the right end of the prominent overlap, pull over the bulge above, and follow a narrow ramp up right for about 10' to join the upper section of **Running of the Bulls**.

FA (TR) 1991, Ken Nichols

15 Running of the Bulls 5.11b PG 140' ★★★★★

Start: At the right end of the Roaches Terrace just before the trail drops down to the right.

P1 5.11b G: Hand-traverse right at chest level to a left-facing flake (bolt), up and right across the face (crux) to a piton, then up to a short right-facing corner. Up the corner, past an overlap to a horizontal (common with the traverse on the **Wald-Calder Route**). 40'

P2 5.9 PG: Continue straight up the face, angle left through a bulge (crux; fragile flake), then up a series of horizontals just right of the **Easy Off** handcrack to a roof. Break the roof at a right-leaning crack and up to a birch tree. 100'

FA Jul 13, 1989, Patrick Purcell, Don Mellor

Raging Raven Area

These routes begin at the low point on the face beneath the orange roofs, down from and right of the Roaches Terrace. To reach this area, take the right fork on the approach trail, which meets the cliff below the roofs. Walk left along the base of the cliff until you come to the routes. You can also access the routes by scrambling down the right end of the Roaches Terrace.

16 Walking the Tightrope 5.12a G 65' ★★

This route ends at the last bolt (it needs a second bolt for an anchor).

Start: 15' uphill from and left of **Raging Raven**, at a flat rock just before the trail begins the 3rd-class scramble up left to the Roaches Terrace, below right-facing, right-rising flakes.

● **P1 5.12a G:** Climb the flakes up and right, then move left onto the overhanging wall and up to a fixed anchor. 65'

Gear: Up to 1.5"; 0.75" cam is mandatory.

FA 1996, George Ide, Hobey Walker

17 Raging Raven 5.11b G 70' ★★★★

This overhanging orange wall is characterized by steep jugs, a few crimps, and big moves between horizontals. Very popular. On the first ascent, the raven's nest right of the anchor had young and Mama Raven was pissed. In 2012, a block pulled from the start of the route, removing a jug and the sole spot of protection. This may be resolved with an additional bolt; until then, use a stick clip, or the route is R.

Start: At the right side of a flaky, orange arching overlap. The start is down from and right of the Roaches Terrace and can be reached from there by scrambling down behind a cedar (3rd-class). It can also be reached from the approach trail, where it meets the cliff under the orange overhangs: walk left on a narrow ledge up against the cliff to a point where the ledge widens.

● **P1 5.11b G:** Climb up and right to break the overlap, then head out right onto the face. Work back left a bit to a large jug, then up to a good horizontal. A brief move right (crux), then back left, leads to a fixed anchor. 70'

FA 1993, Patrick Purcell

*Joe Szot on **P.F. Fliers** (5.10a), with Aya Alt belaying. Photo by David Le Pagne.*

18 Widow Maker 5.12b R 140'

Questionable rock and difficult climbing characterize this route. On the first free ascent, the route nearly lived up to its name—Berzins fell from 25' up, pulling gear and decking, landing on his back, winded. He climbed back up and replaced his gear "with more care." This seems to be a common theme; Mark Synnott describes climbing **Widow Maker** as his very first aid climb: "I got to the roof and learned the hard way about expando nailing. Ripped a lot of pieces and ended up about a foot off the ground right over a jagged rock."

Start: At a handcrack that comes right to the ground, below a large right-facing corner at the left end of the largest roof system. There's an old fixed RURP above the roof.

P1 5.12b R: Climb up the crack to the corner, then up the corner to the roof. Traverse left under the roof and onto the overhanging face with crappy rock (several good nut placements), to a fixed anchor on a ledge, left of the white-streaked raven's nest. 70'

P2 5.11b PG: Traverse right to the anchor on **Dynamo Hum** and then reverse the traverse under the roof to its right end. The route continues rightward, over the raven's nest, to join **Run Higher, Jump Faster**. Move up to a bolt, then straight up following parallel faint seams past another bolt to a belay on a ledge (shared with **The El**). 70'

FA (A3+) Feb, 1981, Alan Jolley, Bill Diemand
FFA (P1) 1992, Martin Berzins

Practice Wall Area

The Practice Wall Area is a lower-angle slab of rock situated below the central section of the cliff—i.e., below the right-facing corners of **Pitchoff Chimney** and **Pete's Farewell**. The area is popular for toproping, as the top is easily accessible with plenty of trees for anchors (and a new fixed anchor on the wall above). The wall is easy for beginners, mainly in the 5.3 range.

To reach the Practice Wall, take the right fork on the approach trail to meet the cliff at the orange overhangs. Walk right along the cliff to a fork: the high path goes to the ledge above the Practice Wall, and the low path goes to the base of the Practice Wall.

Above the Practice Wall Area

The routes in this area begin above the Practice Wall. On the approach trail, take the right fork to meet the cliff at the orange overhangs. Walk right along the cliff to another fork and take the high path up a gravelly chimney to the ledge. Be careful not to knock debris onto the slab below (the Practice Wall).

19 Dynamo Hum 5.9 PG 190' ★★★

The name is harvested from a Frank Zappa song, "Dinah-Moe Humm."

Start: At the left end of the ledge above the Practice Wall before the trail drops down left into the gravelly chimney, below a hanging right-facing corner.

P1 5.9 G: Climb up the hanging corner, then out left to bulging rock to a position below the right end of a ceiling. Traverse left under the ceiling to its left end at a right-facing corner. Step left around the corner to a hanging belay at a fixed anchor. 70'

P2 5.9 PG: Angle up and right to a ledge (optional belay shared with **The El**). Step left and climb past several horizontals to a thin crack (about 15' left of the left-facing corner and crack of **The El**) to an orange spot below a small overlap, then up to a final left-leaning crack that leads to a slabby finish. 120'

History: **Dynamo Hum** was once a single-pitch variation to the finish of **The El** or **Wald-Calder Route**. P1 was added 11 years later and called **Dynamo Direct**. Then, like other routes here, it simply became P1.

FA (P1) Jul, 1992, Don Mellor, Jeff Edwards, Joe Quackenbush
FA (P2) Jun, 1981, Don Mellor, Bob Bushart

20 Run Higher, Jump Faster 5.11b PG 160' ★★★★

There are several routes at Pitchoff with names related to the canvas sneakers PF Flyers, the shoe that, in the 1950s and 60s, "made millions run faster and jump higher" (as depicted by a child leaping over a 5'-high fence). The first ascentionists thought that EBs, the climbing shoe used at that time, provided just the opposite capabilities.

Start: Same as **Dynamo Hum**.

P1 5.11b PG: Climb up the hanging corner, then out left to bulging rock to a position below the right end of a ceiling (same as **Dynamo Hum** to this point). Move up to a bolt, then straight up, following parallel faint seams past another bolt to a belay on a ledge (shared with **The El**). 80'

P2 Death by Minivan 5.11b G: Straight up the crack a few feet, then step right and climb a thin crack just right of the left-facing corner (and left of the **Pete's Farewell** crack) to a good horizontal at the top. Continue straight up the face to the slab and summit blocks. It is possible to "cheat" at various points by reaching into neighboring routes. 80'

History: P2 was eyed for a long time by Don Mellor and Jeff Edwards, but family pressures kept it from happening, so it was dubbed **Death by Station Wagon**. Furman got to it first and changed the name because he was living out of his van at the time.

FA (P1) Aug, 1982, Chuck Turner
FA (P2) 1994, Dave Furman, Don Mellor

21 PF Flyers' Flying Circus 5.7 A2 100'

The route ends at the **Pete's Farewell** anchor; there are several possible finishes (**Pete's Farewell**, **Eurotech**, **PF Flyers**). The first ascent used a taped-on skyhook to protect the free moves to the arête. The name is a play on the title of the BBC comedy show *Monty Python's Flying Circus,* combined with yet another reference to the canvas sneakers PF Flyers.

Start: At the right end of a slab of rock (4' high and 10' wide) that leans up against the cliff below a roof.

P1 5.7 A2: Up the straight-in seam through the bulging roof, then up the face to the right end of the larger roof above. Free-climb right into the right-facing corner, then back left to the arête and follow it up to a belay on a good ledge (shared with **Pete's Farewell**). 100'

Gear: Baby angle, knife blades, small RPs.

History: The aid section of the route had been climbed earlier by Alan Jolley. He either bailed or continued up **Pete's Farewell**. The route was later extended to the arête, making a more independent line.
FA May 12, 1984, Jim Cunningham, Mark Saulsgiver

22 Chuting Star 5.7 A2 40'

Originally envisioned as a direct start to **Star Sailor**.
Start: 15' right of **PF Flyers' Flying Circus**, at a slab that leads to a left-leaning, left-facing corner.
P1 5.7 A2: Climb up the slab to the corner, then follow the very thin seam through the bulging roof to a good horizontal. From here, it is possible to join any of a number of routes (such as **The El**, **Pete's Farwell**, and **Star Sailor**). 40'
FA May 17, 1984, Mark Saulsgiver, Jim Cunningham

23 The Lonely 5.6 G 60' ★

Provides a more direct access to the traverse line of **Pete's Farewell** and can therefore be used as a start to that route as well as other routes (such as **The El**, **Star Sailor**, and **Hidden Constellation**).
Start: Same as **Pete's Farwell**.
P1 5.6 G: Boulder up the left side of a short wall to a ledge. Move left to clean rock at a series of right-facing, left-leaning corners. Climb up left past these corners to a ceiling and break this on the left side, then up a crack to the traverse line of **Pete's Farwell**. 60'
FA Sep, 1980, Bob Bushart, Bill Diemand

24 The El 5.8 G 180' ★★★★★

The second most popular route at the cliff, with many squeezed-in variations.
Start: Same as **Pete's Farewell**.
P1 5.2 G: Same as P1 of **Pete's Farewell**: Boulder up the left side of a short wall to a ledge, then scramble up to the base of the huge chimney in the deep right-facing corner. Climb the left wall of the huge corner, then traverse left to the arête and a good ledge just to its left. 40'
P2 5.7 G: Traverse left across the face to the large right-facing corner. There is a small overlap on the left wall of the corner; hand-traverse left below this to the arête, then around the arête, following a good horizontal that eventually becomes a ledge. (V1, V2) Continue traversing to a belay below a vertical crack. 60'
P3 5.8 G: (V3) Climb straight up the crack and into a left-facing corner capped by an overhang. Follow the cracks above the overhang to a slab and summit boulders. 80'
Gear: To 3".

V1 Pointless and Hard 5.9 G: After moving around the arête onto the main face, climb a thin fingercrack, staying just left of the arête up to the **Pete's Farewell** belay. Finish at will (**Pete's Farewell**, **PF Flyers**, or **Eurotech**).
V2 Beam Us Up, Scotty 5.8 G: From partway across the traverse, climb up into a left-facing corner, then follow it straight up into the finishing crack of **Pete's Farewell** (5.7).
V3 Linkup 5.8 G: From the belay, diagonal up and right across the face to join the finishing crack of **Pete's Farewell** (5.7).
FA Jul, 1976, Grant Calder, John Wald
FA (V1) 1987, Patrick Purcell, Jeff Edwards, Don Mellor
FA (V2) Jun 28, 1981, Pete Benson, Rich Leswing, Chuck Turner
FA (V3) Jun 14, 1983, Steve Larson, Don Mellor

Jesse Williams traversing on P2 (5.7) of The El (5.8). Photo by Rick Levinson.

Above: Jim Cunningham on P2 (5.6) of **Pete's Farewell** (5.7). Photo Jim Cunningham Collection.

Below: Jeff Edwards on **Hidden Constellation** (5.11d). Photo by Don Mellor.

25 Pete's Farewell 5.7 G 165' ★★★★

A high-quality route on clean rock, exposed positions, and varied climbing—an airy traverse, a layback corner, and a stellar finishing crack. One of the most popular 5.7s in the Adirondacks.

Start: At the right end of the ledge above the Practice Wall, just before the trail descends to the right into the vegetated wet area, directly below the giant right-facing corner (the corner that forms the **Great Chimney**). More specifically, the route begins at the left end of a short wall, just right of a low roof 8' up.

P1 5.2 G: Boulder up the left side of the short wall to a ledge, then scramble up to the base of the huge chimney in the deep right-facing corner. Climb the left wall of the huge corner, then traverse left to the arête and a good ledge just to its left. 40'

P2 5.6 G: Traverse left to the large right-facing corner, then layback and stem up a wide crack in the corner. Belay on a good ledge with a small cedar left of the arête. 75'

P3 5.7 G: Traverse left 10' to the left-leaning handcrack. An awkward move starts the crack, which leads past a horizontal with a block and on to a slab and the summit boulders. 50'

Gear: To 3".

History: The route was climbed and named by Pete Gibb and Dave Gilyeat on Aug 24, 1968 on aid (5.6 A1) using wooden wedges. However, Tommy Condon clearly recalls climbing the route in 1950 with Donald Lebeau leading. Condon was 14 years old at the time, climbing in "basketball Converse sneakers" on a face "like that of the Matterhorn," such is the perspective of youth.

FA 1950, Donald Lebeau, Tommy Condon

26 Eurotech 5.11c PG 60' ★★

Named for the European-style tactics used on the first ascent.

Start: At the P2 belay for **Pete's Farewell**.

P1 5.11c PG: Walk left from the belay, then up to a horizontal. Thin moves up the face (bolt) lead to the next horizontal just right of a bush (and the block on **Pete's Farewell**). Up the face to the flake, then up to the top. 60'

Descent: Scramble left along the narrow rib of rock, then make an exposed move down to the summit boulders at the top of **Pete's Farewell**.

FA 1987, Patrick Purcell, Jeff Edwards

27 PF Flyers 5.10a G 60' ★★

A quality boulder problem with a puzzling, well-protected crux. Those who can't do the move simply grab the bolt (5.8 A0).

Start: At the P2 belay for **Pete's Farewell**.

P1 5.10a G: Climb straight up from the belay to a bolt. Make a delicate balance move to a jug, then up to a horizontal. Follow the excellent handcrack to the top. 60'

Descent: Scramble left along the narrow rib of rock, then make an exposed move down to the summit boulders at the top of **Pete's Farewell**.

History: The letters "PF" in the name are the initials of

Tripping Karen

In the autumn of 1979, I climbed the crack system directly above the first pitch belay on Pete's Farewell with my college buddy Mark Arsenault. After we completed the pitch, we hopped across the small chasm formed by the cave, coiled the ropes, and started walking down. Just seconds later, I slipped on a mossy slab and fell off the cliff directly over the finish of Pete's Farewell (how ironic). I landed on the outside corner of the small ledge where the cave route and Pete's join, broke one ankle, then, with arms swinging wildly for balance, I toppled onto the ledge instead of off into space. Mark assumed I had gone to the talus and continued hiking down the trail. He wasn't even going to go to the bottom of the cliff to check my body, but rather he planned to continue into town and report my death. He told me later that when I yelled up to him, he nearly wet his pants. Alan Jolley happened to be at the bottom of the cliff, and he quickly soloed up through the cave, and, with a rope dropped from above by Mark, they got me to the top of the cliff. With their help, I skidded on my butt down the trail, and Mark drove me to the hospital. The next day, in the cafeteria at Paul Smith's College, I intentionally tripped a pretty dark-haired girl with my left crutch. (I had no idea how to meet women.) She fell to the floor with her tray, scattering plates and silverware everywhere, got up, yelled at me, and stomped off. We celebrated our 25th anniversary in October 2007.

- S. Peter Lewis

the route Pete's Farewell, and "flyers" for all the falls being taken; the name PF Flyers started the theme for naming routes after the canvas sneakers popular in the 1950s and 1960s. (The "PF" in the brand name stands for "posture foundation," an insert that made the shoes more comfortable to wear.)
FA Jun, 1981, Don Mellor, Bob Bushart

28 Hidden Constellation 5.11d G 100' ★★★★

A testpiece of climbing thin RP seams. The route is named for the constellation of little crystals in the face that were hidden under the lichen.

Start: At the P1 belay on Pete's Farewell.

P1 5.11d G: Traverse left to an overlap with a short right-facing corner. Climb up the corner and thin crack above to a horizontal. Very thin seams and crimpy edges lead up the face to the next horizontal. Hand-traverse right 10', up to the next horizontal, then up the thin crack to the top. Climb right to the fixed anchor of Disputed. 100'

History: The top bit was climbed earlier by Mellor (Map 16, 1985) by traversing right in a horizontal from the P2 belay on Pete's Farewell.

FA (traversing in from Pete's Farewell) May 25, 1984, Don Mellor, Bill Dodd, Jim Cunningham
FA (complete) May 17, 1985, Don Mellor

29 Star Sailor 5.10c G 60' ★★★

Another gem of steep crack climbing. Mellor took the name, another term for astronaut, from Tom Wolfe's 1979 book *The Right Stuff.*

Start: At the P1 belay on Pete's Farewell.

P1 5.10c G: Traverse left a few feet, then up the face to gain a fingercrack that starts at the right end of a small overlap. Follow the discontinuous crack past a bulge (crux) to the top. Step right to the fixed anchor of Disputed. 60'
FA Apr, 1981, Don Mellor

30 The Disputed (aka Tripping Karen) 5.8 G 60' ★★

An often-overlooked crack, perhaps because it is short. There was a conflict over the first ascent of the route, hence the name.

Start: At the P1 belay on Pete's Farewell.

P1 5.8 G: Climb directly up from the belay to gain a handcrack just left of the arête. Follow the crack through some blocks to a fixed anchor. 60'
FA Oct, 1979, S. Peter Lewis, Mark Arsenault

Great Chimney Area

The Great Chimney Area includes all the routes right of (and including) the Great Chimney. There are many routes in this section, squeezed into the befuddling agglomerate of roofs and corners, all located above an unpleasant jumble of wet, mossy boulders.

Despite the number of routes, all but one route begins at Pete's Farewell. On the approach trail, take the right fork to meet the cliff at the orange overhangs. Walk right along the cliff to another fork and take the high path up a gravelly chimney to the ledge that runs above the Practice Wall. Be careful not to knock debris onto the slab below (the Practice Wall).

Alternatively, you can walk below the Practice Wall (by taking the low path at the second fork) to the wet area below the routes. Scramble up and left to reach the start of Pete's Farewell.

31 Great Chimney 5.6 G 200' ★★★

A historic route and a worthwhile adventure. Climbing (or descending) this chimney gives you an appreciation for the structure of this cliff. The outside face of the cliff is nothing more than a giant flake separated from the main body of the mountain. Once you're in the back of the chimney, there is a hole (aka "the drainpipe") that leads farther into the mountain, but this is more of a caving experience.

Start: Same as Pete's Farewell.

P1 5.6 G: Boulder up the left side of a short wall to a ledge, then scramble up to the base of the huge chimney in the deep right-facing corner. Climb up the corner past chockstones (crux) and into the chimney to a fixed anchor on the right wall (used for descent). 80'

P2 5.5 G: (V1, V2) Scramble over blocks (3rd-class) to a thin vertical crack on the outside (road-side) wall. Stem up the chimney to a notch in the outside wall. Step left to the fixed anchor on The Disputed. 60'

*Jeremy Haas on P2 of **Brrright Star** (5.9+), belayed by Colin Loher. Photo by Bill Sprengnether.*

P3 5.2 G: Step back to the notch, then up the stepped wall to its top. Continue along the ridge of the fin to a short drop, then downclimb it to the summit boulders near the top of **Pete's Farewell**. 60'

V1 3rd class: Scramble over blocks (3rd-class) to the opposite end of the chimney and corkscrew through a constriction to emerge in the summit boulders near the top of **Pete's Farewell**. This is generally used as a downclimb.

V2 Another Crack 5.9 G: On the outside wall opposite the fixed anchor is a fingercrack. Climb up the crack to the giant chockstone, then hand-traverse right (crux) to a notch on the ridge. Step left to the fixed anchor on **The Disputed**.

History: At one time, there was a boulder pile that you could scramble up to enter the chimney with no technical climbing. The top boulder looked a little unsafe, so, in 1979, some local climbers kicked it off, but it got stuck farther down the pile, forcing more boulders to be pushed off. Pretty soon there were no more boulders, and now it's 5.6. The chimney became a popular route for local climbers of that period—Dave Bernays, Stanley Smith, and Tommy Condon. As Condon recalls, they referred to climbing as "running up and down 'em."

FA Jul 16, 1949, Fritz Wiessner, Jim Goodwin
FA (V2) Sep, 1987, Patrick Purcell, Mary Purcell

32 Crack Mechanic (aka The Porcelain Mechanic) 5.11d G 100' ★★★

Excellent thin-crack climbing.

Start: Same as **Pete's Farewell**.

P1 5.1dc G: Begin as for **Great Chimney,** and scramble to a ledge on top of a block (the center of this block forms the offwidth of **Coffee Achievers**). Move up a shallow left-facing corner to its top below an overhang. Over this (bolt) to a sidepull, then up to a good horizontal at an overhang. Finish up the fingercrack (5.8) to the top. 100'

History: The original route climbed **Coffee Achievers** to the bolt, then stepped left to a thin crack. Recently Don Mellor straightened the line, which was subsequently freed by Colin Loher.

FA (original route) Jul 1, 1986, Patrick Purcell
FA (as described) Sep 10, 2009, Colin Loher

33 Coffee Achievers 5.10b G 100' ★★★★

This excellent route climbs the back wall of the depression right of the **Great Chimney**. The obvious feature to look for is the short off-width crack 30' up. (If you don't have a 3" cam, you can avoid the off width by traversing in from higher in the chimney.) The name comes from a bizarre, short-lived ad campaign run in the early 1980s with images of such celebrities as David Bowie and Kurt Vonnegut and a voice-over that said, "Coffee gives you the serenity to dream it, and the vitality to do it. Join the Coffee Achievers."

Start: Same as **Pete's Farewell**.

P1 5.10b G: Boulder up the left side of a short wall to a ledge, then scramble up ledges to below the off-width crack. Up the off width, then step right to a shallow left-facing corner; up this to a ledge, then up to an overlap (bolt). Climb past the overlap on the right (crux), up a discontinuous crack in the left-facing corners to a big horizontal at an overhang, then up the handcrack to the fixed anchor. 100'

Gear: To 3".

FA May 11, 1985, Don Mellor, Mike Heintz

*Emilie Drinkwater on **Star Sailor** (5.10b). Photo by Tomás Donoso.*

34 Wild Man from Borneo 5.10b PG 130'

Wild moves through the roofs will have you swinging like an orangutan.

Start: Same as Pete's Farewell.

P1 5.10b PG: Boulder up the left side of a short wall to a ledge, then scramble up and right on ledges to the large, blocky left-facing corner (the large corner that faces the chimney). Climb up the corner to the roof (level with the base of the off width of Coffee Achievers), around the roof, and into the upper corner. Up the corner to a break in the arête, make a long reach to a jug on the arête, swing around onto the face, and make another long reach right to the belay ledge (shared with Brrright Star). 80'

P2 5.6 G: Same as P2 of Brrright Star: climb up a crack, then up a face, aiming up and left to a wide slot through the headwall. 50'

Descent: Rappel from the Coffee Achievers fixed anchor, just left of the finish crack.

FA Jun 13, 1984, Patrick Purcell

35 Upright and Locked 5.10c R 120'

Originally reported as Early Morning Riser.

Start: Same as Pete's Farwell.

P1 5.10c R: Boulder up the left side of a short wall to a ledge, then scramble up and right on ledges to the large, blocky left-facing corner (the large corner that faces the chimney). Climb up the corner to the roof (level with the base of the off width of Coffee Achievers), then move out right on the right wall of the corner (bolt) to an arête. Pull through using a finger slot and up to the belay ledge (shared with Brrright Star). 70'

P2 5.6 G: Same as P2 of Brrright Star: climb up a crack, then up a face, aiming up and left to a wide slot through the headwall. 50'

Descent: Rappel from the Coffee Achievers fixed anchor, just left of the finish crack.

FA 1990, Patrick Purcell, Dominic Eisinger

36 Brrright Star 5.9+ G 170' ★★★★

An excellent route and a test of one's endurance and footwork. It is so much better than it looks from below. The route was named for Kathy Bright, Jolley's girlfriend at the time; it has three r's because the first ascent was brrrr . . . cold.

Start: Same as Rugosity.

P1 5.8 G: Same as P1 of Rugosity: up the chimney to a ceiling, then a short hand traverse right leads to an awkward (but well-protected) move onto the ledge. 40'

P2 5.9+ G: A real pumper. Head out left from the belay and make a left-rising finger traverse below a ceiling. After 15', move up (crux) into a corner with a small rest stance. Continue in the left-rising crack hand-traversing straight left (2" and 3" cams helpful) to its end. The original belay ledge fell off in the fall of 2013, so an awkward hanging belay is probably the best solution (although you can also run the pitches together). 80'

P3 5.8 PG: From the hanging belay, climb up a crack, then up a face, aiming up and left to a wide slot through the headwall. 50'

Descent: Rappel from the Coffee Achievers fixed anchor, just left of the finish crack.

Gear: A 3.5" cam for P1, then doubles to 2".

FA (5.6 A2) Nov 14, 1982, Chuck Turner, Alan Jolley
FFA 1983, Chuck Turner, Alan Jolley

37 Space Race 5.11b G 120' ★★★★

Good climbing, although dirty.

Start: Same as Rugosity.

P1 5.11b G: Climb up the Rugosity chimney until it is possible to traverse left onto the face under an overhang to its left end. Over this (bolt) and into a shallow left-facing corner. Up the corner past a horizontal at the top to the fingercrack in the left-rising ceiling of Brrright Star (optional hanging belay). Make a big move to a jug on the arête of the left-rising ceiling and swing around onto the face (bolt) and up to belay in a horizontal crack. 80'

P2 5.8 PG: Same as P2 of Bogeyman (which traverses in from the left): climb the cleaned face straight up to a fixed anchor at the top. 40'

History: The roof was climbed earlier by Purcell and Eisinger and called Domineerance.

FA (roof and P2) 1990, Patrick Purcell, Dominic Eisinger
FA (P1) Jun 10, 1991, Don Mellor, Bill Dodd, Jeff Edwards

38 Rugosity 5.8+ R 120'

In the right light, the upper right side of Pitchoff—the slab covered in lichen and green moss—appears wrinkled, hence the name. P1 gets considerable traffic, as it is used to access three other routes. A cleaner finish for this route is P2 of Bogeyman.

Start: At the base of a chimney on the left side of the tower of blocks that rises from the ground and reaches up to the lower right end of the long left-rising ceiling. The best way to get here is to start as for Pete's Farewell, boulder up the slab, then walk right on a vegetated ledge, stepping down across some water and over to the base of the chimney.

P1 5.8+ G: Up the chimney to a ceiling, then a short hand traverse right leads to an awkward (but well-protected) move onto the ledge. 40'

P2 5.8 R: From the topmost boulder on the belay ledge, traverse right 20' across several horizontals, then up to gain a left-rising ledge and crack. Follow this up and left to a grassy ledge with a small birch, then angle up and right on green rock past two good horizontals to the top. 80'

FA 1976, Grant Calder, John Wald

39 Bogosity (linkup) 5.8+ G 120' ★★★★

This linkup is not obvious but worthy of mention as a separate route. It climbs P1 of Rugosity, then P2 of Bogeyman.

Start: Same as Rugosity.

P1 5.8+ G: Same as Rugosity P1. 40'

P2 5.8 G: Same as Bogeyman P2. 80'

40 Etiquette 5.6 G 30'

Start: From the wet vegetated area beneath the Great Chimney, walk right through the woods for 80' to a smooth face on a small buttress that defines the left side of a gully. This route starts on the left side of the buttress, 3' right of a right-facing corner.

P1 5.6 G: Climb the clean crack with good jams to the top of the buttress. 30'

FA Jun 13, 1994, David Lent

41 Rules 5.9 R 30'

This short route is a bit contrived, in that it requires strict avoidance of the crack to the left and the arête to the right.

Start: 2' right of Etiquette at a horizontal crack with a pocket 6' up.

P1 5.9 R: Climb past the pocket to another horizontal break at a small overlap, then up a bulge to the top of the block. 30'

FA Jun 15, 1994, David Lent

42 Bogeyman 5.8 G 160'

A poor start, but interesting chimney and chockstone climbing once you get started. P2 is recommended and can be reached in a straightforward manner by climbing P1 of Rugosity. Watch the flake on P2 next to the first bolt!

Start: From the wet vegetated area beneath the Great Chimney, walk right through the woods for 100' to a gully capped by broken roofs. This is the gully on the right side of the small buttress with the route Rules and Etiquette. Scramble up the wet, unpleasant gully, then left onto blocks on top of Rules and below an obvious break in the roof above.

P1 5.5 G: Climb up lichen-covered rock into a big block-filled chimney-cave and emerge onto a belay ledge on top of the tower (shared with Rugosity). 80'

P2 5.8 G: From the topmost boulder on the belay, work up and left to a bolt, then up to a large horizontal. Traverse left, then go straight up the face to a fixed anchor. 80'

FA 1990, Dominic Eisinger, Patrick Purcell

The Girdles

Every superdeveloped climbing area has one or two girdle traverses, and Pitchoff is no exception. There's a high traverse, which climbs from right to left (Crosstown Traffic), and a low traverse, which climbs from left to right (Low Plains Drifter). Jim Cunningham also created Big Bubble, which makes nearly a complete circle by climbing The Silk Road, then continues on Crosstown Traffic.

43 Crosstown Traffic 5.9 PG 260' ★

Named for a Jimi Hendrix song from the 1968 album *Electric Ladyland.*

Route Description: Climb P1 of Pete's Farewell, then up the crack of The Disputed to a stance on some blocks. Follow the horizontal crack (the one at the top of Star Sailor) leftward, past Hidden Constellation, PF Flyers, and Eurotech, eventually reaching the block on Pete's Farewell. Continue in the same horizontal around the left-facing corner of The El and under the ceiling, then left across some really dirty rock to cross under the final bulge of Wald-Calder Route, and finally reaching the grass near the top of Rainy Night Road Toads.

FA May 25, 1984, Jim Cunningham, Bill Dodd, Rich Leswing

44 Low Plains Drifter 5.9 PG 520'

Start by climbing Uncontrollable Desires to the finger-crack 3' right of the off width. From here, traverse right in a horizontal, crossing Rock and Roll Star, and under the ceiling of Roaches on the Wall. Continue under the ceiling to link with Wald-Calder Route at the top of the left-facing flake. Follow the traverse on Wald-Calder Route to the P1 belay and continue straight right to the belay on The El. Reverse the traverse on The El back to the P1 belay of Pete's Farewell, then slip around the corner and into the Great Chimney. Downclimb to the wet ledges at the base of the chimney and traverse right to the base of the Rugosity chimney and climb that route's P1 to the top of the tower.

45 The Silk Road 5.9 PG 240' ★★★

Perhaps the best traversing linkup on the cliff. Climb P1 of Wald-Calder Route, continue right to the belay on The El, reverse the traverse on The El, then finish up on The Disputed.

GRAND VIEW CLIFF

Location	North side of NY 73 in Cascade Pass, above Lower Cascade Lake
Aspect	Southeast
Height	90'
Quality	★
Approach	25 min, moderate
Summary	Clean, black slab with four low-angle crack routes; somewhat difficult to reach.

-5.6	5.7	5.8	5.9	5.10	5.11	5.12	5.13+	total
2	1		1					4

The mountainside above Pitchoff Chimney Cliff is peppered with small slabs and cliffs, mostly dirty and uninspiring. The Grand View Cliff is an exception. It rises above a steep, open slope with great views, even from the base. The rock is black and waterstreaked, and thus naturally clean. The routes follow cracks in the slab, some cleaner than others.

HISTORY

R.L. Stolz first visited the cliff with Christina Biaggi in the late 1980s to climb ice, then forgot about it for 25 years. Starting in 2012, he made several visits to establish these rock routes. He named the cliff after a hospital in PA, but it fits, as the cliff has good views.

DIRECTIONS (MAP PAGE 353)

The parking for Grand View Cliff is located on NY 73, 4.8 miles from Keene (measured from the intersection of NY 73 and NY 9N) and 9.3 miles from Lake Placid (measured from the intersection of NY 73 and NY 86). It is located below the right end of Pitchoff Chimney Cliff, and there's an information placard entitled "Natural Forces that Shape the Adirondacks" 590852,4898874.

The cliff isn't far from the road, but the terrain is steep and loose, and there is no trail. Direct access is blocked by a wide slab that you must go around. The hiking path begins across the road from the Lake Placid end of the pullout (0 hr 0 min). Hike uphill to the cliff (this is the popular ice climbing area known as Pitchoff Right, and is really just the far right end of the Pitchoff Chimney Cliff). Walk right along the base of the cliff to its right end, then go straight uphill to a wide, 40'-tall slab at 10 min. Walk left along the base, and around the left end of the slab 590735,4898945. Once above the wide slab, contour right (and gently uphill) for 600', past two minor slabs to reach the open area below the main slab 590786,4899108 at 25 min. Scramble up some grassy, low-angle slabs to reach a comfortable, 2'-deep, left-rising ledge below the main slab where the routes begin. The low point on the slab (and the right end of the left-rising ledge) is the route **Withheld Pay**.

1 Wandering and Pondering 5.9- R 85' ★★

Start: 6' left of the prominent full-height crack **Pink Dayglo Tootsie** at a waist-high, 8"-wide horizontal hold below a thin seam.

P1 5.9- R: Go up the thin seam with no protection to reach a fingercrack 16' up. Follow this to its top, then up a slab with knobs trending right to the top. 85'

FA Jul 5, 2012, R.L. Stolz, Nancy Schwartz

Colin O'Connor on the first ascent of **Aquaman** *(5.10a).*

2 Pink Dayglo Tootsies 5.7+ G 90' ★

Start: 20' up and left from the low point of the terrain, below a prominent full-height crack.

P1 5.7+ G: Up the crack to a shallow right-facing corner. Up the corner to its top, then follow a left-leaning, grass-filled crack to the top. 90'

FA Jul 5, 2012, R.L. Stolz, Nancy Schwartz

3 Withheld Pay 5.6 G 95' ★

Start: At the low point of the terrain and the right end of the 2'-deep left-rising ledge, below a full-height crack in a shallow, left-facing corner.

P1 5.6 G: Up the crack in the shallow corner to a small overlap 30' up. Go past some bushes, then up a wider crack to the top. 95'

FA Jul 5, 2012, R.L. Stolz, Nancy Schwartz

4 Jonah Rocks 5.6 TR 90'

Begin uphill and right of **Withheld Pay** at a seam system that breaks the face. Follow the seams to where they disappear, move right 4' and climb a good crack to the top.

FA (TR) Jul 12, 2013, David Shiling

FERN CUBBY

Location	South side of NY 73 in Cascade Pass
Aspect	South
Height	70'
Quality	★
Approach	25 min, moderate
Summary	Small, hidden wall with great views and a good, unique, short route.

-5.6	5.7	5.8	5.9	5.10	5.11	5.12	5.13+	total
1				1				2

This cliff is situated on the ridge across the road above Lower Cascade Lake, but is completely hidden in a small, narrow valley. There are some low-angle slabs and some steeper sections, and a very pretty summit with great views of Pitchoff Chimney Cliff. The gem is the bulging wall on the left end, which is short, steep, and littered with some of the most unusual holds around. The cliff base is open woods with a small stream, and pretty ferns.

HISTORY

The cliff was visited by Jim Lawyer and Tom Yandon in 2013, having discovered it using online resources (Bing's "birds-eye" view).

DIRECTIONS (MAP PAGE 353)

Park as for The Nursery and follow the approach to that cliff. Cross the first seasonal stream and locate the second one. Follow this uphill. The stream disappears, then emerges again, and is braided all over the slope. Persevere, and eventually walk into a narrow, fern-covered valley. The cliff will be on your left 591097,4898626.

1 Aquaman 5.10a G 35' ★★★

Amazing holds, very unlike the Adirondacks, and despite appearances, they are quite solid. Too bad it's not longer.

Start: On the far left end of the cliff is a short, bulging wall above a shallow pond. Use stepping stones to access the starting jugs above the middle of the pond.

● **P1 5.10a G:** Pull up on jugs, swing left, then straight up to the top of the bulging wall. 35'

FA May 31, 2013, Colin O'Connor, Jim Lawyer

2 Alter Weg 5.4 G 70' ★

Provides access to the fantastic summit area.

Start: 40' right of **Aquaman** at a prominent left-facing, right-leaning corner.

P1 5.4 G: Up the corner to a ledge. Continue up and right over ledges to the highest point on the cliff. 70'

History: The name means "Old Route" in German. The East German tradition (from which Fritz Wiessner emigrated) gives this name to the first or easiest route up a formation, which explains why many of the early routes in the Adirondacks are named "Old Route".

FA May 31, 2013, Jim Lawyer, Emi MacLeod, Colin O'Connor

THE NURSERY

Location	South side of NY 73 in Cascade Pass
Aspect	Southwest
Height	50'
Quality	★★
Approach	45 min, moderate
Summary	Small, hidden wall with several vertical fingercracks broken by horizontal cracks.

-5.6	5.7	5.8	5.9	5.10	5.11	5.12	5.13+	total
			1	1	1			3

This cliff sits high above Cascade Lake on the Cascade Mountain side, and has an off-vertical, sheer face split by a few vertical cracks and many horizontal cracks. The established routes are in a 50'-wide section of rock, but the cliff is about 150' wide overall. Good rock quality, great friction, and unlikely—but well-protected—routes. It's relatively pleasant and quiet, with good views from the top, but suffers from a base choked with trees that isn't flat (but not too bad). There's little potential for additional routes on this wall, but there's another wall about 250' left with potential for slab routes.

On the left end of the cliff is a short, 30'-tall chimney, and 40' right of this is a full-height offwidth crack. This offwidth crack is useful for locating the routes.

DIRECTIONS **(MAP PAGE 353)**

The parking for The Nursery is located on NY 73, 4.6 miles from Keene (measured from the intersection of NY 73 and NY 9N) and 9.5 miles from Lake Placid (measured from the intersection of NY 73 and NY 86). When driving from Keene, it is the last parking pullout on the left before the lakes; when driving from Lake Placid, it is the first parking on the right after the lakes 591179,4899031.

Drop down over the side of the parking and cross the outlet stream. Walk towards the lakes, angling uphill; stay away from the shoreline. If you're lucky, you'll find an old road bed that makes for fast walking. Continue through open woods on this roadbed, or just bushwhack, contouring along the hillside, past two seasonal streams (the second of these marks the approach for Fern Cubby), until you are past the Pitchoff Chimney Cliff (which you can easily see across the road), and just about even with the winter routes **Sisters Left** (this is the next cliff past the Pitchoff Chimney Cliff). You should intersect a more substantial stream; follow this uphill and through a notch 0590775,4898451. After this notch, the stream swings left away from the lake; follow it uphill until it dries up. Continue uphill in the same direction until the brook turns to boulders, then eventually talus. The cliff is on your left 0590967,4898253.

DESCENT OPTIONS

The established routes have fixed anchors not easily reachable from above. Above the routes, the cliff angles back and becomes chossy, and trees are way back. To access the top of the cliff, walk right.

1 No Ifs, Ands, or Bolts 5.10a G 40' ★★★

Start: 4' right of the full-height offwidth, starting just right of a good hold at head height,, is a 4'-high fingercrack.

P1 5.10a G: Mantel onto the starting hold, then climb discontinuous vertical cracks (with plenty of horizontal cracks for protection) to the top. Fixed anchor at the top. 40'

Gear: Finger-size cams, small to medium nuts, and a 2" cam.

FA May 18, 2013, Jim Lawyer, Simon Catterall

2 The Optimist 5.9+ G 40' ★★★

Super excellent fingercrack, great protection, great rock.

Start: 15' right of **No Ifs, Ands, or Bolts**, in the center of a horizontal crack at head height. Above the horizontal crack is a seam that widens to finger size, and runs the full height of the cliff.

P1 5.9+ G: Make a hard move to stand in the horizontal crack, place a critical #3 nut, then follow the stellar fingercrack (5.8) to the top. Scramble another 10' up and right to a fixed anchor. 40'

Gear: Nuts and cams to finger size, and a single 2" cam.

FA May 18, 2013, Jim Lawyer, Simon Catterall

3 Peter Croft and the Crime-Fighting Bear 5.11a G 40' ★★★

Continuously challenging climbing with a hard—but well-protected—opening move.

Start: 12' right of **The Optimist** at a small, rounded ledge 4' up.

P1 5.11a G: Stand on ledge, then make a hard move using a lone flared pocket to reach a horizontal crack (crux, bolt). Go straight up the face to the top. Angle left to a fixed anchor shared with **The Optimist**. 40'

Gear: Finger-size cams and nuts.

FA May 18, 2013, Jim Lawyer, Simon Catterall

BETWEEN THE LAKES

Location	Off NY 73 in Cascade Pass, above Lower Cascade Lake
Summary	Several historically-interesting cliffs, but disappointingly overgrown.

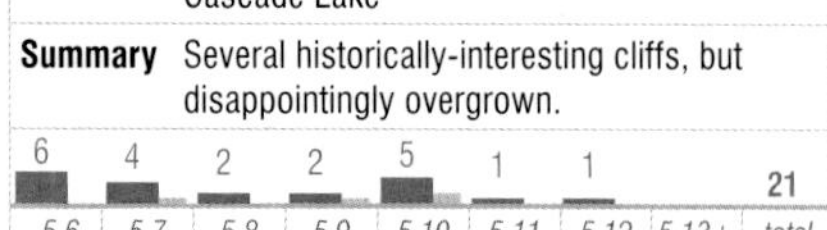

These cliffs are situated above Cascade Lakes and approached from the picnic area on NY 73 between the Upper and Lower Cascade Lakes 589822,4897553. Once the site of a hotel called the Cascade House, today there are several picnic tables, ample parking, an outhouse, and good swimming. Walking south to the Upper Cascade Lake, you can observe the entire right end of Cascade Cliff, rising above jumbled talus on the lakeshore. Left of Cascade Cliff you can just make out the smooth black wall broken by a roof at midheight; this is the Jaws Wall. Walking north to the Lower Cascade Lake, you can see the UFO Wall poking through the trees on the hillside above the lake.

DIRECTIONS **(MAP PAGE 353)**

There is a small unmarked road that accesses the picnic area and parking for the cliffs around the Cascade Lakes, 8.3 miles from Lake Placid on the right (from the intersection of NY 86 and NY 73) and 5.8 miles from Keene on the left (from the center of town where NY 73 and NY 9N split). When you drive from Keene, the left turn is extremely sharp.

Between the Lakes

JAWS WALL

Location	South side of NY 73 in Cascade Pass, above Lower Cascade Lake
Aspect	Northwest
Height	150'
Quality	
Approach	25 min, moderate
Summary	An overgrown cliff with a single overgrown route.

This wall is located left of Cascade Cliff, separated from that cliff by a steep gully. In the winter, the cliff is a playground covered by a veneer of delicious ice. In the summer, this north-facing cliff becomes a vertical jungle of seepage and verdure. The exception is the excellent face that leads to the big roof, the central feature of the cliff.

DIRECTIONS **(MAP PAGE 353)**

Scramble along the base of Cascade Cliff to its left end. Go up a gully about 200' (as if approaching Fig Fuckin' Newton), then contour left to the base of the next cliff. Continue left along the base of this cliff to a section of black rock beneath prominent roofs 70' up 590312,4897803. This is the route Teeth, and there are a number of large sharp-edged talus boulders at the base, about 7 min from Cascade Cliff.

1 Teeth 5.8 PG 150'

Somewhat dirty and often wet, this route climbs the line of the winter route Jaws.

Start: At a slab with a thin right-leaning seam that leads to the roof, where it is double-tiered.

P1 5.8 PG: Climb the black slab on good edges following a right-leaning seam to meet the roof at the right end of the double-tiered section. Pull through the roof on jugs into a left-facing corner, then up a heavily vegetated right-leaning crack to the top. 150'

FA 1976, Todd Eastman, Chris Hyson

Between the Lakes

CASCADE CLIFF

Location	South side of NY 73 in Cascade Pass, above Lower Cascade Lake
Aspect	Northwest
Height	300'
Quality	
Approach	15 min, moderate
Summary	A historically interesting cliff, but, with a few notable exceptions, the routes are mostly overgrown and unappealing moderates.

-5.6	5.7	5.8	5.9	5.10	5.11	5.12	5.13+	total
6	3		1	2	1	1		14

Cascade Cliff is perhaps one of the more visible cliffs in the Adirondacks, as it sits above Lower Cascade Lake at eye level from NY 73 as you travel between Keene and Lake Placid. Despite its proximity to the road, the cliff, with plenty of vegetation-chocked cracks and loose rock, is seldom visited. There are a few worthwhile routes, and a good adventure can be found for those willing to wander to seek out the better pitches.

Once you leave the rather civilized picnic area between the lakes, the terrain immediately takes on an adventuresome feel, with large talus boulders chocked with heavy vegetation. During the winter, the falling ice kills all the trees, making room for leafy head-high saplings that are sloped downward at an inconvenient angle, making foot travel along the base absurdly difficult. The starts of the routes are marked by corners and cracks that are filled to capacity with trees and bushes, so much so that they are nearly undetectable. Allow extra time to find your route, and be prepared to thrash.

The cliff has a few major features, the most obvious being the large right-facing, right-leaning orange corner at the left end; the routes Lichen Delight, Atmospheric Pressure, Super Cell, and Kirby Corner are all located on this corner. Left of the corner and at the upper left end of the cliff is a large expanse of rock with the route Fig Fuckin' Newton. Right of the Lichen Delight corner are a number of right-leaning faults—cracks, chimneys, and corners—often filled with trees. Undoubtedly these would be great rock routes if every bit of vegetation disappeared, but instead, they are an arduous mixture of tree pulling and dirty climbing; Trundle Fodder and Malarkey Direct climb through this terrain. Right of these leaning faults is a large over-

Tom Rosecrans Recollections

My first belay test was with a seventy-five pound cement block that was hoisted into a tree near the Adirondack Loj. I had on leather gloves, to better hold the Goldline rope looped around my back. No harnesses, no belay devices; just a bit of friction, perhaps too much friction, across my lower back. That weekend I became an Adirondack climber, and Mount Jo was the scene of my first climbs.

Shortly after, I met Trudy Healy who knew a great deal about Adirondack climbing, and in fact was a guidebook author. She introduced me to Ken, a transplanted Englishman, who, as a state Health Department Director, had the job of testing the lead content in beer. Beer cans use to have soldered seams back then. Ken and I visited the few developed Adirondack crags, and noticed huge amounts of lichen-encrusted, unclimbed rock. In our travels we discovered a few mistakes in Trudy's guide—notably a picture of Wallface printed backwards. When I asked her about it she countered by saying that perhaps I could do a better job. She followed up that challenge with an invitation to stay at her family's summer home in Keene, so we could do "climbing research" together.

Trudy's guidebook was my invitation to Adirondack climbing. I wore the cover off that little blue guidebook, which I still have. How many people can say their first real climbing partner was a middle-aged mother of four? She passed the authorial responsibility to me, and my guidebook was published in 1976. I last saw Trudy in the late seventies. I still remember sitting on her deck after a great day at an Adirondack crag, watching the afternoon storms roll over the Great Range.

A year after my summer with Trudy, I began student teaching in Saratoga, and it was here I met Joe Szot, a scrawny 9th grader with a broken arm. We discovered a mutual interest in climbing, and over the next 30 years we climbed all over the US and Canada. He seemed oblivious to hardship, setting off on a three-day climbing trip with nothing but a box of sugar donuts and three packets of Kool-Aid. We shared bivys on the Diamond, and thunder snow in the Wind Rivers. He was stubborn and single-minded; he knew what he liked, and he liked what he knew. He moved to Keeseville, and his Memorial Day parties became the stuff of legends.

Joe embodied what I call the Adirondack spirit—bigger than life, powerful, more than a little wild. When he climbed, you got the feeling he was punishing the rock. It wasn't so much a dance as it was a wrestling match. You had to work when you were with Joe. Work to keep up, work to step it up: the easy way out wasn't an option. He called your bluffs. He sniffed out phonies. He dared you to be a better person. We always laughed a lot when we climbed together—he had a distinctive laugh, a full-body laugh.

He introduced me to an engineer from up that way. Dennis Luther and I shared many Adirondack climbs but I most remember the drives across the country for bigger prizes. I liked climbing with Dennis in the big mountains; he was careful and fast. However, Dennis was a sucker for left gear, and once delighted in freeing a fixed nut, while I fumed at the belay with electricity crackling around me. Another time, we spotted a tent, that had blown off the Bugaboo-Snowpatch col, roll down the glacier, and into a crevasse. As we approached the "booty" a helicopter landed near us and one of the passengers hopped out and approached. "Have you guys seen a tent?" he asked. I let my partner deal with his internal struggle, but I was happy when he said "yes".

Dennis Luther was the "anti-Szot". He was deliberate and analytical. The last time I climbed with Dennis and Joe was when Jim Lawyer was doing climbing research, trying to resurrect an old, obscure climb of mine on the Emperor Slab. Dennis and Joe were just "adventure climbing"—no particular route, just climbing. We could hear them at the belays, bantering back and forth—Joe giving it to Dennis—Dennis giving it back.

I sure do miss those days. I sure do miss those people.

- Tom Rosecrans

Pyramid Shield

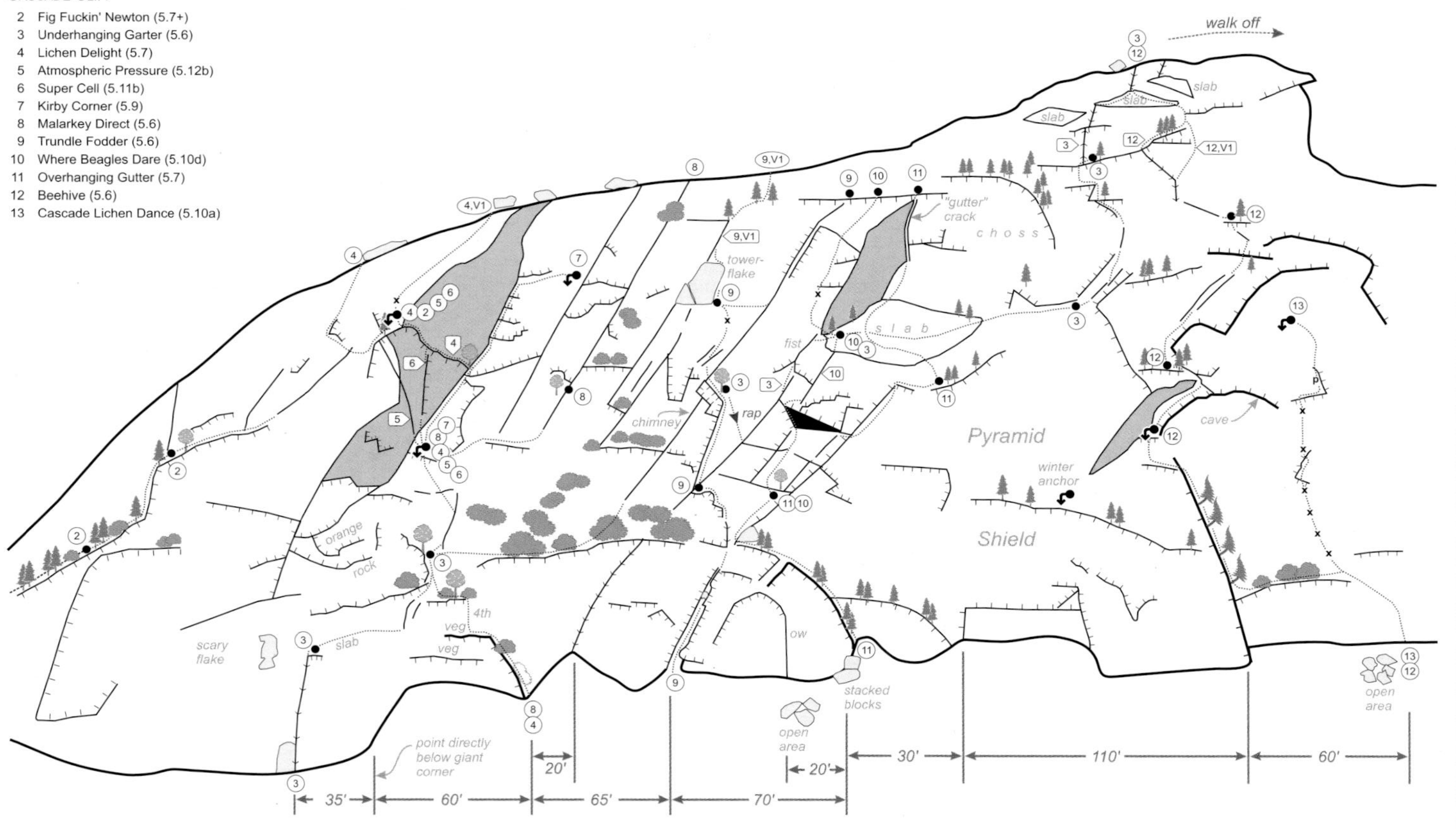
CASCADE CLIFF
2 Fig Fuckin' Newton (5.7+)
3 Underhanging Garter (5.6)
4 Lichen Delight (5.7)
5 Atmospheric Pressure (5.12b)
6 Super Cell (5.11b)
7 Kirby Corner (5.9)
8 Malarkey Direct (5.6)
9 Trundle Fodder (5.6)
10 Where Beagles Dare (5.10d)
11 Overhanging Gutter (5.7)
12 Beehive (5.6)
13 Cascade Lichen Dance (5.10a)
walk off
slab
slab
slab
12,V1
4,V1
9,V1
9,V1
tower-flake
"gutter" crack
choss
slab
fist
rap
chimney
cave
Pyramid
winter anchor
Shield
orange rock
4th
veg
veg
slab
scary flake
ow
stacked blocks
open area
open area
point directly below giant corner
35'
60'
20'
65'
70'
20'
30'
110'
60'

hanging right-leaning wall that rises above a slab, below which is a distinctive triangular roof. Several routes climb these features, such as **Where Beagles Dare** and **Overhanging Gutter**. To the right is a huge triangular section of cliff known as the Pyramid Shield with no summer routes; **Beehive** roughly follows the right edge of this feature. Last, at the right end of the cliff is a vertical strip of white polka dots, the route **Cascade Lichen Dance**.

HISTORY

The cliff is somewhat shrouded in mystery, as many first-ascent parties have reported finding pitons, runners on trees, and other signs of earlier climbers. The earliest reported climbing was in 1949 by Stanley Smith, Donald Lebeau, and Dave Bernays, high school boys from Saranac Lake. By looking at photos in magazines, they made their own pitons and practiced their placement on local cliffs, such as the Charcoal Kiln Quarry at Paul Smiths. In the true spirit of adventure, they took their skills to the larger cliffs, such as Cascade Cliff where they climbed **Beehive** and **Overhanging Gutter**.

Sixteen years later, members of the Penn State Outing Club came on the scene, around the time that Trudy Healy was working on her first guidebook, free climbing **Overhanging Gutter** and **Beehive**. Ten years after that, John Wald and Grant Calder made their mark with **Lichen Delight** and **Malarkey Direct**, and the indefatigable Tom Rosecrans climbed **Underhanging Garter** and **Trundle Fodder** (around the time of his guidebook). Rosecrans reported clean rock and interesting routes; it is possible that the cliff is finally recovering from the fires of the early 1900s that scoured the area of vegetation.

Staying with the "new route every 10 years" theme, Purcell took an interest in the late 1980s and climbed several routes, including one of Cascade Pass's most difficult pitches, **Atmospheric Pressure**. The latest addition is from local guide Jesse Williams with **Cascade Lichen Dance**, climbed in 2001.

DIRECTIONS (MAP PAGE 353)

From the picnic area between the Upper and Lower Cascade Lakes, walk across a wood bridge toward the cliffs, then head toward the shoreline and pick up a fishermen's path that parallels the shoreline. The path quickly fades, at which point simply head uphill through the talus to the base of the cliff at its right end 590142,4897611. The talus is heavily vegetated; if you're lucky, you'll find a section of open talus that leads to the arched roofs at the right end of the cliff.

2 Fig Fuckin' Newton 5.7+ X 280'

This route climbs the right-rising crack on the upper left shield on the cliff. P2 features loose rock, scant protection, and danger for the leader as well as the follower.

Start: Walk to the left end of the cliff, then scramble easily up the gully. Break right onto the lowest ribbon of vegetation and traverse right to a tree belay.

P1 5.5 PG: Continue traversing to the end of the ribbon of vegetation (awful 4th-class), then climb a shallow, broken left-facing corner to a ledge with a cedar below a vertical crack. 90'

P2 5.7+ X: Traverse right on the ledge to its right end, then follow a right-rising crack until it fades into the slab. Step right to a left-facing corner, then up right to a ledge (the top of P2 of **Lichen Delight**). 190'

FA Jun 3, 1989, Patrick Purcell, Jeff Edwards

3 Underhanging Garter 5.6 PG 625'

A wandering line that is just short of a girdle. The name is a play on the name **Overhanging Gutter**.

Start: 35' left of a point directly below the large right-facing, right-leaning corner, directly below a V-groove that leads up to orange, overhanging, shattered rock, at a 10'-high right-facing corner formed by a block. On the left wall of the V-groove is a large, scary-looking perched flake.

P1: Climb the V-groove to its top, exiting right to a sloped stance. 50'

P2: Traverse right beneath a roof, then beneath a headwall to a vertical crack. Up the crack to a slab, then up to a right-facing alcove with a birch tree (on **Lichen Delight** P1). 85'

P3: Traverse right across a slab and into the thick forest. Continue traversing right along the tree ledge to a right-rising crack filled with trees and bushes. Pull and thrash up the right-leaning crack, then over cleaner rock past some overlaps to a niche—a sloped ledge with a birch in a right-facing corner (the same niche mentioned in P2 of **Trundle Fodder**). 110'

P4: Rappel down and right to a right-rising crack, then climb the crack through a ceiling and up a fistcrack to belay at the sloped slab (same as **Where Beagles Dare**). 85'

P5: Traverse the slab to the trees at its upper right end, then continue rightward (and slightly down) beneath a triangular ceiling to a belay 25' to its right below a shallow right-facing, right-leaning corner. 135'

P6: Climb a crack in the slab to the right of the right-leaning corner, then up the corner itself to a shrub. Continue up a crack to its top, then work up and left to a ledge with a single tree. Step right and climb a right-facing corner, exiting left to another ledge, then up to a large sloping ledge beneath a headwall. 120'

P7: Climb up the headwall to a ledge, step right and up a short groove in another headwall to a large triangular slab (the same slab as **Beehive** P4). At the height of the slab, climb a short corner to the trees. 40'

FA Oct, 1974, Tom Rosecrans, Ken Jackson

4 Lichen Delight 5.7 R 320' ★★★

The **Direct Finish** variation is recommended but runout.

Start: At a left-rising tree ramp that is 25' left of a right-rising tree-filled depression and 65' left of the right-leaning chimney of **Trundle Fodder**. This is at a position below and slightly right of the huge right-facing, right-leaning orange corner that dominates the upper section of the cliff here.

P1 5.3 G: Climb up and left, pulling on trees to a ledge. Step left and surmount another short wall by an exposed 4th-class pull on trees to gain another ledge, then move left to gain cleaner rock that leads up and left to a birch tree alcove. Step right and climb up a

short crack, then left to a fixed anchor at the base of the huge right-facing, right-leaning orange corner. 140'
P2 5.7 G: Continue up easy corner to a tree, then make an exposed left-rising traverse following a friable crack and ledge to an exposed perch on the arête with a fixed anchor (shared with **Atmospheric Pressure**). 100'
P3 5.7 R: (V1) From the left side of the ledge, down-climb the tree-filled left-facing corner. Friction left, then up to an overlap and left-facing flake. Unprotected friction leads to the top. 80'
V1 Direct Finish 5.9 R: From a pedestal on the ledge, climb up to a bolt, then progressively easier—but unprotected—climbing for 25' leads to some thin cracks (TCUs), which are followed to the top. If you don't like the protection, be advised that the first ascent didn't have the bolt. 80'
Gear: To 2".
Descent: Walk right 50' to a small cedar in some boulders. A 200' rappel takes you to the birch tree alcove on P1. A second rappel returns to the ground.
FA Aug 28, 1976, Grant Calder, John Wald
FA (V1) 1978, Bob Bushart, Bill Simes

5 Atmospheric Pressure 5.12b TR 85' ★★

This route climbs the amazing fingercrack on the overhanging left wall of the huge right-facing corner that splits the left side of the cliff. Expect some friable rock. It begins at the top of P1 of **Lichen Delight** and climbs to the ledge on the arête with a fixed anchor (the top of P2 of **Lichen Delight**). The lower section overhangs severely with first-knuckle laybacking. The climb is sustained, with a rest found near the arête after the final crux. Purcell was fascinated by weather at the time—a waterspout in Saranac Lake caused some damage, and his shed was struck by lightning and burned down. He named this route and **Super Cell** after weather terms.
FA (TR) Jun 30, 1987, Patrick Purcell

6 Super Cell 5.11b TR 70' ★

This route climbs the crack right of **Atmospheric Pressure**. Beginning at the same fixed anchor at the top of P1 of **Lichen Delight**, climb up the corner a few feet, then up the shallow left-facing corner to its top, then up the face to join the **Lichen Delight** P2 traverse.
FA (TR) 1992, Patrick Purcell, Joe Quackenbush

7 Kirby Corner 5.9 PG 90' ★

This route attempts to climb the major feature of the cliff—the right-facing, right-leaning orange corner. Unfortunately, the crack in the corner peters out before the top. The route was named by Purcell, who, in one of his "neat-freak" moods, was sold on the Kirby vacuum cleaner.
Start: At the top of P1 of **Lichen Delight**.
P1 5.9 PG: Climb the corner to the tree (the handrail out left is **Lichen Delight**). Continue up the corner past two overlaps to a bulge. Traverse right to a fixed anchor just shy of the right-leaning vegetated crack that splits the face. 90'
FA Jul 6, 1987, Patrick Purcell, Rich Leswing

8 Malarkey Direct 5.6 PG 240'

One of the more unappealing lines at Cascade Cliff. Makes an excellent winter route (known as **Early Bird Special**).
Start: At the top of P1 of **Lichen Delight**.
P1 5.4 PG: Climb up and right to a tree, then continue up and right to the left end of a vegetated ledge. Walk right to the right end of the ledge and climb a right-leaning vegetated crack to an alcove with a birch tree. 120'
P2 5.6 PG: Climb the right-leaning crack line to the top. Horribly vegetated and often wet. 120'
FA Aug 14, 1975, Grant Calder, John Wald

9 Trundle Fodder 5.6 PG 330'

Another direct route to the top, with an easy-to-find start. The name comes from an incident in which Jackson threw off a dangerous loose block, which bounced through the talus and shot out into the lake, nearly hitting two spectators in a canoe.
Start: One of the easier routes to find, as the start is distinctive—just left of a low 10'-wide roof, below a 4'-deep right-leaning chimney with a chockstone 25' up where the chimney narrows. This chimney is just right of a right-leaning, right-facing corner and 50' left of an open area with boulders at the base of the cliff.
P1 5.5 G: Up the chimney past the chockstone to some trees, then up and left following a left-leaning open book, then up and left to the base of a right-leaning corner. 110'
P2 5.6 PG: Climb up the corner (and face right of the corner) to its top, then step left to a niche with trees (the P3 belay for **Underhanging Gutter**). Step left from the niche and onto a thin slab, which is followed past a bolt to a sloped ledge at the base of a tower-flake. 120'
P3 5.5 G: (V1) Traverse right across the sloped ledge to a right-leaning vegetated wide crack and chimney, which is followed to a slab finish. 100'
V1 5.5 PG: Chimney to the top of the tower-flake, then follow a right-leaning dirty crack to the top.
History: The bolt preexisted the first ascent, so obviously this section had been climbed earlier.
FA 1975, Tom Rosecrans, Ken Jackson

10 Where Beagles Dare 5.10d G 210' ★★

A wonderfully clean upper buttress. Named after Purcell's beagle, Kato.
Start: At the top of P1 of **Overhanging Gutter**.
P1 5.8 G: Climb the slab to the triangular roof, break through on its left side, then step right above the roof to gain a right-leaning fingercrack, which is followed to a sloping slab bounded on its left side by a smooth, steep wall. 110'
P2 5.10d G: From the lower left end of the slab, step left and climb up to an overlap (bolt). Continue up the face past a left-rising horizontal crack to a slab, which is followed up to the trees. 100'
FA Jun, 1991, Patrick Purcell, Joe Quackenbush

11 Overhanging Gutter (aka Lady's Route) 5.7 PG 380'

The route is named for the final steep corner, dubbed the "gutter," the crux of the route, which had water dripping down (like a gutter) on the first ascent. On that first ascent, it was totally protected by slings around natural chockstones. Goodwin recalls climbing it again in the 1970s and finding that most of the chockstones were gone.

Start: In the center of the Pyramid Shield is a low roof, the left side of which has a right-facing orange corner. At the base of this corner is a left-rising tree ramp. 30' left of this, at the height of a cone-shaped slope, is another vague left-rising tree ramp that marks the start of this route. This is also 30' uphill and right of an open area with boulders at the base of the cliff.

P1 5.5 G: Climb the left-rising vegetated ramp, pulling trees and kicking steps in the sod, to the base of a large right-facing, right-leaning corner. Step out left onto the face and climb up to a break with a birch below a clean slab. The large triangular roof is directly above. 120'

P2 5.6 PG: Up rightward following a crack in the slab to the right end of the triangular roof and good horizontal. Step right, then follow a right-leaning, right-facing corner to where the angle becomes steep. Traverse right to a slab and sloped forest. 110'

P3 5.7 PG: Climb a 10'-high wall to gain a slab, bounded on its left by a large, smooth wall. Traverse left to the smooth wall, then work up and right to the "gutter," a steep vertical off-width crack. Up the gutter to the forested ledge. 150'

History: The general line of ascent was climbed in 1953 by Stanley Smith with Evelyn Comstock, his girlfriend and later wife (thus the name **Lady's Route**). The route was later climbed by a group led by Patterson, who found the remnants of Smith and Comstock's ascents.

FA 1953, Stanley Smith, Evelyn Comstock
FFA Jun, 1966, Craig Patterson, Dave Zimmerman, Tony Goodwin

12 Beehive 5.6 PG 420'

This historic route is largely overgrown with some loose rock, more of a mountaineering adventure than an exercise in aesthetic movement over stone.

Start: Same as **Cascade Lichen Dance**.

P1 5.3 G: Climb up and left on the slab to gain a sloped ledge. Walk left 50' across the ledge to the right-facing, left-leaning corner chocked with trees. Pull and thrash your way up the corner to its top, then climb up and left to a ledge at the base of a right-facing corner with a fixed anchor. 75'

P2 5.4 G: Climb up and right following a right-rising ramp in a right-leaning corner, pulling on cedars. At a position above the arching roofs, follow a left-leaning crack a few feet into a forest of trees. 75'

P3 5.6 PG: Climb up and left to gain a vegetated ramp that leads up and right. Follow the vegetation to two parallel right-leaning cracks that lead to a ceiling with orange lichen on the face below. Climb through the ceiling to a ledge, then up to another ledge with trees. 120'

P4 5.5 PG: Up and left on a slab following a line of vegetation to a large open book. Up the open book, then (V1) continue in a left-rising line to the right end of a large ledge below a headwall. Angle up and right through trees, then up a short wall onto a large triangular slab. At the height of the slab, climb a short corner to the trees. 150'

V1 Fugarwe 5.8 PG: Climb straight up to the right end of a ceiling, around this on its right end, then up and left to join the normal route onto the large triangular slab.

History: The line as described was climbed in 1965 by members of the Penn State Outing Club, who reported finding pitons. These were most likely the work of Stanley Smith and Donald Lebeau, who climbed the line several times using aid when necessary.

FA 1949, Stanley Smith, Donald Lebeau
FFA Sep, 1965, Al Breisch, Craig Patterson, Ronald Dubay
FA (V1) Aug 5, 1987, Butch Kinnon, Jeanne Kinnon

13 Cascade Lichen Dance 5.10a G 130' ★★★★

Aesthetic climbing on a clean face with a puzzling crux headwall. This is perhaps the only route that doesn't involve any thrashing through vegetation and has clean climbing right off the ground. The name is a play on the nearby winter route **Cascade Ice Dance**.

Start: At the right end of the cliff is a slab and face covered with white lichen polka dots, 60' right of a left-rising, right-facing corner chocked with trees and brush, and 30' left of the high arching roofs.

● **P1 5.10a G:** Angle up and left on the slab to a bolt, then straight up the face to a ledge, then over a short bulge to another ledge, then up and left to the base of a right-facing, right-leaning corner. Up this to its top, step left, then up a slab to a headwall, just right of a large arching roof. Move up onto a sloping shelf (crux), then traverse right to a small left-facing corner-flake. Up the corner and slab to a right-facing flake. Step left to sloping ledge with a fixed anchor. 130'

FA 2001, Jesse Williams, Bill Schneider

Dirty Diana Area

Located on the upper right end of the cliff is this short wall with several short routes. The routes are located on a corner, the left side facing the road and the right side facing the Cascade Falls drainage area. On the corner is a large orange roof, facing right (when seen from the road); this is the route **Dirty Diana**. For such an obscure area, the rock is fairly clean, and there are great views from the top.

DIRECTIONS (MAP PAGE 353)

The base of the cliff on its right end is steep, nondescript, and very difficult to navigate. The best approach is to hike the trail from the picnic area across the wood bridge and up to Cascade Falls (about 5 min). This is a low-angle falls with a minuscule drip and the remains of a concrete structure at the base. About 300' before the falls, scramble down left into a ravine and up the other side, then contour left over sloped, rocky terrain to the rock.

DESCENT OPTIONS

Scramble right, then down easy terrain to the base.

14 Dirty Diana 5.3 G 50' ★

Start: On the arête 5' below a ledge and on the right end of a slab.

P1 5.3 G: Traverse left across the top of the slab, then up the corner to the roof. Traverse right under the roof to break through on its right side at parallel cracks, which are followed to their top, then up a slab to a good ledge. 50'

15 Groupies 5.4 G 50' ★

Start: 5' above the start of **Dirty Diana** on a ledge on the arête.

P1 5.4 G: Climb the wide hand- and fistcrack. 50'

Between the Lakes

UFO WALL

Location	South side of NY 73 in Cascade Pass, above Upper Cascade Lake
Aspect	Northwest
Height	120'
Quality	★★
Approach	10 min, moderate
Summary	A small cliff with several cracks, including the excellent **My Favorite Martian**.

-5.6	5.7	5.8	5.9	5.10	5.11	5.12	5.13+	total
			1	2				3

This wall, located above the south end of Lower Cascade Lake, can be seen from the picnic area between the Upper and Lower Cascade Lakes. Look for an arête rising out of the top of the forest canopy; it's the only visible rock above Lower Cascade Lake. The left side of the arête (facing northeast) has **Mr. Spaceman** and **Cosmic Thing**, and the right side (facing northwest) has **My Favorite Martian**.

The cliff has several cracks, the best of which is **My Favorite Martian**, a discontinuous crack on the lake side. The other cracks are shorter and dirty.

DIRECTIONS (MAP PAGE 353)

From the picnic area between the Upper and Lower Cascade Lakes, walk toward the cliffs, over the bridge, then turn right (southwest) to the shoreline of Upper Cascade Lake (the lake nearer to Lake Placid). Walk along the shore to a debris chute and talus below the cliff (marked with a cairn). The cliff is 200' uphill through thick undergrowth 589945,4897350.

DESCENT OPTIONS

From **My Favorite Martian**, walk a few feet back and rappel from trees above **Cosmic Thing**.

16 Mr. Spaceman 5.10a G 50' ★

Don Mellor's first first ascent.

Start: 40' uphill and left from the toe of the buttress, a low horizontal ceiling meets the left-rising slope. This route begins at the right end of this ceiling below a left-leaning crack.

P1 5.10a G: Climb a fingercrack up to the right end of the low roof and into a right-facing corner. Follow a left-leaning crack up the wall to a jutting block, then step right to a ledge at the top of the cliff. 50'

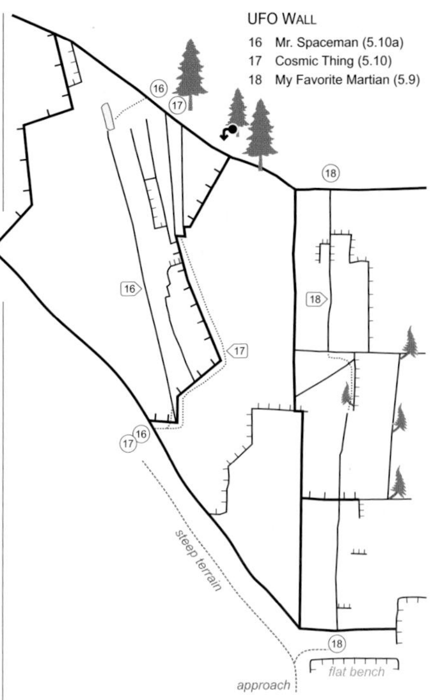

Gear: To 3".

FA Mar, 1979, Dale Frisbey, Tom Coffin

FFA Jul, 1979, Don Mellor, Dale Frisbey

17 Cosmic Thing 5.10 G 60'

Currently very dirty, but a two-star line if cleaned. Named for a B-52's album.

Start: Same as **Mr. Spaceman**.

P1 5.10 G: Climb a fingercrack up to the right end of the low roof and into a right-facing corner to the next roof. Face-climb up and right, following a right-rising ceiling to a right-facing, left-leaning corner. Climb the corner to its top at a roof, over this stepping left, then up parallel cracks to the top. 60'

FA Jun 10, 1990, Tad Welch, John Thackray

18 My Favorite Martian 5.9 G 120' ★★★★

Sustained crack climbing on an exposed wall above the water. Perhaps the best route on this side of the lakes.

Start: At the low point of the buttress, on an open flat bench on the lake side of the wall, below a thin crack 3' right of the arête.

P1 5.9 G: Up the crack to a ceiling, over this (crux), then up the crack to a short left-facing corner with a cedar tree and birch stump. Traverse left in a good horizontal crack, then up following another excellent vertical crack to the top. 120'

FA May 12, 1988, Patrick Purcell, Rich Leswing

Between the Lakes

ICE AGE WALL

Location	North side of NY 73 in Cascade Pass, above Upper Cascade Lake
Aspect	Southeast
Height	50'
Quality	★★
Approach	15 min, moderate
Summary	A small wall with three face climbs of increasing difficulty.

-5.6	5.7	5.8	5.9	5.10	5.11	5.12	5.13+	total
	1	1		1				3

Ice Age Wall is located above the road and Upper Cascade Lake and has a short, nasty approach. There are three routes that share a single fixed anchor. As such, you can lead one route and toprope the others. The wall gets considerable sun, so go on a cool day.

DIRECTIONS (MAP PAGE 353)

From the picnic area between the Upper and Lower Cascade Lakes, return to NY 73 and walk 800' toward Lake Placid to reach the middle gabion—a wire cage filled with rocks used as a retaining wall alongside the road 589473,4897366. From the right (northeast) end of the gabion, head straight uphill (no path) to a small cliff barrier, breaking this on the right to a drainage area. Follow this uphill to the base of the Ice Age Wall, which meets the cliff at the low point near the winter route **Indiscretion**. Walk uphill and left to the routes 589414,4897394.

DESCENT OPTIONS

Rappel from the common fixed anchor.

19 Permafrost 5.7 PG 50' ★

Start: At a flat bench 6' left of the **Meltdown** cedar tree and 6' right of a large, wet, mossy right-facing corner.

P1 5.7 PG: Climb up to a left-facing, right-diagonaling flake. Up the flake to its end, then straight up the face past horizontal cracks to a large tree with a fixed anchor. 50'

FA Apr 30, 1991, Patrick Purcell, Jeff Edwards

20 Meltdown 5.8 PG 50' ★★

Start: At a cedar tree 6' right of **Permafrost** below a horizontal edge 5' up.

P1 5.8 PG: Climb onto the horizontal edge and follow a left-facing, right-rising flake to its end, reach up to another good flake, then up horizontals (joining **The Cave Artist**) to a large tree with a fixed anchor. 50'

FA Apr 30, 1991, Patrick Purcell, Jeff Edwards

21 The Cave Artist 5.10a G 50' ★★★

Start: 20' uphill and left from the low point of the wall and 4' right of the **Meltdown** cedar tree at a fragile left-facing flake.

P1 5.10a G (sport): Up the flake, then step right to a good horizontal edge (bolt). Up the face, angling slightly left to join **Meltdown** past several horizontals to a large tree with a fixed anchor. 50'

FA Apr 30, 1991, Patrick Purcell, Jeff Edwards

UNBALANCED ROCK CLIFF

Location	North side of NY 73 in Cascade Pass, off the Pitchoff Ridge hiking trail
Aspect	Southeast
Height	100'
Quality	
Approach	30 min, easy
Summary	Easily-approached cliff with a couple of routes in a scenic setting.

-5.6	5.7	5.8	5.9	5.10	5.11	5.12	5.13+	total
	1		1					2

DIRECTIONS (MAP PAGE 353)

Park at the Cascade Mountain Trailhead 588867,4896803, located on NY 73 6.6 miles from Keene (from the center of town where NY 73 and NY 9N split) and 7.5 miles from Lake Placid (from the intersection of NY 86 and NY 73). This is a very popular trailhead, and there are pullouts on both sides of NY 73.

The trail begins 220' downhill (towards Cascade Lakes) and across the road from the Cascade Mountain trail, at some steps up a steep embankment 588896,4896854. Follow the red-marked trail for 30 min to a section where the right side of the trail opens up with excellent views of the Cascade Waterfall Slide, Cascade Cliff, and the picnic area between the lakes. The trail makes a left, and descends into a notch; the cliff is directly in front of you. Continue on the trail through some talus to the left end of the cliff, then walk 40' right to the base of **Rotator Complications** 589624,4897788.

HISTORY

The following climbs were reported by R.L. Stolz and Eric Swartz in 2012. Due to the easy approach from one of the most popular hikes in the Adirondack Park, it's difficult to believe that nobody has climbed here before then. The cliff's name relates to Balanced Rock, the local name for the balanced boulder on the south summit of Pitchoff Mountain 1 mile further up the hiking trail.

DESCENT OPTIONS

Walk up, then left, and locate the hiking trail. Follow this downhill to the base of the cliff.

1 Rotator Complications 5.9+ PG 110' ★

Start: 40' from the left end of the cliff (and the hiking trail) at an obvious, wide, right-rising ramp in a corner. The base of the corner is orange.

P1 5.9+ PG: Climb the ramp to its top with good protection. As the terrain steepens continue straight up to a 4'-wide overlap. Make an awkward, reachy undercling move (crux) and follow flakes to the top. 110'

FA Sep 10, 2012, Eric Swartz, R.L. Stolz

2 Virginia Reel 5.7 G 110' ★

Start: 60' right of (and level with) **Rotator Complications** in an open area with a large blocky left-facing corner. The right side of the corner forms a blocky arête.

P1 5.7 G: Climb cracks up blocks to gain the arête. Follow this up to a grassy ledge. Move right into a

Unbalanced Rock
1 Rotator Complications (5.9+)
2 Virginia Reel (5.7)

shallow chimney behind a giant boulder, then straight up a vegetated section to a good tree. 110'
FA Sep 10, 2012, Eric Swartz, R.L. Stolz

PITCHOFF NORTH FACE

Location	Off the Jackrabbit Ski Trail, accessed from NY 73 near the Verizon Sports Complex
Aspect	Northwest
Height	150'
Quality	
Approach	20 min, moderate
Summary	Dirty rock buttress with an easy approach and one adventurous, historic route.

The North Face of Pitchoff is best known for its ice climbing. The first rock buttress on the right (as you approach from Old Mountain Lane) has one reported rock route. The longer slabs at the height of the pass (with the ice routes **Hanging Spoons**, **Screw and Climaxe**, and **Weeping Winds**) are higher but have no reported rock routes, although there are isolated sections of good-looking rock.

The rock here is generally dirty, slow to dry, and friable. The base of the cliff is convoluted, with thick trees; steep, loose terrain; and a forest canopy that absolutely prevents seeing the cliff above. Getting oriented is very difficult.

The central feature of the first rock buttress is the enormous, deep, 30'-wide chimney capped by roofs. Right of this chimney is a buttress with appealing-looking crack lines (they aren't as appealing up close); these are the winter routes **Ground Up** and **Bucking Bronco**. Just left of the opening of the chimney is a face with a large orange spot, above which is a sloping ledge with some trees; this is the P1 belay ledge of **Split Beaver**. Left of this face, the base of the cliff rises up and left, above which are a number of right-leaning cracks and dihedrals, virtually inaccessible from below.

HISTORY

The route **Split Beaver** was originally reported in Don Mellor's 1983 edition but was dropped after that. It was climbed in 1976 by John Wald and Grant Calder, the protagonist behind the superclassic routes on the Pitchoff Chimney Cliff, **Wald-Calder Route**, **The El**, and **Rugosity**. **Split Beaver** probably hasn't seen an ascent in 30 years.

DIRECTIONS

Parking for the Pitchoff North Face is on Old Mountain Lane. From the intersection of NY 73 and NY 86 in Lake Placid, follow NY 73 for 5.6 miles to Old Mountain Lane on the left. If you're driving from Keene, follow NY 73 through Cascade Pass; Old Mountain Lane is on the right, 0.7 mile past the entrance to Mt Van Hoevenberg / Verizon Sports Complex. Drive 1.5 miles down Old Mountain Lane to its end 588148,4898764. There is room for about 10 cars here, but be careful not to block any driveways. From here, hike the yellow-marked Jackrabbit Ski Trail for 10 min to the first beaver pond. The trail stays on the left side of the beaver pond, and the cliff is visible up and right. Just after the beaver pond and on the right side of the trail is a large, flat boulder with the footprint of a large house; surprisingly, it is difficult to see even though it comes right down to the trail. Scramble onto this boulder 589046,4899184 for an unobstructed view of the cliff.

From the boulder, aim for the face with the orange spot. A short but arduous bushwhack steeply uphill through moss-covered and densely vegetated talus leads to the base of the cliff 589113,4899146.

DESCENT OPTIONS

Rappel with two ropes from trees.

1 Split Beaver 5.8 A0 190'

Some loose rock.
Start: The start is nondescript and totally obscured by vegetation. Find a position about 50' left of the enormous, 30'-wide chimney capped by roofs.
P1 5.8 A0 PG: Work up and left, pulling on cedars and other vegetation, aiming for the base of a steep right-leaning corner. The right wall of the corner is wide, steep, smooth, and faces northeast; the left wall is overhanging and covered in white spots. Climb the corner to a 1'-deep overlap on the right wall. Climb out right under the overlap using some tension to the arête. Swing around the arête to a sloping ledge on the right side; belay from trees on the right end of the ledge. 130'
P2 5.8 G: Step left and climb a right-leaning crack to a slab, then follow it up to trees. 60'
FA Jul, 1976, John Wald, Grant Calder

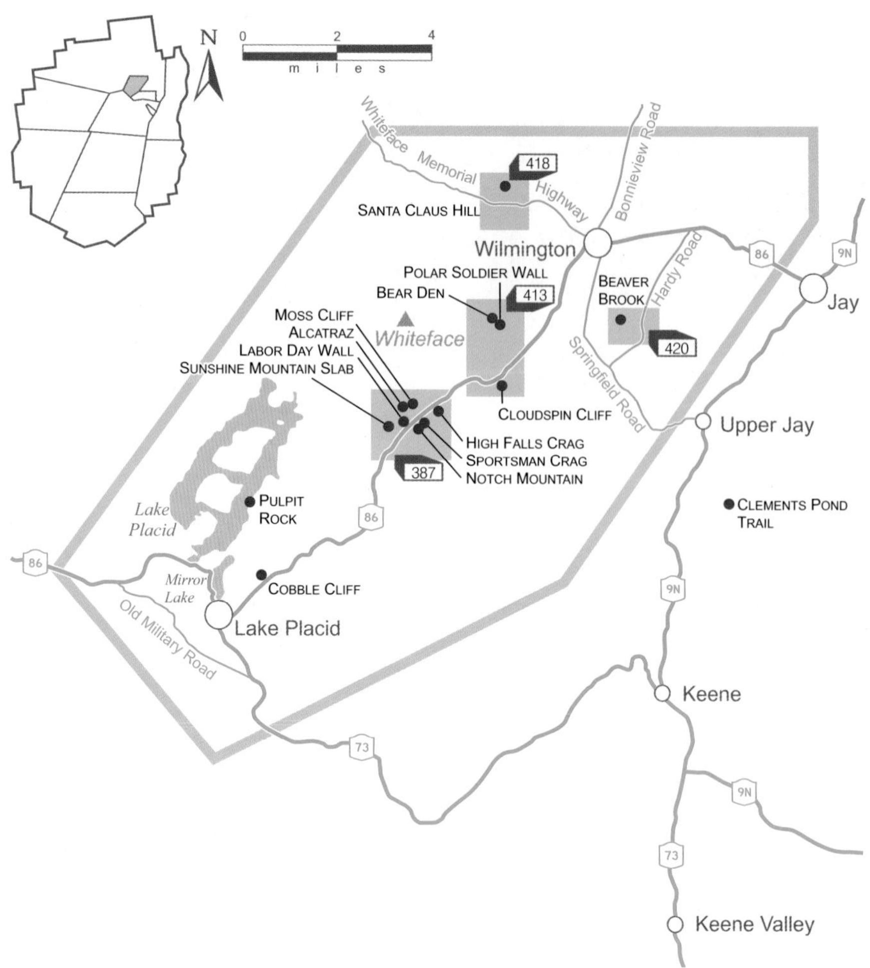
N
0
2
4
miles
Whiteface Memorial Highway
Bonnieview Road
418
Santa Claus Hill
Highway
Wilmington
86
9N
Polar Soldier Wall
Bear Den
413
Beaver Brook
Hardy Road
Jay
Moss Cliff
Alcatraz
Whiteface
420
Labor Day Wall
Sunshine Mountain Slab
Springfield Road
Cloudspin Cliff
Upper Jay
High Falls Crag
Sportsman Crag
387
Notch Mountain
Clements Pond Trail
Pulpit Rock
Lake Placid
86
86
Mirror Lake
Cobble Cliff
9N
Lake Placid
Old Military Road
Keene
73
9N
73
Keene Valley

Wilmington Notch

The cliffs in this section are located along the NY 86 corridor that connects Lake Placid and Wilmington through a narrow mountain gorge called Wilmington Notch. Whiteface Mountain dominates the skyline to the north, the Sentinel Range to the south, and cliffs are scattered liberally on both sides of the notch.

The centerpiece is Moss Cliff, known for superb multipitch crack climbing (among the best in the park), an adventurous river crossing, and more recently, the most difficult route in the park. Moss Cliff is such a prominent and popular destination that the other crags are often overlooked.

Cloudspin Cliff has excellent routes and is worth a visit. There are moderate routes on the slabs of Notch Mountain and Sunrise Mountain, across the valley. The multipitch crack routes on High Falls Crag are unexpectedly good, especially on a hot day. There's an excellent high-end sport route practically in the village of Lake Placid at Cobble Cliff, and there's a cluster of fun sport routes at Beaver Brook. Olympic Acres and Labor Day Wall hold promise for new and resurrected routes.

ACCESS

Annual closures for peregrine falcon nesting affect Moss Cliff (see page 392).

SEASON

The north-facing cliffs (Sportsman Crag, High Falls Crag) take a while to dry out, but the south-facing cliffs on the Whiteface side of the valley can be climbed beginning early in the spring. However, there is a persistent pair of peregrine falcons that take up residence at Moss Cliff every summer, effectively reducing the climbing season there to about six weeks in the fall.

DIRECTIONS **(MAPS PAGES 4 AND 382)**

If you're in the Keene / Keene Valley area, use the shortcut through Upper Jay—north on NY 9N to Upper Jay, left onto Springfield Road (CR 12), left onto Fox Farm Road (CR 63), then southwest on NY 86 into the notch. If you're coming from the north, take the Northway (I-87) to Exit 34, then south on NY 9N to Jay, then southwest on NY 86 into the notch.

WHERE TO STAY

Copperas Pond is located in the notch (see page 387) and has excellent campsites beginning 0.6 mile from the road. Northeast of the notch, where NY 86 crosses the Ausable River, are three designated sites, near the Wilmington Flume. Outside of the town of Wilmington, about 3 miles north on Bonneview Road (CR 19), is a car-camping site at the Cooper Kiln Trailhead. At the top of the Whiteface Mountain Road, just beyond the turnoff to the toll road, is a logging road that leads to an old quarry (winter climb called the **Chiller Pillar**) and another camping option.

Campgrounds: There are two campgrounds in the north: Whispering Pines Campground, in Wilmington (518.523.9322); and Wilmington Notch State Campground (518.946.7172). Other accommodations are listed in the Keene section (page 319).

DIVERSIONS

The Lake Placid area is filled with recreational opportunities. There's great swimming at the village beach on Mirror Lake, and cliff jumps at Copperas Pond and the Wilmington Flume. Bring your mountain bike: Lake Placid has an excellent network of single-track riding, and Whiteface Mountain Ski Area has both downhill and cross-country trails. The river that flows through the notch, the west branch of the Ausable River, is considered one of the best fly-fishing spots in the Northeast.

AMENITIES

Lake Placid has a couple of outdoor shops, gas stations, a grocery store, very good breakfast options, and two brewpubs. Locals favor Lisa G's and Desperados for dining out. Wilmington has a small grocery store (hearty subs), a gas station, and a breakfast option—The Country Bear (518.946.2691).

Pen and ink by Tad Welch.

PG	CLIFF	QUALITY	ASPECT	APPROACH		GRADES	#
385	Cobble Cliff	★	SE	10 min	easy	.6 .7 .8 .9 .10 .11 .12 .13	3
386	Pulpit Rock		NW	20 min	easy boat required	.6 .7 .8 .9 .10 .11 .12 .13	4
387	Sunrise Mountain Slab	★	S	45 min	moderate	.6 .7 .8 .9 .10 .11 .12 .13	2
388	Notch Mountain	★	W	10 min	easy	.6 .7 .8 .9 .10 .11 .12 .13	16
392	Labor Day Wall	★	S	15 min	easy	.6 .7 .8 .9 .10 .11 .12 .13	3
392	Moss Cliff	★★★★★	E & SE	30 min	moderate river crossing	.6 .7 .8 .9 .10 .11 .12 .13	28
408	Alcatraz	★★★★	SE	50 min	difficult	.6 .7 .8 .9 .10 .11 .12 .13	5
410	High Falls Crag	★★★	N	10 min	easy	.6 .7 .8 .9 .10 .11 .12 .13	4
412	Cloudspin Cliff	★★★	N	15 min	easy	.6 .7 .8 .9 .10 .11 .12 .13	6
415	Olympic Acres Polar Soldier Wall		SE	25 min	moderate	.6 .7 .8 .9 .10 .11 .12 .13	3
416	Olympic Acres Bear Den	★★★★	SE	1 hr	moderate	.6 .7 .8 .9 .10 .11 .12 .13	9
418	Santa Claus Hill	★★★	S & E	25 min	moderate	.6 .7 .8 .9 .10 .11 .12 .13	6
420	Beaver Brook	★★★	SE	15 min	easy	.6 .7 .8 .9 .10 .11 .12 .13	7

COBBLE CLIFF

Location	North side of NY 86 near Lake Placid
Aspect	Southeast
Height	60'
Quality	★
Approach	10 min, easy
Summary	A sheer cliff in a stunning setting that offers several climbs, including a single difficult four-star route.

-5.6	5.7	5.8	5.9	5.10	5.11	5.12	5.13+	total
			1			2		3

This is far from a destination crag, but it does have one excellent bolted face climb. The sheer overhanging wall is tucked down in the trees and is invisible from any vantage point. The base of the cliff is level and open with tall trees that form a high, shaded canopy.

The cliff is located on Cobble Hill just outside Lake Placid but is called Cobble Cliff to differentiate it from Cobble Hill in Elizabethtown, an excellent cliff that was documented in Mellor's 1988 guidebook but is unfortunately on private land.

HISTORY

The cliff originally captured the interest of Jeff Edwards while he was working at the Northwood School. Due to its proximity to the school, Edwards brought students here to practice rappelling. He later cleaned and bolted Connection.

DIRECTIONS

From the intersection of NY 86 and NY 73 in Lake Placid, drive northeast on NY 86 toward Wilmington 1.5 miles and park at the first dirt pullout on the right at the crest of a small hill 583151,4904713. (When you're traveling from Wilmington, the pullout is on the left, 1.7 miles from River Road.) Across the street are several DEC signs and a trail that goes into the woods following yellow paint blazes, which quickly fade away. Continue on a bearing of 277° for 10 min to reach the base of the cliff 582784,4904668. Although a more direct route seems possible, it crosses private property.

1 Muscinae 5.9+ PG 60'

Currently an unappealing moss garden.

Start: 20' left of Connection at a left-leaning discontinuous handcrack that begins 10' up.

P1 5.9+ PG: Boulder up to the crack, then up the crack past a horizontal on the left. Before the top, break out right and follow a horizontal crack for 10', then climb up into a mossy depression to a large pine tree. 60'

FA 2001, Jeff Edwards, Don Mellor

2 Reciprocity 5.12d TR 60'

The face to the left of Connection.

FA (TR) Oct, 2003, Derek Amberman

3 Connection 5.12c G 60' ★★★★

Climbs the beautiful, gently overhanging face. Awaits a redpoint.

Start: In the center of the sheer wall, at a flat stone below a zigzag seam that begins 12' up.

● **P1 5.12c G:** Start 3' left of the seam and climb up some sloping holds to the first bolt. Step right into the seam and climb this to a fixed anchor at the top. 60'

History: The line was bolted by Jeff Edwards, then worked by Amberman, a student at Northwood School, who fell repeatedly clipping the anchors.

FA (TR) Oct, 2003, Derek Amberman

PULPIT ROCK

Location	East shore of Lake Placid, accessed from the water
Aspect	Northwest
Height	60'
Quality	
Approach	20 min, easy; boat required
Summary	Four routes that begin out of the water on Lake Placid.

-5.6	5.7	5.8	5.9	5.10	5.11	5.12	5.13+	total
		2		1	1			4

These climbs are located on Pulpit Rock, a rocky point on Lake Placid. The routes begin in the water, and must be led starting from a boat. A calm day and some fancy anchoring are required, as there is no beach or landing zone.

The first rock you come to is a high, low-angle slab heavily covered in moss. To the left, the next section of rock has a distinctive short, parallel-sided, right-leaning chimney. The third and largest section of exposed rock has an obvious right-leaning crack, **Jack in the Pulpit**. The last bit of exposed rock is a small, isolated buttress with a bolted route, **Bully Pulpit**.

The routes are short and currently a bit dirty. The area also has about six ice climbs.

HISTORY

The first reported climbing was by Patrick Purcell in 1985. John Wald may have soloed **Jack in the Pulpit** before that.

DIRECTIONS

In Lake Placid, at the north end of Main Street (NY 86), where NY 86 makes a 90° turn left, continue straight onto Mirror Lake Drive. Go 0.5 mile and turn left onto George and Bliss Lane, which leads to the Lake Placid Fishing Access Site and boat launch 581467,4905482. (You can also get to the parking area by turning into the Lake Placid Marina.)

From the put-in, paddle right (north), following the shoreline around a rocky point. The climbs are on the exposed rock 582298,4907107 just around the rocky point. It takes about 20 min in a canoe to reach the cliff.

DESCENT OPTIONS

Rappel from trees back to the boat.

1 Bully Pulpit 5.8 G 50'

Currently very dirty.

Start: On the leftmost section of exposed rock, at a bolt 3' above the water.

● **P1 5.8 G:** Climb past the bolt to the blunt arête, then up the face, staying right of the arête, past a horizontal to the trees. 50'

FA 1984, Andy Zimmerman, Patrick Purcell

2 Placid Es Pontas 5.11a R 50'

The first ascent was done as a deep water solo (and is probably best climbed this way), so the R protection rating is just an estimate.

Start: 20' left of **Jack in the Pulpit**, at a horizontal crack in an orange section of rock below an overhang.

P1 5.11a R: Climb a faint vertical crack in orange rock to a depression-like hole (a fist-sized offwidth) at mid height. Follow the faint vertical crack up (crux) past several horizontals to a slabby finish. 50'

Descent: Jump (the water at the base is very deep).

FA Jun, 2012, Ross Perrot

3 Jack in the Pulpit 5.8+ G 60' ★★★

Start: In the largest section of exposed rock, at the base of a right-leaning crack that comes out of the water. This is the only bottom-to-top crack in the area, and sits 10' left of a large open book, the left wall of which has tan-colored rock.

P1 5.8+ G: Climb the right-leaning crack to the top. 60'

Gear: Large cams to 4".

History: This route was climbed by walking out onto the ice. Also, it is known that John Wald on-sight soloed the crack out of a canoe (and was distinctly unhappy about the ball bearings near the top), but it isn't known exactly when this occurred.

FA Apr, 1985, Patrick Purcell, Bill Dodd

4 Pulpitted 5.10 PG 50'

Another sketchy solo with multiple attempts (jumps) on the first ascent.

Start: 30' right of the gully that is to the right of **Jack in the Pulpit**, at a right leaning diagonal crack with a bulge that turns into a horizontal crack with a roof.

P1 5.10 PG: Follow the crack up to the horizontal, then to the right, then up and over the roof. 50'

FA Jul, 2013, Ross Perrot

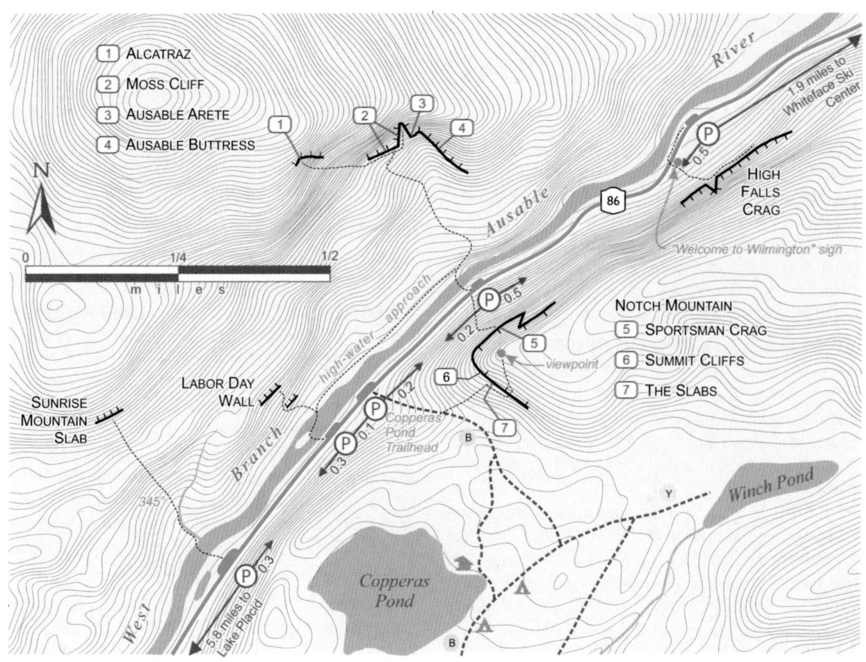

SUNRISE MOUNTAIN SLAB

Location	North side of NY 86 in Wilmington Notch
Aspect	South
Height	200'
Quality	★
Approach	45 min, moderate
Summary	Slab with two interesting moderate run-out routes.

-5.6	5.7	5.8	5.9	5.10	5.11	5.12	5.13+	total
2								2

The Sunrise Mountain Slab sits on the shoulder of Sunrise Mountain above NY 86, obvious to those traveling toward Wilmington from Lake Placid. There are two full-length slab routes here, notable in that they climb fantastically textured rock with knobs, scoops, and flakes; it feels more like rock on a summit in the High Peaks than a roadside crag. There is an adventurous river crossing (best in low water) and no trail, but those who persist will be rewarded with a spectacular spread of High Peaks from Mt Marcy across to Algonquin, and even the deep cleft of Wallface.

As with all seldom-climbed routes, a wire brush is recommended but will be necessary only for the bottom sections of the routes. The bolts are original (of the 0.25" variety and now 25 years old) and probably need replacement.

HISTORY

The cliff was first explored by Jerry Hoover and Dan Gugliantta. Alan Jolley and Andy Helms put in the best route, placing bolts (the few that exist) on lead.

DIRECTIONS (MAP PAGE 387)

Park at a large paved pullout on NY 86 587279,4909207, 5.8 miles from Lake Placid on the left (when you're driving from the intersection of NY 86 and NY 73 in Lake Placid toward Wilmington), and 3.0 miles from the Whiteface Ski Area on the right (when you're driving toward Lake Placid from Wilmington). From the southern trailhead to Copperas Pond, this is the second pullout on the right when you're driving toward Lake Placid.

From the parking area, following a fishermen's path to the Ausable River. Cross the river (knee-deep in summer) and head downstream 200' to a faint opening in the forest on the opposite side. Follow a small stream on a bearing of 345° for 250' to where the stream veers to the right, then continue straight uphill on that same bearing. There is a small knoll about halfway up with views of the slab, and several small mossy slabs that are bypassed on the right. The cliff is reached 45 min from the car 586983,4909585.

DESCENT OPTIONS

There is a fixed anchor in the tree island above the belay. A 200' rappel, diagonally to the left, reaches the ground at the base of **Half-Baked Flake**.

1 Half-Baked Flake 5.4 X 170' ★

A dirty start leads to beautiful dimpled, knobby rock.

Start: 100' left of the lowest point on the cliff, at the highest point of the terrain beneath a wide, frowning ceiling 30' up.

P1 5.4 X: Angle up and right on large flakes (or higher on cleaner friction) to the right end of the frowning ceiling. Step over the ceiling, then follow a right-rising overlap (fixed nut) to its end (last protection). Step right onto featured rock and climb straight up, staying right of a giant gong flake, to a depression below a tree island. Belay here in a good crack (cams up to 3"). 170'

FA 1977, Jerry Hoover, Dan Gugliantta

2 Helms-Jolley 5.6 PG (5.5 R) 200' ★★★

A slightly easier version of **Slide Rules** on Big Slide with incredibly knobby rock on P2. P1 has some decomposing edges that lead to great climbing.

Start: At the low point of the slab where a small drainage area meets the base of the slab, just right of a black streak.

P1 5.6 PG (5.5 R): (V1) Up good edges with no protection to a small overlap 30' up (TCU). Step right past an alarming flexi-flake and up to a bolt, then straight up less featured rock (crux) to a second bolt. Angle right to a shallow right-facing corner at the left end of a vertical headwall. Belay here in the 1" crack. 110'

P2 5.4 R: Step left to a bolt, then straight up a staircase of knobs and scoops to its top (bolt), angle right, then back left to a depression below a tree island. Belay here in a good crack (cams up to 3"). 90'

V1 Best of Friends 5.6 R: Begin on the right end of the slab and climb extremely dirty rock (fur might be a better description) up to a bolt, then angle up and left to the P1 belay.

FA 1982, Andy Helms, Alan Jolley
FA (V1) 1984, Alan Jolley, Kathy Bright

NOTCH MOUNTAIN

Location	South side of NY 86 in Wilmington Notch
Aspect	West
Height	250'
Quality	★
Approach	10 min, easy
Summary	A very scenic cliff that has several distinct sections, including a summit cliff, multipitch slabs, a popular toprope area, and a newly developed cliff with steep rock.

-5.6	5.7	5.8	5.9	5.10	5.11	5.12	5.13+	total
13		1	1					16

Notch Mountain is a minor summit that is visible from the parking area for one of the most popular swimming holes in the Adirondacks—Copperas Pond. The scenery is first-rate, with views across Wilmington Notch to Moss Cliff and Whiteface Mountain, and the High Peaks and Ausable River to the west. Climbing on Notch Mountain is distinctly alpine, with 3rd-class approaches, talus fields, wind exposure, and gnarled conifers. Notch Mountain is divided into several cliff sections: Sportsman Crag is located at the northern end of the mountain and offers the steepest rock on the mountain; the Summit Cliffs are situated below a popular viewing area (the Viewpoint), which is accessed by a herd path that begins at the base of The Slabs (The Slabs are three lower-angled sections of rock arranged side by side and separated by left-facing walls—Daddy Slab, Golfing Slab, and Roast 'n Boast Slab); Southside overlooks Copperas Pond and is accessed from the base of Roast 'n Boast Slab.

DIRECTIONS (MAP PAGE 387)

Parking for Sportsman Crag is the same as for Moss Cliff, at a pullout on the west side of NY 86, 2.5 miles west of the Whiteface Mountain Ski Center and 6.6 miles east of the intersection of NY 73 and NY 86 in Lake Placid 587936,4909931.

Parking for Summit Cliffs, The Slabs, and Southside is at the northern of the two Copperas Pond trailheads, located 0.1 mile farther west than the Sportsman Crag / Moss Cliff parking area. Parking is next to the Ausable River, and the hiking trail (marked with blue discs) is across the road 587666,4909685.

HISTORY

The first climbing occurred here between 1948 and 1953 by Stanley Smith and Donald LeBeau to practice their piton placements. They didn't think much of it and found it crumbly and "too bothersome". Stanley recalls constantly ducking rocks, with no helmets, of course.

Dick Tucker and Tim Riley were next with their ascent of **Return Home** in 1977, followed by Tad Welch and companions in 1985. Tucker saw Welch's route descriptions in Mellor's 1986 guidebook and with renewed interest, returned to establish multipitch routes that led to the Viewpoint near the summit. In the late 1980s, Tucker and Riley rappelled from the Viewpoint into the Ormus Chimney and established some top-down cragging at this scenic cliffband. David Lent and Richard Haffner continued the top-down investigation of the Summit Cliff in 1994. Starting in 2005, Geoff Smith began development of Sportsman Crag by hiking past the Viewpoint and toprope-investigating the steep cliffs at the northern end of Notch Mountain.

Sportsman Crag

As Notch Mountain wraps around to face NY 86 more directly, it becomes overhanging and chossy, separated from the road almost entirely by talus. Development here is in its early stages—there are five pitches of climbing here, only one of which has been led clean . . . but what a pitch! The climbing is steep and demanding. During development of the cliff, Smith noticed the wealth of recreation that takes place in the Notch—including biking, hiking, fishing, running, kayaking, and climbing—so he named the cliff "Sportsman Crag."

DIRECTIONS (MAP PAGE 387)

Walk toward Lake Placid to the end of the pullout, cross the road, then up the loose, rocky bank to find the trail.

The first 20 yards are overgrown, but thereafter the trail is very distinct and well cairned. The trail goes up through moss-covered boulders, then through open talus to the cliff. Walk up and left along the base of the cliff to the highest point of the terrain, at a deep left-rising gully that marks the start of **Wedlock** 587992,4909813.

DESCENT OPTIONS
Rappel **Wedlock** with two 60-m ropes.

1 Wedlock 5.10b A0 250' ★★★
P1 is long and involved. The top pitch is a spectacular roof that hasn't been freed and is one of the remaining prizes of the Notch. The route was named for Gary Allen's imminent marriage.
Start: At the base of a left-rising gully, below a ledge 8' up with a large cedar.
P1 5.10b G: Scramble onto the left end of the ledge, traverse right on the ledge to an arête, and climb it past a bolt to another ledge. Step right and climb a jagged left-facing corner with a steep, gnarly crack (5.9+; overhanging hands). Make airy moves left out of the crack to a stance, then up and right on blocky ledges to the base of an overhanging orange wall. Over the orange wall (crux) to a good stance, then up dirty unprotected rock to a right-facing corner and slot that gains a ledge with some trees and dangerously perched blocks. Traverse left 15' to a fixed anchor below a large roof. 200'
P2 5.10 A0 G: Pull the large roof above the belay to gain a right-rising crack. Follow it to its end, then work up and left across the face to a fixed anchor. 50'
FA 2005, Geoff Smith, Tim Smith, Silas Smith

2 Project
This is one of Geoff Smith's projects, most likely in the 5.11 range, that he worked by rappelling in from the top and fixing ropes on the anchors and intermediate bolts, then toprope-soloing the various pitches. The pitches haven't yet been prepared for leading. Begin as for **Wedlock** by climbing up the arête (bolt) to a ledge. Follow the ledge up and right past a cedar, behind a big flake to its right side below a small overlap. Over the overlap and into a shallow left-facing corner-flake, then up left-facing flakes to a ledge with a fixed anchor. Continue rightward past blocks, move up to the right end of a long overlap, then traverse left under the overlap and up its left side via a left-rising snaking flake. Follow the flake to a crack, which leads to the next fixed anchor and small cedar tree. From the anchor, traverse right under an overlap to gain a vertical crack, then follow it to an open-book niche with a fixed anchor.

Summit Cliffs

At the top of the east end of Notch Mountain, and visible from the Copperas Pond parking area, is a short cliffband of clean rock—the Summit Cliff—situated below the Viewpoint, a popular viewing area. Follow a steep herd path that goes around the right edge of the Roast 'n Boast Slab, then rappel to reach the routes. Finishing to the right of the Viewpoint are the multipitch routes **Fenris**, **Daddy Where Are You?** and **Fat-Free Warrior**.

DIRECTIONS **(MAP PAGE 387)**
From the Copperas Pond Trailhead, follow the trail uphill for 5 min and locate a herd path 587822,4909612 on the left (north) and before a table-sized rock on the left side of the trail. If you reach a large pine tree in the trail, you've gone past the herd path by 30'. Follow the herd path for 5 min as it climbs steeply up a wooded ridge. The herd path ends at the base of the Roast 'n Boast Slab 587873,4909684, a triangular-shaped slab 80' tall. Go around the right end of the Roast 'n Boast Slab and follow a gully to the top of the slab. Go right and follow a steep herd path along the ridge that goes east (left) to the open slabs above the Summit Cliffs. The Ormus Chimney, a deep chimney formed by a detached pillar, is visible 50' east of the open slabs. Rappel from trees to a vegetated ledge at the base of the routes.

3 Scab Slab 5.8 TR 70' ★
Start down from and left of the left side of the Ormus Chimney, at a crack beneath the right end of an overhang. Up the crack, then over a bulge to a stance. Climb a right-rising crack and face-climb to the top of the chimney.
FA (TR) May 26, 1994, David Lent, Richard Haffner

4 Ormus the Viking God 5.4 G 60' ★★
Start: 50' east (climber's left) of the Viewpoint is the top of a detached pillar. Rappel from trees to a ledge on the right side of the pillar.
P1 5.4 G: Up an open book, then left to an off width and a chimney on the right side of the tower. 60'
FA May 13, 1989, Dick Tucker, Tim Riley

5 Flapper 5.9 TR 50' ★
Start as for **Ormus the Viking God** and climb the open book to a right-rising ledge, above which is a widening crack. Climb the crack through tiered ceilings.
FA (TR) May 25, 1994, David Lent, Richard Haffner

6 Zigzag 5.4 G 60' ★
Start: Same as **Ormus the Viking God**.
P1 5.4 G: Up the open book to a right-rising ledge. Follow the ledge to a slab and climb it to a left-facing corner near the top. 60'
FA May 26, 1994, David Lent, Richard Haffner

The Slabs

The approach trail arrives at the rightmost slab, the Roast 'n Boast Slab, which is a popular toproping cliff with several easy routes that are well protected. To the left is a series of slabs that descend in steps past left-facing walls—the Golfing Slab and the Daddy Slab. These slabs contain multipitch routes that cross a 3rd-class traverse ledge that is level with the top of the Roast 'n Boast Slab. With plenty of open rock and exposed 3rd-class traverses, The Slabs feel more like an alpine area than a roadside crag. Aside from the routes on the Roast 'n Boast Slab, expect to climb through bushes and some loose rock.

DIRECTIONS **(MAP PAGE 387)**
From the Copperas Pond Trailhead, follow the trail uphill for 5 min and locate a herd path 587822,4909612 on

the left (north) and before a table-sized rock on the left side of the trail. If you reach a large pine tree in the trail, you've gone past the herd path by 30'. Follow the herd path for 5 min as it climbs steeply up a wooded ridge. The herd path ends at the base of the Roast 'n Boast Slab 587873,4909684, a triangular-shaped slab 80' tall.

To the left is the Golfing Slab, which is 75' down from and left of where the approach trail meets the Roast 'n Boast Slab. A 3rd-class traverse crosses the Golfing Slab 50' above its base and leads to the right side of the Daddy Slab. You can reach the start of **Fenris** by scrambling down and around the base of the Daddy Slab and traversing through trees and ledges for an additional 150'.

DESCENT OPTIONS

For routes that end at the summit ledge (**Fenris**, **Daddy Where Are You?** and **Fat-Free Warrior**), follow a herd path (west) and stay left of the slabs as you descend. Contour around to the top of the Roast 'n Boast Slab and then down its west (climber's right) edge to the base. **Let's Go Golfing**, **Men of Iron**, and **TL** end at a large cedar tree near the top of the Roast 'n Boast Slab. Descend the Roast 'n Boast Slab by following the herd path down along its right side. An alternative descent of the Golfing Slab is a 90' rappel from the cedar tree belay (no fixed anchor).

7 Fenris 5.5 PG 235'

P2 is recommended and can be approached by rappelling directly beneath the Viewpoint.

Start: 300' left of where the approach trail meets the Roast 'n Boast Slab, 150' left of the base of the Daddy Slab. Traverse through tree-covered ledges, staying above cliffs and below a long left-facing wall. The base of **Fenris** is a 25'-wide knob-covered and dark-colored slab.

P1 5.5 PG: Up the slab past a bulge at 75', then left beneath trees to a right-facing corner (optional belay). Up the corner, then right to a belay beneath a tree-filled corner. 150'

P2 5.5 G: Up the corner to a ledge, then left to a wide crack. Climb the crack to the Viewpoint. 85'

FA Jul 9, 1989, Dick Tucker, Tim Riley

8 Daddy, Where Are You? 5.5 G 285'

Start: 150' left of where the approach trail meets the Roast 'n Boast Slab, at the base of the Daddy Slab.

P1 5.5 G: Up the center of the slab to a small pine tree. Follow a right-rising crack toward the long left-facing wall, then left along cracks to a tree-covered ledge. 120'

P2 5.0 G: Up and left to a tree-filled corner that is followed by a short slot. Climb 20' up a dirty, broken slab and belay on a ledge with a short corner and trees to the right. 75'

P3 5.3 PG: Up between trees to an exposed slab. Up the slab to the bulging wall, then go right around the wall and up a dimpled slab to the Viewpoint. 90'

FA Sep 7, 1986, Dick Tucker, Tim Riley

9 Let's Go Golfing 5.4 PG 120' ★

Start: 100' left of where the approach trail meets the Roast 'n Boast Slab. Cross the 3rd-class traverse of the Golfing Slab to a tree belay at the right edge of the Daddy Slab. Start beneath the long left-facing wall.

P1 5.3 G: Up along the left-facing wall for 20' to a small cedar tree. Over the wall, then traverse across the Golfing Slab on a right-rising crack. Climb over bulges and ledges to a belay at a large cedar tree. 80'

P2 5.4 PG: Cross the 3rd-class traverse ledge and climb the dark slab above the belay. Up a short right-facing corner, then scramble to a tree belay at the top. 40'

FA (P1) Aug 20, 1985, Tad Welch, Ali Schultheis
FA (P2) May 25, 1987, Dick Tucker, Tim Riley

10 Fat-Free Warrior 5.6 R 310' ★

It is recommended to skip P1 and instead begin P2 at the start of **Let's Go Golfing**.

Start: 75' down from and left of where the approach trail meets the Roast 'n Boast Slab. Go to the left edge of the Roast 'n Boast Slab, then over blocks to the right edge of the Golfing Slab. The steep slab down and left is P1 of **Fat-Free Warrior**. Scramble down its right edge to the start.

P1 5.6 R: Up and right across the slab to a tree belay. 50'

P2 5.5 G: Step right and climb long, left-rising cracks that follow the left side of the Golfing Slab, and cross the right-rising crack of **Let's Go Golfing**. Belay beneath a short wall with a cedar bush on top. 130'

P3 5.3 G: Climb up and left to the end of the slab, then through the trees to a belay on a ledge with a short right-facing corner (same as **Daddy, Where Are You?**). 40'

P4 5.3 PG: Up and left between trees to an exposed slab. Up the slab to the bulging wall, then go left around the wall and up to the Viewpoint. 90'

FA Sep 25, 1988, Dick Tucker, Tim Riley

11 Men of Iron 5.5 G 80' ★

Start: 50' left of where the approach trail meets the Roast 'n Boast Slab. Go to the left edge of the Roast 'n Boast Slab, then over blocks to the right edge of the Golfing Slab and belay at a tree.

P1 5.5 G: Step left on the 3rd-class traverse of the Golfing Slab, then up the slab and past a couple of shallow right-rising cracks to a prominent right-rising crack. Move right along the prominent crack, then up over bulges and ledges to the cedar tree belay. 80'

FA Apr 12, 1987, Dick Tucker, Tim Riley

12 TL 5.6 G 80'

Named for Tanager Lodge, a children's camp run by Welch's family for more than 80 years on Upper Chateaugay Lake.

Start: Same as **Men of Iron**.

P1 5.6 G: Up past bushes and trees to the long, 12'-tall left-facing wall. Follow the base of the wall to the cedar tree belay. 80'

FA Aug 28, 1985, Tad Welch, Bill Widrig

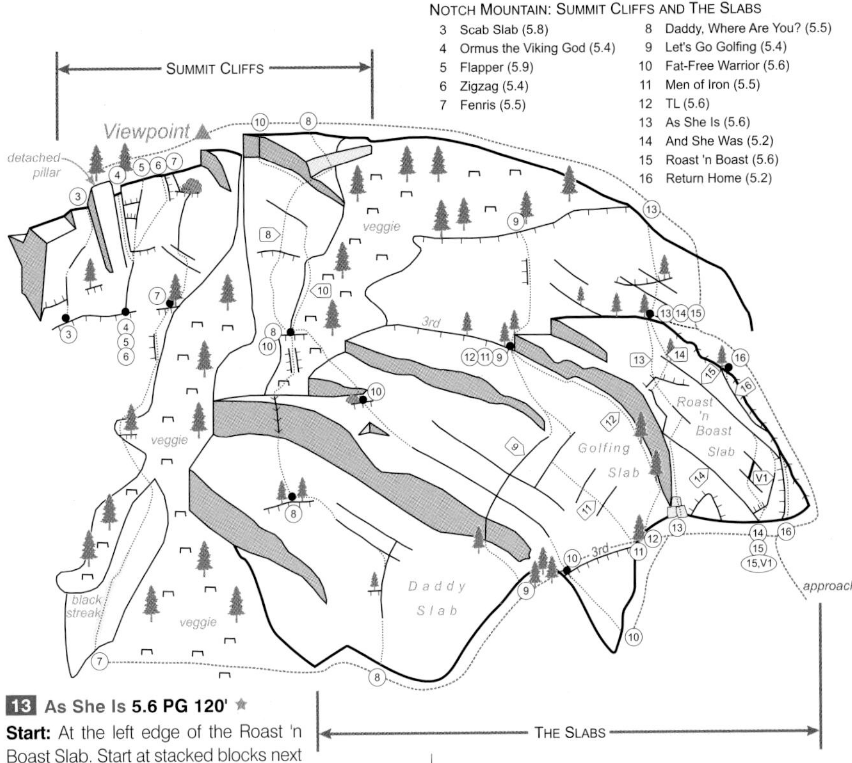

13 As She Is 5.6 PG 120' ★

Start: At the left edge of the Roast 'n Boast Slab. Start at stacked blocks next to the arête.

P1 5.6 PG: Up the arête, then right past the left-rising crack of **And She Was** to thin vertical cracks. Up the cracks, then back left to the overhang. Above the overhang, follow the left arête to a tree belay on the ledge. 80'

P2 5.5 PG: Up shallow vertical cracks on a slab to a steep wall. Over the wall to a tree belay on the top. 40'

FA Jul 3, 1988, Dick Tucker, Tim Riley

14 And She Was 5.2 G 80' ★★

Named for a Talking Heads song from the *Little Creatures* album.

Start: At the center of the Roast 'n Boast Slab, beneath an overlap 10' up and a left-rising crack that comes out of the ground.

P1 5.2 G: Follow the left-rising crack to the left edge of the slab, then up a wide crack to an overhang. Above the overhang, step right and then up to a tree belay on the ledge. 80'

FA Sep 20, 1985, Tad Welch, Ali Schultheis

15 Roast 'n Boast 5.6 G 70' ★★★

Start: Same as **And She Was**.

P1 5.6 G: Up to the overlap, (V1) then face-climb over it to a right-rising crack. Follow the right-rising crack past left-rising cracks to the most prominent crack below the arête. Left along the crack, past a tree, then up to a tree belay on the ledge. 70'

V1 Broil 'n' Brag 5.6 PG: From the overlap, traverse right to the prominent right-rising crack and follow it to the prominent left-leaning crack.

FA Aug 28, 1985, Bill Widrig, Tad Welch
FA (V1) May 25, 1987, Dick Tucker, Tim Riley

16 Return Home 5.2 G 50'

Start: At the right side of the Roast 'n Boast Slab at a right-facing corner.

P1 5.2 G: Up the corner to a spruce tree, then left along the left-rising crack closest to the arête. Tree belay at a notch in the arête. 50'

FA Nov 25, 1977, Tim Riley, Dick Tucker

Southside

DIRECTIONS **(MAP PAGE 387)**

This area is 500' right of where the approach trail meets the Roast 'n Boast Slab. Go around the right edge of the Roast 'n Boast Slab, then traverse the wooded mountainside for several minutes to a right-rising gully.

17 Slippery Needles 5.3 G 90'

Start: Start 10' to the right of the gully and beneath a dirty face.

P1 5.3 G: Up the face past a pine tree at 30', then into the gully and past another pine and a block to the top. 90'

FA Sep 1, 1986, Dick Tucker, Tim Riley

LABOR DAY WALL

Location	North side of NY 86 in Wilmington Notch
Aspect	South
Height	70'
Quality	★
Approach	15 min, easy
Summary	Less-than-vertical crack climbs on a small cliff with a short approach that involves crossing the Ausable River.

-5.6	5.7	5.8	5.9	5.10	5.11	5.12	5.13+	total
	1		1		1			3

This is a small, less-than-vertical cliff with several crack climbs. It is clearly visible from NY 86 south of the Notch Mountain Slab–Copperas Pond Trailhead. Approach during low water. Bring your waders and a fly rod: the Ausable River offers gold-medal fishing.

HISTORY

This small wall was explored by Patrick Purcell and Bill Dodd in 1985 and named Mini Moss Cliff. The wall was rediscovered 10 years later when a party climbed **Dackdation**; they gave the wall its present name.

DIRECTIONS (MAP PAGE 387)

Park at a fishermen's parking area 587576,4909583 on NY 86 that is 2.7 miles from the Whiteface Ski Area (when you're driving toward Lake Placid) and 6.1 miles from the intersection of NY 86 and NY 73 in Lake Placid (when you're driving toward Wilmington). The cliff is visible across the Ausable River.

Ford the river (more shallow 100' downstream) to the grassy bank, then hike 100' into the woods and cross a small talus field. Above the talus, skirt a low cliffband to the left, then traverse to the right above it. The wall is 100' steeply above the low cliffband. Arrive at the cliff at its right end 587507,4909721.

1 Jamie Lee Curtis 5.11d TR 70'

Start at two vertical, pocketed seams that begin at the ground and are 30' left of the approach trail. Up the widening right seam to a bushy topout. Low crux.

FA (TR) Jun, 1985, Patrick Purcell, Bill Dodd

2 Dackdation 5.9+ G 70' ★★

Start: At a right-rising handcrack with a ledge on the right at chest height, and 15' left of where the approach trail reaches the cliff.

P1 5.9+ G: Up the handcrack to the ledge. Above the ledge, the crack narrows to fingertips (crux). Belay at a tree with fixed anchors. 70'

FA Jun, 1985, Patrick Purcell

3 Nuke the Nite 5.7 G 70' ★

Start: Same as **Dackdation**.

P1 5.7 G: Up the handcrack (crux), then step right on the ledge to a vertical handcrack and follow it to a bushy topout. Belay at a tree with fixed anchors as for **Dackdation**. The direct start (5.8 G) begins above the approach trail at a vertical crack 8' up that forks into two cracks that lead to the ledge. 70'

FA Jun, 1985, Patrick Purcell

MOSS CLIFF

Location	North side of NY 86 in Wilmington Notch
Aspect	East and southeast
Height	400'
Quality	★★★★★
Approach	30 min, moderate; river crossing
Summary	A collection of high-quality multipitch crack routes, combined with one of the region's best aid-climbing walls; very scenic.

-5.6	5.7	5.8	5.9	5.10	5.11	5.12	5.13+	total
		2	5	5	4	3	4	28

In a region with an incredible amount of rock, Moss Cliff in particular stands out as a gem. This is the strikingly skyscraperesque rock formation that towers over the West Branch of the Ausable River like an anorthrositic sentinel guarding the passage through Wilmington Notch. The name "Moss Cliff" evokes images of a climber's worst nightmare, but rest assured that the rock is clean with chiseled cracks, stemming corners, and superb multipitch lines. The name is a simple misread of the USGS map by the early climbers, as the real moss cliff is a mossy slab farther on the ridge toward Lake Placid.

Moss Cliff's most distinguishing characteristic is its enormous arêtelike outside corner. The Free Wall is the left side of the arête and faces the road. All of the moderate multipitch free climbing is located on the Free Wall. The right side of the arête, called the Aid Wall, is perpendicular to the road and is traditionally where the aid climbing is found, although this title is somewhat of a misnomer since most of these routes have now been freed.

If you can climb 5.9–5.10 cracks, then Moss Cliff holds some of the best long crack climbs in the region, although there are no easy routes. **Hard Times** and **Touch of Class** are the easiest and have been classics for many years. Stepping up a notch in difficulty are the routes **Fear of Flying**, **No Más**, **The Mossiah**, **Red Zinger**, and **Falconer**. Several linkups allow you to string together some quality pitches; **Fear of Touching Aerie** is a particularly good one.

If you're looking for aid routes, the Aid Wall holds some great projects: **Mosscalito**, **Children and Alcohol**, **Pan Am**, and **Adirondack Black Fly Rancher**. Much of the climbing on these routes has been freed and represents some of the most difficult free climbing yet seen in the Adirondack Park (e.g., **Illuminescence** and **Fire in the Sky**). Even so, these routes are still great projects for the clean aid climber.

Much of the field work, route descriptions, and topos in this section were contributed by Colin Loher.

ACCESS

Moss Cliff presents several challenges. First is the river crossing: wading is an option, but not in high water or late in the fall when it's cold. There is often a Tyrolean cable rigged below the parking, but be aware that this is a nonconforming installation, and may be removed at any time. Use it at your own risk, and please use a

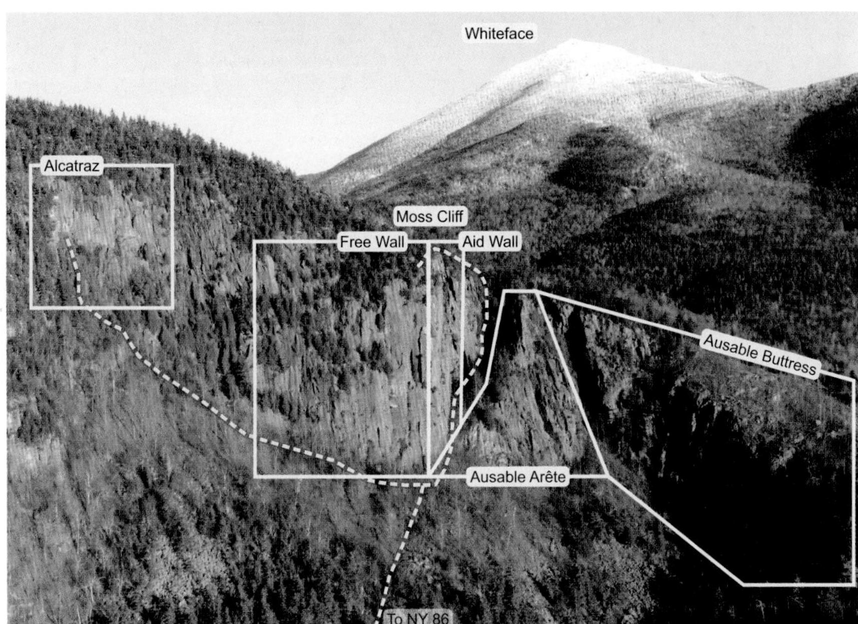

pulley to minimize wear on the equipment.

The second issue is the seasonal closure due to nesting peregrine falcons, which effectively reduces the climbing season to late summer and early fall. Moss Cliff was the first place peregrines were seen in the Adirondacks.

HISTORY

The cliff had some minor explorations in the late 1960s and early 1970s, but the first people to succeed were the informal group of friends known as the Mud and Slush Club, which included Jack Maxwell, Al Rubin, Ben Ales, Rocky Keeler, Bob Harding, Adrian Juncosa, and others who met at Maxwell's house in Wilmington, just down the road from Moss Cliff. Their first forays on the cliff in 1971 included an abortive attempt on the **Red Zinger** corner and the chimney left of the start of **Touch of Class**. Everyone failed. It wasn't until 1974, when Al Rubin teamed up with strongman Al Long, that the first route was climbed—**Touch of Class**, named for the exquisite purity of its line. The Long-Rubin pair continued to chew away at the cliff and produced some of its other super classic lines, including **Hard Times** and **Fear of Flying** (which overlooks the choss pile from hell, the **Ausable Arête**, the second route at the cliff). The Free Wall has continued to see development through to the present day, most notably by Don Mellor, Patrick Purcell, Nick Wakeman, and Dominic Eisinger.

The first route on the Aid Wall was **Coronary Country**, climbed by Long and Rubin in 1977, followed by **Pan Am** and **Children and Alcohol**, which were climbed on the same day in 1981. Thereafter, this wall saw little activity until 2006, when Peter Kamitses freed large sections of these two routes at 5.13c and 5.13d.

DIRECTIONS (MAP PAGE 387)

Park at the Moss Cliff Pullout on the west side of NY 86, 2.5 miles west of the Whiteface Mountain Ski Center and 6.6 miles east of the intersection of NY 73 and NY 86 in Lake Placid 587936,4909931. For road safety reasons, the DOT is planning on removing this pullout; when they do, park at the Copperas Pond Trailhead, 0.1 mile west (toward Lake Placid), next to the Ausable River 587666,4909685.

From the Moss Cliff Pullout, walk toward Lake Placid to where the metal guardrail becomes a stone wall. Drop over the side and follow a herd path steeply downhill to the river. Use the cable rigged between trees (bring a pulley!) to cross to the other side of the river.

If the cable is down and the water is low, park at the Copperas Pond Trailhead, wade across, then walk downstream to the normal crossing. If the cable is down and the water is high, then you'll need a boat.

Once across, follow an unmarked climbers' trail steeply uphill for approximately 30 min to the cliff, arriving at a right-facing flake that forms a chimney—P1 of **Aerie** 587737,4910264.

DESCENT OPTIONS

Central Rappel: Two 50-m ropes are required to rappel from the fixed anchor on top of **Spirit of Adventure** to the shared tree island belay of **Hard Times**, **Aerie**, and **Spirit of Adventure**.

Tree Island Ledge

Moss Cliff: Free Wall

1 The Far Side (5.8)
2 No Más (5.10b)
3 Falconer (5.11a)
4 The Mossiah (5.10b)
5 Red Zinger (5.10a)
6 Hard Times (5.9+)
7 Spirit of Adventure (5.11a)
8 Aerie (5.12a)
10 Touch of Class (5.9+)
11 Fear of Flying (5.10b)
12 Adirondack Black Fly Rancher (A2+)
13 Brass Balls, Steel Nuts, and Sticky Rubber (5.12d)
14 Mistah Luthah (5.12a)

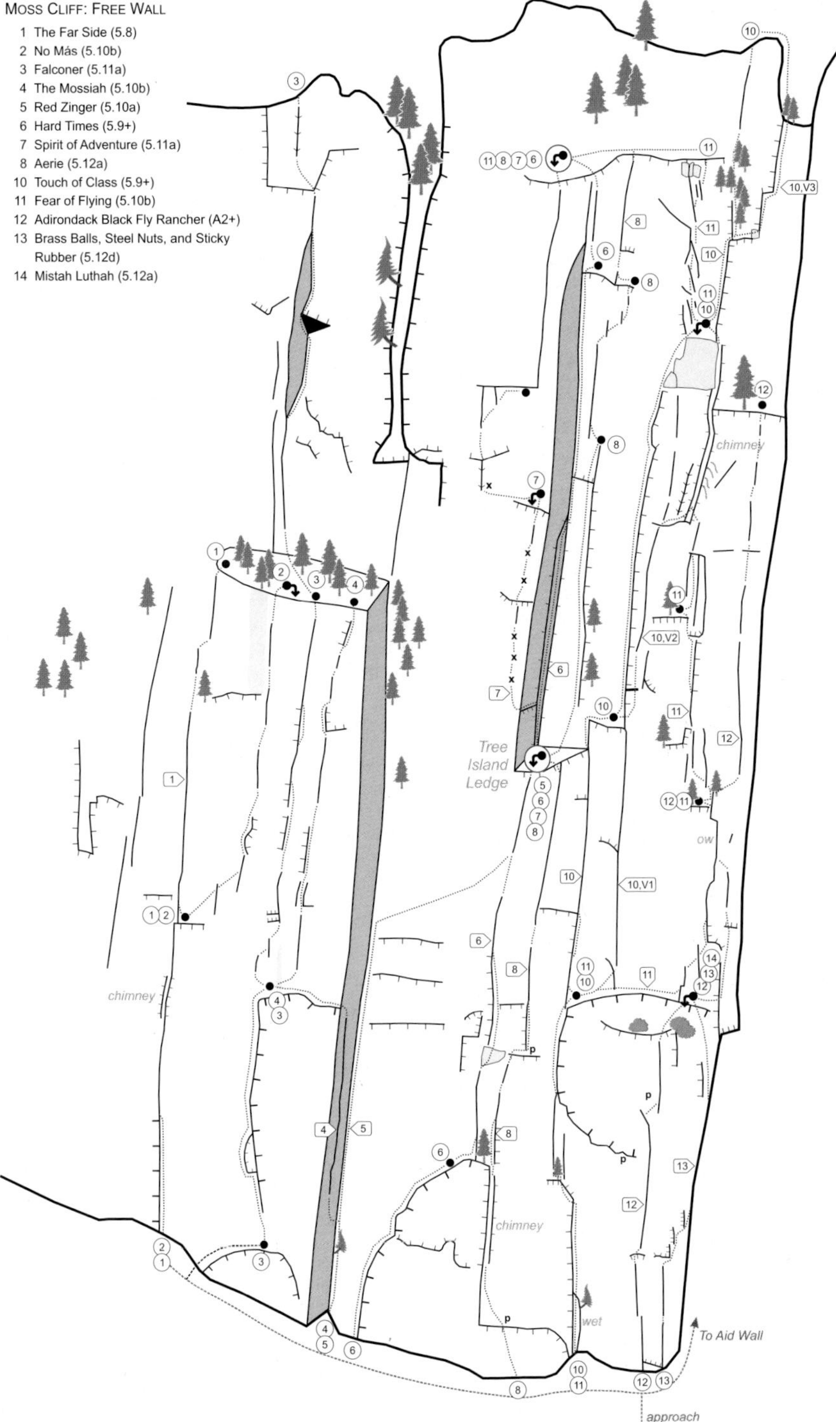

Party Ledge Rappel: For those routes that reach the shared anchor on **Children and Alcohol**, a long 200' rappel reaches the Party Ledge (the wall overhangs, so take precautions not to become stranded in midair). Another 120' rappel reaches the ground.

Walk off: Walk down and right to the top of a gully that separates the Aid Wall from **Ausable Arête**. Descend the gully to reach a fixed rope. Rappel 60' to a forested ledge, scramble down a slab and hug the (skier's) right wall, then downclimb a convenient cedar to reach the base of the Aid Wall near **A Scream from on High**.

Free Wall

The left side of the cliff facing NY 86 is characterized by long free routes that follow cracks and corners—some of the longest crack routes in the region. This is a narrow section of rock for the number of routes it contains, so you don't have to walk far between routes.

The Free Wall has several important features that will help you get oriented. On the left side of the cliff is a 220'-high right-facing corner that is the landmark for the routes **Red Zinger** and **The Mossiah**. Just right of this is a right-rising vegetated ramp and the start of **Hard Times**. Centered on the cliff (and difficult to see from the base) is Tree Island Ledge, which has a fixed anchor where several routes intersect. Above Tree Island Ledge is a 200'-high right-facing corner, the landmark for **Hard Times** and **Spirit of Adventure**. Facing the **Hard Times** corner are several left-facing corners with the routes **Aerie** and **Touch of Class**.

1 The Far Side 5.8 G 210' ★

P1 is better than it looks; P2 is very dirty.

Start: 15' left of **Falconer** at a right-facing corner, hidden behind and left of two large cedars.

P1 5.7 G: Climb the right-facing corner (which is actually pretty good, although the moss makes it look awful) with good gear and holds everywhere, into a chimney (crux). Belay just above on a sloping ledge. 90'

P2 5.8 G: Continue straight up the crack (dirty), past a cedar bush to the left end of a tree-covered terrace (common with **Falconer**). 120'

FA 1984, Tom Rosecrans, Dave Szot, Tom Yandon

2 No Más 5.10b PG 210' ★★

When seen from the road, this route climbs the faint black strip left of P2 of **Falconer**. The name comes from a famous 1980 welterweight boxing match between Roberto Duran and Sugar Ray Leonard; in the eighth round, Duran gave up, saying "No más."

Start: Same as **The Far Side**.

P1 5.7 G: Same as **The Far Side**: Climb the right-facing corner (which is actually pretty good, although the moss makes it look awful) with good gear and holds everywhere, into a chimney (crux). Belay just above on a sloping ledge. 90'

P2 5.10b PG: Traverse 15' right on a right-rising ledge to a shallow left-facing corner 8' left of the **Falconer** crack. Climb steep thin cracks through rolling terrain to the top at the treed terrace. There is a large cedar with a fixed anchor (shared with **Falconer**). 120'

Gear: Many RPs and small nuts.

Descent: A two-rope rappel reaches the ground from the treed terrace.

FA (P1) 1984, Tom Rosecrans, Dave Szot, Tom Yandon
FA (P2) Aug 14, 2006, Don Mellor, Nick Wakeman

3 Falconer 5.11a PG 310' ★★★

Difficult climbing right off the deck leads to pleasant crack climbing above. The name is a tribute to the peregrines that nest at Moss Cliff each year.

Start: At a ledge 15' up (approached from the left) below a small left-facing flake that becomes a left-facing corner midpitch. There is a cedar 25' up the corner system.

P1 5.11a PG: 10' of easy face climbing leads to the flake. Up the flake and into the sustained corner to a nice belay ledge. 70'

P2 5.10b G: Climb straight up from the left side of the ledge to gain a beautiful crack. Follow the crack through several shallow right-facing corners to a final tight-hands crux through a bulge. Belay at a large tree-covered terrace. 140'

P3 5.10d G: (V1) Move the belay to the back of the terrace below two parallel fingercracks in yellowish rock. Up the cracks (crux) to a right-rising ramp that leads to a right-facing corner below a ceiling. Break the roof on the left and continue in the right-facing corner to a ledge with trees. 100'

V1 5.7 G: From the treed terrace, it is possible to bushwhack right 40' to gain some ledges. Walk right on these ledges to the left side of the **Hard Times** chimney-flake (you can see through the chimney to the other side). Up the left-facing corner to the fixed anchor shared with **Spirit of Adventure**. Gear to 5".

Gear: Extra 0.75" and 1" pieces; include RPs for the start.

Descent: Rappel to the treed terrace, then two ropes reach the ground from there.

FA (P1) Jun 15, 1984, Don Mellor, Andy Zimmerman
FA (P2–3) May 29, 1985, Don Mellor, Patrick Munn
FA (V1) Aug 14, 2006, Nick Wakeman, Don Mellor

4 The Mossiah 5.10b G 210' ★★★

Climbs the left side of the right-facing **Red Zinger** corner to a shared belay with **Falconer**, then joins a previously climbed pitch, originally a variation of **Falconer**.

Start: Same as for **Red Zinger**.

P1 5.10b G: Climb the parallel cracks of **Red Zinger** and stay left of a cedar tree to reach the ledge at 15', then break left to gain a fingercrack on the left wall of the right-facing **Red Zinger** corner. Up the fingercrack past some pods, then move left on a ledge to the arête. Up some loose blocks on the arête to gain the belay ledge (shared with **Falconer**). 70'

P2 5.10a G: Above the ledge are two parallel crack lines—**Falconer** climbs the left crack, and **The Mossiah** climbs the right crack. Make a few face moves to gain the right crack, then follow it up stepped right-facing corners to a small overhang. Break the overhang on the left side into a short left-facing corner, then continue up the crack to the treed terrace (shared with **Falconer** and **The Far Side**). 140'

Descent: A two-rope rappel reaches the ground from the treed terrace.
FA (P1) Aug 8, 2006, Nick Wakeman, Don Mellor
FA (P2) Jun 15, 1984, Don Mellor, Andy Zimmerman

5 Red Zinger 5.10a G (5.4 R) 180' ★★

Follows a striking right-facing corner and provides a more aesthetic, alternate start to **Hard Times**. Double ropes necessary. Named after the Celestial Seasonings herb tea, the reddish rock, and the almost "zinger" taken out of the corner.

Start: 15' right of **Falconer** and 15' left of the left-facing, right-rising vegetated ramp of **Hard Times**, in parallel thin cracks to the right of a right-facing corner system; there is a ledge with a small tree 15' up.

P1 5.10a G (5.4 R): Head up thin cracks just right of a right-facing corner system for 15' to a small ledge with a tree. Continue up the corner system for 70' until you can exit to a ledge system on the right. From the ledge, angle up and right (runout) to cracks (joining **Hard Times**) and follow them up to a fixed anchor on the Tree Island Ledge. 180'

Descent: Two ropes reach the ground from the fixed anchor.

History: This corner, so obvious from below, was attempted on another occasion by Rocky Keeler and Al Rubin, but they bailed due to loose rock and dirt.
FA 1981, Todd Eastman, Sparf Ackerly

6 Hard Times 5.9+ G 380' ★★★★★

An amazing route that follows a virtual plumb line up the cliff along cracks and the huge right-facing corner that is visible from the road. This is a true Adirondack testpiece at the grade, and very sustained. Long and Rubin thought the route was "just plain hard" and had to use three points of aid at the crux.

Start: At the base of a left-facing, right-rising vegetated ramp 15' right of **Red Zinger** and 30' left of where the approach trail reaches the cliff.

P1 4th class: Head up the right-rising ramp for 30' to a gear belay behind a prominent birch. Belay here or risk rope drag by linking with the next pitch. 40'

P2 5.9 G: Climb a handcrack for 15' to a small ledge, then continue up a short 8'-high right-facing corner to lower-angled rock. Follow cracks to a right-rising ledge with two birch trees—the Tree Island Ledge—at the base of a large right-facing corner. There is a fixed anchor here on the lower birch. 140'

P3 5.9+ G: Time to cowboy up! Climb the prominent chimney in the right-facing corner until it squeezes down to a hand- and fingercrack (optional belay at the **Spirit of Adventure** fixed anchor on a ledge on the main face to the left). Continue up the cracks in the right-facing corner through an overhanging bulge (crux). Above, the crack diminishes; continue up the somewhat polished face right of the corner to a final short off width to a belay at a flat ledge. 150'

P4 5.9 G: Follow the handcracks to a large ledge system. Traverse left 10' to the fixed anchor of **Spirit of Adventure**. (Continuing up a tree-filled depression to the top is possible but not recommended.) 50'

Descent: Descend via the Central Rappel or walk off.

The Encounter

In the 60s and early 70s, the Adirondacks were a backwater, and, unlike the Gunks and New Hampshire, it was unusual to run into other climbers. Repeats of difficult climbs were rare, and new route activity, particularly on the bigger crags such as Poke-O, was limited. As the 70s progressed, Al Long and I would occasionally make the long drive from Boston to the "Dacks," Leadfoot Long behind the wheel. There we worked our way through the Turner routes and explored possible new areas like Moss Cliff.

In the mid-70s, there were rumors of a group from Plattsburgh putting up bold new routes on Poke-O: a hard group—tough, protective of the cliff, secretive, unfriendly, vehemently antiguidebook, and particularly hostile to outsiders. And we, of course, were outsiders. Over the course of several visits, as we heard more tales of their exploits, our curiosity about these phantom hardmen, tempered by a degree of anxiety, deepened.

One summer evening in 1976, when Al and I hung out in the EMS store in Lake Placid, we noticed three or four other guys with that climber "look." Running into another climber in a Dacks outdoors store was rare. There was something about these guys—maybe their obvious fitness, their well-used attire, or their demeanor—that communicated to us that these guys knew their way around the rock. They were apparently also having similar thoughts as they gave us the once-over. Could these actually be "them," the mystery Plattsburgh crew? We strolled through the store giving them furtive glances. They, too, gave us the same treatment. But no one ventured to break the ice. We had the distinct feeling we were in a scene out of a Western, with gunslingers circling one another. While there was no likelihood of bloodshed in the EMS aisles, the tension increased, as real as it was absurd.

Finally, our friend and store manager Dave Cilley appeared, quickly sized up the situation, and just as quickly introduced us to Geoff Smith and others of the "Ski to Die" tribe. A short time later, tension evaporated over those universal icebreakers, pizza and beer. They weren't unfriendly in the least, though they were concerned about a climber invasion that would turn Poke-O into another Gunks. They freely shared information about their recent creations. Sure, those route descriptions contained a bit of sandbagging, but after all, what else are friends for?

\- Alan Rubin

History: On their climb, Rubin brought a rubber raft to cross the Ausable River but, at the last minute, realized they lacked an oar. Recalling an oar on Andrew Embick's wall, they went to his apartment and borrowed it. Only later, to Embick's horror, did they realize the oar was a trophy of a sculling race win at Oxford.
FA Aug 23, 1975, Al Long, Al Rubin
FFA 1977, Henry Barber, Dave Cilley

7 Spirit of Adventure 5.11a G 210' ★★★

Climbs the beautiful arête left of **Hard Times**. Incredible exposure.

Start: At the Tree Island Ledge (reached by climbing P1 of **Red Zinger** or P1 and P2 of **Hard Times** or **Aerie**).

P1 5.11a G: Climb 15' up the **Hard Times** right-facing corner, then left along a handrail (on the left wall of the right-facing corner) to the arête. Swing around the arête onto the main wall and move up the devious face to a fantastic fingercrack finish. (Careful rope management is necessary here to avoid the rope drag; two ropes are recommended.) 80'

P2 5.11a G: Head down and left to a bolt, then up a groove to an overlap. Make hard undercling moves to a hidden bucket, then up to a horizontal. Hand-traverse right to the right end of the horizontal and belay where it crosses a vertical crack. 50'

P3 5.11a G: Climb the incredible fingercracks just right of the belay to a ledge with a fixed anchor. Awesome positions with good rock. Hard if you're short. 80'

Descent: Descend via the Central Rappel.

FA Aug, 1994, Dominic Eisinger, Patrick Purcell

8 Aerie 5.12a G 400' ★★★★

Another plumb line. P2 (5.10b), a stemming corner, is perhaps one of the most celebrated pitches on the cliff and can be climbed as a variation to either **Hard Times** or **Touch of Class**. The name is another tribute to the peregrine falcons that nest on the cliff each year; an aerie is the nest of a bird of prey.

Start: Where the approach trail meets the cliff, below a right-facing chimney that begins 25' up.

P1 5.11b G: Climb up the face to gain a ledge below the chimney. Up the chimney to a ledge at its top (the same ledge as for the belay of **Hard Times** P1). From the right end of the ledge, climb a thin crack in a shallow left-facing corner to a ledge with a cedar, step right to a shallow right-facing corner, then continue up a thin crack in yellow rock to a slabby ledge (**Fear of Touching Aerie** joins at the point from the right). Continue straight up the crack (5.9) to the Tree Island Ledge and belay at the upper right end of the ledge at the base of a left-facing corner behind a flake. 180'

P2 5.10c G: Climb the amazing left-facing corner via a thin crack to a bulging wave of rock at the top. Belay in the vertical crack just above the wave. 80'

P3 5.12a G: Continue up the increasingly steep vertical crack in black rock, then climb right and connect parallel vertical cracks across the face to a ledge with a large cedar. 60'

P4 5.10b G: Climb up left onto a ledge (the belay ledge for **Hard Times** P3). From the right end of the ledge, climb the thin crack past a small overlap to a ledge. Climb straight up the thicket to the top or, better yet, traverse left 20' on the ledge to a fixed anchor (the top of **Spirit of Adventure**). 80'

Descent: Descend via the Central Rappel.

FA Sep 1, 1988, Don Mellor, Jeff Edwards

9 Fear of Touching Aerie (linkup) 5.10b G 340' ★★★★★

There are many ways to link routes on this cliff, and this is one of the better ones; it combines pitches of **Aerie**, **Touch of Class**, and **Fear of Flying**.

P1 5.9+ G: Same as P1 of **Touch of Class**. 100'

P2 5.9 G: Climb up **Touch of Class** P2 for 10', then traverse left on the slabby ledge to gain the **Aerie** crack and climb it (5.9) to the Tree Island Ledge. Belay at the upper right end of the ledge at the base of a left-facing corner behind a flake. 80'

P3 5.10b G: Climb the **Aerie** corner. At the top of the wavy bulge, starting at a horizontal crack, face-climb up and right and connect vertical cracks (small TCUs) to meet the **Touch of Class** P3 left-facing corner. Climb the handcrack in the corner up to the fixed anchor. 80'

P4 5.10a G: Climb the water-worn fingercracks—i.e., the final pitch of **Fear of Flying**. 80'

Gear: Up to 4".

*Will Mayo on P2 (5.10c) of **Aerie** (5.12a). Photo by David Le Pagne.*

10 Touch of Class 5.9+ G 370' ★★★★★

Arguably the finest multipitch climb at the grade in the Adirondacks, thought by Rubin and Long to be one of the more elegant lines on the cliff. Exquisite corners, splitter cracks, and spacious belay ledges make this a must-do route.

Start: At a right-facing corner (almost always wet) 15' right of the **Aerie** flake-chimney 25' up, and 35' left of the prominent arête's lowest point.

P1 5.9+ G: Follow the obvious crack in the right-facing corner to an angled overhang, around this on the left to a stance, then up parallel cracks and into a left-facing corner with an off-width crack to a belay ledge on the right. 100'

P2 5.9 G: (V1) Above the left end of the ledge, climb a shallow right-facing corner with a crack and follow it with increasing difficulty, past a small overlap, to the right end of the Tree Island Ledge. Crash through trees to a ledge and belay on its right end at the base of a left-facing corner with a handcrack. 80'

P3 5.9: (V2) Strenuous laybacking up a left-facing corner leads to a short chimney section that is followed by a handcrack that will take you up to a belay ledge with a fixed anchor (shared with **Fear of Flying**). (It is possible to rappel from here with two ropes to the fixed anchor at the Tree Island Ledge.) 120'

P4 5.8 G: Exposed cedar climbing: Follow handcracks straight up to a left-facing corner which is followed to a small ledge. (V3) Continue straight up and tunnel through a few cedar jungles in the process. 70'

V1 5.9 PG: Step right from the belay and climb up the face to gain the next crack to the right. Follow this crack straight up to the belay ledge. 80'

V2 Nestlings 5.10a G: From the base of the left-facing corner, traverse right along a horizontal crack (4" cam), around the arête, and onto the main face. A hard mantel leads to easier, well-protected face climbing for 15' that gains thin fingercracks (crux), then up strenuously for 25' past the right side of two trees to a horizontal. Stay in the steepening thin cracks until they fade, forcing a traverse right into the big chimney (join **Fear of Flying** here). Up the chimney to a ledge, then continue up the back side of a large flake to a fixed anchor on top. 125'

V3 5.10b G: Step right from the ledge, then up a shallow right-facing corner to a small, square overhang. Continue up the thin crack above to finish in chossy cedar terrain.

History: Rubin reported finding a piton at 30' in the initial crack. No more is known about it, but it was suspected by the first ascentionists to be the work of Dave Bernays.

FA Sep 8, 1974, Al Long, Al Rubin, Dave Hoffman
FA (V2) Aug 3, 1989, Don Mellor
FA (V3) 1988, Mark Ippolito

11 Fear of Flying 5.10b G 365' ★★★★

Yet another fine line that ascends the rightmost prominent crack line on the free-climbing side. This crack system can easily be seen from the parking area. Lots of wide cracks on this one.

Don Mellor begins the traverse on ***Nestlings*** *(5.10a). Photo by Jeff Edwards.*

P1 5.9+ G: Same as **Touch of Class**. 100'

P2 5.10a G: Traverse 20' right along a ledge system to a shallow right-facing corner with thin cracks. Climb the thin cracks and angle up and right to a curving handcrack. Follow the curving handcrack to a short, overhanging off-hands crack and on to a ledge with small cedars. 75'

P3 5.10b G: There are two cracks above the belay. Start climbing up in the right crack, move to the left crack (crux), then straight up the wide crack capped by a small overhang. Break the overhang on the left and up to a tree ledge. 60'

P4 5.6 G: From the right end of the ledge, climb up a block to a small right-facing corner. Exit left at the top of the corner and tunnel into the bowels of the cliff for 40' to emerge from behind a cedar to belay at a large, flat ledge with a fixed anchor. 50'

P5 5.10a G: Elegant and exposed. Climb water-worn fingercracks on black wall and trend right to a ledge. Traverse left on the ledge 25' to the fixed anchor (shared with **Spirit of Adventure**). 80'

History: The first attempt started to the right (between the normal start and the arête) and used a tree to gain a crack, then used aid (A2) to gain the P1 ledge. Long took a whipper on the fistcrack of P2, hence the route name. After the first ascentionists finally succeeded, Embick recalls driving home in Long's BMW and hitting 115 on the Thruway while brainstorming names for the route.

Gear: Up to 4.5" cam.

FA Sep, 1976, Al Long, Andrew Embick, Al Rubin

24
16
20
17
15
17
20
16
Party Ledge
24
20
16
15
14

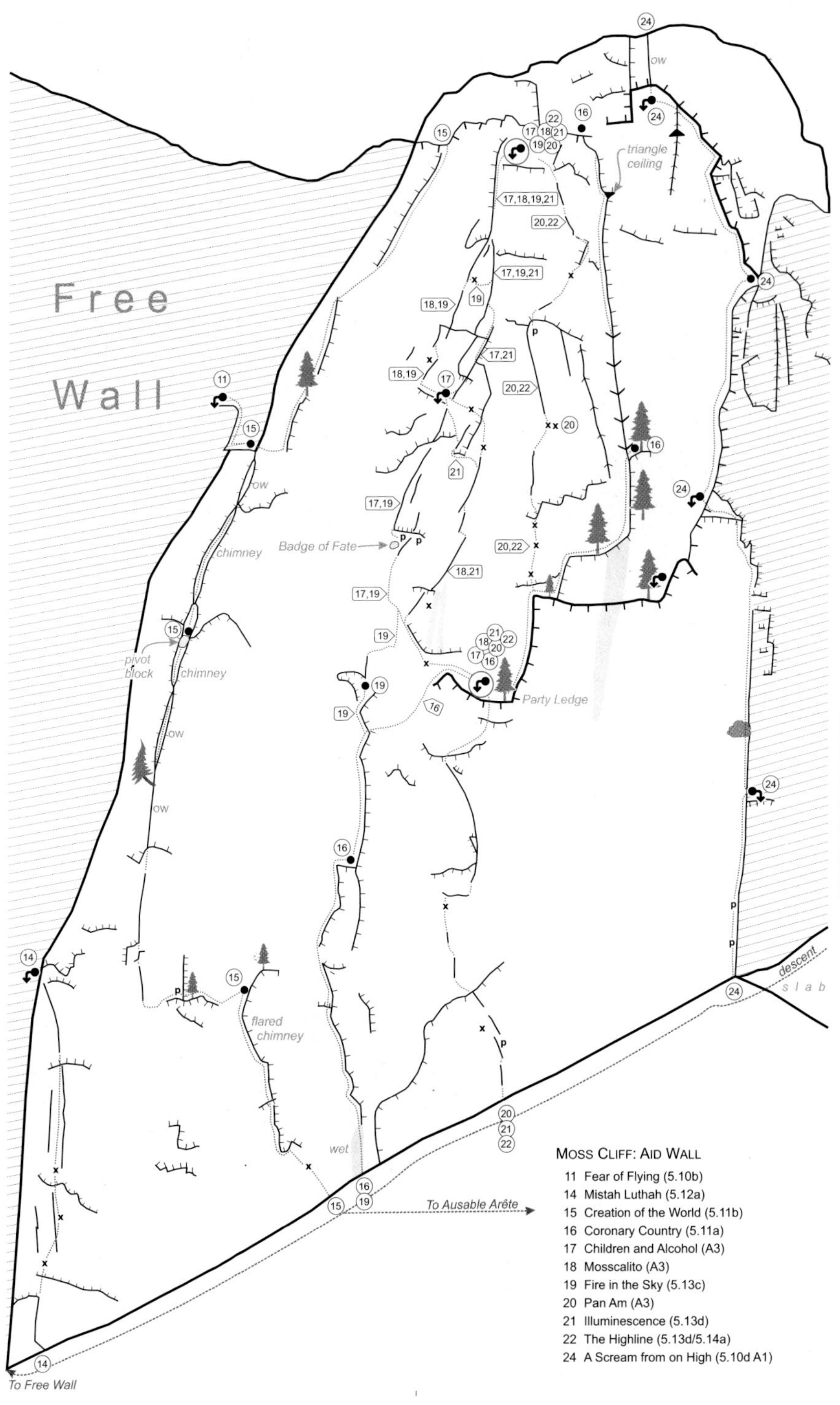
Free Wall
triangle ceiling
Badge of Fate
chimney
pivot block
chimney
flared chimney
wet
Party Ledge
descent
slab
To Ausable Arête
To Free Wall
Moss Cliff: Aid Wall
11 Fear of Flying (5.10b)
14 Mistah Luthah (5.12a)
15 Creation of the World (5.11b)
16 Coronary Country (5.11a)
17 Children and Alcohol (A3)
18 Mosscalito (A3)
19 Fire in the Sky (5.13c)
20 Pan Am (A3)
21 Illuminescence (5.13d)
22 The Highline (5.13d/5.14a)
24 A Scream from on High (5.10d A1)

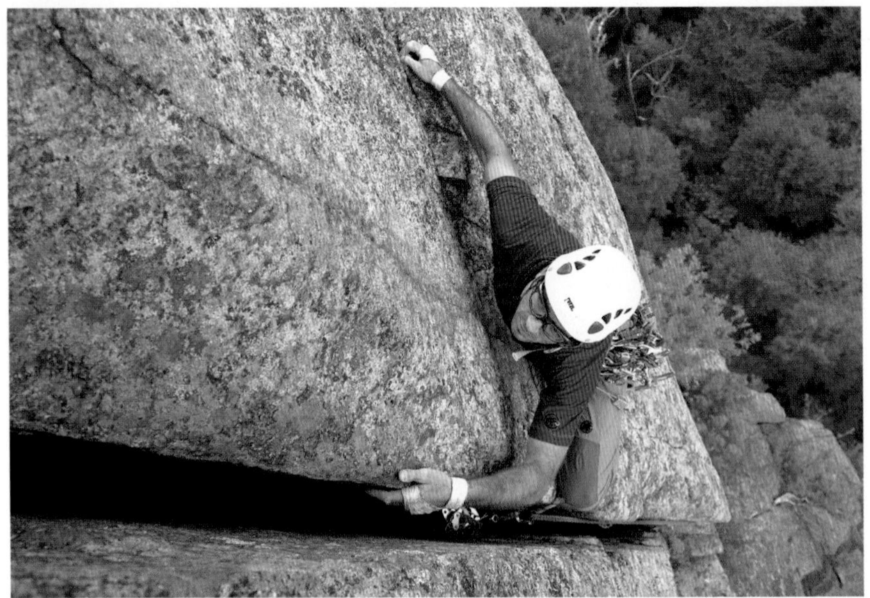

*Will Mayo on P3 (the crux pitch) of **Fear of Flying** (5.10b). Photo by David Le Pagne.*

12 Adirondack Black Fly Rancher A2+ 215' ★

The first ascent was climbed solo with a rescue litter as a portaledge. This route is a good candidate for a free attempt.

Start: 6' left of the arête at an offset finger- and hand-crack that begins on the left side of a knee-high overlap, and directly behind a 15'-high birch stump.

P1 A2+: Climb up the crack to the left side of a small ledge, then continue up the crack, which ascends the wall and arches left at the top. Switch 4' right to another good crack that goes up through a bulge (piton) to a good ledge (the right end of the **Touch of Class** ledge). 90'

P2 A2: Traverse right around an arête to a bush in a corner below some blocky ceilings. Up the corner past two overlaps on the right wall and up thin cracks in orange rock. Traverse left into a curving handcrack (the top of P2 of **Fear of Flying**) up to a cedar tree. 75'

P3 5.7 A2: Step right from the tree to thin discontinuous cracks and follow them to a slab. 5.7 climbing up the slab leads to a good ledge with cedar trees. 50'

FA Sep, 1988, Patrick Purcell (solo)

13 Brass Balls, Steel Nuts, and Sticky Rubber 5.12d PG 80' ★★★★★

Sustained, technical and powerful moves above small intermittent gear; a real testpiece of traditionally-protected climbing. Easily toproped from the **Mistah Luthah** anchor.

Start: At a short fingercrack in a shallow right facing corner, 3' left of the arête that divides the Free Wall and the Aid Wall. Also 3' right of **Adirondack Black Fly Rancher** and 6' left of (and around the corner from) **Mistah Luthah**.

P1 5.12d PG: Up the initial crack to a 2'-wide overlap, surge up to a jug, lieback and gaston up the left-trending flakes, and punch it back right past the crux bulge on crisp crimps. Finish by sidepulling up both sides of the arête to the fixed anchor at the top of **Mistah Luthah**. Have a cigar! 80'

Gear: Cams from purple C3 (#00) to yellow C3 (#2), 2 ea #3 RPs, other small wires.

FA Unknown

FFA Sep 1, 2008, Peter Kamitses, Will Mayo

*Tom Chervenak on P3 of **Creation of the World** (5.11b). Photo by Christian Fracchia.*

Jeff Achey on P2 (5.11a) of ***Creation of the World*** *(5.11b). Photo by Kennan Harvey.*

Aid Wall

The Aid Wall is the sheer 300'-high overhanging wall that forms the right side of the huge arête, named as such because it traditionally contained some high-quality aid routes. These are mostly now free but are still worthwhile outings for those looking for some long, clean aid routes.

The left side of the face has a huge off width and chimney, the line of **Creation of the World**; there is a giant hanging cedar growing from the off-width crack on P2. Right of this is a sea of left-facing flakes (**Coronary Country**) that forms the left edge of a low shield of smooth rock (**Pan Am**). Above the flakes and smooth shield is a large ledge with a fixed anchor, dubbed the Party Ledge and named for a great overnight party that took place here one November. (Don Mellor climbed P1 of **Pan Am** in the dark; Chuck Turner, Alan Jolley, and Kathy Bright jugged and slept on the ledge in the rain, drinking and tossing empty cans into the air.) The right side of the wall is defined by a 300'-high imposing corner with a magnificent roof crack at the top, the route **A Scream from on High**.

14 Mistah Luthah 5.12a G 80' ★★★★

Very cool climbing starting with a crack, then a hard techy face, and finally an amazing 5.10+ fingercrack. Solid for the grade.

Start: 3' right of the arête that separates the Free Wall and the Aid Wall, below a short fingercrack that goes through an overlap to a second overlap 10' up.

P1 5.12a: Up the initial crack, then negotiate a thin, technical face past three bolts (crux) to a striking splitter fingercrack. Follow the fingercrack to its top, which is at the right end of the **Touch of Class** P1 belay ledge at a fixed anchor. 80'

Gear: Double set of cams from green C3 to purple Camalot.

History: The route was established ground up on aid. The first free ascent party found a rusty piton at mid-height, indicating previous passage, most likely by someone thinking it was **Adirondack Black Fly Rancher**. With an unknown history, a name was chosen to honor Dennis Luther, a friend and partner of many local climbers, who perished in a climbing accident at Poke-O in 2007.

FFA Aug 26, 2008, Will Mayo, Peter Kamitses

15 Creation of the World 5.11b G (5.11a R) 350' ★★★★

A spectacular route with multiple sections of off width. A real prize. The route requires a style of climbing that isn't common in the Adirondacks. Peter Kamitses thought it was the hardest route he had ever climbed, and this was after he freed several of the aid lines on the same wall. The route is named in keeping with Nichols's geological theme (**Plate Tectonics**, **Continental Drift**, and so on).

Start: 75' right and uphill of the prominent arête's lowest point is a left-facing chimney-slot 30' up. This route begins uphill from and right of the slot by 15' at a low bolt and some left-slanting corners that lead to the chimney-slot.

P1 5.11a PG: Clip the bolt (while standing on the ground) and make difficult face moves leftward past the bolt to a small overlap with an A-shaped notch. Small TCUs and nuts protect the moves up the shallow left-facing corner and into the "flare." The flare constitutes the crux of the pitch and is easier for small people; awkward moves and good protection in the back of the flare (2.5" cam, nuts) take you to a small cedar and an adequate belay. 80'

P2 5.11a R: Step down and left from the belay onto rounded, green footholds. Move directly left (red Alien) and into a left-facing corner with fixed nuts (optional P1 belay). Continue straight left, then step down once again and climb desperately left (crux) until you finally reach some good cracks. Climb straight up—hands, then fists—to a stance. From here, the crack turns off width (6" cam); hard off-width climbing leads to better holds near the giant cedar. Continue up the off-width crack (another 6" cam) until the crack widens and is filled with flakes and blocks. The crack widens into a chimney; climb deeper into the cliff behind the wedged blocks until you finally emerge onto a giant, flat block the size of a dining room table where you can set a belay. This block is very spooky, as it weighs many tons yet pivots on a center axis. 100'

P3 5.11b G: Stemming and chimney technique allow you to climb up and out from the belay to where the crack pinches down to off-width size. A 6" cam protects the transition from stemming and chimneying to lay-backing. Strenuous laybacking and off-width climbing (another 6" cam) eventually give way to a hand- and fistcrack. Follow the crack to a spacious belay ledge on the arête. 50'

P4 5.9+ PG: (V1) From the belay, traverse thinly out right to gain a left-facing corner (blind nut placement) and follow the corner past a tree to a ledge. Move up to a sloping shelf, traverse right beneath an overhanging face to the arête, and climb the arête to a friction ramp and a short right-facing corner to the top. 120'

V1 5.10a G: A cleaner alternative climbs the top pitch of **Fear of Flying**. From the belay, walk left on the ledge to a large cedar and climb a dirty crack to a ledge with a fixed anchor. Pass this belay, then climb the water-worn fingercracks and trend right to the top.

Gear: Standard rack, including small TCUs, nuts, and cams. For large gear, 2 ea 3", 1 ea 3.5-4.5", 2 ea 6".

Descent: Walk off right to the gully.

History: The route was attempted in the early 1980s by Felix Modugno and Jim Damon, who approached the P2 crack more directly from below, but fell short. The video *Uncommon Ground*[1] has a section showing climbing on this route. The route was also featured in *Climbing* magazine,[2] with a spectacular photo of Jeff Achey leading the handcrack on P2 (this is described as the second ascent, but by that time, it had been climbed twice by Nichols and twice by Rich Romano).

FA Oct 10, 1987, Ken Nichols, Chad Hussey (P1, P4)

16 Coronary Country 5.11a R 320' ★★★

The first route to be climbed on the overhanging "aid section" of the cliff. At the time, Long and Rubin (each of whom took falls on the route) considered it difficult and heart-stoppingly scary. Sustained, with some 5.10 climbing on every pitch. A good adventure but doesn't get climbed very often.

Start: At a wet spot in a 15'-high left-facing, left-arching corner below a sea of left-facing flakes, 20' right of the low bolt of **Creation of the World**.

P1 5.11a R: Climb the left-facing corner and flakes above to a sloping ledge beneath a high left-facing corner. 80'

P2 5.10d PG: Climb up the left-facing corner above the belay for 40', traverse right onto sloping ledges, then up and right to the left end of the Party Ledge. Traverse right to a fixed anchor. 60'

P3 5.10b G: From the right end of the Party Ledge, climb up behind the tree to a left-facing corner. Up the corner (5.10b) to a ledge with a cedar. Step right to a smaller left-facing corner; move up this to a right-rising ledge. Traverse right on the ledge behind an annoying cedar to its right end, then up a left-facing corner to another ledge with a large cedar. 90'

P4 5.10c G: Up the left-facing corner above the belay past a triangular ceiling in the left-facing flake. Up this to the right end of the tree ledge. 90'

FA May 1, 1977, Al Long, Al Rubin

FFA Jul 13, 1984, Bill Dodd, Don Mellor

17 Children and Alcohol A3 170' ★★

Start: At the left end of the Party Ledge.

P1 A2: From the left end of the ledge, traverse left past a white streak to a bolt, then to a right-rising crack; **Mosscalito** follows this crack up and right, whereas **Children and Alcohol** angles up and left, past a white lichen patch, to a ceiling with many pitons on the face just below. Break the ceiling on the left and follow a right-leaning crack to a right-leaning overlap, then up to a ledge with a fixed anchor (shared with **Mosscalito**). 100'

P2 A3: Climb straight up to gain the right-leaning crack, then climb it to its top. Work left (bolt) to another crack and follow it straight up into a right-facing corner and on to a ledge with a fixed anchor. 70'

FA Apr, 1981, Mark Bon Signor, Alan Jolley, Don Mellor

18 Mosscalito A3 170' ★★

Start: At the left end of the Party Ledge.

P1 A3: Begin as for **Children and Alcohol**: From the left end of the ledge, traverse left past a white streak to a bolt, then to a right-leaning crack. **Children and Alcohol** continues up and left, whereas **Mosscalito** follows this right-leaning crack. Where the crack ends, step left to another crack, up past a bolt, then angle left to a right-facing corner. Swing left around the corner (bolt) and up left to the ledge with a fixed anchor (shared with **Children and Alcohol**). 100'

P2 A3: From the left end of the ledge, traverse left to a crack. Climb the crack straight up to where it ends (bolt), then left to a 3"-crack. Move up the crack to parallel thin right-leaning cracks that lead to a left-facing corner (joining **Children and Alcohol** here) and up to a ledge with a fixed anchor. 70'

Gear: Include 2 bat hooks, TCUs, knife blades, RURPs. Some fixed bashies.

FA Sep, 1994, Dominic Eisinger, Patrick Purcell

*Opposite: Peter Kamitses on the top section of **Fire in the Sky** (5.13c), belayed by Dave Sherratt. Photo by Rob Frost.*

1 Second Chance Productions / Rob Frost, 2002.

2 Jeff Achey, "The Rainy Season," *Climbing*, no. 50 (Mar 1995), p. 102.

19 Fire in the Sky
5.13c PG (5.11a R) 290' ★★★★★

This route combines sections of the two aid routes **Children and Alcohol** and **Mosscalito** to make a long totally free route. Named for Kamitses's son Sky Rowan. In Irish lore, *rowan* means "red," and the top of the route features red-colored rock.

Start: Same as **Coronary Country**.

P1 5.11a R: Begin by climbing the first pitch and a half of **Coronary Country**. Climb the left-facing corner and flakes above to a sloping ledge beneath a high left-facing corner. Continue straight up the left-facing crack and chimney (5.9 R). Instead of heading out right (as for **Coronary Country** P2), continue straight up to a belay at a sloping stance with a rotting fixed anchor. 150'

P2 5.13c PG: Climb above the belay to the top of the "teetering choss stack," then balance right 10'. Move up and angle left through overlaps and small flakes (tricky gear) to a small corner beneath a ceiling. Step left to a no-hands rest on top of the Badge of Fate (an odd flake pasted to the face), then over the ceiling via a right-leaning crack. Climb twin cracks to a small overlap (4.5" cam), then over the overlap to a boulder problem (crux) guarding the anchor. Clip a long runner on the anchor bolts, hand-traverse left, move up to a bolt, then layback up to twin cracks (second crux). Slap up the twin cracks, then step right (bolt) and continue up the crack (0.75" cam helpful) to huge jugs that mark the end of the hard climbing. Continue up the wide crack to a ledge with a fixed anchor. 140'

History: Peter Kamitses and Dave Sharratt climbed the route in four pitches on Sep 8, 2006, weighing in at 5.11a, 5.9, 5.12, and 5.13b. Four more days of effort were required for Kamitses to remove the hanging belay between the two top pitches.

FA (as 4 pitches) Sep 8, 2006, Peter Kamitses, Dave Sharratt

FA (complete) Sep 16, 2006, Peter Kamitses

20 Pan Am A3 300' ★★

This is now a totally free route: P1 is part of **Illuminescence**; P2 and P3 are part of **The Highline**. It's listed separately, should you wish to climb this as a clean-aid route.

Start: 30' right of **Children and Alcohol**, at a very thin crack in a sheer wall with a bolt on the left side 18' up.

P1 A3: Up the thin crack, past a ledge at 20', until the crack disappears (bolt). Rail right to a left-arching crack and follow it to the Party Ledge. 120'

P2 A3: From the right end of the Party Ledge, climb up behind the tree to a left-facing corner. Up the corner (5.10b) to a ledge with a cedar. From the left end of the ledge (bolt), aid up a thin crack left of orange rock to the left end of a stepped overhang. Break through the overhang on its left end and into a crack; follow this until it disappears, then up and right to a fixed anchor. 90'

P2 A3: Head up a left-leaning crack to its end at the left end of an overlapping flake. Climb up, angle right to a bolt, then angle up and left to a slab finish. There is a fixed anchor on the left end of this ledge. 90'

History: This route was coincidentally put up the same day as **Children and Alcohol**, making it perhaps the busiest day in this wall's history.

FA Apr, 1981, Mike Heintz, John Sahi

21 Illuminescence
5.13d PG (5.11 R) 260' ★★★★★

Another extreme trad route succumbs to the amazing talent and persistence of Kamitses. The route combines pitches of **Pan Am**, **Mosscalito**, and **Children and Alcohol** in a masterpiece of free climbing, supertechnical and difficult from bottom to top. Named after Kamitses's son Bodhi, which means illuminated or enlightened.

P1 5.13a G (5.11 R): Same as P1 of **Pan Am**: Stick-clip the first bolt and make a hard boulder move up the thin crack, past a ledge at 20', until the crack disappears (bolt). Rail right to a left-arching crack and follow it (with a substantial runout over a #3 RP) to the Party Ledge. 120'

P2 5.13d PG: From the left end of the Party Ledge, angle out left over a white streak, past a bolt, to a right-leaning crack. Up the right-leaning crack past another bolt to a small shelf. Step left and continue up another crack to a preplaced 6' runner on a high bolt. Head left to a hard boulder problem (crux) to gain an overlap, over this (clipping another preplaced long runner on a bolt), then runout up and left to the fixed anchor. Climb past the anchor up the right-angling crack to where the crack pinches off, traverse left on face holds to a bolt, then up a crack to the jugs that mark the end of the hard climbing. Continue up the wide crack to a ledge with a fixed anchor. 140'

FA Oct 5, 2006, Peter Kamitses

22 The Highline 5.13d/5.14a R 140' ★★★★★

This follows P2 and P3 of the aid route **Pan Am** as one long pitch (the first pitch of **Pan Am** was freed as part of **Illuminescence**). Compared to **Ill Fire** to its left, it has easier cruxes, but more pump.

P2 5.13d/5.14a R: From the right end of Party Ledge, climb up the handcrack in the corner behind the cedar tree to gain the top of a pedestal, clip a bolt, then climb up a seam past the initial technical and powerful crux, clipping two more bolts. At a small overlap, run it out to gain the first good nut, and a decent shake. Climb 50' up a twin crack system (good gear), past the old hanging belay station to gain a good rest at two-thirds height. Punch it up through the runout redpoint crux—a big move up and right off a flat undercling protected by an RP in a constriction. Balance up to a good stance (cam at your knees), then do the final 5.11 section past another good RP to a fixed anchor. 140'

History: Kamitses worked the line for several years; it was a year before he finally linked it on toprope. Named for the "balancy, runout and serious nature" of the route, and for its position high on the wall.

FA Nov 22, 2012, Peter Kamitses

23 III Fire (linkup) 5.14a PG 140' ★★★★★

It's a tossup between this route and **Oppositional Defiance Disorder** (the pure trad route of the same grade at the Tsunami Slab at Silver Lake) for the most difficult and demanding climb in the Adirondack Park. Kamitses was finally able to send this after 5 days of effort. Super pumpy and technical.

Start: At the Party Ledge. There are various ways to reach the ledge, the easiest being P1 of **Coronary Country**.

P1 5.14a PG: Climb **Illuminiscence** P2 (5.13d) to where it intersects **Fire in the Sky** (the belay for **Children and Alcohol**). Continue left, and finish on P2 of **Fire in the Sky** (5.13c). 140'

FA Sep 26, 2008, Peter Kamitses

24 A Scream from on High 5.10d A1 350'

This awesome-looking Beaman creation hasn't gone free. This is also the line of the winter route **Bobo the Circus Idiot**.

Start: 75' uphill from and right of **Pan Am** and at the height of land along the base of the cliff, below a huge corner with a splash of orange lichen on the right.

Route Description: For P1, climb the corner past two pitons to a good ledge with a runner around a large fixed block. For P2, continue up the corner, which becomes wider; past a bush to another ledge; then over a bulge to another ledge below the chossy left-arching roofs. Climb up the left-arching chossy roofs (wet and mossy here) to a ledge below a giant pointy flake; traverse left to a left-facing corner and fixed anchor. For P3, continue up the left-facing corner to an alcove on the right with trees. For P4, climb the left-arching orange corner into a chimney, then up to a roof. Aid around the roof to the left following the arching corner leftward, around an arête, to a fixed anchor. For P5, climb out the roof (wow . . . free at 5.10d) via the awesome-looking roof crack, then up the flared crack to the top.

FA 1994, Tim Beaman, Sylvia Lazarnick

Ausable Arete

This is the chossy, wooded arête and broken cliffs right of the Aid Wall. There are several adventure routes reported here.

25 Misadventures on Ausable Arête 5.9 R 255'

Climbs the left side of the broken, chossy, vegetated arête that forms the right side of the descent gully, just right of the main cliff. From the road, this looks more appealing than it is. There are many ways to climb the ridge, but all involve an adventure of loose rock, cedar thrashing, and poor protection. Despite this, the ridge offers an exposed position and excellent views of the overhanging section of Moss Cliff.

Start: From the base of **Creation of the World**, head up and right across the gully to a ledge among the cedars. This makes as good a starting point as any.

P1 5.6 G: Thrash up and right to the crest of the ridge and follow it to a belay ledge at the base of a cleanish wall, left of the ridge crest. 80'

P2 5.9 R: Head up the cleanish wall (5.9 R) above the belay, then right to the ridge crest. Follow the ridge crest up loose blocks and cedars; near the top, the ridge becomes better defined, ending at a beautiful ledge with a giant pine tree perched at the top of the arête. (Incidentally, from the top of the descent gully, you can scramble to this pine tree, which makes an incredible vantage point from which to photograph the big wall.) 175'

History: This ascent was a failed attempt to find the "groove" pitch of **Ausable Arête**. Fixed gear was found on the clean face left of the arête.

ACB Dec 21, 2005, Jim Lawyer, Dennis Luther, Leslie Ackerman

26 Ausable Arête 5.9 R 435'

This historic route, the second route climbed at Moss Cliff, is a disappointing adventure of lichen, dirt, loose rock, and unstable trees. The final pitch is reportedly of better quality and can be reached by traversing right in the gully near **Creation of the World**, then around the arête to the base of the groove.

Start: To the right of the gully that accesses the routes on the Aid Wall is the sharply defined arête. A large dihedral leads up the right-hand base of the arête. Begin in the first corner system left of the main dihedral.

P1 5.9: Fight loose rock, lichen, dirt, unstable trees, and difficult climbing for 140' to a ledge with a pine tree 10' above. Climb a crack in the wall (5.9) to an insecure belay above an unstable pine. 155'

P2 5.7 R: Climb the V-groove behind the pine and exit left onto easier rock, then up right to ledges. 50'

P3 5.9 R: Climb 12' to a ledge below a wide corner, up and left with difficulty out of the corner to a stance, then up and left over a bulge (5.9 R) to easier ground and belay. 50'

P4 5.5 PG: Traverse down right under the base of the arête to the tree below the groove. 20'

P5 5.9 G: Follow the steep, strenuous groove, which leads directly to the crest of the arête. 160'

FA Jul 5, 1975, Al Long, Al Rubin

Ausable Buttress

Right of Ausable Arête, the terrain rises to a gully, then drops downhill to the right along the base of a long wall, the top of which is covered with dead trees from a recent forest fire, and prickly plants. Tim Beaman is rumored to have climbed here, although he can't remember for sure exactly where. Presently, this is an adventure-climbing area, as there's plenty of loose rock and vegetation, with jungle-like terrain at the base.

27 Cream on Top 5.9 TR 100'

A fun splitter handcrack; you pull on a big block to top out. The bottom is a jungle, lower in from the top.

FA (TR) Aug, 2009, Michael Leblanc, Diana Leblanc

28 Don't Give Guns to Children 5.8 PG 200'

This route is located downhill along the base of the long wall several hundred feet, just right of a small buttress of white rock with a cedar tree on top. Just right are two stacked right-facing corners. Climb the corners, then wander up to the top.

FA 1998, R.L. Stolz, Peter Throne

Photo by Michael Leblanc.

ALCATRAZ

Location	North side of NY 86 in Wilmington Notch
Aspect	Southeast
Height	120'
Quality	★★★★
Approach	50 min, difficult
Summary	Steep, intimidating cliff with only difficult routes; a hard-man's playground.

-5.6	5.7	5.8	5.9	5.10	5.11	5.12	5.13+	total
					1	3	1	5

This is the imposing wall up and left of Moss Cliff (when viewed from the road). It's a steep (i.e., overhanging) wall with only six very difficult, high-quality routes, guarded by a difficult approach. The climbs are moderately cleaned, but still with an adventurous feel.

The left side of the cliff has a small but decent base area, but the right side is higher and exposed with slabs beneath you. The entire middle of the cliff is split by an intimidating roof with hanging corners, tooth-like daggers, and stem boxes. The rock quality is excellent. Those that have visited report this as THE place for hard climbing.

ACCESS

The first part of the approach is shared with Moss Cliff, which is usually closed until late summer for peregrine nesting. Alcatraz is not part of this closure, but if you go there, don't linger around Moss Cliff.

HISTORY

Alcatraz Island (aka "The Rock") was America's first maximum security prison, and housed some of the most notorious troublemakers from 1934 to 1963. Although it is not situated on an island, Conor Cliffe found similarities between Alcatraz and this cliff when he began his visits in the summer of 2012: the approach is tough and dangerous, the routes are as hard as the criminals were bad, and the rock has black and white stripes like a prison uniform.

Cliffe spent 12 days at here during the 2012 season. On more than one occasion, he "hucked himself off big cliffs" on the approach, luckily landing in the tops of trees. The approach has since been tamed with several fixed ropes.

In the fall of 2012, Cliffe introduced Matt McCormick to the cliff. He not only climbed **The Great Escape**, but he cleaned up some of the other lines as well, and further tamed the approach.

DIRECTIONS (MAPS PAGES 387 AND 393)

From the parking (0 hr 0 min), approach Moss Cliff (30 min). Continue up and left, staying against the cliff. When the slope steepens, claw straight uphill and find the first fixed handrail at 39 min. At the top of this rope you can see the right end of Alcatraz above you. At 44 min reach a second fixed handrail, and at 50 min reach the base of the cliff at **The Godfather** 587504,4910233.

1 Machine Gun Kelly 5.11+ G 100' ★★

The final 15' fingercrack is very photogenic, overhanging 5'. Could use some additional cleaning.

Start: Located on a separate, orange-colored buttress, walk downhill and left from the main face. Begin at a fistcrack.

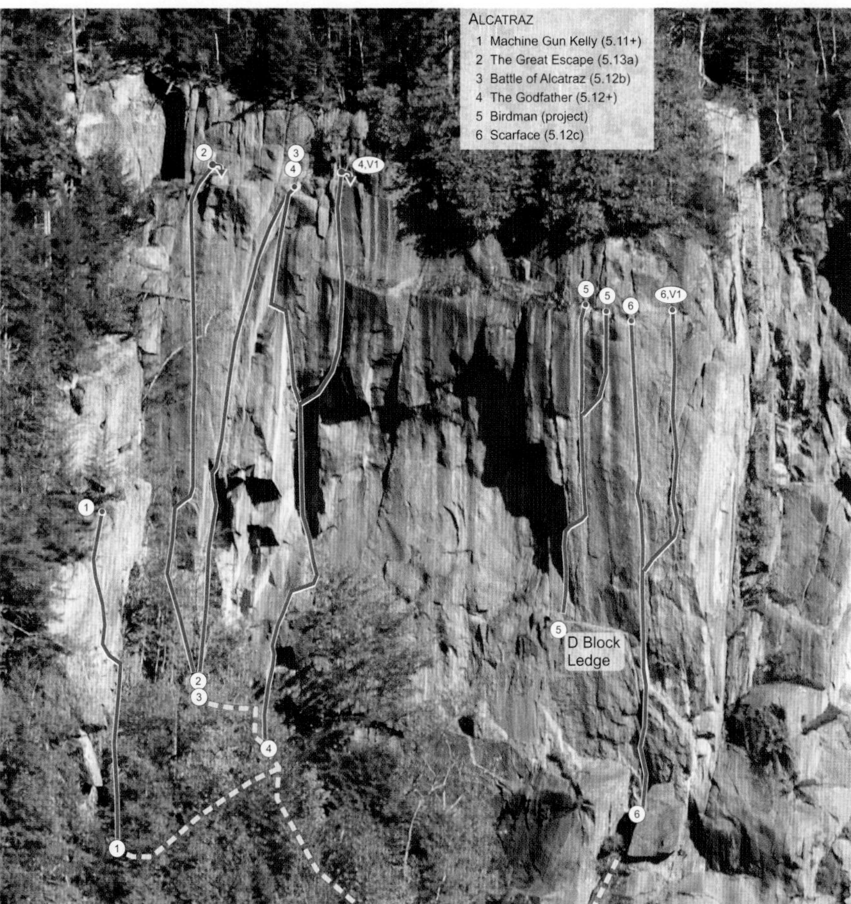

P1 5.11+ G: Follow the fistcrack up and right, duck under a pair of birch trees that nearly touch the rock, up to a small ceiling. Stay in the crack to where it becomes a right-facing corner. Make a tricky step left to gain an overhanging fingercrack which is followed to the top. 100'
FFA Jul 22, 2012, Conor Cliffe, Colin Loher

2 The Great Escape 5.13a G 105' ★★★★★

Reported as "super cool" with the crux at the move into the final fingercrack. High-quality and clean, this route follows a slightly overhanging crack-seam.

Start: In the middle of the main wall (the start of **The Godfather**), go left, and make a 4th-class move up a corner onto a broad ledge. Begin at the left edge of the main wall, in a wide dihedral just left of a right-facing corner capped by roofs (the **Battle of Alcatraz**). There are some trees growing out of the wide dihedral 25' up.

P1 5.13a G: Stem up the dihedral past a small cam placement to a bolt just right of a shallow, 4'-high left-facing corner. Make a bouldery move right to a jug then up to a slot (gear). Punch it above the gear, then climb past 2 bolts to pull into the final, beautiful fingercrack. Fixed anchor. 105'

Gear: A small rack of finger-size cams.
FA Sep 20, 2012, Matt McCormick

3 Battle of Alcatraz (aka BOA) 5.12b G 105' ★★★★

Very clean with physical climbing and good rests. Be aware that the crux is protected by gear in a thin seam on the edge of a huge hollow block, which seems solid but is unnerving.

Start: Just right of **The Great Escape** at a right-facing, right-leaning corner capped by roofs.

P1 5.12b G: Go up the corners into a hanging slot at its highest point. Continue straight up a crack to its end. You can rap from the anchors on **The Great Escape** just to the left. 105'

History: Named for a two-day, unsuccessful escape attempt initiated by Bernard Coy and Marvin Hubbard in May 1946.
FA Jul 22, 2012, Conor Cliffe, Colin Loher

4 The Godfather 5.12+ G 100' ★★★

Amazing stemming guarded by some extremely thin moves near the start. It's worth aiding through these fingernail crimps to gain the better climbing above (which is 5.11+/5.12a).

Start: 10' down and right of **Battle of Alcatraz** (just below the 4th-class move that gains the broad ledge where **The Great Escape** and **Battle of Alcatraz** begin) at a crack that leads into a three-sided box-like alcove (the "missing cell").

P1 5.12+ G: Good holds lead into the three-sided box-like alcove, and then up to a ledge. Step right and go up a series of heinously thin face moves to gain a slightly-overhanging, orange-colored, flared, stem box. Make fun moves up the stem box with a crack on the left (V1) to gain a jug out left. Continue up a right-facing corner, then pull left around an arête. A final right-facing corner leads to the top. 100'

V1 Bookmaker's Variation 5.13a G ★★★★: Clean, fun, and airy. At the top of the stem box, make a series of undercling moves right, then up discontinuous cracks to the top. This variation is prepared for leading, but awaits a redpoint; reported as sustained, and a bit harder than the regular route. Awaits a lead.

History: Named for Ellsworth "Bumpy" Johnson (inmate No. 1117) who was imprisoned at Alcatraz from 1954 to 1963.

FA Oct 13, 2012, Conor Cliffe
FA (V1, on toprope) Oct, 2012, Conor Cliffe

5 Birdman Project

This open project has great gear and is mostly clean except at the finish. Begin on the left side of the "D Block Ledge" at a prominent left-facing corner, on top of a perched block—the "D Block"—which acts as a cheater stone. (You can get here by climbing the first section of **Scarface**, or by rappel.) Go up the corner until the crack fades. Move strenuously right around an arête, then up the arête and crack until you can transfer into a left-facing corner. Go past a "shark fin", then up dirty rock to the top, around 5.12+, 80'. (It's harder—but more classic—to move right before the "shark fin".)

History: Robert Stroud (aka "Bridman") spent seventeen years in solitary confinement on D Block.

6 Scarface 5.12c R 120' ★★★★

Exposed, clean, fun, and full value. Falling at the crux would likely result in an upside-down fall.

Start: From the top of the second fixed handrail, go right. Climb and scramble right (probably want to rope up) to a large boulder in a right-facing corner. This is 35' below the right side of the "D Block Ledge", a ledge with a perched block on its left side (the start of **Birdman**).

P1 5.12c R: Up the crack to a stance out right (5.9, dirty) and then past the D Block Ledge. (V1) Continue straight up the crack to the top. 120'

V1 Bootlegger Variation 5.11a G ★★: 15' above the right side of D Block Ledge, move right and up a series of dirty cracks to the top.

History: Named for the Alphonse Gabriel Capone.

FA Jul 25, 2012, Conor Cliffe, George Clark
FA (V1) Jul 25, 2012, Conor Cliffe, George Clark

HIGH FALLS CRAG

Location	South side of NY 86 in Wilmington Notch
Aspect	North
Height	250'
Quality	★★★
Approach	10 min, easy
Summary	A shaded cliff with big features—roofs, cracks, and corners—and a few high-quality cracks.

-5.6	5.7	5.8	5.9	5.10	5.11	5.12	5.13+	total
				3	1			4

This fearsome-looking cliff towers high above the road and Ausable River with orange roofs, corners, and disconcerting streaks of water. The right side of the face is broken by a deep left-leaning V-gully (the winter route **Multiplication Gully**) and the start of the rock route **High Falls**. Left of the V-gully is a large roof system at midheight on the cliff, below which is the Jeff Edwards Pinnacle. Left of this is a large right-facing corner capped by a right-rising stepped roof; no routes here, but 20' left are the routes **Route of Oppressive Power** and **There Be Dragons**, marked by a bottomless chimney just above tree line.

The real prize at High Falls Crag is **Route of Oppressive Power**, a bottomless chimney and long handcrack.

The cliff is north-facing and rarely visited, so expect some dirt and plan accordingly (e.g., bring material to refresh the anchors).

HISTORY

The first visitor was Rich Romano, ticking the plumb line in 1978. A crew of locals (Don Mellor, Patrick Purcell, Jeff Edwards, and Bill Dodd), thinking the cliff was virgin, climbed all of the lines on this cliff in the mid-1980s. Mellor was particularly proud of **Route of Oppressive Power**, the cliff's best line, only to find that it had been done previously.

DIRECTIONS (MAP PAGE 387)

Parking for High Falls Crag is at a small gravel pullout on the north (river) side of the road 588507,4910343, 5.0 miles from Wilmington (when driving toward Lake Placid), 1.9 miles from the Whiteface Ski Center (again, when driving toward Lake Placid), and 6.9 miles from Lake Placid (when driving toward Wilmington, measured from the intersection of NY 86 and NY 73).

From the parking area, walk toward Lake Placid for 400' to a "Welcome to Wilmington" sign visible to traffic coming from Lake Placid. Cross the road and walk into the woods on a faint trail. The trail improves and goes steeply uphill through pretty moss-covered talus to reach the cliff. The trail then makes a hard left through open talus, then up to the base of a deep, wet gully that breaks the cliff. This is the ice route **Multiplication Gully** and the start of the rock route **High Falls** 588558,4910176.

DESCENT OPTIONS

Rappel the route; walking around is not an option.

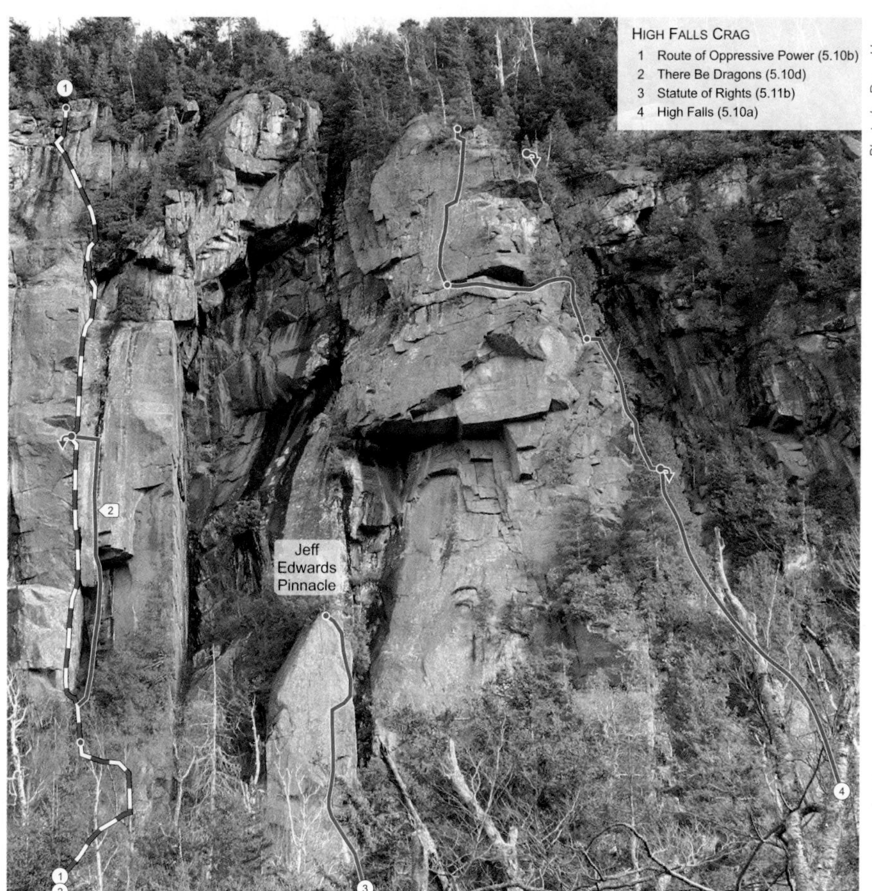

Photo by Drew Haas.

1 Route of Oppressive Power 5.10b G 250' ★★★★

An excellent route and a real North Country prize. Despite its dark and ominous appearance, it is actually much easier and more pleasant than it looks, especially in that it doesn't require pure off-width technique.

Start: Left of the Jeff Edwards Pinnacle is a giant right-facing corner in a large depression beneath high stepped roofs (the hidden left wall of the corner has good-looking unclimbed cracks). 20' left of the corner and at the high point of the terrain is a boulder that marks the start of this route, directly below roofs and the bottomless chimney.

P1 5.7 G: There is an awful-looking straight-up crack that leads to a sloped ledge; don't climb this. Instead, work up and right on a cedar-covered ledge to a shallow right-facing corner with a fingercrack. Up the crack to a sloped ledge, then traverse left to an uncomfortable stance on a wet, sloping ledge. 50'

P2 5.10b G: Climb thin cracks on the left wall of the corner (small nuts and TCUs), working out and left to better holds on the arête. Up the arête (no gear, but easy) to the bottomless chimney. Easy squeeze climbing narrows to off width (6" cam), then finally to hands in a right-facing corner. Up the corner to the "balcony seat," an exposed ledge on the overhanging left wall. There is a fixed anchor in the crack. 80'

P3 5.8 G: Continue up the right-facing corner to a ceiling, which is bypassed on the left wall of the corner, then up to a cedar ledge. Follow a right-facing, left-rising ramp past another ceiling, then up overhanging blocks to the top. 120'

History: For a long time, locals fantasized about the hanging chimney and handcrack of **Route of Oppressive Power**. It was rumored that Jim Dunn and Henry Barber had even talked about the line. This set the stage for Mellor's ascent of the route, an accomplishment that he was particularly proud of, calling the line **There Be Dragons**. In his 1986 suppliment, Mellor enthusiastically declared this one of the best routes in the Adirondacks. Like other routes around the region, it was later learned that Rich Romano had climbed this line 10 years earlier. The "Dragons" name was reused on the neighboring route.

FA 1978, Rich Romano

2 There Be Dragons 5.10d G 80' ★★

Really a single-pitch variation to **Route of Oppressive Power**. "There Be Dragons" was written on ancient maps to indicate dangerous, unknown places.

Start: The top of P1 of **Route of Oppressive Power**.

P1 5.10d G: Just right of the large right-facing corner is a shallow left-facing corner, often wet. Climb the crack in the left-facing corner to the square roof, around this on its right side into a deep right-facing corner. Up the corner to a large multitiered roof. Break through the roof via a good handcrack; follow this to a wide section below some cedars. Traverse left to the fixed anchor (same as for P2 of **Route of Oppressive Power**). 80'

FA Jun, 1985, Don Mellor, Bill Dodd, Patrick Purcell

3 Statute of Rights 5.11b TR 80'

Left of the deep, wet V-gully that splits the cliff is a series of huge orange roofs 150' up (there are two bolts below the roof, courtesy of the winter route **Long-Term Division**). Below the left side of these roofs is a deep gash filled with trees and brush that forms the right side of the Jeff Edwards Pinnacle. The route begins on the right side of the pinnacle, climbs up to a roof, then out the roof via a gnarly crack, which is climbed to its end. Work right to the arête, which is followed to the top.

History: Purcell attempted to lead this route but gave up due to lack of protection.

FA (TR) Oct 28, 1993, Patrick Purcell, Chris Hyson

4 High Falls 5.10a G 230' ★★★

The top pitch is excellent and exposed.

Start: At the height of the cone-shaped slope below the deep, wet V-gully that splits the cliff.

P1 4th class: Step left onto a nice block on the left side of the gully, then angle up and right following the cleanest line to several cedar trees on the left side of the gully, one of which has a fixed anchor. 50'

P2 5.6 G: Step left to a shallow left-facing corner with a 5"-wide zigzag crack. Up the crack to its end, then face-climb for 15' (5.6) to a ledge with a cedar. 60'

P3 5.8 G: Traverse left under a ceiling to a huge hanging flake, then leftward along the top of the flake to a belay at its far side below a vertical fingercrack. 50'

P4 5.10a G: Ascend the beautiful (but somewhat dirty) crack to a horizontal. Work right and continue up a vertical crack to the summit. 70'

Descent: Rappel the gully to the right (the winter route **Multiplication Gully**), which has many fixed anchors.

FA Sep 14, 1988, Jeff Edwards, Don Mellor, Patrick Purcell

Cloudspin Cliff. Photo by Colin Loher.

CLOUDSPIN CLIFF

Location	South side of NY 86, near the Whiteface Ski Center
Aspect	North
Height	140'
Quality	★★★
Approach	15 min, easy
Summary	Small cliff with two very good routes.

-5.6	5.7	5.8	5.9	5.10	5.11	5.12	5.13+	total
1	1	1		2	1			6

As you drive toward Whiteface, you can see this cliff on the hillside above the road after you pass High Falls Gorge. You can also see the cliff from the Whiteface Ski Center. The rock is dirty, as you would expect with a north-facing cliff, but even so, there are two really good routes here (**Frippery** and **Grand Ole Osprey**) that deserve more attention.

For first-time visitors, the routes will be difficult to locate. The left end of the cliff is defined by a large right-facing orange corner. About 90' right of this corner is the base of **Grand Ole Osprey**, and another 25' right is a small triangular cave used as a landmark for **Frippery**. The right side of the cliff, with the routes **Pink Lynch** and **Demolition**, has several large, high roofs above a sea of nondescript rock.

HISTORY

The cliff was first visited by Don Mellor and Jeff Edwards, who were looking for places to bring students of the Northwood School in Lake Placid. Since the cliff is directly in front of your as you drive toward Whiteface, it was an obvious place to investigate. Early explorations focused on the right end, and it wasn't until 1991 that the better sheer face in the center was explored. Mellor named the cliff after the Olympic downhill ski run on Whiteface.

DIRECTIONS (MAP PAGE 413)

Park on the road in front of the state campground in Wilmington Notch 590775,4911342, 0.3 mile southwest (toward Lake Placid) from the Whiteface Ski Center. Walk toward Lake Placid for 250 yards until you encounter a yellow "Campground" sign (visible to cars heading toward Wilmington). Walk 20 yards past this to a cairn and turn into the woods. A mild bushwhack on a bearing of 160° leads to the base of the cliff 590742,4911002, about 15 min. There is a path with cairns, but it's nearly impossible to find on the approach.

DESCENT OPTIONS

Walk off easily to the left.

1 Destined for Obscurity 5.10c PG 150'

Start: 30' uphill and left of the base of the vegetated left-rising ramp (as for **Grand Ole Osprey**) and 60' right of a prominent orange right-facing corner at the left end of the cliff, on a sloped, dirty left-rising ledge below a very dirty handcrack.

P1 5.7 G: Climb the dirty handcrack to a ledge at 30'. Step left and belay at trees. 40'

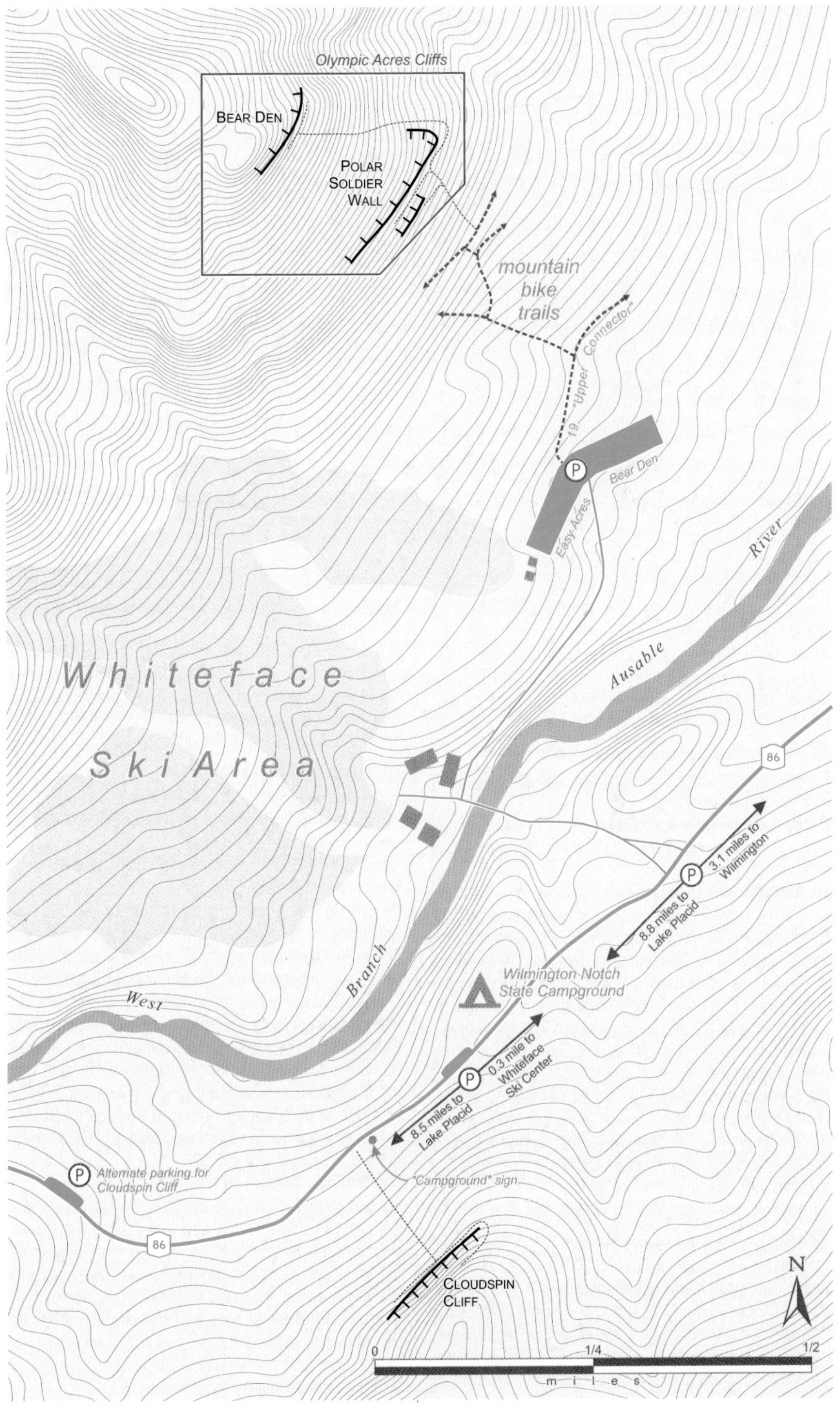

Olympic Acres Cliffs
Bear Den
Polar Soldier Wall
mountain bike trails
19. "Upper Connector"
Bear Den
Easy Acres
River
Ausable
Whiteface
Ski Area
West
Branch
86
3.1 miles to Wilmington
8.8 miles to Lake Placid
Wilmington Notch State Campground
0.3 mile to Whiteface Ski Center
8.5 miles to Lake Placid
Alternate parking for Cloudspin Cliff
"Campground" sign
86
Cloudspin Cliff
N
0
1/4
1/2
miles

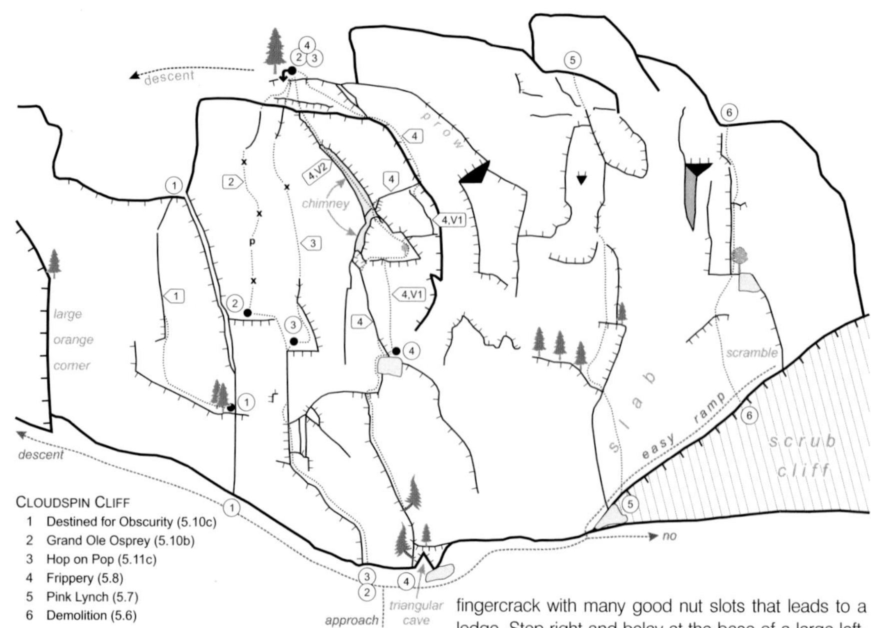

P2 5.10c PG: Traverse up and left on the ledge for 30' to a short, white right-facing corner. Follow a fingercrack straight up, then rightward to the top. 110'
Gear: Standard rack, including RPs.
FA May 14, 1987, Jeff Edwards, Chris Lees

2 Grand Ole Osprey 5.10b G 140' ★★★★

Climbs much better than it looks—great rock, great moves, and unlikely line.
Start: A bit nondescript—25' left of a triangular 5'-high cave at a left-rising vegetated ramp that leads to an orange right-facing corner.
P1 5.10b G: Walk up a left-rising tree ramp to the base of a short right-facing orange corner capped by a 6" overhang. Up the corner to its top, step left onto the face, move back right into a fingercrack with many good nut slots that leads to a ledge, then up another steep bulge to a narrow ledge system. Traverse left 10' to a good belay. (A 3.5" piece works well for the belay, plus an indirect to the follower off the first bolt of the next pitch.) 70'
P2 5.10b G: Climb up right to a bolt, then to a horizontal crack with a piton. Move up right to good holds, then back left (bolt, 2" cam). Several friction moves up the face lead to an undercling out right to the top and a fixed anchor on a tree. 70'
FA May 13, 1991, Don Mellor, Duff Dunlop

3 Hop on Pop 5.11c G 140' ★★★

Named for a Dr. Seuss book.
Start: Same as Grand Ole Osprey.
P1 5.10b G: Same as Grand Ole Osprey: Walk up a left-rising tree ramp to the base of a short right-facing orange corner capped by a 6" overhang. Up the corner to its top, step left onto the face, then back right into a fingercrack with many good nut slots that leads to a ledge. Step right and belay at the base of a large left-facing flake (4" cam). 60'
P2 5.11c G: Climb the left-facing, left-arching overhanging flake to its top, then up the face to a shallow left-facing corner. From the top, clip a bolt, then hand-traverse left to a crack finish. 80'
FA May 6, 1992, Don Mellor, Jeff Erenston

4 Frippery 5.8 G 160' ★★★

A high-quality route with an airy, exposed traverse on P2. Well worth the approach. The route name refers to showy and elaborate clothing.
Start: 3' left of the triangular 5'-high cave, below a V-slot with a cedar at the bottom.
P1 5.7 G: Pull up past the cedar and up the V-groove until it becomes a right-facing corner; up the excellent corner to a ledge. Step right on the ledge and climb the left side of a large detached block, belaying on its top (3" cams for the belay). 80'
P2 5.8 G: (V1) From the ledge, climb up a fingercrack to its top, then head right to the base of the left-leaning off width. Continue up the off width for 10', (V2) then traverse right to a small left-facing corner. Up the corner to a horizontal crack. An exposed traverse leads right for 20' to an arête; step around to the right side of the arête and climb to the top. 80'
V1 Trouser Gallery 5.12a G (5.6 X): Face-climb right of the fingercrack to the ledge (good wire, then runout). Step right to the large left-facing, left-leaning corner that leads to the off width. Step right around the corner, where a strenuous traverse right in a horizontal crack leads to a left-rising fingercrack (crux). Follow it to the next horizontal, then join the normal route to the top. Named for one of four videos in "Sprockets," a *Saturday Night Live* skit in which the audience votes on Germany's most disturbing home video.

V2 1968 Offwidth Pants 5.8 PG: Continue up and left in the off width to its top, then exit left to the top and fixed anchor. A couple of 8" tube chocks will suffice for protection. The name pokes fun at Mellor's pants, which were vintage and clearly not built for off widths.

History: The route was first climbed via the **1968 Offwidth Pants** variation. The first ascent of the route as described occurred later, in a snowstorm.

FA Apr 16, 1992, Don Mellor, Scott Peterson
FA (V1) Jun 12, 1991, Don Mellor, Jeff Edwards
FFA (V1) Jun 24, 1991, Don Mellor
FA (V2) May, 1991, Jeff Edwards, Don Mellor, Brad Hess

5 Pink Lynch 5.7 PG 100'

Start: Walk right 60' from the triangular cave that marks the start of **Frippery** to a narrow right-rising ramp that leads to the upper right section of the cliff. This route begins 30' up this ramp below a clean slab, just right of a right-facing dirty groove.

P1 5.7 PG: Up the clean slab through an angular bulge, then left to a ledge with a tree. Climb a face up and right to the next ledge. Continue up the face just left of an arête to gain an open book, then a crack, which leads to the left end of a huge roof. Break the roof on its left side via a crack, then up an open book. 100'

FA May 4, 1987, Don Mellor, Jamie Bellanca, Tim Lynch

6 Demolition 5.6 PG 90'

Start: Walk right 60' from the triangular cave that marks the start of **Frippery** to a narrow right-rising ramp that leads to the upper right section of the cliff. This route begins near the top of the ramp at a jumble of boulders beneath a large square roof.

P1 5.6 PG: Climb nondescript rock to gain a ledge with a birch, below two right-facing corners. Climb the rightmost of these corners via a good crack to a ledge, then angle up and left to the top. 90'

FA May 4, 1987, Jeff Edwards, Dan Stauft

OLYMPIC ACRES

Location	Whiteface Mountain Ski Area
Summary	Two walls with some obscure crack routes.

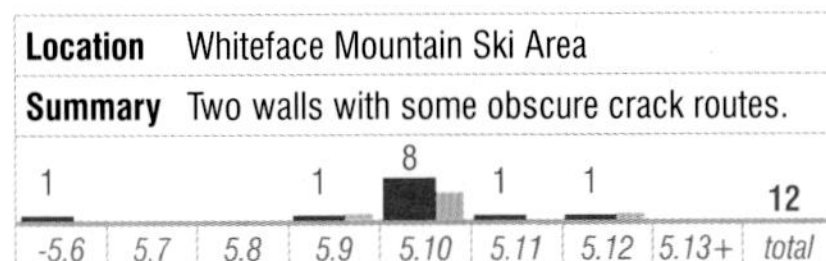

-5.6	5.7	5.8	5.9	5.10	5.11	5.12	5.13+	total
1			1	8	1	1		12

There are two walls on the lower flanks of Whiteface, above and right of the ski area. The lower is the Polar Soldier Wall, and, sitting directly above, is a larger, more prominent wall known as Bear Den.

DIRECTIONS (MAP PAGE 413)

The Olympic Acres cliffs are approached from the Whiteface Ski Area, 3.1 miles from Wilmington on the right (when you're driving toward Lake Placid) and 8.8 miles from Lake Placid on the left (when you're driving toward Wilmington). Drive down the hill toward the ski complex, cross the bridge, then turn right and drive to the highest parking areas (Easy Acres and Bear Den). The approach trail begins on a dirt road that connects the two parking areas, on the uphill side, next to a sand pile enclosed in steel piping 590968,4912434.

Olympic Acres

POLAR SOLDIER WALL

Aspect	Southeast
Height	100'
Quality	
Approach	25 min, moderate
Summary	A wide, mostly overgrown wall with several crack lines.

-5.6	5.7	5.8	5.9	5.10	5.11	5.12	5.13+	total
				3				3

The Polar Soldier Wall is a well-known winter destination but has some interest for rock as well. The only recorded route is **Crime, Fools, and Treasure**, which climbs a chimney and off width through a roof left of the popular **Polar Soldier** ice climb. There are several other possible lines that haven't been explored.

The cliff's most obvious feature is a steep wall with black rock that rises above a ledge system 15' up. This wall is at the low point of the cliff at a small pond in an open area and is the location of **Polar Soldier**.

HISTORY

Patrick Purcell was first attracted to the cliff for the ice and climbed **Polar Soldier** early in 1986. He returned that summer with a young Ian Osteyee.

DIRECTIONS (MAP PAGE 413)

The approach involves navigating a web of mountain bike trails that crisscross the hillside above and right of the ski center. From the parking lot, find Trail 19, "Upper Connector." This begins just right (southeast) of a sand pile enclosed in steel piping. Follow the trail for 600', then take the first left (onto trail #18). Walk 520' and take the first right (onto trail #17). Walk 430' and take the first left (still on trail #17). Walk 345' and take the first right (still on trail #17). Walk for 200' to a small cairn on the left that marks a faint herd path. Turn left onto the herd path and follow it uphill to the base of the cliff 590735,4912964. If you lose the path, simply walk uphill.

DESCENT OPTIONS

Rappel from trees or a long walk to the right.

1 Out for the Boyz 5.10d G 110' ★★★

Start: 50' left of **Crime, Fools, and Treasure** at an open book corner with a small triangular ledge 5' up, and below a left-curving crack.

P1 5.10d G: Climb the left-curving crack through a V-slot to twin cracks. Up these to a ledge, then step right to a fixed anchor. 50'

P2 5.10b G: Step left to a V-slot. Go up the V-slot, then up lower-angled rock to a fixed anchor on a tree. 60'

FA Aug 17, 2012, Will Roth, Dustin Ulrich

2 Crime, Fools, and Treasure 5.10b G 50'

Start: 40' uphill from and left of the low point of the cliff (and the small pond) are three large boulders near the base of the rock. At the left end of these boulders is a flat section of terrain below a steep wall covered in a sea of tiny, thin flakes. This route is 25' left of these boulders below a chimney.

P1 5.10b G: Up the chimney squeeze to a bulge. Up the off width through the bulge to a 4' roof. Through the roof at the V-slot, then up a handcrack to a slab. 50'
Gear: To 4".
FA Apr 1, 1986, Patrick Purcell, Ian Osteyee

3 Hipster Handbook 5.10b G 35' ★

A good selection of everything from finger locks to fist jams.
Start: This route is located on a lower tier, below **Crime, Fools, and Treasure**. As you approach the Polar Soldier Wall, bear left to a short cliffband 50' downhill and left of the lowest point on the main wall (where the Polar Soldier ice climb is located). Begin on a ledge with a flat boulder below an obvious crack in a left-facing open book corner, 20' left of the right end of this cliff.
P1 5.10b G: Up the open book to a 5' roof. Jam over this to a fixed anchor. 35'
FA Jul 13, 2012, Tom Wright, Will Roth

Olympic Acres

BEAR DEN

Aspect	Southeast
Height	100'
Quality	★★★★
Approach	1 hr, moderate
Summary	A large slab with some great long cracks that have escaped popularity for some reason.

-5.6	5.7	5.8	5.9	5.10	5.11	5.12	5.13+	total
1			1	5	1	1		9

Bear Den, also known as the Upper Slab, is the huge slab of rock on the mountainside, clearly visible from the parking area at the Ledge Rock Motel on NY 86 just northeast of the entrance to Whiteface Ski Area.

The central feature of Bear Den is the large depression that narrows to a right-arching chimney higher up, the route **Yard Sale**; this is 40' up from and left of the low point of the cliff—a flat section of terrain that stays dry in the rain. Left of the chimney is a sheer slab with two multi-pitch routes: **Berry Good** and **Bear Necessities**. Right of the chimney is an off-vertical wall with several crack lines. The leftmost of these cracks, on the right side of the low point of the cliff, begins 6' up above a horizontal crack with a bolt; this amazing bottomless crack remains unclimbed. The other routes are to the right of this crack.

The cliff has a beautiful open base with flattish forest at the bottom. The large trees escaped the last ice storm, which devastated much of the region.

HISTORY

The cliff was first visited in 1987 by Patrick Munn, an employee of the Whiteface Ski Center, at the behest of his boss, John Plausteiner. They climbed the most obvious feature visible from below, the arching chimney, **Yard Sale**. Munn returned several more times that summer and climbed the remaining lines with various partners.

DIRECTIONS (MAP PAGE 413)

Bear Den sits directly up the slope from the Polar Soldier Wall. From the Polar Soldier Wall, walk to its right end, then up the steep, forested slope following the right margin of a diminishing cliffband. At the top of the cliffband, angle up and left to reach the base of Bear Den 590478,4913007. There is a path marked with cairns, but the forest is moderately dense, especially since Irene, and the low foliage makes orienting yourself a challenge; a compass is recommended.

DESCENT OPTIONS

Rappel from trees.

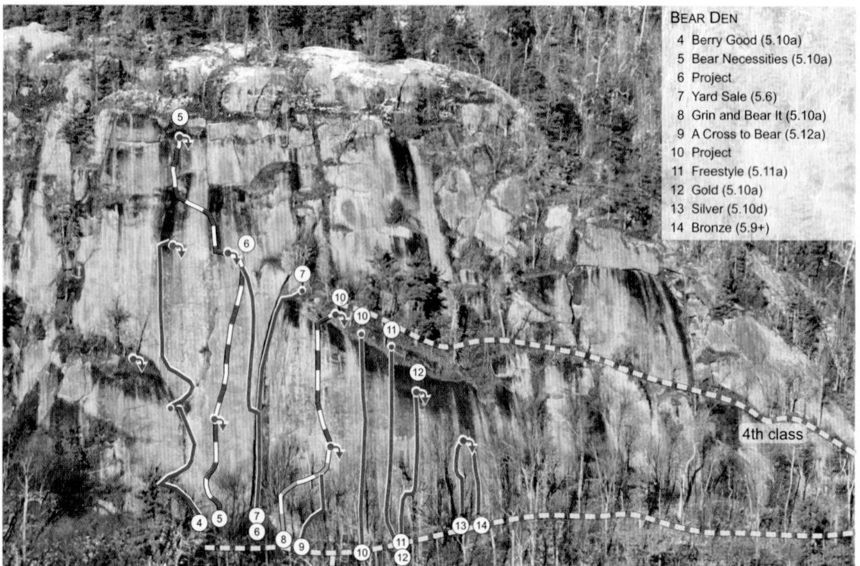

4 Berry Good 5.10a G (5.7 R) 290' ★★★★

An outstanding second pitch that climbs a naturally clean, black water streak. P1 is good, but has a long runout; to avoid this, climb P1 of Bear Necessities, belay, then go left across the slab to the start of P2.

Start: Same as Bear Necessities.

P1 5.9 G (5.7 R): Mantel onto a ledge, then work up and left to a fern ledge. From the ledge, move up to the right-rising "J" crack and climb it to its top (crux) to a series of good flakes and ledges. Continue straight up the slab (runout) to a bolt, then step left to a ledge and tree with a fixed anchor. 100'

● **P2 5.10a G ★★★★:** Move up to the top of a flake, then step left onto the face. Work up and left (crux) to the black water streak, then straight up wonderful knobs to a great belay station on a sloped ledge with a fixed anchor. 110'

P3 5.6 G (5.1 R): Straight up the unprotected slab to the broken crack finish of Bear Necessities. 80'

Gear: Sparse rack to 2".

Descent: Rappel the route with a single 60m rope.

FA Aug 21, 2008, Michael LeBlanc, Diana LeBlanc

5 Bear Necessities 5.10a G (5.2 R) 300' ★★★★

An excellent face climb on knobs and edges that makes its way straight up a deceptively high slab with terrific views of the Wilmington valley. Similar to Freudian Slip, but longer.

Start: 30' uphill and left of the depression of Yard Sale, below right-rising slashes in a steep slab.

○ **P1 5.9 G:** Mantel onto a ledge, then climb a steep wall using good incut jugs to a right-rising seam (gear). From the top of the seam, climb straight up featured rock to a fixed anchor. 100'

○ **P2 5.10a G:** Step right and work straight up the face (crux) to a fixed anchor on top of large flakes. 100'

P3 5.9- G: Step left on flakes, then friction straight up the face to a low-angle area beneath a large left-facing corner. Angle up and left for 60' (unprotected 5.2 friction), then climb a broken crack to a sloped ledge with a fixed anchor. 100'

Gear: Cams and nuts to 1.5".

Descent: Rappel the route with a single 60m rope.

FA Jul 30, 2008, Colin Loher, Jim Lawyer, Emilie Drinkwater

6 Project

There is a project that begins on Yard Sale, then breaks out of the chimney at a horizontal crack and onto the slab. Go up the slab (bolts) to the P2 anchor of Bear Necessities. The project was cleaned, then covered in dirt from rockfall and never completed.

7 Yard Sale 5.6 G 100'

Start: 40' up from and left of the low point of the cliff at the top of a cone-shaped, fern-covered slope, below a depression that narrows to a right-arching chimney.

P1 5.6 G: Climb the chimney to the top. 100'

FA 1987, Patrick Munn, John Plausteiner

8 Grin and Bear It 5.10a G 60' ★★★

Start: On the left end of the flat terrain just before it rises steeply to the left to the chimney of Yard Sale, and 15' left of a straight-up crack–seam, at an overhanging wall with jugs below a short handcrack that breaks a bulge 15' up.

P1 5.10a G: Boulder up the overhanging wall with jugs to the handcrack. Up this to a slab (crux), then up to a giant hanging flake that forms a ceiling. Undercling right along the flake to its right end, then up and right to a fixed anchor. 60'

FA Oct 13, 2013, Jim Lawyer, David Buzzelli

9 A Cross to Bear 5.12a G 60' ★★★

A one-move wonder, but what a move!

Start: 10' left of a crack-seam and 5' right of Grin and Bear It at a jug 6' up.

P1 5.12a G: Stick clip, then move up to a higher incut jug. Make a big 6' dyno up and right to a horizontal edge (crux). Heel hook into a vertical flared crack, then follow this straight up to the fixed anchor shared with Grin and Bear It. 60'

FA Oct 13, 2013, David Buzzelli

10 Project

An open project: this is the attractive bottomless crack that starts 6' up above a horizontal crack. There's a bolt down low, and two more up high where the crack disappears.

Colin O'Connor starts up Gold (5.10a) in the rain.

11 Freestyle 5.11a TR 100'

Begin 15' right of the previous unnamed bottomless crack and 15' left of **Gold** at the point where a horizontal crack goes into the right-rising slope. Climb up a bulge, then up vertical seams through black lichen-covered rock to a small left-facing, left-rising overlap, then up a slab to the top.
FA (TR) Sep, 1988, Jeff Edwards, Don Mellor

12 Gold 5.10a G 100' ★★★★

The best-looking line here climbs a well-protected crack for 70' until it fades into a blank slab.
Start: 30' right of the low point of the face below a vertical crack, and 15' left of a shallow right-facing corner-flake that narrows to a point 25' up.
P1 5.10a G: Climb the crack for 30', then move right and continue up another vertical crack until it fades. Work up a slab (crux, bolts) to a fixed anchor. 100'
Descent: Lower with a 60-m rope, which just makes it.
FA 1987, Patrick Munn

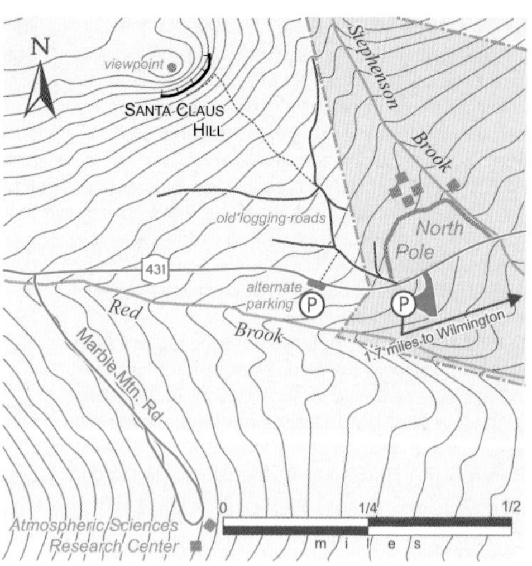

13 Silver 5.10d G 80' ★★

Another good-looking crack line.
Start: At the right end of a pile of stacked flakes, 40' right of **Gold** and 25' right of the shallow right-facing corner-flake that narrows to a point 25' up, are two fingercracks 8' apart. This is the left fingercrack.
P1 5.19d G: Climb the crack, first in a shallow right-facing corner, straight up to its top. Step left to a right-facing flake (bolt), then step right to a fixed anchor shared with **Bronze**. 80'
FA 1987, Patrick Munn, Dave Hough, Mark Meschinelli

14 Bronze 5.9+ G 80' ★★★

Start: This is the right fingercrack, 8' right of **Silver** and 8' left of a deep V-groove.
P1 5.9+ G: Climb the crack to the top, then step left to a fixed anchor shared with **Silver**. 80'
FA 1987, Patrick Munn, Dave Hough, Mark Meschinelli

SANTA CLAUS HILL

Location	Wilmington, accessed from the Whiteface Memorial Highway (NY 431)
Aspect	South and east
Height	70' to 200'
Quality	★★★
Approach	25 min, moderate
Summary	Black slab you can see from Wilmington with high-quality slab and face routes; often wet.

-5.6	5.7	5.8	5.9	5.10	5.11	5.12	5.13+	total
1		2	1	2				6

Despite being obvious from the road (and even downtown Wilmington), this cliff appears to have escaped attention. The summit area above the cliff is a popular hiking destination with good views, a forest road approach, and a large stone fireplace (and grill).

The approach reaches the cliff at its toe. Right of the toe the cliff faces east, is overhanging, dirty, about 70' tall, and has very featured rock, although no cracks. Left of the toe is the "big wall" section that faces south, rises up to 200', and is capped by a roof, the location of **Santa Crux** and its neighbors. Left of the "big wall" are the crack lines **Yes, Virginia** and **Rudolph**.

The cliff is slow to dry after rain.

HISTORY

In 2009, Tom DuBois was hiking nearby, and noticed exposed rock on this hill. He returned a few weeks later to work out the approach, and develop the first couple of routes. He named the cliff for its proximity to Santa's Workshop, the children's theme park in Wilmington. The next year Jim Lawyer and Tad Welch added several high-quality lines.

DIRECTIONS (MAP PAGE 418)

From Wilmington, at the "four corners"—the intersection of NY 86, the Whiteface Memorial Highway (NY 431), and Bonnie View Road—go west on the Whiteface Memorial Highway (NY 431) for 1.7 miles. Park at a pullout on the right (north) side of the road, just past Santa's Workshop, taking care not to block any gravel roads. Alternatively, there is a pullout on the south side of the road 200 yards west of Santa's Workshop.

From the pullout, walk a few feet up a gravel "loop" road to a weed-covered forest road that leaves the loop and goes north. At 1 min, bear left at a fork. At 2 min, the road crosses into state land (there is a Forest Preserve sign on a birch). At 5 min, a road branches to the left at a clearing; continue straight north. At 7 min, another road joins from the right; continue straight. At 9 min, reach a small double clearing. From the second part of this double clearing, two very faint roads branch left (west); take the first one. The road will fade to a lightly traveled intermittent path with some other faint roads branching from it, then fade completely, although there is some flagging. Persist uphill in the same direction on the intermittent path, moderately uphill, to reach the toe of the cliff at 25 min 590924,4917424.

Jim Lawyer on the first ascent of ***Naughty or Nice*** *(5.10a).*

Note: The first section of the approach is private property. At present, there are no private property signs, and it seems obvious that many people use this road to hike up this hill. If there is a concern about crossing private land, it's easy to bushwhack along the heavily blazed property line from NY 431 for a couple of minutes, and reach the forest road where it enters state land.

1 Yes, Virginia 5.8 G 80' ★★

Good gear, but the oddly-shaped crack makes it difficult to place; not a good lead for beginning 5.8 leaders.

Start: Near the left end of the big wall, as the path starts going uphill, a 15'-long tongue of white rock extends from the bottom of the cliff. Left of this, locate an overhanging, flaring, black chimney high on the cliff, with a tan-colored "shark's tooth" boulder jammed in the top of it. 15' feet right of the chimney is a large nose of rock with cracks on either side of it. Begin directly below the nose at an obvious stepped crack, just left of the tongue of white rock.

P1 5.8 G: Step up the crack through some easier climbing to a flat platform below a vertical wall. Climb the crack system on the right side of the nose. At the top of the vertical wall, walk up an easy slope to a tree with a fixed anchor. 80'

FA Aug 7, 2009, Tom DuBois, Ellen DuBois

2 Rudolph 5.5 G 120' ★

Start: Same as **Yes, Virginia**.

P1 5.5 G: (V1) Go up the crack a few feet, then traverse right 20' to a right-leaning crack. Follow the crack for 90' to an easier brushy finish at a beech tree with a fixed anchor. 120'

V1 5.8 R: Begin right of the tongue of white rock, directly below the right-leaning crack. Boulder 10' up to the crack (no gear, bad landing) and join the normal route.

Descent: Rappel with a 60m rope.

FA Jul 12, 2009, Tom Dubois, Ellen Dubois

3 Santa Crux 5.10d G (5.1 X) 100' ★★★

Three hard cruxes separated by easier climbing on brilliant, clean stone .

Start: About 40' right of **Yes, Virginia** is a 20'-tall, overhanging, white wall. Right of this a low-angle slab. Begin on the right side of the slab.

● **P1 5.10d G (5.1 X):** Go up and left across the slab to its left side. Move up to a roof (#2 Camalot), then over this (crux) to a low-angle slab. Run out the slab to the next bulge (trivial climbing, but not a place to fall) and pull this (5.9 G) using great knobs. Continue straight up the slab on great holds and a bit of friction to a final bulge; pull this at a left-facing flake (5.8+ G), then move up super-featured, black, knobby rock to a fixed anchor shared with **Silent Flight**. 100'

Gear: 1 ea #1 or #2 Camalot.

FA Sep 18, 2010, Jim Lawyer, Tad Welch

4 Naughty or Nice 5.10a G 100' ★★★

Start: Same as **Santa Crux**.

● **P1 5.10a G:** Fly up the right side of the slab to blocky steps at its top. Go over a bulge, then leftwards up the slab and over the next bulge. Continue straight up the slab to a right-facing open book in black rock. Up the open book (crux) to a tricky mantel, then move up and left to the fixed anchor shared with **Santa Crux**. 100'

FA Sep 23, 2010, Jim Lawyer, Tad Welch, Martin Villarica

5 Silent Flight 5.8 G 120' ★★★

Varied and interesting.

Start: 25' right of **Santa Crux** at a right-facing, black, frequently wet open book above a three-trunked white ash tree.

● **P1 5.8 G:** Move up the unprotected, frequently-wet corner to a ledge and hidden protection. Mantel left onto the ledge, then go straight up the face to the left side of a distinctive, left-pointed flake below large black roofs. Climb the face left of the left-pointed flake (crux) to a slab below the roof, traverse left under the roof, then pull through the roof on its left side to a fixed anchor shared with **Santa Crux**. 120'

History: Named for the elbow-splitting fall taken by Drinkwater attempting the first lead.

FA Sep 18, 2010, Tad Welch, Jim Lawyer, Emilie Drinkwater

6 Don We Know Wears Gay Apparel 5.9 G 90' ★★★

Varied climbing, and more continuous than the other routes.

Start: From **Silent Flight**, walk right along the base of the cliff, and onto a right-rising ledge. At its highest point is a large tree; from here, scramble up a short 5'-tall wall to the next ledge, then walk right to a huge terrace in a black corner, hidden from below. Begin at the toe of a slab 20' left of the corner.

P1 5.9 G: Move leftwards on the slab to a shallow, right-facing corner. Up the corner to its top, then step left onto a face and climb up past several horizontal cracks. At the highest horizontal, move right 6', then go straight up a knobby face to a fixed anchor. 90'

Gear: To 1.5". The crux is protected by small TCUs.

FA Sep 23, 2010, Tad Welch, Martin Villarica, Jim Lawyer

BEAVER BROOK

Location	Near Wilmington, accessed from Hardy Road
Aspect	Southeast
Height	100'
Quality	★★★
Approach	15 min, easy
Summary	Single-pitch bolted routes on somewhat chossy rock.

-5.6	5.7	5.8	5.9	5.10	5.11	5.12	5.13+	total
			1	4	1	1		7

This cliff is rather unique for the area in that it is primarily bolt-protected climbing on a steep wall, pulling on small holds. The rock was originally quite chossy and is clearner now, but be ready if a hold breaks.

The cliff gets afternoon shade, so it's a good place to come on hot, sunny afternoons. Watch for poison ivy, which is mixed in with other vegetation around the base of the cliff.

HISTORY

The cliff is the brainchild of Colin Loher, a local guide who lives nearby and can see the cliff from his front porch. He laboriously cleaned, prepared, and climbed the routes, often by himself by solo toprope. Royce Van Evera, another local guide, got involved and put up a few lines of his own.

DIRECTIONS (MAP PAGE 420)

Beaver Brook is accessed from Hardy Road. If coming from Wilmington, at the intersection of Springfield Road (CR 12) and Route 86, drive south on Springfield Road. At 1.8 miles, you reach Fox Farm Road on the right (the shortcut to NY 86) and Hardy Road on the left at 2.7 miles.

If coming from Upper Jay, at the intersection of Springfield Road and NY 9N, drive north on Springfield Road 2.7 miles, then turn right onto Hardy Road.

Drive 1.1 miles on Hardy Road and park at a pullout on the right (east) side of the road; there is a memorial plaque mounted on a boulder at the pullout for the Lewis W. Olliffe Preserve 595566,4913023.

Cross the road and follow a logging road for 4 min to a split; go left. Continue another 1 min to a cairn marking a herd path on the right. Turn right and walk 10 min to the cliff 594866,4913086.

DESCENT OPTIONS

Each route is equipped with a fixed anchor.

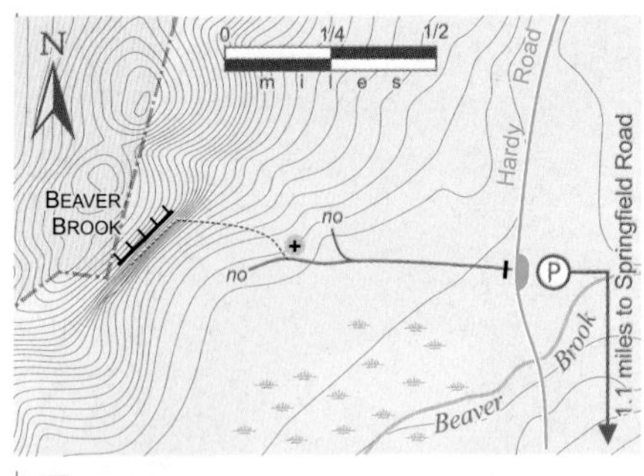

1 Old Guy Shootin' Powder 5.10b G 85' ★★★★

A hard boulder move off the ground, then some balancy climbing after the roof.

Start: 30' left of the two-boulder terrace of **Almost Rectum**, on top of some blocks below several ledges that lead to a bulging face 6' up.

● **P1 5.10b G:** Up the face to the ceiling, breaking it on the left up to a stance. Move back right, then straight up the face to a fixed anchor at the top. 85'

FA Jun, 2006, Royce Van Evera, Eric Nordstrom

2 Save a Tree, Eat a Beaver 5.10d G 90' ★★★★★

Very unusual climbing for the region with two wild overhangs.

Start: 20' right of **Old Guy Shootin' Powder**, on a ledge on the uphill left side of the two-boulder terrace of **Almost Rectum**, below a left-facing, left-rising overhanging corner.

● **P1 5.10d G:** Climb straight up to the overhanging corner, then traverse right through the overhanging corner using a horizontal crack (crux). Continue straight up to a ledge, then pull a second ceiling, bearing right and home to the fixed anchor. 90'

FA Aug 27, 2007, Royce Van Evera, Bill Frazer

3 Castor Canidensis 5.11a G 90' ★★

Start: Same as **Almost Rectum**.

○ **P1 5.11a G:** Up to the top of the left-hand boulder, then up to a ceiling. Angle up and left past two small overlaps to a larger overlap. Break the overlap on the right (crux), then climb straight up the face to a fixed anchor at the top. 90'

Gear: To 1".

FA Jul, 2004, Colin Loher, Erica Loher

4 Beaver Fever 5.10a G 90' ★

Sustained.

Start: Same as **Almost Rectum**.

● **P1 5.10a G:** Up to the top of the left-hand boulder, then up to a ceiling. Step right through the ceiling (crux) and up the face to a fixed anchor. 90'

FA Jul, 2004, Colin Loher, Erica Loher

5 Almost Rectum 5.9+ G 100' ★★

This climb sports many restful ledges. Named for a fall taken on an early ascent when Jeremy Haas slipped off and nearly speared himself on a branch.

*Dennis Luther on **Save a Tree, Eat a Beaver** (5.10d). Photo by Royce Van Evera.*

Start: 35' left of the triangular boulder (**Good to the Last Drop**) where the approach trail meets the cliff are two car-sized boulders leaning up against the cliff with a terrace between them. This route begins on the left side of the terrace at a wide crack in a broken right-facing corner.

P1 5.9+ G: (V1) Climb up the wide crack to a ledge 15' up. Reach out right to the first bolt, then climb straight up the face to a shallow left-leaning, left-facing open book. At its top, continue up the face to a fixed anchor on a tree. 100'

V1 5.10d PG: Straight up the face to the first bolt.

Gear: 1 ea green Alien.

FA Sep, 2004, Royce Van Evera, Dan Stripp, Steve Mergenthaler

6 Good to the Last Drop 5.10d G 90' ★★

This was the original route on the cliff.

Start: On the right side of a 15'-high triangular boulder where the approach trail meets the cliff.

P1 5.10d G: Up the right side of the boulder, then work straight up the face to the top. 90'

FA Jul, 2003, Colin Loher, Emilie Drinkwater

7 Beavers Taste Like Wood 5.12b G 75' ★★★★

An excellent, hard line—bouldery, dynamic, balancy, technical, and straight up hard!

Start: 30' right of **Good to the Last Drop** in a cave-like feature with big holds. You can also begin a little to the left and traverse to the first bolt.

P1 5.12b G: Stick-clip the first bolt. Make bouldery moves out of the cave, then up to a left-facing shoulder. Follow this to its top, then go up the technical face on small holds to a small overhang. Pull this, and gun for the fixed anchor at the top. 75'

FA Jun 27, 2012, Conor Cliffe, Tom Wright

Adirondack Days

I stand in the parking lot and sip warm, sweet coffee from my Big Sky bistro mug while I wait for Erica, my wife and favorite climbing partner, to get her pack ready. Moss Cliff stands before me enshrouded in a fine mist that I associate with gift-wrapping paper. Once the sun gets higher, the fine mist will evaporate, unwrapping itself to reveal Moss Cliff, all 400' of it, and some of the best rock in the park. Like a kid during the holidays, I'm giddy with excitement to see the gift and play with it. Aside from the mist, it's a bluebird day, with temperatures forecast to be in the mid-70s. Erica has a name for these sorts of days: Adirondack days, she calls them. By the time she's ready, the mist has pulled back to a Saturn-like ring around the cliff's midsection.

"Watch me," I stammer, as I struggle with the crux fingercrack section of Nestlings, some 200' up. Once through the hard moves, I am able to take in the scenery—the High Peaks in the distance, the Ausable River 1000' below, Copperas Pond nestled into the crook of Notch Mountain, and the shadowy High Falls Crag. A sudden "swish" startles me from my reverie—a peregrine falcon flashes over my shoulder, its wings cutting surgically through the air. I continue past an easier section to my favorite belay ledge in the Adirondacks. "Off belay," I yell after I've tied in. While Erica makes her way up, I think about how lucky I am to be a climber in the Adirondacks. No crowds, splitter lines, more rock than one could ever hope to climb, and countless different climbing mediums. For some reason, I remember a conversation I had with a well-known Gunks climber who said that no one in their right mind would ever move to the Adirondacks to become a serious climber. Well, I had done just that. Sure, climbing in the Adirondacks has its drawbacks—the short season, a plethora of bloodthirsty insects, and a sparse pool of potential partners—but the Adirondacks also has one thing only a few East Coast climbing venues have: a real sense of wildness and a lifetime's worth of adventure climbing. These qualities are worth the obstacles I face in achieving my full potential as a climber.

Rock climbing in the Adirondacks is a singular experience. I have climbed all over the country, and in the process, I have learned there really is no place like home. I love the pristine quality of most of the climbing venues. Since I moved to this area, I have become adept at digging gear placements out with my nut tool while simultaneously wiping lichen from my eyes. There are definitely more blackflies than people at our cliffs, which suits me just fine.

I am still lost in these thoughts when Erica joins me at the belay. She says something about the pitch we just climbed, and when I don't respond right away, she asks me, "What are you thinking about?" to which I reply, "Oh, I was just thinking there's no place like home." "Okay, Dorothy," Erica says, "why don't you put your ruby-red slippers back on and get us up the next pitch?"

- Colin Loher

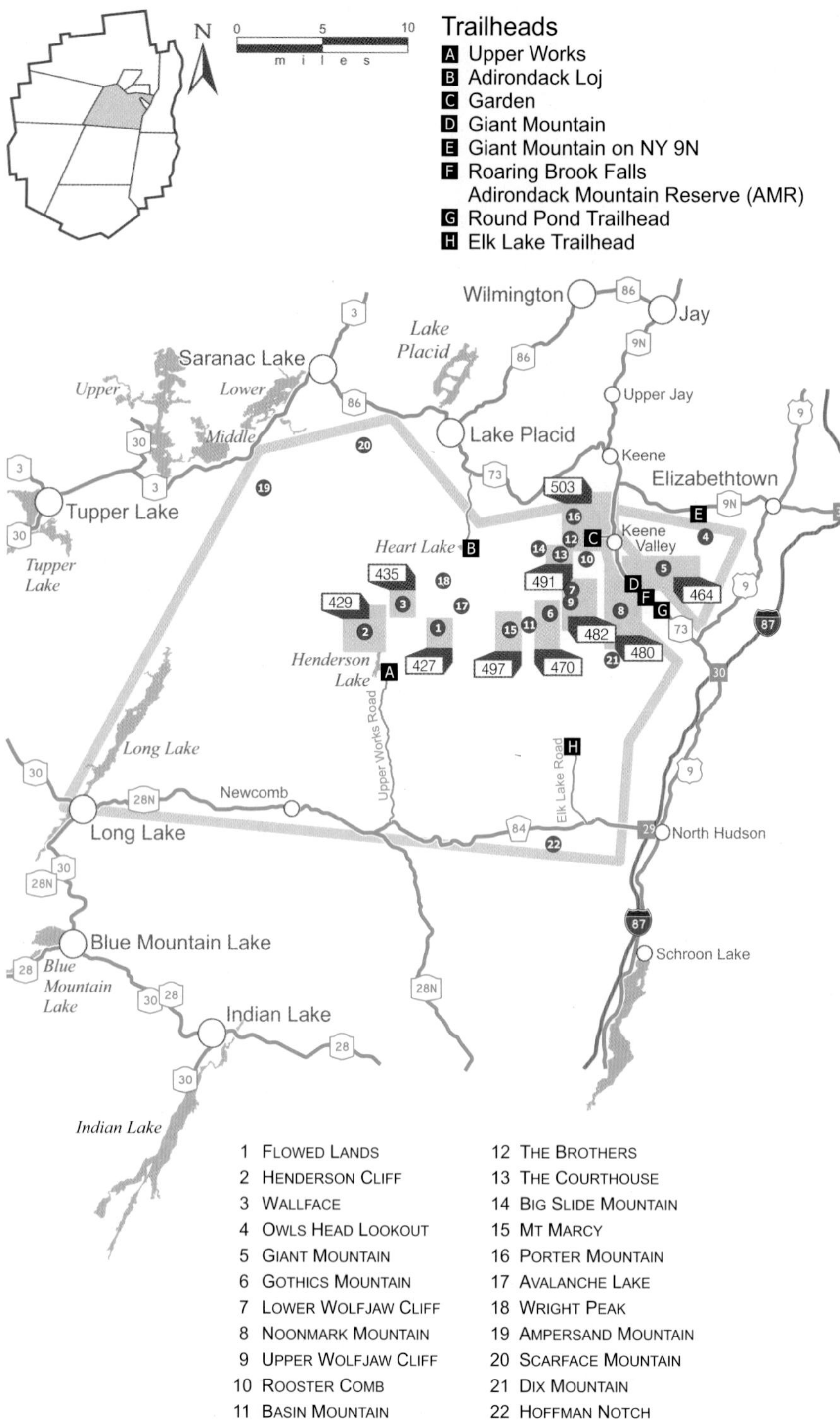
N
0 5 10
miles
Trailheads
A Upper Works
B Adirondack Loj
C Garden
D Giant Mountain
E Giant Mountain on NY 9N
F Roaring Brook Falls
Adirondack Mountain Reserve (AMR)
G Round Pond Trailhead
H Elk Lake Trailhead
Wilmington
Jay
Lake Placid
Saranac Lake
Upper
Lower
Middle
Upper Jay
Keene
Elizabethtown
Tupper Lake
Tupper Lake
Heart Lake
Keene Valley
Henderson Lake
Upper Works Road
Elk Lake Road
Long Lake
Long Lake
Newcomb
North Hudson
Blue Mountain Lake
Blue Mountain Lake
Indian Lake
Indian Lake
Schroon Lake
1 Flowed Lands
2 Henderson Cliff
3 Wallface
4 Owls Head Lookout
5 Giant Mountain
6 Gothics Mountain
7 Lower Wolfjaw Cliff
8 Noonmark Mountain
9 Upper Wolfjaw Cliff
10 Rooster Comb
11 Basin Mountain
12 The Brothers
13 The Courthouse
14 Big Slide Mountain
15 Mt Marcy
16 Porter Mountain
17 Avalanche Lake
18 Wright Peak
19 Ampersand Mountain
20 Scarface Mountain
21 Dix Mountain
22 Hoffman Notch

High Peaks

The High Peaks are the showcase of the largest wilderness area in the Adirondacks. However, the trails and peaks described in this chapter are the most popular destinations for Adirondack hikers. There are 303 miles of trail, and with around 140,000 hikers signing in at the trailheads in 1998 (although this number has been decreasing), expect to share your backcountry experience with others. Thankfully, the climbing areas are off the beaten paths, and they offer much more solitude than the nearby summits. The terrain is steep, rocky, and blessed with coarse anorthosite; climbing here often begins with a long, strenuous approach and sometimes extreme bushwhacking. There is a complex and extensive trail system, well documented in *Adirondack Trails, High Peaks Region,*[1] which includes an excellent hiking map.

Previous guidebooks have given minimal attention to backcountry rock climbing. This book breaks this tradition and describes 147 routes on 25 different cliffs. This is a rugged place: don't underestimate the modest elevations, and be prepared to find your own way even if armed with this new documentation.

Wallface (36 routes, 153 pitches) is one of the most immense cliffs in the Northeast and has historic significance. Despite its difficult approach, it remains a popular cliff. Other lengthy routes are found on Gothics, Giant, Mt Marcy (Panther Gorge), and at Avalanche Lake. Mountaintop destinations include Big Slide, Noonmark, Rooster Comb, and Porter. Backcountry cragging is found at the Courthouse (10 routes), Avalanche Lake (32 routes), Wright Peak (5 routes), Flowed Lands (4 routes), and Henderson (4 routes). For slide climbs, even though there are countless open slabs on the steeper peaks, this book focuses on the classic scrambles and long technical slide climbs on Gothics, Giant, Colden, Dix, and Basin.

Although the approaches to these cliffs are long, they are usually done without an overnight stay. You can save weight by taking a water purifier and filling up at stream crossings. If you are climbing anything other than the most popular routes, bring a wire brush.

This book uses the term *High Peaks* in reference to those areas with peaks over 4000'—i.e., the backcountry areas in the High Peaks Wilderness Area, Giant Mountain Wilderness Area, and Dix Mountain Wilderness Area. Be aware that the regulations are slightly different in each area. If in doubt, contact the local DEC rangers, who are happy to assist (www.dec.ny.gov; search for "Forest Ranger Roster for Region 5"); you can also call the Forest Ranger Office in Ray Brook during business hours (518.897.1300).

SEASON

The High Peaks have perhaps the shortest climbing season in the park. In the summer, the temperature rarely exceeds 90' and can fluctuate as much as 30' during the day. Annual snowfall exceeds 150", and the snowpack in the upper elevations, especially on the northern slopes, lingers until June. Here more than any other area in the park, climbers must be prepared for exposure and sudden changes in conditions.

ACCESS

Before entering the wilderness areas, you are required to sign the trail register. Annual closures for peregrine falcon nesting often affect Wallface.

Day-use group size: In the High Peaks Wilderness Area, day-use groups are limited to a maximum of 15 people. In the Giant and Dix Mountain Wilderness Areas, day-use climbing groups are limited to 10 people with no more than three roped parties at a time. Larger groups need to be separated into compliant groups at least 1 mile apart.

Pets: In the High Peaks, pets are allowed but must be leashed and never left unattended. In the Giant and Dix Mountain Wilderness Areas, pets must be leashed while on marked trails.

DIRECTIONS (MAPS PAGES AND, 422)

No matter which direction you are coming from, the High Peaks are best accessed from the eastern side of the park. With the exception of Upper Works, which is approached via the Blue Ridge Road (from I-87 [Northway] Exit 29), the trailheads are located on the northern side of the region, off NY 73 (I-87 Exit 30).

TRAILHEADS

The following trailheads are used to access the cliffs:

Upper Works Trailhead: Take I-87 Exit 29 and follow Blue Ridge Road (CR 84) west for 17.3 miles to Upper Works Road (CR 25, also posted as the Tahawus Road). This intersection is 1.1 miles east of the intersection of Blue Ridge Road and NY 28N near Newcomb. Turn north onto Upper Works Road and, after 6.3 miles, turn left just before a bridge where the main road enters the old mine, staying on the road for Upper Works. After another 3.5 miles, you reach the trailhead parking area at the end of the road near several abandoned buildings 57557,4882168.

If you're coming from the south, there's a faster way. Take I-87 to Exit 26 in Pottersville (24-hour gas), turn left off the highway, then right onto US 9 to Pottersville. Bear left at the split onto Olmsteadville Road

1 Tony Goodwin, *Adirondack Trails, High Peaks Region,* 13th ed, (Adirondack Mountain Club, 2006).

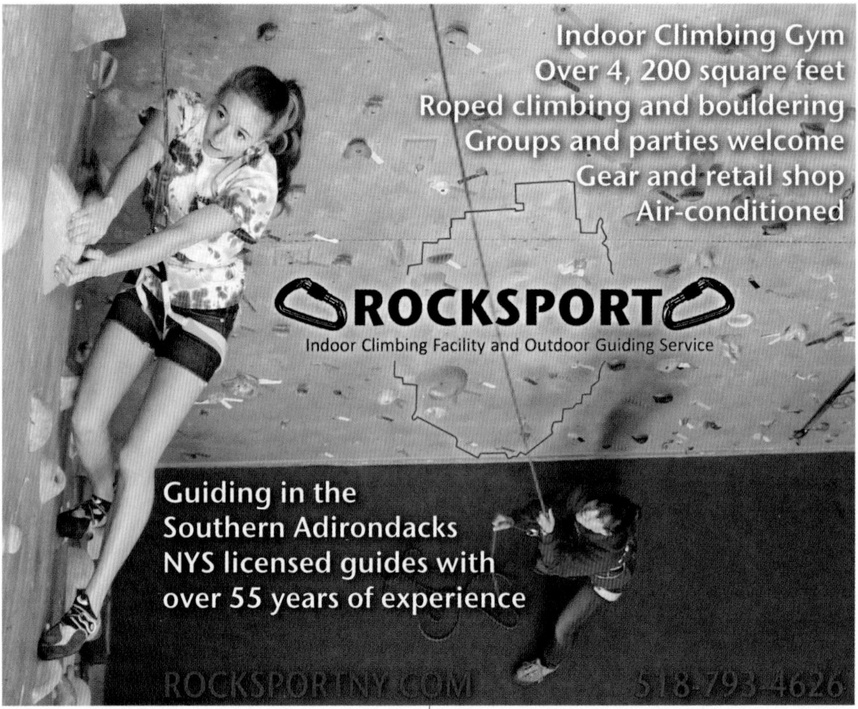

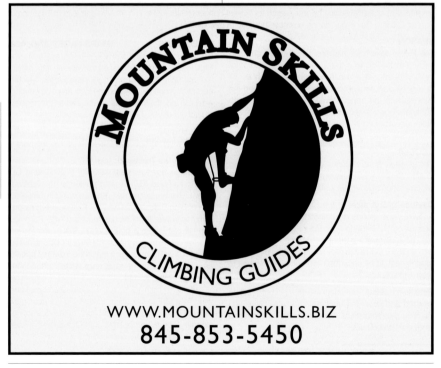

PG	CLIFF	QUALITY	ASPECT	APPROACH		GRADES	#
427	Flowed Lands	★★★	SE	1 hr 50 min	moderate	.6 .7 .8 .9 .10 .11 .12 .13	4
428	Henderson Cliff	★★★	SE	2 hr 30 min	difficult canoe optional	.6 .7 .8 .9 .10 .11 .12 .13	5
431	Wallface	★★★★	E	2 hr	difficult	.6 .7 .8 .9 .10 .11 .12 .13	38
463	Owls Head Lookout	★	SW	1 hr 10 min	moderate	.6 .7 .8 .9 .10 .11 .12 .13	2
465	Giant Mountain West Face	★★★	W	2 hr	difficult	.6 .7 .8 .9 .10 .11 .12 .13	3
467	Giant Mountain East Face	★★	E	3 hr 30 min	difficult	.6 .7 .8 .9 .10 .11 .12 .13	3
469	Gothics Mountain North Face	★	NW	3 hr	difficult	.6 .7 .8 .9 .10 .11 .12 .13	5
473	Gothics Mountain South Face	★★★★	S	3 hr 30 min	difficult	.6 .7 .8 .9 .10 .11 .12 .13	5
477	Gothics Mountain Rainbow Slide	★★★	S	4 hr	difficult	.6 .7 .8 .9 .10 .11 .12 .13	4
479	Lower Wolfjaw Cliff		S	2 hr 30 min	difficult	.6 .7 .8 .9 .10 .11 .12 .13	1
480	Noonmark Mountain	★★★★	SE	1 hr 45 min	difficult	.6 .7 .8 .9 .10 .11 .12 .13	7
482	Upper Wolfjaw Cliff	★★★	SW	2 hr 30 min	difficult	.6 .7 .8 .9 .10 .11 .12 .13	3
485	Rooster Comb	★★	SE	1 hr 30 min	moderate	.6 .7 .8 .9 .10 .11 .12 .13	3
487	Basin Mountain East Face	★	E	4 hr 30 min	difficult	.6 .7 .8 .9 .10 .11 .12 .13	2
488	Basin Mountain Southeast Face	★★	SE	4 hr 30 min	difficult	.6 .7 .8 .9 .10 .11 .12 .13	1
488	Basin Mountain South Face Amphitheater	★	S	4 hr 30 min	difficult	.6 .7 .8 .9 .10 .11 .12 .13	2
489	The Brothers		S	40 min	moderate	.6 .7 .8 .9 .10 .11 .12 .13	2
491	The Courthouse	★★★★	SE	1 hr 10 min	moderate	.6 .7 .8 .9 .10 .11 .12 .13	10
494	Big Slide Mountain	★★★	S	2 hr 30 min	difficult	.6 .7 .8 .9 .10 .11 .12 .13	4
498	Mt Marcy Panther Gorge	★★★	S	4 hr	difficult	.6 .7 .8 .9 .10 .11 .12 .13	8
501	Mt Marcy East Face	★★	SE	4 hr 30 min	difficult	.6 .7 .8 .9 .10 .11 .12 .13	2
502	Porter Mountain	★★	SE	1 hr 30 min	difficult	.6 .7 .8 .9 .10 .11 .12 .13	8
509	Avalanche Lake Avalanche Pass		SE	1 hr 50 min	moderate	.6 .7 .8 .9 .10 .11 .12 .13	1
509	Avalanche Lake West Face of Mt Colden	★★★★★	NW	2 hr	moderate	.6 .7 .8 .9 .10 .11 .12 .13	13
518	Avalanche Lake East Face of Avalanche Mountain	★★★★	SE	2 hr	moderate	.6 .7 .8 .9 .10 .11 .12 .13	20
525	Wright Peak	★★★★	SE	1 hr 30 min	difficult	.6 .7 .8 .9 .10 .11 .12 .13	15
528	Dix Mountain West Face	★★★	W	3 hr	difficult	.6 .7 .8 .9 .10 .11 .12 .13	2
529	Hoffman Notch Long Wall		S	1 hr 10 min	moderate	.6 .7 .8 .9 .10 .11 .12 .13	3

(CR 29) and drive to its end. Turn right onto NY 28N and follow it to Blue Ridge Road (CR 84). Turn right, drive 1.1 miles, turn left onto Upper Works Road, then follow the directions above.

Adirondack Loj Trailhead: The Adirondack Loj is a "hiking center" run by the Adirondack Mountain Club and one of the major trailheads for accessing the High Peaks (with nearly 50,000 visitors in 2008). The Adirondack Loj is reached from NY 73, 3.3 miles southeast of Lake Placid Village (at the intersection of NY 86 and NY 73), or 10.8 miles northwest of Keene (where NY 73 and NY 9N split). Look for a large DEC sign on the south side of the road marked "Trails to the High Peaks" at the intersection of NY 73 and Adirondack Loj Road.

Follow Adirondack Loj Road south for 4.8 miles to the Adirondack Loj. A fee of $10.00 per vehicle per day ($5.00 for club members) is required to park here (as of 2014) 582821,4892715.

Garden Trailhead: From the center of Keene Valley on NY 73, find the DEC sign that reads "High Peaks Wilderness via Johns Brook, Garden Trailhead"; this sign is at the intersection with Adirondack Street, next to the Ausable Inn. Turn onto this street (0.0 mile) and follow the signs to the Garden. After 1.2 miles, there is a snowplow turnaround with "No Parking" signs; continue straight on the dirt road to the parking area at 1.5 miles 594762,4893352.

The parking area at the Garden Trailhead is small (it holds about 60 cars) and fills up quickly; make sure to carpool and get there early (there is no legal parking on the road from Keene Valley). Also, there's a per-day parking fee ($7.00 in 2014). If the lot is full, you can park at Marcy Field (the airfield 1.9 miles north of Adirondack Street on NY 73) and take a shuttle bus to the Garden Trailhead ($5.00 per person round-trip as of 2014; schedule posted at www.townofkeeneny.com).

Giant Mountain Trailhead, on NY 9N: This parking area is located on the south side of NY 9N, 4.3 miles west of Elizabethtown (from the intersection with US 9), and 5.7 miles east of the intersection with NY 73 near Keene. There is a DEC sign on the road indicating mileages for Owls Head Lookout (2.6), Giant Lean-to (5.7), and Giant Mountain Summit (7.4) 605536,4896303.

Roaring Brook Falls Trailhead / Adirondack Mountain Reserve (AMR) Trailhead: These parking areas are located on opposite sides of NY 73 in St. Huberts, 3.2 miles from Keene Valley (from the intersection with Johns Brook Road, when you're traveling toward Chapel Pond), and 5.4 miles from Malfunction Junction (when you're traveling toward Keene Valley). If the lots are full, you can park alongside NY 73 598569,4889323.

Round Pond Trailhead: This parking area is located on NY 73, on the right 1.0 mile from the Chapel Pond Pullout (when you're driving toward Malfunction Junction) and 3.1 miles on the left from Malfunction Junction (when you're driving toward Chapel Pond). If the lot is full, park alongside NY 73 601440,4887318.

Elk Lake Trailhead: The Elk Lake Trailhead is used to access the Dix range and as an alternative southern approach to Panther Gorge. From Northway (I-87) Exit 29, go west on Blue Ridge Road (CR 84) for 4.0 miles, then turn right (north) on Elk Lake Road. Drive 5.2 miles to the trailhead on the right 593945,4874857.

WHERE TO STAY

Camping shortens your approach and can add considerably to the overall experience. In these wilderness areas, it's also highly regulated. No camping above 4000', and camp only in designated sites between 3500' and 4000' (there are only a few such sites anyway). You can camp anywhere below 3500' as long as you are 150' from a road, water source, or trail. Camping at non-designated sites, although legal, is discouraged in the Marcy Dam–Flowed Lands corridor.

Camping group size: In the High Peaks Wilderness Area, overnight groups are limited to a maximum of 8 people. In the Giant and Dix Mountain Wilderness areas, the limit is currently 12 but will soon drop to 8 (depending on when the DEC decides to enforce it). If your party exceeds the limit, you need to split into compliant groups and be at least 1 mile apart.

Length of stay: All camping in the High Peaks Wilderness Area requires a self-issued permit and has a three-night limit (after three nights, you have to move). In the Giant and Dix Mountain Wilderness Areas, you can stay three nights without a special permit and up to two weeks with a special permit. (Special permits are obtained by calling the DEC Forest Ranger Office in Ray Brook: 518.897.1300.)

Bear canisters: In the High Peaks Wilderness Area, overnight users are required to use a bear canister for food, garbage, and toiletries. Canisters are not required in the Giant and Dix Mountain Wilderness Areas.

Fires: No fires are allowed anywhere in the High Peaks Wilderness Area. In the Giant and Dix Mountain Wilderness Areas, fires are allowed only in existing fire rings at designated sites (marked with yellow "Camp Here" disks).

Lean-tos: If you're staying in a lean-to, you must share up to capacity (eight persons), and you can't pitch a tent in a lean-to, although you can tie a tarp to cover the opening.

AMENITIES

There are many lodging, dining, and shopping options in the towns surrounding the High Peaks, some of which are listed in the sections for Chapel Pond Pass (page 177), Keene (page 319), and Wilmington Notch (page 383).

GEOLOGY

Although landslides are a common sight in other mountain ranges, the number of slides in the Adirondacks is unusually large. Gothics, Giant Mountain, Dix Mountain, and Mt Colden have extensive slides, which provide excellent scrambling routes. Most of the slides are located within the High Peaks, but there are a few outside of this region—Snowy Mountain, for example. The High Peaks and Snowy Mountain are largely composed of anorthosite, a rock type that doesn't readily fracture, providing few cracks in which plants can anchor. Further, due to glaciation, the soils are very thin on these mountainsides, and the slopes are steeply inclined. Add heavy rain and moderate seismic activity to this scenario, and you have a perfect recipe for landslides.

FLOWED LANDS

Location	High Peaks Wilderness Area, accessed from the Upper Works Trailhead
Aspect	Southeast
Height	100'
Quality	★★★
Approach	1 hr 50 min, moderate
Summary	Off-vertical face split by several moderate handcracks; unique views of Flowed Lands and the surrounding peaks.

-5.6	5.7	5.8	5.9	5.10	5.11	5.12	5.13+	total
	1	2		1				4

Flowed Lands is the third and southernmost body of water of the Avalanche Pass corridor. It can be approached from the trailhead at Adirondack Loj via Avalanche Pass or, more easily, from the south from the trailhead at Upper Works.

The crag is located at the westernmost tip of Flowed Lands and can be seen from points along the grassy western shore not far from the trail junction and lean-tos. The cliff is approximately 100' high, capped by roofs, and broken midheight by a large tree ledge. Of the four established routes, three are moderate cracks, the most obvious being **Calamity Crack**, a straight-in 70' handcrack. The fourth route is a nice thin-crack/face climb.

HISTORY

Flowed Lands is an area with a rich history. The old dam at the southern tip and sluiceway near the lean-tos were originally built in the 1850s for the mining operation at Upper Works, then improved by loggers in the early 1900s in order to divert water down Calamity Brook to a massive lower dam (the remnants of which can be seen just after you cross Calamity Brook 1.0 mile from the parking lot). These dams were opened each spring to aid in the annual river drives, with the logs targeted for the mills at Glens Falls.

Approximately half a mile before reaching Flowed Lands (from the south), you pass Calamity Pond, where a monument to David Henderson stands poking eerily out of the bog on the north end. In 1845, Henderson was accidentally shot and killed at this small pond while researching the feasibility of diverting the Opalescent River into Calamity Brook to obtain more power for the McIntyre Mines. With Henderson's death, the mines faltered and were ultimately abandoned in 1856. Their remains can still be seen around the Upper Works parking area.

Now to the climbing. The cliff was discovered and developed by Ed Palen; his wife, Teresa Cheetham-Palen; and Laurie Daniels.

DIRECTIONS (MAP PAGE 427)

You can access Flowed Lands from several points, the shortest being from the south at the Upper Works Trailhead (page 423).

From the trailhead, follow the Indian Pass / Wallface Trail (yellow markers) to the intersection with the Flowed Lands / Lake Colden Trail at 7 min. Turn right and follow the Flowed Lands / Lake Colden Trail (red markers); at 37 min, you reach a bridge that crosses Calamity Brook at the intersection with the connector trail from the Indian Pass / Wallface Trail; this section can be boggy. Now following blue markers, continue on the trail to Flowed Lands to reach the two Calamity lean-tos at 1 hr 40 min; this section is very rocky and slow going. From the lean-tos, you can walk 20 yards to the shore of Flowed Lands and see the cliff to the left; walking north along the shore toward the cliff improves the view. (Do not confuse this cliff with the broken cliffs to the southeast on the flanks of Cliff Mountain.)

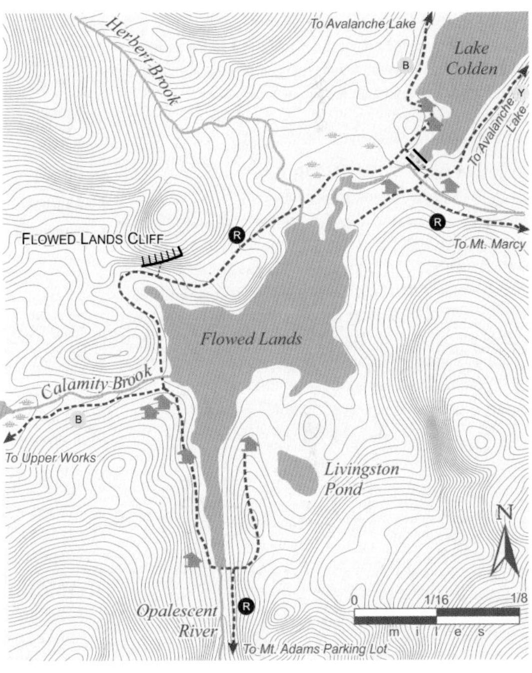

From the lean-to, follow the trail north along the west shore of Flowed Lands (toward Lake Colden) about 10 min to a point where the cliff is clearly visible through the trees on the left 580520,4885254. Bushwhack 200' to the base of the cliff 580542,4885331.

You can make a longer approach from the Adirondack Loj Trailhead, passing Marcy Dam, Avalanche Lake, and Lake Colden. This would double the approach time.

With either approach, there are many camping spots on and around Flowed Lands and Lake Colden.

DESCENT OPTIONS

You can descend the routes with a single rope from the anchor of **Calamity Crack**. The route **Solitude** can be descended with a single rope from its top anchor.

1 C'est la Vie 5.8 G 80' ★★

Start: At the far left end of the main face (at its lowest point) at a short left-facing corner.

P1 5.8 G: Climb the left-facing corner, then move right to gain the crack. Up the crack, parallel to **Calamity Crack**, to a narrow foot ledge. Follow it right to the double-trunked cedar tree anchor. 80'

FA Aug, 1999, Ed Palen, Laurie Daniels

2 Calamity Crack 5.7 G 75' ★★★

The most obvious feature on the cliff is this straight-in handcrack.

Start: At the base of the straight-in crack, 10' right of the left end of the main face, at an island of several small trees, and 25' left of the V-notch of **Millennium**.

P1 5.7 G: Climb the crack to the double-trunked cedar tree anchor on the main ledge. 75'

Gear: Standard rack to #2.

FA Aug, 1999, Ed Palen, Laurie Daniels

3 Millennium 5.10a PG 80' ★★★

A quality face and thin-crack route.

Start: At an inverted V-notch, below and just left of a triangular roof 25' up.

P1 5.10a PG: Climb the V-notch—or the face just to the left—to the thin crack, then up the face and through a bulge left of the triangular roof. Work up to a stance above the triangular roof, then up the thin crack (fixed piton) to a ledge. Follow the ledge leftward to the double-trunked cedar tree anchor on the main ledge. 80'

Gear: Small nuts, TCUs, and cams to 0.75".

FA Sep, 1999, Ed Palen, Laurie Daniels

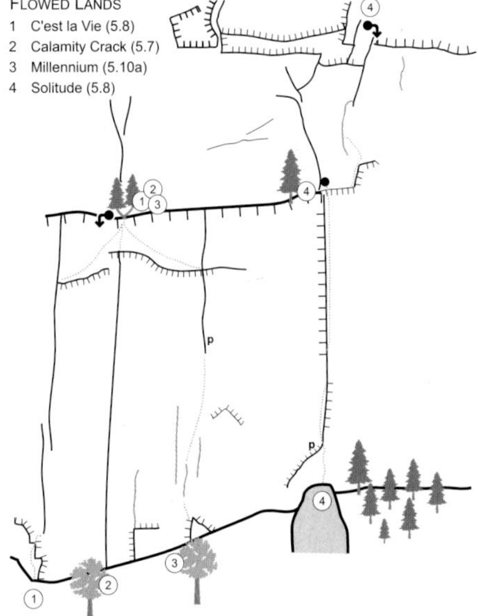

4 Solitude 5.8 PG 100' ★

Start: About 20' right of **Millennium**, scramble to the top of a tree-covered slab, beneath a right-angling 4" flake.

P1 5.7 G: Climb the face just right of the right-angling flake to gain the crack (fixed piton at 15'). Up the crack past a left-facing corner, then up a larger right-facing corner to the main ledge. (You can walk left to the double-trunked cedar tree.) 50'

P2 5.8 PG: From the right edge of the main ledge, go up a 6'-high left-facing corner to a stance. Angle left across and up the face to gain a crack, then follow it to a fixed anchor between the two overlap systems. Often wet. 50'

Gear: Standard rack to #2.

FA Nov, 1999, Ed Palen, Teresa Cheetham-Palen

HENDERSON CLIFF

Location	High Peaks Wilderness Area, accessed from the Upper Works Trailhead
Aspect	Southeast
Height	100'
Quality	★★★
Approach	2 hr 30 min, difficult; canoe optional
Summary	High-quality face and crack climbing in a remote setting; excellent views of Wallface, Indian Pass, and the High Peaks.

-5.6	5.7	5.8	5.9	5.10	5.11	5.12	5.13+	total
	1	1	2	1				5

Standing above Henderson Lake, this little cliff fills a niche in the Adirondack climbing repertoire. Usually thought of as a fun day trip, Henderson really shines when approached as an overnight excursion. A scenic paddle leads to a lakeside camping spot complete with a newly constructed lean-to (2005). The approach from here is about 1.5 hr. Throw in a scenic crag with some interesting climbing and the overall experience is hard to beat.

HISTORY

The starting point for the cliff, namely the Upper Works parking area near Newcomb, was once a mining town, founded in the 1820s. Having plenty of rich iron ore underfoot but no easy means of transporting the ore to market, the town struggled to survive. This combined with the fact that an "impurity" (titanium) made the iron hard to work with led to the eventual failure of the operation in the 1850s. Ironically, the impurity proved more valuable than the ore, and in the 1940s, National Lead bought the old mine and deserted village. The mine closed again, this time in the late 1980s, and in 2004, the Open Space Institute bought the land, which it turned over to the state in 2006.

Ed Palen was the first climber to explore the cliff, camping with Bob Starinsky and Colin Loher.

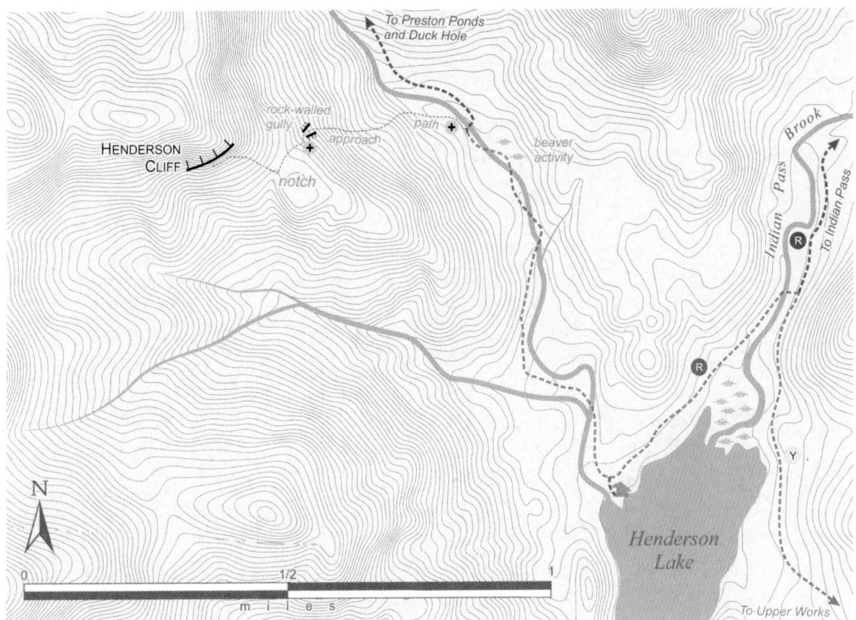

DIRECTIONS **(MAP PAGE 429)**

Access to Henderson Cliff is from the Upper Works Trailhead (page 423). Once you leave the trail, expect some blowdown courtesy of Hurricane Irene in 2011.

From the trailhead (0 min), follow the Indian Pass–Wallface Trail (yellow markers) past Henderson Lake on your left (a slight deviation to the lakeshore provides views of the cliff) to the intersection with the Duck Hole–Preston Ponds Trail, reached at 40 min. Despite recent rerouting around some of the worst sections, this section of trail can be extremely boggy (in fact, the wettest approach in this guidebook). Turn left onto the Duck Hole Trail (red markers) and follow the trail to the intersection near the lakeside lean-to 574590,4883879 at 55 min. (This is a beautiful lean-to.) At this point, the trail continues on relatively flat terrain, crossing many streams and passing a large open meadow (to your right). At 1 hr 15 min—and still on relatively level terrain—look for a bridge that crosses from the left side of a stream to the right side at a 90° angle to the direction of travel 574062,4884960. (There are several such bridges, this is the 6th bridge from the lean-to and the 2nd bridge from the open meadow; if you go too far, the trail begins to climb and passes between two boulders. Another marker is an old yellow "private lands" sign on a tree on the far side of the bridge.)

Don't cross the right-angle bridge; rather, stay on the left side of the brook for 30 yards to a cairn that marks the beginning of the herd path. Follow the herd path steeply uphill, following a faint drainage area, crossing from side to side. Eventually, the drainage area is followed into a rock-walled gully. Exit the gully at its head on the left (cairn) and continue on the herd path up to a notch. The herd path takes a sharp right turn in the notch (just before heading downhill on the other side of the notch) and climbs steeply up to the cliff 573391,4884879, meeting the cliff on the right end. It takes 1 hr to reach the cliff from the 90° angle bridge.

The known routes are located in an amphitheater on the right end of the cliff. To access the routes, you must scramble up to a sloped blueberry terrace.

Ed Palen on the first ascent of ***Topnot*** *(5.7). Photo by Bob Starinsky.*

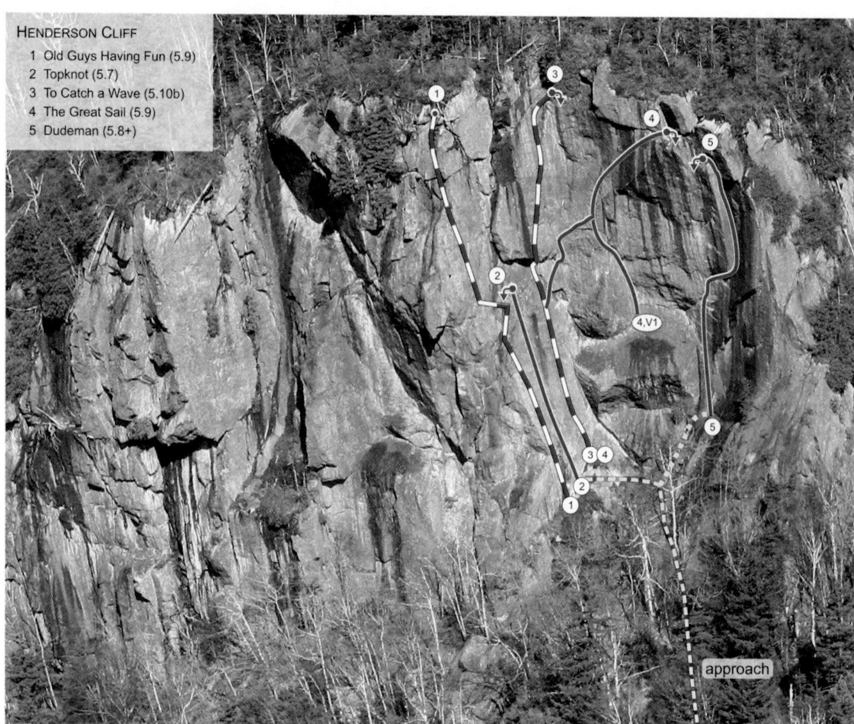

Photo by Drew Haas.

DESCENT OPTIONS

Rappel from fixed anchors with a single 60-m rope.

1 Old Guys Having Fun 5.9 PG 120'

Start: At a 2'-long crack that breaks the right-rising crack on its left end, 4' left of **Topknot**, just right of the arête.

P1 5.9 PG: Climb crack to its top, then face climb (staying left of **Topknot**) to a blocky right-rising ramp. Go up the ramp, then traverse left above a big flake to a steep right-leaning fingercrack (crux). Follow this to its top, then easily left around a left-facing corner to a brushy, blocky crest that leads to the woods. 120'

Gear: To 2".

History: The top half of the route was originally climbed as part of **Topnot**.

Descent: Two raps with a single rope using the anchor on **Topknot**.

FA Jul 12, 2008, Don Mellor, Royce Van Evera

2 Topknot 5.7 G 55' ★★

On the face on the left side of the terrace are two bolted routes, this being the leftmost of the two.

Start: On the left side of the terrace at a widening in a right-rising horizontal crack.

○ P1 5.7 G: Up the clean face along the right-rising horizontal to a second right-rising horizontal. Continue up the clean dimpled face to a fixed anchor 15' below the left end of the roof. 55'

Gear: A few cams to 1".

FA Sep, 2003, Ed Palen, Bob Starinsky

3 To Catch a Wave 5.10b G 100' ★★★★

This is a high-quality route that combines face, crack, and roof climbing. The roof move is height-dependent and could be significantly more difficult for shorter people.

Start: Begin on the left side of the terrace at the base of the clean face, just left of a left-facing corner, 5' right of **Topknot**. The bolts are difficult to see.

P1 5.10b G: Climb the face past two horizontals to a flake beneath the roof. Up the flake and climb through the roof at a bolt at an unlikely spot to a stance above the roof (bolt), then up the crack and face, moving right at the top to a cedar with an anchor. 100'

Gear: Cams to 3".

FA Sep, 2003, Colin Loher, Bob Starinsky

4 The Great Sail 5.9 G 100' ★★★★

This route climbs to the top of the spectacular feature in the center of the amphitheater that resembles a giant sail.

Start: Shares the same start as **To Catch a Wave**.

P1 5.9 G: (V1) Climb the face of **To Catch a Wave** to the flake below the roof. Step right onto the flake and climb the bulge in the roof to a crack in a corner. Continue in the corner until you can foot-traverse right across the face to another crack, which is climbed to its top. Angle rightward across the featured face (the top of the sail feature), to a fixed anchor at a comfortable, exposed belay. 100'

V1 5.9 PG: For an alternate start, scramble up 4th-class rock to the top of the large sloping shelf at the base of the sail feature. From the left side of the shelf, climb the right-facing corner to the top, then swing left onto the face to join the normal route.
Gear: Standard rack to 3".
FA Sep, 2003, Ed Palen, Bob Starinsky
FA (V1) May 7, 2006, Jim Lawyer, Jeremy Haas

5 Dudeman 5.8+ G 100' ★★★
From below, looks like **Frosted Mug** at the Beer Walls.
Start: Begin on the right side of the sloped ledge.
P1 5.8+ G: Climb the right-leaning crescent across the face to the bottom of a right-facing corner. Up the corner, past a small overlap near the top, to a fixed anchor. 100'
FA Sep, 2003, Bob Starinsky, Colin Loher, Ed Palen

WALLFACE

Location	High Peaks Wilderness Area, accessed from the Upper Works Trailhead or the Adirondack Loj Trailhead
Aspect	East
Height	700'
Quality	★★★★
Approach	2 hr, difficult
Summary	Long routes up to 1000', with generally good rock but complex route finding. Most routes are not well traveled.

-5.6	5.7	5.8	5.9	5.10	5.11	5.12	5.13+	total
6	4	4	4	7	4	1		38

Wallface is the largest remote cliff in the Northeast, rising roughly 700' above a talus field of house-sized boulders in the remote Indian Pass in the High Peaks Wilderness Area. David Henderson, credited as the first person to explore Indian Pass, wrote in 1837 that "if Niagara be the prince of waterfalls—[Wallface] exhibits the prince of precipices."[2] The cliff is an intricate patchwork of faces, slabs, corners, and ramps, all laced together with ribbons of vegetation. With a healthy dose of loose, dirty rock, and difficult route finding, this cliff must be approached with an adventurous spirit.

Getting around the base of Wallface isn't easy. The terrain is steep and blanketed by extremely thick, head-high ground cover, most of which is mixed with prickly plants and thistles that hide loose boulders and holes. The base of some routes is more open (like **Diagonal**), but finding the base of other routes can be arduous (with **Rubicon** taking the prize for the most difficult). Some parties turn back without ever finding their routes, frustrated by difficult navigation and nondescript cliff base. In short, allow for extra time to find your route.

One of us once overheard a group of climbers at the Noonmark Diner in Keene Valley discussing their plans for the day over breakfast at 9:00 a.m. Having decided on **Diagonal**, they continued with their leisurely pace because the route was "only 5.8." At this point, they were, at best, 4 hr from the base of the route. The moral of the story: don't be fooled, this is a difficult cliff.

The established routes on Wallface are clustered into six areas. The South Face is on the far left end and is characterized by lower-angled rock, but also some of the cleanest on the cliff. Moving right, the Diagonal Area is the next section and has the highest concentration of routes, including the immensely popular **Diagonal**, a route that climbs a hard-to-miss right-rising ramp that is actually nearly 50' wide in places. Most of the routes in this section intersect this ramp at some point, and most funnel into the exit corners near **Diagonal**. The next section is the Shield Area, characterized by the huge unbroken clean expanse of rock in the midsection of the cliff. The routes in this section climb through the Shield feature, which has some incredible face climbing, then finish through the overhanging dihedrals above. The Central Depression is right of the Shield and includes some of the earliest routes climbed in the Adirondacks—wandering lines that follow vegetated weaknesses for the most part. Farther to the right is the Mental Blocks Buttress, a fist-shaped steep buttress of relatively clean rock configured in a geometric puzzle of corners, ramps, and faces. On the far right is the North End, an uninspiring mess of rock buttresses poking through vegetation; the routes in this section have probably not seen second ascents.

Some notes about gear: The Wallface rack varies depending on the route. A set of cams up to 3" (and sometimes 4", as noted in the route description) will suffice. Small TCUs and wired nuts are also important. You will most definitely want to include a helmet and a headlamp. You will also want to bring extra webbing (and perhaps rappel rings) to beef up or replace existing rappel anchors, especially on routes other than **Diagonal**. The sun and weather here are hard on anchors, and the routes are infrequently climbed. Unless you're climbing in September or later, take bug dope and, if your tolerance is low, a head net. The black flies have been known to make off with small children. Last, bring a wire brush, as the less traveled routes often have a key hold that needs attention.

The main hiking trail weaves a line through the pass, staying high above the jumbled boulders on the east side of the valley. The cliff is approached on one of four herd paths that leave the main trail at various points. About 0.5 mile south of the height of land is Summit Rock, a small outcropping of rock nicely positioned for viewing the routes on the left half of the cliff.

HISTORY

Some of the earliest known climbing, not just in the Adirondacks but in the country, occurred at Wallface. In the fall of 1920, Henry Ives Baldwin, Eastburn Smith, and George B. Happ made a roped, belayed "zigzag climb" up Wallface. We can only guess where this was—perhaps on the brushy slabs on the South Face or perhaps the line that John Case took 13 years later.

The obvious zigzag line up the main face was

2 Arthur H. Masten, *The Story of Adirondac* (Adirondack Museum / Syracuse University Press, 1968), p. 77.

Craig Patterson on P4 (5.5) of the **Diagonal** *(5.8) in 1965. At the time, this was thought to be the first ascent. Photo by Trudy Healy.*

definitely climbed by John Case in 1933 after several attempts. Having been brought up in the British tradition, in which pegs were considered unsporting, Case knew little about piton craft, so his ascents were limited to what he was willing to solo. Wiessner, on the other hand, understood and embraced protection and thus was able to explore more difficult terrain. He began visiting Wallface in the early 1930s and, after initially declaring the cliff unclimbable, returned several times to finally succeed in 1938, starting on Case's route but finishing by a more direct and difficult line of chimneys.

After these early climbs, the history becomes more uncertain. In 1947, Hal Burton writes that the cliff "has been climbed at least a dozen times by four major routes,"[3] and this at a time when there were only two known routes. Among those credited with ascents is Peter Gabriel, a well-known and capable Swiss guide with an impressive résumé; maybe he was responsible for the pitons found by Joseph D. Rutledge in the finish corners of **Diagonal** in 1962. Many "first"-ascent parties have reported finding gear or seeing unexplained gear nearby—the bread crumbs of the earlier explorers who may never be known.

More than any other cliff in the region, Wallface has an allure that has attracted climbers from all over. Perhaps its size and remoteness satiate the desire of young East Coast climbers, stuck in the lowlands and aspiring to loftier goals, a sort of springboard to bigger cliffs out west. The story of the young Frank Abissi and Steve Baker, who were inspired by Royal Robbins and looking for an Everest-like adventure, is very common on this cliff. The high faces above Indian Pass have been a vertical stage for epics, multiday ascents, and climbing projects that spanned months. Take the ascent of **Pleasure Victim** by Michael Dimitri and Michael Sawicky, two young men who worked six days a week. They would drive up the night before their day off, sleep a few hours in the parking lot, then hike in to Wallface to work on their route, pushing it just a little higher each visit . . . for an entire summer. Several first ascents involved wall bivys, such as **Wags on the Wall** and **Diagonal**. When developing the route **Free Ride**, Tim Beaman hiked repeatedly to the summit (which isn't easy) to clean the route on rappel, a project that took three years to complete.

3 Hal Burton, "Rock Climbing is Fun", *Adirondac* 11, no. 2 (Mar–Apr 1947), p. 5.

Wallface Solitude

Fritz Wiessner once wrote this shining endorsement of climbing here: "Wallface, a cliff of about 500 feet, we examined pretty closely. It is steeper than it looks and the rock is not built for climbing. The weathering has not developed holds and the inward corners do not contain the cracks that would be expected from a distant view. The upper part is overhanging. The cliff is probably unclimbable except at the ends, where however it becomes lower and has many trees upon it."[1]

And this was 1 year after John Case had climbed his route in the central depression of the cliff and 14 years after the first known roped ascent of Wallface. One can't be too hard on Wiessner for his statements, though, as he returned three more times to eventually succeed in climbing the second route on the face 4 years later as well as many other routes on cliffs scattered around the region. Fifty years later, he recalled Wallface as his favorite climbing area in all the northeastern United States.[2]

He had this to say about it in 1939: "There is a charm to Wallface, as to all Adirondack rock climbs. It is the charm of solitude. It is beautiful, remote, wild country. There are no cars whizzing by below. There is nothing but unbroken wilderness all around. The views, I might add, are superb. . . . One can forget the city in country like this."[3]

1 Fritz Wiessner and Henry S. Beers, "Rock Climbing: In the Adirondacks," Appalachia 20 (1934), p. 253.
2 Laura Waterman and Guy Waterman, "From Dresden to Wallface: Fritz Wiessner, Dean of American Climbing," Adirondac 52, no. 9 (Oct–Nov 1988), p. 13.
3 Fritz Wiessner, "Wallface: Up the Cliff," Adirondack Mountain Club, High Spots (Jan 1939), p. 50.

Admittedly, for the pure aesthetics of movement, perhaps **Fastest Gun** is a better route than anything at Wallface. But Wallface offers the highest degree of uncertainty and adventure.

Given what is known today, development has been steady since the ascent of **AG** in 1957, with no significant gaps in years for new routes and, with a few exceptions, all climbed by different parties. The first climbers were understandably attracted to the Central Depression, as this afforded the easiest lines to the summit (**Case Route** and **Wiessner Route**). Next was the area around **Diagonal**; this ramp, next to the **Whitney-Gilman Ridge** on Cannon in New Hampshire, is perhaps the most obvious major feature of any large cliff in the Northeast. The first ascent of this feature, although credited to Rutledge, is still uncertain. It wasn't until the early 1980s that the steep and overhanging dihedrals of the Shield Area were explored.

More recently uncovered are the routes on the South Face, which were quietly climbed in the mid-1980s by Bruce Thompson with various partners. The first to explore this face was Rutledge in the early 1960s, although no details of his route are known; maybe he's responsible for the pitons found high on **Wags on the Wall**.

CAMPING

There are many options for camping in and around Indian Pass. If you are approaching from the north, a lean-to and many campsites can be found at Scott's Clearing, about 45 min from the Mental Blocks Approach (there's even a curious three-bolt route—5.7—on the rock buttress attached to the far side of the old dam). If you are approaching from the south, the second lean-to makes a good base and is about 30 min shy of the Diagonal Approach. There are several tenting possibilities across the stream just north of the lean-to.

There are several good bivy sites in Indian Pass itself, listed from south to north:

(a) At the beginning of the Diagonal Approach: When you are approaching from the south, just before the trail crosses to the right side of the stream and climbs into the pass, continue straight on a herd path for 200' to a good campsite. The site accommodates a couple of tents, has a fire ring, and is near the stream; across the stream is an overhanging boulder that makes a good cook spot if it's raining.

(b) Summit Rock: Hike to the viewpoint at Summit Rock, then follow a herd path for 150' north to a grassy site on a promontory. This is also the beginning of the Summit Rock Approach.

(c) At the beginning of the Case Route Approach: There is a good bivy cave just north of the start of the Case Route Approach. Find the giant boulder that marks the start of the herd path, then walk 200' north to a large bivy cave with a flat floor and room for a small tent.

(d) At the beginning of the Mental Blocks Approach: About 100' south of where the Mental Blocks Approach Trail begins is a herd path that leads east to a clearing and a small waterfall.

DIRECTIONS (MAP PAGE 435)

Wallface can be approached from the south from the Upper Works Trailhead (page 423), or from the north from the Adirondack Loj Trailhead (page 425). The approach from the south is shorter and easier, but if you're in the Lake Placid area, you have to weigh the hiking time against the extra driving time to Upper Works. Irrespective of the trailhead, first-time visitors to Wallface will appreciate reviewing the cliff from Summit Rock, although this adds to the approach and increases the difficulty of the final bushwhack to the cliff.

For those familiar with the cliff, the shortest way to reach the cliff is from Upper Works, using the Diagonal Approach for the final section. The exception is for **Mental Blocks** and other routes on the North End; for these routes, the shortest way to reach the cliff is from Upper Works, using the Mental Blocks Approach for the final section.

Upper Works to Summit Rock: This approach is straightforward. However, when you approach via headlamp, some turns, especially at the start, are easily missed, so keep alert for markers and trail signs.

From the trailhead, follow the Indian Pass–Wallface Trail (yellow markers) for 7 min to the intersection with the Flowed Lands–Lake Colden Trail. Bear left (staying on the Indian Pass–Wallface Trail), and, after 40 min, you'll pass the intersection with the Duck Hole–Preston Ponds Trail. Despite recent rerouting around some of the worst sections, this section of trail can be extremely boggy (in fact, the wettest approach in this guidebook). Continue straight, now with red markers, passing two lean-tos and crossing many streams. If you are camping, the second lean-to makes a good base, as do the many flat areas near the stream just after the second lean-to. After 3.8 miles (about 1.5 hr), the valley narrows and the trail crosses to the right side of Indian Pass Brook. Before the crossing, a small path continues 200' to a campsite; this is where the Diagonal Approach begins.

From the stream crossing, continue uphill to the first house-sized boulder. Continue on the steeply uphill hiking trail, eventually overcoming a steep section on a ladder. A few minutes later, and 4.4 miles from the trailhead, you arrive at Summit Rock, a rock ledge with a spectacular view of the southern section of Wallface.

Adirondack Loj to Summit Rock: From the parking area at the Adirondack Loj, walk back to the fee station on the main road; the trail (with red markers) starts across the road. Follow the trail around Heart Lake, passing the trail to Rocky Falls at 2.1 miles (where there is a lean-to) and another lean-to at 3.81 miles. At 4.06 miles, you pass the turnoff for Wallface Ponds and soon reach Scott's Clearing, where the trail has been redirected high on the left, with a frustrating elevation gain and loss. (Hint: If the water is low, you can save 20 min by walking straight into the clearing by the old dam; then stay on the left side and cross the clearing to pick up the main trail on the far end.) At 4.9 miles is the intersection with the Lake Colden Trail, and, at 5.5 miles, you reach a flat, boggy area with views of **Mental**

Blocks on the right and the intersection with the Mental Blocks Approach; it requires about 2 hr to reach this point from the Loj. After another 6 min, the trail passes on the left side of a large rectangular boulder (60' wide, 30' tall, 20' deep) that marks the Case Route Approach. Another 5 min after that is Summit Rock, 6 miles from the Loj.

Diagonal Approach: From the south, this approach is recommended, as it provides the fastest way to the cliff with the fewest hassles. On the hiking trail, immediately before the last stream crossing, continue 200' to a campsite. Stay on the left side of the stream and follow a well-cairned path through a maze of mossy boulders. Eventually, the trail turns away from the river and follows a dried-up drainage area. This drainage area turns uphill and becomes a very rocky streambed, very clear and easy to follow with cairns. Eventually, the trail cuts right out of the streambed (this critical turnoff is not well marked, but there is a large slab in the streambed at this point) and makes its way uphill to the cliff, meeting the cliff at the base of **Diagonal** 577073,4887452. The approach takes about 40 min from the hiking trail.

Summit Rock Approach: This approach is recommended to access routes in the Diagonal Area when you are coming from the north (Adirondack Loj) or if you are camped in the pass. (If you approach from the south, this adds extra elevation gain and loss, and is rougher than the Diagonal Approach.) From the viewpoint at Summit Rock, follow a herd path 150' north along the height of land to a grassy bivy spot. Walk straight downhill into the talus boulders and pick up a line of cairns that weaves through the boulders up to the base of the cliff between **Lewis Elijah** and **Gourmet** 577142,4887486. This trail requires about 20 min, but it isn't well marked, so you may need to allow some extra time.

Case Approach: This approach leaves the hiking trail about 5 min north of Summit Rock and 6 min south of the Mental Blocks Approach (near the height of land in the pass) to meet the cliff at the low point of rock just right of **Case Route**, making this the best approach for the routes in the Central Depression and the Shield Area. The trail begins 20' north of the northwest corner of a huge rectangular boulder (60' wide, 30' tall, 20' deep) that is on the west side of the trail. The hiking trail here is level and boggy and splits briefly to avoid a boggy section; the western split passes within 4' of this boulder. 200' straight north of the boulder is an open area with a boulder cave bivy. There are other boulders in the pass, some the size of small buildings; this boulder is unique in that it is rectangular and close to the trail at a level section.

Follow the herd path through tight boulders and cedars to meet the cliff after about 15 min. Once you are at the cliff, the trail turns left and uphill to the top of a cone of vegetation at the base of **Case Route** 577300,4887663; the 4th-class approach to the base of the Shield also begins here. The routes in the Shield Area begin downhill and left of this high cone of vegetation.

*Tad Welch on P3 (5.6) of **Arch Madness** (5.9), on the South Face.*

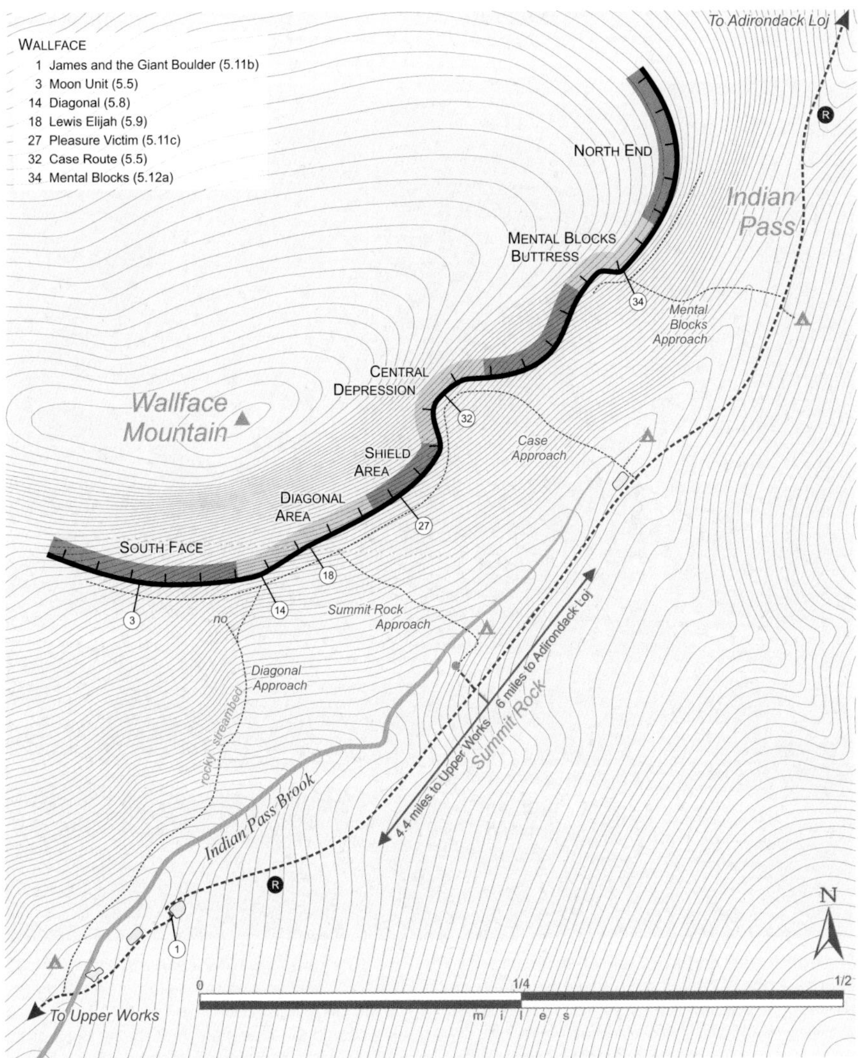

Mental Blocks Approach: This approach is recommended to reach the climbs at the North End—all those right of and including **Rubicon**. The path leaves the main hiking trail about 0.5 mile north of Summit Rock at a flat, boggy section of trail in front of the Mental Blocks Buttress, just south of the height of land in the pass 577676,4887789. The intersection with the main hiking trail is nondescript, but there is a cairn here 20' off the trail; just south of this point is a herd path that leads 100' east to a campsite below a small waterfall, and just north of this point the hiking trail makes a jog through a constriction of mossy boulders. The climbers' path begins fairly level until it reaches a narrow debris strip, which is followed straight up steeply to the base of the cliff 577527,4887809, about 10 min from the hiking trail.

DESCENT OPTIONS

There are several options for descent depending on where you climb; descent options are noted with each route description. It is possible to walk off to the north or south. The southern walk-off returns you to the base of **Diagonal**, whereas the northern walk-off returns you far to the north on the north side of Indian Pass.

Walk-off to the south: The south end of the cliff turns into low-angle slabs with trees. Stay above these and continue west until you're able to drop down on the west end of the slab area. There are tempting ribbons of trees that descend the slabs, all of which dead-end, requiring a rappel or two to return to the cliff base. Either way, once you are at the base of the cliff, follow it down to the base of **Diagonal**.

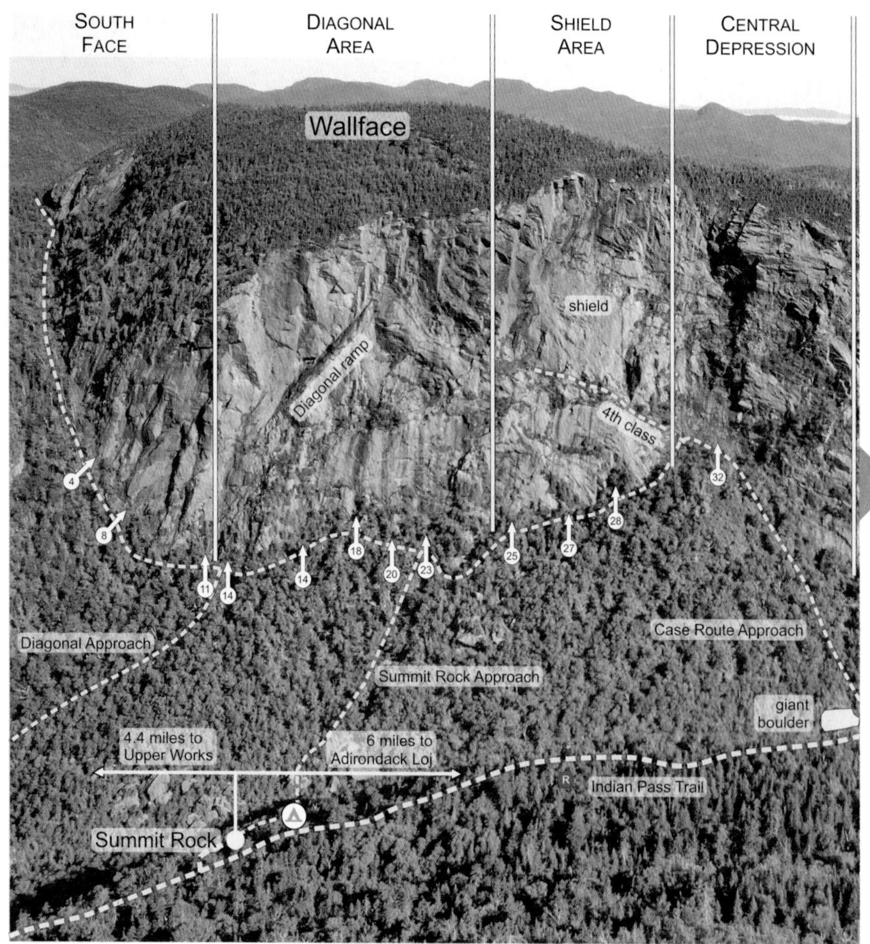

Walk-off to the north: To walk off north, stay back from the edge of the cliff a bit where the growth isn't as thick (the edge of the cliff is nearly impenetrable, requiring hands-and-knees-style bushwhacking). The going is straightforward but arduous due to increased blowdown in recent years.

Diagonal Rappel: From the top of Diagonal, walk left 15' to a fixed anchor on the left wall of a right-facing corner. Rappel to the grassy ledge (P5 of Diagonal) and walk left to a fixed anchor in the left wall of a right-facing corner (the base of P6—the final dihedral of Gourmet). Rappel down the huge overhanging corner below (P5 of Gourmet) to the slab at the base of the corner, then walk right on the slab to a fixed anchor on some birch trees. Another rappel lands on top of the Lewis Elijah slab and another fixed anchor on birch trees. A final rappel (every bit of 200') is required to reach the ground at the base of the Lewis Elijah corner.

Shield Rappels: For routes that reach the top of the cliff in the Shield Area, it is convenient to rappel Free Ride. (The top anchors on Pleasure Victim are in poor condition.) Fight your way to the top of Free Ride and find the long slings attached to several scrubby trees. It is possible to rappel Free Ride to the base of the Shield using a single rope. From there, you can scramble (climber's) right down the 4th-class gully to the base of Case Route (perhaps using an additional rappel if the route is wet). Another alternative: from the top of the Shield, find the P5 anchor of Pleasure Victim, then three double-rope rappels lead to the ground.

Mental Blocks Rappel: From top of the buttress, walk the cliff line 200' left (southwest) and locate an anchor around a chockstone. The first rappel is low-angled and ends at a tree-covered ledge, 150'. Locate a tree anchor for the second rappel, which descends steeply 150' to a broad, vegetated ledge with another tree anchor. The third rappel descends 150' to a vertical forest that is up from and left of the start to Rubicon. Two ropes are required for the descent.

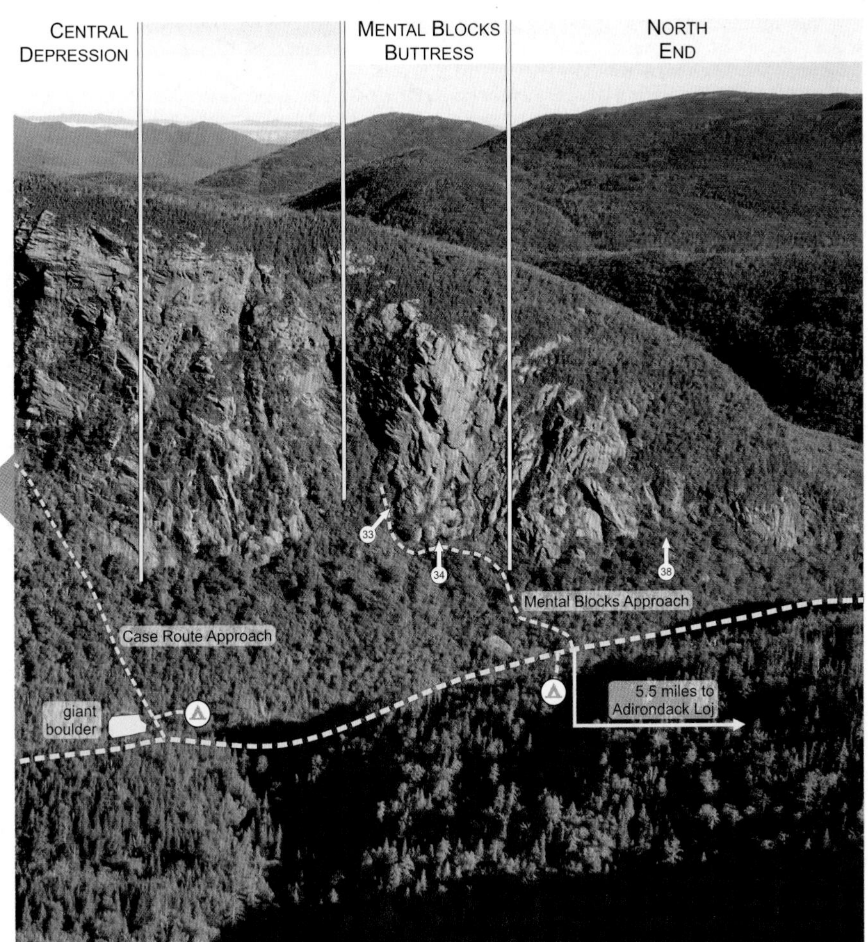

South Face

1 James and the Giant Boulder 5.11b TR 35'

There is some amazing bouldering and toproping to be found below the cliff along the length of the pass. One good toprope problem is very near the campsite on the hiking trail as it ascends to the pass (as you approach from Upper Works). After crossing the stream, the trail ascends gradually past two house-sized boulders. The third boulder is especially large and has a sheer, overhanging wall that faces the trail—this is Small Face Boulder. (Across the trail from the boulder is a good-sized bivy cave.) The route ascends this face.
ACB (TR) Aug, 2006, James Bloch, Colin Loher

2 Travels with Travis 5.5 PG 400'

The western end of the South Face is characterized by low-angle slabs broken by many tree islands. This route finds a relatively clean line, linking cracks among a sea of vegetation.

Start: From the low point of the cliff at the base of **Diagonal**, walk uphill 20 min, passing the Ax of Karma (a house-sized pancake of rock 200' up), the broken right-facing corner used to find **Out with the Boys Again**, and a broken left-facing corner beyond which is the wide section of rock with **Moon Unit**. The route begins about 3 min further uphill and left. Find a high left-facing flake well endowed with cedars that begins 25' up. Begin 30' uphill and left below the left end of a ledge with several clumps of birches. Climb up and right to gain the ledge; belay from its right end below the left-facing flake.

P1 5.5 PG: Stem the left-facing corner or face-climb left of it using the cedars for protection. At its top, head diagonally up and left (runout) over an overlap and slab to a ledge, then up another slab to another ledge at the base of a left-leaning crack. Follow the crack across a slab to a belay at the right end of a crescent-shaped overlap. 200'

P2 5.5 PG: Break through the overlap, and follow a left-leaning crack to its end, then up a vegetated crack that leads to a hanging garden. Before reaching the gar-

den, break right across a slab to a short vertical crack, up this to a left-rising crack, which is followed to an intersection with another crack, forming an X. From the X, follow the right-rising crack to a bushy ledge, then up a right-rising crack in a low-angle slab to a headwall. Follow a left-rising fistcrack up the headwall to the top; find a belay in truly awful vegetation. 200'
History: Some old slings on trees were found at the belays.
Gear: Standard rack plus extra 1-2".
FA Oct, 2003, Jay Harrison, Travis King

3 Moon Unit 5.5 G 150' ★

Incredibly knobby climbing and a wonderful example of the dimpled, textured rock often identified with the High Peaks. Named after the daughter of rock star Frank Zappa.
Start: From **Out with the Boys Again**, continue up the hillside along the base of the cliff for another 3 min to a broken, nondescript left-facing corner with many trees and blocks. Begin 80' uphill and left of the corner at the base of a narrow right-rising grassy ramp.
P1 5.5 G: Scramble out right on the grassy ramp to the highly textured face above. Up higher, the textured face is almost pink in color. Climb up this to a ledge, which is at the right end of a right-rising vein of weeds. Traverse right on scoops and ledges to a shallow left-facing, left-arching corner. Follow this left to an overlap, breaking through on its right side, then angle up and left to the cedar trees. 150'
FA Oct 18, 1986, Tad Welch, Mike Cross

4 Out with the Boys Again 5.7 G 370' ★★

An enjoyable line on relatively clean rock. After several attempts were made to climb a direct route up the imposing South Face, this line was discovered. It bypasses the major difficulties on the wall and offers some very pleasurable climbing. The route takes its name from Mike Thompson's article "Out with the Boys Again," about the southwest face of Everest, which originally appeared in *Mountain*.
Start: From **Diagonal**, scramble left and up along the base of the cliff about 5–10 min to the first large, broken right-facing corner. Just right of this corner, and about 200' up, is the Ax of Karma—a thin, house-sized pancake of rock. The route begins 30' left of this broken corner at a crack in a blank face. About 8' up is a square pocket in the crack.
P1 5.7 G: Follow the crack past the pocket, then angle right, (V1) then back left across the face following a good crack. At its end, make a friction move left (crux) to another crack, then up to a comfortable ledge with trees, about 10' below a tree alcove under a ceiling. 3" cam for the belay. 100'
P2 5.6 G: Climb up staying left of the tree island to the ceiling, pull through on a good left-facing flake, then up blocks to the top of a block pile below a right-arching crack. Walk right 15' to a comfortable ledge below a straight-up vertical crack. 40'
P3 5.7 G: (V2) Up the vertical crack to a right-facing flake, then fight through a cedar to a broken crack and groove to a large cedar. Move left onto the face, then up and left across the face to a vertical garden; belay on a tree with a fixed anchor. A double-rope rappel from this anchor barely reaches the ground. 100'
P4 5.4 PG: Follow a right-rising crack to its end, then straight up a clean, knobby face. 130'
V1 Zigzag Crack 5.10c R: Continue straight up the disappearing crack, then face-climb up and right to a sloped ledge (optional belay). Traverse left across the face, then straight up (crux) to a right-facing, right-arching overlap, then up the face to the comfortable ledge of the normal route.
V2 5.7 G: Step back to the boulder pile and climb a right-arching crack that leads to the right-facing flake of the normal route.
Gear: To 3", 2 ea 0.5-0.75" cams.
History: The route was originally climbed by Bruce Thompson and Ken Eisenberg via the **Zigzag Crack** variation. A year later Jamie Savage and friends added the traverse on P1, which is now considered the "normal" route, as it keeps the grade at a more consistent and moderate level.
FA (V1, P3, P4) Jul, 1985, Bruce Thompson, Ken Eisenberg
FA (P1, P2) May 13, 1986, Jamie Savage, Tad Welch, Bill Widrig
FA (V2) Oct 18, 1986, Tad Welch, Mike Cross

*Tad Welch following P1 of **Out with the Boys Again** (5.7) on the first ascent. Photo by Jamie Savage.*

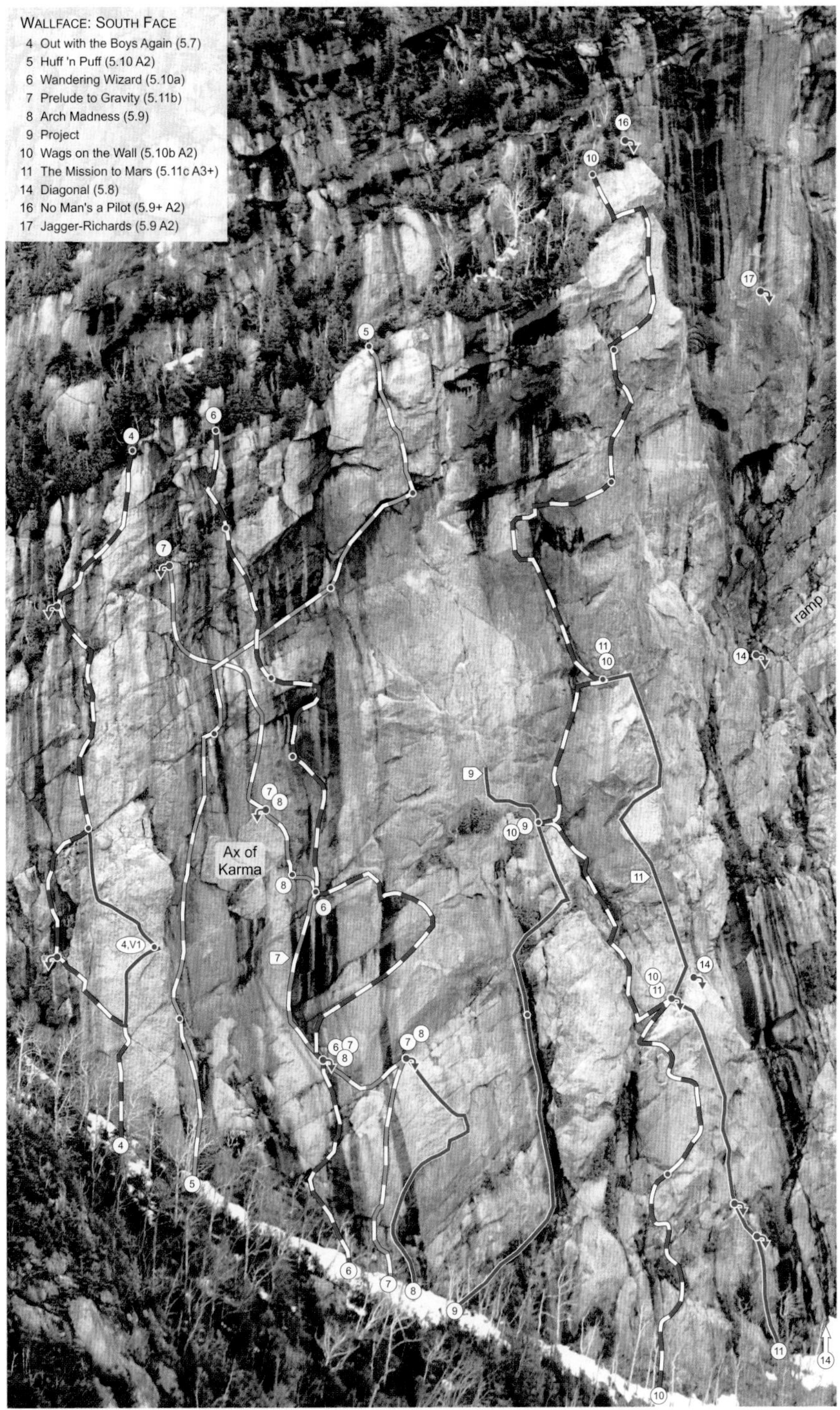
Wallface: South Face
4 Out with the Boys Again (5.7)
5 Huff 'n Puff (5.10 A2)
6 Wandering Wizard (5.10a)
7 Prelude to Gravity (5.11b)
8 Arch Madness (5.9)
9 Project
10 Wags on the Wall (5.10b A2)
11 The Mission to Mars (5.11c A3+)
14 Diagonal (5.8)
16 No Man's a Pilot (5.9+ A2)
17 Jagger-Richards (5.9 A2)
ramp
Ax of Karma
4,V1

5 Huff 'n Puff 5.10 A2 500'

Start: Downhill and right of **Out with the** Boys, left of the Ax of Karma, to the right of a right-facing corner.
P1 5.9 PG: Scramble up bushy terrain to gain a slab. Diagonal left to right-facing corner. Climb corner (crux) to belay tree. 90'
P2 5.10 PG: Start just left of the belay tree. Traverse right over loose terrain to thin crack. Climb crack. Diagonal left to small overlap and climb this. Head toward roof and traverse this to a crack-weakness. Over the roof, then up the crack to top of column. Belay on right side of column. 140'
P3 5.9 C1: Go up column to roof. Traverse right to crack-weakness; aid crack. Continue up crack to slab until reaching a horizontal crack. Traverse horizontal crack to the right 50' to good ledge. Belay at small right-facing corner. 100'
P4 5.10 C1: Climb up to roof. Traverse right using undercling, layback, aid, and cam hooking (stay on the lower crack system). Belay at a pin next to a right-facing corner. 80'
P5 5.7 A2: Aid through roof (using existing knife blades and cam hook, then up crack through corner with bushy tree. Top out left tree. 90'
Gear: Double set of cams from micro to #2, set of nuts, cam hooks.
Decent: Use rappel route for **No Man's a Pilot** a few hundred feet (climber's) right, and slightly uphill.
History: The first ascent was big-wall style over 2 days, bivying in a portaledge below the big roof. No fixed gear was used other than three knifeblades (to facilitate free attempts).
FA Aug 18, 2012, Bryan Kass, Christina Natal, Tony Misuraca (aka Team Team Pig Helmut)

6 Wandering Wizard 5.10a PG 510'

This full-length route shares some pitches with **Arch Madness**. Since modern information is lacking, we've provided a more general description.
Start: 30' uphill and left of **Arch Madness** at a black wall split by horizontal cracks.
P1 5.5 G: Climb up and left to gain a right-rising overlap, which is climbed rightward back into a black streak. Wander up the black streak and up a V-groove to a fixed anchor beneath the black wall. 100'
P2 5.6 G: Same as P3 of **Arch Madness**: Traverse right on a slab below a white wall following a crack to its end. Face-climb up and left to a belay at a cedar below a right-facing chimney. 90'
P3 5.8 G: Begin as for **Arch Madness** by climbing the right-facing corner to the base of the chimney. Step left around a bulging wall (5.8), then traverse left to a right-facing corner. Belay here; **Arch Madness** continues to the left. 60'
P4 5.8: Follow the right-facing corner and right-leaning crack to its end, then climb up and left to a hanging belay below a ceiling. 75'
P5 5.9: Climb out the right side of the ceiling and follow a right-leaning corner to a bush. Step left around the corner and traverse left to a ledge. 60'
P6: Traverse left, then up into a right-facing corner. At its top, follow a left-leaning crack to its end at some trees. 75'
P7 5.10a: Climb a left-leaning crack through a bulge (crux), then head up and right following a right-leaning, left-facing corner to some trees at the top. 50'
FA Jul, 1986, Bruce Thompson, Matt Jasinski

7 Prelude to Gravity 5.11b G 430' ★★★★

High-quality face and crack climbing. The P3 crack is fantastically exposed, but often wet. Named for a Rickie Lee Jones song.
Start: Same as **Arch Madness**.
P1 5.10b G: Climb up and left to a bulge with a bolt. Through the bulge (crux) and up the face (small TCUs) to a right-leaning fingercrack. Follow the beautiful sustained crack (5.9) to its end, then up right to a cedar with a fixed anchor. 100'
P2 5.4 G: Same as **Arch Madness**: Traverse down and left under the steep wall to its left end, then up low-angled rock to a groove below a crack in an overhanging black wall. Fixed anchor on the right side of the groove. 60'
P3 The Black Crack 5.11b G: Power up the right-leaning crack in the overhanging wall to its top. Traverse right on jugs, then up a short shallow right-facing corner (joining **Arch Madness** here). Traverse left to a tree at the base of a right-facing corner, then up the corner to a fixed anchor at the top of the Ax of Karma flake. 100'
○ P4 Rolling the Dice 5.11b G ★★★★: Balance up and left to the top of the Ax of Karma flake, then move up and right onto the steep wall to a short, shallow right-facing corner (gear). Up the corner, then face climb up and right to an imposing, overhanging wave of rock. Pull over the ceiling (crux), up a face, then angle left 40' across several slabs to a steep headwall. Up the headwall (5.10c, much harder than it looks) to a fixed anchor. 170'
Descent: Two 60m rappels to the ground.
Gear: Up to 2.5". P4 requires 2 ea red Alien.
FA (P1, P2) Oct 7, 2006, Jim Lawyer, Simon Catterall, Tad Welch
FA (P3) Sep 23, 2007, Jim Lawyer, Will Mayo
FA (P4) Aug 16, 2008, Jim Lawyer, Emilie Drinkwater

8 Arch Madness 5.9 G 380' ★★★★

Good climbing with excellent protection, extremely clean rock, and exposed situations. The arch is a distinctive feature that just begs to be climbed. The route continues to a high point on the wall right of the Ax of Karma (a thin, house-sized pancake of rock 200' up); what a place to be! Double ropes recommended, as the route traverses quite a bit (it gains only 200' of elevation in five pitches).
Start: At the base of the prominent right-arching overlap. The arch is about 150' long and lies low on the wall, 150' right of a broken right-facing corner (used to locate **Out with the Boys Again**). It is also right of the Ax of Karma flake 200' up and about 2 min left from the base of **Diagonal**.

P1 5.9 G ★★★★: Climb 15' up to the base of the arch, then follow the underside of the arch 90' right, underclinging and face-climbing, to a crux section just before the arch turns vertical (optional hanging belay). Up the vertical section to the top (where the overlap turns horizontal once again), break out left onto the face, and climb (5.6) straight up to a ramp; move left to a fixed anchor at a cedar. 130'

P2 5.2 G: Traverse down and left under the steep wall to its left end, then up low-angled rock to a groove below a crack in a black overhanging wall. There is a fixed anchor on the right side of the groove below **The Black Crack**—the overhanging crack in black rock. 60'

P3 5.6 PG: Traverse right on a slab below a white wall following a crack to its end. Face-climb up and left to a belay at a cedar below a right-facing chimney. 90'

P4 5.8+ G: Up the corner below the chimney, then climb a crack in the left wall that leads left around a bulge to a ledge. Traverse left 30' to a right-facing corner, up this a few feet, then step left across a face to a stance and cedar below a right-facing corner. 70'

P5 5.7 G: Up the right-facing corner (gear to 4") to the top of the flake and a fixed anchor. A spectacular location above and right of the Ax of Karma. 30'

Descent: Two 100' rappels straight down the route.

FA (P1) Sep 30, 2006, Tad Welch, Jim Lawyer
FA (P3) Jul, 1986, Bruce Thompson, Matt Jasinski
FA (P2, P4, P5) Oct 7, 2006, Jim Lawyer, Tad Welch, Simon Catterall

9 Project

This project (5.8+ A3) was an attempt to reach the awesome crack that breaks the shield of rock below the triple-tiered roofs on the South Face. 45' uphill and left of **Wags on the Wall** is a large left-facing corner full of shrubs and trees that begins 75' up. This project begins uphill and left of the corner at a right-leaning crack, which is climbed to low-angle terrain that leads up and right to the large left-facing corner. Climb a left-facing chimney and corner to the top of the buttress, sharing a belay with **Wags on the Wall**. The route then climbs up and left to the top of vegetated ledges, then straight up the face (A3), heading for the base of the crack. A lone bolt marks the high point.

FA Jul, 1986, Bruce Thompson, Matt Jasinski

10 Wags on the Wall IV 5.10b A2 645'

This route climbs the impressive wall left of **No Man's a Pilot**, finishing on the same forested terrace. Since modern information is lacking, we've provided a more general description.

Start: 75' left of **The Mission to Mars** at a point where the cliff bends to become south-facing, below a right-facing corner full of cedars. This is the first large right-facing corner left of **Diagonal**.

P1 5.7: Climb the face right of the corner, over a bulge, then up and right on blocky terrain to a belay at an overlap beneath a smooth shield of rock with a single black streak. 100'

P2 5.9 R: Follow the right-rising overlap, then up the face following the right margin of the smooth shield, aiming for a large flake in the top center of the shield. Climb around the flake, move left into the corner, then immediately up and right to a fixed anchor. 100'

P3: Head back left into the large right-facing corner and climb it to its top. Step left onto the top of the buttress to belay. 100'

P4 5.8 G: Step right and climb a large open book to its top. Join another right-arching open book, which is followed to the top of a buttress. 75'

P5 5.10b G: Step left and climb a left-leaning crack to a sloped ledge, then up a right-facing corner that heads up to an A-shaped roof. Well below the roof, the corner becomes a seam; step left onto the face and climb unprotected flakes (5.9 R) up, then back right to the top of the A-shaped roof. Follow a right-arching crack to a large sloped bivy ledge. 110'

P6 A2: Climb cracks and flakes in an overhanging wall to its top, where the angle eases, then up to a fixed anchor at the base of a large right-facing corner. 60'

Will Mayo on P3 ("The Black Crack") of ***Prelude to Gravity*** *(5.11b).*

P7: Traverse out right on a slab (5.7) to gain a right-facing corner formed by overlapping flaps, just left of the arête that separates the South Face from the **No Man's a Pilot** corner. At the top of the corner, step left and climb a left-leaning crack (same as **No Man's a Pilot** V1) to the forested terrace. 100'

Descent: Rappel **No Man's a Pilot**.

History: Apparently this wasn't the first route on this section of rock, as pitons were found in the roof above the left end of the P5 bivy ledge. The first ascent took two tries over two weekends and involved a bivy on a sloped ledge. "Wags" was an informal group who considered themselves to be scoundrel-climbers, much in the spirit of the Gunks' Vulgarians. The name came about when John Goolrick went to see a talk by Sir Edmund Hillary. At the signing afterward, Hillary asked what club John belonged to. At that time, everyone was part of a club, and being from Fairfield, he replied "Fairfield Alpine Group." Hilary remarked, "Ah . . . Fags," so they changed it to "Westchester Alpine Group."

FA Oct, 1984, Bruce Thompson, Harry Brielmann, Sam Slater

Diagonal Area

11 The Mission to Mars 5.11c A3+ 330' ★★★

A sport route on the buttress left of **Diagonal** that is quick to dry after a rain. P1 features excellent face climbing on a steep wall with solid, clean rock. P2 features a long, crimpy crux on somewhat crumbly rock.

Start: 50' left of the start of **Diagonal**, scramble through trees to the base of the rock; the first bolt is visible just above.

● **P1 5.10d G ★★★★:** Climb the steep wall to a fixed anchor that is just left of a tree-filled gully. Lower from here or continue up and left to a large ledge with a second fixed anchor. 50'

● **P2 5.11c G:** Climb a short slab (right of the orange right-facing V-corner) to a ceiling, over this (5.10d) onto the steep face above. Move up and right to an overlap, then up a right-leaning V-groove. Step back left and up steep rock with crimpy holds and long reaches, leading up and left to a large ledge with a fixed anchor. 120'

P3 5.9 A3+: Continue straight up, and aim for the orange spot. Aid out the arching roof at the top of the orange spot, and at the apex, go straight up past a rivet, then 20' of hooking to a fixed anchor. 160'

Descent: Walk left on the ledge to a second fixed anchor and rappel (two 60-m ropes) to the ground.

History: In the first printing of *Adirondack Rock*, this unclaimed route was named **The Shining Path**. The route has been a multi-year project, initially spotted by Merlin Larsen while climbing **Diagonal**. Larson was a Gunks climber, guide, and worked at the Trapeze Club at the Center of Symbolic Studies in New Paltz. His first attempt in 2001 was thwarted by rain, but he returned later with David Pakenham, the chief instructor at the Trapeze Club, to install P2 and P3. Larsen is still active on this project.

FA (P1) 2001, Merlin Larsen, Thorvald Jacobson
FA (P2-P3) 2001, Merlin Larsen, David Pakenham

12 Dream of Frozen Turkeys 5.8 PG 240'

This is an unfinished line that ascends the buttress left of **Diagonal**. Not quite as classic as **Dream of Wild Turkeys** in Red Rocks. The line was climbed to the midpoint of P5 of **Wags on the Wall** (which had been previously climbed), then abandoned.

Start: Same as **Necessary Risk**.

P1 5.8 PG: Climb up the left side of the depression and left to a right-rising vegetated ledge. Move out left and up the face left of the black streaks and right of the orange right-arching roofs to a point where the arched roofs nearly meet the black streaks. Move up and left in a right-facing corner to a ledge at the top of the buttress (and the fixed anchor of **The Mission to Mars**). 140'

P2 4th class: Climb down and left on a ramp for 20' to join the right-facing corner of P3 of **Wags on the Wall**. 100'

Descent: Rappel the route.

FA 1997, Ian Osteyee, David Lent

13 Necessary Risk 5.6 G 375' ★★

This is a direct approach to the **Diagonal** ramp, avoiding most of the 4th-class cedar pulling. P3 is reportedly very good. Previous guidebooks called this **Diagonal Direct**. Since everybody climbs the lower pitches of **Diagonal** differently, it is likely that portions of this route were climbed earlier. Who knows?

Start: Same as **Diagonal**.

P1 5.5 PG: Climb up the left-facing corner in the right side of the shallow depression, then up and left over a steep face to gain a right-rising vegetated ledge at a point below some black streaks on the face above. Follow this ledge up and right, then step left to a bushy ledge under a large overhang with black streaks. 180'

P2 5.6 G: Traverse left 20' under some black water streaks to a right-facing groove. Up the groove and around a small ceiling 20' up, then up until it is possible to traverse right 40' on a ledge across the face (over the same black water streaks) to a left-facing corner. Up the corner to belay on a tree island. 120'

P3 5.5 G: Traverse right on the tree island, then up a groove to the base of the **Diagonal** ramp and a fixed anchor. 75'

History: Many climbers claim to have done this route before 1983, but nobody knows exactly where they went. The complexity and nondescript nature of the terrain below the **Diagonal** ramp may forever obscure the historic details.

ACB Aug 25, 1983, Ken Reville, George Carroll

14 Diagonal 5.8 G 860' ★★★★

Diagonal is the most popular route at Wallface and for good reason—although the crux pitch is sustained, the rest of the route is 5.7 or easier. This aesthetic route, with exceptional rock quality, follows the low-angled, right-leaning ramp to a thrilling finish in a steep dihedral. As with many Wallface climbs, locating the start of **Diagonal** and deciphering the lower pitches is a challenge.

Start: (V1) The route begins at the south end of the cliff at the low point, just before the cliff bends toward the south. There is an open area here with some birch trees and a flat rock (a barely passable bivy spot), where the approach trail from the south meets the cliff. On the cliff in front of this open area is a shallow depression with a center rib.

P1 5.5 G: Climb up the left-facing corner in the right side of the shallow depression, then up and left over a steep face to gain a right-rising vegetated ledge at a point below some black streaks on the face above. Follow this ledge up and right to belay on a slab to the right of the large roof (below which is the belay for **Necessary Risk**) and below a tree island. 180'

P2 5.5 G: Continue up and right following the weakness for 50', then more directly straight up to a deep groove in steeper rock. Up this to a fixed anchor at the base of the ramp. 180'

P3 5.3 G: The bottom half of the ramp is featured, low-angled rock. Climb to a belay at a block that is 50' above a tree in the corner. 150'

P4 5.5 G: Dodge a bulge above the belay by climbing a right-facing corner that is up from and right of the belay. Regain the main corner, which is followed to the top of the ramp. Belay from fixed anchors at the left end of a traverse ledge. 150'

P5 4th class: Move the belay along the grassy ledge 50' or so to some trees at the base of a right-facing corner, below a slanting ceiling 15' up. 50'

P6 5.8 G: Climb up a thin crack, trending right into a flared chimney, then a right-facing corner. Step back left at the top of the corner onto a grassy ledge (directly above the belay) to the base of a large right-facing corner. 70'

*Ed Palen on P4 (5.5) of the **Diagonal** (5.8). Photo by Olaf Sööt.*

P7 5.8 G: Climb up the steep right-facing corner to the top at a grassy ledge below a black headwall. 80'

V1 5.5 G: An easier (but less aesthetic) approach to the **Diagonal** ramp begins about 300' right of the normal start and involves more 4th-class terrain. At the unusually large birch tree and open area (same as for **Black Plague**), traverse a tree-covered ledge left to its end, then move up over a short face to more cedar pulling. There are many sling anchors dotting this section (used for rappelling **No Man's a Pilot**). Continue up and right following the path of least resistance, eventually heading left over steep, blocky terrain (5.5) to the base of the ramp. In total, there is about 400' of climbing, with a few 5th-class moves just before you reach the ramp. An advantage is that your pack and shoes are very close to the base of the final rappel.

Descent: The recommended descent is to rappel with two 60-m ropes from a fixed anchor that is located 15' left of the exit corner. To hike off, traverse the tree ledge (right) then scramble around the summit cliffband to the woods above. If you are on the ramp and need to retreat, it may be easier to continue to the top of the ramp and join the Diagonal Rappel (rappelling the lower pitches is tedious).

History: The first recorded complete ascent of **Diagonal** was in 1962 by Rutledge and friends. Rutledge had attempted the route solo in Sep 1946 but turned back high on the ramp due to a puzzling "counter-force move." He returned in 1962 with Tom Morgan, Peter B. Andrews, and Cyrus Bryant but ran short of time at the top of the ramp; they escaped by reversing **AG** to the base of the Shield and on to the base of **Case Route** in the Central Depression. On the third attempt, they climbed the route in two days, bivying on ledges at the top of P5. Rutledge reports having found pitons on the top pitch; perhaps this is the lost Gabriel/Burton route mentioned in various issues of *Adirondac*[4], or perhaps **AG** finished here. An interesting sidebar is that it was climbed car-to-car from the Adirondack Loj in 3 hr 14 min by Don Mellor and Jeff Edwards during their children's nap time. They ran in and simul-climbed the route in 35 min (using an 8-mm rope, five wires, five biners, and two slings), then ran off the back side. The record will be difficult to beat due to the recent blowdown.

FA Sep, 1962, Joseph D. Rutledge, Tom Morgan, Jane Morgan

4 Hal Burton, "Adirondack Loj," *Adirondac* 12, no. 4 (Jul–Aug 1948), p. 18; Hal Burton, "Rock Climbing Is Fun!" *Adirondac* 11, no. 2 (Mar–Apr 1947), p. 2.

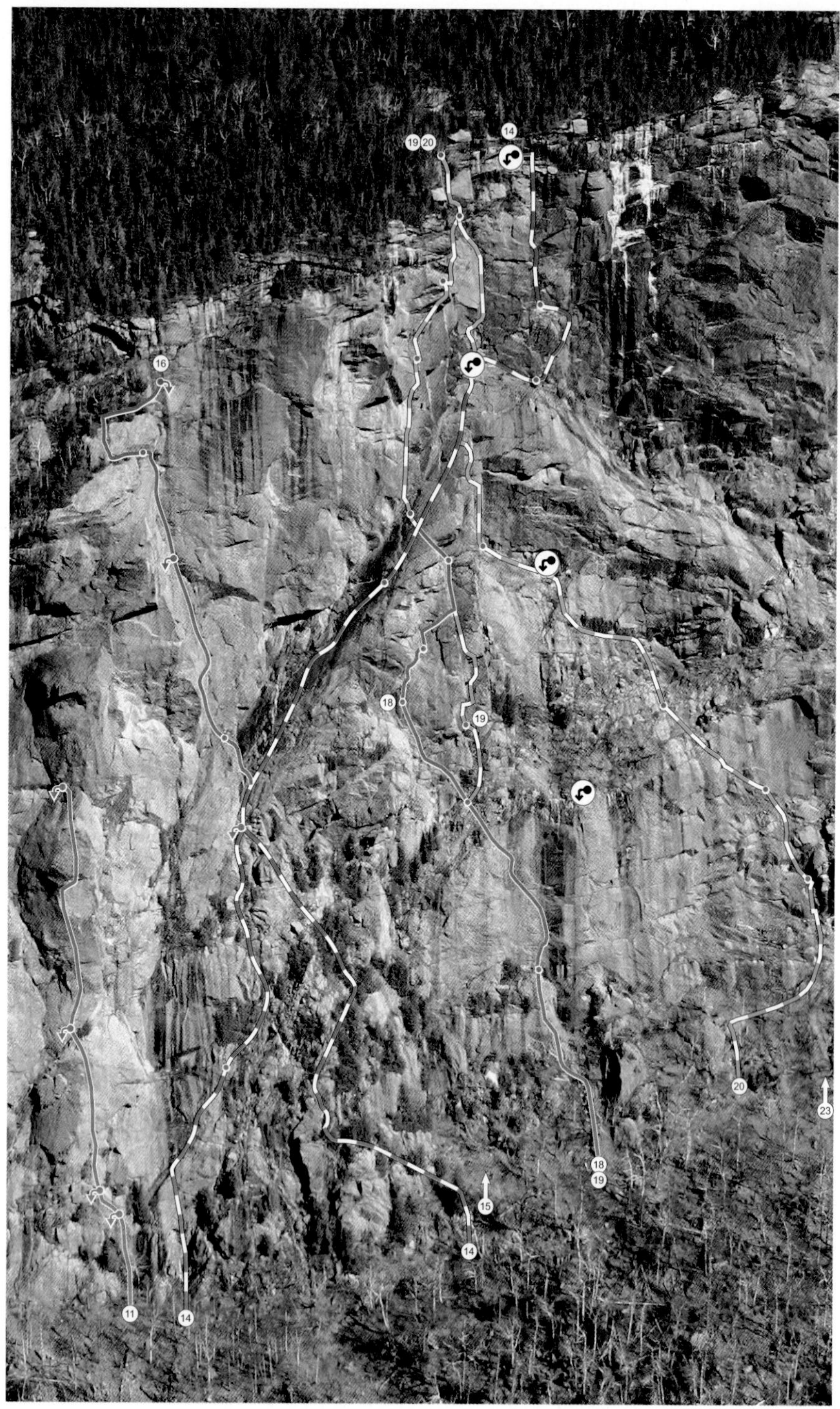

14
19
20
16
18
19
20
23
18
19
15
14
11
14

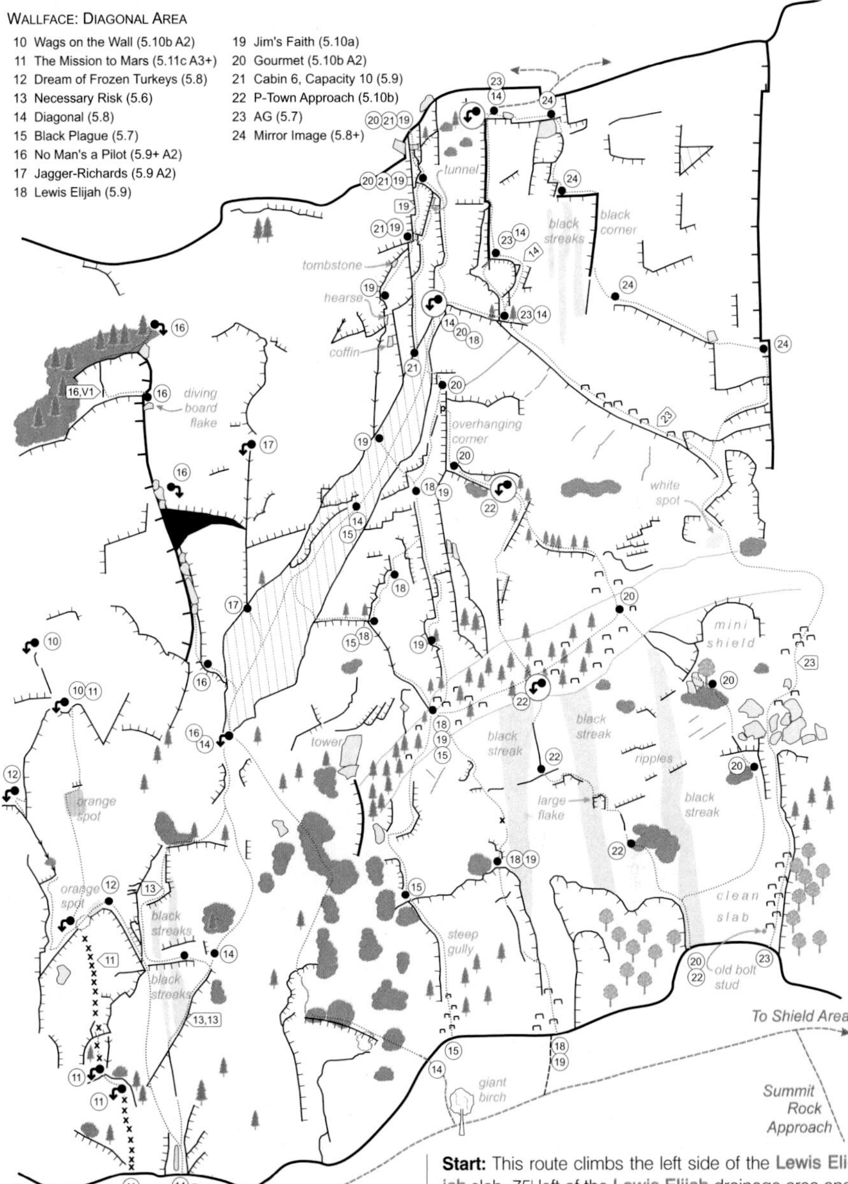

15 Black Plague 5.7 PG 430'

This is a variation to the start of **Diagonal**, joining that route halfway up the ramp. Named for the plague of black flies that eventually drove the first-ascent party from the Adirondacks. For this reason, Webster never returned, making this his first and only climb in the Adirondacks.

Start: This route climbs the left side of the **Lewis Elijah** slab. 75' left of the **Lewis Elijah** drainage area and 300' right of **Diagonal**, the trail passes an unusually large birch near the cliff at a relatively open area. Head steeply uphill here in a small drainage area (pulling on cedars, etc.) to a point where the vegetation ends at a right-facing, shallow chimney filled with blocks and trees. This is also below some orange roofs 200' up with the smooth face of **Lewis Elijah** up and right.

P1 4th class: Climb the chimney and tree-filled corner to the base of the right-facing corner at the lower-left corner of the slab. 100'

P2 5.7 PG: Climb the right-facing corner, then traverse up and right following a groove to a series of left-facing corners. Up the corners to the top of the slab, then trend right on 4th-class terrain to belay at a clump of birch trees, just right of a left-rising ledge system (the same belay as for **Lewis Elijah**). 200'

P3 4th class: (V1) Same as **Lewis Elijah**: climb the left-rising ledge system to a right-facing corner, which is followed up to trees at the base of a right-facing, right-leaning corner. From here, **Lewis Elijah** continues up the corners to the right; instead, **Black Plague** scrambles up left to a nice ledge on the edge of the **Diagonal** ramp. 130'

V1 4th class: It is possible to scramble up and right to join **Gourmet**, then back left to the base of that route's overhanging corner.

History: Webster wrote an account of this route in *Climbing* magazine (no. 27, Sept.–Oct. 1974). The pitches were later climbed by Larry LaForge and Linda Sugiyama (Sep 1982) in an attempt to climb **No Man's a Pilot**, but they instead linked up with **Gourmet**, creating what they referred to as the route **Hang Ten**. They freed the main overhanging corner of **Gourmet** but created no new pitches other than this linkup.

FA Jul 1, 1974, Ed Webster, Ken Nichols

16 No Man's a Pilot 5.9+ A2 370' ★★★

The route climbs the huge right-facing corner starting at the base of the **Diagonal** ramp. Excellent climbing if you like chimneys stuffed with blocks and flakes; however, it is so much better than it looks. Often wet. Most parties climb V1, making the route entirely free at 5.9.

The name "No Man's a Pilot" is a recognition that climbing is a partnership in which decisions are made by the pair rather than the individual .

Start: This route begins at the base of the **Diagonal** ramp (the top of P2 of **Diagonal**).

P1 5.4 G: Climb up the left side of the ramp until it is possible to climb up and left on flakes and ledges into the mouth of the chimney. 90'

P2 5.9+ G: Climb up the flake- and block-filled chimney, through a squeeze section, to a stemming move over the final overhang at the top. Belay above on blocks in the corner. 120'

P3 5.8 G: Climb up the blocky corner to a steeper section of sustained wide crack climbing. Move left at the top to (as Metcalf puts it) a "cupped ledge of delicately balanced boulders"—i.e., the Diving Board flake—below an overhang. 100'

P4 A2: (V1) The original ascent climbed (hammerless using all nuts) the inverted V-slot that breaks the 6' roof above the belay. 60'

V1 5.3 G: From the belay, make an exposed and airy traverse left around the corner to an unpleasant crack in the wall. Up the crack to the trees.

Descent: The route can be rappelled beginning from a fixed anchor on a tree at the top of the corner.

History: The route was originally reported by Spero and Waterman and appeared in Tom Rosecrans's 1976 guide under the name **The Best Climb in the East**, climbing the 5.3 variation to the last pitch.

FA Aug, 1974, Peter Metcalf, Lincoln Stoller (Peter Metcalf is the CEO of Black Diamond Equipment.)
FA (V1) Nov 12, 1975, Alan Spero, Dane Waterman

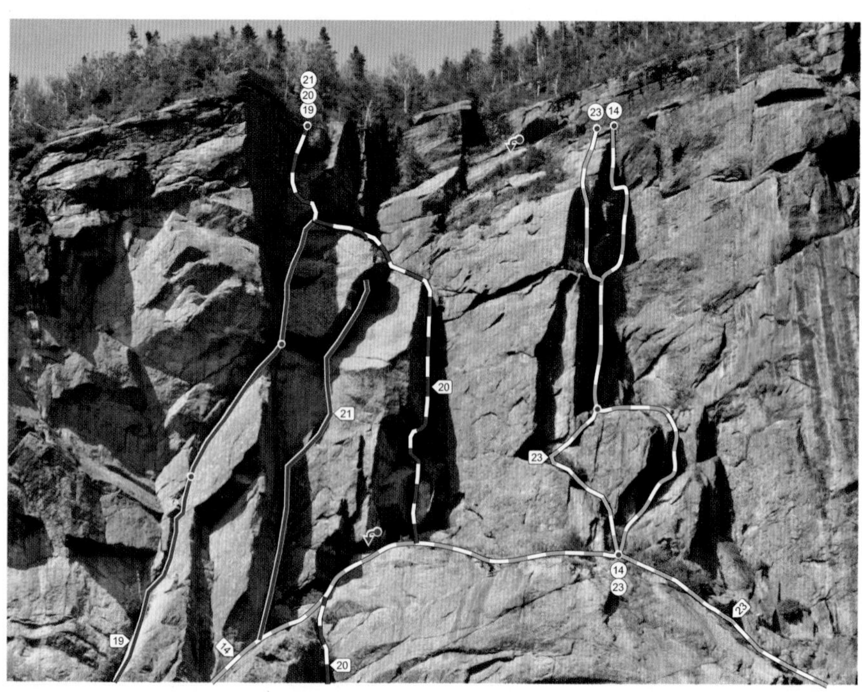

17 Jagger-Richards 5.9 A2 150'

This is an unfinished route that attempts to climb the major right-facing crescent on the sheer face right of No Man's a Pilot and above the Diagonal ramp. Should it ever be completed, this is sure to be an incredible line.

Start: The route begins on the Diagonal ramp. From the base of the ramp, climb up 100' to a belay on the left side below the right-facing corner.

P1 5.9 A2: Climb the corner past a pod. Exciting stemming leads to the base of the right-facing crescent. There is a fixed anchor here, but the rock is rotten. 150'

History: This route was attempted by Michael Sawicky and Michael Dimitri in 1984.

FA Jun, 1986, Tad Welch, Bill Widrig

18 Lewis Elijah 5.9 R 430' ★★★

This route provides a more challenging start to Diagonal and a nice alternative to the start of Gourmet. It has several interesting pitches, including a quality slab (P2) and memorable crux traverse on a knobby face (P5). Lewis Elijah was a Native American trapper who happened upon a small piece of ore in the pass. He was paid "dollar, half, & 'bacco" ($1.50 and a plug of tobacco) to lead David Henderson to the source of the ore in Adirondack Pass (now Indian Pass), which led to the start of mining operations at Upper Works in 1827.

Start: At the base of the cliff and directly below the central section of the Diagonal ramp is a slab with a black streak. This black streak runs down the slab and into a drainage area on the right side of a small buttress. Approach the route up this prominent drainage area to the base of the black streak, at the right-facing corner formed by the buttress. Another landmark to help locate the start is the unusually large birch tree 75' left of the drainage area that marks the start of Black Plague.

P1 5.8 R: (V1) Climb a crack on the rounded arête just left of the unappealing corner to its end. Move slightly right and run it out to the ledge, the crux topout being 15' above the good gear. 75'

P2 5.7 R: (V2) Climb over a small, left-arching overlap-flake, working up and right on scoops and edges to the left side of the black streak, then up past a bolt, angling left to a grassy ledge. From the left side of the ledge, slab-climb up and left to easier blocky terrain. Continue up and left to a vegetated ledge with birch trees, just right of a left-rising ledge system. 100'

P3 4th class: Climb the left-rising ledge system to a right-facing corner, which is followed up to trees at the base of a right-facing, right-leaning corner. (From here, the route Black Plague scrambles up and left, 4th-class, to reach the ramp on Diagonal.) 75'

P4 5.7 G: Climb the right-facing, right-leaning corner, past a jog left, then continue a right-leaning line to a ledge where the corner turns vertical. The rock is very sharp, characteristic of a cheese grater. 50'

P5 5.9 R: Climb the steep corner above the belay until an undercling traverse to the right is possible (5.8+ G). Protect in horizontal pockets before committing to the crux traverse (right) to the vertical crack near the arête. Belay 20' higher at a ledge beneath an overhang (shared with Jim's Faith). 70'

P6 5.5 G: (V3) Go left out of the overhang on easy ground to gain the Diagonal ramp. 60'

V1 4th class: It is possible to begin as for Black Plague. Climb up Black Plague until it is possible to traverse right on a vegetated ledge to the ledge at the top of P1.

V2 5.8 TR: The black streak to the right is an incredible toprope.

V3 5.7 G: Step right around the overhang, continue on the right-rising ramp to a right-facing corner that exits onto the Diagonal ramp. Belay from the fixed anchor at the top of the Diagonal ramp.

FA Aug, 1994, Don Mellor, Ian Osteyee

19 Jim's Faith IV 5.10a PG (5.8 R) 710' ★★★

This route takes a direct line to the top of the cliff, the highlights being the dihedrals of P4 and the right-arching "swoop" on P7. Named in memory of James Weinman, a local mountaineer from Ballston Lake, New York, who disappeared climbing in Chile in 2000. His exploits included solo ascents of difficult routes in the North Cascades and new routes on Mt. Hood and in Patagonia.

Start: Same as for Lewis Elijah.

P1–2 5.8 R: Same as for Lewis Elijah. 175'

P3 5.5 G: Bushwhack up and right through trees and boulders to a gully, then up this to a belay in an alcove under an overhang. 40'

P4 5.8 G: Move up to the overhang above the belay and break it on the right and up into a right-facing corner. Continue up the right-facing corner, around a second overhang, and up to a third overhang. Break this on the left (fixed piton), then step left and up the crack in the shallow, right-facing dihedral to a grassy alcove below an overhang (this belay is shared with Lewis Elijah). 160'

P5 5.5 G: Go left out of the overhang on easy ground to gain the Diagonal ramp. Cross the ramp up and left to the base of nearly vertical flakes at the bottom of an open-book corner system. 60'

P6 5.9 G: Climb up flakes and dihedral past a small cedar tree with loose rocks. Layback up the dihedral to a second cedar, passing an obvious 10" ledge on the right, which holds a coffin-sized block. From the ledge, climb layback to gain jugs and move delicately left under and around a hearse-sized block perched in the corner. Continue in the crack to gain 2" ledges at the start of a prominent swoop (the right-facing dihedral that curves right). 110'

P7 5.9 G: Follow the crack past a detached tombstone-sized boulder below a bush to attain the swoop. Follow the swoop to the arête and hanging belay (positioned at the lower left corner of the Cabin 6, Capacity 10 flake). 50'

P8 5.10a PG: Climb past a right-facing chimney directly above the belay (crux). Follow the right-facing corner above to a small ledge with birch trees. Continue up right-facing flakes to a large sloping ledge; belay on the left end in the overhanging chimney-alcove (same as Gourmet). 85'

P9 5.8 R: Same as **Gourmet**: Make a bouldery move left onto the outside of the flake that forms the left side of the chimney above the belay. Climb up the flake to its top and into another damp chimney. Pull jugs through the chimney, then grab small pine trees to the top. 30'

History: P8 had been climbed earlier as part of the route **The Free Gourmet** (the climbers' attempt to free **Gourmet**).

Gear: 2 ea #3 Metolius 4-cam units (orange), 1 ea #9 Metolius (about the same as Camelot #4) for P7, full set of cams, extra midsize to large nuts.

FA (P8) Mar 8, 1996, Kristian Wild, Bruce Stover

FA Aug 8, 2004, Robert Weinman, Tim Kelly

20 Gourmet IV 5.10b A2 780' ★

This older route is distinguished by the huge overhanging corner on P5; the Diagonal Rappel goes over this corner, allowing full appreciation of its overhanging configuration. The route has a few good pitches but certainly not the artful presentation of fine, discriminating features that the name would suggest.

Start: 200' right of the start of **Lewis Elijah** is another parallel black streak with several angular bulges at mid-height that look like ripples or waves in the rock. The route begins at a short right-facing corner at the base of this black streak. When approaching from **Lewis**

Jim's Faith

"Well, yahoo, partner!" I said, raising my right hand for Tim to return the obligatory high five. He left me hanging. I peered down to our campsite more than 600' below us and thought of the beers waiting for us. "One last pitch and we have a first ascent on Wallface."

"Doesn't count, Bob," he said. "Needs to be a clean single push—bottom to top."

My open hand, still poised for a high five, knotted into a fist.

Noting my mood change, Tim backed up his anchor, then asked, "Do you think Jim would consider this a first ascent?"

My hands were bleeding; my toes were numb, and lodged in my nose were several bales of musty Adirondack moss we had cleaned from cracks in the rock. Six attempts already, yet our goal to establish a route honoring my brother remained unrealized.

In June 2000, my brother James disappeared while climbing solo on a 12,000' peak in Chile. We had deliberated this potential scenario in the past while waiting out weather on mighty mountains in tiny tents, and it angered me that I could not save him. Our family launched a search complicated by floods, blizzards, avalanches, and earthquakes, eventually stopping because we recognized lives were being risked to recover only his body. I yearned for a guarantee that he was at peace, so in 2003, I determined to establish a new climb, an action prayer, in the Adirondacks, where we had shared our first adventures. I supposed such a well-traveled place had little left for new prospects, but hoped I would find some sketchy, slimy, undesirable single pitch to name in honor of my brother. Don Mellor's book and a few Budweisers revised that low expectation. I called him.

"Read up on Wallface," he said. I hung up the phone and read Don's description of Wallface: "a remote and wild place . . . where climbers of all abilities find solitude," consistent with the type of places my brother used to call home. 48 hours later, on a misty August day, I found myself standing with Don on a ledge halfway up the inspiring face of Wallface. "Other than that, a classic line," Don claimed, pointing out some loose blocks to watch out for. On the walk out that evening, he tried to give me some perspective on the difficulties of the project, but I was imagining a one-day jaunt in September.

*Tim Kelly reaches the P7 belay on the first ascent of **Jim's Faith** (5.10a). Photo by Robert Weinman.*

Six humbling attempts and one year later, Tim Kelly and I were standing at the threshold of reaching our goal. The moves we had practiced on crags, climbing walls, and fire escapes gelled for us, removing hesitation as we climbed past various loose blocks and landmarks we had named "coffin," "hearse," "tombstone," and "swoop." I reached a grassy alcove where I found a photo of my brother that had floated down from the top of the climb where earlier I had wedged it. Thinking of the last climb we did together, 700' of granite rising out of dense jungles in Brazil like a giant finger, aptly named Dedo de Deus, meaning "Finger of God," I realized then that my brother's fate had never been in my hands. As a final tribute to a man drawn to rock and the mountains, we named the climb "Jim's Faith."

- Robert Weinman

Elijah, walk right 200' to a point where the vegetation rises higher and the trail drops down below a cliffband. Instead of dropping down, scramble up steep vegetation to its high point at the base of a low-angle slab with the aforementioned black streak.

P1 5.6 PG: Climb up the corner in the black streak for 15' to the top. Traverse right beneath the ripples to the right side of a slab at a ledge beneath an angled overhang with several 8'-tall vertical seams. 110'

P2 5.9 G: Climb through the angled overhang on the right via the thin seams. Step left and scramble up to a clean slab of rock—a "minishield" below arching roofs. Belay on the left side of this clean slab at an overhanging, right-facing corner. 90'

P3 5.8 G: Traverse left to a left-rising crack; up this to easy blocky terrain with many belay possibilities. 80'

P4 5.6 G: Continue in a leftward line following a ribbon of vegetation along the top margin of a slab to the base of the overhanging, right-facing corner. 150'

P5 5.10b G: Spectacular climbing leads up the overhanging, right-facing corner, past a pesky cedar to a "diving board" chockstone. A fingercrack breaking the left wall provides the exit onto a ramp above. 90'

P6 5.9 G: A short crack in the little wall leads to the Diagonal ramp. Continue right to the top of the ramp, and continue to the ledge beneath the "mossy corner," the right-facing corner with moss on the right wall. There is a fixed anchor here used in the Diagonal Rappel. 130'

P7 5.6 A2: This pitch ascends the often wet, always mossy right-facing corner left of the final Diagonal corners. Climb up and into the right-facing corner; up the corner, around the roof, then at the top of the corner, step left to a ledge; belay at the fixed anchor on the right end of this ledge or walk left to the deep chimney-alcove. 100'

P8 5.8 R: From the deep chimney-alcove, make a bouldery move left onto the outside of the flake that forms the left side of the chimney above the belay. Climb up the flake to its top and into another damp chimney. Pull jugs through the chimney, then grab small pine trees to the top. 30'

History: The route has had several misadventures resulting in freeing some of this route. In an attempt to climb No Man's a Pilot, LaForge and Sugiyama free-climbed the Gourmet corner on P5. In 1996, Wild and Stover also attempted to climb No Man's a Pilot and ended up free-climbing portions of Gourmet. They returned over several visits, freeing every pitch of what they thought was Gourmet, calling it The Free Gourmet. Their line of ascent, however, finished on Cabin 6, Capacity 10. The actual mossy corner of Gourmet P7 remains to be freed.

FA Sep, 1964, Ants Leements, Geoff Wood, Dave Isles (Dave Isles climbed the first ascent of the East Ridge of Bugaboo Spire with John Turner, Dave Craft, and Richard Sykes in 1958.)
FFA (P5, P6) Sep, 1982, Larry LaForge, Linda Sugiyama
FFA (P2) Mar 8, 1996, Kristian Wild, Bruce Stover

21 Cabin 6, Capacity 10 5.9 G 190'

This is a two-pitch variation to Gourmet that climbs one of the more obvious features in the upper section of cliff, the huge right-facing chimney formed by a leaning flake, just left of the finish corner of Gourmet. The name is taken from a sign above the door on Cabin 6 in Tuckerman's Ravine, which is appropriate because that's how many people would fit in this chimney.

Start: At the top of the Diagonal ramp, at the base of a right-facing corner, the first corner left of the "mossy corner" of Gourmet P7.

P1 5.9 G: Climb up the corner for 60' to the overlap on the right wall. Climb out right on the overlap, then layback up to the roof formed by the giant flake. Belay under the roof or in the corner on the left side of the roof (as for Jim's Faith). 100'

P2 5.7 PG: Climb up and right into the bottom of the gaping chimney, which is climbed to the chockstone at the top. The first ascent tunneled into the chimney and through a hole behind the chockstone, emerging onto the grassy ledge. Step left to belay in the chimney-alcove. 90'

FA (5.7 A2) May, 1974, Peter B. Harris, Roger Bowman
FFA (P1) Mar 8, 1996, Kristian Wild, Bruce Stover

22 P-Town Approach 5.10b G 370'

Splitting the face below the Diagonal ramp, P-Town Approach offers a fairly direct path to the Gourmet corner, with good climbing on P3 and a few spicy moves punctuating the rest. The route finishes on the Diagonal Rappel where one can descend or walk left to the fantastic Gourmet corner. The route was climbed as practice for a trip to Patagonia, which the first ascentionists dubbed "P-Town."

Start: Same as Gourmet.

P1 5.6 G: Climb up the right-facing Gourmet corner to its top, then scramble up and left to the highest point on the tree ledge. 40'

P2 5.9 PG: Work up a short handcrack to a ledge under a bulge, then step left and climb a small corner to top of large flake. Move left, then make a thin face move to better holds. Step up and left onto a vegetated ledge under bulge (gear), then traverse further left to a hanging belay at a vertical crack. 100'

P3 5.8 G: Follow the vertical crack to its end. Step right onto the face, then trend up and right to a slabby finish. Belay at a fixed anchor shared with the Diagonal Rappel. 80'

P4 5.10b PG: Hike up a drainage path and climb a blocky left-facing corner until it becomes chocked with dirt and the walls of the corner become smooth. Step right and make a hard move (crux) to gain a right-rising ramp that is followed to a vegetated ledge. Step left and follow poorly-protected right-leaning crack on a mossy slab to a fixed anchor on a tree (shared with the Diagonal Rappel). 150'

FA Nov 3, 2007, Dan Ressler, Dave Truncellito

23 AG 5.7 PG 700'

This older route consists of a lot of scrambling with the occasional 5th-class move to finish essentially on **Diagonal**; however, old descriptions of this route are so vague that we'll probably never know exactly where it goes. The description in Rosecrans's 1972 guidebook says that the original ascent went up the corner left of **Diagonal** and to the right of **Gourmet**; if so, the route is much more difficult than 5.7 (perhaps more like 5.10, although there are no recent reports of climbing this corner). If the route finishes on **Diagonal**, then the grade of 5.7 is definitely inaccurate (5.8 would be more like it). The route is named for its protagonist, Art Gran, a well-known East Coast climber.

Start: On the right side of the low-angle slab that marks the start of **Gourmet**, at a point where the slab becomes vegetated and blocky. The trail from Summit Rock meets the cliff at this point. From a distance, a key feature to look for is the "white spot," an obvious scar left of the Shield and level with its base. Below this is a clean slab of rock beneath an arching roof—a "minishield." The route begins directly below the white spot and climbs the blocky terrain right of the clean slab.

Route Description: Climb the vegetated corner (true Adirondack cedar pulling) straight up to where the terrain opens up and becomes very blocky. Continue up and right passing the right side of the clean slab to a vegetated area 100' below the left side of the Shield. Head left toward the white spot, passing under a small tower and up its left side (staying just right of the white spot) to gain a left-rising traverse line. Traverse left for several pitches to the highest grassy bench where the route meets **Diagonal** at the alcove on top of P5. From here, **Diagonal** moves up and right, then back left into the major right-facing corner, whereas **AG** moves up and left on some ledges at the base of a smaller right-facing corner. The route is described as climbing this corner, although recent reports indicate this corner to be exceedingly difficult. Instead, climb out the tilted A-slot to the right and rejoin **Diagonal** until you are even with the ledge on the left wall with a tall cedar growing next to the rock. Climb the cedar to its top and exit left onto the slabs, or continue up **Diagonal**.

History: At the start, if you scramble up about 6' on the right side of the slab where it meets the vegetation, you'll find an old 0.25" bolt stud used to hold a plaque in memory of two men who fell on **AG** in 1981.

FA 1957, Art Gran, Ira Schnall, Mary Sylvander, Bob Graef

24 Mirror Image 5.8+ PG (5.8 R) 370'

This is the first reported route to climb the wall right of the final corners on **Diagonal** and left of the Shield Area and, as such, is more of an exploration of this section of cliff. The route was an attempt to climb the huge arête formed by the right-facing corner left of the Shield. Finding this not to their liking, the first ascentionists traversed left to the next most obvious feature, the large black right-facing corner right of the last pitch of **Diagonal**. There may be a better line by climbing directly into this corner from below (as explored by Ed Palen) instead of 5.8 R traversing. The name was chosen because of a supposed "mirror image" likeness to **Diagonal**.

Start: The route begins at the base of the arête formed by the huge right-facing corner left of the Shield. The first-ascent party climbed **AG** (more or less) to reach this point (from the "white spot" mentioned in **AG**, the base of this corner is up and right 45°), but it's also possible to climb 4th-class terrain by scrambling up to the base of the Shield from the base of **Case Route**, then traversing left under the Shield to the base of this arête.

P1 5.6 PG: Starting just left of the arête, follow a right-rising ramp to the arête. Climb the arête to a ledge (at the point where the arête makes a slight offset to the left). 100'

P2 5.8 R: Traverse left, pass under a small right-facing corner, then gain a large sloped ledge. Traverse left on this ledge to the base of the huge right-facing black corner. 100'

P3 5.8+ PG: Climb the large right-facing corner to its top, then traverse left on a ledge to the base of a right-facing corner capped by a right-facing flake that forms a chimney. (Some fixed gear found at this belay.) 100'

P4 5.5 G: Climb up the chimney behind the flake to its top. Step left onto a tree-covered ledge. 70'

Descent: From the tree-covered ledge, walk left over the top of **Diagonal** to the fixed anchor at the top of the Diagonal Rappel.

FA 1997, Stan Czaplak, Karl Swisher

Shield Area

The largest unbroken section of rock on Wallface is a big slab in the center of the cliff known as the Shield. The rock on the Shield is excellent and provides some high-quality face climbing for those comfortable at the grade. The Shield can be accessed via a 4th-class gully on the right, starting at the base of **Case Route**.

Above the Shield is a jumbled collection of right-facing dihedrals with supersteep corner climbing. Once you are positioned at the top of the Shield, it is possible to move left or right and climb several of these upper dihedrals, rappelling **Free Ride** to return to the top of the Shield. The terrain at the top of the Shield is loose 4th class with virtually no protection other than the established fixed anchors for **Pleasure Victim** and **Free Ride**.

25 Eastern Shield IV 5.10b G (5.8 R) 970'

Wallface seems to offer a number of adventure routes where aspiring climbers first cut their teeth on a big wall. This is another such route, climbed by teenagers who were looking for adventure. The route was the first to climb the Shield, the largest unbroken section of rock on the cliff. The rock quality is generally good, and the route provides a relatively moderate approach to the upper dihedrals, although be aware of some serious runouts on the Shield pitches. There has been some discussion of bad bolts on this route—all but two of the original 0.25" bolts are gone, replaced 20 years ago by a few more solid bolts.

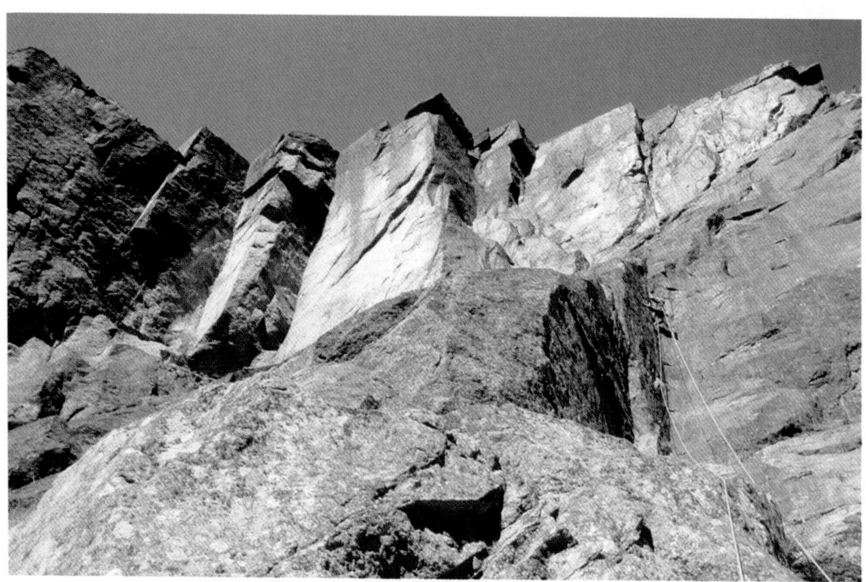

Jeff Achey on P6 (5.11a) of ***Pleasure Victim*** *(5.11c). Photo by Kennan Harvey.*

Start: At a slabby area beneath huge orange overhangs. The base of the route is semiopen and airy large talus, with an especially large slabby block set back 50' from the base of the cliff in front of a clean section of the slab, which is the start of **Hot Metal and Methedrine**; **Eastern Shield** climbs the left side of this slab and begins 20' left of that route's first bolt below a left-facing, right-rising blocky flake with a cedar tree 20' up.

P1 5.5 G: Scramble up the right-rising stepped flake to a ledge below a pointed tan-colored tower. There is a fixed anchor on the right end of this ledge. 100'

P2 5.8 G: Climb up to the top of the tower, then straight up some cracks. At their top, angle sharply right to a low-angled area and fixed anchor. 130'

P3 5.8 R: From the left side of the open ledge, climb a brush-filled, right-facing corner that angles up and left. The corner changes course, angling right; at that point, break out onto the left face (crux, 5.8 R) and climb the face to easier scrambling up and slightly left, running it out over easy rock to a birch tree on the grassy terrace at the base of the Shield, just below a broken left-facing corner that begins 20' up, and 50' left of the highest pile of blocks leaning up against the base of the Shield (the top of P3 of **Pleasure Victim**). 200'

P4 5.7+ R: Be ready to run it out nearly 60' on this pitch. Work up to the base of the corner and climb this to a good ledge at its top (5.6, good gear in the corner but no gear on top). Climb up and right onto the undulating face with no protection to a good flake (crux), then up to a fragile pasted-on block. Work up and right into a left-rising trough, then up this past a small flake (marginal gear, tends to fall out after you pass) until you can step right to a semihanging stance and fixed anchor. 150'

● **P5 5.8+ G:** Climb up and left following a left-rising depression past five bolts to a sloped stance on the left and fixed anchor. The first two bolts are ancient and 0.25", but the climbing is easier; the latter bolts are beefier. 50'

P6 5.8 PG: Climb up the base of the right-facing black corner and large precariously perched black flake. Carefully move up and left onto ledges and into a larger right-facing corner. Up the corner (crux), then up flakes on the right wall to the top. Continue up to belay near the base of the right-facing crack formed by a huge flake with an A-shaped alcove at its base. 140'

P7 5.10b G: (V1) Hard moves up the A-shaped alcove (crux) lead to easier climbing up the widening crack to a belay on the ledge above. (The "dangerous flake" that repelled earlier parties has long since disappeared.) 120'

P8 5.8 PG: Walk to the left side of the ledge and climb the dirty right-facing corner to lower-angled terrain above. 80'

V1 Atlas Shrugged 5.10a PG: This variation climbs the right-facing corner right of the **Eastern Shield** off width. The name is the title of an Ayn Rand novel first published in 1957, chosen by the first ascentionists, who felt the book illustrated their own independence and desire to do their best. The specific corner has been the subject of some mystery; it is reported to be the right-facing corner with orange lichen streaks on the bulging left wall and has a small ceiling at about two-thirds height; this corner also forms the left side of a light-colored face broken in the center by a right-rising overlap. From the belay at the base of the off width, head out right following a right-facing corner that angles back left to form a ledge, just below the orange lichen streaks. Climb the corner above to a vertical section, then up past the roof to the top. 160'

25
25.V1
27
28
29
24
25
26
27
28

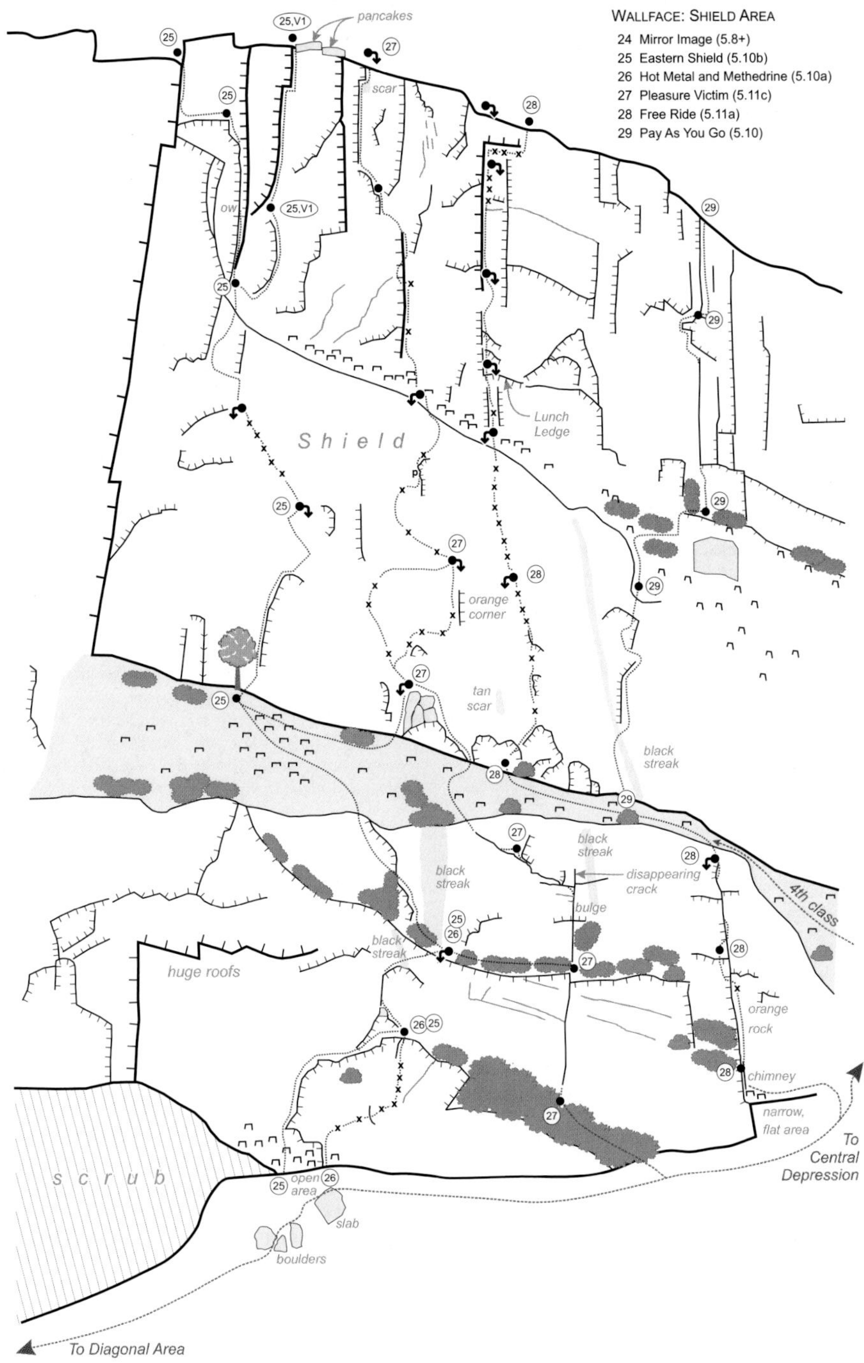
WALLFACE: SHIELD AREA
24 Mirror Image (5.8+)
25 Eastern Shield (5.10b)
26 Hot Metal and Methedrine (5.10a)
27 Pleasure Victim (5.11c)
28 Free Ride (5.11a)
29 Pay As You Go (5.10)
pancakes
scar
ow
Shield
Lunch Ledge
orange corner
tan scar
black streak
disappearing crack
bulge
4th class
huge roofs
orange rock
chimney
narrow, flat area
To Central Depression
scrub
open area
slab
boulders
To Diagonal Area

History: The bolts (some of the worst on the cliff) were placed by Dick Williams, Jim McCarthy, and Dave Craft during an early foray onto the Shield in the mid-60s. They bailed, leaving an original Chouinard biner (stamped "DW") on their high bolt, and never returned to complete their route. Bandorick and Wade found these bolts on their ascent.

FA (5.9 A2) May 23, 1978, Bruce Bandorick, Scott Wade

FA (V1) May, 1979, Scott Wade, Bruce Bandorick, John Kravetz

FFA (P7) 1988, Michael Dimitri, Michael Sawicky

26 Hot Metal and Methedrine
5.10a G (5.8 R) 490' ★★★★

The start of **Pleasure Victim** was altered by rockfall during the summer of the first ascent. In fact, the gear stash of ropes and hardware was buried, never to be found. Given the instability of that section of cliff at the time, the Mikes created a brilliant first pitch starting 200' left of the original start, then joining **Eastern Shield** for a couple of pitches to the terrace below the Shield. This route makes an excellent approach to the Shield. A way to link all the best climbing involves climbing P1 and P2 of this route, then traversing right on the vegetated ledge to the base of the **Pleasure Victim** Disappearing Crack pitch, then continuing with **Pleasure Victim** from there.

Start: The start of the bolt-protected face is beneath the same large orange overhangs that mark the start of **Eastern Shield**. The bolt hangers are rusted, so they blend in with the rock a bit. The base of the route is semiopen and airy large talus, with an especially large slabby block set back 50' from the base of the cliff in front of a clean section of the slab.

● **P1 5.10a G:** Climb up to the first bolt (somewhat hidden in a small left-facing corner), then traverse directly right for three bolts (crux). Continue following the bolts straight up to a good, open ledge with a fixed anchor at the base of a small flake-tower. 100'

P2 5.8 G: Same as **Eastern Shield**: Climb up to the top of the tower, then straight up some cracks. At their top, angle sharply right to a low-angled area and fixed anchor. (From here it is possible to bushwhack right 120' to the base of the Disappearing Crack pitch of **Pleasure Victim**.) 130'

P3 5.8 R: Same as **Eastern Shield**: From the left side of the open ledge, climb a brush-filled right-facing corner that angles up and left. The corner changes course, angling right; at that point, break out onto the left face (crux, 5.8 R) and climb the face to easier scrambling up and slightly left, running it out over easy rock to a birch tree on the grassy terrace at the base of the Shield. 200'

P4 4th class: Move the belay by traversing right on the grassy terrace to a fixed anchor at the top of the highest tower—the top of **Pleasure Victim** P3. 60'

FA (P1) Jun 29, 1986, Michael Dimitri, Michael Sawicky

27 Pleasure Victim
IV 5.11c G (5.10b R) 810' ★★★★

Excellent, varied, long, and demanding, this climb is a real prize. Amazingly, it sees little traffic, perhaps due to off-route bolts that sucker the unsuspecting climber into a dead end. The Shield pitches are excellent, but they wander, and the bolts aren't necessarily placed where the climbing is difficult; there are several places where you simply cannot fall. P1 is of poor quality, so it is recommended to climb **Hot Metal and Methedrine**.

Start: The start is a bit difficult to locate. It begins at a straight-up crack in the wall 50' up and left on a vegetated left-rising ramp 577247,4887556, but locating this ramp can be tricky. Perhaps the easiest way is to find the start of **Hot Metal and Methedrine**, then walk 150' right along the base of the cliff to the first vegetated break; the ramp angles up and back left. Another locator for the ramp is to find the flat bench beneath the steep 50'-wide wall behind trees that marks the start of **Free Ride**; the left-rising ramp is 130' downhill and left from this.

P1 5.7 PG: Climb straight up the crack to the vegetated ledge at the base of a vertical crack through a bulge. 90'

P2 Disappearing Crack 5.9 G: Climb straight up the crack with a tree on the right, through the bulge to where the crack disappears. Climb left following cracks to a belay on a grassy foot ledge below a left-facing corner. 120'

P3 5.1 R: Climb straight up low-angle rock to the grassy terrace below the Shield. Scramble up and left to the top of the highest tower (really a pile of blocks leaning against the Shield proper). There is a fixed anchor here and a good ledge to kick back and relax. 170'

● **P4 5.10b R:** Climb up and left following a weakness to a bolt. Step back down and climb directly right around a bulge (scary 5.10) to a bucket. (V1) Continue rightward for three more bolts to a shallow, nondescript orange corner, which is climbed to the top to a fixed anchor. This brilliant pitch follows the natural weaknesses of the rock and was drilled on lead, on sight, and by hand. Unfortunately, there are at least three places where a fall would result in injury. 70'

● **P5 5.9+ PG:** Step left, then climb directly up to a bolt. Trend left for a couple of more bolts, then traverse directly right following several more bolts. Easier climbing leads up to a fixed anchor at another terrace area below the upper corners. 140'

P6 5.11a PG: Climb directly above the belay into a huge right-facing corner (dirty and often wet), which is followed to its top (fixed wires, one pin, and two 0.25" worthless bolts; green Camalot helpful to back up fixed gear). At the top of the corner, move left to a stance on the arête (crux). Follow the shallow crack (RPs) and crumbly rock (scary 5.10d) straight up until a traverse of 12' can be made leftward into the next right-facing corner. Climb this short corner (5.8) to a large ledge and fixed belay. 160'

P7 5.11c G: Climb up and leftward following a ramp with a crack. At its top, climb straight up into the obvious right-facing corner capped by a roof. Undercling right under the roof (crux), then layback up into the right-facing corner to the bucket at the top of the cliff and a fixed anchor (there's a drift pin driven into one of the bolt holes; the anchor can be backed up to trees

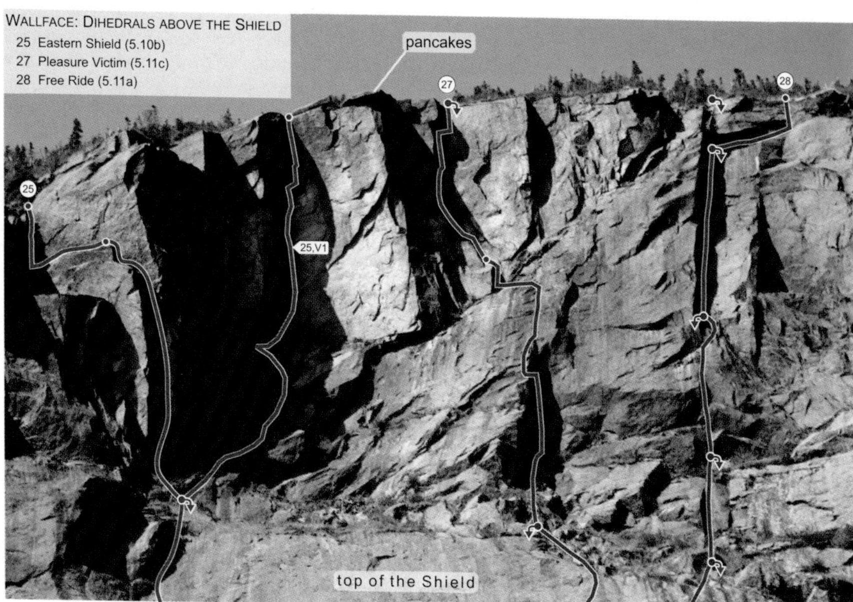

farther back from the cliff). The creaky flake below the roof has fallen off, making the pitch much safer but very slippery on the feet. 60'

V1 5.10a R: Move left up a ramp to two old, bad bolts of unknown origin. Step right to a ledge, then move farther right to the fixed anchor. 70'

Gear: Sparse rack up to 2". Small RPs for P7.

Descent: Due to the condition of the top anchor, it is best to walk (or crawl) right about 100' to the top of **Free Ride**. Either rappel **Free Ride** in its entirety or, if you want to return directly to your packs, do a long 200' rappel to the terrace at the top of the Shield, then scramble left to the P6 anchor and rap **Pleasure Victim** in three more rappels.

History: Dimitri and Sawicky created a masterpiece with this route, one of their first "big" routes and their first experience drilling on lead. Their ascent required many trips to the cliff over an entire summer, when they braved rain, hail, bugs, heat, and rockfall as they launched into the unknown. The route is named for the 1982 album by the punk rock band Berlin and for the "time, energy, and frequency of the thrashings with the weather we received." After completing their route, they were so impressed with its quality that they returned to the cliff in 1986 to replace many of the 0.25" button heads with 3/8" bolts. (These are now 20 years old and are also badly in need of replacement.) Due to this ground-up ethic, bolts needed to be drilled from natural stances, giving the route a reputation for runouts; the route desperately needs an upgrade in hardware.

FA Aug, 1984, Michael Dimitri, Michael Sawicky
FA (P1) Jun 29, 1986, Michael Dimitri, Michael Sawicky
FA (V1) Sep 1, 1986, Jeff Edwards, Don Mellor, Patrick Purcell

28 Free Ride IV 5.11a G 735' ★★★★★

This route has brilliant climbing, good-quality rock, good protection, and exposed situations. The Shield pitches have been called the "best face climbing on the East Coast," and the exposure on the final pitch is jaw-dropping. Some parties skip the lower pitches by scrambling up to the base of the Shield from the start of **Case Route** (4th class).

Start: Begin down from and left of the high vegetated slopes that lead to **Wiessner Route** and **Case Route** (i.e., the same slopes that lead to the 4th-class approach to the base of the Shield). Look for a steep 50'-wide wall behind trees rising from a flat bench, with a right-facing chimney on its left end stuffed with blocks and trees. P1 begins at this chimney below a right-facing corner, the left wall of which is orange.

P1 5.11a G: Climb the right-facing dihedral toward the roof to a bolt on the left face. Move left at the bolt and up to a stance with gear belay. (A block fell from this

*Dennis Luther at the P4 belay on **Free Ride** (5.11a).*

pitch; a tight #3 Camalot provides protection to the bolt; grade unchanged.) 70'

P2 5.10a G: Straight up bulges following a crack past juniper ledges; becoming less steep at the top through a short off-width bulge to a fixed anchor. 70'

P3 4th class: Scramble up low-angle rubble and through vegetation to the base of a subtle pillar at the base of the Shield. 170'

○ **P4 5.10a G:** Climb rightward on a weakness to a stance below the left side of the pillar (bolt). Climb up and left, then back right to gain the base of the left-facing corner (difficult-to-reach gear makes this G; otherwise, it would be R). Continue up past the top of the pillar, moving slightly right, then left and up to a fixed anchor just left of a black streak. 80'

● **P5 5.9+ PG:** Move left from the belay and up a bolt line, moving rightward at the top to a fixed anchor. 70'

P6 5.10a G: Scramble up low-angle terrain to a steep 8'-wide slab between inside facing corners. Climb the outside corner on the left after clipping a bolt and continue up to Lunch Ledge with a fixed anchor. 80'

P7 5.11a G: Climb the overhanging right-facing corner on the left end of the ledge up flaps (crux; easier if you are tall), then past loose plates out right, then back left to a fixed anchor. 70'

P8 Endurance Pitch 5.10d G: Follow the endless right-facing corner to a fixed anchor below the roof. 75'

P9 Perverse Traverse 5.10c G: Traverse right making Houdini moves until past the roof, then straight up the steep face to the top. 50'

Descent: From the top, walk left a few feet (directly above the Endurance Pitch) to a fixed anchor on trees. It is possible to rappel with a single 60-m rope to the bottom of the Shield, then walk right down the 4th-class gully to the base. Two ropes allow you to rappel to the ground.

History: The route required two years to create, then another year to climb it, with all bolts drilled by hand. Dennis Luther and Tom Northrupp put up the Shield pitches, while Sylvia Lazarnick and Tim Beaman did the majority of the cleaning and preparation of the other pitches. One of the biggest challenges, recalls Beaman, was finding the top—each time the top would look different.

FA Sep 12, 1999, Tim Beaman, Dennis Luther

29 Pay As You Go 5.10 PG (5.9 R, 5.8 X) 620'

P3 is classic—nice rock, multiple cruxes, and solid protection—, but the P1 barrier (and its 40+' runouts) will keep away only the most determined.

Start: Follow the 4th class ramp onto the shield terrace. Begin at the right end of the terrace, 30' right of **Free Ride** P4, below the distinct black streak on the shield, and 20' left of a broad, vegetated, left-facing corner.

P1 5.9 R (5.8 X): Climb the face with no protection (5.8 X) to a small overlap and the obvious right-arching crack and corner above. Continue up the corner until it is possible to move back left up and over the corner (5.9 R), then trend right, following an obvious weakness (no pro) to reach a tree island. 160'

*Jim Lawyer follows P8 (5.10d, the "Endurance Pitch") of **Free Ride** (5.11a). Photo by Martin von Arx.*

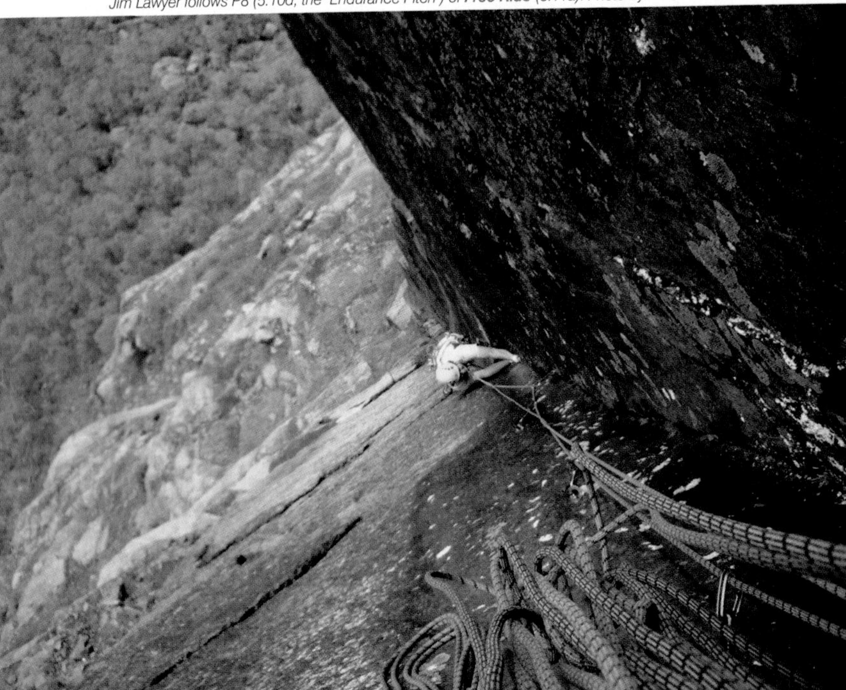

P2 5.1 PG: Continue up easy terrain across the terrace to a birch tree, then traverse right 20' until it is possible to move straight up, then right again to more trees directly below two vertical crack systems. 150'

P3 5.10 PG ★★★: Follow the obvious fist-sized crack off the belay through a bulge. Climb straight up into a shallow, left-facing corner (5.10), then up a larger left-facing corner capped by a roof. Exit out the roof at a crack (5.10) to a semi-hanging gear belay. 130'

P4 5.7 PG: Move up and right to a crumbly crack, and follow this straight up until the climbing eases. Trend left as the cliff merges with krumholtz. Continue up and left until a secure belay can be made at the top of the cliff. 180'

Descent: Tunnel left for 150' to the top of **Free Ride**, and rappel that route.

FA Oct 1, 2010, Christian Fracchia, Rob Mecus

First Epic on Wallface

On August 29, 1933, coincidentally just three days after John Case's first ascent on Wallface, four young boys from Plattsburgh (Tyler Gray, 19; Robert Glenn, 17; William Ladue, 16; and William's young brother Bobby, 14) made an attempt at the "first ascent" of Wallface. Bobby stayed at the bottom while the other three climbed up the face, presumably somewhere in the vicinity of the Case and Wiessner routes. By their account, about 250' from the top, they could "go no further without help." Since their ascent dislodged the rock that had allowed their passage, they could not retreat. They attracted young Bobby's attention and managed to convey their predicament; he immediately left to get help. Racing back to the Loj, Bobby ran into the Loj caretaker, Jed Rosman, and asked, "Mister, would you help a fellow in trouble?"

A rescue party was put together, and a plane was dispatched to do a reconnaissance. It was reported that the pilot shut off the engine and drifted close enough to "shout for the boys to stay put." Relief was not forthcoming that day, so the boys spent a cold night on their narrow ledge, reportedly linking themselves together with shoelaces to a scraggly sapling to keep from sliding off as they dozed. From the pass, rescuers kept the boys company using a megaphone they fashioned from birch bark. In the morning, the rescuers lowered a rope, tied on a boy, and attempted to raise, but the rope broke, dropping the boy back on the ledge. Another rope was airdropped to the rescuers but missed. A third rope (said to be 250 pounds) was dropped, this time successfully, and, with the rescuers coordinating their efforts with revolver shots, the boys were pulled to safety none the worse for wear.

Of the rescue, William's father was heard to say, "If you ever do that again, I'm going to leave you there."

The Central Depression

If you like the mountaineering experience with complex route finding, loose rock, and pulling on cedars with the occasional 5th-class move, then these routes are for you. For those with adjusted expectations, these routes wind through some exposed terrain and are fun adventures, made all the more interesting when you realize these were climbed by some well-known pioneers (Wiessner and Case) in the 1930s.

30 Wiessner Route 5.4 G 500' ★

This route climbs nondescript terrain to a high recessed area bounded by two huge facing corners. From here, it climbs interesting chimneys hidden in the left wall of the left corner, invisible from the trail.

Start: Same as **Case Route**.

Route Description: (V1) Follow **Case Route** to a point where it diverges to the right. Continue up and left to a deep, vegetated depression, which is followed up and left to a point below an orange spot in the rock face above. (This orange spot is just right of the slanting floor of the high recessed area.) Head up toward the orange spot; at the top of a right-facing corner below the orange spot, cut back left across a vegetated ledge to the base of a huge recessed area bounded by facing corners. From here, a pitch or two leads to the top. Angle up and left to a right-facing corner that rises left in a series of steps and ledges just left of a wide roof. Where it meets the major right-facing corner, (V3) continue in chimneys to the top. 500'

V1 Direct Start 5.6 PG: In dry conditions, several pitches can be taken directly up the center of the slab to join the normal route. Start in the center of the slab and climb straight to its top. (V2) Head up and left following a right-facing, left-leaning vegetated groove, then back right to exit onto the lower-angled 4th-class terrain above.

V2 PSOC 5.6 PG: At the top of the slab, head right following a weakness through the steep corners to the right, above an orange face.

V3 More Than One Way to Skin a Cat 5.6 G: Climb the left-facing flake right of the finishing chimneys to a final left-facing corner. A good alternative in wet conditions.

History: Wiessner first attempted the route with Henry S. Beers in 1934 but was driven off by rains. He returned in 1936 but failed due to early snow. His 1937 attempt was thwarted by rain and snow. His determination paid off on the fourth attempt in 1938, in which the route was climbed in 4 hr on a "dismal, foggy day"[5] using two pitons and one belay. This was a busy weekend for Wiessner, as he climbed the first ascent of his route on the Upper Washbowl the day before and his new route on Indian Head (Lower Ausable Lake) the day after. In 1948, Wiessner wrote that "a great deal of vegetation and moss in the chimney make this route a poorer rock climb,"[6] which is perhaps the best rationale

5 "Rock Climbers Route, New Way up Wallface," *Bulletin of the Adirondack Mountain Club* 2, no. 4 (Jun–Jul 1938), p. 8, 14.

6 Fritz Wiessner, "Rock Climbing in the Northeast," Intercol-

for the **More Than One Way to Skin a Cat** variation.
FA May 29, 1938, Fritz Wiessner, Bob Notman, M. Beckett Howorth
FA (V1) Fritz Wiessner
FA (V2) 1966, Penn State Outing Club
FA (V3) Aug 10, 1986, Butch Kinnon, Jeanne Kinnon

31 Forty-niner 5.7 G (5.5 R) 325'

This route has one interesting pitch of climbing—the 5.7 overhanging corner that leads to a small pinnacle.
Start: Follow the **Wiessner Route** to below and right of the final ledges that approach the upper chimneys and below an orange spot on the wall above. Right of the orange spot is a huge, 30'-high, left-facing corner.
P1 4th class: Climb out right on brushy ledges to the base of the left-facing corner right of the orange spot. Continue around the base of this corner on stepped ledges to a belay at the base of the next left-facing corner with a pointed tower at the top. 90'
P2 5.7 G: Climb cracks in the right wall of the corner to the top of the pinnacle. 70'
P3 5.5 R: Step across to the main face and climb up to the slab. Head right to easier ground, then straight up to the trees. 165'
History: In 1941, Gerry Bloch began his quest to climb the pinnacle corner on the buttress of rock between **Wiessner Route** and **Case Route**. He returned many times through the years in an attempt to complete it but was always turned back by weather, route finding, or lack of protection. In 1990, at the age of 72, he roped Mellor into helping him complete his route, 49 years after he started. Mellor was able to unlock the puzzle of the last pitch (by climbing unprotected, dirty slabs no less). Bloch went on to become the oldest person to climb El Cap (in 1999 at the age of 81).
FA Jun 5, 1990, Gerry Bloch, Don Mellor

32 Case Route 5.5 G 1000' ★★

This is by no means a technical rock climb; it's more of a bushwhack with the occasional 5th-class move. Still, it makes an excellent mountaineering objective, ascending a huge buttress of rock with good exposure. The line, visible from the trail, ascends forested ledges, making a number of zigzags up the buttress. It has been said that John Case routinely soloed this route and also used it as a downclimb.
Start: At a flat bench at the highest point of the vegetation, centered below a black slab that has on the right side a huge left-facing corner that arches left into a roof. This is also the beginning of the 4th-class traverse to the base of the Shield.
Route Description: Climb up 30' of unprotected 5.0 slab with good holds, then traverse right to a treed ledge with many blocks, one of which is a nice 8' by 8' platform. Continue right along a bushy terrace, about 200' total, (V1) before grass grabbing upward to begin a leftward traverse. More bushes and trees lead to a point where you can begin traversing right once again (this is where **Case Route** leaves **Wiessner Route** and **Forty-Niner**), this time with some 4th-class climbing, exposure, and areas of freshly loosened rockfall. Use care here. At the end of the rightward traverse is a

legiate Outing Club Association, *IOCA Bulletin* (Winter 1948), p. 46.

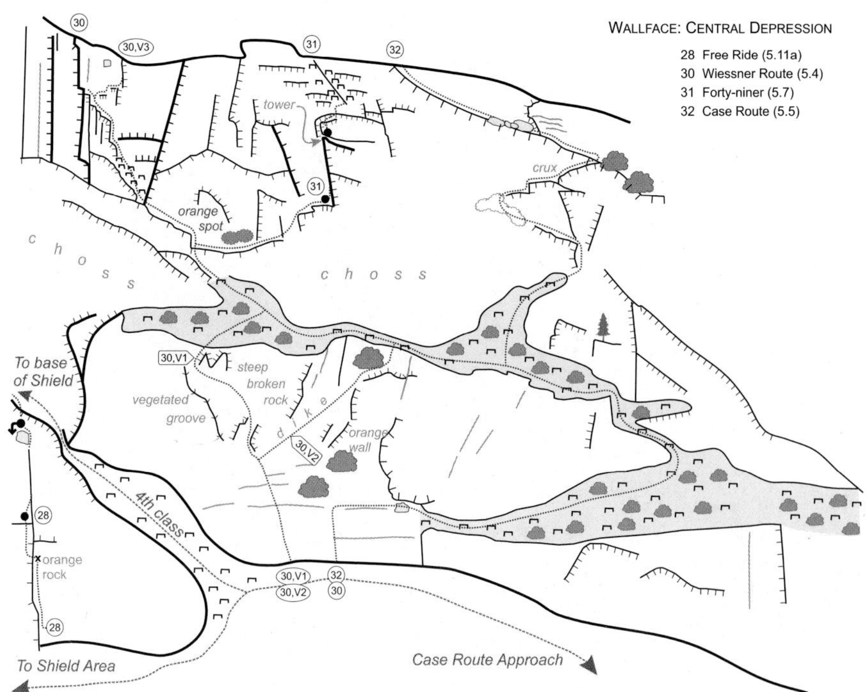

small, 40'-tall blocky buttress with several options, one of which is to make an exposed traverse to the right around the buttress and climb its right side. From its top, continue left to the next forested patch and, at the left side, begin the next rising rightward traverse. The move midway across is out of character with the rest of the route; it's an overhanging 6'-high corner that goes at 5.5. (2.5" cam). Continue right to the next tree island, then begin the final long, rising leftward traverse on a slab (dubbed the "escape route" in early guidebooks). Pass underneath a large right-facing corner and roof, on top of some boulders, and leftward up a beautiful slab to the summit. Alternatively, it is also possible to climb the mossy chimney behind a large flake in the aforementioned right-facing corner.

V1 5.5 G: This variation adds some clean rock climbing by shortcutting the first switchback. About 150' into the traverse, climb a left-facing, left-leaning corner, following a good crack as it rises to the left. At its end, climb a right-leaning crack to a steep wall, then continue the left-rising line, following a ramp to the trees.

Descent: There are some fixed rappels, but these are suspect at best on hideous-looking blocks. Even though it's horrible, the best descent is to bushwhack south or north, depending on where you want to end up.

History: Case made several attempts to climb Wallface before this, once with Jim Goodwin, when they quit after attempting a shoulder stand. He finally succeeded on Aug 27, 1933 with Elizabeth Woolsey (a member of the first women's Winter Olympic Ski Team in 1936) and his son John Case Jr., climbing the route in 1 hr 45 min.[7] An interesting sidebar is that this was three days before the famous incident in which three boys became stranded on Wallface in an attempt to be the first to climb it, requiring a massive rescue effort. In the early days, Goodwin reported the crux of this route being "safer by a rope doubled back around a convenient cedar and held in place by a second man";[8] modern climbers will appreciate a cam. In another account, Henry Ives Baldwin, Eastburn Smith, and George B. Happ made a roped, belayed "zigzag climb" up Wallface in the fall of 1920. It may never be known whether Baldwin's ascent was this route (although the details, few as they are, fit), but it was clearly the first roped ascent up Wallface. **Case Route** was first climbed in the winter of 1951 by Donald J. LeBeau and Stanley "Bud" Smith using one point of aid.

FA Aug 27, 1933, John Case, Elizabeth Woolsey, John Case Jr.

FA (V1) 1978, Bruce Thompson, Bruce Thompson Sr.

7 "Keene Valley" column, *Au Sable Forks (N.Y.) Record-Post*, Sep 7, 1933, p. 3.

8 James A. Goodwin, "Rock Climbs in the Adirondacks," *Bulletin of the Adirondack Mountain Club* 2, no. 5 (Aug–Sep 1938), p. 7.

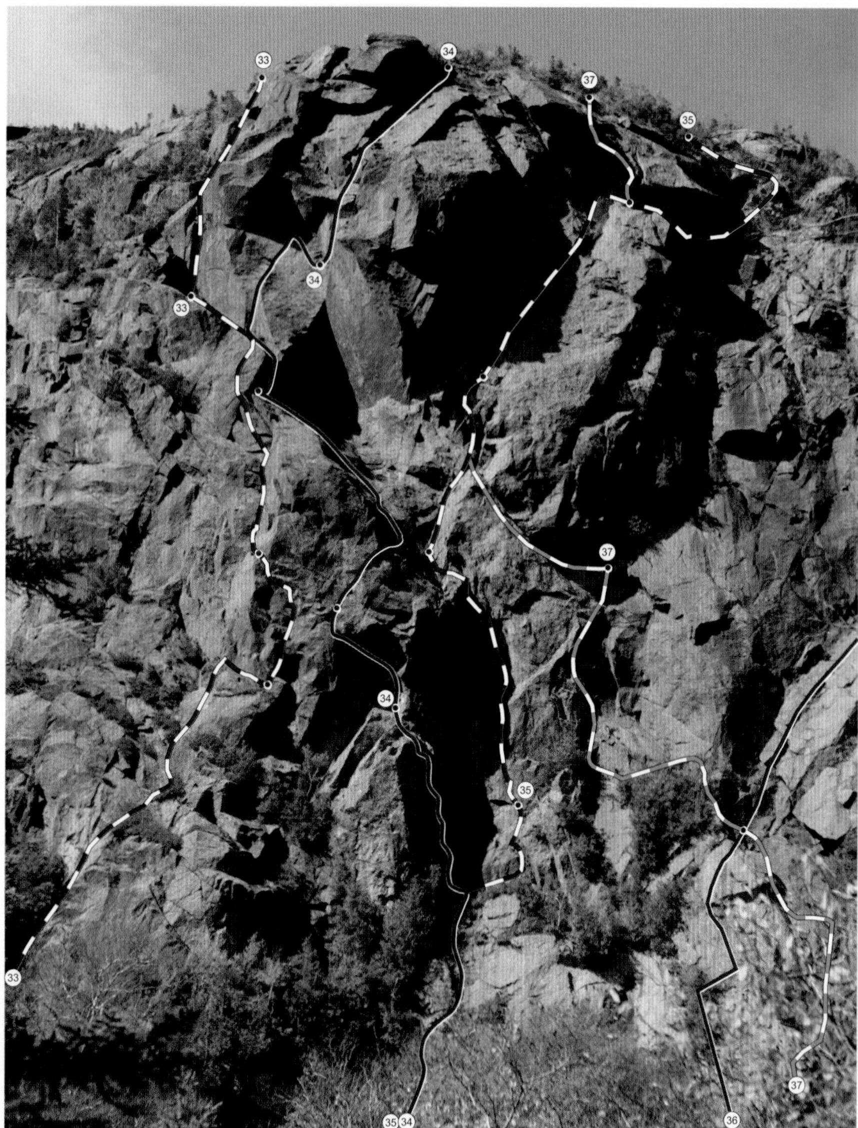

Mental Blocks Buttress

Some of the cleanest rock on Wallface is found on the Mental Blocks Buttress.

33 Rubicon 5.9 R 525' ★★★

Start: From the bottom of the Mental Blocks Buttress, head left and steeply uphill, staying close to the rock on a tree-covered slope. The start is marked by a dirty slab just uphill from and left of a very steep wall.

P1 5.7 PG: Climb up the slab, then angle right up an open book to a vegetated ledge. Climb up and left 10' following a handcrack to a break, then right to a slab. Face-climb up the slab toward a headwall, at the base of which is a flake that forms a point. Traverse down and right to belay at cedars below a three-sided recessed box alcove. 150'

P2 5.9 G: Climb the crack through the left side of the roof of the boxed alcove (strenuous jams), then angle up left by hand-traversing on a flake to a final ramp up and left to a ledge with a vertical crack on its left end. 50'

P3 5.9 R: Climb the crack in the open book to the sharp right-leaning arête. Step left onto the face and up to a stance (bolt), then face-climb up and right (5.9 R)

to a left-rising ramp, which is followed leftward to its top at a right-facing corner. 160'

P4 5.8 G: Climb the crack just left of the right-facing corner to a ledge at its top 30' up. Continue in a sparsely protected low-angle chimney (5.6 R), which is followed to the top. 165'

Descent: Walk left to the Mental Blocks Rappel or walk/thrash off right down through the woods to the trail.

FA Sep 3, 1991, Don Mellor, Brad Hess

34 Mental Blocks 5.12a G (5.7 R) 530' ★★★★★

An intricate puzzle on a buttress with an incredible array of geometric corners, slabs, and roofs. Not only is Mental Blocks a difficult free route, but it is also one of the most sought-after aid routes in the region.

Start: Below the large overhangs high on the cliff, at a brushy area cleared of large trees, at the base of a right-facing white flake that leans right at the bottom and is filled with brush 25' up. The start is also 15' right of two large cedars growing out of the rock 10' up.

P1 5.7 G: (V1) Climb the right-facing flake, then right onto a white face. Up over ledges with trees to the base of the lightning-bolt crack—the zigzag crack on the left wall of the depression (optional belay here). Up the nice crack to a ledge at the top of the small buttress. 140'
P2 (or 5.11c G) C2: Directly above the belay is a left-facing corner capped by a roof. Climb the corner to the roof, then out left 20' to a hanging belay just above the lip of the roof, at the base of a thin right-leaning crack. Easier for tall climbers. 30'
P3 (or 5.10b G [5.7 R]) C2: Climb the right-leaning crack to the arête, then onto the slab on the other side. Climb up and left following the slab (5.7 R) to the top at an overhanging wall with a crack and belay. 120'
P4 (or 5.12a G) C1: Climb up the crack in the steep wall (crux; height-dependent) to a left-rising ramp. Climb up the ramp about 10' to the base of a shallow right-facing corner with a fistcrack. 40'
P5 5.8 A0: Up the fistcrack to the slab, then continue up the right-leaning crack to some fixed gear. Pendulum (or downclimb 5.7) to the right to a hanging belay at a crack in the right wall. 50'
P6 5.7 G: Climb the steep crack to the left-facing, right-leaning corner to the top of some blocks. Step left and up a slab in a large right-facing corner to the top. 150'
V1 King Kan Variation 5.7 PG: This is a two-pitch alternate start. Begin 30' right of the normal start at a brush-filled crack. Climb up the crack and work left to the base of the lightning-bolt crack. Climb the corner up and right of the lightning-bolt crack; this corner arches back left to the ledge at the top of the small buttress. Named for the extralarge (32-oz.) can of Miller beer available at the time.
Descent: Walk left to the Mental Blocks Rappel or walk/thrash off right down through the woods to the trail.
FA Oct 26, 1970, Paul Harrison, Chris Winship
FA (V1) Jul 9, 1987, Jeff Edwards, Adam Clayman
FFA Jul 27, 1991, Don Mellor, Mark Meschinelli

35 Fifth Metacarpal 5.10b PG 615'

Like many routes at Wallface, this route was climbed in an attempt to climb something else, in this case **The B.M.Z.**, but instead covered enough original terrain to be considered a separate route. It does share a pitch up the "twin cracks" on the sheer wall high on the buttress. The rock is consistently poor-quality, and the twin cracks are not the gems they appear from below. From just the right angle, and if you squint using some imagination, the Mental Blocks Buttress looks like a fist; this route climbs the fifth metacarpal of the fist.
Start: Same as **Mental Blocks**.
P1 5.7 PG: Start as for **Mental Blocks**. Climb the right-facing flake and pull on cedars up to a ledge at the base of the lightning-bolt crack. Continue up the corner, then right following a right-rising ramp to some foliage stuffed into a left-facing corner, just below the left side of a pointed tower. 150'
P2 5.10b PG: Step left across the face (bolt) and into a steep open book. Up this to a small overhang, then head left to belay in a bushy V-notch. (**Mental Blocks** passes through this V-notch as well.) 90'
P3 5.8 PG: On the right wall of the V-notch is a face with cracks. Up these to a bulge, broken by a shallow, block-filled chimney on the right. Climb through the chimney (loose) and up to an exposed, semihanging stance at the base of the twin cracks. 90'
P4 5.8 G: Climb the right-leaning twin cracks to a large, sloped ledge on the right. 120'
P5 5.10a PG: From the right side of the ledge, face-climb right to the gully. Easier climbing leads to the top. 165'
FA Jun 6, 1995, Don Mellor, Ian Osteyee

36 Na-my 5.8 PG 430'

Start: 75' right of **Mental Blocks** is a large right-facing corner with a chimney (as described in the start of **The B.M.Z.**). Begin on the face left of this corner.
P1 5.8 PG: Zigzag up the unprotected face (5.6) to a ledge system with trees, then over short rock steps moving up and passing to the left of a short, shallow, left-facing, left-leaning corner. Move up and over a bulge (crux), then traverse 20' right to a spacious ledge (shared with P1 of **The B.M.Z.**). 120'
P2 5.5 G: From here, **The B.M.Z.** goes out left. Instead, go up a short corner (5.5), then head up right following a chimney-like ramp (5.4). Belay in flakes at the top of the chimney. 120'
P3 5.8 G: Go straight up over a bulge (5.7) to a layback under a flake leading left and forming a small, left-facing corner that joins the steep, blank-looking corner coming up from the alcove below. Follow this corner to its top (5.8) where it changes to right-facing. Follow this to a very bushy alcove. 90'
P4 5.8 PG: Do not follow the large and obvious corner leading diagonally up left from the alcove. Instead, ascend a short, overhanging wall at the back of the alcove to a smaller, hidden corner that ascends diagonally up and right. Go up this (5.8, some loose rock) and escape right following a corner (5.4) to a ledge at its top. 100'
Descent: Three more 4th class pitches lead up and right following high-angle brush, and over vertical moss-covered steps. From here, the first ascent party walked (climber's) right and down to the north end of Indian Pass.
History: This route was climbed the day before **No Man's a Pilot**, and named for Nancy and Amy.
FA Sep, 1974, Lincoln Stoller, Peter Metcalf

37 The B.M.Z. 5.9 A2 625'

This was the original route to tackle the "twin cracks" on the sheer wall high on the buttress right of **Mental Blocks**.
Start: About 75' right of **Mental Blocks** is a large right-facing corner with a chimney; this route begins in the dike to the right of the corner. This is also the start of the winter route **Grim and Bear It**.
P1 5.7 PG: Climb up the dike to bushes. Make a friction move left to a corner, then up this to a large ledge. 120'
P2 5.9 A2: Step left from the ledge onto a slab and move diagonally left to a detached flake that leads to a right-leaning, right-facing corner. Climb up the corner to

a ceiling, then aid up and left to a hanging belay below a large roof. 100'

P3 5.8 A2: Move left under the overhang to a left-leaning corner. Traverse leftward following the corner to a blocky chimney, which is climbed to a semihanging stance beneath the twin cracks. 100'

P4 5.8 PG: Climb the right-leaning twin cracks to a large sloped ledge on the right. 140'

P5 5.7 A1: From the left end of the ledge, climb a crack past the left end of a long ceiling. At its top, move left following an overlapping flake to a short right-facing corner. At the top of the corner, claw up grass to the top. 165'

FA Sep 2, 1978, David Martin, D. J. Bouyea, Steve Zajchowski

The North End

38 Right Place, but Must Have Been the Wrong Time 5.5 A2 1000'

Quite an adventure for two 17-year-old kids who felt they could take on the world or, even bigger—Wallface. They were trying to do a "big wall," Royal Robbins–style, which they considered to be 1000' or more, so when it became clear that they were nearing the top after a couple of pitches, they traversed left to get the 1000' they wanted. The reason for the name is that the first ascentionists were "eaten alive by black flies." Not only that, but they approached from the north and the bridge to the Loj was out, increasing the approach by 5 miles. It's difficult to imagine that this route has seen a second ascent.

Start: The route begins well to the right of **Mental Blocks**. Starting at **Mental Blocks**, walk left, then downhill, then steeply uphill to the top of a vegetated cone. Down the other side to a buttress with a prominent left-facing corner and a boulder forming a tower 80' up. Continue right around the base of this buttress (there is a steep, gently overhanging wall here), then uphill to the next, even larger, left-leaning, left-facing corner with a green mossy slab on the left.

Route Description: Begin on the left wall where one pitch leads to a "vegetable ledge." Switch to a nice crack in the right wall, which is aided for a pitch up the corner to a low-angled section with some trees. Mixed free and aid climbing continues up a clean, steeper section of the corner to a point where the right wall merges with the main face. Traverse left aiming for a prow of rock with a bushy ledge at its base. At the prow, drop down onto the face below and continue traversing left around a complex array of corners and steep faces for several pitches. It is possible to top out nearly anywhere, but the first ascent continued left on a nondescript line to finish in the final gully of **Fifth Metacarpal**.

Gear: The first-ascent party carried a selection of knife blades and bugaboos and several standard angles, as well as 25 Kendall Mint Cakes, because "that's what they eat on Everest."

FA Jul 1, 1975, Frank Abissi, Steve Baker

39 North-End Route 5.6 PG 430'

Despite several efforts, details of this route could not be confirmed or reconciled with other routes nearby.

Start: Right of a water-streaked wall with arching roofs, at a shallow corner 40' right of a spring. (The only spring at this end of the cliff, and a seasonal one at best, is left of Mental Blocks.)

P1: Climb the corner on rotten rock for 30' to a ceiling. Traverse left 10' to another inside corner, which is followed for 20' to a ledge. 60'

P2 4th class: Climb up and slightly left to a good stance. 150'

P3: Scramble up a trough for 30' and climb the right-hand of two possible crack-corners in the steep wall above. 100'

P4 4th class: Climb up several steep rock steps, ending with a surprise mantel onto the top. 120'

FA 1972, John Dickson, Gil Griffes, Dwight Bradley, Jeff Rainey

OWLS HEAD LOOKOUT

Location	Giant Mountain Wilderness Area, accessed from Giant Mountain Trailhead on NY 9N
Aspect	Southwest
Height	100'
Quality	★
Approach	1 hr 10 min, moderate
Summary	A "summit cliff" with a single multipitch route on unique and highly featured rock.

-5.6	5.7	5.8	5.9	5.10	5.11	5.12	5.13+	total
		1	1					2

The Owls Head Lookout is a minisummit off the North Trail—the longer and less popular approach to Giant Mountain from NY 9N. The Lookout is also a popular hiking destination with excellent views of the Lake Champlain Valley, the East Face of Giant, Rocky Peak Ridge, and Hurricane (with Hurricane Crag visible on the slopes below). The cliff drops directly below the summit and has the same feeling as other summit cliffs such as Noonmark and Rooster Comb. There is quite a bit of rock, but most is unpleasant-looking and dirty. There are two notable exceptions—the **Fossil Formation Buttress** and the unclimbed 40' crack at the left end of the cliff. The **Fossil Formation Buttress** is a bit of a geologic oddity, with incredibly featured rock.

HISTORY

Patrick Purcell was the first climber to report a route on this cliff, having picked out the most obvious and attractive rock on the cliff.

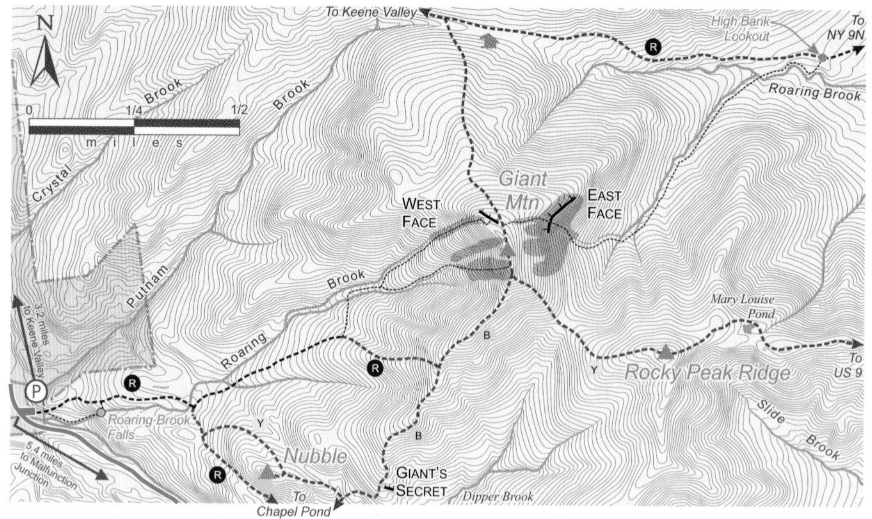

DIRECTIONS **(MAP PAGE 464)**

Park at the Giant Mountain Trailhead on NY 9N (page 426). From the parking area, follow the Giant Mountain Summit Trail (red markers) for 1 hr (2.3 miles) to the intersection with the Owls Head Lookout Trail. The trail is a gradual uphill climb through the forest with several stream crossings. At the intersection, turn left and hike 5 min (0.2 mile) to the Owls Head Lookout, an open area at the top of the cliff.

To reach the route from the top of the cliff, walk (skier's) left to a dirt gully and follow it to the bottom of the cliff. Continue (climber's) left to reach **Fossil Formation Buttress**, the point where the south-facing wall meets the west-facing wall 606334,4893770.

1 Fossil Formation Buttress 5.9 G 120' ★★★

Climbs the beautifully featured chocolate-colored buttress in a scenic setting. Named for a unique feature above the ledge on P1—a raised right-arching rib with many horizontal seams that resembles fossilized vertebrae.

Start: The route is located on a buttress at the junction where the south-facing wall meets the west-facing wall. Locate a level area at the low point of the cliff base. The route begins 20' uphill from and left of this low point at two large boulders that lean up against the chocolate-colored buttress.

P1 5.9 G: Climb the super featured rock (pockets, plates, knobs) to a ledge. 30'

P2 5.8+ G: (V1) Step right and climb a crack, first straight up, then up and right. At its top, traverse left 15' across the top of the vertebraelike feature and under a ceiling to a small ledge on the left side of the buttress. 40'

P3 5.6 G: Climb a broken crack to the nose of the buttress, then scramble to the top. 50'

V1 5.10b TR: Climb directly up the fossilized vertebrae to meet the end of the traverse on P2.

FA Oct 28, 1994, Patrick Purcell, Jen Collins

2 Owl Tail 5.8- G 75'

This route is located on the ridge that runs northeast from Owls Head Lookout.

Start: When approaching Owls Head Lookout from Route 9N, just before the hiking trail swings to the southwest, bushwhack due east 15 min diagonally uphill to the ridge to find a distinct block of rock 607320,4894356. Begin on the northwest side of the block facing toward Knob Lock Mountain, at a flaring moss-filled groove with a small birch tree 12' up.

P1 5.8- G: An insecure start in the groove leads to easy climbing up a network of cracks. Continue up a very aesthetic vertical crack, and finish straight up easier (but questionable) rock to the top. 75'

FA May 17, 2008, Tom DuBois, Ellen DuBois

GIANT MOUNTAIN

Location	Giant Mountain Wilderness Area, accessed from NY 73 and NY 9N
Summary	Easy slide climbs and a few pitches of moderate climbing; **The Eagle** is a classic 4th-class mountain route.

-5.6	5.7	5.8	5.9	5.10	5.11	5.12	5.13+	total
4	1	1						6

Giant Mountain is one of the most popular summits in the High Peaks, and you can approach it from many different trailheads. Of interest to climbers is the fine collection of slides that radiate out from the summit like spokes on a wheel. Although other slides exist on Giant, the technical slides are located on the East and West Faces. Both can be ascended at easy 4th-class, but optional 5th-class pitches offer additional challenges.

The West Face is clearly visible from many of the High Peaks surrounding Keene Valley, and its proximity to the road makes it a popular objective. A tremendous series of slides in 1963 resulted in the formation of **The**

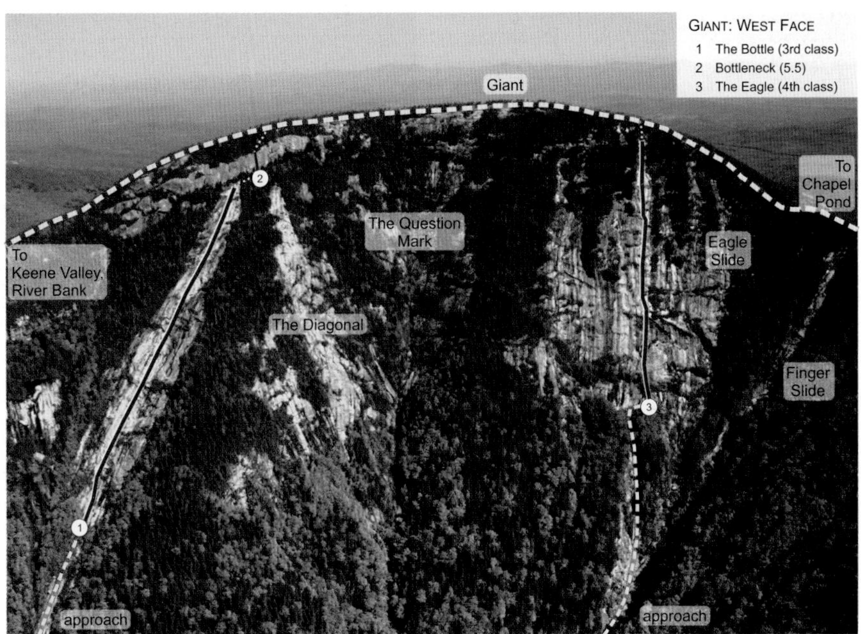

Photo by Olaf Sööt.

Bottle and **The Eagle**, two of the longer and more challenging slide climbs in the Adirondacks. While the other slides on the West Face have begun to grow back, these two remain relatively clean and exit conveniently near the summit of Giant.

In contrast, the East Face is remote, hidden, shorter, and scruffier. The approach is twice as long, and the routes require a long rope and a standard rack. The setting is better than the climbing, as the views extend across Lake Champlain and remind you that Vermont is a close neighbor. Many climbers who drive the Vermont side of the lake, or hike and ski the Green Mountains, marvel at the rocky faces and lofty summits of the Adirondacks. This is the East Face of Giant, and it lives up to that impression.

Giant Mountain

WEST FACE

Aspect	West
Height	1500'
Quality	★★★
Approach	2 hr, difficult
Summary	Easy slide climbs on a high, open summit.

-5.6	5.7	5.8	5.9	5.10	5.11	5.12	5.13+	total
3								3

You can easily view the West Face of Giant Mountain from the golf course of the Ausable Club and access it via a hiking trail above Roaring Brook Falls. The cirque drained by Roaring Brook has several different slides, of which **The Bottle** and **The Eagle** are the cleanest and most challenging. Both slides share the same approach for the first hour. **The Eagle** offers sustained 3rd- and 4th-class friction, which makes it *one of the better* slide climbs in the Adirondacks. Like the **Trap Dike** on Mt. Colden, **The Eagle** slide is a great introduction to East Coast mountaineering and requires off-trail hiking, route finding on the face, and the notion that a rope and sticky shoes may be appropriate. Storm damage, due to Hurricane Irene, has increased the difficulty of the approach to **The Eagle**. **The Bottle** has become more popular in recent years. The exit cliffband has a recommended pitch of 5.5 crack climbing, and the slide is among of the longest in the Adirondacks.

HISTORY

There is a long history of slide climbing in the Adirondacks dating back to the 1800s, as the slides allow the enthusiastic hiker a moderate way to break into mountaineering. The Reverend Joseph Trichell of Harvard was such a person, climbing the open rock on Gothics and Giant and once "saved the guide, Ed Phelps, from a serious fall" on Giant.[9] Unfortunately, it isn't clear exactly where these early explorers went.

DIRECTIONS (MAP PAGE 464)

From the Roaring Brook Falls Trailhead (page 426), hike the trail leading toward the summit of Giant Mountain, marked with red disks. Above Roaring Brook Falls, the summit trail crosses Roaring Brook and turns left at an intersection immediately afterward (25 min). Past practice was to follow Roaring Brook from this point, but the lower portion of the valley has become choked with

9 James A. Goodwin, "Rock Climbing in the Adirondacks," in *The Adirondack High Peaks and the Forty Sixers,* ed. Grace Hudowalski (1970), pp. 142–43.

vegetation, so it is better to continue farther along the hiking trail. Locate a herd path (50 min) 600834,4889932 that goes left (north) and downhill to the brook. If you go too far, you'll pass a car-sized boulder, just left of the trail, a few minutes later. The herd path begins at a cairn in open woods and traverses the hillside, then goes uphill a bit to cross a tributary stream, before it reaches Roaring Brook near some small landslides.

DESCENT OPTIONS

Follow the summit hiking trail back to the parking area.

1 The Bottle 3rd class 1500' ★★★

A classic alpine scramble that rivals **The Eagle** in quality.

Start: Cross to the far side (north) of Roaring Brook, and follow the herd path upstream to an intersection (1 hr 10 min) 601315,4890312 beneath a steep hill. Go left to the drainage area for The Bottle. Alternatively, from the intersection, go right, uphill, then briefly downhill to a small stream. Follow it uphill for another hour to the base of the slide 601784,4890678.

Route Description: From the top of the stream, scramble a landslide and bushwhack a short distance to the base of the clean slide. At the top of **The Bottle**, follow the base of the summit cliffs right, then up to a hiking trail. Go right (south) a few minutes to reach the summit.

2 Bottleneck 5.5 G 80' ★★★

A recommended finish to **The Bottle**. A short herd path leads from the top of the route to a hiking trail. Follow it right (south) to the summit.

Start: 150' right of the top of **The Bottle** at a handcrack in a right-facing corner with a piton 20' up.

P1 5.5 G: Up the clean, steep handcrack to an easy finish and a tree belay. 80'

3 The Eagle 4th class 1300' ★★★

This was once the classic alpine scramble, but is becoming dirtier in recent years.

Start: Follow Roaring Brook upstream to an obvious fork at 1 hr 30 min 601417,4889943. Go left at this fork and avoid the heavily eroded tributary on the right. The brook has several sections with downed trees, and passes smooth slabs that lead to a steep landslide. Climb this to the base of **The Eagle** (2 hr 30 min).

Route Description: The centermost line of the slide begins at a short, dirty wall below a brown water streak. Start left of the water streak and ascend through a sustained section of friction climbing that ends at vegetation below an overlap. Continue straight up the face through easier pitches toward the longest exit slide. In the exit slide, pass some short, 4th-class overlaps that take you to the woods. Follow a herd path past a boulder on a ledge to the summit hiking trail. Turn left and hike a few minutes to the summit. Rock shoes or sticky approach shoes are recommended. When done as a roped climb, there is little protection to be found on the lower pitches (sustained friction). However, a 60m rope will reach secure belays at the numerous tree-covered ledges on the face.

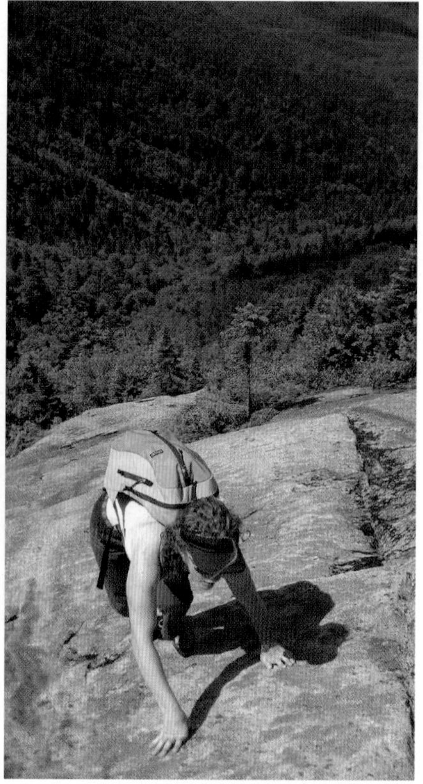

*Michelle Burlitch high on **The Bottle** (3rd class).*

*Bob Hall on **Bottleneck** (5.5). Photo by Ed Palen.*

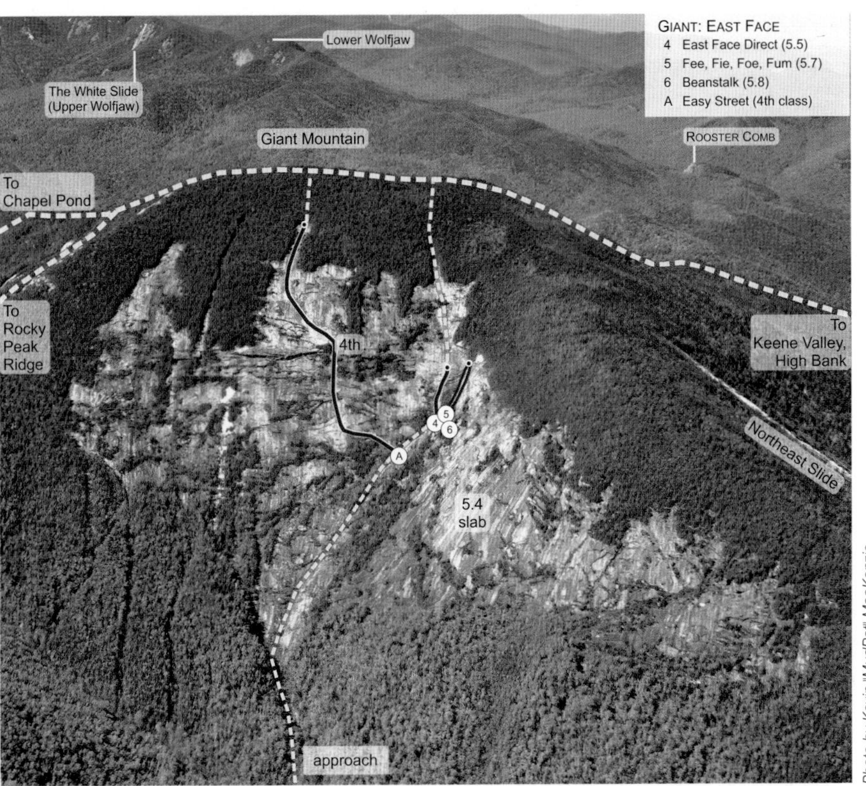

Photo by Kevin "MudRat" MacKenzie.

Giant Mountain

EAST FACE

Aspect	East
Height	800'
Quality	★★
Approach	3 hr 30 min, difficult
Summary	A remote cirque with steep slides that has a long pitch of slab climbing and a short crag pitch halfway up.

-5.6	5.7	5.8	5.9	5.10	5.11	5.12	5.13+	total
1	1	1						3

Despite its being on one of the most popular peaks, the East Face is rarely seen by climbers and seldom visited. Whereas the West Face is easily viewed and approached from NY 73, the East Face requires a long hike and bushwhack with little opportunity to preview the routes. Unlike many Adirondack slides that have headwalls at the base or at the top, the East Face is steepest at its middle. The **East Face Direct** climbs a stepped slab at the right end of the headwall and near a corner with a slab that is farther right. **Fee, Fie, Foe, Fum** climbs the right wall of the corner and accesses an anchor to toprope **Beanstalk**, a steep slab with the best climbing on the face. If you're interested in an obscure mountain route, then this is a worthwhile objective, the approach isn't too hard to follow, and the face has incredible views across Lake Champlain to the Green Mountains of Vermont. Too bad the routes and rock quality aren't on a par with the setting.

DIRECTIONS (MAP PAGE 464)

Although it is possible to drop down to the East Face from the ridge, the bushwhack to the base of the routes would be involved and circuitous. Instead, it is recommended to hike up the drainage area to the base of the face.

Park at the Giant Mountain Trailhead on NY 9N (page 426). From the parking area, hike the trail marked with red discs for 1 hr 30 min to the High Bank Lookout, an open gravel slope above the river, where there is a good view (southwest) of the cirque 604758,4891995. Leave the trail and drop down a loose slope to a brook (Roaring Brook—yes, there are two Roaring Brook's on Giant Mountain). Follow the brook upstream to a junction (2 hr). Follow the left branch (southwest) to a second junction (3 hr), then follow the right branch (southwest) to a third junction (3 hr 15 min). Go right at the third junction and ascend a steep, dry creekbed to the base of the slide (3 hr 30 min) 602628,4890777.

DESCENT OPTIONS

From the top of **East Face Direct**, continue up the slide (2nd class) to the top of the rightmost slide. Bushwhack

(15 min) to the hiking trail along the summit ridge. To return to the parking area, go right (north) and hike down to the junction with the trail that leads back to High Bank (right). You can make a much shorter descent of Giant by hiking left (south) and over the summit to the trail that descends to Chapel Pond. However, this option requires a second vehicle.

4 East Face Direct 5.5 R 190' ★★

Climbs stepped slabs near the right end of the headwall and right of the 4th-class ledges in the center of the headwall. An old piton high on the pitch is of unknown origin.

Start: From the base of the slide, bypass a bulge by staying in the drainage area to the left, then hike up and right across slabs (2nd class) toward the steepest section of the headwall. Scramble alongside a drainage area that leads to a large left-facing corner at the right end of the headwall. Belay on a grassy ledge beneath the large corner with a shallow left-facing corner 5' to the right 602628,4890777.

P1 5.5 R: Up and left over small overlaps to an 8'-tall right-facing corner. (V1) Up the corner to a ledge and traverse left to a shallow right-facing corner (optional belay). Up the corner (crux), or the face to the left, to a right-facing flake. Above the flake, the rock becomes low-angled and dirty. Up and left to a 3'-tall wall (fixed protection), then easy slab climbing up and right for 40' to a belay at a right-facing corner with a 2" crack. 190'

V1 5.6 R: 20' up (5.6 R) to a horizontal (optional belay), then continue on clean rock and move left to a horizontal overlap. Past the overlap on easy slab to a belay at a horizontal crack (3").

FA (V1) 2004, Ed Palen, Bob Hall, Sheila Matz

5 Fee, Fie, Foe, Fum 5.7 PG (5.4 R) 90' ★

Expect to find hollow holds and crumbly rock. Large nuts are recommended for protecting the hollow flakes.

Start: Same as **East Face Direct**.

P1 5.7 PG (5.4 R): Up the shallow left-facing corner—not the large corner to its left—for 20', then right across the face (crux) to hollow left-facing flakes. Up the flakes to a ledge, then up a short left-facing corner (fixed protection). Climb slab (5.4 R) to a fixed anchor. 90'

FA Sep, 2005, Ed Palen, Bob Starinsky

6 Beanstalk 5.8 TR 70' ★★

Climb a black streak that is 30' right of the start of **Fee, Fie, Foe, Fum**. The brown streak to the left is 5.9. Fixed protection, 30' down and right of the **Fee, Fie, Foe, Fum** anchor, is used as a directional for this route.

FA (TR) Sep, 2005, Ed Palen, Bob Starinsky

GOTHICS MOUNTAIN

Location	High Peaks Wilderness Area, accessed from the Garden Trailhead or the Adirondack Mountain Reserve Trailhead
Summary	A backcountry peak with large slides on every side.

-5.6	5.7	5.8	5.9	5.10	5.11	5.12	5.13+	total
7	5			2				14

Gothics has the greatest expanse of technical alpine rock in the Adirondacks. The only other U.S. peak east of the Rockies that exceeds the potential for long mountain routes is Katahdin, Maine. Every side of Gothics has exposed rock. The hiking trails cling to the mountain in the narrow bands of trees that adorn the ridges. Compared to the other slides in the Adirondacks, those found on Gothics are both cleaner and steeper. On most slides, the climber needs to seek out the difficulty. On Gothics, however, technical climbing abounds, and the easy scrambles to the top are not obvious.

Gothics has a broad summit ridge with a sharp, minor summit to the south, Pyramid Peak, which is connected by a narrow ridge. Two southern cirques are located on either side of the narrow ridge: the South Face to the west and the Rainbow Slide to the east. The broad North Face sits on the opposite side of the mountain, directly beneath the ledges of the main summit. The West Face of Gothics is visible from neighboring Saddleback Mountain and saw a couple of solo ascents by Craig Patterson in the 1960s.

*Bob Starinsky follows **Fee, Fie, Foe, Fum** (5.7) on the first ascent. Photo by Ed Palen.*

Gothics Mountain

NORTH FACE

Aspect	Northwest
Height	1200'
Quality	★
Approach	3 hr, difficult
Summary	The Nordwand of the Adirondacks, ominous in appearance but easier to approach and climb than expected. Features slab routes that ascend a complex face riddled with overlaps and moss-covered rock.

-5.6	5.7	5.8	5.9	5.10	5.11	5.12	5.13+	total
2	3							5

This is the biggest, highest alpine face in the Adirondacks. The North Face of Gothics is a sought-after climb in summer conditions, matching its reputation as a winter route. Due to its northern aspect, the North Face is lichen-covered and often wet. Crisscrossing the center of the face are two historic routes for which similar technical difficulties (5.7 R) were reported. The face is filling in with vegetation, and the best line of ascent is not necessarily that of the documented routes. The cleaner **New Finger Slide** is surpassing the older and more difficult routes in popularity. This recent slide is less difficult and provides a direct and interesting way to reach the summit 591417,4886691. Besides **Old Route**, all of the North Face routes finish at the upper right side of the face, which is notoriously wet and moss-covered.

The approach to the North Face is straightforward, as it follows a broad streambed, has modest elevation gain, and requires minimal bushwhacking. A 20'-tall slab that leans against the cliff—the Dugal Slab—and the right-rising corner-ramp on the right side are important landmarks from which to locate the starts of the routes.

DIRECTIONS **(MAP PAGE 470)**

Park at the Garden Trailhead (page 426), hike to Johns Brook Lodge, and take the Orebed Trail past the Orebed lean-to (2 hr). 15 min past the lean-to, and a few minutes past a house-sized boulder next to the trail, you cross the stream from the North Face 590834,4888069. This is a significant streambed, and if you continue past it, the trail begins to climb abruptly. Turn left and follow the stream. Keep right at all branches and choose the major drainage area. After a half hour of rock hopping, you'll see the North Face, and the streambed divides into slide paths. Go left up a wide slide path with bare rock, then up a 3rd-class bulge in the slide path to arrive at the base of the North Face near the start of **The Dugal** at a 20'-tall slab leaning against the cliff—the Dugal Slab 591025,4887286.

*Karen Stolz and Steve Franck on **North Face Direct** (5.7-) in 1984, a route they described as having "big, thick, wet moss." Photo by R.L. Stolz.*

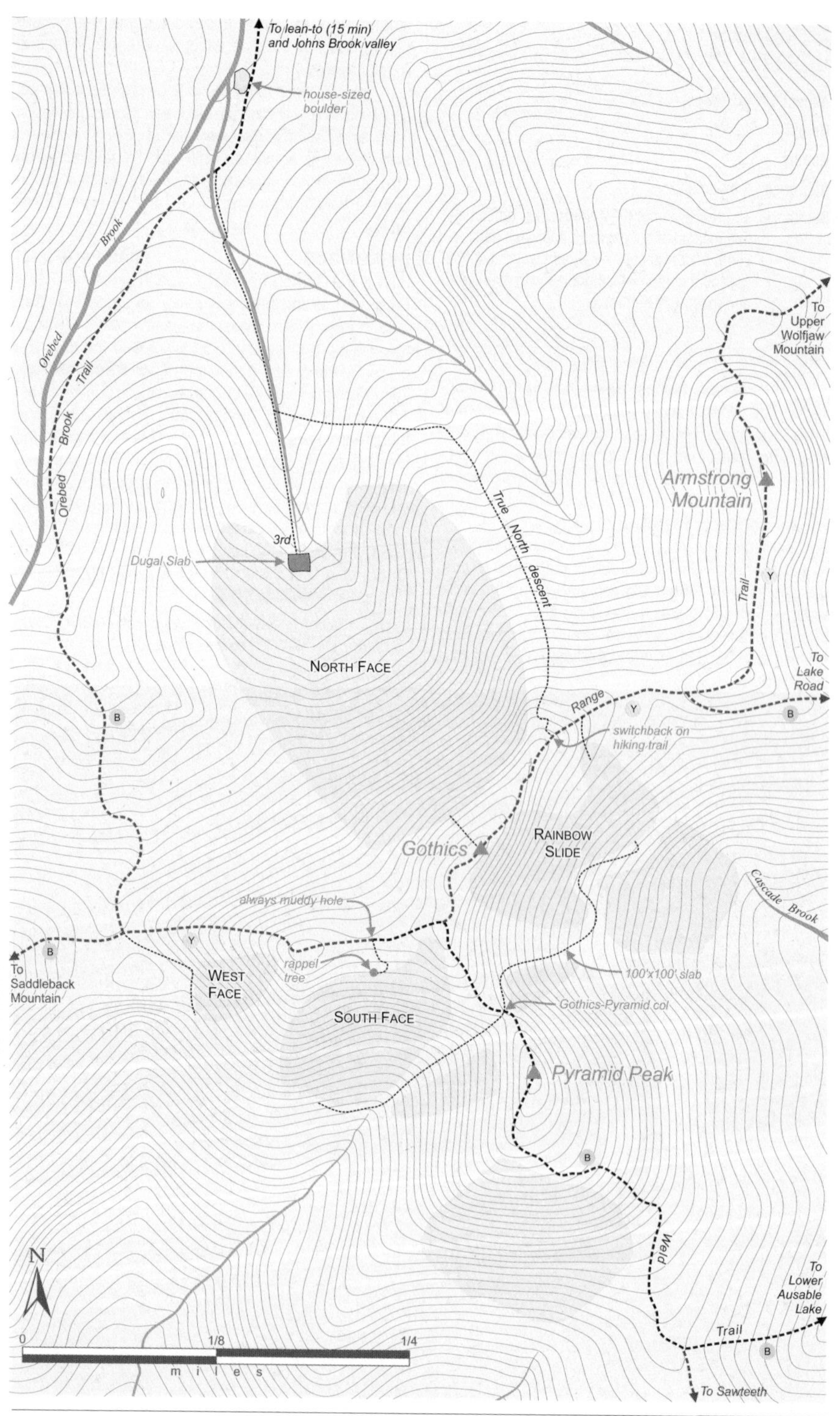
To lean-to (15 min)
and Johns Brook valley
house-sized boulder
Orebed Brook
Orebed Brook Trail
To Upper Wolfjaw Mountain
Armstrong Mountain
3rd
Dugal Slab
True North descent
Trail
Y
North Face
To Lake Road
Range
B
Y
switchback on hiking trail
Gothics
Rainbow Slide
Cascade Brook
always muddy hole
B
To Saddleback Mountain
Y
rappel tree
West Face
South Face
100'x100' slab
Gothics-Pyramid col
Pyramid Peak
B
Weld
To Lower Ausable Lake
Trail
B
To Sawteeth
N
0
1/8
1/4
m i l e s

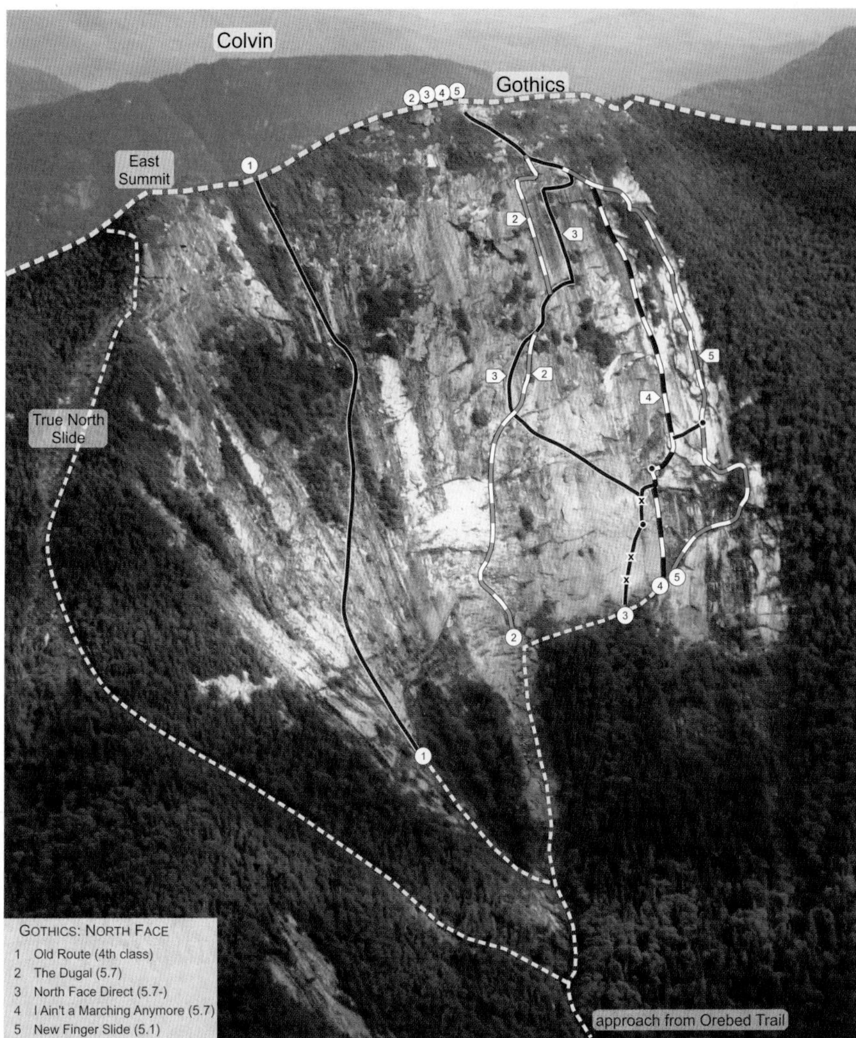

DESCENT OPTIONS

To return by trail to the Johns Brook valley, hike west along the Range Trail to the Gothics-Saddleback Col and the upper junction of the Orebed Trail.

A second option is to return to the base of the North Face via the **True North Slide**, then hike back down the approach drainage area to the Orebed Trail. This is much quicker than hiking down the trail. This descent enters the drainage area below the face; thus, it is recommended that all gear be carried up the route. From the summit, hike east along the Range Trail for less than 5 min until the trail switchbacks to the south and drops over a ledge. At the switchback, leave the trail 591548,4886922 and follow a herd path that goes left (north), and slightly uphill, for 150' to the top of the North Face at its east edge—the North Ridge of Gothics. Hike north, down and (skier's) right along the shrubs to a rock buttress; pass this on the right and continue down to the top of the slide, which is 200' below the buttress. Hike the moss-covered slide for 10 min until it becomes choked with shrubs and a narrow slide path drops down and left. Follow the slide on the left, which becomes a steep streambed, to the wide slide path with bare rock that you encountered on the approach to the North Face.

HISTORY

The first mention of climbing on the North Face was Jim Goodwin's description of **Old Route** in *Adirondac* in 1948.[10] Credit for the first ascent of the main face (Aug 1956) goes to Dick Pitman, Dick Lawrence, and Paul

10 Jim Goodwin, "Keene Valley Chapter," *Adirondac* 12, no. 6 (Nov–Dec 1948), p. 20.

Lawrence, who had an epic day that involved a 2-hr bushwhack from the vicinity of the Gothics-Saddleback Col to the right side of the face. Their harrowing description of the ascent involved 18 pitches of climbing and a near fall by the leader (Pitman) when, 100' out from a poor belay, his feet began to slip. 10 years later, Dugal Thomas and Molly McNutt climbed and reported in great detail **The Dugal**, a direct route up the center of the face. **The Dugal** encounters unprotected slabs, numerous overlaps, and a demanding section of moss-covered rock at the top of the face. In 1973, Tom Rosecrans and Ken Jackson climbed **North Face Direct**, a route that paralleled **The Dugal** to the right and began beneath a bolt of unknown origin that was 30' up the slab. At the right end of the face is a right-rising corner-ramp that may have been crossed by **It'll Probably Be Mostly a Scramble** (5.8; Aug 1, 1988; Butch Kinnon, Jeanne Kinnon). However, on Jun 16, 1990, the right margin of the North Face slid and made many of the features of this route unrecognizable. Shortly after the slide occurred, **I Ain't a Marching Anymore** and **New Finger Slide** were climbed. **I Ain't a Marching Anymore** appears to climb near the line of **It'll Probably Be Mostly a Scramble** and ascends the more challenging rock to the left of **New Finger Slide**. The 1990 slide is still obvious but has begun to grow in.

1 Old Route 4th class 1200'

Popular with winter climbers and skiers, as it follows low-angled slabs and tree-filled depressions to the ridge. Because it has grown in, this route is no longer a rock climb and cannot be recommended. However, it is still the path of least resistance up the North Face.

Start: 200' left of the Dugal Slab and 50' left of a right-rising overlap at the base of the face, beneath low-angled 4th-class slabs that lead up to the minor, east summit of Gothics.

Route Description: Climb up slabs (4th class) that are left of the overlap toward the large stand of trees left of the steeper main face. Go up and right through trees, then climb up dirty slabs to the top of the face near the low point of the ridge and left of the main summit. Battle the brush up and right to the Range Trail.

2 The Dugal 5.7 R 1200'

Start: At the Dugal Slab, above the approach slide.

Route Description: Up and left of the Dugal Slab, then up and right past a long horizontal overlap above the right-rising overlap near the base. Continue up, then over an overlap on the left that has clean white rock beneath it. Break through another overlap, then up and right through a vertical gash filled with vegetation. Above the gash is a low-angled band of vegetation that rises to the left. Climb up and right through the band of vegetation to an overlap beneath a long slab. Break the overlap, then up the slab (crux) to a horizontal overlap. Break the overlap and continue up a higher slab to a small horizontal overlap. Traverse right beneath the overlap, then across overgrown slabs to low-angled rock and shrubs. Angle left through the shrubs to the rock ledges at the main summit.

FA Jul 16, 1966, Dugal Thomas, Molly McNutt

3 North Face Direct 5.7- PG (5.6 R) 1200' ★★

The top of this route is probably unclimbable in its current condition, and it is recommended to traverse over to **New Finger Slide** after P2. P1 climbs some of the smoothest and cleanest rock in the Adirondacks.

Start: 250' right of the Dugal Slab and 50' left of the right-rising, left-facing corner-ramp, beneath an overlap 30' above the ground.

P1 5.7- PG: Up to the overlap (small cam), then step left onto a steep slab (5.7-). Sustained friction climbing up and right past two bolts leads to the bottom of a right-facing corner that is left of a strip of moss and vegetation. Go right across the moss strip and up to a belay at an overlap. 190'

P2 5.4 PG: Up the unprotected slab (5.2) above the belay to a steeper slab protected by a bolt. Above the slab, traverse right on a ledge to the left end of a large overlap and climb up a left-facing corner to a tree belay above the overlap. 190'

P3 5.6 R: (V1) Make a left-rising traverse (dirty) and pass through a notch in an overlap to a belay. 180'

P4 and above: Traverse left beneath the vertical gash filled with vegetation (climbed by **The Dugal**). Climb slabs that are interspersed with vertical cracks to a low-angled band of vegetation that rises to the left. Climb up and right through the band of vegetation to an overlap beneath a long slab (same as **The Dugal**). Traverse right beneath the overlap, then break through the overlap and climb up the slab past several shrub islands. Traverse right from the highest shrub island to avoid climbing the moss-covered slabs above. From the right margin of the face, climb up and left across moss-covered slabs and shrubs (same as **The Dugal**) to the rock ledges at the main summit. 640'

V1 New Finger Connector 5.2 G: This is the recommended finish to **North Face Direct**. Go right across an easy slab to a long left-facing corner. Climb over the corner at a right-rising crack that begins in a wide flare. Follow the crack until it ends, then continue right for 30' to a belay at the left end of a shrub ledge. This belay is directly above the crux pitch of **New Finger Slide**.

History: Rosecrans and Jackson chose this line because it would be one of the longest routes in the Northeast. Beginning at the base of the face, they decided on a start that would ascend a clean, smooth slab that, surprisingly, had a mysterious bolt. The bolt had been reported as missing since the early 1990s and was recently replaced in order to restore this route's superb lower pitches.

FA Oct 7, 1973, Tom Rosecrans, Ken Jackson

4 I Ain't a Marching Anymore 5.7 R 1200'

Start: 300' right of the Dugal Slab, at the base of the right-rising, left-facing corner-ramp and beneath a slab with a large overlap 200' up.

Route Description: Up poorly protected, overgrown slabs (crux) to the left end of an overlap (joining **North Face Direct** at the top of P2). Break the overlap on the left and continue up and right on easier slab (5.4) for two pitches. Up two additional pitches of flakes and corners (5.2–5.6) that stay left of the strip of vegetation and climb to a left-rising overlap. Break the overlap on

the left (5.6) and continue up moss-covered slabs until you can escape right to the right margin of the face. Climb up and left across moss-covered slabs and shrubs (same as **The Dugal**) to the rock ledges at the main summit.
FA Jul 22, 1990, Peter Henner, Nancy Lawson

5 New Finger Slide 5.1 R 1200' ★★

More difficult than **Eagle Slide** on Giant, **New Finger Slide** has a crux pitch of pure friction on clean rock. This is the recommended route for the North Face and a directissima to the summit of Gothics.
Start: Same as **I Ain't a Marching Anymore**.
Route Description: Up the corner-ramp, then right across a tree-covered ledge beneath an overgrown slab. Avoid climbing the overgrown slab by instead climbing a clean, narrow slide to the right that is separated from the main face by a tree island. Traverse to the right beneath the overgrown slab and tree island to an overlap. Climb the overlap (wet) and the narrow slide above to its top. Traverse left across the top of the tree island to the main face. The crux pitch is directly above and is approached by traversing (left) out a vegetated crack until it widens to body-sized. Climb pure friction (crux) for 100' to a ledge. Above the ledge, the technical difficulties ease, and several 4th-class pitches ascend the right margin of the main face. At the top of the slide, make a hard move over an overlap; above this, step left and climb moss-covered slabs and shrubs (same as **The Dugal**) to the rock ledges at the main summit.
FA Jun 26, 1990, Don Mellor, Janet Mellor, Bill Dodd

Gothics Mountain

SOUTH FACE

Aspect	South
Height	600'
Quality	★★★★
Approach	3 hr 30 min, difficult
Summary	The most alluring alpine face in the Adirondacks, with excellent rock quality and routes of all difficulties.

-5.6	5.7	5.8	5.9	5.10	5.11	5.12	5.13+	total
3				2				5

Gracing the steepest face on Gothics are some of the best alpine rock climbs in the Northeast. A tribute to the scouring power of glaciers, the South Face is a deep basin of sculpted rock, not the shattered rock that is commonly encountered at 4500' in the Northeast. The southern exposure enables the face to dry more quickly than the north side of the mountain. However, the vegetation at the top of the cliff will continue to seep for a couple of days after a rain.

DIRECTIONS **(MAP PAGE 470)**

Park at the AMR Trailhead (page 426), hike the Lake Road to Lower Ausable Lake, and then up the Weld Trail to the summit of Pyramid Peak, reached at 3 hr. Pyramid Peak provides excellent views of the South Face of Gothics. An alternative approach from the Garden Trailhead (page 426) is longer, but offers camping and climbing to the main summit via the North Face.

You can reach the base of the climbs on the South

Jeremy Haas follows ***Tea and Biscuits*** *(5.10a), belayed by Robert Livingston on the Piano Ledge. Photo by Rachel Sloan.*

Face either by a bushwhack from the Gothics-Pyramid Col or by rappelling **South Face Direct**.

Bushwhack to base: From the 30' section of level hiking trail in the Gothics-Pyramid Col, leave the trail 591449,4886359 and bushwhack west to a steep, tree-filled drainage area. Hike down the drainage area past one short downclimb to arrive at the base of the face (on the right side, near the start of **Goodwin Route**) within 30 min of the col.

Rappel to base: Locate a herd path on the Range Trail, 0.1 mile west of the main summit and before the open ledges of the minor summit to the west. The landmark for the start of the herd path is a permanently muddy hole on the trail 591191,4886514. Follow the herd path downhill for 5 min to an 80' slab above the South Face. Scramble down the slab, then traverse (skier's) right across the top of the main face (very exposed) for 200'. Locate a tree 20' back from the top of the cliff with long rappel slings 591230,4886456. A 60-m rope is required to make three rappels down **South Face Direct** that end at a 3rd-class left-rising ramp (**Original Route**). Follow it down and (skier's) left to the base of the South Face near the start of **Gothic Arch** 591149,488619.

DESCENT OPTIONS

Don't plan on returning to the base of this face. Carry out whatever gear you descend with.

HISTORY

The South Face is home to one of the oldest technical climbs in North America. **Original Route** climbs the striking crack (4th class) that cuts up and left across

Photo by Kevin "MudRat" MacKenzie.

the wall and involves 5th-class climbing to surmount the bulging rock above it. In 1955, Jim Goodwin made a solo ascent of the right side of the face as a detour while hiking the peak with a friend. Goodwin avoided the steep lower headwall (climbed by **Gothic Arch**) and climbed the longest stretch of rock on the face. More than a century after its original ascent, the South Face got a new look in the new millennium when Ed Palen and Vinny McClelland added four pitches of clean, well-protected face climbing on the steep central section of the face.

6 Original Route 5.4 PG 400'

You can easily see this left-leaning crack from Pyramid Peak. The crack is clean, but the slabs above it are moss-covered. **Tea and Biscuits** and **South Face Direct** start partway up the crack.

Start: From the base of the South Face, hike grassy slopes left and up to the beginning of the crack.

Route Description: The lower portion of the crack is 3rd-class, and fixed protection marks the start at **South Face Direct** and again at **Tea and Biscuits** 50' higher. Near its end, the crack becomes 4th-class, and a step left onto a slab (crux) avoids the steep wall above. Continue up the slabs (4th-class) past shrub ledges to the top of the face. Traverse right across the top of the face for 300' and locate the herd path to the Range Trail.

History: This route was one of the earliest technical ascents in North America. A rope was carried, but there is no mention of its being used.

FA Aug 20, 1896, Newell Martin, Milford Hathaway

7 Tea and Biscuits 5.10a G 120' ★★★

A single-pitch route that begins at the left-leaning crack of **Original Route** and ends at the roof-capped ledge (Grand Piano Ledge) high on the wall. It can be approached either by rappelling **South Face Direct** or bushwhacking to the base and starting up **Original Route**.

Start: At the higher of the two belays, with fixed protection, along the crack of **Original Route**. If you approach the climb by rappel, you'll need to angle the rappels to the left to reach the start.

○ **P1 5.10a G:** Climb past a low overlap to the steep slab (crux) with crystals. Continue toward the steepening headwall and climb to a fixed anchor at the left end of the Grand Piano Ledge. 120'

FA Oct, 2002, Ed Palen, Vinny McClelland

8 South Face Direct 5.10d G 260' ★★★★

Each pitch of this climb is unique, and the climbing gets progressively steeper. The Grand Piano Ledge is one of the most scenic and spacious belay ledges in the Adirondacks. Previously 5.10a, a hold broke near the top of P1 in 2013, making this considerably more difficult.

Start: At fixed protection in the crack of **Original Route** that is 50' below the start of **Tea and Biscuits**. If you approach the climb by rappel, you'll need to angle the rappels to the left to reach the start.

● **P1 5.10d G:** A sustained pitch of low-angled face climbing (fragile flakes) ascends to the left end of a narrow ledge below a steep headwall. Traverse right across the ledge to a fixed anchor. 90'

● **P2 5.9+ G:** Climb nearly vertical rock up and left on positive holds to a thin traverse (right) and easier climbing up to the Grand Piano Ledge and a belay at a fixed anchor. 80'

● **P3 5.9 G:** Step right (V1) and climb up a large boulder to reach the lip of the roof. Over the roof on dimpled rock, then up an easy slab to the top of the cliff. Belay from a tree with fixed anchors. 90'

V1 5.4 R: You can make an easier escape by traversing off the right end of the Grand Piano Ledge toward a tree island and unprotected climbing (5.4) up and left to a tree belay at the top of the cliff.

FA (P1, P2) Oct, 2002, Ed Palen, Vinny McClelland
FA (P3) 2004, Chris Hyson, Tom Yandon
FA (V1) Oct, 2002, Ed Palen, Vinny McClelland

9 Gothic Arch 5.6 PG (5.2 X) 800' ★★★

Ascends the longest line on the South Face; a fantastic alpine climb. Varied climbing and committing position with no fixed gear. The face has three distinct sections: the featured, high-angled slab at the bottom that ends at a vertical headwall; a middle section of low-angled friction that ends at trees; and a narrow slide with overlaps that ends beneath the hiking trail (same as **Goodwin Route**). A 70-m rope is recommended.

Start: Locate a 70'-tall arch at the base of the South Face and a continuous black streak that runs down the face and over the arch. Start at a short slab immediately left of the left end of the arch.

P1 5.6 PG: Climb the slab to a vegetated ledge, then up and right to a spacious ledge with a wide crack on the right. 80'

P2 5.5 PG: Ascend the wide crack, then traverse right on ledges (and across the black streak) and climb flakes toward the right end of a long headwall. Establish a semihanging belay in the featured rock of the headwall. 200'

P3 5.6 G (5.2 X): Climb the steep, pocketed face above the belay and onto a broad slab. Up the slab past a short, vertical crack (optional belay), then easy slab climbing (5.2 X) to a tree belay on the left side of a tree peninsula. 210'

P4 5.4 PG: Step right and go up vegetation to the right of the tree peninsula to a slab beneath an overlap. Up the slab and belay at the overlap as for **Goodwin Route**. 150'

P5 5.6 PG: Same as **Goodwin Route**. Step left and climb the overlap to a crack and then up to the next overlap. Move left 30', then up at a small flake and continue to a third overlap. Climb the overlap, then move up and right to the trees for a belay. 80'

P6 5.6 PG: Same as **Goodwin Route**. Up a slab to an overlap, then climb the overlap to a left-arching crack. Follow the crack left, then climb up and right to the top of the slide. Belay from trees, then bushwhack (50'–100') to the trail that connects Gothics and Pyramid Peak. 80'

10 Goodwin Route 5.6 PG 680' ★

Climbs the right edge of the South Face on low-angled slabs to the narrow slide with overlaps that ends beneath the hiking trail. **Gothic Arch** joins this route for the last three pitches.

Start: At the right side of the face, in a grassy meadow beneath a low-angled white slab left of the trees.

P1 3rd class: Up the white slabs to a tree belay. 200'

P2 3rd class: Up slabs to a belay that is 25' below a tall, black overhanging wall. 200'

P3 5.4 PG: Traverse left beneath a vegetated ledge to a pocketed wall. Up the wall, then back right to a belay in vegetation. 60'

P4 5.4 PG: Up a slab to an overlap, then left along the overlap to a belay. 60'

P5 5.6 PG: Step left and climb the overlap to a crack and then up to the next overlap. Move left 30', then up at a small flake and continue to a third overlap. Climb the overlap, then move up and right to the trees for a belay. 80'

P6 5.6 PG: Up a slab to an overlap, then climb the overlap to a left-arching crack. Follow the crack left, then climb up and right to the top of the slide. Belay from trees, then bushwhack (50'–100') to the trail that connects Gothics and Pyramid Peak. 80'

History: P4 and P5, which were described by Butch and Jeanne Kinnon, make the route harder and more sustained than the easiest line, which is along the right margin of the upper slide.

FA 1955, Jim Goodwin
FA (P5, P6) Jul 18, 1991, Butch Kinnon, Jeanne Kinnon

Gothics Mountain

RAINBOW SLIDE

Aspect	South
Height	600'
Quality	★★★
Approach	4 hr, difficult
Summary	Exceptional friction climbing on some of the cleanest and smoothest rock in the Adirondacks. Phenomenal views of Lower Ausable Lake and the Dix Range.

-5.6	5.7	5.8	5.9	5.10	5.11	5.12	5.13+	total
2	2							4

The Rainbow Slide is the large expanse of rock that can be seen on Gothics when it is viewed from peaks to the southeast. Because hiking trails are found on the adjacent ridges, it is an often-admired wall that can be scoped out easily. Despite its visibility and proximity to popular hiking trails, little climbing has been reported on the Rainbow Slide. Two conditions that may have dissuaded climbers are the apparently long bushwhack up the drainage area and the overgrown appearance of the upper face.

The slide has three sections: a low, clean slab (3rd-class); a steep center slab (where the routes are); and an upper face that has overgrown, low-angle slabs beneath a long, imposing roof. The routes on the center slab involve sustained friction climbing with decent protection. The rock is beautiful—clean, smooth, and golden in color.

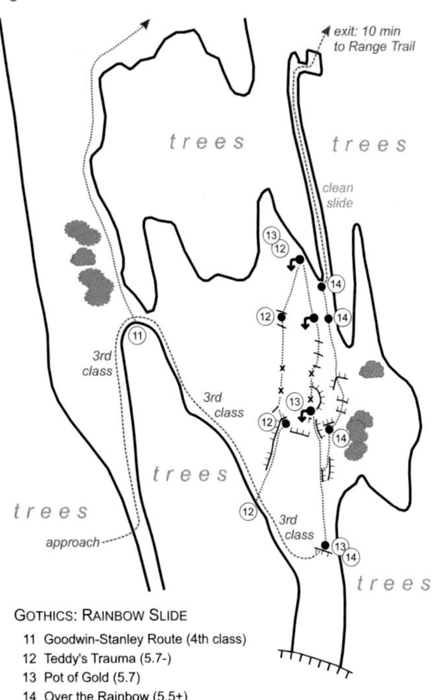

GOTHICS: RAINBOW SLIDE

11 Goodwin-Stanley Route (4th class)
12 Teddy's Trauma (5.7-)
13 Pot of Gold (5.7)
14 Over the Rainbow (5.5+)

DIRECTIONS (MAP PAGE 470)

Due to recent blowdown in the drainage area below the face, it is recommended to approach the Rainbow Slide from the col between Gothics and the minor summit of Pyramid Peak. Park at the AMR Trailhead (page 426), hike the Lake Road to Lower Ausable Lake, and then up the Weld Trail to the summit of Pyramid. Hiking time from the trailhead to Pyramid is 3 hr. At the 30' section of level hiking trail in the Gothics-Pyramid col, locate a break in the vegetation (good views of the face) on the east side of the trail 591449,4886359. Sighting the col between Gothics and Armstrong, set a bearing of 30° and bushwhack past the 30'-tall trunk of a dead tree to a couch-sized boulder that is 100' from the trail. Continue on the 30° bearing for another 100' and change to a bearing of 60°. Follow one of several drainage areas that descend to a 100'-by-100' slab that is 30 min from the hiking trail 591595,4886487. From the bottom of the slab, traverse (skier's) left through woods for 200' to the left edge of the Rainbow Slide, where the slide becomes a streambed. Cross the slide and hike up and around a peninsula of trees to the left side of the steep center section of the Rainbow Slide 591735,4886707.

DESCENT OPTIONS

The recommended exit from the face is to scramble (3rd class) the clean slide up and right of the top of the routes. Follow the slide to its top, then traverse right across ledges before you enter the woods. A 10-min bushwhack up and right ends at the Range Trail. To return to the Lake Road, hike east (right) along the Range Trail for 5 min to a junction with the trail that descends to Beaver Meadow Falls and St. Huberts on the right.

For parties that wish to climb more than one route, **Pot of Gold** can be rappelled from fixed anchors with two ropes. The top anchor is 100' left of the exit slide and above the beginning of the clean slabs that extend to the top of the face.

HISTORY

Newell Martin, a member of the Yale class of 1875, bridged the gap between hiking and mountaineering with his 3rd- and 4th-class scrambles of slides in the region. He is believed to have descended the Rainbow Slide with guide Charlie Beede in that time period.[11] Jim Goodwin's 1938 traverse of Gothics was the first reported ascent of the Rainbow Slide. The traverse involved climbing the left side of the slide to the summit, then descending the North Face. Craig Patterson and Ronald Dubay came next, with their ascent of **Teddy's Trauma** in 1965. Their multipitch route traversed beneath the center of the face before it ascended a committing slab left of center. Several old pitons can be found on the face, perhaps left by the first-ascent party. The remains of their lone belay bolt are still visible high on the face. Activity stalled for nearly 40 years until recently when two new routes were added—**Over the Rainbow** and, more recently, **Pot of Gold**.

11 James A. Goodwin, "Rock Climbing in the Adirondacks," in *The Adirondack High Peaks and the Forty Sixers,* ed. Grace Hudowalski (1970), pp. 142–43.

Photo by Kevin "MudRat" MacKenzie.

GOTHICS: RAINBOW SLIDE
11 Goodwin-Stanley Route (4th class)
12 Teddy's Trauma (5.7-)
13 Pot of Gold (5.7)
14 Over the Rainbow (5.5+)

11 Goodwin-Stanley Route 4th class 600'

Start: At the highest vegetation on the left side of the steep center section of the Rainbow Slide.

Route Description: Up moss-covered slabs left of the steep, clean slabs in the center of the face. Pass through trees and scramble up and right on the vegetated slabs beneath the enormous right-rising roofs to a tree-covered ledge that is level with the right end of the roof. Traverse left toward the roof and beneath a ceiling. Follow a vegetated gash between the enormous roof and the ceiling, then up and right to a short wall. Climb it to the top of the face.

History: The ascent was a section of the traverse of Gothics from Lower Ausable Lake to the Johns Brook valley. Later that day, Goodwin and Stanley descended the North Face to complete the traverse.

FA 1938, Jim Goodwin, Edward Stanley

12 Teddy's Trauma 5.7- G (5.4 R) 360' ★★★

Start: From the highest vegetation on the left side of the face, hike downhill and right, beneath the steepest section of slab, to a belay below a long right-facing, right-leaning corner that begins 25' above the vegetation.

P1 5.5 PG: Up slabs to the right-facing corner, then follow it to a belay at its end. 150'

P2 5.7- G (5.4 R): Climb up to a right-facing flake (protection), then paddle up a 100' stretch of slab (harder for the first half) to a belay at an overlap (small cam and one anchor bolt). 130'

P3 5.0 R: Up and right to a belay at a tree with a fixed anchor (same anchor as **Pot of Gold**). 80'

History: The original ascent began at a low bulge at the base of the center section of the Rainbow Slide. The first-ascent party included Teddy, Patterson's dog, who couldn't send P1 (probably the low bulge). Teddy

would have been a wonder dog to free the crux pitch, which was a very bold lead involving a 100' runout of 5.7 friction. Trying to get the most out of a 120' rope, the first ascentionists placed a belay bolt (still visible) at the base of the crux slab and thankfully reached a belay at rope's end. Longer ropes, small cams, and sticky shoes have changed the seriousness of the route, but the quality still remains.
FA Aug, 1965, Craig Patterson, Ronald Dubay

13 Pot of Gold 5.7 G 400' ★★★★

Start: From the highest vegetation on the left side of the face, hike downhill and right, beneath the steepest section of slab. Continue downhill and cross the low-angle slabs (2nd class) to the right side of the face and belay on a fern-covered ledge.
P1 5.5 PG: Friction up a clean strip that cuts a slab covered in green lichen. Continue up left-facing overlaps, then move left over slabs to a ledge above a long overhang. Belay at a fixed anchor. 150'
P2 5.7 G: Up edges above the anchor to the top of a left-arching overlap; over this, then up and left beneath a bulge. Over the bulge and continue past small overlaps to a belay at a fixed anchor in a scoop. 150'
P3 4th class: Step left and up clean rock that is left of moss-covered slabs to a tree with fixed anchors. 100'
FA Aug 30, 2007, Jeremy Haas, Tom Rosecrans, Robert Livingston

14 Over the Rainbow 5.5+ PG (5.4+ R) 400' ★★

Start: Same as Pot of Gold.
P1 5.4+ R: Friction up a clean strip that cuts a slab covered in green lichen (same as Pot of Gold). Continue up left-facing overlaps, then step right and climb a clean, tan-colored slab to a belay (small cams) at a 10'-long overlap. 200'
P2 5.5+ PG: Up and right for 25' to an overlap, then up another 25' to a second overlap. Up and left on flakes to a shallow right-facing corner and a third overlap. Work up and left across a moss strip to a tree. 200'
FA Jul, 2004, Bob Hall, Sheila Matz, Ed Palen

Gothics Mountain

WEST FACE

The West Face, approached by heading southeast from the Gothics-Saddleback col, has two historic routes that have now become too overgrown to recommend (or even find). **Green Streak: Portside** (5.7 R; Aug 1965; Craig Patterson, solo) frictions up the left side of the slab with long runouts. **Mountain Sunshine** (5.6 G; Aug 1965; Craig Patterson, solo) ascends a long, clean crack system on the right side of the slab.

LOWER WOLFJAW CLIFF

Location	High Peaks Wilderness Area, accessed from the Adirondack Mountain Reserve Trailhead
Aspect	South
Height	150'
Quality	
Approach	2 hr 30 min, difficult
Summary	A short bushwhack to a high cliff that has an incomplete route with good potential for more.

On the south face of Lower Wolfjaw, beneath the wooded summit, is a steep slab above the Wedge Brook Valley. Lots of unexplored, and steeper, rock is visible farther right of the slab. With few cracks and ledges, this is a challenging face with potential for hard friction climbs. The left side of the face has a higher base and a few ledges beneath a ceiling near the top of the cliff. Although Lower Wolfjaw Cliff is without a recommended route, it is a pleasant setting with open, fern-covered slopes beneath a shield of clean rock.

HISTORY

On a hike in the early 90s, DuBois noticed that the exposed rock on Lower Wolfjaw appeared to be more of a cliff than a low-angled slide. He bushwhacked in several times to explore the rock. Most of the cliff is steep and quite featureless, but the one incomplete route follows a line of features up the more moderately-angled left side. Bushwhack explorers rarely encounter other people in their travels, but while the first ascent party was high on the route, they were surprised to see Ed Palen walk out of the woods to say hello.

DIRECTIONS

Park at the AMR Trailhead (page 426). From the parking area (0 hr 0 min), hike the Ausable Lake Road and, at 30 min, reach a footbridge and sign for Canyon Bridge on the right. Cross the footbridge, and follow a trail marked with blue discs to Canyon Bridge. Cross Canyon Bridge, and follow the West River Trail upstream to its intersection with the Wedge Brook Trail, reached at 1 hr. Hike the Wedge Brook Trail and, at 2 hr, reach the intersection with a trail marked with red discs on the right. Follow the red-disc trail for 200' to a view of the cliff where the trail turns left (west). Leave the trail here 0593418,4888611, at 2 hr 10 min, head north, and traverse the mountainside past minor drainage areas and cliffbands. Arrive at fern-covered slopes beneath the left end of the cliff at 2 hr 30 min 0593479,4888813.

DESCENT OPTIONS

Rappel with two ropes from a fixed anchor.

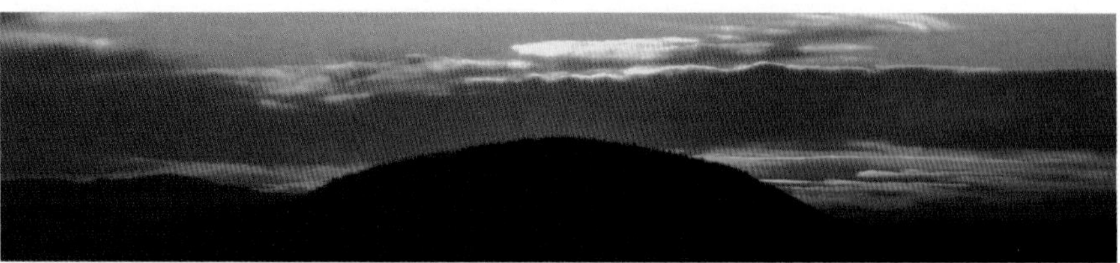

Photo by Jay Harrison.

1 Full Moon 5.7 G 140'

A reconnaissance climb that attempted to ascend the left-facing corners in the center of the cliff and high above the ground. Good toprope routes (5.8 and 5.10) were reported on the slabs beneath the tree belay at the top of P1. The route is begging to be completed to the top.

Start: From the low point of the cliff, which is below the steepest slabs, hike left and up a left-rising vegetated ramp toward the upper left end of the cliff. Start near the left side of the slab, before the cliff becomes a steep wall, at a black streak on the slab that goes up to a horizontal ledge with a clump of cedar trees on its right end.

P1 5.5 PG: Up the black streak to a right-rising crack, then climb the crack to the horizontal ledge. Move right and belay at the clump of cedar trees. 100'

P2 5.7 G: Above the belay is a slab that leads to an overlap with a small tree in it. Move right across the slab to a left-facing corner. The first-ascent party retreated after reaching the left-facing corner, and rappelled from the small tree in the overlap. 40'

FA 1999, Tom DuBois, Morgan House, Rich Arsenault

NOONMARK MOUNTAIN

Location	Dix Mountain Wilderness Area, accessed from the Adirondack Mountain Reserve Trailhead
Aspect	Southeast
Height	100'
Quality	★★★★
Approach	1 hr 45 min, difficult
Summary	The summit cliff on Noonmark Mountain offers incredible views and worthwhile climbing, especially the historic **Wiessner Route**.

-5.6	5.7	5.8	5.9	5.10	5.11	5.12	5.13+	total
3	1	1	2					7

The routes on Noonmark Mountain are clustered together on the summit cliff, follow obvious crack lines, and have steep starts. The summit of Noonmark is a busy place on a clear day, attracting hikers with its bald summit, terrific views, and easy hike, so expect company—i.e., gawking hikers—at the top. It's worth all the fuss, as the views of the Great Range and the Dix Range are especially fine.

The routes can be toproped, and anchors can be created with protection at the top of the routes. Because the cliff turns to slab at the top, long runners are necessary to avoid rope drag.

HISTORY

All of the routes described here were climbed by Fritz Wiessner and various partners at unknown dates, probably in the 1930–1940 era. The bolt at the start of **Wiessner Route** has always been a curiosity. It's not a climber's bolt but rather a 1"-diameter lag bolt hammered into the rock. Too low to use as reasonable protection, when climbing the opening moves, it is very

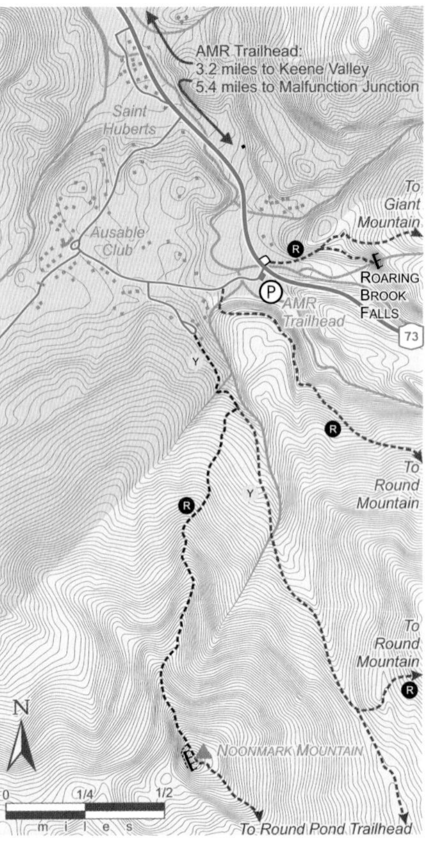

tempting to stand on the bolt, so perhaps it served that function for early climbers. Being the purist, it is unlikely that Wiessner placed such an aid.

DIRECTIONS (MAP PAGE 480)

Park at the AMR Trailhead (page 426). From the parking lot on the west side of the road, walk up the dirt road to the golf course and trailhead for Noonmark (aka the Stimson Trail) on the left, marked with yellow discs. Follow a private road to the beginning of the trail (0.0 mile), then up the trail to a junction at 0.5 mile. Take a right (red markers) and hike steeply toward the summit. 100' before the open slab on top of the summit is a 2nd-class scramble that goes down and right over ledges and along the base of the cliff. Follow the herd path (south) downhill for 150' to a level clearing near the **Wiessner Route** 598152,4886867.

DESCENT OPTIONS

Go left (north) and follow the herd path used for the approach.

1 Crack Chimney 5.3 G 60'

Start: At large blocks uphill from and left of the clearing, beneath a wide crack that begins left of a body-sized detached block 5' up.

P1 5.3 G: Up the slot that becomes a chimney. 60'

2 Kerr Route 5.6 G 80' ★★

Combines a hand traverse with a vertical crack.

Start: Same as Crack Chimney.

P1 5.6 G: Traverse right above the detached block to a stance below the vertical handcrack, then follow it to the top. 80'

FA Douglas Kerr, Fritz Wiessner

3 From Switzerland With Hate 5.9 X 90'

Scary and dangerous; perhaps easier if cleaned.

Start: On the right side of the body-sized detached block mentioned for Crack Chimney, and 5' right of that route.

P1 5.9 X: Move up the right side of the detached block with care, then up a nice, steep crack to its top. Continue straight up the difficult, lichen-covered face to the top. 90'

FA May 29, 2011, Martin von Arx, Martine Schaer

4 Wiessner Route 5.8+ G 90' ★★★★

An early testpiece that still challenges climbers today. This route is Wiessner's most difficult Adirondack climb and arguably one of the best.

Start: At the left end of the level clearing, below a crack with a large bolt 10' up.

P1 5.8+ G: The crack widens from fingers to wide hands (crux) and finishes in a shallow off width. 90'

Gear: To 4".

FA Fritz Wiessner, Garfield Jones

5 High Noon 5.9 PG 90' ★★

Formerly a variation to Center Climb, a direct start straightens out this pitch.

Start: At the middle of the clearing, at a block below a right-facing corner.

P1 5.9 PG: Above the block, climb the right-facing corner to a stance below the left side of the roof. Go up and left to an overlap, then up a vertical crack. 90'

6 Center Climb 5.7 G 90' ★★

Start: At the right side of the clearing, at twin finger-cracks that go past the right side of a roof 30' up.

P1 5.7 G: (V1) Climb the crack on the left, (V2) past the roof to a right-facing corner. Up the corner to a ceiling, then move left and layback a flake to a crack. Follow the crack to the summit. 90'

V1 5.8 PG: Up the crack on the right.

V2 5.9+ PG: At the roof, move left using a fragile flake to the center of the roof. Break through the roof at a vertical crack, and follow this to the top. Gear to 4".

FA Fritz Wiessner

FA (V2), Joe Szot, Bob Witt

7 Old Route 5.4 G 110' ★

Yet another "old route" (the others being at Hurricane Crag, Chapel Pond Gully Cliff, Rooster Comb, and Gothics).

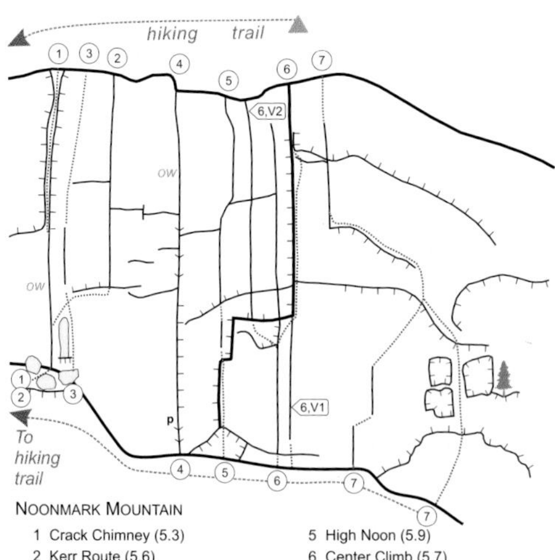

*Stanley Smith on **Center Climb** (5.7) in 1951, belayed by Donald LeBeau. Photo Stanley Smith Collection.*

Start: At the right end of the clearing at a short vertical crack. An alternative start begins 15' farther right just beneath stacked blocks in a depression.

P1 5.4 G: Both starts converge on a left-leaning ramp. At the left end of the ramp, climb through a ceiling (which is right of the handcrack finish of **Center Climb**) and scramble to the top. 110'

UPPER WOLFJAW CLIFF

Location	High Peaks Wilderness Area, accessed from the Adirondack Mountain Reserve Trailhead
Aspect	Southwest
Height	250'
Quality	★★★
Approach	2 hr 30 min, difficult
Summary	A steep, multipitch cliff with 5.10 routes located in a high mountain valley.

-5.6	5.7	5.8	5.9	5.10	5.11	5.12	5.13+	total
				2				3

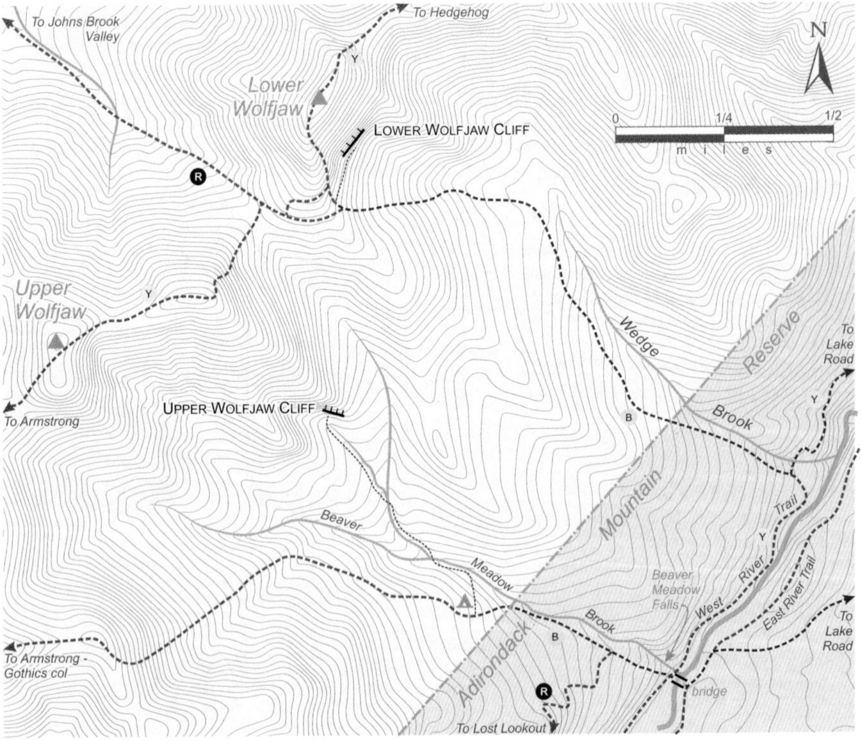

Nestled high in the drainage area whose runoff flows over Beaver Meadow Falls is a sheer cliff visible from the trail to Gothics and Armstrong Mountains. Upper Wolfjaw Cliff is a sunny, protected crag with multipitch routes in the 5.10 range. Although a bushwhack is required, it involves a pleasant rock hop up a wide streambed that becomes a steep waterslide. A tributary leads to a high, wooded valley (good camping) at the base of the cliff. The climbs follow cracks and are adorned with dimples and pinches that are characteristic of anorthositic rock of the High Peaks. The routes share belay ledges, and linking different pitches is easy. The two common ledges are a long, narrow ledge 90' up and a small, sloping ledge—Wolf's Mouth Ledge—that is beneath the summit roofs (known as the Wolf's Mouth).

HISTORY

Ed Palen spotted the cliff from the summit of Noonmark Mountain and staged several trips to the cliff from a camp near the Wedge Brook Trail. He established all the routes here with Mark Scott in 2000 and 2001.

ACCESS

Since bushwhacking and camping are not allowed on Adirondack Mountain Reserve property, hiking up the drainage area from the top of Beaver Meadow Falls is prohibited. The approach described here uses marked trails while on AMR property.

DIRECTIONS (MAP PG 482)

Park at the AMR Trailhead (page 426). From the parking area (0 hr 0 min), hike the Lake Road and, at 45 min, reach the Gothics–Beaver Meadow Falls Trail on the right. Follow the trail to the base of the falls, then to its top at 1 hr 15 min. Continue on the trail as it climbs steadily up the valley above the falls. You reach the State Land Boundary at 1 hr 30 min and then a minor brook a few minutes later. Continue past the brook for 200' and locate a herd path 593935,4887116 that goes east (right) and descends 50' to an unimproved campsite, reached at 1 hr 35 min. Bushwhack north and downhill and, at 1 hr 40 min, reach the major brook—Beaver Meadow Brook. Hike upstream to a junction with a tributary on the right (east) at 1 hr 55 min 593760,4887320. If you encounter a logjam followed by a 100' waterslide, then you've gone too far.

Take the right fork and follow the tributary for 100' to where it becomes a steep, moss-covered waterslide. Follow the waterslide to its top and a stream junction reached at 2 hr. Go left (north) and follow the stream, which is choked with vegetation. At 2 hr 10 min, you reach a small clearing that offers a view of the cliff ahead. Continue north along the stream until it dries up near a room-sized boulder. Hike uphill and right through an easy talus field to the cliff base near its center and lowest point at 2 hr 30 min 593401,4887859.

*Colin Loher on P3 (5.10a) of **Wolfman** (5.10d).*

DESCENT OPTIONS

Rappel **Wolfman** with a single 60-m rope. Long slings on the fixed anchor at Wolf's Mouth Ledge allow for a 100' rappel to the lower ledge.

1 Stanley 5.9+ A1 185' ★

The short aid crack would likely go free at 5.11.

Start: 30' left of and uphill from a low ceiling at the center and lowest point of the cliff base, at a 4'-deep left-facing corner.

P1 5.6 A1 PG: Up the corner on sandy, friable rock for 30' to a tree-covered ledge on the right. From the top of a boulder, aid a steep crack to a long ledge. 65'

P2 5.9+ G: Left across the ledge to a vertical crack, then follow it for 40'. Face-climb right past the top of a second vertical crack to a third vertical crack on the route **Dr. Livingston, I Presume**. Finish as for **Dr. Livingston, I Presume**: follow the third crack to its end, then face-climb right to the left-facing corner of **Wolfman**. Follow the left-facing corner to a fixed anchor on Wolf's Mouth Ledge. 120'

FA Jul, 2001, Ed Palen, Mark Scott

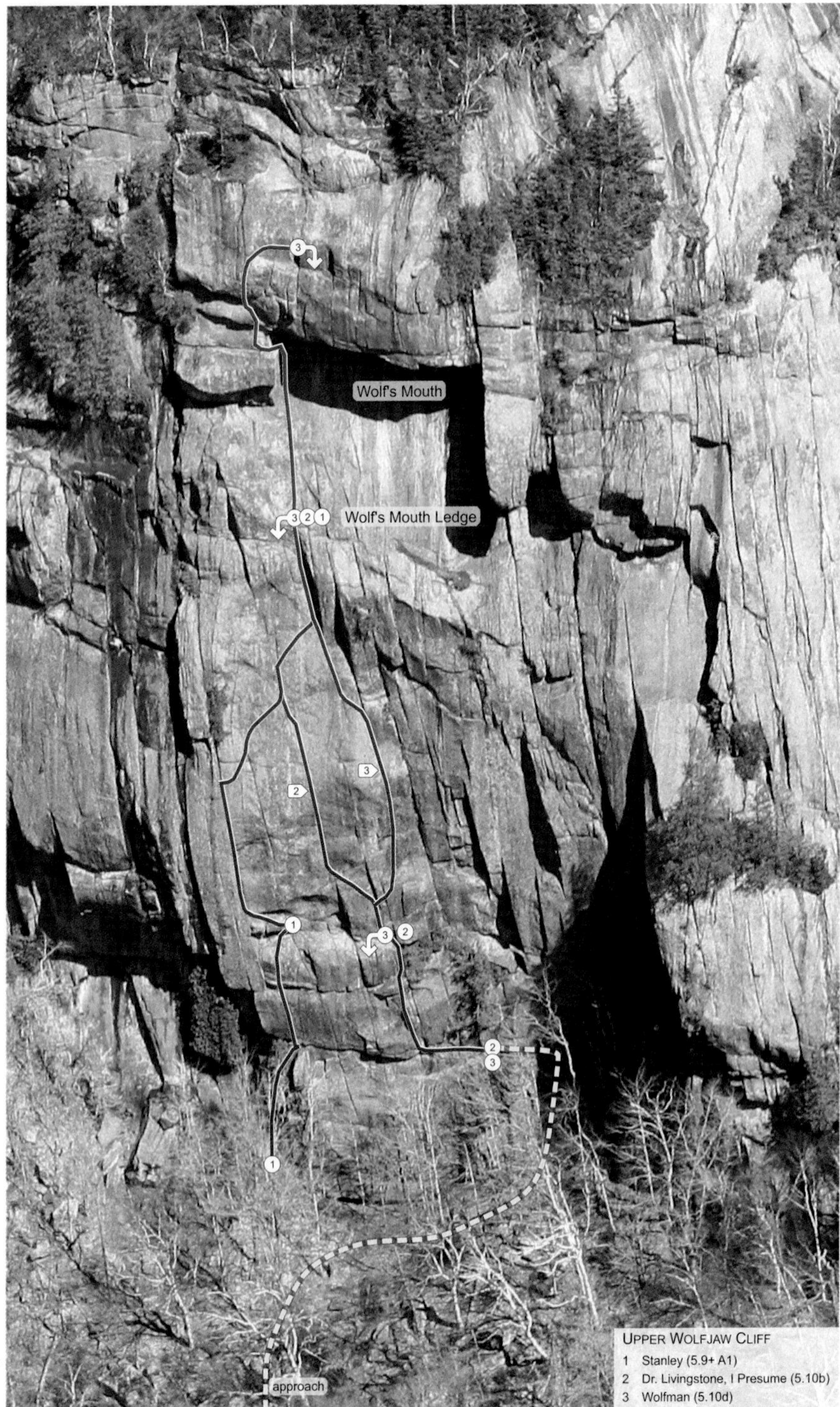

Photo by Drew Haas.

2 Dr. Livingstone, I Presume 5.10b G 180' ★★★

Named for the junglelike approach, similar to that explored in Africa by Livingstone and Stanley, the first Europeans to reach Victoria Falls.

Start: 40' right of and uphill from a low ceiling at the center and lowest point of the cliff base is a dirty left-facing corner. Up the corner, then left along a ledge (4th class) to a belay at a cedar tree that is 30' above the cliff base.

P1 5.9+ G: Left below a ceiling, then over the ceiling at a break to a steep slab. Up the slab to a fistcrack, then climb it to a fixed anchor at the right end of a long ledge. 70'

P2 5.10b G: Face-climb up and left to a vertical crack that begins 20' above the belay. Climb the crack through a bulge and up a slab to its end. Face-climb right to the left-facing corner of **Wolfman** and follow it to a fixed anchor on Wolf's Mouth Ledge. 110'

FA Jul, 2000, Ed Palen, Mark Scott

3 Wolfman 5.10d G 260' ★★★★

Sustained face climbing and an exposed top pitch that traverses out the summit roofs.

Start: Same as **Dr. Livingston, I Presume**.

P1 5.9+ G: Same as **Dr. Livingston, I Presume**. 70'

● **P2 5.10d G:** Above the belay is a shallow crack that breaks a steep wall. Follow the crack to its top, then slightly right across a slab to a left-rising crack. Follow the crack into a left-facing corner and follow the corner to a fixed anchor on Wolf's Mouth Ledge. 110'

P3 5.10a G: Up the slab above the belay to a deep right-facing corner beneath the left end of the summit roof—the Wolf's Mouth. Climb the corner, then hand-traverse left to a ledge (optional belay). From the ledge, climb a steep left-rising crack and make a long reach past an overhang to a jug—exposed and exciting. Step right to a fixed anchor. 80'

FA Aug, 2000, Ed Palen, Mark Scott

ROOSTER COMB

Location	High Peaks Wilderness Area, accessed from NY 73 in Keene Valley
Aspect	Southeast
Height	200'
Quality	★★
Approach	1 hr 30 min, moderate
Summary	A large cliff on top of a pretty summit with good views, but only a few routes.

-5.6	5.7	5.8	5.9	5.10	5.11	5.12	5.13+	total
1		1	1					3

Rooster Comb is a small peak on the end of the Great Range. Its accessibility to Keene Valley, the new trail system, and an exposed summit with pretty views make this a popular day hike. The cliff is relatively large, but there are only a couple of documented routes here, which may explain why there is so little climbing traffic on this cliff. There is certainly more climbing for those willing to explore, and there are several more unexplored outcroppings on the ridge.

The base of the cliff is open and pleasant, slightly sloped, with boulders to sit on. The cliff's main feature is a large buttress that forms a left-facing, left-leaning corner-ramp. There is a sheer face below it with a half-arch overlap 25' up and orange rock beneath it. Just right of this buttress is **Cock-a-doodle-do**. Downhill from and left of this sheer face are several right-leaning corners with **Old Route** and **Woolsey Route**.

HISTORY

Fritz Wiessner and Jim Goodwin were the first to report climbing here in 1949 with yet another "Old Route." Goodwin must have liked the route, as he went back two weeks later and climbed it with his young apprentice Dave Bernays. During those visits, Betty Woolsey climbed a route near **Old Route**, the first "first ascent" (and one of the only ones) done by a woman in the Adirondacks. These two routes, combined with Ed Palen's fantastic **Cock-a-doodle-do**, represent only some of the climbing; other routes have been climbed but remain forgotten.

DIRECTIONS

Park at the Rooster Comb Trailhead 596982,4893207, on the east side of NY 73, 0.4 mile south of Keene Valley (from the intersection of NY 73 and Adirondack Street). Follow the Rooster Comb Trail, and at 2.0 miles, you'll reach a junction with the summit trail. Follow the summit trail to the next intersection; a sign indicates that the summit is 0.3 mile farther. Stay on the summit trail for 3 min to a 90° right turn in the trail (if you go too far, 150' farther is another right turn with a wood ladder). Instead of turning, bushwhack straight down a narrow rock-walled gully to the first break in the cliffs on the right. This position is marked by a unique narrow, 5'-high finger of rock that arches out from the base of the wall. Turn right (now walking climber's left) and bushwhack along the base of the cliff for 5 min to reach the open area at the height of land beneath the central section of the cliff 594882,4891673. Hiking time to the base of the cliff is 1 hr 30 min.

DESCENT OPTIONS

The only expedient descent involves scrambling down the slab left of P4 of **Old Route**, then reversing a few moves (5.2) in the corner to reach the ledge with the tree and boulder at the base of the imposing wall. Tucked into the corner are a few small trees, the lower of which has an anchor, from which you can rappel 100' to the ground. Walking around takes 15 min or so.

1 Woolsey Route 5.8 G 430' ★

P1 has interesting moves on good rock. P2 is a bit dirty and links into **Old Route**'s chimney on P2.

Start: 15' downhill from and left of **Old Route** at the right end of a left-arching roof that begins 12' up.

P1 5.8 G: Climb up knobs to the roof, protect, then traverse left on the face for 10' to the base of a right-rising V-groove. Up the V-groove (crux) to a ledge on the right. 40'

P2 5.5 G: Continue up the right-leaning Woolsey corner to its top (5.5; some grass), step right over loose

rock over the top of the next corner, then continue up and right into the chimney of **Old Route** P2. Up the chimney to a ledge. 110'

P3 4th class: Same as P3 of **Old Route**. 160'

P4 5.2 G: Same as P4 of **Old Route**. 120'

History: Jim Goodwin distinctly recalls Betty Woolsey leading a route near **Old Route**. In Goodwin's words, Woolsey was the "best climber of her day" and "floated up the wall." It isn't known exactly where her route goes, but this corner is the most likely line.

FA 1949, Elizabeth Woolsey, Lewis Thorne

2 Old Route 5.4 G 420' ★★★

This historic route climbs the central feature of the cliff—the large left-facing, left-leaning corner. The route has solid rock, comfortable belays, and airy positions. There are many historic pitons on the route, which should be left in place. The first two pitches can easily be combined.

Start: 200' downhill and left of the high point of the terrain, at a large left-facing open book corner with a ramp on the right wall capped by a roof 25' up. The base of the route is open and has a large flat boulder 10' back from the corner.

P1 5.4 G: Up the broken corner to the roof, then traverse right under the roof (piton) and up a smaller corner near the arête with a good crack (piton). Follow the corner to a good belay ledge. 90'

P2 5.4 G: Climb cracks straight up, passing a bush on its left site. Step left to a chimney and follow it (piton) to a good ledge at its top. Belay off trees. 50'

P3 4th class: Scramble up a few feet, then traverse directly right to a large left-facing, left-leaning corner. (V1) Step around this corner on a narrow ledge and traverse right on a ramp to the larger left-facing, left-leaning corner with an imposing right wall. Belay at a good ledge with a small tree and a large boulder below the imposing wall. 160'

P4 5.2 G: (V2) Climb the corner and ramp to the top. Alternatively, just before the top, climb a short crack in the right wall (5.5). 120'

V1 5.5 G: Climb a right-leaning crack above a tree and up the corner above to the top.

V2 5.10 G: On the imposing wall and just above two small cedars is a system of two parallel cracks. Climb the left crack to a V-slot, then onto a low-angle slab (about 40'). Scramble up the slab to the summit.

FA Jul 17, 1949, Fritz Wiessner, Jim Goodwin
ACB (V2) 2005, Chuck Boyd, Jim Boyd

3 Cock-a-doodle-doo 5.9 G 70' ★★★★

Outstanding climbing up a Devils Tower–like stem box to a fixed anchor—with great gear and excellent jams. It has been climbed through the overhanging open book above, but it is dirty and not recommended.

Start: At the high point of the terrain and at the right end of the half arch 25' up is a large right-facing corner with a chimney in its left wall. This route begins 10' right of the corner at the base of a stem box (two shallow opposing corners 4' apart).

P1 5.9 G: (V1) Climb the cracks in the stem box to a ceiling, breaking it on the left (crux) into a large right-facing corner, then to a ledge with a fixed anchor. 70'

V1 5.7 G: Start in the corner 10' to the left on top of some blocks. Climb to the top of the right-arching corner using several good horizontals, then join the normal route at the crux ceiling.

FA Jul, 1997, Ed Palen, Laurie Daniels

BASIN MOUNTAIN

Location	High Peaks Wilderness Area, accessed from the Garden Trailhead
Summary	A remote summit with several exposed slides and a hidden amphitheater.

-5.6	5.7	5.8	5.9	5.10	5.11	5.12	5.13+	total
3	1	1						5

Basin Mountain is a difficult-to-access summit in the Great Range (the range of summits that extends from Haystack to Lower Wolfjaw). There are several slide pathways with notable scrambles, and a hidden, 200'-tall amphitheater with good potential for new routes.

Basin Mountain

EAST FACE

Aspect	East
Height	900'
Quality	★
Summary	A remote, broad, clean, high-mountain slab directly below the summit of Basin Mountain.
Approach	4 hr 30 min, difficult

-5.6	5.7	5.8	5.9	5.10	5.11	5.12	5.13+	total
2								2

A highly visible face when viewed from Gothics and Saddleback, the east face of Basin Mountain is broad and clean. However enticing this face may be, it is guarded by a very long approach, which thankfully travels some of the most scenic and challenging hiking trails in the Adirondacks. The **East Face** route is a touch more difficult than the **Eagle Slide** on Giant and not as slabby and lichen-covered as the **New Finger Slide** on Gothics.

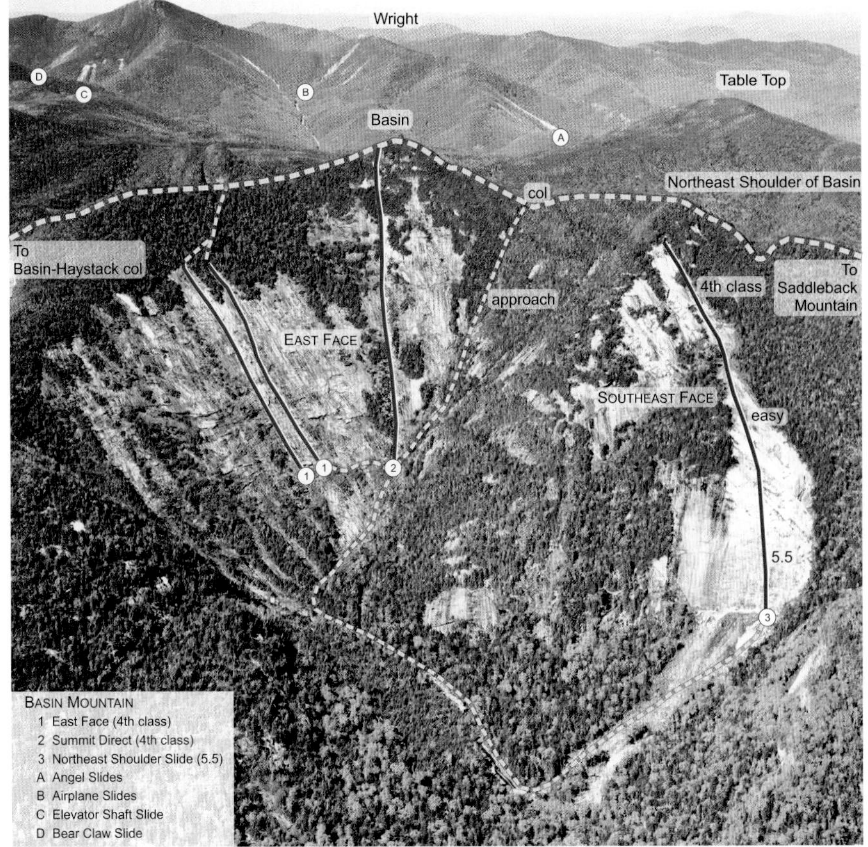

Photo by Kevin "MudRat" MacKenzie.

DIRECTIONS

Get up early for this one. Park at the Garden Trailhead (page 426). Hike to Johns Brook Lodge, and take the Orebed Trail to the Range Trail, meeting it at the col between Gothics and Saddleback. Hike west over the summit of Saddleback where you can view the East Face of Basin Mountain. Leave the Range Trail east of the summit of Basin Mountain (by about 5 min) 589231,4886085. There is a distinct col here located between the summit of Basin Mountain and a small wooded sub-summit (the Northeast Shoulder of Basin Mountain). From the col, bushwack south, heading steeply down in tight vegetation until the drainage area becomes rock-walled on both sides and the going becomes more obvious. A half hour of bushwhacking leads to open rock and grassy slopes. Stay in the drainage area to where it is possible to traverse (climber's) left to the middle of the East Face 589507,4885661.

DESCENT OPTIONS

From the top of the face, continue upward to the Range Trail on the west side of Basin Mountain.

1 East Face 4th class 700' ★★

Climbs up the center of the slab staying left of a black streak. Despite the route being only 4th-class, rock shoes are recommended and some may prefer a rope. Begin just left of a black streak in the center of the face that runs the height of the cliff. Climb easy slabs to a bulge at one-third height of the face. Climb the bulge on positive holds on clean rock, then continue up the slab, staying left of the black streak, to lower-angle terrain. Continue to the highest point of the slab left of center (not the highest open rock, which is far to the right, below the summit). There's a second line further to the left that climbs slightly cleaner rock and finishes up the wider finger to the left.
Descent: At the top of the slab, head up and right to the Range Trail on the west side of Basin Mountain, which requires about 10 min of easier-than-expected navigation. The summit of Basin Mountain is five min right (north), or you can descend the trail left (west) to the Shorey Shortcut Trail and the Johns Brook Valley below.

2 Summit Direct 4th class 900' ★

This narrow route, recently cleaned by rockfall, takes a line directly to the summit of Basin Mountain.
Start: 350' right of the East Face route at the bottom of an obvious line extending to the summit knob.
Route Description: Climb up mossy old-exposure slab for about 150' to the cleaner stone. Continue up a narrow track of slab broken into segments by vegetated cracks. The most challenging and featured rock is at the top on approach to the summit proper.
ACB Jul 14, 2012, Kevin "MudRat" MacKenzie, Richard McKenna, Alan Wechsler

Basin Mountain

SOUTHEAST FACE

Aspect	Southeast
Height	1900'
Quality	★★
Approach	4 hr 30 min, difficult
Summary	A fresh swath of new-exposed rock that leads to the Northeast Shoulder of Basin Mountain.

This set of southeast-facing slides was enhanced by the 2011 Tropical Storm Irene, and is now a fresh, wide swath leading directly to the Northeast Shoulder, a wooded mini-summit of Basin Mountain.

3 Northeast Shoulder Slide 5.5 R 1900' ★★

This route first appeared in *Adirondac*.[12] While equal in quality to the East Face, they are very different. This route has challenging, unprotected, smooth slab at the base, and the East Face is more knobby and featured.
Start: Approach as for the East Face, but continue southeast down the drainage. Follow the drainage as it bends to the east until you encounter the fresh slide debris on the left. Follow the rubble up to the base of the slide, a 500'-wide slab.
Route Description: Friction up the smooth slab for 250. (Slightly easier and cleaner stone to the right below a large left-arching overlap.) Above, the climbing eases through the central segment. The top third is 4th class on well-featured rock. Finish in a narrow debris filled gully at the top. Bushwhack right for 300' through heavy krummholz to the Range Trail.
ACB Sep 18, 2011, Kevin "MudRat" MacKenzie, Mark Lowell

Basin Mountain

SOUTH FACE AMPHITHEATER

Aspect	South
Height	200'
Quality	★
Approach	4 hr 30 min, difficult
Summary	A remote, wide, largely unexplored wall in a high-mountain setting.

-5.6	5.7	5.8	5.9	5.10	5.11	5.12	5.13+	total
	1	1						2

Directly south of the summit of Basin Mountain is a beautiful, south-facing amphitheater. It has received little attention, perhaps due to the many hours of hiking and bushwhacking required for the approach, the density of the vegetation surrounding the rock, or the fact that it's invisible from most vantage points on the surrounding mountains. A visit requires an affinity for the "whole experience" and will exemplify Adirondack-style adventuring. The spectacular setting combined with the strong feeling of solitude make for an unforgettable experience.

12 Kevin MacKenzie, "Basin's Northeastern Shoulder Slide: A Scar from Irene", *Adirondac* (Mar–Apr 2012), p. 20–22.

Photo by Kevin "MudRat" MacKenzie.

In general, the cliff is very clean, with little vegetation. The left side is reportedly loose and unattractive, but the middle and right sides are steep with potential for more traditional lines. There's a new slide (~2012) on the far right side of the Amphitheater.

DIRECTIONS

Approach the cliff from the summit of Basin Mountain 589092,4885956, about 5 hours from the Garden Trail via the Orbed Brook Trail (0 hr 0 min). Follow the trail south from the summit. At 5 min, where the trail turns west 589092,4885636, leave the trail and continue south, staying on the ridge. The bushwhacking is near impenetrable with little visibility; the best advice is to stay on the ridge, and perhaps use a compass. The ridge descends and, at 15 min, splits to form an amphitheater. Continue south down the steepening slope to the tree line at the top of the wall (25 min), then rappel to the base 589260,4885328.

A 60m rappel may not reach the base in the middle section of the wall. The better trees are set back from the edge, so a long cord is helpful.

4 Knock Before Entering 5.8 R 200'

Start: 35' left of Whaamburger.
P1 5.8 R: Climb up the face, then follow a loose ramp up and right to a small roof at 65'. Move off the stance and begin the long traverse right (crux) to a left-facing corner with a small sapling. Pull around the corner (optional belay) and continue up another 80' of unprotected face and overlaps to gain a shrub belay. 180'
P2 4th class: Continue up the tree line to the top. 20'
FA Jul 16, 2011, Jeff Moss, Monica Blount, Matt Oakley

5 Whaamburger 5.7 PG 150' ★★

Start: On the right side of the wall, at a blocky chimney 25' left of a vegetated, left-facing corner formed by an enormous leaning slab.
P1 5.7 PG: Climb the blocky chimney. Pull a small roof and move up a left-facing corner to a prominent horn. Pull around the corner and traverse right, then climb the unprotected face up to a tree. 100'
P2 5.4 PG: Easy climbing leads to the top. 50'
FA Jun 5, 2011, Gil Moss, Jeff Moss

THE BROTHERS

Location	High Peaks Wilderness Area, accessed from the Garden Trailhead
Aspect	South
Height	150'
Quality	
Approach	40 min, moderate
Summary	A largely undeveloped cliff on the side of The Brothers above Keene Valley.

-5.6	5.7	5.8	5.9	5.10	5.11	5.12	5.13+	total
1		1						2

The Brothers is a group of tiny summits on the ridge leading to Big Slide. It offers excellent views of the Great Range with close proximity to the trailhead and is thus a very popular hiking destination as well as an alternate approach to Big Slide.

The climbing is located on the south face of First Brother, near the point where the trail meets the first open ledges. The cliff is largely unexplored but does offer some potential for new routes. The routes described here are historic and were seen as climbs to combine with an outing on Big Slide Mountain farther up the ridge.

HISTORY

The face was first climbed by Jim Goodwin in the 1930s, but details of the specific route are unknown. The routes described here were climbed in the 1960s by members of the Penn State Outing Club (PSOC) for Trudy Healy's first guidebook.

DIRECTIONS (MAP PAGE 503)

Park at the Garden Trailhead (page 426) and follow the trail (blue markers) for The Brothers and Big Slide for 20 min to the first viewpoint at ledges, where there is a large boulder perched on the edge. 30' beyond and below your feet is a large left-facing corner, Pringsheim Chimney 593678,4893551.

From the viewpoint, the hiking trail stays more or less on top of the cliffband. To reach the base of the cliff, continue on the hiking trail another 150' yards (about 2 min); leave the trail and descend 100', then

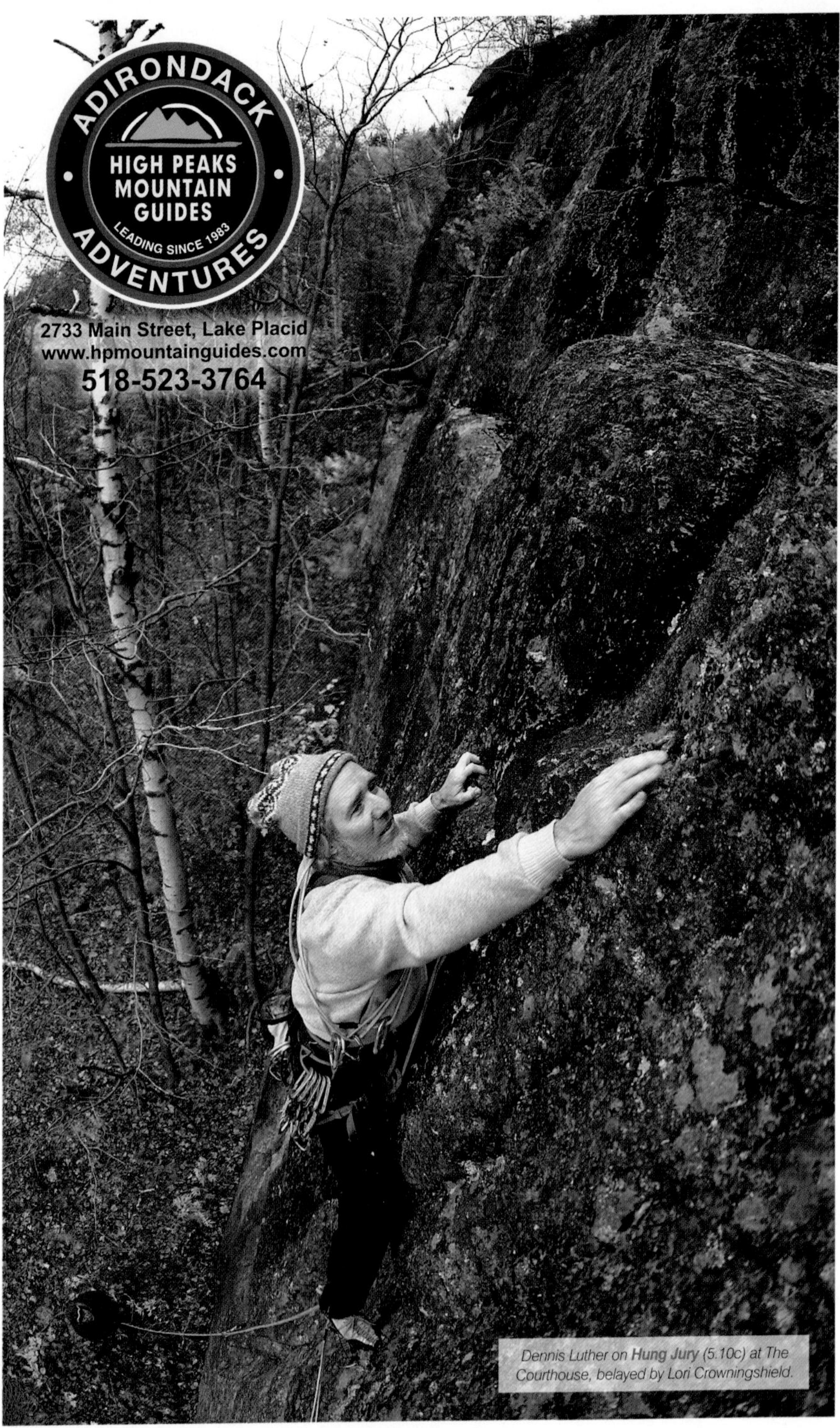

Dennis Luther on ***Hung Jury*** *(5.10c) at The Courthouse, belayed by Lori Crowningshield.*

contour west (parallel to the hiking trail but below the cliff) for 15 min to reach the base of the cliff at its tallest point 593357,4893528. There is a low-angle unbroken flaky slab below a steeper wall 60' up, the start of **Four Plus**. Above and right of this slab is a very steep headwall and a distinctive left-leaning fingercrack that goes through two pods. (Perhaps some future 5.11?)

1 Four Plus 5.5 PG (5.4 R) 180' ★

Start: At the low point of the flaky slab beneath a steeper wall 60' up.

P1 5.4 R: Up and left on flaky, but easy, slab, then up knobs to reach the right end of a long ledge. Traverse left 50' to the widest part of the ledge beneath a vegetated ledge at head height. 100'

P2 5.5 PG: Step right and climb the short wall right of the vegetated ledge. Trend up and right past overlaps to a shallow left-facing, left-leaning corner. At its top, step left and climb a steep right-leaning, right-facing corner to the top. 80'

History: The climb was originally named "F6" because that was the grade (using the historic "F" grading system). Its name was then changed to "Four Plus" because it was regraded at "5.4+."

ACB Jun, 1965, Al Breisch, Trudy Healy

2 Pringsheim Chimney 5.8 G 30' ★

Climbs a distinctive corner, not really a chimney.

Start: First locate the top of the route—where the trail reaches the first viewpoint at ledges, 30' (climber's) left of a large boulder perched on the edge. Walk easily (climber's) right around the east end of the cliff to the base of the corner.

P1 5.8 G: Climb the corner to the top. 30'

History: This was considered a "practice climb," which probably means toprope.

THE COURTHOUSE

Location	High Peaks Wilderness Area, accessed from the Garden Trailhead
Aspect	Southeast
Height	70'
Quality	★★★★
Approach	1 hr 10 min, moderate
Summary	Mostly moderate steep face and crack routes in a beautiful setting above Johns Brook Valley. Toproping is possible.

-5.6	5.7	5.8	5.9	5.10	5.11	5.12	5.13+	total
2	2	2	1	3				10

Located in the Johns Brook Valley on a ridge of the Fourth Brother, this 70' crag can be discerned from Keene Valley. It houses several short but excellent crack and face climbs as well as first-rate views of the Great Range and Giant. On a clear fall day with full foliage color, the views are outstanding.

When you first see the cliff, the routes seem steep and unprotected. Upon closer inspection, you find clean, well-featured rock littered with horizontals, many of which take good—but small—protection.

DIRECTIONS **(MAP PAGE 491)**

Park at the Garden Trailhead (page 426). Follow the Phelps Trail (yellow markers) toward Johns Brook Lodge. You'll reach the first lean-to (Bear Brook) at 15 min and a second lean-to (Deer Brook) at 23 min. From the second lean-to, continue hiking for an additional 5 min to a stream and the beginning of the climbers' path 593033,4892017; if you miss this stream, within 40' you'll pass a boulder in the hiking trail so large that you'll nearly hit it with your left shoulder.

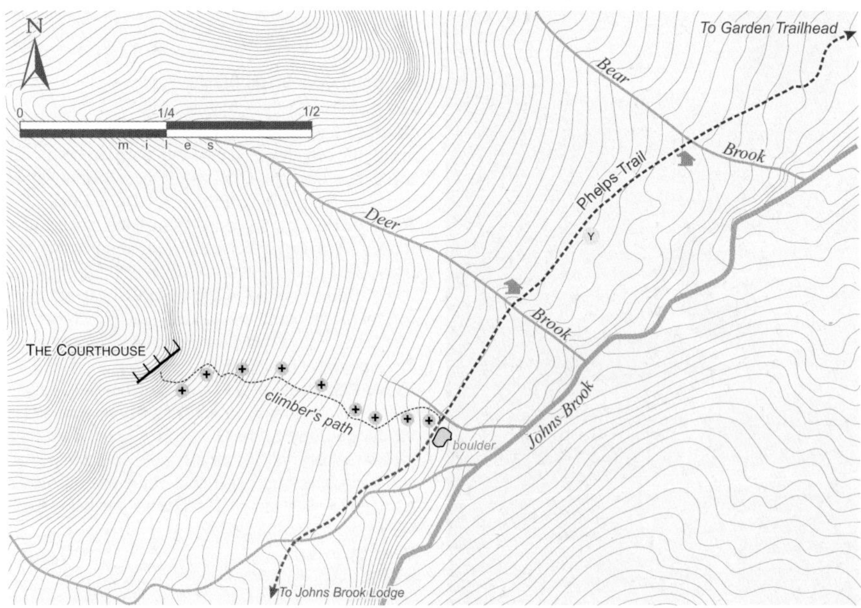

Cross the stream and turn upstream for 10 yards or so until you pick up the climbers' path. This veers leftward away from the stream and uphill to the cliff 592385,4892120, which is reached at 1 hr 10 min. The climbers' path has some cairns, but even so, it is difficult to follow in places. It pays to find the correct path, as it winds through some slabs, and patches of stinging nettles (long pants necessary) that would be troublesome without the path.

Becky Carmen Katz on ***Habeas Corpus*** *(5.8). Photo by Ed Palen.*

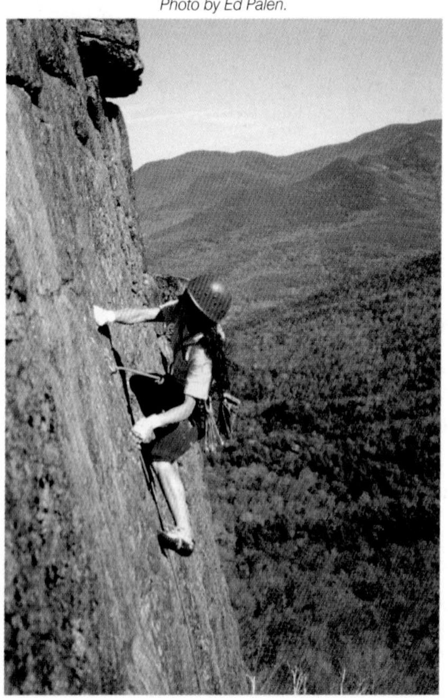

DESCENT OPTIONS

There are few fixed anchors; it's easy to walk left and return to the base of the cliff. It helps to build a rappel anchor and use it for the day, then retrieve it at the end of the day.

1 Dewey, Cheetham, and Howe! 5.6 PG 65' ★★

An easy route on clean, well-featured rock.

Start: About 60' right of the left end of the crag, and left of the block-tower 40' up that you can see behind.

P1 5.6 PG: Climb up stepped rock to a ledge, then into a gray, shallow open book, and past a fixed piton to a ledge. Climb the easy face behind and left of the tower to the top. 65'

FA Apr, 1999, Teresa Cheetham-Palen, Ed Palen

2 Hung Jury 5.10c PG 70' ★

Good climbing, although a little dirty.

Start: 25' right of **Dewey, Cheetham, and Howe!** and left of the arch area, at a face with a zigzag horizontal; this face is beneath a roof at two-thirds height, above which are two parallel cracks.

P1 5.10c PG: (V1) Climb the face off the ground, then move past the zigzag horizontal and through some dirty black rock to a ledge (5.9). Continue up easier rock into a left-facing corner below the roof. (V2) Step right and use the rightmost of two parallel cracks to break the roof (crux). Follow this crack to an off width that leads to the blocks at the top. 70'

V1 5.5 PG: An easier start begins at the shallow right-facing, left-rising ramp 15' right of the normal start.

V2 Judge Judy 5.11a G ★★★: A direct line to the top with a sustained, technical fingercrack interspersed with horizontals. At the left side of the roof, climb the left-hand crack: start with a perfect hand jam and climb the fingercrack to the top.

Gear: Up to 3".

FA Sep, 2005, Jim Lawyer, Jesse Williams

FA (V2) Aug 23, 2008, Chris Yenkey, Jim Lawyer

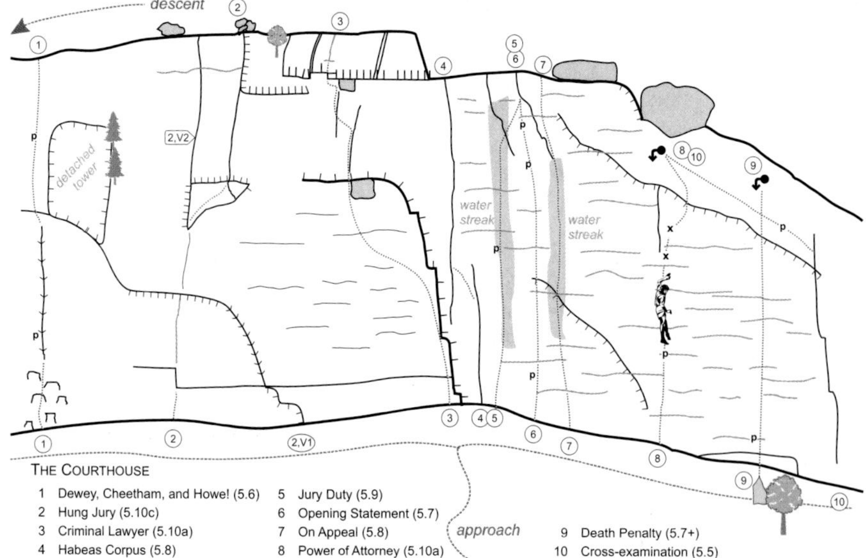

3 Criminal Lawyer 5.10a PG 70' ★★★

Incredible climbing (and clean!) with an unlikely finish. There's a giant raven's nest at the square block that doesn't interfere with the climbing. In the spring when the nest is occupied, well, that's another story.

Start: Begin at the base of the left-facing, left-arching corner in the center of the cliff.

P1 5.10a PG: Up the corner, then left across the face (5.6) to the square block jammed beneath the top of the arch. Use the block to gain a stance on the face above the arch. There are two parallel cracks here; move leftward across the face to the left crack and up to the second roof at a left-facing corner, just left of a jammed block. Move through the roof and make a long reach to a horizontal (crux) on the upper face. 70'

History: This route had been cleaned by Ed Palen but not yet led when Lawyer unknowingly galloped up it.

Gear: Up to 3".

FA Sep, 2005, Jim Lawyer, Jesse Williams

4 Habeas Corpus 5.8 G 70' ★★★★

A first-rate crack that shoots up the middle of the cliff.

Start: Begin 3' right of the left-facing, arching corner of **Criminal Lawyer**, at the base of the first crack.

P1 5.8 G: Climb the fingercrack for 25' (V1), then step left to a thinner crack and follow it to the top. 70'

V1 5.6 G: Start in the left-facing, arching corner of **Criminal Lawyer** until you can step right around the corner and into the upper crack.

Gear: Up to 1".

FA Apr, 1999, Ed Palen, Terry LaFrance

5 Jury Duty 5.9 PG 70' ★

Start: 5' right of **Habeas Corpus** at a fingercrack.

P1 5.9 PG: Climb the fingercrack, then up the gray rock above past numerous horizontals and past a pin at 25' just left of the black streak. Continue up the black streak and, at the top, diagonal right to finish on the next route. 70'

FA May, 1999, Ed Palen, Josh Butson

6 Opening Statement 5.7 PG 70' ★★★★

Briggs was the local D.A. when he and Palen first climbed at the crag. This route was his first first ascent (thus the route name). When asked how he got the day off from work to come climbing, he explained, "Simple. I just told my secretary that I was headed to the Courthouse." The cliff name has stuck ever since.

Start: Begin in chocolate-colored rock 5' right of **Jury Duty** and below a piton 15' up.

P1 5.7 PG: Climb up the face past the piton at 15', then up the gray rock between the two black streaks to the top, past two more pins along the way. 70'

FA Apr, 1999, Ron Briggs, Terry LaFrance, Ed Palen

7 On Appeal 5.8 PG 70' ★

Slightly less enjoyable compared to its neighbors, but still worthwhile.

Start: Begin just right of **Opening Statement** below the second black streak at some right-facing, left-rising stepped ledges.

P1 5.8 PG: Climb up the stepped ledges, then proceed straight up the face and follow the black streak to the top. 70'

FA May, 1999, Ed Palen, Josh Butson

8 Power of Attorney 5.10a PG 60' ★★★★

Challenging face climbing with a short crux.

Start: Begin directly below the anchor that sits beneath the block that overhangs the face.

P1 5.10a PG: Climb the right-facing, left-rising stepped ledges on the chocolate-colored rock, then straight up the face to a bolt. Continue to the second bolt (crux), move slightly right, then back left to the anchor. 60'

Gear: Small gear and a 1" cam.

FA May, 1999, Ed Palen, Dick Drosse

9 Death Penalty 5.7+ PG 65' ★★

A fun line that makes for a good toprope but a serious lead. Since the first ascent was made before the first piton was added, a fall low down was not an option, hence the route name.

Start: Begin on the pointed block 25' right of **Power of Attorney**.

P1 5.7+ PG: Step from the block onto the cliff (piton), then head straight up the face with many horizontals to the left-rising ramp and fixed anchor. 65'

FA May, 1999, Ed Palen, Josh Baker

10 Cross-examination 5.5 PG 65' ★

Baker's first first ascent. It looked easier than it was, especially since he led it in the rain.

Start: Begin below the prominent finger to a handcrack 20' right of the pointed block at the base of **Death Penalty**.

P1 5.5 PG: Climb the crack 30' to a ledge, then traverse left (piton) for 35' to the anchor on **Power of Attorney** (or stop at the **Death Penalty** anchor). 65'

FA May, 1999, Josh Baker, Ed Palen

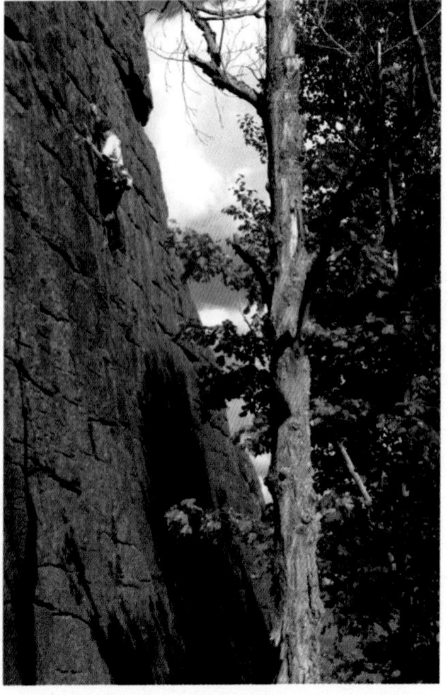

*Tad Welch on **Power of Attorney** (5.10a).*

BIG SLIDE MOUNTAIN

Location	High Peaks Wilderness Area, accessed from the Garden Trailhead
Aspect	South
Height	300'
Quality	★★★
Approach	2 hr 30 min, difficult
Summary	Face climbing on a very scenic summit.

-5.6	5.7	5.8	5.9	5.10	5.11	5.12	5.13+	total
1	1		2					4

One of the best alpine views in the Adirondacks is experienced from the climbs on Big Slide. With the Great Range lined up across the valley, and the north face of Gothics centered perfectly, being on Big Slide embodies summit rock climbing in the High Peaks. When viewed from the nearby summits of Mt Colden or Phelps, the sheer profile of Big Slide is striking, in that it is the only high shield of rock near any of the High Peaks summits. This cliff is hardly a slide; rather, it is a steep helmet of rock that caps the top of a narrow summit.

The most striking feature is the right-facing stepped corner with roofs that bisects the cliff in the middle. **Mustard Sandwich** climbs through this system, and the **Wiessner-Austin Route** begins on slabs to the left. Right of this feature are **Slide Rules** and **Freudian Slip**, the most frequented routes; the first two pitches of these routes are often climbed by themselves. The rock quality on these two routes, after the initial 50', is very good, with leaning dikes and coarse knobs.

HISTORY

None of the High Peaks require technical climbing to reach the summit, but the challenging rock near the summit of Big Slide could have motivated Fritz Wiessner and George Austin to ascend this face in 1953. Considering the number of variations, it must have been a popular route in its day. The **Wiessner-Austin Route** was the only technical climb on Big Slide for 27 years, until Don Mellor and Andy Helms ventured up the intimidating face on the right side of the cliff via **Slide Rules** in 1980. Ed Palen and Joe Seftel's **Freudian Slip** in 1988 was a much-needed addition and, due to its good protection and excellent quality, is currently the most popular route on the cliff.

DIRECTIONS

Big Slide can be approach from two directions, both starting at the Garden Trailhead (page 426). The Slide Brook approach is 1.5 miles longer but has no elevation loss. The Brothers approach is shorter in distance and more scenic, but gains more elevation overall.

Via Slide Brook: Leave the Garden parking area (0 hr 0 min) on the Phelps Trail (yellow disks), heading toward Mt Marcy. Cross Slide Brook to a junction with the Slide Brook Trail (red disks), reached at 3.2 miles (1 hr 20 min), which leads to Big Slide Mountain. Turn right (north) and follow the Slide Brook Trail uphill to a sign

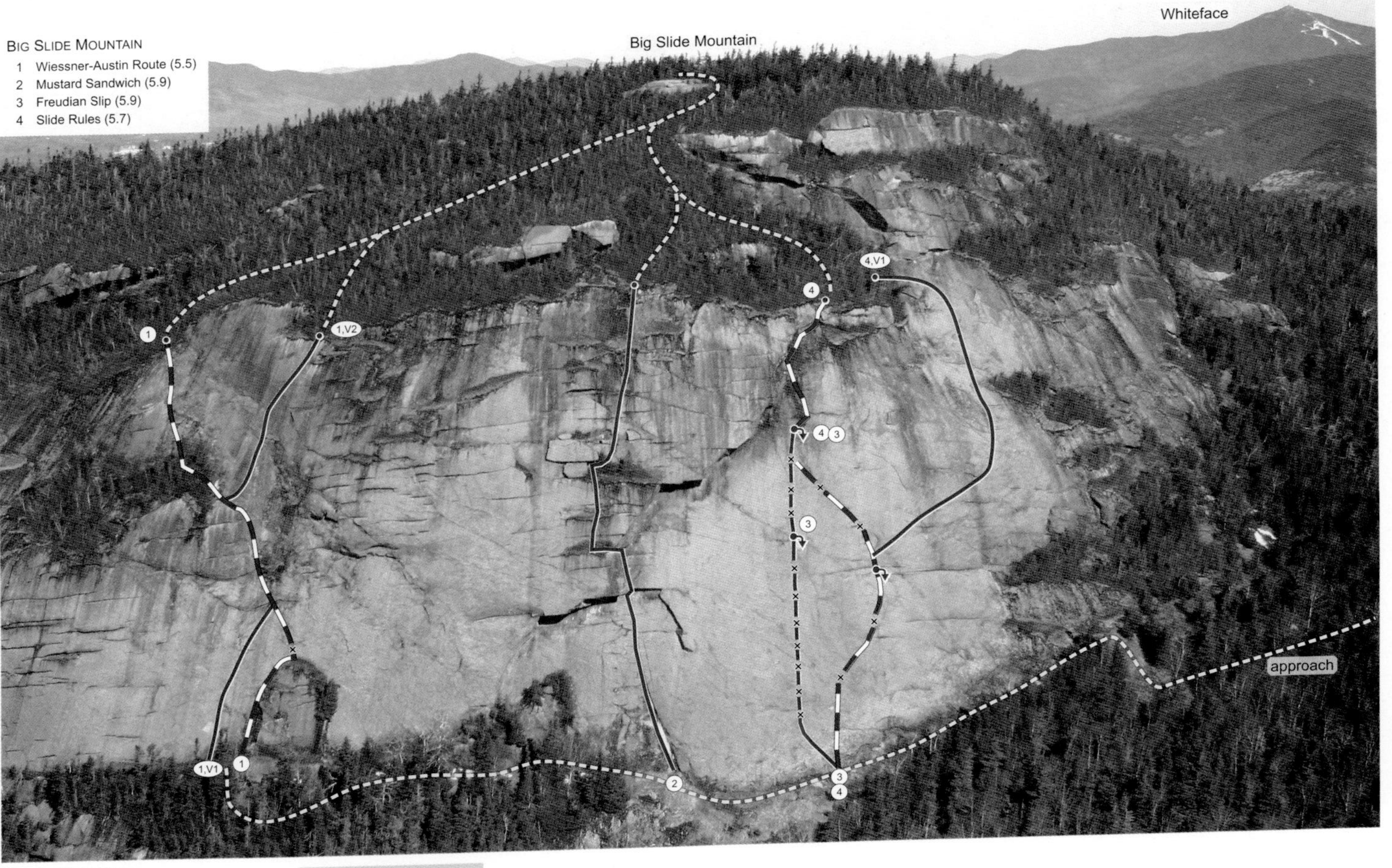

Photo by Drew Haas.

for 3500' camping limit, where an obscure view of the cliff can be seen above and left (2 hr 20 min). Continue on the trail to the junction with The Brothers Trail (blue disks), 5.3 miles from the parking area (2 hr 30 min) 590429,4892725.

Via The Brothers: A more scenic approach follows a semiopen ridge with three little summits (The Brothers), offering views of the Great Range and Big Slide's distinctive profile. From the Garden parking area (0 hr 0 min), follow The Brothers Trail (blue disks) to the junction with the Slide Brook Trail (red disks) at 3.7 miles (2 hr 30 min) 590429,4892725.

From the intersection: Both approaches lead to the same intersection, where a herd path goes west to the cliff. Traverse the mountainside on the herd path to reach a grassy slope beneath the right end of the cliff. Head up to the base of the cliff, then traverse left and down to the open rock at the lowest point of the cliff 590290,4892662.

Descent Options: Besides the fixed anchors on **Slide Rules** and **Freudian Slip**, all other descents would involve bushwhacking to the summit (about 5 min) and hiking down the trail to the herd path used on the approach.

1 Wiessner-Austin Route 5.5 R 300'

The easiest (and dirtiest) climbs on Big Slide are left of the right-facing stepped corner with roofs. Many variation starts and finishes to this route have been climbed.

Start: 300' left of the open rock at the low point of the cliff (and 150' left of the base of the right-facing stepped corner), at a 40'-tall flake with vegetation encircling it. The left-facing corner on the left side of the flake is a cleaner-looking start.

Route Description: (V1) Climb to the top of the flake (old bolt), then cross slabs (crux) angling leftward to the right end of a tree ledge. (V2) Continue leftward on easier slabs to the top of the cliff.

V1 5.6: Up the face, 25' left of the vegetated flake, to the tree ledge.

V2 5.5: From the tree ledge, traverse right, then up and right to the top of the cliff.

FA 1953, Fritz Wiessner, George Austin
FA (V1) Jul, 1965, Craig Patterson, Oliver Jones
FA (V2) Jun, 1970, John Chuta, Trudy Healy

2 Mustard Sandwich 5.9 PG 300'

Climbs through the right-facing stepped corner with roofs, the most obvious feature on the cliff.

Start: 25' uphill from and left of the open rock at the low point of the cliff, at a left-leaning crack that begins in a left-facing corner.

Route Description: Up the crack to an overhang, then over this (crux) to gain a stance in a right-facing corner beneath the right-leaning roof. Break left through the roof and onto vegetated ledges. Climb past several vegetated ledges, and a large block that sits off to the left, then up the dirty face to the trees.

FA 1988, Rob Cassidy, Jeb Wallace-Brodeur

*Gray Watkins on **Freudian Slip** (5.9). Photo by Jesse Williams.*

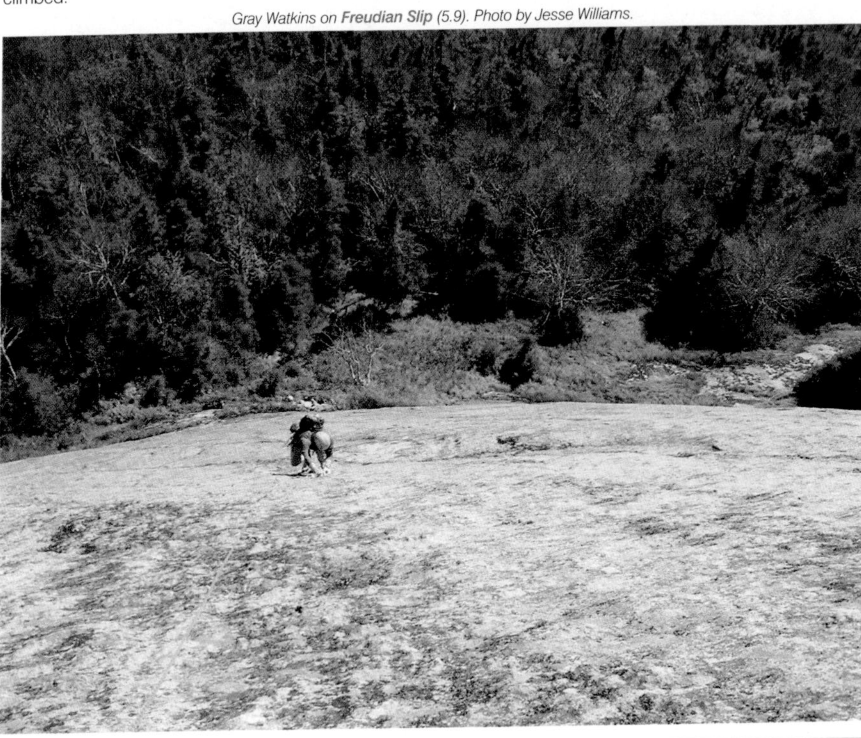

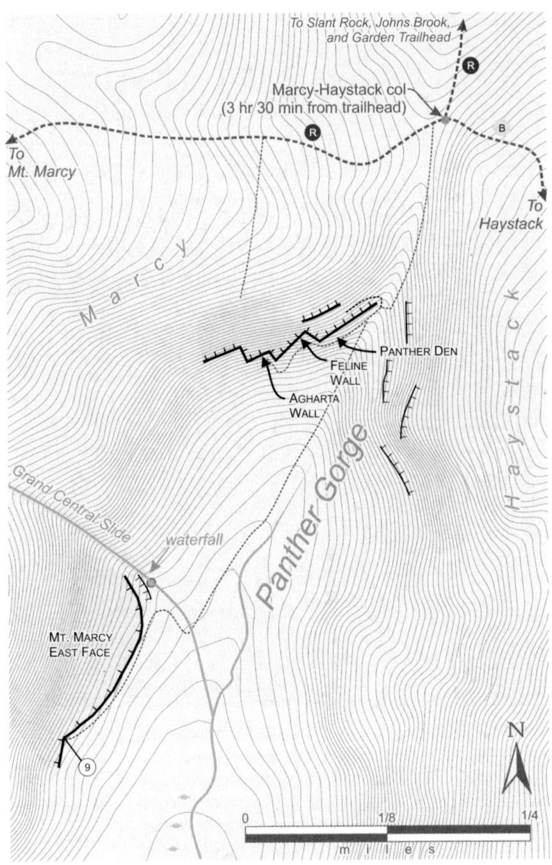

3 Freudian Slip
5.9 G 200' ★★★★

A direct line up the cleanest strip of rock on Big Slide. Always entertaining but never tedious. The initial runout can be protected at a 1" horizontal crack at the start of **Slide Rules**.

Start: 50' right of the open rock at the low point of the cliff, on a fern-covered ledge 30' beneath the first bolt.

● **P1 5.9 G:** Work up and left to the first bolt, then straight up the face. After a few scaly flakes, the quality of the climbing improves, and remains sustained until just below the fixed anchor at a traverse dike. 140'

● **P2 5.8 G:** Straight up steeper and well-featured rock to a fixed anchor that is shared with P2 of **Slide Rules**. 60'

Descent: Rappel **Slide Rules**.

FA 1988, Ed Palen, Joe Seftel

4 Slide Rules 5.7 R 280' ★★

A run-out route, with fragile flakes for the first 60' of the climb.

Start: Same as **Freudian Slip**.

● **P1 5.7 R:** Go up and right on low-angle rock to a horizontal crack 15' up. Trend right on crumbly flakes to the first bolt 50' up. Continue up and right (with improving rock quality) to the second bolt. Angle back left following a left-leaning dike to a fixed belay on a narrow ledge. 120'

● **P2 5.7 PG:** Pull over a bulge to a left-arching crack. (V1) Go left to a beautiful left-leaning dike that converges with the featured face on P2 of **Freudian Slip**. 90'

P3 5.7 PG: Seldom climbed. Move up and right, then straight up on dirty, lichen-covered rock to gain the right-facing, right-leaning corner. Follow the corner to the trees. 70'

V1 Surf and Turf 5.7 X: Head out and right onto unprotected slabs, then straight up to the top. This variation adds a considerable amount of climbing and adventure to the route.

Gear: A few pieces to 1.5" are recommended.

Descent: From the top of P2, you can descend the route by two rappels with a single 60-m rope, angling right on the final rappel.

FA 1980, Andy Helms, Don Mellor

Pen and ink by Tad Welch.

MT MARCY

Location	High Peaks Wilderness Area, accessed from the Garden Trailhead
Summary	The highest peak in New York State with climbing low on its eastern side in the dramatic Panther Gorge.

-5.6	5.7	5.8	5.9	5.10	5.11	5.12	5.13+	total
2	1	3	3	1				10

It's fitting that the highest mountain in the Adirondacks guards the most remote climbing in the High Peaks. Panther Gorge is a cirque that sits between Mt Marcy and Haystack Mountain, two peaks that are well above tree line and 8 miles from the trailhead. The approach is a long one; however, the hiking trail is gradual, and the bushwhack to the first cliff is only 30 min long.

The rock is knobby anorthosite picked clean by nature's gale forces, and the cliffs are surprisingly devoid of loose rock. Despite being below tree line, and somewhat protected, these cliffs are not the place to go in declining conditions.

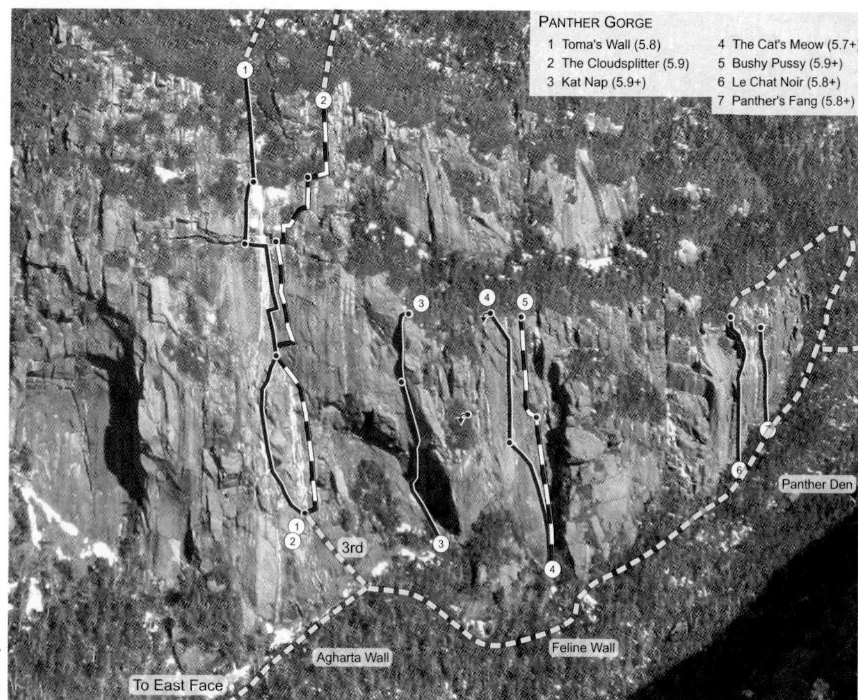

Photo by Drew Haas.

DIRECTIONS **(MAP PAGE 497)**

Two approaches are possible, from Elk Lake and from Keene Valley. Although the approach from Elk Lake passes the outlet stream (and lean-to) from Panther Gorge, this approach is very long, and the added bushwhack up into the cirque through beaver ponds makes this option suitable only for multiday outings. A shorter approach and an easier bushwhack can be made by hiking down the head of the cirque from the Haystack-Marcy col.

Park at the Garden Trailhead (page 426). From the parking area (0.0 mile, 0 hr 0 min), hike the Phelps Trail past Johns Brook Lodge (3.5 miles), Bushnell Falls (5.0 miles), and Slant Rock (6.8 miles). Continue past Slant Rock, following signs for Mt Marcy, to the Range Trail at 7.8 miles. This intersection is just below the Haystack Mountain–Mt Marcy col and is reached at 3 hr 30 min. Continue on the trail toward Mt Marcy for 100' to reach the col proper. As the trail veers toward the right 587600,4885381, go straight (south) and begin the bushwhack down into Panther Gorge. A faint path leads gently downhill, staying in the middle of the drainage area, and crosses many moss-covered boulders. After 20 min of bushwhacking, you will start to see cliffs on both the Haystack and Marcy sides. Leave the middle of the drainage area, and make a rising (skier's) right traverse (west) to reach the Panther Den at its right end 587516,4885086, 4 hr from the trailhead. The last bit involves difficult bushwhacking, but improves greatly once you reach the base of the cliff.

Mt Marcy

PANTHER GORGE

Aspect	South
Height	500'
Quality	★★★
Approach	4 hr, difficult
Summary	A steep single-pitch cliff and two low-angle, multipitch cliffs in a large cirque with good potential for new routes.

-5.6	5.7	5.8	5.9	5.10	5.11	5.12	5.13+	total
	1	3	3	1				8

Three cliff sections are described here, yet many more objectives exist on both the Haystack and Marcy sides of the cirque. On the Mt Marcy side of the cirque is a continuous cliff that is highest at its left end. Three deep left-facing corners, which are hundreds of feet tall and sheer, break the cliff into sections: Agharta Wall, Feline Wall, and Panther Den. When you descend into the cirque from the Haystack-Marcy col, the first cliff section encountered, Panther Den, is a sheer 120' wall on the Marcy side (right). A prominent right-facing corner at the right end (near the start of **Puma Concolor**) is a landmark for locating this section. The next section located downhill and left is the low-angle Feline Wall, with its tall left-facing wall on the right side. 10 min further down and left is Agharta Wall, which has a low bulge below a smooth upper face, and an impressive full-length left-facing wall on its right side.

HISTORY

The first to consider rock climbing in Panther Gorge was Jim Goodwin, who, in the summer of 1936, guided two twelve-year-old boys on a rock climb in the gorge. The exact location isn't known, but Goodwin wrote that he began below the highest section of rock and took several tries to overcome the lower obstacles. Above, he climbed from ledge to ledge with "impressive exposure."[13] This ascent, an adventure Goodwin later recalled as foolhardy, was done before he knew anything about piton craft or proper belaying technique.

The next ascent was done around the time of Trudy Healy's first guidebook in 1965 on a section of rock known as the Panther Den. Craig Patterson and Ronald Dubay's line, **Panther's Fang**, follows a vertical crack up a sheer cliff and was the only reported route in the cirque prior to 2003.

Bill Schneider spent the summers of 2003 and 2004 climbing routes on three separate sections of cliff in the cirque. These were long day trips, spent with local climbers Adam Crofoot, Nic Gladd, Chad Kennedy, and Colin Loher.

13 James A. Goodwin, "Rock Climbing in the Adirondacks," in *The Adirondack High Peaks and the Forty Sixers,* ed. Grace Hudowalski (1970), pp. 142–43.

Agharta Wall

From the streambed that leads up to Feline Wall, hike left for 10 min, going downhill and beneath a 100'-tall slab, then uphill a short distance to grass-covered slopes beneath a tall cliff that bulges at its base. Most of the cliff is less than vertical and has a sheer left-facing wall on the right side. The routes follow the watercourse (where the route **Agharta** forms in winter); have the potential to be wet; and ascend clean, water-worn rock.

DESCENT OPTIONS

It's advisable to carry your pack up this route and hike out of the cirque to the Phelps Trail. The bushwhack from the top begins in tight vegetation but soon opens up as the trees become taller. Don't climb uphill; instead, traverse to the right (north) until you reach the Phelps Trail, about 20 min from the top of the cliff. Turn right and hike down the trail for 10 min to the Haystack-Marcy col.

1 Toma's Wall 5.8 PG 580' ★★★

Ascends the left side of a low black buttress and then follows the watercourse of the winter route **Agharta**. It is named in memory of Toma Vracarich, who died in the massive avalanche on the Angel Slide of Wright Peak on Feb 19, 2000.

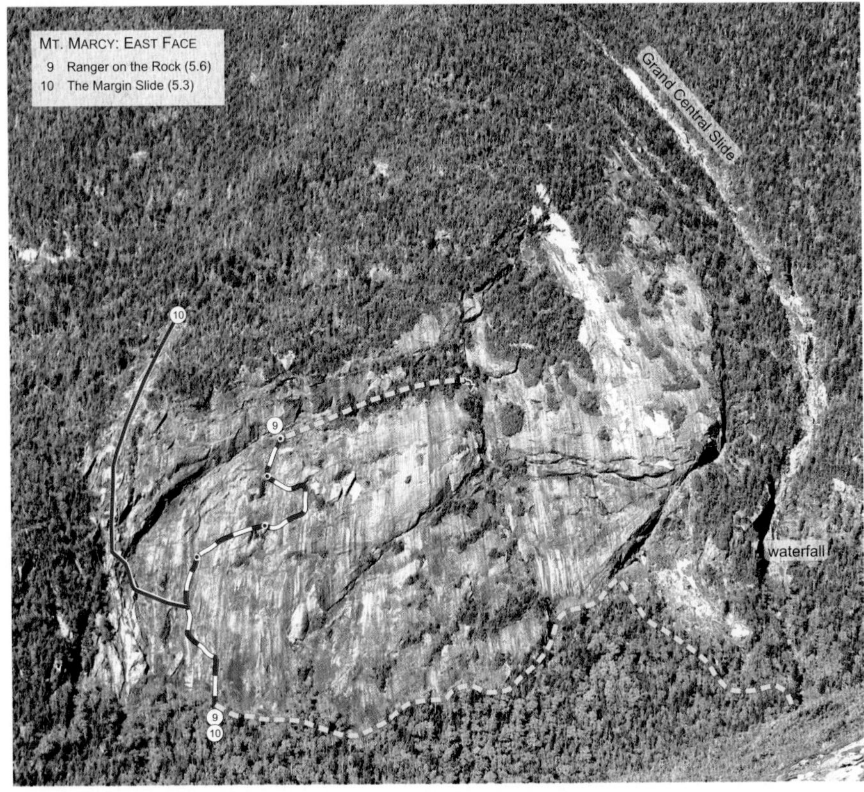

Photo by Kevin "MudRat" MacKenzie.

Start: From the grassy slopes at the base of the wall, scramble up easy 3rd-class rock to a stance beneath a 100'-tall black buttress that is down from and left of the tallest section of the cliff.
P1 5.7 G: Go up a left-rising chimney-slot on the left side of the buttress. The slot steepens and becomes a handcrack through a bulge; above this, follow a right-rising crack to a ledge at the top of the buttress and below a low-angle face with three vertical cracks. 150'
P2 5.8 PG: Start up the centermost crack, then move right and climb a left-rising crack in a left-facing corner, past a steep wall, to a ledge. Traverse left on the ledge to belay at a right-facing wall. 190'
P3 5.7 PG: Break through the steep wall above the belay at a right-facing corner, then go up a slab to a tree belay. 140'
P4 4th class: Go left and climb easy rock to the top of the cliff. 100'
FA 2003, Bill Schneider, Chad Kennedy

2 The Cloudsplitter 5.9 G 600' ★★★

Start: Same as Toma's Wall.
P1 5.8 PG: Go right and up a short vertical crack to a slab, then up and right across the slab to the base of a steep wall between opposing corners. Up the left-facing corner, then up a right-facing corner to easy rock on top of the buttress. Belay below a low-angle face with three vertical cracks (same as Toma's Wall). 150'
P2 5.9 G: Start in the centermost crack, with a short left-facing corner at its bottom. Go up the crack 5', then traverse 20' right to a crack in a left-facing corner. Follow the crack past a steep step (crux), then up a knob-covered wall to a ledge beneath a 30'-tall wall. 170'
P3 5.8 PG: Go to the right end of the ledge, then up broken rock on the right side of the vertical wall. Traverse right through a bush to a slab. Up the slab, then move right to a ledge beneath a clean, steep wall. Go up a vertical crack in the steep wall, then move right past flared cracks to the trees. 180'
P4 4th class: Go right and up a short slab to the trees at the top of the cliff. 100'
FA 2003, Bill Schneider, Nic Gladd

3 Kat Nap 5.9+ PG 280'

Start: At the huge left-facing dihedral that separates the Agharta Wall and Feline Wall.
P1 5.9+ PG: Up a left-leaning crack to a small left-facing corner, then up to a grassy ledge at the base of the main corner system. Follow the main corner system to a belay on a good ledge. 230'
P2 5.8 G: Continue up the corner system to a spruce ledge at its top. 50'
Descent: Rappel the left side of the Feline Wall.
FA Sep 19, 2009, Josh Josten, Conor Murphy, Andrea Hoffman

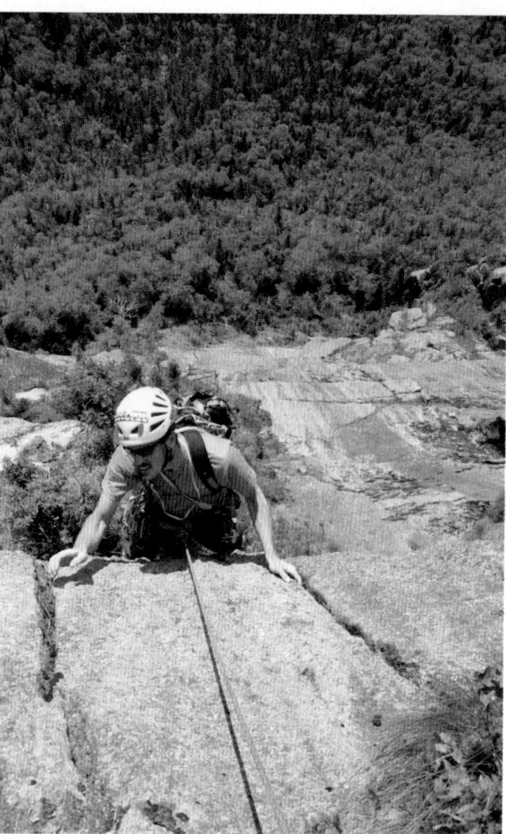

*Bill Schneider follows P3 (5.8) of **The Cloudsplitter** (5.9).*

Feline Wall

From the left end of Panther Den, hike left for 5 min, going downhill and around a small buttress, to a small streambed. Hike 100' up the streambed to a short, dirty slab beneath the start of The Cat's Meow.

DESCENT OPTIONS

Make two long rappels from trees on the left side of the cliff with two 60-m ropes.

4 The Cat's Meow 5.7+ G 380' ★★★

This route has secure climbing on a clean, knob-covered slab with some run-out sections on P1.
Start: Go up and right around the dirty slab to a belay.
P1 5.7 PG: Up and left across slabs to a belay at a vertical crack that is down from and right of stepped ceilings. 190'
P2 5.7+ G: Up the vertical crack that leads toward the left end of a left-facing, left-rising corner. Go over the corner (crux), then continue up cracks that are right of the vegetation. Belay from shrubs on the left side of the cliff. 190'
FA 2003, Bill Schneider, Adam Crofoot, Nic Gladd

5 Bushy Pussy 5.9+ G 640'

On the Feline wall, this route has clean rock and a well-protected crux.

Start: Same as for The Cat's Meow; go up and around the dirty slab to a belay beneath the right side of the tall, low-angled wall.

P1 5.8 PG: Go up vertical cracks on the low-angled wall, stay left of a tall shrub-filled depression, and move slightly right toward an arête at the edge of the wall. Make a tricky slab move, then work up and left to a belay beneath a steep wall with two vertical cracks. 180'

P2 5.9+ G: Climb the crack on the left side of the steep wall (crux), then continue up easier cracks and slabs to the left of some vegetation. Belay from trees at the top of the wall. 160'

P3 3rd class: Bushwhack up and right (northeast) toward a low-angled cliffband with a shrub-filled gully. Go up the gully to the end of the technical climbing. 300'

Descent: From the top of the gully, bushwhack steeply uphill and heading north. Continuing north, the slope and bushwhacking ease, and the Phelps Trail is reached 15 min from the top of the gully.

FA Jul 4, 2010, Mark Toso, Willow Toso

Panther Den

This is the first crag you reach on the approach. It is vertical for nearly 100' and has a base that slopes downhill to the left. It is bounded on its left end by a shallow left-facing corner (the route Le Chat Noir) and a deep right-facing corner on the right end (next to Puma Concolor).

DESCENT OPTIONS

Walk right (northeast) around the top of the cliff.

6 Le Chat Noir 5.8+ G 120' ★★★

A continuous crack and the longest route on this section of cliff.

Start: Begin beneath the shallow left-facing corner marked by a wet spot at its base.

P1 5.8+ G: Up the corner, which leans toward the right and becomes a flared chimney at its top. 120'

FA 2003, Bill Schneider, Adam Crofoot, Nic Gladd

7 Panther's Fang 5.8+ G 110' ★★★★

A plumb line and a stout climb.

Start: Beneath the leftmost of two vertical cracks that have a moss strip between them and are left of a stepped ledge that begins 15' up.

P1 5.8+ G: Up a vertical seam, which widens to 3" and goes past the right end of an overhang 90' up. 110'

FA 1965, Craig Patterson, Ronald Dubay

8 Puma Concolor 5.10a G 90' ★★★

Start: At the base of the prominent 6'-deep right-facing corner on the right side of the cliff.

P1 5.10a G: 8' right of the deep right-facing corner is a blocky left-facing flake. Climb the flake to a narrow ledge. Move up and left to twin vertical fingercracks. Go up the cracks (crux), then traverse right to a wide crack and follow it to the top. 90'

FA 2004, Colin Loher, Bill Schneider

Mt Marcy

EAST FACE

Aspect	Southeast
Height	500'
Quality	★★
Approach	4 hr 30 min, difficult
Summary	Most remote, multi-pitch slab in the park.

-5.6	5.7	5.8	5.9	5.10	5.11	5.12	5.13+	total
2								2

This wide slide is lower in Panther Gorge on the lower east face of Mt Marcy. The views of Mt Haystack and the valley below the Feline and Agharta Walls rate high among the most dramatic views in the High Peaks. The approach is difficult involving substantial bushwhacking over varied terrain.

The slab is capped by a short, right-arching, vertical wall, and bisected in the middle by a tree-filled gully.

DIRECTIONS (MAP PAGE 497)

From Panther Den, bushwhack southwest down to the bottom of the gorge. Take care of the boulder fields; the voids between the moss-covered rock can be substantial. Continue southwest toward the East Face as the terrain becomes more level. Keep an eye out for the drainage from the Grand Central Slide. Cross the drainage and follow it upward towards a spectacular waterfall at a large right-leaning cleft in the cliff. Exit the drainage a few hundred feet before the waterfall to avoid a debris field at the lower right corner of the East Face.

9 Ranger on the Rock 5.6 R 535' ★★

The first pitch features friction climbing up excellent rock to and beyond a small rising corner. Subsequent pitches traverse partway across the slab and up to the cliff band at the top.

Start: Traverse left easily along the bottom of the face to the start of the route 586987,4884408, about 110' from the left end of the slide (where the slab transitions from smooth to blocky).

P1 5.3 PG: Go up easy slab for 80'. Traverse left 20' to a small, vegetated, left-leaning, right-facing corner. Step left around the corner and follow it up until its end (less vegetated toward the top). Climb 30' up and slightly right over small overlaps to an edge with good protection. 210'

P2 5.3 G: Traverse right and up over more small overlaps toward a tree island with a large dead, loose tree. The face becomes more featured on approach to the island. 100'

P3 5.6 R: From the opposite side of the tree island, traverse right to the beginning of a sloping ledge with small evergreens on the far side. The best quality rock is away from the trees. Climb the face up to the base of a large overlap (first good protection). Traverse left to another tree island. 165'

P4 5.3 R: Climb up the face and into the grass to the base of the right-arching cliff band. 60'

Descent: Walk right along the base of the right-arching cliff band, initially through grass, then through trees, to reach a tree-filled gully that splits the face. Six rappels return to the base.

History: A 2009 bushwhack up Marcy via Grand Central Slide led MudRat and friends to a series of long day-trips to the East Face. In August of 2013 they circumnavigated the East Face, and then returned two weeks later for this route. Most of P1 was first climbed during the circumnavigation with local Forest Ranger Scott van Laer, hence the name.[14]

FA (P1) Aug 24, 2013, Kevin "MudRat" MacKenzie, Forest Ranger Scott van Laer

FA (complete) Sep 6, 2013, Anthony Seidita, Kevin "MudRat" MacKenzie

10 The Margin Slide 5.3 R 650'

This is the slide on the left margin of the East Face.

Route Description: Climb P1 of Ranger on the Rock for 100' to the left-leaning, right-facing corner. Step left around the corner and go up and left under the topmost tree island on the left-hand side of the face. The rock gets dirtier on approach to the slide. Climb over a 5'-tall corner to gain the slide proper. Continue up through ledges at a break in the right-arching cliff that caps the slab, then straight up the slide, (mostly 4th class) to the top.

FA May 12, 2012, Kevin "MudRat" MacKenzie, Greg Kadlecik

*Anthony Seidita soloing **Ranger on the Rock** (5.6). The Agharta and Feline Walls are in the background. Photo by Kevin "MudRat" MacKenzie.*

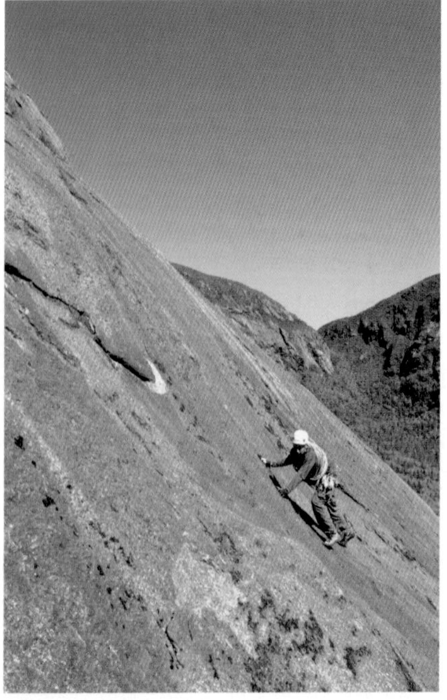

14 Kevin MacKenzie, "A New Route on Mt Marcy: Ranger on the Rock", *Adirondack Life* (May-June 2014), p. 12–15.

PORTER MOUNTAIN

Location	High Peaks Wilderness Area, accessed from the Garden Trailhead
Aspect	Southeast
Height	400'
Quality	★★
Approach	1 hr 30 min, difficult
Summary	Large, remote cliff with generally clean rock that has terrific friction properties; horribly overgrown at the base.

-5.6	5.7	5.8	5.9	5.10	5.11	5.12	5.13+	total
3	2	3						8

The cliff on the east end of Porter Mountain is distinctly visible as you look northwest from the center of Keene Valley. Porter has had the reputation of being a dirty, remote cliff with a long approach and poor documentation. The approach is indeed long, and the final bit of bushwhacking is horrible, but the reward is clean, slabby rock with long spans of highly textured, dimpled rock and generally poor protection. The face is 0.5 mile wide, and the new-route possibilities are numerous.

The most obvious feature on the cliff is the prominent left-facing, left-leaning corner 200' up; this is the **Goodwin-Eastman Route**. The **Goodwin-Stanley Route** begins at the other prominent feature, the large left-facing corner on the right side of the cliff. The base of the cliff is not obscured by trees, so finding your route isn't a problem. Rather, the base is covered in downward-pointing shrubs and prickly raspberry bushes. Traversing along the base of the cliff is . . . well, awful. Perhaps the best time to visit is early spring before these nuisance plants have taken hold.

HISTORY

In the early 1930s, Jim Goodwin was developing an enthusiasm for rock climbing, mostly with his young friends, who included Edward Stanley, Bob Notman, and Jimmy McClelland. Stanley became his best companion for such adventures and, at the age of 16, accompanied Goodwin on their climb up Porter in 1935. This turned into an epic, as this was before Goodwin knew much about protection, and, at the critical moment, it began to rain. Despite climbing later in the Rockies and as an instructor for the Tenth Mountain Division, Goodwin considered this his most difficult rock-climbing achievement.

The second route was climbed 45 years later by Jim Goodwin's son Tony, who, with Todd Eastman, attacked the most challenging feature of the face, the large left-leaning, left-facing corner in the top center. The prolific explorers Butch and Jeanne Kinnon climbed a route here in 1988, taking a line between the two Goodwin routes.

More recently, Ed Palen has explored the right side of the cliff but lost interest due to the awful bushwhacking along the base. Bob Hall and Sheila Matz explored the lower section of the slab left of the Goodwin-Eastman corner, reporting clean, unprotected rock in the 5.6–5.8 range.

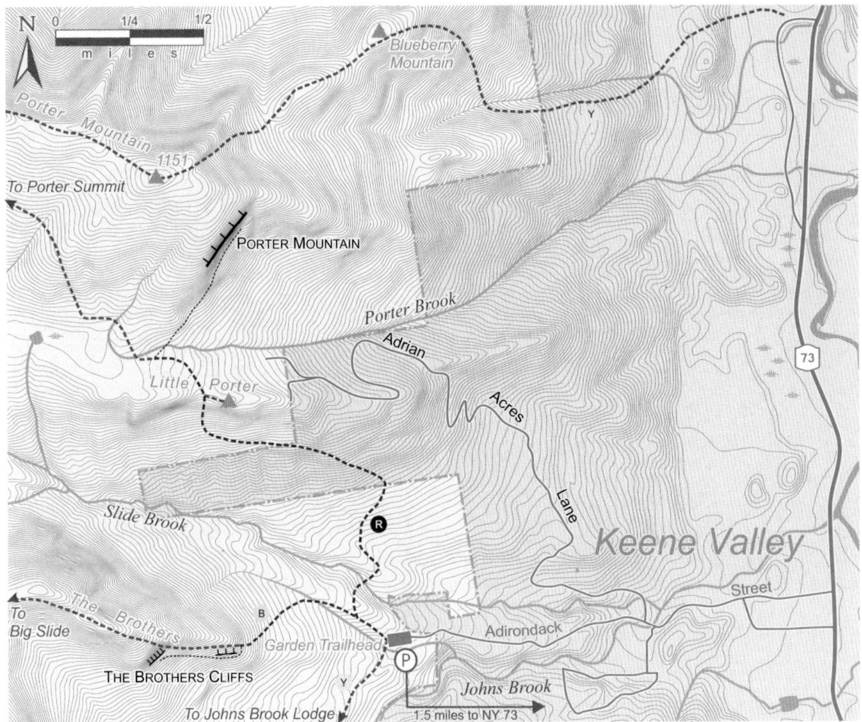

DIRECTIONS **(MAP PAGE 503)**

Park at the Garden Trailhead (page 426) outside of Keene Valley. From the parking lot (0.0), follow the trail for The Brothers and Big Slide (blue markers) to an intersection with the Porter Mountain Trail at 0.2 mile. Turn right and follow the trail (red markers) uphill to the intersection with the Little Porter Trail at 1.8 miles. The summit of Little Porter is 60' to the right and offers excellent views of the cliff. (This spur trail is the old trail up Porter, since redirected because of the private development off Adrian Acres Lane.)

From the intersection, continue toward Porter for 5 min to a flat section with a stream that runs parallel to the trail 20' to the right. There is a small cairn here 593398,4895156. Leave the trail and bushwhack right, following the contour, about 15 min to the base of the cliff 593658,4895634. The going here is rough with tight vegetation.

1 Porter Party 5.8 PG (5.2 X) 365' ★★★

Start: 75' left of the exposed right-rising ramp covered with prickly raspberry and blueberry bushes that marks the approach to the start of the **Goodwin–Eastman Route**, at a right-rising vegetated corner, the left edge of a clean steep slab.

P1 5.2 X: Up bushes in corner for 30', then step out right on good holds and ledges. Belay on the highest ledge. 75'

P2 5.5 PG: Aim for a small, left-rising overlap about 50' up. Up slab past a bolt, then angle left to a second bolt below a small right-facing corner. Gear belay above on a 10"-deep ledge. 125'

P3 5.8 PG: Up black fracture to headwall and a puzzling overlap (crux, bolt). Aim up and slightly right on a long easy run-out to second headwall; break through overlap with good gear to a tree belay. 165'

FA Jul 19, 2009, Don Mellor, Anne Minor

2 Goodwin-Eastman Route 5.8 G (5.7 R) 390' ★★★

Excellent climbing on clean rock with a dramatic corner finish. An excellent outing.

Start: In the center of the cliff is a large left-facing, left-leaning corner that starts 200' up. This corner is visible from various positions along the base of the cliff. Below the corner is an exposed right-rising ramp covered with prickly raspberry and blueberry bushes. Ascend this ramp for 100' to a cluster of birch trees below a broken 200'-high left-facing corner system, 15' right of some flakes stacked 20' high against the face.

P1 5.7 R: Step left onto the face and traverse left to the stacked flakes. Up the stacked flakes, then up a right-facing flake to its top. Traverse right on the face, then follow good holds with no protection up and left to a lone flake that forms a left-facing corner (3" cam). Continue straight up the face, then angle right to the large black left-facing, left-arching corner. Up the corner until you can break right around the corner on hidden holds

*Mark Meschinelli on the **Goodwin-Eastman Route** (5.8). Photo by Dave Hough.*

to a slab of textured dimpled rock. Traverse straight right 25' to the base of the huge left-facing, left-leaning corner that dominates the upper part of the face. 190'

P2 5.8 G: Climb the left-leaning corner through an overlap to where the corner turns vertical (optional belay may reduce rope drag). Up the corner through a crumbly section (crux), then break right into vegetation. Step right onto a slab and follow it to the trees. 200'

Descent: Scramble down and right 30' to a fixed anchor on a pine tree. A rightward rappel of 200' leads to another pine tree with a fixed anchor. The next rappel is 200' and leads down past the ramp to the base of the face.

History: Tony Goodwin originally explored the line with Dick Erenstone in 1979, getting up to the crux high in the corner before turning back. He returned the following year with Todd Eastman to complete the route.

FA 1980, Todd Eastman, Tony Goodwin

3 We Should Have Taken a Left 5.7 G 515'

The name comes from a navigation error on the descent. On the first ascent, a nub of rock broke on the P1 slab, which could have changed the rating of that pitch.

Start: 45' right of the start of the right-rising ramp that leads to the base of the **Goodwin-Eastman Route**.

P1 5.7 G: Climb disconnected cracks to a slab below the tree ledge. Climb the slab (crux), step left near the top, and climb up to belay at a birch on a tree ledge. 145'

P2: Move the belay to the right end of the tree ledge. Climb over right to a left-facing corner. Up the corner and crack above, then climb right to a tree belay. 190'

P3: Diagonal up left past flakes and small ledges, heading for the left-facing break at the top of the face, about 10' right of the right-facing corner at the top of the face. Climb through the left-facing break at the top and diagonal right across the slab (no protection) to a good pine tree belay. 80'

P4: Climb straight up low-angle slab above the belay to an overlap. Climb through the overlap at a break above. Climb the slab above past the left side of a tree island, then continue up the slab to a belay at the top. 100'

FA Jul 2, 1988, Butch Kinnon, Jeanne Kinnon

4 Mellor–Hyson 5.8 R 620' ★★★

Ascends a direct line between the lowest and highest points on the cliff.

Start: At the low point on the cliff, directly below the right end of the prominent, bushy, right-rising traverse terrace (the one from which the **Goodwin–Eastman Route** begins), at a 5'-high, left-facing flake, below a black roof 40' up.

P1 5.8 R: Climb the unprotected face—slightly right, then back left—to roof alcove and some protection. Break roof, then traverse left to a rising overlap at a prominent right-rising crack (#1 or #2 Camalot). Up slab, then right to birch clump. 180'

P2 5.6 R: Climb rock right of grassy pasture to belay at steepening wall. 90'

P3 5.5 X: Move right over flake ledges. Then climb 40' of unbelievably pocketed rock on left-rising ramp; no protection until you reach the headwall (#2 Camalot). Traverse left to short right-facing corner, break headwall at crack above, then go up to trees. 190'

P4 5.4 R: Climb black slab to top. 160'

FA Jul 18, 2011, Don Mellor, Chris Hyson

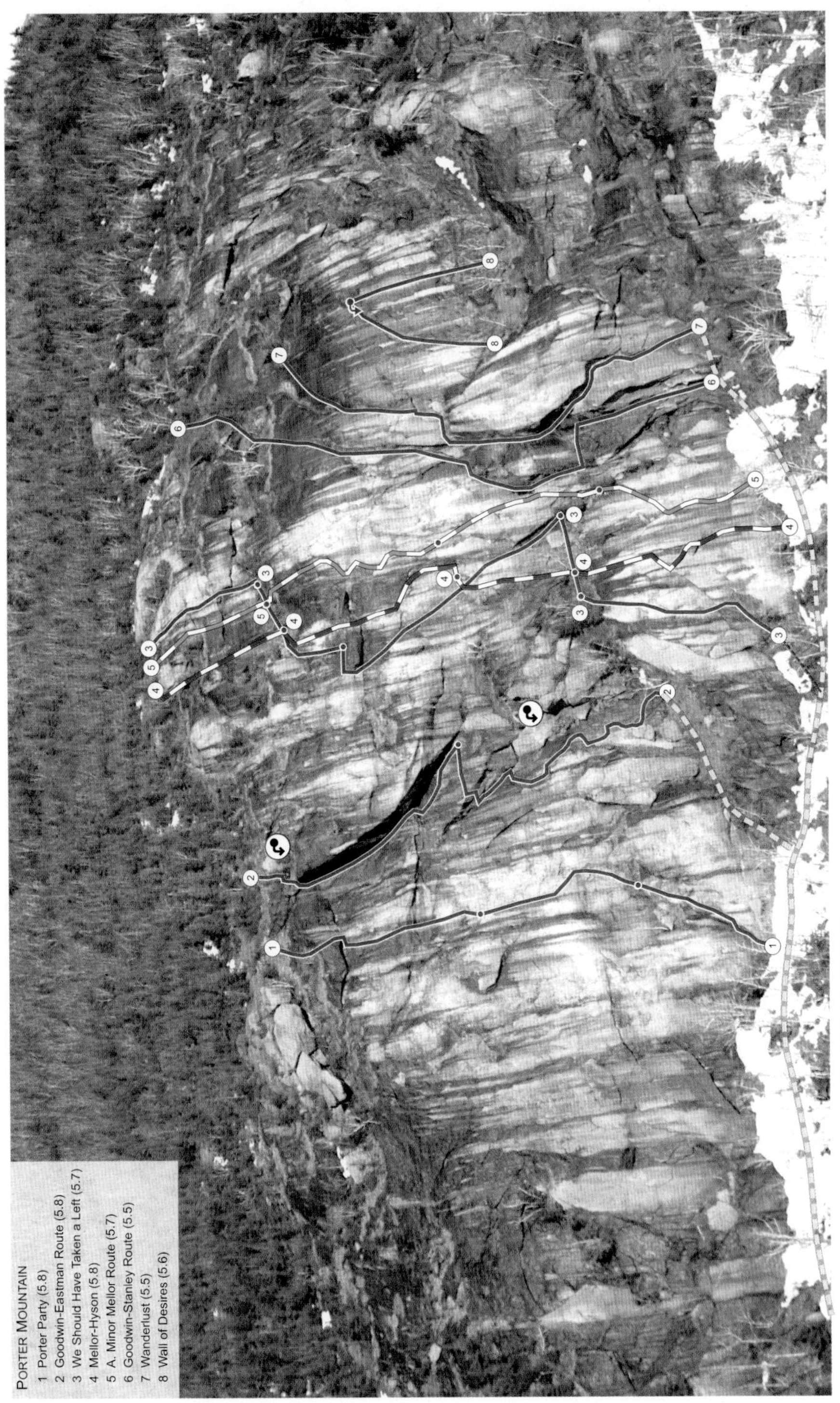
PORTER MOUNTAIN
1 Porter Party (5.8)
2 Goodwin-Eastman Route (5.8)
3 We Should Have Taken a Left (5.7)
4 Mellor-Hyson (5.8)
5 A. Minor Mellor Route (5.7)
6 Goodwin-Stanley Route (5.5)
7 Wanderlust (5.5)
8 Wall of Desires (5.6)

Jim Goodwin's Adirondack Climbs

Jim Goodwin was exposed to the mountains at an early age. As a nine-year-old, he spent his first summer in Keene Valley hiking and exploring, making ascents of various High Peaks with his family, including Marcy, Haystack, and Dix. Because of his familiarity with the trails, three years later, he led his first client up Marcy for $2.00 and became a professional guide. One of his favorite trips was through Panther Gorge, a remote "mini-Yosemite with a spectacular waterfall"—until the 1950 hurricane filled it with debris.

He began technical climbing in 1928, when he made what was then believed to be the first winter ascent of Gothics. This ascent earned him a reputation and led to his introduction to John Case, a well-known European mountaineer who vacationed in Keene Valley. John introduced Jim to technical climbing, first on Sawteeth, then a first ascent on Indian Head, an outcropping above Lower Ausable Lake. Together they tried to make the first ascent of Wallface. After John attempted to overcome an obstacle by standing on Jim's shoulders, they gave up.

With backcountry knowledge and new climbing skills, Jim explored the remote cliffs of the High Peaks. In 1935, he took his friend Ed Stanley, then 15 years old, up the south face of Porter, finishing in the rain on smooth rock and taking tremendous risks—any fall and both would have perished. Later that summer, the pair climbed Gothics (going up the Rainbow Slide and down the North Face), Roaring Brook Falls, and the Colden Slide (beginning just south of the Trap Dike). In 1936, he guided two young boys on a new route in his beloved Panther Gorge. Perhaps most notable was his first winter ascent of the Trap Dike with Ed Stanley in the last days of 1935.

In 1947, Jim started the Adirondack Mountain Club rock-climbing school and invited Fritz Wiessner to serve as an instructor. Fritz loved the challenge of difficult rock climbs, and together they climbed new routes on Rooster Comb and the giant chimney on Pitchoff. His climbing then diminished but resumed when he helped Trudy Healy write the first rock climber's guide to the Adirondacks. Together with Fritz, they repeated many of the old routes for the book. He continued to lead easy climbs and teach rock climbing until he was 70.

- Tony Goodwin

[Authors note: Jim Goodwin was interviewed several times for the first edition of this book. He passed away 2011 at the age of 101.]

5 A. Minor Mellor Route 5.7 R (5.6 X) 515'

There is some really good rock on this high mountain face. And the views (including thirteen 46rs) are as good any in the park. This route holds a direct line to the cliff's high point, running parallel to and about 40' right of **Mellor–Hyson**.

Start: 30' up and right from the cliff's obvious lowest point. The Mellor–Hyson starts just left of this low point.

P1 5.7 R: Face climb up and slightly left to a bolt (25' right of the crux black roof of **Mellor–Hyson**) and up to a right-facing corner. Angle up and right to belay at a pair of balsam firs. 120'

P2 5.6 PG: Climb big blocks and flakes straight up to a faint quartz dike and a bad-stance belay at a left-facing flake (cams to 2") 125'

P3 5.7 R: Weave upward, slightly left at first, to find holds and meager gear, finally breaking the headwall at a little roof 10' right of the obvious right-facing corner–roof. Make a long runout to the trees. This exciting pitch alternates between the good black pocketed rock and the white-yellow to its right. It wouldn't be a good place to try leading for the first time. 170'

P4 5.6 X: Surprisingly good. Aim straight up the middle of the face, breaking a roof about 40' up. This is left of the obvious left-facing corner. Keep the line past another roof to the top. 100'

Descent: Rappel 100' from a good balsam to a tree ledge. Next, 200' to a scarred cedar. Next 170' straight down to base, crossing the **Goodwin–Stanley** traverse.

FA Jul 20, 2012, Don Mellor, Anne Minor

6 Goodwin-Stanley Route 5.5 PG 400'

A written account of this route originally appeared in *Appalachia,*[15] describing features such as a "frowning overhang" and "grassy crack" that have proved difficult to locate. The route described below follows features that roughly match those described in the account, confirmed by Goodwin himself (who is 97 years old at the time of this writing).

Start: On the right side of the cliff below a prominent left-facing corner system. The corner is accessed by scrambling up a right-rising ramp of prickly vegetation.

Route Description: Climb the cracks left of the corner, then up the corner itself until the wall steepens below a chimney. Traverse left to a tree-filled left-facing corner and follow it to its top at a position above the left-facing corner system. Follow a grass-filled crack in a shallow left-facing corner to its top, then friction straight up black rock (crux) to a tree island. Scramble up and right following a line of trees to the top.

History: Being ignorant of piton use, Goodwin and Stanley simply climbed the face with no protection, at one point using a pendulum from a protruding birch to gain better holds. When they got near the top, it started to rain, and, with no retreat possible, Goodwin pressed on past an unprotected friction slab to the top. Stanley was a boy of 16 at the time of this ascent. In Goodwin's memoirs, he writes that he was "negligent for not asking Ed to un-rope. If I had fallen, both of us would have

15 James A. Goodwin, "Climbs in the Adirondacks," *Appalachia* 32 (1938–1939), p. 30.

been killed."[16] Goodwin considered this the toughest technical climb of his career. Stanley returned with John Case to repeat the route but fell on P1 and sustained an injury, leaving the second ascent to Fritz Wiessner.
FA 1935, Jim Goodwin, Edward Stanley

7 Wanderlust 5.5 R 400'

This is a direct start to the **Goodwin-Stanley Route**.
Start: 20' right of the left-facing corner of the **Goodwin-Stanley Route** below a shallow left-facing flake 20' up.
Route Description: Climb up to the left-facing flake, then up into a left-facing corner capped by a ceiling. Traverse left around the ceiling and into a left-facing chimney. Up the chimney, then up a V-groove to the top of the buttress. Step right and climb up to a right-arching overlap, over this, then ascend the face just right of a right-arching corner to some tree islands. Rappel down over **Wall of Desires**.
FA 1993, Ed Palen

8 Wall of Desires 5.6 R 120'

A few exploratory routes have been toproped above a tree ledge on the right side of the cliff. Above this ledge is a shield of excellent, clean, textured, dimpled rock, discovered by Palen when he rappelled **Wanderlust**. An unprotected 5.6 pitch begins on the left side of the ledge and arches up and right to reach a small tree island. The face directly below the tree island has been toproped at 5.8.
FA 1993, Ed Palen

AVALANCHE LAKE

Location	High Peaks Wilderness Area, accessed from the Adirondack Loj Trailhead
Summary	One of the most idyllic climbing locations in the Adirondack Park, with a collection of short routes and some very long mountain routes, including the **Trap Dike**, one of the best alpine scrambles in the Northeast.

-5.6	5.7	5.8	5.9	5.10	5.11	5.12	5.13+	total
3	3	9	10	7	2			34

This stunning locale has long been a favorite of hikers, but only recently has the climbing community embraced it as a destination. The steep walls that bound the narrow lake have beckoned every climber who has set eyes upon them, but up until the mid-1990s, only a handful of routes had been attempted. Old pitons and rotten slings stand as testament to earlier efforts (found during recent "first-ascent" forays), but very little route information has surfaced.

The lake has steep walls on both sides that would make the lake impassable if not for the bridges bolted into the rock above the water, called "Hitch-Up Matildas." As the story goes, in 1868, Matilda Fielding was being carried by Bill Nye across these sections and, as the water became deeper, her husband yelled for her to "hitch up" higher on the guide's back.

The ruggedness of the lake is also what makes the climbing here so special. As you approach from the north, on the left are the steep faces and slabs of Mt Colden that plunge directly into the water, and on the right are the cliffs of Avalanche Mountain that rise very near the hiking trail and, farther down, also drop directly into the water. The lake's orientation makes it easy to follow the sun or shade; simply walk to the other side of the lake to suit your preference. The orientation also makes this a windy spot and sometimes free of black flies even in the thick of the bug season (but don't count on it).

Numerous campsites are available for those seeking to break up the 9 miles (round trip) of walking: Marcy Dam has many sites, as does Avalanche Camp before the pass. There is another tent site at the south end of the lake, 5 min down the trail toward Lake Colden from the outlet bridge. Camping anywhere near the lake is illegal, and the prohibition is strictly enforced.

Avalanche Lake is one of the most popular hiking destinations in the Adirondack Park. It is imperative that climbers keep a low profile here. This means keeping noise levels down and making sure that fixed gear (such as slings on trees) is camouflaged.

HISTORY

Climbing, or perhaps better described as exposed unroped scrambling, began at Avalanche Lake in 1850 with Robert Clarke and Alexander Ralph's first ascent of Mt Colden, which they climbed via the **Trap Dike**. This fantastic feature became a standard outing for those aspiring to a more mountaineering-style approach to an Adirondack summit. More technical variations to the **Trap Dike** were naturally the next to be climbed—the **Wiessner Route** and the **Colden Slide**—although exactly when is uncertain.

Vermont strongman Tim Beaman, shown here in 1997, explored The Fin at Avalanche Lake. Photo by Jim Cunningham.

16 James A. Goodwin, "And Gladly Guide" (privately published memoir), p. 43.

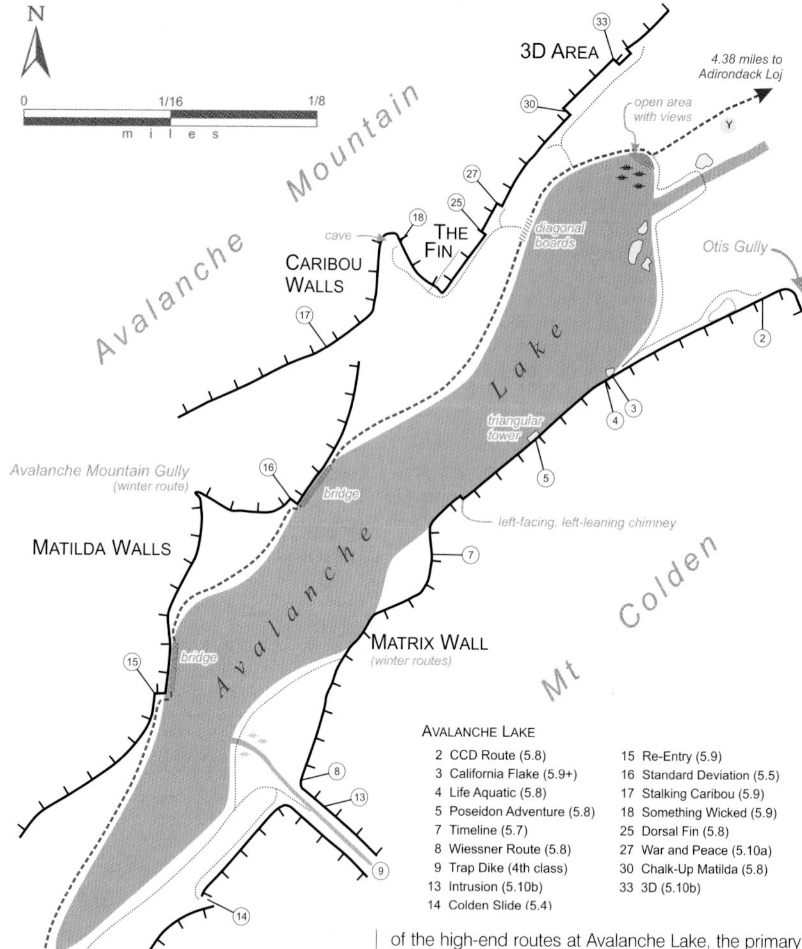

One of the most impressive walls to rise out of the lake is on the east side (on the left as you approach from the Adirondack Loj). This was climbed in 1975 by Robert Lauder and Jeff Vaughan by the route **TV Dinner**, although this feature has since fallen into the lake. Ten years later, in 1985, this wall saw two more routes—**CCD Route** and **Poseidon Adventure**. The face is littered with a chaotic array of very old pitons that tell of earlier explorations that may never be known.

The walls on the west side of the lake (on the right as you approach from the Loj) were first explored in 1984 by Don Mellor, Bill Dodd, and Mark Ippolito with their adventure route **Stalking Caribou**, then again in the late 1980s by Tim Beaman and partners on The Fin. This long wall has been the stage for the majority of the high-end routes at Avalanche Lake, the primary protagonist being Ed Palen. Camping for several days at a time, Palen explored and cleaned many of the best lines at the lake, including **Something Wicked**, **3D**, and **California Flake**, the latter being a 900' technical rock climb.

DIRECTIONS **(MAP PAGE 508)**

Park at the Adirondack Loj Trailhead (page 425) and hike 2.3 miles to Marcy Dam, then continue another 1.1 miles to Avalanche Camp, then another mile to the lake (4.4 miles total). The approach is flat for the most part, except for the last mile, which goes steeply uphill to the pass. Once in the pass, continue gently downhill to a clearing at the north end of the lake 582817,4887438. The approach takes approximately 2 hr.

The outlet at the south end of the lake is another .6 mile and takes about 15–20 min.

An alternative approach is to park at the South Meadow Road and hike the Marcy Dam truck road. This adds 1 mile to the approach but avoids the parking fee and crowds of the Adirondack Loj Trailhead.

Avalanche Lake

AVALANCHE PASS

Aspect	Southeast
Height	60'
Quality	
Approach	1 hr 50 min, moderate
Summary	Small cliff on the trail below a giant slide.

There are several cliffs at the height of the pass just after the avalanche debris, both on the left (the west face of Mt Colden) and on the right. Surprisingly not much has been climbed here.

1 To Pass Or Not To Pass 5.9 X 60'

Start: At the height of the pass, just past the avalanche debris, at a small cliff on the left side of the trail below an obvious zigzag crack 583369,4887847.

P1 5.9 X: Climb the crack to a little bush, traverse right, then head up and slightly left, following the path of least resistance until the bush is straight under you. Unlock the exit sequence (crux) to gain a larger ledge with a system of exit cracks. Belay from the trees. 60'

Descent: Walk off to the left through debris.

FA Jul 11, 2011, Misha Tselman, Boris Itin

Avalanche Lake

WEST FACE OF MT COLDEN (EAST SIDE OF THE LAKE)

Aspect	Northwest
Height	2000'
Quality	★★★★★
Approach	2 hr, moderate
Summary	Long, multi-pitch wall routes and slab climbs on the exposed slide-ridden flanks of Mt Colden.

-5.6	5.7	5.8	5.9	5.10	5.11	5.12	5.13+	total
2	1	4	4	2				13

The steep rock faces of Mt Colden rise above the lake on the east side (on the left when approaching from the Adirondack Loj). To access these routes, from the open area at the north end of the lake, simply follow the shoreline left toward the rock.

Routes will be described starting from the north end of Avalanche Lake on the Mt Colden side, then working clockwise around the lake.

2 CCD Route 5.8 R 390'

From the open area at the north end of the lake, this route is visible high and left on the west face of Colden. Look for a discontinuous crack line that starts near the bottom of the slab and continues up for 400', eventually angling left to end in the tree gully that borders the left side of the slab (Otis Gully).

Start: Walk left from the clearing at the north end of the lake, following the shoreline to a point where the grassy hillside ends and the water begins (the start of California Flake). Follow the grassy slopes left along the base of the cliff for 5 min, crossing some avalanche debris and some raspberry thickets to a large, 20'-high buried boulder up against the cliff. Contour around the boulder, then another 50' to the base of a low-angle slab that is the start of the route. This slab is 20' left of a left-facing, left-arching corner. Just left of the route is a vertical black face and steeper, boulder-strewn terrain that leads into Otis Gully.

P1 5.8: Climb up the slab, angling left into a tree-filled gully, then cut back right to a hanging tree island in a small left-facing corner, which is climbed to gain the start of the crack above. Follow the crack through a bulge in white rock to a belay at a horizontal crack on top of the white rock, just above the right end of a tree island. 70'

P2 5.8 R: Climb the crack above to an overhanging left-facing corner. Step right into the next crack and climb it to its top. Face-climb up to gain another crack, which is followed up to a belay at a sloped ledge. 130'

P3 5.6: Continue in the crack line until it disappears, then run out another 40' of dirty slab to the trees. 190'

Descent: Go left to Otis Gully and make one double-rope rappel.

FA Aug 15, 1985, Dan Costa, David Cason, Kevin Delany

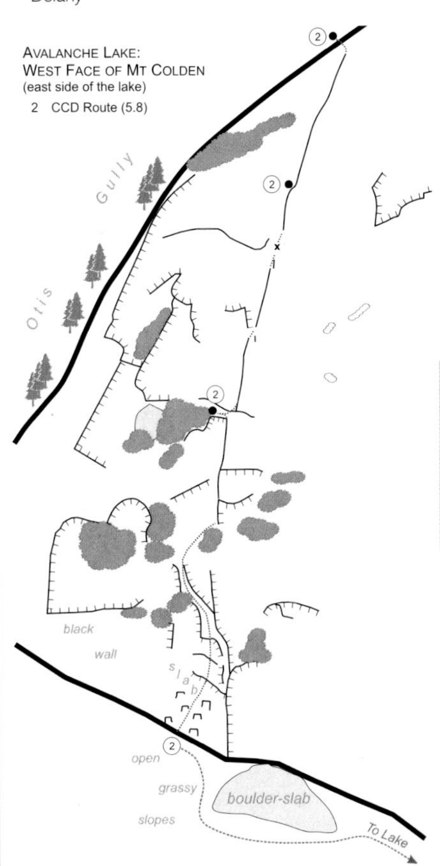

3 California Flake 5.9+ PG 870' ★★★★★

Climbs the right-facing ramps and corners on the sheer left wall as you approach the lake from the north. The lower two pitches climb an enormous flake, the shape of which roughly resembles the state of California, hence the name. P1 and P2 have fantastic climbing and a one-of-a-kind position, although the fixed gear is suspect. In 2012, a large flake fell from under the roof on P2, making this pitch slightly harder.

Start: Walk left from the clearing at the north end of the lake, following the shoreline to a point where the grassy hillside ends and the water begins. There is a large, flat rock just above water level marking the start of the route.

AVALANCHE LAKE: WEST FACE OF MT COLDEN
(east side of the lake)
3 California Flake (5.9+)

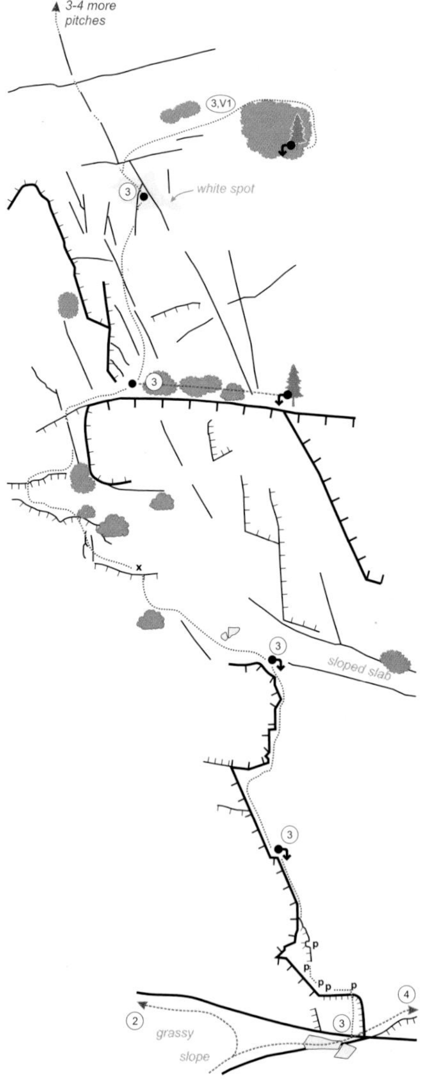

P1 5.9- PG: Climb the face just left of a shallow right-facing corner to a narrow ledge 15' up with a piton. Hand-traverse left to where the ledge meets the narrow right-facing, left-rising ramp; there are two pitons at the base of the ramp. Climb up and left on the ramp 20' (staying well right of the right-facing, dirty off width farther left), then straight up the face to gain a shallow right-facing corner (piton, crux), then up to meet the huge right-facing, left-rising ramp above. Climb up and left on the ramp to an excellent ledge and fixed anchor. 90'

P2 5.9+ G: Continue up the ramp leftward to the top, then up the right-facing corner to the roof. Undercling right (or climb the face just below) to the right end of the roof (crux), then up the right-facing corner above to another ledge and fixed anchor. 90'

P3 5.5 R: Traverse left, then up to a narrow scooped ledge, then continue left to white rock (optional belay higher up in the white rock). Zigzag up the face left of a debris-filled corner, then right around this corner to a huge debris-covered ledge. A rappel station exists in the trees at the right end of the ledge. 180'

P4 5.7 PG: From the left end of the debris-covered ledge, climb the cracks in the white slab to a very white spot (visible from across the lake). Belay in the white spot. 80'

P5–P8 5.3 X: (V1) Wander up the gritty face to the top. Several pitches are required with no gear and good belays at about every 160–180'. 430'

V1 4th class: It is possible to bail off after the white spot. Climb up out of the white spot to a low-angle rock, then traverse right to a large tree island. Walk above the top, then down the right side to a solid tree. A 110' rappel takes you down to the huge debris-covered ledge at the top of P3.

Descent: P1–P3 can be rappelled with a single 200' rope. Above that, two ropes are required to descend tree islands on the right side of the slab back to the top of P3.

Gear: A 4" cam is nice for P1, although small nuts can be arranged.

History: P1 and P2 had been climbed previously and were called **TV Dinner** (so named because Lauder was participating in a diet study involving TV dinners). P1 climbed the manky off-width corner just left of the present line, and a large portion of P2 fell into the lake in the early 1980s, leaving behind a spectacular, clean, Yosemite-like feature. The landslides caused by Hurricane Floyd (Sep 1999) added five to six more pitches of easier climbing on the white slabs above.

FA (portions of P1 and P2, TV Dinner) Jul 26, 1975, Robert Lauder, Jeff Vaughan
FA (complete) Sep, 2004, Ed Palen, Bob Starinsky

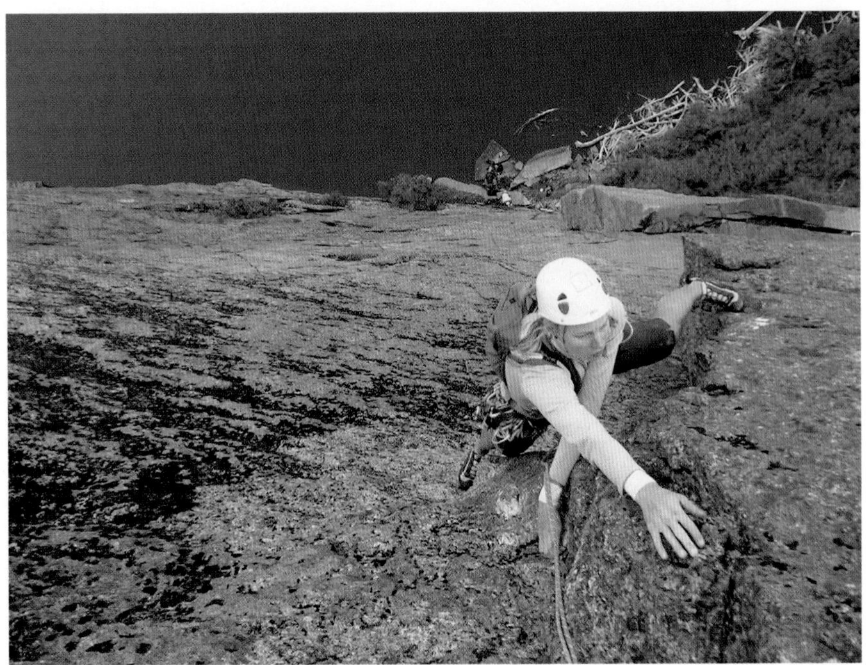

*Emilie Drinkwater on P2 of **California Flake** (5.9+). Photo by Jesse Williams.*

4 Life Aquatic 5.8 R 460' ★

Climbs the sheer wall that plunges into the water on the east side of the lake. It is an adventure route that is recommended only for the competent backcountry climber: it has loose, friable rock; complex route finding; poor gear; and difficult retreat possibilities. The route finishes on the last pitch of **Poseidon Adventure** and shares that route's descent.

Start: From the clearing at the north end of the lake, walk left along the shoreline to its end. This is the base of **California Flake**, marked by a large, flat rock just above water level (formerly a piece of P2). Scramble right from here above the water level on grassy ledges to a 1'-deep ledge with a good belay, 10' above water level. (This point also marks the end of the easy scrambling.)

P1 5.7 PG: Climb up a few feet from the belay, then traverse right and slightly up (passing an ancient ring piton) to the left side of a left-facing corner. Continue traversing right to an extremely fragile 6'-high flake that you can see behind; step down and right around the base of this flake, where some tricky moves farther down and right gain a good crack (crux). Some final moves right gain the Triangle Pillar at its midheight. Climb onto the face of the pillar, then up to belay on its right side just below its top. This is a good pitch and, despite appearances, relatively well protected. 100'

P2 5.7 R: Traverse right from the belay and around a crumbly left-facing, left-arching corner. Climb up to gain the sloped, white-colored ledges, then traverse right and up to a stance at a long left-rising crack. 100'

P3 5.8 R: Traverse right from the belay 30' to the next long left-rising crack and overlap. Make an unprotected move to gain the overlap, then climb up and left following the overlap to a point just above the belay. Climb straight up to break through the overlap, then up easier rock to gain a prominent right-facing corner. Up the corner to the top, then make an exposed move on jugs right to gain the next right-facing corner, which is climbed to the White Block, an alarming car-sized block perched atop the corner. Belay on top of the block. 140'

P4 5.8+ PG: Same as **Poseidon Adventure**: From the belay, step down into the top of the right-facing corner and move 4' right to a mossy jug with good gear. Make a bouldery move up to a stance (5.8 G), then another hard move (5.8 PG) gains a sloped ledge at the base of a right-facing, left-rising corner. Climb up the corner to gain the dirt-filled crack, which is followed to the trees. 120'

Descent: Walk left along a tree slope, passing a short exposed slab, to the ledge at the top of P3 of **California Flake**; look for a tree with a fixed anchor near the end of the ledge. Three 100' rappels reach the ground.

History: The first ascent was an attempt to repeat **Poseidon Adventure**. Ancient pitons were found on P1, evidence of yet other routes on this wall.

FA Sep 18, 2006, Jim Lawyer, Colin Loher

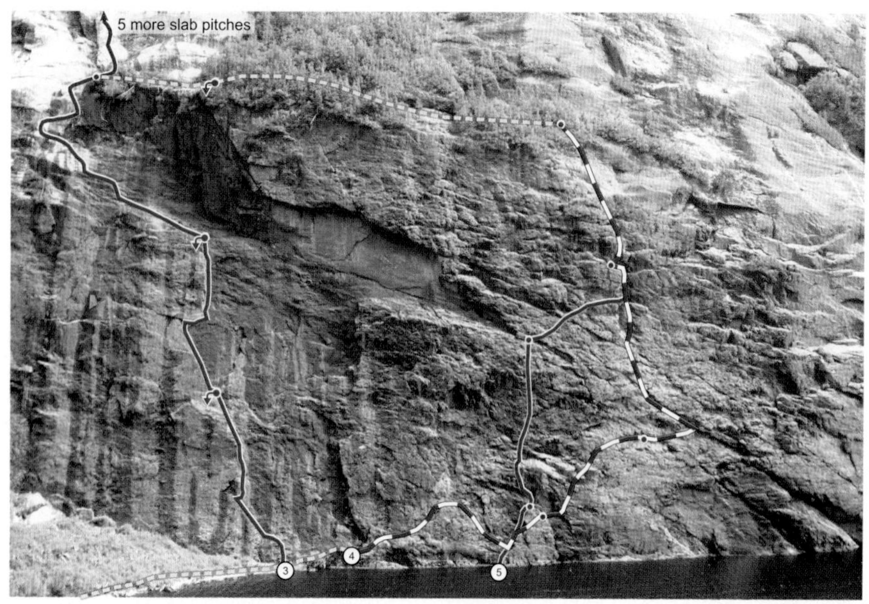

5 Poseidon Adventure 5.8 R 320' ★★

Another route that climbs the sheer wall that plunges into the water on the east side of the lake. An amazing feature of this route is that, from below, it appears black, but from above, it appears white, as the water runoff has polished the tops of all the edges. Be warned: this wall is difficult to navigate, has complex gear and questionable rock, and has a difficult retreat; the second ascent resulted in a new route, despite every effort to link the features described by the first-ascent party. The route begins at the small triangular tower in the center of the face that rises out of the water, known as the Triangle Pillar. On the first ascent, the Triangle Pillar was accessed using an inflatable boat, which was then tied to the rock. Unfortunately, the wind picked up and knocked the boat around, shredding it on the rocks; the route is named for this boating disaster. It is also possible to swim to the Triangle Pillar (perhaps using a dry bag for the gear): there is a ledge on the pillar's left side where you can get out of the water. If you want to stay dry and avoid carrying a boat, climb P1 of **Life Aquatic**.

Start: At the top of the Triangle Pillar, reached by boat, swimming, or climbing P1 of **Life Aquatic**.

P1 5.8 R: The recollection of the first-ascent party was to climb straight up the face from the top of the Triangle Pillar to the Coffin Belay, a coffin-sized block at the right end of the long, sloped ledge that breaks the face under some roofs. 120'

P2 5.8 R: Another nondescript pitch traverses far to the right to gain the right-facing corners, which are climbed to the White Block, an alarming car-sized block perched atop the corner. 80'

P3 5.8+ PG: From the belay, step down into the top of the right-facing corner and move 4' right to a mossy jug with good gear. Make a bouldery move up to a stance (5.8 G), then another hard move (5.8 PG) gains a sloped ledge at the base of a right-facing, left-rising corner. Climb up the corner to gain the dirt-filled crack, which is followed to the trees. 120'

Descent: Walk left along a tree slope, passing a short exposed slab, to the ledge at the top of P3 of **California Flake**; look for a tree with a fixed anchor near the end of the ledge. Three 100' rappels reach the ground.

FA Jul, 1985, Don Mellor, Bill Dodd

*Bill Dodd follows P1 of **Poseidon Adventure** (5.8) on the first ascent. Notice the rubber dinghy. Photo by Don Mellor.*

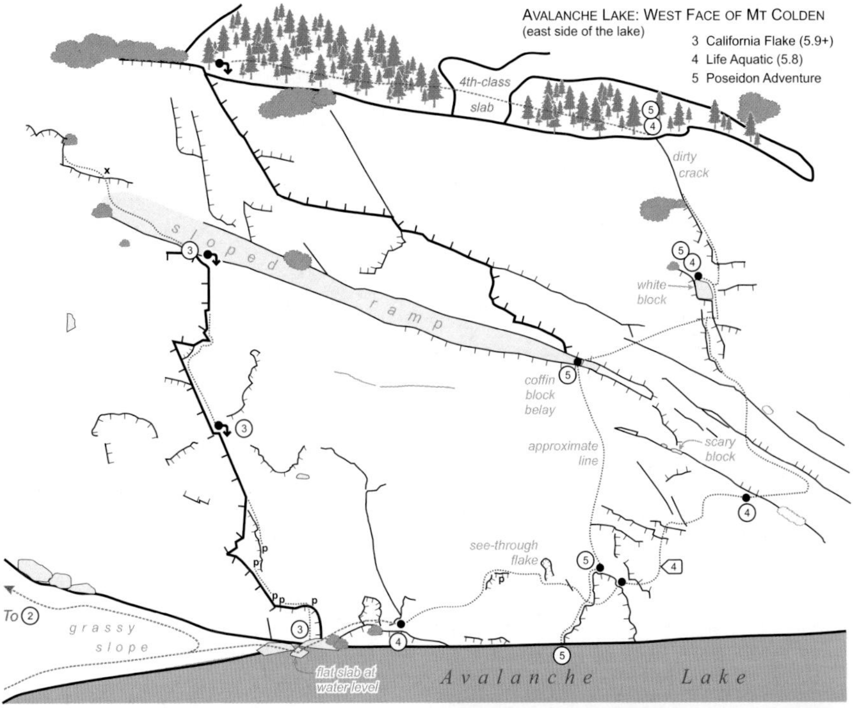

Avalanche Lake: West Face of Mt Colden
(east side of the lake)

3 California Flake (5.9+)
4 Life Aquatic (5.8)
5 Poseidon Adventure

4th-class slab
dirty crack
sloped ramp
white block
coffin block belay
approximate line
scary block
see-through flake
To ②
grassy slope
flat slab at water level
Avalanche Lake

6 Wish You Were Here 5.10a PG 210'

Named in memory of the day, and for climbers who are no longer with us.

Start: Approach as for the Trap Dike and continue (climber's) left along the shore to the Matrix Wall. Wade across (knee deep) to the next tree island (the one with the route **Timeline**, and the winter route **Adirondike**). Begin on the (climber's) left side of the tree island, where the land disappears into the water.

P1 5.10a PG: Walk five feet left on boulders in the water to a faint rib that turns into a small right-facing edge–flake. Up this, step right to a right-leaning crack, then move up to a left-leaning, right-facing flake system. Move up the flake to a thin horizontal crack, traverse 5' left, then move up to a left-leaning fingercrack and follow this 15' to an alcove. Place small cams in a right-rising horizontal, then mantel onto a sloping ledge (crux). Move up and left along a handrail past a small cedar. Face moves lead to a hand- and fist-crack; up this excellent feature for 15' to a ledge with birch trees. 130'

P2 5.6 G: Scramble through the trees to the base of a wide crack. Up the wide crack for 50' (wide gear necessary). At the end of the crack angle up and right 30' to an anchor on cedars. 80'

Descent: Rappel 200' down and right to a cedar, then another short rappel to the start of the route.

FA Sep 11, 2010, Bob Starinsky, Mark Scott

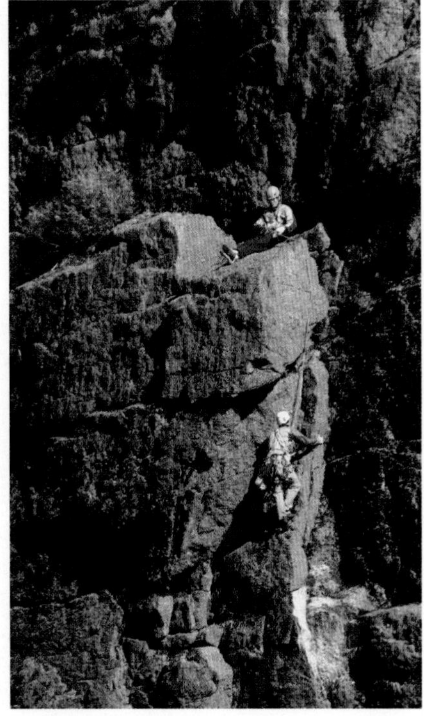

*Colin Loher follows P3 of **Life Aquatic** (5.8) on the first ascent, belayed by Jim Lawyer. Photo by Drew Haas.*

Mt. Colden

North Summit

To Lake Arnold

col

To Lake Colden

upper exit

lower exit

second waterfall

first waterfall

routes 10-13

MATRIX WALL

To Outlet (5 min)

AVALANCHE LAKE: WEST FACE OF MT. COLDEN

8 Wiessner Route (5.8)

9 Trap Dike (4th class)

14 Colden Slide (5.4)

(A) Trap Dike Slide

(B) Colden Slide

7 Timeline 5.7 PG 230'

Climbs a right-facing chimney and corner system on the east side of the lake and makes for a fun adventure. The route begins on the tree "island" that lies on the east side of the lake, about halfway down; this is the only water-locked tree island at Avalanche Lake (the winter route Adirondike begins from the top of this tree island). To access the tree island, you will need to use a boat, swim (walk left from the base of the Trap Dike and swim under the Matrix Wall), or traverse in from the Trap Dike.

Start: At the left end of the tree island is a huge flake that forms a straight-in chimney facing the water. Begin on the flake, 40' above and right of the bottom of the chimney.

P1 5.7 PG: Climb to a stance on top of the flake at 30' (crux). From here, the chimney formed by the flake continues up to the right, and another, larger chimney-cave begins on the main wall. Step across to the main wall and enter the larger, broken chimney-cave and belay above the cave in a large depression. 90'

P2 5.5 PG: Continue in the depression into the huge low-angle, right-facing corner above. Climb the corner to within 10' of its top, then climb up and left out of the corner following a left-rising crack (which is formed by a huge triangular block at the top of the corner) past some loose rocks, finishing at trees to the right. 140'

Descent: Options for descent include (a) rappel from the top or (b) continue the adventure up slabs and tree islands to a point where you can traverse left to California Flake, then rappel that route.

8 Wiessner Route 5.8 G 300'

Start: 20' left of the opening to the Trap Dike, on a ledge with a couple of cedars, below a left-facing corner with a handcrack.

Route Description: Climb up the corner (5.8 G) to the trees at 40'. Continue rightward through trees to the very rim of the Trap Dike, then follow open rock on a narrow strip of slab above the abyss to a point level with the top of the first waterfall, and descend a 4th-class ramp into the dike.

History: The description above was pieced together from various accounts, namely those written by Jim Goodwin in *AdirondacAdirondac*[17] and Trudy Healy in the 1972 printing of her guidebook.[18] Wiessner himself even wrote a description.[19] As unlikely as it seems that Wiessner climbed this particular dirty crack, it is the only possibility that begins left of the opening of the Trap Dike and reenters the dike at a reasonable point higher up, which are details shared by all of the accounts. Regarding the year, all that is known is that it was before 1947.

FA 1947, Fritz Wiessner, Werner Bachli

17 11, no. 2 (Mar–Apr 1947), p. 5.

18 Trudy Healy, *A Climber's Guide to the Adirondacks* (1972).

19 Fritz Wiessner, "Rock Climbing in the Northeast," *IOCA Bulletin*, Intercollegiate Outing Club Association (Winter 1948), p. 46.

9 Trap Dike 4th class 2000' ★★★★★

This feature is a spectacular dike that runs from the lake directly up the northwest face of Mt Colden, splitting the Colden Slide with a deep, steep-walled chimney. The dike leads to a "long slab of scenic splendor"[20] that leads to the very summit of Mt Colden with almost no bushwhacking. In many ways, this is where Adirondack mountaineering began and, incidentally, was also the first ascent of Mt Colden. For most Adirondack climbers, this is their first backcountry introduction to slide climbing. The Trap Dike begins in a deep, rock-walled chasm formed by the erosion of the less resistant dike rock. Tremendous slides ripped down the northwest face of Mt Colden, and one of them, the Colden Slide, poured into the dike, creating a clean route to the very summit of the mountain. A "no bushwhacking" approach and a hiking trail descent add to the popularity of this climb. In 2011, Hurricane Irene swept through with devastating floods that significantly altered the backcountry landscape, including the west face of Mt Colden. A new slide was created from the Mt Colden summit to the upper Trap Dike. The debris scoured the dike, stripping it clean of vegetation and dumping the resultant slurry into a debris cone that extends halfway across Avalanche Lake. Not only did this create a new and most excellent slide climb—the Trap Dike Slide—but it improved the exposed alpine feel of the dike itself, making this modest scramble feel like a big mountain route.

Start: Hike to the south end of the lake to a bridge over the outlet. Cross the bridge and leave the trail, roughly following the shoreline along the Mt Colden side of Avalanche Lake. The herd path enters the woods briefly, passes behind the house-sized boulder perched above the shore, then drops back down to the shore (the site of the old Caribou lean-to, destroyed by a massive slide in September 1942, which temporarily raised the water level of Avalanche Lake by 6'). Continue on the path roughly following the shore to the clean avalanche path, then up a rocky streambed into the dike.

Route Description: The first waterfall (3rd class) is encountered immediately once you enter the steep-walled section of the dike. Above this is a flat section, then a second waterfall (4th class). There are fewer climbing options when the waterfalls are gushing and the footing becomes slick. Consider bringing a 100' section of rope if you have any concerns about your group's ability or the conditions that may be encountered on a wet day. There is no longer any vegetation in the dike, so you'll need gear for anchors atop the waterfalls. There are several popular exits from the dike.

Lower Exit onto Colden Slide: Immediately right of the top of the second waterfall traverse right 50' to a left-facing corner that leads into the 5th-class section of the Colden Slide, at the top of P3 of that route.

Upper Exit onto Colden Slide: Continue up the dike with several 3rd-class slots, most of which you can avoid with short slab scrambles on the left. Approximately 30 min above the second waterfall, the rock walls on either side of the dike lessen in height, and you

20 Ibid.

reach the base of the **Trap Dike Slide**, the clean, white slide that enters from the right. 100' before the slide, leave the dike and bushwhack right for 100' to a 3rd-class step that gains the **Colden Slide**. The upper section of the **Colden Slide** is mostly 2nd-class friction with a few exposed 3rd-class overlaps. Once established on the slide, you can see a boulder on the summit, a nice beacon to aim for. The summit is reached after 45 minutes on the slide.

*Colin O'Connor inspects a dike intrusion on the **Trap Dike** Slide.*

Exit onto Trap Dike Slide: Continue up the dike to the **Trap Dike Slide**, the clean, white slide that enters on the right. The base of the slide has a steep wall with a left-rising crack. Climb this (exposed 3rd class) to clean, white, dimpled rock. Friction up the board slide past several steep bulges to the summit headwall. The headwall (exposed 3rd class) can be wet and sandy, but there is vegetation nearby. From the top, bushwhack 100' up and right to the summit which is reached after 45 min on the slide.

Stay in the Dike: A final option is to stay in the dike drainage. From the base of the Trap Dike Slide, simply bushwhack another 30 min to a notch to meet the hiking trail between Colden and the mini-summit to its northeast.

Descent: Take the hiking trail to Lake Colden (to the right) or Lake Arnold (to the left); most parties make a loop from the Adirondack Loj, up the **Trap Dike**, down to Lake Arnold, then back to the Loj.

History: The first ascent of the dike was described by Clarke in a letter to his mother. In it, he recounts a very full, action-packed day beginning with 9 or so miles of hiking; a thwarted attempt to shoot a deer; the first ascent of the dike, which they climbed in 1 hr 30 min from the south end of the lake; downclimbing the dike; hunting for minerals and filling one of their packs; shooting a deer (and dressing it); then hiking another 4 miles to a camp, where they proceeded to cut a "cord of wood" for the evening fire. All this armed with, among other things, an ax, a rifle, and a brandy bottle they called "the admiral."

FA Jul, 1850, Robert Clarke, Alexander Ralph

Trap Dike Wall, Left Side

The following routes are located in the entrance to the **Trap Dike** on the left side. This is an especially scenic place to climb, but the rock quality is not as good as it appears. A toprope can be set up by scrambling to the top of the first waterfall, then climbing a left-rising ramp (4th class) to gain the open area at the top of the wall.

The walls on the right side of the dike look especially appealing but have no reported routes.

10 Trapped in the Dike 5.9- PG 40' ★

Start: 60' from the left end of the wall (from the entrance to the **Trap Dike**) is a 20'-high black open book. 20' right of this is a 30'-tall blocky broken right-facing corner that ends on a right-rising ledge. 10' right of the blocky corner is a right-facing flake that begins 20' up; this is the central feature of this route. Begin 20' right of the flake at a crack that leads to a right-facing corner (of the route **NCS Crack**).

P1 5.9- PG: Climb up the crack to a ledge and get high gear, then step down and traverse left 15' to jugs at the base of the right-facing flake. Up the flake to its top at a little point. Swing around left onto a right-rising ledge to a tree anchor. 40'

Gear: To 2.5".

FA Aug 13, 2007, Jim Lawyer, Ed Palen

11 NCS Crack 5.9 TR 40' ★

Named for North Country School (NCS), which Hochschartner heads. Begin as for **Trapped in the Dike** and climb up to a ledge, then up a right-facing flake to its top, finishing with a few face moves to reach the right-rising ledge.

FA (TR) 1989, David Hochschartner, Tom Hughes

12 Hochschartner Highway 5.9 G 90' ★

A good route for the first 40', but the teetering blocks in the middle section are unnerving.

Start: At a flat area in the stream, 45' uphill and right of **Trapped in the Dike**, below a shallow right-facing flake and open book that leans left.

P1 5.8 G: Climb up through an off-width V-groove (5.8) to a good ledge, then up an easy open book with a fingercrack to some blocks. Climb to the top of the teetering blocks below a ceiling. (V1) Downclimb left along a ramp to cedars, then lower to the ground. 90'

V1 5.9 G: Pull the roof and face-climb to a fist-sized hole (crux) to a friable jug finish.

Descent: Rappel from a cedar.

FA 1989, David Hochschartner, Tom Hughes
FA (V1) Jul 20, 2007, Larry Robjent, Sam Cowan

13 Intrusion 5.10b TR 100'

The most impressive line on the left side is a crack that breaks a gently overhanging wall. It remains to be led and has good gear—that is, if the friable rock holds. Extremely pumpy. Begin 75' downhill and left of the first waterfall at a crack in a right-facing layback flake that splits the highest point on the wall. It is the rightmost of several climbable cracks and begins in the water (i.e., not a good route to do in high water). Climb up the crack past a pod at two-thirds height to a large horizontal and broken area. Continue up a shallow right-facing flake over a bulge to the top.

FA (TR) 2005, Ed Palen

End of Trap Dike Wall, Left Side

14 Colden Slide 5.4 R 980' ★★★

A (mostly) clean and surprisingly easy ascent of Mt Colden can be made directly from Avalanche Lake by breaking through the lower cliff band and diagonaling across the slide to the right edge of the **Trap Dike**. The climbing is predominately 4th class with significant slab exposure and has decent protection and belays. Descend as for the **Trap Dike**.

Start: Hike to the south end of the lake to a bridge over the outlet. Cross the bridge and leave the trail, following the shoreline along the Mt Colden side of Avalanche Lake. The herd path enters the woods briefly, passes behind the house-sized boulder perched above the shore, then drops back down to the shore. Continue along the shore to a marsh (well before the avalanche path from the 2007 slide) to a herd path that cuts right to a 40'-tall rock slab beneath the steep cliffs that are to the right of the entrance to the **Trap Dike**. Scramble its left side, then traverse right, beneath the 100'-tall cliff band that guards the slide above. About 100' right of the rock slab, next to a table-sized boulder, are three weaknesses (5.5–5.7) in the cliff band that gain the slide directly. The easier, cleaner, and preferred approach is to continue right for several hundred feet to a tree-filled slope that breaks through the cliff band. Traverse (left) above the cliff band and climb a short slab to a tree-filled ramp that heads out (left) onto the slide. Approach time from the outlet is 30 min.

P1 5.0 R: From the left end of the tree-filled ramp, traverse left for 100' to a belay on a foot-wide ledge positioned 100' below several islands of cedar trees. 100'

P2 5.0 R: Continue left heading toward the left side of the slide where it empties into the **Trap Dike**. Belay at one of the cedar islands. 150'

P3 5.0 R: Climb up and cross through the lichen strip, staying close to the **Trap Dike** and below the steeper slabs on the right. Belay from trees near the **Trap Dike**. Escape into the **Trap Dike**, above the second waterfall, is possible from this point. 200'

P4 5.0 G: Step left to gain a vertical handcrack that extends out of a left-facing corner. Follow this crack to a stance below a bulge. Climb the bulge and crack above to a belay at the very edge of the **Trap Dike**, below two left-facing ramps. 150'

P5 5.2 G: Undercling to gain the upper of the two left-facing ramps and follow the corner to a belay at a horn beneath a clean, featured slab. 80'

P6 5.4 R: Two possibilities exist for the crux pitch: traverse right to gain a long left-arching flake, which is climbed to a tree belay on the left, or climb the slab directly to its intersection with the flake at the top of the arch. 150'

P7 5.0 PG: Step left to avoid the bulging slab above and continue left on low-angle terrain beneath a steep left-facing wall. Step down into the **Trap Dike** (3rd class), arriving in the dike at a point a few minutes below where one typically leaves the dike. From here, continue up the Trap Dike to the summit, or descend the dike to the lake. 150'

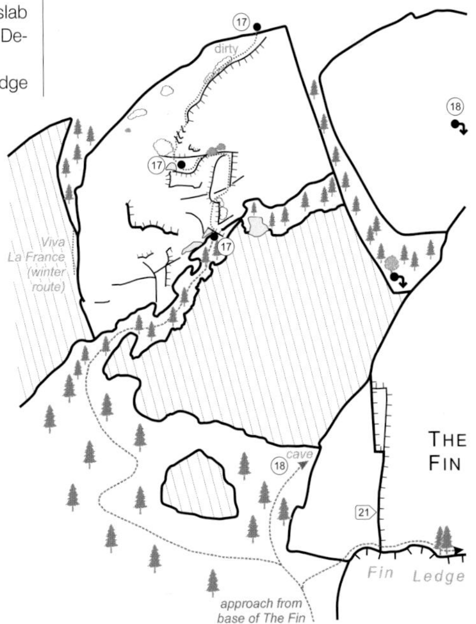

AVALANCHE LAKE: EAST FACE OF AVALANCHE MOUNTAIN (west side of the lake)
17 Stalking Caribou (5.9)
18 Something Wicked (5.9)
21 Affliction (5.8+)

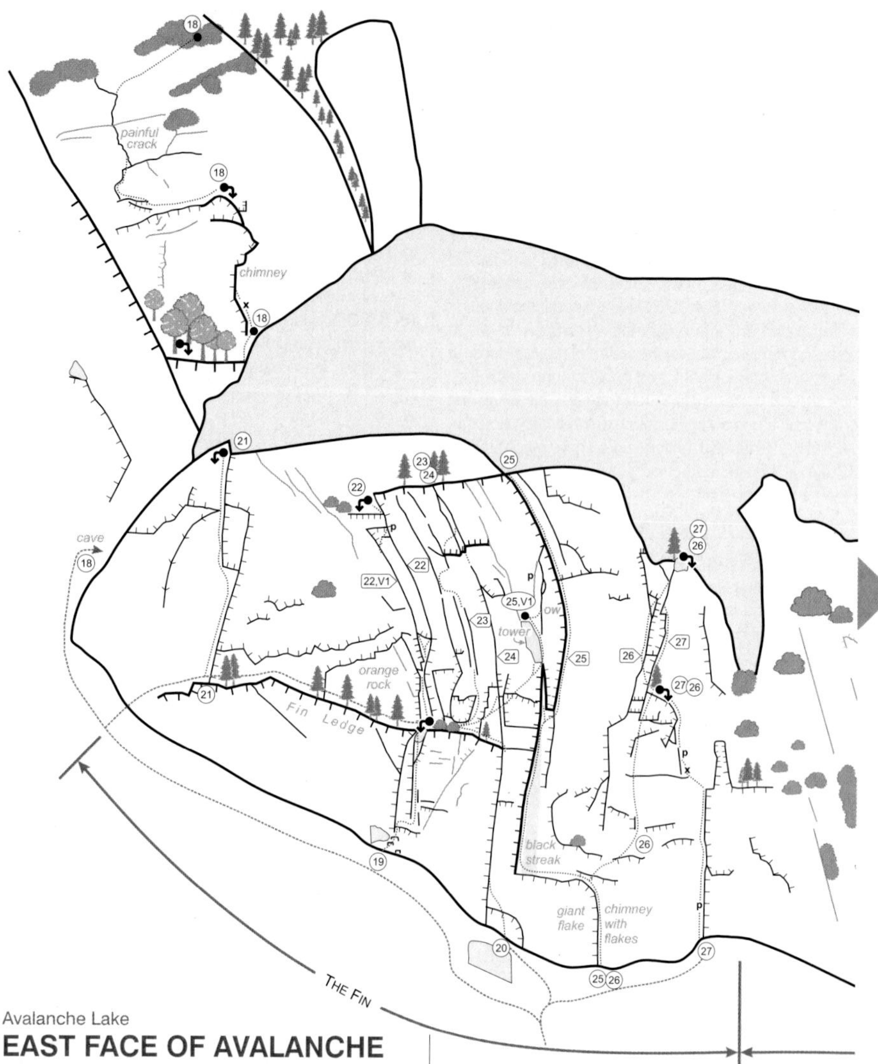

Avalanche Lake

EAST FACE OF AVALANCHE MOUNTAIN (WEST SIDE OF THE LAKE)

Aspect	Southeast
Height	400'
Quality	★★★★
Approach	2 hr, moderate
Summary	One to two-pitch crack climbs on a steep wall above a stunning lake.

-5.6	5.7	5.8	5.9	5.10	5.11	5.12	5.13+	total
1	2	5	5	5	2			20

Avalanche Mountain rises above the lake on the west side (on the right when approaching from the Adirondack Loj). There are several cliffbands, the most continuous being the lower cliff immediately to the right of the open area when you reach the lake. On the left side of this cliff is The Fin (the collection of left-arching cracks in orange rock), and on the right are the steep stepped dihedrals of **3D**. Up and left of The Fin are some large, high cliffs, the Caribou Walls, and down by the water at the south end of the lake are the Matilda Walls.

Matilda Walls

These routes are located on the west side of the lake, on the south end, near the two Hitch-Up Matilda bridges.

AVALANCHE LAKE: EAST FACE OF AVALANCHE MOUNTAIN
(west side of the lake)

18 Something Wicked (5.9)
19 Grand View (5.8)
20 Entrance (5.8)
21 Affliction (5.8+)
22 Sheer Failure (5.10d)
23 Magic Flute (5.11a)
24 TG Farm (5.11b)
25 Dorsal Fin (5.8)
26 The Flying Dutchman (5.9)
27 War and Peace (5.10a)
28 Bad Karma (5.10a)
29 Root Explosion (5.7)
30 Chalk-Up Matilda (5.8)
31 Shaky Flakes Traverse (5.7)
32 Downtown Brown (5.10a)
33 3D (5.10b)
34 Straight A's (5.9)

15 Re-Entry (aka Mrs. Clean) 5.9 G 75' ★★★

Climbs a nice corner very near the trail.

Start: On the left end of the southernmost Hitch-Up-Matilda (the second bolted-on bridge when approaching from the north) is a prominent left-facing corner above a dirty chimney-slot directly above the end of the Hitch-Up-Matilda. Begin 15' uphill and left from this corner, just right of an opposing right-facing corner.

P1 5.9 G: Climb up the face, angling right to a narrow ledge 20' up with a small tree. Step right to gain the left-facing corner with the wide crack. Follow the continuous wide crack up to a sloped ledge at the top of the buttress and a fixed anchor. 75'

Gear: Up to 5", with an extra 4" cam.

History: This was climbed in 2004 and named Mrs. Clean until R.L. Stolz discovered an old photo of himself leading it 19 years earlier.

FA May, 1985, R.L. Stolz, Karen Stolz

16 Standard Deviation 5.5 G 90' ★★★

Climbs a left-facing, right-leaning corner-gully very near the hiking trail.

Start: 40' beyond the northernmost Hitch-Up-Matilda (the first bolted-on bridge when approaching from the north) at the base of a low-angle, left-facing corner.

P1 5.5 G: Climb the corner and face on the right with many solid flakes (V1) to a tree ledge with a fixed anchor. 90'

V1 5.5 G: Halfway up, step left onto the left wall and into another left-facing corner, which is followed to the top; step right to the fixed anchor. 90'

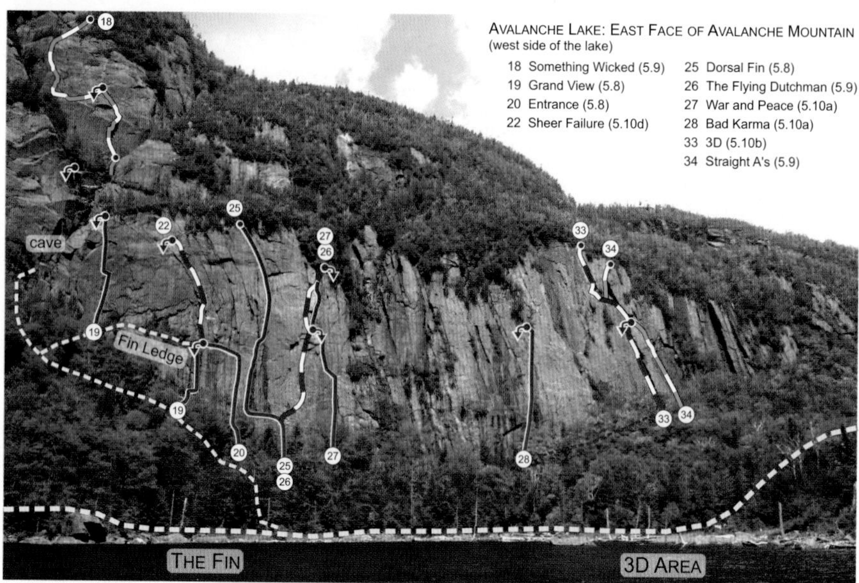

Caribou Walls

Up and left of The Fin are some large, high cliffs with the following routes.

17 Stalking Caribou 5.9 PG 310'

Above and left of The Fin is a high shield of rock split horizontally across its lower third by a right-rising line of trees and vegetation. This route explores the shield, taking the path of least resistance to the top. Avalanche Mountain was once known as Caribou Mountain, hence the name.

Start: Climbing begins after a challenging approach. Bushwhack up and left from The Fin and gain the left end of the ribbon of vegetation that breaks the face. Follow the ribbon of vegetation up and right across the face to a point level with and right of a roof system out on the face to the left. Begin on a ledge at the start of a crack that arches up and left across the face.

P1 5.9 PG: Climb up and right across the face to a right-facing corner with vegetation. Continue up and right into a prominent left-facing corner that is followed to its top. Move left past two small trees, then down and left following a ledge to belay at a large block below the right side of a bush. 140'

P2 5.7 PG: Up and right from the cedar island past several overlaps to gain a left-facing flake. Follow this into the tree-filled depression above and up increasingly dirty rock to the trees. 170'

FA Jul 9, 1984, Bill Dodd, Mark Ippolito, Don Mellor

18 Something Wicked 5.9 G 390' ★★★★

An incredible line that corkscrews up a deep chimney with a spectacular exit to a perch high above Avalanche Lake. P1 and P2 are highly recommended.

Start: Approach as for the Fin Ledge, but continue up the gully another minute to a cave with a stream in the back. Begin at the base of a crack in the right wall (just right of the cave), 2' left of a block-filled chimney.

P1 5.6 G: Climb up the crack, which widens to off width, then into a chimney. At the top of the chimney, traverse left 30' over sloping ledges to a short wall that breaks through a notch and onto the tree island above the cave. 160'

P2 5.8 G: Move the belay to the back of the ledge at the mouth of the right-facing chimney formed by a giant flake. Start up the right-facing chimney, staying in a wide crack on the left side of the chimney. Continue up and right into the narrow chimney (possible belay), which is followed to the top past a final chockstone (passed on the left) to gain a good ledge and fixed anchor. The chimney has good protection in cracks hidden from below. 120'

P3 5.9 PG: Walk left on the huge flake, step across to the main wall, and traverse 20' left to the base of an obvious crack. Up the crack (dirty and painful), eventually heading right to the tree island directly above the belay. 110'

FA Oct, 1996, Ed Palen, Laurie Daniels

The Fin

This cliff is very near the trail on the north end of the lake. The cliff resembles the dorsal fin of a fish and has multiple crack lines that arch left with some orange rock. The right side of The Fin is defined by the right-facing, left-arching corner of **Dorsal Fin**.

Fin Approach: To approach The Fin from the open area at the north end of the lake, walk on the hikers' trail for a minute or so to the boards placed diagonally across the trail 582751,4887377. Turn right and walk away from the lake on a climbers' path up to the base of the cliff. The path meets the rock in the vicinity of **Entrance**.

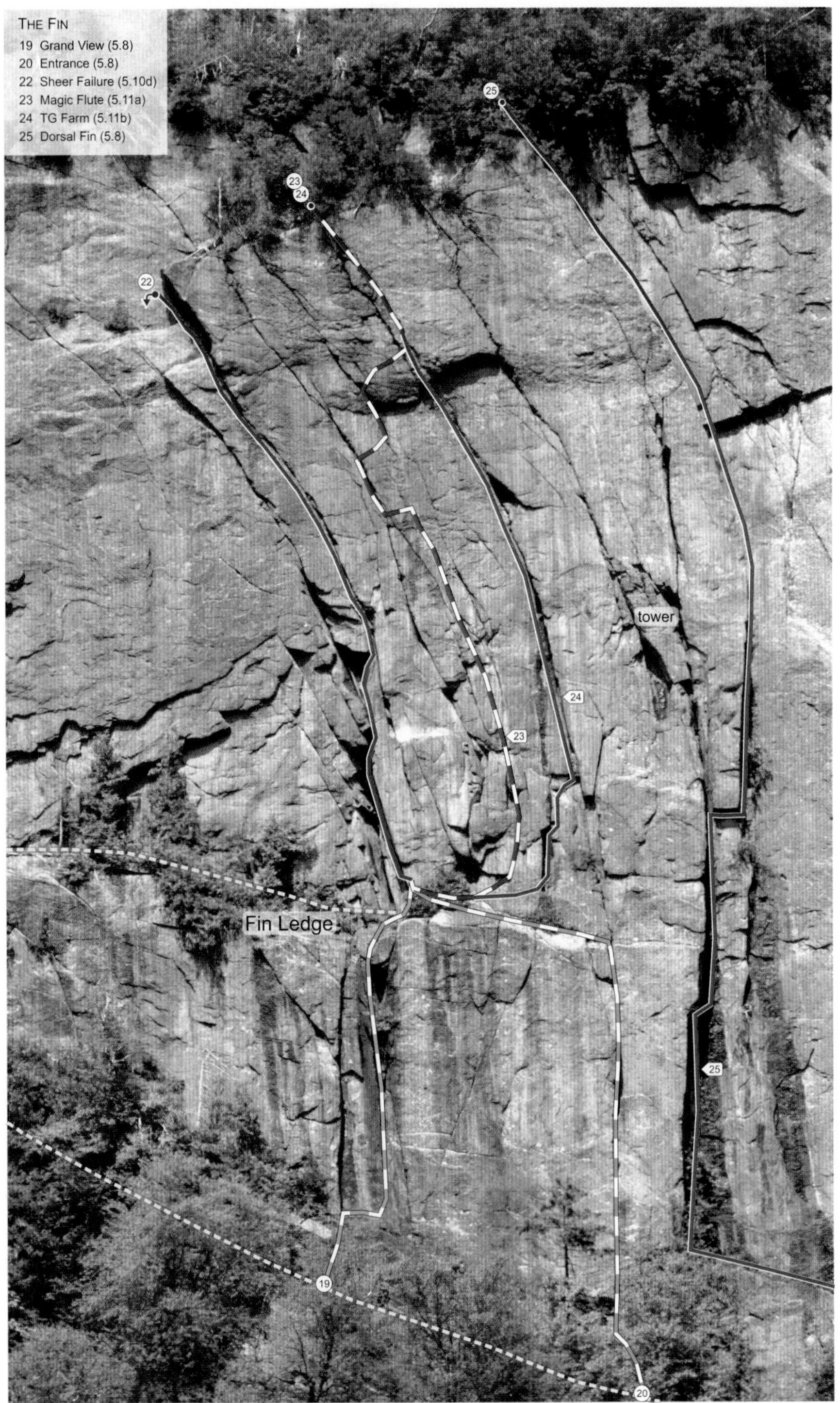
THE FIN
19 Grand View (5.8)
20 Entrance (5.8)
22 Sheer Failure (5.10d)
23 Magic Flute (5.11a)
24 TG Farm (5.11b)
25 Dorsal Fin (5.8)
25
23
24
22
tower
24
23
Fin Ledge
25
19
20

Fin Ledge Approach: The Fin is broken at midheight by a horizontal ledge—the Fin Ledge—which can be accessed by climbing **Grand View** or **Entrance**, or by walking left along the base of the cliff into the gully on its left side, then cutting back right onto the ledge. Once on the ledge, walk right with some exposure to the fixed anchor just right of a prominent chimney. This is a spectacular spot where you can sit in the morning sun and view the routes across the lake. It also makes a private perch to escape the hiker traffic below.

The first two routes (**Grand View** and **Entrance**) are located below the Fin Ledge. The next four routes begin on the Fin Ledge. The remaining routes (right of **Dorsal Fin**) begin on the ground.

19 Grand View 5.8 G 75'

Climbs the wall below the Fin Ledge.

Start: At some blocky, vegetated steps, 40' left of a point directly below the **Dorsal Fin**.

P1 5.8 G: Scramble up the steps until a step out right can be made to the base of a right-facing corner. Traverse right and slightly downhill on a narrow ledge to another right-facing corner. Then follow this corner and a crack to the Fin Ledge. 75'

History: This route was climbed as the first pitch of a full-length route, the second pitch of which climbed a variation to **Sheer Failure**, a route climbed earlier by Beaman.

FA Sep, 1990, Eric Wahl, Ken Nichols

20 Entrance 5.8 G 75' ★★★

This excellent crack and corner climb is the best approach to the Fin Ledge.

Start: Directly above where the climbers' path meets the cliff, on a ledge below a shallow right-facing corner that is hidden by a few cedars. (Not to be confused with the larger right-facing corner of the **Dorsal Fin**, which defines the right margin of The Fin.)

P1 5.8 G: Climb the corner using several horizontal ledges on the right wall to the right end of the Fin Ledge. Traverse left 20' to the fixed anchor just right of the chimney on the Fin Ledge. 75'

Gear: To 4".

History: This pitch was originally climbed as the first pitch of **TG Farm** but has become the standard way to reach the Fin Ledge.

FA 1989, Tim Beaman, Sylvia Lazarnick

21 Affliction 5.8+ G 110' ★★

Start: On the left side of the Fin Ledge, below the left-facing corner system that defines the left margin of The Fin.

P1 5.8+ G: Climb the left-facing corner 30' to a square roof. Step left under the roof (crux) and continue in the left-facing corner to a fixed anchor. 110'

FA Aug, 1997, Ed Palen, Paul Brown

22 Sheer Failure 5.10d G 90' ★★★★★

Incredible crack climbing in an awesome position; one of the best at the lake. A five-star linkup when combined with **Entrance**.

Start: On the Fin Ledge, below a chimney and just left of the fixed anchor.

P1 5.10d G: Climb up the chimney, past a constriction, and into a V-slot capped by a ceiling. There are two cracks that exit the slot; (V1) exit using the right-hand crack up to a stance above. Follow the fingercrack that arches up and left to a steep left-facing, left-leaning corner (crux) and a foot ledge with a fixed anchor. 90'

V1 5.9+ G: Exit the slot using the left crack. Stay in the lower crack to a small left-facing, left-leaning corner. At the top of the corner, rail right on a horizontal to the larger left-facing corner of the normal route (just above its crux) and follow the corner to the foot ledge with a fixed anchor.

FA 1988, Tim Beaman, Sylvia Lazarnick
FA (V1) 2001, Jesse Williams, Emilie Drinkwater

23 Magic Flute 5.11a PG 100' ★

Another upper pitch possibility that breaks The Fin. Very continuous and demanding. Named for a Mozart opera, but inspired by an annoying hiker below who kept warbling on a flute during the first ascent.

Start: On the Fin Ledge, at the fixed anchor just right of the chimney.

*Michelle Burlitch on P2 (5.8) of **Something Wicked** (5.9).*

P1 5.11a PG: Move right on the ledge, then up on large hollow blocks to the base of a prominent 2" crack. Step right and follow two thin parallel cracks 20' up the unrelentingly steep face until it is possible to step left to the 2" crack. Continue up the 2" crack for a few feet, then back right to the original crack system just below the overlap. Pull over the overlap and hand-traverse right to a left-facing corner (joining **TG Farm** here) that angles up left to the top. 100'

History: This route was originally climbed as the top pitch of a full-length route that started with the first pitch of **TG Farm**, which had been done earlier.

FA Sep, 1990, Ken Nichols, Eric Wahl

24 TG Farm 5.11b PG 100' ★★★

Climbs the left-arching crack that breaks through the center of the ceiling high on The Fin. "TG" refers to temperature gradient snow, and "TG Farm" is a nickname for the ski resort Big Sky in Montana.

Start: On the Fin Ledge, at the fixed anchor just right of the chimney.

P1 5.11b PG: Step right from the anchor and up to a short left-facing corner. Up this, then continue right on flakes to the base of the crack. Climb up the thin crack that arches left past a pod (often wet) to an A-shaped flare in the crack, then up to the center of the ceiling. Break through the ceiling at twin cracks in a left-facing, left-leaning corner to the cedar ledge above. 100'

FA 1989, Tim Beaman, Sylvia Lazarnick

Gear: To 4".

25 Dorsal Fin 5.8 G 160' ★★

Climbs the long, continuous right-facing corner that curves left and defines the right side of The Fin. The corner is offset in the middle with a small, square ceiling. Often wet. The more difficult variation is recommended.

Start: Same as **The Flying Dutchman**.

P1 5.8 G: Climb the chimney formed by the detached flake for 30'. At its top, step across the void to the main cliff and traverse left into the right-facing corner. Climb the corner to the square ceiling at midheight, then (V1) step right into the main corner and climb past exceedingly dirty rock to a point where the corner begins to lean left. Follow the corner past a ceiling on the right wall and up to the cedar jungle. 160'

V1 Avalauncher 5.10d G: This is a recommended variation, but bring some 4" cams for the off width. The variation can also be accessed from the Fin Ledge. At the square ceiling, continue straight up through a slot (5.8), then up the right side of the left-leaning tower (the left side of the left-leaning tower has also been climbed at 5.10a) to its top (optional belay). The tower, balanced on a tiny stance, is a dangerous-looking and eerie feature; use good judgment here. From the top of the tower, step right into an off-width crack (crux), which is climbed to its top (at the wide section, there is a smaller crack with a piton on the left wall). Step right to the arête and swing into the right-facing corner of the normal route.

FA 1988, Tim Beaman, Jim Cunningham, Sylvia Lazarnick

FA (V1) Unknown

26 The Flying Dutchman 5.9 G (5.7 R) 160' ★

Start: Just right of where the approach trail meets the cliff, 40' left of the prominent left-facing corner of **War and Peace** at the base of a detached flake that forms a right-facing chimney filled with loose flakes.

P1 5.9 G (5.7): Climb the chimney formed by the detached flake for 30'. At its top, step across the void to the main cliff and head right, then up to a rotten right-facing corner. Avoid the rotten corner by traversing right and up 20' to a shallow right-facing corner 15' to the right of the rotten corner. Step left at a right-rising overlap with a pin (crux) and climb up to steep cracks that lead to the cedar and first belay shared with **War and Peace**. 100'

P2 5.7 PG: Directly above the cedar is a right-facing, right-leaning corner of **War and Peace**. Step left and climb the left side of this pillar (very dirty) to a flared alcove at the top with a small tree. Step right and join **War and Peace** to a cedar with a fixed anchor. 60'

FA Sep, 1996, Ed Palen, Laurie Daniels

27 War and Peace 5.10a PG 160' ★★★

Good-quality corner and face climbing.

Start: 50' right along the cliff from the approach trail, at the base of a large left-facing corner.

P1 5.9 PG: Climb the off width in the left-facing corner (large gear appreciated) for 65' until just below a possible belay stance on the right. Hand-traverse left (crux) gaining a small ledge, then up a thin crack to a short right-facing corner. Climb up the corner, then head left on the ramp to a belay at a large cedar (shared with **The Flying Dutchman**). 100'

P2 5.10a PG: Follow the clean right-facing corner above the belay (crux) to a stance. Continue up and right over easier ground to a cedar with a fixed anchor. 60'

History: The first-ascent party found an old 50s-era piton 20' up the first pitch, indicating that the initial corner had most likely been climbed.

FA Sep, 1996, Ed Palen, Laurie Daniels

3D Area

The 3D Area is the collection of routes on the right end of the lower band of cliffs near the hiking trail at the north end of the lake. The most distinctive features are the huge right-facing, left-leaning ramp-corner (this is the **Chalk-Up Matilda** corner) and the three dihedrals 70' to its right. The upper two dihedrals form a deep A-shaped alcove (these are the dihedrals of **3D** and **Straight A's**).

To approach this area, from the clearing at the north end of the lake, stay on the hiking trail in the woods (instead of walking through the marshy area along the shoreline) for about a minute, looking for a point roughly even with the end of the lake where you can clearly see the cliff on the right 582800,4887399. A good path leads 60' up and right to the base of the cliff. The main feature to help locate climbs is the **Chalk-Up Matilda** corner, a 10' deep right-facing corner, the left wall of which forms a ramp, 50' right and uphill from where the approach trail meets the cliff.

28 Bad Karma 5.10a TR 120'

This toprope problem begins 70' left of the **Chalk-Up Matilda** corner (and 20' left of where the approach path meets the cliff) at the base of a shallow right-facing corner with a birch tree growing out of the rock. The route climbs the right-leaning corner through an A-shaped notch in a ceiling 30' up. Continue up the right-leaning crack (5.8) to a cedar tree with a fixed anchor. The top of the route is accessed by climbing the first half of **Chalk-Up Matilda**, then climbing left to reach the cedar.

FA (TR) Aug, 1995, Ed Palen, Bob Harris

29 Root Explosion 5.7 PG 200'

Start: Same as for **Chalk-Up Matilda**.

P1 5.7 PG: Follow **Chalk-Up Matilda** up the ramp 80' or so to the ledge below the headwall with the distinctive fingercrack. Step left and gain a blocky left-rising 3" ledge, which is hand-traversed to a stance at the base of the handcrack. 140'

P2 5.6 G: Follow the wide crack to the trees and fixed anchor. 60'

Descent: Rappel to the **Bad Karma** tree, then to the ground with a single 60-m rope.

FA Aug, 1995, Ed Palen, Bob Harris

30 Chalk-Up Matilda 5.8 PG 160' ★★★

The highlight of this climb is the fingercrack that snakes up the blank wall high on the route. The name is a reference to the Hitch-Up Matildas—the bridges bolted into the rock face over the water on the hiking trail.

Start: At a clearing at the base of a huge right-facing, left-leaning, 10'-deep corner, the left wall of which forms a ramp. The corner is 50' right of where the approach trail meets the cliff and 70' left of the left-facing dihedral of **3D**.

P1 5.8 PG: Climb the left wall of the corner to a ledge. While a belay here would be optimal, the route continues up due to lack of an adequate anchor. Leave the ledge and follow a steep crack to a fixed anchor at a cedar. Two ropes are needed to rappel. 160'

FA Nov, 1994, Ed Palen, Paul Brown

31 Shaky Flakes Traverse 5.7 PG 150'

A rising traverse from the **Chalk-Up Matilda** corner to the final corner of **3D**. From the end of P2, you can join the last pitch of **3D** (5.10b), the last pitch of **Straight A's** (5.9), or rappel.

Start: Same as **Chalk-Up Matilda**.

P1 5.5 G: Climb up the corner past a couple of cedar stumps until it is possible to break out right to gain a ledge with a cedar on its right end. 80'

P2 5.7 PG: Climb the left-facing, right-rising corners and flakes across the face to belay at the base of the final left-facing dihedral of **3D**. The crux involves laybacking an off-width crack, so some wide gear will be appreciated. 70'

Gear: To 4".

FA Oct, 1994, Ed Palen, Bob Martin

32 Downtown Brown 5.10a TR 150'

Halfway between **Chalk-Up Matilda** and **3D** is a left-facing, left-leaning edge. This is climbed for 40' to face climbing up to a cedar (with a fixed anchor), then up to the Shaky Flakes off width, finishing on that route. This can be toproped by climbing **Shaky Flakes Traverse**.

FA (TR) 1994, Ed Palen, Paul Brown

33 3D 5.10b G 220' ★★★★

This recommended route climbs a series of three left-facing, left-leaning dihedrals on the right side of the face. P3 is especially good.

Start: 70' right of **Chalk-Up Matilda** at a large left-facing, left-leaning corner.

P1 5.9 G: Climb the corner past two "petrified" cedar stumps to a fixed anchor at the top of the pillar. 90'

P2 5.8 G: Straight up the face gains the bottom of the next left-facing dihedral. Climb toward the A-shaped alcove, then traverse left across the face to a cedar at the base of the next left-facing dihedral. 70'

P3 5.10b G: Climb the left-facing dihedral to tricky moves at the top. Step right to belay in trees. 60'

Descent: From the top, walk right 100' to where a short rappel gains the top of a tree-filled ramp, which can be downclimbed to the ground, 100' right of the start of the route.

FA Oct, 1994, Dominic Eisinger, Ed Palen

34 Straight A's 5.9 PG 200' ★★

Climbs the right side of the **3D** pillar, then up to the A-shaped cave formed by the second and third pillars of **3D**.

Start: On the right-facing corner formed by the right side of the **3D** pillar.

P1 5.7 G: Climb cracks in the left wall of the corner to a wider section before the top of the pillar. 90'

P2 5.9 PG: Straight up the face gains the bottom of the next left-facing dihedral. Climb into the A-shaped alcove (old piton), then out an overhanging crack in the right wall to gain a left-facing, right-rising corner, which is followed to the trees. 110'

Gear: To 4".

Descent: Rappel as for **3D**.

History: The first-ascent party found a 50s-era piton in the A-shaped cave.

FA Oct, 1994, Ed Palen, Dominic Eisinger

Watercolor by Lucie Wellner.

WRIGHT PEAK

Location	High Peaks Wilderness Area, accessed from the Adirondack Loj Trailhead
Aspect	Southeast
Height	65'
Quality	★★★★
Approach	1 hr 30 min, difficult
Summary	Highly featured steep face and crack climbing in an idyllic alpine setting.

-5.6	5.7	5.8	5.9	5.10	5.11	5.12	5.13+	total
4	4	3	2	1	1			15

This small cliff—about 140' long—is located on a tiny summit below the summit of Wright Peak and is approached using the extremely popular hiking trail to Algonquin and Wright. The rock is steep and laced with vertical cracks and amazing incut horizontal cracks. It is also unusually clean, with no lichen, dirt, or moss, and extremely coarse, with excellent friction properties; you could probably climb anywhere. The terrain at the base is supertight waist-high spruce with a herd path and several open grassy areas that make moving about easy. The top of the cliff is a large, flat, open rock summit with excellent views of Lake Placid, Whiteface, Cascade Pass, and the summits of Big Slide, Wright, Algonquin, Street, and Nye. It's a great place to spend the afternoon enjoying the views, basking in the sun, and perhaps climbing.

Since there are no trees on the summit, gear anchors are required but must be placed in exposed positions below the summit. Thus, the cliff is difficult to toprope. When leading routes, build an anchor on ledges below the summit, bring up the second, then scramble to the top.

HISTORY

Not much is known about climbing at this cliff. It certainly gets noticed by hikers, but very few climbers have bothered to carry gear. Don Mellor and Jeff Edwards are known to have brought groups from the Northwood School. What was toproped, led, or soloed may never be known. Jim Lawyer and Lori Crowningshield made a trip here in 2007 to come up with some route descriptions for the first edition of *Adirondack Rock*. After publication, this spurred Ken Nichols to make several visits with various partners and pick off the remaining lines.

DIRECTIONS

The approach, beginning at the Adirondack Loj, follows very popular trails for 3.1 miles to within 75' of the cliff. Navigation is easy, but the terrain isn't—steep and very rocky.

Park at the Adirondack Loj Trailhead (page 425). From the parking area (0 hr 0 min), follow the Van Hoevenberg Trail toward Marcy Dam. At 20 min, you'll reach the intersection with the trail to Algonquin and Wright; turn onto the trail to Algonquin and follow it over rolling terrain, which then becomes steeper and more rocky. At 1 hr 30 min, you'll reach a short, flat section where the cliff is visible to the right, about 75' from the trail. Follow a herd path over to the base of the cliff 581033,4889654.

DESCENT OPTIONS

Walk right and descend a short 3rd-class chimney that returns easily to the base.

1 Lost in the Thicket 5.6 G 40'

Start: At the left end of the cliff, 80' to the left of the chimney, at a crack that begins at the ground as a seam, and widens to hand-size at a horizontal crack 15' up.

P1 5.6 G: Follow the crack to some ledges, step right, then climb another short vertical crack just left of a short left-facing corner. 40'

FA Sep, 2008, Ken Nichols, Boris Itin

2 Spruce Crack 5.7 G 40' ★★

Start: At a ledge at waist height that has a 2'-wide gap with a vertical fingercrack that disappears 15' up.

P1 5.7 G: Follow the crack, then face climb to a wide horizontal crack. Traverse right and go up a left-facing corner then move right to finish. 40'

FA Sep, 2007, Ken Nichols

3 Happy Trails to You 5.9 G 45' ★★

Start: At a vertical seam with a horn at head height that is at the right end of a waist-high ledge.

P1 5.9 G: Follow the seam, then move right to another seam in a right-facing corner. Move up to a bulge that is climbed to a horizontal crack. Finish in a bottomless, left-facing corner. 45'

Gear: Standard rack plus a pink Tricam and a #3 Friend below the crux.

FA Sep, 2007, Ken Nichols

4 Ranger Danger 5.6 G 50' ★★

Start: 50' to the left of the chimney at a crack that begins 5' up and has a 6"-wide section at 8'.

P1 5.6 G: Up the crack to a ledge that is capped by an overhang, continue up the crack (in a right-facing corner) and climb a short chimney to a rounded right-facing corner at the top. 50'

FA Sep, 2007, Ken Nichols, Fausta Esguerra

5 Fogbound 5.7 G 50' ★★

Start: At the left end of a long, waist-high ledge, below a left-rising crack that goes to a ledge 20' up (the ledge is shared with **Ranger Danger**).

P1 5.7 G: Up the crack and go past the ledge to an overhang that is climbed to a wide crack that widens to offwidth near the top. 50'

FA Sep, 2008, Boris Itin, Ken Nichols

6 Gorillas in the Mist 5.8 G 65' ★★

Start: Same as **Fogbound**, at a crack that ends at two horizontal cracks 25' up.

P1 5.8 G: Up the crack to the highest horizontal crack. Move up right along another thin crack, then exit up left at the top. 65'

FA Sep, 2008, Ken Nichols, Boris Itin

7 The Wright Crack 5.7 G 65' ★★★

Start: 30' left of the left-leaning chimney of **Wright Wrong Chimney** are two parallel left-leaning cracks 20' apart. This route climbs the rightmost of these cracks and begins on a narrow ledge at the base of the crack just above the thick jungle of balsams.

P1 5.7 G: Up the left-leaning crack with many small ledges and horns, then through a short, overhanging hand-sized section (crux) to a ledge. Step right and up a left-facing corner to the top. 65'

ACB Aug 29, 2007, Lori Crowningshield, Jim Lawyer

8 The Wrong Crack 5.9 PG 65' ★★

Hard if you're short.

Start: Same as The Wright Crack, below a thin vertical crack.

P1 5.9 PG: Up the crack to a ceiling 8' up. Pull over the ceiling and go up to a stance below a bulge. Make long reach toward a horizontal crack that is broken by a short vertical crack. Follow ledges up and left, and finish in a right-facing corner that is 7' right of The Wright Crack. 65'

FA Sep, 2008, Boris Itin, Ken Nichols

9 Knock the Cairn Down 5.8+ TR 65'

Begin 20' right of The Wright Crack and 15' left of Wright Wrong Chimney at a short left-slanting crack above a sharp right-pointing end of a long narrow ledge. Follow the crack to a steep face that leads to another short crack. Work up past a series of ledges and short faces to the highest part of the cliff.

FA (TR) Sep, 2008, Ken Nichols

10 Wright Wrong Chimney 5.3 G 65' ★★★

A pleasant outing with easy climbing and good protection on a steep wall. Named after the popular ski descent on the other side of the mountain.

Start: In the center of the cliff below a left-leaning chimney that begins 25' up. This is 20' left of a large white spot 8' up.

P1 5.3 G: Up a jagged discontinuous crack in black rock past numerous horizontals and ledges to gain the chimney, then climb it to the top. 65'

ACB 1984, Jim Lawyer (solo)

11 The Hole 5.8 G 65' ★★★★

An unlikely line with incredible incut horizontals on a steep face.

Start: In the center of the cliff is a large white spot 8' up, with a zigzag 10'-high right-facing corner bordering its left side. This route begins on the face 5' left of the zigzag corner and 5' right of a left-facing corner. Another marker is the cantilevered triangular block at the top of the cliff that sits between this route and the left-leaning chimney of Wright Wrong Chimney, which begins 15' to the left.

P1 5.8 G: Up the face past a good incut horizontal crack to a ledge, then up to a left-rising horizontal crack. Continue up the steep wall to another horizontal crack, (V1) then to an incredible bottomless hole (3" cam fits perfectly). Above is a short, jagged black crack. Follow it to a large ledge. Step right to the next ledge and belay (same as for B-47). 65'

V1 Lizard Head 5.6 G: On the face below the hole, work up and left to finish on the left side of the cantilevered triangular block.

ACB Aug 29, 2007, Jim Lawyer, Lori Crowningshield
FA (V1) Sep, 2007, Ken Nichols, Fausta Esguerra

12 Disappearing Act 5.6 G 65' ★★

Start: At the base of a zigzag 10'-high right-facing corner, 5' right of The Hole.

P1 5.6 G: Up the corner, or the face to the left, then over a bulge to a stance. Step right and follow a right-rising crack to a prominent horizontal crack. Finish in a short, shallow left-facing corner. 65'

FA Sep, 2007, Ken Nichols, Fausta Esguerra

13 B-47 5.7 G 65' ★★

Named in memory of the B-47 that crashed into the summit of Wright Peak in 1962.

Start: 60' left of the descent chimney at the right end of the cliff, at a 10'-high left-facing, left-leaning corner that arches left at its top. The corner is 6' right of a large white spot 8' up.

P1 5.7 G: Climb the corner, swing right onto the face, then follow a discontinuous left-leaning crack to a ledge. Step right and up to another ledge (cams to 0.75" for the belay). There is a cool hueco-pocket on the right face just before the top. 65'

ACB Aug 29, 2007, Lori Crowningshield, Jim Lawyer

14 The Wright Stuff 5.11b TR 65'

Begin 8' right of B-47 and 5' left of Perilous Journey at the right-hand of two short left-leaning cracks. Climb past the crack to a ledge, then traverse 5' left to within 2' of the right-facing corner of B-47. Work straight up the face past a small overlap to a shallow vertical scoop on the upper part of the cliff, then to the top above the left side of the scoop.

FA (TR) Sep, 2007, Ken Nichols

15 Perilous Journey 5.10d G 65' ★★★★

Another unlikely line made possible by the amazing incut nature of the horizontal cracks on this cliff.

Start: 20' right of B-47 and 40' left of the descent chimney at the right end of the cliff, 4' left of a 12'-high shallow left-facing corner, below a short left-leaning black crack.

P1 5.10d G: Up the face past the black crack to a stance below an overhanging black wall with a vertical seam. Up the seam (crux; good small nuts) to a horizontal, then straight up past several incredible incut horizontal cracks to the top. 65'

ACB Aug 29, 2007, Jim Lawyer, Lori Crowningshield

AMPERSAND MOUNTAIN

At the top of this popular peak is an open summit with several small cliffbands and some large boulders. This is a very scenic location, and the rock is surprisingly clean. However, the climbing potential is limited because the cliffs are small and scattered. There are currently two routes.

Park at the Ampersand Mountain Trailhead at a widened shoulder along NY 3, 12.4 miles east of downtown Tupper Lake (where NY 3 and NY 30 split) or 8.2 miles west of Saranac Lake (from NY 3's intersection with NY 86). Follow the steep trail (red disks) toward the summit for 2.5 miles (about 1.5 hr). A few minutes

Photo by Kevin "MudRat" MacKenzie.

before reaching the open slabs on the summit, the trail squeezes between two boulders, the landmark for finding the routes.

To reach **Summit Snacks** (5.11b TR; 40'; May 1993; Patrick Purcell), hike around the house-sized boulder on the right to the opposite side of the boulder (its east face) 563552,4898186. The route begins in a rock-walled gully and goes up a dirty crack to a stance beneath a clean fingercrack. Follow the crack as it jogs to the right then goes left onto a slab. **Table Scraps** (5.6 G; 40'; 1992; Dave Furman) is visible to the right of the trail, after it squeezes through the boulders but before it emerges on the open slabs on the summit. Start beneath the left end of a low roof. Go up to the roof, traverse right, and move over a bulge to a belay on a spacious ledge.

SCARFACE MOUNTAIN

This northwest-facing slab 573260,4902252, which overlooks the village of Saranac Lake, is clearly visible as you drive on NY 86 toward Lake Placid. The slab is a bit of a disappointment, low-angle and extremely dirty. The earliest climbing was done between 1949 and 1950 by Stanley Smith and Donald LeBeau, who used the slab as a practice area to prepare for bigger things. Tom Condon also recalls climbing this in 1951, as it was the place where he learned to fall. In more recent times, Don Mellor reported leading an unroped ascent of the central line with kids from the Northwood School. He recalls peeling off carpets of moss and using a dog leash as a handrail at the crux.

DIX MOUNTAIN

Location	Dix Wilderness Area, accessed from the Elk Lake Trailhead or the Round Pond Trailhead
Summary	A vast wilderness area with long slab climbs and scrambles.

-5.6	5.7	5.8	5.9	5.10	5.11	5.12	5.13+	total
2								2

Dix Mountain, the highest point in the namesake range, is a remote peak with good trails and more open rock slides than any other mountain in the park. Most of the slides can be ascended at 3rd class, but the steepest ones—the **Hunters Pass Slide** and the **Buttress Slide**—have good 4th- and 5th-class friction climbing.

Dix Mountain

NORTHWEST FACE

Visible from NY 73 between Keene and Keene Valley, this face has five slides that are arranged like a left handprint known as the **Finger Slides**. Park at the Round Pond Trailhead. Follow the trail marked with blue discs past Round Pond, then past a four-way intersection to reach the Boquet River lean-to at 4.2 miles. Continue another 1.6 miles to where the trail crosses the debris area at the base of the slides 597070,4882898. From the top of the slides (the top of the longest "finger") there is a faint herd path to the hiking trail. Another option is to descend one of the neighboring slides back to the base.

Dix Mountain

WEST FACE

Aspect	West
Height	1500'
Quality	★★★
Approach	3 hr, difficult
Summary	Long slide climbs in a remote location.

-5.6	5.7	5.8	5.9	5.10	5.11	5.12	5.13+	total
2								2

Invisible from any road, this face has an excellent collection of slides approached from the Elk Lake Trailhead.

DIRECTIONS

From the Elk Lake Trailhead, follow the trail marked with red discs past Slide Brook Lean-to, Lillian Brook Lean-to, and Dix Pond to a junction with the Beckhorn Trail (yellow markers) at 4.3 miles. Continue straight (red markers) toward Hunters Pass.

1 Hunter's Pass Slide 4th class 2300'

This route is mostly 2nd-class, but other options exist on this face. An option for 5th-class climbing is encountered at a dihedral in a bowl near the center of the slide. The 2011 Tropical Storm Irene also created two new, clean fingers on the right-hand side.

Route Description: Walk 25 min past the Beckhorn Trail junction to where the trail levels out, parallel to a stream on the right. The west face cirque (the North and South Fork Slides) is visible to the right, with a steep buttress on its north side. Continue walking past the buttress and find a tributary coming into the stream from the right. Leave the trail 595821,4881760, cross the brook, and follow the tributary past a debris field to a 30'-tall waterfall below the slide. The lower section of the slide offers the most sustained climbing before it splits into several fingers near the top. Go up the left finger slide (4th-class), bushwhack a few minutes, and reach the hiking trail above Hunter's Pass, about 500' above the intersection with the Round Pond trail, and well below the summit of Dix Mountain.

2 Buttress Slide 5.4 R 1450' ★★★★

Created in 2011 by Tropical Storm Irene, this 900'-tall slide is considered by some to be one of the most difficult in the park. The approach is easy (the slide debris nearly intersects the hiking trail) and begins just few minutes before the Hunter's Pass Slide. The rock quality is generally excellent, although there is still some loose debris from the storm.

Start: From the Beckhorn Trail junction, follow the trail towards Hunter's Pass. The slide is on the right just beyond a stream flowing down from the eastern slopes of Nippletop Mountain (to your left), about 20 minutes from the junction. Walk about 300' along the debris to a footwall—a nearly vertical cliff with twin roofs 596021,4881802. Don't climb between the roofs (heavy debris above); instead, bushwhack left, then back right to the slide path above the roofs.

Route Description: Begin with 2nd class scrambling beside a hulking bulge of anorthosite. There are two slide paths; go up the left one for 400' until it converges with the right. Continue up the slide to the upper dihedral—a steep, 80'-tall, stunning corner with a fingercrack. Up this, then traverse left (crux) below an overlap. Continue up, go over some overlaps, then stay near the right side as the slide narrows near the top. Traverse left around a triangular roof to finish the route.

Descent: Follow the ridge down a few hundred feet, then bushwhack roughly parallel to the slide, weaving a line downhill. Another option is to bushwhack southeast over and down the ridge to the drainage from the North Fork Slide. A short walk up leads to the slide proper, then scramble to the summit.

FA Aug 18, 2012, Kevin "MudRat" MacKenzie, Richard D. McKenna

HOFFMAN NOTCH

Location	North Hudson, accessed from the Hoffman Notch trailhead on Blue Ridge Road
Summary	A collection of backcountry cliffs in a remote setting, but uninspiring routes so far.

-5.6	5.7	5.8	5.9	5.10	5.11	5.12	5.13+	total
	1	2						3

The Hoffman Notch trail runs 7.4 miles in a north-to-south direction. The area is an explorer's dream, accessed by a well-maintained trail and surrounded by a vast wild forest—the Vanderwhacker Mountain Wild Forest—about 2 miles south of Blue Ridge Road.

The cliffs are on the lower reaches of Washburn Ridge. So far there are three named cliffs: The Trailside Wall, the Long Wall, and the Outback Wall.

The Trailside Wall faces east and parallels the trail, about 100'–200' to the right (west). Towards the left (south) end, at the point nearest the trail is a section with potential for some steep cracks routes (the location of the winter routes **Adventure Party** and **Twisted Sister**).

At the far left (south) end of the Trailside Wall is a waterfall where the cliff bends to the south 591752,4864929 and turns uphill. This south-facing wall is the Long Wall. This is the largest and sunniest of the cliffs, and has potential for new routes.

The Outback Wall is steeply uphill, west of and above the north end of the Trailside Wall. The Outback Wall is not visible from the trail, and takes an additional 35 minutes of strenuous uphill hiking to reach 591694,4865434. There is some potential here for rock routes.

HISTORY

The cliffs were located by Tom DuBois in Autumn 2009. After the cliffs were identified and publicized, the area saw extensive ice climbing development during winter 2009–2010, and now features more than 35 ice routes (from WI2 through WI5+, and mixed up to M7). DuBois returned in August 2010 to begin cleaning and climbing rock routes.

DIRECTIONS

From Northway (I-87) Exit 29, go west on Blue Ridge Road (CR 84) 5.4 miles. The trailhead parking is on the left (south) side of the road, across from a "Ragged Mountain Fish and Game Club" sign. The small pullout will accommodate 5 cars.

Follow the Hoffman Notch trail south through relatively level terrain. After the last of several bridges, the trail makes a series of gentle climbs alongside Hoffman Notch Brook, and then descends slightly and levels off close to the brook. Large boulders appear by the right side of the trail, and soon you'll see sections of the Trailside Wall through the trees. The trail passes through a tight section very close to the stream and crosses a seasonal brook with a giant boulder on the right. This is the Bucket Boulder named for an old rusty bucket sitting on its south side. The path starts directly behind this boulder, and is marked with cairns.

Hoffman Notch

LONG WALL

Aspect	South
Height	200'
Quality	
Approach	1 hr 10 min, moderate
Summary	A very wide cliff with mediocre rock quality and some route potential; the huge roof holds promise.

-5.6	5.7	5.8	5.9	5.10	5.11	5.12	5.13+	total
	1	2						3

DIRECTIONS

From the Bucket Boulder (0.0 min), follow the path up the bed of a seasonal brook, and follow this to the waterfall at the far left end of the Trailside Wall. Walk left along the base of the cliff to its left end, then go uphill and around the corner to the Long Wall. At 10 min, the path reaches a large cairn about 80' from the base of the Long Wall, a position directly beneath the route Summer Rules.

To reach the top of the Long Wall, from the large cairn, follow the path right (east). Climb along a ledge, then make an improbable left turn to climb steeply up to the top of the wall. This is the only hiking route to the top of the cliff for 1000' in either direction.

DESCENT OPTIONS

Rappel. There may be some fixed anchors in place on trees. Longer routes may require two ropes for the rappel.

1 The Pretty Good Dihedral 5.8- G 100' ★

Start: Walk uphill and left along the base of the cliff, and locate the huge, 100'-wide roof 40' up. Near the left end of the roof, the path steps away from the cliff, around a small buttress, then climbs up steep open woods to return to the base of the cliff below an enormous left-facing corner. Begin on top of a bushy ledge a few feet up at the bottom of the dihedral.

P1 5.8- G: Climb through a low crux, and then continue up the dihedral to finish at a medium-sized cedar. (A second pitch appears possible above and left.) 100'

FA Aug 7, 2010, Tom DuBois, Ellen DuBois

2 Peregrine Project

An open project. 35' left of The Cockpit, is a pile of recent rock fall at the base of two left-facing corners. The right-hand corner is loose and orange, and the left-hand corner is black and solid. 20' left of these is another group of smaller left-facing corners, with a large cedar growing on a ledge 20' up. Begin 6' left of the large cedar on a small sloping platform at the base of the cliff. Climb blocky rock, passing 6' left of the large cedar, and up a left-facing corner. Step right around a bulge at 60', and left around another bulge at 70' to a fine, exposed ledge. Continue up the corner to the top. Definitely the most appealing rock up here.

3 The Cockpit Project

An open project. 35' left of Three Way at a section of blocky, white rock with a large roof about 30' above. This cleaned route begins at the left edge of the blocky white rock, under a small "octopus" cedar. Go up the blocky white rock, and then traverse to the right under the roof into a cramped stance. Turn the roof where it is smallest, a few feet left of a tiny evergreen that sprouts about 5' above the roof. Move up and right to finish straight up a vertical crack in white rock.

4 Three Way 5.8 PG 150'

Start: At a left-facing corner, 40' left of Summer Rules.

P1 5.8 PG: Easy climbing up the corner leads to a steeper section about 20' up with some loose rock to climber's right. Climb up and left to a weedy ledge, then step up left and continue on a clean, exposed face, and a vertical groove, to finish up the left side of a blank buttress with a wonderfully exposed perch at its top. 150'

FA Aug 20, 2010, Tom DuBois, Ellen DuBois

5 Summer Rules 5.7 G 150'

Not recommended due to loose and scary rock.

Start: From the right end of the cliff, walk 300' or so uphill and left, and locate blocky rock with a small, cave-like overhang at its base. Above is a square, 6'-wide, chimney-like feature that continues up the cliff. (This is the line of the winter route Don't Fall or Go to Hell.

P1 5.7 G: Climb straight up, with ledges interspersed among steeper sections, finishing at the trees. The crux wall at 30' is loose and scary. 150'

FA Aug 20, 2010, Tom DuBois, Ellen DuBois

Appendix A: Grade Conversion

Legend: safe (G protection) / bold (R or X protection)

YDS	V	UIAA	FR	AUS	SAX	SCA	BRA	UK (1)	UK (2)	UK (3)	UK (4)
5.2		II	1	7-8	II	3					
5.3		III	2	9-10	III	3+		D difficult			
5.4		IV-	3	11-12		4			VD very difficult		
5.5		IV IV+		13		4+				HVD hard very difficult	
5.6		V-	4	14		5-		HS	4a		S severe
5.7		V V+		15	VIIa	5		hard severe	VS		
5.8		VI-	5a	16	VIIb	5+	4 4+		5a very severe	4c	
5.9		VI	5b	17	VIIc	6-	5 5+			HVS	5a
5.10a	V0	VI+	5c	18	VIIIa	6	6a	5b		5b hard very severe	E1
5.10b			6a	19	VIIIb		6b				
5.10c		VII-	6a+	20		6+		E2	5c		5c
5.10d	V1	VII	6b	21	VIIIc		6c	6a	E3	6a	
5.11a		VI+	6b+	22	IXa	7-	7a				6a
5.11b	V2		6c	23	IXb	7	7b		6a	E4	
5.11c		VIII-	6c+	24		7+					
5.11d	V3	VIII	7a		IXc		7c	6b		6b	E5
5.12a		VIII+	7a+	25		8-	8a				
5.12b	V4		7b	26	Xa	8	8b	E6	6c		6c
5.12c	V5	IX-	7b+	27	Xb	8+	8c			6c	
5.12d	V6	IX	7c	28			9a		E7		7a
5.13a	V7	IX+	7c+		Xc		9b	6c			
5.13b	V8		8a	29		9-	9c			E8	
5.13c	V9	X-	8a+	30		9	10a	7a	7a		
5.13d	V10	X	8b	31	XIa		10b				E9
5.14a	V11	X+	8b+	32	XIb		10c		7a	7a	
5.14b	V12	XI-	8c	33		9+	11a	E10			
5.14c	V13	XI	8c+	34	XIc		11b		E11		7b
5.14d	V14	XI+	9a	35			11c				
5.15a	V15	XII-	9a+	36			12a	7b			
5.15b	V16		9b	37			12b		7b		

Appendix B: Cliffs by Category

Canoe Approach Crags

A boat is required, or highly recommended, to reach these cliffs:

CLIFF	REGION	PAGE
Baldface Mountain	Indian Lake	*253*
Bluff Island	Northern Mountains	*424*
Grass Pond Mountain	Cranberry Lake	*392*
Jolly Roger Slab	Lake George	*87*
Long Pond	Indian Lake	*240*
Pulpit Rock	Wilmington Notch	386
Rogers Rock, Rogers Slide	Lake George	*92*

Canoe-Optional Crags

These cliffs have paddling opportunities nearby, or an approach by water is preferred to hiking the entire distance. In many cases, the boat approach is faster and more pleasant.

CLIFF	REGION	PAGE
Barn Rock	Lake Champlain	145
Cat Mountain	Cranberry Lake	*396*
Good Luck Mountain	Southern Mountains	*323*
Henderson Cliff	High Peaks	428
Hitchins Pond Cliff	Cranberry Lake	*390*
Lake Lila	Cranberry Lake	*387*
Mitchell Ponds	Old Forge	*362*
Palisades	Lake Champlain	141

Backpacking and Climbing

These destinations offer the opportunity to backpack into a campsite near the cliff—at the base or on the top. While it is possible to camp nearly anywhere and at almost every cliff, these destinations are far from the road and have excellent camp spots. Most of the cliffs in the High Peaks make excellent backpacking destinations.

CLIFF	REGION	PAGE
Barn Rock	Lake Champlain	145
Barton High Cliff	Lake George	*117*
Cat Mountain	Cranberry Lake	*396*
Good Luck Mountain	Southern Mountains	*323*
Grass Pond Mountain	Cranberry Lake	*392*
Huckleberry Mountain	Indian Lake	*214*
Long Pond	Indian Lake	*240*
Middle Settlement Lake	Old Forge	*353*
Pharaoh Mountain	Lake George	*122*
Snowy Mountain, Main Face	Indian Lake	*248*
Washbowl Pond	Chapel Pond Pass	250
West Canada Cliff	Southern Mountains	*331*

Areas Near Water

These cliffs, and areas, are close to water and afford the opportunity to combine climbing and swimming.

CLIFF	REGION	PAGE
Avalanche Lake	High Peaks	507
Between The Lakes	Keene	372
Bluff Island	Northern Mountains	*424*
Boquet Canyon	Chapel Pond Pass	181
Boxcar	Chapel Pond Pass	183
Buck Mountain	Lake George	*67*
Chapel Pond Gully Cliff	Chapel Pond Pass	223
Chapel Pond Slab	Chapel Pond Pass	213
Eagle Falls	Old Forge	*364*
Grass Pond Mountain	Cranberry Lake	*392*
Gull Pond Cliff	Lake George	*132*
Hitchins Pond Cliff	Cranberry Lake	*390*
Hudson River Crag	Lake George	*79*
Lake Lila	Cranberry Lake	*387*
Middle Settlement Lake	Old Forge	*353*
Otter Lake	Southern Mountains	*303*
Pilot Knob	Lake George	*74*
Pitchoff Chimney Cliff	Keene	352
Roaring Brook Falls	Chapel Pond Pass	316
Rogers Rock	Lake George	*87*
Shelving Rock	Lake George	*38*
Tilmans Arete	Chapel Pond Pass	234
Washbowl Pond	Chapel Pond Pass	250
Whitewater Walls	Chapel Pond Pass	183

Toprope Areas

The areas listed here have easy access to the top for setting topropes, an accessible cliff base, and few obstructions for dropping ropes. Plan on building your own anchors with long cord and/or protection. Review the regulations in the relevant section regarding group size, and be sure to share the cliff with others.

CLIFF	REGION	PAGE
Baker Mountain	Northern Mountains	*425*
Beer Walls	Chapel Pond Pass	285
Bluff Island	Northern Mountains	*424*
Brain, The	Lake George	*78*
Chapel Pond Viewpoint	Chapel Pond Pass	251
County Line Mountain	Northern Mountains	*420*
Courthouse, The	High Peaks	491
Crane Mountain, Measles Group	Indian Lake	*164*
Crane Mountain, The Prows	Indian Lake	*159*
Creature Wall	Chapel Pond Pass	236
Eagle Falls	Old Forge	*364*
Flatrock Mountain	Old Forge	*213*

CLIFF	REGION	PAGE
Grass Pond Mountain	Cranberry Lake	*392*
Jewels and Gem Wall	Chapel Pond Pass	**198**
King Philip's Spring Wall	Lake Champlain	**147**
Lake Pleasant Quarry	Southern Mountains	*338*
Ledge Mountain (Nobleboro)	Old Forge	*349*
Lost T	Southern Mountains	*306*
Middle Settlement Lake	Old Forge	*353*
New Buck	Lake George	*69*
Noonmark Mountain	High Peaks	**480**
Notch Mountain, The Slabs	Wilmington Notch	**389**
Outlet Wall	Chapel Pond Pass	**256**
Owls Head Mountain	Keene	**349**
Panther Mountain	Southern Mountains	*334*
Pitchoff Chimney Cliff, Practice Wall	Keene	**362**
Silver Lake, Midway Cliff	Northern Mountains	*464*
South Bay Roadcut	Cranberry Lake	*392*
South Colton	Northern Mountains	*406*
Spruce Hill Crag	Keene	**330**
Stewarts Ledge	Lake George	*74*
Tanager Face	Chapel Pond Pass	**230**
Wright Peak Cliff	High Peaks	**525**

Mountaintop Destinations

These cliffs are positioned on top of a mountain or pointed viewpoint. In other words, when you reach the top of the climb, you're on top of a summit.

CLIFF	REGION	PAGE
Bald Mountain, Summit Cliff	Old Forge	*360*
Castle Rock	Indian Lake	*279*
Cat Mountain	Cranberry Lake	*396*
Catamount Mountain	Northern Mountains	*433*
Chimney Mountain	Indian Lake	*257*
Crane Mountain, Summit Cliffs	Indian Lake	*153*
Good Luck Mountain	Southern Mountains	*323*
Gothics	High Peaks	**468**
Hitchins Pond Cliff	Cranberry Lake	*390*
Mt Colden	High Peaks	**509**
Noonmark Mountain	High Peaks	**480**
Notch Mountain, The Slabs	Wilmington Notch	**389**
Owls Head Lookout	High Peaks	**463**
Owls Head Mountain	Keene	**349**
Poke-O Moonshine, Summit Cliff	Lake Champlain	**115**
Rooster Comb	High Peaks	**485**
Silver Lake, C Chimney Cliff	Northern Mountains	*447*
Silver Lake, Potter Mountain	Northern Mountains	*470*
Silver Lake, Summit Cliff	Northern Mountains	*447*
Wright Peak Cliff	High Peaks	**525**

Multipitch Climbing Areas

These cliffs offer mostly multipitch climbing, or have at least one noteworthy multipitch climb. Note that many scrambling routes in the High Peaks should be treated as multipitch climbs (for example, Mt Colden, Giant Mountain, Basin Mountain, Marcy East Face, and Dix Mountain).

CLIFF	REGION	PAGE
Avalanche Lake	High Peaks	**507**
Barton High Cliff	Lake George	*117*
Big Slide Mountain	High Peaks	**494**
Chapel Pond Gully Cliff	Chapel Pond Pass	**223**
Chapel Pond Slab	Chapel Pond Pass	**213**
Crane Mountain, Bellavista Slab	Indian Lake	*174*
Crane, Beaverview	Indian Lake	*146*
Deer Pass	Northern Mountains	*417*
Gothics, South Face	High Peaks	**473**
Hurricane Crag	Keene	**321**
Marcy, Panther Gorge	High Peaks	**498**
Moss Cliff	Wilmington Notch	**392**
Pharaoh Mountain	Lake George	*122*
Pitchoff Chimney Cliff	Keene	**352**
Poke-O Moonshine, Main Face	Lake Champlain	**31**
Poke-O Slab	Lake Champlain	**106**
Porter Mountain	High Peaks	**502**
Rogers Rock, Rogers Slide	Lake George	*92*
Silver Lake, Center of Progress	Northern Mountains	*453*
Silver Lake, Outback Slab	Northern Mountains	*467*
Silver Lake, Potter Mountain	Northern Mountains	*470*
Silver Lake, Summit Cliff	Northern Mountains	*447*
Sugarloaf Mountain	Indian Lake	*263*
Upper Washbowl	Chapel Pond Pass	**240**
Upper Wolfjaw Cliff	High Peaks	**482**
Wallface	High Peaks	**431**

Slab Climbing Areas

These cliffs offer friction climbing.

CLIFF	REGION	PAGE
Avalanche Lake	High Peaks	**507**
Basin Mountain	High Peaks	**487**
Big Slide Mountain	High Peaks	**494**
Chapel Pond Slab	Chapel Pond Pass	**213**
Crane Mountain, Bellavista Slab	Indian Lake	*174*
Crane, Beaverview	Indian Lake	*146*

CLIFF	REGION	PAGE
Emperor Slab	Chapel Pond Pass	**209**
Giant Mountain, West Face	High Peaks	**465**
Gothics, Rainbow Slide	High Peaks	**477**
Marcy East Face	High Peaks	**501**
Moss Lake Slab	Old Forge	*360*
Mt Colden	High Peaks	**509**
Notch Mountain, The Slabs	Wilmington Notch	**389**
Poke-O Slab	Lake Champlain	**106**
Rogers Rock, Rogers Slide	Lake George	*92*
Silver Lake, Outback Slab	Northern Mountains	*467*
Silver Lake, Potter Mountain	Northern Mountains	*470*
Snowy Mountain, Lower Slabs	Indian Lake	*252*
Sugarloaf Mountain	Indian Lake	*263*

Quick-to-Dry Areas

These cliffs dry quickly after a rain.

CLIFF	REGION	PAGE
Ark Wall	Lake George	*60*
Beer Walls	Chapel Pond Pass	**285**
Chimney Mountain	Indian Lake	*257*
Deadwater	Lake Champlain	**155**
Lake Pleasant Quarry	Southern Mountains	*338*
Notch Mountain, The Slabs	Wilmington Notch	**389**
Owls Head Mountain	Keene	**349**
Pitchoff Chimney Cliff	Keene	**352**
Potash Cliff	Lake George	*80*
Shelving Rock	Lake George	*38*
Silver Lake, C Chimney Cliff	Northern Mountains	*447*
Silver Lake, Potter Mountain	Northern Mountains	*470*
Snowy Mountain, Main Face	Indian Lake	*248*
Spider's Web	Chapel Pond Pass	**258**
Stewarts Ledge	Lake George	*74*
Tilmans Arete	Chapel Pond Pass	**234**
Typhoon Wall, Ward Cleaver Buttress	Keene	**331**

Areas with Sport Routes

These cliffs have several sport routes or at least one notable sport route.

CLIFF	REGION	PAGE
Ark Wall	Lake George	*60*
Beaver Brook	Wilmington Notch	**420**
Beer Walls	Chapel Pond Pass	**285**
Brain, The	Lake George	*78*
Charcoal Kiln Quarry	Northern Mountains	*423*
Crane Mountain, Measles Group	Indian Lake	*164*
Eagle Falls	Old Forge	*364*
Good Luck Mountain	Southern Mountains	*323*
Gothics, South Face	High Peaks	**473**
Green Lake	Southern Mountains	*301*
Honey Pot, The	Lake Champlain	**145**
Huckleberry, Hard Guy Wall	Indian Lake	*226*
King Wall	Chapel Pond Pass	**200**
Little Crow Mountain	Keene	**337**
Little Johnson	Lake Champlain	**169**
Lost Hunters	Southern Mountains	*315*
Makomis Mountain	Lake Champlain	**151**
Martini Wall	Chapel Pond Pass	**236**
McMartin Cliff	Southern Mountains	*319*
New Buck	Lake George	*69*
Otter Lake	Southern Mountains	*303*
Poke-O Moonshine, Main Face	Lake Champlain	**31**
Potash Cliff	Lake George	*80*
Rogers Rock, Campground Wall	Lake George	*88*
Santa Claus Hill	Wilmington Notch	**418**
Shanty Cliff	Indian Lake	*231*
Shelving Rock	Lake George	*38*
Silver Lake, Mud Pond	Northern Mountains	*486*
Silver Lake, Potter Mountain	Northern Mountains	*470*
Snowy Mountain, Main Face	Indian Lake	*248*
Spanky's Wall	Chapel Pond Pass	**190**
Stewarts Ledge	Lake George	*74*
Typhoon Wall, Ward Cleaver Buttress	Keene	**331**
Wild Pines	Lake George	*106*

Areas with Good Cracks

These cliffs have excellent cracks, or at least one exceptional crack.

CLIFF	REGION	PAGE
Alcatraz	Wilmington Notch	**408**
Avalanche Lake, The Fin	High Peaks	**520**
Bald Mountain	Old Forge	*356*
Barkeater Cliff	Keene	**339**
Bear Den, right side	Wilmington Notch	**418**
Beer Walls	Chapel Pond Pass	**285**
Cat Mountain	Cranberry Lake	*396*
Crane Mountain	Indian Lake	*140*
Creature Wall	Chapel Pond Pass	**236**
Deadwater	Lake Champlain	**155**
High Falls Crag	Wilmington Notch	**410**
Hurricane Crag	Keene	**321**
Jewels and Gem Wall	Chapel Pond Pass	**198**
Long Pond	Indian Lake	*240*

CLIFF	REGION	PAGE
Lost Hunters	Southern Mountains	*315*
Lost T	Southern Mountains	*306*
Moss Cliff	Wilmington Notch	392
Noonmark Mountain	High Peaks	480
Owls Head Mountain	Keene	349
Pinnacle Mountain	Southern Mountains	*295*
Pitchoff Chimney Cliff	Keene	352
Poke-O Moonshine, Main Face	Lake Champlain	31
Poke-O Moonshine, Upper Tiers	Lake Champlain	114
Polar Soldier Wall	Wilmington Notch	415
Silver Lake, Mud Pond	Northern Mountains	*486*
Silver Lake, Summit Cliff	Northern Mountains	*447*
Silver Lake, Tsunami Wall	Northern Mountains	*461*
Spider's Web	Chapel Pond Pass	258
Starbuck Mountain	Indian Lake	*282*
Tongue Mountain	Lake George	*111*
Twin Falls	Northern Mountains	*399*
Upper Washbowl	Chapel Pond Pass	240

Bug-Free Areas

Unfortunately, there's no such thing as bug free, but these areas have fewer bugs due to insect control, elevation, or wind.

CLIFF	REGION	PAGE
Chapel Pond Pass	Chapel Pond Pass	177
Eagle Falls	Old Forge	*364*
Owls Head Mountain	Keene	349
Pitchoff Chimney Cliff	Keene	352
Rogers Rock, Rogers Slide	Lake George	*92*
Shelving Rock	Lake George	*38*
Stewarts Ledge	Lake George	*74*

Areas to Visit When it's Hot

These areas have shade and stay cooler.

CLIFF	REGION	PAGE
Avalanche Lake	High Peaks	507
Barkeater Cliff	Keene	339
Lost Hunters	Southern Mountains	*315*
Lost T	Southern Mountains	*306*
Martini Wall	Chapel Pond Pass	236
McMartin Cliff	Southern Mountains	*319*
Notch Mountain, The Slabs	Wilmington Notch	389
Pinnacle Mountain	Southern Mountains	*295*
Tanager Face	Chapel Pond Pass	230
Wild Pines	Lake George	*106*

Areas to Visit When It's Cold

These areas are good when it's cold due to sun exposure, elevation, or protection from wind. On a sunny, windlesss day, you can climb at many of these late or early in the season. Check the cliff's aspect to determine the best time of day.

CLIFF	REGION	PAGE
Beaver Brook	Wilmington Notch	420
Deadwater	Lake Champlain	155
Eagle Falls	Old Forge	*364*
Gull Pond Cliff	Lake George	*132*
Hurricane Crag	Keene	321
Pitchoff Chimney Cliff	Keene	352
Poke-O Moonshine, Main Face	Lake Champlain	31
Poke-O Slab	Lake Champlain	106
Potash Cliff	Lake George	*80*
Rogers Rock, Rogers Slide	Lake George	*92*
Shelving Rock	Lake George	*38*
Silver Lake, Potter Mountain	Northern Mountains	*470*
Spider's Web	Chapel Pond Pass	258
Stewarts Ledge	Lake George	*74*

Areas to Visit in Light Rain

These cliffs stay dry in a light rain.

CLIFF	REGION	PAGE
Ark Wall	Lake George	*60*
Beer Walls, Clutch and Cruise Cave	Chapel Pond Pass	309
King Wall	Chapel Pond Pass	200
Moss Cliff, Aid Wall		392
Potash Cliff	Lake George	*80*
Shelving Rock	Lake George	*38*
Shelving Rock, Main Face	Lake George	*44*
Silver Lake, Mud Pond	Northern Mountains	*486*
Spider's Web	Chapel Pond Pass	258

Areas with Clean Aid Routes

These areas are good for clean aid climbing.

CLIFF	REGION	PAGE
Beer Walls, Upper Beer Wall	Chapel Pond Pass	289
High Falls Crag	Wilmington Notch	410
Moss Cliff	Wilmington Notch	392
Poke-O Moonshine, Main Face	Lake Champlain	31
Spider's Web	Chapel Pond Pass	258
Wallface	High Peaks	431

Appendix C: Private Land Crags

The cliffs listed below are not documented in this book but have a known climbing history. All of these cliffs are on private land. Access to these cliffs requires permission from the landowner, whether it be an organization, a hunting club, a paper company or an individual. A few cliffs, such as Mt. Jo (Adirondack Mountain Club) and Indian Head (Ausable Club), are of historic significance, and climbing is permitted by membership in those clubs. Other cliffs are frequently visited because climbers have been granted permission by the landowner.

Do not trespass at these cliffs. Trespassing may compromise the access for those climbers who were mindful enough to contact the landowners beforehand. If you ask permission, the worst that can happen is a "no" from the landowner. If you are declined access, respect the landowner's decision and go climb somewhere else. This book has no shortage of destinations that are accessible to the public.

Some of these cliffs may become accessible in the future through conservation easements or direct acquisition by the state. Be sure to check www.AdirondackRock.com for updates.

8 Eyes Wall
Anthony's Nose
Antone Mountain
Aunt Mary's Kitchen
Broughton Ledge
Cartehena Cliff
Cartoon Cliff
Clear Pond
Crane Mountain, Northernmost Wall
Crane Mountain: Putnam Farm Wall
Diameter Mountain
Ebenezer Mountain
Hadley Pond
Knob Mountain
Mosher Cliff
Moxham Quarry
Otis Mountain
Realty Wall
Sherwood Forest
Shippee's Ledge
South Bay
Super Face Wall
The New New
Willsboro

Private cliffs described in previous guidebooks

Cobble Hill
East Keene Hill
Haystack Mountain
Indian Head
Moxham Dome
Mountain Shadows
Mt Gilligan
Mt Jo
Petit Mountain

Appendix D: Advertiser Index

Appendix E: Local Resources

Gear Shops

These gear shops are located in the Adirondack Park:

Eastern Mountain Sports: Lake Placid, www.ems.com (518.523.2505)

High Peaks Cyclery (vol. 1, 490): Lake Placid, www.highpeakscyclery.com (518.523.3764)

The Mountaineer (vol. 1, 178): Keene Valley, www.mountaineer.com (518.576.2281)

Near the park are the following shops:

Eastern Mountain Sports: Saratoga, www.ems.com (518.580.1505)

Fountain Square Outfitters (vol. 2, 138): Glens Falls, www.fountainsquareoutfitters.com (518.932.8355)

Outdoor Gear Exchange (see cover flaps): Burlington, www.gearx.com (802.860.0190)

Rock and Snow (vol. 1, 16; vol. 2, 404): New Paltz, www.rockandsnow.com (845.255.1311)

Wear on Earth: Potsdam, www.wearonearth.com (315.265.3178)

Climbing Gyms

Gyms are a good place for partners, limited gear, posting, and perhaps cliff updates.

Albany Indoor Rock Gym: Albany, www.airrockgym.com (518.459.7625)

The Crux (vol. 1, 57): Willsboro, www.ClimbTheCrux.com (518.963.4646)

The Edge Halfmoon (see inside back cover): www.theedgehalfmoon.com (518.982.5545)

Petra Cliffs (vol. 2, 16): Burlington, www.petracliffs.com (866.657.3872)

Rocksport (vol. 1, 424; vol. 2, 36): Queensbury, www.rocksportny.com (518.793.4626)

Guide Services

There are many guide services for the park, all of which have licensed guides.

Adirondack Mountain Guides: www.adirondackmountainguides.com (518.576.9556), Ian Osteyee

Adirondack Rock and River Guide Service, Inc.: www.rockandriver.com (518.576.2041), Ed Palen

Alpine Adventures: www.alpineadven.com (518.576.9881), R.L. Stolz

Alpine Development Koncepts (vol. 2, 16): www.alpinedevelopmentkoncepts.com (518.524.3328), Stephen Mergenthaler

Alpine Endeavors (vol. 1, 28; vol. 2, 294): www.alpineendeavors.com (845.658.3094), Marty Molitoris

Cloudsplitter Mountain Guides (vol. 1, 180): www.cloudsplitterguides.com (518.569.8910), Jesse Williams

Eastern Mountain Sports: www.emsclimb.com (800.310.4504), Matt Wiech

High Peaks Mountain Adventures (vol. 1, 490): www.hpmountainguides.com (518.523.3764), Brian Delaney

Mountainside Adventures (vol. 2, 162): www.mtnsideview.com (518.623.2062), Jay Harrison

Mountain Skills (vol. 1, 424): www.mountainskills.biz (845.853.5450), Doug Ferguson

Petracliffs (vol. 2, 16): www.petracliffs.com (518.657.3872), Steve Charest

Rocksport (vol. 1, 424; vol. 2, 36): www.rocksportny.com (518.793.4626) Tom Rosecrans

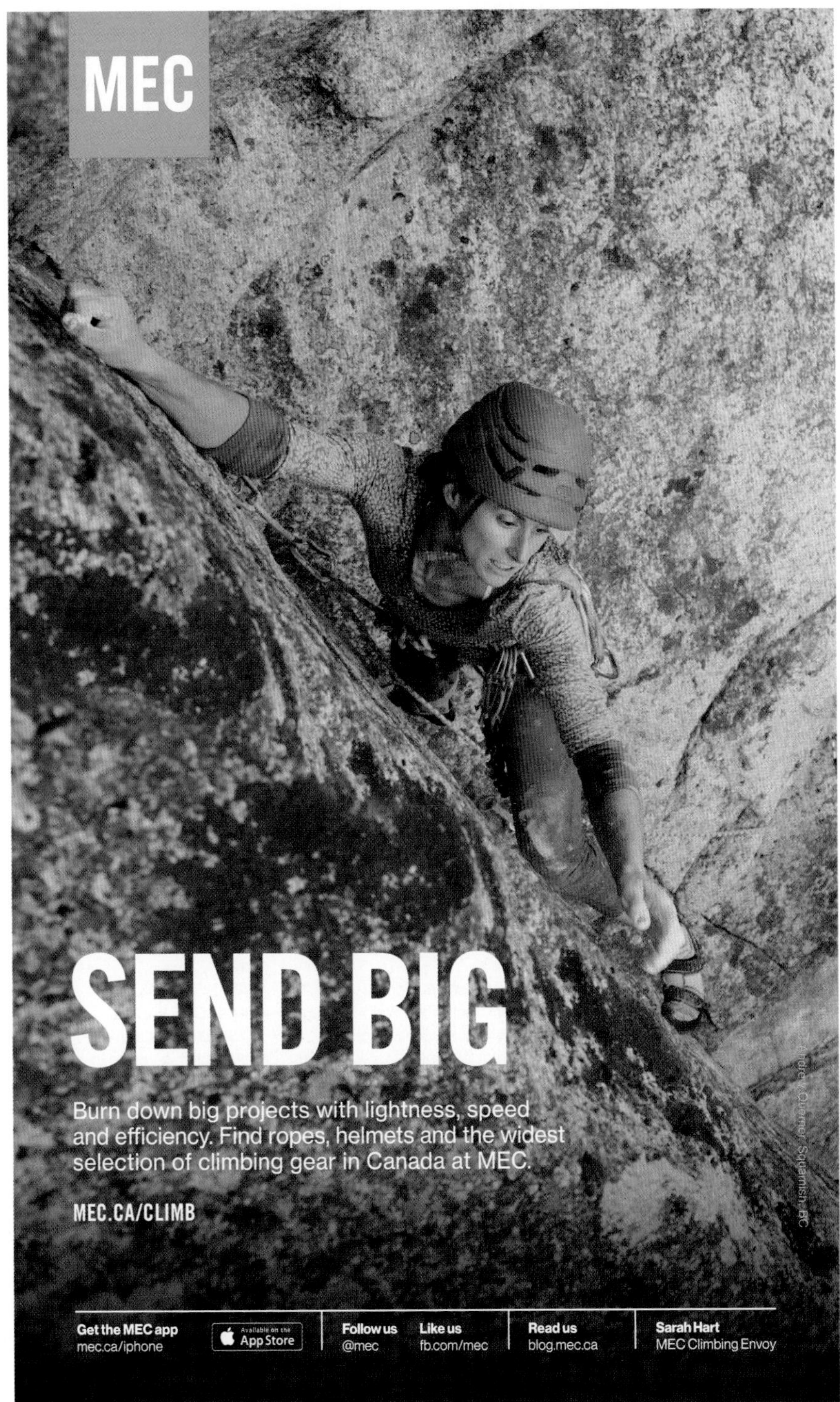
MEC
SEND BIG
Burn down big projects with lightness, speed and efficiency. Find ropes, helmets and the widest selection of climbing gear in Canada at MEC.
MEC.CA/CLIMB
Get the MEC app
mec.ca/iphone
Available on the App Store
Follow us
@mec
Like us
fb.com/mec
Read us
blog.mec.ca
Sarah Hart
MEC Climbing Envoy
Andrew Querner, Squamish, BC

Index

Page numbers in this volume *Page numbers in Volume 2*

C

D

E

F

G

M

N

O

P

Q

R

S

T

U

Page numbers in this volume *Page numbers in Volume 2*

X

Y

Z

Drawing by Colin O'Connor.

Acknowledgments

Producing this guide was a monumental effort, involving the collaboration of many individuals.

Those who made first ascents deserve the ultimate credit. It's because of their dedication and perseverance that we have so many routes to climb. We contacted many first ascentionists, who have our deep appreciation for accepting our cold calls and dredging their memories to recount route details of long-ago climbs.

We thank those who helped with background research. Don Mellor was always accessible and willing to share his insights, opinions, and historical recollections. Without his "blue bin"—and, no, not the recycling bin, but rather his collection of notes, correspondence, and route reports dating back to Trudy Healy— this project would not have been possible. Dick Tucker deserves special mention for his generous diligence in uncovering historical gems.

Since the first edition, many people have contributed material that has served as a basis for our work. Special thanks to Kevin "MudRat" MacKenzie and his excellent photos of the High Peaks; Justin Sanford and his topos of the Southern Adirondack areas; and Gary Thomann and his online mini-guides.

Of our many contributors, Jay Harrison tops them all. Not only is he a prolific route developer, but he spent many countless hours poring over aerial photos, editing and reediting route descriptions, and running up to the cliff from his house to confirm route details. If you see him at the cliff, be sure to shake his hand, and thank him for his many years of scrubbing routes.

Many climbers contributed essays to the first edition that portrayed Adirondack climbing in a variety of voices. This second edition offers new additional essays from Tad Welch, Tom Rosecrans, Peter Kamitses, Dick Tucker, Conor Cliffe, David Buzzelli, Dave Hough, and Colin Loher. Thanks guys!

The Department of Environmental Conservation was very helpful with their contributions on peregrines and timber rattlesnakes, and their reviews of backcountry rules and regulations. In the 6 years since the first edition, New York State has purchased huge tracts of land, and coincidentally many cliffs. Special thanks to Dan Levy, Robert Daley, and Allison Buckley, who, along with Connie Prickett at The Nature Conservancy, kept us in the loop, assisted with field research, and reviewed draft materials.

A special thanks goes to our production team: Karen Kwasnowski for her GIS expertise; Sara Catterall and Sue Cohan for copy editing; and Colin O'Connor, Tad Welch and Lucie Wellner for their drawings and watercolors. Lucie Wellner in particular went above and beyond by color correcting hundreds of photos and assisting with nearly every aspect of book design.

There's also a long list of photographers, many of whom donated their photos. Those that deserve special recognition are Jim Cunningham, Joel Dashnaw, Drew Haas, Keenan Harvey (www.kennanharvey.com), David Le Pagne (www.davidlepagne.com), Rick Levinson (www.rlphoto.com), Mark Meschinelli, Olaf Sööt (www.osphoto.com), Dave Vuono (www.davevuono.com), Carl Heilman II (www.carlheilman.com), and Tomás Donoso (www.tomasdonoso.com).

We thank those who accompanied us on forays into the mountains to research this guide. Like all climbing partnerships, we depended upon you to show up, navigate the woods, share the rope, and be willing to do it again (and again).

Lastly, we offer the deepest gratitude to our wives who know us well enough to realize that our bellyaching was mostly a facade, and for being on call as both editors and therapists. Lucie and Erika, you knew you were marrying climbers, but this was a whole new level. Thank you both.

About the Authors

JIM LAWYER

Jim began bagging peaks in the Adirondacks at the age of 5, during a family vacation in 1970. His love of wild places and the escape they offer led him to long-distance hiking in his teens. After that, rock climbing was a natural extension. Over the last 30 years, he has dedicated his life to climbing extensively around the world. With an education in computer science from Syracuse University, he helped found Summit Software in 1989. He and his wife Lucie split their time between Pompey, NY, and their hut in the High Peaks.

JEREMY HAAS

Jeremy began climbing at the age of 14, and promptly abandoned his childhood dream of becoming an Olympic gymnast. His first Adirondacks weekend was an epic: wasp nests on Poke-O; freaky runouts on Big Slide; and a struggle up Wallface after he'd left all the slings in the car. A graduate of the University of New Hampshire, with a Masters in Education from Cornell, he teaches science at Saratoga Springs High School, and in his spare time is a guide for Adirondack Rock and River. Jeremy and his wife Erika live in Glens Falls, NY.